Personality Theory & Research

AN INTERNATIONAL PERSPECTIVE

GORDON L. FLETT
YORK UNIVERSITY

JOHN WILEY & SONS CANADA, LTD.

Library and Archives Canada Cataloguing in Publication
Flett, Gordon L. (Gordon Leslie), 1957-
Personality theory and research / Gordon L. Flett. 1st ed.

Includes bibliographical references and index.
ISBN 978-0-470-83550-0

1. Personality--Textbooks. 2. Personality development—Textbooks. I. Title.
BF698.F54 2007 155.2 C2006-906035-5

Production Credits
Acquisitions Editor: Michael Valerio
Publishing Services Director: Karen Bryan
Editorial Manager: Karen Staudinger
Developmental Editor: Gail Brown
Marketing Manager: Joan Lewis-Milne
Editorial Assistant/Permissions Coordinator: Sara Dam
Editorial Assistant: Sheri Coombs
Media Editor: Elsa Passera Berardi
Design & Typesetting: Mike Chan, Adrian So
Cover Design: Swap Advertising & Design
Cover Photographer: Jarret Anderson
Wiley Bicentennial Logo: Richard J. Pacifico
Printing & Binding: Quebecor World Inc.

Printed and bound in the United States of America.
1 2 3 4 5 QW 11 10 09 08 07

John Wiley & Sons Canada, Ltd.
6045 Freemont Blvd.
Mississauga, Ontario L5R 4J3
Visit our website at www.wiley.ca

This book is dedicated to my wife Kathy and my daughters Hayley and Alison, as well as my parents Mary and Gordon. I would also like to thank Kathy, Hayley, and Alison for their unwavering support and patience throughout the process of writing this book.

I would also like to dedicate this book to the memory of Norman Endler, a great personality researcher and theorist, but more important, my colleague, friend, and mentor.

ABOUT THE AUTHOR

Gordon L. Flett is Professor of Psychology at York University in Toronto. He received his B.Sc., M.A., and Ph.D. from the University of Toronto, and he began his appointment at York University in 1987. Dr. Flett has served as Director of Undergraduate Studies in York's Department of Psychology, and received the Outstanding Teaching Award from the Faculty of Arts at York University in 1993 and again in 1997. Dr. Flett has taught courses on personality psychology, personality theory, and behavioural disorders at the undergraduate level, as well as courses in personality theory and research and in the self-concept at the graduate level.

In 2004, Dr. Flett was awarded a Tier I Canada Research Chair in Personality and Health. In 1999, he received the Dean's Award for Outstanding Research from the Faculty of Arts at York University. In 1996, Dr. Flett was recognized by the American Psychological Society as one of the top 25 scholars in psychology, based on the number of publications over a five-year period.

Dr. Flett's research interests include the role of personality factors in depression and the interpersonal aspects of anxiety. Dr. Flett is most recognized for his seminal contributions to research and theory on the role of perfectionism in psychopathology. His collaborative work with Dr. Paul Hewitt of the University of British Columbia on perfectionism has received widespread national and international attention and has been the subject of numerous media stories, including coverage on CTV, CNN, and the BBC. This work has been supported by major research grants from the Canadian Institutes of Health Research and the Social Sciences and Humanities Research Council of Canada.

Dr. Flett has written more than 130 journal articles and book chapters. He co-edited the first academic book on perfectionism, entitled *Perfectionism: Theory, Research, and Treatment*, published in 2002. Dr. Flett has also teamed up with Dr. Hewitt to create the Multidimensional Perfectionism Scale. They have also collaborated on the development of several other measures, including the Child-Adolescent Perfectionism Scale, the Perfectionism Cognitions Inventory, and the Perfectionistic Self-Presentation Scale. Dr. Flett is also the co-creator of the newly developed Endler Multidimensional Anxiety Scales (EMAS)–Social Anxiety Scales.

PREFACE

The field of personality continues to grow, and significant developments have occurred over the last 10 years. One notable factor, for example, is that the study of personality is much more international in its scope and focus. Due to its expansion, the challenge for the undergraduate instructor and reader is to have a clear and authoritative presentation of this dynamic field that encompasses its breadth, and to have a resource that is engaging.

This author has taught many personality courses at the university level for more than 20 years, and it has become apparent that a new approach is needed in order to facilitate instruction and to stimulate interest. So what then constitutes an "ideal textbook" on personality, and what are the guiding principles of this text to try to approximate this goal? The following guiding principles provide a framework that facilitates teaching and a critical appreciation of personality for the reader.

Balance between Theory and Research

This textbook strikes a meaningful balance between theory and research, and the importance of theoretical explanations is discussed throughout the textbook. Some personality textbooks focus heavily on classic personality theories, which is acceptable if the course focuses primarily on theories. However, due to the proliferation of research and its importance in informing these theories, scant commentary on research findings does not give the reader a full appreciation of this crucial aspect in personality studies. On the other hand, a text that over-emphasizes research does so to the detriment of not revealing the richness of key personality theories.

Balance between the Contemporary and the Historical

The ideal textbook must have the proper balance of "the new" and "the old." At present, the personality field is quite dynamic, and several innovative research advances have emerged in recent years. It is vitally important to recognize these developments. Thus, up-to-date accounts have been provided in this textbook. At the same time, it is important not to lose sight of key developments, both empirical and theoretical, from many years ago. One of the concerns stemming from the current proliferation of psychology journals is that it is difficult to keep up with current developments without losing sight of past contributions. That is, we do not benefit as much as we should from the knowledge and wisdom of earlier authors. The contributions of these scholars are recognized where appropriate in this textbook by locating the empirical findings and theories within a historical context.

An International Perspective and Approach

Without a doubt, one of the most significant developments in the personality field over the past 10 years is that the field has become much more international in its scope and focus. Historically, most areas of psychology, including personality, have been dominated by contributions from the United States. However, several authors have noted that the personality field is becoming more global, and, as such, it is important for this to be reflected in the content of contemporary textbooks. From its inception, this textbook was designed and intended to be international in scope, suitable for use around the world. Accordingly, this textbook includes descriptions of research conducted in numerous regions of the world. The aim was to provide a textbook that appeals to a wide target audience and will be embraced by users from various regions. This decision is based, in part, on the recognition that existing textbooks often do not provide this more global perspective, sometimes to the extent that the case study examples are of limited relevance for an international audience.

In light of this goal, attempts have been made in every chapter of this textbook to highlight contributions from around the world. Most notably, each chapter has at least one International Focus on Discovery feature that examines an issue from a cross-cultural perspective (e.g., the nature of the self-concept across cultures).

Maximize Student Interest in and Engagement with the Material

The ideal textbook has material that is interesting and engaging for students. It is important to remember that most students who are interested in the study of personality are not simply interested in learning about variables and associations; they also have a natural interest in people. Personality is about studying people; so this textbook, wherever possible, includes examples of actual people to supplement the description of personality variables and the correlates of these variables.

Two clear biases were adhered to in an attempt to maximize students' interest and engagement. First, there was a tendency to favour research topics that students have shown substantial interest in over the years. This was accomplished, in part, by selecting topics that students can relate to, such as research on constructs such as procrastination and perfectionism, or broader themes that are reflected in entire chapters. These themes include (1) personality and the self; (2) interpersonal factors in personality; (3) personality, stress, coping, and health; and (4) personality and psychopathology. In short, there is a focus on topics that matter to students.

The second bias was the decision, early on, to include case illustrations as a way of highlighting the complexity inherent in any individual. Also, the inclusion of case material is in response to the interest that students have in people and their unique personalities. So, for instance, we examine the projective test responses of Mark David Chapman when he was assessed after killing John Lennon. We also examine the personality and cognitive constructs of Ted Kaczynski, also known as The Unabomber. This focus on the personalities of specific people is examined in great detail in Chapter 14. This chapter examines the role of personality factors in psychobiographies and includes brief psychobiographical sketches of Salvador Dali, Sylvia Plath, Anne Sexton, and Ozzy Osbourne.

Personality Psychology from a Scientific Perspective

It is stated from the outset of this textbook that personality research and theory will be addressed from a scientific perspective. This focus on personality as a science is maintained throughout the textbook by including up-to-date empirical articles and by including a chapter that focuses explicitly on the methods of assessing personality and associated research designs.

Part of fostering a scientific perspective is encouraging students to develop critical thinking skills and to reach their own conclusions about the phenomena being presented. Accordingly, in keeping with this goal, descriptions of key personality theories are accompanied by a critical evaluation of these theories. These critical evaluations aim to strike a balance between the contributions of these theories and their shortcomings and limitations.

An Applied Perspective that Highlights Practical Knowledge

Just as Zimbardo (2004) has argued that psychology matters and has made a real difference in people's lives, there is also no denying that personality matters, and it matters in many respects, as illustrated by a recent review paper (see Ozer & Benet-Martinez, 2006). In fact, one reason for renewed interest in the study of personality is that there has been a steady stream of research investigations that show the practical importance and significance of individual differences. There is perhaps no better way to establish the importance of personality factors than to illustrate how they are associated meaningfully with "things that matter" to most people. Accordingly, each chapter also has one or more Applied Perspective feature that illustrates the relevance of personality factors in the lives of people (e.g. personality factors as part of "the criminal personality").

As for practical knowledge, one goal was to provide pragmatic information whenever possible. For instance, experience with the development of personality tests and an awareness of their properties is essential given that most students will either be taking a personality test or will likely be given an opportunity at some point to evaluate research findings derived from personality measures. Thus, a key focus of the textbook is on the assessment of personality. Students learn what constitutes a good personality measure. The process of developing a personality measure according to the construct validation approach is outlined, and psychometric principles of reliability and validity are described. Finally, several personality scales are included in the textbook. These scales serve as illustrations, but students also have an opportunity to acquire practical knowledge about themselves and their own personalities.

Personality from the Student Perspective

It is important for textbook authors never to lose sight of a textbook's target audience—in this case, undergraduate students. It is important to present material in a way that is suitable for students taking their first course in personality theory and research. Students who decide to take a personality course want information that is relevant and useful to their future studies and life experiences. In addition, students want to be able to learn as much as possible and to do as well as possible in the course, so it is important for the textbook to have a clear yet engaging style and to provide students with learning aids that will help them achieve their goals.

This textbook has many topics that should resonate with students. Extensive material was included because it involves topics that students can relate to without difficulty. Four relevant examples among many are research and theory on (1) procrastination (surveys indicate that 45% of students suffer from chronic procrastination); (2) perfectionism; (3) the role of personality in dating relationships; and (4) the role of coping styles in psychological adjustment and health outcomes. Also, as alluded to above, material tends to have more impact when it is presented within the context of a "people focus." Accordingly, this textbook has several case examples, including accounts of the psychological functioning and personality features of many famous and infamous people (e.g., Adolf Hitler, The Unabomber, and Mark David Chapman). In fact, the textbook culminates with a chapter on psychobiography. This chapter serves two purposes. First, it provides a detailed analysis of some well-known people (Salvador Dali, Sylvia Plath, Anne Sexton, and Ozzy Osbourne) and in so doing, reminds us of the need to focus on the whole person rather than on isolated personality variables. Second, the chapter provides an opportunity to illustrate how the various personality constructs and theories described in the earlier chapters can be applied within the context of actual people with actual lives!

FEATURES AND SUPPLEMENTARY MATERIALS

For the Student

Key Terms and ***Key Theorists*** Key terms and key theorists are highlighted throughout each chapter as well as compiled at the end of the chapter, with page numbers for easy reference.

Glossary Key terms are defined in the glossary at the end of the text.

Key Points Summary key points are provided throughout each chapter to help students focus on the main points of the material covered in each section.

Applied Perspective Each chapter includes one or more Applied Perspective feature that illustrates the real-world relevance and significance of personality factors.

International Focus on Discovery This textbook highlights contributions from around the world and discusses personality issues from a cross-cultural perspective. These are highlighted by the International Focus on Discovery feature, which is included in each chapter.

Chapter Summary and Questions to Consider Each chapter concludes with a summary of the chapter material as well as questions to help students further their analysis and understanding of the material covered. Students are encouraged to make their own summaries as they go through each section.

Student Companion Website The textbook's website **www.wiley.ca/go/flett** contains numerous resources for students, including the glossary of key terms and links to websites related to issues in personality.

For the Instructor

Instructor Companion Website The textbook's website **www.wiley.ca/go/flett** contains a full suite of resources for instructors using the textbook, including an instructor's manual, PowerPoint slides, and a computerized test bank.

ACKNOWLEDGEMENTS

It is a great pleasure to acknowledge the contributions and support of numerous people who provided valuable support, comments, and feedback. First and foremost, many thanks to the staff at John Wiley & Sons Canada, Ltd. for their creative vision, support, and enthusiasm. Specifically, I would like to express my gratitude to Acquisitions Editor Michael Valerio and Editorial Manager Karen Staudinger for their unwavering belief in this project. A special thank you to Michael for overseeing and managing all aspects of this textbook from its inception. Michael has been a model of professionalism and enthusiasm and this has substantially enhanced this textbook. Thank you to Gail Brown, the Developmental Editor, for her patience, good nature, energy, and of course, ability to improve ambiguous content into much clearer material. I would also like to thank Laurel Hyatt for her superb and thorough copyediting of this textbook. Gail and Laurel have substantially enhanced the content and structure of this textbook. Gratitude is also expressed to Leanne Rancourt, the initial Development Editor, who led the way and helped get this textbook off to a good start.

I would also like to thank the various family members who have served as my assistants throughout the process of writing this textbook. In particular, I am very grateful for the assistance of my local "team," which consists of Alison Flett, Hayley Flett, Kathy Flett, and Karen Flett. Given their contributions to this textbook, I am hoping that Alison and Hayley will take a personality course some day!

I would especially like to thank those colleagues who provided comments and suggestions for the initial proposal for the text and those who reviewed chapter material. Their insights and feedback were invaluable and constructive and helped to shape the text.

John Allbutt, *University of Teesside*
Sunaina Assanand, *University of British Columbia*
John Barresi, *Dalhousie University*
Allan Blunt, *Carleton University*
Michael Cowles, *York University*

Richard Day, *McMaster University*
Teresa DeCicco, *Trent University*
Greg Fouts, *University of Calgary*
Trevor Gilbert, *Athabasca University*
Kim Goddard, *Red Deer College*
Richard Goffin, *University of Western Ontario*
Verena F. Gosse, *Memorial University of Newfoundland*
Peter Hall, *University of Waterloo*
Barry Ledwidge, *Simon Fraser University*
Han Li, *University of Northern British Columbia*
Bertha Mook, *University of Ottawa*
Sampo V. Paunonen, *University of Western Ontario*
Terry Prociuk, *University of Calgary*
Alexandra Rutherford, *York University*
Guus L. van Heck, *Tilburg University*
Patty Witzel, *University of Saskatchewan*

I would also like to take this opportunity to thank the professors who taught me a great deal about personality theory and research while I was a graduate student. Specifically, I would like to thank my Ph.D. supervisor Patricia (Patty) Pliner, Kirk Blankstein, Janet Polivy, and Harvey Skinner. I would also like to thank my colleagues in the Psychology Department at York University, both current and past. These colleagues with interests and expertise in the study of personality and associated processes include Norman Endler, Ray Fancher, Esther Greenglass, Paul Kohn, Igor Kusyszyn, Clarry Lay, Doug McCann, Ian McGregor, Myriam Mongrain, and Krista Trobst. Of course, I would also like to thank my research colleagues Paul Hewitt, Avi Besser, Marnin Heisel, and my current post-doctoral students Edward Sturman and Abby Goldstein for their assistance and suggestions.

Finally, I would like to thank my many students over the years, both at the undergraduate and graduate levels. The students I have worked with are too numerous to mention, but I would like to say that just as personality development is bidirectional, learning is also bidirectional, and I am proud to say that I have learned many things from my students over the years. Their enthusiasm is infectious, and it has provided a source of inspiration for me throughout my career. I look forward to continued interactions with my current students and I want to thank them for being very patient and supportive of this project.

Gordon Flett
Mississauga, Ontario
March 2007

BRIEF TABLE OF CONTENTS

TABLE OF CONTENTS

chapter one

PERSONALITY: AN INTRODUCTION

- The Goals of Chapter 1
- What Is Personality?
- The Goals of Personality Research
- Overarching Themes in the Personality Field and in this Book
- Organization of this Book

Trait psychology .... minimizes the importance of physiological occurrences, irrational impulses and beliefs, infantile experiences, unconscious and inhibited drives as well as environmental (sociological) factors...It stops short precisely at the point where a psychology is needed, the point at which it begins to be difficult to understand what is going on.

—HENRY MURRAY (1938, P. 715)

Arguments about whether personality is consistent over time and context, arguments about the proper units of personality, and arguments about the utility of different types of measures have all had one common and unfortunate effect: They have obscured the reasons why proponents of different positions cared about personality in the first place, and first and foremost among these reasons is that personality matters.

—DANIEL OZER AND VERONICA BENET-MARTINEZ (2006, P. 416)

HOW OLD WERE YOU when you first started noticing ways that you are different from other people? Can you remember the first person you met who made you think about the personality differences between people? Maybe you had two very different friends while you were growing up and you couldn't help wondering why they were so different. Or perhaps you had a nice family member and a not-so-nice family member and you said to yourself, "Just how is it that two people from the same family can be so different?"

Most people have an interest in personality because they are very much aware that there can be some big differences among people. Students are often interested in taking a personality course as a way of finding out more about themselves and other people. Also, students are very aware that personality differences are on display just about wherever you go. For instance, you can see personality differences when you go to a movie. Perhaps you have had the misfortune of sitting behind the one or two people who are talking out loud during the movie despite requests by others to keep quiet. What is it about these people that makes them different from the considerate people who just keep quiet and put up with these individuals?

Personality differences may have been on display while you were travelling to the theatre to see the movie. If you arrived by car, you likely encountered many drivers who were quite considerate of others on the road and who obeyed the law. These "good citizens" can be distinguished from "those other people" who displayed the Type A driving style. Type A people are characterized by speed, impatience, and aggressive tendencies, while Type B people are less impatient and tend to be more co-operative than other people (see Friedman & Rosenman, 1957). In fact, Type A people have been described as "hard-driving." Is this reflected in their driving behaviour? It seems so. A study of bus drivers in India and the United States showed that in both countries, Type A drivers had more accidents than Type B drivers (Evans, Palsane, & Carrere, 1987). Another recent study conducted in France showed that once potential confounding factors (demographic factors and alcohol consumption) were controlled, the risk of being involved in a road traffic accident increased proportionally with Type A scores (Nabi et al., 2005).

Personality differences might have even influenced your decision of which movie to attend. Clearly, people differ in their interests: some people are interested primarily in comedies, while others prefer action-adventure movies or horror movies. Personality may also have come into play if you read some movie reviews prior to making your selection. You can find extensive information on the Internet about the qualities of a movie before deciding whether to watch it. You may have noticed that even with the same movie, expert reviewers can differ widely in their opinions of it, which could reflect different personality styles.

The data in Table 1.1 illustrate this point. The data were taken from a popular Internet site. Table 1.1 lists six movie critics. Each movie is given a rating between "0" and "100" based on the review given by each critic. Ratings are provided for seven well-known movies: (1) *Ocean's 12*, starring George Clooney and Matt Damon, among others; (2) *Pirates of the Caribbean*, starring Johnny Depp; (3) *The Terminal*, starring Tom Hanks; (4) *Closer*, starring Julia Roberts and Jude Law; (5) *Harry Potter and the Prisoner of Azkaban*, starring Daniel Radcliffe; (6) *Troy*, starring Brad Pitt; and (7) Mel Gibson's *The Passion of the Christ*.

Two conclusions can be derived from these data. First, for most films, there is substantial variability among reviewers. Almost uniformly positive reviews were given to the Harry Potter film, but there was great variability in responses and reactions to *The Passion of the Christ*. Ratings for Mel Gibson's movie ranged from the highest possible (100) to a low of 25.

The second point that can be gleaned from Table 1.1 is that, at least to some extent, movie reviews reflect the critics' own personality characteristics and evaluative standards. For instance, the reviews given by Roger Ebert are consistently more positive than the ratings given by some other reviewers represented in this table. Interestingly, this website tabulates how each reviewer compares with other reviewers as new movies are released. Whereas Roger Ebert has given reviews that are more favourable than others about 71% of the time, Rick Groen, a reviewer for Canada's *The Globe and Mail* newspaper, has given reviews that are more favourable than other reviewers only about 45% of the time. Thus, just as some people in our lives are sterner critics, certain movie reviewers are also more demanding in their expectations and appraisals.

Table 1.1 Movie Ratings by Critic (on a scale of 0 to 100)

	Ocean's 12	***Pirates of the Caribbean***	***The Terminal***	***Closer***	***Harry Potter and the Prisoner of Azkaban***	***Troy***	***The Passion of the Christ***
Critic							
Roger Ebert (*Chicago Sun-Times*)	75	75	88	100	88	50	100
Claudia Puig (*USA Today*)	75	88	75	63	88	75	75
Kenneth Turan (*Los Angeles Times*)	50	30	80	60	80	50	50
Richard Corliss (*Time*)	40	90	50	90	80	80	80
Peter Travers (*Rolling Stone*)	50	50	50	88	88	75	75
Rick Groen (*The Globe and Mail*)	50	50	38	75	63	50	25

Source: Data retrieved from www.metacritic.com January 9, 2005. Critics are listed according to their levels of difficulty. Website statistics indicate that the degree to which critics have given above average ratings to movies across all of the movies in the database is as follows: Roger Ebert (71%), Claudia Puig (65%), Kenneth Turan (59%), Richard Corliss (59%), Peter Travers (57%), and Rick Groen (45%).

Given that personality is a topic of great interest to most people at one time or another, this book is designed to inform readers about personality research and theory. And you should learn a fair bit about other people as we go along. There is one important caveat that must be stated from the outset, however. The personality field is enormous and is continually evolving; thus, even though this book attempts to be as comprehensive as possible, it cannot cover everything. Theories and specific themes have been selected for coverage because of their impact on the field or because of their potential relevance and ability to provoke readers into thinking in greater detail about personality topics. Of course, you are encouraged to seek out other sources to find out more about personality.

THE GOALS OF CHAPTER 1

This initial chapter has four main aims. The first goal, obviously, is to define what is meant by "personality." Personality is defined and discussed in terms of the various ways that it can be measured and studied.

The second aim is to outline the goals and purposes of personality research. Multiple goals operate, and it is not enough to merely describe personality differences because we also want to be able to explain how these differences came about in the first place.

The third purpose of this chapter is to outline and highlight several of the key themes that run throughout this book. In total, seven specific themes are identified, including the need to see personality development as the mutual influence of multiple factors, and the need to evaluate personality theory and research from a critical perspective. Try to think back to these themes as you read this book.

Finally, an overview of subsequent chapters is also provided in this chapter. This overview will illustrate the immense scope of the personality field. When it comes to studying personality, there is something for everybody! If you have limited interest in the classic theories that are outlined in the first half of this book, perhaps you will be more interested in some of the more applied chapters later in this book, such as personality and interpersonal relationships, or personality and health.

WHAT IS PERSONALITY?

Personality refers to the external styles of expression that are displayed for others to see.

We have discussed personality but not defined it. So, what is personality? **Personality** refers to relatively stable individual differences that are believed to present early in life and involves characteristics that generalize across time and across situations. We usually discuss personality in terms of the dispositioned factors and associated behaviours that distinguish us and make us different from other people, but there are some personality characteristics and processes that may be at least somewhat similar across individuals.

The term "personality" is derived from the ancient Greek word meaning **persona**. Persona refers to the masks that Greek actors would wear according to which character they were portraying. Thus, although much of our personality lurks inside us and we carry our personality from place to place, the term "personality" actually refers to the external styles of expression that are on display for other people to see.

Although personality researchers focus mostly on the differences between people, we are interested in more than just the differences. In their classic paper, Clyde Kluckhohn and Henry Murray (1953) emphasized different levels of analysis and inquiry by noting that "Every man is in certain respects (a) like all other men, (b) like some other men, (c) like no other man" (Kluckhohn & Murray, 1953, p. 53). Today, of course, it would be more appropriate to state this in more gender-neutral terms as, "Every person is in certain respects (a) like all other people, (b) like some other people, (c) like no other people."

Figure 1.1 is adapted from Runyan (1983). Runyan noted that, in keeping with the views of Kluckhohn and Murray, the scope of personality research includes things that apply to *all people*, things that apply to *defined groups of people*, and things that apply to *specific people*. Universal themes are represented in some of the theories described in subsequent chapters, such as psychodynamic, humanistic, and cognitive theories. As you can see in Figure 1.1, salient group differences come in many different forms. Sex, race, and social class are key demographic factors that are group difference factors of importance. Other important group differences reflect cultural differences and historical differences. The need to consider cultural differences is described in more detail in a subsequent section of this chapter. Finally, anyone (including you) can be studied when the focus is on particular individuals.

Figure 1.1 Levels of Personality Inquiry

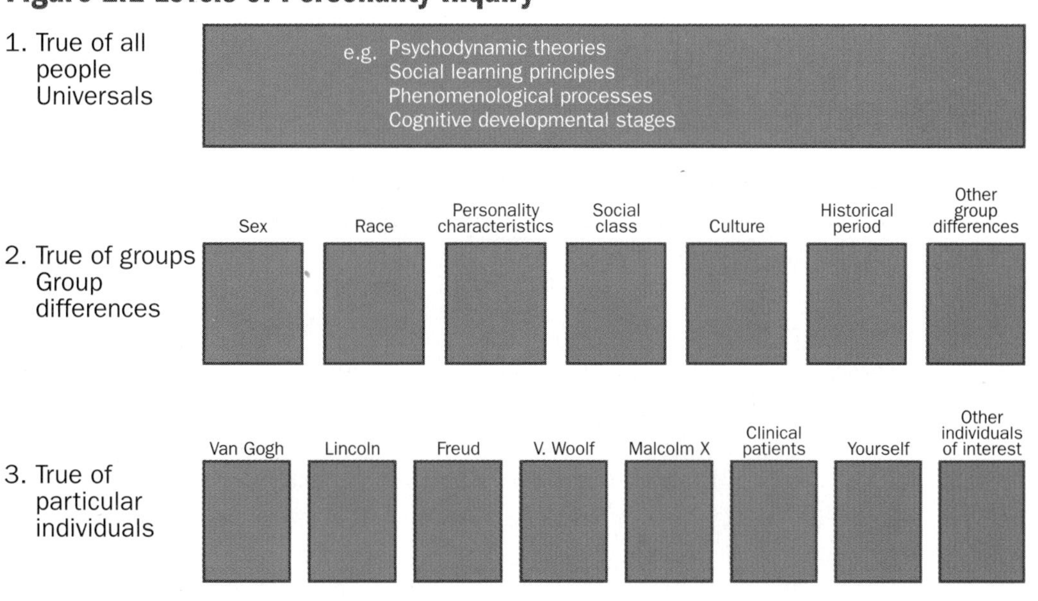

Source: Adapted from Runyan, 1983.

KEY POINTS

- Personality is defined as stable individual differences that are usually detectable early in life and that generalize across time and situations.
- When examining someone's personality, we primarily focus on the ways that they are different from other people, but we sometimes also consider commonalities and similarities among people.
- The term "personality" comes from the word "persona." Persona stems from the public masks that were used to display and express different personalities.

An important aspect of Figure 1.1 is that it emphasizes that, in many respects, to have an interest in the study of personality is the same as having an abiding interest in the study of *people*. A person interested in the study of personality is called a **personologist**, though it would be entirely appropriate to use the term "people-ologist." Personologists have a great interest in finding out how people differ and why they differ. If you are interested in the study of personality, then people probably matter to you a great deal as well!

THE GOALS OF PERSONALITY RESEARCH

Most personality research is guided by three main goals or objectives: description, explanation, and prediction. The first goal is to describe personality differences as completely as possible. What are the key features of personality? How are these features related and to what degree are they related?

The second goal is to explain personality differences. Where did they come from? How did they originate? Why do some people have certain characteristics that are not shared by other people? This desire to explain personality differences is the main reason why we have personality theories.

The third goal is to make predictions about personality in the future based on what is currently known about personality. Will the personality factors in question predict positive outcomes or negative outcomes? Will the personality characteristics prove to be stable over time? What can we expect about a person's future behaviour based on what we know about his or her personality? All of these questions reflect our need to reduce uncertainty about the future by being able to predict future outcomes.

In his classic text on personality and prediction, Jerry Wiggins (1973) discussed the important role that personality assessment plays in prediction. Specifically, Wiggins, a researcher and theorist who spent many years at the University of British Columbia, observed that "Personality assessment has the quite applied aim of generating predictions about certain aspects of behavior that will contribute to decisions concerning the disposition or treatment of individuals" (p. 6). This is a vitally important point because personality measures are used in many parts of the world to make decisions about people based on expectations about their future behaviours.

Regarding these goals of description, explanation, and prediction, it is likely the case that explanation is the most important goal. Many highly regarded personologists have made strong cases for injecting as much theory as possible into the field of personality because theories provide us with explanations. For example, Rotter (1990) argued that it is vitally important to consider theory when developing a measure to assess a new personality variable. He suggested that not only is it important to have clear notions about the theoretical properties of the variable being considered, but it is also important to have formulated a theory of behaviour, including a theory of test-taking behaviours of the people who will ultimately take the personality test designed to tap this new variable. This sentiment was echoed by Canadian personologist Douglas Jackson. As an expert in personality test construction, Jackson (1970, 1971) argued convincingly for the need for personality assessment measures to be derived from theory. According to Jackson, the first general principle of personality scale construction is that "personality measures will have broad import and substantial construct validity to the extent, and only to the extent, that they are derived from an explicitly formulated, theoretically based definition of a trait" (Jackson, 1971, p. 232).

The need to go beyond description to include a focus on explanation is a challenge analogous to that faced by the clinician who must assess, diagnose, and treat abnormal behaviour. When a clinician encounters someone with one or more personality disorders, for instance, the goal is not simply to describe the symptoms and manifestations of these personality disorders; it is to understand these disorders' developmental origins and the personality dynamics that have taken place and are currently taking place within the individual. If recovery due to treatment is to occur, then the disorder's core, underlying causes must be accurately understood and fully addressed in treatment.

Personality Goals from an Idiographic versus a Nomothetic Perspective

> The chances of a hypothetical average man for survival or death are all the insurance business wants to know. Whether Bill himself will be one of the fatal cases it cannot tell—and that is what Bill wants to know.
>
> —*Gordon Allport*

When it comes to the goals of description, explanation, and prediction, the focus can be on a group of people or on a specific individual. The above quote was provided by legendary personologist Gordon Allport. In noting that "Bill" wanted to know the implications for him, Allport alluded to the important distinction he first made in 1937 between the **idiographic** and the **nomothetic** approach to studying personality (see Allport, 1937). As we will see in subsequent chapters of this book, much of personality research is focused on a nomothetic approach.

The nomothetic approach involves gathering a small amount of data from a relatively large sample in the hopes of identifying general laws or principles. The nomothetic approach can be regarded as a variable-centred approach that may tell us, for instance, whether one variable relates to another variable. It looks at personality from a normative perspective.

In contrast, the idiographic approach involves gathering a large amount of data from one person or only a few people (i.e., a case study method). The idiographic approach can be regarded as a person-centred approach because the ultimate goal is to understand the entire person (their traits, life goals, values, personal experiences, and so on). Allport (1962) later suggested replacing the term "idiographic" with **morphogenic** to reflect a greater focus on the pattern or structure that exists within the individual. Allport (1937) made an important plea for personologists to get to know the entire person. This plea has been repeated by various personologists throughout the years.

Information about average trends, the nomothetic approach, does not tell us much about unique individuals such as Shaquille O'Neal. These individuals are best understood according to an idiographic approach.

The goals of description, explanation, and prediction tend to be addressed in very different ways in the personality field depending on whether a nomothetic or idiographic research approach is adopted. A nomothetic approach could, for example, involve describing the extent to which two variables are related, and then seeking to understand why these variables are related. Prediction could also be involved when trying to ascertain the relative ability of these variables to predict a third variable. (For example, are height and weight related to points scored in a basketball league?) In contrast, the idiographic approach would focus on the various characteristics of a particular person, and any attempts at understanding would try to focus on how this person came to have these particular characteristics. For example, in the case of basketball, we could focus on Shaquille O'Neal, perhaps the best player in the National Basketball Association (NBA). Issues involving him possibly being overweight became a central focus in his final year with the Los Angeles Lakers prior to being traded to the Miami Heat in 2004. At a descriptive level, we could chart O'Neal's scoring to determine whether it varied as a function of variability in his weight. An explanatory focus would have us shift the emphasis perhaps to a consideration of the motivational factors that may have influenced his scoring output, and his weight fluctuations. What intrinsic factors and extrinsic factors could explain his performance? Did a conflict with another player (e.g., Kobe Bryant) decrease his motivation to exercise? Finally, based on existing data, we could then try to predict what O'Neal's future performance would be for the Miami Heat.

The important thing to keep in mind when reading research findings derived from a nomothetic approach is that general laws derived from large samples of people may not be useful when seeking to predict the outcome for a particular person. There is no doubt that as a basketball player, Shaquille O'Neal is without peer, so overall averages for the NBA probably tell us very little about what he will be able to accomplish.

KEY POINTS

- Personality involves the goals of description, explanation, and prediction. Explanations come in the form of theories and measures designed to assess personality and should have a theoretical basis that guides scale construction.
- The nomothetic approach involves gathering a small amount of data on a large group of people to identify general themes and principles that apply broadly to the overall group.
- The idiographic approach involves gathering a large amount of data on a small number of people, or indeed, on just one person. The goal here is to fully understand the complexity of these individuals, and there is little concern with generalizing to other people.

The Five Ws: Who, What, When, Where, and Why

One way to make sure that there is an equal focus on the three goals of description, explanation, and prediction is to consider five key questions (the five Ws) for any personality phenomenon of interest. The first question relates to *who*. Who is the person? And from a descriptive perspective, who are the people this person differs from? If this question were examined at a nomothetic level, of course, then the focus would be on identifying a group of people, in terms of who they are, relative to other people.

The next question relates to *what*. In what ways does the person differ? In what ways is he or she similar to others? Or, from a nomothetic perspective, in what ways does a group of people or a sample of people differ from another group of people (e.g., males versus females)?

The third question relates to *when*. It is important to recognize that there is a temporal side to personality. Implicit in the definition of personality and its presumed stability is the notion that people usually differ in some key respects across most points in time. However, there may be some temporal fluctuations that can have an impact on behaviour as well as the association between personality and behaviour.

Revelle (1989) has conducted extensive work on the importance of temporal factors in personality research. For instance, Revelle reminded us that if we are interested in the link between personality and levels of arousal and levels of seeking stimulation, we must acknowledge that there is diurnal variability that must be taken into account. Specifically, people tend to be more aroused in the afternoon and the evening when they are seeking stimulation, while in the morning, they are less likely to be seeking stimulation.

Revelle underscored his point about the need to consider within-person variability across time periods by studying the associations among impulsivity, caffeine, and performance. Impulsivity is a broad and complex personality construct with many characteristics (see McCown, Johnson, & Shure, 1993). If someone is impulsive, they tend to act and react quickly to situations without considering the long-term consequences of inappropriate actions, whereas someone with low impulsivity would be more deliberate and thoughtful. Revelle, Amaral, and Turriff (1976) examined individual differences in performance on the Graduate Record Exam (GRE), an ability-based test that is often used to help select students who have completed their undergraduate degrees and who then wish to pursue graduate studies. Revelle et al. (1976) found that the GRE performance of highly impulsive students is facilitated by caffeine, while the performance of students with low impulsivity is hindered by caffeine when the test is written in the morning. A very different pattern emerges when the test is written in the afternoon or evening. As the day wears on, caffeine begins to facilitate the performance of low impulsive students who benefit from the increased arousal, while the performance of highly impulsive students is hindered in the afternoon or evening. Thus, it is important to consider when personality is being evaluated, in addition to whom and what is being considered. In this instance, whether caffeine improves performance varies as a function of time of day and personality.

The fourth W, which relates to *where*, reflects the fact that behaviours will often be a joint reflection of the personality characteristics involved as well as the situations in which people find themselves. This is a central theme that will be re-examined in Chapters 2 and 3, as well as in other segments of this book. One example of the importance of situational differences is to compare the reactions of people in controllable versus uncontrollable situations (see Endler, Speer, Johnson, & Flett, 2000). According to the goodness of fit model (see Felton & Revenson, 1984; Forsythe & Compas, 1987), coping responses when faced with a problem may vary in their adaptiveness depending on whether the situation is controllable (a situation that favours task-oriented attempts to solve the problem as being adaptive) or the situation is uncontrollable (a situation that favours the emotion-oriented expression of negative emotions as being adaptive). Consideration of the issue of *where* is important because the environmental contexts we find ourselves in can have a substantial impact on our behaviours.

Finally, as indicated earlier, the ultimate W question relates to *why*. As noted above, it is not sufficient to simply describe personality phenomena; we must also attempt to explain it. The theories described in subsequent chapters of this book are important because they represent concepts and processes that may help us understand how certain variables are related, or how a particular person came to have certain characteristics.

OVERARCHING THEMES IN THE PERSONALITY FIELD AND IN THIS BOOK

In addition to the points already raised, there are several other important themes that pervade the study of personality and seem to encompass many aspects of the field. We will now consider seven of these themes as a way of further introducing the topic of personality.

Personality Is a Science

Without a doubt, the study of personality is a science, and the typical personologist can be regarded as a social scientist. However, many people are reluctant to regard the study of personality as a science, and some of this may have to do with the fact that personality is something that can be seen as deep, dark, and mysterious inside each individual, and it is not easy to observe "personality" much of the time. It may also have to do with the fact that the lay public already has some clear ideas about the nature of personality, and personality differences among people, and these beliefs about personality flourish among everyone, including people with little or no scientific background.

This awareness of personality among members of the general public is reflected by a number of sayings that are familiar to most people. These sayings include the notion of a "split personality" to connote someone who is quite inconsistent in their behaviours, as well as the notion of someone having a "magnetic personality" if they are charismatic and attract other people. Other well-known phrases include "no personality" to describe someone who is bland and uninteresting, and "chameleon personality" to describe someone who intentionally changes his or her self-presentation as situations change. Another phrase that emphasizes interpersonal awareness is the notion of a "personality clash"—a long-standing quarrel between two or more individuals.

Most people are characterized by well-articulated **implicit personality theories**. That is, we have developed a tendency to link together certain personality characteristics in our minds. Thus, for example, if we are told that a blind date has "a lot of personality," it is common for people to assume that this person is ugly or at least unremarkable in physical appearance, and the personality description is an attempt to compensate for a lack of physical attractiveness. Anderson (1995) has noted that one implicit theory that causes distress when it is violated is the belief that friendly people are not liars. This belief is particularly inaccurate when it is applied to some of the most infamous psychopaths who have roamed the planet. Serial killers such as Ted Bundy have been described as exceptionally charming and seemingly friendly, so some friendly people may be capable of reprehensible, immoral behaviours. The accuracy of our implicit personality theories is itself a worthy topic for scientific investigation, and this has been the subject of numerous studies.

The degree to which a personality study is regarded as scientific likely varies as a function of the methods used and the topics under investigation. The prototypical study (having a group of students circle responses to items on a questionnaire) does not seem particularly scientific. This contrasts sharply with recent research on the psychobiological aspects of personality. A growing number of investigators are examining the association between personality differences and related neuropsychological differences involving brain structure and brain activity (see Canli & Amin, 2002; Kumari, ffytche, Williams, & Gray, 2004). For instance, Schmidt (1999) from McMaster University in Hamilton, Ontario, examined electroencephalograms (EEG; a measurement of brainwave activity) in undergraduate women who varied in trait levels of sociability and shyness. Schmidt found that sociability was associated with greater left frontal EEG activity. Schmidt also found that a measure of shyness was associated with greater right frontal EEG activity, so he was able to use physiological measures to confirm past suggestions that shyness and sociability are separate dimensions, with shyness reflecting a fearful form of avoidance.

Regardless of whether personality is accepted as a science, the field relies extensively on empirical research findings. These findings have been derived from experimental and correlational studies that are designed in accordance with accepted standards and principles of science.

Personality Is Not Just Common Sense

The willingness to acknowledge that the study of personality is a science is important because many people regard many of the things being studied as "just common sense," and this feeds into the notion that personality is not a science. Cacioppo (2004) observed astutely that when students begin taking a course in most sciences, they typically enter the course with a very limited knowledge of the subject matter. Personality is quite different. Students entering a personality course have had a lifetime of observing personality differences and noting the characteristics that seem to go along with these differences.

This lifetime of experience can foster a great deal of scepticism among some students about the information value of material presented in a personality course (because, after all, they "knew it all along"). Cacioppo (2004) has summarized the problem as follows:

> Because deep-seated prior beliefs and folk theories about personality and social behavior are grounded in years of observation and prior experience, students new to the field may have difficulty feeling that their theories of social behavior are any less valid or substantiated than are those they may learn while reading a textbook or hearing a lecture. Personal testimonials for many of these students continue to carry more weight than statistics evidence about a cherished social attitude or belief. Intuitions constructed from a lifetime of experience are not easily dismissed. (p. 116)

However, there are several problems with equating much of what is studied in personality as just common sense. First, and foremost, one key purpose of empirical research is to determine whether common sense beliefs turn out to be correct. It is sometimes the case that accepted common sense beliefs are false, or at least appear to be false. One clear example of this is the "Blue Monday" phenomenon, which has been reflected in popular songs such as "I Don't Like Mondays" by the Boomtown Rats and "Manic Monday" by the Bangles. These songs reinforce the belief that Mondays are simply a drag. Moreover, it is usually not too difficult to find people who promote the general view that Monday is a bleak day. But is this confirmed by research? Although people have indicated that Saturday is their favourite day and Monday is their least favourite day (see Farber, 1953), a prospective personality study of daily mood reports found no evidence whatsoever of the Blue Monday phenomenon (see Stone, Hedges, Neale, & Satin, 1985).

Another problem involving the notion that personality is "just common sense" is suggested by the results of a survey conducted by noted Yale University psychologist Robert Sternberg. He found that common sense is surprisingly uncommon by and large, and many people overestimate their own degree of common sense. Sternberg conducted an on-line survey in 2004 for a well-known corporation. The sample consisted of 1,000 Americans who were selected via representative sampling. The survey showed that 74% of respondents felt that they had more common sense than most people, and 43% felt that they had a lot more common sense than most people. These overestimates are in keeping with self-positivity biases that have been documented by numerous researchers. In fact, Sternberg analysed responses to his ability test and determined that only about 7% of the sample actually had a high level of common sense perception, with more women than men having exceptional common sense. Thus, common sense is not all that common!

Personality Must Be Viewed from a Critical Thinking Perspective

The ultimate hope is that research training in personality methods and the other psychological methods will prove to be beneficial in creating increasing numbers of critical thinkers who demand to see the data; that is, we need to carefully evaluate theoretical assumptions before accepting claims about the nature of personality. The study of personality is a lot like going through life in that it is better to be a critical thinker who questions and examines information and broad claims rather than simply accepting the proclamations of other people. It is important for students to accept that there is good science and bad science and there is good research and bad research. No study is without limitation, and it is important to consider whether the limitations undermine the conclusions reached by the investigators.

Fortunately, a study conducted at Bishop's University in Quebec showed that research training in psychology does indeed seem to diminish students' willingness to endorse erroneous assertions such as "Clear evidence exists to show that a very small percent of people can receive the thoughts of others and predict the future" (see Standing & Huber, 2003). However, the authors cautioned that progress in reducing myth acceptance by having students take psychology courses is "slow."

One exercise in particular may be especially useful in convincing students of the need to adopt critical thinking skills and regard personality as a science that is more than common sense. The **Barnum effect** is named after P. T. Barnum, the famous circus owner credited with the phrase, "There is a sucker born every minute." The Barnum effect refers to the widespread tendency for people to accept personality feedback provided to them as accurate, even though the feedback itself is quite general and vague. Dickson and Kelly (1985) demonstrated the Barnum effect in the following manner: They administered a personality test to a group of students and then provided each participant with a personality profile that presumably described them. In fact, all students were given the exact same feedback. They found that the vast majority of participants rated the feedback as either a good or excellent description of their personality, even though the feedback was standard and not at all tailored to their actual personalities!

A more recent study by Boyce and Geller (2002) did provide a glimmer of hope, however. These researchers showed the benefits of preparing students by instructing them about the Barnum effect and teaching them research methods and ways to develop critical thinking skills. This preparation had the effect of lowering their belief that graphology (the analysis of handwriting samples) is a science. This effect held for both psychology majors and non-psychology majors!

Readers of this book are encouraged to use a critical thinking perspective and apply it to the material in this book. To help do this and to engage you in learning the material, each chapter is concluded by a summary and a series of questions, for further consideration. Take the time to carefully consider each question because working through this material should not only foster an evaluative mode, it should also help with your initial learning and subsequent retention of the material in memory.

KEY POINTS

- Personality is a science, and is based on theories and empirical research rather than common sense notions. Some common sense notions are supported by research, but many are not.
- Theory and research in personality should be carefully evaluated to determine whether the conclusions reached are valid. Students who receive training in research methods and critical thinking are less likely to endorse beliefs that are not supported by data.
- The Barnum effect reflects the tendency for people to perceive that general, ambiguous feedback about personality actually applies to them.

Personality Development Reflects Multiple Influences

The next section discusses the fact that many personality features involve a complex array of factors. As we will see in Chapter 3, these complexities often go well beyond common sense and everyday accounts of personality factors.

It is generally accepted that personality development reflects factors inside of the individual as well as the external circumstances. Interactionists accept the notion that behaviour reflects the complex interplay of the person and situational factors, and then the consequences of behaviour shape and influence the person and the situation in an ongoing sequence. Contemporary developmental accounts view personality as due to multiple influences. For instance, Thompson and Goodvin (2005), in their description of "the individual child," argued that personality reflects the complex interplay of temperament, emotion, and the development of the self, and these, in turn, are influenced by and exert an influence on the social world. A key point to emphasize is that other people are part of the environment, and the environment changes readily as a function of whom we encounter in our daily lives. A central issue here is whether a person's temperament fits with the environment and there is a match or mismatch (E.g., does a highly active child have parents who can keep up this pace?).

Note that the factors that influence personality development may themselves have multiple determinants. For example, in a recent review, Belsky and Jaffee (in press) document the multiple determinants of parenting. Parenting contributes directly to personality development. Parenting itself can be influenced by a host of factors, including the parent's temperament, the amount of experience as a parent, the quality of the relationship between the parents, socio-economic status, and so on.

To underscore the roles of multiple factors, consider the many factors that can influence self-esteem differences in adolescents. Adolescence has been described as a life period of "storm and stress" because of the numerous changes that occur, and many of these changes can contribute to differences in self-esteem. The list of factors that play a role include physical maturation and pubertal changes, peer influence, family influence, cultural influences, temperament, and actual levels of ability (for discussions, see Robins, Trzesniewski, Tracy, Gosling, & Potter, 2002; Rosenberg, 1986). Given the numerous possible influences, it is evident that two adolescents might have a similar level of self-esteem, but how they arrived at that same level could be very different.

Factors influencing personality development may themselves have multiple determinants. For example, adolescence, which contributes to differences in self-esteem, is affected by factors such as pubertal change and peer influence.

Personality Must Be Studied from a Cross-Cultural Perspective

It was seen earlier in Figure 1.1 that the role of culture is included as one important group difference factor that must be taken into account in "the study of lives." One feature of this book (and the personality field in general) is that wherever possible, an attempt has been made to incorporate a cross-cultural emphasis.

What is the link between personality and culture? **Clyde Kluckhohn** (1954) provided an excellent overview of the topic of personality and culture. Although this research is dated in some respects, most of the points made by Kluckhohn hold up very well over time. Kluckhohn argued that there is a functional interdependence between culture and personality. He also stated that culture should not be equated with personality because culture is only one part of personality. He probably felt that it was necessary to make this point in response to the National Character Studies that were in vogue at the time (see Chapter 2). Table 1.2 consists of an overview of nine points about personality and culture made by Kluckhohn (1954). Review these assumptions because they are valid points about personality and culture and how culture relates to personality development.

In recent years, one of the most exciting developments in the personality field is the growth of research on personality from a cross-cultural perspective. Much of this has to do with the increasing popularity of models such as the five-factor model (see Chapter 2), which is based on the assumption that there are universal personality frameworks that can be applied to everyone, no matter their country of origin. Regardless of whether you agree or disagree with this bold statement, it is clear that this kind of thinking has served as a major catalyst for research with an international scope. This has been facilitated by the advent of the Internet, which has made it increasingly possible to contact researchers around the world and perhaps engage in collaborative research with them. The research we have conducted in our laboratory on perfectionism, for example, has been enriched and strengthened considerably by collaborative investigations with Avi Besser from Israel (see Besser, Flett, & Hewitt, 2004).

Table 1.2 Kluckhohn's Assumptions about Personality and Culture

1. There is a functional interdependence between personality and culture.
2. Total cultures never completely determine individual personalities, but prevailing beliefs about different ideal personalities and associated training practices have their effects on personality.
3. A culture may influence personality long after the external and observable aspects of culture are apparently gone.
4. Culture is not behaviour. It is only one aspect of behaviour. People behave, not cultures.
5. Certain cultures influence people by generating tensions and thwarting basic human needs.
6. We need to distinguish between the explicit culture (the objectively defined culture) and the implicit culture (the subjectively defined culture).
7. Cultures are invariably more complex than how they are reflected in both dated stereotypes and current conceptualizations.
8. We should be aware of both the universals and divergences across cultures.
9. Cultures condition individuals, but individuals also condition cultures.

Diener and Scollon (2002) reviewed major trends in the personality field and argued that the link between personality predispositions and culture and society is one topic that merits increased attention. At the same time, they noted that the personality field has taken on much more of an international focus in recent years. Specifically, they stated that:

> For many of the past decades, North America has dominated the field of psychology. Although there have been pockets of strengths beyond US borders, such as Eysenck's laboratory and personality research in continental Europe, the majority of empirical work has come from the US. We believe that this is changing, and that personality psychology is now truly an international science. Several groups of personality scientists exist in Europe, while Canada, Israel, and Australia possess a number of outstanding laboratories. (Diener & Scollon, 2002, p. 633–634)

The conclusions reached by Diener and Scollon are quite reasonable, and it is likely that personality science will become even more international in the future. There has been unprecedented growth of cross-cultural research in personality over the past five years. Accordingly, to underscore this theme, whenever possible in this book, research examples from around the world will be used to illustrate key points as inclusively as possible. Substantive findings derived from research with a cross-cultural emphasis are described in several segments of the book, and consideration is also given to the role of cultural factors in personality assessment and in personality development. Moreover, each chapter in this book will have at least one International Focus on Discovery feature, which examines a personality issue from an international perspective.

Consider the material presented in International Focus on Discovery 1.1. There are widespread differences in the extent to which people believe that there is a link between physical attributes and personality. As illustrated, some people strongly endorse the belief that blood type characteristics relate to personality characteristics.

One final comment about studying cultural differences needs to be expressed at this point. Once it is established that cultural factors are relevant to a particular personality phenomenon, it is not enough to stop there. It still has to be determined which aspect of culture is important and why it is important. Ideally, when acknowledging the role of culture, there is a need for a focus on both description and explanation. According to Heine and Norenzayan (2006), there are at least three different types of explanation for cultural group differences: (1) **evoked culture** (people occupy different ecological niches that evoke different cognitive tendencies in people); (2) **transmitted culture** (differences are transmitted from one generation to the next via processes such as social learning and imitation); and (3) **genetic variation** (the more controversial notion that psychological differences between cultures reflect genetic differences). Heine and Norenzayan (2006) presented evidence in favour of their conclusion that group differences are mostly due to cultural transmission.

International Focus on Discovery 1.1 Personality and Blood Type in Japan

In Japan, some people believe that personality differences are determined, at least in part, by a person's blood type. That is, it is believed that there are differences between people according to whether they have blood type A, B, O, or AB. According to Ando (1995), a psychology professor, a majority of Japanese university students answer "yes" when asked whether blood typing reveals a man's personality.

Maruko (2001) traced this view back to 1916 when a Japanese doctor named Kimata Hara published a paper linking blood group to personality. In 1925, the Japanese military gathered blood type information to help identify the strengths and weaknesses of soldiers.

Extensive media coverage in Japan is one factor that has contributed to the continuing fascination with blood type and personality among certain segments of the population (Maruko, 2001; Miller, 1997).

Note that beliefs in the link between blood type and personality have spread to other regions besides Japan. For instance, in 2005, a popular romantic comedy in South Korea was the movie *My Boyfriend Type B* (his girlfriend had Type A blood).

According to Maruko (2001), the theoretical link between blood type and personality was outlined originally by Furakawa Tajeki, a professor at Tokyo Women's Teacher's School, in an article entitled "The study of temperament through blood type." Type A blood is associated with being reserved, mild-mannered, and full of worry. Tajeki labelled people with Type A blood as "farmers" who are cautious and calmly obey rules.

Type B blood is associated with being cheerful, independent, and light-hearted. The adventurousness of people with Type B blood led Tajeki to label them as "hunters."

Type O blood leads to being calm, patient, strong-willed, self-controlled, and full of confidence along with a calm and quiet outward appearance. According to Tajeki, these people are romantic and proud and share the features of "warriors."

Finally, Type AB blood is associated with the external presentation of Type B characteristics on the outside, but Type A features on the inside. Tajeki referred to people with this blood type as "humanists" who are sensitive to their surroundings and the needs of others.

Do you accept the possibility that personality may be determined by blood type? Do you even know your own blood type? Here we see the value of empirical research. Investigations have yielded some evidence of a link between blood type and personality, but there is no substantial association. Extensive work on this issue was conducted in Japan by Nomi (1985), who reported numerous associations, including a tendency for people with Type O blood to be overrepresented among people who hit a pedestrian while driving. Research on personality and blood type has also been conducted in North America. Raymond Cattell and his associates conducted extensive work on this issue, and did find some evidence of links between personality and blood type. For instance, they found that anxious characteristics did differ according to blood type in the predicted manner (Cattell, Brackenridge, Case, Propert, & Sheehy, 1980), and other research suggested that blood type O was associated with a more tense personality style (Swan, Hawkins, & Douglas, 1980).

Overall, even when associations are found between blood type and personality, they tend to be relatively low in magnitude. Regardless of whether you believe that personality is linked with blood type, it is important to be aware that many people in Japan do believe in these associations. Some have suggested that if you visit Japan, it is more likely that you will be asked about your blood type than your astrological sign. More importantly, this information has been used to group people in various settings and to differentially treat people. For example, according to Miller (1997), a nursery school in Saitama used blood type information to divide young children into groups, and Mitsubishi Electronics used blood type information to form product development teams composed solely of employees with the AB blood type.

Finally, according to Thatcher (2005), it is now possible in Japan to purchase blood type chewing gum, soft drinks, calendars, and condoms. The condoms are the same but instructions vary on how to use them based on your blood type.

Personality Differences Are Expressed in Many Ways

Individual differences in personality can be expressed in myriad different ways. In this section, five modes of personality expression are briefly described. Specifically, personality can be reflected or expressed by individual differences in emotions, behaviours, cognitions, motivational properties, and social tendencies. People differ in their actions, but they also tend to differ in their characteristic emotional tendencies. For example, some people tend to have intense emotions, while others have emotions of mild or moderate intensity. Individual differences in emotional intensity are assessed with the Affect Intensity Measure (Larsen & Diener, 1987). People can also differ in their level of emotional expressiveness, with some people being very expressive, while other people are less likely to show their emotions. People can also differ in their cognitive styles and thinking patterns, their needs, personal goals, and motives, and in their typical interpersonal styles.

The multiple forms of personality expression are illustrated by the trait hostility personality construct. Someone who is usually antagonistic and harsh toward other people would be high in trait hostility. Trait hostility is a complex construct that has affective, behavioural, cognitive, motivational, and social features. First, the affective or mood component of trait hostility has been demonstrated in countless studies. One common finding is that people who are typically high in trait hostility (i.e., hostile personalities) also tend to be high in state hostility (i.e., current levels of hostility in specific situations), especially when they have encountered a situation that invokes feelings of anger and hostility (see Anderson, Anderson, Dill, & Deuser, 1998).

Regarding the behavioural component, hostility reflects antagonistic behaviours toward other people (Smith, 1992). These behaviours were documented by Smith, McGonigle, and Benjamin (1998) in a study of adult male twins. They showed that those with high self-reported levels of hostility were described by their twin siblings as engaging in hostile and controlling behaviour at times, while being neglectful at other times.

At the cognitive level, hostile people have been described as suffering from a fundamental inability to trust other people. Trait hostility is associated with a cynical perception that other people are unreliable and are likely sources of mistreatment (see Smith, 1992). Hostile people have a negative attributional bias that involves blaming negative outcomes on the dispositions and actions of other people (see Pope, Smith, & Rhodewalt, 1990). This extends to having hostile expectations about other people and interpreting their ambiguous behaviours as hostile (Dill, Anderson, Anderson, & Deuser, 1997).

At the motivational level, it is usually assumed that hostile people are characterized by elevated levels of arousal and malevolent motives such as the desire to retaliate against others for some presumed misdeed. Indeed, thoughts of revenge constitute one element of the Hostile Automatic Thoughts Questionnaire (see Snyder et al., 1997). Hostile people are also motivated to engage in the fight or flight response. Cannon (1932) described a sympathetic nervous system response to either aggress (fight) or to hide (flight) when confronted with a stressful situation that involves perceived harm or the possibility of harm. A series of experiments by Lindsay and Anderson (2000) confirmed that students high in trait hostility did indeed have increased fight and flight tendencies when threatened. Thus, trait hostility can reflect the desire to retaliate (fight) but it can also reflect a desire to escape, perhaps because hostile people expect others to also engage in hostile behaviour.

Note that the fight and flight motives among hostile people contribute to apparent differences in interpersonal behaviour. Shelly Taylor and her associates have argued that the tendency to flee or to fight and confront other people is primarily a male tendency, while females of various ages are much more likely to be motivated by a desire to "tend-and-befriend" during stressful times. This affiliative response reflects females' greater investment in attachment and caregiving systems (see Taylor et al., 2000). This apparent difference serves as a reminder to consider possible gender differences in personality.

Overall, we have seen that trait hostility can be examined in terms of affect, behaviour, cognition, motivation, and social factors. This should give you some sense of the many different ways to express individual differences.

The Practical, Applied Side of Personality

As suggested earlier, personality theory and research has many practical applications. While efforts to gain knowledge simply for the sake of knowledge are noble and certainly have their place, personality research seems particularly impressive when it can enhance peoples' lives.

Personality factors have importance in a variety of domains that pertain to our daily roles (such as in the workplace) and the important relationships in our lives. Ozer and Benet-Martinez (2006) have summarized many of the practical aspects of personality in a contemporary review paper titled "Personality and the prediction of consequential outcomes." Their paper highlights the role of personality at three different levels: (1) the individual; (2) interpersonal relationships; and (3) society. Personality outcomes at the individual level include happiness, physical health, psychological health, and personal identity. Personality relates to a wide range of interpersonal relationships, including family relationships, peer relationships, and dating and marital relationships. Finally, at the societal level, personality can have an impact on community involvement and engaging in pro-social or anti-social and criminal activities.

Accordingly, each chapter of this book includes a special feature called Applied Perspective, which highlights the practical applications of personality. Applied Perspective 1.1 focuses on the role of personality factors in the selection of astronauts.

KEY POINTS

- Personality has multiple determinants both inside and outside the person.
- Personality has many practical applications. Personality has consequences for the individual, for social relationships, and for society.
- Personality is expressed (or revealed) in many ways. Personality is expressed in terms of related differences in affect, behaviour, cognition, motivation, and interpersonal tendencies.

Applied Perspective 1.1 Individual Differences in Space and the "Right Stuff" Personality

Evidence continues to indicate that personality differences can predict outcomes in space exploration, and it is becoming increasingly obvious that psychologists can play a vital role in space flight and exploration (see Suedfeld, 2003). Endler (2004) suggested that psychologists in general and personality researchers in particular can have input at four specific stages in space flight to help to ensure successful missions. Specifically, they can play a role in (1) personnel selection; (2) training; (3) real or simulated space missions; and (4) post-flight problems as they return to their families. There is a need to conceptualize space flight as a process that begins with the selection of astronauts (or cosmonauts) and their training via various forms of assessment, including personality testing, and culminates with what occurs during space flight (simulated or real), and post flight factors and adjustments (i.e., psychological re-entry).

Peter Suedfeld from the University of British Columbia and Gary Steel from Lincoln University in New Zealand have also discussed how personality factors are linked with environmental psychology. That is, personality is linked with the ability to cope with living in confined capsule habitats (see Suedfeld & Steel, 2000).

Psychological investigations have focused extensively on the role of personality factors in space flight. This research has either examined samples of actual astronauts (e.g., McFadden, Helmreich, Rose, & Fogg, 1994; Rose, Fogg, Helmreich, & McFadden, 1994) and astronaut candidates (e.g., Sekiguchi, Umikura, Sone, & Kume, 1994) or people in physically isolated, terrestrial environments (e.g., Sandal, 1998), with the assumption that these **analogue situations** provide the sorts of challenges encountered in space. Helmreich and associates have used the Personal Characteristics Inventory to identify desirable personality characteristics and undesirable personality characteristics (see Bishop & Primeau, 2002; Helmreich, 2001).

Favourable characteristics of astronauts have been referred to as the **right stuff personality** while unfavourable characteristics have been described as the **wrong stuff personality**. The term "right stuff" is derived from the famous book on the original Mercury astronaut program by author Tom Wolfe, which was turned into the movie *The Right Stuff*. According to Bishop and Primeau (2002), the "right stuff" personality includes high levels of task focus, positive interpersonal orientation, and achievement motivation, and low levels of hostility, aggressiveness, and competitiveness. In contrast, the "wrong stuff" personality includes low levels of task focus, interpersonal orientation, and achievement motivation, and high levels of hostility, aggressiveness, impatience, and competitiveness. Hostility, aggressiveness, impatience, and competitiveness are all features of the Type A personality described at the beginning of this chapter.

Favourable personality characteristics of astronauts include high levels of task focus, positive interpersonal orientation, and low levels of hostility, aggressiveness, and competitiveness

A third category involving the "no stuff" personality has also been detected. The "no stuff" personality shares many of the negative personality characteristics of the wrong stuff personality, but it is also relatively low in the mastery, work, and competitiveness orientations.

Research has shown that the right, wrong, and no stuff personalities predict meaningful performance differences in astronauts (McFadden et al., 1994; Rose et al., 1994). These various personalities have also predicted performance differences among aircrews, submariners, and military recruits (see Palinkas, 2001, for a review). An illuminating book by Santy (1994) summarizes earlier research involving personality factors and their role in assessment and evaluation.

Bishop and Primeau (2002) also illustrated how measures of broad personality traits reflecting the five-factor model (see Chapter 2) can reveal whether a person is capable of high functioning in extreme environments. Analyses have also been done of the interpersonal climates associated with actual space missions (e.g., Kanas et al., 2001) and other settings characterized as extreme environments (see Suedfeld & Steel, 2000).

Although salient personality differences have been identified and seem to relate to performance difference, a study of applicants by Musson, Sandal, and Helmreich (2004) suggests that personality factors may be underused or underemphasized in astronaut selection. They found that the three types of applicants (right stuff, wrong stuff, no stuff) were clearly evident when responses to the Personal Characteristics Inventory and a five-factor personality inventory were analysed. However, the personality information did not have an impact on which of the 63 out of 259 applicants were eventually selected as astronauts. If personality factors are important, then it follows from this finding that personality information is under used.

The complex interplay of personality and cultural factors continues to be of great interest, in part because of the International Space Station, which is arguably the most complex international science project in history. It involves 16 nations: the United States, Canada, Japan, Russia, Brazil, and the 11 nations of the European Space Agency. Clearly, the ability of representatives from these nations to get along with each other will be a key factor in determining the station's success. In fact, one simulation study conducted by researchers representing the Canadian Space Agency found that real and perceived cultural factors interacted with non-cultural factors to precipitate conflict situations (Tomi, Rossokha, & Hosein, 2002).

Other research conducted by graduate student Suzan Kiesel from Western Kentucky University appears to illustrate many important themes involving the associations among culture, environment, and personality (see Myers & Perkins, 2001). Kiesel interviewed astronauts and cosmonauts at the Johnson Space Center in Houston, Texas. The results showed some salient differences between Americans and Russians in workplace communication, but some key similarities also emerged. In terms of differences, Kiesel learned that Russian cosmonauts tend to operate from a top-down model in which the team leader is at the top of a hierarchy, and this person has substantial control over other team members. This was described as "boss-oriented instruction." In contrast, American astronauts use an approach with more of an emphasis on equality and shared responsibilities. Another difference that was noted is that astronauts seemed more task-oriented, while the Russian cosmonauts were more interested in developing strong personal bonds and relationships.

As for similarities, the astronauts and cosmonauts reported that they had grown to appreciate the things they have in common, such as a love of flying, a great drive for success, and, of course, strong interest in space exploration. They characterized themselves as "cut from the same cloth" (Myers & Perkins, 2001, p. 10).

How did personality factors enter into the picture? Kiesel reported that almost all of the astronauts and cosmonauts felt that individual personality traits had the most significant impact on their interactions. One NASA astronaut summed this up as follows:

> There's so much variation ... from person to person that it's not clear to me that, you know, you can say well *all Russians* are like this or *all Americans* are like this and that it *means* anything ... some people are certainly easier to get along with than others and I think it's more up to the person ... it's more important *whom* you fly with than what the *mission* is. (Myers & Perkins, 2001, p. 11)

The personality measures studied thus far have provided some useful information, but further developments can be obtained by including a focus on other personality measures (such as coping factors) that have received little empirical attention in space research thus far.

ORGANIZATION OF THIS BOOK

As promised, this chapter concludes with a brief overview of the organization of the book and the subsequent chapters. The first four chapters are designed to introduce what is meant by personality and the broad scope of personality research and theory. Chapter 2 highlights the differences between personality traits and types and the ways that they are conceptualized and studied. Chapter 3 addresses how personality develops. The numerous factors, both inside and outside the person, that contribute to personality development are described. The roles of these various factors are illustrated by considering the development of Type A behaviour in children. Chapter 4 is designed to provide some important background on research methods in personality. This chapter describes various research methods, and also discusses the current predominant types of personality research being conducted.

The next six chapters focus on the various theories that have been formulated to explain individual differences. The emphasis is on classic theories and how they differ in the factors and processes used to account for individual differences. Chapter 5 focuses on psychodynamic theories, beginning with the highly influential and controversial views of Sigmund Freud. Freud's views are contrasted with classical neo-Freudian theorists such as Alfred Adler, Karen Horney, and Carl Jung. In many respects, Chapter 6 is an extension of Chapter 5 because its focus on motivational theories is centred on the contributions of Henry Murray. Like the theorists in Chapter 5, Murray emphasized the role of the unconscious, but he examined personality in terms of individual differences in personal needs. Murray's list of needs and his theorizing about motivational differences has provided the basis for many well-known personality inventories.

Chapter 7 acknowledges the contributions of humanists such as Carl Rogers and Abraham Maslow. These humanists are also known as "self-actualization theorists" in that they emphasize the need for people to maximize their full potential. These theorists are also represented because they provided us with an important message about the goodness of people and the need to focus on positive outcomes and well-being, rather than continuing the general preoccupation that psychology has with maladjustment. The current movement in psychology is the study of **positive psychology**, and Rogers and Maslow provided much of the original impetus for us to analyse growth, personal development, and well-being rather than analysing such things as tension, anxiety, and dysfunction.

Chapters 8 to 10 reflect three of the ways that personality can be expressed, through behaviour, cognition, and interpersonal tendencies. Chapter 8 reflects the great influence of the behavioural and learning theorists who predominated in the 1960s and 1970s. Classic behaviourists such as B. F. Skinner and John Watson were not personality theorists per se, but they had many useful and insightful things to say about how regularities and consistencies in behaviour are acquired. Our analysis of learning factors and processes is quite broad, and, accordingly, Chapter 8 also includes a description of social learning theory and the process of learning via imitation as part of social cognitive theory.

Individual differences in cognitive factors and cognitive processes are examined in Chapter 9. In addition to examining key personality constructs with a cognitive emphasis (e.g., field dependence versus independence, cognitive rigidity), Chapter 9 also includes an overview of the personal construct theory put forth by classic theorist George Kelly. Kelly's work is especially important because it has formed the basis for much work on the practical applications of personality theory.

Chapter 10 reinforces the fact that much of personality is social. In this chapter, we discuss the role of personality in interpersonal functioning by examining such topics as personality and adjustment in dating and marital relationships. Equally important is the focus in this chapter on interpersonal theories and models, such as the interpersonal circumplex and Harry Stack Sullivan's interpersonal model.

Although the specific theories examined vary across Chapters 5 to 10, common features can be found throughout these chapters. For instance, these theories have often provided the impetus for extensive research designed to test the theorists' assertions. Research findings testing these assertions are cited throughout these chapters. In addition, the various theoretical orientations outlined in Chapters 5 through 10 are evaluated from a critical perspective that highlights both the strengths and limitations of each theory. Consistent with our critical thinking perspective, you are encouraged to evaluate each theory and reach your own conclusions about the merits of its theoretical orientation.

Chapters 11 to 13 focus on specific topics and themes that tend to be of great interest to students, either because of their personal relevance, or because the topics highlight the role of personality in adaptive and maladaptive tendencies. Chapter 11 is a detailed analysis of personality and the self. Research and theory on personality and the self is quite extensive, so some difficult choices had to be made in Chapter 11 about what material could be covered, given space limitations. The breadth of available topics on personality and the self-concept is indicated by the mere fact that this topic can be a course on its own.

Chapter 12 examines the role of personality factors in stress, coping, and health outcomes. This is a topic that has gained in importance over the past decade as findings continue to emerge that link personality with good and bad health outcomes. There are many factors that contribute to a person's health status, but for many people, their personalities and associated behaviours play a vital role.

Chapter 13 reflects the role of personality factors in mental health by examining personality and psychopathology. It discusses personality dysfunction in the form of personality disorders, and the merits of examining personality dysfunction from a categorical versus dimensional perspective. In addition, we consider the role of personality factors in specific forms of maladjustment (depression and binge drinking). These areas of maladjustment were selected because they represent common problems for many students.

The final chapter of this book serves two purposes. Chapter 14 examines personality from a psychobiographical approach that entails case studies of specific people. The first aim of Chapter 14 is to return to a theme expressed earlier in the book about the need to study the whole person as a complex and unique entity rather than focusing on personality variables in isolation. The strengths and limitations of psychobiography are described, and brief psychobiographical sketches of well-known people are provided.

The second purpose of Chapter 14 is to serve as a mini-review. Concepts and theories introduced in earlier chapters are invoked to describe and explain the personalities of the people featured in Chapter 14. This will underscore the fact that the same person can be viewed from many different theoretical perspectives.

In closing Chapter 1, it is important to emphasize that people are very complicated beings, and the study of personality is just as complicated. Although personality has been studied formally and informally for many decades, a strong case can be made that we are just in the early stages and, to paraphrase the noted poet Robert Frost, we have "miles to go before [we] sleep." It is the hope of this author that you will enjoy the voyage and maybe continue this journey in your future studies.

Summary

Personality is the study of individual differences. Although much of the field focuses on factors and variables that can be used to distinguish individuals, there are universal factors and processes that are shared by everyone. Research at different levels of analysis can focus on how all people are similar or how certain people are similar (versus other dissimilar people), or research can focus on the uniqueness of a particular individual.

Personality research is guided by the goals of description, explanation, and prediction. Explanation is seen as vitally important because there is a need to understand why people are different and how different personalities emerge.

Most personality research adopts a nomothetic perspective. The focus is on identifying general laws and normative principles that apply to large groups of people. Allport and others have argued for more of an idiographic focus that seeks to examine the complexities and intricacies of the individual person.

The personality field is guided centrally by a number of overarching themes. Themes discussed in this chapter include the notion that personality is a science and requires a scientific approach, and personality is much more than common sense. Students are encouraged to adopt a critical thinking perspective when interpreting theory and research in the personality field. It was also noted that personality differences are expressed and revealed in many different ways, and it is important to consider the respective roles of emotional, cognitive, motivational, behavioural, and interpersonal factors. Similarly, personality development is seen as the product of multiple influences that contribute dynamically to individual differences. It was also emphasized that there is a growing emphasis on studying personality from a cross-cultural perspective, and the personality field is being increasingly international in scope. Finally, the practical and applied aspects of personality were emphasized, and this was illustrated by a consideration of the role of personality factors in the selection of astronauts and adaptation to space travel.

Questions to Consider

1 Reflect on the descriptions provided above of the "right stuff," "wrong stuff," and "no stuff" personalities. Based on your self-observations, if you were selected for astronaut or cosmonaut training, do you think you have the right stuff, the wrong stuff, or regrettably, no stuff? Do you think that personality makes a real difference in astronaut selection?

2 Imagine that you are in charge of the International Space Station and you can choose anyone you want to participate. Would you select people who are very similar in their personalities ("birds of a feather"), or would you want people with different personalities and different

skills ("opposites attract")? How important are personality factors in your choices? Do you think the personality factors would become more important or less important over time?

3 Now that you know about the Barnum effect, are you willing to accept general feedback as descriptive of your personality? You can test yourself with the personality profile feedback that Boyce and Geller (2002) gave to their students as part of their demonstration of the Barnum effect. Students were told:

> You have a strong need for other people to like and to admire you. You have a tendency to be critical of yourself. You pride yourself on being an independent thinker and do not accept other opinions without satisfactory proof. You have found it unwise to be too frank in revealing yourself to others. At times you are extraverted, mild-mannered, and social; at other times you are introverted, wary, and reserved. Some of your aspirations tend to be pretty unrealistic. It seems like you are nursing a grudge against someone; you really ought to let that go. You worry about things more than you let on, even to your best friends. You are adaptable to social situations and your interests are wide ranging.

Does this personality profile describe you? Of course, there is always the possibility that it is a highly accurate description of you, and, of course, you are one of the exceptions because Barnum must have been referring to "other people."

4 What would you tell someone who questioned the scientific aspects of personality? What would you say if they claimed that personality, like much of psychology, is just common sense?

5 Think about the person whom you identify as your best friend. List some factors that might have played a role in shaping your friend's personality.

Key Terms

analogue situations, p. 21
Barnum effect, p. 13
explicit culture, p. 16
evoked culture, p. 17
genetic variation, p. 17
idiographic, p. 7
implicit culture, p. 16
implicit personality theories, p. 11
morphogenic, p. 8
nomothetic, p. 7
persona, p. 5
personality, p. 4
personologist, p. 6
positive psychology, p. 23
right stuff personality, p. 21
transmitted culture, p. 17
wrong stuff personality, p. 21

Key Theorists

Clyde Kluckhohn, p. 15

chapter two

UNITS OF PERSONALITY: TYPES VERSUS TRAITS

Because a concern for traits and individuals has been the dual concern of trait psychologists, it has been easy simply to accept traits and situations as adversaries in accounting for variance, whereas it is more appropriate to juxtapose the individual and the situation. Traits are inventions, and there is no reason for believing that they should account for all of the person variance.

—KENNETH BOWERS (1973, P. 325).

It is easy to forget, when considering human behavior, how similar we all are to each other.

—WILLIAM REVELLE (1995, P. 301)

SUPPOSE YOU ARE ASKED to describe the personality of a woman you have known for many years. When describing her outlook on life, you could say, "She's an optimist," or "She's a pessimist." Or would you be more likely to say, "She's a bit of an optimist," or "She's a bit of a pessimist?"

When asked how outgoing she is, would you say, "Wow—she really likes to be with people, she's a real extrovert," or "She likes to keep to herself. She's an introvert"? Does this sound realistic? Might you be more likely to say, "She's a little bit extroverted; she can be outgoing at times and reserved at other times"? Categorizing someone as either a pessimist or an optimist or as an extrovert or introvert reflects a type approach to personality. In contrast, characterizing someone as somewhat optimistic or as being a little bit extroverted or a lot extroverted reflects a dimensional trait approach. The type approach is now described.

PERSONALITY TYPES

Personality types are discrete categories that differ qualitatively in kind rather than in degree. Personality types are categories that can involve a constellation of personality characteristics that are present in an all-or-none fashion. Can you recall an example from Chapter 1 of a personality type?

One benefit of the categorical approach is that the types usually consist of multiple personality characteristics that cluster together and the combination of characteristics predicts certain outcomes (e.g., the risk of violence, aggression, and abuse). Studies that examine personality traits from a dimensional trait perspective often focus on specific traits in isolation and do not consider how multiple personality factors combine within the same person to create a qualitatively distinct type that predicts behavioural outcomes.

If two types are being used to characterize a group of people, then everyone must fall into one or the other category. Unfortunately, the use of discrete types may obscure some important differences among people within the same category; that is, there may be substantial heterogeneity among people with the same type.

Sheldon's Somatotype Theory

Sheldon (1942) provided a famous example of personality types. He posited a link between body types and personality temperaments. This work built on observations made by two ancient Greek physicians—Hippocrates in 400 BC, and Galen in 160 AD—about the link between temperament and the balance of four bodily humours. According to Hippocrates, the four bodily humours of importance are blood, black bile, yellow bile, and phlegm. According to Galen, too much blood results in a passionate and fiery temperament. Too much black bile results in a melancholic, sad temperament. Too much yellow bile contributes to a choleric, angry temperament. Finally, too much phlegm contributes to a lethargic, easygoing temperament. The next time you come across someone who is depressed, see if it cheers them up by telling them that they might be suffering from too much black bile!

Rather than being interested in bodily fluids, Sheldon (1942) focused on somatotypes or body types. It is a type theory because Sheldon studied three main body types and associated personality characteristics. These body types and their associated features are summarized in Table 2.1. The three body types involve being excessively thin (the ectomorphic body type), medium and somewhat muscular (the mesomorphic body type), or overweight (the endomorphic body type). People characterized by ectomorphy were hypothesized to be high in cerebrotonia, which involves being socially restrained and high in the need for privacy. People characterized by mesomorphy were hypothesized to be high in somatotonia, which included an emphasis on physical assertion and high activity level. Finally, the larger size of endomorphy was believed to be associated with viscerotonia, which is a love of relaxation and comfort.

KEY POINTS

- Personality types are discrete categories that differ qualitatively from each other. In a personality typology, everyone must fit into one and only one of the categories.
- Sheldon's theory is a type theory because it postulates three body types and associated personalities.
- The three somatotypes postulated by Sheldon are ectomorphs (underweight), mesomorphs (muscular and average weight), and endomorphs (overweight).

Sheldon coined the term "constitutional psychology" to reflect the link between personality and physical attributes. Sheldon (1942) conducted his empirical research by capitalizing on the fact that male students at Yale University had to get photographed individually in the university gymnasium. Sheldon assessed the somatotype of each student, who was photographed in the nude, and then rated their temperament characteristics after studying each student. As an aside, Sheldon continued this practice of photographing students for many years, and, in 1950, he was asked to leave the University of Washington at Seattle when photographs were also taken of female undergraduates and one young woman complained to university officials! This practice of photographing incoming students continued for many years in the Ivy League schools in the eastern United States, and photos were taken of several well-known people, including Diane Sawyer and Hillary Rodham.

Sheldon reported strong empirical support of his theory. However, critics pointed out rightfully that his findings were highly suspect because Sheldon conducted all the research himself and he may been biased in his ratings of personality characteristics. Ideally, ratings of this type should be done by someone who is naïve to the hypothesis to reduce the possibility of biased evaluations.

Concerns about the possible role of bias led Child (1950) to conduct a follow-up study at Yale with a subset of the students who were somatotyped originally by Sheldon (1942). Child (1950) administered a self-report questionnaire to more than 400 students. This questionnaire consisted of 60 self-report statements about temperament. A subset of the items is shown in Table 2.1.

Table 2.1 Somatotypes and their Characteristics According to Sheldon

Somatotype	Characteristic	Characteristics
Ectomorph	Cerebrotonia	Does not withstand pain easily and willingly. Is not characterized by amiability and goodwill toward everyone he/she meets. Lacks real desire for strenuous physical exercise. Does not like to swim nude. Prefers to have a few very intimate friends to having many friends. Does not like to participate in strenuous or dangerous physical adventure.
Mesomorph	Somatotonia	Withstands pain easily and willingly. In talking with another person, looks at him/her right in the eye. Has real desire for strenuous physical exercise. Likes cold showers. Likes to participate in strenuous or dangerous physical adventure.
Endomorph	Viscerotonia	Gets to sleep easily. Is not easily awakened in the middle of the night. Is inclined to eat more than is really needed to maintain weight and growth. Tends to be apprehensive, insecure, or worried. Tends to be complacent about himself/herself and his/her relations with the world. Is characterized by amiability or goodwill toward everybody he/she knows or meet.

Source: Scale items assessing cerebrotonia, somatotonia, and viscerotonia are adapted from Child, 1950.

Child (1950) found some evidence to support Sheldon's theory but the associations were less robust than those found by Sheldon. Subsequent studies provided, at best, only very limited support for Sheldon's theory. The lack of support likely reflects the fact that if you were to take a room full of overweight people, or a room full of underweight people, you would still find a wide range of personality differences. Some people would resemble the characteristics described by Sheldon, but many others would not.

When it comes to formulating discrete groups, the philosopher Plato advanced the notion that science should "carve nature at its joints" like a good butcher does because theoretical explanations and subsequent research can be designed to try to account for the differences between groups. The process of classifying people into discrete type groups has also been described as "carving nature at its joints" by American researchers (see Gangestad and Snyder, 1985) and European researchers (Asendorpf, Borkeneau, Ostendorf, & van Aken, 2001). Gangestad and Snyder (1985) examined whether the construct of self-monitoring fits the criteria for being a personality type. If you are high in self-monitoring, you tend to be very attentive to situational cues and adjust your behaviour in a chameleon-like way according to changes in the situation (see Snyder, 1974). In contrast, low self-monitors are relatively unchanging and are much less sensitive to external cues. They could be described as somewhat inflexible in that they do not change their behaviour as the situation changes. Their focus is on internal cues and thoughts.

Gangestad and Snyder's (1985) data analyses supported their contention that self-monitoring is a class variable that reflects a personality type. Some authors (e.g., Miller & Thayer, 1989) questioned their conclusion on the grounds that Gangestad and Snyder (1985) used an inappropriate statistical procedure. However, von Davier and Rost (1997) addressed this issue and still found evidence of discrete types of high versus low self-monitors; evidence of heterogeneity was also obtained in that not one but two subgroups of self-monitors were identified.

Taxometrics is the term given to the complex statistical approach used to test for personality types or discrete categories in general. A **taxon** is an identified category. Meehl (1992) noted that the word "taxon" comes from the Greek word for arrangement or ordering. He emphasized that the goal is to establish taxons that really do exist in nature; they are natural types rather than arbitrary classes or arbitrary distinctions that do not correspond to a meaningful and observable difference.

In reality, most personality research focuses on traits rather than types, and some theorists who have posited types have had to make adjustments after reviewing the data. The classic example is Jung's theory (see Chapter 5) that initially made a clear, categorical distinction between introverts and extroverts. Jung felt initially that we are extroverts (outgoing and sociable) or introverts (reserved and not outgoing). However, Jung changed his thinking when he realized that the majority of people are **ambiverts**, with characteristics of both introversion and extroversion. Presumably, an ambiverted style is most adaptive because people with this orientation should be able to change their behaviour so that they are comfortable when they are with other people or by themselves.

It is often overlooked in the history of personality theory and research that in addition to psychologists, anthropologists have discussed personality types at length. Anthropologists have attempted to examine the personalities of entire societies of people. Their views are discussed in International Focus on Discovery 2.1.

International Focus on Discovery 2.1 Cultures as Personality Types: The Anthropological View

Prominent anthropologists conducted much of the early work on personality and culture. They were interested in the similarities and differences across cultures, and they recognized that there were differences across cultures that were reflected in the society's overall personality.

Ruth Benedict was one of the leading figures. In her book *Patterns of Culture*, Benedict (1934) described several cultures and the personality characteristics that accompanied these cultures. Benedict referred to the culture's personality as "a personality writ large." Benedict categorized cultures as four personality types: (1) Apollonian; (2) Dionysian; (3) Paranoid; and (4) Megalomaniac. The Apollonian type was a culture that was calm and reserved (e.g., the Pueblo Indians of New Mexico). The Dionysian type was an impulsive and expressive culture that engaged in excess (e.g., the Plains Indians). The Paranoid type had a preoccupation with possible betrayals and attacks (e.g., the Dobu Islanders of New Guinea). The Megalomaniac type (e.g., the Kwakiutl from the northwest coast of British Columbia) had an overemphasis on wealth, social prestige, personal glory, and superiority.

Benedict has been criticized for ignoring the developmental aspects of personality, and for demonstrating a limited understanding of individual psychology (see Inkeles & Levinson, 1954). As an anthropologist, she focused on the psychological aspects of societal institutions rather than the personalities of people per se.

Cora Du Bois was another prominent anthropologist interested in personality. As part of her analysis of the inhabitants of Alor Island in Indonesia, she introduced the notion of **modal personality** and suggested that various cultures could be contrasted in terms of the modal personality (Du Bois, 1944). In statistics, the **mode** is the number that occurs the most times. Although Du Bois introduced the notion of the modal personality, she also recognized that individual differences do indeed exist among the people in a society. For instance, she analyzed eight autobiographies of people from the preliterate society of Alor, and she found that they shared many characteristics but each person had unique features as well.

Margaret Mead suggested that personality types could be represented graphically as if they were the north, south, east, and west points of a compass.

Margaret Mead also had an abiding interest in personality types and at one point postulated that there were four personality types. She suggested that types could be represented graphically as if they were the north, south, east, and west points of a compass (see Sullivan, 2004). Continuing with the compass analogy, Mead described the paternal, male personality as a possessive type that represented the Northern personality. The maternal personality was the Southern personality and involved responsiveness to possession. The Eastern position was associated with avoidance and detachment, while the Western position was associated with engagement and acting pro-socially in a conservative, traditional manner.

The outbreak of the Second World War led anthropologists such as Benedict, Mead, and Bateson (Mead's husband) to focus their interests on personality and culture by undertaking evaluations of the prevailing national character or personality of countries, with much of the impetus for these studies coming from the United States military. These national character studies entailed sweeping evaluations of all the people in a particular country such as the United States, England, Germany, Japan, and the Soviet Union (for a review, see Inkeles & Levinson, 1954). Benedict (1946) observed that "to the anthropologist, the study of national character is the study of learned cultural behavior" (p. 274), and that given the focus on all the people from a country, the emphasis is on *the common personality aspects* of these people. But how accurate were these assessments?

The concerns of personality scholars about these studies and the assumptions guiding these studies was summarized aptly by Klineberg (1949), who observed that:

> When an anthropologist tells us about a cultural pattern and its relationship to individual behavior, we would also like to know, and this is what we miss in these studies, does *everybody* do this? Is this the sort of thing people *should* do, or what they *actually* do? Do *you* do this? Do you *always* do this? Do you *usually* do it? (p. 135–136)

In other words, Klineberg felt that we need to move beyond generalities to fully understand how nations and cultures have an impact on the individual.

Anthony Wallace's book *Culture and Personality* went a long way toward combatting the tendency to make sweeping characterizations about the modal personalities of cultures. Wallace (1961) argued that the proper way to characterize the differences is to compare cultures by the various individual differences within the culture. He had become "increasingly annoyed by the neglect of behavioral diversity" (Wallace, 1985, p. 24). The book by Wallace coincided with a decline in interest in anthropological assessments of personality and culture. Oishi (2004) noted that "the field was nearly abandoned after 1960, as both anthropology and personality lost their intellectual influence on other disciplines" (p. 69).

In general, personality theorists were quite critical of these national character analyses. Hans Eysenck made this point. Eysenck was one of the most vocal critics of these national character evaluations. In his controversial and popular book, *Uses and Abuses of Psychology*, Eysenck (1959) summarized his views as follows:

> It is certainly possible to make a genuinely empirical study of national differences; indeed, it may be said that such a study would be of the utmost importance in the future development of the United Nations and the effective implementation of the resolutions passed by many internationally-minded bodies. Yet no such empirical studies are likely to be undertaken or financed while those in power remain convinced either that the correct answer can be obtained by arm chair theorizing, or else that social science is incapable of giving any answer at all. (p. 260)

In addition to the lack of supporting data, national character studies are questionable in that great heterogeneity must exist among the people in a particular culture, and an emphasis on the national character fosters a stereotypical view that does not apply to many individuals in the culture. Indeed, Eysenck (1959) issued a call for factual thinking instead of "adding new stereotypes to the old" (p. 260).

Finally, anthropologists have been criticized for making limited use of personality theory in general. A related criticism is that they relied far too heavily on psychoanalytic concepts (see Chapter 5) that were predominant at the time (see Inkeles & Levinson, 1954).

Eysenck's call for an empirical approach is being addressed many years later by an increasing number of researchers who are examining personality from a cross-national perspective. Eysenck himself conducted some of the initial research in this area. Barrett and Eysenck (1984) examined responses to the Eysenck Personality Questionnaire from respondents from 24 nations. Researchers from Ireland extended this analysis by adding data from 13 other nations (see Lynn & Martin, 1995, 1997). Specifically, they reported the levels of extroversion–introversion, neuroticism, and psychoticism for 37 nations in total. The highest scoring countries in terms of mean levels of extroversion were Nigeria, Israel, and India, and the lowest scoring countries were China and Iran. The United States was among the more extroverted nations, while Canada was much lower in extroversion. As for neuroticism (low trait emotional stability), the highest levels of neuroticism were found in Egypt, Japan, and Russia, while the lowest levels were in such nations as Israel, Nigeria, Norway, and the Netherlands.

The main intent of Lynn and Martin (1997) was to examine possible gender differences. The most consistent gender difference was that women had higher levels of neuroticism than did men in all 37 countries, while men had higher levels of psychoticism in virtually all the countries. The fact that these gender differences appeared across nations, regardless of economic differences, led Lynn and Martin (1997) to conclude that these gender differences in personality may have a genetic basis. For our purposes, these findings illustrate the individual differences within cultures, and provide us with much more information than would have been the case if nations had simply been stereotyped as modal personalities or national characters.

Peabody (1985) conducted an analysis of national character in 20 countries. He found widespread agreement and consensus about perceived national characteristics.

His assessment of actual features led him to conclude that there is some overlap between perceived national character and actual personality characteristics for most countries. The one dramatic exception was the discrepancy in perceived and actual characteristics for Russians (Peabody & Shmelyov, 1998).

More recently, Terracciano and McCrae and their colleagues (see McCrae & Terracciano, 2006; Terracciano et al., 2005) re-examined this issue in a collaborative study with data from 49 countries on six continents. The researchers created a new measure known as the National Character Survey (NCS). The NCS consists of 30 scales with two or three items each. The scales tapped the facets of Costa and McCrae's NEO-PI-R five-factor measure. Overall, the results showed once again that there was consensus in how national characters are perceived. However, in terms of actual personality characteristics, these views of national characters were determined to be unfounded stereotypes. That is, national character differences are more apparent than real. For instance, people from countries such as Canada and the United States were perceived as very different (Canadians were seen as relatively lower in neuroticism and relatively higher in agreeableness). However, the actual personality profiles of Canadians and Americans were quite similar.

This research is important because it discounts national character stereotypes. While there is no question that national stereotypes are inaccurate oversimplifications, better data are needed to more fully evaluate this issue. This new study is flawed because although it was designed to assess national character and perceptions of national character, this research relied almost exclusively on college and university students from each nation as participants. If you want to assess the personality of a nation, you need to assess each country with a nationally representative sample. This is particularly important in Canada, where there is a need to also include French Canadians, especially in Quebec. However, it appears that only data from Ontario and westwards were obtained. In addition, it can only be concluded at present that the national stereotypes have been refuted solely based on the personality dimensions assessed by the NCS. What happens when other personality characteristics and psychological needs are evaluated?

Contemporary Research on Personality Types

Although the trait approach described below is predominant, the type approach has become much more prominent in recent years. It is possible now to find a growing number of researchers both in the United States and throughout Europe who are convinced about the importance of certain personality types, and they seem to have the data to support this position. Much of this research stems from the original work conducted by Block and Block (1980) and Block's (1977, 2002) model of personality processes. The Blocks posited that personality could be couched in terms of ego control and ego resiliency. **Ego control** is a person's degree of impulse control, including control of emotional and motivational tendencies. **Ego resiliency** is the ability to alter behaviours according to situational demands. If the high self-monitors described earlier in this chapter are actually good in the ability to self-monitor, then high self-monitors would have high levels of ego resiliency.

Block and Block (1980) posited various combinations of people based on having very high versus very low levels of ego control and ego resiliency. People would be controlled or undercontrolled and resilient or brittle. The four possibilities are represented in Table 2.2.

Table 2.2 California Q-Sort Items Associated with the Four Ego Resilience and Ego Control Conjunctions

	Resilient	Brittle
Undercontrolled	Energetic, Active Curious, Exploring Recoups, Resilient Interesting, Arresting	Restless, Fidgety Undercontrolling of impulse Externalizing, Vulnerable Brittle, Narrow margin of integration Manipulative
Over-controlled	Compliant Calm, Relaxed Empathic	Inhibited, Constricted Worrying, Anxious Intolerant of ambiguity Rigidly repetitive under stress Interpersonally reserved Withdraws under stress Manifests inappropriate affect Manifests behavioural mannerisms

Source: Adapted from Gramzow et al., 2004. Based originally on Block & Block, 1980.

The four possible categories displayed in Table 2.2 are based on the premise that the ego control and ego resiliency dimensions are orthogonal (independent). However, an influential study by Robins, John, Caspi, Moffitt, and Stouthamer-Loeber (1996) focused on three types or categories. They analyzed data from 300 adolescent boys from the United States and, rather than being orthogonal, there was an inverted U-shaped function between ego control and ego resiliency. This led the researchers to posit the existence of three types: (1) the **resilient type**; (2) the **overcontrolling type**; and (3) the **undercontrolling type**. The resilient type has the best adjustment. The resilient adolescent boys were described as having respect for themselves and others and they accepted personal responsibility for their actions. They have a well-integrated ego structure and are open to new experiences. They were deemed to be intelligent and successful in school, and they were relatively free of internalizing symptoms of

The overcontrolling type, one of the types identified by Robins et al., in their study of adolescent boys, is described as uneasy, introverted, passive, and likely to have internalizing problems.

maladjustment (e.g., anxiety and stress) and externalizing symptoms (e.g., aggressiveness and behavioural conduct problems directed against other people).

In contrast, the overcontrolling type seems inhibited in many respects. They were described as highly constricted, tense, uneasy, introverted, and passive. Those with the overcontrolling type experienced some of the positive outcomes experienced by the boys with the resilient type, but they also had internalizing problems (e.g., proneness to depression).

Finally, the undercontrolling type seemed to consist of boys who, in some respects, were simply out of control. They were characterized as hostile, irritable, and lacking in consideration for others. They were also seen as tense, dominant, and having fluctuating moods. They also had low levels of academic, behavioural, and emotional functioning and were high in both internalizing and externalizing symptoms (see Robins et al., 1996).

Research using various measures and methods has provided general support for the existence of these three personality types. Particularly influential has been work by Asendorpf and his colleagues in Germany, who have provided extensive evidence of the three types (see Asendorpf et al., 2001; Asendorpf & van Aken, 1999). For instance, Asendorpf et al. (2001) used self-reports and parental ratings to identify three clusters representing resilient children, overcontrolled children, and undercontrolled children, and they confirmed that overcontrolled children had internalizing symptoms (e.g., depression) while undercontrolled children had externalizing symptoms (e.g., acting out aggressively).

Other revealing findings have emerged from analyses in the United States of data obtained in the Children of the National Longitudinal Survey of Youth, 1979. The results are fully outlined in a research monograph written recently by Hart, Atkins, and Fegley (2003). Their results essentially demonstrate that the three types are replicable. Moreover, group membership is relatively stable over time, and the three types predict meaningful outcome variables. In addition, they showed that personality type interacts with participation in the American Head Start program to predict outcomes. Head Start is a preventive program designed to enhance the learning and achievement of children with disadvantaged family situations.

Still, some nagging questions remain to be addressed. First, several studies have yielded types other than those identified by Robins and associates (Barbaranelli, 2002; Caspi & Silva, 1995; Pulkkinen, 1996; York & John, 1992). For instance, a study of 199 university students who completed Block's (1978) Adult California Q-Sort measure (see Gramzow et al., 2004) identified four discrete types: (1) high resilience and moderately low control; (2) above average resilience and high control; (3) low resilience and low control; and (4) low resilience and high control. Essentially, these researchers found heterogeneity among the resilient types, as would be expected based on the ideas advanced by Block and Block (1980).

Other research has failed to distinguish resilience from overcontrol or undercontrol, and there seems to be a blending of personality types. Weir and Gjerde (2002) analyzed parental ratings of preschoolers and once again found three clusters, but the clusters were identified as (1) overcontrolled resilients; (2) resilient undercontrollers; and (3) "brittles."

Overcontrolled resilients were described as reflective and dependable, while resilient undercontrollers were described as aggressive, self-assertive, dominating, and emotionally expressive. Brittles were described as shy and reserved, fearful and anxious, and easily offended. Longitudinal investigation of the preschoolers who were now adolescents found few correlates of the brittle type, with the exception of a demonstrated link between being "brittle" and having lower levels of intelligence (relative to the other two types). In contrast, participants in the overcontrolled resilient group were rated as adolescents as high in shyness and low in activity level and low in drug use. The resilient undercontrollers were just the opposite. They were low in shyness and high in activity level and high in drug use. While it is intriguing that personality features assessed during preschool can predict level of drug use during adolescence, the main point to be taken from this study is that resiliency was not distinguished from overcontrol or undercontrol in this study.

Logically, some subtle but important differences likely exist within some of the other personality type categories. For instance, within the undercontrolling type, there are individuals who have little control and little remorse, much like is the case with cold-hearted psychopaths, while others have little control over their behaviour but can be quite remorseful and self-critical. This is an important distinction.

KEY POINTS

- Most personality research and theory focuses on personality traits rather than personality types.
- The work of anthropologists resulted in attempts to characterize the personality of nations (i.e., national characters). People agree on personality stereotypes about nations but there is little evidence of actual personality differences.
- Contemporary research has found that there is evidence of the validity of general personality types reflecting resilient, undercontrolled, and overcontrolled people. However, variability has been detected because other types reflecting variations on these categories have been found.

Briefly, to further illustrate the heterogeneity issue, consider the research on conduct disorder and persistent physical aggression in boys that was conducted by Canadian researchers Nagin and Tremblay (2001). All of the participants would be considered aggressive if they were sorted into high versus low aggression categories. Analyses focused on **developmental trajectories**. Developmental trajectories are the levels of a particular behaviour over time. Does the behaviour increase, decrease, or stay at about the same level over time? Detailed analyses of the boys from the age of 6 to 15 years led Nagin and Tremblay (2001) to distinguish four types of boys: (1) those 4% who had a "flat" trajectory due to chronic physical aggression; (2) another 28% who started out with high levels of physical aggression but who declined steadily in this behaviour over time; (3) another 52% who had lower levels of physical aggression over time but who also experienced declines over time; and (4) another 16% of boys who seldom exhibited physical aggression once the study was underway. Clearly, when it comes to highly aggressive boys, one size does not fit all!

Finally, whenever types are identified, the developmental antecedents of these types must be studied. Personality development is discussed at length in Chapter 3. Regarding the different types, a study conducted in the Netherlands found that lower levels of perceived parental rejection were reported by adolescents who were deemed to be resilient, versus both the "overcontrollers" and the "undercontrollers" (Akse, Hale, Engels, Raaijmakers, & Meeus, 2004). Other research indicates "resilients" receive higher levels of social support from their family and friends, while the undercontrolled report greater family coercion (van Aken & Dubas, 2004). This finding runs counter to the common misperception that undercontrolled children have parents who have "checked out" and have given up on trying to control them.

As noted, the trait approach still dominates the personality field. Personality traits are examined at length in the next section.

PERSONALITY TRAITS

What is a trait? This question was the title of an influential conference paper delivered by **Gordon Allport** in 1929. Allport was a Harvard University psychologist, and he is regarded as the father of personality trait psychology. Accordingly, his views will be described at length. His distinction between an idiographic and nomothetic approach was already described in Chapter 1. Readers who are interested in finding out more about the history of the trait concept and about Allport himself are advised to read a compelling book by Ian Nicholson (2002), who is at St. Thomas University in New Brunswick.

Allport's Bold Assertions

Allport (1968) stated that many of his thoughts about personality traits were contained in "eight bold assertions" (p. 44) he made in 1931:

1. *A personality trait has more than a nominal existence.* Allport believed that personality traits are real entities that reside within people. The concept of a trait is not simply a metaphor or symbol. Rather, it represents a tendency that lies within the individual.
2. *A personality trait is more generalized than a habit.* Allport believed that personality traits tend to be manifest across situations and life circumstances. This assertion has resulted in research on the cross-situational consistency of personality traits.
3. *A personality trait is dynamic, or at least discriminative, in behaviour.* Allport sensed that whether a personality trait is activated will depend greatly on the situation, and, depending on the circumstance, some traits will seem to come and go in terms of whether they are reflected in behaviour.
4. *A personality trait may be established empirically.* This assertion acknowledges the need to measure traits in quantifiable ways in research investigations.
5. *A personality trait is only relatively independent of other traits.* The content and processes associated with certain traits often overlap (e.g., kind and altruistic) and co-exist within

a person or sample of people. The same behaviour could be due to the activation of two or more traits.

6. *A personality trait is not synonymous with moral or social judgement.* This assertion attempts to distinguish personality traits from aspects of character and morality but also allows for the possibility of anti-social traits.
7. *A personality trait may be viewed either in the light of the personality which contains it or in the light of its distribution in the population at large* (i.e., the idiographic versus nomothetic approach). This assertion reflects the distinction made earlier in this book between studying an individual and a group of people.
8. *Acts, and even habits, that are inconsistent with a trait are not proof of the nonexistence of the trait.* Allport acknowledged that people can sometimes act in an inconsistent manner, especially if they attempt to create a specific impression in a situation. For example, a timid person may wish to seem courageous when confronted by a knife-wielding attacker.

This last point is Allport's response to those who take a more situational view of personality and who believe that differences in behaviour reflect the different characteristics of different situations rather than enduring personality traits. Situationism is discussed in a subsequent segment of this chapter.

As noted earlier, a personality trait is believed to reflect a continuous dimension that applies to everyone. It involves differences *in degree* rather than in kind. So, returning to our earlier example, we would refer to a person's degree of optimism (i.e., a little bit versus a moderate amount versus a lot) instead of saying he or she is an optimist or pessimist.

Allport's Conceptualizations of Traits

In just a few pages of his seminal 1937 book, Allport makes a number of extremely important distinctions between different types of traits, or different ways of thinking about traits. These distinctions are outlined briefly below.

Common Traits versus Unique Traits

Allport acknowledged that certain personality traits are shared by other people. These are referred to as **common traits**. Although common traits are important, Allport placed greater emphasis on **unique traits**. Unique traits can also be called individual traits because they are unique to a particular individual. As a way of underscoring the difference between common and unique traits, Allport advised it might be better not to refer to unique traits at all, and instead use the term "personal disposition." Personal dispositions are unique to the person, and these dispositions provide an accurate representation of personality structure.

Phenotypical versus Genotypical Personal Dispositions

Allport incorporated the distinction between phenotypes versus genotypes by stating that a phenotypical disposition is involved when the focus is on describing behaviour in a situation in the here and now. Allport regarded phenotypical dispositions as part of personality in that they show some consistency in someone's behaviour. An example of a phenotypical disposition could be providing a descriptive account of a person's behaviour at a party. In contrast, a genotypical disposition involves an explanatory account of a more fundamental and deeper disposition (i.e., a person's core). Allport (1937) advised that we could only get at genotypical dispositions by studying a person's entire life because this would clarify deep-seated motives and needs, and perhaps even provide an awareness of conflicting dispositions within the same person.

Pseudotraits

Allport also emphasized the usefulness of studying a person's life as a way of distinguishing between true personal dispositions and pseudotraits. Allport (1937) acknowledged that we sometimes develop erroneous beliefs about a person's personality because we fail to discern that a person has acted in a false way in order to create a particular impression or appearance to others. Note that the concept of pseudotraits goes back to our discussion in Chapter 1 about not relying on common sense. Allport (1937) observed that by distinguishing true dispositions from pseudo dispositions, psychology becomes more than just common sense.

Cardinal, Central, and Secondary Dispositions

Allport (1937) also suggested that any one person could be characterized by one or two cardinal dispositions that are central to their personality, as well as 5 to 10 central dispositions that are less obvious and less generalized but nevertheless key components of their personality. He also posited secondary dispositions that are more peripheral and more akin to habits or smaller regularities in behaviour that a person exhibits, but some sparingly (e.g., a student who tends to chew on a pencil while pondering the answers to multiple choice questions).

Creativity was one of writer Ernest Hemingway's cardinal dispositions.

It is usually possible to consider famous people in terms of one or two truly defining attributes (cardinal dispositions), followed by five or so central dispositions that also are relevant. For example, let us consider the famous American author Ernest Hemingway, who won the Nobel Prize in literature in 1954. He contributed such works as

For Whom the Bell Tolls, To Have and Have Not, and *The Old Man and the Sea*. He was a writer for various newspapers, including the *Kansas City Star* and the *Toronto Star*, prior to writing his classic novels. He was one of the most remarkable, complex, and colourful figures of the first half of the twentieth century. Tragically, Hemingway suffered at times from severe depression, and he took his own life in 1961.

Hemingway's cardinal traits would include his great creativity and his self-destructiveness, such as alcohol binges and womanizing. Examination of biographical and autobiographical material reveals several other central dispositions. Hemingway displayed a hypermasculinity that is a form of overcompensation. His hypermasculinity as an adult could probably be traced to the fact that his mother dressed and raised him as a girl for a significant portion of his childhood and referred to him as "Ernestine" (see Grauer, 1999). His hypermasculine activities included boxing, wrestling, hunting, and running with the bulls. He also survived two plane crashes. Hemingway had a high level of bravery and was given a medal for bravery from the Italians because he served as a Red Cross ambulance driver during the First World War. He was severely wounded in both legs and acted boldly to save another man's life. Another obvious central disposition was Hemingway's hostility, although he had many friends. For instance, he enjoyed upsetting and being exceedingly critical of his good friend, fellow author F. Scott Fitzgerald, who penned classics such as *The Great Gatsby* and *Tender Is the Night*. Finally, it could be stated that Hemingway was high in attention-seeking and effectance. Effectance motivation is derived from White's (1959) effectance theory. White argued that we have a basic drive to be competent and a drive to have a demonstrable impact on other people, objects, and the self (for an overview, see Kusyszyn, 1990). That is, some people have a great need for others to react to them.

The late Diana, Princess of Wales, is another public figure who can be described in terms of her cardinal and central dispositions. Princess Diana's cardinal dispositions would likely include her compassionate, altruistic spirit as well as her personal vulnerability and low self-esteem, some of which stemmed from her parents' divorce. As for central dispositions, her other main characteristics noted by biographers, and sometimes noted by herself, included her charisma, interpersonal sensitivity, moodiness, neuroticism, perfectionism, and strong maternal devotion (see Bedell Smith, 1999).

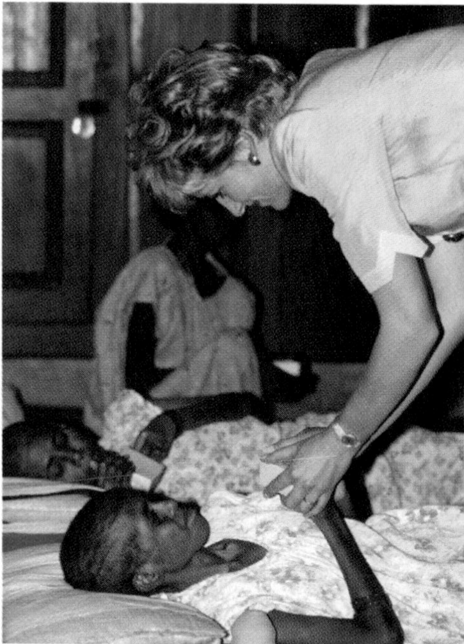

Princess Diana's cardinal dispositions would likely include her compassion and altruism.

KEY POINTS

- According to Allport, each person has unique traits and common traits shared with others.
- As part of his assertions about traits, Allport observed that traits are dynamic and discriminative in terms of being in a situation that elicits the behaviours associated with the trait.
- Allport postulated that people are characterized by one or two cardinal dispositions that are central to who they are, as well as 5 to 10 central dispositions that are less generalized but still highly relevant to the individual.

Traits versus Types

Now that the concepts of types and traits have been introduced, their relative properties need to be evaluated. Strube (1989) cogently noted some key differences between types and traits in terms of their implications and associated assumptions. First, according to Strube, types differ from traits in their perceived antecedents. Types are believed to arise from a small number of necessary conditions that must be entirely present, while a trait continuum, by definition, involves the gradual or incomplete acquisition of certain behaviours. Thus, there may be differences in the developmental sequences for types versus traits.

Second, because types exist in an all-or-none fashion, this has important implications when treating adjustment problems linked to a personality type, as opposed to a trait. Strube (1989) posited that it may be more difficult to change a personality type, but when change does occur, it should be more complete and dramatic.

Mischel's Challenge to the Trait Approach

A dramatic turning point in the history of the personality field occurred with the publication of a journal article by Walter Mischel in 1969. Mischel provided an exceedingly critical review of existing research on personality traits and the assumptions guiding this research. Mischel's critique contributed to personality research falling out of favour for many years (in the 1970s and early 1980s). In fact, Goldberg (1992) characterized this era as a time when "we had no personality."

What were Mischel's primary objections? Briefly, Mischel (1968, 1969) reviewed the available evidence and reached the following conclusions: (1) Traits are poor predictors of behaviours in situations, with the correlations between trait measures and behavioural measures in situations being relatively low; (2) The situation is better than personality traits when seeking to account for individual differences in behaviour; and (3) If you change the situation, you often change behaviours in a way that is inconsistent with the trait assumption that personality involves stable and long-lasting individual differences that generalize across situations. Mischel (1969) concluded that at best, the correlation between personality traits and behaviours was .30, which, according to the statistical formula, indicates that personality factors can account for only 9% (.30 × .30) of the variability in behaviours. He referred to this .30 value as the **personality coefficient**. Nisbett (1980) later suggested that the upper ceiling of the personality coefficient was .40. Subsequent authors noted that there are various ways to increase the apparent link between personality traits and behaviours, including increasing the reliability of measurement by aggregation (i.e., collecting repeated measures, which has the effect of decreasing measurement errors). Still, the extent of the association between personality traits and behaviours is not as great as many personality researchers would desire.

KEY POINTS

- Mischel argued that traits are poor predictors of behaviours in situations.
- Mischel noted that changes in situations result in changes in behaviour and these behavioural changes are not in keeping with the presumed stability of personality traits and associated behaviours.
- Mischel estimated the personality coefficient to be .30. This suggests that only 9% of the variance in behaviour expressed in situations is predicted by personality traits.

SITUATIONISM

Mischel's observations facilitated an approach known as **situationism** (the impact of situational factors and their role in contributing to differences in behaviour). Some dramatic findings from the social psychology literature contributed to the emphasis on the role of the situation over personal characteristics. One example is the famous Stanley Milgram obedience study conducted in the 1960s. Milgram (1975) conducted an experiment in which he showed that the majority of men in his experiment would deliver seemingly fatal electrical shocks to another person who was making mistakes on a learning task simply because they were instructed by the experimenter to deliver the shock. Briefly, if you were in Milgram's experiment, you would arrive with another person and be told that one of you would be the teacher and one of you would be the learner presented with an intellectual task. The other person was a confederate of the experimenter's and was always assigned the learner role. You would get the teacher role, and then be told to pose questions to the learner. Whenever a mistake was made, you would be asked to administer an electric shock to the learner. The shocks increased by 15 volts each time up to a maximum of 450 volts. The participants did not realize at the time that the experiment did not involve administering the electrical shock; rather, it was set up so that the men believed they were administering the shock. Note that the mistakes were pre-planned, and the key dependent variable was whether the person playing the role of teacher would keep administering shocks up to the maximum possible, simply because the experimenter insisted that it had to be done. The shocks increased by 15 volts each time the "learner" made a (preplanned) mistake. Although the men showed visible signs of distress when asked to deliver the shock to the learner, who was providing audible signs of distress and pain, 26 of the 40 participants were willing to administer up to 450 volts. They were willing to do this even though the learner screamed in pain at the 375 volt mark and stopped responding altogether because he was now presumably unconscious.

This famous experiment showed the clear impact that a strong situation (in this case, an authority figure demanding that you obey) can have on behaviour. However, there are still individual differences in this powerful situation that leave room for the possible impact of personality factors. That is, roughly two thirds of the participants gave the maximum shock, but one third did not and openly refused to do so. Could it be that there was something in their personalities that made them take a stand? Some authors believe that this is indeed quite possible. Blass (1991) suggested that those who refused to obey might have been low in a widely studied personality trait known as authoritarianism. People high in authoritarianism can be dogmatic and domineering, but they also tend to respect moral authority figures and will conform to expectation (see Chapter 10 for a broader description). Blass (1991) cited later research by Elms and Milgram (Elms, 1972; Elms & Milgram, 1966) that confirmed that those who refused to administer the full extent of the shock were indeed low in authoritarianism. Blass (1991) also suggested that nonconformity might have reflected individual differences in interpersonal trust and social intelligence. That is, you would be less like to comply with the authority figure if you tended to be distrusting of what other people told you and what they wanted you to do, and if you were higher in social intelligence, you would be less likely to obey because you would be more cognitively capable of sizing up the situation and finding some way to make it easier for you to disobey. Research by Gisli Gudjonsson and his colleagues in Iceland has focused on individual differences in the compliant personality (see Gudjonsson et al., 2004). The least compliant people tend to be stable extroverts. Stable extroverts would probably be the ones who would refuse to administer the maximum shock in the Milgram obedience experiment.

It is generally accepted that strong and compelling situations like that in the Milgram study leave less room for personality differences to be reflected, while weak and ambiguous situations leave much more room for the impact and expression of personality differences. Still, as was suggested above, personality may play some role even when we are in situations that have a dramatic impact on us.

Mischel's observations sparked a raging debate about the relative importance of personality factors versus situational factors in predicting individual differences in behaviour. For many, Mischel's views represented an assault on the core assumptions of the trait approach. This assault diminished, for a time at least, the perceived importance and relevance of traits, thereby making it very difficult to conduct and publish research based on personality traits. One response to Mischel's challenge was to demonstrate that situational factors are also important, but they also only account for a relatively small proportion of the variability in behaviour. An important paper by Funder and Ozer (1983) was based on their re-analysis of classic social psychological studies such as Milgram's that showed the power of the situation. Funder and Ozer (1983) concluded that, at best, situational factors had a correlation of only .40 with behavioural differences. Note that this value is identical to the upper value of the personality coefficient according to Nisbett (1980). Although Funder and Ozer (1983) did not refer to it, this could be called the **situation coefficient**. Funder and Ozer (1983) explicitly stated in their discussion of their findings that they did not wish to suggest that situational differences are not important. Rather, both person and situation factors are important and, depending on the specific context, may be relatively comparable in their ability to predict behavioural differences.

The ultimate response to Mischel's challenge came from personality theorists and researchers who promoted the view that differences in behaviour often reflect the interaction of personality traits and situational factors. This view is known as **interactionism**, which is discussed below.

THE TRAIT–SITUATION INTERACTION IN PERSONALITY RESEARCH

Norman Endler's research is one of the most extensive series of studies of interactionism.

Norman Endler from York University in Toronto established an international reputation as one of the leading proponents of the interactionism approach, along with his colleague David Magnusson from Sweden (Endler & Magnusson, 1976). Although many other researchers have adopted the interactionist view and provided supporting evidence (for reviews, see Magnusson, 1999; Magnusson & Stattin, 1998), and some authors discussed it prior to Endler and Magnusson (1976), we will focus on Endler's conceptualizations and empirical work, in part because his research represents one of the most extensive series of studies testing interactionism. In addition, his research incorporated some very compelling situations to test his theories.

Endler (1983) distinguished between mechanistic and reciprocal models of interactionism. Mechanistic models focus primarily on how situations influence certain people's behaviours (Endler & Magnusson, 1976). In contrast, **reciprocal interactionism models** allow for the possibility that not only does the situation have an influence on the person, but the person can also have an influence on the situation (e.g., whom we choose to be with; where we go and don't go). That is, we can select or change the situation by behaving in a particular way. The reciprocal interactionism model accounts for dynamic changes in the associations among persons, situations, and behaviours.

Emmons, Diener, and Larsen (1985) discussed this aspect of the reciprocal interactionism model at length and suggested that the influence of personality factors in these models is often underestimated. They maintained that not enough weight is given to the fact that people opt for certain situations and avoid others based on their personalities (also see Snyder, 1983).

Personality factors are also underestimated because we also know that people often differ in their perceptions of situational cues (see Endler, 1982). Given the same situation, not all people see the same thing.

Most of Endler's work evaluated his interaction model of trait anxiety. This model incorporated Spielberger's (1972) distinction between trait and state anxiety. The term "**trait anxiety**" refers to a person's usual or typical level of anxiety (how anxious you usually feel).

For instance, someone who is a chronic worrier would be exceptionally high in trait anxiety. The original interaction model of anxiety proposed by Endler (1983) maintains that there are four distinct elements or facets of trait anxiety: social evaluation anxiety, physical danger anxiety, anxiety in ambiguous situations (ambiguous anxiety), and daily routines anxiety. The model predicts that levels of state anxiety will be a joint function of levels of trait anxiety and situational experiences. **State anxiety** is the current or momentary feeling of anxiety experienced at a specific point in time (how anxious you feel *right now*). The model suggests that high state anxiety occurs when a person with an elevated level of congruent trait anxiety experiences a threatening event that matches this component of trait anxiety.

A version of Endler's interaction model of anxiety, stress, and coping is depicted in Figure 2.1. The far left side of the diagram represents person variables (including traits, cognitive styles, and internal vulnerabilities and susceptibilities), and it also represents situations in terms of stressful situations (e.g., life events, life traumas, daily hassles, etc.). Trait anxiety is represent by the term "A-trait." Both person and situation variables then are related to perceptions of the situation as dangerous or threatening (or benign, of course). If the situation is recognized as dangerous or threatening and it reflects a relevant personality disposition, elevations in state anxiety (i.e., A-state) are experienced. An increased level of state anxiety is then reacted to in a variety of possible ways. The tendency to be very distressed and emotional may elicit an avoidance-oriented form of coping by a person with high state anxiety; but if a person regarded the situation as a challenge, he or she would probably have less state anxiety and may be less avoidant in his or her coping response.

When examining Figure 2.1, it is important to note that it reflects a process model. That is, our reactions to increased state anxiety can also have an influence on person variables and stressful situations (e.g., using avoidance coping can make a situation more stressful). Endler was a proponent of a dynamic interactionism approach that acknowledges that people create outcomes but behaviours and outcomes can also influence people.

Figure 2.1 Interaction Model of Stress, Anxiety, and Coping

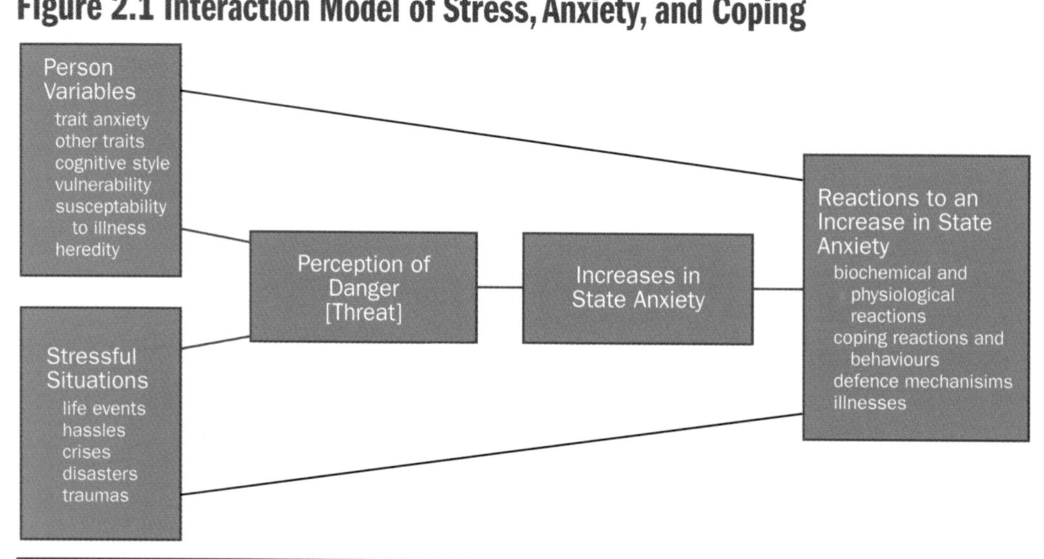

Source: Endler & Parker, 1999.

KEY POINTS

- The interactionism models view behaviour as a joint function of the person and the situation. Reciprocal interaction models allow for the person, situation, and behaviour to all have an influence on each other in a dynamic sequence.
- Person factors are likely underestimated in interaction models because people choose and structure situations according to their personalities. Also, people differ in how they perceive and cognitively appraise situations.
- Endler's interactionism model of anxiety distinguishes trait and state anxiety. High state anxiety results when there is a match between an element of trait anxiety (e.g., physical danger anxiety) and a congruent situation (e.g., a situation involving physical threat).

The validity of the interaction model of anxiety has been tested in many naturalistic situations. For instance, Lobel, Gilat, and Endler (1993) examined the reaction of Israeli citizens who were under attack by Iraqi Scud missiles during the Persian Gulf War in 1991. Participants in the Lobel et al. study were obtained from workplaces and shopping centres within 30 km of Tel Aviv. Imagine that you are worried about Scud missiles being launched in your direction, and researchers come and ask if you would be willing to fill out some personality questionnaires! Lobel et al. (1993) confirmed the predictions of the interaction model by showing that people who were high in the physical danger component of trait anxiety and who were under attack had understandably high levels of psychological distress, especially on a measure constructed by the authors to assess war-related distress.

Other tests of the interaction model of anxiety have included such situations as taking a driving test (King & Endler, 1990) and undergoing medical and dental procedures (King & Endler, 1992). Most studies have yielded strong support for the model. For instance, Endler and Magnusson (1977) measured anxiety among students taking an exam at the University of Stockholm. They found that students high in trait social evaluation anxiety (who were presumably worried about what failure would look like to significant others) had greater physiological arousal as assessed by pulse rates during the examination. Another study of trait and state anxiety in Canadian military recruits undergoing parachute-jumping training also supported the model (Endler, Crooks, & Parker, 1992). Higher state anxiety was detected among those recruits who felt a sense of threat and who were relatively higher in both physical danger anxiety and social evaluation anxiety. The role of social evaluation anxiety reflected their concerns about being embarrassed in front of their peers.

Another test of the model examined an event in Canada that took place on October 30, 1995. The province of Quebec conducted a referendum that asked whether it should separate from the rest of Canada. The possibility of separation has been a constant threat for several decades, with many possible political, social, and economic implications. Public opinion polls in October 1995 indicated that Quebec would indeed opt for separation, though the vote's outcome was the opposite. The Quebec referendum represented an opportunity to test the interaction model because the event was viewed by many as a threatening situation characterized by ambiguity and uncertainty. Students' reactions to this event confirmed predictions from the interaction model (see Flett, Endler, & Fairlie, 1999). If the interaction model is valid, then those people with high trait anxiety in circumstances involving novelty and uncertainty should have higher levels of state anxiety as a result of the threat to national unity, as perceived by them; this should not be the case for individuals with low levels of this facet of trait anxiety, or individuals who are high in the other facets of trait anxiety. This hypothesis was supported by the data.

How has the interactionist viewpoint in general fared in research? For this answer, we can go back to one of the first investigations of this issue. Kenneth Bowers (1973), a long-time faculty member of the University of Waterloo in Ontario, provided a rousing and spirited critique of the situationism movement in psychology. In addition, he reported the results of a review he conducted of 11 studies in articles published since 1959 that had tested the relative impact of personality factors, situational factors, and their interactions. He determined that personality factors accounted for about 10% of the variance in behaviour, while situational factors accounted for almost 13% of the variance. More importantly, the interaction of personality and situational factors accounted for approximately 21% of the variance in behaviour!

Endler and Parker (1992) observed that generally, the debate has been resolved and personologists accept the fact that behaviour is a joint product of the person and the situation. This was reiterated in a new review paper by Swann and Seyle (2005), who stated that "the traditional distinction between personal, situational, and interactional determinants of behavior continues to be useful within appropriate contexts" (p. 155).

BEYOND TRAITS

Personality Capabilities and the Maximal versus the Typical Personality

When we assess traits, we ask people about their usual or typical characteristics over time. We don't tend to ask them about how often they demonstrate these characteristics, and perhaps more importantly, we don't tend to ask them about what behaviours they are capable of (what behaviours exist in their behavioural repertoire). The important point here is that the personality field permits researchers to define individual differences in many different ways, and we do not need to restrict ourselves to the usual trait approach.

An analysis of **personality capabilities** illustrates the usefulness of measuring individual differences from different perspectives. Wallace (1966) observed astutely that certain personality characteristics could be measured as abilities or capabilities. The notion of capability incorporates the distinction between a person's typical tendencies in a domain (their traits) versus their maximum possible response in this domain (their capability). The trait approach requires research participants to describe their personality characteristics in terms of their *usual* personality characteristics. The **maximal approach** requires research participants to describe their personality characteristics in terms of their *possible* personality characteristics. The distinction between typical and maximal with respect to procrastination, for instance, would involve asking the person to rate himself or herself in terms of their typical level of procrastination (e.g., the extent to which you usually submit your essays on time) versus the range of their behaviour (e.g., the extent to which you could hand your essays in on time if you really had to).

Consider how capabilities apply to interpersonal tendencies. In the case of agreeableness, for instance, someone may usually be a disagreeable person. But perhaps this same person has shown a range of responses to other people, and he or she could be a warm and friendly individual in situations that require a more agreeable disposition or when he or she is with certain people who bring out or elicit more agreeable behaviours. This person differs from the disagreeable person who is incapable of being any other way.

Paulhus and Martin (1987, 1988) illustrated the usefulness of assessing personality capabilities. They showed that capability and trait ratings of interpersonal characteristics are relatively orthogonal, and both capability and trait ratings are associated with low self-esteem and anxiety. The implications of these findings are clear: individual differences in trait ratings and capability ratings are quite different in their nature, and judgements of personality capabilities may play a prominent role in the adjustment process.

Other research supports the usefulness of additional research on personality assessment from a maximal perspective, consistent with the notion of personality capabilities. Unfortunately, however, relatively little research has incorporated this approach.

Metatraits and Traitedness

A vexing problem when the same personality trait measure is administered to a sample of participants is that the construct being assessed will be very important and highly relevant to some people, while others do not see the construct as being very pertinent to them at all. For the current author, this was illustrated poignantly during data collection for one study when one participant put up his hand and said loudly, "Professor, should I fill out this scale if I just don't give a damn?" This was a clear reminder that a person may be circling items on a scale but the dimension being tapped has little meaning for him or her. In contrast, another person might circle the same responses, and the construct being assessed has great personal importance or relevance.

The concept of metatraits has been incorporated into research as a way of trying to inject a bit of an idiographic focus into nomothetic research. **Metatraits** are those traits that are highly relevant to an individual. Another term for the metatrait concept is traitedness. If a concept is "traited," it is said to be high in trait relevance. Trait relevance has been defined by Britt and Shepperd (1999) as "the degree to which a trait is *consequential* in influencing an individual's thought, affect, and behavior" (p. 109).

Various types of validity are involved in personality assessment (see Chapter 4). Britt and Shepperd (1999) introduced the concept of **trait relevance validity**. This is the degree to which the construct being assessed is pertinent and relevant to the target population being studied.

Metatraits can be assessed quite simply by asking people to evaluate the importance of a trait dimension. The presumption here is that more relevant traits are given higher importance ratings. Another way of measuring metatraits is to evaluate the inter-item variability in responses across a series of items all purporting to tap the same construct.

The assumption here is that people who are rating a dimension that is highly relevant to them will show less variability in their answers across a group of relatively similar items, while people who are low in traitedness will be "all over the map" and inconsistent in how they respond to the set of items. The second form of assessment has an advantage over the first type of assessment (i.e., ratings of importance) because it does not require people to be consciously aware of their traitedness on a dimension.

Cognitive measures have also been used to evaluate trait relevance. Cynthia Fekken and Ronald Holden from Queen's University in Kingston, Ontario, have conducted research based on the premise that people will respond faster to material and they will make quicker judgements if the stimulus material is relevant to their self-concepts (see Fekken & Holden, 1992). A stimulus that is quite relevant to your personal identity and how you see the world should elicit a faster response or reaction from you than a stimulus that is simply not on your personal "radar screen."

There is relatively little research on the concept of metatraits, but existing research indicates that traitedness is important. Baumeister and Tice (1988) showed that the predicted effects for a variable known as locus of control (which is a trait described later in this chapter) were evident only among the subset of people who indicated that issues of control represent a key part of their personalities. Britt (1993) showed that the correlation between two personality constructs was much greater among the subset of participants who were deemed to be "traited" on both personality constructs.

KEY POINTS

- Individual differences exist in personality capabilities. Whereas traits focus on what a person typically does, capabilities refer to maximal tendencies in the range of behaviours a person can exhibit.
- A metatrait is one that is highly relevant to an individual. Metatraits can be assessed by self-reports of trait importance, the amount of variability in responses to items assessing the same trait, or the speed of responding to trait-related stimuli.

HOW MANY SUPERTRAITS ARE THERE?

When cardinal traits are considered in a sample of people or samples of people across various nations, they are often referred to as **supertraits**. Supertraits are the main traits that are universal and that capture the major proportion of variance in behaviour. To use an analogy, if you were to go shopping for supertraits, these would be the "big ticket items" because we are talking about the huge personality trait dimensions that are broadly applicable. In the next section, classic and somewhat contentious frameworks of these supertraits are outlined.

Eysenck's Big Three

The story of the search for supertraits begins with Allport and Odbert (1936), who identified thousands of personality-related adjectives. The researchers decided that a good way to identify these dimensions would be to start by identifying all of the personality terms in the English language. In total, they amassed 36,000 terms and adjectives reflecting personality characteristics. This tendency to identify the personality differences represented in language is known as the lexical approach.

Cattell (1943) reduced these thousands of adjectives to 132 terms, and then reduced them further to just 35 terms. He eventually used the statistical procedure known as factor analysis to reduce these items to the 16 trait dimensions that compose Cattell's Sixteen Personality Factor System (16 PF) (Cattell, Eber, & Tatsuoka, 1970).

Critics suggested that these 16 factors could be reduced to more sweeping trait categories. **Hans Eysenck** (1947, 1967, 1970) postulated a hierarchical model of personality that had four levels. Specific cognitions and behaviours in specific situations were the first level (i.e., personality states). The second level was composed of habitual acts or cognitions (e.g., an individual has frequent headaches or is frequently tardy). The third level was described as the trait level and was defined as significant intercorrelations between habitual behaviours with a related theme. For example, a trait such as sociability encompasses things such as going to parties, enjoying talking to other people, being bored when alone, and preferring listening to someone to reading alone. The fourth level has received the most attention. It involves higher order traits or broad dimensions of personality (i.e., supertraits).

The third level of Eysenck's hierarchical model of personality is the trait level, which involves intercorrelations between behaviours with a related theme. For example, sociability would include enjoying talking to other people.

In initial versions of Eysenck's model, only two supertraits were included, but subsequent versions consisted of three broad dimensions. Eysenck and Eysenck (1985) presented evidence that these broad dimensions could be found and measured reliably in many different countries.

The first broad dimension is extroversion–introversion, which encompasses second-level traits including sociable, lively, active, assertive, sensation-seeking, carefree, dominant, surgent, and venturesome. This broad trait dimension is tapped by such scale items on the Eysenck Personality Questionnaire as (1) Do you usually take the initiative in making new friends? and (2) Can you easily get some life into a rather dull party?

The second broad dimension is neuroticism–emotional stability, which encompasses second-level traits such as anxious, depressed, guilt feelings, low self-esteem, tense, irrational, shy, moody, and emotional. It is measured by scale items such as (1) Does your mood often go up and down? and (2) Are your feelings easily hurt?

Although he advocated a dimensional approach to personality traits, Eysenck (1970) argued that the various combinations of these first two trait dimensions (neuroticism versus emotional stability and introversion versus extroversion) yielded four combinations that correspond to the temperaments described by Galen. Unstable introverts were seen as melancholic while stable introverts were seen as phlegmatic. Unstable extroverts were seen as choleric and stable extroverts were seen as sanguine.

Psychoticism versus superego control is the third broad supertrait dimension, which was the factor added in later versions of Eysenck's model. The psychoticism factor encompasses second-level traits such as aggressive, cold, egocentric, impersonal, impulsive, anti-social, unempathic, creative, and tough-minded. It is reflected by items such as (1) Do you prefer to go your own way rather than act by the rules? and (2) Would you like other people to be afraid of you? The second item is reverse-keyed, meaning that people high in psychoticism would not agree because they are relatively unconcerned about what other people think of them. The psychoticism dimension is clearly the most controversial trait proposed by Eysenck. Various authors (e.g., Claridge, 1993) have questioned some of the core assumptions of this construct, but psychoticism is able to predict some key individual differences (see Applied Perspective 2.1).

Scores on these broad trait dimensions tend to be quite stable, even over many years, consistent with the general definition of personality traits (Eysenck & Eysenck, 1985). Eysenck maintained that the individual differences in these broad traits can be traced to biological and genetic differences, and there is a clear physiological basis to personality traits. In fact, by linking his theory with the Greek temperaments, Eysenck (1970) found a way to reiterate his belief that personality traits stem from biological factors.

Consistent with this biological emphasis, Eysenck argued that introverted and extroverted people differ in their levels of arousal. That is, introverts are overaroused, and their more reserved behaviours reflect their need to keep stimulation from arousal to a minimum. In contrast, extroverts are underaroused physiologically, and their outgoing tendencies reflect a need to try to increase their level of physiological activation.

KEY POINTS

- Eysenck traced personality differences to underlying biological differences.
- The three traits studied by Eysenck and measured by the Eysenck Personality Questionnaire are neuroticism, extroversion, and psychoticism.
- The PEN model reflects Eysenck's belief that criminals have elevated levels of psychoticism, extroversion, and neuroticism.

Five-Factor Models and the Big Seven

While Eysenck focused on developing and testing his model, attempts to analyze the personality descriptors in language continued. Several different researchers reported that they had identified five broad superfactors.

In particular, Norman played an important role in the emergence of the five-factor model. For example, Norman (1963) advanced the argument for including conscientiousness as one of the supertraits. In addition, Norman and his associates analyzed the adjectives found in language and confirmed the presence of five factors (see Norman & Goldberg, 1966; Passini & Norman, 1966). Independently, Tupes and Cristal (1961) also

Applied Perspective 2.1 The Criminal Personality and Eysenck's Theory

One potentially important application of Hans Eysenck's model is the study of the role of personality factors in criminal behaviour and criminal sentiments. If it can be established reliably that certain personality factors are linked with criminality and malevolent behaviour, then it may be possible to identify youth at risk of becoming criminals and to design preventive interventions that will minimize the damage these people can do to themselves and others.

In his book *Crime and Personality*, Eysenck (1977) postulated that the criminal personality is characterized by high levels of psychoticism, extroversion, and neuroticism (known as the **PEN model**), and people with these personality traits are prone to criminality and delinquency. People high in extroversion are theorized to be more likely to engage in criminal and delinquent behaviours because they are high in sensation seeking and they need the arousal associated with engaging in risky and socially unacceptable activities. In addition, conditioning studies have shown that people who are high in neuroticism and extroversion are less able to learn from their mistakes by linking behaviours with the consequences that follow. These individuals are said to have poor **conditionability**. The reduced conditionability of extroverts stems from having a level of arousal that is too low for optimal conditionability, while people high in neuroticism are less "conditionable" because they are overwhelmed by feelings of anxiety. As for psychoticism, certain characteristics believed to compose the psychoticism construct (i.e., aggressive, hostile, low in empathy, and impulsive) are also believed to be characteristics shared by criminals and delinquents.

What does the current research show? Unfortunately, there is limited and mixed evidence to support the PEN model. A comprehensive review of personality predictors of anti-social behaviours in children found strong evidence of a link between psychoticism and anti-social behaviours, but not support for the predictiveness of neuroticism and extroversion (Center & Kemp, 2002).

So, is there a criminal personality? Contemporary researchers have focused on other personality factors. Psychopathy is one such factor linked with criminality. The most highly regarded measure of psychopathy as a personality characteristic is the Psychopathy Checklist-Revised (PCL-R; Hare, 1991). This measure was developed by Robert Hare from the University of British Columbia. It assesses two main factors. The first factor taps the egocentricity, manipulativeness, and callousness of those who are prone to violence and other anti-social acts. The second factor taps the extent to which a person has an unstable and anti-social lifestyle marked by impulsivity and irresponsibility.

Gretton, Hare, and Catchpole (2004) analyzed longitudinal data and concluded that high levels of psychopathy in adolescents is a predictor of risk for violence in early adulthood, and it remains a strong predictor of subsequent risk, even after controlling for other factors such as a known history of conduct disorder and violent offending. Still, some authors have questioned the ability of psychopathy to predict general crimes (Walters, 2004), and there is little doubt that other personality factors probably play a role.

There is limited and mixed evidence to support the theory of a link between personality and the likelihood of becoming a criminal.

If you subscribe to the theory that personality factors are primarily due to biological and genetic factors (see Chapter 3), then you might interpret these data linking crime and anti-social behaviours with psychopathy as evidence that some people are "born criminals" and aggressive tendencies may be inbred. However, the possible role of environment and learning factors should not be discounted, especially given the link between subsequent delinquency and lack of exposure to nurturant parenting (see Scaramella, Conger, Spoth, & Simons, 2002).

detected five factors, and comparable results were later obtained in a re-investigation by Digman and Takemoto-Chock (1981).

What five factors did Norman identify? They are extroversion, agreeableness, conscientiousness, emotional stability, and culture. Culture in this context refers to being a cultured and sophisticated individual versus relatively unsophisticated (i.e., artistically sensitive versus insensitive, intellectual versus unreflective and narrow). An important aspect of Norman's original work and the subsequent evaluations of this work by Digman and Takemoto-Chock (1981) is that the five-factor structure was evident both in self-reports and in informant ratings.

Any list of scholars who have made important contributions in this field would also include such researchers as Goldberg (1993), as well as Costa and McCrae. In addition to his extensive empirical work, it was Goldberg who coined the term the "Big Five" to refer to the five-factor model (see Goldberg, 1981). Meanwhile, Costa and McCrae set out to develop a personality scale that could measure these supertraits without having to use the adjectives found in language (i.e., the lexical approach). The end result is a highly influential personality scale called the NEO-PI-R (Costa & McCrae, 1992b). Initial versions of this scale assessed only three of five factors in the five-factor model, but the remaining traits were added subsequently when the measure was expanded. The five factors, or major dimensions, of personality on the NEO-PI-R are neuroticism, extroversion/introversion, openness to experience, agreeableness/antagonism, and conscientiousness. Six specific facets further define each broad trait dimension. For instance, the facets of conscientiousness are achievement striving, competence, deliberation, dutifulness, order, and self-discipline. The six facets of neuroticism are anxiety, angry hostility, depression, impulsivity, self-consciousness, and vulnerability.

Table 2.3 presents some questionnaire items from the supertraits measured on Costa and McCrae's NEO-PI-R inventory. You can acquire a better sense of what each dimension consists of by reading the table.

Table 2.3 Sample Items from the Revised NEO Personality Inventory Assessing the Five-Factor Model

Neuroticism	I am not a worrier (–) I often feel tense or jittery (+)
Extroversion/ introversion	I'm known as a warm and friendly person (+) Many people think of me as somewhat cold and distant (–)
Openness to experience	I have a very active imagination (+) I don't like to waste my time daydreaming (–)
Agreeableness/ antagonism	I believe that most people will take advantage of you if you let them (–) I think most people I deal with are honest and trustworthy (+)
Conscientiousness	I keep myself informed and usually make intelligent decisions (+) I often come into situations without being prepared (–)

Source: Costa and McCrae, 1992b.

Eysenck (1992) and Costa and McCrae (1992a) squared off and engaged in a lively debate about how many supertraits are needed. Eysenck (1992) maintained that only three factors are needed (his three factors) and that conscientiousness and agreeableness are subsumed by the psychoticism trait. Costa and McCrae (1992a) reiterated that five factors are essential and illustrated the replicability of the five-factor model across many cultures.

Digman is a key figure in this field; he has conducted several studies that have confirmed the presence of five factors. In addition, however, Digman (1997) conducted supplementary analyses on various datasets composed of adults and children and he concluded that the five factors could be represented by two higher order factors that incorporate the five factors. The first super-superfactor was identified as *alpha* and incorporated agreeableness, conscientiousness, and emotional stability. The second super-superfactor was identified as *beta* and incorporated extroversion and intellect. So, based on Digman (1997), we are now down to two factors, but these are exceptionally broad. And what do these two super-superfactors represent? Digman (1997) suggested that the alpha factor represents socialization, while the beta factor represents personal growth. Other researchers have taken to refer to alpha and beta as the "Big Two" (see DeYoung, Peterson, & Higgins, 2002). A team of researchers at the University of Toronto confirmed the presence of the Big Two in a sample of university students and in a sample of community volunteers (DeYoung et al., 2002). DeYoung et al. (2002) interpreted the alpha factor as representing stability and the beta factor as representing plasticity, and showed that conformity is associated positively with stability and negatively with plasticity. They used the factors of the Big Two to suggest that people with high levels of conformity are high in stability but also quite rigid.

In contrast to the Big Two, other researchers have identified seven superfactors! Evidence for the "Big Seven" came from a lexical analysis of the Hebrew language. In addition to identifying five factors that resembled those posited in the five-factor model, Almagor, Tellegen, and Waller (1995) found a "positive valence" factor and a "negative valence" factor. The positive valence factor had trait adjectives such as "fabricator" and "devilish." The negative valence factor had trait adjectives such as "sophisticated," "impressive," and "witty." These evaluative factors likely reflect our tendency to make self-evaluative judgements of ourselves (our "goodness" versus "badness") that get reflected in our sense of self-esteem. Based on their data, the authors concluded that a five-factor model is not extensive enough to represent the valid factors that can be detected in language.

Benet-Martinez and Waller (1997) also reported clear evidence of seven factors when they administered 299 personality descriptors to a sample of 894 Spanish university students. In addition to the usual five factor dimensions, they, too, found a large factor that included adjectives reflecting a positive evaluation, as well as another factor with adjectives reflecting negative evaluation. They concluded that the Big Seven are robust, both cross-culturally and cross-linguistically, and the factors of positive valence and negative valence are relatively independent of each other and are not redundant with the prevailing Big Five. At the same time, some culture-specific findings did emerge. For instance, they found that openness incorporated aspects involving indiscretions that entailed talking too much (e.g., gossiping, disclosing too much). Indeed, other studies have found that it is the openness factor that seems to vary substantially in its content, interpretation, and meaningfulness across cultures (see Bond, 1979; Yang & Bond, 1990).

Saucier and Goldberg (2001) summarized lexical studies conducted in 13 different languages, and they concluded that what is referred to as the Anglo-Germanic Big Five is found more clearly in some languages than others. Although there is substantial agreement across studies, there is substantial variability as well. Saucier and Goldberg (2001) attributed some of this variability to the fact that by using personality descriptors in different languages as the starting points, different researchers are starting with different variables, making cross-study comparisons difficult. Still, it is evident that complete uniformity does not seem to exist.

KEY POINTS

- The five-factor model is seen as pervasive across cultures. It was identified based on the lexical analyses of words. The five factors are openness, conscientiousness, agreeableness, extroversion, and neuroticism.
- Researchers have identified a seven-factor model with additional factors reflecting positive self-evaluations and negative self-evaluations.
- Two even broader super-superfactors have been found based on analyses of the five-factor model. The alpha factor is a combination of conscientiousness, agreeableness, and lack of neuroticism. The beta factor reflects openness and extroversion.

Readers who are new to the field of personality must be starting to feel overwhelmed by the many alternative conceptualizations available of the supertraits. Although the search for supertraits is important and has provided much new information, this emphasis on supertraits is dangerous if we lose sight of the potential importance of more narrow, specific traits. The next section illustrates this point by considering individual differences in trait procrastination. The importance of studying procrastinators from an applied perspective is also illustrated.

The Predictiveness of Specific "Narrow" Traits

The ability of smaller, specific factors to predict outcome measures is an important theme of research conducted on procrastination. Procrastination is defined as an irrational tendency to delay tasks that should be completed (Lay, 1986). One way to conceptualize procrastination is that it is a personality trait that involves an extreme lack of conscientiousness. The close association between procrastination and low conscientiousness has been confirmed by research on the correlations between trait procrastination and the facets of the five-factor model. Several relevant studies have been conducted over the years. For instance, Watson (2001) examined academic procrastination in a sample of students from Alberta and showed that academic procrastination was associated with facets of low conscientiousness (i.e., low levels of competence, order, discipline, achievement striving, self-discipline, and deliberation) and high neuroticism (i.e., anxiety, depression, self-consciousness, impulsiveness, and vulnerability).

Recently, van Eerde (2004) from the Netherlands reported the results of a meta-analysis on the association between procrastination and the five-factor model. A meta-analysis is a quantitative review that involves tabulating the average effect sizes across all of the available studies that have examined a particular topic. In this instance, van Eerde included data from 45 samples across 41 different articles with more than 9,000 people. Overall, 87% of samples consisted of university or college students, and 71% of the samples came from North America. The largest association was a strong negative association between conscientiousness and procrastination. In addition, there was a smaller but still significant association between procrastination and neuroticism. Negligible associations were obtained with the other trait dimensions of the five-factor model.

Given the strong association between low conscientiousness and procrastination, perhaps the predictive usefulness of procrastination measures is relatively unimportant once the conscientiousness superfactor is considered. Research by Clarry Lay at York University in Toronto indicates that this is definitely not the case. Lay (1997), one of the world leaders in the study of procrastination, demonstrated that once the five-factor model is taken into account, his trait measure of procrastination is still a robust predictor of scores on a checklist assessing dilatory behaviours (i.e., delaying tendencies tapped by items such as "I phoned or visited friends when I should have been studying"), over and above trait conscientiousness.

Extreme procrastination can be debilitating, and perhaps even life-threatening for some people who are chronic procrastinators. Accordingly, it is the subject of Applied Perspective 2.2.

Applied Perspective 2.2 Trait Procrastination and the Counselling of Procrastinators

Procrastination has been described by a team of researchers from Israel as "a dysfunction of important human abilities" in routine daily tasks and critical life tasks (Milgram, Sroloff, & Rosenbaum, 1998, p. 210). The extent of the dysfunction is reflected by estimates indicating that at least 25% of students suffer from severe levels of procrastination (see McCown, Johnson, & Petzel, 1989).

Contemporary research on procrastination has addressed several interrelated questions. These questions include (1) What are the characteristics and correlates of procrastination? (2) To what extent is procrastination associated with maladjustment? and (3) What can be done to help the troubled procrastinator?

Before these issues are examined, an important question needs to be asked: Are you a procrastinator? Table 2.4 lists the items that compose the Procrastination Cognitions Inventory, which was developed by Stainton, Lay, and Flett (2000). Consider each thought statement and indicate how often you have experienced this thought in the past week, by giving yourself a "0" if not at all and a "4" if you experienced it all the time, and somewhere in between if you experienced the thought but not all the time.

Your score would be the sum of the 18 items on the Procrastination Cognitions Inventory. The average score is approximately 29 with a standard deviation of about 17. This means that if your score is 46 or higher (or stated in another way, you averaged at least a 2 on each item), you are relatively high in the frequency of cognitions involving procrastination.

What are some of the things that have been learned thus far about the procrastination construct? First, not all procrastinators are alike. Lay (1987) found that most procrastinators are distressed and tend to be pessimistic about the future, but there is a subset (about one third) who are "optimistic procrastinators." These procrastinators seem to require and may perhaps even enjoy the increased arousal that is experienced as deadlines loom large. The two main motives for procrastinating are fear of failure

Table 2.4 Thoughts Assessed on the Procrastination Cognitions Inventory

1. Why can't I do what I should be doing?
2. I need to start earlier.
3. I should be more responsible.
4. I should be doing more studying.
5. No matter how much I try, I still put things off.
6. People expect me to work and study more.
7. Why can't I just get started?
8. I know I'm behind but I can catch up.
9. I'm behind in my studies this time, but next time it will be different.
10. I'm letting myself down.
11. This is not how I want to be.
12. It would be great if everything in my life were done on time.
13. I'm such a procrastinator, I will never reach my goals.
14. I need deadlines to get me going.
15. I can turn it in late.
16. I really don't like studying.
17. Why can't I finish things that I start?
18. Why didn't I start earlier?

and having a task that is so aversive and overwhelming, you would rather delay (Solomon & Rothblum, 1984). It is also possible that some people delay as a reactive form of rebelliousness (they don't like other people telling them what to do).

Second, there are some obvious negative consequences for students who are extreme procrastinators. Tice and Baumeister (1997) showed that procrastinators, relative to non-procrastinators, took longer to hand in their term papers and assignments and received lower grades. Analyses of indices of stress and illness showed that procrastinators reported less stress and less illness at the beginning of the term, but the pattern had reversed by the end of term. Procrastinators experienced more stress and illness in the long run.

Jennifer Lavoie at Simon Fraser University in Vancouver and Tim Pychyl at Carleton University (2001) have investigated trait procrastination and cyberslacking. Cyberslacking is the tendency to excessively use the Internet as a way of avoiding other work. Lavoie and Pychyl conducted a survey on the Internet with respondents from around North America. They found that approximately one half of the respondents reported frequent Internet procrastination and acknowledged that they spent time online as a way of engaging in procrastination. Internet procrastination was correlated significantly with trait procrastination, and those who engaged in Internet procrastination tended to feel that it was a way of relieving stress. This is ironic, however, because there is little doubt that some of these people probably made their lives even more stressful by either missing deadlines or by becoming more anxious about looming deadlines.

So, what problems have been linked with procrastination? Extensive research has established that procrastination is associated with depression, anxiety, low self-esteem, and stress (Flett, Blankstein, & Martin, 1995; Stainton et al., 2000). Accordingly, it is not surprising that procrastination is a topic that has been discussed at length by clinicians and counsellors. Growing awareness of the difficulties experienced by procrastinating students culminated in a book entitled *Counseling the Procrastinator in Academic Settings* (see Schouwenburg, Lay, Pychyl, & Ferrari, 2004). This book illustrates the inextricable links among personality theory, personality research, and practical applications. Various chapters in this book outline the problems associated with procrastination and counselling techniques and strategies for combating procrastination. Contributing authors discuss such topics as self-management and self-control techniques for procrastinators (van Essen, van den Heuvel, & Ossebaard, 2004), behavioural interventions (Tuckman & Schouwenburg, 2004), and cognitive-based interventions (Mandel, 2004). Collectively, these interventions emphasize learning specific skills but also developing a more positive and self-confident orientation toward academic work.

Careful reading of this counselling book and the burgeoning literature on procrastination leaves the unmistakable impression that theory and research are vitally important, but even more significant is the ability to take these conceptualizations and empirical findings and translate them into interventions that may help the struggling, procrastinating student. This book on procrastination is a good starting point, and seeking counselling is another advised step for readers who may been alarmed by the score they obtained when they answered the Procrastination Cognitions Inventory.

Supertraits across Cultures

An assumption of personality theorists who have hypothesized supertraits is that they apply universally across cultures. This reflects a growing interest in psychology in identifying "universals" or commonalities across people throughout the world (see Norenzayan & Heine, 2005).

Research on the universality of the five-factor model has tended to provide general support for the model when participants from various countries have been assessed. For instance, evidence suggesting the validity of the five-factor model was obtained in a study of samples of Filipino high school and university students (Church, Reyes, Katigbak, & Grimm, 1997). Church et al. (1997) found factors that were comparable to agreeableness, conscientiousness, extroversion, and intellect, as well as a self-assurance factor that resembled neuroticism. A follow-up investigation found evidence that the five-factor model was applicable to participants from the Philippines (Katigbak et al., 2002).

The Five-Factor Personality Inventory (Hendriks, Hofstee, & De Raad, 1999) is another measure that appears to have a substantial degree of cross-cultural generalizability. This measure was developed via the lexical approach. The five factors include four that overlap with and resemble those included in other frameworks (extroversion, agreeableness, conscientiousness, and emotional stability). However, rather than having a culture, intellect, or openness factor, the Five-Factor Personality Inventory has an autonomy factor. Hendriks et al. (1999) noted that the initial intent was to have an openness factor, but the end result was a fifth factor that seemed to be more representative of individual differences in autonomy (self-sufficiency and freedom from influence). The emergence of this factor and work emphasizing it is interesting given that developmental theories often include stages of development where autonomy issues are very salient, and self-determination models of motivation also place a great emphasis on individual differences in autonomy. The Five-Factor Personality Inventory does seem to have factors that generalize across cultures. Hendriks et al. (2003) compared the responses of participants from 13 countries, including Israel, Japan, Germany, Italy, Spain, England, and the Netherlands. Analyses provided clear evidence of the existence of five factors in all cultures except the United States, and the authors attributed this problem to low sample size in the American subsample. Overall, then, we have a situation where a five-factor measure is generalizable. However, factors specific to certain regions also exist. This topic is explored in more detail in International Focus on Discovery 2.2.

International Focus on Discovery 2.2 The Five-Factor Model across Cultures and Indigenous Characteristics

Cross-cultural psychologists make an important distinction between an *emic* approach and an *etic* approach (see Kim, 2000). One criticism of much research is that it follows an **etic approach** because this involves exporting supposed universal findings and models and applying them to specific cultures. Etic represents imported concepts imposed on a culture. This may involve some gross overgeneralizations and mistaken beliefs that concepts relevant in one culture are also relevant in other specific cultures. In contrast, an **emic approach** involves establishing and identifying culture-specific factors and processes. It is an indigenous approach. It incorporates the impact of local and regional influences that have an impact on the development of the emerging personality.

Researchers investigating indigenous personality factors are interested in the differences within a defined region for their own sake, and generalizability issues are not of central importance. That is, **indigenous personality research** is based on the premise that an understanding of individual differences in a particular culture is a worthy goal in its own right. There is little immediate concern with generalizability because the purpose is to establish the important concepts with a specific culture.

Thus far, much of the existing research on personality from an indigenous perspective has been conducted in China. Important work is being conducted by Fanny Cheung and Kwok Leung and their colleagues (see Cheung et al., 2001; Cheung & Cheung, 2003). They created the Chinese Personality Assessment Inventory (CPAI) to assess behavioural and emotional problems and four broad personality characteristics: (1) social potency; (2) dependability; (3) accommodation; and (4) interpersonal relatedness. The specific subscales of the revised Chinese Personality Assessment Inventory-2 (Cheung, Leung, Song, & Zhang, 2001) that contribute to these four broad factors are shown in Table 2.5.

Dr. Fanny Cheung and her colleagues created the Chinese Personality Assessment Inventory (CPAI) to assess behaviour and emotional problems and personality characteristics.

Cheung et al. (2001) reported three studies of the degree of association between the constructs assessed by the CPAI and the five-factor model, as assessed by Costa and McCrae's NEO-PI-R. The first two studies were conducted with Chinese students and Chinese managers, while the third study was

Table 2.5 Factors and Subscales of the Chinese Personality Assessment Inventory-2

Factor	Subscales
Social Potency	novelty, diversity, divergent thinking, leadership, logical versus affective orientation, aesthetics, extroversion versus introversion, enterprise
Dependability	responsibility, emotionality, inferiority versus self-acceptance, practical mindedness, optimism versus pessimism, meticulousness, face, internal versus external locus of control, family orientation
Accommodation	defensiveness, graciousness versus meanness, interpersonal tolerance, self versus social orientation, veraciousness versus slickness
Interpersonal Relatedness	traditionalism versus modernity, Ren Qing (Relationship Orientation), social sensitivity, discipline, harmony, thrift versus extravagance

conducted with Hawaiian students. Cheung et al. (2001) found that the indigenous factor composed of interpersonal relatedness (see Table 2.5) was unique and not captured by the NEO-PI-R. The interpersonal relatedness assesses the degree of interrelatedness that people have (the connection between the self and others). This factor predicted a variety of outcomes such as trust, persuasion tactics, and communication styles, even after taking into account the ability of the measures from the five-factor model to predict these outcomes.

Lin and Church (2004) tested whether the indigenous personality constructs found in research in China could be detected in other samples. They had Chinese American and European American participants complete the CPAI and when it was assessed, they found that the interpersonal relatedness factor was clearly evident in their Western sample. Thus, this interpersonal relatedness factor is indigenous to Chinese participants but it is generalizable and detectable in other samples. Studies such as those conducted by Lin and Church (2004) have resulted in Cheung et al. (2001) re-naming the CPAI-2 so that now it is being referred to as the Cross-Cultural Personality Assessment Inventory (see Cheung & Cheung, 2003).

Indigenous factors have been identified with various measures. We noted earlier that Church et al. (1997) found general support for the five-factor model after analysing data from Filipino participants. However, two other factors emerged. One factor described as "Filipino temperamentalness" had some overlap with dimensions of the five-factor model but was nevertheless regarded as a distinct, indigenous factor.

It seems intuitively reasonable that certain factors and personality processes involve broad themes that may be universal, or at least mostly universal. However, certain factors and personality processes of significance will exist in specific cultures, and any attempt to describe, understand, and predict someone's behaviour in a specific culture must also place substantial importance on these indigenous characteristics.

Challenges for the Five-Factor Model

The five-factor model and other broad trait schemes face several other challenges. Revelle (1987) and McAdams (1992) criticized five-factor models, arguing that they are primarily descriptive rather than explanatory, and they lack the conceptual basis that must be present to be considered a theory. McCrae and Costa (1996) responded with an extended theoretical account that incorporated the notion that neuroticism, extroversion, openness, agreeableness, and conscientiousness are basic tendencies that are rooted developmentally in biological bases. However, it can be argued that a more extensive explanation of the origins of the five-factor model is still required.

A specific criticism of the five-factor model comes from clinical psychologists and researchers interested in the study of psychopathology (for a review, see Shedler & Westen, 2004). Several authors have questioned the five-factor model's utility when applied to severely disturbed individuals, and they have suggested alternative frameworks involving five factors that they have deemed to be more relevant to individual differences involving psychopathology. They have argued correctly that describing someone as having "disagreeableness" does not capture the extreme anti-social tendencies of the psychopath. Some alternative conceptualizations such as the PSY-5, a five-factor model derived from the Minnesota Multiphasic Personality Inventory, are outlined in Chapter 13, which examines the role of personality factors in psychopathology.

Recall the challenge stated earlier that involves the apparent importance of more narrow, specific traits. We have already discussed this issue with respect to the predictiveness of procrastination versus conscientiousness. More generally, are narrow personality factors able to predict criteria after already taking into account the broad personality factors that comprise the five-factor model? Saucier and Goldberg (1998) analyzed clusters of personality trait descriptors that capture important individual differences yet are not highly correlated with existing traits in the five-factor model. The general conclusion that emerged from their study was that although it was possible to identify these seemingly distinct personality attributes, most characteristics could be readily interpreted as correlates of the five-factor model.

This conclusion was disputed by Paunonen and Jackson (2000), who reanalyzed the original data gathered by Saucier and Goldberg (1998). They showed that a greater proportion of personality adjectives fell outside the purview of the five-factor model when more relaxed criteria were used. Overall, they identified 26 personality trait clusters that could be grouped into nine distinct personality categories that do not seem to fit readily into the five-factor model. These categories included factors tapping religiosity (e.g., religious, devout, reverent), sexuality (e.g., sexy, sensual, erotic), and fiscal conservatism (e.g., thrifty, frugal, miserly). Perhaps you have known a religious person, an overaroused person, or a cheap person. If asked, Paunonen and Jackson (2000) would probably have suggested that the salient attributes of these people in your life are not easily captured by the factors of the five-factor model.

Paunonen and his associates went on to examine this issue in an international investigation with a newly created measure known as the Supernumerary Personality Inventory (SPI) (see Paunonen, Haddock, Forsterling, & Keinonen, 2003). The co-authors provided data from Canada, Wales, Germany, and Finland. The SPI scales are illustrated in Table 2.6. The SPI is composed of factors that Paunonen and Jackson (2000) deemed to be relatively independent of the five-factor model. This measure was pitted against a measure of the five-factor model (the NEO-FFI) to ascertain their relative ability to predict 19 criterion variables, including grade point average, getting regular exercise, drinking alcohol, and driving too fast.

Both the SPI and NEO-FFI predicted several criterion variables, but the SPI was much better at predicting the criteria, and this pattern was evident across all four datasets from the four countries. Importantly, the SPI factors predicted unique variance in certain outcome variables (e.g., use of alcohol and tobacco) even after statistically controlling the variance attributable to the five-factor dimensions.

Although several findings were common to all four cultures tapped in this study, Paunonen et al. (2003) noted that many findings did not hold across all four cultures. The general pattern they observed was that results were similar for the English-speaking participants in the Canadian and British samples, relative to the participants from Germany and Finland. They concluded that it is important to keep an open mind about possible cultural differences because "different cultures could have different behavioural determinants, and consequently, different personality-behaviour correlations" (Paunonen et al., 2003, p. 430).

Another challenge to the five-factor model's validity is the claim that it does not capture other broad personality trait dimensions of importance. For instance, Ashton and his associates have provided empirical evidence that a trait dimension involving honesty is

Table 2.6 Scales on the Supernumerary Personality Inventory (SPI)

Scale	Description
Conventionality	Wants to preserve existing traditions and institutions Is opposed to radical change or innovation
Seductiveness	Engages in behaviours intended to attract the romantic or sexual interests of others Can be charming and flirtatious
Manipulativeness	Tries to use others to achieve his or her goals May use diplomacy, flattery, ingratiation, or even deception
Thriftiness	Does not waste resources of self-gratification Is economical and not given to extravagances
Humour	Has the ability to arouse amusement and laughter in other people Is also quick to see the humour in situations
Integrity	Shuns behaviours involving stealing, cheating, or deceiving Believes that such behaviours are never acceptable
Femininity	Is considered feminine for his or her own sex Displays behaviours and emotions that might be considered effeminate
Religiosity	Is devoted to some ultimate reality or deity, a higher power that is believed to control one's destiny Is spiritual
Risk-Taking	Seeks out and is stimulated by situations involving risk of bodily harm Is positively aroused by danger
Egotism	Has an exaggerated sense of self-importance Feels superior to others and may be contemptuous of them

Source: Adapted from Paunonen et al., 2003, p.418.

empirically distinguishable from the five-factor model (see Ashton, Lee, & Soon, 2000). Thus, it can be argued that a morality factor should also be considered (note that this factor would help detect psychopaths). Evidence of this honesty or "morality" factor has emerged in lexical analyses of personality terms in various languages, including English, French, German, Hungarian, Italian, and Korean (Angleitner & Ostendorf, 1989; Boies, Lee, Ashton, Pascal, & Nicho, 2001; Hahn, Lee, & Ashton, 1999; Peabody, 1987; Peabody & Goldberg, 1989).

Saucier (2002) has criticized research by Ashton and his colleagues on the grounds that an honesty dimension involves evaluative judgements and that lexical analyses of the five-factor model were supposed to be based on personality descriptions rather than words with evaluative content. However, there can be no doubting that exceedingly moral people can be found in the real world, both now and throughout history, and the potential importance of a morality trait dimension is underscored by considering some of the exceptionally immoral acts that certain world leaders have perpetrated throughout history.

However, Saucier's criticisms do underscore the fact that a great deal of subjectivity is involved when evaluating the adequacy of trait schemes; there are no established statistical or conceptual criteria for determining whether a trait dimension should be considered a supertrait. How big does a factor have to be in order for it to be super? And who gets to decide the best way to identify these traits?

KEY POINTS

- A challenge to broad schemes such as the five-factor model is that more narrow and specific traits such as procrastination account for a significant degree of unique variance in outcome variables, above and beyond the variance attributable to the traits of the five-factor model.
- The five-factor model does not capture indigenous traits of importance in individual cultures.
- The five-factor model has been criticized for being descriptive rather than explanatory.
- It has been argued that the five-factor model has limited clinical utility, and five-factor models specific to psychopathology have emerged.
- There is an apparent need to expand the five-factor model to include broad dimensions reflecting themes such as morality and honesty.

When one reads studies that assess constructs that seem to go beyond the five-factor model, one cannot help being reminded of a significant point raised initially by Cattell (1965). Cattell suggested that our overarching goal should be to get an unbiased estimate of "the whole" in terms of "the totality of human behaviour." He coined the term "**personality sphere**" to refer to the totality of human behaviour. While the identification of supertraits is an important goal in its own right, other traits, perhaps more narrow, deserve consideration as well, especially when they are highly pertinent to people's daily lives. As a way of underscoring this key point, the next section focuses on individual differences in locus of control.

The locus of control construct has not been mentioned as a supertrait, and it is garnering less attention recently. However, the locus of control construct is vitally important to the salient differences that exist among people, either within a culture or from different cultures. This chapter concludes with a description and overview of the locus of control construct.

ANALYSIS OF A KEY PERSONALITY TRAIT: LOCUS OF CONTROL

It is assumed by some theorists that all humans are characterized by a universal drive to have control over their environments (Schulz & Heckhausen, 1996) because a life filled with chaos is simply too unsettling and distressing. Although the importance of control is widely recognized and may indeed be a universal theme, a focus on control has not been incorporated into the broad schemes that tap personality superfactors. Do individual differences involving a sense of control deserve to be incorporated into these frameworks? This is a topic for future research. Some research has tied locus of control to neuroticism (Judge, Erez, Bono, & Thoreson, 2002), but whether locus of control is a distinguishable dimension remains to be determined. What is clear at the moment is that a strong case can be made that the control construct represents a core theme for many people in the issues they face in their daily lives. Feeling out of control or in control can have a profound influence on our other thoughts, feelings, and behaviours. As Lefcourt (1966) from the University of Waterloo, Ontario, noted in his influential review paper, feeling that we are pawns of chance and fate can lead to a profound state of apathy and susceptibility to stress. However, Lefcourt (1979) also noted that a sense of control leads to great vitality. Specifically, he observed that

"When people believe that outcomes flow from their actions, then behavior becomes more purposive, and, to others, they seem to be much more alive" (p. 197).

Jerry Phares and Julian Rotter are two very prominent theorists in this area. They identified and developed the locus of control construct. **Locus of control** refers to individual differences in internal versus external control of reinforcement (Rotter, 1990). Phares (1993) recounted the intriguing story of how theory and research on locus of control came about. As colleagues, Phares encountered a patient named Karl and contacted Rotter to be a consultant on the case. Eventually, they came to realize that Karl suffered from the perception that he had little personal control over the reinforcements in his life. Phares and Rotter went on to develop a theory about individual differences in locus of control, and Rotter (1966) constructed his famous Locus of Control Scale, which is reproduced in Table 2.7. You can assess your own locus of control. Scoring information is also given in Table 2.7.

Table 2.7 Rotter's Locus of Control Scale

1a.	Children get into trouble because their parents punish them too much.
1b.	The trouble with most children is that their parents are too easy with them.
2a.	Many of the unhappy things in people's lives are partly due to bad luck.
2b.	People's misfortunes result from the mistakes they make.
3a.	One of the major reasons why we have wars is because people don't take enough interest in politics.
3b.	There will always be wars, no matter how hard people try to prevent them.
4a.	In the long run people get the respect they deserve in this world.
4b.	Unfortunately, an individual's worth often goes unrecognized no matter how hard he/she tries.
5a.	The idea that teachers are unfair to students is nonsense.
5b.	Most students don't realize the extent to which their grades are influenced by accidental happenings.
6a.	Without the right breaks, one cannot be an effective leader.
6b.	Capable people who fail to become leaders have not taken advantage of their opportunities.
7a.	No matter how hard you try, some people just don't like you.
7b.	People who can't get others to like them don't understand how to get along with others.
8a.	Heredity plays the major role in determining one's personality.
8b.	It is one's experiences in life which determine what they're like.
9a.	I have often found that what is going to happen will happen.
9b.	Trusting fate has never turned out as well for me as making a decision to take a definite course of action.
10a.	In the case of the well prepared student there is rarely, if ever, such a thing as an unfair test.
10b.	Many times, exam questions tend to be so unrelated to course work that studying is really useless.
11a.	Becoming a success is a matter of hard work; luck has little or nothing to do with it.
11b.	Getting a good job depends mainly on being in the right place at the right time.
12a.	The average citizen can have an influence in government decisions.
12b.	This world is run by the few people in power, and there is not much the little guy can do about it.
13a.	When I make plans, I am almost certain that I can make them work.
13b.	It is not always wise to plan too far ahead because many things turn out to be a matter of good or bad fortune anyhow.

14a. There are certain people who are just no good. 14b. There is some good in everybody.
15a. In my case getting what I want has little or nothing to do with luck. 15b. Many times we might just as well decide what to do by flipping a coin.
16a. Who gets to be the boss often depends on who was lucky enough to be in the right place first. 16b. Getting people to do the right thing depends upon ability—luck has little or nothing to do with it.
17a. As far as world affairs are concerned, most of us are the victims of forces we can neither understand, nor control. 17b. By taking an active part in political and social affairs people can control world events.
18a. Most people don't realize the extent to which their lives are controlled by accidental happenings. 18b. There really is no such thing as "luck."
19a. One should always be willing to admit mistakes. 19b. It is usually best to cover up one's mistakes.
20a. It is hard to know whether or not a person really likes you. 20b. How many friends you have depends upon how nice a person you are.
21a. In the long run the bad things that happen to us are balanced by the good ones. 21b. Most misfortunes are the result of lack of ability, ignorance, laziness, or all three.
22a. With enough effort we can wipe out political corruption. 22b. It is difficult for people to have much control over the things politicians do in office.
23a. Sometimes I can't understand how teachers arrive at the grades they give. 23b. There is a direct connection between how hard I study and the grades I get.
24a. A good leader expects people to decide for themselves what they should do. 24b. A good leader makes it clear to everybody what their jobs are.
25a. Many times I feel that I have little influence over the things that happen to me. 25b. It is impossible for me to believe that chance or luck plays an important role in my life.
26a. People are lonely because they don't try to be friendly. 26b. There's not much use in trying too hard to please people; if they like you, they like you.
27a. There is too much emphasis on athletics in high school. 27b. Team sports are an excellent way to build character.
28a. What happens to me is my own doing. 28b. Sometimes I feel that I don't have enough control over the direction my life is taking.
29a. Most of the time I can't understand why politicians behave the way they do. 29b. In the long run the people are responsible for bad government on a national as well as on a local level.
Score one point for each of the following: 2.a, 3.b, 4.b, 5.b, 6.a, 7.a, 9.a, 10.b, 11.b, 12.b, 13.b, 15.b, 16.a, 17.a, 18.a, 20.a, 21.a, 22.b, 23.a, 25.a, 26.b, 28.b, 29.a. Higher scores reflect a more external locus of control. Original norms reported by Rotter (1966) indicate that the average score for students is approximately 9, with an approximate standard deviation of 4, suggesting that scores of 15 and above would clearly suggest an external locus of control, while scores of 5 or less connote an internal locus of control.

Source: Rotter, 1966.

The process of interacting with real people, sometimes in a therapeutic context, is how many research ideas are born. Much of the appeal of the locus of control concept and its focus on people who feel a sense of control over the reinforcements in their lives (i.e., the internals) versus those people who feel that control over reinforcements are outside of themselves (i.e., the externals) is that we often encounter events and situations that make us feel either in control or out of control. And Rotter (1990) suggested that another reason why the locus of control construct has received great interest over the years is because the construct was embedded within a theory and measurement was guided by theoretical principles and hypotheses.

Rotter's Locus of Control Scale is a 29-item forced choice scale that was designed to be a unidimensional measure. That is, it was supposed to measure one factor and provide one score to assess the extent to which a person has an internal versus external locus of control. However, one study detected six smaller factors that contribute to a more general, higher order factor (see Marsh & Richards, 1987). Given this evidence of different factors within the Rotter scale, Marsh and Richards (1987) suggested that focus on locus of control as a global, generalized solitary dimension may not be warranted.

Spheres of Control

Rotter's Locus of Control Scale has been supplemented by measures that view the construct as multidimensional. The Spheres of Control Scale by Paulhus (1983) is a 30-item measure that assesses three locus of control dimensions. The first dimension is personal control, the second is interpersonal control, and the third dimension is socio-political control. A more recent version of the scale can be found in Paulhus and Van Selst (1990).

A similar measure is Levenson's IPC Locus of Control Scale (Levenson, 1981). It consists of three eight-item scales that measure beliefs in internality (e.g., "When I make plans, I am almost certain to make them work"), powerful others (e.g., "I feel like what happens in my life is mostly determined by other people"), and chance (e.g., "To a great extent, my life is controlled by accidental happenings").

One important caveat about the locus of control construct is that it is vitally important to assess this issue from a cross-cultural perspective and to use measures that are culturally sensitive. This need to create culturally sensitive and relevant measures is a key assessment issue that is discussed at length in Chapter 4. In terms of locus of control, comparative studies have identified differences between representatives of different cultures. One common finding is that Asians, relative to Americans, typically have scores that suggest a more external locus of control (Hamid, 1994; Hui, 1982; Smith, Trompenaars, & Dugan, 1995). A similar pattern has emerged in research on a construct known as work locus of control (the sense of internal versus external control of reinforcements in the job setting). Spector and associates compared levels of work locus of control with samples representing 24 nations (Spector et al., 2002). They found that participants from the People's Republic of China, Hong Kong, and Taiwan tended to have more external scores than most other countries sampled, including those in North America and Europe.

However, in a study, Spector, Sanchez, Siu, Salgado, and Ma (2004) showed that these results are biased, in part, because there are other ways to frame the locus of control construct such that Asian participants score in a more internal direction. Specifically, they advanced the construct of socio-instrumental control in the work context. This is the notion that we can develop a sense of control via our interpersonal relationships at work, and socio-instrumental control should be elevated in cultures that emphasize the connection between self and other people. Indeed, the Asian participants in this research scored higher in this type of locus of control, relative to the American participants. That is, they were more likely to endorse items such as "It is important to cultivate relationships with superiors at work if you want to get ahead," and "You can get your own way at work if you learn how to get along with other people." Asian people may have a more internal locus of control than first believed, but it is fostered through developing relationships with other people.

Another important consideration is that it appears that the locus of control scores vary by age cohort. Absolute levels of locus of control have been shown to vary over time in a manner suggesting that there are **cohort effects**, which involve differences associated with the historical period of assessment. Doherty and Baldwin (1985) evaluated scores on Rotter's Locus of Control Scale throughout the 1970s for a sample consisting of older and younger men and women. They found that as the decade progressed, the scores of women increasingly reflected an external locus of control, while the scores of men did not vary substantially over time. The authors suggested that this shift toward externality reflected an increasing awareness among women of the external constraints on their ability to meet their employment goals. More recently, Twenge, Zhang, and Im (2004) studied samples of American college students and children who were assessed between 1960 and 2002. They confirmed that locus of control scores have become progressively more external in subsequent generations for both men and women. In fact, they concluded that the typical college students evaluated in 2002 would have a more external locus of control than 4 out of 5 college students evaluated in the early 1960s. The authors suggested that this is "uniformly negative" (p. 308) in its implications because other research has linked an external locus of control with such outcomes as poorer school achievement, stress, and depression (see Benassi, Sweeney, and Dufour, 1988; Ganellen & Blaney, 1984).

Locus of control scores also seem susceptible, at least temporarily, to world events in general. Chia, Allred, Hall, and Smith (2003) compared responses to Levenson's IPC Locus of Control Scale in successive samples of university students over a three-year period, including a sample of participants who completed the scale about 10 days after the terrorist attacks in the United States on September 11, 2001. As expected, levels of internal control went down after the incidents and levels of external control went up. However, six months later, mean scores returned to levels comparable to before 9-11.

KEY POINTS

- Locus of control reflects differences in perceptions of control over reinforcements. Internal locus of control sees control as stemming from inside the person. External control sees control as being outside the self (i.e., in the environment or due to other people or chance).
- The locus of control construct is multi-faceted. It can be assessed based on perceptions of personal control, socio-political control, work locus of control, and so on.
- Cohort analyses indicate that locus of control scores have become increasingly more external over the past several decades.

The Desire for Control

Research on locus of control tells us whether the person feels that he or she is in control of outcomes or is controlled by factors outside the self. It does not tell us about who wants control the most. We have all heard stories of people who have been described, often in a derogatory manner, as "control freaks." These people must have a sense of personal control, and it is very threatening to them when they do not. These people are clearly different from individuals who seem relatively unfocused on control issues and are seemingly unperturbed by circumstances that are not controllable.

The Desire for Control Scale (Burger & Cooper, 1979) is a 20-item measure of the level of motivation to have control over the events in one's life. The measure's predictive utility has been demonstrated in numerous contexts (see Burger, 1984, 1990). One of the most compelling investigations here examined the interplay of locus of control and desire for control in predicting depression and suicidal tendencies (see Burger, 1984). A sample of students from Wake Forest University in North Carolina completed measures of locus of control, desire for control, and depression. These same students completed another measure of depression six months later. It was found that depression was associated with an external locus of control focused on the belief that events are due to chance. In addition, if students had this external locus of control but they also had a high desire for control, then they were more likely to seek help for their depression from non-professional sources. Thus, locus of control *interacted* with desire for control to predict help-seeking behaviour. Students with a high need for control but an external locus of control were also more likely to experience suicidal thoughts.

A study from the Netherlands confirmed that it is meaningful to assess the desire for control in that country, and the researchers also reported that the Desire for Control Scale has acceptable measurement qualities when administered to their sample of Dutch participants (Gebhardt & Brosschot, 2002). Moreover, these researchers isolated three factors within the Desire for Control Scale: (1) a desire to be in charge of and control others; (2) a desire to establish a sense of control over personal outcomes involving the self; and (3) a willingness to relinquish control to other people. These researchers also showed that there was a positive, moderate correlation between an internal locus of control and the desire for control, but the correlation suggested that these constructs are associated but not redundant with each other. Other correlates of desire for control in this research included elevated levels of dominance, higher self-esteem and active problem-solving, and low levels of fear of failure and worry. People with a high desire for control were also less likely to use avoidant coping when faced with stress.

So, the message here from the research on control is quite clear: there is a substantial difference between trait locus of control and individual differences in needs and motives, and both merit consideration.

Summary

This chapter began with a description of personality types, with personality types being illustrated by considering the three somatotypes outlined by Sheldon. Types were described as all-or-none categories. They are qualitatively distinct and differ in kind rather than in degree.

Historical and contemporary research on types was described. The work of anthropologists was focused on establishing the national character of various countries. Current research indicates that there is consensus among students of their perceptions of the personalities of countries, but these stereotypes are not reflected in differences in the personalities of people from various countries.

Other contemporary research of personality types distinguishes among resilient, overcontrolling, and undercontrolling people. Although different types have emerged from various investigations, there is substantial evidence of these types' long-term stability and meaningfulness.

Types were then differentiated from traits, which are continuous dimensions. Traits differ in degree rather than in kind and refer to personality attributes that you have more or less. Allport's various assertions about personality traits were outlined, including his important distinction between central and cardinal dispositions.

The chapter examined criticisms of the trait approach raised by Mischel about the notion that traits represent stable individual differences that generalize across situations. A focus on situationism was presented and it was noted that the relative impact of personality traits and situational factors is comparable. An alternative that focuses on the interaction between traits and situations was presented, and it was noted that there is a need to differentiate between mechanistic and dynamic interactionism models. The concept of interactionism was further elaborated upon by describing Endler's interactionism model of anxiety.

The issue of personality traits was then discussed within the context of competing theoretical frameworks that emphasize three superfactors (Eysenck) versus five superfactors (Costa and McCrae and others) versus a seven-factor model. Various objections to the five-factor model were then raised, including findings from emic research testing of the lexical hypothesis (i.e., the structure of personality factors found in language). Finally, the viability of focusing on specific traits was illustrated by looking in detail at research and theory on trait constructs such as procrastination and locus of control.

Next, this chapter discussed alternatives to the current way in which personality traits are studied. Personal capabilities are an assessment of what people are capable of and the range of behaviours they can display. Personality capabilities reflect a maximal approach to personality assessment (as opposed to a trait focus on "typical" personality features).

Metatraits were described along with the associated notion that each person differs in the relevance or central importance of personality trait dimensions.

Questions to Consider

1 Review the personality typology and the factors that were used to form the categories described in Table 2.2. Because it is a typology, it should apply to virtually everyone. Which category do you feel most applies to you? Do you have features of more than one of the four categories?

2 Review Allport's distinctions among cardinal, central, and secondary traits; then reflect on your own cardinal and central dispositions. If Allport asked you to list your cardinal and central dispositions, what would you tell him? What would you tell him if he asked you whether the distinction between cardinal and central dispositions is useful?

3 Describe the five supertraits of the five-factor model. Do you see each trait as relevant to you? Do you endorse the Big Two, the Big Three, the Big Five, or the Big Seven? Or none of the above?

4 As a budding personality researcher, you should be able to raise several objections to and criticisms of these attempts to describe the national character of an entire country. What questions would you have for someone who was purporting to be able to characterize the personality of an entire nation?

5 Review the concept of trait capabilities. Think about this concept in terms of your own sense of how introverted or extroverted you usually are. Do you sense a discrepancy between how outgoing you are most days and how outgoing you could act if you encountered someone you were interested in being with?

6 Do you believe that locus of control scores have become more external over time? What factors might have contributed to this dramatic shift toward externality?

7 Do you see a difference in your sense of locus of control with respect to academic versus interpersonal matters? What about your perceived control over health outcomes? Are you external or internal?

Key Terms

ambiverts, p. 31
cardinal disposition, p. 40
central disposition, p. 40
cohort effect, p. 68
common trait, p. 39
conditionability, p. 53
constitutional psychology, p. 29
developmental trajectory, p. 37
ego control, p. 34
ego resiliency, p. 34
emic approach, p. 60
etic approach, p. 60
factor analysis, p. 51
genotypical disposition, p. 40
indigenous personality research, p. 60
interactionism, p. 45
lexical approach, p. 51
locus of control, p. 65
maximal approach, p. 48
meta-analysis, p. 57
metatraits, p. 49
modal personality, p. 32
mode, p. 32
overcontrolling type, p. 35
PEN model, p. 53
personality capabilities, p. 48
personality coefficient, p. 42
personality sphere, p. 64
personality type, p. 28
reciprocal interactionism model, p. 45
resilient type, p. 35
situation coefficient, p. 44
situationism, p. 43
somatotype, p. 29
state anxiety, p. 46
supertrait, p. 50
taxometrics, p. 31
taxon, p. 31
trait anxiety, p. 45
trait approach, p. 28
trait relevance validity, p. 49
type approach, p. 28
undercontrolling type, p. 35
unique trait, p. 35

Key Theorists

Gordon Allport, p. 38
Norman Endler, p. 45
Hans Eysenck, p. 51

chapter three

THE DEVELOPMENT OF PERSONALITY

- Personality Differences in Children
- Personality Stability: Plaster, Plastic, or Both?
- Personality Development
- External Influences on Personality Development
- The Role of Culture in Personality Development
- Type A Behaviour in Children: An Illustration of Multiple Developmental Influences

The same temperament that can make for a criminal can also make for a hot test pilot or astronaut ... That kind of little boy—aggressive, fearless, impulsive—is hard to handle. It's easy for parents to give up and let him run wild, or turn up the heat and the punishment and thereby alienate him and lose all control. But properly handled, this can be the kid who grows up to break the sound barrier.

—DAVID LYKKEN (1998, P. 49)

Almost any trait that can be measured is about 40 to 60 percent heritable. Even things like choice of vocation. But that means that 40 to 60 percent of a trait is also affected by environment.

—THOMAS BOUCHARD (2004)

WHERE DO WE GET our personalities? How does personality develop? Many factors influence us. Consider the following example of a student with the condition known as the impostor phenomenon. As you read this person's self-description, reflect on how she might have reached this point.

> I knew I wanted to become a psychologist. I applied and was accepted to the Ph.D. graduate program in psychology at Temple University.
>
> When I arrived at Temple, I had no formal academic training in psychology. I didn't know the academic vocabulary of psychology or the procedures for research. I hadn't even been in a classroom in years. Even though I'd had a lot of practical experience in my work, I felt that I knew far less than everybody else. They had studied psychology in undergraduate school and were familiar with all the jargon and statistics. And I was afraid the other students were just plain smarter than I was. I thought that if I were going to survive in graduate school, I would have to act as if I knew just as much as the others. I began to feel like I was a fake.
>
> This feeling became almost overwhelming in one seminar I was taking. Anyone could sign up for these seminars, so as a newcomer, I was thrown in with third- and fourth-year students. The other students were so articulate. They seemed so knowledgeable. I didn't understand half of what they were saying (because, of course, I hadn't gotten as far in my studies as they had). Yet, I sat there pretending to comprehend absolutely everything.
>
> At the end of the term, we were all required to give a presentation before the rest of the class. I was terrified. I felt my speech had to be perfect, and that *I* had to be perfect when I stood up to give it. I managed to get my presentation scheduled as the last one of the semester. But I began working on it before any of the other students had started theirs. (Harvey & Katz, 1985, p. 30–31)

So what happened? This student's speech received a very good response, despite her anticipations of doom and disaster. This excerpt was taken from the personal reflections of Joan Harvey, who went on to become a leading theorist on the impostor phenomenon. This example was selected, in part, because many students feel exactly the same way. Students often say to themselves, "They must have made some mistake when they accepted me into this school. They are going to find out, sooner or later! It's only a matter of time!" If you are one of these students, take some solace from the fact that many other students also feel like they are about to be discovered as not up to par, even though they may exhibit a calm exterior. But how do people get to the point where they feel like impostors or "poseurs"? Does it reflect our family upbringing? Does it reflect a genetic predisposition to react this way? What other factors are involved? In the case of the impostor phenomenon, one suggestion is that people who feel like impostors have been raised in a family that has encouraged them to act in ways that are not consistent with their true selves. People are also likely to feel like impostors if they compare themselves with perfectionistic standards (see Clance & Imes, 1978; Harvey

& Katz, 1985). Or maybe they have been raised in a cultural milieu where modesty is norm. Overall, it is likely that several other factors also play a role. This is in keeping with the central theme of this chapter; namely, that personality development reflects multiple influences that operate not only in childhood, but also throughout the lifespan.

This chapter focuses on personality from a developmental perspective. In Chapter 3, we will invoke a central theme from the previous chapter: the need to distinguish between factors within the person versus outside the person. The previous chapter concluded with a description of the locus of control construct and its distinction between an internal and external locus of control. Developmental factors that are intrinsic or extrinsic to the self and their complex interplay will be discussed at length in this chapter. First, however, we examine research on personality differences among children, and the related issue of whether early individual differences in childhood reflect stable personality factors over the lifespan. We then return to a description and analysis of the various developmental factors that influence the contents and the structure of personality.

PERSONALITY DIFFERENCES IN CHILDREN

In Chapter 2, we introduced personality differences among children through the personality types of overcontrolled, undercontrolled, and resilient children. Several questions about personality differences in children remain. For instance, at what age is it possible to detect personality differences? And are broader trait frameworks applicable to children?

What is the origin of personality differences in children, and how soon can these differences be detected?

Some individual differences can be detected shortly after babies are born. If these differences have a genetic origin, then differences go back to the moments when children are first conceived. Birth circumstances and experiences may even come into play, given the findings of a recent British study that showed that babies born "very pre-term" (after fewer than 33 weeks' gestation time) have relatively high neuroticism scores and low extroversion scores on the Eysenck Personality Questionnaire when assessed as adults (Allin et al., 2006)

Research on Type A behaviour in children (which is described in more detail later in this chapter) suggests that personality differences can be detected among three- and four-year olds. The early presence of personality differences is in keeping with the definition of personality traits as stable and long-lasting personality differences that can be detected very early in the lives of individuals. So, what evidence is there of supertraits in children?

Supertraits in Children: The Five-Factor Model

Does the five-factor model described in Chapter 2 apply to children? Recall that the five personality traits of this model are agreeableness, conscientiousness, extroversion, neuroticism, and openness to experience. A clue about the five-factor model in children was supplied in the previous chapter. Recall the earlier reference to Digman's work. He conducted a comprehensive evaluation of whether the five-factor model exists among children (see Digman, 1989, 1990). He had teachers from Hawaii describe the personality features of more than 2,500 students in six different samples between 1959 and 1967. The existence of the five-factor model was confirmed (see Digman & Inouye, 1986; Digman & Takemoto-Check, 1981). These five factors were also detected in a sample of Russian children (Digman & Shmelyov, 1996). Follow-up analyses of Digman's Hawaiian data by Goldberg (2001) showed that all five factors were evident in every sample. The youngest participants were in Grades 1 and 2, so the five factors are detectable among six-year-olds. Subsequent work by Mervielde had teachers rate students on bipolar adjectives reflecting the five factors, and this also yielded evidence suggesting that the five factors can be detected in children beginning elementary school (Mervielde, 1992, 1994; Mervielde, Buyst, & de Fruyt, 1995).

John and associates have evaluated what they came to refer to as the **Little Five** (see John, Caspi, Robins, Moffitt, & Stouthamer-Loeber, 1994). The term "Little Five" connotes the test of the five-factor model in young people. John et al. (1994) tested mothers' perceptions of their 12- and 13-year-old boys' personalities by having mothers complete the California Child Q-Set (Block & Block, 1969/1988). This study confirmed the existence of the five factors and two other factors identified as irritability and activity. Irritability and activity are believed to reflect temperament.

Another study had mothers in Sweden complete the California Child Q-Set to describe their toddlers, who averaged 2.3 years of age (Lamb et al., 2002). The personalities of these children were reassessed until they were 15-year-olds. Lamb et al. concluded that the extroversion, agreeableness, and neuroticism factors were "incoherent" (not clearly distinguishable), and they suggested that these aspects of personality are either not well-defined in early childhood or they do not become readily apparent to parents until their children are older. Additional evidence suggested that the openness to experience factor was not a meaningful dimension until the children reached adolescence. However, the results of another study cast doubt on the existence of the openness dimension during adolescence. Markey, Markey, and Tinsley (2004) found that there were significant correlations between maternal ratings of their adolescent's personality and observer ratings of trait-relevant behaviours exhibited by adolescents for four of the five dimensions. However, openness was not identified as a meaningful dimension.

Another study conducted in Belgium had students from Grades 3 through 6 use a peer nomination procedure to identify the classmates who most reflected or least reflected 25 personality characteristics selected to represent the five-factor model (Mervielde &

De Fruyt, 2000). Analyses of the data yielded three factors: (1) an agreeableness factor; (2) a combined extroversion and neuroticism factor; and (3) a combined factor that reflected conscientiousness and the intellect aspect of openness. This general pattern of results was replicated in two samples. However, it is possible that the peer nomination data did not yield the five-factor model because the cognitive abilities required to make accurate assessments of other children's personalities may not be fully developed. Similar difficulties in identifying the five factors based on peer nominations of adolescents were reported by Scholte, van Aken, and van Lieshout (1997). Scholte et al. (1997) posited that the peer nomination data were biased in that the peer nomination approach is heavily influenced by global evaluations of the group reputations of each adolescent being described.

Are the five personality factors evident when parents are asked to give free and spontaneous descriptions of their children? Do the five factors resemble categories that are used naturally? Free descriptions that parents gave of their children's personalities were obtained in Belgium, China, Germany, Greece, The Netherlands, Poland, and the United States. Mervielde (1998) reported that about three tenths of parents spontaneously described their children in ways that touched on all five factors, and almost seven tenths of the parents provided descriptions that touched on four factors. The use of four categories was the most common outcome. At least three categories were used by almost all the parents.

Another comparative study of parents' free descriptions found evidence of the five factors, but the salience of trait dimensions varied by culture. Zhang et al. (2002) compared descriptions provided by Chinese parents and Dutch parents. Overall, 86% of the statements provided by Chinese parents touched on all five personality dimensions (versus 77% for the Dutch parents). One particularly salient group difference also emerged. The Chinese parents spontaneously generated more descriptions that reflected the conscientiousness category. The Chinese parents, relative to the Dutch parents, gave more positive descriptions of conscientiousness (7.1% versus 4.3%) and more negative descriptions of conscientiousness (12.1% versus 2.4%), with the overall evaluative tone being much more negative. The top three categories for the Chinese parents were extroversion (27.2% of all statements), conscientiousness (19.4%), and agreeableness (17.4%). The top category for Dutch parents was also extroversion (28.5% of all statements), but the next two most commonly mentioned categories were agreeableness (18.9%) and intellect/openness (12.2%). These data suggest cross-cultural differences in the salience or importance of certain personality dimensions.

KEY POINTS

- The elements of the five-factor model are detectable in children, with the exception of the openness dimension.
- Peer nomination data find little evidence of the five-factor model in adolescence.
- Spontaneous "free" descriptions usually result in at least four traits from the five-factor model being mentioned by parents.
- The personality factors in children and adolescents are found across cultures, though the salience of certain dimensions may vary by culture, as shown by the greater emphasis on conscientiousness among Chinese parents.

Eysenck's Big Three in Children

Independent research has examined the viability of assessing among children the three personality dimensions posited by Hans Eysenck. As noted in Chapter 2, these three dimensions are neuroticism, extroversion, and psychoticism. Research has been conducted with the Eysenck Personality Questionnaire – Junior (EPQ-J; Eysenck & Eysenck, 1984). The EPQ-J assesses these three dimensions and includes a lie scale. In contrast to much of the research on the five-factor model in children, most research with the EPQ-J assesses the child's self-reports instead of ratings by parents or teachers.

Collectively, research with the EPQ-J has attested to the presence of reliable individual differences in extroversion, neuroticism, and psychoticism. Research has been conducted with children from such countries as Britain and Hong Kong (Eysenck & Chan, 1982), The Netherlands (De Bruyn, Delsing, & Welten, 1995), and Iran (Eysenck, Makaremi, & Barrett, 1994). Caruso and Edwards (2001) summarized the data from 23 studies that used 44 samples of children. The general use of the scale was supported, but they found that the psychoticism dimension has low reliability, and the scale's psychometric properties seemed to vary as a function of the sample's gender composition and participants' age. The assessment and conceptualization of psychoticism in children may require modification (see Corulla & Corulla, 1990; De Bruyn et al., 1995).

Comparative cross-cultural research has shown that children from Hong Kong, relative to children from Britain, have lower levels of extroversion and neuroticism, but higher lie scores (Eysenck & Chan, 1982). Children from Iran also have significantly lower levels of extroversion, neuroticism, and psychoticism than children from Britain (Eysenck et al., 1994). Gender differences also exist, with boys scoring higher on psychoticism, but lower in neuroticism and extroversion (Eysenck et al., 1994). Overall, these data suggest that there are valid individual differences among children in neuroticism and extroversion.

In summary, the existing data suggest that the five-factor model has received limited support when evaluated in children because the openness factor is not clearly evident. However, by the time children reach elementary school, individual differences exist in agreeableness, extroversion, neuroticism, and conscientiousness. So how stable over time are these individual differences?

PERSONALITY STABILITY: PLASTER, PLASTIC, OR BOTH?

William James (1890) was among the first to question whether personality is stable or changing. He discussed the issue of personal character in terms of whether it is plastic and changing (i.e., the plasticity hypothesis) or is like plaster and enduring (i.e., the plaster hypothesis). James (1890) defined plasticity as "the possession of a structure weak enough to yield to an influence, but strong enough not to yield at once" (p. 105). He felt that plasticity in personality is reflected by gradual, evolving change. The plaster hypothesis reflects James' notion that the habits associated with character take hold and become permanent.

James (1890) favoured the plaster hypothesis and suggested that "It is well for the world that in most of us, by the age of thirty, the character has set like plaster, and will never soften again." However, note that James referred to "most of us," not "all of us," so he left some room for individual differences among people in the stability of their personalities. And, if we continue with the plaster analogy, most people will acknowledge that even plaster can fall apart if it takes enough of a pounding!

James went on to suggest that the period between 20 and 30 years of age is critical for developing the intellectual and professional habits that will be reflected from the age of 30 years and older. The period before the age of 20 is the time for the formation of personal habits.

Robert McCrae and Paul Costa are among the most vocal proponents of the plaster hypothesis. They analyzed data available at the time and concluded that personality is pretty well fixed by the age of 30 (see McCrae & Costa, 1994). If they are correct, then people who are older than 30 and who dislike their personalities appear to be somewhat doomed. This would suggest that older adults receiving psychotherapy for personality deficiencies cannot achieve personality change. Do you think this is the case? Even so, there is still the possibility that they may learn more adaptive ways of interacting with their environment, including the people in their lives.

Factors that Promote Personality Stability

You can probably think of several reasons why personality can change. We will see in research described below that new life experiences may have an impact. Why might personality remain relatively stable over time? One possibility is the continuing influence of genetic factors. Caspi and Bem (1990) outlined three other ways that personality stability may result. First, people are proactive. That is, they may actively seek out situations and life experiences that are in keeping with their personalities.

Second, people are characteristically reactive. That is, people tend to react in unique but predictable ways to environmental stimulation, and these styles of reaction will be repeated over and over again.

Finally, people are evocative. That is, certain personal characteristics will elicit similar reactions from other people time and time again.

Methods of Evaluating the Consistency of Personality Traits

The issue of whether personality is stable can be evaluated in several ways. The least satisfactory way to test this issue is to simply evaluate whether there are differences in mean levels of personality traits among people of various ages. Age differences at a particular point in time are evaluated. This is a very indirect way of assessing stability; clearly, it is better to conduct a longitudinal investigation in which the same sample of participants is followed over time and means are compared across time. This is known as a test of **mean-level stability**.

Another test is to assess relative stability by the correlations between scores when a sample of participants is retested at subsequent time intervals. The main statistic involved here is known as the **test–retest correlation**. Researchers have referred to this way of looking at this issue as evaluating **rank-order stability** or differential stability. That is, when a sample of people is retested, in the overall distribution of scores, do people tend to maintain their rank in personality dimension scores relative to other people also evaluated on this personality dimension?

Conley (1984) reported on personality stability over a 45-year period and found that extroverts tended to remain extroverts, while people high in neuroticism tended to remain high in neuroticism over time. An important feature of Conley's research is that multiple traits and types of assessment were used to show that the findings for various traits were comparable across various forms of assessment. Block (1981) also determined from his longitudinal study that personality is essentially stable over time.

The most comprehensive assessment of personality stability was a review conducted by Brent Roberts and Wendy DelVechhio (2000). They performed a meta-analysis, which was described earlier as a quantitative review of previous studies. This meta-analysis of 152 longitudinal studies yielded several important results. First, they found that the rank-order consistency of personality traits over time was much higher than previously believed, and the apparent stability of personality traits increased with age. The meta-analysis estimated that the mean test–retest reliability of personality traits was .31 for participants in childhood, .54 for participants in college, .64 at 30 years of age, and .74 between ages 50 to 70. They suggested that there was a "step-like linear increase" in the rank-order consistency of personality traits over time before it reached a plateau in the 50 to 70 years age range. It can be inferred from this study that previous estimates of .30 cited in the Mischel (1969) critique were dramatic underestimates of the stability of personality.

A third way of testing stability was illustrated by Soldz and Valliant (1999), who investigated the stability of personality traits over a 45-year period. This study is remarkable for two reasons. First, it involved the longest time period used to assess the stability of the traits of the five-factor model. Second, it showed that conclusions about personality stability may vary depending on how stability is conceptualized and measured. Participants were from the Harvard Longitudinal Study, which assessed personality and lifestyle variables for samples of young men from classes at Harvard University in 1939 to 1944, and then followed them for more than 45 years and re-evaluated them when they were 67 or 68 years old. Soldz and Valliant (1999) evaluated the stability of the traits in the five-factor model using conventional methods, and found only weak evidence of rank-order stability. Specifically, small but significant associations were found over time between neuroticism at Time 1 and at Time 2, as well as between extroversion at Time 1 and Time 2, and openness at Time 1 and Time 2. The greatest rank-order stability was found for openness. In contrast, rank-order stability was not found for agreeableness and conscientiousness.

However, these researchers also investigated another form of stability known as **ipsative stability**. The term "ipsative" is applied generally to measures where the focus is on comparing one variable with another variable, and the level of one variable limits possible values of the other variable. Ipsative scoring occurs when the score that a person obtains on one measure somehow has implications or constrains how that person can score on another measure. This abstract concept is best illustrated by showing its use by Soldz and Valliant (1999). They examined ipsative stability by assessing each participant's *profile of scores* on the five factors at Time 1 and their profile of scores on the five factors at Time 2. Ipsative stability exists if it is found with most people that the *pattern of scores* across the five factors was generally similar over time. It is ipsative because if one trait (e.g., conscientiousness) is the highest, obviously, one of the other traits cannot be the highest. What did this analysis reveal? In contrast to their relatively weak evidence of differential stability, the researchers found strong evidence of ipsative stability. Thus, if someone tended to be high in conscientiousness but low in neuroticism at Time 1, they also tended to be high in conscientiousness but low in neuroticism 45 years later. The assessment of ipsative stability implies that there can be fluctuations over time in personality scores, but the score profile across traits is generally similar over time.

KEY POINTS

- There is at least a moderate degree of stability in personality over time.
- Meta-analysis indicates a step-like increase in the rank-order consistency of personality traits over time, peaking among 50- to 70-year-olds.
- Stability exists because people are proactive in seeking out or evoking situations that fit their personalities. People also react in characteristic, predictable ways to similar situations.

Research at McGill University in Montreal by Debbie Moskowitz and her colleagues has examined individual differences in the dynamic stability of interpersonal tendencies. These investigators have suggested that there is a regularity or predictability over time in fluctuations in interpersonal variability, and there are individual differences in this dynamic stability. That is, there is a regularity to being an "up-and-down" person. Brown and Moskowitz (1998) used daily event recorders and event sampling and found that behaviours tended to be cyclical throughout the course of a week, and it is even possible to identify stable patterns of changing behaviours when focusing on a 24-hour period. Thus, our interpersonal behaviour varies according to a weekly and a daily cycle. In this instance, extroverts, relative to introverts, had greater variability (greater daily cyclicity) in their interpersonal behaviours. One indication of this is that extroverted people had a greater number of different interactions with different people, especially at night.

Moskowitz and Zuroff (2004) conducted a subsequent study that resulted in the introduction of the concepts flux, pulse, and spin. These terms are complicated concepts that all refer to different ways of characterizing intra-individual variability in interpersonal behaviour (i.e., fluctuation is treated as an individual difference variable). Flux refers to the amount of variability that a person has around their mean score on an interpersonal dimension. This concept can be illustrated by contrasting two hypothetical people.

If someone were high in interpersonal sensitivity and quite reactive to feedback from others by responding in kind (i.e., if criticized they returned the criticism), this person would probably be high in flux. Another person might be relatively indifferent to praise and criticism and would be low in flux, at least in terms of the interpersonal sensitivity dimension. Pulse and spin are related concepts. Pulse is the individual differences in the overall extremity of interpersonal behaviours. Spin is the individual differences in the use of different interpersonal styles (e.g., hostile toward one person versus warm and agreeable to another person).

Moskowitz and Zuroff (2004) analyzed the data from event recordings, and several unique findings emerged from their research. For instance, they found that individuals had greater flux in dominant behaviour toward others if they had many unique interaction partners. Overall, there was a high stability of flux in submissive, agreeable, and quarrelsome behaviours, but there was less stability of flux in dominant behaviours. Moskowitz and Zuroff also reported moderate to high stability in pulse and spin. Overall, this research suggests that there are predictable individual differences in "dynamic stability" in the interpersonal domain. Thus, we can conclude that people differ in how predictable they are with their fluctuations in behaviour.

Is Personality Set by Age 30?

Recently, Roberts and his associates provided seemingly definitive evidence on the issue of long-term stability of personality (see Roberts, Robins, Trzesniewski, and Caspi, 2003; Roberts, Walton, & Viechtbauer, 2006). They summarized the empirical research on changes in mean-level personality scores across the lifespan. Roberts et al. (2006) conducted a meta-analysis of the data from 92 samples.

The initial conclusions reached by Roberts et al. (2003) are reproduced in Table 3.1. The results are presented separately for one-time (cross-sectional) studies and longitudinal studies of the same individuals over time. In general, it can be seen that substantial personality change occurs after age 30.

It can be seen in Table 3.1 that the results for extroversion vary depending on how extroversion is assessed as a form of social dominance or social vitality. Social dominance involves a sense of power or authority over other people. Social vitality involves the degree of social contact and outgoingness. It can be seen that in both cross-sectional and longitudinal research, social dominance increases with age, while social vitality decreases with age.

Table 3.1 also shows that both agreeableness and conscientiousness tend to increase with age. Thus, stereotypes of cranky old people are inconsistent with existing data that show instead that we tend to mellow with age. Cross-sectional research tends to indicate that neuroticism decreases slightly with age, and this pattern is evident when longitudinal research assessed young adults and middle-aged adults, but the evidence for older people suggests no change.

The subsequent meta-analysis by Roberts et al. (2006) confirmed many of the findings of the earlier review. They focused on six trait categories listed in Table 3.1 and concluded that

Table 3.1 A Summary of Personality Change across the Lifespan

	Cross-Sectional Studies		Longitudinal Studies	
Personality Domain	**Ages 18 to 80**	**Young Adulthood (20–40 years)**	**Middle Age (40–60 years)**	**Midlife to Old Age (Over 60 years)**
Extroversion				
Social dominance	+	+	+	?
Social vitality	–	–	–	–
Agreeableness	+	+	+	+
Conscientiousness	+	+	+	+
Neuroticism	–	–	–	0
Openness to experience	–	+	0	0

A "+" denotes a developmental increase in mean scores, a "–" denotes a developmental decrease in mean scores, a "0" signifies no change, and a "?" signifies that no conclusion could be drawn because more research is needed.

Source: Adapted from Roberts, Robins, Trzesniewski, & Caspi, 2003.

all six trait categories had significant change among people older than the age of 30, and four of the six trait categories showed significant change in middle and old age despite there being substantial long-term stability overall, as measured by rank-order stability (i.e., people's scores relative to each other). Most notably, they concluded that the period of most dramatic change in personality was early adulthood. Finally, Roberts et al. (2006) suggested that the changes across the lifespan were due primarily to life experiences and life lessons.

According to Roberts et al. (2006), personality continues to change throughout the lifespan, with the greatest change occurring during early adulthood.

Overall, it seems that a conclusion reached more than a decade ago still applies. Weinberger (1994) summarized existing knowledge by concluding quite reasonably that "There is substantial evidence for both personality stability and change. The trick is to understand what changes and what does not, when to expect stability and when to expect change, and why stability and change occur as they do" (p. 336).

KEY POINTS

- It was predicted that personality is "set in plaster" by age 30. However, personality continues to change throughout the lifespan.
- The greatest change in personality occurs during early adulthood.
- The amount of change in personality over the lifespan varies by trait; for instance, different patterns are found for two different facets of extroversion.

Another Way of Examining Stability: The Stability of Character

Valliant (2002) suggested that the answer to whether personality is stable or unstable depends, in part, on how personality is defined. He suggested that personality should be seen as the sum of individual differences in temperament and character. Character is reflected in lifestyle and life choices, including health habits and the selection of a mate. He acknowledged that temperament does not change very much, but character can change in some profound ways because it is influenced by the environment and by developmental maturation. Valliant then demonstrated his point that character evolves by describing the life histories of individuals who had lives that were seemingly unpredictable because their lives turned out much better or much worse than anticipated.

Vaillant (2002) based his conclusions on the results of three long-term longitudinal investigations designed to assess adult development. For instance, he described the life of Zelda Maus, who was an intellectually gifted young woman in the famous Terman study. The Terman study was a longitudinal study of gifted children started in 1921 by famous Stanford psychologist Lewis Terman (see Shurkin, 1992). His participants came to be known as "Termites." There were substantial personality and life circumstance differences among the Termites even though they were all intellectually gifted (see Shurkin, 1992).

What about Zelda? Zelda Maus was a highly accomplished young woman who captained her high school basketball team and was editor of her school yearbook. She got married when 21 years old, but was divorced at the age of 25, and went downhill from there. She married three times, and her third husband developed chronic alcoholism prior to his death. When she was interviewed at the age of 78, Zelda was a recluse and isolated from others. She had experienced five bouts of major depression in her lifetime, each resulting in electroconvulsive shock therapy. Valliant attributed her sad outcome to marrying badly along with ruminating on the losses in her life and never developing the capacity to see the goodness in other people.

Zelda's story has some themes that are quite similar to another Zelda who had an exceptionally unhappy life, Zelda Fitzgerald, the wife of famous author F. Scott Fitzgerald. Zelda Fitzgerald's story included going from a state of being immensely popular with a very bright future as a young adult to eventually suffering from mental illness while coping with a famous husband who suffered from extreme forms of alcoholism. The life outcomes of both Zeldas illustrate the strong impact that psychosocial stressors can have on an individual over time.

Valliant (2002) concluded in general that negative personality change over time is likely if the person has a bad marriage, bad habits, debilitating disease or illness, and maladaptive psychological defences (see Chapter 5). Valliant (2002) also identified four personal qualities that are resiliency factors that enhance long-term outcomes. Positive aspects of character that contribute to success include (1) developing a future orientation that involves the ability to plan and to hope; (2) fostering a capacity for gratitude and forgiveness; (3) having a sense of empathy and imagining how the world seems to other people; and (4) developing a desire to do things *with* people as opposed to doing things *to* people or becoming cognitively preoccupied with things done to us.

In essence, Valliant has accounted for both continuity (temperament) and change (character). Caspi and Roberts (2001) have argued that both continuity and change occur and both can be documented.

Personality Stability and Change in Older People

Interesting new information is emerging from research on personality stability among older adults. A new study by Johnson, McGue, and Krueger (2005) examined 833 twins from the Minnesota project when they were approximately 59 and 64 years old. Personality scale scores in this study were found to be extremely stable over time. Two factors contributed to this extreme stability. First, there was the strong, lasting influence of genetic factors. However, stability also stemmed, in part, from greater constancy in environmental influences; that is, their environments did not change very much.

When personality changes do take place in the elderly, newly introduced life events are indeed important (see Maiden, Peterson, Caya, & Hayslip, 2003). This longitudinal investigation assessed the stability of three personality traits (neuroticism, extroversion, and openness) in 78 elderly women. These same women were interviewed on two occasions, with the second assessment occurring six to seven years later. Moderate stability in rank-order stability was found for all three personality traits, though the authors did note that the attained level of stability was typically lower than that found in other studies. In addition, the experience of negative life events predicted changes in levels of two of three personality variables. Neuroticism increased and extroversion decreased as a function of negative life experiences, while openness did not change. Specific life experiences of importance included health problems, social interactions, and problems in meeting essential personal needs. Thus, self-reported levels of personality, while moderately stable, may be responsive to or influenced by life circumstances. This was illustrated earlier when in the discussion on the two Zeldas.

Elder and Caspi (1988) postulated the **accentuation principle** as a way of accounting for the role of life experiences. They believe that the experience of life stressors tends to increase the stability of personality traits over time because people respond to life stress by returning to familiar ways and tendencies. They exaggerate or accentuate existing psychological features when transitional life experiences take place. However, some stressors may be highly incongruent with existing personality tendencies, and these can result in substantial change for some people.

One final point needs to be mentioned before moving on to an analysis of factors that contribute to personality development. Although there is overwhelming evidence for at least moderate personality stability, a recent longitudinal study of university students found that most participants perceived that they had changed substantially over the course of their university careers (Robins, Noftle, Trzesniewski, & Roberts, 2005). Interestingly, Robins et al. (2005) also found that there was a correspondence between perceived personality change and actual personality change. So, if you think you have changed, maybe you really have.

PERSONALITY DEVELOPMENT

The following sections describe various factors that influence personality development. As suggested earlier, it is presumed that there are factors within the person and factors outside the person (e.g., other people, the environment, cultural factors) that combine to influence personality development throughout the lifespan. Factors that originate within the personality are primarily genetic in origin and are best reflected in individual differences in temperament. It is also assumed that the individual is an active agent in his or her personality development and, as such, the individual can act in ways that influence and structure the external environment.

At the same time, external factors play a role. People who influence our personality development include our parents (and their parenting style), our peers, and the environments that we encounter. Cultural orientation also plays a role. Thus, overall, it is evident that the process of personality development is exceedingly complex. We begin with an overview of the role of genetic factors in personality development.

Genetic versus Environmental Factors

Are people born wicked or do they have wickedness thrust upon them?

—*From the hit musical* Wicked

If you have been fortunate enough to have seen the hit musical *Wicked* or have read the book that inspired it, you will know that the answer, via the protagonist Elphaba (The Wicked Witch of the West), is that wickedness is a result of how one is treated by other people. Elphaba has a good nature but is shunned by others who cannot handle her being born with green skin. In terms of her innate characteristics, she is not at all wicked but she takes on this persona over time.

But what does the research literature say about the role of genes versus environment in personality development? Before describing some findings, it is first necessary to describe the primary method used to test this issue, and introduce some key terms. Genetic factors are assessed with twin research. Comparisons are made between monozygotic twins, also known as identical twins, and dizygotic twins, also known as fraternal twins. Monozygotic twins have 100% of their genetic makeup in common, while fraternal twins share 50% of their genetic makeup. Fraternal twins are similar to family members in general in that we share 50% of our genes with family members who are direct blood relatives. Thus, if you have a younger sister, for example, you share 50% of your genes with her.

Another key distinction is made between the **genotype** and the **phenotype**. The genotype is a person's unobservable genetic constitution in the form of inherited genes; it is someone's potential according to genetic background. The phenotype is the person's behavioural expression of this genetic potential, and the phenotype can and usually is influenced by experience. The genotype can be described as fixed but not static in that the range of possibilities is limited by genotype, but genes can become activated at certain times as a function of the person's stage of development and life experiences. The phenotype can be quite variable over time and is a reflection of the interaction between the genotype and the environment.

The term "**heritability**" refers to the proportion of phenotypic variation in a sample or population that is attributable to genetic factors. If something is said to be 100% heritable, then the variability would be entirely due to genetic factors.

When twins are similar in their behaviours or other characteristics, they are described as being high in **concordance**. Generally speaking, if genetic factors play a role in contributing to a specific behaviour or tendency, the degree of concordance should be significantly higher for monozygotic than dizygotic twins.

One reason why there may be greater similarity among monozygotic twins is that not only do they share their genetic makeup, but they may also be treated similarly by other people, including caregivers. That is, there may be a violation of what is known as the **equal environment assumption**. If we wished to compare monozygotic and dizygotic twins, an implicit assumption is that environmental factors have operated to a similar degree in contributing to the behaviour of both types of twins. However, this assumption often doesn't apply. It is much more likely that two dizygotic twins or two siblings who are not twins will be treated differentially depending on their unique characteristics, relative to the treatment received by monozygotic twins. One way to determine the role of genetic versus environmental similarities and differences is to compare the characteristics of twins (both monozygotic versus dizygotic) who share genes but have been reared apart (i.e., they have been raised in different settings, perhaps by entirely different families). The **adoptees method** involves comparing children who have no genes in common but who were adopted by the same parents. The term for common environmental influences is **shared environment**, while **nonshared environment** refers to unique influences. Finally, when researchers refer to **nonadditive genetic effects**, they are indicating that personality does not depend on single genes in isolation, but on clusters or combinations of genes that coexist in the same person.

How much of personality is genetic? You may have heard of some of the remarkable stories of identical twins who were reared apart (usually adopted by separate sets of parents) and who met each other years later and discovered that many aspects of their lives, their interests, and their personalities are virtually identical. In some instances, it almost seems as if they have lived parallel lives. These stories have been compiled in a book titled *Entwined Lives* by Nancy Segal, a researcher who is a twin herself (see Segal, 1999). Her book recounts the stories of several sets of identical twins who were separated virtually at birth. For instance, two identical twins named Daphne Goodship and Barbara Herbert met 41 years after being separated at birth. They discovered that they had identical physical symptoms (a heart murmur and enlarged thyroid gland) and they had similar life experiences. That is, both broke their ankle at the age of 15 years old. Both sisters met their respective husbands at 16 years of age. Both sisters were mothers of two boys and one girl after first suffering a miscarriage. Both sisters were also deathly afraid of heights.

Minnesota psychologist Thomas Bouchard first reported another remarkable case. Jim Springer and Jim Lewis were born in 1940. The boys were given the same first name by their adoptive parents, but the similarities did not end there. The twins both married twice to wives with the same first names. They each had sons also named James. Their favourite beer and cigarette brands were identical, and they drove the same kind of car. They also both served as police deputies. Finally, they even had dogs that shared the same name (Toy)! This degree of overlap between the brothers points to the strong influence of genetic factors.

So, do research findings confirm the apparent role of genetics? There are many prominent research teams around the world that have used the data from twin registries to empirically assess the role of genetic versus environmental factors. Numerous large scale research programs have already taken place or are currently underway. By and large, this research has provided extensive evidence of the role of genetic factors in personality. Table 3.2 was adapted from a comprehensive review paper by Bouchard and McGue (2003). This table summarizes the heritability estimates for the traits from the five-factor model based on the results from four large investigations between 1996 and 1998. It also contains the estimates that emerged from Loehlin's (1992) review of kinship studies and Bouchard's (1997) summary of the literature. The twin studies included were conducted in Canada, Germany, and the United States. The Canadian data are from a behaviour genetics research program at the University of British Columbia, led by Kerry Jang and John Livesley. This research program focuses on the heritability of personality traits and their role in behavioural disorders, including personality disorders.

It can be seen in Table 3.2 that the heritability estimates for the various personality traits were quite comparable across the four studies. The fifth column in Table 3.2 represents the mean heritability estimates across the four studies. The heritability estimates ranged from .42 for agreeableness to .54 for extroversion and .57 for openness. These values signify that about 50% or more of the variance in most broad personality trait dimensions can be attributed to genetic factors. Thus, most broad personality dimensions have a large heritable component. This general conclusion has been supported by research on the role of genetic factors in personality in several other countries, including Australia, Britain, Sweden, and Russia. Also, as indicated by Bouchard and Loehlin (2001), the degree which genetic factors play a role is comparable for men and women.

Bouchard (2004) reviewed existing data and suggested that all five personality trait domains show strong evidence of nonadditive genetic effects (i.e., personality clusters are inherited), and all five personality trait domains are not influenced substantially

Table 3.2 Broad Heritabilities of Self-Report Measures of the Big Five Factors Based on Twin Studies and Comprehensive Reviews of the Twin Literature

	Twin Studies Reviews						
Trait	Jang et al. (1996) (Canada)	Waller (1999) (U.S.)	Loehlin et al. (1998) (U.S.)	Riemann et al. (1997) (Germany)	Mean (4 studies)	Loehlin (1992)	Bouchard (1997)
Extroversion	.53	.49	.57	.56	.54	.49	.54
Agreeableness	.41	.33	.51	.42	.42	.35	.52
Conscientiousness	.44	.48	.52	.53	.49	.38	.40
Neuroticism	.41	.42	.58	.52	.48	.41	.58
Openness	.61	.58	.56	.53	.57	.45	.52
Monozygotic Pairs	123	313	490	660	–	–	–
Dizygotic Pairs	127	91	317	304	–	–	–

Source: Adapted from Bouchard & McGue, 2003.

by shared environmental effects. Extroversion was identified by Bouchard (2004) as the only trait dimension that may involve sex differences in heritability. Finally, Bouchard (2004) compared the heritability of personality traits with the heritability of other types of individual differences and suggested that the heritability of intelligence was substantially greater than the heritability of personality traits, but the heritability of psychological interests was slightly but noticeably lower than the heritability of personality traits.

Other classic research by Loehlin, Willerman, and Horn (1985) examined the association between the personality of children and the parents who adopted them. This research confirmed the role of genetic factors by finding little resemblance in the personalities of children and their adoptive parents, as well as little resemblance between adoptive siblings.

One limitation of past research on heredity and personality is that virtually all of these investigations have been based on self-report personality measures. However, at least one study conducted with self-reports and informant ratings confirmed the role of genetic factors in personality development and expression (see Heath, Neale, Kessler, Eaves, & Kendler, 1992).

A critically important issue that has emerged from this research is the estimated role of environmental factors. Research has found that the role of environmental factors is relatively weak and accounts for little variability in personality traits. This was illustrated in investigations conducted by Eaves and his associates. One study of almost 30,000 participants from the state of Virginia examined genetic and environmental factors in their relative contribution to personality differences and differences in social attitudes (Eaves et al., 1999). As expected, there were strong genetic effects for both personality and social attitude variables. In addition, the results indicated that there was substantial evidence of cultural transmission of social attitudes via the family environment, but personality

Although they look identical, the Olsen twins are actually fraternal twins, which would explain why one twin (Mary-Kate, right) developed anorexia nervosa and her sister Ashley didn't.

differences were not attributable to differences in family environments.

Although environmental factors are relatively less important than genetic factors, in individual cases, environmental factors in the form of differential treatment from parents may still play a very significant role and result in different personality orientations and life outcomes. Otherwise, how can we explain situations like the Olsen twins, Mary-Kate and Ashley, where one twin (Mary-Kate) develops anorexia nervosa and the other twin does not? In this instance, even though they look identical, the Olsen twins are actually fraternal twins, not identical twins. Thus, they are not genetically identical, and this difference may account, at least in part, for their different outcomes. More difficult to explain is the remarkable case of the Genain quadruplets, born in 1930 in the Midwestern United States. All of the Genain sisters developed schizophrenia by the time they reached 24 years of age. The story of these sisters is fascinating for various reasons. Genain is a pseudonym meaning "dire birth" that was used to protect the sisters' identity. First, it was estimated in 1963 that the odds of identical quadruplets all developing schizophrenia were one in 1.5 billion births. They have a shared genetic vulnerability that resulted in the development of schizophrenia and associated personality characteristics (for summaries, see Mirsky et al., 2000; Rosenthal, 1963). However, what is particularly fascinating is that the sisters had different life outcomes despite sharing the same genetic background. One sister (Hester) could not function independently, experienced severe impairment, and did not finish high school. Two other sisters named Nora and Iris had better functioning but never got married nor did they have substantial careers. Finally, the fourth sister, Myra, married and had a family and she was able to hold a job. Why did they experience dramatically different outcomes? Mirsky and other scholars have suggested that the key variable was the cruelty of the girls' father. He was particularly cruel to Hester and Iris and more responsive to Nora and Myra. Also, accounts suggest that the girls' mother was concerned about the tendency of Hester and Iris to masturbate, so these two were forced to undergo female circumcision at the age of 11. Now, it could be argued that the differences stemmed from the girls themselves; perhaps Nora and Myra had better functioning in general and this resulted in less parental frustration. Although this is certainly possible, there is no denying that the girls grew up to be women who were identical in some ways, but very different in other key respects, despite being genetically identical.

KEY POINTS

- The genotype is our inherited, genetically determined potential. The phenotype is the expression or realization of this potential based on life experiences.
- Some identical twins have remarkable similarities even when reared apart. However, other cases illustrate differences among identical twins raised together.
- Heritability estimates of personality traits are quite comparable across studies; about 50% of the variance in traits reflects genetic factors.

Historically, one of the greatest debates in psychology is the extent to which behaviour reflects nature (genetics) versus nurture (experience). Some feel that enough data have now accumulated to lay this debate to rest. In a recent review paper, Plomin and Asbury (2005) concluded that we should now simply frame this issue as nature *and* nurture. Both genetics and environment play a role. We will see that this is the case even when it comes to examining temperament, which is believed to mostly reflect hereditary factors, but is also responsive to experiential factors.

Although it is recognized that there is a genetic component to personality, important challenges need to be addressed by researchers. Most notably, it remains for researchers to identify the specific genes that account for personality development. According to Caspi, Roberts, and Shiner (2005), for complex personality traits, genetic influence will likely involve multiple genes that have relatively small effect sizes when individually examined.

Temperament

Temperament is a concept that was introduced in Chapter 2 when Hippocrates' views were outlined. Recall that Hippocrates suggested that there are four basic temperaments (sanguine, melancholic, choleric, and phlegmatic) that reflected the balance of four bodily humours (blood, black bile, yellow bile, and phlegm).

Current research on temperament is also based on the notion that individual differences among people are largely attributable to biologically based differences, and these differences are detectable when children are born or shortly thereafter. The next time you are in a hospital, go to the viewing window where newborns are on display. At first glance, they all look alike. If you take a closer look, you will notice some obvious physical differences that distinguish these babies. If you could actually interact with them, you would notice some salient differences in how they respond to stimulation and how they interact with people. The most logical explanation for these differences, even after taking into account differences in the uterine environment and whether they benefited from a full-term pregnancy, is that genetic differences are at play.

Contemporary theory and research on temperament is derived primarily from the seminal work of Thomas and Chess and their colleagues as part of their work on the New York Longitudinal Study (Thomas et al., 1963). Their initial interest in temperament differences stemmed from observations of their own children. They observed that,

> ...like innumerable other parents, we were struck by the individual differences in our own children, even in the first few weeks of life. There were differences in the

> regularity of biological functions such as sleep and hunger, in levels of motor activity, in the intensity of laughter or crying, in the initial reactions to new stimuli, in the ease with which the baby's reactions could be modified. (p. 3–4)

You might think that siblings would have great similarities in their temperaments and subsequent personalities given that they originate from the same parents and they share genes. In most cases, you would be wrong! This lack of similarity had been confirmed in many studies, and it led Plomin, Asbury, Dip, and Dunn (2001) to write a review paper that asked the question, "Why are children in the same family so different?" Differences can be attributed to a variety of factors, including non-shared environmental experiences as well as idiosyncratic, chance experiences that occur for only one sibling (Plomin et al., 2001). Also, the impact of siblings and how they differentially treat each other (e.g., one sibling continually picking on another sibling) cannot be discounted.

So, what is temperament? Rothbart and Putnam (2002) defined **temperament** as constitutionally based differences in reactivity and self-regulation. Temperament often refers not to the "what" of behaviour, but the "how" of behaviour. That is, temperament differences are often reflected in differences in the style of expressing behaviours. Even in cases where two people exhibit the same general behaviour, how they outwardly express the behaviour (the frequency, intensity, and tempo or speed) may be quite different as a result of temperamental differences.

The difficult child is active, irritable, and often reacts negatively to changes in routine, while the slow-to-warm-up child is typically inactive, displays passive forms of resistance, and is less demonstrative.

Originally, Thomas and Chess identified nine temperament dimensions in total. These temperament dimensions were then used to distinguish three types of children: (1) the easy child; (2) the difficult child; and (3) the slow-to-warm-up child. The easy child represented about 40% of their sample of infants. The easy child is described as even-tempered and typically in a positive mood. This child is quite open and adaptable to new experiences, and tends to have habits that are regular and predictable.

About 10% of their sample was composed of difficult children. The difficult child is described as active, irritable, and irregular in habits. They often react vigorously and negatively to changes in routine, and they are relatively slow to adapt to new people and new circumstances.

Case Study 3.1 The Slow-to-Warm-Up Child and the Difficult Child

One young man, Edward, was a slow-to-warm-up child temperamentally (negative reactions to new situations with slow adaptability). His shyness with new situations was handled well by his parents, with support, encouragement, and lack of excessive pressure to adapt quickly. As a result, Edward never developed a major behaviour problem and went through college and professional school successfully, though not brilliantly. When we last interviewed him at age 29, he was functioning in his profession, in an area devoted to community services to the poor. This position was underpaid and offered little opportunity for material advancement. It did require him to act quickly and assertively in all kinds of complicated new situations and with new people. This he accomplished without excessive stress. His shyness with social situations had, however, not only continued but had grown worse to the point where he was socially isolated, had no close male friends, and was severely sexually inhibited. How do we explain this dichotomy of functioning? He had high moral and ethical standards, which he learned from his parents. These appeared to be the motivating force that overcame his shyness at work. Socially, these standards were not as meaningful and did not serve to counterbalance his temperamental pattern, as they did at work. He talked openly about his problems and was eager to obtain professional help which we arranged.

By contrast, there is Ronald, whose slow-to-warm-up temperament as a child was more extreme than Edward's, even resulting in a school phobia in the early grades. His parents also managed his problem well, with our advice, and his difficulties with new situations improved gradually. He went through college with the ambition to make his way up the ladder in the corporate world. This he is doing successfully, and his ambitions outweigh any temptations to withdraw from any new situation that, if he did, might affect his career adversely. He is married and has a number of friends. However, he refuses to discuss any of his discomfort … and insists that he never had a school problem as a youngster. He is using the defence mechanism of denial successfully so far, though the future is unpredictable.

Then there is Bernice, a girl with high activity, positive mood, and quick adaptability as a child. She ran eagerly and cheerfully to perform any errand requested by parent or teacher, and was a favoured child at home and at school. Her eagerness to gain the praise her quick compliance brought turned, however, progressively into the characteristic of impulsivity as she grew into middle childhood. She began to plunge thoughtlessly into a number of actions that were embarrassing and damaging. Her parents set strict rules for her as to what was permissible activity, and she basically complied. At age 13, however, impulsive behavioural difficulties again appeared in relation to increased academic demands, the onset of puberty, and the new complexities of adolescent peer interactions. Within a few months, her father, who had been a stabilizing authoritative (but not authoritarian) figure in the family, died suddenly and unexpectedly. We had given the same advice for quiet consistent limit-setting, but this time the mother could not follow our advice. Bereft of her husband and his influence, stretched to her limits physically by having to return full-time to a demanding and difficult job, she was unable emotionally to cope with her daughter's crises and outbursts, in addition to attending to the needs of her three other young children. The girl's problems escalated, her interaction with her mother and sibs became increasingly hostile and disruptive, and she developed a severe sociopathic behaviour disorder, including truancy, sexual promiscuity, stealing, and lying. Several attempts at psychotherapy were unsuccessful.

Bernice left home at 18, and her behaviour, now at age 30, is essentially unchanged. She supports herself at a job much below her potential, admits she behaves impulsively, and at times puts on an air of repentance and determination to change. This lasts only to the next anti-social activity that attracts her, which now includes severe drug abuse. Bernice's impulsivity, which derived from her childhood temperament and the praise she received for it, had been her downfall.

Source: Thomas & Chess, 1989, p. 255–256.

Finally, the slow-to-warm-up child is typically quite inactive and moody. He or she is similar to the difficult child in being slow to adapt to new people and situations. However, unlike the difficult child, the slow-to-warm-up child may resist attempts to be cuddled and may display passive forms of resistance when others try to interact with him or her. Overall, they are much less demonstrative than "difficult" children.

The next section contains descriptions of children with various temperaments taken from the case files of Thomas and Chess (1989). These excerpts not only highlight the individuality of children, but also illustrate that children with a similar temperament style can experience dramatically different life outcomes. Thomas and Chess (1989) attribute these outcomes to goodness or poorness of fit in terms of the child's characteristics and environment.

Temperament Dimensions

Various theorists have differed in the number and type of temperament dimensions they postulate. Although the exact number of temperament dimensions has been debated, it is generally accepted that the nine dimensions posited by Thomas and Chess had to be revised for two reasons. First, certain temperament dimensions had limited variability (i.e., widespread individual differences were not apparent). Second, the expression of temperament was too situationally specific for some dimensions and did not generalize across contexts.

The six temperament dimensions used by a team of researchers from Concordia University in Montreal are outlined in Table 3.3 (see Karp, Serbin, Stack, & Schwartzman, 2004). These investigators developed an observational framework known as the Behavioural Style Observation System (BSOS), and identified six dimensions: activity level, adaptability, approach to toys, mood, mood consistency, and vocal reactivity. Like Thomas and Chess (1977), Karp et al. (2004) focused on temperament in descriptions of the child's behavioural style. The behavioural style of children is observed and coded following three separate tasks. These tasks are a free play period in which the mother and child are asked to play normally as if they were at home, an interference task that requires the mother to complete a questionnaire and does not directly interact with her child, and an unstructured free play period. Each child's behaviour is given a three-point rating in six temperament domains, reflecting such characteristics as mood, activity, adaptability, and approach-avoidance (see Table 3.3).

The use of the BSOS enabled Karp et al. (2004) to conclude that there is a significant association between behavioural observations of temperament and maternal reports of temperament. This is important to establish because while behavioural observations of temperament are preferred, studies often rely on parental descriptions of temperament. We have often found in our own work that depressed parents provide more negative reports of their child's temperament, and, in the absence of behavioural observations, it is impossible to determine whether the link between parental depression and negative temperament ratings is a general reflection of the negative cognitive style that often accompanies depression or whether depressed parents actually have young children with difficult or unresponsive temperament styles.

Table 3.3 Description of the Temperament Dimensions Composing the Behavioural Style Observational System

Code	Description
Mood	1 = negative: whining, frowning, screeching, tantrums, crying 2 = neutral: neither positive nor negative 3 = positive: laughing, positive vocalization, smiling
Activity Level	1 = child who sits for entire period without getting up 2 = child who gets up once or twice 3 = child who gets up three or more times
Vocal Reactivity	1 = low reactivity: even-tempered child, very calm, not bothered by little things 2 = somewhat reactive at times but calms down on own (more than once) 3 = high reactivity: expressed by loud verbalizations, crying, whining and can't calm down on own
Approach to Toys	1 = child who resists playing with toys, sulks, wants to be alone 2 = child who takes some initiative to play but mostly follows mom's lead 3 = child who actively seeks out toys to play with, takes initiatives to get toys, starts games
Mood Consistency	1 = consistent: no fluctuations for majority of the time 2 = fluctuates once or twice, from positive to negative, or negative to positive 3 = fluctuates three or more times
Adaptability	1 = child who becomes quite upset at beginning of interference task, whines, cries 2 = child who becomes fussy, tries to get mom's attention, does not try to play with toys immediately 3 = child who moves easily into interference task without making a fuss, starts to play with toys right away

Source: Adapted from Karp et al., 2004.

Contemporary surveys of research and theory on temperament (e.g., Buss & Plomin, 1984; Goldsmith et al., 1987; Rothbart, 1981) usually acknowledge five main temperament dimensions: (1) activity level; (2) irritability/negative emotionality; (3) soothability; (4) fearfulness; and (5) sociability. Several of these dimensions overlap with the BSOS dimensions.

The Stability of Temperament

Overall, dimensions of temperament are relatively stable over time. Thomas and Chess (1986) observed that initial differences in temperament sometimes do continue and are reflected later in life. They observed that parental treatment can reinforce or exacerbate pre-existing differences in temperament, but, by the same token, parental treatment can extinguish or mute temperamental characteristics. Indeed, research has confirmed that temperament can change as a function of the goodness of fit between temperament and the approach to childrearing adopted by parents (Cohen, Kasen, Brook, & Hartmark, 1998).

Overall, longitudinal research indicates that several temperament dimensions (e.g., activity level, sociability/shyness) are moderately stable from infancy through to the adult years (see Caspi & Silva, 1995; Lemery, Goldsmith, Klimert, & Mrazek, 1999). Much of this information comes from the long-term longitudinal investigation of temperament conducted by Caspi and Silva and their colleagues (Caspi & Silva, 1995; Newman, Caspi, Moffitt, & Silva, 1997).

Although temperament is moderately stable over time, the meta-analysis conducted by Roberts and DelVechhio (2003) suggested that trait and temperament factors differ in their longitudinal stability. Overall, traits were deemed to have greater evidence of longitudinal stability.

KEY POINTS

- Temperament reflects how behaviours are expressed. Temperament differences are believed to have biological origins and are detectable among infants.
- Temperament dimensions combine to reflect three types of children: easy, difficult, and slow-to-warm-up children.
- Temperament dimensions are moderately stable over time, but less stable than trait dimensions, according to a recent meta-analysis.

These comparative findings notwithstanding, studies such as the one performed by Newman, Caspi, Moffitt, and Silva (1997) attest to the long-term stability of temperament. This study assessed children from Dunedin, New Zealand, when they were 3 years old and then again when they were 21 years old. Newman et al. (1997) found some remarkable long-term differences related to initial differences in child temperament. They suggested that it was astounding that meaningful differences could be detected 18 years later after measuring temperament based on only a 90-minute observational period with an observer who was unfamiliar with each participant. These differences were characterized as modest, but significant, effects in terms of the ability of individual differences at 3 years of age to predict differences at 21 years of age. What differences were found? Initially, five distinct groups of children were identified: well-adjusted children, confident children, undercontrolled children, reserved children, and inhibited children. Analyses of tendencies in young adulthood showed that undercontrolled and inhibited children, as young adults had relatively low levels of interpersonal adjustment and high levels of interpersonal conflict. Whereas the undercontrolled had interpersonal problems and were more likely to be the victims of crime and to be seen by others as unreliable, the inhibited children had interpersonal problems only in specific contexts as an adult, and they were described as generally conscientious and reliable.

What about cultural differences in temperament? The influential program of research led by Mary Rothbart has identified temperament dimensions that do seem to generalize across cultures (Rothbart, Ahadi, Hershey, & Fisher, 2001). They developed the Children's Behavior Questionnaire (CBQ) to assess temperament differences in children between the ages of three and seven. Analyses of 15 primary temperament dimensions identified three temperament dimensions: (1) extroversion/surgency; (2) negative affectivity; and (3) effortful control. The **effortful control** dimension has recently received a great deal of empirical attention. It reflects a cognitive tendency to focus attention and to not respond in an impulsive manner. Comparative research by Rothbart and associates (2001) established that not only were the three temperament dimensions evident in their North American samples, but they also existed among children from China and Japan.

Researchers such as Jerome Kagan focus on temperament in the form of individual differences in behavioural inhibition (shyness). This concept, as well as cross-cultural work on behavioural inhibition, is outlined in International Focus on Discovery 3.1. Practical issues involving differences in temperament are addressed in Applied Perspective 3.1.

International Focus on Discovery 3.1 Temperament and Behavioural Inhibition in Asia, Europe, and North America

Behavioural inhibition is an accepted temperament dimension. Behavioural inhibition is often expressed in social situations and is closely linked with shyness and low sociability. The pioneering work of Jerome Kagan and his colleagues has studied infants and toddlers in behavioural situations and has shown that about 10% of children are severely inhibited, while up to one fifth of children are exceptionally low in behavioural inhibition, and most children are moderate in behavioural inhibition (see Garcia-Koll, Kagan, & Reznick, 1984; Kagan & Snidman, 1991). Indicators of behavioural inhibition include lack of spontaneous interaction with others and an unwillingness to approach unfamiliar people. Extreme behavioural inhibition has some clear negative consequences. For instance, Kagan was part of a team that showed that behavioural inhibition is associated with a greater frequency of social anxiety disorder in children (see Biederman et al., 2001).

Behavioural inhibition has been associated with greater frequency of social anxiety disorder in children.

One hypothesis is that behavioural inhibition is due, at least in part, to differences in emotionality that reflect brain structures and processes. Louis Schmidt from McMaster University in Hamilton, Ontario, has shown that adults who report high levels of shyness can be distinguished by resting electroencephalogram (EEG) activity that suggests that there is an EEG asymmetry in the right frontal area of the brain (Schmidt & Fox, 1994). A study of temperamentally shy seven-year-olds by Schmidt, Fox, and Schulkin (1999) showed that shy children also had this right frontal EEG asymmetry, and it was exacerbated in a stressful situation. Schmidt has teamed with Nathan Fox to show that infants who consistently display behavioural inhibition over a four-year period also tended to display right frontal EEG asymmetry and this pattern of brain activation could be detected in infancy as early as nine months of age (see Fox et al., 2001).

Although worldwide differences in behavioural inhibition have been detected, the degree of significance and the correlates of behavioural inhibition seem to vary in meaningful ways across cultures. Research on behavioural inhibition has been conducted in countries such as Canada, China, Sweden, Switzerland, and the United States. Kerr, Lambert, and Bem (1996) contrasted the academic and social consequences of shyness in Sweden and the United States by comparing their findings with data from the United States gathered by Caspi, Elder, and Bem (1988). The reason for possible differences is that Kerr et al. (1996) observed that shyness is much more socially acceptable in Sweden. The similarities and differences are summarized in Kerr (2001). They found that shy boys in both Sweden and the United States, relative to boys who were not shy, got married later in life and had children later, perhaps due to less frequent social interaction opportunities. However, in terms of achievement goals, it was found in Sweden that shy and non-shy boys grew up to be similar on education and career outcome measures, but in the American sample, shy boys entered stable careers about three years later than their non-shy counterparts. Kerr and associates argued that shyness is less likely to be rewarded in the United States and may be a more detrimental factor than in Sweden. According to Kerr (2001), another interesting finding specific to Sweden is that 44% of the non-shy girls went on to earn university degrees while none of the shy girls earned degrees! Thus, even though behavioural inhibition is less problematic in Sweden in some respects, it is deleterious in other respects.

Another important line of research has been conducted by Xinyin Chen from the University of Western Ontario and by Kenneth Rubin from the University of Maryland and their associates. This research team has investigated behavioural inhibition in children from China and Canada. Their basic premise is quite simple: behavioural inhibition is disapproved of in countries such as Canada but it is approved of in countries such as China where self-promotion and expressive displays of emotion are less desirable. Their initial study examined two-year-olds who were evaluated for their levels of behavioural inhibition based on observational data (see Chen et al., 1998; Chen et al., 1999). This research involved giving the Chinese and Canadian toddlers the opportunity to interact with an unfamiliar adult female without a parent being present. Toddlers rated as high in behavioural inhibition were indeed more fearful and inhibited in this situation. It was also found that the Chinese toddlers with high inhibition were significantly more fearful and inhibited in this situation. Analyses of maternal attitudes showed that behavioural inhibition displayed by the Canadian toddlers was associated with a punitive orientation and lack of maternal acceptance, while behavioural inhibition by the Chinese toddlers was associated with greater maternal acceptance, protection, and concern. Thus, cultural values are intertwined with temperament differences.

Subsequent research has shown that even though behavioural inhibition is regarded less positively in North America, prolonged inhibition in Chinese children can have serious consequences. Recently, the results of a seven-year longitudinal study showed that initial levels of sociability in Chinese children predicted better psychosocial adjustment in adolescence (Chen et al., 2002). Moreover, a comparative study of Swiss and Chinese children by Stoeckli (2002) found that teacher ratings of shyness in Grade 4 students were associated with lower scholastic achievement and peer popularity in Swiss girls and boys, and in Chinese girls. These data combine to suggest the need to consider the predictiveness of differences in behavioural inhibition from a cultural perspective.

Applied Perspective 3.1 Accommodating Temperament Differences in the Individual Lives of Children

Several authors have outlined the practical applications of temperament differences. The education field represents one area of application. Martin (1989) linked certain temperaments with underachievement. Children differ in the levels of attentional control, activity, and adaptability, and this can have a dramatic influence on their educational outcomes. It has been suggested that teachers need to remain cognizant of temperament differences among children so that they can predict and prevent problems (Keogh, 1989).

A strong case can also be made for the importance of evaluating temperament when making clinical assessments of children who may suffer from some form of psychopathology. A team of researchers including Kagan found, for instance, that persistent behavioural inhibition was a potent predictor of subsequent anxiety disorders (Hirschfeld et al., 1992). The constellation of temperament factors may assist with the diagnosis of a disorder and suggest the most effective forms of treatment.

Finally, Bates has described the importance of educating parents about temperament differences among children, and the need to tailor parents' behaviours to their child's characteristics (see Bates, 1989; Bates, Wachs, & Emde, 1994). Bates has demonstrated the need for parental sensitivity by outlining some compelling case studies, including the following:

One case example involves a 6-year old boy whose mother initially complained of frequent tantrums, coerciveness, and inconsiderate and risky behavior. Part of my approach involved recasting the child's behavior in temperament-like terms. I described the child as high in negative emotionality, demanding high levels of social and other kinds of stimulation, and resisting outside control. I described how the mother and the boy's older brother were getting upset by the negative emotionality aspect of the boy's attempts to act in accord with his temperament, and falling into coercive traps. I told the mother that the child needed attention, action, and a sense of control, and that she needed to make sure that the boy got extra doses of these things. However, the boy also needed to learn ways to control himself and to be more aware of other's needs. The mother's defensiveness was reduced by attributing her son's coerciveness to relatively neutral needs for attention and action rather than relatively negative excesses and deficits in the child or her. This made it possible for her actually to use specific recommendations to change her behavior with the child. She was able to give the child more warmth and positive control and less reactive, negative control. She was also made aware of the likelihood that the basic challenges with her child would probably continue for quite a few years

In the case of a fearful, inhibited child, I tend to frame the problem in terms of the child being sensitive and highly aware of environmental changes. I emphasize that this can be good, but the child needs help in managing novel and intense stimuli. I then show the parents how to help the child manage these stresses through standard clinical techniques of redirecting attention, direct coping behaviors and cognitive self-statements, graded exposure exercise, and muscular and mental relaxation. Again, the advantage of a temperament formulation is that it can deflect the parent from attributions based on negatively valenced attributes of the child or themselves... (Bates, 1999, p.345)

In both externalizing and internalizing problems, it is sometimes helpful to imply genetic inheritance for the temperamental roots. This allows for one or both parents more closely to identify with the child despite the chronic conflicts they have been having with the child.

Given that temperament variables are meaningful and important, top personality researchers such as Jan Strelau from Poland have criticized the neglect of the temperament construct by trait researchers. Strelau (2001) suggested that temperament refers to:

> ...basic, relatively stable personality traits which have been present since early childhood, occur in man, and have their counterparts in animals. Being primarily determined by inborn neurobiochemical mechanisms, temperament is subject to slow changes caused by maturation and individual-specific genotype-environment interplay. (p. 312)

Although Strelau places great importance on individual differences in temperament, he sees these differences within the context of situational factors and psychological and physiological states that can all combine to have an impact on behaviour. Figure 3.1 represents Strelau's hypothetical view of the factors that contribute to temperament and how temperament traits are but one of several sets of factors that can have an influence.

Strelau (1998) was particularly interested in the link between temperament and stress reactivity. He observed that temperament is present before stressors are experienced, and it was his view that temperament traits are factors that modify various kinds of stress-related phenomena. Regarding the important role of the environment, as illustrated in

Figure 3.1, Strelau (1998) suggested that the goodness of fit hypothesis, especially if viewed from a cross-cultural perspective, allows for the possibility that a difficult temperament can actually have adaptive value! That is, when ruggedness, toughness, and assertiveness are needed for reasons of survival, those who are prepared via their temperament will have an adaptive advantage.

Figure 3.1 The Complex Interplay of Temperament Factors with Other Factors

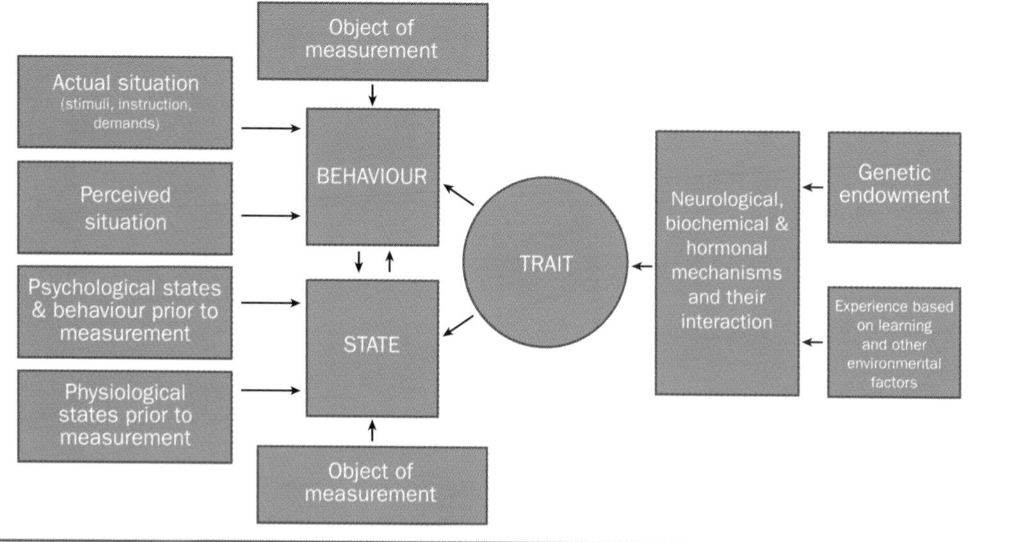

Sorce: Strelau, 2001, p. 319.

Strelau (1998) illustrated this point by citing work by de Vries (1987) on the Maasai children of Kenya. A sub-Saharan drought led the Maasai to migrate to a new location. Differences were found in infants' ability to withstand the physical demands of the migration. Children with a "difficult temperament" were more likely to survive. De Vries attributed their enhanced survival rates to the squeaky wheel hypothesis, which is the tendency to allocate more resources to those who are more likely to fuss and make their needs known to caregivers.

EXTERNAL INFLUENCES ON PERSONALITY DEVELOPMENT

Parenting Styles

In her classic work, Diana Baumrind (1971) identified three parenting styles: authoritarian, permissive, and authoritative. The authoritarian and permissive styles lead to negative outcomes in children, but for different reasons. Authoritarian parents tend to be restrictive, punitive, and overcontrolling. Children respond to the perceived harshness of their parents with externalizing problems or internalizing problems (Hetherington & Martin, 1986;

Patterson & Stouthamer-Loeber, 1984). Exposure to authoritarian parenting also leads to poorer intellectual and social development (see Clarke-Stewart & Apfel, 1979). Whereas authoritarian parents are overinvolved with their children, permissive parents show little involvement and may seem disinterested in their children. This type of parenting style is also associated with internalizing and externalizing symptoms in children. An authoritative approach is most adaptive. Authoritative parents use discipline in conjunction with reason and warmth. That is, guidelines are set out for the child but the rationale is communicated in a matter that signifies a warm, caring attitude.

American parenting expert Barbara Colorosso talks about these same distinctions in terms of three types of families (Colorosso, 1994). The authoritarian family is the brick wall family. Here the parent has absolute control and strict rules, and the child develops a contingent sense of self-worth (i.e., parental approval only comes when expectations are met). The permissive family is referred to as the jellyfish family. Here there are no recognizable rules or guidelines, as anarchy and chaos reign free in the environment. Also, punishments and rewards are doled out arbitrarily. Finally, the authoritative family is referred to as the backbone family. In this family, rules are clearly stated in simple terms, and there are reasonable but undeniable consequences for irresponsible behaviour. However, the goal is to raise children who are taught to think and feel for themselves and to develop a clear level of self-determination.

The Parental Authority Questionnaire (Buri, 1991) is a 30-item measure to assess the three parenting styles. It consists of three subscales with 10 items each that tap the authoritative parenting style (e.g., "My mother has always encouraged verbal give-and-take whenever I have felt that family rules and restrictions were unreasonable"), the authoritarian parenting style (e.g., "As I was growing up my mother would get very upset if I tried to disagree with her"), and the permissive parenting style (e.g., "As I was growing up, my father seldom gave me expectations and guidelines for my behaviour").

The Personality of Parents

Increasingly, researchers are examining the extent to which parenting styles are predicted by pre-existing personality differences among parents. It is presumed that certain parents have a personality style that is reflected by poor parenting behaviours. Children are at risk if they have parents with less than optimal personalities (e.g. they have high hostility) and presumably, preventive programs designed to improve the parenting of these mothers and fathers should prove to be quite effective.

There are some caveats about research in this area. First, only a limited number of personality characteristics have been evaluated thus far, and more research is required. Belsky and Barends (2002) have been particularly critical of the limited scope of research on personality and parenting thus far. Second, as is often the case, there is less research with fathers than with mothers, as fathers are sometimes not included. Finally, results may differ across parents; the link between personality and parenting seems stronger for mothers than for fathers (see Belsky, Crnic, & Woodworth, 1995).

In general, research on this topic suggests that certain traits in the five-factor model are at least moderately predictive of maladaptive or adaptive parenting. Belsky et al. (1995) assessed parents' personality when first-born infants were 10 months old, and then subsequent observational ratings of mothering and fathering behaviours were obtained when the child was 15 months old and 21 months old. Neuroticism, agreeableness, and extroversion were studied. Neuroticism in mothers and fathers was associated with poorer parenting behaviours. For instance, neuroticism in mothers was associated with less maternal sensitivity, less cognitive stimulation of the infant, greater expression of negative affect, and greater intrusiveness. Extroversion and agreeableness in mothers was associated with greater sensitivity and cognitive stimulation. This same general pattern of findings was also found for fathers.

Neuroticism is usually associated with maladaptive parenting, and extroversion and agreeableness are associated with optimal parenting behaviours (see Clark, Kochanska, & Ready, 2000). Conscientiousness also plays a role in some studies. For instance, Clark et al. (2000) found that maternal conscientiousness, neuroticism, and extroversion predicted responsiveness and power assertion techniques in subsequent behavioural interactions between mothers and their young children.

In a study conducted in Montreal, Ellenbogen and Hodgins (2004) found that higher parental neuroticism was not only associated with poorer parenting but also associated with greater maladjustment among their children. Another recent investigation found that conscientiousness and low neuroticism in parents was associated with less externalizing problem behaviours (e.g., aggressiveness, acting out) among their four-year-old boys and girls (Prinzie, Onghena, & Hellinckx, 2005).

Another study by Kochanska and her associates at the University of Iowa sought to replicate findings involving the five-factor model, but the researchers also wanted to test the impact of other personality factors that receive substantially less attention in the research community (Kochanska, Friesenborg, Lange, & Martel, 2004). Their study showed that the personality factors that predicted parenting behaviours were quite different for mothers and fathers. Specifically, mothers higher in neuroticism displayed less positive affect when interacting with their infants. Maternal responsiveness was predicted by a measure of empathy included in this study. For fathers, positive emotional expression was associated with agreeableness and openness to experience. Openness was also linked with fathers' responsiveness to the infant.

Research indicates that personality factors such as high extroversion and openness to experience and low neuroticism were predictors of parental nurturance.

One intriguing study conducted in Finland looked at personality dimensions and parenting behaviours, but it also went a step further because it examined the extent to which parents' personality was linked with the parenting styles outlined by Baumrind (1989). In addition to the three parenting styles delineated by Baumrind (the authoritative, authoritarian, and permissive parenting styles), Metsapelto and Pulkkinen (2003) identified three other groups of parents: engaged parents, emotionally involved parents, and emotionally detached parents.

Personality factors were assessed when the parents were approximately 33 years old, and parenting tendencies were evaluated when the parents were 36 years of age. The main results linking personality and parenting tendencies are displayed in Figure 3.2. It can be seen that parental nurturance was predicted by high extroversion and openness to experience, and low neuroticism. Parental restrictiveness was predicted solely by openness to experience. Finally, parents high in neuroticism had decreased parental knowledge. None of the parenting factors were linked with conscientiousness and agreeableness.

Figure 3.2 Personality Traits and Parenting Behaviours

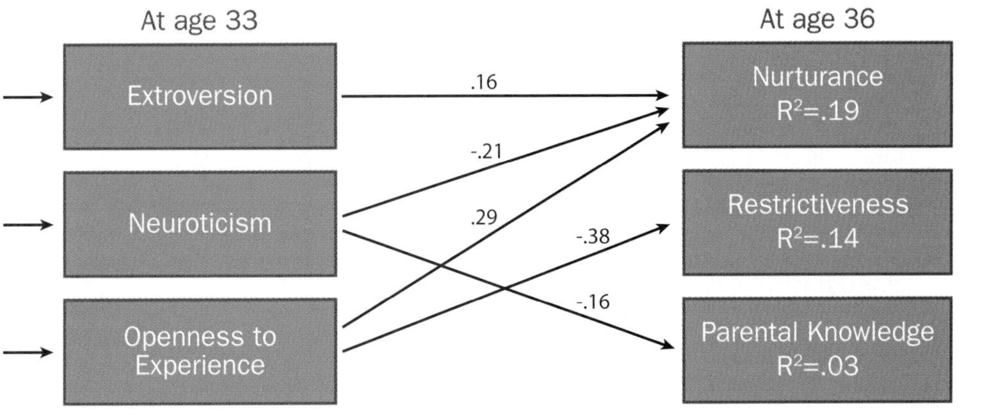

Source: Metsäpelto & Pulkkinen, 2002, p. 67.

As for the parenting style classifications, authoritative parents were high in extroversion and openness. In contrast, authoritarian parents and emotionally detached parents were exceptionally low in extroversion and openness. Also, consistent with Belsky et al. (1995), comparisons of mothers and fathers showed that personality factors were more predictive of parenting tendencies for mothers.

Collectively, these findings suggest that parenting behaviours and parenting styles are driven, in part, by pre-existing personality differences among parents. One clear limitation of this research is that the link between personality and parenting in various cultures is largely unexplored.

Parenting Styles and Child Outcomes across Cultures

It was noted above that certain parenting styles contribute to adjustment levels in children. One particularly remarkable study examined the association between parental characteristics and the children's personality with data from eight international, urbanized locations

(Canberra and Brisbane in Australia; Winnipeg, Canada; Phoenix, United States; Berlin, Germany; Hong Kong; Taipei, Taiwan; and Osaka, Japan). This study by Scott, Scott, and McCabe (1991) also was unique in that it obtained data not only from the children themselves, but also from their parents and their teachers. The children were in Grades 7 to 12. One intriguing finding that emerged from this study was that parental nurturance was associated with higher self-esteem and lower anxiety in all eight samples when the focus was exclusively on the self-reports of the children. There were no differences across cultures! However, two other important findings were noteworthy. First, parental punitiveness was associated with hostility in children, according to parental reports, but not according to the ratings provided by the children. Second, the cross-source correlations were quite low both in personality variables and family variables. Thus, there was little correlation between parental characteristics reported by children and their teachers' ratings of their personality features. Scott et al. (1991) concluded that there may be substantial same-source bias in the children's data, but it is also equally plausible that bias influenced the data provided by parents and teachers. We will revisit this methodological concern in Chapter 4.

The Directionality Issue

One problem in focusing on the impact of parenting styles and parental personality factors is that this can incorrectly foster a model of unidirectional influence (the parent influences the child). Bell and Chapman (1973) made the important point that influence is bidirectional (the parent and child each influence each other). The **directionality issue** is the term used to describe personality models prior to the 1970s that focused on the impact of the parent on the child without taking into account the child's role in shaping outcomes and experiences. The concept of **self-socialization** is based on the realization that the developing child can make choices and act in such a manner as to influence the feedback received from others and the situations that he or she experiences. That is, each child is an active participant in his or her development and learning experiences. Bell and Chapman (1986) noted that children's behaviour may force parents to act, may selectively reinforce or increase the likelihood of certain parental behaviours, or may create expectations that then guide parental behaviours.

Today, psychologists acknowledge that the influence in social relationships is typically reciprocal. That is, parents influence their children and children influence their parents. In his developmental model, Jay Belsky (1984) posits mutual, interdependent influences in which each member of a system affects and is affected by the others.

There are numerous examples of how the child's temperament can have an impact on the parental behaviour, which in turn will have an impact on the developing child. Observational research indicates that temperamentally difficult children may get more assistance from their mothers, but they also garner more maternal disapproval and they are given less freedom to discover problem-solving strategies on their own (Gauvain & Fagot, 1995). Other research shows that mothers show more sensitivity if infants have "easy" temperaments (Feldman, Greenbaum, Mayes, & Erlich, 1997), and they adjust their play behaviour as a function of the child's temperament (Dixon & Smith, 2003). The need to jointly consider the characteristics of the child and the parent was illustrated by Bugental and Shennum (1984). Their research monograph describes research on how "difficult" and "easy" children have an impact on parents and how parents, in turn, behave toward these children. Their research was based on a **transactional model** that allows for the various individuals to have an impact on each other in an ongoing sequence of behaviours.

KEY POINTS

- The three parenting styles identified by Baumrind are authoritative parenting (discipline with reason), authoritarian parenting (overcontrolling and harsh), and permissive parenting (uninvolved). Authoritative parenting is most adaptive in terms of child outcomes.
- Parents high in neuroticism and low in extroversion and agreeableness tend to display less optimal parenting.
- The directionality issue refers to the child's influence on the parents. Transactional models reflect the mutual influence of the parent and child on each other.

The Unimportance of Parents?

The notion of mutual influence of parent and child on each other is not in keeping with the claim by Judith Harris that parents' actions or inactions contribute little to their child's personality development (see Harris, 1998). Instead, Harris suggests that the main contributing factors are genetic factors (temperament) and the influences of the peer group. The message that "parents don't matter" is a highly controversial one that has garnered much attention in the media. However, we should at least be grateful to Harris for reminding us of the powerful influence of peers.

There can be no denying that peers play a very significant role in influencing and shaping us, and peer influence is particularly strong during certain life periods, such as adolescence. But can we conclude that parents play no role? Harris (1998) herself acknowledged that there are some indications that parents have some impact. These are summarized by Harris (1998) in her Generalization 1 and Generalization 2. Generalization 1 is, "Parents who do a good job managing their lives and who get along well with others tend to have children who are also good at managing their lives and getting along well with others" (p. 20). Generalization 2 is, "Children who are treated with affection and respect tend to do better at managing their lives and their personal relationships than those who are treated harshly." If these generalizations are correct, how can Harris argue that parents have no impact? If stated in personality trait terms, essentially Harris (1998) concluded that conscientious and agreeable parents tend to have conscientious and agreeable children (Generalization 1), and children who are treated with dignity and not mistreated tend to cope better and have more self-control, and by extrapolation, have lower impulsivity and neuroticism.

Parental harshness has a very deleterious effect on personality development. Rogosch and Cicchetti (2004) compared 135 maltreated children with 76 children without a history of maltreatment. The maltreated children had documented histories of child abuse and/or neglect. The prototypical child in this study was six years of age and had already experienced multiple forms of abuse, including physical abuse, emotional maltreatment, and neglect. The participants were from a camp for maltreated and non-maltreated children from low-income families. Personality assessments were provided by camp counsellors who evaluated children at the end of each week on the California Child Q-Set, which can be scored according to the five-factor model. The analyses showed that there were significant group differences on four of the five factors. Maltreated children were rated as having comparatively higher levels of neuroticism and lower levels of agreeableness, conscientiousness, and openness to experience. Extroversion levels did not vary significantly for the two groups. The largest group differences were in conscientiousness.

Another issue to consider when evaluating peer influence versus parental influence is that we must also allow for the possibility that parents can have an indirect impact on personality development because the way in which parents interact with their children can come to be reflected in how their children interact with their peers. Socialization research has revealed that interactions between mothers and their children can indeed predict subsequent interactions that children have with their peers (e.g., Kochanska, 1992).

One reasonable conclusion is to suggest that with certain children, perhaps parents will indeed have little impact. However, for other children, parents may have a great deal of impact. Indeed, parenting seems to play a much greater role for children who were highly negative as infants, and plays less of a role for children who had a more appealing, positive temperament (Park, Belsky, Putnam, & Crnic, 1997).

Another way of evaluating this issue is to examine research findings that have emerged since Harris (1998) suggested that parents have little role to play. Several findings suggest that parents have some role to play, within the context of other factors (such as temperament). Two such areas are outlined below.

One area of investigation involves the concept of **gender schemas**. Gender schemas are cognitive categories that people have as a means of thinking about themselves and others in terms of gender and gender-related characteristics. Someone who has a highly developed gender schema would be cognitively attuned to differences between males and females and factors that distinguish masculinity and femininity. Other people who lack this gender schema would be less aware of gender-related differences and would place less importance on using gender as a way of interpreting events in his or her world. In the current context, what is the link between the parents' gender schemas and the gender schemas in their children? A meta-analysis of 43 articles on this topic led to the conclusion that there is a small but significant link between the gender schemas of parents and their children (Tenenbaum & Leaper, 2002). For instance, parents with very traditional gender schemas were more likely than parents with non-traditional gender schemas to have children with similar gender-typed cognitions about themselves and other people. The authors concluded that parents may indeed have an impact on self-concepts and attitudes reflecting gender, but they appropriately cautioned that this conclusion is based on correlational data, and the causal impact of parents is yet to be demonstrated.

Research on anxiety in children represents another area where parental treatment seems to contribute to personality differences. It has been suggested that parental treatment that is overcontrolling fosters a dependency on the parent and conveys to the child the message that events are beyond his or her personal control (Chorpita & Barlow, 1998). In contrast, parents who foster a sense of autonomy in their children are less likely to have children with high trait anxiety. A review indicated that parenting style in general is not associated with trait anxiety, shyness, and anxiety disorders in children, but exposure to specific parenting behaviours and overcontrolling practices predicts anxiety in children (Wood, McLeod, Sigman, Hwang, & Chu, 2003). Parental overcontrol fosters a lack of mastery in children.

THE ROLE OF CULTURE IN PERSONALITY DEVELOPMENT

The significance of cultural differences has already been introduced in this book. In this section, the association between personality and culture is described in more detail, and the role of cultural factors in personality development is outlined.

Contemporary theorists can have some dramatically different viewpoints on the link between personality and culture, and the role of culture in personality development. For instance, McCrae (2004) endorsed the view that culture does not have an effect on personality, but personality traits can sometimes influence culture. McCrae acknowledged that this view (culture does not influence personality) is extreme and may ultimately be shown to be inaccurate, but it is a reflection of his belief that biological differences account for personality traits.

Shigehiro Oishi adopted a radically different perspective (see Oishi, 2004). Oishi endorsed the view that cultural factors do indeed influence the development of personality, but also, it is not enough to merely compare participants from different countries by their mean score on a personality measure or measures. It is also important to assess the heterogeneity and differences within one culture and compare this with the heterogeneity and differences that exist within other cultures.

Cultural differences can be represented in many different ways. There can be differences between cultures in mean levels of personality variables. Also, as noted above, there may be cultural differences in the amount of variability and heterogeneity that exists within the culture, with some cultures accommodating more widespread differences among people.

There can also be cultural differences in the relevance or importance of personality dimensions. Cultural differences may also exist in the hypothesized and actual correlations that a personality variable has with other variables. This may be a reflection of extant differences in cultural values. Deater-Deckard and Dodge (1997) used differences in cultural values to help explain why parental physical discipline is associated with aggressive behaviour in European-American children, but these variables are either not associated or are associated negatively in African-American children. They suggested that the key element is whether physical discipline is seen as atypical and inappropriate or, as is the case among African-American people, it is seen as normative and reflective of parental involvement and concern. Another example they cited is that physical discipline in Sweden is absolutely forbidden and is regarded as a clear indicator of poor parenting.

The most extensive focus on the role of cultural differences in personality development is Hofstedt's distinction between idiographic and collectivist cultures. Hofstedt (1980) is a researcher from the Netherlands who conducted an international investigation of IBM employees from 40 countries and identified four dimensions, including the critical dimension of individualism versus collectivism. **Individualism** involves an extensive self-focus on the individual and his or her immediate family. The emphasis is on the self in relation to the self, and the emphasis is on personal goals and achievements. **Collectivism** involves much more of a group emphasis and fostering the connection between the self and other people. People are more integrated, interdependent, and cohesive in a collectivist society. Hofstede's (1980, 2001) results indicate that collectivism is higher in less developed countries. In general, individualism prevails in Western cultures and collectivism prevails in less well-developed Eastern cultures, and some cultures such as Japan are in the middle of this dimension. As noted by Hofstede and McCrae (2004), the use of IBM employees was a strength of this research because the employees included across countries were comparable in education and work experience, so this factor likely did not bias the results.

Hofstede (2001) has examined the link between individualism–collectivism and personality traits. His work indicates that the there is a robust association between individualism and extroversion, and little link between individualism and the other traits of the five-factor model. Extroverts tend to be higher in individualism, suggesting that part of their orientation toward other people is to establish their sense of identity among their associates.

Subsequent work on individualism versus collectivism has been conducted by a number of highly influential researchers such as Harry Triandis. Triandis and Gelfand (1998) established that individualism and collectivism can take many different forms, and, as such, subtle yet important differences may exist among cultures that all share a general emphasis on either collectivism or on individualism.

Clearly, cultural factors are associated with personality differences. Before concluding this section, two important caveats about the role of cultural differences need to be acknowledged. First, it is important to regularly evaluate a culture's characteristics rather than rely on past stereotypes about the culture. The need to evaluate and re-evaluate preconceived ideas was dramatically underscored by David Matsumoto in his 2002 book *The New Japan: Debunking Seven Cultural Stereotypes*. Matsumoto challenged seven key beliefs about Japan, including many stereotypes that have been accepted uncritically by previous researchers. Matsumoto questioned the extent to which the emerging Japan is high in features that are directly relevant to personality research, such as collectivism, interdependent self-construal, interpersonal consciousness, and control of emotion. He also questioned the current applicability of traditional beliefs about employment, lifestyle, and marriage. In essence, Matsumoto argued that in contrast to Hofstede's (1984) conclusion that Japan is moderately collectivistic in orientation, more current research suggests that individualism is much higher than would be expected. He also suggested that there is a shift toward less interdependent self-construal and interpersonal consciousness, and reduced control of emotion, so previous stereotypes do not apply to an increasing proportion of the Japanese population.

In addition to the ongoing need to evaluate a culture's characteristics, it is also important to recognize the great heterogeneity that may exist within a culture. Even cultures that are exceptionally high in collectivism have widespread differences among people. The differences among people was revealed in research on Japanese women and conducted by Holloway and Behrens (2002). As part of a broader analysis of the parenting self-efficacy of these women, Holloway and Behrens interviewed 40 women from Sapporo about the parental treatment they received as they were growing up. One belief is that Japanese children are treated with indulgence (the concept "*amae*") by their parents (see Rothbaum et al., 2000). However, interviews revealed widespread differences among the women in the parental treatment they received, and overall, much less indulgence was found than was expected.

When asked to describe their own mothers and their parenting styles, nine women characterized their mothers as being high in warmth and kindness and involvement. Another eight women described their mothers as being quite strict but having a "fundamental kindness." For instance, one participant with siblings said in her interview that her mother was "strict to us three children, but she was also kind. I am still afraid of her sometimes [laugh]. She just never accepted lies. If you lie and she finds out about it, she doesn't speak to you" (Holloway & Behrens, 2002, p. 33).

Finally, the largest group consisted of the 16 women who described their mothers as being either very strict (*kibishii*) or scary. This is the antithesis of indulgent parenting. The accounts of these women are compelling.

> "When I was a child, I remember feeling that she was scary. I feel that I was always being scolded. Now, today, they say that we should raise our children by praising them. But it wasn't like that. I was scolded or I just wonder if she ever accepted me, when I think back now. It was very strict or tough. My father was very scary. I don't think I ever had a normal conversation with him. In any event, I don't remember that I was ever loved much at all by my parents, both my mother and father."
>
> "My mother was very controlling. She was, like, I can't do this, and I can't do that. She was very rigid and really intimidating. Always, even when my friend was bad, I was the one who got scolded, like that. She had a very strong will, and so she could really persevere at things and also didn't know how to ask for indulgence. Maybe she wanted to complain and show her weakness, but she couldn't. So I thought, like, for things like that, it was her loss. Also for her children too,

> she demanded strictness, but like, because I was controlled, maybe I went in the opposite direction."
>
> "She was like a devil. She would scold totally depending on how she felt, and then although she'd get mad based on her feelings, she did insist on what's wrong is wrong, and would stand up with a medal of honor. She was like hysterical. Every day, I kept being scolded in any event. I was spanked, thrown out of the house, beaten with [inaudible], and pushed in water. I mean really! Now if anyone did such a thing, it'll be considered a crime. All my siblings experienced this kind of thing. Now we all laugh at it. Honestly, I didn't like her. I hated and hated her so much."
>
> "She was so strict. Regarding education and child rearing, she wasn't strict, but about playing ... She never did anything with children. Well, those days were, it was the period for advanced economic growth. As the name tells, it was the period for work, work, work. Even at harvest time, there was no extra help. She was always yelling. I guess she didn't really have the emotional capacity. And so I resisted and disobeyed. During my rebellious period, I totally hated my parents with all my guts. Everything she said totally ignored my human rights. She said everything, using parental rights as the excuse, 'What do you think you're saying toward your parent?'" (Holloway & Behrens, 2002)

In addition to the differences in parenting styles, the Holloway and Behrens (2002) study yielded other findings that emphasize the need to be careful in generalizing findings from one culture to another culture. In general, research indicates that being in a warm and responsive family promotes a sense of **parenting self-efficacy** (i.e., viewing the self as a competent parent). However, much of this research has been conducted with participants in North American samples. Holloway and Behrens (2002) found that harsh parental treatment in Japan was associated with *increased parenting self-efficacy* when the children who were treated harshly were evaluated as adults. It was presumed that this harsh parental treatment included demands to be extremely involved in childcare of siblings, and this higher amount of experience facilitated a sense of competence about parenting duties and responsibilities. Although parenting self-efficacy was perhaps boosted by harsh parental treatment, it is likely that this also took a negative toll on general self-esteem.

Other research has examined whether concepts and themes that exist in Eastern cultures have some relevance in Western civilizations. For example, investigators have evaluated whether the concept of ***guan*** is meaningful in the United States (see Stewart, Bond, Kennard, Ho, & Zaman, 2002). *Guan* was a term suggested by Chao (1994) to refer to a mode of parenting among Chinese parents that is focused on training. It is a more directive form of parental behaviour that, according to Chao (1994), does not fit well into Baumrind's parenting typology (authoritarian, authoritative, and permissive parenting). It is represented by test items such as, "My father/mother pointed out good behaviours in others as a model for me," and "My father/mother emphasized self-discipline." Stewart et al. (2002) concluded that *guan* was "exportable:" individual differences in *guan* were found across their three samples (drawn from the United States, Pakistan, and Hong Kong). *Guan* in mothers and fathers was correlated in all three samples, and mothers received higher *guan* scores than fathers in all three samples. However, differences emerged in the health implications of *guan*; that is, *guan* was a positive predictor of life satisfaction in Hong Kong participants, but *guan* did not predict life satisfaction among the participants from the United States.

TYPE A BEHAVIOUR IN CHILDREN: AN ILLUSTRATION OF MULTIPLE DEVELOPMENTAL INFLUENCES

This chapter concludes with an analysis of the developmental of Type A behaviour. Type A behaviour as a personality style was described briefly in Chapter 1. This personality construct was selected because it has been the subject of extensive developmental research over the past three decades. Moreover, it is obvious that research in this area supports the general contention that personality development must consider several factors inside and outside the individual. Finally, research on Type A behaviour in children shows that personality differences exist at a very early age.

While growing up, you probably encountered some children who were always striving and seemingly always on the go, versus other children who were more laid back and calm. You might have been one of these continually striving children with the Type A behavioural pattern. What do we know about Type A behaviour in children? Because it is a personality construct, individual differences in Type A characteristics should be detectable even among very young children.

The main attributes of Type A behaviour found in adults also seem to exist in children (for an overview, see Nay & Wagner, 199). Central features include (1) highly competitive achievement striving; (2) speed and time urgency; (3) chronic impatience; and (4) hostility. These Type A characteristics have been identified in children as young as four or five years of age (Corrigan & Moskowitz, 1983; Lundberg,

Type A characteristics such as highly competitive achievement striving and speed and time urgency have been identified in children as young as four years of age.

Rasch, & Westermark, 1992). Imagine being the nursery school teacher for a group of Type A preschoolers! Research from Sweden indicates that Type A boys and boys with attention deficit hyperactivity disorder (ADHD) both respond with speed and impatience; but unlike the boys with ADHD, Type A boys do not have cognitive deficits in inhibitory control and executive functioning (Nyberg, Bohlin, Berlin, & Janols, 2003). An earlier study had also linked Type A behaviour with hyperactivity (Whalen & Henker, 1986).

Type A features in children interact with situational demands. There is evidence, for instance, that Type B children respond more slowly when working on a task without a time constraint, but they more closely resemble Type A children when time limits and incentives are put in place (Corrigan & Moskowitz, 1983). Lundberg et al. (1992) found in a Swedish sample of young boys that Type A features are more evident when these boys were playing a computer game with "Type-A relevant challenges." Presumably, Type A computer games that focus on speed, competition, and aggressiveness would be particularly engaging for Type A children.

Familial Factors

What is the role of familial factors in Type A behaviours in children? Meyer Friedman, one of the doctors who originally identified the Type A pattern, and his co-author Diane Ulmer suggested that Type A behaviour is designed to compensate for feelings of inferiority and that Type A behaviours are attempts to gain approval from significant others (see Friedman & Ulmer, 1984).

There is a positive association between Type A behaviour in parents and Type A behaviour in their offspring, but this association is only moderate in magnitude and varies as a function of the Type A component being assessed (e.g., Raikkonen, 1993). Vega-Lahr and Field (1986) found that Type A in children was related only marginally to their mothers' levels of Type A characteristics and their levels of impatience. As for fathers, there was a moderate link between fathers' impatience and overall Type A scores in their children. However, additional analyses showed that higher impatience in children was associated negatively with parental competitiveness (i.e., more impatient children had less competitive parents).

Genetic Factors

Regarding genetic factors, several studies suggest that Type A behaviour has a biological component and has its roots in individual differences in temperament (Raikkonen & Keltikangas-Jarvinen, 1992; Steinberg, 1985). Heft et al. (1988) found that temperament differences did not predict subsequent Type A behaviour in children, but they did find that Type A children had elevated levels of emotionality (e.g., depression, anxiety, and anger) and emotion reactivity. They suggested that Type A behaviour may gradually emerge from a diffuse pattern of emotional arousal and arousability. Steinberg's (1985, 1987) research on the temperament factors in early childhood that serve as antecedents to Type A behaviour in adulthood involved an analysis of the temperament factors identified by Thomas and Chess. Steinberg reported that the achievement striving component is elevated among adults who had temperaments characterized by high adaptability, high approach tendencies, negative mood, and low rhythmicity. The impatience–anger component was found among adolescents with temperaments involving low adaptability, low persistence, and low sensory threshold.

The role of genetic factors may vary according to which Type A component is assessed. Earlier research by Rosenman and colleagues found no evidence that Type A behaviour has a genetic component, but a reanalysis of these data suggested that the hostility component might be heritable (see Matthews et al., 1984). A subsequent study of parents and their young children by Matthews et al. (1992) found no family resemblance in hostility. Weidner et al. (2000) reasoned that family resemblance in hostility may emerge over time, and it is necessary to examine this issue in adult offspring and their parents rather than in young children and their parents. Secondary analyses by Weidner et al. (2000) suggested that the inherited biological component is most evident in individual differences in cynical hostility. Cynical hostility involves pessimistic beliefs about the world and other people. It is measured by such items as, "I think most people would lie to get ahead" and "No one cares much about what happens to you."

A study of twin pairs found that overall Type A scores did indeed have a heritable component (Meininger, Hayman, Coates, & Gallagher, 1988). However, there was also substantial evidence of the role of environmental factors. The results of this and other research (e.g., Sallis, Dimsdale, & Caine, 1988) promoted a model in which Type A behaviour was seen as a learned response to stressors and the family's tendency to respond intensely when confronted with stressors and other challenges.

Karen Matthews is a pioneer in the field of personality and developmental factors linked with long-term vulnerability to health problems. Matthews has conducted extensive research on the antecedents of high levels of Type A behaviour in general and the hostility component in particular.

Karen Matthews developed the most widely used measure of Type A behaviour in children, the Matthews Youth Test for Health (MYTH).

Her accomplishments include developing the most widely used measure of Type A behaviour in children, the Matthews Youth Test for Health (MYTH; Matthews, 1978). This instrument consists of 17 statements that are used to rate the child on two characteristics: (1) competitiveness; and (2) impatience–aggression. This scale has been used to assess children of various ages, including preschoolers; Type A differences can be identified among three- and four-year-old children, and scores on levels of Type A are moderately stable over time (Matthews, 1978; Vega-Lahr & Field, 1986).

Matthews has analyzed the role of family environment in the development of the hostility component. Why focus on hostility? Hostility seems to be "the active ingredient" in health problems. A study by Woodall and Matthews (1989) provided evidence that children with high levels of hostility and an amplified heart rate in response to stressors presented in a laboratory setting came from families characterized by low positive affiliation combined with parents with an authoritarian personality (i.e., dogmatic and domineering).

Recent research indicates that developmental theories that focus on exposure to a Type A family environment need to be modified because there is great heterogeneity among Type A families; that is, there are different Type A families and different Type A family environments. An important longitudinal study by Keltikangas-Jarvinen and Heinonen (2003) from the University of Helsinki in Finland studied children and their parents, and they found that there were three distinct family types: (1) a family that was not Type A; (2) a family that was described as "a positive Type A family"; and (3) a family that was described as "a negative Type A family." The key distinguishing factor between the two Type A families is that the parents in the positive family had moderate or high life satisfaction (defined as a combination of marital satisfaction and work satisfaction), while the parents in the negative Type A family had low life satisfaction. What difference did this make? Keltikangas-Jarvinen and Heinonen (2003) reported that parental Type A characteristics had a vastly different impact in that hostile attitudes and trait irritability developed primarily in the children who were exposed to dissatisfied parents, and there was little evidence of hostile attitudes and trait irritability in the children raised in positive Type A families. However, the children's early characteristics also played a role in determining whether the family was deemed subsequently to be a positive or negative Type A family. Children in the positive Type A family were seen as being higher in leadership responsibility and this served a protective role. The main characteristic of children in the negative Type A family was at least an average level of impatience and aggression during childhood. This study illustrates the complex interplay between parent and child factors in personality development, but it also emphasizes the need to examine possible heterogeneity among parents who might be similar in some but not all respects.

One final study by Matthews (1977) deserves mention because it reiterates the need to remain cognizant of the child's role in his or her self-socialization. Matthews had boys act in a Type A manner or Type B manner. The level of Type A behaviour in the mothers was also assessed with a self-report measure. Each mother was required to instruct and assist a boy who was performing block design and block-stacking tasks. Boys enacting a Type A role accomplished this through various ways, including continually interrupting the experimenter with questions as initial instructions were being given. In contrast, boys enacting the Type B role waited and posed their questions after the instructions had been given.

So, what difference did the child's behaviour make? The two key outcome measures were the number of positive performance evaluations that the adult delivered to the child and the amount of pushing (i.e., remarks the adult designed to spur the child on and motivate him to attain higher achievement). The findings indicated that the Type A female caregivers tended to respond quite similarly to the boys enacting a Type A or Type B role. However, the Type B caregivers delivered more performance evaluations and pushing for boys enacting the Type A role. This study suggests that Type A boys may actually shape their own caregivers by getting parents without Type A characteristics to interact with them in a manner that is more in keeping with Type A tendencies.

It was noted earlier that, in general, as children get older and become adolescents, peer influence becomes increasingly important. While it is likely that peer influence (at least as a form of competitiveness) has a substantial impact on escalating or decreasing Type A tendencies, depending on the person, there is an apparent lack of research on peers and Type A behaviour.

A Role for Culture?

Finally, the possible role of cultural differences in the etiology and expression of Type A behaviour must be considered. Relatively little research has been done on Type A behaviour from a cross-cultural perspective, especially in children. However, studies with adults suggest that cultural differences exist and must be given consideration. Findings in Japan by Hokaka and Tagawa (1987) led these researchers to posit a Japanese Type A behaviour pattern. This form of Type A places much less emphasis on hard-driving competitiveness because this is an element that is too individualistic for Japanese culture. Instead, the focus is on Type A as hard-working workaholism and perfectionistic, compulsive striving that may be designed to improve organizational outcomes rather than individual outcomes. However, as might be expected, there appear to be clear consequences for individuals from Japan who exhibit this Type A orientation. Yoshimau (2001) confirmed the emphasis on workaholic striving as part of the Type A construct, and then demonstrated that Type A behaviour is a risk factor for heart attacks in both male and female workers. Personality and health is explored in more detail in Chapter 12.

The developmental factors associated with Type A behaviour were selected, in part, because the research as a whole highlights the multitude of factors that must be considered from a developmental perspective. Genetic and temperament play a role, but exposure to Type A environments and parental models of Type A must also be considered, along with the extent to which cultural factors promote the Type A orientation.

Summary

The purpose of this chapter was to illustrate the many influences, both internal and external, that are involved in personality development. First, however, we revisited the issue of personality differences in children. It was established that stable individual differences in at least four of the five trait dimensions of the five-factor model can be detected in relatively young children. All of the factors, with the exception of openness, can be found, and most parents spontaneously mention three of four trait domains when describing their children. Similarly, individual differences in the traits outlined by Eysenck can also be identified in young children from various countries.

Research on the stability of personality trait differences across the lifespan was then outlined. Various ways of assessing the stability issue were described. It was demonstrated that personality trait differences are moderately stable across the lifespan. Recent evidence that personality can change in middle and late adulthood was described. It was concluded that there was little support for the suggestion that personality is set in plaster by the age of 30.

What factors contribute to the development of personality throughout the lifespan? First, the role of genetic factors was documented. It was shown that most major personality traits are high in heritability. Individual differences in temperament were then described. Temperament differences are genetic in origin and are clearly distinguished in the three types of children described by Thomas and Chess (the easy child, the slow-to-warm-up child, and the difficult child). The child's role in being an active agent that shapes his or her experiences, and socialization was also emphasized.

Several external influences on development were then noted. Different parenting styles as outlined by Baumrind were delineated (authoritarian, authoritative, and permissive parenting styles). In addition, we examined the link between the personality features of mothers and fathers and their parenting behaviours. This segment concluded with an analysis of the argument that parents are relatively unimportant in shaping personality, relative to the influence of peers. It was suggested that parents continue to have a direct and indirect influence on their adolescents.

Cultural factors were then explored. The important distinction between individualistic and collectivist cultures as described by Hofstede was then described. Finally, the multiple influences contributing to Type A behaviour in children were discussed. It was concluded that individual differences in Type A behaviour reflect the complex interplay of factors stemming from the child and his or her family, as well as the broader society.

Questions to Consider

1 Recall the study by Robins et al. (2005) that found that most participants perceived that they had changed substantially over the course of their university careers. Have you changed much since you began university, or are you the "same old person" you used to be?

2 Where do you stand on the nature versus nurture debate? We will see when we discuss the behaviourists that theorists such as Watson believe that a child can be shaped by reinforcement and punishment. Do you agree with this notion or do you feel that genetic background places a limit on personality change?

3 Do you accept that children from the same family can be very different? Why might this occur? To what extent do the children act in a way to create differences?

4 Review the five main temperament dimensions that have been endorsed in recent reviews of this field. How do you see yourself with respect to these temperament dimensions? To what extent do you have an easy versus a difficult or slow-to-warm-up temperament?

5 Did your parents have an authoritative, authoritarian, or permissive parenting style? Perhaps you are a parent or plan to be one some day. What style will characterize your parenting behaviour? And where do you stand on the issue of whether parents matter?

6 Think about the five traits that compose the five-factor model. Do you think these traits have similar or different developmental origins? Which trait, if any, is more likely to be influenced by life experiences?

Key terms

accentuation principle , p. 85
adoptees method, p. 87
behavioural inhibition, p. 97
collectivism, p. 108
concordance, p. 87
cynical hostility, p. 113
directionality issue, p. 104
dynamic stability, p. 81
effortful control, p. 96
equal environment assumption, p. 87
flux, p. 81
gender schemas, p. 106
genotype, p. 87
guan, p. 110
heritability, p. 87
impostor phenomenon, p. 74
individualism, p. 108
ipsative scoring, p. 81
ipsative stability, p. 80
Little Five, p. 76
mean-level stability, p. 79
nonadditive genetic effects, p. 87
nonshared environment, p. 87
parenting self-efficacy, p. 110
phenotype, p. 87
plaster hypothesis, p. 78
plasticity hypothesis, p. 78
pulse, p. 81

rank-order stability, p. 80
self-socialization, p. 104
shared environment, p. 87
spin, p. 81
temperament, p. 92
test–retest correlation, p. 80
transactional model, p. 105
twin registries, p. 80

Key Theorists

William James, p. 78
Karen Matthews, p. 113

chapter four

PERSONALITY RESEARCH METHODS AND ASSESSMENT ISSUES

- Experimental Research
- Correlational Research
- Personality Research Trends
- Different Types of Data
- Issues in Personality Assessment

An essential ingredient in the research process is the judgment of the scientist. He or she must decide by how much a theoretical position has been advanced by the data, just as he or she decided what to study, what data to get, and how to get it. I believe that statistical inference applied with informed judgment is a useful tool in this process, but it isn't the most important tool: It is not as important as everything that came before it.

—JACOB COHEN (1990, P. 1310–1311)

You can see a lot just by observing.

—YOGI BERRA, HALL OF FAME NEW YORK YANKEES BASEBALL CATCHER AND COACH

Personality psychology's preoccupation with statistics and methodology is routinely criticized, and many psychologists continue to sense, as Allport did in the 1930s, that the field is being driven more by its allegiance to scientific method than by its commitment to subject matter.

—IAN NICHOLSON (2003, P. 226)

THE QUOTE FROM IAN Nicholson underscores that personality research methods are a means to end; the ultimate goal of personality research should be to yield information that enables us to describe and understand personality constructs. However, we should remain aware that the quality of knowledge obtained is influenced by the quality of the methods and types of assessment used to gain that knowledge. This was stressed by a critical review of research on personality and depression by Flett, Hewitt, Endler, and Bagby (1995). In that review paper, it was argued that research on personality and depression had great potential. It could be possible, for instance, to pinpoint personality vulnerability factors associated with the development of depression, and then identify vulnerable people and provide preventive interventions designed to lessen their likelihood of becoming depressed. However, the authors concluded that conceptual and practical advances will emerge only if researchers adopt a more sophisticated and refined approach to the use of research methods and the creation of personality assessment measures. They highlighted the limitations of measures designed to assess personality vulnerabilities and expressed their concern that the proliferation of these measures could provide a misleading view of the link between personality and depression.

Thus, issues involving research methods and personality assessment are quite important. Accordingly, Chapter 4 explores these issues in more detail. This chapter addresses such questions as: What are the various ways to conduct personality research? How should individual differences be measured? And how should personality tests be developed? Some themes have already been discussed in previous chapters (e.g., the distinction between the nomothetic and idiographic approach) and will not be reiterated here. Other themes and issues are newly introduced in this chapter. We begin by comparing and contrasting experimental research and correlational research.

EXPERIMENTAL RESEARCH

Independent versus Dependent Variables

Personality research sometimes takes the form of an experiment in which independent variables are evaluated by their influence on a dependent variable. An **independent variable** is the variable that is manipulated in an experiment. It is regarded as the causal variable as it is the one that creates change. The **dependent variable** is the outcome variable that is measured in an experiment. The dependent variable represents the effect in a cause–effect relationship, and it responds to changes in the independent variable.

Personality researchers study two types of independent variables. Most experimental studies include an independent variable that is a **manipulated variable** where one level or form of the variable is applied by the experimenter to a subset of the experiment participants, but a different level or form of the independent variable is applied to another subset of participants. For instance, if you wanted to examine the effects of reward versus punishment on behaviour, the independent variable would be whether the participant is in the **experimental condition** that involves exposure to punishment or in the experimental condition that involves exposure to reward.

Random assignment is a key part of experiments that are designed to make inferences about cause and effect relations. That is, participants should be allocated randomly to either the subgroup receiving reward or the one receiving punishment. If participants are allocated randomly to one group or the other, any additional variables that might influence behaviour (e.g., age differences) are spread out evenly across the groups.

The independent variable always has at least two different conditions (e.g., reward and punishment). Some studies include independent variables with three or more conditions. For instance, the Bobo doll study by Bandura, Ross, and Ross (1963) included three levels of the manipulated independent variable. Children in this study were assigned randomly to witness either a live adult aggress against the Bobo doll, a filmed adult aggress against the Bobo doll, or a cartoon character (Herman the Cat) aggress against a cartoon Bobo doll.

When one level of an independent variable is applied to some study participants but not others, it is a **between-subjects variable**. That is, there is a difference between subjects or between participants in the experimental conditions they experienced. The independent variable in the Bobo doll study is a between-subjects variable because the children in this study were exposed to *only* one of three possibilities (live adult model, filmed adult model, or cartoon model). Other studies involve a manipulation of a **within-subject variable**, also known as a **repeated measures** design. In this type of experiment, a person is measured each time after being exposed to two or more levels of the independent variable. In the Bobo doll study, the participant is exposed eventually to *all* of the possibilities. A within-subject variable would be operating if a child was measured after witnessing the live adult model, and then was retested on another occasion after witnessing the filmed adult model. One benefit of a repeated measures study is that the participant is the same each time. After all, it is the same person being studied across experimental conditions, so variability reflecting the person's characteristics is not an issue. One potential drawback is that the investigator may create an **order effect**. That is, when the same person is used repeatedly across different experimental conditions, the order that the conditions are experienced in may create a source of bias. Accordingly, researchers remove this concern by presenting the various experimental conditions in a randomly determined order so that participants receive different orders.

Personality research of an experimental nature is different from most experiment research in psychology because we can also study independent variables in the form of **subject variables**: classification variables that are not manipulated. Subject variables can involve comparing people who differ in demographic characteristics (e.g., males versus females, younger versus older participants), but they can also involve comparing people who differ in personality features. For instance, an independent variable as a subject variable could involve a comparison of procrastinators versus non-procrastinators or perfectionists versus non-perfectionists.

As noted above, the dependent variable is the measured outcome variable. It is called a dependent variable because it is assumed that the value of the dependent variable will depend or co-vary as a function of differences in the independent variable. Thus, in the case of the Bandura et al. (1963) Bobo doll study, the dependent variable was the amount of aggression displayed by children after being exposed to the independent variable. In addition to the manipulated variable (the type of aggression witnessed), another measured independent variable of interest was whether the child was male or female (i.e., a subject variable).

Hans Eysenck was one of the leading advocates of using experimental procedures to test hypotheses involving personality traits. Eysenck wanted to test predictions involving traits in his model, such as introversion–extroversion, but he also wanted to establish that experimental manipulations would not have the same effect on all people, depending on the phenomenon being investigated, because the manipulated independent variable might operate differently as a function of the individual's personality.

KEY POINTS

- The independent variable is manipulated in an experiment and is seen as the cause in a cause–effect relationship.
- The dependent variable is measured in an experiment and is regarded as the effect.
- Participants in experiments must be assigned randomly to an experimental condition.
- Independent variables can be subject variables (personality variables used to group participants).

The findings from one of Eysenck's experiments are shown in Figure 4.1. This experiment by Howarth and Eysenck (1968) should be of particular interest to students who consider themselves either extreme introverts or extroverts. Differences in cognitive performance between introverts and extroverts have been postulated, and these differences are believed to reflect the fact that introverts are more arousable physiologically than are extroverts. The theory of action decrement (see Kleinsmith-Kaplan, 1963) is based on the notion that heightened arousal during the initial learning of material facilitates recall of material in the long run, but instantaneous memory performance will be low because cognitive attention is focused on developing and strengthening the memory itself. If introverts are more arousable, they should show poorer memory at first, relative to extroverts, but better memory over time.

The results displayed in Figure 4.1 support this theory. The Howard and Eysenck (1968) experiment showed that over a 24-hour period, introverts displayed substantially better memory than extroverts. The dependent measure in this experiment was recall score. The two independent variables were introversion–extroversion and the length of the recall interval (ranging from one minute to five minutes).

Moderator and Mediator Effects

The effect shown in Figure 4.1 is known as an **interaction effect**, also called a **moderator effect**. This means that the effect of an independent variable is moderated or influenced by the level of another independent variable. That is, the dependent variable is influenced by the combination of particular levels of independent variables in a way that leads to a qualitative change in the dependent variable. In this instance, the personality trait interacted with the recall interval to produce a unique change in the pattern of recall scores.

Moderator effects need to be distinguished from **mediator effects**. If a factor is a mediator, this suggests that the link between a variable and another variable exists primarily

Figure 4.1 Recall as a Function of Introversion versus Extroversion and Delay (Howarth & Eysenck, 1988)

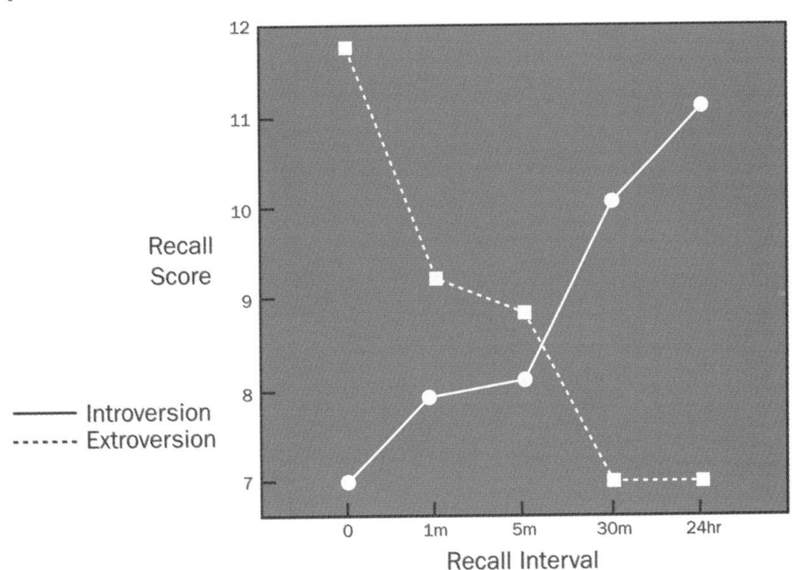

Source: Eysenck, 1996, p. 429.

because of their mutual link with another intervening variable that influences both of these variables (see Baron & Kenny, 1986). Coping variables are often assessed as potential mediators of the link between personality and psychological distress (Hewitt & Flett, 1996). That is, personality is linked with psychological distress because personality variable is associated with maladaptive, self-defeating coping styles, which in turn are associated with psychological distress.

According to Baron and Kenny's (1986) criteria for mediation, three general conditions must be present: (1) a significant association between the predictor variable (e.g., the personality trait) and the criterion variable (e.g., distress); (2) a significant association between the predictor variable (e.g., the personality trait) and the mediating variable (e.g., the coping style); and (3) the mediator (e.g., coping) must be a significant predictor of the criterion variable (e.g., distress). Mediation would be suggested if the initial link between the predictor and criterion variables is significantly reduced (perhaps to the point of being negligible) after statistical tests are done that take into account the link that the mediator variable has with both the predictor and the criterion variable.

As one example, consider the associations among self-criticism, avoidance coping, and depression. Self-criticism is associated with avoidant forms of coping. If self-criticism is no longer associated with depression after considering the predictive role of avoidance coping, then this suggests that avoidance coping acted as a mediator of the link between personality and depression in this example.

Note that personality variables can be mediated by the influence of other variables, but sometimes personality variables themselves may serve as mediators. For instance, a Canadian study showed that changes in self-criticism mediated the extent to which group cognitive behaviour therapy resulted in lower depression. That is, therapy reduced self-criticism, which in turn led to reduced depression (Enns, Cox, & Pidlubny, 2002).

Another recent study showed that prior exposure to verbal abuse from parents in childhood was associated with subsequent self-criticism, which in turn was associated with depression in adulthood (Sachs-Ericsson, Verona, Joiner, & Preacher, 2006). Self-criticism was identified as a full mediator because the association between abuse and depression depended entirely on self-criticism. If taking self-criticism into account had resulted in a significant reduction in the association between abuse and depression, but abuse and depression still had a significant but lower association, then partial mediation would have occurred. That is, the link between abuse and depression depends partly or somewhat on the intervening influence of self-criticism.

Figure 4.2 illustrates three types of effects involving personality variables, coping variables, and maladjustment. The top panel of Figure 4.2 shows a mediational model in which the link between personality and maladjustment exists because personality is associated with coping, which in turn is linked with maladjustment. In this model, personality does not have a direct link with maladjustment; it has an indirect link via its association with coping.

The bottom panel of Figure 4.2 shows a moderator model. This signifies that personality and coping combine and interact in a unique way, and it is the combination of these variables that predicts maladjustment.

The middle panel of Figure 4.2 shows a simpler model in which personality and coping make unique contributions in an additive model. They are additive since both types of factors are significant but contribute independently to the prediction of levels of maladjustment. An additive model is also known as a main effects model, as both factors make independent contributions to the prediction of the outcome variable (i.e., maladjustment).

Figure 4.2 Additive, Mediator, and Moderator Models Linking Personality, Coping, and Maladjustment

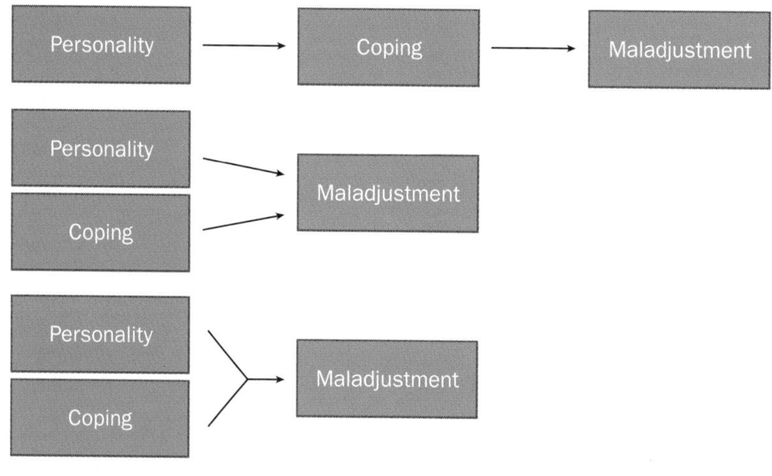

Source: Adapted from Hewitt & Flett, 1996 from Zeidner & Endler, 1995.

KEY POINTS

- If a variable is a moderator variable, it interacts with or combines with another variable to produce change in the measured variable. That is, the outcome is a function of a combination of at least two variables.
- If a variable is a mediator variable, it is an intervening variable that accounts for the association between two other variables. One variable is associated with the mediating variable, which is in turn associated with a third variable.
- In an additive model, two variables make independent and significant contributions in predicting an outcome variable.

Benefits and Limitations of Experimental Research

Experiments have both benefits and limitations. The chief advantage of experimental research is that it may enable the researcher to draw some conclusions about cause and effect relationships. If participants are assigned randomly to experimental conditions, and analyses of the dependent variable shows that being in one condition results in affect, behaviour, or cognitions that is significantly different from those exhibited by people in another experimental condition, this points to the possibility that the differences reflect the causal variable that was manipulated.

With cause–effect relationships, it is easier to suggest that a manipulated independent variable is a causal factor than it is to suggest that a subject variable is a causal variable. Even when a subject variable is associated with a significant difference in the measured variable (i.e., the dependent measure), other factors that are linked with the subject variable may be the actual cause. For example, if we find that some dependent variable differs for males and females (say, the established tendency for females to be more orderly and organized than males), all we really know is that the gender difference exists. We don't know whether the significance difference was caused, at least in part, by biological differences or by differences in socialization experiences, both inside and outside the family unit. Thus, the ability of experimental research to shed light on cause–effect associations between variables is restricted to experiments with manipulated independent variables. This limitation reflects the fact that you can't manipulate a person's personality!

Experimental research enables researchers to draw conclusions about cause-effect relationships.

An important benefit of experimental research that takes place in a laboratory setting is that it affords the researcher a degree of control that is lacking in natural settings. It is possible to structure the experiment so that all other factors and possible sources of influence are held constant, so that the only thing that differs for participants in a between-subjects experiment is the level of the independent variable received (e.g., did they witness a live model or film model aggressing against a defenceless Bobo doll?). This degree of control is important because it reduces ambiguity. Other extraneous factors are not influencing the measured outcome.

Unfortunately, this increased control must be weighed within the context of the limitations of experiments. One significant problem is the issue of **demand characteristics**. Martin Orne was a prominent psychologist who suggested that most people in experimental studies have a great desire to please the experimenter (they want to "do the right thing") (see Orne, 1962) As a result, they will try to fulfill the role of "good participant" by trying to figure out the experimental hypothesis and pleasing the experimenter by acting in a manner that will support the hypothesis. (As a budding personologist, you should immediately respond to this by saying, "Yes, but some people will be much more interested in pleasing the experimenter than other people will!").

Orne (1962) reached his conclusion based on his research indicating that participants in hypnosis experiments act in a manner consistent with their preconceived notions about the effects of hypnosis on people. Demand characteristics are clues in the experimental setting or procedure that enable the participant to figure out the hypothesis and act in a manner to support the hypothesis. Whereas Orne (1962) argued that research participants value and identify with the goals of scientific research, Berkowitz and Donnerstein (1982) pointed to the participants' "evaluation apprehension" and fear of negative evaluation. That is, participants are trying "to impress the experimenter by appearing smart, sophisticated, or healthy" (p. 251).

The greatest limitation of experimental research is that it is low in **external validity**. That is, the differences in behaviours that are obtained in the laboratory setting may be quite artificial and not reflect what happens in real-world settings. If external validity is a problem, then an experiment is said to be low in **generalizability**. That is, it cannot be generalized beyond the laboratory setting to more naturalistic contexts.

KEY POINTS

- Experiments suffer from key limitations, including concerns about whether the results of lab studies are artificial and low in generalizability to real-life settings.
- Demand characteristics influence participants in experiments who wish to be seen favourably and try to act in accordance with the experimenter's hypotheses. These participants are attuned to subtle cues in the experimental procedure.
- Experiments use random assignment to conditions to control extraneous variables that may influence the results and make interpretations more complicated.

Linear versus Non-linear Effects

The problems outlined above apply to experimental research in general. Other issues are specific to the use of subject variables as independent variables in personality experiments. Researchers in experimental personality research usually categorize people into groups based on some personality characteristic (e.g., introverts versus extroverts) and then evaluate them on other factors to establish whether significant group differences exist. Although this seems quite straightforward, there are at least two possible problems. First of all, in studies that compare just two subgroups of individuals, it is assumed that the personality variable is associated with the measured variable or variables in a linear fashion. That is, as the personality dimension goes from extroversion and shifts toward introversion, the measured variable is presumed to shift to a similar degree in the corresponding direction. Once again, an example will help clarify this. Some research has examined the association between introversion–extroversion and levels of intelligence. Eysenck suggested originally that higher levels of intelligence would be associated with introversion (see Eysenck & Cookson, 1969). If this reflects a linear association, as scores vary and become increasingly reflective of introversion, there should be a corresponding rise in intelligence scores. However, research by Eysenck and his colleagues and by Don Saklofske from the University of Saskatchewan has found that there is not a strong association between extroversion–introversion and intelligence (Eysenck & Cookson, 1969; Saklofske, 1985).

One possible reason for the lack of a strong association is that we also need to consider levels of intelligence in ambiverts. Recall that ambiverts are people who are characterized both by introversion and extroversion, and these people tend to fall toward the middle of the introversion–extroversion dimension. Robinson (1989) argued that ambiverts have an optimal level of arousal, and optimal functioning in terms of intelligence; extreme introversion or extroversion have associated levels of arousal that limit intelligence. If so, then there would be a non-linear association (also known as a curvilinear association) between introversion–extroversion and intelligence. Some support for this has been obtained. A study by British researchers found that ambiverts had higher intelligence test scores (an average of 120) than did introverts (a mean of 109) and extroverts (a mean of 112). However, a recent study conducted by Australian researchers did not support this possibility; they found that introverts had significantly higher levels of intelligence than ambiverts (Luciano, Leisser, Wright, & Martin, 2004). Whatever the case, the middle group has to be taken into account! The main point to take from this example is that we cannot assume that people in the middle of a distribution of scores will have characteristics that support the assumption that personality variables are associated in a linear fashion with other variables. Non-linear or curvilinear effects may be present.

Unfortunately, personality researchers often do not analyze their data in a way that could detect non-linear effects. However, there are numerous illustrations of non-linear effects in the personality literature.

For instance, in a study by Gjerde, Block, and Block (1988), male and female adolescents provided self-reports of depression and various personality characteristics, and their personality characteristics were also rated by four psychologists. Gjerde et al. (1988) found clear evidence of curvilinear effects based on observer ratings of personality. That is, depression was associated with being either exceptionally high or low in terms of having an antagonistic, hostile personality. Very hostile males could have been depressed because they alienated other people, while those low in hostility may have been depressed because perhaps they were too agreeable and didn't stick up for themselves.

The message of importance to take from this discussion of non-linear effects is that if an experiment is conducted and only two groups of participants (e.g., introverts and extroverts) are compared, then some very valuable information may be lost. Also, it is possible that misleading and inaccurate conclusions may be drawn about how one personality variable relates to another. This problem was illustrated by Chabot (1973), who conducted a critical evaluation of research on repression–sensitization. The repression–sensitization construct was first described and assessed by Byrne (1961). If you are a repressor, you tend to rely on an avoidant and defensive coping style when in threatening situations. Repressors tend to deny and distort the situations in a way to make them seem less problematic. Sensitizers, on the other hand, are oriented toward threatening situations. They are people who tend to ruminate and obsess over a situation and analyze it thoroughly. The repression–sensitization distinction is relevant to this issue because Chabot (1973) conducted a re-analysis of the data from 26 studies that compared repressors and sensitizers, but also included an intermediate group. Chabot (1973) found that in 15 of the 26 studies, the intermediate group acted in a manner that was clearly like either the repressor group or the sensitizer group. That is, they were not intermediate as they would be if the data had been representing linear associations. This suggests the need to consider non-linear effects when studying this personality construct.

Another concern about two-group comparisons of people is the sometimes difficult process of determining whether a particular person does or does not merit inclusion in a group. To continue with the same example, researchers would have to determine just how extroverted or introverted a person has to be in order to be considered an extrovert or an introvert. Some criterion must be used to enable the researcher to determine that a person does or does not warrant inclusion in a defined personality group. Common procedures that are used may be sample-specific. If the researcher is interested in comparing three levels of a grouping variable, he or she may perform what is known as a **tertial split**. That is, the sample is divided into three based on the distribution of personality scores. The top one third could represent extroverts, the middle one third could represent ambiverts, and the bottom one third could represent introverts. Although this may seem straightforward, for the sake of argument, consider what would happen if the researcher somehow happened to study a sample of people that was dominated by a huge overabundance of introverts (e.g., 80% of the people were exceptionally high in introversion). In this instance, if a tertial split was conducted, some of the people who would be classified according to the three-way split as ambiverts would, in fact, actually be introverts.

If a researcher was interested in creating only two groups, then a **median split** is often performed. The researcher establishes a midpoint in the range of scores on the variable in question; people above this midpoint would be in one group and those below the midpoint would be in the other. Although median splits are often performed on a distribution of scores, potentially valuable information is lost because a range of scores is transformed into a categorical variable. This may have some unintended and misleading effects, as shown by research indicating that the use of median splits can create spurious effects that do not exist in reality (for an illustration, see Bissonnette, Ickes, Bernstein, & Knowles, 1990).

If group assignment to personality categories must be done, it is preferable to assign participants to groups based on established cut-off scores that have been previously determined based on the norms for personality measures. Cut-off scores should be derived from personality measures that have themselves been the subject of extensive research and development. If researchers do not rely on some common cut-off score in assigning participants to groups, comparisons of the findings across studies becomes quite difficult, if not impossible. In his review of repression–sensitization research, Chabot (1973) was quite critical of researchers using different cut-off points that often seem quite arbitrary. Consider the case of extroverts. Although two researchers might be both studying "extroverts," how can we compare their findings if one researcher used a less stringent criterion and included in the extrovert group some people whom the other researcher would have considered ambiverts?

One final point about the use of cut-off scores needs to be mentioned. The actual practice of research is seldom ideal for many pragmatic reasons. However, in an ideal research world, group assignments based on cut-off scores would be based on administering two or more measures of the personality characteristic in question (i.e., two measures of perfectionism) or alternatively, group assignment would be based on administering the same measure on two or more occasions (i.e., retesting the same people with the same perfectionism measure). Why? We must also be cognizant of a statistical phenomenon known as **regression to the mean**. This refers to the fact that in most, if not all, distributions of scores, some people will have high scores because they are actually high on the attribute in question, but other people will appear to have high scores simply because their scores have been inflated by **measurement error**. Measurement error is present when a number that has been measured and counted is not an accurate reflection of the true value. At best, a measured number is only an *estimate* that may or may not be entirely accurate.

Regression to the mean has been discussed in the literature of emotional adjustment with respect to assigning a participant to a group of depressed people, solely based on a single administration of a self-report depression scale, such as the Beck Depression Inventory (BDI) (see Flett, Vredenburg, & Krames, 1995). Some people are not actually depressed but appear to be depressed because their scores have been influenced unduly by measurement error. When groups of high and low scorers are retested on a second occasion, the average score of the high group tends to decrease to a significant degree, while the average score of the low group tends to increase to a significant degree (i.e., the mean scores tend to gravitate and get pulled toward the middle). Regression to the mean implies that extreme scores, upon retest, become more reflective of the actual mean for the overall sample as a whole. Flett et al. (1995) demonstrated this with depression by showing that, upon retesting, the BDI scores of students with initially high BDI scores tend, as a whole, to go down over time, while the BDI scores of students with initially low BDI scores tend, as a whole, to go up over time. Although this is what happens for the two groups overall, an identifiable proportion of people in each group did not change substantially upon retest. A person who had a BDI score that was elevated according to both assessments is someone who likely has depressive characteristics.

In summary, there are some clear benefits associated with conducting experiments in the personality field. Experiments allow us to test certain issues with control and precision, and may allow us to obtain insights about cause and effect associations. At the same time, we must be aware of concerns about low external validity and lack of generalizability, and when experiments use personality variables as grouping variables, we must consider possible complexities (e.g., non-linear effects, problems in the assignment of people to groups).

CORRELATIONAL RESEARCH

If you are a betting person, you would be likely to win your bet if, without knowing specific details, you wagered that a personality research study was a correlational study. Most personality research is in the form of a correlational investigation in which two or more personality scales are administered to a sample of participants and the scores on these scales are compared to determine if they are significantly associated with each other. Before discussing correlational research in more detail, it is first necessary to discuss the concept of correlation, which has been used repeatedly in the preceding chapters of this book.

A correlation involves the degree of association between two variables. The correlation coefficient is a statistic that evaluates how much a series of data points co-vary in a linear manner so that the data points lie on or near a straight line. The most well-known statistical test to evaluate the magnitude of a correlation is the Pearson product-moment correlation, which is represented by the letter "*r*." The absolute value of *r* when two variables are entirely unrelated is zero. When there is a perfect correlation between two variables, the absolute value of *r* is 1 and this is as high as it can go.

Positive and Negative Correlations

A **positive correlation** exists when there is a linear association between variables, such that as one variable tends to increase, the other variable tends to increase to a corresponding degree. Thus, if there were a positive correlation between procrastination and length of time to hand in an essay, this would mean that as levels of trait procrastination increase, there is a corresponding increase in the amount of time it takes to hand in an essay. If two variables are perfectly and positively correlated, then *r* equals 1.

A **negative correlation** exists when there is a linear association between variables, such that as one variable tends to increase, the other variable tends to decrease to a corresponding degree. Thus, if a negative correlation existed between procrastination and conscientiousness, this would mean that as levels of procrastination increase, there is a corresponding decrease in trait levels of conscientiousness. If two variables are perfectly and negatively correlated, then *r* equals –1.

Figure 4.3 consists of scatterplots that illustrate what is meant by a positive correlation versus a negative correlation. The top half of the illustration shows a positive correlation between grade point average and the number of hours spent studying. The bottom half shows a negative correlation between grade point average and the number of hours spent goofing off.

Returning to the correlation topic, Cohen (1988) identified criteria to help characterize the magnitude of correlational effects. Cohen suggested that correlational coefficients in the order of .10 are small. Correlation coefficients of about .30 are medium, while correlations of about .50 are large in their magnitude and associated effect sizes.

James Hemphill from Simon Fraser University in Vancouver noted recently that the values selected by Cohen were determined subjectively based largely on Cohen's extensive experience (Hemphill, 2003). Hemphill observed that in reality, very few large effects in well-known research studies meet Cohen's criterion of .50. Hemphill also reported the results of a survey of more than 100 senior undergraduate students and graduate students who were asked to indicate how large a correlational coefficient had to be in order to be considered large. They identified .60 or greater as the criterion for the presence of a large correlation. Hemphill (2003) concluded by noting that even though the correlation between taking an aspirin and preventing a heart attack is only $r = .03$, this statistically small correlation can have great social significance because taking aspirin can save lives. Thus, even small correlations can have practical significance.

Figure 4.3 Illustrations of a Positive and a Negative Correlation

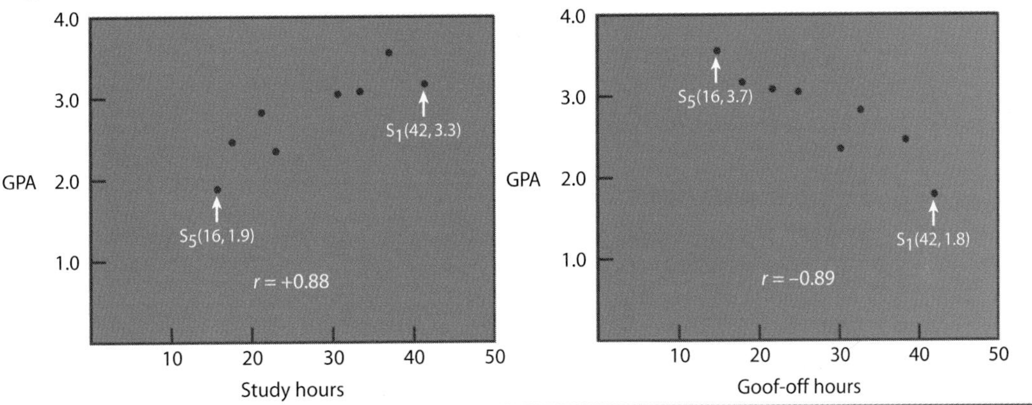

Source: Goodwin, 2005, p. 288.

What are the limitations of correlational research? The most meaningful limitation is that establishing a significant correlation between two variables does not allow us to make any assumptions about causality. Two variables are merely correlated, and we cannot presume that one variable is the cause of the other variable. Because personality traits are believed to be present early in development (in early childhood), and temperament differences can be detected soon after a child's birth, there is a tendency to regard personality and temperament factors as the variables that cause other differences to occur. However, it is not possible to assume causality because of the **third-variable problem**. It is possible that there is an association between two variables because both of these variables have been influenced by some other variable that is related to both variables.

The Directionality Issue

Another reason for not inferring causality is the **directionality issue**. If two variables are related, all that can be stated is that they are associated with each other; it cannot be assumed that the variability associated with one variable caused or contributed to the variability of the other variable. Correlational research can be informative in its own right, but it cannot help us disentangle and understand cause–effect relationships. In fact, correlational research can be downright misleading since it promotes a distorted view of the importance of certain personality traits that are seen as causal when, in fact, they are not.

The directionality issue refers to the fact that correlational research cannot tell us which variable comes first when two variables are significantly correlated. Flett,

Vredenburg, Pliner, and Krames (1985) illustrated the directionality issue with respect to the association between sex roles and depressive symptoms. Most previous research in this area assumed implicitly that levels of masculinity and femininity cause levels of depression, and research findings indicate that low levels of masculinity in both men and women are associated with depression. However, the test–retest data obtained by Flett et al. (1985) indicated that, if anything, the experience of elevated levels of depressive symptomatology was a cause of sex-role self-concept rather than vice versa. That is, the experienced feelings of depression seemed to reduce masculinity. Thus, the direction of the effect was the exact opposite of what had been presumed! The data supported a phenomenon known as the scar hypothesis, which is the notion that a bout of depression can change a personality variable (Hirschfeld & Cross, 1987). However, even in this case, causality cannot be ascertained because some third variable may have influenced depression and lowered masculinity.

KEY POINTS

- With a positive correlation, two measures are associated such that as one increases, the other tends to increase as well.
- With a negative correlation, two measures are associated such that as one increases, the other tends to decrease.
- Correlation values can range from +1 to −1.
- Correlational studies are limited because they cannot establish cause and effect relationships. The directionality issue makes it unclear which variable came first.

PERSONALITY RESEARCH TRENDS

In the early history of the personality field, one of the most influential research programs was conducted more than 50 years ago on the construct of authoritarianism. Authoritarianism is defined as a rigid personality style involving a need to dominate and control others in a manner suggesting that you have authority over them. The concept of authoritarianism is described in more detail in Chapter 10. Here it is cited to make a point about how research methods and strategies have changed in the personality field.

The initial research on authoritarianism by Adorno and his colleagues was exemplary in that it used a variety of methods and participants. Rather than relying on self-report questionnaires, as is often the case in contemporary research, initial research on authoritarianism used the type of in-depth interviews that are in keeping with a psychoanalytic perspective (see Adorno, Frenkel-Brunswik, Levinson, & Sanford, 1950). Also, although self-report measures of authoritarianism were constructed and developed initially based on the responses of available undergraduate students, this research expanded to include a wide range of participants, including military officers, veterans, and the League of Women voters. However, over time, this broad approach gave way to an extensive focus on university and college students as research participants (for a review, see Sears, 1986). The reliance on students in personality research is discussed in more detail below.

Historically, one of the most widely cited papers on research methods in personality reported a study conducted by Rae Carlson (1971). Carlson evaluated existing studies in the 1968 issues of the *Journal of Personality and Social Psychology* and concluded that 71% were based on student samples. She also expressed concern about the fact that almost four fifths of the studies were experimental in nature, and this raised concerns about external validity of the findings. The title of the article posed the question, "Where Is the Person in Personality Research?"

A subsequent review by Craik (1986) confirmed the preponderance of research based on self-reports and conducted in laboratory settings. Canadian researchers Endler and Speer (1998) provided a concise and more up-to-date overview of trends in personality research by examining the articles published in five leading personality journals from 1993 to 1995. They also reported comparative analyses of their findings and the results found previously in similar studies (see Carlson, 1971; Endler & Parker, 1991). One clear finding that emerged is that there is a continuing trend in the personality field to publish fewer laboratory studies. Whereas Carlson (1971) found that 78% of papers in the *Journal of Personality*and the *Journal of Personality and Social Psychology* included laboratory studies with an experimental manipulation, Endler and Parker (1991) found that only 37% of studies in three journals in 1986 to 1988 included an experimental manipulation, and this dropped to 34% in the same three journals in 1993 to 1995.

Endler and Speer (1998) also found a small decrease in the proportion of studies that relied on university students as participants. They found that when compared with studies reviewed by Carlson (1971), the decrease in the use of students as research participants was not statistically significant. Overall, two thirds of the studies reviewed by Endler and Speer were based on data provided by university students.

Most studies of personality rely on university student participants, as they are more convenient and available to researchers. However, some question whether findings obtained with students are generalizable to other groups in the general population.

However, one encouraging trend did emerge from this study. Endler and Speer reported a statistically significant five-fold increase over the last 25 years in the use of older, non-student adults in research. Thus, although there is still a tendency to focus on students as research participants because they are more convenient and available to researchers, the use of non-student samples is increasing.

This tendency to rely on university and college students as participants in most studies is not unique to the personality field. The analysis by Sears (1986) of social psychology research studies also concluded that the vast majority of participants were students. This study examined research investigations published in 1980 and found that 70% of the studies in the *Journal of Personality and Social Psychology* (JPSP), and 81% of the studies in the *Personality and Social Psychology Bulletin* involved students from American institutions. As high as the numbers are for personality psychology, a study of articles in JPSP found that even more social psychology studies are based on data from students. Sears (1986) found that 51% of the studies published in the JPSP's "Personality Processes and Individual Differences" section were based on students, while more than 80% of studies in the journal's social psychology sections were based on students. Still, most studies used data collected from students.

What is unfortunate about relying on student samples? Why is it a concern? Concerns have been raised about whether findings obtained with students are generalizable to other groups of people from the general population. Sears (1986) argued that we must break this dependence on what he referred to as "a narrow database," and he went on to outline a number of ways that university and college students differ from the general adult population. He presented evidence that university and college students as a whole represent a highly unique group in that they have been pre-selected for compliance with authority figures and they have elevated cognitive skills. In addition, they are egocentric in their self-focus, and their sense of self-definition has not been fully crystallized. Although Sears (1986) focused on the implications of his findings for the field of social psychology, he also noted that the personality of these students is still evolving and is not fully developed. He concluded by issuing a call for "research on persons from life stages other than late adolescence" (Sears, 1986, p. 527) and suggested that there is a need to branch out by conducting less laboratory research and more study in various behavioural settings.

Another concern is the continuing tendency for personality researchers to emphasize one-shot cross-sectional studies. Consistent with past findings, Endler and Speer (1998) also established that relatively few studies are longitudinal. The vast majority of published studies used a cross-sectional "snapshot in time" research design, with only 3% of studies being longitudinal.

Also, consistent with past trends, only a relatively small number of personality studies use research methods that go beyond structured self-report questionnaires. Endler and Speer (1998) found that 74% of papers published in North American personality journals and 81% of papers in European personality journals were based on questionnaire data. Finally, they reported that the most predominant statistical method used was the correlation, which was found in approximately three quarters of all studies, followed by an analysis of variance (or multivariate analysis of variance).

Mallon, Kingsley, Affleck, and Tennen (1998) conducted a related study that supplemented the analysis by Endler and Speer (1998). They analyzed 150 randomly selected *Journal of Personality* articles between 1970 and 1995. They concluded similarly that the prototypical study was cross-sectional rather than longitudinal (a one-time assessment), and used self-report measures administered to undergraduate students. They also confirmed the claim by West, Newsom, and Fenaughty (1992) that statistical techniques are becoming increasingly complex. That is, there is an increasing proliferation of highly sophisticated multivariate approaches.

KEY POINTS

- Review papers have assessed research trends in the personality literature.
- There are relatively few experiments in the personality field. Most studies are self-report, correlational studies.
- Most studies are cross-sectional and use a one-time assessment of a large sample of students. Only a small proportion of research is longitudinal.

To summarize, the modal personality study is a cross-sectional, correlational investigation that is based on a student sample. These students are most likely to be completing self-report questionnaires.

DIFFERENT TYPES OF DATA

The next section examines different types of data, with a particular focus on limitations of self-report data. Given the numerous problems associated with self-report personality studies (Kagan, 1988), other forms of assessment should be used more often. The range of possible measures was described by Block (1977). He made important distinctions among S-data (self-reports), L-data, O-data, and T-data. L-data represent the life record and include an individual's family, occupational, and marital pasts. O-data are ratings of an individual by his or her peers or family members. Finally, T-data include performance tests, measures of behaviour, and other objective laboratory measurements. These distinctions among types of data underscore the wide range of measures that can be employed in personality research.

Structured versus Unstructured Assessments

Another way to characterize types of data is to distinguish between structured and unstructured personality assessments. **Structured assessments** are close-ended scales in which the scale content has already been determined by the people who have constructed the measure, and participants indicate their response to each item by selecting options from the ones that have been provided. The hope here is that the items that are being responded to are relevant for the respondent. Some people may circle items on a personality scale while realizing that the issues being tapped are not very important to their personality structure and sense of self-definition.

In contrast, **unstructured assessments** are open-ended since people generate their responses. Unstructured assessments can be in the form of verbal responses given during an interview. Another example of an unstructured assessment is to perform a content analysis of writing samples. For instance, attributional studies have employed content analyses of the causes of events identified spontaneously by people in order to see if depression-prone people are more likely to blame themselves for negative events (Peterson, Seligman, & Vaillant, 1988). A third form of unstructured assessment involves thought-listing data in which people are asked to report concurrently their ongoing, conscious thoughts (see Singer & Kolligian, 1987). They can be asked to report their thoughts out loud (think aloud data) or asked to list their thoughts on paper.

Unstructured assessments are open-ended and can be in the form of verbal responses given during an interview.

The projective techniques described in Chapters 5 and 6 represent one of the most widely acknowledged forms of unstructured assessments. These measures tap the various responses that people generate when given an ambiguous stimulus (e.g., an inkblot or a depicted scene), and they are free to say anything in response.

Self-Report Measures and Their Limitations

Structured self-report measures represent a paradox in the personality field. As we have seen above, self-report measures are relied on extensively and form the basis of much of the personality research literature. Nevertheless, the validity of self-report measures is regarded with scepticism and sometimes derision. Why? Several factors and biases operate to limit the accuracy of self-report measures.

One general problem is that people often lack sufficient insight and self-awareness to accurately evaluate themselves. The problem of insufficient self-awareness was demonstrated in compelling research conducted by Kruger and Dunning (1999). This research will be described despite the risk that it might frighten you, or, at the very least, make you feel quite self-conscious. Kruger and Dunning's research identified a very substantial proportion of college students who are objectively unskilled yet seemingly unaware of their lack of ability. These investigators showed across a series of studies that students scoring in the bottom quartile of the sample on a variety of ability tests tapping use of logic and grammar tended to grossly overestimate their test ability and performance. Moreover, the ones with the lowest ability levels were most likely to do this!

Some people may simply lack self-awareness, while other people may be characterized by a personality orientation known as **self-deception** (Sackeim & Gur, 1979). Self-deception is an intrapsychic phenomenon that involves overly positive self-evaluations that the person actually believes. Self-deception is seen as a trait form of self-enhancement that is similar to but distinguishable from other forms of self-enhancement such as narcissism (see Paulhus, 1998).

Although self-deception may seem to have adaptive features (see Taylor & Brown, 1988), recent research led by Jordan Peterson from the University of Toronto showed that self-deceivers are actually less responsive to negative feedback and they keep persisting at a task when they shouldn't (Peterson et al., 2003). It is as if their self-enhancement leads them to believe that they can overcome challenging situations even when there is no possibility of doing so. This finding runs counter to the notion that self-deception is adaptive, because in this instance self-deception reflected poor adaptation to a losing situation. Related research by Edward Johnson from the University of Manitoba and his associates has shown that individuals high in self-deception are able to minimize the impact of threats that have an element of ambiguity, but high self-deceivers who experience a clear and unambiguous threat tend to respond very poorly in their performance on anagram tasks and intelligence tests (Johnson, 1995; Johnson, Vincent, & Ross, 1997).

Self-deception may also be maladaptive since it may alienate other people. Unfortunately, high self-deceivers may be seen as annoying by others. A longitudinal study conducted by Paulhus (1998) showed that at the end of seven weeks, people high in self-deception were rated by acquaintances as arrogant, hostile, low in warmth, and overconfident about their true abilities. People high in narcissism were seen as having these same characteristics. These negative impressions became more evident over time and were much more apparent at the end of the study. Yet these same individuals rate themselves as high in self-esteem and ego resiliency. Although not considered a response style per se, personality self-reports may be overinflated by people high in self-deception.

The biggest concern with personality self-reports is that they may be influenced by a social desirability response bias. People have a general tendency to create a positive impression in the eyes of other people, and one way they can accomplish this goal is to answer personality items in a way that makes them appear desirable and important. The need to write and select personality test items that are not too highly contaminated by social desirability bias is discussed later in this chapter.

Delroy Paulhus at the University of British Columbia is a leading authority on impression management and self-deception.

Various authors have developed measures to tap social desirability response bias (see Edwards, 1957, 1964; Stober, 2001). Historically, the Marlowe-Crowne Social Desirability Scale has been the most well-known scale (Crowne & Marlowe, 1960, 1964). In more recent years, the predominant measure of response styles is the Balanced Inventory of Desirable Responding (BIDR) by Delroy Paulhus from the University of British Columbia (see Paulhus, 1994). The BIDR includes a 20-item impression management scale designed to tap socially desirable responding and a 20-item self-deception scale. The latest version of these measures is now referred to as the Paulhus Deception Scales (Paulhus, 1998). Representative items from the impression management and self-deception scales are shown in Table 4.1.

Table 4.1 Sample Items of Self-Deception and Impression Management from the Paulhus Deception Scales

Impression Managment
I always pick up litter on the street.

Self-Deception (Enhancement)
Many people think that I am exceptional.

Self-Deception (Denial)
I never regret my decisions.

Note: Self-deception comes in two forms. Endorsing positive things (enhancement) and not acknowledging bad characteristics (denial).

Source: Paulhus, 1998b.

Currently, Paulhus is regarded as the leading authority on impression management and self-deception. His work has established that socially desirable responding can come in the form of endorsing positive self-statements (self-enhancement) and rejecting negative self-statements (denial) (see Paulhus & Reid, 1991; Paulhus, 2002).

To what extent do impression management and self-deception overlap? An informative experiment by Tomaka, Blascovich, and Kelsey (1992) provided clear evidence showing that it is possible to empirically distinguish impression management and self-deception. This study examined the extent to which three measures of defensiveness (self-deception, social desirability, and repressive coping) were associated with physiological and psychological reactions of 64 male college students. Participants engaged in contiguous mental arithmetic tasks that were quite challenging. The physiological measures included indices of heart range change, pulse change, and skin conductance change. The results indicated that self-deception was adaptive in that people high in self-deception appraised the looming tasks as less threatening, and objective measures showed that people high in self-deception were less reactive physiologically during the actual task. However, self-deception was not entirely adaptive in that post-task ratings showed that men high in self-deception, relative to those low in self-deception, reported higher levels of post-task stress. In contrast, social desirability, as assessed by the Marlowe-Crowne Social Desirability Scale (Crowne & Marlowe, 1960, 1964), was unrelated to the perceived threat associated with the looming tasks, but participants with high social desirability had great physiological reactivity during the task. Perhaps they were physiologically reactive because they were placed in a demanding situation that could be embarrassing depending on their level of performance. Overall, this study used physiological data to show that self-deception and impression management are independent and have little in common.

A pilot study of 25 medical students illustrates how self-report measures may be susceptible to biases (Evans, Leeson, & Newton-John, 2002). A pilot study is a preliminary investigation that typically leads to a more complicated follow-up study. The results of this study showed that 80% of the trainees scored high or very high in levels of impression management. In contrast, 32% of the respondents had exceptionally high self-deception. The authors concluded that self-deception was clearly evident, but the impression management findings reflected the pressure on trainees to portray themselves in the best possible light.

These findings notwithstanding, there is a longstanding, vigorous debate in the field about how to interpret evidence of social desirability (see Rorer, 1965; Rundquist, 1966). Could social desirability scales reflect an important individual difference variable rather than just a response style? McCrae and Costa (1983), among others, have argued that individual differences in social desirability reflect a personality trait that is of interest in its own right, and not simply a "nuisance variable." They based their arguments on evidence indicating that validity coefficients actually decreased rather than increased when social desirability was statistically taken into account, so the social desirability construct must be measuring something of importance. This accords with results reported by Borkenau and Ostendorf (1989). They found that participants with high levels of social desirability were rated both by themselves and by informants as being high in trait levels of conscientiousness and low in neuroticism. It is revealing that peer ratings of these personality traits were associated with socially desirable responding. Meston, Heiman, Trapnell, and Paulhus (1998) also evaluated social desirability and the dimensions in the five-factor model. They analyzed BIDR responses and found that impression management was correlated positively with conscientiousness in women and men, as well as agreeableness in women. Another study of personality and social desirability found evidence of both substance and style (see Morey et al., 2002). Thus, social desirability can reflect a personality construct of importance.

Response biases may operate in many contexts, and it is important to evaluate empirically the extent to which the results have been influenced by response styles. For instance, two studies by Flett, Blankstein, Pliner, and Bator (1988) showed that both impression management and self-deception influence self-reports of emotional experience. The measures in this study were the Self-Deception Questionnaire (SDQ) and Other-Deception Questionnaire (ODQ) created by Sackeim and Gur. Higher levels of impression management were associated with the reported experience of negative emotions that were less frequent and intense, and shorter in duration. While impression management was not associated with the ratings of positive emotions, self-deception was associated with less negative ratings of negative emotions and more positive ratings of positive emotions.

There is extensive evidence indicating that personality measures are being used increasingly to make employment decisions when selecting personnel (see Hogan, Hogan, & Roberts, 1996; Hough & Oswald, 2000). How effective are personality measures in predicting job-related outcomes? Is the effectiveness of personality measures undermined by response biases? The use of personality measures for employee selection purposes is discussed in Applied Perspective 4.1.

Applied Perspective 4.1 The Use of Personality Measures to Select Employees

Personality measures are used in many countries to help select people for jobs. Are they useful? Should they be used? A growing body of research does suggest that personality inventories have merit in this context.

Extensive research has focused on the utility of the five-factor trait model in the work context. An initial meta-analysis by Barrick and Mount (1991) examined three job performance criteria for five occupational groups and found that conscientiousness was a significant predictor of job success. Subsequent research showed that both high conscientiousness and low neuroticism were predictors of job performance. Comparable findings emerge from data gathered in North America and Europe (Salgado, 1997, 1998). Most importantly, conscientiousness and low neuroticism had significant incremental validity in their ability to predict job performance, over and above the effects of general measures of mental ability.

A more recent meta-analysis by Salgado (2003) from the University of Santiago de Compostela in Spain focused on research conducted after the Barrick and Mount (1991) meta-analysis. Salgado identified 92 relevant papers (72 from the United States and 20 from Europe). The criterion measure was supervisor ratings of job performance. Salgado's new meta-analysis showed that there were significant validity coefficients of .28 for conscientiousness and .16 for emotional stability when standard five-factor measures were used. Salgado concluded that these personality constructs should be used to make personnel decisions.

Another alternative approach by Judge and his associates focuses on dispositional traits that reflect *core evaluations* involving the self (see Judge, Erez, Bono, & Thoreson, 2003). This approach is based on the premise that the value judgements that people make about themselves and other people, either positive or negative, help determine job success. Four main individual difference variables central to self-worth are focused on here: self-esteem, generalized self-efficacy, locus of control, and neuroticism. A review by Bono and Judge (2003) led to the conclusions that these four individual difference factors reflect a higher order construct that represents individual differences in core evaluations, and these factors are associated with both job satisfaction and job performance. Accordingly, Judge, Bono, and Thoreson (2003) represented the four themes of self-esteem (e.g., "Overall, I am satisfied with myself"), self-efficacy (e.g., "I complete tasks successfully"), locus of control (e.g., "I determine what will happen in my life"), and neuroticism (e.g., "There are times when things look pretty bleak and hopeless to me") in a 12-item scale that reflects the broad core evaluations factor. They showed that their new one-factor measure predicted job performance, job satisfaction, and life satisfaction, and it accounted for substantial variance in these measures not accounted for by the traits of the five-factor model.

Collectively, you might conclude that these areas of research represent rather compelling evidence of the usefulness of personality measures to select employees. However, some cautions must be raised. First, although personality tests may be useful in general, there is no guarantee that personality tests will be useful when applied to a particular individual, and the types of decisions made. For instance, would someone who is deemed to be high in conscientiousness but also high in neuroticism be found suitable for a particular job? And how might this vary as a function of the type of job?

Perhaps the biggest concern here is whether personality measures are still useful once we consider the possibility that response sets and response styles might undermine the validity of these personality assessments. The impact of response bias is addressed typically in two different ways. One approach is experimental and involves recruiting a sample of participants who either complete the personality measures in the usual manner or who are instructed to "fake good." That is, they are told explicitly that they should answer the scale items in a way that will create a good impression. In essence, then, the independent variable in this research is the presence or absence of "fake-good" instructions, and the dependent variables are the personality scale scores.

The second approach is to simply administer measures of response bias along with a set of personality measures and job-related measures. Specific criterion variables, including objective indicators of job performance, are also obtained. Initially, researchers examine the correlations between the personality measures and job-related indicators, as well as the extent to which the response bias measures are also linked with the personality measures and the job-related indicators. Next, the associations between the personality measures and the job-related indicators are re-examined after conducting statistical analyses (e.g., partial correlational analyses) that first remove the measured impact of response bias by statistically removing the variance attributable to impression management.

Should an employer consider these job applicants' personalities when deciding which one to hire? Although research indicates that personality tests could be useful when selecting employees, there is no guarantee that personality tests will be useful when applied to a specific individual and specific jobs.

Research on faking-good instructions has shown that personality measures used in job contexts may be quite susceptible to attempts by respondents to try to create a positive impression, as would be the case in people looking for a job. A meta-analysis of 51 studies showed that all five dimensions of the five-factor model are equally susceptible to faking (Visweswaran & Ones, 1999). Research has shown that not only do instructions to "fake good" inflate mean scores on desirable personality attributes, but they can also influence the content of trait factors (Ellingson, Sackett, & Hough, 1999). Research with the NEO-PI-R, for instance, has found that the typical factor structure of the measure is altered following fake-good instructions (Griffith, 1997). However, the degree to which faking has an influence needs to be evaluated measure by measure. Another study by Smith and Ellingson (2002) tested their contention that personality measures have been portrayed as worse than they actually are because previous studies were conducted in artificial laboratory settings. They reported that the items from the Hogan Personality Inventory were not substantially influenced by response distortion when completed by real job applicants in more naturalistic settings.

Various solutions have been offered to reduce susceptibility to faking in job contexts. Jackson, Wroblewski, and Ashton (2000) reported that measures are less susceptible to faking if forced-choice options are used rather than continuous rating scales. Ronald Holden and his associates have adopted a more sophisticated approach by applying cognitive information processing principles and techniques to the study of response styles. The basic premise of this work is that the validity of responses to self-report items is reflected by the speed with which the respondent answers the personality test item (Holden, 1998). That is, at a cognitive level, it takes time to lie when completing inventories, and measures tapping this are called **latency-based validity indices**. Holden and his colleagues have used response latencies to derive "faking indices" in a wide variety of contexts involving several different groups of participants, including unemployed Canadians looking for work (Holden, 1995, 1998), prisoners taking a test to measure psychopathy (Holden & Kroner, 1992), and university students responding to a test of "normal" personality (Holden & Hibbs, 1995). A recent experiment confirmed that greater concern with social desirability results in longer latency times when evaluating personal characteristics (Holtgraves, 2004).

KEY POINTS

- Self-report measures are susceptible to social desirability response bias due to impression management.
- Impression management and self-deception are independent and are associated with different phenomena.
- Authors have argued that individual differences in socially desirable responding reflect a substantive personality variable of importance and not just a response bias.

Supplementing Self-Reports with Observer Ratings

One important alternative to self-reports is to take advantage of the fact that people tend to be highly aware of the personality differences among the key people in their lives, and these people can be evaluated on trait dimensions. The ability to evaluate others was demonstrated recently in an interesting study of perceived social support by Lakey, Lutz, and Scoboria (2004). This study could have been nicknamed the "I'll Be There for You Study" because it required participants to use the five-factor model to rate the personalities of four main characters from the television show *Friends*. Personality ratings were made of Phoebe, Ross, Monica, and Joey. If you are familiar with this show, you know that the friends have quite distinct personalities. Who would you rate highest in conscientiousness? Who is highest in openness? As might be expected, predictable differences were found. For instance, Ross

Observer ratings can provide crucial data, as shown in the study of the characters on the television show *Friends*, all of whom had distinct personalities.

and Monica were seen as equally high in neuroticism, but Ross was rated as more agreeable than his sister Monica. Your own ratings of Phoebe and Joey would likely reflect the fact that both characters are agreeable and outgoing, but not high in openness if openness is defined by intellectual capacity.

The personality impressions we have of other people represent a crucial source of data, and, if possible, self-reports should be supplemented with observer ratings of personality characteristics. Observer ratings can be provided by parents or peers. Ratings can be provided by the partners of people who are married or cohabiting.

Just as self-reports can be influenced by response biases, the data provided by informants can also be influenced by response styles (see Klonsky, Oltmanns, & Turkheimer, 2002). Will best friends be entirely truthful when assessing their friends? It is for this reason that members of the dyad should independently complete the questionnaires in separate locations.

Research by Funder (1980) found that agreement between self-reports and informant ratings is higher when traits high in social desirability are being rated. According to Funder (1980), this greater tendency to ascribe more desirable traits to the target person who is being evaluated has been referred to as a positivity bias or the leniency effect.

So what is the overall degree of correspondence between self-reports and observer ratings of personality? Kenny (1994) found across four studies that the median correlations for neuroticism and conscientiousness were .44 and .39, respectively. The self-other agreement for workaholism, a form of excessive conscientiousness, has been estimated at $r = .45$ (Ready, Clark, Watson, & Westerhouse, 2000). Research by Watson and Clark (1991) on self-reports and peer ratings for negative and positive emotional traits found that the mean correlation across eight affect scales was .27. This value is quite reasonable given that emotional experience has an internal, subjective quality that is difficult for other people to rate with a high degree of accuracy. Overall, evidence that the correlations between self-reports and informant ratings are only modest in magnitude attests to the fact that the respective sources of data are not redundant with each other, and studies are strengthened by having both types of information.

Methodological factors influence the degree of association between self-reports and informant ratings. The use of multiple informants tends to result in more accurate assessments and, as a result, higher levels of concordance (see Klonsky et al., 2002; McCrae & Costa, 1987). The degree of acquaintance is also important (see Funder, Kolar, & Blackman, 1995). Greater length and closeness of acquaintance enhances the correspondence between self-reports and informant ratings, so levels of agreement are substantially higher among spouses. McCrae, Stone, Fagan, and Costa (1998) found that the correlations between self and spousal ratings ranged between .46 and .74 for the traits of the five-factor model, with extroversion having the highest correlation.

However, perfect agreement does not exist even among spouses. Although it is not exactly news that spouses don't necessarily agree, we are still left to wonder why there is not greater agreement than research has shown. What factors do you think account for the lack of agreement? McCrae et al. (1998) found no evidence suggesting that the lack of agreement was due to response styles such as social desirability bias. The main factor that seemed to be operating is that husbands and wives were like other people in that they had very idiosyncratic and personal interpretations of personality adjectives, and this fits with other research showing that one of the most salient forms of individuality is the definitions and understanding of personality words (Dunning & McElwee, 1995).

Researchers have also evaluated whether certain personality characteristics in the perceiver operate as a source of bias. Heath, Neale, Kessler, Eaves, and Kendler (1992) found that neuroticism in the rater was not linked with bias, but this was not the case for extroversion. A modest rater bias was found. Extroverted people tended to overestimate levels of extroversion in others, while introverted people underestimated extroversion in others.

A critical issue is whether parents are accurate when rating the personalities of their children. Many studies of personality in children are based solely on parental reports. How accurate are parental reports? A recent personality study paints a bleak picture. Researchers from Boston University set out to explore past research suggesting that parents of non-twins tend to exaggerate the differences between siblings when they rate temperament (Saudino, Wertz, Gagne, & Chawla, 2004). The temperament characteristics of siblings between the ages of 3 and 8 years were evaluated with a variety of measures. The assessment included parental ratings, observer ratings, and objective measures of the child's shyness in a laboratory setting. The degree of resemblance between siblings was quite substantial according to observer ratings and objective measures. In contrast, not only did parental ratings of the siblings show little agreement, but their ratings were also negatively correlated! Parents saw the siblings were very different, but this did not fit with the other data collected. Thus, parental reports of their children may be very biased. Saudino and associates concluded that if we just focus on the parental reports, siblings are as different as night and day.

To some extent, parental inaccuracies in ratings of child personality characteristics could reflect identifiable aspects of the parent's personality. An investigation found that psychological distress in both mothers and fathers contributed to discrepancies across raters in terms of how the children were evaluated (Treutler & Epkins, 2003). Perhaps some parents project their own attributes on to their children when evaluating the children's personalities.

The main point here is that many studies of personality in children may be highly limited because they are based solely on parental reports. Parental reports are relied on because children must attain a certain level of cognitive development before they can meaningfully complete personality measures, and the assumption is that parents have great insight into their children based on the extensive interaction they have had with their children. However, parental preconceptions may be operating.

The safest bet to enhance reliability and validity of assessment is to use multiple measures and methods within the same study. This is consistent with observations about the need for a **methodological pluralism** (Campbell, 1986; Craik, 1986). A multimethod approach is preferable for many reasons, not the least of which is that findings based on only one method are less likely to be replicated (see Campbell, 1986).

KEY POINTS

- Given their limitations, self-report personality measures should be supplemented with behavioural measures and observer ratings.
- The correlations between self-reports and informant ratings are only moderate at best.
- Higher levels of self-other agreement are found when rating visible traits among people we have more contact with.
- Authors have argued that individual differences in socially desirable responding reflect a substantive personality variable of importance and not just a response bias.
- Parental reports of child personality features are often inaccurate and, in part, seem to reflect the personality of the parent doing the rating.

Current Innovations: Data Collection via the Internet

A recent innovation in the personality field (and in other fields of psychology) is to use the Internet to collect data. This method has some clear advantages, and various authors have observed that the personality field is well-suited to this method (e.g., Buchanan, 2000; Buchanan & Smith, 1999). It is a way to obtain a sample that is much larger than usual. In addition, as shown by Pasveer and Ellard (2004), generalizability may be increased by obtaining a more diverse sample than is typically the case (compared with the usual tendency to rely on student samples). Diverse samples of people from various nations will increase the international focus of personality research. It is a relatively economical way of gathering data, as it is quick and saves photocopying costs. Also, it is fairly easy in Internet studies to randomize the order in which questions are presented and thereby minimize concerns that question order might have influenced how people responded (for a discussion, see Fraley, 2007). For instance, having everyone complete a depression inventory at the beginning of a test package could induce a negative mood orientation as respondents read statements reflecting hopelessness and suicidality. Although paper-and-pencil questionnaires are supposed to be arranged randomly, researchers often use two or three orders (or stick to the same order) because it is time consuming to physically randomize the questionnaires.

However, there are also some drawbacks to Internet data collection. First, the sample will be restricted to individuals with computer access who happened to be in an area of the Internet that somehow drew their attention to the study.

Also, in many respects, researchers relying on the Internet are at the mercy of individual respondents who presumably are completing the measures with the best intentions and are not being capricious and whimsical in their responses. Care must also be taken to make certain that the respondent does not complete the online measures more than once, either by design or by accident. A new study by Johnson (2005) tested four research protocol problems by comparing Internet responses and traditional paper-and-pencil responses. Four research protocol problems were evaluated: (1) submission of duplicate protocols; (2) failure to fully read the items; (3) an unacceptable number of missing responses; and (4) careless completion of the protocols, resulting in inconsistent responses. Analyses showed that the Internet data reflected a greater incidence of three of the four problems, with only the problem of inconsistent responses not being greater on the Internet.

Still, by and large, the findings that emerge from Internet studies seem valid, and the measures seem to hold their psychometric properties. Valid and reliable measures of the five-factor model can be administered via the Internet (Buchanan, Johnson, & Goldberg, 2005). Similarly, Buchanan and Smith (1999) examined the psychometric properties of the Revised Self-Monitoring Scale (see Snyder & Gangestad, 1986). They found that the psychometric properties of the measure completed by their online sample were actually slightly better than previous assessments of the scale via traditional approaches. They suggested that the use of the Internet may have facilitated a level of honesty and self-revelation not present in traditional laboratory settings.

Although data collected from the Internet has reflected greater incidence of problems, such as duplicate protocols, research indicates that there is a higher level of honesty and self-revelation in data collected on the Internet than in traditional approaches.

Intriguing new findings have also emerged from Internet-based studies that likely would have not been possible without this technology. For example, Robins and associates examined age differences in levels of global self-esteem as assessed by their one-item measure (Robins, Trzesniewski, Tracy, Gosling, & Potter, 2002). Their research found that self-esteem levels were relatively high in childhood and lower in adulthood. Levels of self-esteem increased with age throughout adulthood, and then declined greatly in old age. The highest levels of self-esteem were reported by participants in the 9- to 12-year-old group, followed by the participants in the 60- to 69-year-old group. The lowest self-esteem was reported by the 80- to 90-year-old group. Another interesting finding was that decrease in self-esteem in adolescence was much more evident for girls than boys, and this fits with the reported gender difference in depression, which is more prevalent among adolescent girls than boys. Regarding the age differences, it is important to reiterate that this research used a large cross-sectional sample; thus, age group differences could reflect either developmental trends or age-related cohort effects.

A study by Srivastava, John, Gosling, and Potter (2003) examined possible age and gender effects in personality variables. The analyses of age differences were designed to test the plaster hypothesis described in Chapter 3. Their comparisons of Internet versus traditional data collection from more than 130,000 participants from the United States and Canada identified great similarities in the findings across types of assessment. Gender differences were apparent with both forms of assessment; neuroticism and extroversion declined substantially with age for women but not for men. In addition, comparable age differences were found for most of the five personality factors relative to the age trends detected via other forms of assessment. Additional results showed that the internal consistencies (Cronbach alpha coefficients, Cronbach 1951) were quite comparable across assessment methods, and the intercorrelations among the five personality dimensions were also quite similar across the two forms of assessment.

When a new technique is just beginning to take hold, several related issues require investigation. In this instance, additional research is needed on possible biases that characterize the people who volunteer for Internet-based studies. Could it be that people who participate via the Internet are elevated in introversion and shyness? Are introverted people overrepresented in these investigations? This possibility is suggested by research linking excessive Internet use with shyness and loneliness (see Davis, Flett, & Besser, 2002). Gosling et al. (2004) described findings suggesting that levels of introversion and neuroticism are not significantly different in samples of university students who completed measures via the Internet or the more typical paper and pencil measures.

Ethical issues also abound with Internet data collection and need further consideration. Questions include how feasible is it to provide participants with informed consent and a meaningful debriefing period after they have participated in the study (see Fraley 2007). One particularly vexing issue is the inclusion of children and adolescents in Internet studies. Typically, children only participate in research after parental consent has been obtained. What safeguards can be put in place so that children do not participate in personality research and other forms of research without proper consent?

Finally, a practical concern is that certain personality measures probably cannot be used in Internet research because these measures are copyrighted, and testing companies who own the copyrighted materials are not likely to make these measures available online. Unfortunately, some online research in our laboratory has simply not been feasible with certain measures due to the restrictions imposed by publishing companies. This is not a large problem when alternative, public domain measures of key constructs are available, but it is a very significant problem when there is no other measure. Of course, this reflects the more general issue of what happens when a researcher is unable to purchase a personality measure due to limited financial resources.

These problems and issues notwithstanding, it cannot be denied that the use of the World Wide Web has enabled researchers to study some significant issues that would otherwise go unexamined. It will be intriguing to witness the effects of this methodology on the personality field in years to come.

ISSUES IN PERSONALITY ASSESSMENT

The next section of this chapter explores issues in personality assessment. This section not only describes the steps to be taken in creating a new personality measure, it also provides a platform for introducing and elaborating on key concepts such as the validity and reliability of personality assessments.

Construct Validity and the Construct Validation Approach

Currently, in the personality field, the construct validation approach is one of the most widely accepted frameworks for the development of personality scales. Several authors have described aspects of the construct validation approach in detail (e.g., Cronbach & Meehl, 1955; Hogan & Nicholson, 1988; Jackson, 1970; Loevinger, 1957). **Construct validity** and the construct validation process will be described in detail because of its importance.

In their classic paper, Cronbach and Meehl (1955) observed that there is a joint need to assess the validity of the construct and the validity of tests assessing the construct. This point was reiterated by Fiske (1973), who observed that, "The investigation of construct validity must study a construct-operation unit, not a construct and casually selected procedure for its measurement. The specific measuring procedure must be involved integrally in the total conceptual framework being subjected to empirical test" (p. 89).

Fiske (1973) underscored his point by noting that scales that share the same construct name may differ in item content by having very different correlations with other variables. He referred specifically to a study by Edwards, Abbott, and Klockars (1972), which found substantially different results depending on whether the Edwards Personal Preference Scale (EPPS) or Personality Research Form (PRF) was used. The results involving the correlates of endurance are summarized in Table 4.2. It can be seen that the correlations between endurance and both achievement and dominance are much stronger with the PRF. In contrast, the correlation with order was stronger with the EPPS; and there was a negative association between endurance and affiliation with the EPPS, while the PRF had a negligible correlation with affiliation. The results shown in Table 4.2 are so different, it is almost possible to forget that these results were obtained with the same sample of participants!

Table 4.2 Psychological Needs Correlated with Two Measures of Endurance

	EPPS	PRF
Achievement	.21	.68
Affiliation	-.25	.03
Dominance	-.09	.39
Order	.42	.13

(Note: Based on the same sample of participants.)

Differences in scale content with measures that purport to assess the same construct imply that individual measures may not fully assess broad personality constructs. This issue was illustrated by the results of a recent study that examined the conscientiousness construct by administering seven conscientiousness measures to participants (Roberts, Chernyshenko, Stark, & Goldberg, 2005). Analyses identified six facets to the conscientiousness construct: industriousness, order, self-control, responsibility, traditionalism, and virtue. Importantly, none of the seven conscientiousness measures tapped all six of these characteristics. Thus, if a researcher used only one of these measures, he or she would not be fully assessing the entire construct.

KEY POINTS

- Construct validity is supposed to reflect an underlying theory.
- Measures may have the same name but have different associations with other variables because the content of measures with the same name is quite different.
- Measures may not assess the entire breadth of a construct.

The Sequential System of Test Construction

Superb personality tests reflect sophisticated conceptual schemes and a diligent and systematic approach to test construction. **Douglas Jackson** from the University of Western Ontario wrote an influential paper that is an excellent summary of the process of creating a scale according to the construct validation (see Jackson, 1970). The construct validation approach is regarded as a sequential system used to refine questionnaires.

As part of this paper, Jackson identified four principles as essential to personality test development: (1) the overriding importance of psychological theory; (2) the need to suppress response style variance; (3) the importance of scale homogeneity and generalizability; and (4) the importance of establishing the convergent and discriminant validity of the measure at the start of the test development process.

Regarding the first principle, according to Jackson (1970), the first and arguably most important step in developing a personality measure of a psychological construct is to describe the theoretical construct in question in as much detail as possible. The psychological construct is a hypothetical, abstract entity that can only be inferred from more observable indicators (such as the answers that a person circles on a personality test). This step is vitally important because personality scales should reflect theories and should never be constructed in an atheoretical manner.

The **nomological network** must be outlined as part of this initial process. The nomological network consists of the factors and variables that are theoretically related to the construct in question. The nomological network of variables needs to be defined fully with respect to the hypothesized interrelations among variables (Loevinger, 1957). In addition, when seeking to describe a psychological construct, the factors and characteristics that are not part of the construct should also be described.

The next step in this process is the rational generation of a large pool of items (Jackson, 1970). The items are then evaluated on their clarity in wording and their relevance (how closely they match the description of the theoretical construct). Next, in keeping with the second principle (the need to suppress response style variance), items are evaluated for their susceptibility to response styles.

These next goals are achieved by administering the items to a large sample of participants. Item selection and factor analytic techniques are used systematically to examine the empirical qualities of the item on a personality scale (Jackson, 1970). Items high in infrequency are eliminated. Items are rejected if they were endorsed at too high a level (i.e., agreed to by 90% of respondents) or at too low level (i.e., refuted by 90% or more of respondents as a form of nea-saying). This criterion is employed because personality scale items are only useful if they yield substantial individual differences. They are not informative if virtually everyone in a sample agrees or disagrees with the items. Also, items that are endorsed at too high a level may be susceptible to an **acquiescence response bias** (also known as yea-saying).

As alluded to above, a critical factor is the examination of the extent to which the various items have incorporated a social desirability bias. Items are to be retained only if they are not correlated highly with social desirability measures, unless it can be argued, as noted earlier, that social desirability is an inherent aspect of the construct in question (McCrae

& Costa, 1983). Jackson (1970) introduced a statistical test known as the **differential reliability index** to evaluate whether a particular test item has too high a correlation with a measure of social desirability. The differential reliability index is a statistic that takes into account the extent to which an item is correlated with social desirability and the extent to which an individual item is correlated with its intended scale. Preferred items are highly correlated with other intended scale items, and they are minimally correlated with social desirability.

The resultant scales are also evaluated to ensure that they have adequate degrees of reliability and validity. The third principle of test construction outlined by Jackson (1970) involved a scale's homogeneity. Homogeneity exists if all scale items are tapping the same construct, and there are high correlations between the item and the total score of the items that make up the intended factor being measured. The level of homogeneity is assessed with a type of reliability known as **internal consistency**. **Lee Cronbach** (1951) introduced this concept and created a statistic known as the **alpha coefficient**, which is based on the degree of intercorrelations among scale items. The alpha coefficient is based on the average intercorrelation among the items and the total number of scale items involved. The alpha coefficient can range between 0 and 1. There is no established criterion to determine whether a scale has acceptable internal consistency, though Nunnally (1978) suggested that an alpha coefficient value of .70 or greater is acceptable for scales in the initial stages of development.

The internal consistency of a scale has to do with the scale's internal structure, and this type of reliability is very different from another type of reliability known as **test–retest reliability**. Test–retest reliability is the stability of test scores over time, and this type of reliability is vitally important to establish, given that scales tapping personality traits are assessing individual differences that are supposed to be relatively stable over time. A key thing about test–retest reliability is that it does not mean that a person's scores cannot vary over time. Here it must be remembered that the focus is on the scores for a sample of many participants. The key issue is whether the person's scores place him or her at about the same point in a distribution of scores.

Additional Test Construction Guidelines

Other authors have also provided some helpful guidelines that can be used to evaluate personality assessment measures. Burisch (1984) from the University of Hamburg in Germany outlined four criteria: (1) the validity of the scales; (2) communicability; (3) economy of measurement; and (4) nonarbitrariness and representativeness. "Communicability" refers to the meaning and interpretation of test items being unambiguous; test constructors should avoid using "double-barrelled" items that tap more than one theme because this may result in confused responses that are difficult to interpret.

Burisch also advocates developing brief measures rather than measures with redundant items. He introduced the economy issue by noting that some scales have taken years to construct, yet "it cost me two hours and a bottle of wine to write an aggression and a depression scale that turned out to be of equal or superior validity" (p. 219) compared with existing measures. Brief measures with high internal consistency are preferred. Finally, when discussing nonarbitrariness and representativeness, Burisch (1984) argued for the importance of sampling from all possible item content while keeping arbitrary decisions about scale content to a minimum.

Types of Validity in Personality Assessment

When considering the concept of validity, Burisch's advice seems particularly important. Burisch (1984) stated that he agreed with scholars such as Messick (1980) that it is best not to think of validity as a generic and abstract concept. Instead, it should be remembered that validity has many facets, but the bottom line is that all forms of validity involve "our ability to generalize from test scores to the way a person acts, thinks, and feels outside the testing room" (p. 217). In this context, if a personality measure is valid, then to some extent, it accurately reflects reality.

There are several types of validity. The concept of test validity itself was advanced considerably from 1950 to 1954 by the American Psychological Association Committee on Psychological Tests. This committee's mandate was to establish principles that should be in place before a psychological test is published. As part of its recommendations, this committee introduced four types of validity: construct validity, content validity, concurrent validity, and predictive validity. Concurrent validity and predictive validity are criterion-oriented validation procedures (see Cronbach & Meehl, 1955). Various types of validity are summarized in Table 4.3.

Table 4.3 Types of Validity

Construct Validity	To what extent does a measure reflect an abstract, hypothetical personality difference?
Content Validity	Does a measure have breadth because it has items that fully assess the personality construct in question?
Criterion Validity	Is the measure associated with other measures it should be related to, either measured at the same time (concurrent validity) or later in time (predictive validity)?
Discriminant Validity	Is a measure unrelated to a measure that it should not be related to?
Ecological Validity	Does the measure predict meaningful outcomes in the environment?
Face Validity	Through visual inspection, do test items seem relevant for measuring the construct?
Factorial Validity	Does the hypothesized factor structure of the measure replicate when tested via factor analyses?
Incremental Validity	Does the measure predict significant unique variance in an outcome variable, above and beyond the variance attributable to another predictor variable?

As stated earlier, construct validity is an abstract concept that reflects the need for personality measures to stem from a theory. Construct validity involves a theory of a set of hypotheses about a psychological construct. Assumptions and beliefs about this abstract entity are tested via the gathering of observable data and operationally defined measures.

The issue involved in **content validity** is whether test items are adequate and representative samples of the universe that make up a particular construct. For instance, if you wished to assess the content validity of a measure of dependency, you wish to know whether the dependency test items fully reflect the various forms of psychological dependency that have been identified. Content validity is related to another type of validity known as **face validity**. There is no established statistical test to evaluate face validity. The only things you can use to judge face validity are your eyes and your thoughts. Face validity involves the question, "On the surface or face of the test itself, do the items seem to measure the construct?" This most basic form of validity is quite important because personality researchers sometimes encounter measures with item content that seems to have very little to do with the stated description of the construct in question. This sometimes occurs because researchers retain items in a scale simply because they were highly correlated with other items on this scale, but in fact, they measure quite different trait concepts.

KEY POINTS

- Reliability reflects the consistency of measurement. Consistency can refer to whether the items in a scale are responded to in a similar way (internal consistency) or whether the responses are relatively stable over time (test–retest reliability).
- Validity occurs when a measure assesses in reality what it purports to measure.
- There are many forms of validity, including the validity of the hypothesized psychological variable (construct validity) and whether the items seem visually, on the surface, to reflect the construct (face validity).

As noted, both **concurrent validity** and **predictive validity** are criterion-oriented. These types of validity pertain to the fourth principle outlined by Jackson (1970). When evaluating concurrent validity, you seek to establish that there is a significant association between the personality measure and a criterion variable that it should be associated with, according to theory, and both measures are assessed at the same time. Predictive validity is quite similar, but in this instance, the goal is to determine that the personality measure can predict measures that it should be related to when assessed in the future.

Recall that Jackson's (1970) fourth principle of test construct involved **convergent validity** and **discriminant validity**. Personality test items are favoured if they are highly correlated with measures of the intended construct (i.e., similar measures converge on each other), but they have minimal correlation with other constructs. A personality scale has discriminant validity if it is unrelated to a measure with which it theoretically should not be correlated. For example, if you were creating a new measure of procrastination, you would want to establish in a sample of participants that it was correlated with other measures of procrastination (i.e., convergent validity), but not associated with scores on a seemingly unrelated construct (e.g., openness).

The **multitrait–multimethod matrix** is an essential aspect of test construction and refinement that is used to evaluate concurrent and discriminant validity. The logic behind the multitrait–multimethod matrix was outlined in the seminal paper by Campbell and Fiske (1959). This matrix is used to examine the validity of the measures after removing variance that may be due to the procedures used to assess the construct, such as the biases associated with self-report measures. Two or more personality traits are evaluated with two or more methods (e.g., self-reports and observer reports). It is then possible to use sophisticated statistical techniques such as confirmatory factor analysis to determine how much variability is attributable to individual differences in the personality traits, and how much variability is **method variance** due to the manner in which personality was assessed.

The value of adopting a multitrait–multimethod approach was demonstrated recently in an investigation conducted by Biesanz and West (2004). They were interested in testing the associations among the five dimensions that make up the five-factor model. Different measures tapping the Big Five were completed by the participants, their friends, and their parents. They found that whether intercorrelations exist among the five dimensions depends largely on the research methods used. When the focus is on just one informant (e.g., the individual's self-reports or ratings from a parent or a friend), then there is substantial overlap among the five dimensions and the intercorrelations are evident. However, when more sophisticated analyses were conducted with the multitrait–multimethod matrix and method variance was taken into account, the five factors were relatively independent (also known as orthogonal). Thus, more extensive analyses indicate that the five dimensions are not related. This contemporary study represents a compelling example of how measurement issues directly influence research conclusions.

Several other forms of validity have been identified. **Factorial validity** occurs when an assessment measure based on a construct that is conceptualized as having several different factors does indeed seem to have these factors when factor analyses are conducted. In the initial stages of test construction, exploratory factor analyses are constructed just to determine if the general factor structure being proposed is evident. However, in the latter stages of test construction, **confirmatory factor analyses** are performed. Confirmatory factor analyses involve multivariate statistics in which the researcher stipulates that the proposed factor structure (including whether the factors are correlated with each other or are independent) and the data are evaluated to determine whether the item responses fit the theoretical model that was postulated from the outset of the test construction process.

Ecological validity is another kind of validity. The concept of **ecological validity** was introduced by Brunswick (1955). Research has ecological validity if it employs a representative sample of situations and participants drawn from the general population. Ecological validity is a probabilistic notion that involves the degree to which the research reflects the actual phenomenon in nature. **Experience sampling** is one emerging technique designed to increase the ecological validity of psychological research. In experience sampling, participants are required to record their behaviours, cognitions, and emotions at various points throughout their day as a way of assessing their individual difference tendencies in specific contexts. For instance, this technique was used in a recent study to compare and contrast the emotional experiences of participants from five cultures (Scollon, Diener, Oishi, & Biswas-Diener, 2004) and to compare the daily emotional experiences of participants differing in attachment styles (Torquati & Raffaelli, 2004). Experience sampling can involve the use of the Electronically Activated Recorder (see Mehl, Gosling, & Pennebaker, 2006), a device that automatically records ambient sounds throughout a period of several days.

What are the advantages of experience sampling? It is a form of time sampling that is done in specific situations, which increases the generalizability of the findings. In addition, experience sampling involves collecting multiple measures of the same phenomenon. The acquisition of many measures is known as **aggregation**, and it is useful because multiple assessments tend to result in more reliable assessments with less measurement error.

Incremental validity is a relatively new form of validity that has its roots in the clinical literature (see Haynes & Lench, 2003). The key question in incremental validity is, does a newly introduced measure predict a phenomenon more accurately than an already existing measure? There are many forms that incremental validity can take, but the key issue is whether a new measure can predict a significant degree of additional variance in a criterion measure, over and above the variance attributable to already existing measures. For instance, in our work on perfectionism, we established the incremental validity of a new measure of perfectionistic thoughts by showing that this new measure predicted significant variance in levels of psychological distress after already considering the variance attributable to pre-existing trait measures of perfectionism (Flett, Hewitt, Blankstein, & Gray, 1998).

It should be evident by now that personality assessment can be quite complex. Things become even more complex when personality assessment is examined from a cross-cultural perspective. This topic is explored in International Focus on Discovery 4.1.

International Focus on Discovery 4.1 Personality Assessment across Cultures

There are many issues that need to be considered when examining personality assessment from a cross-cultural perspective. These issues involve both the content of measures as well as the conceptualizations that are reflected in personality scale development.

The first important consideration is **conceptual equivalence**. Does a personality concept in one culture have the same conceptual meaning in another culture? The same general personality construct may vary substantially across cultures. This is perhaps most evident with respect to the dependency construct. People who are high in dependency have a great need to maintain contact with the significant people in their lives. There are differences across cultures in whether dependency is a positive or negative attribute. Dependency is regarded negatively in North American cultures where there is a focus on individualism and self-reliance. Accordingly, when measures of dependency are administered, dependency tends to be linked with depression. (Zuroff, Mongrain, & Santor, 2004).

In contrast, cultures that tend to place a higher premium on the ability to connect with significant others tend to value dependency, and dependency is a protective personality orientation. According to Rothbaum et al. (2000), people in countries such as Japan value connectedness and the interdependencies of children and their parents.

If the meaning of dependency and healthy attachment varies across cultures, then perhaps dependency is not universally maladaptive. Indeed, research in Israel has shown that rather than dependency being correlated positively with postpartum depression, dependency is associated *negatively* with postpartum depression (Priel & Besser, 1999, 2000). Moreover, dependency is associated with adaptive forms of coping and receiving social support from significant others (Priel & Besser, 2000).

The importance of not assuming conceptual equivalence across cultures was also illustrated by research on Machiavellianism. Machiavellianism is a tough-minded orientation with the general belief that it is acceptable to take advantage of others and use ingratiation for personal gain (Christie & Geis, 1970); see Chapter 10. Machiavellianism is tapped by such test items as, "It is safest to assume that all people have a vicious streak and it will come out when they are given a chance." Kuo and Marsella (1977) compared the properties of a measure of Machiavellianism administered to Chinese and American college students because they noted that there is no concept equivalent to Machiavellianism in Chinese culture. They confirmed that Machiavellianism items completed by Chinese students were not in line with the intended nature of the construct. If anything, the scale was now tapping the Chinese concept of "Li-Chi," which is a willingness to profiteer for personal gain, but this is supposed to be restricted to marketplace transactions and is not a broad-based disposition to use other people.

Cross-national differences in response styles also exist. Some research has explored differences in social desirability response bias. As might be expected, cultures that place greater importance on collectivist goals and the connection between the self and other people tend to be higher in levels of social desirability and deception. Research has found that people from a collectivist orientation are more likely to engage in impression management lying, deception, and face-saving behaviour (Triandis & Suh, 2002). In contrast, the individualistic orientation is linked with self-deceptive enhancement. This research was summarized by Johnson and van de Vijver (2003).

Differences exist even in whether people exhibit extreme response tendencies versus more moderate tendencies. The tendency for extreme responses to occur (i.e., excessive use of the scale endpoints) was first identified by Cronbach (1949). Research on the acquiescence bias (excessive yea-saying) indicates that people from certain cultures are more likely to use the endpoints of a scale when responding to personality items, while people from other cultures are more likely to use the midpoint when provided with several alternatives. One study analyzed data from marketing surveys and found that people from Mediterranean countries (e.g., Greece and Italy) had consistently higher levels of acquiescence and extreme responding relative to people from Britain, Germany, and France (van Herk, Poortinga, & Verhallen, 2004).

The tendency for Chinese people to excessively use the midpoints is believed to reflect the **moderation norm**. Hamid, Lai, and Cheng (2000) found in a sample of university students from Hong Kong that the midpoint was used disproportionately by people high in public self-consciousness. Another analysis of culture and response styles in 19 countries across five continents confirmed that individualism is associated with an acquiescent response bias (Johnson, Kulesa, Lic, Cho, & Shavitt, 2005).

Normative equivalence is another important consideration (see Marsella, Dubanoski, Hamada, & Morse, 2000). It remains to be determined whether the scale means as well as the degree of variability in responses is comparable across geographical regions, and subgroups of individuals within geographical regions. For many measures, local norms have to be developed.

Perhaps language issues represent the biggest hurdle confronting personality researchers. A thorough process known as **back translation** is performed when translating a scale into another language in order to maximize **language equivalence**. Ideally, one language expert translates a scale and then one or more other experts takes the translated version and puts it back in the original language to see if the language used in the item content has changed. Even subtle differences as a result of the translation process can significantly alter the meaning of an item.

The linguistic equivalence of measures means that measures are also needed in different languages to tap the diversity found within countries. In Canada, for instance, measures are needed for both English-speaking and French-speaking respondents. A recent investigation by van de Vijver and Jeanrie (2004) assessed whether it was feasible to create a French language version of Gough's (1996) California Psychological Inventory (CPI) that is equivalent to the English version. Extensive care was taken in the translation process, and then the CPI was administered to more than 1,000 English-speaking and 1,000 French-speaking Canadians. It was determined that the CPI was structurally equivalent (i.e., comparable factor structure). Item-level analyses identified several items with small amounts of bias, but their removal did not influence the results. Thus, comparable measures can emerge when care is taken to develop such measures.

As the personality field continues to adopt a more international focus, issues surrounding cross-cultural differences in personality assessment will become increasingly apparent. Such issues will stand as a constant reminder of the need to develop sound measures and understand how these measures influence the findings of subsequent research.

We will conclude this discussion with an excerpt from Marsella et al. (2000). Marsella has extensive experience in using personality measures across cultures. Marsella et al. (2000) observed that:

> The simple fact of the matter is that asking self-report questions is a complex task. This is made even more complex when psychologists move across cultural boundaries to ask questions of people whose perceptions of the task and whose motivations to participate differ from those on whom the scale was constructed. (p. 55)

Summary

Chapter 4 provided an overview of the issues in conducting personality research and assessment. The chapter began with an overview of experimental research in personality. A clear distinction was made between independent variables and dependent variables. It was noted that experimental personality research is focused on moderator effects, and the differences between moderator and mediator effects was discussed. The need to remain cognizant of the benefits and limitations of experimental research was noted. While the experimental approach is more suited to examine cause and effect associations, limitations of the experimental approach include the key issue of whether experimental research is generalizable to real-world contexts.

Next, the process of conducting correlational research was described. Concerns about correlational research were discussed, including the inability of correlational research to test cause and effect relationships, and the directionality issue.

This general description of approaches to personality research was then discussed within the context of surveys of the actual types of personality research conducted by investigators. It was noted that contemporary surveys suggest that the modal or typical investigation is a correlational study with self-report measures completed by university or college students. Studies on actual research methods used then led to a discussion of various types of data and forms of personality assessment, including the differences between structured and unstructured forms of assessment. An important theme of this chapter was the limitations of self-report measures.

The final segment of this chapter can almost be considered to be a "how-to manual" with established principles of personality test construction and assessment. The sequential system of test construction advocated by Jackson was outlined, along with other recommendations provided by authors such as Burisch. This description of test construction principles provided the platform for introducing the concepts of reliability and validity and the various forms they may take (e.g., face validity, construct validity, concurrent validity, discriminant validity, and incremental validity). The chapter concluded by examining issues of personality assessment from a cross-cultural perspective.

Questions to Consider

1 Review the benefits and limitations of experimental studies of personality. Do you believe that the benefits outweigh the limitations? Do you think that correlational studies are more predominant simply because they are easier and less time-consuming to conduct?

2 Using one of your favourite television shows, rate the main characters according to the five-factor model. Get a friend to do the same and compare your ratings. Did your ratings match your friend's rating? Why or why not?

3 What is the difference between impression management and self-deception? Which is the bigger threat to personality test validity?

4 You are conducting a study and you suspect that the student who is participating is totally disinterested and is simply doing it for a reward (e.g. getting experimental credit to improve grades). What measures could you include in your study to check your suspicions?

5 Do you agree that parents are not accurate raters of their children's personality? What personality and experiential factors might predict different levels of accuracy among parents?

6 Review the different types of validity. What kind of validity is it if a measure appears visually to have items that are relevant? What types of validity are involved if a measure is associated with another variable that it should be associated with, and this second variable is measured (a) at the same time and (b) one month later?

7 Do you think it is appropriate to administer personality measures when seeking to hire someone for a job? What three personality traits would you most like to measure?

Key Terms

acquiescence response bias, p. 148
additive model, p. 124
aggregation, p. 153
alpha coefficient, p. 149
back translation, p. 154
between-subjects variable, p. 121
conceptual equivalence, p. 153
concurrent validity, p. 151
confirmatory factor analyses, p. 152
construct validity, p. 146
content validity, p. 151
convergent validity, p. 151
demand characteristics, p. 126
dependent variable, p. 120
differential reliability index, p. 149
directionality issue, p. 131
discriminant validity, p. 151
ecological validity, p. 152
experience sampling, p. 152
experimental condition, p. 120
external validity, p. 126
face validity, p. 151
factorial validity, p. 152
generalizability, p. 126

incremental validity, p. 153
independent variable, p. 120
interaction effect, p. 122
internal consistency, p. 149
language equivalence, p. 154
latency-based validity indices, p. 141
main effects model, p. 124
manipulated variable, p. 120
measurement error, p. 129
median split, p. 128
mediator effects, p. 122
methodological pluralism, p. 143
method variance, p. 152
moderation norm, p. 154
moderator effect, p. 122
multitrait–multimethod matrix, p. 151
negative correlation, p. 130
nomological network, p. 148
normative equivalence, p. 154
order effect, p. 121
positive correlation, p. 130
predictive validity, p. 151
random assignment, p. 121
regression to the mean, p. 129
repeated measures, p. 121
self-deception, p. 136
social desirability response bias, p. 137
structured assessments, p. 135
subject variables, p. 121
tertial split, p. 128
test–retest reliability, p. 149
third-variable problem, p. 131
unstructured assessments, p. 135
within-subject variable, p. 121

Key Theorists

Lee Cronbach, p. 149
Douglas Jackson, p. 148

chapter five

PSYCHODYNAMIC THEORIES

- Psychodynamic Theory and Sigmund Freud
- The Neo-Freudians: Carl Jung's Analytical Psychology
- The Neo-Freudians: Alfred Adler
- The Neo-Freudians: Karen Horney
- Psychodynamic Assessment Techniques

... we might say that the reserve, or downright hostility, that academic psychologists have customarily shown to psychoanalytic theory has both a rational and an irrational component. The rational component focuses upon psychoanalysts' slight concern for carefully controlled experimental evidence, the absence of adequate empirical definitions, and the frequent statement of relationships in such a manner that they are not subject to proof or disproof. The irrational component derives from a kind of professional jealousy that strongly resents contributions made by individuals not trained in the discipline of psychology.

—CALVIN HALL AND GARDNER LINDZEY (1959, P. 143-144)

... psychoanalysis has not evolved scientifically. Specifically, it has not developed objective methods for testing the exciting ideas it had formulated earlier. As a result, psychoanalysis enters the twenty-first century with its influence in decline. This decline is regrettable, since psychoanalysis still represents the most coherent and intellectually satisfying view of the mind. If psychoanalysis is to regain its intellectual power and influence, it will need more than the stimulus that comes from responding to its hostile critics. It will need to be engaged constructively by those who care for it and who care for a sophisticated and realistic theory of human motivation.

—ERIC KANDEL, 2000 NOBEL LAUREATE (KANDEL, 1999, P. 505)

SIGMUND FREUD IS WELL-KNOWN for his case histories of clients and his psychoanalytic theory. Many clients suffered from physical illnesses and associated forms of distress. Consider the case of Dora (a pseudonym for Ida) and Freud's interpretation:

> Freud enthusiastically greeted Ida as a patient who would provide him with a suitable test of his theories of hysteria, his technique of analysis and of the interpretation of dreams. The picklock he took to Ida's case was his claim that "sexuality is the key to the problem of the psychoneuroses ... No one who disdains the key will ever be able to lock the door." But he wished also to demonstrate how "dream interpretation is woven into the history of a treatment and how it can become the means of filling in amnesias and elucidating symptoms." (Appignanesi & Forrester, 2005, p. 149)

The case history of Dora (Ida) is regarded as perhaps Freud's greatest failure, in part because of his attempt to interpret all of her problems in terms of sexual issues. For instance, Freud concluded on the basis of little evidence that Dora's asthma reflected her repressed, now forgotten memory of hearing her parents have sex. Dora's own breathing problems symbolized her parents' heavy breathing during the act itself. Interested students can find many accounts and critiques of Freud's treatment of Dora.

Freud's psychoanalytic theory is very provocative, not only because of the theory itself, but also because it provided the impetus for other psychoanalytic theorists to formulate their own theories, which are examined in detail in this chapter. First, however, note that Chapter 5 marks an important shift in emphasis in this book. Much of the material in the previous chapters looked at personality from a descriptive perspective. That is, the focus of previous chapters was mostly on the "what" of personality. Basic issues examined from this perspective included: (1) What is personality? (2) What broad traits have been hypothesized as accounting for personality? and (3) What principles need to be considered when conducting personality research and assessing personality? In contrast, in Chapter 5, we begin to focus more on the "why" questions, for it is here that the focus shifts to classic theories of personality. The main goal of these theories is to explain why individual differences come about.

Psychoanalytic theorists tend to emphasize internal and unconscious motives and drives that interact dynamically to influence our behaviours. Although some themes are common to all theorists in this camp, we will see that there are substantial differences among the theorists within this domain in their main tenets and beliefs.

We begin with Freud's classic theory. It is important to reiterate that the views espoused by Freud and the subsequent "neo-Freudians" are quite controversial, and certain concepts have been met with strong objections over the years. These objections extend to the measures that have emerged to assess psychoanalytic concepts. Regardless of whether you agree or disagree with Freud's theoretical notions, there can be no denying that Freud has had a remarkable impact on the public's awareness of psychological principles. Also, despite the criticisms of the psychoanalytic approach, psychoanalytic therapists operate in great numbers throughout the world, and assessment measures representing the psychoanalytic perspective are considered to be standard and are used extensively in clinical assessments. An overview of the classic beliefs of Sigmund Freud is provided below.

PSYCHODYNAMIC THEORY AND SIGMUND FREUD

Theorists with a psychodynamic orientation share certain core assumptions. First, they believe that personality is a reflection of the dynamic interplay of internal motives and conflicts. They also endorse the importance of unconscious influences on our conscious behaviours, thoughts, and feelings. They also place stock in the introspective method. Introspection is an analysis of internal thoughts and images, including dreams. Several theorists in this orientation have based their theories, at least in part, on their personal introspections and self-analyses. The theorists we will focus on in this section are Sigmund Freud, Carl Jung, Alfred Adler, and Karen Horney.

Sigmund Freud believed that personality is composed of about 10% conscious awareness and 90% unconscious or preconscious.

Sigmund Freud is undoubtedly one of the most famous people of the twentieth century. His provocative views promoted a great deal of interest in psychology in general, and clinical psychology and developmental psychology in particular.

Freud was born in 1856 in what is now the Czech Republic. In his autobiography, Freud noted that he and his parents were Jewish, and he remained a Jew throughout his life. At the age of 4, Freud and his family moved to Vienna, Austria. Freud's theory is based in large part on the Viennese people who were the subjects of his case studies over the years.

Freud was trained as a medical doctor but soon gravitated toward the field of psychiatry. Other famous theorists described in this chapter were also psychiatrists. Before becoming a psychiatrist, Freud received research training in the laboratories of scientist Ernst Brucke, and this background in experimental work led Freud to hope to establish that psychoanalysis is a science. This proved to be one of many controversial aspects of his work because, as documented by Storr (1988), Freud's version of psychoanalytic theory became increasingly subjective over time and lacked the objectivity typically associated with science.

A subjective approach was necessary to test Freud's strong belief in the importance of the dynamic interplay of unconscious factors. He used the analogy of an iceberg to convey his belief that about 10% of ourselves is above the water in conscious awareness, but the other 90% of personality is below the surface, in the form of the unconscious or the preconscious, which is the feeling just prior to waking. The goal is to bring the unconscious to the surface and into conscious awareness so it may be interpreted by a psychoanalyst.

KEY POINTS

- The psyche reflects the dynamic interplay of factors inside the self that are amenable to introspection.
- Freud emphasized most of personality resides in the unconscious and is not conscious.
- Personality development, for Freud, reflects early life experiences in the family context.

Components of the Psyche

One of Freud's most compelling ideas is that our psyche (our mind and self) has three components: the id, the ego, and the superego. The **id** is present at birth and is the primitive and least rational part of our selves. The id is unconscious and operates according to the **pleasure principle**. That is, the id is a demanding structure that seeks pleasure and immediate gratification without concern of the possible consequences for inappropriate thoughts and actions. Initially, Freud regarded the id as being driven by biological urges involving the need for food, water, sex, and so on. The id is the reservoir for the **libido**, which is the individual's psychic energy that demands expression. Libido is an important concept because Freud believed that much of our behaviour is fuelled by psychosexual energy. The id strives to be satisfied by engaging in behaviours that provide pleasure, but when this is not possible, it must be satisfied via other means. According to Freud, one way to achieve temporary satisfaction is via **primary process thinking**. That is, the person generates cognitive images of pleasurable stimuli. This would occur, for instance, when fantasizing about sexual activities with someone who is appealing yet unavailable. Primary process thinking often comes in the form of **wish fulfillment** as fantasies reflect the wishes and baser desires of the id.

Wish fulfillment may result in **catharsis**, the reduction of tension by engaging in processes (e.g., primary process thinking, wish fulfillment) that provides some temporary relief. Catharsis is often mentioned in the debate over the effects of television violence on children. The typical argument by those who wish to claim that witnessing televised violence does not actually create an aggressive person is that simply watching violence portrayed in television and movies is enough to reduce built-up aggression.

The id is regarded as the "reservoir of psychic energy." The libido reflects **eros**, which is the life instinct postulated by Freud. Eros reflects both the sex instinct and the self-preservation instinct.

The id also reflects the death instinct known as **thanatos**. Initially, Freud rejected the concept of an instinct toward aggression; however, he added this concept to his theory in later years after witnessing the effects of the First World War and the events building toward the Second World War. He saw our willingness to be destructive toward ourselves as part of a death instinct that is constantly in conflict with eros, the life instinct. He equated the differences between eros and thanatos to the differences between the emotions love and hate. Our emotions are often ambivalent (i.e., mixed feelings) because we can both love and hate another person at the same time, or we can grow to hate someone we used to love (or vice versa). An example of the death instinct operating during pleasure seeking would be dangerous activities such as extreme use of dangerous drugs.

Whereas the id is believed to be present at birth, the **ego** develops out of the id, and this process starts to occur in the second half of the baby's first year. The ego is mostly but not entirely conscious. The ego's main purpose is to address the demands of the environment and reality. As such, the ego operates according to the **reality principle**. The ego tries to balance the primitive urges of the id with the reality of the situation. It uses a form of thinking known as **secondary process thinking**. This involves planful thoughts and decisions that consider environmental contingencies and challenges. The ego is determined primarily by a person's experiences including accidental events and contemporary events. Freud suggested that the experience of the ego will include not only exposure to the parents' personalities and the family as a whole, but also the experience associated with racial, cultural, and national traditions.

The **superego** is the final component of the psyche. It begins to emerge at approximately the age of three or four. The superego is the moral part of personality. The superego requires us to act according to accepted societal standards, rules, and principles. People with a strong superego are punished by thoughts of shame and guilt when they do not act according to prescribed standards of acceptable behaviour. The superego operates according to the **perfection principle**: the notion that we must act perfectly by meeting societal dictates, which often come in the form of endorsing and internalizing our parents' values.

Freud indicated that both the id and superego are influenced by the past. The id reflects the impact of heredity, while the superego reflects the influence of significant others early in life (i.e., one's parents). Freud also stated, however, that the superego could also reflect the influence of later successors, such as teachers and public figures, who come to represent social ideals.

The superego is one of Freud's most controversial notions only because it is linked with one of the most provocative (and to most people, unacceptable) aspects of Freud's theory. Freud suggested that we come to internalize parental values as a way of resolving the **Oedipus complex** for boys and the **Electra complex** for girls. Freud borrowed concepts from Greek mythology and suggested that as children reach the age of approximately four years old, at an unconscious level, they covet the opposite-sexed parent. In the case of a boy, his desire for his mother must be balanced by his fear that his father will find out and will respond by punishing him. The punishment leads to **castration anxiety** because the boy fears that his father will remove his penis. Freud's famous case of Little Hans was cited as an example of the Oedipus complex and castration anxiety. Little Hans reported a phobia of being bitten by a horse. At the same time, according to his father, Little Hans had a great interest in touching his "widdler." Freud interpreted this phobia and fascination as a reflection of Hans' fearfulness of his father, and claimed that Little Hans was remarkably cured after only one meeting with Freud. Simply hearing Freud's explanation and having the unconscious conflict brought to conscious awareness was supposedly enough for a miraculous recovery! Two prominent clinical researchers and theorists, Joseph Wolpe and Stanley Rachman, have scoffed at Freud's interpretation of the horse phobia. They were particularly critical of Freud's claim that Little Hans improved immediately upon hearing Freud's insights (see Wolpe & Rachman,

1998). In fact, Little Hans did improve but it was gradual and not directly attributable to Freud's insights.

Karen Horney (1937) was also quite critical of Freud's willingness to generalize from his specific subgroups of neurotic patients to all people. Horney argued that it is very unlikely that the jealousies and interpersonal problems that Freud identified in his patients as reflections of the Oedipus complex could be generalized to other people within the same culture, and to individuals from other cultures.

According to Freud, the way to resolve the Oedipal complex is through identification with the father. It is through this process of identification that the boy comes to internalize his father's values. This process of **introjection** is implicated directly in superego development, which is the structure that eventually emerges.

As for girls, the Electra complex is a girl's desire for her father. As controversial as this is, it became worse when Freud suggested that girls suffer from **penis envy** and they can compensate for their own lack of a penis by developing a relationship with the father. Whereas boys were assumed to fear castration and were fearful of their fathers, a comparable fear for girls did not exist. Nevertheless, they were believed to identify with the opposite-sex parent but this resulted in weaker internalization, and, ultimately, a weaker superego.

How many objections can you raise to this hypothesized scenario? Aside from the general absurdity of children having this kind of interest in their parents, research on morality suggests that, if anything, females have a stronger superego than males, and it is females who have a more developed superego, on average. Also, the scenario posited by Freud is highly sexist, and it has led some critics (e.g., Macmillan, 1998) to suggest that Freud's views were more representative of prevailing cultural stereotypes at the time in Vienna rather than accurate interpretations of the women receiving treatment. Karen Horney challenged Freud and suggested that if anything, males suffer from **womb envy** because of their inability to bear a child.

KEY POINTS

- Our psyches reflect three internal structures (the id, ego, and superego) that are in constant conflict.
- The id is primitive and irrational and operates according to the pleasure principle.
- The ego plays the role of mediator as it balances the respective wishes of the id and superego with the ongoing demands of the physical environment.
- The superego is formed as a result of the Oedipus complex (boys) and the Electra complex (girls). Societal standards and dictates are represented in parental feedback about proper behaviour. The superego emerges following identification with the same-sex parent as a way of resolving the Oedipus or Electra complex.

Although Freud deserves credit for focusing attention on how children come to internalize values and develop a personal conscience (a sense of what is right versus wrong), he can also be criticized for not realizing that development of conscience actually occurs much earlier than he suggested. Investigations indicate that by the end of their second year, children display signs of shame and guilt when they commit a transgression (Barrett, 1998;

Lewis, Sullivan, Stanger, & Weiss, 1989; Zahn-Waxler, 2000), and developmental theorists believe that children of this age already have a developing sense that their transgressions do not meet with standards and expectations (Lewis et al., 1989; Kochanska, Casey, & Fukumoto, 1995).

Contemporary research by Grazyna Kochanska and colleagues has established that internalization and the development of conscience involves many factors, including the mutual responsiveness of the mother and the child, as well as the child's temperament (Kochanska & Aksan, 2004; Kochanska, Forman, Aksan, & Dunbar, 2005). One study showed that young children with a fearful temperament are higher in guilt proneness, and the fearful temperament, which is at least partly biological in origin, is associated with a decreased propensity to violate rules and norms (Kochanska, Gross, Lin, & Nichols, 2002). A key variable is a personality construct known as effortful control. This is assumed to be a personality trait, in part, because it is high in longitudinal stability and it generalizes across different situational contexts (Kochanska & Knaack, 2003). Effortful control is higher among children with a temperament high in positive emotionality. Children with high effortful control at the age of two have demonstrably stronger consciences when they are almost five years old. Although excessive maternal power assertion as a parental style tends to impede the development of conscience in general, effortful control in children mediates this association such that children with high effortful control who are exposed to maternal power assertion are less likely to have poor conscience development (Kochanska & Knaack, 2003). These explanations seem more reasonable than the far-fetched Oedipus and Electra complexes.

Freud's Views on Culture

We also need to consider Freud's views of culture. These were outlined in his 1930 classic book *Civilization and its Discontents*. Here, Freud described the concept of thanatos and the death instinct.

According to Freud (1930), the words "culture" and "civilization" are the same. He defined culture as "the sum of achievements and institutions which differentiate our lives from those of our animal forebears" (p. 49). Although affiliation with groups and with culture affords some protection to people, Freud focused on culture as a source of dissatisfaction and unhappiness for people because it restricts the id's search for pleasure and desire for freedom of expression. Overall, there are four sources of dissatisfaction: (1) the individual must give up his or her power to the broader group; (2) civilization restricts individual freedom; (3) the biological instincts of eros and thanatos must be renounced in favour of co-operation and affiliation; and (4) cultural limitations are placed on sexuality. Examples of culturally imposed limitations identified by Freud include the concepts of monogamy (as opposed to having many partners) and the cultural demand for heterosexuality.

Two other points deserve mention here. First, Freud suggested that the process of id, ego, and superego development occurs not only at the level of the individual person, but also at the societal level. As societies evolve, they must develop a superego, and the morals involved must become internalized and widely accepted without question.

Second, cultures differ in their blends of the eros and thanatos instincts, and this accounts for why some cultures appear to be much happier and more pleasant than other cultures. By extension, it can be concluded that cultures differ in their superego development. Cultures also differ in the extent to which they employ sublimation, which is the tendency to channel aggressive and sexual instincts into socially approved outlets (e.g., works of art).

Freud's Stage Theory of Psychosexual Development

Another distinguishing aspect of Freud's theory is his belief that personality develops during a series of **psychosexual stages**. Four stages and a latency period are postulated. Freud suggested that the timing and sequence of these stages is believed to be universally applicable. They are called psychosexual stages because for each stage, a particular area of the body is the main source of pleasure and sexual gratification for the id and its impulses.

Freud believed that it is important to get just the right amount of gratification at each age. A **fixation** results from getting too much or too little gratification. If a fixation develops, psychosexual development has become stuck or fixated at a particular stage, and the adult personality is a reflection of how these early stages of childhood are dealt with and resolved. One theme that binds Freud with the other theorists in this chapter is the importance of early childhood experiences. Freud was particularly deterministic; for him, personality is determined by how we resolve early conflicts during childhood. He would reject the notion that personality is set in plaster by the age of 30 because he believed it is fixed much sooner than this.

Fixations involve too little or too much gratification at each developmental stage. Thus an oral fixation can reflect too much or not enough stimulation when pleasure is centred around an infant's mouth. Similarly, an anal fixation can also reflect too much stimulation or too little stimulation during the period where toilet training is a central task and pleasure is centred around the anus region.

The theory of psychosexual stages begins with the notion that everyone starts in the **oral stage**, which stretches from birth to 18 months of age. Pleasure is centred around the mouth and involves the activities of feeding, sucking, and biting. Oral fixations reflecting understimulation are believed to contribute to a need for more support and dependency on others (oral dependent personality). Too much gratification results in later adult problems with pleasurable activities involving the mouth such as overeating and smoking (oral aggressive personality).

The **anal stage** is next. It stretches from approximately 18 months to 3 or 4 years of age. Here pleasure is centred around the anus. Too much gratification results in an anal retentive personality, which is rigid and orderly and focused on cleanliness. Too little gratification results in an anal expressive personality. This could apply to someone who is expressive, disorganized, and careless.

To illustrate how this would work, consider the obsessive–compulsive disorder (OCD) of Canadian comedian Howie Mandel, the host of the television show *Deal or No Deal.*

A Freudian would attribute Canadian comedian Howie Mandel's obsessive compulsive disorder to an intense fixation in the anal stage of psychosexual development.

Mandel's OCD includes an unwillingness to shake other people's hands (even when he is greeting them on television). A Freudian would attribute this to an intense fixation and too much gratification in the anal stage.

The most controversial stage is the **phallic stage** because it includes the aforementioned Oedipus and Electra complexes. It occurs normally during the ages of four to six years. Libidinal pleasure is now focused on the genital area, which would account for Little Hans' apparent fascination with his "widdler."

If the child has successfully resolved the issues and conflicts of each stage and received the proper amount of gratification, the next period is known as the **latency period**. This stretches from 6 to 12 years old. This is a period when psychosexual urges seem relatively dormant and are sublimated into a focus on school activities and achievements and developing and maintaining friendships.

The final stage is the **genital stage**. It coincides closely with adolescence and the physical changes that accompany puberty. Here psychosexual pleasure is refocused on the genital area with the goal of establishing healthy heterosexual relationships (as opposed to unconsciously lusting after the opposite-sexed parent as a young child).

Besides the notion of the Oedipus complex, there are several highly contentious issues of the psychosexual theory of development. The most problematic aspect is the notion that our personalities are fixed at a fairly young age and will not be modified by adult experiences. Still, Freud deserves credit for promoting the notion that development occurs in stages because this helped paved the way for developmental psychology as a separate area within psychology.

KEY POINTS

- Freud maintained that personality development involves working through a series of psychosexual stages, each of which requires resolving a particular conflict specific to each stage.
- The stages are invariant and universal. They are the oral stage, anal stage, phallic stage, latency stage, and genital stage.
- Fixation (becoming stuck in an earlier stage) occurs when the developing child experiences too much or too little sexual gratification. Adults regress to the stage where fixation occurred.

Defence Mechanisms

Freud postulated different types of anxiety depending on whether the id, ego, or superego was prevailing. If the id is predominant, then neurotic anxiety is experienced. If the ego is in control, then realistic anxiety is experienced. This is also referred to as objective anxiety. Finally, if the superego is predominant and is ready to punish us for misdeeds, then moral anxiety is experienced.

According to Freud, objective anxiety can be lessened by changing the situation or environment so that real threats are no longer a problem. Neurotic anxiety is addressed via defence mechanisms. A defence mechanism is an unconscious strategy that helps the ego by warding off anxiety, so defence mechanisms are often referred to as ego defence mechanisms. Because they operate at an unconscious level, people should not be able to directly tell you about their defence mechanisms. Defence mechanisms help the id express some of its energy so that the id does not get out of control and become too overwhelming.

What are the most well-known defence mechanisms? Table 5.1 contains a fairly comprehensive list of postulated defence mechanisms and their definitions. These defence mechanisms reflect not only the work of Freud but also of his daughter, Anna Freud, who is almost as famous as her father because she is regarded by many as the founder of the child psychoanalysis movement. Anna Freud dedicated much of her life to promoting her father's views and testing and refining them. She elaborated on defence mechanisms through her work with children and adolescents (see Freud, 1966).

Table 5.1 Descriptions of Various Defence Mechanisms

Defence Mechanism	Definition	Example
Denial	Refusing to recognize objective events in conscious awareness	Not accepting the death of someone who has been missing at sea
Displacement	Redirecting distress from original target to someone/something else	Yelling at your partner because of your frustration with your boss
Projection	Attributing personally undesirable thoughts/feelings to others	Addressing erotic urges by accusing your friend of being "a skank"
Reaction Formation	Transforming unacceptable thoughts/urges into their exact opposite	Having left-wing values and working for ultra-conservatives or vice versa
Regression	Retreating to an earlier stage when life was presumably simpler	Dealing with work stress by asking for milk and cookies and having a nap at work
Repression	Being unable to remember or reflect on past events or impulses	A child who was sexually abused unable to remember the abuse
Sublimation	Channelling unacceptable impulses into positive behaviour or artistic forms of expression	Former US president Bill Clinton playing the saxophone

Repression is regarded as one of the most significant defence mechanisms. Repression resembles the act of forgetting; distressing impulses and past experiences are submerged into the unconscious, where they continue to operate. Recall the example of Dora and Freud's contention that her asthma reflected the repressed memory of hearing her parents have sex. The suggestion that children have overheard parental sex acts is one of Freud's most frequent claims. He suggested the same thing in the case of the Wolf Man, a Russian who related a dream involving white wolves sitting in a walnut tree. He was terrified that the wolves were going to eat him.

Conflicts and traumas from early childhood that have been repressed can continue to have a strong impact on adult functioning. When adult functioning is aberrant and maladaptive, the therapist's goal is to uncover repressed conflicts and traumas and have the adult work through and resolve issues from their past.

Denial is a tendency to reject and refuse to acknowledge past traumas that have taken place. Although the psychoanalytic approach focuses on the denial of childhood events, a common tendency for anyone, including adults, is to initially use denial when faced with overwhelming traumas that seem impossible to accept. Denial may be useful in the short term as a protection against extreme stress, but long-term use of denial is a form of defensiveness that can be highly self-defeating. When denial is in the form of a defence mechanism, it involves unconscious processes and is not the same as knowing the truth but simply refusing to acknowledge the truth in public. So, in 1998, when U.S. President Bill Clinton referred to Monica Lewinsky by saying "I did not have sexual relations with that woman, Ms. Lewinsky," he was certainly denying the truth, but it was not an example of denial in the Freudian sense.

Projection is a tendency to displace unacceptable aspects of the self on other people or other things. Projection occurs because admitting unacceptable aspects of the self to oneself at a conscious level is too threatening. A common manifestation of projection is to refuse to take personal blame for negative outcomes and instead externally project the blame onto someone else. Tennen and Affleck (1990) argued that a tendency to chronically blame other people for personal misfortunes is a clear indicator of psychological distress and perhaps psychopathology.

Reaction formation is a defence mechanism that converts an unacceptable impulse, image, or thought into its exact opposite. An example of reaction formation could be falsely reacting in a sweet and agreeable manner toward someone whom you actually despise.

Displacement is a defence that involves channelling a negative emotional reaction away from the true source of the negative emotion and instead directing it toward a less threatening target. People often realize when they are taking out their frustration with someone on someone else or something else, but often they do not realize what they are doing. An example where displacement likely occurs is the concept of stress spillover. It is well known that stress at work can contribute to stress at home and vice versa. This has often been investigated within the context of the family lives of working mothers (Barnett & Marshall, 1992), but of course, this phenomenon applies to both men and women.

The defence mechanism of **regression** refers to retreating unconsciously to an earlier stage of development that was presumably not as threatening as the current age. If a behaviour that you have outgrown (e.g., sucking your thumb) suddenly returns for no apparent reason, perhaps regression is occurring. According to Freud, regression is more likely if more extreme fixation has occurred.

Defence mechanisms vary in how much they are adaptive or maladaptive. Highly maladaptive defence mechanisms are said to be **immature defences**, while adaptive defence mechanisms are **mature defences**. One relatively mature defence is **sublimation**. Sublimation is on display when aggressive or sexual impulses that would be shocking to others if openly revealed are instead channelled into socially acceptable behaviours and outlets of expression, such as works of art. A possible example of sublimation is the highly regarded artwork of Chris Sizemore, the woman with dissociative identity disorder (multiple personalities) who was the subject of the book and movie *The Three Faces of Eve*.

Rationalization is another more adaptive form of defence. It involves coming up with a cognitive explanation to counter unacceptable thoughts, impulses, and behaviours.

Baumeister, Dale, and Sommer (1998) reviewed evidence from the social psychological literature to determine whether evidence could be found for the existence of the more moderate defence mechanisms. This article was part of a highly informative series of articles on defence mechanisms published as a special issue of *The Journal of Personality*. Baumeister et al. (1998) reported that they found ample evidence of such defence mechanisms as reaction formation and denial. They also found evidence of a defence mechanism known as undoing, but this did not seem to help defend people against threat. Undoing involves a cognitive attempt to reconstruct the past so it appears that an event did not actually take place. Finally, Baumeister et al. also found evidence of projection but concluded that projection seemed to be an after effect of the defensive responsive, and they found little evidence of displacement.

Experiments by Schimel, Greenberg, and Martens (2003) have qualified the conclusions reached by Baumeister and associates by providing clearer evidence of the defensive functions of projection. They focused on people who were given anger-inducing feedback and who were then allowed to project their anger on to other people. People who were allowed to project their anger onto others had the lowest levels of anger accessibility on a subsequent word completion exercise. A second experiment showed that participants made to feel dishonest who could then project this dishonesty onto someone else seemed to be purged of their own sense of dishonesty when reassessed. Thus, there also appears to be clear evidence of projection.

According to contemporary researchers, adaptive and maladaptive defences differ not only in terms of their maturity, but also in terms of their conscious awareness. Less mature defence styles are conceptualized as unconscious responses to life stressors and only more mature defences are accessible in conscious awareness (see Paulhus, Fridhandler, & Hayes, 1997).

Contemporary Theory and Research on Repression and Other Defence Styles

Contemporary research has focused on individuals known as "repressors" who are believed to rely on repression as a defence. Repressors are identified as self-deceptive individuals who report high levels of social desirability on the Marlowe-Crowne Social Desirability Scale but low scores on trait anxiety as measured by the Taylor Manifest Anxiety Scale. Collectively, research on repressors indicates that they are quite good at avoiding exposure to emotional information; they are less likely to recall negative emotional information in the short term, and they are quick to recall happier times after watching unpleasant, upsetting stimuli (Boden & Baumeister, 1997). Current results indicate that repressors may cope better in the short term after a negative life event; for instance, they are less likely to experience symptoms of post-traumatic stress disorder after being in a motor vehicle accident (Palyo & Beck, 2005). However, the expected advantages of being a repressor, such as being protected from negative emotional states, are sometimes not found (e.g., Jorgenson & Zachariae, 2006). Other recent findings indicate that repressors are good at repressing emotion in the short term, but there is a "rebound effect," and they are more likely to suffer from intrusive emotional memories in the long run (see Geraerts, Merckelbach, Jelicic, & Smeets, in press). In addition, rather than having a healthy, adaptive style, repressors tend to have reduced levels of immune system functioning (Jamner & Leigh, 1999), and a heightened stress response in terms of cortisol levels (Brown et al., 1996), which could eventually result in health problems.

Other research has compared various defence styles within the same investigation. **Defence styles** are the typical ways that people respond when feeling anxious and challenged. Although most defence styles are unconscious, they are often assessed subjectively via self-report questionnaires. Is this appropriate? How meaningful are self-reports on unconscious processes? A similar problem applies to other research on individual differences in phenomena that reflect intrapsychic processes (i.e., does it make sense to use self-report measures to assess self-deception?). Various researchers have been critical of self-report measures of defence mechanisms and have recommended the inclusion of observer ratings (see Davidson & MacGregor, 1998; Perry & Ianni, 1998). This suggestion is supported by evidence indicating that there are only moderate correlations between self-reports and informant ratings of defence styles (Bronnec et al., 2005; Flett, Besser, & Hewitt, 2005).

There are several well-known measures of defence styles, including the Defense Mechanism Inventory and Defense Styles Questionnaire-40 (DSQ-40; Andrews et al., 1993). The DSQ assesses mature defence styles (e.g., anticipation, humour, rationalization, sublimation, and suppression), neurotic defence styles (e.g., idealization, passive aggression, pseudoaltruism, reaction formation, and undoing), and immature defence styles (e.g., acting out, autistic fantasy, denial, devaluation, displacement, dissociation, isolation, projection, somatization, and splitting). Although defence styles can be evaluated with questionnaire measures, other researchers (e.g., Cramer, 1991) have been able to assess defence mechanisms by relying on the projective tests that are introduced in subsequent segments of this chapter and in Chapter 6.

George Vaillant and Phoebe Cramer are two prominent theorists and researchers who study defence styles. Much current work is based on Vaillant's (1977, 1992) hierarchical model of defence mechanisms. According to this model, defence styles vary in their relative levels of maladaptiveness versus adaptiveness, as well as their associated levels of developmental maturity. The four levels described by Vaillant (1994) are psychotic defences (delusions and distortions), immature defences (projection, denial), neurotic defences (reaction formation), and mature defences (sublimation). Whereas immature defences are evident early in development (Cramer, 1987, 2006), when mature defences do emerge, they are believed to occur later in development (for a summary, see Punamaki, Kanninen, Qouta, & El-Sarraj, 2002). Clearly, however, some adults continue to retain an immature defence style that renders them vulnerable to various forms of psychological distress (Vaillant & Vaillant, 1992).

Vaillant's and Freud's views of defence mechanisms differ in three key respects. First, as alluded to above, whereas Freud regarded most defences as primarily maladaptive, Vaillant acknowledges the adaptiveness of certain defences. Second, both authors focus on the role of early experiences in developing defences, but Vaillant allows for current experiences to also have a role. Finally, whereas Freud focused on the internal, intrapsychic origins of defences, Valliant accepts that external events also can have an impact.

Phoebe Cramer has been in the forefront of important research and theory on defence styles for the past two decades. She has outlined a developmental model of defence styles that is based on the notion that certain key defences are dominant depending on one's age. Denial is the predominant defence among preschool children, and then denial becomes less evident (Cramer, 1991). Middle childhood and late adolescence is characterized by a gradual increase in projection. Finally, among college-aged participants, the predominant psychological defence is identification, which presumably requires age-related advances in cognitive development and self-awareness.

KEY POINTS

- Defence mechanisms ward off anxiety and help the ego maintain control over the id and superego.
- There are relatively mature defence mechanisms (e.g., sublimation) and immature defence mechanisms (e.g., displacement). Mature defences are more open to conscious awareness.
- With the exception of displacement, contemporary empirical work attests to the validity of postulated defence mechanisms.

Evaluation of Freud's Contributions

The research just described indicates that Freud continues to have a lasting influence on the personality field. Still, Freud's theory has been criticized on many grounds. Salient criticisms include the scientific basis of psychoanalysis, such as the apparent abstractness and untestable aspects of certain concepts (see Eysenck, 1985). This concern was referred to in the quotes that opened this chapter. These criticisms are understandable given Freud's explicit goal of establishing psychoanalysis as a science. However, in the interest of fairness, certain concepts (such as defence mechanisms) are amenable to empirical research, and authors such as Westen (1998) have mounted spirited defences of the scientific status of Freud's theory based on extant research.

Another overarching concern of Freud's work is the great importance that he placed on the concept of libido and psychosexual energy. Motives may be more general and may not involve sexual drives. Indeed, Freud acknowledged this somewhat when he incorporated the death instinct and aggression.

Another limitation is Freud's reliance on the case study method. This chapter has already mentioned the case studies of Dora and the Wolf Man. The Wolf Man case is relatively unique as a study of a male because Freud's insights were derived primarily from case studies of middle-to upper-class women in Vienna. A general problem with case studies is that they are not generalizable to the population as a whole. Of course, other theorists such as Allport would applaud the case study method in that Freud was interested in studying the whole person and did not restrict his focus to a small number of isolated variables studied across a group of people.

One criticism of psychoanalytic treatment is that in the Freudian approach, the agent of change is the therapist himself or herself. The psychoanalyst's job is to analyze and provide interpretations to clients. In contrast, subsequent theorists such as Rogers and Maslow emphasize the importance of the client's self-discovery and self-awareness, and how each person has to act as the agent of change.

Another concern is Freud's patronizing view of women, including the notion that women lack a strong superego. Related to this concern is the tendency for most sceptics to regard the Oedipus and Electra complexes as patently absurd.

Finally, many authors have taken issue with the notion that personality is fixed and is based on early childhood experiences. Even psychoanalytic theorists such as John Bowlby, the attachment style theorist, allow for the possibility that subsequent life experiences as an adult can influence personality development.

Although Freud is a highly controversial figure, there is no doubt that he made several important contributions. First, his developmental theory paved the way for subsequent advances in the study of children, and although he was not the first to discuss the concept, he certainly drew attention to the importance of unconscious factors.

Second, contemporary research leaves little doubt that the unconscious exists and can have a profound influence on us (e.g., Najstrom & Jansson, 2006). Canadian researcher Mark Baldwin and his associates provided one of the clearest laboratory demonstrations of the role of the unconscious (Baldwin, Carrell, & Lopez, 1990). In their initial study, these investigators used a tachistoscope to present graduate students with either the image of the scowling face of the chair of the psychology department or the image of a more pleasant visage, but below the participant's conscious level of awareness. A second study involved presenting devout Roman Catholic women with either a photograph of the Pope making a disapproving face or an unfamiliar person displaying a more pleasant expression. Baldwin et al. (1990) reported that being exposed to negative expressions from the departmental chair or the Pope had the effect of increasing the participants' levels of anxiety and caused them to endorse more negative self-evaluations. Yet they couldn't verbalize why they felt anxious nor did they make any mention of the photos that were presented to them! Westen (1998) summarized other evidence showing that there is compelling evidence for the existence of the unconscious, and that there are multiple unconscious processes that involve various neural systems.

Freud also deserves to be commended for his role in linking personality and culture. His book *Civilization and Its Discontents* focused on how personalities exist within and are linked to a broader culture. Also, recall that Freud's theory was used by anthropologists who compared the modal personality and the national character of various cultures.

Finally, Freud should be commended for attempting to provide a comprehensive, controversial theory that drew the public's attention to the importance of psychological factors. Freud also deserves credit for training and influencing a host of other theorists who went on to make their own major contributions. The work of some of these theorists is described in subsequent sections of this chapter.

THE NEO-FREUDIANS: CARL JUNG'S ANALYTICAL PSYCHOLOGY

> In "Wrapped Around Your Finger" there's the classic line where he goes, "Things they would not teach me of in college." Sting, I just want to say, I went to college and I learned all of this Jungian shit. It's just Psych 101: It had no mystique for me at all.
>
> —*Stewart Copeland of The Police, taking issue with the influence of Carl Jung's theory on Sting and the album* Synchronicity *(in Gabarino,* 2000)

Carl Jung accepted some of Freud's core beliefs, but rejected others.

Some people have argued that **Carl Jung's** theory has had as much impact as Freud's theory. Jung was a Swiss psychiatrist who grew up in Basel, Switzerland. He was the son of a church pastor, and this may have led to his great interest in religious symbols. Jung died in 1961 at the age of 85. In his final year, he published his autobiography *Memories, Dreams, Reflections*, which contained his own self-analysis.

He is regarded as a neo-Freudian because he accepted many of Freud's core beliefs, yet rejected others. Freud and Jung were close associates for many years. They first met in 1907. Freud came to regard Jung as his successor, and he referred to Jung as his "crown prince." He also asked Jung to never waver in his belief in the psychosexual theory. Jung's many contributions include becoming the first president of the Psychoanalytical Society.

In his autobiography, Jung (1961) acknowledged that he was warned by many scholars that he should not become affiliated with Freud if he wished to obtain an academic career. He noted that Freud was *persona non grata,* and at academic conferences, Freud's views were discussed in the corridors, but not on the main floor. However, Jung admired many aspects of Freud's work, including his emphasis on the unconscious and the importance of defences such as repression, as well as the impact of early experiences. Jung also believed in the significance of dreams and the general usefulness of the projective techniques described below. Jung found that the study of dreams and Freudian dream analysis was particularly helpful in understanding "schizophrenic forms of expression" (p. 169).

At the same time, Jung was troubled by certain aspects of Freud's theory. He questioned the presumed basis for repression and the nature of unconscious conflicts. Jung rejected the notion that conflicts reflect psychosexual energy. Specifically, he observed that Freud "considered the cause of the repression to be a sexual trauma. From my practice, however, I was familiar with numerous cases of neuroses in which the question of sexuality played a subordinate part, other factors standing in the foreground—for example, the problem of social adaptation, of oppression by tragic circumstances of life, prestige considerations, and so on" (p. 170). Thus, Jung rejected the notion of psychosexual energy and instead focused on psychosocial energy. He endorsed the concept of libido but saw it as a general form of psychic energy that was not exclusively sexual in origin.

Jung also rejected Freud's notion that dreams have a deceptive aspect to them. Jung regarded dreams as a natural form of self-expression, and although the symbols in dreams still required interpretation and understanding, they were not a reflection of psychosexual conflicts.

In his autobiography, Jung also expressed negative views of Freud's personal qualities. Jung felt without a doubt that Freud was blind to his own human failings. He felt that Freud was in the grips of his own neurosis and was far too preoccupied with sexual matters, which blinded him to other possibilities. He was dogmatic and stubborn and refused to consider other possibilities (i.e., he was low in the openness trait). This rigidity was especially problematic with respect to Freud's views of spirituality. Jung placed a great deal of importance on spiritual matters, and this led ultimately to Jung's emphasis on the collective unconscious, which is described below. But how did Freud regard spirituality?

Jung indicated that whenever there was an indication that intellectual spirituality was being reflected, either in a specific person or displayed in a work of art, Freud attributed it to repressed sexuality. And, if sexuality was not directly implicated, Freud said it reflected "psychosexuality." In his autobiography, Jung said:

> I protested that this hypothesis, carried to its logical conclusion, would lead to an annihilating judgement upon culture. Culture would then appear as a mere farce, the morbid consequence of repressed sexuality. "Yes," [Freud] assented, "so it is, and that is just a curse of fate against which we are powerless to contend." (Jung, 1961, p. 172–173)

Unfortunately, Jung and Freud eventually came to a parting of the ways as Freud became increasingly disenchanted with Jung's unwillingness to accept some of his core beliefs and instead propose alternative beliefs. Freud actually developed a tendency to have fainting spells when in the presence of Jung, and the final straw was when Jung did indeed refute Freud's sexual theory in published form. At this point, Jung became an outcast as former friends and associates of Freud no longer accepted him, and this caused Jung to have significant personal distress for many years. Out of this distress, however, grew one of the more compelling personality theories in existence.

The Personal and the Collective Unconscious

Jung believed that we have a personal unconscious that reflects our unique experiences and conflicts, with the above noted caveat that these experiences were not exclusively sexual. It is the personal unconscious that distinguishes us and makes us unique.

The personal unconscious is composed of feeling-toned complexes that reflect personal conflicts and tensions. Jung is credited with introducing the term "complex" (Storr, 1988), meaning a highly emotional image of a certain psychic situation. This image is unified, powerful, and autonomous, and has a theme that is inconsistent with the typical attitude of consciousness. Jung suggested that an unconscious complex acts like "an animated foreign body" injecting itself into the consciousness. In general, the personal unconscious consists of forgotten or repressed memories that were previously conscious.

Jung also postulated a collective unconscious and suggested that this is his most controversial and least understood concept. The collective unconscious is a shared experience that makes us similar to everyone else. Jung observed as a part of his own self-analysis, including his assessment of his own dreams, that certain symbols continually reappeared. At the same time, he became deeply interested in the myths and legends of various cultures. He came to believe that there is a collective unconscious that accounts for the seemingly spiritual influences that Freud saw as sexual in origin. Where does it come from? Jung argued that it is inherited.

The collective unconscious is composed of archetypes. Archetypes are symbols that reflect our instincts and how they are expressed. Jung suggested that archetypes are primordial images that reflect the themes that stretch back to our early ancestors. Because these images go back thousands of years, Jung suggested that our unconscious psyche is "immensely old."

Storr (1988) suggested that Jung got the initial idea for the collective unconscious from his work with schizophrenics. He was puzzled by the bizarre hallucinations and delusions reported by these patients, and the reoccurring themes that could be found in them. He realized that the hallucinations and delusions did not reflect actual experiences of these patients, so he came to believe that they reflected experiences passed on from previous generations.

Specific Archetypes

There are many archetypes. The most central archetype is the Mandala, which is represented by images of circles. Jung spent extensive periods painting and drawing the Mandala. The Mandala reflects the ultimate goal of developing a complete, whole, unified self. Because it is part of the collective unconscious, the goal of a complete and whole self applies to everyone. However, everyone is to have a unique self, so a key process here is **individuation**, which occurs when a person becomes a psychological individual by achieving a separate unity or whole. Jung's focus on the unity of personality is directly attributable to his experiences with his 15-year-old female cousin, who later became the subject of his doctoral thesis (see Storr, 1988). His cousin claimed to be a medium who was controlled by different personalities (i.e., she had multiple personality disorder). This is one of the earliest recorded cases of this phenomenon. Jung inferred from this case that mental health occurs when the person has a unified, organized sense of themselves. In contrast, mental illness reflects a fragmented self where there are several incomplete personalities lurking in the unconscious.

Besides the Mandala, other prominent archetypes include the mother, the wise old man, the hero, the trickster, and the anima/animus. The **anima/animus archetype** is a highly significant one because the anima refers to the hidden, feminine side of men, and the animus refers to the hidden, masculine side of women. According to Jung, regardless of biological sex, we all have both masculine and feminine characteristics. Both the anima and the animus have positive and negative features, and, according to Jung (1961), it is the positive side of the anima that communicates aspects of the unconscious to the conscious.

The sex role personality literature incorporated this notion into the anima/animus concept of androgyny. Androgynous individuals are characterized jointly by the instrumental characteristics associated stereotypically with masculinity, and the expressive characteristics associated stereotypically with femininity. Androgyny is believed to be highly adaptive because someone with high androgyny is capable of acting masculine or feminine when required.

David Bowie, as Ziggy Stardust, embraced androgyny displaying both masculine and feminine characteristics.

Finally, the **shadow archetype** also deserves special mention. The shadow archetype refers to a dark side of personality that is in all of us, according to Jung. Whereas Freud postulated thanatos (the death instinct) to account for aggression, war, and mistreatment of others, Jung suggested that the shadow is responsible. Other authors have picked up on this theme. Stevens (1995) discussed the relevance of Jungian archetypes in explaining widespread societal tendencies for human aggression in the form of war. He suggested that nations engage in conflict and war when their shadows are projected outward onto others and mutual shadow projection takes place. One pessimistic aspect of this notion is that since the collective unconscious will always include the shadow, it is likely that wars will continue throughout history.

KEY POINTS

- Jung distinguished the personal unconscious (accounting for individual uniqueness) and the collective unconscious (accounting for similarities across people).
- The collective unconscious consists of archetypes, which are universal symbols. The collective unconscious with its archetypes is genetically inherited.
- The Mandala archetype, according to Jung, reflects the ultimate goal: the development of our own unified, whole sense of self.
- The shadow archetype reflects the dark side of personality. The anima/animus reflects the masculine and feminine aspects of personality. According to Jung, everyone has a dark side and everyone is capable of masculine and feminine tendencies.

Popular Applications of Jungian Concepts

It has been argued by many scholars that immensely popular books and movie series have such widespread appeal because they include characters who represent the archetypes of the collective unconscious. When we find certain movies appealing, for example, it is because we are recognizing elements in the movie that are also located deep within our collective unconscious. Movies that have been analyzed from this perspective include the George Lucas series of *Star Wars* movies as well as *The Lord of the Rings* films. The hero archetype in *Star Wars* is represented by Luke Skywalker and Han Solo (see Phipps, 1983). The mother archetype is represented by Princess Leah. The shadow archetype is represented by Darth Vader, and the wise old man archetype is, of course, represented by Yoda. Archetypes represented in *The Lord of the Rings* include the child (pick any Hobbit here), the hero (Aragorn), the shadow (Sauron and the Nazgul), the trickster (Gollum), and the wise old man (Gandalf).

Movies such as *The Lord of the Rings* are appealing because they contain recognizable archetypes, such as the hero archetype Aragorn, portrayed by Viggo Mortensen.

Jung's archetypes have also been represented in popular music, such as the album *Synchronicity* by The Police, one of the most popular albums of all time.

Jung was greatly influenced by Chinese thought and the classic text *I Ching*, and the concept of synchronicity is derived from the impact of Chinese concepts on his thinking (see Stein, 2005). **Synchronicity** is a term suggested by Jung to refer to the coincidental co-occurrence of two things that are actually paired randomly but seem to go together. As an example, Jung told the story of a female client who was recounting a dream in which she was given a golden scarab, an Egyptian symbol of birth or rebirth. As she was describing her dream, Jung heard a tapping on his window. The noise was made by a greenish-tinged gold beetle. This beetle closely resembles the scarab in appearance. Jung opened the window, grabbed the beetle and presented it to the woman, telling her that her scarab had just arrived.

Introversion–Extroversion

In his autobiography, Jung acknowledged that he came up with the insights that formed the basis of his 1921 book *Psychological Types* because he was eager to develop concepts that clearly distinguished him from Freud and Alfred Adler. It was noted earlier in this book that Jung was the first personologist to highlight the differences between the psychological types of introversion and extroversion. He remarked that "it is one's psychological type which from the outset determines and limits a person's judgment" (p. 233). Recall that extroverted people are oriented outward toward other people, while introverted people are oriented inward toward their own thoughts and perceptions and are often quite reserved individuals. Jung suggested that extroversion is libido (psychic energy) turned outward, and introversion is libido turned inward. Extroversion or introversion reflects a psychological type only when this tendency becomes habitual.

According to Jung, introversion and extroversion have associated cognitive differences. Introverts tend to focus their attention inward on their own thoughts and perceptions. In contrast, extroverts focus their attention outward and are constantly scanning the environment. While other people often capture their attention, Jung argued that the cognitive style of extroverts is more general and they will also focus on objects in the environment. Because they are more attuned to what is happening in their surroundings, Jung suggested that extroverts are more objective in their approach to life, while introverts are more subjective and guided by their own intuitions.

Jung was among the first theorists to tie personality differences to cultural differences. He had a great interest in societies around the world, in part due to his desire to identify universal archetypes. While archetypes are common to all cultures, Jung suggested that cultures differ in terms of whether they are extroverted or introverted. He suggested that Western societies are extroverted, while Eastern societies, including Asian cultures, are introverted. He went on to suggest that there are associated differences in thinking, especially thinking about the self. Western society has a conscious awareness of the ego and its role in the environment, while the goal in Eastern society is to transcend consciousness and, at an unconscious level, attain an "ego-less mental condition." Eastern society incorporates a focus on transcending the self, and this is more likely to be accomplished by withdrawing from the realities of the external world. The Eastern goal is self-liberation.

In addition to introversion–extroversion, Jung also posited other individual differences that reflect unique ways in which a person relates to other people, the world, and information available in this world. He referred to these as "psychological functions" and there are four functions altogether. These are referred to as preferences for how to interact with and engage our worlds.

The four functions are sensing, intuition, thinking, and feeling. Jung distinguished between sensing and intuition (taking in sensory information versus coming up with insights that may not be obvious). Jung suggested that sensing and intuition were two irrational functions. He contrasted these with the two rational functions of thinking and feeling (a more logical analysis of information according to either unconscious thoughts or feelings).

Jung indicated that extroversion and introversion combine with the four functions to produce eight psychological types. These are described briefly in Table 5.2, along with some of Jung's observations about these types.

Table 5.2 Jung's Psychological Types

Extroverted Rational Types
Extroverted Thinking Type • Objective thinking about stimuli in the environment; more common in men than women
Extroverted Feeling Type • Feelings used as a guide to external life realities; more common among women than men
Extroverted Irrational Types
Extroverted Sensation Type • Guided by sensation of concrete object • Enjoyment of knowing things through one's senses • Accepts that things will happen and wishes to enjoy their sensation; more common in men
Extroverted Intuitive Type • Focus on external objects, but to assess these rely on personal judgements and intuitions • Most complicated extroverted type intuits the possibilities of the external stimuli in the environment; may be highly creative as a result
Introverted Rational Types
Introverted Thinking Type • Influenced greatly by ideas, but ideas come from inward, subjective thought inside the self • May have little bearing to reality of external world • Would be a poor teacher due to unawareness of students as external objects; inability to relate to students' experiences
Introverted Feeling Type • Deeply felt conscious images kept inside the self seem cold because of inability to focus on emotions of other people, but personal emotions are intense • More common in women; tendency to be silent about emotions and linked with melancholy
Introverted Irrational Types
Introverted Sensation Type • Relies on arbitrary associations between subjective sensations and objective stimuli • Unconscious focus on the sensations of a mythological world • Oriented not by sound judgement but by what happens
Introverted Intuitive Type • Professing or proclaiming without reason • A person who is aloof from tangible reality • Most of all, represses the sensations of the external object

The Myers-Briggs Type Indicator

The Myers-Briggs Type Indicator (MBTI) is one of the most widely used personality measures in the world. It was developed by a mother-daughter team in the 1940s and is based on Jung's theory. It uses the four dimensions outlined above. In total, 16 possible combinations exist and each person would fall into 1 of 16 type categories. For example, a person deemed to be the ISFJ type (introverted, sensing, feeling, judging) is quiet, conscientiousness, and quite perfectionistic, while the ESTJ type (extroverted, sensing, thinking, and judging) is practical, reliable, and likes to run and organize group activities.

How popular is the MBTI? Estimates indicate that it was administered to more than 3 million people in 1993 (Paul, 2004; Webb, 1990). Currently, it is used by 89 of the Fortune 100 companies throughout the world (Paul, 2004). Student applications include using the inventory to pair up college roommates and to maximize the benefits of career counselling.

It seems that the MBTI can be used to analyze just about anyone. In fact, recently, Howell (2004) reported students' perceptions of the personality structure of Jesus Christ based on their beliefs about how Jesus would score on the MBTI and another popular measure tapping Jungian beliefs, the Kiersey Temperament Sorter II (Keirsey, 1998). The results showed that Jesus was regarded as being an Extroverted Feeler. Students who felt they should model Jesus were more likely to regard him as a Judger, while students who placed less importance of modelling Jesus saw him as a Perceiver. Not surprisingly, Jesus has also been analyzed from a five-factor model perspective, and determined to be somewhat introverted yet agreeable.

The measure's validity is shown by research linking MBTI measures of judgement and intuition with social information processing (Edwards, Lanning, & Hooker, 2002). This research established that the MBTI predicted performance on a social–cognitive task, above and beyond the effects of the traits of the five-factor model. Thus, the MBTI has "incremental validity."

But is the use of the scale warranted? In her popular book *The Cult of Personality*, Annie Murphy Paul was highly critical of the applied use of personality tests in general, and she devotes extensive coverage to the concerns associated with the MBTI in particular. According to Paul (2004), the most damning criticism reflects the fact that the scale leads to decisions reflecting a categorical approach instead of focusing on continuous personality dimensions. Test–retest studies indicate that anywhere between 39 and 76% of respondents actually change personality types when re-evaluated! How can this be if personality is supposed to be relatively stable? Many of these changes could be due to ambiverts who score as extroverted at one point and introverted at another.

According to Paul (2004), the MBTI has now been translated into 16 languages. Research has highlighted the problems of translating the MBTI. Past research found with Chinese versions that an unacceptable number of items were associated with the wrong factors following factor analyses, and several items could not be directly translated because a literal translation changed the item's true meaning. Also, the sensing–intuition scale divided into three distinct factors instead of the intended factor (Osterlind, Danmin, Yanyan, & Chia, 2004).

Evaluation of Jung's Contributions

Carl Jung's theory is subject to the same general criticism that applies to the psychoanalytic field; that is, he conducted no empirical tests of his notions and, as was the case with Freud, it is regarded as unscientific. Also, certain assumptions seem questionable. For instance, can part of the psyche really be inherited from ancestors? Is it really the case with archetypes such as the shadow that there is a dark side lurking in everyone, or is it that only certain people are capable of evil? Do all people have both a masculine and feminine side (anima/animus)? In general, some themes reflecting the collective unconscious may not apply to everyone.

These problems notwithstanding, it can be argued that Jung has not received his fair due, so it is difficult to be too critical of his work. Jung has had a great impact on personality assessment by providing the theoretical basis for the MBTI. In addition, he was the first to identify the distinction between introversion and extroversion as a personality type, and this dimension is now afforded a central place in the predominant five-factor trait model. In addition, the lay public has a very clear understanding of what is meant by an introvert and extrovert. A third point is particularly relevant to one of the central emphases of this book—that is, the study of personality from a cultural perspective. Jung's concept of the collective unconscious and his analysis of archetypes across cultures, both contemporary and historical, helped promote the study of commonalities among people in addition to individual differences. And he provided a very testable hypothesis by suggesting that extroversion characterizes Western tendencies and introversion characterizes Eastern tendencies. Finally, Jung also helped promote the study of cognitive factors in personality by suggesting that extroverts focus attention outward on the environment, while introverts focus attention inward. Of course, he also postulated a personality type dominated by thinking (as opposed to feeling and perception).

THE NEO-FREUDIANS: ALFRED ADLER

Alfred Adler created the movement of individual psychology to reflect the fact that each person is unique.

Alfred Adler was born in Vienna, Austria, in 1870. He was another psychiatrist with medical training. Initially, Adler played a central role in the Vienna Psychoanalytic Society, but when it became increasingly apparent that his views were greatly at variance with Freud's, he was forced to leave this society in 1911. He then set up his own movement known as individual psychology. Other noteworthy developments included working as a physician in the First World War and moving to the United States in 1935. Adler died at age 67 in 1937.

Alfred Adler's movement is called **individual psychology** to reflect the fact that each person is unique and no previous theory adequately reflects this individuality. According to Adler, the term "individual psychology" captures the uniqueness of each individual in developing his or her own style of life.

Adler was also a close friend and associate of Freud for almost a decade. Nevertheless, in the end, according to Ansbacher (2004), Adler claimed to have learned nothing of value from Freud. Adler began as a psychoanalyst and was the editor of the first psychoanalytic journal (Ansbacher, 2004). He accepted Freud's notion that people are motivated by biological factors, but the biological factors of importance are not sexual urges, but instead are determined to overcome organ inferiority, which is explained below.

The Inferiority Complex

> George Harrison: *You've got an inferiority complexity, haven't you?*
> Ringo Starr: *It's why I play the drums. It's my act of compensating.*
> —*From the* 1964 *Beatles movie* A Hard Day's Night

Adler originated the concept of the **inferiority complex**. Adler (1958) defined this as a condition that "appears before a problem for which an individual is not always properly adapted or equipped, and expresses his conviction that he is unable to solve it" (p. 52). The inferiority complex is a sense of not measuring up to expectations and not being on par with other people.

According to Adler, inferiority feelings always produce a palpable sense of tension. Inferiority feelings are not necessarily abnormal and can be the catalyst for dramatic improvements that ultimately benefit mankind. Adler further suggested that inferiority feelings are highly idiosyncratic. In fact, he felt that inferiority feelings can be expressed in at least 1,000 ways!

Of course, for many, inferiority feelings contribute to a deep sense of neurosis. Adler (1958) suggested that neurotics will often openly deny their feelings of inferiority, so we must analyze behaviours to see evidence of inferiority complexes. This goes back to our previous discussion of the extent to which personality self-reports correspond to actual behaviours.

Initial versions of Adler's theory focused on his belief that everyone suffers from **organ inferiority** (biological weaknesses), while subsequent versions of his theory also allowed for a sense of inferiority in a psychological sense. Inferiority can be manifest in various ways. For instance, Adler suggested that show-offs act in an exaggerated way to overcompensate for feelings of inferiority.

Adler argued that we seek to overcome this sense of inferiority by striving for superiority and perfection. Superiority striving is, in essence, a quest to be godlike. Superiority is seen as a dynamic, life-striving tendency that reflects a continuous process. Adler suggested that striving for superiority is behind every human creation and is the source of all contributions to culture.

Superiority striving via perfectionism is a driven form of existence that is overcompensation for feelings of being inferior to other people. Specifically, Adler (1938/1998) stated that "individuals, perpetually comparing themselves with the unattainable ideal of perfection, are always possessed and spurred on by a sense of inferiority" (p. 35–36). Although organ inferiority and the inferiority complex were regarded by Adler as universally applicable concepts that we all must deal with, he noted explicitly that not all people are created equal. He attributed individual differences to differences in health, biological constitution, and environments.

Styles of Life and the Meaning of Life

As noted above, Adler also claimed that each person has a unique style of life. Styles of life are forms of individual expression that derive from early life difficulties and the ways in which an individual strives to achieve goals. In his compelling book *What Life Should Mean to You*, Adler (1931/1958) suggested that each person's existence depends upon finding his or her own unique meaning in life, and this "useful life" flows from co-operation with and a commitment to other people. He then went on to identify three situations that can result in "gravely mistaken" meanings in life: (1) organ inferiority; (2) pampered children; and (3) neglected children. He suggested that children with an identifiable physical deficiency could grow up to feel humiliated by the world, and this is exacerbated by making social comparisons with children without a similar affliction. While this may foster a defensive and cynical stance, Adler noted that many people overcome organ inferiority and go on to greatness, so this situation can be overcome.

As for pampered children, Adler (1958) suggested that these children have been made to feel prominent without having to work for it. He suggested that when the pampered child becomes an adult, this type of individual may become among the most dangerous class of people in our communities because they will not react well when they are no longer pampered and life experiences no longer make them feel prominent. Adler went on to suggest that if an Oedipus complex does exist, being pampered is at the root of it. Pampering limits social excursions outside the home and promotes a heightened focus on family relations.

Finally, as for neglected children, because they have experienced a life without friendliness, Adler suggested that they grow up to expect a hostile interpersonal world that will always be cold to them. This contributes to a lack of trust of others.

Because difficulties early in life are important, Adler emphasized the need for therapists to focus on an individual's old remembrances. He said that old remembrances are the key to understanding styles of life because our childhood memories are the early prototypes for adult styles of life. Accordingly, the primary goal of individual psychology is to understand the causes of a person's style of life.

He proposed four styles of life, with three of the four styles being highly maladaptive or "mistaken." Mistaken styles include the ruling types, the getting types, and the avoiding types. The positive style of life is the socially useful type. These various types are described below.

The three negative styles of life seem to be precursors of similar concepts suggested by Karen Horney. The ruling type refers to an individual who needs to control others. If one seeks to dominate and rule over others, it is important to be competitive, so the ruling type tends to apply to higher achievers with a great desire for control. The ruling types of the world have little hesitation in letting other people know about their successes. They will let other people know about their triumphs in a way that mocks or belittles these people. Adler has referred to this as the deprecation complex.

The getting type is a person who is very dependent on others and lets other people take the lead with various things, including activities that need to get completed and decisions that must be made. The getting type is the end result of being a pampered child.

The third type of person is the avoiding type. As might be expected, these people are highly avoidant and they try to run away from problems so that they will not be defeated or undermined in some way. People who are the avoiding type are regarded as socially avoidant and isolated people who do not mix well with others. According to Adler, these individuals convince themselves that they are superior to other people, but this is not a deep-seated conviction since it is very fragile, and the avoiding type can be hypersensitive to the experience of negative feedback.

Finally, the socially useful type applies to people who perceive a sense of self-control, and they have a great desire to contribute to the general welfare of society. A high degree of social interest is an important feature of this type of person, and this concept is afforded a prominent role in Adler's theory. It is described in more detail below.

Social Interest

Social interest grows out of a person's ability to master three basic tasks of life: work, love, and social interaction (Adler, 1938). Adler traced the early roots of social interest back to the impact of the mother on the child and suggested that poor social interest was due to two possibilities: (1) the mother makes social contact with others difficult or does not regard it as important; and (2) the mother pampers the child and smothers him or her with affection so that contact with other people is not necessary for the child.

How critical is social interest? Adler concluded that increasing social interest and social co-operation could actually save an individual. Adler would be very much in favour of volunteering to help others because ultimately this will help the self. Indeed, volunteerism research attests to the boost in self-esteem that comes from helping others.

Unfortunately, empirical research on social interest has been restricted by some key limitations. Particularly noteworthy is a meta-analytic study that found exceptionally low intercorrelations among five well-known measures of social interest (Bass, Curlette, Kern, & McWilliams, 2002). That is, the five measures differ substantially in their content. However, on a positive note, the meta-analysis also confirmed that a wide variety of theoretically relevant constructs are associated with social interest, so the construct itself seems to have validity.

As indicated above, as a supplement to the inferiority complex, Adler also suggested the presence of a superiority complex that is designed to mask the presence of the inferiority complex. The superiority complex involves a complete lack of social interest as the individual "aims for the glitter of personal conquest" (p. 38). The superiority complex involves a conscious sense of possessing superhuman gifts and abilities and a tendency to make extreme demands of both self and others. According to Adler, the superiority complex can involve many negative attributes, including arrogance, snobbishness, boastfulness, and a tendency to disparage and domineer over weak others while fawning on prominent people. Adler identified depreciating others as a by-product of the superiority complex.

KEY POINTS

- Adler suggested that most people have an inferiority complex. Initial versions of his theory focused on inferiority stemming from the body (organ inferiority). We resolve a sense of inferiority by developing a superiority complex and striving for perfection.
- Mistaken styles of life (reflected by the ruling, getting, and avoiding types) can be overcome by developing social interest.
- Measures of social interest are not highly correlated with each other, but they have validity in their links with predicted outcomes.

Adlerian Analysis of the Unabomber

The journal *Individual Psychology* (which is dedicated to Adler's views) contains a paper by Leeper, Carwile, and Huber (2002) that was an Adlerian analysis of Theodore Kaczynski, who is also known as the Unabomber. Kaczynski is notorious for expressing his upset with technological developments by sending mail bombs, which resulted in the deaths of 3 people and injuries to 29 others over a span of two decades. Kaczynski was the subject of the most extensive manhunt in the history of the Federal Bureau of Investigation. He was captured when his brother turned him in after recognizing the writing in the *Unabomber's Manifesto*, a document that summarized the Unabomber's beliefs.

Leeper, Carwile, and Huber (2002) argued that this is a classic example of what happens in extreme cases of the superiority complex. Kaczynski suffered from a profound lack of social interest, even though he believed that he was acting in the public's best interests. He responded to his sense of inferiority by overcompensating in a way that is very much in keeping with the superiority complex and his grandiose goals. These grandiose goals and thinking patterns are clearly on display in the content of the Unabomber's Manifesto, a copy of which is easy to locate on the Internet. Leeper and colleagues also noted that, in keeping with grandiose goals, Kaczynski belittled others, confirming the depreciation tendency identified by Adler. We will return to his case in the next chapter because of Kaczynski's connection with Harvard University and noted personality theorist Henry Murray.

Birth Order and Personality

Adler's theory included his deep conviction that birth order and personality are associated. Adler maintained that first-borns are overly conservative and too willing to bow to authority, which they learned as a way to placate their parents. Adler also maintained that only children were deficient, in part because they were likely to be pampered, and the lack of siblings could mitigate against developing social interest.

Second-born children are seen as ideal because the parents have learned from their mistakes. Do you think it is a coincidence that Adler was a second-born child who was described as jealous of his older brother?

International Focus on Discovery 5.1 extends Adler's views on personality and birth order by examining the implications of the one-child policy in China. Many people believe that birth order makes a difference, and books for the public on birth order tend to sell well. What does research tell us about the empirical link between birth order and personality? Consistent with the theme expressed in Chapter 1, here is an example of a topic where it is important to supplement common sense with empirical data.

International Focus on Discovery 5.1 The One-Child Policy in China and the "Little Emperor Phenomenon" in Only Children

Are you an only child? It was noted that Adler had particular disdain for the attributes and characteristics of only children. Does research support these views? In general, empirical analyses of the personality characteristics of only children have found few differences between only children and other children, and most stereotypes about only children (that they are self-focused prima donnas who are unable to interact with others) have not been supported (Falbo & Polit, 1986). One of the leading researchers in this area is Toni Falbo from the University of Texas at Austin. Falbo is an only child and the mother of an only child (Randall, 2004). Falbo traces the stereotypes about only children back over 100 years to the historical views of G. Stanley Hall, American child psychology expert, who concluded that "being an only child is a disease in itself" (see Randall, 2004). Falbo argued that if her research had confirmed that only children were, in her terms "sick, sick, sick," then this would have been award-winning data that would have "skyrocketed" her career. In fact, evidence of dysfunction among only children is quite limited.

Toni Falbo at the University of Texas at Austin is a leading researcher in the study of only children.

The issue of the personality characteristics of only children has become prominent once again due to the one-child policy implemented in China in 1979. It was decided that China simply did not have the resources to become a superpower if overpopulation was to continue, so families were restricted to having only one child. Quite naturally, researchers became interested in whether raising an entire nation on only children had a significant impact on the personality characteristics and other features of the children involved. In particular, researchers became interested in testing what became known as the Little Emperor Phenomenon. That is, according to stereotypes, would there be a generation of "spoiled, dysfunctional 'little emperors'" (Guo, 2000, p. 10)? It has been suggested that this notion is derived, at least in part, from the fact that Chinese people, relative to American people, place greater emphasis on a child's position relative to his or her siblings, and birth order is more central to a person's identity (see Falbo & Poston, 1993).

Various studies have allayed concerns about the creation of a generation of "little emperors." A sample of 1,000 children from four provinces in China was compared with first-born and later-born children in terms of their academic achievements, personality characteristics, and physical characteristics (Falbo & Poston, 1993; Poston & Falbo, 1990). This study included personality evaluations by peers. Results showed some differences in academic achievement, with only children having higher levels of verbal achievement. Few personality differences were found; only children received more negative personality evaluations in only one of the four provinces studied, and this was restricted to boys. The researchers expected that only children would have inflated self-evaluations, but this was not confirmed.

Analyses of audio taped descriptions of children by their parents found some evidence of the Little Emperor Syndrome among very young children (aged 3 to 5 years), but little evidence of this among older children (Zhang, Kohnstamm, Cheung, & Lau, 2001). Another study found that only children in the equivalent of Grade 1 were cognitively superior to their Grade 1 counterparts with siblings, but this cognitive superiority was less evident among the Grade 5-age students in the study (Jiao, Ji, & Jing, 1996). The authors suggested that differences could have been less evident among Grade 5 students because for their cohort, the one-child family program was not being strictly enforced, and parents might have treated these children similarly to children with siblings.

A sample of 126 Chinese university students without siblings and 134 with siblings completed the Zuckerman-Kuhlman Personality Questionnaire, and it was found that the students with siblings had higher levels of neuroticism–anxiety and aggression–hostility (Wang, Du, Liu, Liu, & Wang, 2002).

At present, Adler's negative characterizations of only children do not seem to apply to children in China. Failure to confirm the existence of the Little Emperor Syndrome is not surprising when one considers the diversity of experiences involved, and the role of other influences, such as genetic factors, that contribute to personality development (see Chapter 3).

Scholars disagree quite vehemently on the degree of association between personality and birth order. Ernst and Angst (1983) conducted a comprehensive review of existing studies and concluded that there is very little association between personality and birth order. They also identified several methodological factors that undermined previous research, including the failure to control for related individual differences in socio-economic status and the number of other siblings in the family. They found that evidence in keeping with a link between birth order and personality was restricted primarily to studies in which parents rated the personality features of their own children.

Sulloway (1996) questioned the criteria used by Ernst and Angst to determine whether a study did or did not support the association. He conducted his own tally of available findings and concluded unequivocally that birth order and personality were associated. There are two problems associated with his conclusion. First, as noted by Sulloway, there are many studies that show no link between personality and birth order. If there is a strong association, then how can these non-effects be explained? Second, subsequent authors have tried to replicate Sulloway's conclusion by conducting their own tally, and they have been unable to reproduce the same numbers that were reported by Sulloway's findings (see Harris, 2002).

Sulloway (1996) reported evidence from a meta-analysis indicating that being first-born was associated with higher levels of extroversion and conscientiousness and lower levels of agreeableness, emotional stability, and openness. A more recent study (Michalski & Shackelford, 2002) conducted with university students in Florida confirmed the link between low agreeableness and being first-born, but in contrast to Sulloway (1996), first-borns had comparatively higher levels of openness. Birth order was not associated with significant differences in the other traits of the five-factor model. Earlier research with both self-reports and informant ratings also provided only limited support for the birth order effects described by Sulloway (1996). Jefferson, Herbst, and McCrae (1998) found no evidence of self-reports on the NEO-PI-R, thus replicating the non-findings reported by Parker (1998) in a sample of gifted children. Although peer ratings suggested that later-born children had higher agreeableness and openness, an analysis of spousal ratings of partner personality characteristics did not confirm this pattern. Jefferson et al. (1998) concluded that birth order has only subtle effects on perceived personality.

Sulloway (1996) is also a controversial figure because of his **niche model of birth order**. He proposed that second-borns are rebellious because this is one way of gaining parental attention and distinguishing them from first-borns who are higher in achievement orientation and more accepting of parental dictates. Empirical research led by a team of

Canadian researchers found consistent evidence to support Sulloway's model (see Paulhus, Trapnell, & Chen, 1999). Specifically, across four studies, first-borns were nominated as most achieving and conscientious, while later-borns were seen as more rebellious. The tendency for first-borns to have higher achievement is consistent with the confluence model postulated by Zajonc and Markus (1975). Other data from Belgium support a link between rebelliousness and being a later-born (Saraglou & Fiasse, 2003), but another study of adults found no evidence indicating that first-borns were more conservative and supportive of authority (Freese, Powell, & Steelman, 1999).

Overall, the effects of birth order on personality are modest at best and seemingly inconsistent across studies. Nevertheless, beliefs about birth order are quite important and salient. It seems that birth order is important because of people's beliefs about the link between birth order and personality and related outcomes. That is, people hold the strong conviction that that there is a link between birth order and personality characteristics. Research conducted jointly at Stanford University in California and the University of Warsaw in Poland has shown that people believe that first-borns are more intelligent and less creative (Herrera, Zajonc, Wieczorkowska, & Cichomski, 2003). People also believe that first-born status is linked with higher occupational status. This turns out to be true! The final study conducted by these investigators confirmed that higher birth order status is linked with greater occupational attainment and completing more years of schooling.

KEY POINTS

- Adler's birth order theory sees second-born children as most adjusted. Parents learn from their mistakes with the first-born, but pamper later-born children.
- Research indicates little objective link between birth order and personality.
- Research supports the greater achievements of first-born children and the rebelliousness of second-born children, a phenomenon postulated by Sulloway.
- Birth order and beliefs about birth order are central to how people see themselves.

Evaluation of Adler's Contributions

Adler is to be commended primarily for three contributions. First, his notion of the inferiority complex is regarded as a highly valid phenomenon that is a key part of the identity process. The phrase "inferiority complex" is a wildly popular notion that has been embraced by the public. Second, Adler reminded us of the significance of social interest and its role as a potential buffer of maladjustment (or a contributor to maladjustment among those lacking social interest and a co-operative orientation). In general, he provided some much needed balance after Freud by highlighting psychosocial factors rather than psychosexual factors. Third, his statements about parents who pamper or neglect their children set the stage for volumes of subsequent work on parental styles and the influence of child maltreatment on subsequent personality development.

However, there is much to be critical of when considering Adler's work. First, when assessing his contribution, it is almost impossible to avoid the conclusion that his views were highly subjective and too influenced by his own personal experiences. While this same problem applies to many theorists, it is most obvious with Adler, who suffered from physical problems as a child (organ inferiority) and who, as a second-born child, was reported to have been very jealous of his older brother. His views on birth order are highly subjective, and he is largely responsible for the mistaken beliefs that the lay public has about the influence of birth order on personality. Finally, in contrast with Freud, Jung, and Horney, among others, Adler's theory is relatively narrow and lacks comprehensiveness. It is not enough to simply state that there are at least 1,000 ways that an inferiority complex can be expressed without making more of an effort to detail different types of inferiority complexes and the motives related to these complexes.

THE NEO-FREUDIANS: KAREN HORNEY

Karen Horney was born and raised in Hamburg, Germany. She graduated with a medical degree from the University of Berlin in 1913, and then studied psychiatry. She taught at the Berlin Psychoanalytic Institute for approximately 15 years, and then went to the United States in 1934. There she worked as a psychoanalyst and she became dean of the American Institute of Psychoanalysis. She died in New York in 1952.

Horney and the Importance of Culture

Karen Horney believed that individual differences in personality could be traced back to cultural factors.

Readers of Karen Horney's work are typically impressed by her deep insights into the nature of people, and there can be little doubt that her theoretical ideas are clear reflections of the people she encountered as a psychoanalyst. Horney's personality theory fits well with the emphasis of this book on cultural factors in personality development and expression. One of her main tenets is that individual differences in personality and psychic disturbances can be traced back to cultural factors. The role of culture is outlined clearly in her book *The Neurotic Personality of Our Time* (Horney, 1937). Horney took issue with Freud's emphasis on the biological determinants of behaviour, object relationships, and intrapsychic conflict, and she was particularly critical of Freud's lack of emphasis on cultural factors. Specifically, she noted that, "Freud's disregard of cultural factors not only leads to false generalizations, but to a large extent blocks an understanding of the real forces which motivate our attitudes and actions" (Horney, 1937, p. 20–21).

Horney (1937) acknowledged that there are widespread differences between cultures. What is considered normal will not only vary across cultures, but will also vary within a culture as things change over time.

Horney also felt that a particular culture at a particular point in time tends to exert a similar influence on all members of that culture, so that the differences between "normal" and "neurotic" people were quantitative rather than qualitative. That is, people differ more in degree than in kind, and everyone in the culture is faced with the same conflicts; neurotic people have more intense reactions to the same challenges faced by "normal" people. Thus, the essential difference between normal and neurotic individuals within the same culture is their ability to cope with similar conflicts and similar problems.

Regarding her own culture, Horney (1937) outlined three main contradictions that confront everyone. The first contradiction is the need to be competitive and successful versus the need for love, affiliation, and humility. This is the classic conflict between focusing on our own accomplishments and yielding to others and promoting their welfare.

The second contradiction is the stimulation of our idealistic needs versus the frustration associated with being unable to attain these ideals. Horney (1937) recognized that we are bombarded with cultural images and messages about what constitutes an "ideal life" but we are troubled by the fact that most people's lives fall far short of this ideal. There can be little doubt that if she were alive today, Horney would have much to say about the negative impact of culture on fostering unrealistic ideals, especially with respect to unattainable body images that are at the root of eating disorders such as anorexia nervosa and bulimia nervosa.

The final contradiction emphasized by Horney (1937) involves what she refers to as "the alleged freedom of the individual" (p. 289). Although people are told that they are free agents who are independent and can decide their own fates, situational and contextual constraints may substantially limit this freedom.

Although she gave Freud great credit for his contributions, Horney's emphasis on cultural factors reflected her belief that Freud overemphasized the importance of biological factors (e.g., libido) and underemphasized the role of cultural and social factors in creating individual differences. Horney was among the first of the analysts affiliated with Freud to place stock in the research on personality by cultural anthropologists such as Ruth Benedict that was described in Chapter 2. Horney also differed from Freud in that she was much more optimistic about human nature and believed that personality could change. In contrast, Freud was very cynical and felt that personality was fixed as a result of early experiences.

Basic Anxiety and Basic Hostility

According to Horney (1937), anxiety is "the dynamic center of neuroses" (p. 41) and much of our behaviour is guided by **basic anxiety**. Basic anxiety is a fear of helplessness and worries about possible abandonment. It occurs when our basic needs are not met.

Horney further suggested that some children develop a sense of **basic hostility**: a reaction to parental indifference and neglect. Because the child is fearful about what will happen after expressing basic hostility, this hostility is not openly displayed.

Like Freud, Horney believed in a basic conflict, and she applauded the attention that Freud focused on our desire to resolve a basic conflict. However, she rejected the notion that the conflict was a battle among the id, ego, and superego. According to Horney, the basic conflict was the source of neurosis, and the conflict involved the contradictory orientations that the neurotic has toward other people. These distinctive orientations are described next.

Moving Toward, Against, and Away from People

The neurotic person has desires to move toward, against, and away from other people. This is clearly evident in the neurotic's stance toward his or her parents. Everyone has a desire to move toward parents, away from parents, and against parents (see Horney, 1945). Horney discussed these conflicting desires by referring to the classic story by Robert Louis Stevenson of Dr. Jekyll and Mr. Hyde. Dr. Jekyll is kind toward people, while Mr. Hyde is anti-social and has a mutual desire to distance himself from others and to hurt others.

Horney (1945) refers to moving toward, against, or away from people as attitudes. Moving toward people reflects helplessness. An excessive tendency to move toward people reflects the compliant type personality. There is an excessive need for attention and approval and a willingness to self-sacrifice to please others. These tendencies are common among people high in the dependency personality trait. Horney suggested that they operate according to the **self-effacing solution**. This "solution" requires them to forestall their own desires to satisfy the desires of others. The main appeal for these people is the appeal of love. According to Horney, they often adopt the "poor little me" personality.

Former U.S. President Bill Clinton has been identified as someone with an extreme tendency to move toward people (see Renshon, 1994). Note that this analysis was provided and identified prior to the Monica Lewinsky affair. Moving toward people is reflected by Clinton's outgoingness and large circle of friends, as well as a great eagerness to please others and seek validation of self-worth through the positive reactions of others. As a leadership style, moving toward people is seen as contributing to an overconcern with public appearance, and when negative information may come to light in the public arena, it could develop into a tendency to "shade meaning, and be less than forthright" (Renshon, 1994, p. 384).

The tendency to move against people is a neurotic style that reflects basic hostility. In essence, the person has decided to act aggressively to hurt others before they can hurt him or her. Thus, this reflects the aggressive personality type. Horney suggested that such individuals believe in a Darwinian world where it is survival of the fittest, and fitness requires aggressiveness. People moving against others operate according to the expansive solution. The main appeal for these people is the appeal of mastery over others.

Horney noted that basic hostility and the tendency to move against people can be taken to an extreme and be reflected in a sadistic personality. The essence of the sadistic person is a desire to enslave other people in general, and one's partner in particular. Horney's description of the sadistic personality is frighteningly accurate in describing extremely sadistic individuals such as Canadian killer Paul Bernardo. He and his wife Karla Homolka kept at least two young women as sex slaves prior to murdering them.

As for Horney, she pointed to Adolf Hitler as an example of moving against people (see Horney, 1950). She attributed his actions and his hateful attitudes of Jews to the self-hate and fear of defeat that Hitler developed as a result of childhood humiliations. This created a search for glory by shaming and dominating others.

Finally, the third attitude of moving away from people represents a sense of detachment and alienation from others. Moving away from people reflects the sense of isolation inherent in basic anxiety. This person is hypothesized to operate according to the resigning solution. The main appeal for these people is the appeal of freedom (Horney, 1950).

Caspi, Elder, and Bem (1987, 1988) conducted studies in which they isolated temperament patterns consistent with Horney's descriptions of moving away from people and moving against people. They also confirmed that these are highly maladaptive responses. They equated the difficult temperament with "moving against the world." Caspi et al. (1987) found that moving against people in childhood predicted lower occupational status, more erratic work histories, and less stable marriages among adult men. Moving against people in childhood was associated with women tending to marry men of less occupational status, having less stable marriages, and becoming more ill-tempered as mothers. A related study by Caspi et al. (1988) examined shy children and found that moving away in boys was associated with delayed entry into marriage, parenthood, and stable careers. For girls, a moving away style was associated with a greater subsequent likelihood of adopting conventional and stereotypical patterns of marriage, childbearing, and homemaking.

KEY POINTS

- Horney suggested that neurotic tendencies are rooted in culture and social experience.
- Children have basic anxiety and basic hostility. They suffer neurosis because they cannot express their hostility to parental figures.
- Conflict ensues from the simultaneous desires to move toward, against, and away from others.

Ten Neurotic Needs

Horney identified ten neurotic needs, which are displayed in Table 5.3. The various needs reflect the themes of moving toward, away from, or against people. Two needs that reflect moving toward people are the neurotic need for a partner and the neurotic need for affection and approval.

Table 5.3 Neurotic Needs Identified by Karen Horney

Neurotic Need	Example
For affection and approval	Refusing to criticize someone out of fear that it will hurt the relationship
For a partner	Going back to a past lover despite evidence that it simply will not work
Restricting one's life to narrow borders	Trying a less difficult task in a competition and settling for second place
For power	Running for student president despite not being well-suited to the job
To exploit others	Conning elderly people out of their life savings
For social recognition	An actor or actress who will do anything to stay in the headlines
For personal admiration	Truly believing the lies and inaccuracies in your resumé
For personal achievement	Being a workaholic to win an unspoken competition with your co-workers
For self-sufficiency and independence	Refusing to accept help from a neighbour because you feel it would be a sign of weakness
For perfection and unassailability	Refusing to admit a stock manipulation so you go to jail for lying to federal prosecutors

Moving away from other people is represented by a different set of needs. This is reflected by the neurotic need to narrowly restrict one's life and to be inconspicuous and out of the mainstream. The neurotic need for self-sufficiency and independence also reflects this desire to distance the self from others.

Most of the neurotic needs described by Horney can be regarded as moving against other people in a way that increases personal dominance. This includes the neurotic need to have power, the neurotic need to exploit others, and the needs for personal achievement and recognition of these achievements, perhaps as a result of being hypercompetitive with others. Another relevant need here is the need for perfection and unassailability, which may result in demanding perfection not only of the self, but from other people as well.

Each need has a dreaded outcome associated with it, which makes sense because people high in neuroticism are often focused on avoiding negative outcomes. For instance, those who need recognition dread being ignored by others. The dreaded outcome for someone high in the need for a partner is being alone. Horney described the concern that people have with what they should do to satisfy these needs as "the tyranny of the shoulds."

The theoretical beliefs that both Adler and Horney outlined about the need to strive for perfection have provided the theoretical impetus for contemporary research and theory on perfectionism. Current developments in perfectionism as a personality trait are now described.

Extension of Psychoanalytic Theory: Perfectionism as a Multidimensional Personality Construct

Recall that Adler suggested that all humans are motivated by a drive for perfection to compensate for feelings of inferiority. Similarly, Horney discussed the neurotic need for perfection and the hypercompetitiveness that often accompanies this excessive striving. In many respects, it was these psychodynamic theorists who drew attention to this important personality trait. Recall as well that Freud also suggested that the superego operates according to the perfection principle.

Contemporary theory and research on perfectionism has confirmed that there are widespread individual differences in perfectionism, and individual differences in perfectionism can be detected in young children. Perfectionism was studied as a general construct prior to 1990, but perfectionism is now studied as a multidimensional construct.

Randy Frost and his associates from Smith College in Massachusetts created a multidimensional perfectionism scale with six dimensions (see Frost, Marten, Lahart, & Rosenblate, 1990). Their measure assessed four aspects of perfectionism directed toward the self (high personal standards, doubts about actions, concern over mistakes, and organization) and two aspects of perfectionism that reflect the perceived presence of parental demands on the self (high parental expectations and high parental criticism). Factor analyses confirmed that the scale is indeed multidimensional, but the exact number of factors is at issue. Joachim Stober (1998) from Germany found that the Frost Multidimensional Perfectionism Scale was best represented by four factors rather than six, with the two parental factors combining to form one factor and the doubts about actions and concern over mistake factors also being joined.

Hewitt and Flett (1991, 2004) completed their Multidimensional Perfectionism Scale at about the same time as Frost and his associates completed their measure bearing the same name. The Hewitt and Flett measure is much more interpersonal in focus. They identified dimensions involving perfectionism directed toward either the self (self-oriented perfectionism) or others (other-oriented perfectionism) as well as a third dimension that involves the belief that others are imposing unrealistic demands on the self (socially prescribed perfectionism). Representative items reflecting these three perfectionism dimensions are shown in Table 5.4. Other-oriented perfectionism can be traced back to Horney's observations that people who demand absolute perfection from themselves also tend to demand perfection from others.

Table 5.4 Sample Items from the Multidimensional Perfectionism Scale

Self-Oriented Perfectionism
One of my goals is to be perfect in every thing I do.
Other-Oriented Perfectionism
If I ask someone to do something, I expect it to be done flawlessly.
Socially Prescribed Perfectionism
My family expects me to be perfect.

Source: Hewitt & Flett, 1991, 2004.

The Hewitt and Flett Multidimensional Perfectionism Scale was developed in Canada with the sequential construct validation approach outlined by Jackson (1970) (see Chapter 4). This process begins with making detailed theoretical statements about the nature of perfectionism and its specific dimensions, followed by generating a large pool of items that are gradually reduced by administering the items and related measures to samples of participants, and then empirically evaluating item properties.

The validity of these perfectionism dimensions has been demonstrated in various ways. As might be expected, measures with similar content on the respective MPS instruments are highly correlated, and this attests to the concurrent validity of the measures. That is, the Frost et al. high personal standards subscale is highly correlated with self-oriented perfectionism, and the parental measures are correlated significantly with socially prescribed perfectionism.

As for the correlations with the five-factor model, various studies have shown that self-oriented perfectionism is associated primarily with conscientiousness and its facets, as expected (Hill, McIntire, & Bacharach, 1997). Other-oriented perfectionism is associated with low trait agreeableness. Finally, socially prescribed perfectionism is associated with high levels of neuroticism.

Unfortunately, research has established that extreme levels of self-oriented and socially prescribed perfectionism are implicated in a variety of adjustment problems. Self-oriented perfectionism has been linked with clinical depression and elevated symptoms of depression in psychiatric patients (Hewitt & Flett, 1991; Hewitt, Flett, & Ediger, 1996) and with eating disorders such as anorexia (Cockell et al., 2002). Socially prescribed perfectionism is perhaps the most deleterious form of perfectionism since it has been associated with a host of problems including anxiety, depression, personality dysfunction, and marital problems (see Hewitt & Flett, 2004: Sherry et al., in press). Research with the Frost et al. MPS has shown that concern over mistakes is the most deleterious aspect of perfectionism measured by this inventory (see Frost & DiBartolo, 2002).

Most existing research has focused on perfectionism from a variable-centred approach. It is important to recognize that perfectionism can also be studied with a person-centred approach that focuses on extreme perfectionists. Their personal stories often show that any potential benefits of perfectionism are often accompanied by some severe costs. For instance, consider Blatt's (1995) seminal paper entitled "The Destructiveness of Perfectionism." He described three prominent people who were all very successful but they killed themselves, in part because they were extreme perfectionists who appeared to lack a sense of self-satisfaction as a result of pursuing impossibly high standards. These people included Vince Foster, who was a close friend of Bill Clinton and Hilary Rodham Clinton.

Another sad example is the case of Asian superstar Leslie Cheung, who was described by all of his friends as an extreme perfectionist. His accomplishments as a musician and actor did not stop Cheung from committing suicide in 2003.

Unfortunately, other examples abound of perfectionists with adjustment problems. In Canada, for instance, prima ballerina Karen Kain has acknowledged that she is an extreme perfectionist. Kain has suffered from depression and symptoms of anorexia. Her lack of self-satisfaction is reflected by her acknowledgement that she enjoyed only 12 of her more than 10,000 public performances because she was striving for absolute perfection.

Evaluation of Horney's Contributions

As with Jung's work, this author finds it difficult to be too critical of Karen Horney's work, aside from the general concerns about the scientific merits of the work of all psychoanalytic theorists. Horney was a pioneer in establishing the importance of examining social conflicts and related factors (cultural and familial influences) rather than psychosexual conflicts. In addition, her identification of the concepts of moving toward, against, and away from other people was a key development that set the stage for the extensive research we have today on interpersonal styles. Her suggestion that high neuroticism may involve a simultaneous desire to engage in all three styles seems a very accurate description of people with borderline personality dysfunction (see Chapter 13) who badly need to be with other people yet can't seem to stand to be with people at the same time. One gets the clear sense when reading Horney's work that she had amazing insight into the problems and personalities of her patients seen in clinical practice. Third, Horney's concepts of neurotic needs and "the tyranny of the shoulds" served as an early precursor for subsequent theory and research on irrational beliefs by Albert Ellis and his followers. In essence, it can be argued that she paved the way for rational–emotive behaviour theory and therapy. Finally, she also deserves extensive praise for asserting a feminist position and having the courage to voice her objections to patronizing views of women.

Others have been more specific in their criticisms of Horney's theories. For example, Allport (1968) suggested that Horney's notion of moving toward, against, or away from people is too broad or coarse. That is, in reality, there are more than three interpersonal orientations and it is too easy to lose sight of the individuality of each unique person by relying on these three interpersonal stances. Others have suggested that the 10 neurotic needs postulated by Horney are too abstract to be measured. The bigger problem is that it simply appears that no one has attempted specifically to create a measure to assess all 10 needs. As we will see in the next chapter, certain needs, such as the need for power and affection from others, have been the subject of extensive work.

PSYCHODYNAMIC ASSESSMENT TECHNIQUES

A variety of psychodynamic assessment techniques have been used. All are based on the **projective hypothesis**, which is the notion that unconscious themes that reveal the self will be projected on to ambiguous stimuli and that differences in responses reflect meaningful individual differences among people. **Free association** is the classic psychoanalytic technique that has often been satirized in cartoons. The patient is put into a state of relaxation while reclining on a couch and then is asked to freely associate by telling whatever thoughts come into mind. The process of relaxation is important because this is akin to lowering one's defences so that unconscious conflicts can come out into conscious awareness.

A **word association test** developed by Jung has also been used. Here, people are asked to respond as quickly as possible to 100 stimulus words and to report whatever comes to mind for each word. Any resistances are given particular attention. That is, when the person seems to have difficulties in providing a response or takes an inordinately long time to respond, this is noted because it is believed to reflect distressing unconscious conflicts.

Dream Analysis

> There's a very limited audience of people interested in your dreams. That's why they're only showing in your head.
>
> —*Comedian and political commentator Bill Maher*

Dream analysis is another projective technique. It is believed that our defences are relaxed during sleep so unconscious conflicts can be expressed through the themes inherent in our dreams. Each major theorist in this chapter believed in the importance of dreams, though dreams are typically associated with Freud, who referred to dreams as "the royal road to the unconscious." Freud's classic book *The Interpretation of Dreams* includes his own recounting and analyses of 46 of his own dreams.

A classic Freudian approach distinguishes between a dream's **manifest content** and **latent content**. Manifest content is the symbols or images in the dream while latent content is the deeper meaning or significance of the dream. In the Wolf Man's dream described earlier, the white wolves in the walnut tree are the manifest content, and the latent meaning is that the wolves symbolize the angry father of the Wolf Man. To cite another example, if you lived in Toronto and you dreamed about the CN Tower and the retractable roof of the nearby domed stadium, a Freudian psychoanalyst would say that the latent content of the dream is that the CN Tower reflects a preoccupation with phallic symbols, while the opening of the dome symbolizes a preoccupation with female genitalia. Of course, the manifest content would simply be these well-known structures in Toronto.

The examples above were selected intentionally to reflect Freud's (1955) **dream symbolism theory**. Certain objects in dreams are supposed to represent male and female forms of sexuality. Although the dream symbolism theory per se has not met with much empirical support, research does show that people who are anxious tend to be more likely to have dreams with sexual content (see Robbins, Tanck, & Houshi, 1985). It is suggested that dreams allow anxious people to express sexual themes that they would not otherwise express in their conscious day-to-day activities. So, once they get to sleep, perhaps there is an upside for worriers!

The process of transforming the latent dream content into manifest content is known as **dream work**. The psychoanalyst's goal is to interpret the manifest content and tell the dreamer what the dream signifies.

Adler was highly critical of Freud's dream theory (Adler, 1958). Whereas Freud suggested that there may be an apparent discrepancy between unconscious conflicts represented in dreams and conscious awareness of dreams, Adler maintained that there does not have to be a contradiction and that the conscious is an extension of the unconscious. Adler suggested that we are most likely to dream about things that we consciously reflect on. That is, the unconscious is an extension of concerns and desires that the person values and thinks about daily.

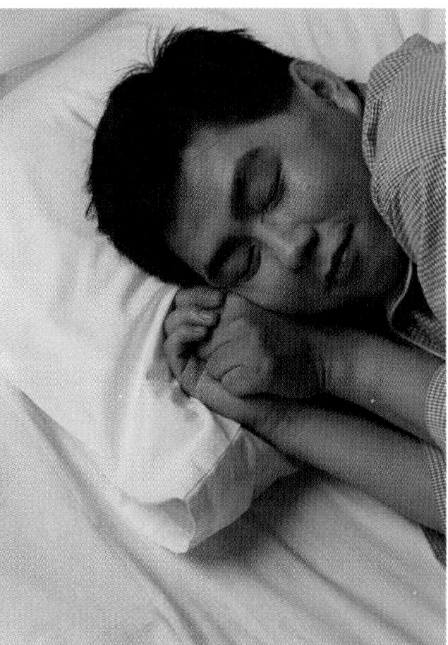

It is believed that because our defences are relaxed during sleep, our unconscious conflicts can be expressed in our dreams.

Most public libraries contain many popular books that help us analyze our dreams. But how useful is dream analysis from a clinical perspective? Reiser (2001) has evaluated the role of dreams in contemporary psychiatry. He noted that Freudian dream analysis was predominant in psychiatry in the 1950s, but it became much less popular as the influence of the psychoanalytic approach decreased. More recently, however, there is a renewed focus on dreams in psychiatry in light of research on the neurobiology of dreams. Extensive research has confirmed that emotional events are encoded in memory and then become reflected in the symbols and themes that emerge in dreams. Reiser (2001) noted that Freud, as a trained doctor, recognized that biological mechanisms in the brain would be implicated in dreams, and his views are consistent with a more contemporary psychobiological conceptualization of dream processes.

Freud also believed that relatively common mistakes, jokes, and slips of the tongue are meaningful; essentially he felt that there are no accidents. The most common example of a slip of the tongue, according to Freud, is saying the exact opposite of what was intended. Mistakes, jokes, and slips of the tongue are attempts by unconscious material to break into conscious awareness. He referred to this as "the psychopathology of everyday life."

KEY POINTS

- The projective hypothesis is the notion that unconscious images are revealed by the conscious responses given to ambiguous, abstract stimuli.
- Three well-known projective techniques are free association, word association, and dream analysis.
- For Freud, dreams have manifest content (the symbols in the dream) and latent content (the underlying meaning of the dream).

The Rorschach Inkblot Test

In terms of more systematic approaches, Hermann Rorschach developed the most well-known projective test. He based it on the different answers his children gave when they were looking at clouds and reporting what symbols and images they could detect. The **Rorschach Inkblot Test** involves presenting respondents with 10 inkblots, some of which are in colour and others that are in black and white. For each inkblot, people list as many things as they can see in these ambiguous stimuli. (Perhaps you are familiar with the inkblot designs because you saw them in the video for the song *Crazy* by Gnarls Barkley.) Personality is projected because even though people are given the same stimulus, they tend to see and report different things.

The second most popular projective test is typically the **Thematic Apperception Test** (TAT). This test requires the respondent to tell stories when presented with black-and-white photographs that depict various scenes. The TAT is described in more detail in the next chapter.

What do psychometric evaluations tell us about the strengths and limitations of tests such as the Rorschach Inkblot Test? This is an important question given the extensive use of this test in various settings. The use of the Rorschach Inkblot Test is the subject of Applied Perspective 5.1. Overall, it is possible to identify both strong supporters and harsh critics when it comes to the use of this test and the systematic scoring system that was developed by Exner (see Hunsley & Bailey, 1999; Lilienfeld, Wood, & Garb, 2000; Meyer, 2001). For instance, it has been said by one critic that "the Rorschach is a very poor test and has no practical worth for any of the purposes for which it is recommended by its devotees" (Jensen, 1965, p. 501), while staunch proponents of the test, such as Irving Weiner, have stated that "those who currently believe the Rorschach is an unscientific or unsound test with limited utility have not read the relevant literature of the last 20 years, or having read it, they have not grasped its meaning" (Weiner, 1996, p. 206). Weiner served for many

Applied Perspective 5.1 A Blot on the Court? The Use of the Rorschach in Legal Settings

One of the seemingly ironic things about the legal system is that the same courtroom that is used to introduce sophisticated biological evidence in the form of DNA tests may be used more often to introduce testimony based on projective tests such as the Rorschach Inkblot Test and the Thematic Apperception Test. Rigid testing standards must be in place for DNA test results to be used as evidence. What standards exist for introducing projective personality test results in court proceedings? Are projective tests valid in this context? And how often are they used?

Although current statistics are unavailable, the most recent surveys suggest that projective tests are extensively used, and it is likely that this pattern has continued. Weiner, Exner, and Sciara (1996) surveyed 93 Rorschach clinicians about their experiences in the five years prior to conducting the survey. Collectively, these clinicians reported that Rorschach Inkblot Test results had been used in 7,934 cases in 32 states in the United States. The Rorschach was used in criminal cases, custody cases, and personal injury cases.

More detailed analyses of the use of the Rorschach Inkblot Test in child custody evaluations also suggest that projective measures are relied on extensively. Three surveys of the methods used to assess adults and children in child custody cases (see Ackerman & Ackerman, 1996; Keilin & Bloom, 1986; Quinnell & Bow, 2001) indicate that administration of the Rorschach test to adults ranged from 42 to 48%. The Rorschach Inkblot Test was also administered to children in about one quarter of the cases. More common was the use of the Children's Thematic Apperception Test, which was used in 35 to 39% of the child custody cases.

Weiner et al. (1996) reported that testimony relating to the Rorschach was seriously challenged in only 6 of the 7,934 cases, which is less than 1%. Meloy, Hansen, and Weiner (1997) also evaluated what they referred to as "the authority of the Rorschach." That is, they sought to determine whether the Rorschach made a difference in the outcome of legal proceedings. The Rorschach test was included in legal citations in 247 cases between 1945 and 1995. A subset of 26 cases were examined in detail, and by and large, it was found that the test findings were deemed by legal authorities to be reliable and valid to the point of seemingly being of use. When the Rorschach testimony was not seen as useful, it was because the person interpreting the results had reached questionable conclusions.

So, what concerns have been raised? Some people simply object to the notion that responses to inkblots can tell us anything useful about meaningful individual differences among people. Meloy et al. (1997) related the transcript of one trial in which a prosecuting attorney expressed his contempt for the test by saying, "Rorschach. My pen leaks and I have a Rorschach ink spot on my shirt with a matching t-shirt!" (p. 57). In terms of more tangible concerns, research suggests that individuals motivated to fake their responses or respond in a socially desirable manner are able to alter their answers to portray high psychological health (Exner, 1991). Exner found that people being evaluated in child custody trials tend to provide answers reflective of high intellectualization, and they give more popular answers.

Malingering is another problem. Malingering is the tendency to "fake bad," perhaps by trying to seem mentally ill in order to not be criminally responsible for misdeeds. McCann (1998) noted that there are no clear diagnostic cut-offs established to detect malingering and dissimulation. Nevertheless, he concluded on the basis of the overall body of evidence that the Rorschach meets professional and legal standards for admissibility of evidence, and the Rorschach has "maintained a very high level of acceptance and use" (p. 140–141).

The most damning criticisms of the use of the Rorschach in general have come from Garb and his colleagues (for a current review, see Garb, Wood, Lilienfeld, & Nezworski, 2005). Garb (1999) has gone so far as to call for a moratorium (a suspension of use) on employing the Rorschach in forensic settings. Specific concerns include evidence suggesting that positive Rorschach findings are seldom replicated in follow-up studies, and there is little evidence for the incremental validity of Rorschach assessments. Also, it is difficult to develop criteria to distinguish between valid and invalid responses. Garb noted further that proponents of the Rorschach have relied on unscientific impressions and the overall popularity of the measure, and this is no substitute for empirical data. Available data, in Garb's estimation, fall short of the mark and do not support such extensive use of the Rorschach.

years as the editor of *The Journal of Personality Assessment,* and this journal is dedicated, in part, to research on the psychometric properties of projective measures.

Proponents of projective techniques such as the Rorschach argue that it is less susceptible to faking and dissimulation than structured personality measures such as the Minnesota Multiphasic Personality Inventory (MMPI). Minimization is the tendency to portray oneself in a way that minimizes psychopathology to influence treatment and placement decisions. A comparative study of sex offenders confirmed that a structured personality measure showed little evidence of dysfunction, but Rorschach responses revealed significant levels of psychopathology (Grossman, Wasyliw, Benn, & Gyoerkoe, 2002). In terms of limitations, concerns have been raised about the inter-rater reliability (the agreement between two or more scorers) when scoring Rorschach responses, and the general validity of the test itself. Although these concerns have been raised, Meyer (2004) provided a unique defence of the use of the Rorschach Inkblot Test by showing in a series of meta-analyses that there is "reasonable evidence" of the test's reliability and validity based on contemporary research. More importantly, he concluded that the psychometric properties of the Rorschach were comparable to the psychometric properties of other types of personality tests and other tests used in medical research. He concluded that tests such as the Rorschach and TAT are "not noticeably deficient in their psychometric properties relative to the other assessment procedures commonly used in psychology, psychiatry, and medicine" (Meyer, 2004, p. 331). Of course, a purist or sceptic would argue that validity coefficients are lower than they should be in general, so comparative conclusions across different forms of personality tests may have reduced significance. Perhaps the most important issue is whether the Rorschach has incremental validity relative to these other measures. In this regard, a study by Blais and associates showed that there is little correspondence between the Rorschach Inkblot Test and the MMPI-2, but the Rorschach did have incremental validity when predicting symptoms of borderline personality disorder and narcissistic personality disorder. The Rorschach did not have incremental validity in predicting anti-social personality disorder symptoms, however (see Blais, Hilsenroth, Castlebury, Fowler, & Baity, 2002).

Different people see different things in a Rorschach inkblot, thus reflecting their different personalities. What do you see in these inkblots, and what do you think this says about your personality?

Summary

This chapter began with an introduction to psychodynamic concepts by outlining Freud's theory. The components of the psyche (id, ego, and superego) were described, including the types of anxiety that are experienced depending on whether the id, ego, or superego is predominant. The ego's mechanisms of defence were noted and contemporary theory and research on ego defence styles was cited to highlight some of the current applications of the defence mechanisms concept. Freud's theory of psychosexual development was then described in detail, including radical concepts such as the Oedipus and Electra complexes and the notion of penis envy. It was noted that people become fixated if the task of a particular stage is not resolved and this early childhood experience is reflected in the adult personality. Although Freud has made numerous contributions, several problems associated with his theory were also noted.

The differences between Freud's theory and the beliefs of neo-Freudians were then listed. Carl Jung's *analytical psychology* theory was described including his important distinction between the personal and the collective unconscious, and his notion that the collective unconscious consists of primordial images in the form of archetypes (universally applicable symbols). Universal symbols such as the shadow, the wise old man, and the mother are believed to exist in everyone's unconscious.

The section on Jung also included a detailed description of introversion versus extroversion and the four functions of sensing, intuition, perception, and thinking. Next, the Myers-Briggs Type Indicator was described because it is based on these perceptions. The various uses, either rightly or wrongly, of this measure were then examined.

Just as Freud and Jung have had significant impacts on contemporary society, so have Alfred Adler and Karen Horney. Adler's notions of the inferiority complex and the superiority complex were presented, as well as his notion of different styles of life that account for the individuality among people. In addition, Chapter 5 also included an assessment of Adler's predictions about the importance of birth order as a predetermining factor of personality. This issue was also examined in light of the one-child policy in China. In general, empirical research does not support the view that there is a strong link between birth order and personality. Empirical links are modest at best, though birth order and the perceived importance of birth, order seem to be prominent in how people see themselves.

Next, Horney's criticisms of Freud's theory were discussed, including his neglect of cultural factors. Horney's unique concepts of basic anxiety, basic hostility, and neurotic needs were also presented. Horney postulated that people with neurotic tendencies are caught in a conflict due to their desires to move toward people, against people, and away from people. This segment concluded with a description of current theory and research on perfectionism that is derived from the theories of Adler and Horney.

The final section of this chapter examined various forms of assessment that reflect the projective hypothesis. Topics that were addressed include dream analysis and the use of projective measures such as the Rorschach Inkblot Test. The debate about the merits and limitations of projective measures was examined within the context of their widespread use in forensic and legal settings.

Questions to Consider

1 Can you recall a dream you had? What is the manifest content of this dream, and what do you see as the latent meaning of this dream? How would Freud interpret your dream? How would Adler differ in how he would explain your dream?

2 Do you accept Jung's notion of the collective unconscious? List the archetypes that are potentially most relevant to your daily experiences. Can you identify the folk tales or symbols in your culture that resemble the archetypes?

3 Re-examine Adler's theory and Sulloway's views on birth order. Do you agree with these authors? To what extent has your own birth order influenced your personality?

4 Review the three kinds of anxiety posited by Freud and the intrapsychic mechanisms believed to be responsible for these types of anxiety. How would Freud explain the continual and pervasive anxiety of someone suffering from generalized anxiety disorder, which is characterized by chronic worry?

5 Consider someone who you know quite well. Does Freud's developmental theory apply to that person? Does that person have any habits or tendencies that could reflect fixation in a particular stage? Do you have any habits or tendencies that could reflect fixation? Or do you regard Freud's developmental model as unrealistic?

6 Adler's concept of the inferiority complex seems to be well-established. Do you think that most people have some sort of inferiority complex? Can you think of a public figure (besides the Unabomber) who seems to have developed a superiority complex to overcompensate for feelings of inferiority? Review the neurotic needs postulated by Horney. How many of these needs apply to you?

Key Terms

anal stage, p. 166
anima/animus archetype, p. 177
archetypes, p. 176
avoiding type, p. 185
basic anxiety, p. 191
basic hostility, p. 191
castration anxiety, p. 163
catharsis, p. 162
collective unconscious, p. 176
complexes, p. 176
defence mechanism, p. 168
defence styles, p. 171
denial, p. 169
displacement, p. 169
dream analysis, p. 197
dream symbolism theory, p. 198
dream work, p. 198
ego, p. 163
Electra complex, p. 163
eros, p. 162
fixation, p. 166
free association, p. 197
genital stage, p. 167
getting type, p. 185
id, p. 162
immature defences, p. 170
individual psychology, p. 182
individuation, p. 177
inferiority complex, p. 183
introjection, p. 164
introspective method, p. 161
latency period, p. 167
latent content, p. 198
libido, p. 162
manifest content, p. 198
mature defences, p. 170
moral anxiety, p. 168
neurotic anxiety, p. 168
niche model of birth order, p. 188
Oedipus complex, p. 163
old rememberances, p. 184
oral stage, p. 166
organ inferiority, p. 183
penis envy, p. 164
perfection principle, p. 163
personal unconscious, p. 176
phallic stage, p. 167
pleasure principle, p. 162
primary process thinking, p. 162
projection, p. 169
projective hypothesis, p. 197
psychosexual stages, p. 166
rationalization, p. 170
reaction formation, p. 169
realistic anxiety, p. 168
reality principle, p. 163
regression, p. 170
repression, p. 169
Rorschach Inkblot Test, p. 199
ruling type, p. 184
secondary process thinking, p. 163
self-effacing solution, p. 192
shadow archetype, p. 177
social interest, p. 185
styles of life, p. 184
sublimation, p. 170
superego, p. 163
superiority complex, p. 185
synchronicity, p. 178
thanatos, p. 162
Thematic Apperception Test, p. 199
wish fulfillment, p. 162
womb envy, p. 164
word association test, p. 197

Key Theorists

Alfred Adler, p. 182
Sigmund Freud, p. 161
Karen Horney, p. 190
Carl Jung, p. 174

chapter six

MOTIVATIONAL THEORIES AND PSYCHOLOGICAL NEEDS

- Henry Murray and Psychological Needs
- The Assessment of Psychological Needs
- Alternative Measures of Psychological Needs
- Specific Psychological Needs
- Contemporary Theory and Research on Motivation

Since Freud, psychologists have accepted the fact that a simple act can be variously motivated. In the economic sphere, advertisers have long since taken advantage of Freud's findings in recognizing that a man doesn't buy a car just because he "needs" one in a rationale sense, but the possession of a particular kind of car may satisfy other motives—for power, prestige, or even sexual display.

—DAVID MCCLELLAND (1961, P.38)

TAKE A MOMENT TO reflect on the following questions: What matters to you so much that it propels you into action? What makes your behaviours persist over time? And how does this make you different from other people? Chapter 6 focuses on motivational theories and concepts. Motivational theorists address such questions as why behaviours occur. Personality theorists are interested in identifying and explaining common motivational factors that are shared by people and the unique motivational factors that distinguish people. Chapter 5 introduced psychoanalytic theories. For the Freudians, motivation is provided primarily by the unconscious conflicts inside a person. The primary theory described in Chapter 6 is derived from psychoanalytic theory but is different enough to warrant being in a separate chapter. Specifically, we focus on Henry Murray's theory of psychological needs. We also discuss other motivational approaches to the study of personality that have emerged in recent years.

HENRY MURRAY AND PSYCHOLOGICAL NEEDS

Henry Murray is one of the most fascinating figures in the history of the personality field. He made important contributions to personality theory, as well as to the assessment of personality and its applications. He also introduced the term **personology**: the study of human lives and the factors that influence their development, with a particular emphasis on differences among individuals and their personality types. He coined the term, in part, because he felt that a term such as the psychology of personality was too cumbersome.

Murray from a Psychoanalytic Perspective

Murray is affiliated with the psychoanalytic perspective for several reasons. Consistent with Freud and Jung, Murray believed that psychological needs were located in the unconscious, but it is possible to study their manifestations in conscious thoughts and reactions. Murray felt that all experience has an impact on us, including our experiences as a fetus, and that experiences before language ability is developed become represented in the unconscious. He introduced the concept of the **habit system** to describe customary modes of behaviour that have become almost automatic and occur repeatedly without conscious thought. The habit system accounts for overly rigid behaviours that persist over time.

Murray also accepted the existence of the id, ego, and superego and saw them as shaping the habit system, but he differed slightly from Freud's description of these structural aspects of personality. For Murray, the id contained not only the instincts described by Freud, but also more acceptable instincts that reflected psychological needs. He felt that the id is not always active and energized and suggested that it sometimes needs to be stirred up. While the id can sometimes reflect irrational and inappropriate tendencies, it also has a positive side and is responsible for fantasies, faith, and creative inspirations (Murray, 1938). For Murray, the ego is part of a broader ego system. The ego is conscious and is focused primarily on perceived aims, goals, and plans of action. Finally, the superego is mostly unconscious, and, similar to Freud, he saw it as a cultural by-product of internalized expectations. Its first goal is to inhibit anti-social tendencies, and its second goal is to present cultural and religious norms as "the highest good."

A third factor that ties Murray to the psychoanalytic camp is that he also endorsed the general concept of defence mechanisms. In particular, he accepted the influence of the defence mechanisms of repression and resistance (Murray, 1936, 1938).

Murray was particularly taken with Carl Jung and his work. Triplet (1992) suggested Murray's interest in psychology (he was trained as a medical doctor) was sparked in 1923 when he picked up a copy of Jung's book *Psychological Types*. Murray's appreciation of Jung's eight types and psychoanalytic concepts in general converted him to this theoretical orientation. Murray made pilgrimages to Europe to meet and study with Jung, who, among other things, encouraged Murray to express his anima, the feminine side of his personality. It was here that Murray not only learned to explore his unconscious, but also came into contact with Christiana Morgan, who was one of Jung's patients, and a budding analytical psychologist herself. Morgan and Murray began a 40-year affair (both were married to other people), and she played a vital role in assisting Murray with the development of his theory. They were also co-creators of the Thematic Apperception Test, which was introduced briefly in Chapter 5, and is described in more detail later in this chapter.

Henry Murray's approach, which is referred to as the multiform method, involves the use of multiple assessments and assessments of participants in actual situations.

Several sources have provided some exceptionally revealing glimpses of Henry Murray (see Robinson, 1992; Triplet, 1992). He was based at Harvard University, so his colleagues included Gordon Allport. Like Allport, Murray has had an enormous impact on the personality field. One thing that Allport and Murray had in common was they emphasized studying the whole person. Murray maintained that the whole person should be studied across his or her lifespan and not just at one point in time. This desire to study the whole person is why Murray and his colleagues went to great lengths to extensively study participants with as many different forms of assessment as possible. His classic book *Explorations in Personality* incorporates many psychoanalytic concepts and is based on the results of studying a sample of 50 men over a two and a half year period. Each participant was evaluated with more than 25 forms of assessment! They were evaluated by different observers in as many naturalistic situations as possible. Murray's methodological approach is referred to as the **multiform method**. Triplet (1992) pointed out that this use of multiple assessment forms including assessments in actual situations has provided the basis for employee assessment techniques that are used by major corporations in the United States and throughout the world.

The Importance of the Situation: Press

Although he is known primarily for his emphasis on psychological needs, Murray was a remarkable scholar who included many elements and concepts in his theory. Murray recognized that a multitude of factors, both conscious and unconscious, must be taken into consideration to fully understand a person. He also acknowledged the role of the biologically inherited characteristics, as well as the importance of the environment in influencing behaviour.

Murray's concept of press refers to the role of situational factors that operate like a pressure on the individual and contribute to his or her behaviour. There are two types of press. Alpha press is the actual situation as it objectively exist. Beta press is an individual's perception or appraisal of the situation. Murray's inclusion of the beta press concept was the forerunner of current research on the role of personality factors in the cognitive appraisal of situational cues.

Murray was similar to Allport in that he, too, incorporated the concept of interactionism. Murray's concept of thema refers to the combination of press (the environment) and the personality factors that combine to produce regularities in behaviour. The interaction of internal factors within the individual and external factors outside the individual meant that the person's individuality can become quite complex and can be expressed in many ways (Triplet, 1992). Behaviour can reflect internal factors (e.g., needs, drives) or external factors (e.g., press) or some combination of internal and external factors.

A thema reflects a single episode (in Murray's words, a creature by environment interaction). However, episodes may repeatedly follow each other in a sequence, and this would involve a complex episode and a complex thema.

KEY POINTS

- Murray believed in psychoanalytic concepts such as the id, ego, and superego. These personality structures served slightly differed functions than the id, ego, and superego described by Freud.
- Murray emphasized the importance of unconscious processes. Defence mechanisms also operate, according to Murray.
- The concept of press reflects the influence of the situation, either the objective situation (alpha press) or the perceived situation (beta press). Themas reflect the combination of person factors and situational press.
- Murray promoted a multiform method that involved assessing people with many measures to get a clear sense of each individual as a whole person.

Interdependence of Personality from a Cultural Perspective

Murray is also noteworthy for his emphasis on the role of cultural factors. Murray and Kluckhohn (1953) teamed together to examine the role of culture in personality development. This occurred, in part, because Kluckhohn was an anthropologist, but it was also due to Jung's influence on Murray and to his emphasis on symbols and themes in various societies.

Murray and Kluckhohn stated that personality reflected both inherited dispositions and environmental experiences. Environment was defined broadly and included the physical, biological, and social environment, and all of these types of environment were seen as influenced by culture.

Murray and Kluckhohn (1953) identified four sets of determinants in personality development: (1) constitutional determinants (genetic structures); (2) group membership determinants; (3) life role determinants; and (4) situational determinants. Cultural factors play an important role in group membership determinants, but Murray and Kluckhohn (1953) added the appropriate caution that cultural influences are experienced quite differently within a culture, and each person's selection of cultural influences and reactions to cultural differences may have a very individual quality to it. They also noted that these four sets of determinants are mutually interdependent, and although it is important to acknowledge the link between culture and personality, we should not lose sight of the influence of constitutional and life role determinants.

Murray as a Motivational Theorist: Needs

A reasonable question is "Why is it that Murray is usually considered primarily as a motivational theorist?" There are two main reasons. First, he emphasized directionality. That is, he maintained that the most important thing when seeking to know a person is to discover the factors that determine the specific direction of mental, verbal, and physical activities. For Murray, behaviours are directed by motives and drives inside people, and people are complex because they have complex motives.

Second, the concept of "need" is at the heart of Murray's theory. It is discussed in detail below and is examined in terms of physiological and psychological needs.

Murray (1938) defined a need as follows:

> A need is a construct (a convenient fiction) or hypothetical concept which stands for a force (the physicochemical nature of which is unknown) in the brain region, a force which organizes perception, apperception (expectation), intellection, conation and action in such a way as to transform in a certain direction an existing, unsatisfying situation. (pp. 123-124)

There are many remarkable ideas incorporated into this definition. First, for Murray, needs are internal, abstract, and hypothetical because they cannot be directly observed. Needs can be inferred by looking at one or more pieces of evidence: (1) the analysis of the aftereffects of behaviours; (2) the typical mode or pattern of behavioural expression; (3) the selection or avoidance of certain situations (i.e., press); (4) characteristic emotional expressions; and (5) expressions of satisfaction or dissatisfaction following an effect.

Second, Murray's focus on the need as being located in the brain region is a reminder of his initial training as a medical doctor. Murray (1938) introduced the concept of **regnancy** to indicate that psychological needs always had a biological manifestation as well.

A need that is prepotent is one that has become "regnate," meaning reigning or ruling (i.e., dominant). Regnate needs must be satisfied with some degree of urgency because there is some overarching physiological requirement involved, and these physiological demands drive the motivational system. In subsequent years, Murray (1968) further underscored the biological roots of personality by suggesting that genetics plays a vital role in determining the course of maturation and the timing of key stages across the lifespan.

The other remarkable thing about Murray's definition of a need is his belief about the various functions served by a need. A need influences our perceptions, cognitions, and actions and is most evident when there is a recognizable deficit between our current status or state and where we would like to be. Behaviours and thoughts directed toward satisfying a need are thus designed to alleviate a deficiency that exists within the person.

Murray observed that needs that are aroused but not satisfied will persist for quite a while. Individuals with unsatisfied needs enter situations with a **need set** such that there is a readiness to respond in a way to satisfy the need. Murray was highly cognizant of the temporal course of needs. He identified three periods as part of his description of the **periodicity of needs**. First, there is a refractory period when the need is essentially dormant and virtually no incentive will elicit it (e.g., a male's lack of interest in sex immediately after ejaculation). There is also an inducible period when the need is inactive but is ready to respond to an exciting stimulus. Finally, there is an active period when the need is almost, if not entirely, determining ongoing behaviour.

According to Murray, one action can satisfy two or more needs at the same time. The satisfaction of two or more needs reflects a phenomenon known as **fusion of needs**.

The **subsidation of needs** occurs when other needs are recruited to promote another need that is more powerful (at least for the time being). The recruited need is known as the subsidiary need, and the more powerful one is the determinant need.

Murray also noted that two needs within the same person could be in conflict, and this can become "a spiritual dilemma" that can account for much misery and neurosis in the world (Murray, 1938). To further underscore the link between motivation and cognition, Murray (1951) postulated the term **ordination** to describe the process of planning and implementing **schedules** in order to reduce conflict among two or more goals that are seeking expression at the same time. Thus, for Murray, a schedule exists to help us satisfy our different needs at different times.

There are many ways of subdividing or classifying types of needs. For instance, Murray differentiated focal needs (ones that apply to specific objects in specific settings) and diffuse needs (global, pervasive needs that operate across many settings). He also discussed proactive needs (ones that stem from inside the person) and reactive needs (ones that are triggered by environmental press). Thus, needs can reflect a "push" from inside the person or an environmental "pull" from the external setting. Murray also distinguished between manifest needs and latent needs. Manifest needs are overt and reflected directly by behaviours or actions. Latent needs are more abstract and are represented in symbolic form.

Murray also differentiated conscious and unconscious needs. Conscious needs are retrospective but immediately available in awareness, and can be verbally described. Murray observed that unconscious needs are opposed to a person's social or public personality. They combine to form what he referred to as the alter ego, which is a dissociated aspect that is kept apart from the conscious self and is not "let out" in everyday life. The example he used to illustrate this concept is the story of Dr. Jekyll and his alter ego, Mr. Hyde.

Murray acknowledged that unconscious needs are particularly difficult to change, more so than conscious needs. Accordingly, he felt that a key step in the development of a healthy personality is to make unconscious needs become conscious. Murray believed, like Freud, that unconscious needs were revealed by the conscious in a variety of ways, including consciously remembered dreams, visions, absent-minded gestures, compulsions, projections, psychiatric symptoms, and mistakes and slips of the tongue. So Murray, like Freud, would find a deeper significance to potentially innocent events. An example would be when actress Sienna Miller (who was engaged to actor Jude Law) went public in 2005 with the story that she had lost one of the diamonds on her engagement ring in a mitten. Rather than just being bad luck, this missing diamond could be a conscious reflection of an unconscious need to avoid a lasting relationship with Law, who was later discovered to have had sexual relations with the nanny hired by Miller.

Types of Needs

Needs have been distinguished by whether they are physiological or psychological. Physiological needs are referred to as primary needs. They are primary because they are essential for survival and relate to internal bodily processes. Psychological needs are referred to as secondary needs. They are secondary because they reflect emotional and psychological concerns.

Primary needs were described as viscerogenic. Murray (1938) identified 13 viscerogenic needs: (1) air; (2) water; (3) food; (4) sex; (5) lactation; (6) urination; (7) defecation; (8) harm avoidance; (9) noxavoidance; (10) heat avoidance; (11) cold avoidance; (12) sentience; and (13) passivity. Murray suggested that these needs could be grouped into things we lack that we need (e.g., food), distensions that lead to outputs (e.g., urination), and possible harms (e.g., noxavoidance). The secondary needs are psychological and, according to Murray, are presumably dependent on the primary needs first being satisfied.

It is not surprising that Murray would identify primary needs such as the need for sex. As noted earlier, it is well-documented that Murray and Christina Morgan had a 40-year extramarital affair. There are also sources indicating that their sexual activities were highly aberrant and unusual and involved sado-masochistic activities. You will see this pattern of behaviour reflected in the psychological needs presented below.

Psychological Needs

Summaries of Murray's theory of psychological needs usually indicate that Murray listed 20 psychological needs, but it is evident in his 1938 book that many more psychological needs were identified. A more complete list of needs and definitions of these needs is provided in Table 6.1. The needs are grouped according to the themes identified by Murray (1938).

Table 6.1 Psychological Needs Identified by Murray

Needs Associated with Inanimate Objects	
Acquisition	To gain possessions and property; to grasp, snatch, or steal things; to bargain or gamble
Conservance	To collect, repair, clean, and preserve things; to protect against damage
Construction	To organize and build
Order	To arrange, organize, put away objects; to be tidy and clean; to be scrupulously precise
Retention	To retain possession of things; to refuse to give or lend; to hoard; to be frugal, economic, and miserly
Needs Associated with Ambition and Desire for Accomplishment	
Superiority	To have an ambitious attitude, reflected by needs for achievement and recognition
Achievement	To overcome obstacles, to exercise power, to strive to do something difficult and as quickly as possible
Exhibition	To attract attention to one's person; to excite, amuse, stir, shock, thrill others; self-dramatization; the opposite of the need for seclusion
Recognition	To excite praise and commendation; to demand respect; to boast and exhibit one's accomplishments; to seek distinction, social prestige, honours, or high office
Needs Associated with Defending Status and Avoiding Humiliation	
Inviolacy	Desires and attempts to prevent depreciation of self-respect; to preserve one's good name Includes needs for infavoidance, defendance, and counteraction
Infavoidance	To avoid failure, shame, humiliation, ridicule
Defendance	To defend oneself against blame or belittlement; to justify one's actions
Counteraction	To proudly overcome defeat by restriving and retaliating; to select the hardest tasks; to defend one's honour in action
Needs Associated with Exerting or Yielding to Power	
Autonomy	To resist influence or coercion; to defy an authority or seek freedom in a new place; to strive for independence
Contrarience	To act differently from others; to be unique; to take the opposite side; to hold unconventional views
Dominance	To influence or control others; to persuade, prohibit, dictate; to lead and direct; to restrain; to organize the behaviour of a group
Deference	To admire and willingly follow a superior; to cooperate with a leader; to serve gladly
Similance	To empathize; to imitate or emulate; to identify oneself with others; to agree and believe

Needs Reflecting the Sado-Masochistic Dichotomy	
Aggression	To assault or injure; to murder; to belittle, harm, blame, accuse, or maliciously ridicule a person; to punish severely
Abasement	To surrender; to comply and accept punishment; to apologize, confess, atone' self-depreciation; masochism
Need Associated with Inhibition	
Blamavoidance	To avoid blame, ostracism, or punishment by inhibiting asocial or unconventional impulses; to be well-behaved and obey the law
Needs Reflecting Affection for People	
Affiliation	To form friendships and associations; to greet, join, and live with others; to cooperate and converse socially with others; to love; to join groups
Rejection	To snub, exclude, or ignore; to remain aloof and indifferent; to act discriminatingly
Nurturance	To nourish, aid, or protect a helpless other; to express sympathy; to "mother" a child
Succorance	To seek aid, protection, or sympathy; to cry for help; to plead for mercy; to adhere to an affectionate, nurturant parent; to be dependent
Play	To relax, amuse oneself, seek diversion, and entertainment; to "have fun"; to play games; to laugh, joke, and be merry; to avoid serious tension
Needs to Ask and to Tell	
Cognizance	To explore (moving and touching); to ask questions; to satisfy curiosity; to look, listen, inspect; to read and seek knowledge
Exposition	To point and demonstrate; to relate facts; to give information, explain, interpret, lecture

KEY POINTS

- Murray's theory is often known as a needs theory and is a motivational approach. Needs can be physical (primary needs) or psychological (secondary needs).
- Needs emanate from the brain and reflect physiological structures.
- The force of a need has an impact on and organizes perceptions, thoughts, and actions.
- Needs can be interrelated and may even conflict. Two needs can be satisfied by one behaviour (fusion of needs), or one need can become subservient to another need (subsidiation of needs).

The Personal Needs of Henry Murray

It is probably not surprising that an analysis has been conducted of the psychological needs of Henry Murray himself. This analysis by Anderson (1988) showed that Murray had a depressive core to his personality. In fact, he blamed his mother for his troubles because of his stated awareness that he was not his mother's favourite child. Murray was high in narcissism and had a powerful need for intimacy, particularly with women. However, he would be characterized as someone high in hostile depression because he was an outwardly angry person who often made scathing comments about his colleagues at Harvard University. It was generally accepted that Murray was very high in narcissism (a vulnerable form of excessive self-admiration). How narcissistic was he? Theorist Erik Erikson suggested that if given the opportunity, Murray would have replaced Napoleon's statue in France with a statue of himself.

This narcissism likely reflected one of Murray's most dominant needs: the need for uniqueness (see Anderson, 1988). Although not part of Murray's theory per se, the need for uniqueness has received extensive attention in the personality literature. This need was studied by Fromkin and Synder and is assessed by the Need for Uniqueness Scale (see Snyder & Fromkin, 1977, 1980). It is assessed by such self-report items as "People often say I am a nonconformist." People high in this need tend to be independent, inventive, and willing to incur disapproval to establish their uniqueness (Fromkin & Lipshitz, 1976).

Snyder and Fromkin (1980) postulated that there is a cultural aspect to the need for uniqueness. Indeed, recent research by Tafarodi, Marshall, and Katsura (2004) showed that Canadian and Japanese students did not differ in their overall level of need for uniqueness, but they did differ in how the need was expressed. Japanese students are less likely to act in a way that makes them stand out. This study highlights cultural differences in motivation, and reminds us that there are individual differences not only in needs and motives, but also in how these needs and motives are outwardly expressed in behaviours.

Although he was narcissistic and had a need to be unique, Murray also demonstrated his commitment to broader causes. Murray joined the U.S. Army Medical Corps in 1943, and it was there that he established the Office of Strategic Services, the forerunner to the Central Intelligence Agency (CIA). As part of his work, Murray conducted a personality analysis of Adolf Hitler (Murray, 1943). This analysis is described in Applied Perspective 6.1.

Applied Perspective 6.1 Personality Assessment Goes to War

The Office of Strategic Services (OSS) Assessment Unit was designed to conduct the physical and psychological screening of OSS candidates from around the world. Their work is summarized in the book *The Assessment of Men* (OSS Staff, 1948). Although based initially in the United States, assessment centres were developed in other parts of the world, including Calcutta, India and several locations in China (Handler, 2001).

The psychologists and psychiatrists that were part of this assessment used several of Murray's techniques described in his 1938 book *Explorations in Personality* (see Katz, 1989; Morgan, 1957; OSS Assessment Staff, 1948; Robinson, 1992). Potential candidates were screened for their suitability in a variety of roles, including possible spies, saboteurs, or propaganda experts. Various techniques were used, including a projective form of assessment known as **psychodrama**. Psychodrama examined how people responded when placed in lifelike situations. Some of these situations were exceptionally challenging and involved such things as replicating the stress and duress of an interrogation session. According to Handler (2001), more standard forms of assessment such as the TAT and Rorschach were also used initially, but these took too much time to administer and were subsequently dropped.

In his overview paper, Handler (2001) identified seven factors that were considered in selecting candidates. Several of these factors were related directly or indirectly to personality differences. These factors were (1) motivation for the assignment; (2) energy and initiative; (3) practical intelligence; (4) emotional stability; (5) social relationships (including teamwork); (6) leadership; and (7) security (e.g., discretion, ability to dissimulate).

As noted, in addition to conducting assessments of candidates, personologists such as Murray conducted personality evaluations of Adolf Hitler. Murray listed three purposes for compiling his "memorandum" about Hitler: (1) to present an analysis of Hitler's personality with a hypothetical formulation of the manner of its development; (2) to make a few predictions as to Hitler's conduct when confronted by the mounting successes of the Allies; and (3) to offer some suggestions as to how the U.S. government might influence his conduct and behaviour (at the time of the assessment in 1943).

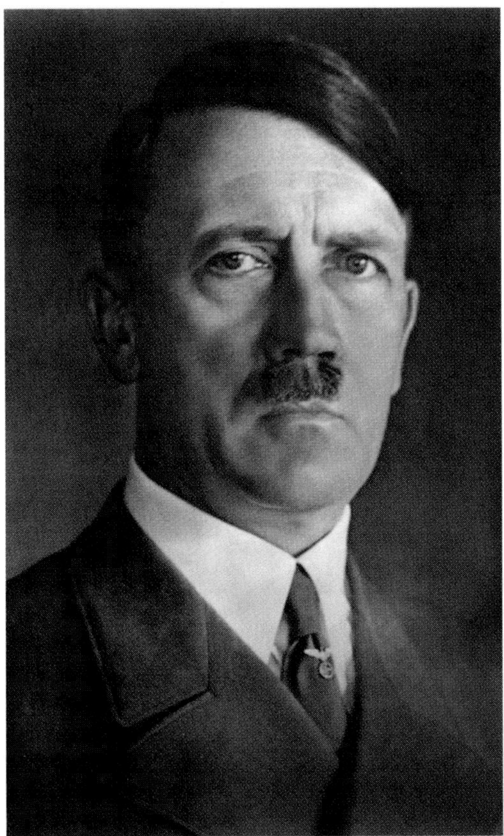

Murray's assessment of Adolph Hitler's personality identified the psychological needs for dominance, superiority, and aggression.

Murray (1943) suggested that to analyze Hitler was to take a crucial step in identifying and understanding the psychological makeup of the typical Nazi. Murray also reasoned that an analysis of Hitler's personality could go a long way to understanding the needs of most German people at the time because, according to Murray, Hitler must have been providing something that fulfilled their psychological needs.

Murray based his analysis on inside information provided by the OSS, as well as the content of Hitler's book *Mein Kampf*, and four other books written about Hitler. Murray's entire report has been declassified and is now available on the Internet (see Cornell, 2005).

Briefly, Murray summarized Hitler's personality by identifying four main themes. He identified two sets of psychological needs and two primary defence mechanisms. The psychological needs reflected the general need for counteraction (overcoming defeat by retaliating). The first psychological need was Hitler's "Counteractive Need for Dominance, Superiority." Hitler's need for dominance and superiority was a response to a deep-seated and neurotic sense of inferiority. This notion is in keeping with Adler's notion that feelings of inferiority are overcompensated for by a superiority complex.

The second psychological need was "Counteractive Aggression, Revenge." Murray suggested that this factor was needed to account for Hitler's "immeasurable hatred" and cruelty that went beyond his need for dominance. It was suggested that Hitler had suffered extensive humiliation and wounded pride, primarily because of the cruelty and tyranny of his father. Murray went to great lengths to explain that this psychological need was tied to repressing the common Oedipus Complex suggested by Freud, and instead substituting highly ambivalent feelings toward both the father and the mother. That is, it was suggested that Hitler hated his father but also greatly admired his father's powerfulness. Similarly, he hated his mother because she was quite weak and submissive, especially around Hitler's father, but at the same time, he still loved his mother.

Regarding defence mechanisms, the first one was "Repression of Conscience, Compliance, Love." Murray posited that Hitler had a more feminine side to his personality and his acts of domination and hatred were often followed by pangs of neurotic anxiety, which was Hitler's repressed conscience trying to assert itself.

Finally, the second defence mechanism was "Projection of the Criticizable Elements of the Self." According to Murray, Hitler frequently projected his own "wicked impulses" and weaknesses on to other people. This projection was interpreted as Hitler's paranoid way of maintaining his self-esteem by seeing his own failings in other people.

We conclude this segment with some excerpts from the memoirs of James Grier Miller, who was reflecting on his work for the Office of Strategic Services (see Miller, 1996). Miller, who was educated at Harvard University, is regarded as the originator of the term **behavioural science** and he served for over 30 years as the editor of the journal *Behavioral Science*. He was recruited by Murray and he joined the assessment department of the OSS. He took over as military commander of the OSS Assessment Branch when Murray left and performed in this role until the end of December 1945.

The excerpts from Miller below contain some interesting insights about the types of assessment being conducted by the OSS.

> We had to determine for three classes of about 30 candidates every two weeks whether or not each one could function successfully as an intelligence agent on a specific mission. All of our assessments had to be done very quickly. We developed some methods that are still used today. Our effort was to use a more dynamic approach to the study of the psychology of individuals, and to make it as quantitative as possible … In the assessment program we had a battery of about 78 tests that were given in four days. Before he or she came to Area S, each candidate was trained to prepare a cover story. Each one had to come under a false name with a false life history. All candidates were called students, and had names like Student Rex of Class 22. They were told to dress in GI fatigues, without any signs of rank or means of identification. They were never to tell the truth about themselves except when they were alone behind a closed door in a room with only one staff member, and that staff member took the initiative, saying "We are now talking under X conditions." When that was said, they were supposed to tell the truth, but under no other circumstances.
>
> When the candidates arrived they were very quiet and very careful. As they rode out in the truck together, they did not speak … We started to test the next morning. The tests came thick and fast. There were physical tests, and intellectual tests, and field tests. The probstacle test was a combination of problems and obstacles. First, candidates had to climb 20 feet of sheer wooden wall. Most of them got to the top one way or the other and then they walked out about 20 feet on a board measuring 2 by 6 inches. At the end of the board was written a problem: Prove that all mathematical statements of the form "abcabc" are divisible by 13, and then proceed. After one minute, if they could not answer, a staff member on the ground below would say, "I will give you a hint. The hint is the number 1001." All numbers "abcabc," for instance (123123), are multiples of 1001, and 1001 is divisible by 13. About 25 or 30 percent of the people figured it out. Then all went on to the next test.
>
> One of the tests we used was the "construction test." Ostensibly this was a test of the candidate's ability to direct two helpers in building with him a frame structure out of simple wooden materials. The test actually was one of emotional stability

and frustration tolerance. The candidate was told what sort of structure was required and how long he had to complete it. He was given two helpers who were to do the actual labor under his direction. Two members of the junior staff played these parts, under the pseudonyms of Kippy and Buster. Kippy did nothing at all unless specifically ordered to, whereas Buster was aggressive, made impractical suggestions, and criticized every order given him. They were to obey every instruction specifically but to present as many obstructions and annoyances as possible. As it turned out, they succeeded in frustrating the candidates so thoroughly that the construction was never once completed in the allotted time.

The test was an opportunity for the candidate to demonstrate leadership, controlled and sensible action, and tolerance for frustration and stress. In addition to such tests, we used two-hour interviews with trained psychologists and psychoanalysts. The results of the entire battery of tests were considered in the final evaluation.

Ten percent of our candidates were women, and they were all asked if they would be willing to use sexual means to obtain information. Without exception they said yes. However, this was against national policy, and to the best of my knowledge women were never used in such a capacity. But we did ask the question. And we were somewhat surprised when we never got a negative response.

Later we moved our headquarters from Paris to Versailles, near the office of the French intelligence organization, DGER. I was invited to see how they analyzed, as they called it, their candidates. I sat in on a few sessions with ever-increasing amazement. The entire evaluation concerned their candidates' attitudes toward sex. Each candidate was asked about his preferences in various areas—arts, clothing, food, and others—as related to his sexual attitudes. They never once asked any practical questions. Certainly Freud was the major influence in the selection of French intelligence agents even though he came from the German side of the world. The French believed they could determine from a candidate's sexual attitudes how self-confident he was, how much of a leader he was, how aggressive or passive he was, and how intelligent he was in solving problems. Unlike the Thematic Apperception Tests devised by Henry Murray, their tests used only sexual objects and pictures. They assumed that sex was the basic dynamic of life. They were looking for somewhat the same variables that we Americans were, but they were looking at it very differently! (Miller, 1996, pp. 247-248)

There can be little doubt that Murray played a vital role in helping to establish that the personality field has vitally important applications in the real world. Murray and his associates, with their applied work, provided the field with much credibility in the eyes of the public.

Although Murray is highly regarded for his contribution to the war effort, and the developments in personality assessment that emerged from the military work of Murray and his colleagues, Murray's work has been a source of controversy in recent years, and Murray's reputation has suffered. Why? Strangely enough, it has to do with the Unabomber.

Murray and the Unabomber

The Unabomber's anti-social activities have been extensively documented. At one point, the Unabomber topped the Federal Bureau of Investigation's most wanted list. The Unabomber, Theodore Kaczynski, made and deployed 16 bombs over a 17-year period, beginning in 1978. The bombs were often sent to university professors in packages, and the bombs would explode when the packages were opened. A bomb also exploded on an airplane. (Note that "UNA" in Unabomber stands for universities and airlines). In total, the bombs killed three people and maimed at least 23 others. The main concerns of the Unabomber are outlined in *The Unabomber's Manifesto*. The Unabomber was concerned about the increasing role of technology in taking control over people, and his bombs were designed to illustrate the destructive effects of technology, as well as anti-social reaction to perceived attempts to restrict a personal sense of autonomy.

Theodore Kaczynski, the Unabomber, was a participant in Henry Murray's personality study while attending Harvard University in the 1950s.

The possible role of Henry Murray in influencing the Unabomber came to light in 2000 with a provocative article in the *Atlantic Monthly* by Alston Chase, who was a Harvard student who went to school with Ted Kaczynski. Recently, Chase has expanded on his analysis in his even more provocative 2003 book titled *Harvard and the Unabomber: The Making of an American Terrorist.*

When Kaczynski was a student at Harvard, in 1959, he was one of 20 young men who volunteered to take part in a study by Henry Murray. Murray conducted a replication study and extension of his original study described in the book *Explorations in Personality.*

Several aspects of the 1959 research study are troubling because of the ethical violations that were apparently committed. Clearly, the study violated the right of every research participant to be fully informed about the research and associated risks prior to giving informed consent. Some of the problems included the fact that procedures were not outlined in detail to participants, and risks were not identified. In addition, the actual length of the study was misrepresented. Although it was billed as research that would take place over a year, the study took almost three years to complete!

The most problematic aspect is that participants were subjected to various procedures designed to induce extreme stress and distress. Tactics included a task known as "The

Dyad" in which a trained confederate sought to interrogate and humiliate the student participant with the allegation that this involved techniques developed by the OSS. This does not seem to fit with the ethical guideline of research participants not experiencing any physical or psychological harm.

What effect did this have on Kaczynski? Although Chase (2003) noted that Kaczynski was deemed to be psychologically vulnerable and was included in the study for this reason, he seemed to be relatively healthy from a psychological perspective at the beginning of the study. In fact, his Thematic Apperception Test scores were considered to be quite normal, according to Chase (2003). The Thematic Apperception Test is described in more detail in the next section of this chapter. Unfortunately, the Unabomber-to-Be seemed to deteriorate over the course of Murray's study, and many point to his involvement in Murray's research as the turning point. We can never know for sure whether harsh and coercive treatment in this study contributed to the Unabomber's desire to exert freedom from the control of technology and his subsequent behaviour, but the possibility certainly exists.

Evaluation of Murray's Theory

Murray is one of the most colourful characters in the personality field and his influence is enduring. Murray was instrumental in finding ways to conduct empirical research on psychoanalytic concepts. His theory of needs paved the way for extensive research on individual differences in motivational factors, and by introducing the concepts of press and thema, Murray paved the way for an interaction approach that reflected the impact of situational factors on behaviour. Also, as we continue to see in the next segment of this book, Murray had an undeniable influence on personality assessment. Murray and Morgan provided us with the widely used Thematic Apperception Test, and Murray's theory provided the framework for several of the high profile personality inventories described in the next section. Also, with his work in the OSS, Murray showed the possible applications of personality theory and research. The profile conducted of Hitler also gave impetus to the field of psychobiography (see Chapter 14).

KEY POINTS

- Murray's applied contributions include contributing to the war effort and providing a theory that formed the basis for many well-known personality inventories.
- Although Murray was a pioneer in establishing the applications of personality theory and research, his research may have influenced and contributed to the problems of the Unabomber.
- All research must be ethical. Murray's study involving the Unabomber appears to have violated the principles of informed consent and that no harm should come to the participants.

A strength of Murray's theory is also a potential limitation. Murray provided a broad theory that had many elements (e.g., the unconscious; the id, ego, and superego; needs;

schedules). Perhaps Murray's theory has too many elements, and it might have been better to focus on certain unique aspects of the theory and develop them in more detail. For instance, the developmental factors that contribute to specific needs should have been elaborated in more detail. What contributes to a need for exhibition or a need for order? Why is it that some people have a great number of needs, while other people have relatively few? These questions were not adequately addressed.

Most criticisms of Murray's theory focus on the initial 20 needs he identified. It is hard to deny claims that he based these needs on his own subjective and potentially arbitrary decisions. What criteria were used to determine whether a need was included? Reiss and Havercamp (1998) defined fundamental motives as those that were (1) universal motivators; (2) psychologically important; and (3) intrinsic (internal) motives that result in the voluntary initiation of behaviour. Empirical research resulted in the identification of 16 basic desires that met these criteria (for a review, see Reiss, 2004). Of course, many needs identified by Murray were not represented in this research, so some of them may be of only marginal importance.

Finally, both Murray and subsequent theorists such as David McClelland (1985) accepted the notion that needs have an unconscious component. However, McClelland placed a greater influence on the role of learning in terms of the strength and potency of a need or motive (McClelland & Friedman, 1952).

THE ASSESSMENT OF PSYCHOLOGICAL NEEDS

As noted above, many measures have been designed to assess the psychological needs Murray identified. This section describes an unstructured test (The Thematic Apperception Test) and the structured tests (self-report personality inventories) that are shaped by Murray's theory.

The Thematic Apperception Test

Murray and Morgan developed the Thematic Apperception Test (TAT; Murray, 1943), which can assess an individual's personality and self-understanding. In its original form, the TAT consists of a series of black and white pictures depicting scenes, and respondents are required to provide a story that fits with the picture being shown. It is a projective test in that the story generated to an ambiguous stimulus allows the person to project his or her personality into conscious awareness. Each scene in the pictures was selected to represent a specific psychological need described by Murray (1938).

The manner in which personality is projected is illustrated below in the projective test responses given by Mark David Chapman, who shot and killed John Lennon in New York City. Chapman was delusional and suffered from anti-social and narcissistic tendencies. He idolized the fictional character Holden Caulfield from J. D. Salinger's classic book *The Catcher in the Rye*. He indicated that he shot Lennon, in part, because the voices of "the little people" in his head were instructing him to do so.

The biography of Chapman written by Jones (1992) includes excerpts from the projective testing conducted as part of Chapman's psychiatric evaluation. Excerpts from this Rorschach and TAT responses are provided below. The TAT response was provided in reaction to a picture showing a boy in the foreground while a team of surgeons is attending to a patient in the background of the picture. The TAT card being referred to was designed to tap the need for achievement. Common stories provided by TAT participants include the young boy envisioning himself as a doctor some day. Instead, as illustrated in the excerpt below, Chapman provided a story that no doubt reflected his own struggle with the theme of good versus evil, and his need to resolve his aberrant sense of morality and the fact that he had shot and killed a member of one of the most popular musical groups of all time.

TAT responses of Mark David Chapman, who shot and killed John Lennon, reflected a need to distance himself from someone who is 'evil.'

> This key—this boy is the key to the story. He's very intelligent. But look at him closely. He's a very evil person. He just shot him. He just shot him and he's waiting here for the trial to come. In the back you can see they're operating on the patient. I don't think he's going to make it. He's a very evil boy. They're operating right on the stomach and chest of this patient and if you look at the boy's face, he's got a very noncompassionate look. This guy's a phony and he's no good. He's strange. When I shot John Lennon I had this dream that they were opening up his chest and going inside with their hands and trying to make his heart work well. Anyway, this boy is evil and he has no compassion. I want you to know that when I shot John Lennon I was concerned and I chose the right type of bullet so that it expanded inside him rather than going in and just laying there. This way the expansion of the bullet, it instantly damaged more of his internal organs and death was quicker there for him. But you know it's real strange, when I shot him he managed to walk a couple of steps and then he fell. The blood was all over the place … Anyway, this is an evil boy and I am not. (Jones, 1992, pp. 80–81)

Despite his undeniably heinous act, Chapman's responses to this TAT reflected a need to distance himself from the type of person who would act this way.

TAT testing can show how current crises get reflected in projective responses (Jaques, 1955). This study involved four cases of TAT testing conducted with Canadian military personnel in a military hospital. A soldier's TAT responses are reproduced below:

> This was a 22-year-old private, admitted to hospital because of fainting attacks. He had a life-long history of timidity and recessiveness, and had never adjusted properly in the army. Electroencephalogram was negative. Although the attacks appeared to be clearly related to disturbances in his mood, nevertheless the actual precipitating factors were not elicited in the interview. A TAT was done, and among others the following two stories with a repeated theme were obtained.
>
> Picture 6: Looks like somebody has attempted suicide. Looks like a soldier serving away from home. Probably got involved in some way. His conscience got the best of him and he decided to end it all. (What led up to this?) Whatever he got involved in. (Make up a story about it. Fill in more detail). He got in trouble with say, a woman and he's married back home and he just couldn't face it.
>
> Picture 12: Looks like a person being hypnotized. Probably a doctor putting a patient under hypnotism to see what his reactions are. After a few minutes he comes out of it and maybe the doctor has found something that has a bearing on the case and he is able to cure the patient. (What does the doctor find out?) Found out what was worrying him. Maybe he was troubled—we'll go back to the woman—and he was a married man and it just kept working on him and so the vision always seemed to be in front of him and he wasn't in the best of health and it just kept wearing him down. It was something he hadn't told the doctor before and, by hypnotizing him, he found out. (What is the final outcome?) The patient is cured. No, I wouldn't want to say he'd be cured because (pause) the doctor will probably suggest something for him to do, but don't know what he could suggest. Say the fellow admits being the father of the child and then it's born and lives and they put him in a home. (Jaques, 1955, p. 80)

Jaques noted that this soldier's responses were focused predominantly on themes involving guilt and heterosexual activity. It was suggested that the soldier may have been projecting his own guilt over an extramarital affair or some other dalliance. The soldier denied this vehemently, but subsequently under hypnosis, he revealed that he had been sexually involved with his cousin and this was a source of great distress.

Although the TAT seemed to yield very useful information in the cases outlined above, critics of the measure abound. Concerns have been raised about psychometric properties, with very low test–retest reliabilities being reported. Test–retest reliabilities for TAT-derived measures of need for achievement and need for affiliation range typically from .20 to .40 (for a review, see McClelland, 1985). Concerns have also been raised about the measure's validity, though it was noted in Chapter 5 that Meyer (2004) conducted an empirical review that failed to show that the TAT had poorer validity relative to other forms of assessment.

Others have argued that the TAT has "considerable validity" (Woike & McAdams, 2001). Supportive evidence includes established links between implicit motives and the ability to recall life events (McAdams, 1982; Woike, Gershkovich, Piorkowski, & Polo, 1999). As for the low test–retest reliabilities, it has been noted by several authors that the low temporal stability may, in part, be a reflection of the TAT instructions, which require respondents to answer with stories that reflect being as creative as possible. Test–retest reliabilities tend to increase to approximately $r = .60$ when respondents are told to repeat their original story (also see Lundy, 1985; McClelland, 1985).

Proponents of the TAT raise a number of other points that merit consideration. First, David McClelland has amassed evidence showing that implicit measures of motivation such as the TAT have only minimal correlations at best with self-report measures of motivation, and they relate to different measures.

Second, various authors have suggested that responses to the TAT are very useful in measuring variables of clinical importance because of their relevance to psychopathology. For instance, Phoebe Cramer, who was mentioned in Chapter 5, has developed a system that scores the defence mechanisms of children based on their responses to select TAT cards. She has focused on the defences of denial, projection, and identification (see Cramer, 1987, 1997). Cramer has argued that there is a wealth of evidence that supports the use of the TAT as a measure of defence mechanisms. For instance, TAT responses provided support for Cramer's development model of defence mechanisms. She posited and demonstrated empirically that denial is predominant in early childhood but gives way to projection as children mature. The more adaptive defence of identification is the last to develop because it requires a level of cognitive maturity that begins to emerge in adolescence. Cramer (1991) has also used TAT cards to show that experimental manipulations are reflected in subsequent predicted changes in defences. Other research with responses to TAT cards has confirmed the link between defence mechanisms and certain forms of psychopathology (Cramer, Blatt, & Ford, 1988).

The TAT has also been used to assess individual differences in variables derived from **object relations theory**, which stems from the psychoanalytic perspective. Object relations emphasizes how people come to view relationships with other people, and incorporates such things as our interpersonal wishes and our emotional responses to other people. Drew Westen (1991) devised a scoring scheme that focuses on responses to select TAT cards. He noted that the TAT is ideally suited to this purpose because many TAT scenes include other people. Westen's scoring scheme assesses four factors: (1) the complexity of representations of people; (2) the affect-tone (emotional tone) of relationship paradigms; (3) the capacity for emotional investments in relationships and moral standards; and (4) understanding of social causality.

Westen (1991) demonstrated how his object relations factors could be applied to a case study of a woman with borderline personality disorder. People with borderline personality disorder typically have very unstable and changing interpersonal relationships, and this is accompanied by a very negative self-concept and vulnerable sense of self-esteem. This personality disorder is described in Chapter 13.

The object relations scoring scheme should be particularly effective in identifying highly aberrant responses in TAT stories with unusual interpersonal content. It would have certainly been able to identify the problems in the following example. When the current author was an undergraduate student, a professor recounted a recent story that took place in Brampton, Ontario. The professor administered the TAT to a young man and was puzzled by a response to a particular card. The scene on the card depicts what seems to be a man in a trench coat under a streetlight. Typical responses to this scene reflect stories such as the man is a detective and he is following someone, or he is a secret agent (or it is Humphrey Bogart's character in the classic movie *Casablanca*). In this instance, when asked to provide a story, the young man told an elaborate story about the streetlight and made no mention of the person under the streetlight! He stuck to this story despite being asked explicitly to say something about the shadowy figure under the streetlight. He was unable to do so. This provided the vital clue about his personality that led to the young man's arrest for a series of sex offences committed in the nearby neighbourhood. The object relations scoring scheme would certainly have reflected this failure to incorporate the interpersonal cues in the picture.

The same professor who recounted this story also critiqued the merits of projective tests of the TAT, stating they do not have the required levels of reliability and validity. Indeed, many others have criticized the unscientific nature of projective tests (see Hunsley & Bailey, 2001). However, the professor also noted that he would never forget the time that the TAT aided directly in the capture of a suspected sex offender.

KEY POINTS

- The Thematic Apperception Test is a projective measure in which people's needs are revealed by the content of the stories they tell in response to depicted scenes.
- Concerns have been raised about the reliability and validity of the TAT. The TAT appears to suffer from exceptionally low test–retest reliability.
- A recent review suggests that the TAT's validity is comparable to other measures. Also, the test–retest stability of TAT scores is influenced by the way the TAT is administered.

ALTERNATIVE MEASURES OF PSYCHOLOGICAL NEEDS

As noted above, Murray's theory has been extremely influential in providing the theoretical basis for several well-known personality inventories besides the TAT. These personality inventories are similar in that they tap many of the same needs. They differ from the TAT in that they are structured self-report inventories that are not projective. These measures are described below.

The Edwards Personality Preference Schedule

The Edwards Personality Preference Schedule (EPPS; Edwards, 1959) is a widely used measure in clinical and counselling situations. It consists of 135 distinct statements. There are 9 items for each of the 15 needs tapped by the inventory. The 15 needs are abasement, achievement, affiliation, aggression, autonomy, change, deference, dominance, endurance, exhibition, heterosexuality, intraception, nurturance, order, and succorance. Piedmont, McCrae, and Costa (1992) compared scores on the NEO-PI-R and EPPS and found evidence for the concurrent validity of the EPPS. For instance, the EPPS order scale was highly correlated with trait conscientiousness, and the needs for affiliation and nurturance were associated with trait agreeableness.

Unfortunately, the EPPS suffers from one significant limitation that often undermines its usefulness. The EPPS uses **ipsative scoring**, which tends to bias scores. The respondent is given a forced choice between two items that reflect different personality scales. For example, the person must decide between "I am very goal-directed" and "I love to be with other people." The alternatives are not independent because only one score can be counted, and it would be particularly biased for the person who is high in both achievement and affiliation motives. Overall, Edwards (1959) created 225 forced-choice items based on creating pairs of the 135 needs statements. The ipsative scoring format of the EPPS is believed to have a negative impact on the scale's validity, and it points to the need to consider other available measures of psychological needs (for a discussion, see Piedmont et al., 1992).

Recall in Chapter 4 that work by Fiske (1973) was cited to illustrate that personality inventories purport to measure the same personality construct but their degree of association is sometimes quite low when empirically evaluated. Fiske relied on data from the EPPS to make this point. Perhaps the lower than acceptable correlations among measures designed to tap the same construct was due not only to differences in item content, but also the ipsative scoring method used with the EPPS.

The Adjective Check List

The Adjective Check List (ACL) by Gough and Heilbrun (1965) consists of 300 adjectives arranged in alphabetical order. The ACL was designed for use in a variety of ways. The adjectives can be used to describe the self or other people. Also, the ACL was created initially to rate the personality of individuals who were in group interactions. These same adjectives could be applied when assessing the personality of groups as well (see Williams & Best, 1991).

In terms of its actual content, the ACL measures the same needs as the EPPS, but it also contains a number of unique scales that were derived from the adjective ratings. For instance, the ACL also provides measures of the degree to which a person has a creative personality, and the extent to which the person has the characteristics associated with military leadership. Other measures include indices of self-control, self-confidence, and personal adjustment. The ACL also permits an assessment of extreme response bias based on the total number of unfavourable and favourable adjectives endorsed.

Analyses have confirmed some correspondence between the psychological needs assessed on the ACL conform and components of the five-factor model (see FormyDuval, Williams, Patterson, & Fogle, 1995; Piedmont, McCrae, & Costa, 1991). Piedmont et al. (1991) sought to establish the extent to which the five factors captured by the NEO have motivational aspects in terms of associated psychological needs. They found that succorance was a primary need associated with neuroticism. Extroversion was associated with needs involving dominance, heterosexuality, and exhibition. Overall, there were relatively few correlations involving openness, though openness was associated with a need for change and, to a lesser extent, a need for autonomy. Agreeableness was associated with a need for deference and nurturance and low levels of need for autonomy, aggression, and dominance. Finally, trait conscientiousness showed the expected link with need for achievement, endurance, and order.

The versatility of the ACL is illustrated by research with the measure using it to evaluate cross-cultural personality stereotypes involving age and gender. Williams (1993) assessed personality impressions and age stereotypes by asking students from 19 countries to identify the ACL adjectives most associated with old adults and young adults, and it was found that comparable adjectives were selected across all 19 countries. Follow-up analyses (FormyDuval et al., 1995) showed that younger adults were attributed ACL adjectives reflecting extroversion, neuroticism, and openness, while older adults were attributed ACL adjectives reflecting agreeableness and conscientiousness.

Data from another ACL study in 32 countries (see Williams & Best, 1990) found that gender stereotypes were much more variable across countries. This implies that there are substantial cross-cultural differences in the extent to which gender stereotypes get incorporated into our self-concepts and expressions of our personality. The ACL comparison of the United States and Pakistan, for instance, showed that males in the U.S. were stereotypically higher on only conscientiousness, while the male stereotype in Pakistan had them significantly elevated on not only conscientiousness, but also on extroversion and openness. As for the female stereotype, in the United States, agreeableness was linked with being female, but in Pakistan, agreeableness was replaced by neuroticism (FormyDuval et al., 1995). Evidence that gender role stereotypes are not generalizable across cultures is in keeping with research suggesting that personality measures of masculinity and femininity are culture-specific. Conceptions of masculinity and femininity seem to reflect indigenous beliefs and needs (for examples, see Sugihara & Katsurada, 1999; Zhang, Norvilitis, & Jin, 2001).

The Personality Research Form

The Personality Research Form (PRF) created by Douglas Jackson and his associates at the University of Western Ontario is one of the most highly regarded personality measures of the psychological needs described by Murray (see Jackson, 1974). The PRF was developed according to Jackson's (1970) sequential approach to test creation and reflects the construct validation approach outlined in Chapter 4. It consists of 20 scales tapping a range of psychological needs, as well as two validity scales assessing socially desirable responses and infrequent responses (measured by the infrequency scale). The PRF subscales are relatively uncontaminated by social desirability response bias and this is due, in large part, to a careful item selection process that involved the rejection of items that were too highly correlated with a social desirability measure. This degree of care in test construction and existing empirical results led Wiggins and Broughton (1985) to conclude that the PRF is probably the most promising measure designed to tap the needs outlined by Murray.

Various forms of the PRF have been created as the scale has been updated and improved over several decades. Skinner, Jackson, and Rampton (1976) examined the factor structure of Form E of the PRF in a sample of Canadian men who were applying for non-commissioned service in the Canadian Armed Forces. The men spoke either English or French as their first language. Skinner et al. (1976) commented that this study was a challenging test of the PRF in this sample because it extended original work with the scale beyond the university student population, and it involved an evaluation of the equivalence of an English language and French language version. They noted that equivalent personality inventories are required in Canada, especially if the measure is used for selecting French-speaking and English-speaking members of the Canadian military. Their factor analyses of PRF responses yielded comparable six-factor solutions for both English-speaking and French-speaking men. They concluded that there was a "marked similarity" in the factor structures. A separate factor representing the infrequency scale occurred in both samples. The five other factors that emerged were deemed to reflect (1) an Aesthetic-Intellectual Factor (sentience and understanding); (2) Dependence versus Autonomy (succorance and social recognition versus autonomy); (3) Orientation toward Work versus Play (achievement and endurance versus play); (4) Outgoing Social Leadership (exhibition, affiliation, and dominance); and (5) Self-Protective versus Submissive Orientation (defendance and aggression).

Other work has focused on the comparability of the PRF across cultures. This work is discussed in International Focus on Discovery 6.1.

Costa and McCrae (1988) found the expected links between the PRF factors and the NEO factors. The strongest associations were between the Outgoing Social Leadership factor and trait extroversion and between Orientation toward Work versus Play and trait conscientiousness. There was also a robust association between the Aesthetic-Intellectual Factor and trait openness. Costa and McCrae (1988) concluded that broad personality traits have explicit motivational aspects.

In light of these associations, it is logical to ask to what extent individual differences in needs or motives add unique information, above and beyond what we know from a person's traits. The position taken by Winter and associates is that traits and motivational variables are related, but both types of variables are important because they play different roles in regulating behaviours (see Winter, John, Stewart, Klohnen, & Duncan, 1998). Their data showed that traits and motives can *interact* to predict behaviour. That is, there is a substantial difference between the person who has a strong need to be with other people and is extroverted and another person with an equally strong need to be with other people but who is an introvert. In this instance, the personality trait will influence how the same underlying need is publicly expressed and revealed. So, it is important to know a person's traits and his or her needs.

Omnibus personality measures such as the PRF and ACL assess many needs at the same time. Various theorists have focused on individual needs of interest and conducted research on specific needs. In addition to the need for control described in Chapter 2, the

International Focus on Discovery 6.1 The Personality Research Form (PRF) across Cultures

Little is known about individual differences in psychological needs from a broad cross-cultural perspective. Aside from the work conducted by McClelland, most of the information we do have comes from research conducted with the PRF in various countries. At present, the PRF is available in 16 languages.

Dion and Yee (1987) examined the PRF scores of 635 University of Toronto students who were classified into Asian, European, and Anglo categories. The placement of students into groups was less than ideal in that it was based solely on a retrospective analysis of the students' surnames. Also, as a result of this procedure, no attempt could be made to determine if students were born in Canada. This study found that students with an Asian background, relative to the other students, had greater needs for order, harmavoidance and social recognition, and lower needs for dominance, exhibition, nurturance, and affiliation. It is interesting that these students desired social recognition but not to the extent that it reflected a more flagrant need for more exhibition.

Research by Cynthia Fekken and her associates at Queen's University in Kingston, Ontario, explored the measurement of psychological needs by administering the PRF to a sample of Filipino university students (Fekken, Holden, Jackson, & Guthrie, 1987). This study also incorporated self-ratings and peer-ratings on adjectives corresponding to the PRF subscales. Overall, evidence for validity was found, but Fekken et al. (1987) characterized the validity coefficients as "modest, lower than ideal, and lower than reported elsewhere" (p. 405). They posited that test items may reflect common behaviours but relatively weak examples of these needs for people from the Philippines. Previously, Guthrie, Jackson, Astilla, and Elwood (1983) raised the possibility that obtaining peer ratings of personality via adjective ratings may also be problematic and difficult for people from the Philippines because Filipinos tend focus on situations and personal relationships as determinants of behaviour rather than personality traits.

Another team of researchers examined the PRF's psychometric properties with a sample of 156 students from Zimbabwe (Wilson, Doolabh, Cooney, Khalpey, & Siddiqui, 1990). This study found that internal consistencies of the PRF subscales were only slightly lower than those obtained with North American students. However, the validity coefficients between the PRF and adjective self-ratings were acceptable in overall magnitude but appreciably lower than those found with North American samples. The most glaring problem was the Zimbabwean students endorsed the PRF infrequency scale to a much greater degree. The authors recommended that special instructions may be needed to increase the understanding and motivation of students completing a measure being adapted for use.

More recently, Moneta and Wong (2001) sought to redress a lack of research on "thematic motivations" in China by examining the possibility of translating four PRF scales (achievement, affiliation, dominance, and nurturance) into Chinese and then examining their correlates in a sample of Hong Kong college students. An important component of this study is that they investigated whether the Chinese version of the PRF subscales would reflect the themes that emerged in students' daily experiences. That is, an experience sampling component (see Chapter 4) was included. What did they find? Evidence for the construct validity of these PRF subscales was found in that only the affiliation subscale was associated with more positive associations in face-to-face communications with other people. Analyses of other questionnaire measures showed that people high in affiliation and nurturance needs were more likely to think of themselves in terms of their relationships with other people. This is known as **interdependent self-construal**, and this will be explored in more detail in the subsequent chapter on the self-concept.

The most comprehensive comparative study thus far was conducted by Heinrich Stumpf from Germany (Stumpf, 1993). He examined the attributes of the PRF in 18 samples, including two European countries (The Netherlands and Germany) and the Philippines. Data were also compared from English-speaking and French-speaking Canadians. Stumpf showed high similarity across cultures in the PRF factor structure when the same statistical procedure was applied across the various samples. We can infer that many basic needs are shared across cultures.

three needs that have received the most attention are the need for achievement (achievement motivation), the need for affiliation or intimacy, and the need for power. These needs are now examined in greater detail.

SPECIFIC PSYCHOLOGICAL NEEDS

Achievement Motivation

A voluminous literature has examined the characteristics and correlates of the need for achievement, and much is known about this need. Some of this research was conducted by personologists, but understandably, research on achievement motivation is also of great interest to educational psychologists. In general, achievement motivation refers to the drive and determination that a person has to attain goals involving work (school or job performance).

David McClelland is the leading theorist in this area, and it is most fitting that his work was conducted at Harvard University, where Murray was based. McClelland's primary way of assessing the achievement motive was to examine people's fantasies. Fantasies were assessed by examining the content of the stories generated by respondents. McClelland identified three reasons for assessing motives with fantasies instead of behaviours. First, he noted that anything can happen in fantasies, but behaviours are constrained by the realities and dictates of life situations. Second, he argued that fantasies are easier to influence and are more responsive to experimental manipulations than other kinds of behaviours. Finally, behaviours can be due to many factors; it is not always apparent why a behaviour occurred. Fantasies are more amenable to determining which particular motives or motives were aroused in the fantasy.

Fantasies can be assessed in stories obtained through a variety of means. The main focus has been on the stories that have been provided in response to the scenes displayed in TAT cards. McClelland (1961) outlined how it is possible to examine individual differences in achievement motivation by analyzing folk tales and children's stories. The current author is often reminded of this by being married to a Grade 3 teacher who spends many nights marking stories written by her students. There is great variability in the stories that Grade 3 children write in response to a specific theme or when allowed to write about anything they want at all. Some children seem preoccupied with achievement themes, while other children seem devoid of any concerns with achievement. Of course, achievement themes often reflect the goals of middle-class children in the new millennium. That is, achievement may come in the form of conquering some villain in the latest video game, but it is achievement nonetheless!

McClelland refers to the TAT assessment as an evaluation of needs with **implicit measures** because the person is not required to consciously reflect on his or her motives. Motives are inferred when derived from implicit measures. Structured self-report measures are referred to as **explicit measures** because the respondent is instructed to reflect on his or her motives. Typically, measures of implicit and explicit motives are not correlated significantly with each other (see Koestner, Weinberger, & McClelland, 1991; Woike, 1995). Koestner et al.'s experiments at McGill University in Montreal showed that an implicit measure derived from fantasies was not correlated significantly with self-reported motives. They suggested that the two forms of assessment involved different motivational systems that are responsive to distinctly different factors in a performance situation.

High versus Low Achievement Motivation: A TAT Illustration

As a way of illustrating achievement motivation and how the TAT is involved, consider the following responses given in a study conducted in Brazil (see De Vos, 1997). The answers provided are in response to a TAT picture (Card #1) that shows a boy playing a violin. High achievement motivation is reflected in the following story:

> When I look at this picture, I see a boy who wants to learn the violin. But by his face, the way he is looking at the violin, he is having difficulties ... Why is he having difficulties? Because he is still a youth, and at his age, all that is different is difficult, but with time, it will become easier for him. In the future, I perceive that he will eventually be able to play this violin—it is simply a matter of time. It is hard at first, but becomes more easier later. (De Vos, 1997, p. 448)

Keep the above response in mind when reading the next one. This response to the same picture was deemed to be low in achievement motivation:

> It was a boy who tried to play the violin. Maybe he was not able to do it for various reasons: for knowing not how to play or for having not learned it right. He quit playing and became very frustrated. He felt incapable of accomplishing something. This shows everybody's fight, the profits or the frustrations that the person's day had. He quit playing the instrument because a person who feels incapable once does not try to do it again. (De Vos, 1997, p. 450)

We see from these examples that not only do people project their motives and needs, but this is also often accompanied by cognitive beliefs about outcome expectancies.

Achievement Motivation from a Societal Perspective

Recall that McClelland placed great emphasis on the acquisition of motives via learning experiences. The acknowledgement of learning experience is important because it suggests that just as cultures differ in the experiences provided to children, they will also differ in the normative motives that operate. McClelland and Friedman (1952) demonstrated this by exploring the association between child-training practices and achievement motivation in eight Native American cultures (Navajo, Ciricahua Apache, Western Apache, Comanche, Flatheads, Hopi, Paiute, and Sanpoil). Achievement motivation was assessed by coding the achievement imagery in the ancient folk tales in each culture. The eight cultures differed greatly in the achievement motivation embedded in their folk tales. The main hypothesis of this study was confirmed: that cultures that placed a greater emphasis on independence-training and autonomy also had higher levels of achievement motivation, which presumably became reflected in the personal features of the members of these cultures.

Considering possible cultural differences, McClelland (1961) concluded that there were more similarities than differences when the achievement motive is aroused in the various cultures. He theorized that when achievement motivation is heightened, similar reactions are displayed regardless of whether the focus is on Navahos, Brazilian students, or high school students from radically different socioeconomic backgrounds. That is, the person tends to have thoughts of doing well by meeting an elevated performance standard, as well as thoughts of being blocked from attaining this standard. In addition, people of various cultures will consider various means of obtaining their goal and will anticipate joy or sadness depending on whether their efforts result in the achievement goal being attained.

McClelland demonstrated that it is possible to examine the fables and legends of ancient societies and determine the extent to which the achievement motive was present in these ancient societies. In his analysis of "achieving societies in the past," McClelland evaluated apparent changes in achievement motivation in various societies, including ancient Greece, Spain in the late Middle Ages, and England from the Middle Ages through to the Industrial Revolution. For example, regarding ancient Greece, McClelland posited that achievement motivation would have been high during its period of maximum growth but would then have fallen precipitously in conjunction with the decline of Greek civilization. He substantiated this by analyzing written documents from a variety of eras.

Although McClelland has pointed to similarities across cultures and societies, well-known achievement researcher Janet Spence has taken issue with this perspective. She pointed to some important differences as part of her critique of the benefits and costs of the individualistic focus on personal achievements that permeates most segments of North American society (see Spence, 1985). She suggested that excessive commitment to individualistic achievement is responsible for business and stock market scandals, for instance. She made a strong case for examining the achievement motive within the framework of prevailing cultural values; mainstream theories of achievement motivation apply to individualistic cultures, but may not apply to cultures where there is a greater emphasis on belonging to a group and fitting in. Specific examples cited by Spence (1985) include studies by Ramirez and Price-Williams (1976) and Gallimore, Boggs, and Jordan (1974). The first study showed that black children and Mexican-American children, relative to white children, gave answers to projective tests that were more focused on family achievement than individual achievement. The second study by Gallimore et al. (1974) showed with a sample of young Hawaiians that achievement motivation seemed to vary as a function of the values endorsed by various subcultures. Similarly, data from a Canadian study of occupational and achievement values show that French Canadian workers, relative to English-speaking workers, place a higher premium on being able to pursue their achievement goals in a work setting with a secure interpersonal environment (Kanungo & Bhanagar, 1978). This difference emerged even though participants in both groups had similar aspiration levels. Thus, there is clear evidence that the expression of achievement motivation, especially in how individual accomplishments reflect relationships with others, can indeed vary across cultural groups.

More generally, on the basis of a rather voluminous literature, what are some of the things that we know about people high in achievement motivation? Atkinson worked with McClelland and is another major theorist in this area. Atkinson's (1957) theory predicted and subsequent research confirmed that people with high achievement motivation have an overwhelming preference for tasks of moderate difficulty (see Heckhausen, 1977). Tasks of extreme difficulty have negative implications for the self if failure occurs, while easy tasks lack information value. Other research indicates that students with high need for achievement have a strong preference for a job in the business world, with stockbroker, office manager, and sales manager being their top three choices (McClelland, 1955). Given these data, you can imagine just how aversive and embarrassing it must have been for high need achievers to hear "You're fired!" from Donald Trump as they were dropped from his TV show *The Apprentice*.

KEY POINTS

- McClelland argued that implicit motives were best studied through fantasies and projective techniques rather than by studying actual behaviour.
- People with high achievement motivation prefer tasks of moderate ability because this provides them with more information than extremely difficult or extremely easy tasks.
- McClelland argued that motives are influenced by experiences and that cultures vary in the experiences provided.
- McClelland concluded that when it comes to achievement motivation, cultures are more similar than they are different. Spence has contested this and suggested that there are substantial differences for cultures with an individualistic versus collectivist orientation.

Affiliation Motivation

Extensive research has also examined affiliation motivation. Byrne, McDonald, and Mikawa (1963) used a scoring format for TAT responses reflecting affiliation motivation that enabled them to distinguish between approach responses and avoidance responses. Their analyses showed that people with high affiliation motivation produced stories reflecting high approach tendencies and low avoidance tendencies, and, as might be expected, people with low affiliation motivation generated stories reflecting high avoidance tendencies and low approach tendencies. People with moderate levels of affiliation motivation provided stories that were a mix of both approach and avoidance tendencies.

Most contemporary research in this area focuses on a specific form of affiliation motivation known as intimacy motivation. This is the need to establish intimate relations with others. Given its focus on intimacy, it seems to have a connotation of greater urgency and intensity than does the concept of affiliation motivation in general (note that a person with high intimacy motivation is described later in this chapter in Table 6.3).

The complexities and nuances of affiliation motivation have been demonstrated in other ways. Hill (1987) created a self-report measure known as the Interpersonal Orientation Scale to demonstrate that there are different motives that may operate within the same motivation domain. As a result, two people with high levels of a particular type of motivation may behave in a seemingly similar manner but for very different reasons. He suggested that two people can have an equal need to be with other people but this need can be expressed in very different ways. Hill (1987) identified four dimensions that make up the need for affiliation: (1) attention; (2) positive stimulation; (3) social comparison; and (4) emotional support. Affiliation motivation can result from needing attention and having one's accomplishments or life situation recognized and acknowledged by other people. Alternatively, it could simply be due to a craving for positive stimulation from other people as a source of social comparison. Festinger (1954) indicated that when we are unsure of our opinions and attitudes or whether our performance is good or bad, we engage in **social comparison** to establish whether we are similar to other people or atypical in some respects. Festinger's (1954) **similarity hypothesis** is the belief that we prefer to compare with similar others based on general characteristics. A male university student, for instance, would prefer to compare with another male university student rather than with a female university student.

According to Hill, one dimension of the desire to be with others (affiliation motivation) is the need for emotional support.

Finally, much of Hill's research has been focused on affiliating with others to gain emotional support. He showed that people prefer to obtain support from others who are interpersonally warm and expressive, but this preference was particularly strong among people who were in this component of affiliation motivation (Hill, 1991). Another investigation showed that people high in this component of affiliation motivation were more satisfied with warm and expressive partners. These people also reported actually seeking more emotional support in their daily lives. Finally, they reported deriving greater benefit from the emotional support provided by other people. Thus, they had a greater sense of relief by seeking comfort from other people (see Hill, 1997).

Are you high or low in affiliation motivation? If you have high affiliation motivation, which component or components are elevated? You can get some sense of this by considering how you would answer the sample items from the Interpersonal Orientation Scale found in Table 6.2.

KEY POINTS

- The affiliation motive is the need to be with other people.
- There are various forms of affiliation motive. Intimacy motives are a more urgent and intense form of motivation.
- Hill's research indicates that people can have a similar level of desire to be with others, but the reasons for this desire may vary between people. It could be due to the need for social comparison, for instance, or it could be a need for emotional support.

Table 6.2 Sample Items by Subscale from the Interpersonal Orientation Scale

Attention

I like to be around people when I can be the centre of attention.

I mainly like people who seem strongly drawn to me and who seem infatuated with me.

Positive Stimulation

One of the most enjoyable things I can think of that I like to do is just watching people and seeing what they are like.

I seem to get satisfaction out of contact with others more than most people realize.

Social Comparison

I find that I often have the desire to be around other people who are experiencing the same thing I am when I am unsure of what is going on.

I prefer to participate in activities along side other people rather than by myself because I like to see how I'm doing on the activity.

Emotional Support

If I feel unhappy or kind of depressed, I usually try to be around other people to make me feel better.

One of my greatest sources of comfort when things get rough is being around other people.

The Need for Power

The need for power is the third need that has received extensive empirical and theoretical attention. Much of this work has been conducted by David Winter, who defined the need for power as a need to have an impact on others or the world at large (see Winter, 1973). It is related to another psychological term known as effectance, which is a need to have an impact on people, places, and objects.

Participants are shown five pictures. They then must write a story for each picture. The five pictures were images of a ship captain, a bicycle race, a boxer, women in a laboratory, and trapeze artists. They have five minutes for each story (see Schultheiss, Dargle, & Rohde, 2003). Power and other motives (e.g., affiliation motive) are then assessed by scoring the content of each story according to Winter's (1994) *Manual for Scoring Imagery in Running Text*. Schultheiss et al. (2003) used this procedure to show that undergraduate students with higher power motive reported more frequent sexual intercourse. This finding was obtained for both men and women. In contrast, students with high affiliation motive reported significantly less sexual intercourse.

Not surprisingly, people who need power are more likely to engage in actions that reflect their focus on power attainment. Power has been linked to higher levels of aggressiveness (Mason & Blankenship, 1987) and gambling (Hirschowitz & Nell, 1983). People who need power seem to be quite persuasive in convincing others that they should adopt their approach or point of view (Schultheiss & Brunstein, 2002). This study conducted on persuasion at the University of Potsdam in Germany found that greater persuasiveness could be traced, in part, to the use of a variety of nonverbal behaviours, including gestures and well-timed eyebrow lifts.

One particularly salient finding is that the need for power is associated with heavy drinking (McClelland, Davis, Kalin, & Wanner, 1972). Alcohol has the subjective effect of increasing feelings of power and personal efficacy, despite ultimately being a depressant, so it is quite rewarding to someone who needs to feel powerful. This link between need for power and drinking applies to students. One study conducted in South Africa showed that male undergraduates with a high need for power tended to have a greater number of drinks, more consumption of alcohol, and they were more likely to have their first drink before the age of 16 (Nell & Strumpfer, 1978). They were also likely to have poorer academic performance. Chapter 13 contains a more extensive discussion of the need for power and the role of other personality factors in excessive drinking behaviour.

As might be expected, demographic and cultural factors are related differentially to motives. Women have higher levels of affiliation motive, relative to men, but consistent gender differences in power have not been found (Pang & Schultheiss, 2005; Schultheiss & Brunstein, 2001). A comparative study showed that African American students had higher levels of achievement motivation that either Asian American or white students. This study also showed that, in general, U.S. students had higher levels of achievement motivation and lower levels of power motivation than did a comparison sample of German students (Pang & Schultheiss, 2005).

Winter (2002) has been particularly interested in the levels of the need for power and need for achievement displayed by American presidents and their subsequent political outcomes. Psychological needs are measured by examining the content of presidents' speeches, books, and other printed material (see Winter, 2005). In general, a high need for achievement does not translate into political success, in part because events are often not controllable. However, a high need for power does relate to political success, in part because the need for power is associated with other desirable characteristics such as charisma and persuasiveness.

As for individual presidents, Winter (2002) has argued that Bill Clinton struggled in his first year in office, in part because he was high in achievement motivation but his need for power was low. However, analyses suggest that Clinton's need for power increased steadily throughout his eight years in office.

Research into the psychological needs of former U.S. presidents Bill Clinton and Richard Nixon indicated that Clinton had a growing need for power throughout his terms in office while Nixon, though high in his need for achievement and affiliation, was only moderate in his need for power.

Research on psychological needs of presidents includes an intriguing analysis of the psychological needs of Richard Nixon, who ultimately resigned his post as president as a result of the Watergate scandal in the 1970s. Winter and Carlson (1988) analyzed the content of Nixon's inaugural speech and concluded that Nixon had high needs for achievement and affiliation, but he was only moderate in the need for power. They also analyzed the memoirs of six Nixon aides who described the former president in great detail, and the same pattern emerged. Winter and Carlson suggested that Nixon's high need for achievement may have been his ultimate undoing in that the tapes provided information that was used against him instead of being used to document his achievement. His high affiliation motivation accounted for his willingness to remain a part of his college football team for four years despite being a "benchwarmer" and never getting to play in a game. Winter and Carlson (1988) also noted that Nixon's high need for affiliation could have accounted for his tendency to react in a paranoid manner. They observed that high need for affiliation is positive when it can be expressed within the context of safe and satisfying interpersonal relationships, but it can result in highly defensive behaviour when a person feels threatened.

Subsequent research by Winter and associates compared the psychological needs and other personality attributes of former U.S. President George Bush Sr. and the leader of the

Soviet Union, Mikhail Gorbachev (see Winter, Hermann, Weintraub, & Walker, 1991a, 1991b). This research is intriguing because it compared the personalities of the leaders of two world "superpowers." The motivational analysis suggested that both leaders had a fairly similar profile (high achievement and affiliation motives, average to low power motives), with Bush being distinguished somewhat by being more emotionally expressive and impulsive than Gorbachev.

Given these two profiles, the authors concluded in their first paper that "there is reason to be optimistic about the impact of Bush and Gorbachev on world peace and international cooperation, at least between the superpowers. Their motives seem benign" (Winter et al., 1991a, p. 241). However, in 1991, Iraq invaded Kuwait, and this resulted in the Persian Gulf War, led by the United States! These analyses highlight the fact that personality factors must be viewed within the context of ongoing events and situational factors, which may impinge on personal motives.

Contemporary research on power has sought to establish its links with physiological indices. Research by Schultheiss and colleagues at the University of Michigan examined how people high in power motivation responded to personal victories versus personal defeats by people engaged in a contest (see Schultheiss et al., 2005). This study found that in men with high power motivation, victories resulted in increases in the hormone testosterone, while losses resulted in decreases in testosterone. Another recent study examined how participants as a whole would respond when they experienced a manipulation that either increased their level of power motivation or their level of affiliation motivation (Schultheiss, Worth, & Stanton, 2004). How were motives manipulated? Here the researchers turned to movies that colloquially would be referred to according to stereotypes as "a movie for guys" or "a chick flick." Motives were manipulated experimentally by watching 30 minutes from a movie that either increased power motive (*The Godfather, Part II*) or affiliation motive (*The Bridges of Madison County*). It was hypothesized that increases in affiliative need would increase the hormone progesterone, while increased power motive would increase testosterone. The hypotheses were only partially supported. Levels of progesterone did increase as a result of watching *The Bridges of Madison County*. However, the manipulation of power need had a varying impact depending on the participant's gender and initial level of testosterone at the start of the experiment. It was found that men who were already high in testosterone had further increases in testosterone as a result of watching *The Godfather, Part II*. In contrast, women with initially high levels of testosterone had *decreases* in these levels after watching this movie. This research seemed to confirm McClelland's assertion that situational experiences influence motives.

Research has debunked some longstanding myths about the need for power. One such myth is that females are lower than males in the need for power. This has not been supported in research; mean level differences in the need for power are typically not found. Moreover, research shows that the same procedures that arouse the need for power in men have a similar effect on women (Stewart & Winter, 1976).

CONTEMPORARY THEORY AND RESEARCH ON MOTIVATION

We conclude this chapter with an overview of some current approaches to the study of individual differences in motivation. Theory and research has focused on the personal goals and projects that influence people daily. Current developments are represented below.

Personal Strivings

In the past 20 years, the personality literature has included several studies that focus on personal action constructs or life task constructs as motivational variables (Cantor, Norem, Niedenthal, Langston, & Brower, 1987; Emmons, 1986; Emmons & King, 1988; Little, 1983;).

One emphasis is on personal strivings, as described by Robert Emmons (1986, 1989). Personal strivings have been defined as "idiographic, goal-directed units that represent what the person is typically or characteristically trying to do" (Emmons & McAdams, 1991, p. 649). In other words, our personal strivings reflect our personality traits and other personal characteristics. Table 6.3 lists the personal strivings for three types of people: one who is high in intimacy motivation and the need to be with other people; one who is high in power motivation and is striving to dominate people and life events; and one who is high in achievement motivation and is striving to meet achievement-based goals. Inspect the strivings of these three people and see if you can detect how the themes of the various strivings vary according to the types of motivation involved.

A person high in achievement motivation strives to follow through on goals and to be successful.

The predictive utility of individual differences in personal strivings was illustrated in a study of personal strivings, life events, and well-being by Emmons (1991). Participants listed 15 personal strivings and then recorded life events and moods over a three-week period. Subsequent analyses showed that power strivings were associated with reduced well-being, while affiliation strivings were associated with increased well-being. Type of striving did not interact with type of life event to predict individual differences in mood state.

Table 6.3 Personal Strivings for Three Types of People

Strivings of Person High in Intimacy Motivation
Make my mother proud of me
Give people the benefit of the doubt
Help my friends
Study for tests ahead of time
Understand others
Maintain good relationships with siblings
Enjoy free time
Get along with roommates
Make things easier on my mother whenever possible
Complete the tasks expected of me at work
Be a good friend
Stay interesting during conversation times
Strivings of Person High in Power Motivation
Be assertive when I feel violated or taken advantage of
Be honest in my speech and behaviour
Use "I" messages when communicating
Be disciplined in my study habits
Avoid confrontations
Force friendships into deeper intimacy than others are willing or ready for
Not get defensive when I'm confronted
Be responsible for my actions
Arrange things so I get my own way
Take care of my body—stay in shape
Be the peacemaker in a crowd or relationship
Make myself look like the "good guy"
Maintain too many friendships
Strivings of Person High in Achievement Motivation
Be successful in everything I do
Be an understanding and caring person
Be a patient worker
Help my friends and family when I'm needed
Enjoy life
Express an opinion on issues when I'm in a discussion
Push myself to my fullest potential
Keep up with latest fashions
Look at life without anxiety
Follow through on my promises and goals
Not draw too much attention to myself

Source: Emmons & McAdams, 1991.

A recent study of personal strivings and binge drinking in university students showed that personal strivings may be protective or associated with risky behaviour depending on the nature of the striving. Simons, Christopher, and McLaury (2004) had participants generate a list of personal strivings, and then they returned 30 days later and provided accounts of their drinking behaviour. Raters tabulated the number of personal strivings reflecting achievement, affiliation, health, and self-presentational issues.

Students with greater achievement strivings reported fewer alcohol-related problems and slightly lower levels of binge drinking behaviour than students with fewer achievement strivings. In contrast, students who were preoccupied with self-presentational strivings involving their image to others reported more alcohol-related problems. Perhaps this reflects greater self-focused attention and ego involvement on the part of these students.

Personal Projects

A central focus in this area is research on the personal projects that are pursued and how personal projects are cognitively appraised (Little, 1983). Brian Little introduced the personal projects concept. Little is a Distinguished Research Professor at Carleton University in Ottawa, Ontario, and has conducted research as a visiting professor at Harvard University. A personal project is defined by Little (1983) as "a set of interrelated acts extending over time, which is intended to maintain or attain a state of affairs seen by the individual" (p. 276). Personal projects are similar though not identical to related concepts such as current concerns, life tasks, and personal strivings in that they all focus on issues that are relevant and central to a person's daily life (see Klinger, 1989). Because the focus is on the personal goals and issues of importance for each unique individual, investigation in this area typically entails an open-ended and idiographic assessment of central themes that reflect each person's issues of importance (see Little, 2005).

Personal projects have been described as "a mid-level construct." This is a construct that is more responsive to ongoing concerns (as opposed to a static personality trait). It is a process-oriented construct that reflects proximally how a personality trait is expressed in terms of current goals. Thus, it is reasonable to expect that a mid-level construct, relative to a more distal personality trait, will have a stronger association with daily behaviours.

The specific projects that people pursue may be quite stable, but they should change as a function of life experiences and temporal changes in life stage. While it is best to demonstrate this with a longitudinal investigation, cross-sectional research confirms age-related changes in personal projects (see Ogilvie, Rose, & Heppen, 2001). Ogilvie and associates asked samples of adolescents, middle-aged adults, and elderly adults to identify their personal projects and the main purpose for each project. In general, people listed five to six personal projects. Ogilvie et al. then developed a personal projects taxonomy that entails classifying each project according to four motives: (1) acquire (obtain a desired outcome); (2) cure (overcome an existing negative condition); (3) prevent (avoid a possible negative outcome) and; (4) keep (avoid the loss of an existing positive condition). Illustrations of each category are provided in Table 6.4. Age group comparisons showed that the acquire category was the most common one for all age groups, but there was an age-related stepwise decline in the number of projects reflecting the acquire category. Not surprisingly, the elderly participants had a substantially higher number of projects in the keep category. The number of projects in the cure category was significantly higher for the middle-aged and oldest groups, relative to the adolescent group. These data illustrate how projects tend to vary as a function of developmental stage, as would be expected if they reflected current concerns.

Table 6.4 A Taxonomy of Personal Projects Categories

Project Category	Goal	Example
Acquire	Obtain positive outcome	Exercise to get a new partner
Cure	Remove negative condition	Exercise to improve poor heart condition
Prevent	Avoid negative condition	Floss three times a day to avoid tooth decay
Keep	Avoid losing positive condition	Compliment and show caring for appealing mate

Research has confirmed some expected associations between individual differences in personality traits and personal project dimensions. For example, Blunt and Pychyl (2000) have shown that procrastination can be associated with all phases of personal projects, but, not surprisingly, procrastination in students is particularly likely to influence the initial orientation toward a project. A previous study by Lay (1990) examined the personal project appraisals of 72 students from York University in Toronto. Each student listed and evaluated 12 personal projects. Various dimensions were rated, including the aversiveness of the project and the likelihood that the project would be completed and would be successful (i.e., the likelihood of failure). Trait procrastinators regarded their projects as being more aversive and higher in the likelihood of failure. Supplementary analyses showed that only those projects that had a deadline were seen as aversive; open-ended projects without a deadline were not regarded this way.

Another recent study established that people high in trait optimism had more positive personal project appraisals (Jackson, Weiss, Lundquist, & Soderlind, 2002). Specifically, higher trait optimism was associated with rating projects as being lower in strain, and higher in mastery control and positive identity fulfillment.

A five-factor analysis of personal projects has yielded some fairly predictable findings (see Little, Lecci, & Watkinson, 1992). Neuroticism is related to negative project appraisals, while conscientiousness is associated with positive project appraisals. This fits with the Blunt and Pychyl (2000) finding that procrastination (a specific form of low conscientiousness) is linked with a negative orientation toward starting projects. It was also found that extroversion and agreeableness were linked with positive project appraisals, but particularly if the projects involved interpersonal goals. Collectively, these data suggest that those people who have certain personality traits are more likely to be doing particular projects, and adaptive personality styles are linked with more positive cognitive evaluations of important personal projects.

Extensive research on personal projects has examined their association with psychological distress. The general premise of the research on personal projects and adjustment is that negative appraisals of personal projects are associated with a variety of forms of negative affectivity, including symptoms of anxiety and depression. Existing research has provided support for this view (Lecci, Karoly, Briggs, & Kuhn, 1994; Omodei & Wearing, 1990; Palys & Little, 1983; Ruehlman & Wolchik, 1988; Salmela-Aro, 1992). Research conducted in Canada established that happiness is linked with perceived goal efficacy for personal projects (McGregor & Little, 1998). In their initial study, Palys and Little (1983) tested the hypothesis that reported life satisfaction is associated with the manner in which individuals "structure and organize their projects and concerns" (p. 1221). Palys and Little (1983) used the personal projects methodology developed by Little (1983) to establish that people with relatively low life satisfaction tended to pursue projects that were high in difficulty and low in enjoyment.

Ruehlman and Wolchik (1988) provided further evidence of the importance of personal projects in psychological adjustment. They had 229 university students rate their four most important projects on the 17 appraisal dimensions formulated by Little (1983). Factor analyses of project ratings yielded three summary factors representing project mastery, project strain, and project self-involvement. Project mastery consisted of such dimensions as project progress, time, absorption, outcome, control, and enjoyment. Project strain included such dimensions as difficulty, stress, challenge, and negative impact. Finally, the self-involvement factor included the perceived value and degree of self-initiation associated with the project. Correlational analyses with measures of well-being and psychological distress established that greater distress and lower well-being were associated with projects rated as high in strain and low in mastery and self-involvement.

In related research, Omodei and Wearing (1990) examined the associations among positive affect, negative affect, need satisfaction, and involvement in personal projects in a small sample of 39 adults. It was found that greater involvement and greater absorption in personal projects were associated significantly with higher levels of positive affect and lower levels of negative affect.

Lecci et al. (1994) examined the link between personal project dimensions and symptoms of depression and anxiety in 152 university students. Consistent with earlier research, it was found that negative project appraisals were associated jointly with depression and anxiety symptoms. Specifically, distressed students rated their personal projects as more stressful and difficult and low in enjoyment. They also perceived that they were low in degree of control and deficient in the skills required to complete the project. Collectively, the findings described above indicate that the types of projects that are pursued and the types of appraisals associated with these projects are key factors in personal adjustment; greater distress is reported by people who perceive that they are confronted with difficult and challenging projects that do not promote feelings of personal mastery. These findings serve to underscore and emphasize the importance of the things that matter in people's lives. Personal strivings and personal projects represent a potent source of individual differences that can make a difference in how we feel every day.

KEY POINTS

- Personal strivings and personal projects are mid-level constructs. As opposed to more distal traits, they reflect current concerns and how traits are expressed in everyday actions and behaviours.
- Personal strivings and personal projects are idiographic because they focus on the unique themes of a particular individual. Personal project appraisals indicate that projects can be rated by positive features and negative features, such as the strain of a project.
- Positive appraisals of personal projects contribute to greater well-being. Personal projects are associated in meaningful ways with other personality traits (e.g., optimists have more positive appraisals of their projects).

Summary

Chapter 6 provided an overview of individual differences in motivation. Much of the chapter was an extension of the previous chapter on psychoanalytic theories in that Henry Murray's theory of psychological needs included the role of unconscious. Indeed, Murray endorsed some key Freudian concepts, but also distinguished himself by providing a complex theory of physical and psychological needs in his book *Explorations in Personality*.

Various aspects of Murray's theory were outlined, including his concept of situational press and the need to consider the complex interplay of personal and situational factors that combine with cultural factors to produce individual differences in behaviour. The complexity of needs was addressed in such themes as conflicting needs and a need hierarchy where one need enlists the aid of another.

Chapter 6 illustrated how psychological needs and related motivational factors can be represented in individuals. Infamous people such as Adolf Hitler, Mark David Chapman, and the Unabomber were used to illustrate key concepts.

In addition, the assessment of psychological needs was examined through a description and review of the Thematic Apperception Test, as well as structured self-report personality scales based on Murray's theory (e.g., the Adjective Check List and Personal Research Form).

In addition to describing needs in general, Chapter 6 included a more detailed analysis of specific psychological needs. Individual differences in the need for achievement, affiliation, and power were discussed. These were analyzed in the needs of specific political leaders with high levels of achievement and affiliation motivation, and moderate levels of the need for power.

Finally, more contemporary research was described to illustrate how individual differences in motivation can be reflected in our daily concerns. This theme was illustrated through a description of research on personal strivings by Emmons and his colleagues and research on personal projects by Little and his colleagues.

Questions to Consider

1 Do you accept that both personality traits and personal needs are important? What are your three top needs? How do they fit in with the list of needs outlined by Murray or the other themes identified in this chapter?

2 List your top five personal projects. What were your top five personal projects in high school? In your estimation, how much do your projects reflect your personality versus the current situation or situations you find yourself in?

3 Was there a time when you were with a group of people and you all had a similar situation to deal with? Is your view of this situation an example of alpha press or beta press?

4 Do you think that all politicians are essentially the same, or they can be differentiated by their needs for power, affiliation, and achievement motivation? To what extent does the politician role take precedence over these motives? If you were a politician, what would be your levels of power, affiliation, and achievement motivation?

5 What are your views on the roots of needs and motives? Do you agree with Murray that the focus should be on physiological processes in the brain and the role of the unconscious? Or do you subscribe to McClelland's position that experience plays a major role in establishing motives?

Key Terms

alpha press, p. 208
alter ego, p. 211
behavioural science, p. 216
beta press, p. 208
effectance, p. 234
explicit measures, p. 229
fusion of needs, p. 210
habit system, p. 206
implicit measures, p. 229
interdependent self-construal, p. 228
ipsative scoring, p. 225
multiform method, p. 207
need set, p. 210
object relations theory, p. 223
ordination, p. 210
periodicity of needs, p. 210
personology, p. 206
press, p. 208
primary needs, p. 211
psychodrama, p. 214
regnancy, p. 209
schedules, p. 210
secondary needs, p. 211
similarity hypothesis, p. 233
social comparison, p. 233
subsidation of needs, p. 210
thema, p. 208
viscerogenic, p. 211

Key Theorists

David McClelland, p. 229
Henry Murray, p. 206

chapter seven

HUMANISTIC THEORIES AND SELF-ACTUALIZATION

- Common Themes of the Humanists
- Maslow's Humanistic Theory
- Carl Rogers
- The Assessment and Measurement of Self-Actualization
- The Contemporary Focus on Well-Being

Our first baby changed me as a psychologist. It made the behaviorism I had been so enthusiastic about look so foolish that I could not stomach it any more. It was impossible. Having a second baby, and learning how profoundly different people are even before birth, made it impossible for me to think in terms of the kind of learning psychology in which you can teach anybody anything.

—ABRAHAM MASLOW (1971, P. 163)

It is through hearing people that I have learned all I know about individuals, about personality, about interpersonal relationships…I mean of course, hearing deeply. I mean I hear the words, the thoughts, the feeling tones, the personal meaning, even the meaning that is below the conscious intent of the speaker.

—CARL ROGERS (1995, PP.7–8)

CONSIDER THE CASE OF Ellen West, a troubled young woman who was not helped by therapy. Quoting from her diaries, classic theorist Carl Rogers wrote:

> "I am isolated. I sit in a glass ball, I see people through a glass wall. I scream but they do not hear me." Ellen's words ring in my ears. No one *did* hear her as a person. Beyond her childhood years—and perhaps not even then—neither her parents, nor her two analysts, nor her physicians ever seem to have respected her enough to hear her deeply. They did not deal with her as a person capable of meeting life, a person whose experiencing is trustworthy, whose inner feelings are worthy of acceptance. How, then, could she listen to herself or respect the experiencing going on within her?
>
> Reading this tragic case angers me (as will have been evident), but it also encourages me. I feel angry at the tragic waste of a human being, encouraged because I feel that we have learned enough during the intervening years that if Ellen West came today to my office, or to the offices of many therapists I know, she would be helped. (Rogers, 1961; reprinted in Kirschenbaum & Henderson, 1989, p. 165)

The case of Ellen West is disturbing. She committed suicide at the age of 33. West suffered from symptoms of anorexia and depression though she was diagnosed initially with schizophrenia. A key precipitating event in her demise was falling deeply in love with a man deemed unsuitable by her father, who then insisted that the engagement be terminated. According to Rogers (1961), West had an extensive history of living her life according to the dictates of others rather than according to her own wishes. Rogers also felt that West was the victim of preconceived ideas because her true desires were never really probed nor were they understood.

Humanistic theories of personality are the focus of Chapter 7. At the root of these theories is the notion that we need to focus on the individual experience of each human rather than how these people are interpreted by others. In the case of Ellen West, for instance, Carl Rogers asked, "Did anyone ever really try to look at things through Ellen's eyes?" Or were they simply too preoccupied with evaluating her according to their own biased hypotheses? As we will see below, the theme of living according to the dictates of other people is a central one in Rogers' theory.

In addition to emphasizing personal experience, humanistic theories stress the innate goodness of people and their continual striving for self-improvement.

The theories described in this chapter are also regarded as **organistic theories** or holistic theories. Organistic theories focus on the development of the entire organism. The leading proponent of this focus was Kurt Goldstein, a psychiatrist who studied the brain injuries of First World War soldiers. Goldstein (1939) felt that the specific symptoms of these soldiers could only be understood and treated within the context of the entire organism (the person), and the organism was motivated primarily by a drive for **self-actualization**. Self-actualization is a continuous and unrelenting striving to develop one's full potential. It reflects a desire for both self-improvement and self-completion.

We will explore the concept of self-actualization in more detail by examining the theories of Abraham Maslow and Carl Rogers. Both influential theorists continue to have an enormous impact on society, with legions of devout followers around the world. Although both theories have many unique aspects, some common themes can also be detected. These themes are outlined briefly below.

COMMON THEMES OF THE HUMANISTS

Shared themes among humanists include (1) the central role of personal growth; (2) the importance of openness to personal experience; (3) living in the here and now; (4) personal responsibility; and (5) the inherent goodness of people.

Theorists in this area place prime importance on the central theme of personal growth. They argue that we rarely cease striving when our immediate needs have been met; rather, we are motivated to continue to develop in a positive manner and try to better ourselves. This growth process is part of the human experience. Life problems may derail the growth process but we are still motivated to grow and achieve a more satisfying existence. This theme will be discussed at length below.

As noted above, theorists in this area also emphasize the importance of openness to personal experience. Maslow discusses openness to experience as part of his description of self-actualization and the characteristics of healthy people. This is also illustrated in Rogers' theory with its emphasis on how the person as a whole is the source of all experience. As we saw in his interpretation of the plight of Ellen West, Rogers highlighted the perceptual experiences of the organism and how various aspects of the self-concept combine to form an overall sense of self. Thus, there is an emphasis on the phenomenology of the individual and the unique perceptions and viewpoints of each person as the appropriate unit of analysis. Even in situations where the person's perceptions and viewpoints are entirely incorrect, this is how this person sees the world, and it is accepted as the starting point for a humanistic therapist who realizes that it is how this person defines his or her world. Thus, there is a belief that no one knows the person better than the person knows himself or herself. As a result, it is absurd for therapists to tell people what their behaviour really means. Similarly, Rogers (1947) reminded us that behaviour is not directly influenced by cultural or organic factors; rather, it is our *perception* of these factors that wields the influence.

Although striving for growth and self-actualization inevitably focuses on the future self, as part of the openness to experience, theorists in this area emphasize that it is essential to be attentive to the here and now rather than becoming preoccupied with the past or consumed with future possibilities. People focused on the here and now have a life process approach that allows them to experience daily events. Individuals who are too concerned about previous problems or possible threats in the future are not able to fully experience and appreciate their current experiences, and if taken to an extreme, a lack of focus on the here and now can contribute to various forms of psychological distress. This point has been illustrated by Canadian researchers Darcy Santor and David Zuroff. They created two subscales assessing individual differences in accepting the past and reminiscing about the past (Santor & Zuroff, 1994). Accepting the past was defined as an ongoing process involving an internal cognitive representation of one's past as satisfying. Reminiscing about the past is simply the frequency with which people reflect on past life experiences. They found that depression and health problems were strongly associated with a failure to accept the past, but were not associated with simply reminiscing about the past.

The theme of **personal responsibility** is another prevailing view among theorists in this area. Although we may deny it, we are ultimately responsible for what happens to us. The notion of personal culpability for actions is one of the cornerstones of this approach, and we should reject a person's mechanistic views that promote the idea that we are unable to exercise self-control and achieve a sense of self-determination. In essence, then, our behaviours are consciously made personal choices of what we want to do at a particular moment. This stance is quite different from the Freudian view that we are controlled by early childhood experiences. Accordingly, the message in this kind of therapy is that people do indeed have the power to become whatever they want.

Clearly, the theories described in Chapter 7 reflect a very positive view of people. Maslow and Rogers both emphasize the basic goodness of people. You might find their views to be a refreshing change from other theorists and psychology in general, which tends to emphasize negative themes (e.g., stress and psychopathology). Maslow and Rogers both emphasized what people are capable of and the potential levels of greatness that may be possible to achieve. Maslow is credited with providing the early impetus for a current movement within psychology known as the **positive psychology** movement. Contemporary theorists such as Martin Seligman have embraced the general theme of positive psychology, and they have argued that it is time for psychology to have less of an interest in the negative (maladjustment) and focus instead on positive adjustment and the factors that maximize well-being and self-satisfaction. This is in keeping with the views of humanistic psychologists such as Maslow who also emphasize the inherent goodness of people and the unique positive features of each individual.

This strength of the humanistic approach is also one of its drawbacks. Many people take exception to the notion espoused by theorists such as Rogers that there is a good side to some of the most heinous characters in history. It is difficult to identify and consider the positive features of infamous killers Ted Bundy and Paul Bernardo, for instance. However, it is still important to cling to the notion that everyone is human and the vast majority of people at least have a capacity for goodness.

KEY POINTS

- Humanists believe people are basically good and capable of great things.
- Humanistic theories recognize our capacity for growth and our need to realize our full potential. Growth and self-development require that we are open to experience.
- Openness means living in the present (the here and now) and not being too preoccupied with the past or future.
- Humanistic theorists emphasize self-determination and establishing a sense of personal responsibility.

MASLOW'S HUMANISTIC THEORY

Abraham Maslow was born in Brooklyn, New York in 1908. He died in California in 1970. Although he had a relatively short life, Maslow made a number of important contributions. He was the first-born son of immigrants from Russia who lived in New York. His parents were very demanding and had high expectations, but Maslow rose to the challenge and became a very successful academic.

Abraham Maslow developed a universal hierarchy of human needs, which progressed from basic health and safety needs required for survival to upper level needs for love, esteem, and self-actualization.

Maslow attended University of Wisconsin, where he became Harry Harlow's first graduate student. In his last interview, Maslow indicated that he was eager to attend graduate school because he had just discovered Watson's behaviourism and he had become enamoured with it. In this same interview, Maslow recounted his various life experiences and noted that his interest in humanism grew out of the events of the Second World War and wanting to develop a psychology that would help us understand others and human nature in general when we are at the peace table. He recounted that "I wanted to prove that humans are capable of something grander than war, prejudice, and hatred. I wanted to make science consider all the people: the best specimen of mankind I could find" (Hoffman, 1992, p. 4).

Maslow has had an enormous impact on contemporary society. His humanistic theory has been applied to education and business contexts, and his beliefs have had a resonance with the general public. Maslow was the only psychologist to be included on *Esquire* magazine's 1982 list of the 100 most influential people.

Maslow's key concepts include the distinction between deficiency motives and growth motives, as well as his famous hierarchy of needs. He is also well-known for his analysis of the characteristics of psychologically healthy people. These concepts are described in more detail below.

Deficiency Motives and Growth Motives

The difference between deficiency and growth motives is a central aspect of Maslow's theory. Maslow believed that neurosis can be regarded as a deficiency disease. That is, the neurotic individual desperately needs something that is absent. Maslow emphasized ungratified wishes for safety, belongingness and identification, love relationships, and respect and prestige. Psychological health, on the other hand, is associated with the pursuit of growth motives and actions that will help us realize our full potential.

Neurosis is a lack of personal growth and neuroticized needs represent a loss of capacity or capability. "It is a falling short of what one could have been, and even, one can say, what *should* have been... Human and personal possibilities have been lost" (Maslow, 1971, p. 32). Conflict is an indicator of health in the sense that hopeless and apathetic people have given up entirely, but conflict reflects some desire to achieve a more favourable level of existence. The person who experiences conflict is bothered by it, and rather than packing it in, has a need to renew a sense of growth, but must experience some painful experiences along the journey to a higher level of self-development.

The General Characteristics of Needs

In many respects, Maslow's name has become synonymous with the hierarchy of needs. Maslow proposed a universally applicable hierarchy of needs, consisting of five types of needs arranged by their relevance to survival: survival needs, safety needs, the need for belonging and love, esteem needs, and the need for self-actualization. These needs are described below and are displayed in Figure 7.1. First, however, some general aspects of needs are discussed.

Lower needs (e.g., physiological) are stronger than higher needs (e.g., self-actualization). When more than one need is frustrated, the lower needs are predominant and stronger. Lower needs are more relevant for survival, and survival needs take precedence. In addition, lower needs are described as more localized, tangible, and specific than higher needs.

The notion of a hierarchy signifies that lower level needs must be satisfied before the individual can proceed to the next level. This seems entirely logical: a person who has an imminent threat to his or her survival is not going to be worried immediately about developing a positive sense of self and maximizing personal potential.

Gratification of the higher needs has important consequences in terms of positive health outcomes. That is, higher needs have both survival value and growth value.

Importantly, gratification of higher needs has great civic and social consequences. This reflects an unselfish approach that can enhance the well-being of others. However, Maslow maintains that gratification of needs, while contributing to society, can still foster greater individualism. He believed that individualism does not preclude collectivism; both can be fully developed within the same person. There is a close link between trying to improve one's culture and trying to improve oneself. Maslow maintained that the betterment of culture fosters personal growth and represents movement toward self-actualization.

The Hierarchy of Needs

The hierarchy of needs is shown in Figure 7.1. Note that the higher needs are believed to have evolved later in human development. Maslow noted that all living organisms have a need for food, and there is evidence that both apes and humans have a need for love, but the need that humans have for self-actualization is not found in other animals.

Higher needs also occur later in personal development. Maslow stated that, for example, "As for self-actualization, even Mozart had to wait until he was three or four" (Maslow, 1987, p. 57).

Most of the lower needs reflect deficiency motives. However, self-actualization is a reflection of growth motives.

Figure 7.1 Maslow's Hierarchy of Needs

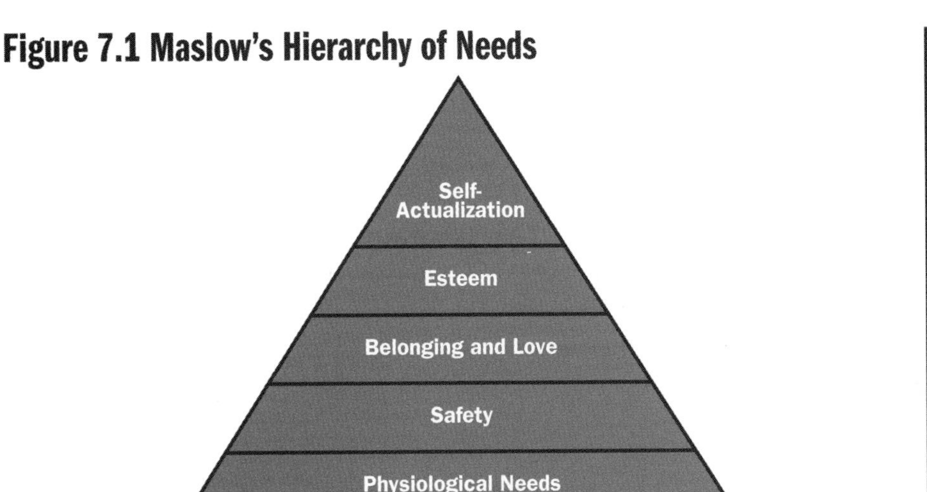

The first level of physiological needs incorporates many of the primary needs that were included in Murray's theory of needs (see Chapter 6). These are the basic biological needs (e.g., to satisfy thirst, hunger, need for air) that must be addressed for survival reasons. Physiological needs predominate in underprivileged societies.

The hierarchy's second level (safety needs) can be quite general and include both physical safety and emotional safety. Just as an infant must have basic physiological needs met, he or she also needs to feel safe and actually be safe.

The first two needs are both deficiency needs and are satisfied once the desired object or goal has been obtained. Maslow suggested that the lower level needs are basic needs and they are instinctual or instinctoid needs. He outlined five characteristics of long-term deficiency-related basic needs. A basic need exists when (1) its absence breeds illness; (2) its presence prevents illness; (3) its restoration cures illness; (4) in free choice situations, it is preferred over other choices; and (5) it is inactive and seemingly not present in the psychologically healthy person.

Maslow postulated that once our basic survival and safety needs have been addressed, our interests turn to social connections and fostering a sense that we belong with others and we are loved. **Belonging and love needs** reflect a need for sustained intimacy with others, either in the form of knowing that we fit in with significant others, or establishing a mutual loving relationship. Maslow distinguishes between selfish and unselfish forms of love and suggests that there are two substages to this level of the hierarchy that reflect D-love versus B-love. D-love is a deficient form of love that involves satisfying personal needs and gratifications. B-love is a love for another person's being, and feelings of affection are focused on enhancing the well-being of one's person without regard to personal needs and gratifications. We must work through our need for selfish love before we can develop a much more adaptive form of love. Maslow (1962) went so far as to suggest that no ideal relationship could ever be established with anyone, especially children, if the person in question was not able to reach a state of B-love. The presence of a selfish, deficiency-based love is significant. People who are high in deficiency motives have been described by Maslow as highly self-conscious, egocentric, and oriented toward gratification.

Maslow's observations about selfish versus unselfish love helped paved the way for theory and research on different love styles. Clearly, unselfish love is associated with self-actualization. An earlier study conducted on the love experiences of university students confirmed the existence of a strong correlation between the degree of healthy, unselfish love experiences and levels of self-actualization (Dietch, 1978). Additional analyses showed that among people who had terminated love relationships, resentment toward the former partner was associated negatively with self-actualization. The degree of B-love was unrelated to the length of the relationship, but females had higher levels of B-love than did males.

These data accord with observations made by Maslow (1970) about psychologically healthy people. He stated that living one's life according to higher level needs contributes to many positive outcomes, including greater biological efficiency, greater longevity, less disease, better sleep, and a happier and rich "inner life." He observed further that psychologically healthy people have led loving lives, and they have both given and received extensive love. He noted paradoxically that these people need love less than the average person because they have already experienced enough love. Maslow extended this concept to his distinction between B-cognition and D-cognition. He argued that our cognitive styles and mental preoccupations could be either focused on deficiency-related thoughts or a higher level of cognition and awareness that involved an appreciation of self and others in an unselfish manner.

Although the need for love has received most of the attention in extant research, there is an increasing focus among researchers on the need to belong. Baumeister and Leary (1995), in their informative review paper, suggested that the need to belong is a core need that "has multiple and strong effects on emotional patterns and cognitive processes" (p. 497), and it was distinguishable from other constructs such as attachment styles. They were somewhat critical of Maslow for positing this need because he did so without reviewing existing literature or reporting new data on this need.

Extensive research indicates that people who have not satisfied their need to belong are at great risk for emotional and physical problems. The most well-known theory is Durkheim's (1963) theory of **anomic suicide**: that people are prone to suicide if they feel alienated from others and lack a sense of belonging and ties with other people. One of the worst feelings a person can have is that he or she is "a misfit" who feels disconnected from other people.

Baumeister and Leary's review (1995) provided the theoretical impetus for measures assessing individual differences in the sense of belonging, and this, in turn, has sparked empirical research on the correlates of the need to belong. For instance, contemporary research has established that people who are high in the need to belong are more accurate in non-verbal tasks that involve identifying vocal tones and facial emotions (Pickett, Gardner, & Knowles, 2004). Another recent study of 194 retirees from Australia showed that the need to belong was associated with a greater participation in physical activities with others and actually achieving a sense of belonging (Bailey & McLaren, 2005). Moreover, the need to belong predicted greater mental health among retirees! So, just like the old song says, "People who need people are the luckiest people in the world."

The fourth level of Maslow's hierarchy is **esteem needs** that reflect feelings of prestige and recognition through personal accomplishments. This is the need for people to perceive themselves as competent and achieving. Failure to satisfy esteem needs results in feelings of inferiority, helplessness, and discouragement. The placement of esteem needs at a higher point in the hierarchy than the love needs implies that there is more to life than love.

The self-actualization level is the final level of attainment in the hierarchy. Maslow (1962) defined self-actualization as an episode in which the person experiences intense enjoyment and a sense of being fully functioning and integrated. The person who is self-actualized is recognized as being highly open to experience. Recall that openness to experience is one of the five trait dimensions of the five-factor model. Self-actualization, according to Maslow, is a state of ego-transcendence that involves actualizing potential and feeling closer to one's actual being. It is process and state rather than a static endpoint, and it can come at any time for a person, but self-actualized people attain this state more regularly than others.

KEY POINTS

- Behaviour is motivated by deficiency motives and growth motives.
- Maslow postulated that there was a universal hierarchy or stage-like sequence of human needs.
- The needs progress from basic health and safety needs required for survival to the upper level needs for love, esteem, and self-actualization.
- Higher level needs emphasize self-completion and self-development through realizing potentials that we may not know we have.

Maslow believed that only a fraction of 1% of the population achieve self-actualization. Maslow predicted that if 7% of a culture were able to attain self-actualization, profound changes would improve the lot of everyone in that culture.

Also, Maslow adopted a process-oriented view, so a person could reach a state of being self-actualized but not stay self-actualized. Why are so few people able to attain self-actualization and stay at this level? Maslow (1962) suggested that part of the problem is the belief that our inner nature has an evil, anti-social aspect, and working toward self-actualization could arouse concerns about activating this evil component of the self. The main reason suggested by Maslow (1962) is that we have lost the strong instincts that tell us what to do, and when, how, and where to do it.

Motivation may also be a factor. When asked to list what makes most people happy, wealthy and non-wealthy participants mentioned the love category most often (Diener, Horwitz, & Emmons, 1985). Self-actualization needs were mentioned next by the wealthy respondents, but physiological needs were second for non-wealthy respondents.

Self-actualization also loses its importance due to world events. Safety needs become especially important during times of war and strife, such as during the horrific events in the United States on September 11, 2001. This point was illustrated dramatically in a survey of the personal values of 500 aviation industry employees before and after the attacks (see Murphy, Gordon, & Mullen, 2004). In terms of the ranked importance of values, family security was the top value before and after September 11. Health and freedom were also highly rated before and after the attacks. In contrast, self-actualization values such as a sense of accomplishment were highly rated (6th overall out of 18) before the attacks but this dropped to 16th out of 18 after the attacks. In contrast, hoping for a world at peace went from 16th before the attacks to 3rd place afterwards. A reasonable question is why world peace wasn't ranked higher to begin with, but the main point to draw from these data is that world events that raise safety concerns can decrease, at least momentarily, the importance of self-actualization goals and values.

Maslow was very much a realist. He recognized that even highly self-actualized people are not perfect, and he recognized further that environmental factors may determine whether a person can pursue higher level needs. Favourable conditions outside the self enable people to pursue self-actualization and very good conditions must exist. He noted that familial, economic, political, and educational stressors and problems might make it impossible, at least for the time being, to strive for self-actualization.

The Psychological Characteristics of Healthy, Self-Actualized People

Maslow developed his concept of self-actualization through a variety of means, including analyzing the characteristics of famous people he considered to have attained self-actualization. This included such individuals as social reformer Jane Addams, Albert Einstein, Aldous Huxley, William James, Thomas Jefferson, Abraham Lincoln, Eleanor Roosevelt, and Albert Schweitzer. The psychological characteristics of healthy, self-actualized people as deemed by Maslow are shown in Table 7.1.

Table 7.1 Maslow's Characteristics of Healthy, Self-Actualized People

Superior perception of reality
Increased acceptance of self, of others, and of nature
Increased spontaneity
Increase in problem-centring
Increased detachment and desire for privacy
Increased autonomy and resistance to enculturation
Greater freshness of appreciation, and richness of emotional reaction
Higher frequency of mystical, peak experiences
Increased identification with the human species
Changed interpersonal relations
More democratic character structure
Greatly increased creativeness
Certain changes in the value system

One of the most noteworthy attributes in Table 7.1 is the tendency to have peak experiences. These are moments when the person feels heavenly, and there is a sense that time and space and the self have been transcended. People having these experiences are free, at least for the moment, from feelings of fear and self-doubt. Maslow suggested that virtually all of us have peak experience moments at one time or another, though not everyone is consciously aware of them.

KEY POINTS

- Self-actualization involves transcending the ego. It is a state or process rather than an endpoint.
- Everyone has moments of self-actualization at some point, though attaining the self-actualization level is rare and occurs for less than 1% of people, according to Maslow.
- Peak experiences invoke feelings of ecstasy and wonderment and are moments of self-actualization.

Maslow suggested that peak experiences are often equated with amazing sexual experiences, though he also found that music led him to have the occasional peak experience. Peak experiences may occur in a variety of contexts based on what is meaningful to the individual. For example, Michael J. Fox, the well-known Canadian actor, seemed to feel a peak experience while testifying before a U.S. Senate Appropriations Subcommittee. Fox was part of a lobby group seeking to increase research funding for Parkinson's Disease, which he has. Fox recounted that:

> Later that day, when I finally got a chance to see the hearing broadcast in its entirety on C-SPAN, I was struck too, but by a transformation of a completely different kind. Sure, the symptoms were severe—I looked as though an invisible bully were harassing me while I read my statement. My head jerked, skewing my reading glasses as if the back of my skull were being slapped. I was fighting to control the pages of my speech, my arms bouncing as if someone were trying to knock the paper out of my hands. But through it all, I never wavered. I saw in my eyes an even, controlled sense of purpose I had never seen in myself before. There was, ironically enough, a steadiness in me, even as I was shaking like a leaf. *I couldn't be this still until I could no longer keep still.* The bully attacked from every angle, even from within my own body, but I wasn't about to give in, or be distracted from what I had come there to do. (Fox, 2002, p. 247–248)

Carl Rogers, whose theory is discussed later in this chapter, described his own peak experiences, felt during the altered states of consciousness that he sometimes experienced when facilitating group therapy. He reported that:

> When I am at my best, as a group facilitator or as a therapist, I discover another characteristic. I find that when I am closest to my inner, intuitive self, when I am somehow in touch with the unknown in me, when perhaps I am in a slightly altered state of consciousness, then whatever I do seems to be full of healing. Then,

> simply my *presence* is releasing and helpful to the other ... it seems that my inner spirit has reached out and touched the inner spirit of the other. Our relationship transcends itself and becomes a part of something larger. Profound growth and healing and energy are present. (Rogers, 1980, p. 129)

These peak experiences tap into a previously untapped potential. The end result is a profound sense of revelation and wonderment as the person experiences self-development and self-completion.

Have you had any peak experiences so far? Fewer than 1% of university and college students are at the level of self-actualization when assessed in broad surveys (perhaps because self-actualization likely follows from developmental experiences and insights), but recall that Maslow said that everyone has moments of peak experience at some point, so perhaps you have had these as well.

Maslow included people on his list of healthy, self-actualized individuals based on his subjective appraisals, and you might take issue with one or more of these choices. For instance, although Abraham Lincoln made enormous societal contributions, he suffered from personal problems, including a depression that plagued him for much of his life. In general, critics have reacted to the fact that Maslow based his observations on a subjective holistic analysis that is not very scientific. Also, Maslow selected these people after the fact and it would be much more informative to study people over time and see how they become self-actualized. We can get some insight into the self-actualization process by studying the lives of people who have achieved their potential. This is illustrated in Case Study 7.1 on cyclist Lance Armstrong.

In his final book, *The Farther Reaches of Human Nature*, Maslow (1971) identified eight behaviours leading to self-actualization:

1. Experiencing fully with vividness and complete concentration.
2. Making personal choices that are growth choices rather than fear-based choices.
3. Developing a sense of self and letting the self emerge without being influenced too much by other people, including our parents.
4. Being honest with oneself and with other people.
5. Being courageous and making wise life judgements according to personal preferences.
6. Recognizing that self-development is an ongoing process of actualizing potential at many points in time.
7. Having peak experiences and being open to them.
8. Being aware of ego defences and stopping the use of them.

Regarding this last behaviour, Maslow maintained that self-actualization occurs when people, especially younger people, give up the defence mechanism of **desacralizing**. Desacralizing is a defensive way of minimizing and ignoring the sacred value of being needs. Maslow attributes this in younger people to their contempt for their parents because they fail to see the potential in their parents and instead focus on those times when parents have been hypercritical and have not acted in accordance with values and beliefs that they espouse.

Case Study 7.1 Lance Armstrong Cycles toward Self-Actualization

In 2005, Lance Armstrong won his seventh consecutive Tour de France, which is regarded as the world's most prestigious and gruelling road cycling event. The magnitude of this accomplishment is difficult to comprehend. Armstrong has not only defeated highly competitive world-class athletes, he also defeated cancer. Armstrong was diagnosed with an advanced form of testicular cancer in October 1996. The intense challenges and struggles associated with recovery are detailed in his inspirational autobiography *It's Not About the Bike*. In this book, Armstrong outlines the many things he faced, included the severe side effects of chemotherapy and having to undergo brain surgery because his cancer had spread.

Lance Armstrong's life story illustrates that Maslow's hierarchy of needs is a process through life stages and life circumstances.

Armstrong's story reminds us that when considering the hierarchy put forth by Maslow and the level of accomplishment that is achieved, new challenges can come along and this can reactivate lower level needs. Issues involving personal health and safety can come at any time and can make someone become focused entirely on personal survival. Thus, the hierarchy should be viewed from a process approach that takes life stages and emerging life circumstances into account.

Armstrong's life story reminds us to focus on the entire organism as a complex being and the complex issues that people may face. There are many sides to most individuals. The cover of Armstrong's autobiography, for instance, describes him as winner of the Tour de France, cancer survivor, husband, father, son, and human being. Life roles, life goals, personality traits and temperaments, and situational and cultural factors all combine to foster a unique individuality.

Armstrong's personal account illustrates clearly that once a lower level basic need is satisfied, then it does indeed become possible to address higher level needs and take on the characteristics of psychological health as described by Maslow. Armstrong noted in his book that one by-product of his experience is that he became much less judgemental and much more accepting of both himself and other people.

Other characteristics of psychologically healthy people that Armstrong developed included a problem focus rather than a personal focus and a reduced concern with social approval. He stated that, "Since the illness I just care a lot less if people like me or not" (Armstrong, 2001, p. 288). He also discussed his growing appreciation of life experiences and his richer emotional reactions and his unwillingness to get too upset about life stressors. He noted that, "Above all, I've learned that if I have a tough week, all I have to do is sit back and reflect. It's easy to say, 'These things don't bother me anymore'" (p. 289).

Most important, it is evident that Armstrong experienced changes in his personal value system and developed a sense of commitment to others that transcended his own personal needs. A stronger identification with the human species is a clear indication of psychological growth. As a cancer survivor, Armstrong has dedicated himself to raising research funds for cancer through his charitable foundation. Sales of his Livestrong wristbands have helped raise more than $33 million. It can be argued that Armstrong reached his full athletic potential, but it is this charitable work that suggests a different form of self-actualization and self-completion. Much of this came to him in a moment of revelation during a race while climbing (perhaps symbolically) through a mountain range. Armstrong recounted that, "As I continued upward, I saw my life as a whole. I saw the pattern and the privilege of it, and the purpose of it, too. It was simply this: I was meant for a long hard climb." (p. 197)

Although he is retired from racing, Armstrong's personal climb is continuing and valleys have sometimes followed peaks. It is important to remember that striving for needs is an ongoing process and significant changes can occur. In Armstrong's case, the problems that ensued in his life no doubt made it difficult to maintain a focus on self-actualization.

A lack of psychological health can occur in the form of neurosis. Maslow stated that neurosis may develop instead of self-actualization, due in part to what he referred to as the **Jonah Complex**. Maslow defined the Jonah Complex as a fear of greatness and a fear of our own destiny. Perhaps this proposed complex reflected Maslow's awareness that people are frightened by the possibility that they may attain perfection, perhaps because this may create very high expectancies for levels of attainment in the future. It could also result in a sense of arrogance and boastfulness about accomplishments. The complex reflects the Biblical story of Jonah, the prophet who did not heed the call to reform the city of Nineveh, and, as a result, he fled in a boat on the sea. Because he did not answer the call and use his talents, storms rained down on him. Jonah tried to throw himself into the sea but instead landed in the mouth of a whale.

One way to get closer to either a momentary or long-term state of self-actualization is to engage in meditation. International Focus on Discovery 7.1 outlines the various meditative influences on Maslow's theory and describes research on the benefits of meditation.

International Focus on Discovery 7.1 Buddhist Psychology, Meditation, and Self-Actualization

Several aspects of Maslow's theory have their roots in the principles of Buddhism. Maslow was influenced greatly by Buddhism, Hindu spiritual philosophy, and other religions (see Miovic, 2004). Buddhism includes the concept of enlightenment as an ultimate goal, and this is similar to the concept of self-actualization. Hindu philosophy incorporates the transpersonal goal of transcending and going beyond the self (Miovic, 2004). Maslow's conceptualization of self-actualization as a form of selflessness is entirely in keeping with the tenets of Buddhism and Hinduism.

Maslow introduced this emphasis on spiritual elements near the end of his illustrious career and life. His views provided much of the basis for **transpersonal psychology**, which is definedv as the psychological study of spirituality and mystical, spiritual experiences. Transpersonal psychology goes beyond the self and, according to Maslow, is centred in the cosmos rather than in the self.

Maslow's theory of self-actualization is similar to the concept of enlightenment found in meditation and Buddhist philosopy.

The peak experiences described by Maslow were referred to as a special feeling of Nirvana, a Buddhist term meaning an ideal state and sense of wonderment where time and space are transcended. Parenthetically, given the term's meaning, it is more than ironic that Kurt Cobain, the leader of the grunge group Nirvana, was exceptionally creative but also exceptionally disillusioned by life in a way that seems antithetical to the concept of Nirvana.

Buddhism incorporates various forms of meditation as a means of attaining a sense of transcendence and personal healing. Meditation uses heightened awareness of sensory and cognitive experience and learning to detach oneself from these experiences to achieve a sense of selflessness (see Emavardhana & Tori, 1997). According to Epstein (1995), this approach combines **mindfulness** (awareness of the moment as it emerges) and the **Vipassana meditation** (focused concentration). If meditation is designed to achieve a state of being that resembles self-actualization, then people who habitually engage in meditation should have higher levels of self-actualization. This hypothesized link has been evaluated in several studies.

Research on the effectiveness of various forms of meditation supports the notion that meditative thought can facilitate a state of self-actualization. For instance, Zika (1987) examined scores on a measure of self-Research on the effectiveness of various forms of meditation supports the notion that meditative thought can facilitate a state of self-actualization. For instance, Zika (1987) examined scores on a measure of self-actualization in a sample of participants. Two groups of participants received instruction in meditation techniques, and their self-actualization scores were compared with two other groups of participants (a group that received hypnosis and a control group that received no intervention). Meditation was associated with slightly higher levels of self-actualization, but the hypnosis group had even higher levels of self-reported self-actualization.

Previously, Seeman, Nidich, and Banta (1972) gave a measure of self-actualization (The Personal Orientation Inventory) to a sample of 15 people who were about to take a transcendental meditation program, and a 20-person control group. Self-actualization was also assessed after the program. It was found that the meditation group had higher self-actualization scores on six variables assessed by the Personal Orientation Inventory.

The definitive study in this area was conducted by Alexander, Rainforth, and Gelderloos (1991). They conducted a meta-analysis of 42 available studies on the link between transcendental meditation and self-actualization. This meta-analysis of previous findings showed that this form of meditation was much more effective than relaxation training in raising levels of self-actualization, and it was more effective than other forms of meditation.

A subsequent study by Emavardhana and Tori (1997) evaluated the impact of Vipassana meditation on changes to the self-concept and ego defences. Research in Bangkok, Thailand compared participants who did or did not take part in retreats including meditation sessions. Those who participated in the retreats had improved overall self-esteem, feelings of worth, and self-acceptance. They were also less likely to use maladaptive psychological defences such as displacement, projection, and regression.

Although various forms of meditation seem effective overall, some authors have reported a failure to increase levels of self-actualization (e.g., Klein, Docherty, & Farley, 1982). In addition, significant cautions were raised by a study by Zuroff and Schwarz (1980). They compared the effects of relaxation versus meditation and found no differences at follow-up. More alarming is the fact that fewer than one quarter of the participants reported at longer term follow-up that they had even moderate satisfaction with the technique, and fewer than one fifth of students were practising meditation at least once a week. Thus, although meditation may be useful, it is certainly not recognized as helpful by everyone, and in terms of the key question for any intervention (i.e., how much is the technique practised after the intervention), there was little evidence of long-term use. If this study were repeated today, the techniques would probably be used by only a limited number of students. Still, given the hectic pace of most people's lives, it seems that the relaxation afforded by meditation would probably have substantial benefits if used more regularly.

The B-Values

Maslow (1971) also postulated that there are meta-motivations (which he referred to as **B-values**). Meta-motivations must be realized in order to avoid illness and realize one's full potential. Failure to realize and attain these values results in "metapathologies" or illnesses of being human (see Maslow, 1971).

Table 7.2 lists 15 B-values. Each value is accompanied by a "pathogenic outcome" if it has been deprived, as well as one or more metapathologies that can ensue. These values do not form a hierarchy, as Maslow regarded them as equally important to the realization of our intrinsic nature. However, one important source of individuality is that these B-values can be arranged in a hierarchy or framework where some are more important than others based on a person's unique talents, temperaments, and capabilities.

Table 7.2 Maslow's B-Values and Associated Metapathologies

B-Value	Pathogenic	Specific Metapathologies
Truth	Dishonesty	Disbelief, mistrust, cynicism
Goodness	Evil	Utter selfishness, hatred, disgust
Beauty	Ugliness	Vulgarity, specific unhappiness
Unity, wholeness	Chaos, atomism, lost connectedness	Disintegration, arbitrariness, "The world is falling apart"
Dichotomy-Transcendence	Black and white dichotomies, loss of degrees	Black-white thinking, low synergy, simplistic view of life
Aliveness, process	Deadness mechanizing of life	Deadness, robotizing, loss of emotion, boredom
Uniqueness	Sameness	Loss of feeling of self-individuality
Perfection	Imperfection	Discouragement, hopelessness
Necessity	Accident, inconsistency	Chaos, unpredictability
Completion, fullness	Incompleteness	Feelings of incompleteness, no use trying, cessation of striving and coping
Justice	Injustice	Insecurity, anger, cynicism
Order	Lawlessness, chaos	Insecurity, wariness, loss of safety
Simplicity	Confused complexity	Overcomplexity, confusion, conflict
Richness, totality, comprehensiveness	Poverty, coarctation	Depression, uneasiness, loss of interest in the world
Effortlessness	Effortfulness	Fatigue, strain, striving, clumsiness
Playfulness	Humourlessness	Grimness, depression, loss of zest
Self-Sufficiency	Contingency	Dependence, others' responsibility
Meaningfulness	Meaninglessness	Meaninglessness, despair, senselessness

Source: Adapted from Maslow, 1971, p. 308–309.

Young people tend to mistrust the B-values, which Maslow specifically identifies as the types of values that people over 30 years of age have come to trust and accept as important. There is no hierarchy with respect to the B-values; they are equally important, and each one has unique value. B-values are as necessary as "vitamins and love" (Maslow, 1971, p. 186).

It is beyond the scope of this book, but note that there is a fairly extensive literature composed of theory and research on individual differences in personal values. Most certainly, Maslow's work on B-values has provided theoretical impetus in this area. And research shows that just as it is possible to assess individual differences in traits and needs, meaningful individual differences also exist in personal values.

Associated Research on the Nature of Self-Actualization

What has been learned about self-actualized people from research findings? First, people high in self-actualization are low in death anxiety and other types of anxiety (Ebersole & Persi, 1993), and they are high in self-acceptance. Pufal-Struzik (1999), for example, established that self-actualization and self-acceptance were positively correlated in a sample of intellectually gifted students.

Second, though it might seem paradoxical at first, striving for perfection is associated with less self-actualization, not more. Flett et al. (1991) examined the link between dimensions of perfectionism and self-actualization in Canadian university students and found a negative association between self-oriented perfectionism and self-actualization. Further analyses showed that the main reason for a negative association was the component of self-actualization that involved an inability to tolerate failure. Those individuals with an excessive fear of failure tend to doubt themselves and are not open to current experiences and opportunities that hold the possibility of failure.

Research on the downside of "The American Dream" also sheds light on the key to self-actualization. The American Dream includes working hard to achieve high levels of wealth and prosperity. Kasser and Ryan (1993, 1996) showed that the pursuit of external goals (such as to become wealthy and get the approval of others) is *associated negatively* with self-actualization, while pursuing intrinsic goals and goals (such as contributing to one's community) are associated with increased self-actualization. Carver and Baird (1998) qualified this finding by showing that self-actualization was not lower for people who pursued external goals such as becoming wealthy if they did it for self-determined reasons that reflected a sense of personal autonomy and self-control. They clarified that it's not what you want that matters, it's why you want it. Overall, however, the main finding reported by Kasser and Ryan still holds. So, it seems the popular Beatles song ("Can't Buy Me Love") needs to be modified; not only can't love be bought, but material success also can't buy inner peace, fulfilment, and personal growth.

Finally, there has been an unfortunate paucity of research on the developmental antecedents of self-actualization. One exception is a study with students by Dominguez and Carton (1997). They examined self-actualization and reported parenting styles. Students who reported that their parents had an authoritative parenting style had higher scores on the Short Index of Self-Actualization by Jones and Crandall (1986). Authoritative parenting from both parents was reported, though the link was substantially stronger when the father had an authoritative parenting style.

KEY POINTS

- Ego defences must be lowered for self-actualization to take place.
- Anxiety and fear of failure are antithetical to the goal of achieving self-actualization.
- Self-actualization requires the pursuit of personal goals according to personal choices rather than trying to please others and live up to social expectations.

Maslow's Views on Personality

What did Maslow say specifically about personality? As might be expected, his views include a focus on the whole person. Maslow concluded that the person is composed of various "personality syndromes." As such, any one behavioural act is the product of multiple personality syndromes, and acts reflect the integrated personality; an integrated personality, according to Maslow (1971), is one of the keys to psychological health. According to

Maslow, our inner nature or personality is an important determinant of behaviour, but cultural factors and the immediate situation also play important roles. For him, personality syndromes are not isolated systems but exist within situational and cultural contexts. The salience and strength of the situation will have an impact on the extent to which there is a correspondence between inner character (personality) and outwardly expressed behaviours. Maslow (1987) noted specifically that there is often a small correlation between character and outwardly expressed behaviours because of environmental factors; however, there is a stronger correlation between character and impulsive behaviours because impulsive behaviours are less influenced by situational and cultural factors.

Regarding the role of the environment in personality development, Maslow (1949) observed that some psychologically healthy people live in far from perfect environments. Although Maslow endorsed the general view that good environments contribute to "good personalities," he also suggested that how we define a good environment should have less emphasis on objective economic and materialistic conditions and much more emphasis on the spiritual and psychological aspects of the environment.

According to Maslow (1987), the various personality syndromes are highly resistant to change and will typically withstand extremely stressful and traumatic experiences. He stated that when change does occur, it may be temporary and personality syndromes will revert to their previous form. However, in the event that lasting change does occur, there will be concomitant changes across a number of personality syndromes, and a holistic change in the organism will take place (i.e., changing as a whole).

KEY POINTS

- Maslow believed that studying personality meant looking at the whole person.
- Personality is composed of multiple personality syndromes.
- Any one behaviour is the end product of multiple personality syndromes as well as the influences of the immediate situation and culture.
- Personality syndromes are highly resistant to change, but when change does occur, it is dramatic and pervasive.

Evaluation of Maslow's Theory

There are several controversial aspects of Maslow's proposed theory, with most critics focusing on his hierarchy of needs. Research has provided general support for the notion that basic needs must be realized before more psychological needs can become a focus (Wicker, Brown, Wiehe, & Hagen, 1993). A study of managers and professionals in an industrial organization in Israel provides evidence that confirmed the need hierarchy (see Porat, 1977). This study included performing what is known as a **Guttman scale analysis**, a statistical technique that tests whether hypothesized stages can be detected in empirical data. Porat's study found that the needs are "scalable" in a manner that conformed generally to the hypothesized need hierarchy.

Overall, research on this topic has provided an equivocal picture, with support being obtained in only some studies (see Yang, 2003). From a conceptual viewpoint, you, the reader, ought to be able to raise some serious concerns of your own. Is it not possible, for instance, that some people would place a higher premium on love and belongingness rather than self-esteem needs, so their hierarchy would have a different order of stages? Also, how do we account for people who make heroic sacrifices and demonstrate the ultimate act of altruism? These people give up their own lives to promote the well-being of others. It seems for these remarkable people, personal safety and survival needs are no longer relevant. Maslow would likely argue that these people have attained self-actualization and demonstrated this through their selflessness. While this is no doubt the case, what does this mean to the lower needs of the hierarchy?

Another concern that has been raised is the need for more precision with respect to the self-actualization construct. In particular, Maslow has been criticized for not being more explicit about how a person advances from the self-esteem level to the self-actualization level (see Heylighen, 1992). Many people have self-esteem, but few attain self-actualization. What are the critical differences?

More general concerns have been raised about the need to clarify and refine the self-actualization concept. A team of researchers from Quebec decided that the time had come for a complete review of the self-actualization concept, so they surveyed Canadian, American, French, and Belgian experts about the characteristics and indicators of self-actualization (Leclerc, Lefrancois, Dube, Hebert, & Gaulin, 1998). That is, they sought to maximize the content validity of the self-actualization construct. In total, 36 different indicators were identified, and 30 indicators were mentioned by more than 85% of the experts. These 30 indicators are outlined in Table 7.3. Leclerc et al. (1998) noted that their findings reiterated in general that self-actualization is a dynamic process rather than an end state and that it can take unique forms in each self-actualized person. And it involves high functioning rather than high performance per se. These same researchers used this information to develop their own measure of self-actualization (see LeFrancois, Leclerc, Dube, Hebert, & Gaulin, 1997). This scale taps two higher order aspects of self-actualization: self-reference (autonomy) and openness to experience (openness to self, to others, and to life itself).

Table 7.3 Thirty Characteristics of Self-Actualization

Self-Actualized People:

1. Give meaning to their life
2. Have positive self-esteem
3. Consider themselves responsible for their own life
4. Give a meaning to life
5. Are capable of establishing meaningful relationships
6. Take responsibility for their actions
7. Are aware of their feelings
8. Have a realistic perception of themselves
9. Are capable of commitment
10. Accept the consequences of their choices
11. Act according to their own convictions and values
12. Are able to resist undue social pressure

13. Trust in their own organism
14. Are capable of insight
15. Feel free to express their emotions
16. Are able to accept contradictory feelings
17. Are open to change
18. Enjoy thinking for themselves
19. Are aware of their strengths and weaknesses
20. Are capable of spontaneous reactions
21. Behave in a congruent, authentic way
22. Maintain contact with themselves and the other person
23. Are capable of empathy
24. Have a well-developed sense of ethics
25. Are capable of not focusing on themselves
26. Are not paralyzed by the judgement of others
27. Feel free to express their opinions
28. Use personal criteria to evaluate themselves
29. Live in the present (the here and now)
30. Have a positive perception of human life

Are these 30 characteristics valid and exhaustive? Are there any attributes you would add?

Maslow's Views on Culture

How does the need hierarchy fare across cultures? Maslow adopted the view that his hierarchy could be applied universally, and one of the defining features of self-actualization is that the self-actualized person has somehow become independent of his or her culture. Maslow maintained that self-actualized people have transcended the values of their culture. They are citizens of the world rather than a particular nation because they see themselves as part of the human species.

Maslow had several other observations about the role of culture and other environmental factors. He wanted to promote Ruth Benedict's (1970) concept of synergy, which she applied to different cultures or societies. A culture with high synergy has people and systems where the focus is on mutual rewards and well-being; a society with low synergy is composed of people and cultures where one person's advancement and wealth occurs at the expense of many other people. Maslow expanded this concept to discuss synergy at the level of the individual person. He related this to his concept of selfish versus unselfish love. The person with high synergy is mutually interdependent with another person in a highly unselfish way. That is, one person's advantage is also to their partner's advantage and vice versa.

Several critics have responded by suggesting that the need hierarchy is far from universal. For instance, Hofstede (1980) pointed to Maslow's hierarchical model as an example of over-extrapolating models with an individualistic orientation to non-Western people. Similarly, on the basis of his perceptions of people and life experiences in mainland China, Nevis (1983) identified the need to belong as the critical level of personality development for people from China. The ultimate goal for these individuals is to make significant contributions to their community and to society in general.

Some authors have argued convincingly (e.g., Hanley & Abell, 2002) that Maslow's views need to be altered to allow for a communal, interpersonal form of self-actualization that reflects the emphasis on relating to others in more collectivist societies. Yang (2003) has provided the most detailed analysis of this issue thus far. He concluded that Maslow's theory is "a culture-bound, linear theory" that has generated great interest but has limited applicability around the world (p.175). He suggested that it is popular theory because it has great face validity but has not been successfully validated in other forms. Yang (2003) proposed the need for different hierarchical models for people from individualistic and collectivist cultures. The collectivist alternative was provided, in part, because Yang wanted to emphasize the tendency for some people to define their self-worth not in terms of individual accomplishments but in terms of maximizing potential by becoming a successful social being.

An anecdote related by Kabat-Zinn (1994) illustrates the concerns that these scholars have about the universal applicability of Maslow's hierarchy. Kabat-Zinn is renowned internationally as the developer of mindfulness meditation as a technique for enhancing personal well-being. Kabat-Zinn described the Dalai Lama's perplexed reaction when he learned of the typical North American view of the self while attending a cross-cultural meeting. Kabat-Zinn (1994) related that the Dalai Lama:

> … did a double take when a Western psychologist spoke of low self-esteem. The phrase had to be translated several times for him into Tibetan, although his English is quite good. He just couldn't grasp the notion of low self-esteem, and when he finally understood what was being said he was visibly saddened to hear that so many people in America carry deep feelings of self-loathing and inadequacy. (p. 163)

Michalon (2001) observed that Buddhist psychology is based on a highly positive view of the self but the ultimate goal is to achieve a state of selflessness. People who fail to maintain a positive self-view and who are preoccupied with their personal failings are very difficult for Easterners to comprehend and, as a result, they are regarded as being quite foolhardy.

Other scholars have criticized Maslow because he never really addressed the important topic of gender differences in personality. Should the same principles be applied equally to men and women? While some have suggested that a focus on connecting with people and interpersonal needs involving love and belongingness are more relevant to females and should be reflected in Maslow's theory, a relatively new analysis by Hyde (2005) suggests that gender differences have been overstated. She obtained support for her **gender similarities hypothesis** by examining 46 prior meta-analyses. This examination found that males and females are similar on most psychological variables and there are far more similarities than differences between the sexes.

Now that Maslow has been discussed in detail, we turn to the second major theorist described in this chapter: Carl Rogers. Rogers was also a humanist who saw mostly the good in people and their potential. His story and accomplishments are outlined next.

KEY POINTS

- The hypothesized sequence of stages in Maslow's hierarchy has been questioned and not consistently supported in research studies.
- Maslow's theory has been criticized for being culture-bound. As well, it does not address gender differences.

CARL ROGERS

Carl Rogers felt that the ultimate goal was to become a fully functioning person.

In many respects, it seems that the theoretical views of **Carl Rogers** are a reflection of his personal history. Rogers came from a very religious, overcontrolling farm family from the American Midwest. His autobiographical writings acknowledged that throughout his childhood, he had very little contact with the outside world. Also, his family did not encourage the expression of emotion. This environment had a profound effect on the young Carl Rogers. He developed an ulcer by the age of 15 and admitted to feeling wicked when he had his first bottle of soda pop. The theoretical views outlined below seem, at least to some extent, to be a rebellion to this overcontrol. Increasingly, through his life experiences, Rogers eschewed his previously accepted religious beliefs and came to emphasize the importance of freedom, autonomy, and self-determination.

Rogers felt that an individual's ultimate goal was to become a fully functioning person with characteristics that are described below. First, however, we must discuss Rogers' views on personality and two needs that he felt must be satisfied for someone to be fully functioning.

The Organism, the Self, and Personality Structure

Rogers argued that personality reflects "the organism" and that the organism is the source of our experiences. The experience of the organism combines to form the phenomenal field that reflects the totality of our existence (see Rogers, 1959). The phenomenal field is the perceptual field of awareness and cognition. Note that although we tend to focus on conscious perceptions and experiences, Rogers allowed that there is an unconscious aspect of experience that is not accessible to conscious awareness.

An explicit goal of therapy is to restore a sense of trust in one's own organism instead of accepting and endorsing the perceptions of other people. It is restoring a sense of "reality-as-perceived" by the individual. As Rogers (1980) noted in *A Way of Being*, his semi-autobiographical book,

> The only reality I can possibly know is the world as I perceive and experience it at this moment. The only reality you can possibly know is the world as you perceive and experience it at this moment. And the only certainty is that those perceived realities are different. There are as many "real worlds" as there are people! (p. 102)

The self, according to Rogers, is a segment of the phenomenal field that forms over time and eventually becomes a distinguishable entity by itself. Rogers (1947) argued that the self is "a basic factor in the formation of personality and in the determination of behavior" (p. 361).

Rogers (1959) argued that the self is something that can change over time. He defined the self as:

> [an] organized, consistent conceptual gestalt composed of the perceptions of the characteristics of the "I" or "me" and the perceptions of the relationships of the "I" or "me" to others and to various aspects of life, together with the values attached to these perceptions. It is a gestalt which is available to awareness though not necessarily in awareness. It is a fluid and changing gestalt, a process, but at any given moment it is a specific entity. (p. 200)

By highlighting the potential dynamic aspect of the self, Rogers provided a view of the self that has received extensive empirical support over the past 30 years.

How important is the self? Rogers went so far as to suggest that clinical improvements in behaviour as a result of therapy are almost always reflected by positive changes in the self-concept. These changes were often structural (as opposed to the contents of personality) because Rogers saw the self as being capable of reorganization.

The Need for Self-Regard

As indicated above, two needs are essential, according to Rogers. The first need is for unconditional positive regard. Self-regard is a positive orientation toward the self that is experienced independently of a person's interactions with other people (Rogers, 1959). In fact, to underscore our autonomy, Rogers argued that the person becomes his or her own significant social other. Rogers maintained that we all have a need for self-regard. The need for self-regard is a learned need that develops out of personal experiences that satisfy or frustrate this need. Self-regard can be formed from specific experiences, but these specific experiences combine at a global level to form what Rogers (1959) referred to as a self-regard complex.

Conditions of worth represent the primary threat to self-regard. Conditions of worth emerge when a person's self-experiences are discriminated against and reacted to by other people who respond to the person based on what they themselves find desirable. If self-experiences are either sought or avoided based on the anticipated reactions of other people, so that the self-regard is now contingent on their actions and reactions, then conditions of worth have emerged. The antidote to conditions of worth is to experience unconditional positive regard from the significant others in our life. That is, the person receives positive feedback and love from other people regardless of his or her behaviour. This would mean that a mother or father would convey to his or her child that no matter what they do or say, they will be unconditionally loved. In real life, of course, parents often convey to their children that rewards and punishments are tied to meeting expectations about appropriate behaviours and goals. This is reflected in perfectionism research by the general concept of socially prescribed perfectionism (see Hewitt & Flett, 1991) and parental pressures to meet high expectations or suffer the consequences of parental criticism for failing to meet these expectations (Frost, Marten, Lahart, & Rosenblate, 1990).

The problem that emerges from conditions of worth is that it fosters an incongruence between the self and experience. That is, the person exposed to conditions of worth will increasingly fail to act in accordance with their true nature and inclinations and will instead act in a non-authentic way to satisfy the conditions of worth. Thus, conscious behaviour is a distortion of the true self.

Rogers (1961) suggested that distortion of the true self takes the form of a person displaying a mask. His concept of mask is very much in keeping with the root of the word "personality" and the idea that we adopt a persona. In this instance, Rogers discusses masks in terms of the "false fronts" that people put on to cover up their true selves. A key task for the therapist is to "get under the mask" and help the person start to express their true aspects of themselves.

According to Rogers (1959), the larger the gap between the actual self and the true self, the greater the level of dysfunction in a person. The true self often takes the form of an ideal self, and there is great distress associated with the growing realization that there is a large discrepancy between how one actually is (the actual self) and how one would like to be (the ideal self).

Rogers used the Q-sort technique to evaluate the degree of overlap between the actual self and the ideal self. This technique requires sorting a pile of 100 cards into 9 categories. It can be used to tap the actual versus ideal self because a person can be asked to derive categories that reflect the current self and then reorganize the cards to reflect the ideal self.

KEY POINTS

- Rogers felt that becoming a fully functioning person is the ultimate goal.
- Fully functioning people have satisfied two needs: the need for unconditional positive regard and the need for self-actualization.
- An absence of unconditional positive regard fosters conditions of worth.
- Conditions of worth contribute to psychological distress because a lack of authentic experience contributes to a gap between the self and actual experience.

People who are tormented by a gap or discrepancy between the actual self and the ideal self can manifest a variety of psychological problems. We will return to this concept in Chapter 11 when we discuss self-discrepancy theory. A goal of therapy is to reduce the size of the gap. Rogers (1961) noted that initially he felt that positive changes would involve modifications to the ideal self, but the ideal self seems to change only a little, if at all, and it is the perceptions of the actual self that show the greatest change.

The Need for Self-Actualization

The need for self-actualization is the need to enhance and develop and become one's best possible self. This need was reflected for many years in the recruitment message for the American military ("Be all that you can be in the army!"). This need reflects the basic motive to change and grow.

A key aspect of this need is the **actualizing tendency**. Rogers argued that everyone has an internal **organismic valuing process**. That is, our internal nature includes a knack for intrinsically knowing the things that are good for us and the things that are bad for us. It is "an inherent tendency of the organism to develop all of its capacities in ways which serve to maintain or enhance the organism" (Rogers, 1959, p. 196). This actualizing has four main characteristics (and it gives rise to other motivations): (1) it is organismic (it is a natural, biological predisposition); (2) it is an active process, which is why people are always exploring and initiating behaviour; (3) it is directional and pointed toward growth; and (4) it is selective (a person has many capabilities but only select capabilities are developed). Rogers believed that given an atmosphere of respect and freedom to make choices, the organismic valuing process would operate in the same way across cultures (see Rogers, 1989).

The Fully Functioning Person

If these needs for positive regard and self-actualization are satisfied, it is then possible for the individual to become "a fully functioning person." Consistent with the themes outlined at the beginning of this chapter, the fully functioning person is open to experiences in the here and now. They also strive to live their life to the fullest. Finally, they have learned to trust their own feelings, so they follow their own intuitions and emotional cues. If you are fully functioning, then you are open to your ongoing existence. However, this is a continuous process rather than an end state.

If you are fully functioning, this also has implications for the use of psychological defences. Rogers believed that defence mechanisms are used to combat anxiety. Anxiety arises when we become aware of information and feedback that does not jibe with our self-perceptions. This awareness is at a subconscious level and reflects a process that Rogers referred to as **subception**. The fully functioning person does not resort to the use of psychological defences and is open to experience and information about themselves. The reliance on psychological defences would detract from their ability to live life to the fullest.

Contemporary Research Reflecting Rogers' Theory

The theory outlined by Rogers has provided the impetus for many current lines of investigation. For example, consider his notion that it is distressing when the actual self is discrepant from the ideal self. This notion has led to research on the cognitive aspects of perfectionism, distress, and discrepancies from the ideal self. As a supplement to the trait perfectionism measures of self-oriented, other-oriented, and socially prescribed perfectionism described in Chapter 5, Flett, Hewitt, Blankstein, and Gray (1998) developed the Perfectionism Cognitions Inventory (PCI). Cognitive rumination over mistakes and imperfections has been noted often in the perfectionism literature, and the PCI is designed to assess individual differences in these thoughts.

Flett et al. (1998) based the PCI on the premise that perfectionists who sense a discrepancy between their actual self and the ideal self will tend to experience automatic, negative thoughts that reflect perfectionistic themes and their personal sense of not being perfect. It is believed that perfectionists with high levels of perfectionism cognitions are especially susceptible to negative affect in the form of depression about failure to attain perfection in the past, as well as in the form of anxiety about the likelihood of failing to attain perfection in the future.

Representative thoughts from the 25-item PCI are shown in Table 7.4. This scale has a range of item content that reflects direct thoughts about the need to be perfect, as well as thoughts of an individual's cognitive awareness of his or her imperfections. Respondents are asked to make five-point ratings of the frequency with which they have experienced these thoughts throughout the previous week.

Table 7.4 Thoughts Assessed by the Perfectionism Cognitions Inventory

Why can't I be perfect?
I should never make the same mistake twice.
I have to be the best.
People expect me to be perfect.
I can always do better, even if things are almost perfect.
My work should be flawless.
It would be great if everything in my life was perfect.

If we extrapolate from Rogers' notion that the discrepancy between the actual and ideal self predicts psychological distress, then elevated scores on the PCI should be associated with various forms of stress and distress. High scorers have stated a need to be perfect and are constantly ruminating about their inability to be perfect. As expected, Flett et al. (1998) reported that the PCI was correlated significantly with indices of anxiety and depression, and it accounted for unique variance in distress, even after using existing trait measures of perfectionism and general measures of negative automatic thoughts to remove variance in adjustment scores.

Although the discrepancy between the actual and ideal self is associated with distress, Rogers maintained that the real root of the problem are the conditions of worth that start the person down the path toward a less than genuine existence. So, in essence, it is the conditions of worth that represent the catalyst and true source of the person's distress.

Self-Worth Contingencies

Some contemporary research has explored how conditions of worth become reflected in self-worth contingencies. This research shows that conditions of worth can exist in various life domains and life themes.

Various authors have examined the possibility that people are vulnerable to distress due to their self-worth contingencies. For example, Kuiper and his associates at the University of Western Ontario have formulated a model of vulnerability to depression based on the premise that dysfunctional self-worth contingencies become associated with depression following the experience of stressful life events (see Kuiper, Olinger, & MacDonald, 1988).

DiBartollo and associates at Smith College in Massachusetts have created two brief measures of conditional self-worth (DiBartollo, Frost, Chang, LaSota, & Grills, 2004). The first measure assesses self-worth contingencies in terms of success-based self-worth. It is measured by items such as "I normally think of myself as a worthwhile person, but when I do badly at something, I sometimes feel worthless." The second measure examines self-worth contingencies in terms of the need to feel busy or active all of the time in order to be a worthwhile person. This measure of "activity-based self-worth" is tapped by scale items such as "It seems I always have to be working toward a goal or accomplishment to feel right about myself," and "When I have free time, I feel guilty about not doing something productive." This study showed that higher levels of both forms of conditional self-worth were associated with psychological distress and daily life hassles. It was also found that perfectionists are higher in conditional self-worth.

Jennifer Crocker and her associates (Crocker, Luhtanen, Cooper, & Bouvrett, 2003) have identified self-worth contingencies in six different areas. Their measure taps contingent self-worth in seven domains, with the domains varying in the degree to which they reflect factors that are internal and external to the individual. The seven areas with illustrative sample items are shown in Table 7.5. This measure establishes quite clearly that there are self-worth contingencies that can be measured in various ways and reflect the many different ways that people come to view and evaluate themselves.

Table 7.5 Factors on the Contingencies of Self-Worth Scale

Factor	Representative Scale Item
Academic Competence	Doing well in school gives me a sense of self-respect.
Appearance	My self-esteem is influenced by how attractive I think my face or facial features are.
Competition	I feel worthwhile when I perform better than others on a task or skill.
Others' Approval	I can't respect myself if others don't respect me.
Family Support	When I don't feel loved by my family, my sense of self-esteem goes down.
God's Love	My self-esteem would suffer if I didn't have God's love.
Virtue	My self-esteem would suffer if I did something unethical.

Research in Crocker's laboratory has provided some convincing evidence that university students with a sense of contingent self-worth are at risk for a variety of negative outcomes. For instance, Crocker and Luhtanen (2003) conducted a longitudinal study of first-year university students and found that academic competence contingency predicted academic and financial problems, even after controlling for personality traits from the five-factor model. Another study examined something that many professors and students are familiar with. It examined the daily emotions of graduate school applicants responding to whether they heard good news or bad news from the places they had applied to (Crocker, Sommers, & Luhtanen, 2002). Of course, anyone who receives an acceptance is elated and, by the same token, rejections elicit a host of negative moods. This study showed that the typical reactions were even stronger among students who acknowledged basing their sense of self-worth on academic competence.

Another investigation with a general measure of contingent self-esteem illustrated how young women can be vulnerable to the social comparison information that they are being exposed to advertisements featuring women who are exceptionally thin (Patrick, Neighbors, & Knee, 2004). This study showed that when asked to rate advertisements showing women who were thin, university women characterized by high contingent self-esteem, relative to women without contingent self-esteem, had greater increases of negative mood. This suggests that being bombarded constantly by advertisements in magazines and on television should have a very strong negative impact on young females who have based their self-worth on trying to emulate people with unrealistic body images. This form of contingent self-worth likely plays a role in the etiology of eating disorders such as anorexia nervosa and bulimia nervosa.

Recent research by Assor, Roth, and Deci (2004) is important because it not only showed the deleterious effect of parents' conditional self-regard, but also suggested that there is intergenerational transmission of this conditional self-regard. In their first study, they showed that mothers who reported that they were exposed to conditions of worth had lower well-being and they themselves had a more controlling parenting style. Reports from their college-aged daughters showed that these mothers who had themselves been exposed to conditions of worth had a tendency to use this same approach in socializing their daughters. Intergenerational transmission in this context means that conditions of worth could be passed on from generation to generation. Their second study (Assor, et al., 2004) examined perceptions of parents' conditions of worth in four domains: sports, academics, pro-social behaviours, and the control of emotions. A sense that parents had created conditions of worth in these four areas was linked with students' reports of resentment toward parents, a sense that parents disapproved of them, feeling compelled to meet parental expectations, and predictable fluctuations in self-esteem.

Personality Change and Client-Centred Therapy

Rogers believed that dramatic personality change is quite possible, and the key is for the therapist to provide the type of setting and relationship that has been missing in the distressed person's life. Key concepts include the therapist being warm and genuine with the person (i.e., congruent), and providing unconditional positive regard.

The Rogerian approach to therapy has been referred to as non-reflective and client-centred. Rogers believed that it is up to the individual to find ways to change the self, and it is not up to the therapist to provide the control and direction that would be provided by a Freudian therapist who must interpret the person and provide deep clinical insights. To

Rogers, the therapist's role is to assist the client who is in the process of self-discovery. The Rogerian therapist reframes the themes of importance identified by the client and simply reminds the person of what he or she has learned thus far. A heavy emphasis is placed on the client's ability to verbalize key issues and themes, and experience these feelings as they work toward a growth state.

Consistent with his general theory, Rogers' client-centred therapy rests on the basic premise that people can be understood only from their own phenomenology—the immediate experience that they have of themselves and their world—and that they become disordered when they fail to attend to their own inner nature and instead guide their behaviour according to what others wish. Client-centred therapy places great emphasis on people's freedom to choose and on the responsibility that comes with having that freedom. We are what we make of ourselves, according to Rogerian and other humanistic and existential therapists.

The therapist's principal role is to create conditions in therapy that are totally accepting and non-judgemental, doing so by being empathic rather than directive. The result is that the client gradually comes to understand better his or her own wishes, needs, fears, and aspirations and gains the courage to pursue his or her own goals rather than the goals that others have set. The importance of the level of empathy shown by the therapist is a general humanistic principle from Rogers that has been incorporated into various therapeutic approaches.

In Carl Rogers' client-centred therapy, the therapist's role is to assist the client by being accepting and non-judgemental, and empathic rather than directive.

Table 7.6 provides a summary of the key challenges in therapy that were outlined by Rogers (1961) in his classic book *On Becoming a Person*. This table also summarizes the characteristics of the "person who emerges" as a result of successful treatment. Note that one characteristic is a greater openness to experience, which is one of the five traits in the five-factor model.

Table 7.6 Challenges and Positive Consequences of Person-Centred Therapy

Key Challenges
No longer rely on false "fronts" (i.e., the mask)
Move away from "oughts"
Move way from a focus on meeting expectations
Move away from pleasing others
Positive Consequences for the Person Who Emerges
Heightened openness to experience
Increased trust in one's organism and self
Now evaluating the self according to an internal locus of evaluation
Now willing to be a process
Greater acceptance of self and others

KEY POINTS

- In client-centred therapy, the therapist's main task is to be non-directive and assist the client in his or her voyage of personal discovery. The therapist must be warm, genuine, and full of empathy for the client.
- Client-centred therapy is as effective as other therapies.
- The notion that the therapist should be empathic and genuine has been incorporated as a principle of general importance in various therapies.

Watts (1998) made some interesting observations about Rogers' concept of empathy. He suggested that it is no coincidence that the core conditions for therapeutic change outlined by Rogers bear a strong resemblance to Alfred Adler's views on the importance of social interest. It turns out that Rogers studied with Adler in the late 1920s. Watts (1998) made a compelling case to link Adler's beliefs with the emphasis that Rogers placed on developing genuine care and empathy for another person.

Evaluating the Contributions of Client-Centred Therapy

Many efforts have been made to evaluate client-centred therapy, largely because Rogers became a pioneer by insisting that the therapy process be operationalized and empirically assessed. Rogers is regarded by many scholars as the originator of the field of psychotherapy research. Currently, the field of clinical psychology is becoming increasingly focused on the need for research to demonstrate the effectiveness of clinical interventions. That is, there is a need for empirically supported treatments and evidence-based treatments (for discussions, see Davison, Neale, Blankstein, & Flett, 2005; Hunsley & Lee, 2006).

What about the specific tenets of Rogerian theory? How have they fared when evaluated in research? The central research focus has been on the personal qualities of therapists and the effects of empathy. Equivocal, inconsistent findings have emerged, and this has tempered the assumption that positive outcome is strongly related to the therapist's empathy and genuineness (see Greenberg, Elliott, & Lietaer, 1994). Still, Davison et al. (2005) concluded that it makes a great deal of sense to train clinicians to instill the kind of therapeutic atmosphere and qualities advocated by Rogers. As shown in a widely cited study by Lafferty, Beutler, and Crago (1989), the clinical effectiveness of a therapist, regardless of their theoretical orientation, is linked directly with the client's sense that the therapist understands them and knows where they are coming from.

A meta-analysis of studies on client-centred therapy revealed only eight that had a control group and concluded that after such intervention, clients were better off than about 80% of comparable people who had not received any professional therapy (see Greenberg et al., 1994). Although this level of improvement is impressive, comparative research needs to be conducted before it can be concluded that client-centred therapy is superior to other treatment approaches. Clearly, however, there is a role for empathy. A meta-analysis of psychotherapy studies found a moderate effect size of $r = .32$ between therapist empathy and positive outcomes of therapy (Greenberg, Elliott, Watson, & Bohart, 2001).

Note that a Rogerian emphasis by therapists on empathy and acceptance has seemingly resulted in improvements of some of the most difficult to treat individuals. The importance of the therapeutic relationship is central to Marsha Linehan's (1987) dialectical behaviour therapy. Linehan has shown that specific cognitive-behavioural techniques can be implemented with patients who have borderline personality disorder when they are explored in an atmosphere of acceptance and empathy. Borderline personality disorder is one of the most extreme forms of personality dysfunction (see Chapter 13) and is usually very difficult to treat. Recent research on sex offenders who are also notoriously difficult to treat shows that an atmosphere of empathy and warmth facilitates their recovery process (see Marshall et al., 2003). In a recent review, Marshall (2005) re-affirmed the importance of therapist empathy. He concluded that empathy promotes positive behaviours, and sex offenders respond well to praise and encouragement, but they react poorly to confrontational techniques and criticism. Marshall (2005) stated that Rogerian nondirectiveness will simply not work with some sex offender patients, but directiveness can also go too far in undermining the sense of personal responsibility for actions.

According to Horvath (2000) from Simon Fraser University in Vancouver, other data support the Rogerian emphasis on subjective, phenomenological experiences. That is, the patient's perception of the therapist behaviour is more important for predicting therapy outcome than the therapist's actual behaviour in the therapeutic relationship! Thus, the patients' cognitive appraisals are quite important.

In addition to the therapeutic context, Rogers also made important contributions to education and learning situations in general. These contributions are highlighted in Applied Perspective 7.1.

Applied Perspective 7.1 Humanistic, Student-Centred Learning Environments

Both Carl Rogers and Abraham Maslow identified the need to apply their theoretical concepts to educational settings. The typical university and college classroom is based on the traditional model where the instructor is the authority who pre-selects and determines what material will be covered, how it will be covered, and how student learning will be evaluated. In many ways, it is a very "top-down model" as students must find ways to please their instructors and meet their expectations in order to attain the highest grades possible. Conditions of worth when expressed by teachers are not effective. Wentzel (2002) conducted an interesting study of the extent to which good teachers have the same characteristics as good parents, and found that negative feedback from teachers in the form of criticism and scolding was the most consistent negative predictor of school performance and appropriate social behaviour in a sample of sixth grade students.

Rogers had extensive advice for professors and universities and colleges. He suggested that there is a great need for a humanistic learning environment that is focused on self-determined learning. In this environment, professors should be open and genuine and should be transparent "real people" who are not afraid to state their personal views, even if this includes expressing anger when anger is warranted (Rogers, 1989). Most important, professors should strive to create an atmosphere of unconditional positive regard and should never demean a student by treating him or her in a disrespectful manner. Accordingly, conditions of worth should be removed. While this last component sounds good in theory, it is difficult in practice to minimize a focus on performance goals and maximizing grades. Maslow was also quite vocal in his criticisms of the prevailing educational models. He stated that, in his estimation, education is focused on the wrong things. It would be much more valuable from a societal perspective to focus efforts on the development of growth and self-actualization. Instead, schools tend to punish the student who tries to be creative. The way to succeed is to "jump through the hoops" by striving for extrinsically defined rewards and avoiding punishments without concern for intrinsic rewards and personal growth.

The basic concepts outlined by Rogers and Maslow seem to be quite effective in other performance contexts. Research and theory on job enrichment in work contexts has embraced some of their core notions (see Hackman & Oldham, 1976; 1980). Three of the five core job dimensions outlined by Hackman and Oldham (1980) reflect principles espoused by Rogers and Maslow. They suggested that jobs are enriched to the extent that they have: (1) skill variety (different skills are required); (2) task identity (workers identify with work that has visibility and is recognized by others); (3) task significance (the work is seen as personally meaningful because it benefits others); (4) autonomy (workers are free from constraints on scheduling and decisions); and (5) feedback. Task significance, autonomy, and self-determined feedback are all in keeping with a humanistic approach.

Farmer (1984) is among several authors who have argued that a more humanistic approach to education will yield many benefits. A humanistic focus is designed to not only educate but help the growth and development of the whole person. There are also potential implications in the type and sheer amount of learning that takes place. An overarching concern with the traditional approach to education is whether students are learning material they are really interested in. Conventional approaches to education focus on attaining grades merely to maximize rewards and minimize punishments. Does long-term learning take place and does intrinsic interest get developed? Research indicates that student learning and interest is maximized when the student has adopted mastery goals. Mastery goals involve an intrinsic desire to master the material rather than to achieve a particular performance goal. It is learning for the sake of learning rather than learning for the sake of a grade. For instance, compare the thesis student who simply wants the highest grade possible with the thesis student who is primarily interested in testing a research idea because he or she is genuinely interested in the topic and wants to embrace the process of learning to be a researcher. In your estimation, which student is most likely to have a positive thesis experience?

Both Rogers and Maslow suggested that a humanistic approach represents a very viable alternative to prevailing approach and they believe that, in the long run, a humanistic approach will result in substantially greater "real learning." What does this mean in terms of how classrooms are structured and how the learning process unfolds? First, instructors must try to remove conditions of worth and counter the tendency for students to try to maximize their grades by seeking ways to gain the instructor's approval. Conveying and modelling an attitude of acceptance to the student, who, in turn, can develop an unconditional sense of self-acceptance, can achieve this. Second, students must be allowed the opportunity to develop a sense of autonomy and self-determination. The instructor's role is to be a resource for the student and assist the student in the process of self-discovery. Third, instructors must have the same characteristics as the ideal therapist. That is, he or she is genuine, real, non-judgemental, and empathetic.

A revealing account by Samuel Tenenbaum (see Rogers, 1961) illustrated how attempts to implement a student-centred approach can lead to great confusion at first among students who are used to learning in an atmosphere that is shaped and directed by their instructor. However, the end result if the process is continued is a highly engaging learning experience. Tenenbaum participated in a four-week course being taught by Rogers on "The Process of Personality Change," and he provided his overview of his experience after the course had concluded. He recounted that the class did not start out well when Rogers turned the class over to the participants and refused to implement his own preconceived structure. Tenenbaum related that:

> The class was not prepared for such a totally unstructured approach. They did not know how to proceed. In their perplexity and frustration, they demanded that the teacher play the role assigned to him by custom and tradition; that he set forth for us in authoritative language what was right and wrong, what was good and bad. Had they not come from far distances to learn from the oracle himself? (Tenenbaum, 1961, p. 301)

Although there was initial frustration, the end result was highly rewarding. What Tenenbaum found most impressive were the new insights that students learned about such concepts as the importance of acceptance, both for the self and others, as well as the sheer amount of participation that took place as students learned to "talk and talk."

There is no shortage of student testimonials to the benefits of student-centred learning, but student-centred classrooms are the exception rather than the rule. In practice, few classrooms have historically been based on a person-centred approach, but technological advances bring new opportunities. Several authors have noted that a person-centred approach may be quite compatible with web-based course instruction and virtual reality learning environments. Various forms of e-learning require the instructor to be a facilitator who helps the student achieve his or her own learning objectives, and then the student will be primarily responsible for evaluating his or her own learning experience (Miller, 2001). The case analysis by Motschnig-Pitrik and Holzinger (2002) of the program, known as **person-centred e-learning**, led them to conclude that student-centred teaching at the University of Vienna can indeed result in deeper learning of material, while at the same time, facilitating personal growth and the development of personal skills. More recently, Motschnig-Pitrik and Mallich (2004) concluded unequivocally that person-centred e-learning is "truly effective and rewarding" (p. 178).

Finally, one important caveat about person-centred learning needs to be mentioned. We return to the insightful account of Tenenbaum (1961). He noted that the Rogerian approach was highly successful overall, but he also reported that the non-directive teaching approach was not entirely successful. It seems that there were four students "who found the whole idea distasteful" (p. 307). As a budding personologist, you should not be too surprised by this! Some people are low in a personality construct known as **tolerance of ambiguity**. Tolerance of ambiguity refers to whether a person perceives an ambiguous situation as upsetting and threatening or energizing and interesting. On a related note, Sorrentino at the University of Western Ontario has identified individual differences in **uncertainty orientation**. Some people simply cannot tolerate uncertainty, while other people seem to thrive on it because it affords an opportunity for stimulation and creativity. Someone who has difficulty with uncertainty and tolerating ambiguity would likely not respond well to the more open approach advocated by Rogers.

Evaluation of Rogers' Theory

The conditions outlined by Rogers have had a great impact overall, but it is important to recognize that not everyone has endorsed his approach. Some people object to the positive view of people promoted by Rogers and suggested that he was naïve if he truly believed that people with anti-social and sadistic tendencies had an inherent goodness that they just needed to discover.

Other concerns have been raised about the generalizability of his techniques. Usher (1989) observed that certain aspects of the Rogerian approach are not well suited to cross-cultural counselling. Specifically, the approach is not appropriate for clients who come from a background where the self is not an extensive focus, and it is difficult for people who find it tough to verbalize their feelings. Poyrazli (2003) has expanded on these themes by criticizing the widespread use of Rogerian therapy in Turkish culture. This therapy is a poor fit for Turkish people, according to Poyrazli, because Turkish culture is traditional and collectivist and can be quite authoritarian. That is, people are used to being told what to do. Thus, the nondirective approach is simply a recipe for confusion. Also, they are not used to revealing themselves through verbal means and instead rely on the expression of nonverbal cues. Are they expressive enough to benefit from the client-centred approach?

One of the most salient criticisms of Rogers' theory (and, by extension, Maslow's theory) stems from a cross-cultural focus. The notion that there is a universal need for positive self-regard has been challenged by an impressive team of researchers consisting of Steven

Heine and Darrin Lehman from the University of British Columbia, Hazel Markus from Stanford University, and Shinobu Kitayama from Kyoto University (see Heine, Lehman, Markus, & Kitayama, 1999). In their comprehensive review paper, they focused on how the need for positive self-regard does not apply to Japanese culture. They outlined various ways in which Japanese people are focused on self-criticism rather than self-enhancement. The essential difference they note is that whereas North American people tend to be focused on being as good as possible, Japanese people are focused on being better rather than good, and this takes the form of an incessant drive toward perfection. The Japanese concept of *hansei* requires reviewing events and trying to find ways to improve in the future to more closely approximate the ideal way of behaving or performing. Thus, there is a "never-ending drive toward improving one's skills" (p. 771) and using self-criticism as motivation with the ultimate goal of completing the self. This self-critical orientation is extended beyond the self to include criticisms of close others, institutions, and the country itself. Heine et al. (1999) concluded by arguing that the need for self-regard must not be culturally invariant "because the constructions of *self* and *regard* themselves differ across cultures" (p. 766). We will return to a broad discussion of cross-cultural differences in the self-concept in Chapter 11.

For now, we will close this part of our analysis by noting that it should not necessarily be assumed that this self-criticism and pressure to perfect the self is adaptive among Japanese people. Ohtani and Sakurai (1995) translated the Multidimensional Perfectionism Scale (Hewitt & Flett, 1991, 2004) into Japanese and showed that high socially prescribed perfectionism (the pressure to attain imposed demands to be perfect) is associated with depression and hopelessness in Japanese students.

THE ASSESSMENT AND MEASUREMENT OF SELF-ACTUALIZATION

Historically, self-actualization has been regarded as a diverse personality construct with many facets (Maslow, 1971). Although there is some debate about certain components of self-actualization, there is general agreement about more general characteristics of the fully functioning person. Ellis (1991) summarized 14 attributes that are generally regarded as aspects of self-actualization. These attributes include self-awareness, nonconformity, tolerance, creativity, and social interest.

The complexity of the self-actualization construct is clearly reflected in the two best-known measures of self-actualization: the Personal Orientation Inventory (POI) by Shostrom (1964) and the Personal Orientation Dimensions (POD), also by Shostrom (1975). Both the POI and POD have been used by researchers and have provided a great deal of insight into the self-actualization construct. Both measures are useful instruments that provide total scores as well as subscale scores tapping such dimensions as inner-directedness and time competence. The distinction between inner-directedness and outer-directedness is a main focus of these measures. Inner-directed people are more self-actualized; they are guided by their own motives and goals. Outer-directed people are highly sensitive to external cues and dictates, so they respond to external pressures. The time competence measure examines how much the person is focused primarily on the present (low self-actualization) versus how much they are able to maintain a balance and sense of coherence to the past, present, and future (high self-actualization).

Unfortunately, the length of both instruments is prohibitive for most uses. The POI consists of 150 forced-choice items, while the POD is composed of 260 forced-choice items. Crandall, McCown, and Robb (1988) observed that the format and length of these instruments may result in several negative consequences, including a tendency to engender feelings of hostility and resentment among respondents. Of course, the same criticism will apply to any personality measure that is overly long and creates a sense of fatigue and frustration.

These problems led Jones and Crandall (1986) to develop the Short Index of Self-Actualization (SI). The SI consists of 15 items derived from the POD and POI. Items were selected and written to represent most of the subscales found on these instruments. The SI represents a significant improvement in that it is considerably shorter and the items are much easier to respond to because the forced-choice has been removed and respondents simply make six-point dimensional ratings of the extent to which they agree with each item. The 15 items that comprise the SI are shown in Table 7.7.

Table 7.7 Items of the Short Index of Self-Actualization (SI)

I do not feel ashamed of my emotions.
I feel that I must do what others expect of me.*
I believe that people are essentially good and can be trusted.
I feel free to be angry at those I love.
It is always necessary that others approve of what I do.*
I don't accept my own weaknesses.*
I can like people without having to approve of them.
I fear failure.*
I avoid attempts to analyze and simplify complex dimensions.*
It is better to be yourself than be popular.
I have no mission in life to which I feel especially dedicated.*
I can express my feelings even when they may result in undesirable consequences.
I do not feel responsible to help anybody.*
I am bothered by fears of being inadequate.*
I am loved because I give love.
*These items are worded in the opposite direction to self-actualization. The highly self-actualized person would disagree with these items.

Source: Flett, Blankstein, & Hewitt, 1991.

The SI's usefulness has been demonstrated in a variety of contexts (Schelle & Bonin, 1989). The scale appears to have adequate concurrent validity in that it is correlated significantly with concurrent measures of self-actualization (Jones & Crandall, 1986). The SI has also proved useful in differentiating between people with high versus low levels of self-actualization as determined by other measures (Jones, 1980). Also, Crandall et al. (1988) reported that total SI scores rose following a clinical intervention designed to raise levels of assertiveness, and this improvement was maintained a year later.

Other psychometric evaluations indicate that the SI has adequate internal consistency, with coefficient alpha values ranging from .65 to .75 (Jones & Crandall, 1986; Schelle & Bonin, 1989). This is close to the threshold of .70 that Nunnally (1978) suggested for measures in the initial stages of development. Other data indicate that the scale has acceptable test–retest reliability of .69 (Jones & Crandall, 1986), so there is temporal stability to scale responses.

Perhaps the SI's most problematic aspect is its factorial validity. Initially, Jones and Crandall (1986) conducted a factor analysis and found that the SI consisted of four interpretable factors reflecting autonomy, self-acceptance, acceptance of emotions, and trust in interpersonal relationships. They also identified an unclear fifth factor that seemed to reflect a willingness to confront undesirable aspects of life. Tucker and Weber (1988) reanalyzed these same data with more sophisticated factor analytic techniques. They confirmed the existence of the five factors but suggested that new items should be rewritten to more rigorously assess the factors. A subseqeuent factor analysis by Flett, Blankstein, and Hewitt (1991) with data from 799 university students confirmed that the SI is multidimensional with three factors being identified, but only the tolerance of failure factor had an adequate degree of internal consistency.

The concerns about the SI's factorial validity are unfair to some extent because the measure was never intended or conceptualized to tap self-actualization as a multidimensional construct. Rather, Jones and Crandall (1986) simply wished to create a brief measure of key self-actualization themes so that researchers interested in assessing self-actualization would have a brief and practical measure. However, it is possible that some researchers desire a brief but multidimensional measure of self-actualization, and there remains a need for one.

Given the clear theoretical basis provided by Maslow, it is surprising that there have been few attempts to create a self-actualization measure that taps the five levels of Maslow's hierarchy. The exception is a measure created by Lester et al. (1983), which does have five self-report subscales tapping the degree to which physiological, safety, belongingness and love, esteem, and self-actualization needs have been met. Lester et al. (1983) used this measure to show that students who had their needs satisfied were lower in trait neuroticism. Unfortunately, this measure has not had widespread popularity.

KEY POINTS

- The two well-known measures of self-actualization appear to be valid, but they are quite lengthy and this has impeded their use in research.
- A brief measure of self-actualization is associated with other constructs in a meaningful way but suffers from concerns about factorial validity.
- There is no measure that is commonly used to assess Maslow's needs hierarchy.

THE CONTEMPORARY FOCUS ON WELL-BEING

Although it is evident that the theoretical viewpoints of Maslow and Rogers are far from immune to criticism, we probably owe a debt to them and their followers because of their focus on the positive aspects of human functioning. As was noted earlier, this has provided much of the impetus for the current "positive psychology" movement. It has also provided the impetus for lines of research on subjective well-being and psychological well-being.

Examination of the current research on domains of well-being reveals how current researchers have been influenced by the theories advanced by Maslow and Rogers. This is particularly evident in the work by Carol Ryff and her colleagues. Ryff and her associates have noted that there are widespread individual differences in psychological well-being (see Ryff, 1989), defined as the person's perception of engagement with the existential challenges of life. Ryff (1989) has identified six components of psychological well-being.

The first component is autonomy. People high in autonomy are self-determining and independent. They are similar to self-actualized people in that they are able to resist social pressures to act in certain ways, and they evaluate themselves according to personal standards rather than social standards. They acknowledge such scale items as "Being happy with myself is more important to me than having others approve of me."

The second component is environmental mastery, which is a sense of mastery and competence in managing the environment. A person high in this dimension of well-being is able to choose or create contexts to suit his or her personal needs, in a manner in keeping with the personal responsibility theme. A relevant scale item here is "I have been able to build a home and a lifestyle for myself that is much to my liking."

Personal growth is the third component. This person has a feeling of continued development, and sees the self as growing and expanding (and it has nothing to do with waist size!). Personal growth is a sense of realizing potential and recognizing improvement in self and behaviours over time. A scale item tapping personal growth is "With time, I have gained a lot of insight about my life that has made me a stronger, more capable person."

The fourth component is positive relationships with others, which, of course, reflect the need to belong, as identified by Maslow. People high in this characteristic have warm, satisfying, and trusting relationships with other people. They have a concern about other people's welfare, and they are capable of empathy and affection. A sample item from Ryff's measure is "People would describe me as a giving person, willing to share my time with others."

Purpose in life is the fifth component. A person with purpose in life has defined goals and a sense of directedness as reflected by their aims and objectives for living. This person feels that there is a meaning to his or her present life and past life. A sample item here is "I enjoy making plans for the future and working to make them a reality."

Finally, the sixth component is self-acceptance, and once again, this is a theme relevant to self-actualization theories, which regard self-acceptance and other-acceptance as being very important. Obviously, the self-accepting person possesses a positive attitude

Carol Ryff's six components of psychological well-being are autonomy, environmental mastery, personal growth, positive relationship with others, purpose in life, and self-acceptance.

toward the self, but this means that this person can acknowledge and accept multiple aspects of the self, including both their good and bad qualities. A sample item reflecting self-acceptance is "When I look at the story of my life, I am pleased with how things have turned out."

Ryff's (1989) initial research with these six domains has shown that they combine, via factor analyses, to reflect a broad higher order construct of psychological well-being (also see Ryff & Keyes, 1995). Thus, there is a broad construct with different facets that represents individual differences in self-esteem. These six domains have been the subject of extensive research (see Ryff, 1995; Ryff & Singer, 1998), including a new study confirming that all six well-being domains can be detected in a sample of Japanese university students (Kishida et al., 2004). Other research has shown that higher well-being is associated with lower levels of trait neuroticism and higher levels of conscientiousness and extroversion (Keyes, Shmotkin, & Ryff, 2002). The most recent work by Ryff and colleagues foreshadows Chapter 12 in this book on personality and health. Investigation of a sample of aging women revealed that higher levels of well-being are linked with lower levels of cardiovascular risk, lower daily salivary cortisol (a stress index), and longer duration of REM sleep (Ryff, Singer, & Love, 2004). Related research on the neural components of well-being showed that greater well-being was linked with left hemisphere activity in the brain, which is regarded as a healthy sign of being positively engaged and motivated (see Urry et al., 2004).

One clear theme emerging from this new research is that well-being has a strong interpersonal component. Indeed, another study of social conditions that used data from a national survey of Americans found that exposure to perceived discrimination was associated with lower well-being, but this link was gender specific (Ryff, Keyes, & Hughes, 2003). Women, regardless of minority status, reported less well-being in terms of growth, mastery, autonomy, and self-acceptance if they perceived that they were the targets of discrimination.

KEY POINTS

- The humanist orientation has promoted research on positive psychology with an emphasis on topics such as well-being.
- Well-being is a complex construct with six factors that combine to form an overall, higher order construct. The six factors are autonomy, environmental mastery, personal growth, positive relationships with others, purpose in life, and self-acceptance.

Summary

In Chapter 7, we examined the phenomenological theories of personality outlined by humanistic psychologists Abraham Maslow and Carl Rogers. Theorists from this school of thought endorse some common themes such as the basic goodness of people and, in keeping with positive psychology, they focus on ways of maximizing psychological health rather than focusing on psychopathology and neurosis. Key concepts here include realizing one's potential and being open to experience.

We began with an overview of Maslow's theory. Maslow distinguished between deficit needs and growth needs and incorporated this distinction into his hierarchical model. Maslow posited a universal sequence of needs that begins with the basic needs of survival and safety. If these needs are met then the person focuses on needs with a more psychological basis. If needs for belongingness and love are met, then the person progresses to the level of self-esteem. The healthiest people, albeit less than 1% of the population, achieve the level of self-actualization. Maslow also posited a set of being needs that are guides for the attainment of growth and working toward self-actualization. Criticisms of Maslow's model tend to focus on whether the stages are invariant and whether the concept of self-actualization is culturally biased and not reflective of an interpersonal form of self-actualization.

Carl Rogers also endorsed the concept of self-actualization. Rogers identified the organism and the self as two key aspects of personality and suggested that these structures are directly implicated in our overall perception of experience (the phenomenal field). Rogers hypothesized that everyone has a need for positive self-regard. Ideally, positive self-regard occurs if the person experiences people who are genuine and who provide unconditional positive regard. Rogers suggested that people become inauthentic and get away from their true nature when they experience conditions of worth. Conditions of worth are perceived or actual contingencies whereby the person must act or behave in a certain way (or perform at a certain level) in order to get rewards, which can be either tangible rewards (e.g., money) or praise from others. Rogers also introduced the notion of self-discrepancy and suggested that people are prone to psychological distress when they are aware of the gap between the actual self and their ideal self. Rogerian therapy is client-centred and seeks to address problems in psychological health by providing a setting where the therapist is genuine and empathetic, and provides unconditional positive regard. Empathy shown by the therapist has been confirmed as a general feature that enhances the client–therapist relationship and the effects of therapy in general.

This chapter also included extensive discussion of whether the theoretical concepts advanced by Maslow and Rogers are applicable across cultures. In addition, the practical applications of the humanistic approach in education settings were discussed.

The chapter concluded with an evaluation of the primary measures designed to tap individual differences in self-actualization and a discussion of current research on psychological well-being. The main measures were found to be wanting in several respects, and this is why alternative measures have been created in recent years. The final focus on the contemporary approach to the conceptualization and assessment of well-being illustrated how several themes advanced by Maslow and Rogers are reflected in the well-being construct. Research highlighting the role of well-being in positive health outcomes was described, and it was noted that the humanistic perspective has contributed to a recent emphasis on positive psychology.

Questions to Consider

1 Review the hierarchy of needs outlined by Maslow. Where do you fall on this hierarchy? Recall that fewer than 1% of students attain the level of self-actualization. Is this finding accurate, or could it reflect a measurement bias? Do you think it is ever possible for a young person to become self-actualized, or does it require more life experience?

2 Maslow's list of famous self-actualized people is now getting quite dated. Can you think of a contemporary person you would consider to be self-actualized? Or do you think this is an impossible standard that no one can reasonably attain? To help with your determination, review the list of 30 specific attributes associated with self-actualization in Table 7.3.

3 Review the list of B-values from Maslow's theory in Table 7.2. Select three values from this list that you embrace as most personally meaningful. Are there values not on this list that you see as very important? Do you think the importance of values remains relatively stable or does it change as we get older?

4 Marshall's work on the treatment of sex offenders indicates that when it comes to Rogerian principles, they respond well to treatment approaches based on empathy but may require a more directive approach than would be advocated by Rogers. Do you think that sex offenders have a capacity for goodness and they, like most people, should respond reasonably well to being treated with empathy?

5 Assume that you have an unlimited budget and you are given the job as an administrator of a school system. What steps could you or would you take to make the system into a person-centred approach reflecting the beliefs of Rogers? Do you believe that this would result in increased learning? Note that some authors have characterized our schools as abysmal failures because they have not produced a greater number of self-actualized people. Do you think it is possible to increase self-actualization through educational training?

6 The family is often seen as the primary source of conditions of worth. To what extent do you think that societal messages delivered via the media (e.g., promoting the "thinness is good" stereotype in young women) also play a role? Why do you think some people

internalize these conditions of worth and try to live up to them while others reject these same conditions of worth?

7 List the six domains of well-being. Which domains do you see as reflecting the views of Rogers and which reflect the views of Maslow?

Key Terms

actualizing tendency, p. 269
anomic suicide, p. 252
belonging and love needs, p. 251
B-values, p. 259
client-centred therapy, p. 273
conditions of worth, p. 267
desacralizing, p. 256
esteem needs, p. 253
gender similarities hypothesis, p. 265
Guttman scale analysis, p. 262
Jonah Complex, p. 258
mindfulness, p. 258
organismic valuing process, p. 269
organistic theories, p. 246
peak experiences, p. 255
person-centred e-learning, p. 277
personal responsibility, p. 248
phenomenal field, p. 266
positive psychology, p. 248
Q-sort technique, p. 268
self-actualization, p. 246
subception, p. 269
tolerance of ambiguity, p. 277
transpersonal psychology, p. 258
uncertainty orientation, p. 277
unconditional positive regard, p. 268
Vipassana meditation, p. 258

Key Theorists

Abraham Maslow, p. 249
Carl Rogers, p. 266

chapter eight

BEHAVIOURAL AND LEARNING THEORIES

- Ivan Pavlov and Classical Conditioning
- Radical Behaviourism and John B. Watson
- Operant Conditioning and B. F. Skinner
- Dollard and Miller's Social Learning Theory
- Rotter's Social Learning Theory
- Bandura's Social Cognitive Theory
- The Aggressive Personality and the Learning of Aggressive Behaviour

A psychiatrist told me once that he had used "operant therapy" in a U.S. Army hospital in Vietnam. He had called the patients together and told them that if they did not go to work they would get electric shock therapy! That, he said, is the kind of therapy that people understand.

—B. F. SKINNER (1980, P.7)

WE BEGIN THIS CHAPTER with an excerpt from John Watson's classic book *Behaviorism*, which was originally published in 1924. This excerpt titled "How to Change Personality" tells us much about Watson and how a behaviourist views the environmental origins of individual differences. He observed that:

> Even we "normal ones" after having looked ourselves over and decided that we'd like to slough off a few of our worst carryovers, find that making these changes in our personalities is no easy task... it is doubly difficult when you have to unlearn a vast organized system of old habits before you can put on the new. And yet this is what the individual faces who wants a new personality. No quack can do it for you, no correspondence school can safely guide you....
>
> What do you have to do to change personality? There must be both *unlearning* the things we have already learned (and the unlearning can be an active *unconditioning* process or just *disuse*) and *learning* the new things, which is always an active process. Thus the only way thoroughly to change personality is to remake the individual by changing his environment in such a way that new habits are to form. The more completely they change, the more personality changes. Few people can do this unaided. That is why we go on year in and year out with the same old personality. Some day we shall have hospitals devoted to helping us change our personality because we can change the personality as easily as we can change the shape of a nose, only it takes more time. (Watson, 1970, p. 301–302)

We will discuss Watson and his beliefs in more detail below. For now, there are two main themes to take from this excerpt. First, personality is a reflection of learning; as such, what has been learned can be unlearned. Second, personality differences stem from contingencies in the environment; thus, we should focus on the external factors and their influence on us.

Previous sections of this book focused on stable, internal personality traits as the sources of individual differences (i.e., personality lurks somewhere inside the self). During the 1960s and 1970s, the concept of personality traits fell out of favour. Instead, alternative explanations took hold, including the learning perspective, which focuses on factors outside the person as being responsible for individual differences. That is, contingencies in the environment and situational factors account for differences among people.

Although the main catalyst for this shift away from internal personality attributes inside people was Mischel's (1968, 1969) influential critique of the trait concept, historically, the roots of this change in emphasis had taken place several decades earlier with the classical conditioning experiments of Ivan Pavlov. This was followed by the radical behaviourism advocated by John Watson. We will examine their work as well as other classic theorists such as B. F. Skinner, John Dollard and Neal Miller, Julian Rotter, and Albert Bandura.

IVAN PAVLOV AND CLASSICAL CONDITIONING

Although he did not outline a personality theory per se (which also applies to Watson and Skinner), **Ivan Pavlov** deserves consideration here for outlining how new behaviours can develop. Pavlov and his dogs rival Freud in popularity and the level of awareness shown by the general public. Sometimes famous contributors are not only ingenuous, they are also very lucky. In this instance, Pavlov, a Russian physiologist, accidentally discovered the kind of learning known as classical conditioning. He received the Nobel Prize in 1904 for his work in this field.

As a physiologist, Pavlov had a great disdain for unscientific psychology, and, according to Fancher (1990), Pavlov banned the use of psychological terminology in his laboratory with threats of immediate dismissal for any employee caught using psychological terminology or trying to explain phenomena in psychological terms.

Pavlov studied the digestive system of dogs by presenting them with meat powder to make them salivate. It became apparent that dogs started to drool simply at the sight of the person who fed them, even before the actual meat powder was presented. Pavlov referred to the salivary responses as "psychic secretions." Pavlov decided to conduct controlled experiments of this phenomenon. The first study involved ringing a bell behind the dog just prior to placing the meat powder in the dog's mouth. Repeated pairings resulted in the dog eventually starting to salivate as soon as the bell was rung.

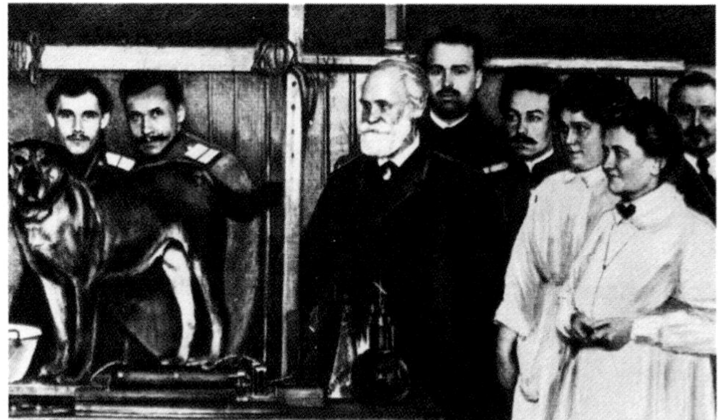

Ivan Pavlov discovered and developed the theory of classical conditioning by conditioning dogs to salivate at the sound of a bell.

A similar phenomenon occurs regularly in the current author's home. Our family dog Toby has developed his own version of Pavlovian conditioning. He has a great desire to share in breakfast bagels. The sound of the bell ringing on the toaster oven is a cue that will bring him running each and every time he hears it.

The Unconditioned and Conditioned Stimulus and Response

Pavlov first introduced the concept of conditional reflexes and the processes involved in his 1904 address while accepting his Nobel Prize. Pavlov described several new terms to account for the various factors that operate in classical conditioning. The meat powder is referred to as the unconditioned stimulus (UCS). The seemingly automatic, hard-wired drooling response of salivation is known as the unconditioned response (UCR). The bell

Figure 8.1 The Process of Classical Conditioning

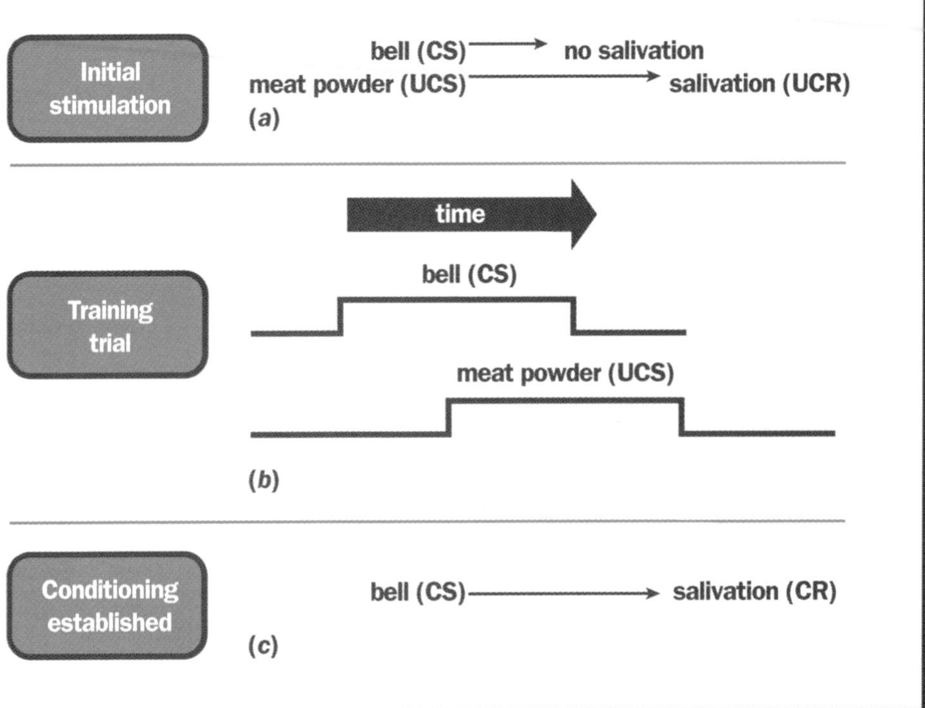

a) Before learning, the meat powder (UCS) elicits salivation (UCR), but the bell (CS) does not. b) A training or learning trial consists of presentations of the CS, followed closely by the UCS. c) Classical conditioning has been accomplished when the previously neutral bell elicits salivation (CR).

Source: Kring, 2007, p.23.

that eventually comes to elicit the saliva response is known as the conditioned stimulus (CS). Figure 8.1 illustrates the sequence of events leading up to the conditioned response. Whereas the saliva response was an unconditioned response when it appeared almost as a reflect action in response to the meat powder, when it now occurs dues to the presentation of the CS, the saliva response is known as the conditioned response (CR) .

If the bell is eventually rung repeatedly, but the meat powder now doesn't follow, then the phenomenon of extinction will eventually occur. Extinction means that the CR eventually disappears because the pleasurable stimulus (the meat powder) is no longer evident and eventually the organism adapts to this new reality.

Extinction is at the root of a clinical intervention technique known as flooding. Flooding is a behaviour modification technique used to treat extreme phobias of specific objects. The person is exposed to the feared object and is not permitted to escape. Someone with a snake phobia might have to watch the movie *Snakes on a Plane*, for instance, or have to touch a live snake. The usual avoidance response is no longer reinforced and eventually, fear lessens because the imagined or anticipated catastrophe after being exposed to the feared object does not happen.

The concept of **differentiation** (also introduced by Pavlov) occurs when the organism learns to respond specifically to the exact CS and does not respond to a highly similar stimulus. Why? The organism has learned that similar stimuli are not followed by the UCS. However, when these similar stimuli do resemble the CS enough to elicit the response, then **generalization** has occurred. That is, the CR occurs in response to stimuli that resemble the original CS.

Rescorla's (1987) extensive research on Pavlovian conditioning showed that a UCS is more effective in conditioning a response if it is surprising and unexpected (Rescorla & Wagner, 1972). An unexpected UCS has the potential for large increases in associative value. His work also established that the reinforcing aspects of instrumental responses in stimulus–response paired learning are cognitively encoded in memory. That is, "the reinforcer is not just a catalyst, but is itself encoded" (Rescorla, 1987, p. 129). Contemporary cognitive neuroscience research is examining the physiological processes that take place in the brain when reinforcement and punishment are experienced. Extensive evidence now indicates that the brain responds differentially to positive and negative feedback. Research on reinforcement learning theory has established the role of neurons (the basal ganglia at the base of the brain and dopamine in the midbrain) in learning via reinforcement. The experience of reinforcement leads to changes in dopamine activity, and this is recorded by the basal ganglia as well as the firing of neurons in the frontal cortex (for a review, see Niewenheis, Holroyd, Mol, & Coles, 2004).

Earlier basic work on classical conditioning and the UCS qualities uncovered a phenomenon known as the **blocking effect** (see Kamin, 1968, 1969). The blocking effect is the introduction of a second UCS once another UCS has already been used to create a conditioned response. The response to the second UCS is suppressed (blocked) by the already established conditioning link. Thus, whether a UCS can facilitate a conditioned response depends on prior conditioning. The blocking effect in conditioning responses with humans was shown in a study by Lanzetta and Orr (1980). They showed that facial images conveying fear and anger acquired excitatory strength when paired with a UCS (in this case, a small electrical shock), but images of happy faces could not elicit a conditioned response. Thus, the fear and anger expressions overshadowed the happy expressions when they appeared together, and this was interpreted as evidence of the blocking effect.

KEY POINTS

- The process of classic conditioning was described by Russian physiologist Ivan Pavlov.
- In classical conditioning, a conditioned stimulus acquires the ability to elicit a conditioned response by being paired with and immediately preceding an unconditioned stimulus.
- Conditioned responses are extinguished and no longer present once an organism learns that the unconditioned stimulus no longer follows the conditioned stimulus.
- Classical conditioning is more likely when we are biologically prepared to express the conditioned response.
- Cognitive neuroscience has focused on the basal ganglia and frontal cortex as areas of the brain that are activated by rewards and punishments.

Personality Differences among Pavlov's Dogs

One often unrecognized aspect of Pavlov's work was his strong conviction that there are individual differences in temperament, and these differences reflect inherited differences in biological response systems and related tendencies. Regarding temperament, Pavlov (1927, 1928) observed that he could identify four distinct types of dogs. They had differences in their nervous systems that led them to closely resemble the four temperament types outlined by Hippocrates (see Chapter 2).

Another chance event helped Pavlov recognize these individual differences. Pavlov's laboratory got flooded. This exposed his dogs to grave danger as the water poured in. Afterwards, Pavlov reflected on the event and remarked on the clear differences among his dogs. He recounted that:

> A big flood which occurred in Petrograd on the 23rd September, 1924 afforded us an opportunity to observe in our dogs prolonged neuro-pathological disturbances which developed as a result of the extremely strong and unusual external stimuli consequent on the flood ... During the terrific storm, the breaking of the waves of the increasing water against the walls of the building and the noise of breaking and falling trees, the animals had to be quickly transferred by making them swim in groups from the kennels into the laboratory, where they were kept on the first floor, all huddled up together indiscriminately. All this produced a very strong and obvious inhibition in all the animals, since there was no fighting or quarrelling among them whatever, otherwise a usual occurrence when the dogs are kept together. After this experience some of the dogs on their return to the kennels showed no disturbance in their conditioned reflexes. Other dogs—those of the inhibitable type—suffered a functional disturbance of the cortical activities for a very considerable period of time, as could be disclosed by experiments upon their conditioned reflexes. (Pavlov, 1927, p. 314)

This chance event illustrated the need to consider the personality differences among dogs.

Pavlov studied individual differences in his research on **experimental neuroses**. Experimental neuroses refer to the confusion and distress that Pavlov's dogs experienced when they were required to make a choice between expressing two or more conditioned responses of equal strength and magnitude. The precise manner in how dogs responded to this choice depended on the dogs' temperament. Highly active dogs became even more active and demonstrative in their clawing and snapping behaviour (thus expressing frustration and anger), while less intense and active dogs seemed to become depressed and helpless, as if they were paralyzed by indecision. These differences led Pavlov to introduce the concepts of **excitation** and **inhibition**. The first set of dogs have a physiological system dominated by excitatory energy and related processes, while the second set of dogs have a physiological system dominated by inhibition and the suppression of possible responses.

Pavlov's increasing awareness and appreciation of individual differences throughout his career led to some clear changes in his thinking over time. Pickenhain (1999), in an article detailing Pavlov's contribution to neuroscience, concluded that in his waning years, Pavlov eschewed a deterministic view and instead came to view "the organism and its environment as a self-organizing system" (p. 85).

KEY POINTS

- Pavlov focused on personality differences among his dogs, with some dogs being active and excitable and others being listless and inhibited.
- Experimental neuroses result when dogs must choose between two conditioned responses of equal magnitude and strength.
- Personality differences among animals are stable over time and are reflected in everyday behaviours.

RADICAL BEHAVIOURISM AND JOHN B. WATSON

John B. Watson (1878–1958) was a key theorist who became increasingly disenchanted with the psychoanalytic approach and its focus on introspection as a way of elucidating unconscious processes. It can be argued that his dramatic statement in 1913 essentially "rocked the world" of psychology. Specifically, he stated that:

> Psychology as the behaviourist views it is a purely objective experimental branch of natural science. Its theoretical goal is the prediction and control of behaviour. Introspection forms no essential part of its methods, nor is the scientific value of its data dependent upon the readiness with which they lend themselves to interpretation in terms of consciousness. (p. 158)

Watson was influenced greatly by research on learning in the form of experiments conducted on observable animal behaviours. He favoured **behaviourism** as an approach that focuses on the study of observable actions rather than cognitions and internal stimuli. Watson argued that only observables in the form of behaviour should be the proper subject matter for psychology if it is to attain the status of being a science. Introspective thoughts and cognitions are not observable, and, as such, there is no reason to study them, he maintained. That is, because subjective feelings cannot be objectively observed, they have no room in psychology.

Watson's views have been characterized as **radical behaviourism** because the exclusive focus is on overt behaviour that can be observed, predicted, and controlled. Moreover, other concepts such as words and language need to be redefined in behavioural terms. For instance, verbal behaviour is not words or concepts; instead it is the movement of vocal cords. In subsequent work, Watson (1924) supplemented the concept of radical behaviourism by introducing the concept of **radical environmentalism**: that the environment is a much more important determinant of behaviour than is heredity or temperament.

What is it about the environment that is important? The other key assumption of Watson's approach is that the process of conditioning or learning is the key to understanding human behaviour, and these learning conditions are located in our environments. This was demonstrated by Watson and Rayner (1922) in their classic case of Little Albert. Little Albert, the 11-month-old son of a hospital worker, was used to demonstrate that it is possible to use conditioning principles to create a fear of white, furry objects. Watson and Rayner (1920) created this fear by hitting a steel bar behind Little Albert's head every time a white rat was presented to him. Eventually, after repeated pairings of the white rat with the startling noises, Albert came to display significant distress at the initial presentation of the rat, and this was extended to white furry objects in general. This is an illustration of generalization, which was described earlier.

Unfortunately, due to circumstantial events, the trials with Little Albert were terminated, so there was no deconditioning phase. Thus, there was no **extinction phase**, so perhaps poor Little Albert carried this fear of white furry objects with him throughout his life. In their work, Watson and Rayner (1920) chided the Freudians about how they would interpret Little Albert's dysfunction years later when he is suffering from a seemingly inexplicable phobia. They suggested that:

> The Freudians 20 years from now ... when they come to analyze Albert's fear of a sealskin coat, will probably tease from him a recital of a dream which upon their analysis will show that Albert at three years of age attempted to play with the pubic hair of his mother and was scolded violently for it. If the analyst had sufficiently prepared Albert to accept such a dream, he may be fully convinced that the dream was a true revealer of the factors which brought about the fear. (Watson and Rayner, 1920, p. 14)

Watson and Rayner's experiment is often cited as an illustration of classical conditioning. However, in the strictest sense, this is not classical conditioning because the loud noise only occurred after Little Albert reached for the rat. It was Little Albert's actions that met with aversive consequences. Thus, in some ways, it represents another form of conditioning, operant conditioning, which is described in more detail below (see the section Operant Conditioning and B. F. Skinner), as part of our analysis of Skinner's theory.

Although Little Albert's case is not a pure instance of classical conditioning, his example provided the impetus for a subsequent model of how phobias develop. Mowrer's (1947) two-factor theory about phobias identifies two phases: (1) Classical conditioning occurs as a person comes to identify a neutral stimulus (e.g., a bumble bee) with a frightening or painful stimulus (the UCS). The neutral stimulus is the CS. (2) The person learns to escape the CS (e.g., by avoiding bumble bees) and is rewarded by the reduction in fear that comes with avoiding the phobic object. This second phase reflects a process known as avoidance conditioning, an example of operant conditioning.

Is Mowrer's two-factor theory supported by empirical evidence? There is clear evidence that avoidance conditioning does indeed contribute to the development of fears and phobias (Siddle & Bond, 1988). However, there are two important caveats. First, only certain people develop debilitating phobias. Some vulnerability factor reflecting personality and temperament is likely involved. Second, only certain stimuli are likely included in the development of phobias. The concept of prepared learning is that we are biologically prepared to fear only certain stimuli and not others (see Marks, 1969; Marks & Tobena, 1990). That is, from an evolutionary perspective, a bee phobia makes sense given the existence of killer bees and the fact that some people have allergies and could die from a bee sting. A phobia of pigs makes little sense because they pose no obvious or apparent threat to us.

Why do some things generate phobias in some people and not in others? Some factor of personality is likely involved.

Watson's Views on Personality

Finally, how did Watson view personality? In general, Watson downplayed the possibility of constitutional factors that contribute to subsequent life outcomes and interests. For him, a few key conditioning principles could explain almost any human behaviour. In essence, the characteristics of people could be shaped and controlled by the environmental contingencies that operate on the individual. This basic view is reflected in Watson's famous and most controversial quote. He suggested the following:

> Give me a dozen healthy infants, well-informed, and my own specified world to bring them up in and I'll guarantee to take anyone at random and train him to become any type of specialist I might select—doctor, lawyer, artist, merchant-chief, and yes, even beggar men and thief, regardless of his talents, penchants, tendencies, abilities, vocations, and race of his ancestors. (Watson, 1924, p. 82)

In essence, then, Watson suggested that the power of conditioning is so great that we can create any type of person.

So where does personality enter into the picture? Watson believed that personality is merely the end product of our habit systems. It is behaviour that is repeated as environmental contingencies continue to recur. As such, he claimed that, "Personality is the sum of activities that can be discovered by actual observation of behavior over a long enough time to give reliable information" (Watson, 1970, p. 274).

Watson was certainly not shy about stating his views on most matters, and the nature of personality was no exception. "Personality" was the title of the final chapter in his classic book *Behaviorism*. In this chapter, Watson adopted the previous view espoused by James that personality is mostly fixed by the age of 30. Watson maintained that personality changes very slowly if at all by the time we reach 30 because our habit patterns have become set. People, according to Watson,

> [u]nless constantly stimulated by a new environment, are pretty well settled into a humdrum way of living .... If you have an adequate picture of the average individual at 30 you will have it with few changes for the rest of that individual's life—as most lives are lived. A quacking, gossiping, neighbor-spying, disaster-enjoying woman of 30 will be, unless a miracle happens, the same at 40 and still the same at 60. (p. 278)

Of course, as we learned in Chapter 3, contemporary research indicates that the stability of personality is not at issue, but changes in personality occur throughout the lifespan, and there is nothing magical about the age of 30.

Watson also had some clear views about how personality should be studied. He felt that habit systems could be detected by sampling broadly from a person's "activity stream." Personality should be observed in various situations and life roles because, according to Watson, "the situation that we are in dominates us always and releases one or another of these all-powerful habit systems" (p. 276). He felt that there was no quick way of studying the behaviour or psychological characteristics of individuals. He felt that, at a minimum, a person had to be evaluated based on (1) their educational chart (educational history); (2) their yearly achievements and accomplishments; (3) their preferences in recreational activities and use of spare time; and (4) their emotional "make-up" in terms of their practical situations and responses to daily life events.

Watson acknowledged that some personalities are healthier than others, and a personality may require changing. He attributed weaknesses in personality to our inferiorities, our susceptibility to flattery, and a constant desire to become "a king" or "a queen" (superiority striving). However, the most important factor is the carryover of unhealthy habit systems established in infancy and early childhood. He argued that we can develop very unhealthy and overlapping strong attachments (positive conditioning) and dubious habit systems. He referred to these early habit systems as "nest attachments." Here Watson was not at all hesitant about placing the blame on mothers. This is revealed by the following hypothetical scenario of nest habits outlined by Watson (1970):

> Suppose by the time you are 3 years of age your fond and doting mother has got you into the following ways of behaving. She waits on you hand and foot. You are an angel child and anything you do or say is perfectly wonderful. Your father must not correct you. Your nurse is always wrong if she scolds you. Three years

> later you start school. You are a problem child all through. Soon you play hookey; your mother backs you up. You steal and lie repeatedly, and your teacher sends you home and closes the school to you. Your mother gets a tutor—but a tutor over who she has control. He educates you. You are "finished off" by travel. One meets people everywhere of this kind. (p. 293)

It seems that Watson's views of women were less than favourable. As we will see below, this abhorrence of pampering was foreboding in terms of Watson's treatment of his own sons, and the fates that they experienced.

Although Watson believed that habit systems were mostly in place by the age of 30, he suggested that it is difficult but not impossible to alter these habit systems. Change, according to Watson, could only occur as a result of the unconditioning of bad habit systems and the conditioning of new, more appropriate habit systems. He felt that this was vastly superior to psychoanalysis, which he saw as having "no virtue." That is, he concluded that:

> I venture to predict that 20 years from now an analyst using Freudian concepts and Freudian terminology will be placed on the same plane as the phrenologist. *And yet analysis based upon behavioristic principles is here to stay and is a necessary profession in society—to be placed upon a par with internal medicine and surgery*... New habits, verbal, manual, and visceral, of such and such kinds, will be the prescriptions the psychopathologist will write. (Watson, 1970, p. 297)

Watson was correct in one sense. Behavioural principles involving learning and conditioning became a very popular form of treatment in the 1960s and 1970s, largely as a result of the work on operant conditioning by Skinner. However, other forms of treatment, including psychoanalysis and modern versions of it incorporating object relations theory, have also remained quite popular.

KEY POINTS

- Watson's radical behaviourism focused on only observable actions and not cognitions hidden inside the person.
- Little Albert was used to show how fears and phobias can be conditioned.
- Mowrer's two-factor model showed how phobias reflect both operant and classical conditioning.
- Watson felt that personality did not really exist in that environmental contingencies could shape the person into anything or anybody.
- According to Watson, personality is the end product of our habit systems and is essentially in place and fixed by the age of 30.

As a postscript, it is difficult, if not impossible, to evaluate Watson's radical behaviourism and some of his more contentious observations without taking into consideration the effect that Watson's own behaviour had on those around him. Most notably, he was involved in a scandalous extramarital affair with his graduate student, Rosalie Rayner. This affair became the talk of Baltimore society and led eventually to Watson being dismissed from his academic position at Johns Hopkins University. Watson and his wife, Mary Watson, were divorced, and he subsequently married Rosalie Rayner. They had two sons together. What became of their sons? The rest of the story was aptly summarized by actress Mariette Hartley, the granddaughter of Watson from his first marriage. Hartley's autobiography contains an excerpt that suggests Watson was quite misguided. Specifically, she recounted that:

> Billy became a highly respected psychiatrist in New York, fulfilling his father's dream. Ironically, that same Billy, brought up with "minimal fixations," took an overdose of pills in his office in Manhattan … His second suicide while in his thirties was successful. Little John, brought up with "minimal fixations," became a deeply religious man but continued to have a queasy stomach and intolerable headaches. Taking about twenty aspirins a day, his stomach went; he died in his early fifties of bleeding ulcers. (Hartley & Commire, 1990, p. 43).

This account suggests that there is a clear need to temper parental behaviour with love and affection, but Watson decided that this display of emotion was simply frivolous and unnecessary.

Classical Conditioning with People

The experiment with Little Albert mentioned earlier was a precursor of contemporary research on classic conditioning of people. For instance, contemporary research has been conducted by Martin Lalumière, who is currently at the University of Lethbridge in Alberta. Lalumière and Quinsey (1998) conducted research with males, pairing slides of partially nude females with highly arousing tapes of heterosexual interactions, and found subsequently that there was enhanced genital responding to the slides.

In another study, Plaud and Martini (1999) paired a slide of a penny jar with slides of partially or fully nude females, and this resulted in increases in penile circumference from viewings of the previously neutral penny jar. Although classical conditioning has been demonstrated in men, similar attempts to show classically conditioned sexual responses in females have been largely unsuccessful (Hoffmann, Janssen, & Turner, 2004; Letourneau & O'Donohue, 1997).

Sadly, there are indications that classical conditioning may have played some role in heinous acts by killers. Michael Briere abducted, sexually assaulted, and then killed 10-year-old Holly Jones from Toronto shortly after becoming aroused by child pornography that he downloaded from the Internet. In his court statement, he indicated that, "I don't know how it is for other people, but for myself, I would say that, yes, viewing the material does motivate you to do other things ... the more I saw it, the more I long for it in my heart" (Leclair, 2004). Infamous serial killer Ted Bundy, who once served as a suicide crisis line worker in the United States, granted an interview prior to his execution. Bundy attributed his actions to seeking out pornography during his adolescence. Specifically, he stated that, "The most damaging kind of pornography—and I'm talking from hard, real, personal experience—is that which involves violence and sexual violence. The wedding of those two forces—as I know only too well—brings about behavior that is too terrible to describe". You, as a budding personality theorist, would likely respond to Bundy by asking whether there was also something about his personality or character that interacted with pornography exposure to contribute to his behaviour. After all, Bundy acknowledged that at least initially the pornography was not in his house. He admitted to finding it in trash cans and the like after searching for it, suggesting that he had an inclination and personal need for it. Still, the classical conditioning studies described above suggest that exposure can contribute to an enhanced sexual response in males.

If classical conditioning can create inappropriate behaviours, it can also be used in treatment to reduce unhealthy and inappropriate behaviours. Applied Perspective 8.1 provides an overview of how conditioning has been used to treat dysfunctions.

Applied Perspective 8.1 Aversion Therapy and Behavioural Treatments of Clinical Dysfunctions

A general maxim in this area is that the same conditions and principles that were involved in the acquisition of a behavioural style can also be used to remove or "unlearn" this behavioural style. Thus, classical conditioning and operant conditioning can be used to remove inappropriate behaviours and replace them with appropriate behaviours. For instance, **aversion therapy** entails an attempt to reduce a behaviour by pairing it with a highly noxious stimulus. Regarding sexual disorders in Canada, for instance, deviant fantasies have been paired with punishing stimuli, such as a small yet painful self-administered electric shock (Marshall & McKnight, 1975; Rice, Harris, & Quinsey, 1990).

Aversion therapy can also be used to treat other problems. For instance, exposure to a noxious chemical has been used to successfully treat addiction to crack cocaine (Bordnick et al., 2004). Earlier research involved problem drinkers being shocked or made to feel nauseous while reaching for a drink or beginning to drink alcohol. **Covert sensitization** requires drinkers to simply imagine becoming extremely ill as a result of their drinking (Cautela, 1966).

Aversion therapy is used less frequently today than when it was first introduced in the 1960s, primarily due to ethical concerns around exposing already distressed people to harmful stimuli. However, it has still been employed in extreme cases when other options have not worked. For example, contingent shock was administered as a form of treatment to a mentally challenged woman as a way of reducing her extreme levels of self-injurious behaviours (Williams, Kirkpatrick-Sanchez, & Crocker, 1994). The treatments were successful in that she averaged 25 self-injurious acts prior to treatment and only two acts after treatment. Moreover, this treatment gain was maintained over a six-year period.

Another dramatic case was a nine-month-old baby who had been hospitalized on three occasions for chronic vomiting and chronic rumination. Rumination is a tendency to vomit food and then rechew it. Several alternatives were tried to no avail (see Lang & Melamed, 1969). The failure to keep food down was resulting in this infant wasting away to the point that a feeding tube was inserted that went from his nose directly to his stomach. As a last result, the therapists paired the beginning of vomiting with one second long shocks administered to the infant's leg. It took only two sessions for the infant to learn this contingency, and all vomiting had stopped after just six sessions!

Not all behavioural treatments rely on such extreme interventions as aversion therapy. **Exposure therapy** is one of the most common techniques for treating anxiety disorders in the form of phobias. Exposure to the object or situation associated with the phobia (e.g., making a snake-phobic patient touch a snake) while the patient is put into a relaxed state has been highly effective. Wolpe's (1958) **systematic desensitization** procedure is highly effective; it requires the person to imagine frightening events in a fear hierarchy while being relaxed. A patient with

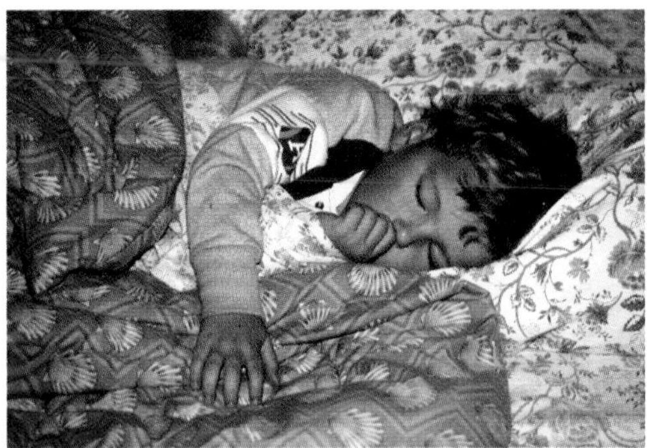
To stop thumb sucking, a parent may resort to a form of aversion therapy—rubbing the child's thumb with something that tastes unpleasant.

a fear of elevators, for instance, could imagine approaching an elevator, getting on, and then closing the door. Eventually, actually going on an elevator could be paired with being placed in a relaxed state. Contemporary technological developments have led to some sophisticated new approaches involving virtual reality exposure treatments that are based on simulated situations and computer-generated imagery (see Emmelkamp et al., 2002).

Finally, it should be noted that other forms of learning may also play a role. Classic experiments by Bandura and his associates have shown that not only can anxiety be learned by witnessing the aversive consequences experienced by a model, but a positive therapeutic response can also be displayed by a model, and this can have a positive effect on a person suffering from anxiety (see Bandura & Rosenthal, 1966).

Sensitivity to Punishment and Reinforcement

Pavlov's views on individual differences in the ability to condition dogs provided the initial theoretical impetus for contemporary research on individual differences in conditioning and sensitivity to punishment and reinforcement. **Hans Eysenck** and **Jeffrey Gray** are the two most prominent theorists in this area. Eysenck (1959) postulated that there are important personality differences in the ease of conditioning. Specifically, Eysenck (1959) hypothesized that introverts, relative to extroverts, can be conditioned more easily and readily. Eysenck (1947) drew analogies between introversion versus extroversion and Pavlov's construct of the strength of the nervous system with introverts having a weaker nervous system. The relative ability to condition introverts versus extroverts is also related to Eysenck's (1967) connection between levels of arousal and introversion versus extroversion, with introverts having higher levels of arousal.

Eysenck's initial views on personality and conditioning were summarized in two main postulates. The postulate of individual differences was stated as follows:

> Human beings differ with respect to the speed at which excitation and inhibition are produced, the strength of excitation and inhibition produced, and the speed at which inhibition is dissipated. These differences are properties of the physical structures involved in making stimulus-connections. (Eysenck, 1957, p. 114)

The postulate of individual differences identified the general possibility of personality differences in conditioning. The typological postulate tied these differences to introversion and extroversion and clinical conditions of hysteria and dysthymia. Eysenck postulated that:

> Individuals in whom excitatory potential is generated slowly, and in whom excitatory potentials so generated are relatively weak, are thereby predisposed to develop extraverted patterns of behavior and to develop hysterical-psychopathic

> disorders in cases of neurotic breakdown; individuals in whom excitatory potential is generated quickly and in whom excitatory potentials so generated are strong, are thereby predisposed to develop dysthymic disorders in case of neurotic breakdown. (Eysenck, 1957, p. 114)

Subsequently, Eysenck (1981) postulated that individual differences in this personality dimension relate to the cortical arousal system, which is modulated by reticulothalamic-cortical pathways. One implication is that there should be associated cognitive performance differences between introverts and extroverts. A recent neuroscience experiment by Kumari, ffytche, Williams, and Gray (2004) that compared introverts and extroverts provided strong support for Eysenck's claims. This experiment incorporated the fact that a neural circuit including the dorsolateral prefrontal cortex (DLPFC) and anterior cingulate (AC) cortex has been identified via research that has applied functional magnetic resonance imaging (fMRI) to people engaged in cognitive tasks. Kumari et al. (2004) compared the fMRI activity of introverts and extroverts. They found that extroversion was associated negatively with resting fMRI signals in the thalamus and Broca's area of the brain. Also, consistent with predictions derived from Eysenck's (1981) theory, when a cognitively demanding task began, higher levels of extroversion were associated with greater changes in the DLPFC and AC areas, as detected by fMRI recordings.

Like Eysenck before him, Jeffrey Gray is based at the Institute of Psychiatry at the University of London. Gray (1972, 1981) extended and refined Eysenck's views in several respects. First, in his initial work, Gray suggested that reinforcement versus punishment must be distinguished. That is, he suggested that introverts can be more easily conditioned under threatening environments with the possibility of punishment, but extroverts are sensitive to rewards and are more easily conditioned when there is the possibility of rewards and reinforcement.

Gray also made clear predictions about the neuroticism and individual differences in the ease of conditioning. He suggested initially that neuroticism was linked with high susceptibility to both punishment and to reward. However, Gray (1981) later modified his views somewhat based on his discovery from factor analyses that slightly rotating Eysenck's dimensions of extroversion and neuroticism resulted in two other factors (impulsivity and anxiety) that were conceptually and empirically more meaningful in their links with conditioning responses. High impulsivity reflects elevated levels of both neuroticism and extroversion. High anxiety reflects high levels of neuroticism and low levels of extroversion.

The personality traits of impulsivity and anxiety stem from two neurophysiological systems postulated by Gray (1981). The **behavioural approach system** (BAS) accounts for individual differences in impulsivity. It is linked with an appetitive orientation and involves a sensitivity to reward (and situations involving non-punishment). The **behavioural inhibition system** (BIS) accounts for individual differences in anxiety. It is linked with a defensive orientation and elevated sensitivity to punishment and non-reward.

Over the last 15 years or so, questionnaire measures have been developed to assess the BIS and BAS and related concepts. The Gray-Wilson Personality Questionnaire (Wilson,

Barrett, & Gray, 1989) was designed to tap six individual difference dimensions in humans based on animal research paradigms: (1) approach; (2) active avoidance; (3) passive avoidance; (4) extinction; (5) fight; and (6) flight. Although the six dimensions were assessed with an adequate degree of internal consistency (reliability), the measure was somewhat of a failure from a construct validation perspective. Why? The researchers' ultimate goal was to establish that their six dimensions were linked in a conceptually meaningful way with Gray's personality theory, but several anomalous results were found in the subscale intercorrelations. For instance, it was predicted that the approach and active avoidance subscales would be positively correlated because both are activation orientations, but these two subscales were negatively correlated. It was also expected that the flight and fight subscales would be correlated positively and reflect the same neurological system, but these subscales were not significantly correlated.

Stronger support for Gray's theory was obtained when Carver and White (1994) created a brief self-report measure to assess the BIS and BAS. They developed one general BIS measure and three subscale measures of BAS activation: (1) reward responsiveness (e.g., "When I get something I want, I feel excited and energized"); (2) drive (e.g., "When I want something, I usually go all-out to get it"); and (3) fun-seeking (e.g., "I will often do things for no other reason than that they might be fun"). The BIS general factor is tapped by such items as "If I think something unpleasant is going to happen I usually get pretty worked up," and "I worry about making mistakes." Although the BIS and BAS are supposed to be independent, research suggests that the BIS and reward responsiveness factors are, in fact, correlated (see Jorm et al., 1999).

In general, the BAS is believed to be linked with the willingness to approach others, while the BIS predicts the need to distance oneself from other people. A recent study of attachment styles and relationship threat confirmed that these factors are differentially associated in the predicted manner with approach versus avoidance tendencies (Meyer, Olivier, & Roth, 2005).

The same Meyer et al. (2005) study also showed that the BIS predicted reports of emotional distress when participants were asked to imagine their reactions if their partner was going to spend time with a highly attractive member of the opposite sex. One issue that has received extensive empirical attention in this area is the role of the BIS and BAS in emotional distress and various forms of psychopathology. Depressed individuals tend to have low BAS scores and high BIS functioning (Rottenberg & Gotlib, 2002). A study conducted with Australians selected from Canberra's electoral roll showed that BIS scores are linked with neuroticism, while BAS scores are linked with extroversion (Jorm et al., 1999). In addition, BIS scores were linked with both depression and anxiety. Another Australian study also confirmed a positive association between the BIS and neuroticism and a negative association between the BIS and extroversion (Gomez & Gomez, 2005). The BIS has also been linked with higher social anxiety (Harmon-Jones & Allen, 1997).

Researchers at the University of Barcelona in Spain have created other measures derived from Gray's theory. These measures assess sensitivity to reward (Torrubia, Avila, Molto, &

Grande, 1995) and sensitivity to punishment (Torrubia & Toben, 1984). A modified version of these scales has been published recently (Torrubia, Avila, Molto, & Caseras, 2001). This new questionnaire (SPSRQ) has shown good reliability and validity properties and has been used in several behavioural studies with good results (see Avila & Parcet, 2000).

The sensitivity to reward and punishment measures were designed for use with adults. Colder and O'Connor (2004) recently modified the items to tap parental reports of sensitivity to reward and punishment in children. The child's sensitivity to punishment is tapped by such items as "Your child often refrains from doing something because of fear of being embarrassed." Sensitivity to reward is tapped by such items as "Your child often has trouble resisting the temptation of doing forbidden things." The initial evidence attests to the reliability and validity of these two subscales. For instance, scores on the sensitivity to reward scale were associated with the child's level of heart-rate reactivity while experiencing reward during a task.

KEY POINTS

- Eysenck's postulate of individual differences highlights differences in the speed and strength of excitation and inhibition.
- Gray qualified Eysenck's claim by showing that introverts are more easily conditioned with punishment and extroverts are more easily conditioned with rewards.
- Gray linked conditioning with impulsivity and anxiety and tied them to the behavioural activation system (impulsive seeking of sensations) and the behavioural inhibition system (responsiveness to anxiety).

OPERANT CONDITIONING AND B. F. SKINNER

The roots of operant conditioning were laid by research conducted prior to 1900 by Edward Thorndike. His animal research with cats in cages led him to realize that actions that generate positive consequences are repeated. In this case, Thorndike's cats figured out how to get out of their cages, and they quickly repeated these actions when they experienced the joys of escaping (something my next door neighbour's cats figured out a long time ago).

Thorndike's work led him to postulate his most important concept: the **law of effect**. The essence of this law is demonstrated by billions of people in millions of contexts each and every day. That is, behaviour that is followed by positive outcomes is repeated, and behaviours that are followed by negative outcomes are less likely to be repeated. In his autobiography, American psychologist **B. F. Skinner** (1980) gave packing a suitcase as one example of the law of effect. People who pack their suitcase often are quite unsystematic at first, but once they realize that they don't have enough room for all of their belongings, they find a way to repack the suitcase in a much more organized way and repeat this procedure later when packing the suitcase again.

Initially, learning a behaviour because it was rewarded was known as **instrumental conditioning**. The research conducted by Skinner throughout most of the last half of the

B. F. Skinner introduced the idea of operant conditioning, which refers to a person operating on the environment through his or her actions to generate consequences.

20th century led to instrumental conditioning becoming known as operant conditioning. The term "operant" refers to the person operating on the environment through his or her actions to generate consequences, either positive or negative.

Skinner was born in Pennsylvania in 1904. He was raised by conservative parents who were not thrilled with his career goal of becoming a writer. Skinner was quite determined and even sought feedback about his work from such noteworthy figures as Robert Frost (see Skinner, 1980). He did not experience the success he had anticipated, and, as a result, over time, his interests shifted to science and the study of behaviour. As a result of his interest in the work of Pavlov and Watson, Skinner enrolled as a graduate student in psychology in the fall of 1926, and he was on his way to becoming famous.

How influential is Skinner? Surveys typically identify Skinner as one of the most famous psychologists if not the most famous psychologist ever. His goal was to focus on observable behaviours and approach phenomena with experimental paradigms that reflect psychology as a science. Skinner is responsible for adding many terms to the psychology lexicon; one of his most famous is S–R learning. This refers to stimulus–response paired learning. A particular stimulus becomes associated with a particular response as a function of whether positive consequences follow the response.

There are two different types of reinforcement that increase the likelihood of a response being repeated when a stimulus is presented. Positive reinforcement increases the likelihood of a behaviour being repeated due to the occurrence of positive, pleasurable outcomes after the behaviour has been expressed. An example would be developing an effective studying plan and being rewarded with a high grade, which is a positive reinforcer. Negative reinforcement also involves an increase in the likelihood of a behaviour being repeated, but in this case, the behaviour results in the termination of an aversive, unpleasurable event. The most common example from learning experiments would be a rat learning to make the correct choice in a maze in order to terminate the mild electric shock being applied to its feet. The termination of the shock is a negative reinforcer. Returning to our earlier example, the negative reinforcer could be developing an effective studying plan so that your parents stop frowning at you.

Another distinction is between primary reinforcers and secondary reinforcers. A primary reinforcer is something that has inherently rewarding properties in its ability to reduce a drive state. For instance, water is a primary reinforcer because it reduces thirst and water is needed for survival. A **secondary reinforcer** is a reinforcer that has acquired rewarding properties through its association with primary reinforcers. For instance, money is a secondary reinforcer because students, like most other people, have learned that money on a Friday or Saturday night can buy you the pizza that satisfies your basic need for food.

Skinner differentiated reinforcers and punishments. A common error made by students is confusing negative reinforcement and punishment. Both involve aversive events. However, punishments serve to *decrease the likelihood that a behaviour will be repeated.* Reinforcers, even negative reinforcers, serve to *increase the likelihood that a behaviour will be repeated.* Punishment is performing a behaviour and having that behaviour lead to negative consequences. An example with the earlier context is developing an effective study plan that results in your parents frowning at you because you forgot to pick them up at the airport.

The issue of whether the stimulus–response sequence leads to reinforcement or punishment helps establish the specific properties of a stimulus. Skinner's notion of a **discriminative stimulus** involves the ability that develops over repeated stimulus–response outcomes to identify a specific stimulus and its associated response to lead to rewards or punishments. For example, the type of course you take could be a discriminative stimulus if you learn that developing an effective study plan results in higher grades in your personality course, but the study plan does not result in higher grades in your statistics course because the professor likes to set exams requiring the application of the learned material to totally different situations. In this instance, you would learn to tailor your studying behaviour to the course that is linked with the reward, and you would probably decrease your studying behaviour for statistics exams. (Of course, this was just a hypothetical example because the effective studying plan should also help in the statistics course).

As discussed earlier, **stimulus generalization** is present when any stimulus that is similar to the originally conditioned stimulus will evoke the same response. Recall that Little Albert provided one of the earliest illustrations of stimulus generalization. Watson and Rayner reported that poor Little Albert demonstrated his fear response to not just the rat, but also to anything that was white and furry, including a rabbit, a dog, a fur coat, and even a Santa Claus mask. Typically, there is a stimulus generalization gradient such that the more dissimilar a stimulus becomes, relative to the original stimulus, the weaker the response.

Gradations are also involved in the gradual acquisition of a response through the process of **shaping**. Shaping entails providing rewards in a gradual sequence to responses that are **successive approximations**. For instance, a music teacher would initially reward any attempt on the part of a child to sing. Over time, rewards are applied only for specific improvements in singing.

Schedules of Reinforcement

Skinner and other behavioural theorists recognized that in the real world, reinforcement and punishment often do not immediately follow behaviours and instead are delayed.

The external environment contains different schedules of reinforcement. Reinforcement schedules were postulated to vary as a function of (1) whether the reinforcement is fixed or variable and (2) whether the key factor is the number of responses that must occur in order for reinforcement to follow or whether it is the amount of time that must have elapsed before the reinforcer became available. In a **fixed ratio schedule**, the number of responses occurring between one reinforced response and the other reinforced response is held constant. A FR5 schedule would mean that every fifth response would be rewarded. It is sometimes possible to figure out the type of reinforcement schedule, if any, in effect, based on the pattern of behaviour that the respondent displays over time. For instance, in a fixed ratio schedule, responses occur at a high and steady rate until the reinforcement is provided. The respondent pauses and then resumes the pattern. An example would be a child who discovers that he or she gets candy on Halloween from every fifth house that is visited, so there is persistent responding until the reinforcer (candy) is obtained after visiting the fifth house. The child sits under a tree and eats the candy and then vigorously starts the process all over again.

With a **fixed interval schedule** the key factor is the amount of time involved; the amount of time between reinforced responses is held constant. To continue with our earlier example, assume that the child is now being reinforced after every five minutes of going to houses. How do you think this child would respond once the pattern became clear? The predicted response would be relative inactivity, followed by a period of intense activity, as the time of the reinforcement's availability gets closer. If the child was on a FI10 schedule (reinforcement after every 10 minutes), he or she would probably go back to the treat, rest for about nine minutes, and then run to a nearby house at the 10-minute mark.

Hopefully, your own studying for tests does not follow this pattern. Some professors have suggested that students study on a fixed interval schedule. That is, there is very little studying in the prolonged interval prior to a test, followed by frenzied cramming the night before the test. This pattern is reinforced by the reality (but more likely the perception) that last minute cramming actually helps retention. Generally speaking, distributed studying done in an effective manner is likely to result in higher grades (i.e., more reinforcement) than leaving things to the last minute. Nevertheless, cramming tends to prevail. A 2004 Canadian survey found that two thirds of university students admitted to cramming and not studying at all until a test was one week away (Ipsos-Reid, 2005). The prevalence of cramming has resulted in the inappropriate use of Ritalin as a stimulant to keep students awake. Ritalin is normally prescribed for children suffering from attention deficits and hyperactivity, but there are growing reports of its use by university and college students who have found that the drug keeps them awake while they are cramming for a test or exam.

The fixed reinforcement schedules outlined above are relatively straightforward, but they are problematic since things are seldom fixed in real life. That is, reinforcement is often quite variable in terms of when it is obtained. In a **variable ratio schedule**, reinforcement occurs based on a set number of responses, on average. Thus, a VR5 schedule could mean that a child on Halloween gets candy at the first house, ninth house in succession, and fifth house in succession. A variable ratio schedule could apply to the rate of reinforcement from casino gambling using slot machines (assuming that eventually somebody wins).

The variable interval schedule requires a certain amount of time to elapse (on average). For instance, to use our same example, the child on Halloween on a VI5 schedule might receive candy at the ninth minute, the fifth minute, and the first minute, so that it averages out to five minutes that typically pass prior to receiving reinforcement. Variable interval schedules usually result in behaviour that is highly resistant to extinction, at least at first, because the reinforcement is not entirely predictable and may or may not be available. Also, because responses that are too early are not reinforced, but a subsequent response is reinforced, this contributes to creating a condition known as **partial reinforcement**. Partial reinforcement grants rewards on only certain trials following certain responses. Behaviours that are learned according to a partial reinforcement schedule are quite resistant to extinction because it is never immediately apparent that reinforcement is no longer available at all. In contrast, if someone is on a FI2 schedule that provides reinforcement every two minutes, the first or second time where this no longer occurs quickly fosters the impression that the chance to obtain reinforcement has come and gone.

Skinner and Lindsley were the first psychologists to extrapolate operant conditioning principles derived from animal research to the treatment of human problems, with reinforcement schedules put into effect. Their efforts are summarized in an engaging review paper by Alex Rutherford from York University in Toronto (see Rutherford, 2003). In 1954, Skinner and Lindsley used operant procedures in an attempt to change the behaviours of patients suffering from psychosis. Various reinforcers were used, including candy and cigarettes, and on occasion, pinup photographs of young women (see Lindsley, 2001; Skinner, Solomon, & Lindsley, 1954). The behaviours they hoped to increase involved the pulling of a plunger. They reported that two schedules of reinforcement were implemented: a one minute variable interval schedule and a fixed ratio 20 schedule. It was concluded that the effects of reinforcement were comparable for humans and animals, and the program was expanded to a 1-minute variable interval, and a fixed-ratio of 20. They concluded that the effects of different schedules of reinforcement on the behaviour of the subjects were similar to those found in rats, pigeons, and dogs. The program was expanded due to possible funding from drug companies to show that with certain patients, the administration of therapeutic drugs could serve as a reinforcer for plunger-pulling behaviour.

Skinner's faith in operant conditioning was so strong that he tried to apply it to a wide range of phenomena, including verbal learning (see Skinner, 1957). That is, he argued that the vocabulary we develop is largely a reflection of our reinforcement histories. This view of language was refuted vociferously by linguists such as Noam Chomsky (1959), who argued that the empirical evidence was lacking. Chomsky also maintained that the usual meaning of the concepts of reinforcement and conditioning were stretched by Skinner in a way that renders these concepts of little value. Stated simply, it would take too long for children to learn language through operant conditioning sequences involving rewards and punishments. Instead, it is believed that language is a by-product of cognitive development as well as forming general rules and axioms that guide us when forming new sentences and comprehending new words.

KEY POINTS

- Reinforcement schedules can be fixed or variable.
- Reinforcement schedules can reflect the number of responses required or the time that must elapse before the reward becomes available.
- Partial reinforcement schedules yield the greatest resistance to the extinction of a behaviour.
- Skinner believed that language was acquired via operant conditioning, a claim that was strongly rejected by linguists.

Skinner's Views on Personality and Individual Differences

Skinner was like other behaviourists in that he had little interest in personality. Berlyne (1968) analyzed this phenomenon and suggested that behavourists' interest in stimulus–response contingencies led them to focus on universal principles that applied to everyone rather than focusing on the unique differences among people.

Skinner suggested that personality should not be interpreted as a series of instincts or drives. Rather, behavioural differences are a joint focus of genetic factors that have evolved to maximize the chances of survival as well as the individual's unique history of reinforcement.

Skinner (1971) stated that he did not believe in personality questionnaires and instead favoured assessing behaviour. Much of Skinner's disdain for self-report measures stemmed from the fact that he felt people lacked insight into their own reinforcement histories when they are selecting scale items. For instance, he stated that, "The juvenile delinquent does not feel his disturbed personality" (p. 13). According to Skinner, people cannot fully describe the influential reinforcements and punishments they have experienced going back to earlier childhood and people are much better at reflecting on current experiences from a phenomenological perspective. Thus, for Skinner, personality self-reports are too heavily influenced by current subjective feelings.

Skinner was particularly adamant about the unimportance of needs. He stated that he didn't see any necessity to postulate needs (see Evans, 1969). In fact, he suggested that he could even make a pigeon into a high achiever by putting it on the proper reinforcement schedule, but he couldn't do anything with the pigeon if it required reordering the bird's needs. He concluded that: "If you want people to be productive and active in various ways, *the important thing is to analyze the contingencies of reinforcement, not the needs to be satisfied*" (Evans, 1969, p. 10). Regarding the issue of sexual needs, Skinner argued, "Sexual contact is not reinforcing because it feels good. It feels good because it is reinforcing" (Skinner, 1974). This was Skinner's way of saying that sexual contact is a reinforcer, not a need as psychodynamic theorists suggest. Perhaps it is a need *and* a reinforcer.

Skinner's views on personality were reflected clearly in his depiction of a hypothetical young man who had graduated from college and then was inducted into the army (see Skinner, 1971). If the young man feels insecure, this means that his behaviour is weak and inappropriate. If he is dissatisfied or discouraged, this means he is seldom reinforced, and, as a result, his behaviours are extinguished. If he feels uneasy or anxious, then, according to Skinner (1971), this means that his behaviour has unavoidable aversive consequences that have emotional effects. In short, all characteristics can be explained by behaviours and the consequences of these behaviours.

One criticism of Skinner's views on personality is that it is difficult to use operant conditioning to explain how a person will act in an entirely novel situation. Many exhibited behaviours do not seem to stem from a person's learning history. This was discussed earlier in terms of alternative views of language development. Perhaps novel behaviours reflect drives and motives, but Skinner would persist and argue that if you go back far enough in an individual's past, you should be able to locate reinforcers and punishers that account for the novel behaviour.

Skinner's Views on Culture

> If students do not learn, is it their fault? No, their teachers have not arranged effective contingencies. Is it then the teachers' fault? No, the culture has not arranged effective contingencies for them.
>
> — *B. F. Skinner*

As shown in the above quote, Skinner also had some strong views about the nature and role of culture. Skinner suggested that culture can be equated with the social environment, and that it is via culture that people acquire much of their behavioural repertoires. The overarching effect of culture, according to Skinner (1990), is that cultures shape and maintain operant behaviours. Cultures differ primarily in the different contingencies that exist and operate.

As for the cultures themselves, Skinner argued that whether they survive and thrive depends largely on operant conditioning. He stated that the most important function of culture is to assist the members of the culture to solve their personal problems. He maintained that "the strength of the culture in solving its problems will depend upon the behaviour it encourages and sets up in its members; a culture which induces its members to behave in effective ways will be a stronger culture". As a way of underscoring this point, Skinner wrote his controversial book *Walden Two* to depict a Utopian society that is made better through the principles of reinforcement and punishment. This book was controversial, in part, because some objected to the position that people were controllable based on the reinforcements and punishments they received.

According to Skinner, conflict ensues between cultures because they have evolved different repertoires based on operant conditioning, and thousands of different repertoires reflecting different contingencies have emerged. Just prior to his death, Skinner (1990) remarked, "The fact that a culture prepares a group only for a world that resembles the world in which the culture evolved is the source of our present concern for the future of a habitable earth" (p. 1207). Clearly, new contingencies, perhaps radically different, have to be created at a time when other rewards and punishments that may be entirely inconsistent with these new contingencies are still operating.

What is the relative importance of culture versus genetic factors? Skinner placed much more emphasis on culture. Skinner (1989) stated that:

> We can trace a small part of human behavior ... to natural selection and the evolution of the species, but the greater part of human behavior must be traced to the contingencies of reinforcement, especially to the very complex social contingencies we call cultures. Only when we take those histories into account can we explain why people behave the way they do. (p. 18)

Recall Skinner's earlier quote about problems in students' learning being attributable to a culture that fails to establish effective contingencies. Do you believe this is the case? How important is it for students to develop a sense of self-determination and personal responsibility along with an intrinsic interest in their own achievements? Clearly, situational and cultural factors play a role, but it still seems that some people have a level of achievement motivation and drive that seems to stem from them and may have little to do with past reinforcements and punishments. In other words, the reinforcement history may have a greater impact on some people than on others.

KEY POINTS

- According to Skinner, individual differences primarily reflect individual learning histories and reward contingencies, though evolutionary factors and genetic influences also play a role.
- Culture, according to Skinner, is essentially the social environment. Operant conditioning can be used to create better cultures.

Skinner's Views on Humanistic Psychology

In 1972, Skinner received the Humanitarian of the Year Award from the Association of Humanistic Psychology, and he gave a presentation entitled "Behaviorism is a Humanistic Psychology" as part of the award ceremony. Skinner used this opportunity to argue compellingly that behaviourism is indeed humanistic, and he expressed some resentment that behaviourism has been portrayed as non-humanistic by those who wish to focus on how reward and punishment contingencies can be used to control people. He made three main points: (1) it is only through a careful analysis of rewards and punishments that we can truly understand why people behave in certain ways; (2) with enough foresight and determination, it is possible to design the most effective environments and reward contingencies to bring out the best that mankind is capable of; and (3) self-actualization theories are misguided because they exaggerate the importance of the individual and his or her well-being. Skinner felt that a focus on self-actualization is misguided, and he posed the question "Isn't all this emphasis on the self a selfish view?" That is, it promotes the individual and not society as a whole.

Skinner died of leukaemia in 1990. Because he knew he was dying, he dedicated himself to one final, full-fledged attack on theories and approaches that were not very behavioural. These views are summarized in his final article entitled "Can psychology be a science of mind?" (see Skinner, 1990). He argued that psychotherapy and cognitive psychology were co-conspirators because they had lured psychologists away from the only thing that really mattered: the study of behaviour and its consequences. Skinner went so far as to suggest that people from these alternative theoretical camps could be equated with "creationists" who believe that the world is only a few thousand years old. His last speech was given just eight days before he died. It was during this presentation that he expanded the creationist label and applied it to anyone who was not a behaviourist. Right to the end, he espoused that a focus on behaviour is essential if psychology is to be regarded as a science.

DOLLARD AND MILLER'S SOCIAL LEARNING THEORY

Social learning theory represents the highly integrative, combined expertise and interests of **Neal Miller** and **John Dollard**. Miller's background was in experimental learning theory and he worked with famous learning theorist Clark Hull. Dollard's interest was in social science, including social psychology, cultural psychology, and sociology. Their combined theory reflects experimental and learning themes as well as social behaviours.

The concepts in this theory are outlined below. While reviewing these concepts, remember that they provide the basis for an influential personality theory with important applications. This is reflected in the title of Dollard and Miller's classic 1950 book *Personality and Psychotherapy*.

The social learning theory revolved around four key terms introduced earlier by Hull: (1) drive; (2) cue; (3) response; and (4) reinforcement. The drive concept is similar to the concept of needs espoused by theorists such as Murray. It is the motivational state that propels behaviour and creates a readiness to respond. Regarding the questions outlined at the beginning of this book, it provides the "why" component. A cue is another term for the stimulus that helps determine where and when the behaviour is expressed. Cues are signals that can elicit behaviour if they are accompanied by the drive state that requires expression.

Response is simply another term for the behaviour that is expressed, with the caveat that Dollard and Miller, like Skinner, defined behaviours in broad terms that included verbal behaviours. When it comes to a particular person, Dollard and Miller acknowledged that people are complex and are capable of various responses. The term **response hierarchy** was introduced to acknowledge that the same cue for a particular person can have multiple responses associated with it, with one response being more dominant than another.

Finally, reinforcement refers to the positive consequences that follow the performance of a behaviour. Reinforcement, of course, is critical in establishing and strengthening the link between the cue and the behaviour.

International Focus on Discovery 8.1 Learning and Display Rules for Expressing Emotions across Culture

It is widely acknowledged that there are salient individual differences between people in various aspects of emotional experience. One line of research on individual differences involves examining cultural differences in emotional experience and emotional expression.

Display rules represent one explanation for these cultural differences in emotional expression. Display rules have also been called "feeling rules" (Hochschild, 2001). The concept of display rules was first introduced by Ekman and Friesen (1969). Display rules fit with a social–cognitive view of the role of learning in the development of new behaviours. Display rules are learned and socialized. They are rules that indicate when it is appropriate to express emotions in social situations, with appropriate emotions being reinforced and inappropriate emotions being punished. Display rules also have a clear cognitive component. That is, display rules involve beliefs and outcome expectancies about the contingencies linked with the appropriate and inappropriate display of emotion.

As noted by Ekman (1997), display rules not only include a sense of what kind of behaviour is appropriate, but also convey information about when and where emotional displays are appropriate. And because they are learned, cultural variations in the nature of display rules have been postulated, not only across cultures, but also within subgroups in a culture (Ekman, 1997).

What role does learning play? A growing number of studies have investigated the parents' role in the socialization of emotion. Parents shape their child's emotional displays by how they react to them, particularly when negative emotions are involved (see Eisenberg, Cumberland, & Spinrad, 1998). Parents have been characterized as emotion coaching (or encouraging) or emotion dismissing (Gottman, Katz, & Hooven, 1996). While this can sometimes be in the form of direct rewards or punishments (e.g., scolding), it can also be in a contingent response. That is, the child learns that a particular emotion is followed shortly thereafter by a parental reaction. Malatesta-Magai (1996) identified five different ways in which parents can socialize emotions, via: (1) reward; (2) punishment; (3) override (dismissing the child's emotion by telling the child to stop feeling a particular way); (4) neglect (simply ignoring emotion); and (5) magnifying (matching and amplifying the child's emotion). The same parent may respond differently to the emotions shown by sons and daughters (Birnbaum & Croll, 1984; Radke-Yarrow & Kochanska, 1990). Of course, we should also consider the possibility that the child eventually learns to imitate a parent's emotional displays. It has been argued, for instance, that chronic exposure to a depressed mother is one way that children take on the characteristics of a depressed person.

At present, research has focused for the most part on documenting differences across cultures in the display or expression of emotion. Typically, relevant studies compare people from different countries who are given the opportunity to express emotion in a public situation, and this is sometimes contrasted with the emotions expressed in a private situation. In the first study in this area, for instance, no significant differences in facial expressions were found when Japanese versus American participants watched films while alone (see Friesen, 1972). In contrast, when in the presence of an authority figure, the Japanese participants were much more likely to cover up their negative emotions by hiding them behind their smiles. The term given to this activity is masking, and the link with personality is obvious since the original interpretation of the word "personality" involved the concept of mask. More recent research compared Americans who had ancestors from Norway with those with backgrounds from Ireland and found that the latter were more emotionally expressive (Tsai & Chentsova-Dutton, 2003).

As noted, until recently, research has been restricted to cultural differences in expression, without

Research has shown that the Japanese are more likely to cover up or mask negative emotions when in the presence of an authority figure.

attempting to directly compare the display rules themselves. Matsumoto and associates created the Display Rule Assessment Inventory (DRAI) so that it is now possible to conduct research that directly examines individual differences in display rules among people within a culture and across different cultures (see Matsumoto et al., 2005; Matsumoto, 2006). The DRAI requires participants to indicate what they would do if they experienced seven different emotions in four different social contexts: (1) with family members; (2) with friends; (3) with colleagues; and (4) with total strangers. Participants must include what they should do and what they would actually do. Six modes of expression are evaluated based on the various possibilities outlined by Ekman and Friesen (1969, 1975): (1) uninhibited (expressing the feeling with no inhibitions); (2) deamplifying (expressing the feeling with less intensity); (3) amplifying (expressing the emotion with greater intensity); (4) neutralizing (expressing nothing); (5) qualifying (expressing the emotion accompanied by a smile); and (6) masking (expressing nothing but a smile).

An earlier study with the DRAI compared display rules across people from four countries (Japan, South Korea, Russia, and the United States), and differences within people from the same country were also evaluated as a function of how individualistic versus collectivistic they were in their orientation (see Matsumoto et al., 1998). A general factor identified as control was found by analyzing the various DRAI dimensions, and it was in found in display rules that Russians reported the highest control over emotional expression and Americans reported the lowest control over emotional expression. The differences held across all rating domains, emotions, and social situations.

Finally, a new study in this area by Matsumoto (2006) points to an important issue that applies to cross-cultural research on personality in general. He showed in a comparative study of participants from the United States and Japan that there were cross-national differences in emotion regulation, as expected. He then went on to show that these differences were actually attributable to related individual differences in personality. Matsumoto (2006) cautioned that it is important when conducting cross-cultural research to explore the extent to which differences across cultures actually reflect "aggregate differences in personality" (p. 421). Thus, when it comes to establishing display rule differences across culture, we must also ask whether these display rule differences reflect, at least in part, related differences in personality.

Types of Imitation

The nature of imitation is a central theme in social learning theory and subsequent versions of this theory by scholars such as Bandura. Miller and Dollard made this topic the focus of their 1941 book *Social Learning and Imitation*. Overall, they identified three types of imitative behaviour.

The first type is called **same behaviour**. This occurs when two people independently experience the same cue and end up making the same response. Recently, the concept of "same behaviour" was on display among teenagers after watching the 2002 movie *The Ring* starring Naomi Watts. The plot of this suspense film includes characters getting a phone call foretelling death in exactly seven days after having watched a videotape with eerie, frightening images. Same behaviour was a reported reluctance of movie watchers to answer their own phones right after viewing this movie! The same cue elicits the identical response (or non-response in this case).

The second type of imitation is called **matched-dependent behaviour**. This requires two people to be together, and the second person imitates the behaviour of the first person. The cues for these two people are different. The first person is responding to some cue, but the cue for the second person is the behaviour of the first person, hence the description of it as "matched-dependent" behaviour. An example of matched-dependent behaviour was discussed in Chapter 4 in the description of children imitating their parents' behaviour and driving a car despite being of very young age.

As for Dollard and Miller's theory, it has been noted that people often swear as a response to some event, but the swear word then becomes a cue that elicits responses from other people (see Geiwetz, 1969). An example would be road rage where one driver swears at another driver, who then retaliates.

Copying, such as Jamie Foxx's portrayal of Ray Charles in the movie *Ray*, is a type of imitation.

Copying is the third type of imitation. It is slightly different from matched-dependent behaviour because here a person is trying but is not entirely successful at imitating the actions of another person. An example of copying would be Jamie Foxx's exacting portrayal of performer Ray Charles in the movie *Ray*. Miller and Dollard (1941) indicated that the issue of sameness versus difference is what helps demarcate copying versus matched-dependent behaviour. Specifically, they observed that:

> The essential difference between the two processes is that in matched-dependent behavior the imitator responds only to the cue from the leader, while in copying he responds only to the cues of sameness and difference produced by stimulation from his own and model's responses. (Miller & Dollard, 1941, p. 159)

Thus, there are some subtle but important differences between matched-dependent behaviour and copying.

Drives, Motives, and Conflicts

Miller (1944) is also noteworthy for focusing attention on one of the most basic conflicts that people experience. The approach versus avoidance conflict was alluded to earlier in discussing how we sometimes simultaneously want to be with someone and yet want to be away from them. There are many times in life when we are faced with two opposing options. Miller's (1944) work was extrapolated from research with animals and highlighted other forms of the conflict, in addition to the **approach–avoidance conflict**. We can also have an approach–approach conflict when faced with two equally desirable alternatives. An avoidance–avoidance conflict exists when there are two unpleasant options to consider.

Can you think of an example of an approach–avoidance conflict? Dollard and Miller (1950) pointed to the example of the strong sex conflict when there is the awakening sex drive of teenagers along with the intense fears of talking about sex or actually doing something about it. They recounted the case of Mrs. A, a married woman with an intense anxiety disorder that included a need to count her own heartbeats. She was deemed to be neurotic; that is, she was unable to resolve a conflict. The conflict is often unconscious and it is repressed so that it becomes a great source of confusion and misery. In the case of Mrs. A, Dollard and Miller attributed her disorder to a strong desire for sexual expression along with anxiety about sexual expression as a result of repressive sex training while growing up (the sex–fear conflict). Recall that reinforcement is part of this model. In this instance, it was argued that the anxiety was reinforced because Mrs. A. would flee interpersonal situations that could involve satisfying her need for sex (including avoiding her husband). In Mrs. A's case, the conflict not only persisted, it flourished until she sought treatment.

Miller's (1944) theoretical views on approach versus avoidance incorporated other findings from the animal literature that showed that the proximity of the goal must also be taken into account. Specifically, goals have more impact as we get closer to attaining them. Thus, for proximal goals, the competing effects of approach versus avoidance tendencies are stronger and have more impact. The significance of the closeness of the goal is reflected in two similar terms. The approach gradient reflects a stronger pull toward the goal as we get closer to it, while the avoidance gradient reflects a stronger need to avoid the goal as we get closer to it. An example of this would be a dieter who orders a pizza for pickup. The dieter would feel a much stronger attraction to the pizza as he or she gets closer to the pizza store, but also feels a stronger feel of guilt and wanting to get away from the pizza at the same time.

Finally, Dollard et al. (1939) focused on frustration as a particular stimulus situation and incorporated this into their **frustration–aggression hypothesis** (which holds that all acts of aggression are the result of frustration, and all frustration leads to aggression). Frustration is said to occur when the organism is blocked from acquiring a goal or source of gratification and must delay attaining the gratification, and then the aggression that ensues is seen as an intentional act of harming or hurting someone else or something else. Subsequently, Miller (1941) softened the original position by suggesting that frustration gives rise to a variety of possible responses, one of which is aggression.

Overall, Dollard and Miller are given credit for translating the terms and principles derived from learning experiments with animals into testable terms that form the basis of a personality theory. It is probably a little too easy to forget their sophisticated contributions to behavioural and learning models of personality.

KEY POINTS

- Dollard and Miller combined experimental and learning principles with social factors.
- Social learning is a broad process that reflects drives, cues, responses, and reinforcements.
- The responses we have reflect social learning in that they are imitated. Imitated responses vary in whether they resemble the behaviours of other people or are exact copies.

ROTTER'S SOCIAL LEARNING THEORY

Julian Rotter subsequently expanded the theory outlined by Dollard and Miller. Rotter's views were introduced earlier in the book because he was the theorist and researcher who was instrumental in drawing attention to the locus of control construct (Rotter, 1966).

Rotter's social learning theory is centred on five basic concepts: (1) behaviour potential; (2) expectancy; (3) reinforcement value; (4) psychological situations; and (5) needs (see Rotter, 1954, 1982; Rotter, Chance, & Phares, 1972). Each concept is discussed below.

Behaviour Potential

Behaviour potential, a relatively straightforward concept, is the potential of a behaviour occurring in a situation as a function of a reinforcement or set of reinforcements. In contrast to radical behaviourists, Rotter suggested that there could be a focus on explicit, overt behaviours, as well as implicit behaviours that are less observable, such as rationalizing or repressing an event. Thus, covert cognitive activity can be evaluated on its "behaviour potential."

Expectancy

Some have suggested that Rotter's social learning theory is a misnomer and it should be called a social–cognitive learning theory because of the emphasis that he placed on expectancies and cognitive appraisals. Specifically, he stated that,

> Expectancy may be defined as the probability held by the individual that a particular reinforcement will occur as a function of a specific behavior on his part in a specific situation or situations. Expectancy is systematically independent of the value or importance of reinforcement. (Rotter, Chance, & Phares, 1972, p. 12)

Expectancy is the concept that provided the theoretical basis for individual differences in locus of control. People with an external locus of control expect that reinforcers are controlled by factors outside of themselves, while an internal locus of control entails the expectation that reinforcers are determined by personal influence and are influenced by the self.

Reinforcement Value

Rotter defined reinforcement value as the degree of the person's preference for that reinforcement to occur if the possibility of occurrence of all alternatives were equal (Rotter, 1960). In short, reinforcement value is the importance that the reinforcement has come to take on for the individual. The concept of differences in value has been extrapolated to other areas. For instance, extensive research on goals and goal commitment is based on the premise that certain goals are more important to one person than another. These goals have become associated inherently with greater reinforcement potential, and are more likely to result in persistence and other goal-directed activities.

Note that reinforcement value combines with the other concepts outlined above in a statistical formula. Rotter postulated the following equation: $BP = f(E \,\&\, RV)$. In other words, the behaviour potential is a joint function of both expectancy and reinforcement value. For Rotter, expectancy and reinforcement value are independent concepts. That is, a person can strongly value something, but have a negative expectation that it will be obtained. In that instance, behaviour potential is low.

Psychological Situations

Rotter also recognized the importance of the situation. He concluded that the psychological situation is very important, and he criticized trait theorists who focused on trying to identify the stable aspects of personality without also placing more emphasis on the psychological situation. Rotter regarded reinforcement value and cues that provide signals about reinforcement value as key components of the psychological situation.

Rotter's view of the situation is that each psychological situation provides a range of cues that, in turn, activate the various expectancies that reinforcement will follow specific behaviours. He went on to suggest various ways to categorize situational differences, including conducting a survey of the reinforcement-related expectancies that people have across situations, as well as evaluating the objective characteristics of situations. Situations can also be grouped together according to their tendency to evoke similar behaviours from people. Finally, Rotter suggested that generalizability could be evaluated by seeing what follows a behaviour that is performed across several situations.

Needs

One factor that clearly distinguishes Rotter from other learning theorists is the recognition of individual differences in needs. Recall that Skinner was particularly critical of the concept of needs and felt that reinforcement and punishment contingencies could account for most behaviours. In contrast, Rotter endorsed the views of Murray and others about the importance of including a focus on individual differences in needs. Rotter's views were based on his realization that learning theories typically focus on how personality is formed without much regard for the specific contents (e.g., traits, needs) that make up personality. Unlike Murray, however, Rotter suggested that the term "need" is not some state of deprivation but is simply a construct that accounts for the directionality of behaviour. Because it is a social learning theory, the six needs all have an interpersonal emphasis:

1. *Recognition–Status*: The need to be considered competent or good in a professional, social, occupational, or play activity
2. *Protection–Dependency*: The need to have another person or group of people prevent frustration and punishment, or satisfy other needs
3. *Dominance*: The need to control or direct the actions of other people, including family and friends
4. *Independence*: The need to make one's own decisions and to rely on oneself (including developing personal skills that provide self-satisfactions rather than relying on the intervention of other people)
5. *Love and Affection*: The need for acceptance and indication of liking and the warm regard of other people
6. *Physical Comfort*: The learned need for physical satisfaction that is associated with gaining security

In addition to his specific views, Rotter (1989) made some important observations about personality constructs in general. In particular, he made a strong argument for the importance of theory. He saw the locus of control construct as an outgrowth of social learning theory and felt that atheoretical efforts were largely misguided.

BANDURA'S SOCIAL COGNITIVE THEORY

The possible role of social learning in general was demonstrated in classic research conducted by **Albert Bandura** and his colleagues. According to Haggbloom et al. (2002), Bandura is the world's greatest living psychologist and ranks only behind Skinner, Piaget, and Freud in his overall influence. Regardless of whether you agree with this conclusion, there is no denying that Bandura's work has had a remarkable influence on the personality field as well as on developmental psychology and clinical psychology. Bandura was born in Alberta in 1925 and completed his graduate work at the University of British Columbia and the University of Iowa. He has conducted his influential work while serving as a faculty member of the prestigious psychology department at Stanford University.

Initially, Bandura accepted that Skinner's denouncement of the many internal mechanisms posited by Freudian theorists was justified. At the same time, however, he argued that the basic concepts of radical behaviourism are inadequate to explain complex human behaviour. Trial and error learning is too slow to explain the acquisition of complex human behaviours that do not allow room for error (e.g., swimming, a surgeon learning to operate).

Bandura's social learning theory (later known as social cognitive theory) is that the behaviours that make up our personality are obtained via operant conditioning and observational learning. Operant conditioning refers to the rewards and punishments discussed earlier. With this observational learning component, Bandura is similar to Dollard and Miller and to Rotter in acknowledging that new behaviours are learned not only by classical and operant conditioning, but also by observing, reading, or hearing about other people's behaviours.

Albert Bandura's social learning theory is that the behaviours that make up our personality are obtained via operant conditioning and observational learning.

Bandura's work coincided with other research emphasizing how personality and our behaviour are influenced by external factors in the environment. The essence of this theory is that other people provide us with a range of behaviours that can be imitated, such as actual people in our lives or televised images of models.

Bandura's initial research was described in books co-written with his first graduate student, Richard Walters (Bandura & Walters, 1959, 1963). Their 1963 book *Social Learning and Personality Development* not only promoted a focus on the role of imitation, but also included a critical analysis of the psychodynamic approach to development (see Chapter 5).

Research on social learning theory is synonymous with the classic Bobo doll studies performed by Bandura, Ross, and Ross (1961, 1963). In the Bandura et al. (1963) study, the independent variable was one of four experimental conditions. Children either saw (1) a live adult model being highly aggressive with a plastic Bobo doll; (2) a filmed version of the adult model being aggressive with the doll; (3) a cartoon of a cat being aggressive with the doll; or (4) no model being aggressive (i.e., the control condition for comparison purposes). The dependent measure was the level of aggressive behaviour expressed subsequently by the children when given the opportunity to play with other children. Those children who witnessed the aggression were subsequently much more aggressive, and this was found for both the real-life and film versions (see Figure 8.2). In the original Bandura et al. (1961) study, the level of aggressive behaviour was seven times higher than the level of aggression displayed by children not exposed to the aggressive model! Bandura et al. (1963) reported that girls exposed to an aggressive model were also more aggressive, relative to the control condition, but they were significantly less aggressive than boys (see Figure 8.2). This research points to the possible role of the social learning of aggression as a result of exposure to violence on television and elsewhere.

Figure 8.2 The Effects of Imitation on Aggression (Bandura, Ross, and Ross's Bobo Study, 1963)

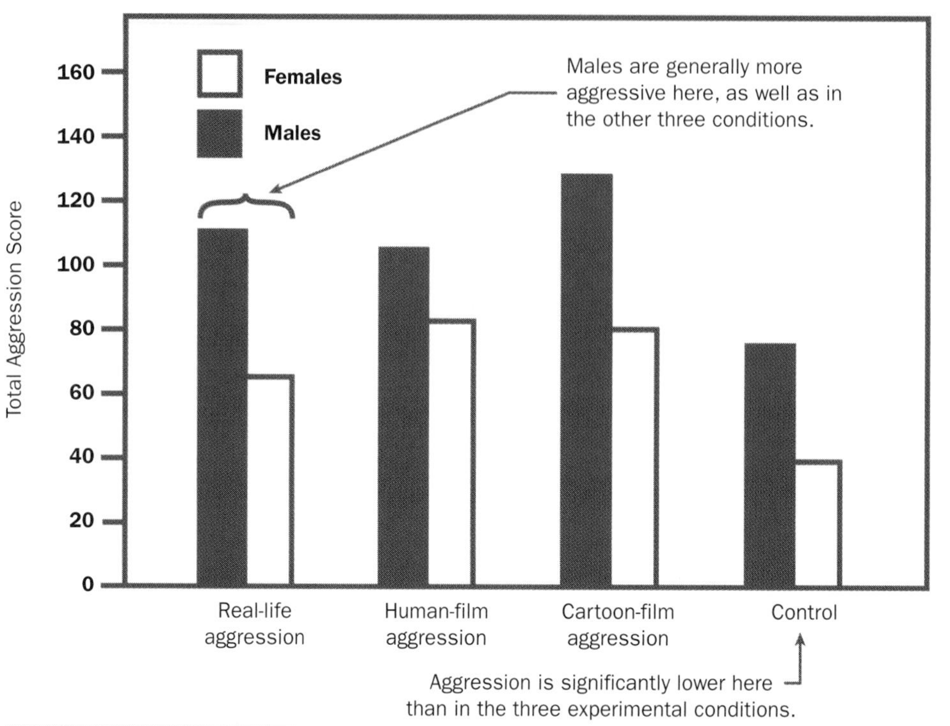

Source: Goodwin, 2005, p.158.

Subsequent research by Bandura and his associates showed that children are more likely to imitate models who are seen as powerful and personally rewarding. People also tend to imitate those who are seen as similar to themselves (see Bandura, 1986). Other research showed the scope of imitation by showing that children imitate and embrace the evaluative standards modelled by others. For example, in the Bandura and Kupers (1964) experiment, children were exposed to an adult model who had high or low standards that had to be met in order to engage in self-reward. Bandura and Kupers found that children exposed to models who rewarded themselves only after meeting high standards were unlikely to reward themselves unless they met high standards as well. In contrast, children exposed to models who rewarded themselves for meeting lower standards imitated this pattern of self-reinforcement.

In related research, Bandura, Grusec, and Menlove (1967) conducted an experiment that examined several factors in social learning. They found that the most extreme, stringent style of self-reward is evident among children who experience (1) an adult model with unrealistic standards; (2) an adult model who does not indulge the child; and (3) non-exposure to peers who reward themselves for lower levels of performance. Bandura et al. (1967) conducted this research to demonstrate the many factors that may influence the setting of high standards and related aspects of self-evaluation.

Baby You Can Drive My Car: Observational Learning in Action

Powerful illustrations of observational learning are when very young children drive their parents' automobiles without an adult being present! A recent example occurred in 2005 near Grand Rapids, Michigan. A four-year-old boy drove his mother's car to the video store just after 1 a.m., only to find the store closed, so then he returned home. The boy wanted to rent a video game after having his video game confiscated by his mother as a form of punishment for a misdeed. The car got the attention of a police officer on the boy's return trip. The officer witnessed the car hit a parked car. The boy then put the car in reverse and hit the police officer's car. According to the officer, the boy had learned to drive by watching his mother shift the car into forward and reverse, and the boy knew how to drive because his mother had let him sit on her lap while she was driving. As might be expected, the boy's mother did not know that her son was up and had gone on his midnight joyride. How remarkable was this trip? The video store was located about one quarter of a mile away from the apartment building where the family lived!

Although this incident is a clear reflection of observational learning, we should not lose sight of the role of personality factors. Many children witness a parent's driving behaviour, but only a few actually attempt to drive. What is it about the children who drive that distinguishes them from other children? Temperament and personality traits also operate at some level.

Bandura conducted several other classic studies designed to establish when and how observational learning and imitation takes place and is reflected in the child's own behavioural displays. These studies led Bandura to conclude that there are four key processes in observational learning: (1) attention (noticing the model's behaviour); (2) retention (remembering the model's behaviour); (3) reproduction (personally expressing the behaviour); and (4) motivation (repeating imitated behaviours if they receive positive consequences). This last aspect reflects Bandura's recognition of the need to combine social learning with the principles of reward and punishment that form the basis for operant conditioning.

The last two processes are particularly important. The third phase involves reproduction processes. In other words, is the person now able to translate into action what he or she has attended and remembered? Someone could watch an exceptional performer, such as the soccer player Ronaldo from Brazil or tennis player Serena Williams, and still not have the skill level and personal capability to perform the behaviour.

The fourth phase involves motivational processes that guide the potential imitator by his or her sense that imitating the behaviour is actually worth it. A key factor in incentive value is the aforementioned issue of whether the model has been rewarded or punished. Once the behaviour is imitated, the issue then becomes whether the imitated behaviour meets with pleasurable consequences, negative consequences, or no consequences at all. The motivational phase is significant in terms of the distinction between learning a behaviour and actually engaging in the behaviour (i.e., performance). A behaviour may be learned but not repeated right away because there is no immediate incentive for the behaviour.

Children exposed to angry interactions between their parents will likely translate this into increased aggressiveness with their own peers.

Extensive evidence attests to the role of social learning in personality and social development. For instance, research suggests that exposure to parental anger and hostility tends to result in higher levels of hostility and anger among children. Cummings, Iannotti, and Zahn-Waxler (1985) found that children exposed to angry interactions between their parents translated this into increased aggressiveness with their own peers. Similarly, exposure to media violence tends to foster aggressive behaviour in children, but the impact of media violence can be mitigated if children are exposed to feedback designed to foster a negative attitude toward violence and aggression (see Huesmann, Eron, Klein, Brice, & Fischer, 1983).

Social Learning, Imitation, and Sex Role Development

The need for a sophisticated approach that includes cognitive factors in learning is shown by research on imitation and learning in terms of sex role development. Sex role development is the process of acquiring the affective, cognitive, motivational, and behavioural attributes that are defined culturally as appropriate for one's biological sex. Several different theorists have argued that sex role development and socialization involves imitating the same-sex parent to some degree (see Bandura & Walters, 1963). Extensive research has been conducted on this issue. Two influential reviews conducted in the 1970s led to the conclusion that the available evidence was inconsistent with the claim that we imitate our same-sex parent (see Barkley, Ullman, Otto, & Brecht, 1977; Maccoby & Jacklin, 1974).

Perry and Bussey (1979) argued that past research on this issue suffered from several methodological weaknesses and conceptual limitations. They showed in their experimental research that in keeping with Bandura's emphasis on the need to consider cognitive factors in observational learning, cognitive mediators must be taken into account. Specifically, they found that children are more likely to imitate a same-sex parent only to the extent that they believe that the parental model's behaviour is appropriate for their sex. That is, children are more likely to imitate a parental model if they regard the parental model as "a good example" and accurate representation of how people of their gender should behave. Thus, cognitive appraisals of the extent to which a behaviour should be imitated must be considered.

Self-Efficacy

Bandura's theory became more complex over time and was extended to include the concept of self-efficacy (see Bandura, 1977, 1986, 1997). Self-efficacy is the individual's sense that he or she is capable of something (high self-efficacy) or incapable of something (low self-efficacy). This concept will be discussed in much more detail in Chapter 12. It is described there because of the many important applications involving self-efficacy in the field of personality and health. For now, it is important to note that Bandura suggested that the motivational incentive for imitating a behaviour may eventually come in the form of self-reinforcement and involve the process of cognitive self-regulation. Thus, whereas most work on operant conditioning has focused on rewards and punishment that are outside the person and in the environment, Bandura expressed the view that rewards and punishments also can be internal and come from ourselves based on our personal standards and evaluative reaction to our behaviours. Self-reinforcement is a form of self-talk in which the person praises themselves by saying such things as "Hey, I must be pretty good after all" after they have learned to perform a certain behaviour. Unfortunately, some people are better at self-punishment than they are at self-reward. Failures to perform a behaviour can be accompanied by nasty self-talk in the form of statements such as "I'm a loser" and "Why can't I keep up with other people?" Not surprisingly, this form of thinking is quite common among people prone to depression (Hollon & Kendall, 1980). Depression is associated with frequent negative thoughts about the self and a low frequency of positive thoughts (Ingram et al., 1994). People who experience frequent thoughts about the need to be perfect also tend to have frequent negative self-thoughts and infrequent positive self-thoughts (Flett, Hewitt, Blankstein, & Gray, 1998).

Self-reward and self-punishment reflect the self-regulation process. In general, self-regulation is the process of taking personal control over thoughts and actions through various means, including self-rewards and self-punishments.

You can imagine the controversy that would have ensued if Bandura had emphasized the concept of self-efficacy in the 1960s, when the focus of Skinnerians was on observable behaviours. Bandura's emphasis shifted to include individual differences in internal cognitive processes related to the self in the form of beliefs about personal efficacy or agency. This is more in line with the introspective approach that was criticized heavily by radical behaviourists such as Watson. Bandura included an emphasis on self-efficacy not only because of the cognitive revolution that took place in psychology throughout the 1970s and 1980s, but also because of his awareness of the powerful impact that self-efficacy has on moods and behaviours.

Note that Bandura's work on self-efficacy is paralleled by and reflected in the social–cognitive theory advanced by Walter Mischel, Bandura's colleague from Stanford University. A key aspect of Mischel's theory is its focus on the competencies or skills that distinguish people (see Mischel & Shoda, 1995). According to this view, a person's behaviour varies across different situational contexts as a function of their specific competencies, their awareness of their competencies, and the general expectancies that have developed as a result of previous life experiences. Social cognitive theories such as those put forth by Mischel and Bandura adopt an agentic perspective to human development, adaptation, and change.

Although Bandura focuses primarily on the individual and his or her sense of personal agency, it is important to realize that he has incorporated a broader perspective that includes looking at the concept of efficacy or agency from a societal or cultural perspective. Bandura (2002) postulated three modes of agency: (1) personal agency; (2) proxy agency (getting what you want and need by getting others to act for you as your proxy); and (3) collective agency (people working together in a form of common social interest to effect change). Bandura (2002) maintained that there are differences across cultures in the determinants of these three forms of agency, but he argued that notwithstanding these cultural differences, all three modes are needed for people from various cultures to "make it through the day" (Bandura, 2002, p. 269). That is, all agentic modes are needed, regardless of the cultural context in which one resides. Cultures are diverse and dynamic social systems, not static monoliths. Intracultural diversity and intra-individual variation in psychosocial orientations across spheres of functioning underscore the multifaceted dynamic nature of cultures.

Reciprocal Determinism

A final point about Bandura deserves mention. His model is based on the concept of reciprocal determinism (see Bandura, 1978). That is, he believes in the constant interaction of a person's characteristics and behaviours, and the environment. This concept is represented in Figure 8.3. It has also been referred to as triadic reciprocal causation. The arrows going to and from each component reflect the fact that each of three components has an impact on the other components, and they are also influenced by the other components. This is an ongoing sequence so that changes in the person, his or her behaviour, and the situation will continue to feed back and have an influence on the other aspects of the model.

Figure 8.3 Bandura's Model of Reciprocal Determinism

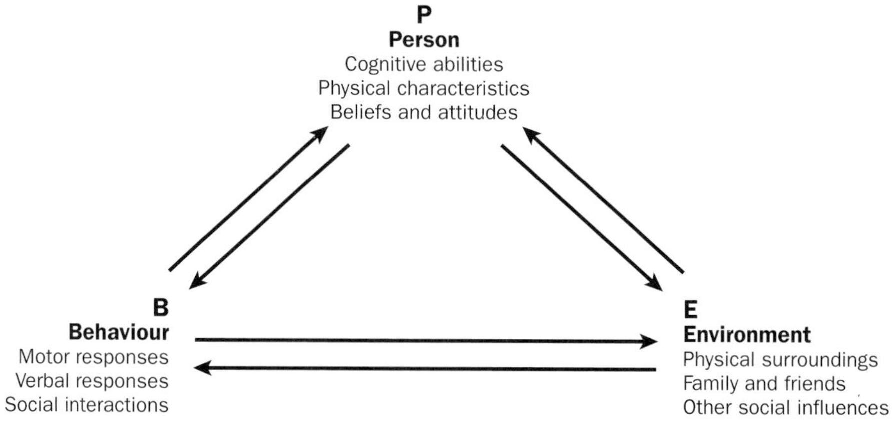

Source: Shaffer, 1996.

According to Bandura (1986), it should not be assumed that the three elements of the triad are always equal in their influence. Environmental influences as a form of situational constraint will vary in their strength or salience. Bandura illustrated this by contrasting how a person's behaviour would be influenced by trying to select a book from a library with vast resources versus a library with only a small number of books.

Bandura (1986) illustrated the concept of reciprocal determinism by referring to television shows. He observed that what we see on television is an ongoing and dynamic reflection of viewer preferences (the person), viewer behaviours (behaviours), and initial televised offerings (the available environment). How else can we explain the current proliferation of crime scene investigation shows (*CSI: Crime Scene Investigation, CSI Miami, and CSI New York*)? The first CSI show aired in 2000. Apparently, this show reflected a strong preference among millions of viewers, and it resulted in a high degree of viewing behaviour. The television industry responded (i.e., the environment) by adding more offerings of a similar nature. In this instance, people's behaviours clearly shaped the environment!

Note that the personal factors include cognitive aspects such as cognitive abilities and beliefs and attitudes. Physical characteristics are included in recognition of the structural and constitutional limitations that place an upper limit on the behaviours we are able to imitate. Note that Bandura later extended this concept to cultures by arguing that cultures are also dynamic and both have an affect on and are affected by global forces (see Bandura, 2002).

KEY POINTS

- Bandura suggested that learning involves trial and error via rewards and punishments as well as observational learning that entails the imitation of others.
- Imitation of others depends on paying attention to their acts, remembering their acts, and then being able to perform the behaviour. Imitated acts are more likely to be repeated if followed by rewards.
- Powerful and likeable models are more likely to be imitated.
- According to Bandura, rewards and punishments can also be internal in the form of self-talk. A powerful determination of the self-regulation of behaviour is whether the person has developed a sense of self-efficacy (that they are capable of the behaviour).

THE AGGRESSIVE PERSONALITY AND THE LEARNING OF AGGRESSIVE BEHAVIOUR

This chapter concludes by illustrating the role of learning in the development of individual differences in aggressive behaviour. A superb review paper by Leonard Eron provides an overview of his impressive research program on the development of aggression from a behavioural perspective (see Eron, 1987). It summarizes the main findings of his 22-year longitudinal investigation of the aggressive personality. Aggression was studied, according to Eron (1987), not only because of its societal importance, but also because it is "definable, observable, and measurable" (p. 435). Thus, it fits with the behaviourist focus on overt acts.

Aggression in this study was not defined in terms of intent. An act was deemed to be aggressive if it injured or irritated another person, regardless of intent. It was defined in this manner because it is often very difficult to establish whether what seems to be an aggressive act was intended or was accidental.

The main themes from Eron's (1987) paper are as follows: (1) aggression reflects the confluence of multiple learning processes and influences; (2) cognitive factors play a vitally important role in the learning of aggression and the long-term development of the aggressive personality; (3) there are substantial changes over time in the predictors of aggression when aggression and related outcomes are assessed over a 22-year period; and (4) there is substantial long-term stability in aggressive behaviour when people are studied as children and continue to be studied as adults.

A key aspect of this study was the extent to which aggressive tendencies learned in the family would be reflected in the child's aggressive behaviour at school. In terms of the first theme outlined above (multiple learning processes play a role), the study's initial phase showed that children were more aggressive at school if their parents provided low reinforcement (their parents were less nurturing and accepting), but high levels of punishment (including physical punishment). Children were also more aggressive at school if they were low in the extent to which they cognitively identified with their parents. Children who did not want to be like their parents were more aggressive.

Additional results indicated that levels of parental punishment interacted with parental identification to predict the child's aggression (see Eron, 1987, p. 37). High punishment resulted in less school aggression only if the child identified with the father.

How might this work? Consider an example of a boy who is from a divorced family. The boy is now being punished physically by a stepfather whom he despises and with whom he has little in common. This would foster a level of resentment and frustration that would be displaced (to use a Freudian term) in the form of directing violence and aggression toward the boy's classmates. Contrast this with the boy who is receiving punishment from a father or stepfather whom he has come to worship. This boy would be more likely to internalize the ultimate message that aggression is good, and, hopefully, he would develop the ability to restrain the urge to aggress.

It has been often mentioned that parents who engage in physical punishment of their children actually provide an aggressive model of behaviour that can be imitated by the child. Eron's findings suggest that the extent to which the child imitates the parent will depend, in part, on the respect held for the parent.

Other results reported by Eron (1987) showed that modelling played a role in terms of the amount of televised violence watched as a child. This was a robust predictor of subsequent aggression in adulthood. Witnessing violence can contribute to the development of subsequent aggression. Imagine the following scene that illustrates this point: An audience witnesses a marathon 12 hour festival of Kung Fu movies at an all-night theatre. As they are leaving the theatre the next morning, a 10-year old boy who was not provoked goes up to his 10-year old friend and kicks him in the place where no male wishes to be kicked. Unfortunately, accounts of similar incidents are relatively commonplace and show how violence and aggression can be imitated.

Eron's (1987) review also makes the point that the characteristics of the child make a difference here. This research established that the causal direction of the link is bi-directional. That is, television violence creates aggression, but aggressive people, by nature, are also drawn to televised violence and seek it out. So, perhaps the 10-year-old aggressor described above already had highly aggressive tendencies prior to watching the movie marathon.

It was noted above that cognitive factors also played a role in whether televised violence contributed to aggressive behaviour. How were cognitive factors important? This was best illustrated by the results of an intervention that the researchers employed in an attempt to curtail the behaviour of a subset of boys who watched an extremely high level of televised violence. Eron (1987) reported that subsequent aggressive behaviour in these children was lower only to the extent that these children eventually developed less positive attitudes about televised violence and aggressive behaviour in general as a result of the intervention. Thus, even in a study that started out with an exclusively behavioural focus, cognitive factors played an important mediating role.

The third theme noted above was that the predictive significance of various factors changed over time. For instance, exposure to physical punishment from parents predicted initial aggression, but this factor diminished over time in its ability to predict aggression by adults. In other words, aspects of the home environment were more proximal in contributing to aggression by children in Grade 3, but more generalized factors become more salient over time.

Perhaps the most striking finding of Eron's (1987) investigation was the long-term persistence of aggressive behaviour and the ability of initial measures of aggressive behaviour to predict subsequent outcomes. Analyses of the 10-year follow-up data showed that those who were rated at Time 1 by their peers as the most aggressive as children were also rated this way by their peers 10 years later. Self-reports showed the same pattern; at the age of 18, those who rated themselves as more aggressive were the ones deemed most aggressive in Grade 3. They also rated other people as more aggressive and tended to see their world as a more hostile place.

A subset of 300 participants were followed up again 22 years later. This included interviews with their spouses as well as with their children, if they had any. This long-term follow-up revealed that aggression during peer interaction in Grade 3 was a significant predictor of criminal behaviour, number of moving traffic violations, convictions for driving while intoxicated, aggressiveness toward spouses, and the severity of punishment used with one's own child. The link with punishment of one's own child suggests that there is a generational transmission of aggressive behaviour.

Summary

If you were to compare the various theorists represented in this chapter, it should become evident to you that there are some behavioural and learning theorists who focus almost exclusively on the role of external factors, while other theorists have a joint emphasis on external factors in the environment and internal factors reflecting the self. Overall, it is unlikely that we can be shaped into any type of person because personality, at least to some degree, is biologically based, according to the studies of genetic factors cited in earlier segments of this book. Still, the work of theorists represented in this chapter indicates that habits can be modified according to the learning and conditioning contingencies that we encounter.

The classical conditioning findings of Ivan Pavlov were described first. Classical conditioning entails a process through which a neutral stimulus develops the ability to elicit behaviours by being paired with an unconditioned stimulus. Although Pavlov's work on classical conditioning has received extensive theoretical and empirical attention over the years, his observations about the personality differences among his dogs are less well known but equally important. These observations provided the impetus for the research and theory on personality and conditioning by Eysenck, who suggested that it is easier to condition introverts as opposed to extroverts. Research and theory by Gray showed that introverts can be more easily conditioned under threatening conditions with the possibility of punishment, but extroverts are sensitive to rewards and are more easily conditioned when there is the possibility of rewards and reinforcement. Gray also postulated two physiological systems, with the behavioural inhibition system reflecting anxiety and sensitivity to threats and punishments, and the behavioural activation system reflecting excitement seeking and a tendency to approach rewarding stimuli.

Pavlov's work set the stage for the radical behaviourism of John Watson and the illustration of radical behaviourism in the form of the experiment that Watson and Rayner conducted with Little Albert. Radical behaviourism is an approach that focuses on the study of observable actions rather than cognitions and internal stimuli. Watson later emphasized radical environmentalism, a belief that the environment is a much more important determinant of behaviour than is heredity or temperament. Watson also equated personality with learned habits and suggested that most of our habits are in place by the age of 30.

Next, we considered the operant conditioning model of B. F. Skinner. Whereas classical conditioning involves reflexive reactions to conditioned and unconditioned stimuli, operant conditioning involves behaviours that are freely emitted by the organism in response to the rewards and punishments that have followed past expressions of the behaviour. Skinner extrapolated learning research with animals and showed that the same general principles of reinforcement and punishment could also be applied to humans. Skinner argued that personality differences primarily reflect people's learning histories (past reinforcers and punishments) as well as differences due to genetic factors that reflect evolutionary development.

Both classical conditioning and operant conditioning have provided concepts and principles that have been incorporated into clinical treatments designed to treat various forms of dysfunction. Behaviour modification is the field of clinical psychology that reflects the conditioning approaches.

This chapter concluded with an overview of the classic social learning theorists of Dollard and Miller, Rotter, and Bandura. Dollard and Miller's theory was derived, in part, from research and theory on learning conducted by Clark Hull. In addition to emphasizing the roles of cues, drives, responses, and rewards, Dollard and Miller highlighted the role of different types of imitation. They also focused specific motivational states and cues by postulating the frustration–aggression hypothesis: that a state of frustration leads inevitably to aggression.

One of the primary contributions of Rotter's theory is the importance he placed on individual differences in expectancy. In addition, his theory incorporated earlier theories that focused on individual differences in psychological needs by suggesting that there are six needs that distinguish people: recognition–status, protection–dependency, dominance, independence, love and affection, and physical comfort.

Finally, Bandura's social cognitive theory focused initially on acquiring new behaviours via imitation and social learning, but subsequent versions of his model also placed importance on internal cognitive processes. Bandura acknowledged that some behaviours are too complex to learn via the relatively slow process of trial and error learning. Observational learning and the performance of imitated behaviours was possible to the extent that the potential imitator had developed the cognitive capacity to attend to and remember a model's behaviour. Cognitive factors also play a role in developing the belief that a person is capable of performing a certain behaviour or achieving a certain outcome (self-efficacy). Feelings of self-efficacy and the tendency to engage in self-reward versus self-punishment were postulated by Bandura in recognition of the fact that there are external rewards and punishments in the environment, but there are also internal rewards and punishments, with the things that we say to ourselves as part of our attempts at self-regulation.

Finally, Chapter 8 concluded by showing how the various principles of learning and conditioning seem to play a role in the development of the aggressive personality. Longitudinal research suggests that operant conditioning (low reinforcement and high punishment from the parent), social learning (the child learns to imitate an aggressive parent and/or imitate televised portrayals of violence), and cognition all play a role.

Questions to Consider

1. Some personality books have limited or no coverage of Pavlov and Watson because they are not considered to be personality theorists. Do you believe that the types of learning these theorists identified play a role in personality development? How do you rate the importance of learning processes versus the influences of personality traits in expressions of behaviour?

2. Imagine that you have a time machine. You go back in time to chair a debate between Watson and Freud. What would Watson say about the Oedipus complex? What would Freud say about behaviourism?

3. Do you agree with Watson's claim that people could be shaped and moulded into anybody? Could an agreeable person be trained to be disagreeable?

4. Do you agree with Watson's claim that personality is essentially fixed by the time most people reach the age of 30 years old? Could it be that personality is fixed for some people but not others? Can you think of someone who seemed to have a characterological change in the later stages of his or her life?

5. Review the description of the behavioural activation system and the behavioural inhibition system. Also review the concepts of sensitivity to reward and sensitivity to punishment. Are you more sensitive to reward cues or punishment cues? To what extent do you feel that reward and punishment cues influence your behaviours?

6. Skinner interpreted the acquisition of language from a behavioural perspective, and his views were critiqued at length by Chomsky. Where do you stand on this issue? Do you think it is possible to teach a new language to someone via operant conditioning? What about the notion of a critical period and that new languages must be learned at a relatively early age? How would Skinner respond to the notion of a "critical period"?

7. Review the statements about imitation made by Dollard and Miller and by Bandura. Children often imitate others. In your estimation, to what extent are adults susceptible to and influenced by imitation?

Key Terms

approach–avoidance conflict, p. 315
aversion therapy, p. 299
behavioural approach system, p. 301
behavioural inhibition system, p. 301
behaviourism, p. 293
blocking effect, p. 291
classical conditioning, p. 289
conditioned response, p. 290
conditioned stimulus, p. 290
copying, p. 314
covert sensitization, p. 299
differentiation, p. 291

discriminative stimulus, p. 305
display rules, p. 312
excitation, p. 292
experimental neuroses, p. 292
exposure therapy, p. 299
extinction, p. 290
extinction phase, p. 294
fixed interval schedule, p. 306
fixed ratio schedule, p. 306
flooding, p. 290
frustration–aggression hypothesis, p. 315
generalization, p. 291
inhibition, p. 292
instrumental conditioning, p. 303
law of effect, p. 303
masking, p. 312
matched–dependent behaviour, p. 314
negative reinforcement, p. 304
operant conditioning, p. 304
partial reinforcement, p. 307
positive reinforcement, p. 304
postulate of individual differences, p. 300
prepared learning, p. 295
primary reinforcer, p. 304
radical behaviourism, p. 293
radical environmentalism, p. 293
reciprocal determinism, p. 324
response hierarchy, p. 311
same behaviour, p. 314
secondary reinforcer, p. 305
self-efficacy, p. 323
self-regulation, p. 323
self-reinforcement, p. 323
shaping, p. 305
S–R learning, p. 304
social learning/cognitive theory, p. 319
stimulus generalization, p. 305
successive approximation, p. 305
systematic desensitization, p. 299
triadic reciprocal causation, p. 324
typological postulate, p. 300
unconditioned response, p. 289
unconditioned stimulus, p. 289
variable ratio schedule, p. 306

Key Theorists

Albert Bandura, p. 318
John Dollard, p. 311
Hans Eysenck, p. 300
Jeffrey Gray, p. 300
Neal Miller, p. 311
Ivan Pavlov, p. 289
Julian Rotter, p. 316
B.F. Skinner, p. 303
John B. Watson, p. 293

chapter nine

COGNITIVE THEORIES AND COGNITIVE FACTORS

- George Kelly's Personal Construct Theory
- Kurt Lewin's Cognitive and Field Theory of Personality
- Cognitively Based Personality Differences
- The Need for Cognition
- Attributions
- Cognitive Rigidity

... what was meant in Kelly's central paradigm of "man-the-scientist" (or the "personal scientist") was not in fact an accomplished *scientist, one who always did relevant experiments, but an "incipient scientist" — one whose experiments are often irrelevant, uninformative, or self-mystifying, and who thus needs training in how to conduct experiments of a more personally relevant kind. But how might such a training in the "science of life" be given?*
—JOHN SHOTTER (1985, P. 273)

People put things and other people in mental boxes, give each box a name, and thereafter treat the contents of the box the same. But if our fellow humans are as unique as their fingerprints and no two snowflakes are alike, why the urge to classify?
—STEVEN PINKER (1997, P. 306)

A YOUNG, OVERWEIGHT MAN in ratty clothes, including mismatched socks and a hat worn backwards, enters a classroom of 10-year-old children. These children are at a summer workshop being taught by a graduate student in psychology. The young man, after circling the room a few times, presumably in search of audiovisual equipment, then steals the wallet of the graduate student instructor, which was left on a table. He then bolts out of the room with the stolen wallet. The students scream in unison to the graduate student "He stole your wallet!" and one boy takes off in hot pursuit, but can't keep up with the surprisingly nimble young man.

What does the ripped off instructor do? Rather than getting upset, she calmly turns to the children and says, "Take out your pencils and some paper. I'm going to ask you some questions about the person you just saw and the event you just witnessed."

The scene described above occurred many years ago when I took part in a staged scene designed to demonstrate individual differences in eyewitness testimony to a summer class of young psychology students. This example and previous empirical experiments on eyewitness testimony show that despite having equal access to the same situational information, there are widespread differences in how people perceive and remember situational events. It is unsettling when someone develops an unshakable belief in an eyewitness situation, but this belief is entirely incorrect. In the example described above, the children were asked subsequently to identify the perpetrator from a makeshift police lineup. Each child dutifully went to a one-way mirror to identify the culprit from a lineup of five young men. Two thirds of the children concluded (correctly) that the culprit was not actually in the lineup. The other children selected a lab technician named Roger who was nowhere near the crime scene. This led to an unexpected opportunity to introduce another area of research to the children: the study of prejudice. Roger was the only black person in the lineup and he was selected by these children, all of whom were white! We prefer to think that this had nothing to do with skin colour and instead was due to the fact that Roger had a beard, as did the actual thief. Still, the remarkable thing is that these children refused to change their mind even after being presented with information that ruled out Roger as the thief.

Extensive pieces have been written about the fallibility of eyewitness testimony. Personality research on this topic is limited. Existing data suggest that there is some evidence linking traits such as self-monitoring (see Chapter 11) with the ability to accurately identify faces. Overall, however, this association is relatively small in magnitude, and the overall research on personality and recognition accuracy is "largely inconsistent" (see Narby, Cutler, & Penrod, 1996). Still, it is important to recognize that people differ substantially in how events are perceived and recalled.

The scenario introduced above also serves as our introduction to individual differences in cognition. Chapter 9 consists of a more detailed analysis of cognitive factors in personality theory and research. Cognitive and perceptual factors have already been mentioned in several areas of the book. In the first chapter, for instance, we began with a discussion of how movie critics often differ greatly in their perception and evaluation of the same move. Cognitive factors were also mentioned in Chapter 7 in terms of Maslow's distinction between deficiency cognitions and being cognitions. As another example, in Jung's theory and in the description of the Myers-Briggs Type Indicator (MBTI), the thinking orientation was contrasted with sensing and intuiting.

An excellent way to conceptualize the role of cognitive factors in personality is by distinguishing between "having" and "doing" (see Allport, 1937; Cantor, 1990). The personality field has been dominated by the trait approach (especially the five-factor model). The trait approach emphasizes "what a person has" in terms of the structure and specific facets of personality. In contrast, the cognitive approach emphasizes "what a person does." According to Cantor (1990), the doing side of personality focuses on how "dispositions are cognitively expressed and maintained in social interaction" (p. 735). The focus here is on how events are perceived and expectations are formed each and every day, and there are predictable individual differences in this cognitive activity.

Relative to stable personality traits, cognitive variables are more flexible and dynamic. Cantor (1990) highlighted the dynamic aspects of personality and cognition by posing the question of just how much and under what circumstances people change their cognitive orientations in response to their daily experiences. The degree of change itself is a key individual difference variable; as we will see in this chapter, some people are high in cognitive rigidity and are resistant to change.

Chapter 9 begins with an overview of George Kelly's personal construct theory of personality and its applications. This is followed by a discussion of Kurt Lewin's field theory and its cognitive elements. Both Kelly and Lewin emphasize the phenomenology of the individual; that is, there is a focus on how individuals cognitively appraise and mentally represent their ongoing experiences and the situations that occur.

We then examine some personality constructs that reflect individual differences in cognitive styles (e.g., the need for cognition). Next, the link between cognition and well-being is explored through a description and assessment of research of attributional style and attributional complexity. Finally, we illustrate differences in cognitive structure by describing how people differ in their level of cognitive rigidity.

Before we begin, it is important to point out that cognitive factors are linked inextricably with related individual differences in motivation, emotion, and social behaviour. How people experience and interpret the events in their lives has a direct bearing on their levels of motivation and their emotional reactions, and their orientations toward, away from, or against people. Kelly, for instance, focused on cognitive factors in the form of personal constructs, but emphasized that these constructs serve as guides for action. The choice itself is based on our cognitive expectancies and beliefs about the relative merits of both choices.

GEORGE KELLY'S PERSONAL CONSTRUCT THEORY

George Kelly was born in 1905 and raised in Kansas in the Midwestern United States. Kelly went to the University of Kansas, and he earned a Bachelor of Education degree from the University of Edinburgh in Scotland. His doctoral degree was obtained in psychology at the University of Iowa.

George Kelly felt that although people differed in their constructs, there were certain "universals" in the structure, nature, and development of constructs.

As a psychologist, Kelly worked in pilot training during the Second World War. In subsequent years, he was appointed as Director of Clinical Psychology at Ohio State University, and it was during his 20 years there that he made his major theoretical contributions. In 1965, he accepted a research chair at Brandeis University, a position he held until his death in 1967. (Abraham Maslow was at Brandeis at the same time). Kelly's influence continues; in 2005, the International Congress on Personal Construct Psychology was held at Ohio State to commemorate the 50-year anniversary of Kelly's greatest work, his book *The Psychology of Personal Constructs*.

George Kelly would certainly have explained the differences in eyewitness testimony given by the summer workshop students by attributing them to variability in the personal constructs among these children. **Constructs** are psychologically meaningful cognitive categories. They are unique and personal, and as such, they are very much in keeping with the view of European personologists Kreitler and Kreitler (1990), who suggested that personality traits can be seen entirely in cognitive terms and are unique patterns of meaning preferences. Kelly felt that although people differed in their constructs, there were certain "universals" in the structure, nature, and development of constructs. These beliefs are outlined below.

What did Kelly suggest about constructs? First, constructs are bipolar with two different poles. One end (the more accessible end) is called the emergent pole. The other end of the construct is called the implicit pole. These two ends have also been called the likeness pole and the contrast pole. Sometimes the implicit pole becomes submerged. Submergence results when a person becomes cognitively preoccupied, even obsessed, with a theme that reflects the emergent pole of a construct.

Constructs also differ in the extent to which they are accessible to conscious awareness. While most constructs have at least one pole that is conscious, Kelly did allow for some constructs to exist but not be entirely conscious. Specifically, he referred to **preverbal constructs**, **submerged constructs**, and **suspended constructs**. According to Fransella and Neimeyer (2005), Kelly agreed with Freud that many things take place outside of our conscious awareness, but rather than postulating the unconscious, Kelly discussed this in terms of varying levels of awareness. Preverbal constructs should not be equated with the unconscious because they reflect a conscious feeling of knowing but the person cannot put the thought or image into words. The term "construing" was used to refer to preverbal constructs. Preverbal constructs are likely involved in the tip-of-the-tongue phenomenon that occurs when you can almost but not quite put something into words.

In a submerged construct, one or both ends of the construct are not available for conscious reflection and verbalization. A suspended construct is similar to repression in that current events have made the previously accessible construct now forgotten.

Regarding the notion of preverbal constructs, Fransella and Neimeyer (2005) stated that a central goal of personal construct therapy is to identify and explore preverbal constructs. They also highlighted Kelly's influence on current research by observing that:

> ... those who call personal construct theory a traditional "cognitive" theory—meaning that it deals only with verbally or intellectually accessible thought processes—are taking no account of the majority of what Kelly calls construing. It is interesting to note that in this respect Kelly foreshadowed more contemporary cognitive theories, which now routinely recognize the limits of consciousness in grasping the "metacognitive basis" of much human functioning. Clearly, people "know" much more than they can tell, in the sense that some of the bases on which we construe events in our lives can only be inferred rather than directly reported. (p. 11)

Recall our earlier analysis in Chapter 5 of the unconscious and how research by Baldwin and others has shown how events represented in our subconscious can influence our conscious thoughts and feelings, even though we cannot verbalize these unconscious events.

KEY POINTS

- Personality and cognition involves a focus on "the doing" of personality as opposed to the focus of the trait approach on "the having" of personality.
- Constructs are cognitive categories with psychological meaning.
- According to Kelly, people differ in how they see the world because there are differences in personal constructs.
- Constructs are bipolar. The more accessible end of the construct is the emergent pole.
- Constructs vary in the extent to which they are open to cognitive awareness; preverbal constructs cannot be articulated but involve a "feeling of knowing."

The Person as Scientist

Kelly used the metaphor that each person is a scientist who is motivated to make as much sense as possible out of life events. We feel anxious when we encounter information and circumstances that do not fit with our personal constructs and are not readily understood. When this happens, we need to form newer, healthier constructs.

Kelly identified three specific conditions that undermine the ability to form new constructs. Threat is the first limiting condition. We are all familiar with the general meaning of threat, but here it means that a specific construct is part of a higher order construct that is incompatible with another higher order construct that is necessary for living. For example, Kelly observed that for most people, death constructs are threatening because they are incompatible with constructs representing life.

The second limiting condition was identified in the therapy context. Some people are so preoccupied with old constructs, they are not able to form new, more representative constructs. An example would be someone who has a history of extensive paranoia and continues to reflect on past events that are taken as evidence of some plot against him or her, when in fact no plot exists. This person would be better off to develop healthier, newer constructs to deal with day-to-day existence.

The final limiting condition is when a person essentially has "no laboratory." Here Kelly was referring to his notion that we are all naïve scientists, but, unfortunately, some people lack access to situations that would allow them to test out and update their constructs as experiences unfold. Thus, the person who is highly isolated from other people does not get to update his constructs.

Failure to update constructs results in hostility. Hostile people are frequently at odds with their environment; they are distressed and frustrated by their inability to make sense out of their world. Kelly (1991) further noted that constructs are more likely to change when used to predict immediate events rather than future events because of the feedback provided by immediate events.

Kelly (1991) summarized his views on the modifying constructs in the following passage: "Constructs cannot be tossed about willy-nilly without a person's getting into difficulty. While there are always alternative constructions available, some of them are definitely poor implements. The yardstick to use is the specific predictive efficiency of the system of which it would, if adopted, become a part" (p. 11).

Kelly (1955) used the concept **constructive alternativism** to refer to how two people can have different interpretations of the same event. Constructive alternativism can also refer to changes in how the same person interprets a reoccuring situation or event over time.

Kelly (1955) did not perceive a need to list a series of motives or needs like others before him, such as Henry Murray. He believed that people are naturally active simply because they are alive, and it is not necessary to postulate unconscious conflicts that propel our behaviours. In his estimation, it was quite simple: at a cognitive level, we want to understand as much as possible and be able to predict what will happen next. We are developing our own "anticipatory theory of behaviour."

KEY POINTS

- Kelly described people as scientists who are trying to describe and understand their world and associated life experiences.
- Constructs must be changed and updated when they no longer help a person to construct meaning out of his or her life experiences.
- People who lose contact and fail to interact with their environment are most likely in need of developing new constructs.
- Kelly rejected a list of motives and focused on our desire to accurately understand current events and predict future events.

Kelly's Corollaries

George Kelly expanded on his theory by stipulating a series of corollaries. A corollary is a proposition or statement that follows readily or easily from a theory. In this instance, corollaries are the specific principles that emerge from Kelly's theory.

Kelly identified several corollaries that derive from his **Fundamental Postulate**, which is that "a person's processes are psychologically channelized by the ways in which he anticipates events." It is fundamental, according to Kelly, because it is this basic notion that feeds into each of the other theoretical beliefs, and the corollaries outlined below. Because it involves the anticipation of events, the fundamental postulate sees people as being very future-oriented. In fact, Kelly described this as an anticipatory theory of future behaviour. Constructs provide us with a guide of what will happen, and this can be a strong source of motivation as we look forward to positive outcomes or perhaps work hard to avoid undesirable possibilities.

Arnold Schwarzenegger, movie star and Governor of California, had an unwavering sense of self-efficacy. He was confident that he would "make it."

As an example of a fundamental postulate, consider Arnold Schwarzenegger's unwavering sense of self-efficacy. In his autobiography (see Schwarzenegger & Hall, 1977), the future Governor of California reported that "Never was there even the slightest doubt in my mind that I could make it … I knew I had what it took" (p. 67–68). This reflects a self-confidence that involves highly favourable images of future events and possibilities.

The **construction corollary** is that a person anticipates events by construing their replications. The construction corollary reflects Kelly's notion that our constructs exist, in part, because they help us to predict what will happen in the future. And the anticipation here is tied to the anticipation of real events, not hypothetical or imagined ones (Kelly, 1955).

The **individuality corollary** accounts for the differences between people; that is, persons differ from each other in their construction of events. This included Kelly's observation that individuality stems, in part, from differences in cultural experiences.

The **organization corollary** is that each person characteristically evolves a construction system that includes ordinal relationships between constructs. This system is created due to the person's desire to easily anticipate and understand future events.

The **dichotomy corollary** is that a person's construction system is composed of a finite number of dichotomous constructs. Each theme is represented by endpoints of a dichotomy, and sometimes, but not always, the endpoints are polar opposites. The inclusion of the notion of a dichotomy is one aspect that distinguishes the term "construct" from the term "concept."

The **choice corollary** is that a person selects the option in a dichotomized corollary that is anticipated to provide the best possibility for extending and defining the construct system. Implicit here is the notion that the poles of a construct may have very different properties and associated characteristics.

The range corollary describes a construct that is convenient for anticipating a finite range of events. It is also suggested that each construct has a range of convenience, which essentially refers to all of the things that the person with the construct feels would apply to the construct. The range of convenience is one source of individual difference because the range for a specific construct ought to vary from person to person.

The experience corollary reflects the change in the construction system as a person successively construes the replication of events. Given the experience corollary, the personal constructs we have in childhood may be quite different than the ones we have in adulthood. Whether this is the case, however, depends in part on the modulation corollary and the permeability of our constructs.

The modulation corollary involves the evolution of the construction system. It is the notion that variation in the construction system is limited by the permeability of the constructs in the construction system; that is, to what extent new elements are assimilated (permeable) or not assimilated (impermeable).

The fragmentation corollary acknowledges that a person can simultaneously use two or more construction subsystems even though these subsystems may seem logically incompatible. Kelly (1955) felt that the fragmentation corollary was necessary to account for those times when the person seems to be acting in a manner that is inconsistent with her or his previous behaviour.

The commonality corollary accounts for similarities between people. People will have similar psychological processes and perceptions to the extent that they rely on similar constructions of experience. According to Kelly, this corollary has implications for how culture is interpreted. For Kelly, similarities among people are due, in part, to culture, and culture reflects the tendency for a group of people to construe their experiences in the same way.

Kelly provided the sociality corollary to reflect the fact that being from the same culture is not enough to ensure social harmony. This corollary involves the idea that a person may play a role in a social process involving one or more other people to the extent that he or she is able to accurately construe the construction processes of other people. It is not essential to see the world in the same way; what is essential, according to Kelly, is to understand how the world is perceived by someone else.

The unique construction system of the Unabomber is outlined below to illustrate further what is meant by personal constructs. Clearly, the Unabomber had a way of looking at the world that was entirely unique and atypical.

Personal Constructs of the Unabomber

Kelly's theory can be used to get a reasonably good understanding of the personality structure of the Unabomber and his aberrant ways of thinking. Recall that the story of Theodore Kaczynski was introduced in Chapter 6 to illustrate Murray's theory of psychological needs.

Although the Repertory Grid approach is the most common way of identifying psychological constructs, it is also possible to identify constructs by analyzing textual and narrative data (see Green, 2004). The Unabomber's Manifesto (UM) has enough material to allow readers to get a clear sense of the constructs that make up Kaczynski's personality. This 35,000 word essay, titled "Industrial Society and its Future," was published in *The Washington Post* and *The New York Times*. It was published as part of a bargain made by the Unabomber, who pledged to end the attacks (the mailed bombs) if his lengthy essay was published. Additional insights are provided in the 1998 court ordered psychiatric report by Dr. Sally Johnson. This public document reflects her analyses of autobiographical material written by Kaczynski, including his autobiographical statement obtained by Murray in the experiment conducted at Harvard University. It is also based on Dr. Johnson's clinical interviews with Kaczynski.

Certain section headings in the UM provide a clear indication of elements of Kaczynski's construction system. Many of these themes are supported in the psychiatric assessment conducted by Dr. Johnson. Figure 9.1 is an analysis of the Unabomber's construction system.

Figure 9.1 An Analysis of the Unabomber's Construction System

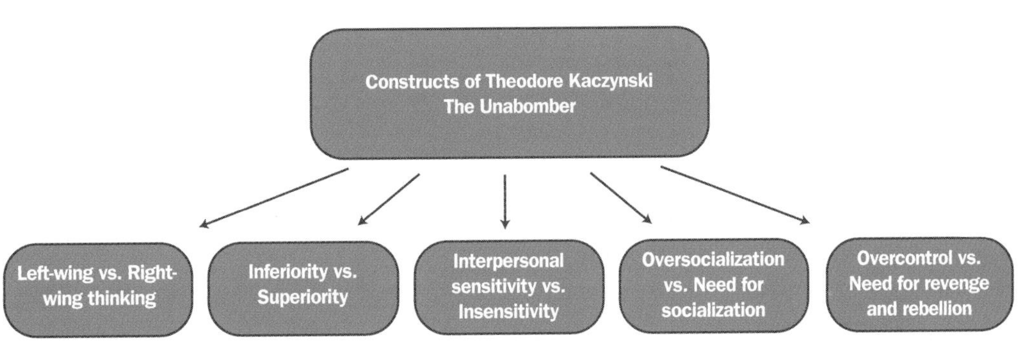

The first theme reflects the construct of left-wing versus right-wing thinking. The relevant section heading in the UM is "The Psychology of Modern Leftism." The Unabomber attributed many of the world's ills to the psychology of leftists, and he stated that they tend to hate white males. He interpreted external events as either left-wing or right-wing thinking. His views are summarized in his statement that "Almost everyone will agree that we live in a deeply troubled society. One of the most widespread manifestations of the craziness of our world is leftism, so a discussion of the psychology of leftism can serve as an introduction to the discussion of the problems of modern society in general."

The theme of inferiority versus superiority forms the second construct. The UM contains the heading "Feelings of Inferiority," which Kaczynski interpreted as an outgrowth of leftism. However, it is clear from Dr. Johnson's report that Kaczynski struggled with the perception of himself as inferior. Specifically, she observed the following:

> Throughout his writings and conversations, he focuses on the fact that he was moved from the fifth to seventh grade. He identifies this as the cause of his lack of development

> of social skills, a problem that continues with him to the present. Between the seventh and 12th grade, he perceived "a gradual increasing amount of hostility I had to face from the other kids. By the time I left high school, I was definitely regarded as a freak by a large segment of the student body." He describes a number of incidents in his junior high and high school years, including a discussion of making a small pipe bomb in chemistry, which gained him some notoriety. He described himself as having "frustrated resentment towards school parents, and the student body" which often was given outlet through "snotty behavior in the classroom which often took a sarcastic or crudely humorous turn."

This tendency to be perceived as "a freak" signals a deep-seated cognitive concern about inferiority in a way that accords with Adler's theory (see Chapter 5), and it suggests that the Unabomber may have overcompensated by trying to establish a superiority complex.

Another related construct is interpersonal sensitivity versus insensitivity. Dr. Johnson noted that Kaczynski was hypersensitive to even the slightest form of criticism and had a capacity to feel a deep-seated sense of humiliation. He would be attentive cognitively to indications of being slighted.

The fourth construct is oversocialization versus need for autonomy. This construct is likely the most important in explaining Kaczynski's behaviour. He actually noted in his manifesto that psychologists have extensively studied the phenomenon of oversocialization and how feelings of shame have been internalized by children, who instead desire personal freedom and autonomy.

The fifth construct is overcontrol versus the need for revenge and rebellion. The Unabomber's murderous acts are related directly to this construct. His bombs represented a form of freedom of expression that was denied to him in real life. Dr. Johnson noted this as a salient aspect of his personality. She specifically observed the following:

> He also claims that during high school and college he would often become terribly angry because he could not express that anger or hatred openly. "I would therefore indulge in fantasies of revenge. However, I never attempted to put any such fantasies into effect because I was too strongly conditioned ... against any defiance of authority. To be more precise, I could not have committed a crime of revenge even a relatively minor crime because of my fear of being caught and punished was all out of proportion to the actual danger of being caught."

Power versus powerlessness is another related construct. The UM incorporates the belief that people are able to maintain some semblance of psychological health by responding to efforts at control by industrial–technological society by developing a sense of personal power.

Note that each of the identified constructs is bipolar, consistent with Kelly's views. Although the identified constructs seem fairly obvious, they are based primarily on verbal information, and an assessment of preverbal constructs could lead to the identification of other constructs.

The case of the Unabomber illustrates the problems that arise when, as Kelly suggested, a person has "no laboratory" and cannot update personal constructs in a way that becomes more representative of reality. The Unabomber lived in isolation as a miser in Montana, and, as such, had very limited human contact. Once he made the decision to live this type of life, opportunities were lost to take in new information and modify constructs. Thus, abnormal views on the world were able to flourish as the destructiveness continued.

Empirical Research on the Nature of Personal Constructs

Extensive research has examined the nature of personal constructs. One theme that has emerged goes right back to Kelly's emphasis on *personal* constructs. This is a highly idiographic approach; research findings tend to be much more informative and easier to comprehend when research methods are designed to elicit the constructs from the people themselves rather than have the construct categories supplied by the researchers (see Adams-Webber, 1998). This point was emphasized in an insightful review of personal construct theory by Mischel (1964), who suggested that a nomothetically based statistical approach was not really applicable to the personal construct approach. Mischel argued that focusing on personal constructs with an idiographic approach would surpass the emphasis of the statistical approach on *prediction* and would get us closer to our ultimate goal of *understanding* people and their unique differences.

Extensive research has been conducted by Jack Adams-Webber, a longstanding member of the psychology department at Brock University in Ontario. Adams-Webber studied with George Kelly, and he has dedicated much of his career to research and theory on personal construct theory.

Jack Adams-Webber

Jack Adams-Webber has also conducted research on the concept of cognitive complexity postulated by Bieri (1955). Cognitive complexity reflects the structure and interrelation of cognitions rather than the actual content or theme of the cognitions. Bieri analyzed the constructs used to judge other people and determined that some people are high in cognitive complexity and can simultaneously invoke several constructs when forming their impressions, while other people are low in cognitive complexity.

Jack Adams-Webber has conducted research on the concept of cognitive complexity.

Cognitive complexity is also known as integrative complexity. According to Suedfeld (1994), integrative complexity reflects whether cognitions are *differentiated* (the person recognizes two or more legitimate perspectives or dimensions that apply to an issue) and *integrated* (the person recognizes the interconnectedness of perspectives or dimensions). Suedfeld (1994) tested U.S. President Bill Clinton's integrative complexity based on quotes during the early stages of his presidency and expected to find a high level of integrative complexity but instead found that Clinton had one of the lowest levels of integrative complexity relative to other U.S. presidents.

Zalot and Adams-Webber's (1997) work on cognitive complexity found that people who were more cognitively complex in terms of how they rated their neighbours actually had more frequent social interactions with their neighbours. In separate research, Adams-Webber also found evidence to support Crockett's (1965) **familiarity hypothesis**. This is the hypothesis that "an individual's constructs relative to others with whom he interacts frequently and intimately will be more complex than his constructs relevant to categories of persons with whom he interacts less frequently" (p. 63). Adams-Webber (2001) found in a study of couples that there was a high correlation between partners in their level of cognitive complexity. In general, people tend to be high in cognitive complexity to the extent that they have confidence in their own self-evaluations (Adams-Webber, 2003).

Roles and Fixed Role Therapy

Kelly defined a "role" as a psychological process and ongoing pattern of behaviour that reflects a person's understanding of the ways of thinking of those people the person is associated with. Kelly stated that a person's understanding of a role is tied to his or her personal construct system. A role is not to be equated with the self-concept because playing and understanding a role is not necessarily a part of an individual's identity. Still, it is important because our awareness of roles helps us gain a better appreciation of how other people regard things. By assuming someone else's role, we are better able to understand how they view things (i.e., by putting yourself in the other person's shoes).

Kelly has much in common with Rogers because he, too, believed that the client needs guidance and assistance from the therapist, but, ultimately, the client is the scientist who must find a way to update his or her constructs (Kelly, 1955). The primary focus in therapy is on the client's self-construct, and how the client sees the self as different from other people. The main goals of treatment are to improve and strengthen the self-construct so that the person essentially becomes a better scientist for events involving the self.

Modifications to the self-construct occur in response to the main form of treatment advocated by Kelly: **fixed role therapy**. The client is required to act a role for a particular period of time, and this is believed to facilitate the process of not only gaining a better appreciation of how other people view things, but also examining the self from a different perspective or point of view (see Adams-Webber, 1981; Kelly, 1973). The fixed role therapy allows the client to identify the constructs of other people in his or her life, and gives them the chance to try out these constructs as a different way of construing and interpreting reality.

Scott Miller (2003) recounted one of his cases that serves as a dramatic illustration of how assuming a role can help a client see things from a different perspective and can ultimately lead to personality change. It is a story of a 19-year-old mental patient who had received training for a religious mission he was about to embark on. This young man started to suffer delusions and was diagnosed with "brief reactive psychosis." His primary delusion was that he was a famous character from the Arnold Schwarzenegger movies. When asked to introduce himself, he said, "I'm the Terminator… You know, I have to save John Connor" (Miller, 2003, p. 98). "The Terminator" also believed that he was being held against his will in a prison. He needed to escape to continue his mission, so that is why he had led several "prison breaks" that included several other mental patients!

Therapeutic progress was slow, as might be expected. The key to improvement was getting the young man to assume other roles. One day, Miller got a brilliant insight after recalling another famous case in which a patient assumed someone else's identity. Miller approached the young man and angered him initially by saying the following:

> "I've been wondering if you really are the Terminator? … Wait, wait … It's just that, as I've been listening to you talk, I've had the sneaking suspicion that you really aren't the Terminator after all… Aren't you really Arnold Schwarzenegger?"
>
> "How did you know?!" the boy said in true astonishment. "How did you know who I really am?"
>
> Sitting opposite this huge, underwear-clad, grinning guy, Miller thought to himself, "Just damn lucky," and then wondered how he'd guessed this might be a good thing to try.
>
> "So," he said, "what should I call you? Do you prefer to be called the Terminator or Arnold Schwarzenegger?"
>
> "My friends call me Arnold," the boy grinned again, then licked his lips.
>
> "Well, OK Arnold, thanks. So, aren't you married to Maria Shriver?"
>
> "Yeah, isn't she great?" (Kottler & Carlson, 2003, p.100)

After Miller achieved this breakthrough by recognizing his client as Arnold Schwarzenegger, he then told him, "You're obviously a great, great actor, Arnold," and he asked him to demonstrate his amazing acting ability by playing the role of a cooperative mental patient on a ward. As the next week unfolded, as a result of playing the mental patient role, the patient began to reassume his actual identity and there were no further escape attempts.

According to Kelly (1991), it is important for therapists to be highly cognizant of the client's subjective reality, and this includes recognizing the cultural differences among clients. He maintained that people are not simply the product of their cultures because they play a part in how the culture is perceived. That is, it is "the client's culture as he sees it" (p. 92). However, culture is very important because it provides much of the data used to evaluate and possibly update the personal construct system. Also, Kelly stated that cultural similarity between people occurs when they have constructs in common and they share similar beliefs and views about what is expected of them.

Try a version of fixed role therapy for yourself. Assume you are frustrated with your teaching assistant because she is not giving you enough time to finish your test. You might conclude that the teaching assistant is mean-spirited and enjoys mistreating people. Now imagine that you have been asked by the professor to replace the teaching assistant because the teaching assistant has become ill. There still isn't enough time for students to finish their tests. Do you rely on the construct that "teaching assistants are mean people," or do you develop a new construct with the theme, "I wish the situation could be changed so that students could have more time"? Typically, the **actor–observer attribution bias** is such that we blame negative things on other people's personal characteristics but are much more likely to make attributions to situations and circumstantial factors when we are put in the same position. Perhaps assuming someone else's role would make someone less likely to automatically blame negative things on the other person's dispositional features.

Karst and Trexler (1970) conducted an interesting experiment that demonstrated the usefulness of fixed role therapy. This study focused on the treatment of a problem that is common among university students: speech anxiety. Typically, surveys indicate that people give higher fear ratings to the fear of public speaking than they give to the fear of death! The study involved a comparison of the efficacy of fixed role therapy versus the rational–emotive therapy devised by Albert Ellis. Ellis (1961, 2002) believes that psychological distress stems from the personal endorsement of irrational beliefs such as "In order to be loved and respected by others, I must be perfect." These two interventions were contrasted, in part, because Karst studied fixed role therapy with Kelly while Trexler studied rational–emotive behaviour therapy with Ellis. The fixed role therapy involved, among other things, observing people speaking in public and projecting themselves being in that role, including their thoughts and feelings.

Comparisons of those treated via fixed role therapy and via rational–emotive behaviour therapy and a control group showed that it was the fixed role therapy that led to the greatest improvements on dependent measures (i.e., anxiety self-report scale responses). Karst and Trexler (1970) also found that the fixed role therapy patients gave higher ratings when asked to indicate the usefulness of the intervention.

Adams-Webber (1986) summarized the results of many experiments on self-concept change and social cognition following the type of role playing advocated by Kelly. He concluded that "the results of these experiments indicate that role playing temporary changes in moods, states, and self-image can lead to systematic changes in the way in which we construe ourselves and others" (p. 300).

Roles and the Person–Situation Interaction

Although Kelly's definition of roles is more elaborated and a bit different from how the term "role" is typically used, it is important to take this opportunity to discuss how life roles can influence behaviour. Cattell (1963) made an important but often overlooked theoretical contribution by suggesting that the person–situation interaction needs to be expanded to also consider life roles. Specifically, he suggested a model that included both roles and affective states as "modulators" of the link between personality and behavioural responses. Roles were described as operating across several specific situations. Cattell (1965) also observed that no behavioural act occurs without being influenced to some extent by a role. Finally, Cattell also suggested roles are powerful because they "whether temporary or permanent, common or unique, involve the capacity to react to a focal stimulus differently in a global situation" (p. 16).

There is little doubt that roles are important to our interest in cross-cultural differences in personality, especially the expression of personality differences. Cultures may differ in the nature, significance, and impact of roles, and there may be differences in how roles interact with personality traits and needs. The current author became acutely aware of how roles have an impact on personality, cognition, and behaviours due to personal experiences when first hired as a professor. Because there was still some graduate work to be completed, many days I found myself performing the role of professor in the morning at York University and then re-assuming the student role at the University of Toronto in the afternoon. The role demands of being a professor elicited a very different set of responses to the expectations associated with the graduate student role. Consistent with Kelly's theory, it is almost certain that the different roles also evoked different cognitive orientations and associated concepts and constructs. Clearly, given that roles often represent recurring situations that are personally important, a focus on roles represents an important way of extending research on the personality–environment interaction and the fit between the person and his or her environment.

At present, there is very little systematic research on personality, life roles, and behaviours, but extant research is quite informative. Roberts and Donahue (1994) examined self-perceptions of middle-aged women across a variety of roles (parent, friend, worker) and found salient differences across social roles. However, in each instance, role-specific views of the self were related to the general view of the self, suggesting that role-specific views each contribute to an overall sense of the self. Other research has examined personality attributes in specific role contexts. Mitchelson and Burns (1998) assessed levels of perfectionism at home and at work in a sample of working mothers. Levels of perfectionism were significantly higher at work than at home, though perfectionism in either role location was associated with greater stress and distress.

Sheldon and associates from the University of Rochester (see Sheldon, Ryan, Rawsthorne, and Ilardi, 1997) performed perhaps the most revealing study in this area thus far. Previous research had identified five life roles as particularly salient for students: (1) student; (2) employee; (3) child; (4) friend; and (5) romantic partner. Sheldon et al. (1997) had students rate adjectives from the traits from the five-factor model in terms of how the expression of these traits would vary according to the role being performed by student. Differences by role were found across all five factors. For instance, conscientiousness was highest in the employee role, while extroversion was highest in the friend or romantic partner role. Agreeableness was highest in the employee and in the friend roles. Neuroticism was highest in the student role. Finally, openness to experience was highest in the friend and romantic partner roles.

The Role Construct Repertory Test and Repertory Grids

There are many different versions of the Role Construct Repertory Test. In its original form, the test requires the respondent to identify 15 people according to 15 specific labels. The same labels are given to everyone. People are listed according to such cues as: (1) someone you look up to; (2) someone you dislike; (3) someone who is successful; (4) someone who is not successful; (5) someone who has authority over you; and (6) someone who is inferior to you. Different three-person sets of these people are then identified, and the respondent has to indicate how two of these people are similar and how the third person is different from the first two people. For instance, a person could be asked to identify someone they like and someone who is successful and compare these people with someone they dislike. One end of a construct is represented by how the liked person and successful person are deemed to be similar, and the other end of the construct reflects the ways in which the disliked person is different. It is called a grid because it is possible to geometrically represent the constructs once various three-person sets are identified and described.

You could do a similar exercise. Think of three of your professors. Pick a professor you admire and another professor who is successful. Compare them and select a word or two that describes how they are similar. Now think of the third professor and how she or he is different from the other two. You might have identified two female professors and suggested that they are both female, and contrasted them with a male professor (or vice versa). If so, according to personal construct theory, the category of female versus male is one of your personal constructs.

When constructs are identified with Repertory Grids, they are then analyzed to see if they can be grouped into some higher order factor or theme. This was illustrated in McCoy's (1980) analysis of "culture-shocked marriages." A culture-shocked marriage is an intercultural marriage that often results from a couple meeting and marrying while the man is a temporary resident in a foreign country. The partner experiences adjustment difficulties if the couple then returns to the husband's homeland.

McCoy (1980) recounted the case of Maria and "Mr. H." Maria was from Eastern Europe and had moved to Canada at a young age. As an adult, she met Mr. H., who was from Hong Kong, while he was receiving medical training in Canada. Maria did not cope well when they eventually moved to Hong Kong. She was very dissatisfied and felt alienated from Mr. H.'s family and the culture in general. Her attempts to learn Cantonese were not helpful. Also, she resented it when Mr. H.'s sister and family moved in with them because of financial problems. Most importantly, she and Mr. H. were having extreme marital problems. They had a daughter together, but Maria perceived that her husband had changed and was no longer the sympathetic and modern man she married. She felt rejected, in part due to his apparent lack of sexual interest, and they grew apart as a couple. She wanted to return to Canada but he did not; she saved enough money to leave and go back to her parents. She returned as they tried to "patch up" the marriage, in part because her parents insisted that she must try to salvage the marriage because divorce went against their religious convictions. According to McCoy (1980), Maria continued to nag for a return to Canada. Mr. H. responded by becoming passive and withdrawn and going out on expensive entertainment binges with his friends. To Maria, this simply took away the money needed for another return to Canada.

Maria received counselling and she completed two Repertory Grid analyses. Her 12 elicited constructs from her first assessment are shown in Table 9.1. Empirical analyses found that all but two of these constructs reflected a higher order construct identified as "The Modern Canadian viewpoint versus traditional Chinese culture." It was deemed that her construct system had "tightened" in response to extreme culture shock and was focused almost entirely on her perceptions of cultural differences.

Table 9.1 Maria's Elicited Constructs

Construct Number	Constructs		
9	Sees marriage as a role	vs.	Sees marriage as sharing
11	Self-centred	vs.	Giving
12	Culture bound	vs.	Open to other cultures
3	Victim	vs.	Personally responsible
2	Old-fashioned	vs.	Modern Canadian
1	Authorities (older generation)	vs.	Equals (my generation)
8	Hong Kong people	vs.	Others
5	Chauvinistic	vs.	Free
10	Have superficial relationships	vs.	Having sincere relationships
7	Unfeeling	vs.	Warm of heart
6	Having sexual problems	vs.	No sexual problems
4	Content with own life	vs.	Dissatisfied

Note: Constructs are listed in terms of their empirical contribution (weight) on the broad overall factor. Constructs 6 and 4 were not part of this factor.

It is important to state that these unfavourable views of traditional Chinese culture reflected Maria's subjective perceptions as a visitor with extreme adjustment issues, including a profound sense of loneliness. Her overarching construct is illustrated in globe graphs that were derived from her grid responses. These globe graphs are three-dimensional representations of her predominant construct and are based on the themes associated with the 15 people nominated by Maria. Although the globes shown in Figure 9.2 clearly reflect a modern Canadian orientation versus a traditional Chinese orientation, it is interesting to note that the traditional Chinese orientation that is associated with Maria's unhappiness also was found to empirically capture her feelings about her father and her ex-boyfriend. Note that Maria's husband appears on both globes to reflect the husband she perceived in

Figure 9.2 Maria's Globe Graphs Showing Modern Canadian versus Traditional Chinese Cultures

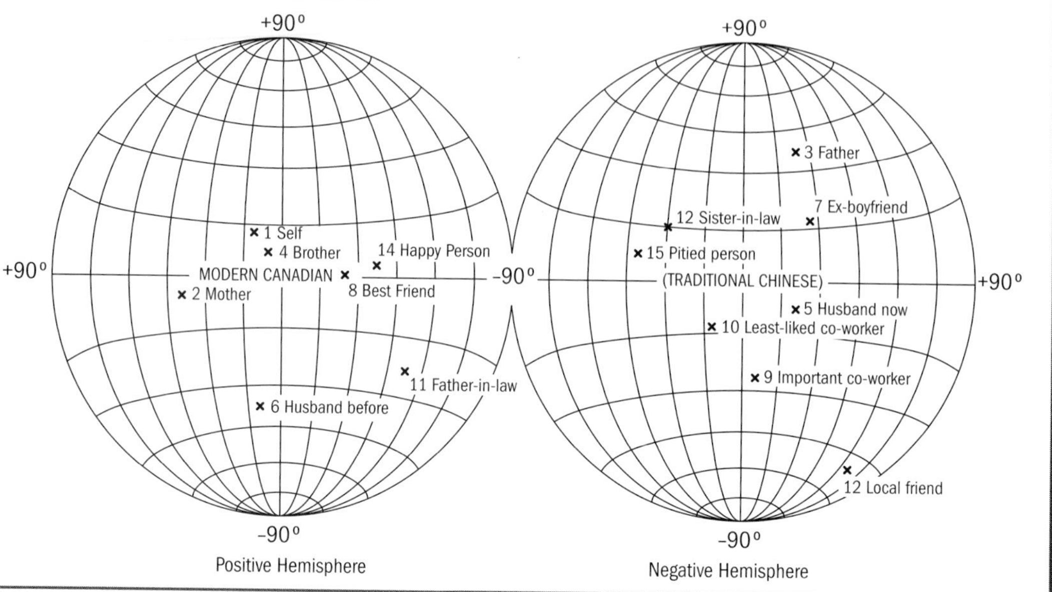

Source: McCoy, 1980, p. 152.

Canada versus the husband she perceived in Hong Kong.

It is interesting that when Maria was re-assessed two years later, she no longer suffered from profound culture shock (though there was a recent extramarital encounter), and her constructs were very different. Three constructs were identified: (1) warm and friendly versus cold and unexpressive; (2) generous and tractable versus domineering and self-promoting; and (3) felicitous (accepting, considerate) versus manipulative. Her construct system was now deemed to be relatively culture-free, though McCoy (1980) observed that the lack of emotional expressiveness seen in the first construct could be a reflection of traditional Chinese culture.

Repertory tests come in many different forms. For instance, Crockett's (1982) Role Category Questionnaire requires the respondent to identify a list of people (e.g., people you like, people you don't like) and then take each person and describe him or her as fully as possible for three minutes each. The themes that reappear reflect personal constructs. The generated responses are also used to assess individual differences in cognitive complexity.

Grids have been used extensively in research. For instance, according to Neimeyer (1985), the Repertory Grid was used in approximately 96% of the studies that were conducted between 1954 and 1981 to test Kelly's model. There have been many practical applications of the original and modified versions of repertory grid techniques. Some of these applications are outlined in Applied Perspective 9.1. Some applications examine the constructs of people suffering from psychopathology. For instance, one study compared 19 depressed patients, 19 psychiatric controls, and 19 control participants without psychopathology (Space & Cromwell, 1980). Analyses of responses to the Role Construct Repertory Test showed that the depressed patients were unique in that they had a self-description that was highly negative but also had positive features (i.e., a mixed self-characterization); but they also had constructs that reflected they were highly different from others. This is something that the author experienced while testing depressed psychiatric patients from Hamilton, Ontario. These patients often stated that no one could understand their unique situation and the things that only they had to deal with. The irony was that this sense of uniqueness was mentioned by patient after patient, yet their expressed issues were often quite similar to those expressed by other patients. For each person, however, their sense of being unique was their reality.

Fransella and Neimeyer (2005) noted that although the Repertory Grid garners the attention, Kelly deserves recognition for other contributions in the assessment area. For instance, Kelly also used a technique known as self-characterization. This involves writing a description of the self from the perspective of favourable third person observer. This is a qualitative form of assessment that represents a rich source of data. This type of assessment helped provide the impetus for contemporary research on life narrative accounts (see Chapter 14).

Applied Perspective 9.1 Practical Applications of Role Construct Repertory Grids

A cursory search of references on the Internet yields an astounding number of references to Kelly's work. This type of search not only underscores the widespread appreciation of Kelly's theory, but also illustrates the extensive applications of role construct theory. The general technique used in a typical construct grid (identifying two things as similar and determining how these two things are different from a third thing) can be modified to assess not only people, but also organizations and systems (and presumably cultures).

New uses of construct grids are continuing to emerge. For instance, Sewell and Cruise (2004) devised a Psychopathy Grid to assess psychopathy in adolescents. The psychopathic grid assessed self-construals and assessments of peers on specific psychopathy symptoms. This enabled the authors to determine the extent to which the psychopathic role was adopted by two boys who were analyzed as case studies.

Many applications involve developments in the information technology sector. One study conducted in New Zealand used the Repertory Grid technique to evaluate business–information technology alignment, which is how the IT goals outlined in a business plan actually became reflected in the IT deployment (Tan, 1999). Hassenzahl and Trautmann (2001) used a Repertory Grid technique to evaluate websites. Comparisons of how two websites were similar yet differed from a third provided valuable insights about both their design and content.

The Repertory Grid has been used by employers to assess prospective employees and facilitate personnel decisions.

By far and away, the majority of applied uses involving repertory grids involve the business sector (for summaries, see Fransella, 2003; Jankowicz, 1987; Stewart & Stewart, 1981). According to Stewart and Stewart (1981), from a chronological perspective, the first business use of the Repertory Grid assessment was by marketing research experts who sought to compare their clients' products and the products of competitors. The Repertory Grid was next used to facilitate personnel decisions. The personal constructs of prospective employees were evaluated. In addition, the Repertory Grid has been used to appraise the management potential of current employees.

Finally, Mildred Shaw and Brian Gaines from the Knowledge Science Institute at the University of Calgary in Alberta examined how the Repertory Grid can be used to identify the personal construct system of the expert computer system programmer (see Gaines & Shaw, 2003). Repertory Grids have proven to be enormously useful to identify the constructs involved in knowledge acquisition. In short, the Repertory Grid helps identify the construction systems of experts so that this knowledge can be used to develop more expertise.

Green (2004) has provided a comprehensive view of the various content analysis frameworks that have been created to systematically analyze construct content. He noted that there are two approaches: one data-driven and one theory-driven. The data-driven approach simply involves taking the concepts that are generated, placing them on index cards, and seeing what categories can be formed by independent raters. The theory-driven approach is different in that various authors have derived conceptual schemes designed to identify specific constructs, so the repertory grid data are analyzed by the categories and scoring schemes that have been developed to tap these theories.

What kinds of category schemes have been developed? Some are much more complex than others. One simple approach is to examine the number of constructs that reflect external factors outside the self (Bieri, Bradburn, & Galinsky, 1958). Another framework distinguished whether the constructs represented people or life problems and whether the constructs were global, higher order constructs or subordinate constructs (Walker, Ramsey, & Bell, 1988). This scheme also included an assessment of the number of impermeable constructs. Yorke (1989) devised an approach to distinguish between constructs with endpoints that are antonyms (polar opposites) versus the number of what Yorke referred to as bent constructs (constructs with poles from seemingly different constructs). Finally, to reflect his particular research interests, Neimeyer and associates developed a 25-category framework to analyze death themes (Neimeyer, Fontana, & Gold, 1984).

In theory, an astounding number of constructs can be identified, given the vast cognitive differences among people. This is underscored by the development of a computer program known as the AUTOREP program (see Murphy & Neimeyer, 1986), which provides automatic computer scoring for approximately 1,500 personal constructs. This program was used most recently to identify the personal constructs of female survivors of sexual abuse (Harter, Erbes, & Hart, 2004). Another computerized scoring program that has been developed is called OMNIGRID (Mitterer & Adams-Webber, 1988). These programs have been created to try to reduce subjectivity and maximize the degree of objectivity in identifying personal constructs.

KEY POINTS

- Fixed role therapy was designed by Kelly to enable people to develop new constructs and modify old constructs by trying out new roles and experiences.
- Research indicates that fixed role therapy can be quite effective and is as effective as rational–emotive therapy.
- Cattell postulated that behaviour often reflects the interaction of personality and life roles.
- Roles in various life domains contribute to our overall sense of self and well-being.
- Broad personality traits reflecting the five-factor model vary in their relevance across specific life roles.
- The Role Construct Repertory Test and Repertory Grids are idiographic measures of personal constructs.

Kelly's Contemporary Influence

Many points raised by Kelly retain a certain resonance and appeal because they seem reasonable and show common sense, and there is no denying that people have abstract mental categories that guide their interpretation of their world and life events. Kelly's theory helped promote the cognitive revolution in clinical psychology in the 1970s and 1980s, and his influence on clinical psychology remains quite strong in certain areas of the world (e.g., Great Britain). His work also stimulated an area of psychology known as constructivist psychology.

A contentious issue involving Kelly is whether he should be regarded as a cognitive theorist or a humanistic theorist (see Chapter 7). A strong case can be made for both. The cognitive aspect of his theory is beyond debate, but as noted by Raskin (2002), Kelly was a humanist due to (1) the emphasis he placed on personal choice; (2) the emphasis he placed on the creation of personal meaning; and (3) the general disdain he expressed for anti-humanistic diagnostic traditions. Raskin (2002) maintained that Kelly was believed to be working on a more humanistic version of his theory at the time of his death. Some authors (e.g., Fransella & Neimeyer, 2005) have concluded that Kelly's focus on personal choice and personal meaning was a reactive response to the conservative religious ideology espoused by Kelly's parents.

Evaluation of Kelly

Overall, Kelly deserves credit for providing one of the first purely cognitive theories of personality. He helped promote a focus on the unique individual as a whole person and his emphasis on personal constructs helped paved the way for the subsequent cognitive revolution in psychology. Kelly also deserves enormous credit for developing the Role Construct Repertory Test and for this influence on therapy.

His theory is not beyond criticism, however. It was mentioned earlier that Kelly's theory focused more on the structure of personality and had little to say about the content of personality, in part because of his emphasis on the uniqueness of each person. Kelly's theory has also been criticized because he did not examine personality from a developmental perspective (Fransella & Neimeyer, 2005). He was relatively silent about the origins of how constructs are initially established and why some people have much more elaborate and extensive construct systems.

Other concerns involve challenges to specific aspects of his theory. For instance, Bruner (1956) questioned the choice corollary and the notion that when it comes to the two endpoints of a dichotomous construct, people choose the alternative that allows for the greatest extension of the construct system. Bruner argued convincingly that this aspect of the theory sees people as highly rational at all times, but we know that people often act according to strong emotions; during these times, they are not concerned with expanding their constructs. Also, how can the theory apply to people who suffer from extreme forms of irrationality (e.g., the young man who thought he was the Terminator)?

Another issue involves whether each construct is dichotomous with two identifiable endpoints. Certain constructs represent cognitive categories that may exist without having two endpoints. Consider for example the apparent dichotomy of optimism–pessimism (or hope–hopelessness). Research has established that optimism and pessimism are not two endpoints of the same continuum; in fact, separate dimensions of optimism and pessimism can be identified (perhaps because optimism and pessimism have very different motivational orientations). So, when optimism applies to someone, should it be paired with pessimism? Or should optimism and pessimism be represented by two separate constructs? Kelly emphasized the dichotomy but this may not apply across all of a person's constructs.

Although these are viable concerns, there is no doubt that Kelly provided a valuable contribution that has resulted in extensive research on personality and cognition. His work opened the door for major theoretical developments on cognitive factors in the decades that followed, and he continues to have a widespread influence on applications.

KURT LEWIN'S COGNITIVE AND FIELD THEORY OF PERSONALITY

Kurt Lewin, who is regarded as the primary founder of social psychology, also made contributions to the field of personality.

Kurt Lewin was born in Prussia in 1890 and emigrated to the United States prior to the outbreak of the Second World War. Although Lewin is regarded as the primary founder of social psychology, his contributions to the personality field should not be overlooked. His 1935 book *A Dynamic Theory of Personality* set the stage for the interactionism approach to the study of personality and behaviour. His contributions are outlined briefly here in Chapter 9 in recognition of the fact that an emphasis on cognitive factors was also central to his personality theory. This emphasis on cognitive appraisal means that Lewin should probably be considered along with the phenomenological theorists, though Lewin is distinguished by his **Gestalt** focus. The term "Gestalt" typically signifies a coherent whole. The Gestalt focus is based on the general concept that if we want to understand or appreciate how a particular object or stimulus is perceived, we need to examine the object in the total context or configuration that surrounds it. For Gestalt theorists, the whole and the global impact that it has on us is "greater than the sum of its parts." Lewin defined Gestalt as "a system whose parts are dynamically connected in such a way that a change of one part results in a change of all other parts" (Lewin, 1935, p. 214).

Lewin (1935) illustrated his focus on unity and wholeness rather than constituent parts of a person by emphasizing that our sense of self is part of a broader whole, and there is more to us than the conscious aspects of ourselves. Specifically, he observed that:

> The question of the unity of consciousness is not identical with the question of the unity of the whole region of psychical forms and processes .... Further, it is at least questionable whether that which may be called ego or self, the unity of which is important for many problems, is not merely one system or complex of systems, a functional part region within this psychical totality. (p. 56)

According to Sheehy (2004), the essential starting point in understanding Lewin's views is the distinction that Lewin made between the contrasting views of nature espoused by Aristotle and Galileo. Lewin rejected Aristotle's views that objects (e.g., people) can be placed into different categories based on their natural tendencies (e.g., instincts) and that individual differences occur when environmental events interfere with and distort natural tendencies. Rather, Lewin favoured Galileo's contention that behaviours and personal development are a product of the total forces that influence us, and these forces are dynamic in nature.

Lewin expanded on Einstein's concept of fields of force, and Lewin is generally seen as the one who provided the theoretical impetus for the popular phrase from *Star Wars*, "May the force be with you."

Lewin (1935) argued that behaviour reflects the person and the situation. Specifically, he stated that:

> In psychology one can begin to describe the whole situation by roughly distinguishing the person (P) and the environment (E). Every psychological event depends upon the state of the person and at the same time on the environment, although their relative importance is different in different cases. Thus, we can state our formula B = f(S) for every psychological event as B = f(PE). (Lewin, 1936, p. 11)

Lewin went on to clarify that the whole situation consists not only of the state of the environment at the time, but also of the state of the person at the time. Thus, he made a clear distinction between the traits of a person and his or her momentary states in specific situations. For him, the word "situation" should not refer to just the environment; it also includes the person's psychological situation at the time of assessment.

According to Lewin, a person's needs represent a key source of individual differences. Needs are defined by Lewin as tension systems within someone's inner-personal region. Needs play several roles. They influence behaviour, cognitions and perceptions. To underscore the impact that the person can have on the environment, Lewin stated that the structure of the environment as well as its "constellation of forces" will vary with the needs, desires, and general state of the person, which become reflected in the person's behaviour.

Lewin introduced the term **life space** to summarize all of the factors that have an impact on a person. Consistent with his Gestalt emphasis, the life space refers to the whole psychological field, and a person's behaviour must be interpreted within the context of their entire life space. Life space includes all possible events that a person may experience. It includes internal events inside the person (e.g., hunger cues), external events (the situation), and a person's recollection of prior situational experiences (perceptions and cognitions).

Lewin preferred to represent his concepts with topographical maps that outlined how his concepts were interrelated. Figure 9.3 represents how Lewin came to view the person and his or her interrelation with the environment (see Lewin, 1951). It can be seen in Figure 9.3 that the small circle represents the boundary of the person, and included in this small circle are the needs and abilities of the person. The boundary reflects Lewin's concept of differentiation and our need to keep some distance between ourselves and the outside environment. The small circle is embedded within a larger oval that reflects the boundary of the life space, and inside the oval, the factors include the psychological environment. Experiences that are beyond the person and the situations they encountered were described as "the foreign hull of the life space" (see Figure 9.3).

Figure 9.3 Lewin's Topographical View of the Person

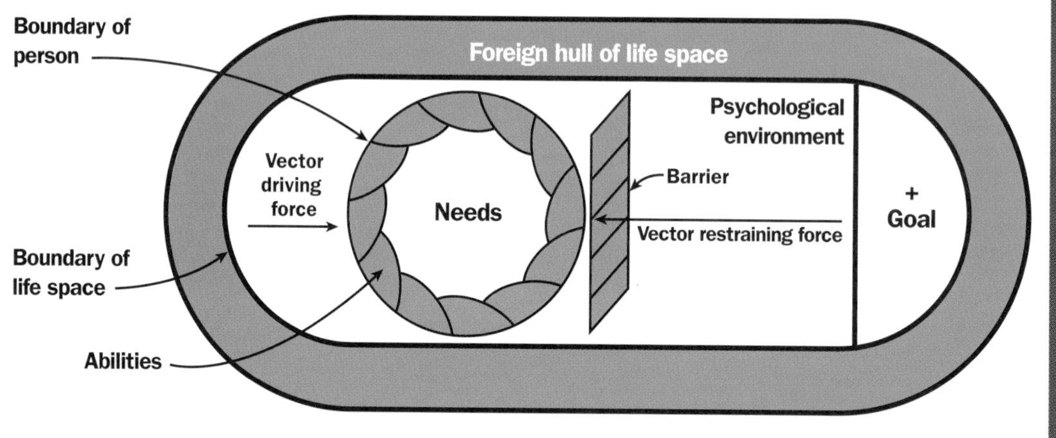

Source: Lewin, 1951.

The dynamic component is reflected by Lewin's belief that, over time, events outside the personal life space can come into the life space. Also, things that were once in the life space can lose their relevance and move out of the life space.

So why is Lewin's theory regarded as a cognitive theory? Several aspects make it extensively cognitive in origin. First, the life space is divided into separate regions or fields and fields are similar to constructs in that they reflect how the person has come to cognitively organize his world and experiences. Lewin placed importance on psychological descriptions of the field, and these descriptions were based on how individuals cognitively represented their fields.

Second, as illustrated in Figure 9.3, the life space also includes reference to goals. Lewin argued that behaviour is often goal-directed and whether a person pursues a goal is a joint function of the person's cognitive expectancy that the goal will be attained and of the value or importance that the person attaches to the goal and its attainment. The cognitive expectancy is a highly subjective evaluation of the probability of goal attainment.

Note that Lewin's notion of cognitive expectancies is the forerunner of subsequent social–cognitive theories that placed great emphasis on individual differences in expectancy. Social–cognitive expectancy theories such as those outlined by Rotter and Bandura can be regarded, at least in part, as extensions of Lewin's personality model. This is not too surprising given that Lewin taught at the University of Iowa and his students included both Rotter and Bandura.

Tension and force are two other key concepts in Lewin's theory. Lewin posited that our psychological makeup is composed of a field of tensions. Tensions derive from our needs and build up if barriers in the environment tend to block the satisfaction of these needs. Our thoughts (and ultimately our actions) are shaped by our psychological tensions. Force is an inner drive caused by tension. Goals are approached to the extent that the person perceives that the goal is positive and goals are avoided if they are perceived as negative. This is represented in Figure 9.3 by the concept of positive valenced forces (driving forces) and negatively valenced forces (restraining forces).

KEY POINTS

- Gestalt personality theorists emphasize the whole or totality of personality ("the sum of a person is greater than the parts").
- Lewin was a Gestalt theorist who is credited with introducing the notion that behaviour is a joint function of the person and the situation.
- Lewin believed that personal needs account for individual differences among people; needs operate on the environment and are reflected in differences in the constellations of forces in the environment.
- The life space reflects our entire psychological field and all the events experienced. Each life space consists of several specific fields.

According to Lewin and his associates, important changes occur in personality structure over time (see Barker, Dembo, & Lewin, 1943; Lewin, 1935). The six key changes are:

1. *Differentiation*: The developing child's various characteristics become more differentiated over time; that is, in Lewinian terms, it is our fields that become more differentiated.
2. *Complexity*: With advancing age, there is greater complexity in the overall organization of the life space.
3. *Expansion*: There is expansion in the aspects of life related to the child's personality.
4. Rigidity: The boundaries between different aspects of a child become stronger and more rigid.
5. *Realism*: Behaviours become more realistic as there is increasing assimilation to the environment.
6. *Integration*: Consistent with the Gestalt emphasis on wholeness, we become increasingly integrated over time (i.e., we do "get our acts together").

In terms of evaluation, note that Lewin was not a personality theorist in the typical sense. Lewin emphasized the general structure of personality and its link with external events, but he had little interest in the specific contents of the personality (i.e., specific traits). As such, it is not a full-fledged theory in the usual sense, and valid criticisms have been raised. As was the case with Kelly, Lewin's views on personality result in a theory that is very descriptive but does not tell us much that enables us to predict an individual's behaviour. A related criticism is that it is not very specific in how a person's life space relates to situational environments.

Still, Lewin's theory deserves recognition not only because it is often overlooked, but also because it highlighted the need for a cognitive emphasis, the need for a dynamic approach, and the need for jointly considering the person and the situation.

COGNITIVELY BASED PERSONALITY DIFFERENCES

Although George Kelly's theory is more detailed than Kurt Lewin's theory, both emphasize the role of cognitive representations in personality differences. The rest of this chapter continues this theme by focusing on some specific cognitive concepts that have been put forth to characterize individual differences between and among people.

The role of personality differences in cognition can be evaluated in many different ways. The theories of Kelly and Lewin suggest that there are important individual differences in cognitive content, and this guides the perception and appraisal of information in the environment.

Contemporary research highlights the role of personality factors in information processing and memory. For instance, research in the United Kingdom suggests that extroverts, relative to introverts, have better short-term and long-term **prospective memory** (Heffernan & Ling, 2001). Prospective memory is remembering that you will have to do something in the future (e.g., recalling that you have to phone your bank manager next week). This study on prospective memory focused on self-reported memory ability. Other studies examine actual differences in cognitive information processing. For example, Michael Eysenck from the University of London has conducted research on introversion and extroversion and cognitive information processing (see Eysenck & Eysenck, 1979). Eysenck and Eysenck (1979) used a standard procedure known as the Sternberg paradigm to show that extroverts were faster than introverts at cognitive scanning of semantic information (i.e., determining whether a stimulus word reflects a particular category). Other research on working memory also points to advantages associated with extroversion. Research using Sternberg's memory scanning task showed that extroverts have faster working memory because they are faster at comparing the contents of working memory with an external target or stimulus (Lieberman, 2000).

Other research suggests that extroversion promotes better **episodic memory**, which is the ability to remember events from one's past. A study of 287 healthy elderly people showed that after controlling for age differences, extroversion was associated with higher episodic memory performance. In contrast, neuroticism was associated with lower episodic memory performance (Meier, Perrig-Chiello, & Perrig, 2002).

Episodic memory is tapped when researchers assess **autobiographical memories**, which are a person's recall of earlier life events. In general, we know that past life events are more likely to be remembered if the events involved intense emotional experiences. **Flashbulb memories** refer to the tendency for people to remember small details with exacting recall—details that might otherwise seem trivial or mundane when people first learn of horrific events such as political assassinations or natural or unnatural disasters such as the events of September 11, 2001 (see Luminent, 2004). The reason why these mundane details are remembered is that the intense emotion enhances the initial encoding and subsequent recall of the information details.

Given the role of emotional intensity in autobiographical recall, it follows that people who are dispositionally high in emotional tendency should have better recall for the emotional events from their past. The Affect Intensity Measure (AIM; Larsen & Diener, 1987) is used to assess personality differences in emotional intensity. It contains such items as "When I am happy, I am so happy, I feel like I am in heaven." Obviously, someone high in affect intensity would endorse this item. Flett, Boase, McAndrews, Pliner, and Blankstein (1986) reasoned that high AIM scorers would report better recall of both positive and negative emotional experiences from their past, and this was indeed found. High AIM scorers also report greater emotional expression (Flett, Bator, & Blankstein, 1987). Subsequent unpublished research in our laboratory has found that high AIM scorers are quicker at recalling emotional autobiographical events and greater reported vividness of emotional images from past events.

How good are you at remembering the emotional events of your past? Do you think your ability to remember is tied to your personality attributes? Table 9.2 contains The Autobiographical Memory Questionnaire by Rubin and Siegler (2004). Think back to a particularly happy event from your life and then respond to the items shown in Table 9.2.

What other individual differences related to the emotional experience influence the ability to remember things? People who tend to suppress their emotional expression are actually involved in a cognitively demanding exercise that impairs their ability to recall newly presented information (see Richards & Gross, 2000). Richards and Gross (2000) examined this phenomenon in an experiment by showing participants a highly emotional scene from the movie *Fatal Attraction* (in which Michael Douglas' character tells his wife that he has been cheating on her with a mentally unstable woman). Participants who were given instructions to suppress their emotions were less able to recall new information presented in the experiment. It seems that the concentration and attention required to limit emotional expression limits the ability to develop new memories.

Your own ability to recall autobiographical memories could reflect your level of trait openness. People who are high in the openness to feelings facet of the openness to experience supertrait actually report better recollection of autobiographical memories based on their answers to the questions shown in Table 9.2 (see Rubin & Siegler, 2004). So, if you had especially vivid memories when you recalled the happy event from your past, perhaps you are high on openness to feelings.

Incidentally, the type of event you are likely to recall will probably vary depending on other factors, such as your cultural background and your sense of connectedness to significant others. A new study of autobiographical memory in European American and Chinese adults found striking group differences (Wang & Conway, 2004). The American adults provided more memories that highlighted their individual experiences and unique personal qualities, while the Chinese participants were more likely to recall social events involving other people and events that emphasized themes of morality. Cultural differences are also explored in the next section on a perceptual and cognitive variable known as field dependence versus field independence.

Table 9.2 The Autobiographical Memory Questionnaire

For questions 1 through 6 and 14, the scales range from 1 (not at all), to 3 (vaguely), to 5 (distinctly) to 7 (as clearly as if it were happening right now). For questions 8 through 12 and 15, the scales range from 1 (not at all), to 3 (vaguely), to 5 (distinctly), to 7 (as much as any memory). Questions 7, 13, and 16 through 18 have unique scales, which follow each of these items. Think about a happy event and respond to the following:

1. As I remember the event, I feel as though I am reliving the original event.
2. As I remember the event, I can hear it in my mind.
3. As I remember the event, I can see it in my mind.
4. As I remember the event, I or other people are talking.
5. As I remember the event, I can feel now the emotions that I felt then.
6. As I remember the event, I can recall the setting where it occurred.
7. To what extent is your memory of the event distorted by your beliefs, motives, and expectations rather than an accurate reflection of the event as a neutral observer would report it? (Scale: 1 = 100% distorted; 7 = 100% accurate)
8. Sometimes people know something happened to them without being able to actually remember it. As I think about the event, I can actually remember it rather than just knowing that it happened.
9. As I remember the event, it comes to me in words.
10. Would you be confident enough in your memory of the event to testify in a court of law?
11. As I remember the event, I feel that I travel back to the time when it happened, that I am a participant in it again, rather than an outside observer tied to the present.
12. As I remember the event, it comes to me in words or in pictures as a coherent story or episode and not as an isolated fact, observation, or scene.
13. If another witness to the event, whom you generally trusted, existed and told you a very different account of the event, to what extent could you be persuaded that your memory was wrong? (Scale: 1 = not at all; 3 = in some details; 5 = in some main points; 7 = completely; reverse scored as 8 – value given).
14. As I remember the event, I know its spatial layout.
15. This memory is significant for my life because it imparts an important message for me or represents an anchor, critical juncture, or turning point.
16. Since it happened, I have thought or talked about this event (Scale: 1 – not at all; 7 = as often as any event in my life)
17. I believe the event in my memory really occurred in the way I remember it and I have not imagined or fabricated anything that did not occur (Scale: 1 – 100 % imaginary; 7 = 100% real)

To the best of your knowledge, is the memory of an event that occurred *once* at one particular time and place, a summary or *merging* of many similar or related events, or for events that occurred over a fairly continuous *extended* period of time lasting more than a day? (Scale: 1 = once; 2 = merging; 3 = extended)

Source: Adapted from Rubin & Siegler, 2004, p. 929–930.

KEY POINTS

- Personality has been linked with associated differences in prospective memory, short-term working memory, and autobiographical memory for past life events.
- Supertraits such as extroversion and openness predict enhanced memory.
- People have better autobiographical memory if they are high in affect intensity, but the suppression of emotional expression is linked with poorer memory.

Field Dependence versus Field Independence

Field dependence versus field independence is a personality style that was first identified by **Herman Witkin**. It began when Witkin first became fascinated in the late 1930s with a phenomenon involving pilots. Pilots who would fly their planes into clouds sometimes discovered that the plane was flying upside down when it came out of the clouds! Witkin suggested that whether this occurred is largely a function of a cognitive–perceptual individual difference variable he and his associates called field dependence versus field independence (see Witkin, Dyk, Faterson, Goodenough, & Karp, 1962). Field-dependent people are described as being global in their perceptual and cognitive functioning, while field-independent people focus on specific details and are relatively uninfluenced by the surrounding context. Specifically, Witkin (1967) observed that "In a field-dependent mode of perception, the organization of the field as a whole dominates perceptions of its parts; an item within the field is experienced as fused with the organized ground. In a field-independent mode of perception, the person is able to perceive items as discrete from the organized field of which they are a part" (p. 103). According to Witkin et al. (1962), field-independent people have greater "psychological differentiation." While field-dependent people tend to rely on external cues in the environment to orient themselves, field-independent people are more likely to rely on internal sensations within themselves.

Witkin (1967) regarded field dependence versus independence as a continuous personality dimension rather than a type, with most people falling in the middle of the distribution. A 14-year study by Witkin, Goodenough, and Karp (1967) found strong evidence of the long-term stability of field dependence versus independence. Nevertheless, a subsequent study found that field-dependent people could become more field independent with training (Globerson, 1985).

Do you think it is more adaptive to be field dependent or independent? It is presumed that field independence is more adaptive than field dependence, but several authors, including Witkin himself, cautioned that the issue of which style is more adaptive depends greatly on task and situational requirements. Still, field independence is regarded as a more advanced form of development than field dependence (see Witkin, 1967), and most research outcomes show benefits for those who are field independent. For instance, a study of students from Hong Kong showed that field independence was associated with better academic learning in distance education courses (Luk, 1998). Also, adult students learning English as a second language tend to have higher levels of English language proficiency if they are field independent (Jamieson, 1992). A meta-analytic study also showed that field independent people perform better in facial recognition studies designed to tap the accuracy of eyewitness testimony (Shapiro & Penrod, 1986).

Consistent with the original phenomenon studied by Witkin, limited research on pilots suggests that field independence confers a performance advantage. One study involved having pilots fly in a helicopter simulator and track an airborne target. A strong correlation was found between perceptual style and tracking performance such that pilots higher in field independence were able to track the target for a substantially longer period

(Atchley, 1991). However, this study must be interpreted with caution because it included only four pilots.

How is this dimension measured? Witkin (1967) described three tests: (1) The Rod and Frame Test; (2) The Embedded Figures Test; and (3) The Body Adjustment Test. The Rod and Frame Test requires a participant to be in a dark room where he or she must adjust a luminous rod so that it is upright. The rod is located within a tilted luminous square frame. Field-independent people are able to adjust the rod without being influenced by the tilted frame; instead, they rely on their own body position.

The Embedded Figures Test requires the participant to identify a previously seen geometric figure that has been placed subsequently in a complex figure containing other shapes and figures. Field-independent people are able to parse the complex figure into separate components and locate the target figure. Field-dependent people have more difficulty because the simple figure has become fused with the overall organization of the complex figure.

Finally, the Body Adjustment Test involves placing the participant in a tilted room. Similar to the Rod and Frame Test, the participant must now keep his or her own body in a perfectly upright position without being unduly influenced by the perceptions and sensations emanating from the tilted room. Contemporary research in Ian Howard's Human Performance Lab at York University in Toronto is based on more sophisticated versions of the Body Adjustment Test. Howard has created a rotating sphere (cylinder) and two versions of "The Tumbling Room" to test static versus dynamic visual orientations while participants are strapped into a chair and experience the rotating sphere or tumbling room. Howard and associates have conducted this research as part of a project for NASA to provide insights into the perceptual experiences of astronauts while tumbling in weightlessness conditions. Astronauts often report experiencing visual reorientation illusions (e.g., seeing another crew member who is upside down can make other astronauts feel upside down even though they are right side up). Presumably, field-independent astronauts would be much less influenced and would adjust better to these illusions.

Witkin (1967) made the important observation that unlike many personality tests, the measures of field dependence versus independence are objective and lend themselves to precise measurements. Also, the tests of field independence are non-verbal. These attributes are noteworthy because by not relying on language proficiency, these tests facilitate cross-cultural comparative research. Some of this research is described below.

Research on field dependence–independence has focused primarily on the cognitive and interpersonal processes and factors associated with this dimension. Research by Pascual-Leone at York University in Toronto has shown that field dependence decreases as short-term memory improves (Pascual-Leone, 1979; Pascual-Leone & Goodman, 1979). A more recent experiment of working memory (short-term memory) confirmed that differences in field dependence versus independence can be traced to the visuospatial and executive components of working memory (Miyake, Witzki, & Emerson, 2001).

A study of children's behaviour while playing indicated that field-dependent children were more socially oriented than their field-independent counterparts.

As for the interpersonal aspects, research has linked field independence with introversion and field dependence with extroversion (Witkin, 1967). A study of children's behaviour while playing games showed that field-dependent children were more socially oriented and responsive to interpersonal cues than were their field-independent counterparts. Field-independent children were more task-oriented (Ruble & Nakamura, 1972). Although a gender difference was predicted, with girls being more field dependent, this pattern of findings was similar for boys and girls.

As noted earlier, there is a cultural component to field dependence versus independence. Research on cultural differences is explored in International Focus on Discovery 9.1.

Regarding the role of personality and information processing, terms such as **schema** and prototype have been advanced as trait-like cognitive structures that guide our attention and cognitive retention. A schema is a hypothesized, internal cognitive structure that contains knowledge about concepts, objects, events, and people, both other people and ourselves. We will return to the concept of schema in the form of self-schemas in the chapter on the self-concept (Chapter 11). A prototype is similar to a schema. It is an abstract, internal cognitive framework for a category that is used to determine the extent to which a new stimulus represents the category and warrants being included in the category (Rosch, 1970). Cantor and Mischel (1977) suggested that personality traits can serve as cognitive prototypes that influence the judgement of new information, especially in the context of forming personality assessments of other people. They showed that when people are given information about another person (in this case, whether the person is an introvert or extrovert), people will falsely recognize new trait information consistent with the trait category as information they have seen already (e.g., words reflecting introversion). In other words, the personality trait acted as a cognitive prototype and became activated such that new information was also deemed to be part of the category.

This section highlighted the fact that individual differences in emotional and cognitive factors are often linked with each other. The next section, on the need for cognition which is demonstrates that motivational and cognitive factors are often linked inextricably as well.

International Focus on Discovery 9.1 Field Dependence versus Field Independence from a Cultural Frame Perspective

So how do cultural factors come into play in field dependence versus independence? Herman Witkin and John Berry, at Queen's University in Ontario, have identified four antecedents that contribute to field dependence–independence (see Witkin & Berry, 1975). These four factors are (1) ecological and cultural adjustment; (2) social pressures for conformity; (3) parent–child relationships; and (4) biological factors (possible genetic differences that have arisen from adaptive selection). Regarding the first factor, Witkin and Berry (1975) contrasted children from hunter and gatherer societies with children raised in farming and pastoral societies. They confirmed their prediction that children from a hunting and gathering society would be more field independent, while those raised in a farming and pastoral society would be more field dependent. Dawson (1967) examined field independence–dependence in two contrasting tribal groups in Sierra Leone, Africa. The Temne are raised in a manner that involves severe pressure to conform and rigidly adhere to parental authority, while the Mende are raised by parents who emphasize personal responsibility and who are less likely to rely on physical punishment. As expected, Dawson confirmed that the Temne children were substantially higher in field dependence. These data accord with other research linking pressure to conform with field dependence. Witkin (1969) reported that Orthodox Jewish boys, relative to more secular Jewish boys, had higher levels of field dependence and he felt that this reflected their stronger social role obligations. Similarly, being raised by domineering parents tends to promote an orientation toward field dependence.

In related research, Berry (1966) predicted and confirmed that the Inuit (then known as Eskimos) from Baffin Island in northern Canada, relative to the Temne, would be much more field independent. This prediction was based on the fact that as part of adapting to their environment, the Eskimos must learn to make fine perceptual discriminations in snowy environments. Indeed, the role of visuospatial experience was confirmed in a recent study of the play behaviour of children from Quebec. This study found that the degree of current and previous spatial manipulation play behaviour predicted superior performance on the Embedded Figures Test (Robert & Heroux, 2004).

These initial findings have provided the impetus for intriguing new research on culture and cognition and related personality factors (for reviews, see Nisbett & Miyamoto, 2005; Norenzayan & Nisbett, 2000). This research suggests that the Western mentality is analytic and focused on the details of individual objects, while the East Asian mentality is holistic and is focused on the context or field (Norenzayan & Nisbett, 2000). A study by Ji from Queen's University and associates compared Caucasian American students and Taiwanese Chinese students from the University of Michigan (see Ji, Peng, & Nisbett, 2000). The study was based on their belief that there are culturally related habitual differences in how people attend to their environment. They suggested that North Americans have an analytic attentional style and North Americans are more likely to operate cognitively in a field-independent manner that involves the ability to identify and separate objects from their environment. In contrast, Chinese people have a holistic attentional style and are more likely to operate in a field-dependent manner as a result of being raised in a culture that emphasizes interrelatedness and connectedness to others. Ji et al. (2000) used the Rod and Frame Test and found that East Asians, relative to European Americans raised in North America, made more errors indicating that they had trouble ignoring the frame; that is, the whole field influenced them. They also confirmed that the students raised in North America made fewer errors on the Group Embedded Figures Test, confirming that they are higher in field independence. Kitayama et al. (2003) developed a test similar to the Rod and Frame Test known as the Framed-Line Test, and they confirmed that the East Asians were more field dependent. In addition, they have stronger memories of the contextual field as they seem to "cognitively bind" target objects to features of the field.

Masuda and Nisbett (2001) linked culture and cognitive style via "the fish tank experiment." Participants were shown eight scenes of a fish tank composed of a focal fish on a background of other fish, rocks, plants, coral, and so on. This research found that Japanese participants, relative to American participants, were much more influenced by environmental and contextual cues. Participants were required to describe the scene after a second showing. Japanese participants made over 60% more references to background features. Also, when subsequently shown 96 objects, half of which had been presented earlier, Japanese participants were substantially better at identifying a previously viewed object if it was displayed in its original scenario, suggesting that they closely link objects with the surrounding context (the other fish, coral, and rocks) (also see Nisbett & Masuda, 2003).

Similar differences should be detectable with other stimuli. Indeed, a search of past studies revealed a comparative study of Rorschach Inkblot responses by Chinese participants born in either China or in America (see Abel & Hsu, 1949). The China-born participants were more likely to provide responses that used the whole pattern of the inkblot, while those born in the United States were more likely to focus on individual inkblot details.

Important advances on personality, culture, and cognition have also resulted from insightful work on people with a **bicultural identity**; that is, they have two or more cultural identities. These people are also referred to as "biculturals." Research on this topic is vital given increasing trends toward multiculturalism and the increasing prevalence of bicultural people.

How is bicultural identity determined in concrete terms? Hong, Benet-Martinez, Chiu, and Morris (2003) studied 100 Chinese-born students attending the University of California at Berkeley. These students met three criteria. First, they had spent at least five years living in the United States and five years living in the People's Republic of China, Taiwan, Hong Kong, Macao, or Singapore (i.e., the residency requirement). Second, they were proficient in both English and Chinese. Finally, they indicated on a six-point Likert Scale that they had internalized both the American identity and the Chinese identity.

Research by Hong and associates with these students supports the **dynamic constructivist approach** to personality and cognition, and it does so in a way that is quite compatible with Kelly's focus on personal constructs (see Hong, Morris, Chiu, & Benet-Martinez, 2000; Hong et al., 2003). Each culture is seen as a cultural frame, and students report changes in how they see the world as a function of shifting between cultural settings (i.e., cultural frame switching). It is these changes that underscore the dynamic (as opposed to static) aspects of cognition and related aspects of personality. Hong and associates have shown experimentally that when biculturals are in situations where constructs are made *cognitively accessible* (via priming) and their *applicability* is made highly salient (by changing situational parameters), their perceptions and reactions also change in a way that reflects cultural differences. Specifically, activating the Chinese identity highlights a group agency construct, while activating the American identity highlights an individual agency construct.

Recent follow-up work by Benet-Martinez and colleagues has linked biculturalism with cognitive complexity (Benet-Martinez, Lee, and Leu, in press). They found that Chinese-American biculturals, relative to people with only one cultural identity, have substantially more complex and integrated descriptions when describing American and Chinese cultures. A key factor here is whether the bicultural people have conflicted culture identities (two identities that do not mesh well) or they have compatible cultural identities. The most complex descriptions were provided by participants with conflicted cultural identities. Presumably, these individuals have spent a great deal of time thinking about their respective cultures, and this rumination is reflected by more complex descriptions of the nature of each culture.

It is unfortunate that we cannot ask George Kelly for his interpretation of these emerging findings. Kelly might suggest that when people have two cultural identities, the identities represent different ends of a dichotomy and one identity is submerged when it is not activated by priming. One thing is most certain, however. Kelly would applaud the demonstration of how the activation of personal constructs influences how we see and interpret other stimuli. He would probably also caution us that there is great heterogeneity within the group of biculturals and it is important to focus on the constructs of each individual person.

As the originator of the concept, Witkin was the central figure who was responsible for much of the initial research on field dependence versus independence. After his death in 1979, there has been less empirical attention on this construct. However, it is clear that research on culture and cognition and related individual differences is now thriving and this is due largely to Witkin's work.

THE NEED FOR COGNITION

Research on the need for cognition can be traced back to an experimental investigation by Cohen, Stotland, and Wolfe (1955), who focused on the need for some people to understand and make reasonable their experiential world. Failure to achieve this goal results in tension and discomfort. The need for cognition was defined by Cacioppo and Petty (1982) as "the tendency for an individual to engage in and enjoy thinking" (p. 116).

The items from the abbreviated version of the Need for Cognition Scale (NCS; Cacioppo, Petty, & Kao, 1984) are shown in Table 9.3. Consider the statements, and ask yourself, "Why should I care about my need for cognition?" Two reasons are that higher NCS scores have predicted higher course grades (Sadowski & Gulgoz, 1996), and higher need for cognition in students has been linked with higher life satisfaction (Coutinho & Woolery, 2004). If you find that you are answering the items in a manner that suggests a low need for cognition, it might be time to re-examine your cognitive style! This might not be so easy to do, though, considering that the need for cognition is a personality variable that should reflect a long-term pattern. It seems that high need for cognition (NFC) is associated with the type of planful, self-regulated approach to learning and studying that has been found to facilitate learning and subsequent recall of academic material (Evans, Kirby, & Fabrigar, 2003). This research was conducted with students from Queen's University in Kingston, Ontario. Although you may not be able to change your trait level of NFC, you can learn and be counselled on how to develop this planful and thoughtful approach to learning school material.

Cacioppo and Petty (1982) developed the NCS in part due to their interest in the judgements people make when exposed to persuasive messages. Subsequent research confirmed that people high in NFC are particularly responsive to the quality of persuasive messages, and they are more likely to take this into account when evaluating a message designed to persuade them (Cacioppo, Petty, & Morris, 1983). The potential implications of this cognitive tendency were demonstrated in an intriguing study of the decisions made by legal jury members (Sommers & Kassin, 2001). Analyses showed that people with high NFC are much more likely to use information that has been deemed to be "inadmissible evidence" if they perceive that this information should be used in reaching a just verdict. In fact, they show signs of "a bias overcorrection" if they feel that important information has not been given enough weight because it was seen as inadmissible evidence. Subsequent research using a hypothetical murder case confirmed that high NFC participants were less likely to convict the suspect even when the prosecutor had a very strong case, presumably because these people wanted even more evidence (Leippe, Eisenstadt, Rauch, & Seib, 2004).

Research at the University of Waterloo in Ontario shows that people high in the need for cognition are less concerned and less ambivalent about holding personal attitudes that conflict with each other, and this is especially the case if it involves an issue that they are highly involved with (Thompson & Zanna, 1995). Other research indicates that people with high NFC tend to prefer complex as opposed to simple tasks, and they have higher levels of intelligence than people low in the need for cognition (Cacioppo & Petty, 1982).

Table 9.3 The Abbreviated Need for Cognition Scale

1. I would prefer complex to simple problems.
2. I like to have the responsibility of handling a situation that requires a lot of thinking.
3. Thinking is not my idea of fun.*
4. I would rather do something that requires little thought than something that is sure to challenge my thinking abilities.*
5. I try to anticipate and avoid situations where there is a likely chance I will have to think in depth about something.*
6. I find satisfaction in deliberating hard and for long hours.
7. I only think as hard as I have to.*
8. I prefer to think about small, daily projects to long-term ones.*
9. I like tasks that require little thought once I have learned them.*
10. The idea of relying on thought to make my way to the top appeals to me.
11. I really enjoy a task that involves coming up with new solutions to problems.
12. Learning new ways to think doesn't excite me very much.*
13. I prefer my life to be filled with puzzles that I must solve.
14. The notion of thinking abstractly is appealing to me.
15. I would prefer a task that is intellectual, difficult, and important to one that is somewhat important but does not require much thought.
16. I feel relief rather than satisfaction after completing a task that required a lot of mental effort.*
17. It's enough for me that something gets the job done; I don't care how or why it works.*
18. I usually end up deliberating about issues even when they do not affect me personally.

* These items require reverse-scoring.

Source: Cacioppo, Petty, & Kao, 1984, p. 307.

High NFC is also linked with trait curiosity (Olson, Camp, & Fuller, 1984) and a greater tendency to use the Internet for information searches (Das, Echambadi, McCardle, & Luckett, 2003).

Research on the personality correlates shows that high NFC is associated with elevated levels of general self-esteem and social self-esteem, and it is linked with less social anxiety and self-consciousness (Osberg, 1987). A five-factor analysis of need for cognition showed that elevated NCS scores are associated positively with traits of openness and conscientiousness (Sadowski & Cogburn, 1997), and, not surprisingly, the most robust correlation is with trait openness. There was also a negative correlation between neuroticism and NFC.

ATTRIBUTIONS

Attributions are the causal explanations we come up with in seeking to understand why an event occurred. Attributions are reflected when blame or responsibility is allocated. In the case of the 1999 animated movie *South Park: Bigger, Longer, & Uncut*, the song "Blame Canada" reflected the movie's plot of the United States blaming Canada for its difficulties and deciding to invade its neighbours to the north. Attributions are most likely when we experience negative events that are unexpected (Weiner, 1985).

Attributional Style

For our purposes, individual differences in the types of attributions that people make represent another very viable way of illustrating personality differences that are rooted in cognition. The term attributional style refers to an aspect of personality that involves the characteristic way that people tend to explain events. Explanatory style is another term for attributional style. People with a hostile attributional style tend to blame others for their misfortunes. In a classic review paper, Tennen and Affleck (1990) argued that an irrational tendency to externalize blame by blaming other people is one of the most robust indicators of psychopathology.

People with a hostile attributional style tend to blame others for their misfortunes.

Research on attribution and depression has been a predominant theme in the personality literature. Most previous research tested the validity of the reformulated attributional learned helplessness model of depression postulated by Abramson, Seligman, and Teasdale (1978), and the subsequent hopelessness of model of depression (Abramson, Metalsky, & Alloy, 1988). According to these models by Abramson and her colleagues, stable individual differences in attributional style or explanatory style are related differentially to depression. Abramson et al. (1978) postulated that depressed individuals are more likely than non-depressed people to attribute negative outcomes to internal, stable, and global causes (suggesting that chronic aspects of themselves are to blame). Conversely, depressed people are more likely than non-depressed people to attribute positive outcomes to external, unstable, and specific causes (suggesting that any credit is due to environmental events and do not reflect the self). Note that attributional style is considered a vulnerability factor (often referred to as a diathesis). **Lynn Abramson** and her colleagues indicated that this vulnerability is only activated when negative events have occurred and then attributions are made. Diathesis–stress models are discussed in more detail in the subsequent chapter on personality and health (Chapter 12).

Consider the attributional pattern of the depression-prone person who is about to take a test to get a driver's licence. The attribution patterns for success versus failure are shown in Figure 9.4. Success would mean not taking the credit and attributing the outcome to uncontrollable factors outside the self, while failure means self-blame for the driving candidate.

Although the primary focus has been on attribution and depression, research has also linked attributional style with academic performance in university students. Gibb and associates found that students who tend to show elements of the depressive attributional style (i.e., they attribute negative outcomes to internal and stable causes) tended to have

Figure 9.4 Self-Statements Reflecting the Depressive Attributional Style at the Driver's Licence Office

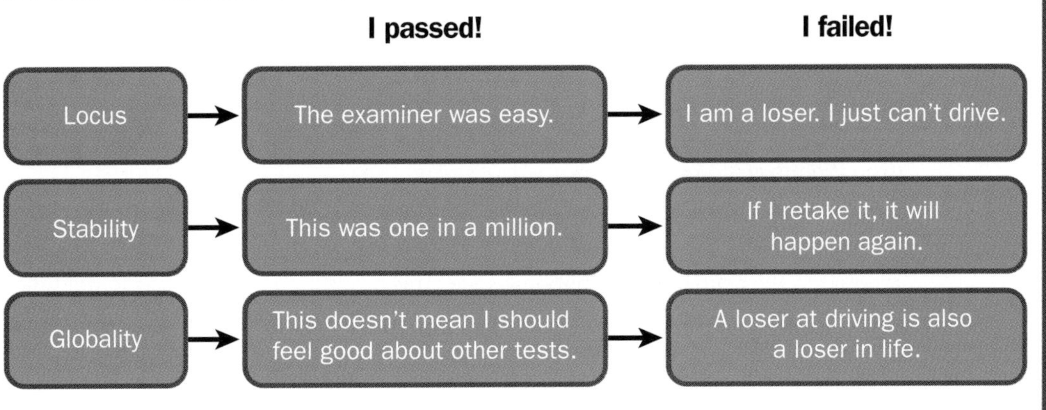

lower cumulative grades if they also had lower SAT (Scholastic Aptitude Test) scores (see Gibb, Lin Zhu, Alloy, & Abramson, 2002). In contrast, students who had lower SAT scores but attributed negative outcomes to external or unstable causes not reflecting themselves did not have lower grades. Thus, recognizing that limited capabilities are a reflection of the self tends to undermine performance.

Regarding the link between attribution and depression, Sweeney, Anderson, and Bailey (1986) conducted an extensive meta-analysis of 104 studies with 15,000 participants in total. They confirmed the expected pattern for both negative events and positive events. The findings held for attributions for both hypothetical and real events and for both mildly depressed students and clinically depressed patients. Sweeney et al. (1986) summarized their findings by noting that "a not-so-valuable addition to the literature would be further studies in which researchers simply examine whether attributional style is related to depression" (p. 987). Instead, they issued a call for new studies that clarify, explain, and expand upon existing findings.

One such study was conducted by Peterson and Vaidya (2001), who established that the link between attributional style and depression is mediated by a person's general expectancies; that is, the depression attributional style is linked with depression through a pessimistic outlook on life problems. This is in keeping with the theoretical views of Abramson et al. (1988), who suggested in their hopelessness model that a sense of helplessness becomes transformed into a sense of hopelessness when the person develops a condition known as **depressive predictive certainty**. That is, the person comes to believe that negative events are absolutely certain to occur and there is nothing they can do to avoid them.

Research on the developmental origins of attributional style confirms what we learned in Chapter 3; that is, multiple determinants contribute to individual differences. A negative attributional style reflects a complex array of factors that can include social learning and imitation of the maternal attributional style (Seligman et al., 1984), developing a pattern of self-blame in response to emotional maltreatment and other forms of negative parenting (Bruce et al., 2006; Gibb et al., 2001), and even genetic factors, as shown by a recent study of twins that found a moderate effect of genetic factors (Lau, Rijsdijk, & Eley, 2006). Previous research indicated that explanatory style was 50% heritable (see Schulman, Keith, & Seligman, 1993), but this study did not focus on identical twins reared apart. The heritability dropped to 25% when studying identical twins reared apart (Pedersen et al., 1991; Plomin et al., 1992).

The Penn Prevention Program led by Seligman has reported impressive results in the use of cognitive–behavioural techniques to encourage an optimistic explanatory style, as opposed to the depressive attributional style. This prevention program has found much lower rates of depression among children given the prevention, relative to a control group, and these results have been maintained and are even greater at a two-year follow-up (see Seligman, Reivich, Jaycox, & Gillham, 1995). What does this tell us? Certain cognitive styles associated with less risk for depression can be taught, and presumably this will apply to children who already have this heritable risk factor.

Unfortunately, one criticism of research on attributional style and depression is that it has paid little heed to possible cross-cultural differences in attributional style. The importance of considering this issue from a broad perspective that allows for variability in typical attributional tendencies is illustrated in International Focus on Discovery 9.2.

KEY POINTS

- People seek to explain unexpected negative events.
- People have typical and stable ways of explaining events and this is known as "attributional style" or "explanatory style."
- The depression-prone attributional style involves attributing negative events to internal, stable, and global causes reflecting perceived deficits in the self.
- Depressive attributional style is also linked with poorer performance.
- Attributional models of depression suggest that a sense of helplessness becomes hopelessness when a person is characterized by depressive predictive certainty; that is, negative future events are unavoidable and absolutely certain to occur.

International Focus on Discovery 9.2 Attributional Style across Cultures

One assumption that seems to guide research and theory on attributional style is that there is cultural invariance: the individual differences in attributional style are manifest similarly across cultures. The limited amount of evidence suggests otherwise. It seems that there are cultural differences in mean scores on the various attributional dimensions, and there is some evidence to indicate that the link between attributional style and depression also tends to vary across cultures. Research in this area is summarized below.

Some researchers have simply sought to establish whether the predictions derived from the attributional style model of depression are supported in specific countries. For instance, one investigation showed a pessimistic attributional style for both negative events and positive events was associated with depression in participants from Turkey (Aydin, & Aydin, 2001). Other studies have included two or more groups within the same study, and this has afforded a more meaningful test of possible group differences in how events are attributed. For instance, Nurmi (1992) compared the responses of Finnish and American students on the Attributional Style Questionnaire. Overall analyses confirmed the self-serving attribution bias exists in both countries. That is, positive events were more likely to be attributed to internal causes reflecting the self, and negative events were attributed to external causes outside the self. However, the strength of this bias varied according to nationality. American students were slightly more likely to attribute positive events to the self and they were slightly less likely to attribute negative events to the self. A similar pattern was reported by Kashima and Triandis (1986), who found that Japanese students made fewer self-serving attributions than their American counterparts. The self-serving bias may apply more broadly to North America because Fry and Ghosh (1980) found that Canadian children made more self-serving attributions than Asian-Indian participants.

A key factor is whether attributions are being made for negative events or positive events. A study of attributional style in Japanese undergraduates found that the usual link between attributional style and depression was not evident when making attributions for negative events, but there was a significant association when making attributions for positive events (Sakamoto & Kambara, 1998). Sakamoto and Kambara (1998) observed that the self-serving tendency is usually comparatively weaker in general in Japan than in the United States, but "in a society where many people are unassuming, as is the case in Japan, those with a self-enhancing attributional style may be more obvious and may more effectively foster their self-esteem" (p. 238).

Craig Anderson (1999) from the University of Missouri at Columbia examines attributions from a more differentiated perspective because he distinguishes between attributions for interpersonal events and non-interpersonal events (i.e., achievement outcomes). His comparative study of American students and Chinese students from Shanghai found that Chinese students, relative to American students, took more responsibility for both interpersonal and non-interpersonal failures. They also took less credit for interpersonal success. The Chinese students had significantly higher scores on both depression and loneliness (perhaps as a reflection of the attribution differences).

The most dramatic evidence thus far of cultural differences in attributional or explanatory style is a study that was conducted by Oettingen and Seligman (1990). They performed an analysis of newspaper accounts of the 1984 Winter Olympic Games. Comparisons were conducted of the accounts found in newspapers in East Berlin and West Berlin in Germany. Because East Berliners were confined inside the Berlin Wall, the researchers predicted a more depressive attributional style would be found among East Berliners.

Attributional accounts from newspaper articles were analyzed via the CAVE (Content Analysis of Verbatim Explanations) technique developed by Peterson, Luborsky, and Seligman (1983). This technique can be used to measure the attributions found in such sources as newspapers, diaries, and audiotapes of therapy sessions. Oettingen (1995) argued that the CAVE technique is well-suited to cross-cultural personality research because it can be applied in a similar fashion to all types of texts from various cultures and does not require the equivalent use of language.

The results of the CAVE analysis in this study are reproduced in Figure 9.5. Essentially, it was found with both composite scores (combining internal, stability, and globality indices) and with scores on the stability dimension for positive events that Western Berliners had a less depressogenic attributional style than did East Berliners.

This study is not without interpretive difficulties. We have to assume, for instance, that there were no related group differences in self-presentation and societal demands that may have influenced how the events were portrayed in the newspapers. Also, there is no basis for assuming that these same attributional tendencies found in newspaper reporters would extend to people other than sportswriters. Still, this study represents an interesting example of the apparent existence of cultural group differences in spontaneous attributions.

Oettingen and associates have also used the CAVE technique to examine the attributional statements in the writings from the religious versus secular domains of nineteenth-century Christian peasantry and in the writings of the nineteenth-century Russian Jewish culture (see Oettingen, 1995). It was hypothesized and subsequently confirmed that more optimism would be found in the religious written materials. Regarding Russian Jewish culture, Oettingen (1995) reasoned that the "religious written materials were expected to evidence an optimistic explanatory style, because the Jewish religion promises the arrival of the Messiah, and religion in general serves the function (among other things) of providing relief from a dismal earthly existence by instigating hope for salvation" (p. 213).

Before concluding this segment, it is important to acknowledge the very real difficulties associated with assessing attributions across cultures. Unintended sources of variability can come in two forms, and this can make it difficult to draw conclusions. First, most attributional measures involve presenting hypothetical events to respondents. To what extent are these hypothetical events meaningful for people from various cultures? A team of Canadian researchers showed appropriate sensitivity to this issue in their comparative study of attributional style in students from India versus Canada (see Higgins & Bhat, 2001). These investigators realized that certain hypothetical events on typical inventories and scales would have very low meaning in India, so events such as "You go out on a date and it goes badly" were changed to "Your engagement breaks off." An event such as "There is harmony in your family" was also used for the same reason. Because these authors tried to provide events that were equally meaningful for both groups, they could have more faith in the subsequent significant differences they found. These differences included a stronger self-serving bias among the students from India, and a greatest tendency for the students in India to make use of contextual cues. Unfortunately, other investigators have not been as sensitive to the need for respondents to make attributions for events that are equally meaningful across cultural groups.

Second, as alluded to in discussing the advantages of the CAVE technique, it is well-known that language cues can bias the attributions that people make (see Brown & Fish, 1986). It is important to evaluate attributional measures that have been translated into various languages to make sure that they are equivalent and that subtle differences in implied causality have not been introduced across measures.

Figure 9.5 Causal Statements in East and West Berlin Newspaper Reports

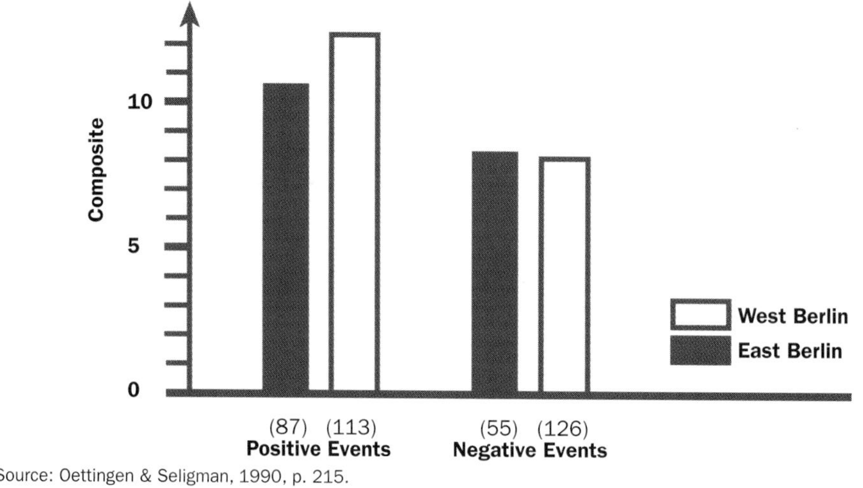

Source: Oettingen & Seligman, 1990, p. 215.

Attributional Complexity

The call for innovation that was issued by Sweeney et al. (1986) was answered by researchers interested in the attributional complexity construct. Attributional complexity is the tendency to make complex attributions to two or more causes when presented with an environmental outcome that requires explanation (Fletcher, Danilovics, Fernandez, Peterson, & Reeder, 1986). Research by Fletcher et al. (1986) has confirmed the existence of consistent individual differences in attributional complexity. Whereas certain individuals tend to make one or no attributions for life outcomes, other individuals tend to rely on complex causal schemata and perceive that the events experienced by themselves and others are due to a combination of factors.

The Attributional Complexity Scale (Fletcher et al., 1996) consists of seven subscales with four items each. The seven subscales and a representative sample item are shown in Table 9.4. The seven subscales are (1) motivation to explain behaviour; (2) preference for complex explanations; (3) presence of causal metacognition; (4) awareness of the causal importance of social interactions; (5) tendency to infer complex internal attributions; (6) tendency to infer complex external attributions; and (7) use of a temporal dimension.

Table 9.4 Dimensions of Attributional Complexity

Dimension	Sample Item
Motivational component	I really enjoy analyzing the reasons or causes for people's behaviour.
Preference for complex explanation	I have found that the causes for people's behaviours are usually complex rather than simple.
Presence of meta-cognition	I give little thought to how my thinking works in the process of understanding or explaining people's behaviours (reversed item).
The causal importance of social interactions	I believe that to understand a person you need to understand the people who that person has close contact with.
Inferring complex internal attributions	I have thought a lot about how the different parts of my personality influence other parts.
Inferring complex external attributions	When I try to explain other people's behaviour I concentrate on the person and don't worry too much about all the external factors that might be affecting them (reversed item).
Use of a temporal dimension	When I analyze a person's behaviour I often find the causes form a chain that goes back in time, sometimes for years.

Source: Scale names and items from Fletcher et al., 1986.

Attributionally complex people have been found to provide more accurate responses when given a challenging problem (Fletcher, Rosanowski, Rhodes, & Lange, 1992). Attributionally complex people, relative to people low in this attribute, also tend to seek more information and actually use more information in making their judgements (Murphy, 1994). And, consistent with the research linking need for cognition with jury decisions, research on attributional complexity and mock jury decisions shows that people low in attributional complexity are less likely to find someone guilty in the face of ambiguous evidence, and they are more likely to weigh external causes that may have influenced the perpetrator's behaviour (Pope & Meyer, 1999).

A focus on attributional complexity is a potentially important way of extending work on attribution and depression. Flett, Pliner, and Blankstein (1989) supported their contention that attributional processing and complexity variables should be incorporated into depression models by showing that individual differences in attributional complexity are related differentially to depression. In their first study, Flett et al. (1989) administered the Attributional Complexity Scale (ACS) and a measure of depression to 208 university students. It was found that depression was related to increased attributional complexity, both in total ACS scores and in ACS subscale measures of motivation, complex external explanations, and use of a temporal dimension. It was concluded that these findings might reflect a motivated attempt by depressed students to protect their already low self-esteem by invoking the discounting principle (Kelley, 1973). According to Kelley (1973), the perceived presence of two or more causes creates a situation of attributional uncertainty whereby it is difficult to determine whether any one cause is responsible for an outcome. Thus, the depressed person can try to avoid the hit to self-esteem that comes with the realization that he or she is solely responsible for a negative outcome by instead making complex attributions involving factors related to the self and to the environment.

Independently, Marsh and Weary (1989) administered the ACS and the Beck Depression Inventory to a sample of 564 students. Similarly, they found that mild and moderate depression in college students was associated with elevated levels of attributional complexity. A small but significant positive correlation between the ACS and depression in students was also reported by a team of researchers at Concordia University in Montreal (see Conway, Giannopoulos, Csank, & Mendelson, 1993).

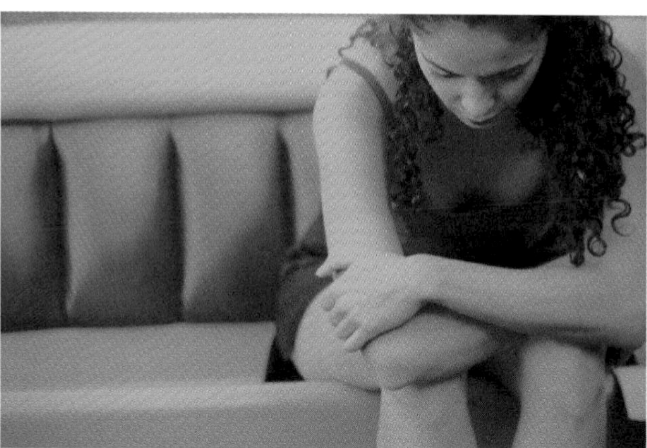

Research has linked mild and moderate depression to high attributional complexity, and extreme depression to low attributional complexity.

Further investigation suggests that elevated attributional complexity may hinder mild and moderate depression from escalating into very severe levels of depression. Marsh and Weary (1989) actually reported a curvilinear association; mild and moderate was associated with the highest ACS scores, but the lowest ACS scores in their sample were reported by the severely depressed and the non-depressed students. Likewise, a follow-up report by Flett and Hewitt (1990) confirmed in a sample of people suffering from extreme levels of clinical depression that severe depression is associated with low attributional complexity.

Marsh and Weary (1989) observed that these results are in keeping with a control motivation interpretation of attributional processing. It is believed that mildly and moderately depressed individuals are high in control motivation while non-depressed and severely depressed people are low in control motivation. Whereas the mildly depressed individual wishes to gain a sense of control and understanding over unexpected, negative events (i.e., has a need for cognition), the severely depressed person suffers from a lack of motivation due to a sense of learned helplessness over a perceived incontingency between actions and outcomes.

Research with alternative measures has confirmed that mild and moderate depression is linked with attributional complexity. For instance, Flett, Blankstein, and Holowaty (1990) used a measure created by Janoff-Bulman to illustrate a link between depression and complex attributions of blame to external factors and internal factors reflecting blaming one's behaviour and one's character (characterological self-blame).

The practical implications of these findings merit comment. Applied research on attribution focuses on interventions in the form of attributional retraining. That is, cognitive interventions try to change the way the person cognitively explains events. The results linking depression with attributions to internal and external causes suggest that individuals with adjustment problems do not simply suffer from a tendency to blame themselves for negative life situations. These individuals tend to attribute blame to a wide variety of factors. They internalize blame and see themselves as responsible, but at the same time, they also externalize blame and see other people and external circumstances as also responsible. Perhaps these people need to learn to stop this destructive pattern and stop playing "the blame game," but therapeutic efforts should also be focused on developing a more positive sense of self-esteem and personal control in these people.

KEY POINTS

- People vary in their attributional complexity, with some people more likely to make complex attributions to two or more causes when trying to explain why an event occurred.
- Mild and moderate depression is linked with higher attributional complexity, but extreme depression is associated with low attributional complexity.
- Marsh and Weary suggest that related differences in control motivation underscore the curvilinear association between attributional complexity and depression.

COGNITIVE RIGIDITY

Unfortunately, we have all probably had the misfortune of encountering people who are so rigid, both in terms of their cognitions and their behaviours, that it seems that they would not bend and be flexible even if their life depended on it. What do we know about these people?

Rigidity can be defined generally as an unwillingness to adapt by making even slight changes to one's thoughts or behaviours. The opposite of rigidity is cognitive flexibility. According to Martin, Anderson, and Thweatt (1998), cognitive flexibility consists of three elements: (1) a person's awareness in any situation that options and alternatives are available; (2) a willingness to be flexible and adapt to the situation; and (3) a sense of self-efficacy or self-confidence about the tendency to be flexible.

According to Schultz and Searleman (2002), individual differences in rigidity versus flexibility represent one of the longest standing areas of research in psychology. They provide evidence indicating that rigidity has been studied for over 100 years. In their review, they noted that there are disparate measures and definitions of rigidity, so this tends to make it more difficult to compare across studies.

Some insight into the nature of cognitive rigidity was obtained by an experiment conducted by Pally (1959). This experiment involved the manipulation of threat, and the dependent measure was the cognitive ability to change mental set on a cognitive problem-solving task. Pally found that experimental conditions associated with higher threat were associated with less cognitive flexibility. Threat may operate in two respects. The anxiety and distress usually engendered by stress may make people rely on already established cognitive patterns and styles. In addition, people may find that abandoning their usual cognitions and beliefs may simply add to an already high level of tension and sense of threat.

Consistent with the role of perceived threat, rigidity is associated with perceptions of low self-control (Reiter, 1976). Related research has found that rigid learners are higher in tenseness, compulsivity, and group dependency (Dean & Garabedian, 1981). Given that extreme perfectionists have been described as highly defensive individuals, it is perhaps not surprising that perfectionism has been linked with cognitive rigidity.

Ferrari and Mautz (1997) examined the correlations between the Multidimensional Perfectionism Scale (Hewitt & Flett, 1991, 2004) and the Schaie measures of psychomotor speed, attitudinal inflexibility, and motor-cognitive rigidity in a sample of college students. They found that both self-oriented and other-oriented perfectionism were associated with attitudinal inflexibility. Self-oriented perfectionism was also correlated with motor-cognitive rigidity.

Evidence exists for the long-term stability of cognitive rigidity. An eight-year longitudinal study of cognitive and behavioural rigidity found an exceptionally high level of stability in the test–retest reliability for a measure of cognitive rigidity (Schaie, Dutta, & Willis, 1991). This research was based on a measured developed by Schaie (1955), who conducted a factor analysis of eight measures of rigidity and found three distinct factors: (1) psychomotor speed; (2) personality–perceptual rigidity (low mental and attitudinal flexibility); and (3) motor–cognitive rigidity (difficulty in shifting attention and going on to a new activity). The Schaie et al. (1991) study described earlier found that there was a very high correlation between personality–perceptual rigidity and motor–cognitive rigidity ($r = .81$).

The excellent review paper by Schultz and Searleman (2002) that was described earlier lists a number of conclusions about rigidity of thought and behaviour based on a quantitative review of the literature. Their seven main findings are as follows:

1. There is a curvilinear association between age and rigidity. It seems that rigidity decreases between the ages of 5 to 18, and then levels of rigidity are fairly stable between the ages of 18 to 60. However, after the age of 60, there is a linear increase in rigidity.
2. There is a positive link between rigidity and authoritarianism, but the association between authoritarianism and rigidity becomes stronger during periods of stress.
3. There is a negative association between cognitive rigidity and intelligence.
4. No firm link has been established between rigidity and mental retardation.
5. Men are significantly higher in rigidity than are women.

6. As indicated, obsessive–compulsive symptoms are linked with rigidity.
7. People with schizophrenia, relative to non-schizophrenic controls and non-schizophrenic siblings, have higher levels of cognitive rigidity, and this significant difference becomes lower in magnitude but is still evident even when medication is provided.

And, finally, where does cognitive rigidity come from? An intriguing study that involved gathering measures of cognitive and behavioural rigidity from parents and their four-year-old children provided us with some clues. Blum (1959) found that there were salient individual differences in rigidity among children. It should be possible to detect these differences in temperament if theorists are correct in including a focus on individual differences in rigidity versus flexibility. More important, however, Blum (1959) also found significant positive correlations between rigidity in children and rigidity in both their mothers and fathers. Thus, there seems to be some evidence to indicate that rigidity runs in the family.

Summary

Chapter 9 provides an overview of personality and individual differences in cognition. The chapter begins by illustrating that there are widespread individual differences in such phenomena as eyewitness testimony, and the same stimulus can be perceived and recalled quite differently by different people.

These individual differences were interpreted within the context of the cognitive theories of personality outlined by George Kelly and Kurt Lewin. Both theorists emphasized the total experience and unity of the unique individual and how it is essential to acknowledge the role played by how the individual perceives events (i.e., the phenomenology of the individual).

Our detailed analysis of Kelly's theory focused on his view of each person as a scientist who developed personal constructs to make predictions about his or her world. These constructs have several properties, including two poles, and they may exist at different levels of cognitive awareness. Kelly outlined a series of corollaries to further elucidate his construct notion. Measures designed to assess constructs that involve repertory grids have been extremely popular in a variety of applied settings. A focus on personal constructs has also been introduced in clinical settings. Fixed role therapy is designed to help the client form new constructs.

Chapter 9 also included a description of Lewin's cognitive and field theory. Though known primarily for his contributions to social psychology, Lewin's personality theory clearly delineated the importance of both personal and situational factors, and this set the stage for viewing behaviour as joint interaction of the person and the environment. Lewin introduced the concepts of the personal field and a Gestalt focus on the entire life space of the individual. Overall, he was not a typical personality theorist in that he focused on the structure of personality and demonstrated little interest in the contents (traits and needs) that make up personality.

The second half of Chapter 9 illustrated various ways of representing personality and individual differences from a cognitive perspective. This segment began with an overview of research that links key personality traits with related differences in prospective memory (remembering things that still have to be done), short-term memory (working memory), and autobiographical memory (episodic memory of previous life events). Better memory is associated with traits such as extroversion and affect intensity.

Next, the association among perception, cognition, and personality was examined in a description of theory and research on field dependence versus independence, which is a dimension introduced by Witkin and his colleagues. Field-independent people are good at focusing their attention on specific details and ignoring contextual cues, and this typically confers several advantages. It was then established that individual differences in field dependence versus independence are a reflection of several factors, including cultural and ecological factors, family background, and the pressure to conform. In addition to individual differences in general cognitive style, there are also individual differences in people's specific beliefs. This was shown with respect to individual differences in attributional style and attributional complexity (the tendency to attribute events to two or more causes). The role of attributional style in depression was outlined. A tendency to attribute negative events to internal, stable, and global causes is associated with elevated levels of depression.

Chapter 9 concluded by showing that it is also possible to examine cognitively based differences in the motivation for cognition (the need for cognition) and the overall flexibility versus rigidity of their cognitive systems. People high in the need for cognition have a cognitive style that reflects their desire to understand their experiences. As for cognitive rigidity, it has been found that individual differences in cognitive rigidity are stable and long-lasting, and rigidity seems to be an anxiety-based response to feeling threatened. Cognitive rigidity measures have been found to reflect three types of rigidity: (1) psychomotor speed; (2) attitudinal rigidity; and (3) motor-cognitive rigidity (the shifting of attention).

A pervasive theme throughout this chapter is that individual differences have widespread implications in terms of other factors and processes. That is, cognitive differences are linked inextricably with related differences in emotion, motivation, and social behaviour, and these cognitive differences may involve both conscious and unconscious aspects.

Questions to Consider

1 George Kelly advocated a "person as scientist" model. This is supposed to apply to everyone. Do you agree with the view of people as scientists who form cognitions to make sense of their

world? Do all of the people in your life conform to this view, or do some people seem more focused on explaining things than others? Do you see this view of people as totally different from or complementary to a trait approach to the study of personality?

2 Review the description of the Role Construct Repertory Test. What are your personal constructs? What themes represent the main ways that you look at the world? Do you think your constructs are similar or very different from the constructs of other students or family members?

3 Recall that one study of life roles involved the roles of being a student, an employee, a child, a friend, and a romantic partner. Think how these different roles apply to you. Would you expect differences in how you present your personality (your mask) when in these various roles? What constructs might be activated when you are in one role (e.g., with your fellow students) but are not activated when you are in another role (e.g., with other friends who did not go to university or college)?

4 Review the concepts of prospective memory and autobiographical memory. What is your earliest autobiographical memory? What prospective memories do you have that apply to the next week in your life? Do you think that your mood state (emotion) plays a role in the encoding and ability to recall these memories?

5 Describe the differences between field dependence and field independence. Are you the type of person who remembers specific details, or are you a "big picture" person? Do you know people in your life who seem field dependent versus independent?

6 Consider your performance on the first test in this personality course. Did you meet your performance expectations? Illustrate your awareness of the attributional style concept by determining whether your test performance reflected internal or external causes, and stable or unstable causes.

7 In terms of your explanatory tendencies, do you favour complex attributions, or is one explanation sufficient? Look over the various attributional complexity subscales to see how you might respond to this inventory. To help resolve this issue, think about how you would explain the breakup of a famous couple. What is due to him, her, or both? And to what extent does it depend on the specific couple you selected?

8 On the basis of your reading and your personal experience, what personality factors seem to apply to people who are high in cognitive rigidity? Recall the gender difference in cognitive rigidity. Do you agree with the idea that men and women differ in their levels of cognitive rigidity?

Key Terms

actor–observer attribution bias, p. 346
attribution, p. 367
attributional complexity, p. 372
attributional style, p. 368
autobiographical memories , p. 358
bicultural identity, p. 365
choice corollary, p. 339
cognitive complexity, p. 343
commonality corollary, p. 340
construction corollary, p. 339
constructive alternativism, p. 338
constructivist psychology, p. 353
constructs, p. 336
depressive predictive certainty, p. 369
diathesis, p. 368
dichotomy corollary, p. 339
dynamic constructivist approach, p. 365
episodic memory, p. 358
experience corollary, p. 340
explanatory style, p. 368
familiarity hypothesis, p. 344
field dependence versus field independence, p. 361
fields, p. 356
fixed role therapy, p. 344
flashbulb memories, p. 358
force, p. 357
fragmentation corollary, p. 340
Gestalt, p. 354
individuality corollary, p. 339
Kelly's Fundamental Postulate, p. 339
life space, p. 355
modulation corollary, p. 340
organization corollary, p. 339
preverbal constructs, p. 336
prospective memory, p. 358
range corollary, p. 340
range of convenience, p. 340
schema, p. 363
self-serving attribution bias, p. 370
sociality corollary, p. 340
submerged constructs, p. 336
suspended constructs, p. 336

Key Theorists

Lynn Abramson, p. 368
Jack Adams-Webber, p. 343
George Kelly, p. 335
Kurt Lewin, p. 354
Herman Witkin, p. 361

chapter ten

INTERPERSONAL THEORIES AND INTERPERSONAL STYLES

- Harry Stack Sullivan
- The Interpersonal Dimensions
- The Interpersonal Circumplex
- The Machiavellian Personality
- The Authoritarian Personality
- Attachment Styles
- Personality in Dating and Marital Relationships

I never loved another person the way I loved myself.
—MAE WEST, US ACTRESS AND DRAMATIST

It is only when we no longer compulsively need someone that we can have a real relationship with them.
—ANTHONY STORR, BRITISH PSYCHIATRIST

Always remember there are two kinds of people in this world: those who come into a room and say "Well, here I am!" and those who come in and say "Ah, there you are!"
—FREDERICK L. COLLINS, AUTHOR AND HISTORIAN

Like the characters in the movie *When Harry Met Sally*, starring Meg Ryan and Billy Crystal, our personality and interpersonal styles can play a significant role in our interpersonal relationships.

THE 1989 COMEDY *When Harry Met Sally* explores whether a man and a woman can be "just good friends," and illustrates many important themes found in the literature on personality and interpersonal relationships. In the movie, Harry and Sally illustrate the differences between a person high in neuroticism (Harry) versus a person who is cheerful and optimistic (Sally).

Our interpersonal styles and how people view our interpersonal traits can play an enormous role in life outcomes and the quality of our relationships. In this chapter, we consider interpersonal styles and how these styles contribute to our interactions with people. Specifically, Chapter 10 examines personality from the perspective of interpersonal theories and interpersonal styles, including a description of personality traits that are rooted in how we relate to and respond to others. Interpersonal factors have already been examined in numerous places throughout this book, and this signifies the pervasive influence that interpersonal factors have on personality phenomena. For example, many psychological needs outlined by Murray (1938) have a clear interpersonal emphasis. Needs such as affiliation, aggression, and recognition all reflect our reliance on other people and the interpersonal expression of our needs. Similarly, a key element of Maslow's hierarchy is the belongingness and love stage, while Adler discussed developing social interest.

To further underscore the relevance of interpersonal factors, refer to Chapter 3, which discussed the role of interpersonal factors in personality development, including the role of parental styles and peer influences. And, of course, no overview of interpersonal aspects of personality would be complete without acknowledging the role of interpersonal factors in psychodynamic theories. While the Freudian concept of psychosexual conflict is most likely to come to mind, the neurotic tendencies of moving toward, against, and away from people identified by Horney (1950) are probably more relevant to our daily social interactions. Finally, this would probably be a good place to reiterate that the word "persona" in personality refers to the masks worn when we publicly express our personalities to other people. Thus, personality is highly interpersonal.

In Chapter 10, we explore personality from an interpersonal perspective in more detail. We begin with the influential theory of Harry Stack Sullivan and how this provided the theoretical impetus for research on interpersonal styles and the interpersonal circumplex. Next, we discuss the Machiavellian and authoritarian personalities and contemporary theory and research on social dominance orientation.

At present, a central theme in the theory and research is attachment styles as personality factors. Accordingly, attachment styles are described in detail, including research on attachment styles across cultures, and the importance of attachment styles in therapeutic contexts.

Finally, Chapter 10 concludes with a review of contemporary research on the link between personality factors and satisfaction with close relationships, including the link between personality traits and destructive behaviour in the form of relationship violence.

HARRY STACK SULLIVAN

The personality theory of **Harry Stack Sullivan** is not always found in personality texts. It should be, however, because of its elegance, its relevance, and its having served as the initial catalyst for important developments that are predominant today. Sullivan's views are summarized in his 1953 book *The Interpersonal Theory of Psychiatry*. His theory rests on the basic premise that relationships are not just critical—they are vital. It was noteworthy because it was arguably the first systematic personality theory that was entirely interpersonal. At the heart of Sullivan's theory is the notion that personality has meaning only in how people interact with each other, and in the initial stages of development, parents play a crucial role. He defined personality as "the relatively enduring pattern of recurrent interpersonal situations which characterize a human life" (Sullivan, 1953, p. xi).

Thus, Sullivan asserted that interpersonal relationships shape personality. Variability across people and across time is due to changing social situations and the people we encounter. He went so far as to suggest that a person has "as many personalities as he has interpersonal relations" (Sullivan, 1964, p. 221).

Generally speaking, Sullivan placed greater emphasis on communal, common experiences and felt that individuality was not as important as most people imagined. He felt that people often delude themselves about how unique they are. "the self-system from its nature—its communal environmental factors, organization, and functional activity—tends to escape influence by experience which is incongruous with its current organization and functional activity." (Sullivan, 1953, p. 190).

According to Sullivan, personality has meaning only in how people interact with each other, and in the early stages of personality development, parents play a crucial role.

Sullivan felt that we were shaped by communal social experiences. Personality development is experiential and reflects the social situations in which we find ourselves. However, the self-system is somewhat resistant to change, according to Sullivan's theorem of escape, which incorporates the notion that we resist experiences that evoke feelings of anxiety. For Sullivan, anxiety is central to the self, but this anxiety is also interpersonal in its nature and origin. He stated that:

> The self-system is derived wholly from the interpersonal aspects of the necessary environment of the human being; it is organized because of the extremely uncomfortable experience of anxiety; and it is organized in such a way as to avoid or minimize existent or foreseen anxiety. (Sullivan, 1953, p. 190)

Sullivan's work focused on the precursors and the manifestations of anxiety. He was particularly concerned with the way in which early social relationships set the stage for anxiety. He suggested that lack of love and caring from significant others results in insecurity and anxiety because the young child is totally dependent on significant others. The interpersonal aspects of anxiety are reflected in Sullivan's theorem of reciprocal emotions, which is the notion that other people influence our emotions, and we, in turn, influence their emotions as well (Sullivan, 1953).

Like Freud, Sullivan saw anxiety as playing a key motivational role, and he also followed the Freudian tradition by incorporating a series of developmental stages. Initially, the child is socialized through interactions with his or her parents, but as the child gets older, parents become less important as peers become more central. In keeping with some recent findings in developmental psychology, Sullivan maintained that it is not that parents become unimportant; rather, they simply become less important over time. The developmental theory continues by suggesting that the focus then shifts to the formation of intimate relationships in young adulthood.

Culture also plays an important role. Sullivan regarded the cultural context as a broad interpersonal situation. Culture is represented by social expectations and dictates that may be quite dissonant with the developing child's actual desires. For Sullivan, culture often serves as a trap stemming from unfortunate circumstances that hinder personal growth.

Sullivan's emphasis on key developmental stages could be a reflection of his own personal history while growing up in New York State. Sullivan was an only child and led a very isolated existence. He felt detached from his peers and suffered from profound loneliness. Given that he was an only child, his statements about birth order are particularly revealing. He commented that only children are almost always pampered and restrained from developing a realistic self-appraisal system, and this contributes to a lack of acceptance by one's peers. He suggested that this makes full personality development only a remote possibility (see Perry, 1982).

The notion that maladjustment reflects how earlier developmental stages were handled is interesting considering that there is evidence that Sullivan suffered from bouts of schizophrenia as a young man to the point of requiring hospitalization (see Perry, 1982). His views on anxiety and different components of the self reflect his own self-analysis and the insights that he gained into his own developmental influences and their subsequent manifestations.

The Developmental Epochs

Sullivan (1953) identified six developmental "epochs" or stages that must be worked through before becoming an adult. The six epochs were: (1) infancy; (2) childhood; (3) the juvenile era; (4) preadolescence; (5) early adolescence; and (6) late adolescence. Infancy stretches from birth to approximately 30 months of age, as speech begins to appear. Childhood then occurs and is focused on relationships with friends and companions. The juvenile era stretches throughout the elementary school years and sees the gradual focus of a need for intimacy with a similar other. Preadolescence continues this trend as there is a keen interest in issues involving the genitals, sexuality, and puberty, and establishing an intimate relationship with a member of the opposite sex. The process of moving from adolescence to late adolescence to adulthood is a process of transforming lust urges into a loving relationship with another person.

Initially, the need for security is evident in infancy and is a critical motivating factor that facilitates the developing self-system. Other prime motivating forces throughout development are the need for satisfaction and the need for intimacy. Various needs, primarily biological, create a tension that must be satisfied. The initial tension in the infant creates a corresponding tension in the mother that is experienced by the mother as a syndrome called **tenderness**. This tenderness compels the mother to satisfy the infant's needs. Sullivan also postulated that the experience of anxiety in the mother creates a maternal tension that ultimately induces anxiety in the infant.

The desire for tenderness, security, and intimacy all reflect our need to connect with other people. Sullivan (1953) also emphasized the infant's sense of powerlessness and an agentic need to develop a sense of power. The need for power results from success experiences and becoming increasingly aware of how expressing certain behaviours results in positive consequences.

Recall that the shift from infancy into childhood occurs at the age of 30 months, according to Sullivan (1953). Perry (1982) noted that no explicit reason was given for why this age was selected, but Sullivan was this age when his own personal situation changed. He was sent away to live with his maternal grandmother because his mother was quite ill. At this time, he developed a morbid fear of spiders after his grandmother put a spider at the top of the basement stairs due to superstitious beliefs. This could have contributed to his focus on how anxiety in maternal figures gets transmitted to young children.

For Sullivan, early social experiences shape the self-concept in keeping with the symbolic interactionism view (see Chapter 11). That is, we construct our self-images from the appraisals provided to us by significant others. Thus, a person who perceives that others are being hostile will incorporate this into a negative self-view, and a person who perceives that others are responding with respect and affection will incorporate this into a positive self-view.

KEY POINTS

- In Sullivan's interpersonal theory of psychiatry, personality reflects exposure to enduring interpersonal situations.
- We all have interpersonal needs reflecting desires for communion (tenderness) and personal capability (power).
- There are six developmental stages or epochs, from infancy to late adolescence.

The Good Me, the Bad Me, and the Not Me

One of Sullivan's central concepts is the distinctions among "the good me," "the bad me," and the "not me." He suggested that each child develops a sense of the good me versus the bad me as a result of the feedback received from and the pressures of the socialization process. Anxiety stems from the sense of the bad me that follows from negative reactions from significant others. The "not me" is the unknown and unintegrated aspects of ourselves that are often repressed. The "not me" component is believed to exist right from infancy.

Eventually, people try to protect themselves from their anxiety. They attempt to do this by not attending to and finding ways to avoid their bad me. How? People try to stop attending to their own bad me component by constructing their own self-system that includes the good me. A central purpose of the self-system is that it is designed to protect them from anxiety.

Sullivan, like Carl Rogers, was greatly concerned about a lack of congruity between the actual experiences and the person's perceptions of events. Like Rogers, he felt that this incongruity could only serve to accentuate maladaptive behaviour and ways of interacting.

Personifications

Sullivan's concept of personifications is a key aspect of his theory. It provided the early theoretical basis for contemporary research on the self and cognitive processing of interpersonal information and the self in relation to others. Personifications are mental prototypes (cognitive categories). These prototypes are similar to the concept of schemas. These mental prototypes are formed early in life and are used as a guide that assists us with the perception of current relationships. These personifications influence our perceptions of the self, others, and the self in relationships.

Contemporary research focuses on something quite similar known as relational schemas or relationship schemas (see Baldwin, 1992). Relationship schemas are also hypothesized cognitive structures that guide perception and cognition. Relationship schemas, once activated, have been associated with changes in self-evaluation and levels of social anxiety.

Sullivan (1953) suggested differences between personifications may account for the profound disagreements between people when asked to report on the same event. This would occur if differences in their personifications led them to attend to and remember different types of information.

Keep in mind that, first and foremost, Sullivan was a psychiatrist and his was a theory of interpersonal psychiatry. Accordingly, he discussed mental illness at length; mental disorder results in situations that are simply not relevant to and understandable through our personifications. Sullivan further suggested that paranoid schizophrenics experience their symptoms in part because their "not me" component has become personified or if they are extremely fearful, they have developed personifications of evil creatures. The focus of interpersonal therapy is on alleviating problematic relationships and on ways to cognitively view these relationships.

Evaluation of Sullivan's Theory

When evaluating Sullivan, we must keep in mind his role as a catalyst. As a by-product of Sullivan's interpersonal theory, other researchers began to focus on interpersonal factors and processes. Leading theorists in this area include Leary, Kiesler, Wiggins, and Benjamin. Sullivan deserves extensive accolades by being among the first to emphasize the importance of considering personality as intertwined with social situations. His focus on the fundamental needs for power and needs for tenderness and intimacy also set the stage for subsequent work on agency and communion. This work is described in the next section.

Although Sullivan made extensive contributions, his overall contribution has been limited because many of his tenets are quite abstract and difficult to test via empirical research. In this sense, he closely resembles earlier psychoanalytic theorists who also had provocative ideas that were very difficult to operationalize and investigate. As a result, there is little research that directly tests aspects of his theory. Still, this criticism is probably overestimated because Sullivan's work provided the general impetus for research on the effects of social situations on people and for research on themes involving agency and communion. Sullivan may also be criticized like other psychoanalysts with a stage theory for failing to extend it throughout adulthood and the life cycle.

Another issue that must be raised is whether Sullivan's theory is overextended because of its purely interpersonal emphasis. According to Sullivan, all motives, thoughts, and images reflect interpersonal processes and interpersonal situations. While interpersonal influences have a pervasive influence, it is hard to accept, for instance, that all of our thoughts stem from interpersonal factors. This was illustrated by research testing Sullivan's views of anxiety. It was found that social relations do contribute to anxiety, but anxiety also reflects non-social factors and anxiety is not exclusively interpersonal (see Ingraham & Wright, 1987).

KEY POINTS

- Sullivan postulated the good me, the bad me, and the not me. The bad me contributes to anxiety.
- Personifications (mental prototypes) are cognitive categories that influence our perceptions of the self in relation to others.
- Sullivan contributed to the field by making it impossible for us to ignore the interpersonal roots of personality. However, aspects of his theory were untestable, and his developmental theory was limited.

THE INTERPERSONAL DIMENSIONS

Other significant contributions were made by **Timothy Leary** and his colleagues. (Leary later became well-known for his advocacy of hallucinatory drugs.) Leary (1957) tried to incorporate Sullivan's views on interpersonal differences into his work. He also derived many of his theoretical concepts from witnessing how patients interacted in group therapy sessions. He theorized that every interpersonal behaviour could be interpreted with respect to two primary axes or dimensions representing affiliation versus hostility, and power versus submission. He provided a diagram of how two orthogonal interpersonal dimensions (dominance versus submission, hate versus love) could form to provide a rudimentary circumplex (see Laforge, 1985; Wiggins, 1996).

Leary also used his theory as a springboard for arguing that two people have a reciprocal influence on each other. This concept was elaborated by Carson (1969), who is credited with introducing the complementarity principle. This is the notion that the specific type of interpersonal behaviour expressed by one person will elicit a corresponding or supplementary behaviour from another person, similar to opposite poles on the circumplex dimensions. For instance, if one person exhibits a dominant behaviour, their partner is hypothesized to respond with a submissive behaviour. While general evidence of complementarity has been found (see Kiesler, 1983), it depends on the specific behaviour expressed. Rather than eliciting a passive and submissive response, hostility often elicits hostility, and as shown by Widom (1989), violence begets violence.

Agency versus Communion

Another influential theoretical statement was formally introduced by **David Bakan** from York University in Toronto. Bakan (1966) followed Sullivan's lead by positing two meta-orientations known as agency and communion, which formed the basis for subsequent work (see Wiggins, 1991). Agency and communion have been described as "axes around which the social world revolves" (Wiggins & Trobst, 1991, p. 659). Agency refers to an achievement orientation and the need to have an instrumental impact on outcomes. High agency reflects the drive to be dominant and establish status, while low agency reflects passivity, weakness, and submission. A high degree of agency characterizes someone who is independent and autonomous. In contrast, communion involves connecting with others and establishing interdependencies. Elevated communion reflects nurturance, warmth, solidarity, and union with other people, while low communion involves dissociation, remoteness, and perhaps coldness.

Personal adjustment stems from having a healthy balance of the agency and communion orientations. An excessive preoccupation with either agency (e.g., workaholism) or communion (e.g., being overly dependent on others) can be a recipe for disaster. This has been demonstrated by the work of Vicki Helgeson (Helgeson & Fritz, 1999, 2000). Excessive agency is referred to as **unmitigated agency**. It has been described as a focus on self to the exclusion of others. Unmitigated agency is assessed by socially undesirable forms of instrumental, masculine traits as assessed by items from the Extended Personal Attributes Scale (Spence, Helmreich, & Holahan, 1979). This cluster of traits includes such attributes as arrogant, boastful, cynical, dictatorial, egotistical, greedy, hostile, and self-promoting.

Unmitigated communion is a focus on others to the exclusion of the self (Helgeson & Fritz, 2000). On Helgeson's measure, unmitigated communion is tapped by such items as "I always place the needs of others ahead of my own." It's almost as if people high in unmitigated communion are interpersonal martyrs in the service of other people.

What has research told us thus far about unmitigated agency and communion? Both unmitigated agency and communion predict low social support, low help-seeking, and poor health behaviours and outcomes (Helgeson & Fritz, 2000). In addition, unmitigated communion is linked consistently with psychological distress, while a more balanced and less extreme form of communion is not (see Helgeson & Fritz, 2000).

THE INTERPERSONAL CIRCUMPLEX

Wiggins (1991) regarded agency and communion as central to the main dimensions of the interpersonal circumplex. Agency involves the sense of power and mastery inherent in dominant interpersonal behaviour. Positive communion is reflected by a high degree of interpersonal warmth. The relevance of these interpersonal tendencies in a model known as the interpersonal circumplex is outlined in Figure 10.1.

Data tend to show a **circumplex** configuration when the variables are organized in a circle, or perhaps a diamond shape. The most robust correlations are found near the diagonal of the circumplex. As the distance gets farther from the diagonal, the correlation coefficients decrease steadily and systematically until they reach a point where they start to increase systematically. Adjacent variables in the circumplex tend to be highly correlated, while two variables that are distant from each other in the circumplex can be negatively correlated. Orthogonal variables at 90 degrees from each other tend to be uncorrelated.

Circumplex models are especially appropriate when the variables are evenly distributed around or about the circumference of a two-dimensional plot. The interpersonal circumplex has two major dimensions. The first one involves themes of love, warmth, and nurturance, while the second dimension involves themes of power and dominance. The horizontal axis or dimension is represented by cold and quarrelsome at one end or pole versus warm and agreeable at the other end. The vertical axis or dimension reflects being dominant and ambitious at one end or pole versus lazy and submissive at the other end. Note that these two dimensions resemble the distinction made in the parenting literature between parental control (dominance) and parental warmth and supportiveness.

The interpersonal circumplex is further divided into eight major octants. These octants are located off the main dimensions, and they represent blends of varying degrees of the nurturance and dominance dimensions.

Historically, the interpersonal circumplex has been assessed by two measures. The Interpersonal Adjective Scales developed by Wiggins and Trapnell consist of 124 items with 64 items measuring the eight octants of the circumplex. Extensive psychometric evidence has confirmed that these adjective scales do indeed form a meaningful interpersonal circumplex involving the dominance and warmth axis. The eight octants of the circumplex are shown in Figure 10.1. The eight octants are each represented by two letters, signifying that an octant is a blend of two underlying coordinates. The eight octants beginning at the top and moving clockwise are ambitious–dominant, gregarious–extroverted, warm–agreeable, unassuming–ingenuous, lazy–submissive, aloof–introverted, cold–quarrelsome, and arrogant–calculating.

Figure 10.1 The Interpersonal Circumplex

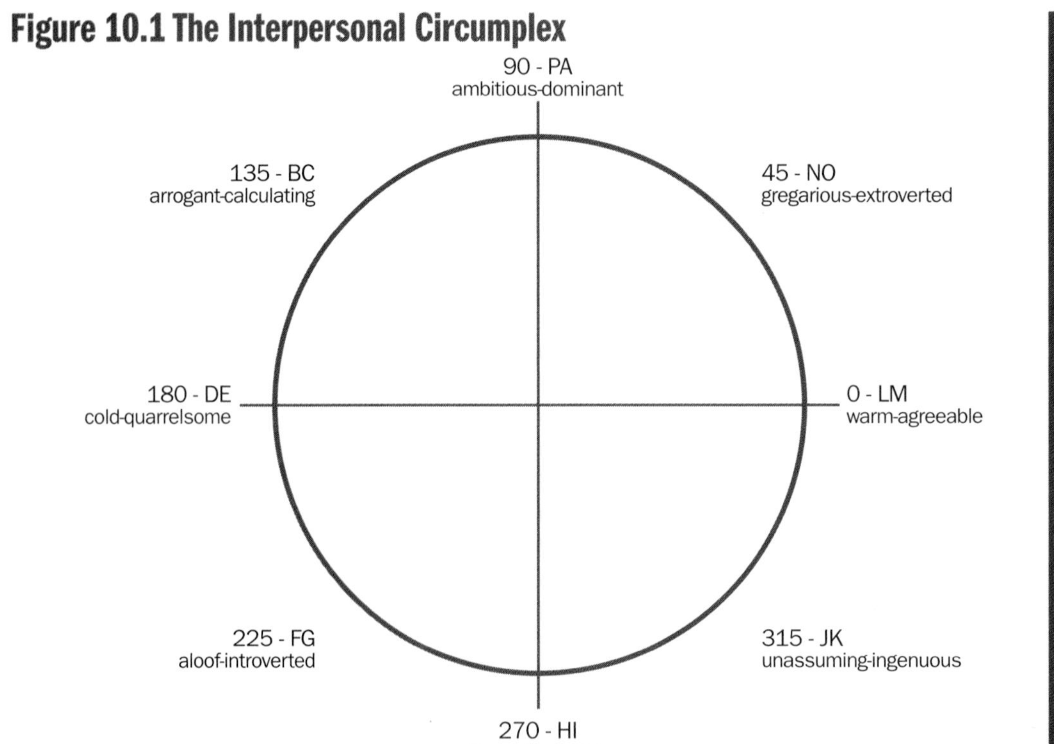

Source: Retrieved and adapted from http://www.interpersonalcircle.com/overview.html. Based on Kiesler, 1983.

The circumplex works such that a respondent gets a score for each of the eight dimensions. Each interpersonal style is assessed and represented by a line that is known as the vector length. The length of the line represents the intensity with which the prototypical octant is expressed. Longer lines emanating from the middle indicate a more intense interpersonal style. If the dimension is not very salient and distinctive for this individual, he or she would get a score that is closer to the middle of the circumplex. That is, if all eight interpersonal styles were not that relevant, the person's scores would be clustered toward the middle of the circumplex, as if trying to hit the bull's eye on a dartboard. If a dimension is highly relevant and very distinctive for a person, then he or she would receive a score that is in the direction of the outside perimeter of the circumplex. To reiterate, then, the farther the score is from the middle of the circumplex, the more central this interpersonal style is to a person's personality. It is also an interpersonal style that is more intense as well as more rigid and inflexible. In addition to scores for the eight octants, a statistical formula can be used to assess the person's levels on the main dimensions of dominance and warmth (sometimes referred to as "love").

The other primary circumplex measure is derived from the Inventory of Interpersonal Problems (IIP) created by Horowitz et al. (1988). The IIP was based on the interpersonal problems that were related to Horowitz by psychiatric patients receiving treatment. Alden, Wiggins, and Pincus (1990) isolated a 64-item subset from the IIP and showed that these items representing interpersonal problems also formed a circumplex structure. The first octant is located at 0 degrees and represents people who are overly nurturant. This octant assesses the tendency to try too hard to please others, as well as being too trusting, generous, and caring. Representative sample items are shown in Table 10.1.

Table 10.1 The Interpersonal Circumplex Octants from the Inventory of Interpersonal Problems

Octant	Description	Representative Item
PA	Domineering	I try to change other people too much.
BC	Vindictive	I fight with other people too much.
DE	Cold	I keep other people at a distance too much.
FG	Socially avoidant	It is hard for me to socialize with other people
HI	Non-assertive	It is hard for me to be assertive with another person.
JK	Exploitable	I let other people take advantage of me too much.
LM	Overly nurturant	I put other people's needs before my own too much.
NO	Intrusive	It's hard for me to stay out of other people's business.

Source: Alden et al., 1990.

The intrusive octant is located at 45 degrees. It represents people who are inappropriately self-disclosing and attention seeking.

The domineering octant is at 90 degrees. These people are too controlling and manipulative and are always trying to change others.

Sample items from the Interpersonal Adjective Scales are shown in Table 10.2 to illustrate the eight interpersonal styles represented by the eight octants of the circumplex.

The vindictive octant is located at 135 degrees. This reflects problems in trusting people and being suspicious and aggressive toward others.

The cold octant is at 180 degrees. People with this difficulty, not surprisingly, are unable to express affection and feel love toward other people. They may also have chronic difficulties getting along with and forgiving other people.

The socially avoidant octant is located at 225 degrees. These people suffer from profound feelings of shyness and social anxiety. They are easily embarrassed in the presence of other people. As a result, they tend to have extensive problems initiating social contact and expressing their feelings.

Table 10.2 Sample Items for the Interpersonal Circumplex from the Interpersonal Adjective Scales

Octant	Description	Sample Adjectives
PA	Domineering	Assertive, firm, forceful, self-assured
BC	Vindictive	Tricky, calculating, wily, cunning, crafty
DE	Cold	Ruthless, hardhearted, cruel, unsympathetic
FG	Socially avoidant	Introverted, unneighbourly, distant, unsociable
HI	Non-assertive	Timid, meek, unaggressive, unauthoritative
JK	Exploitable	Unargumentative, undemanding, unsly, uncalculating
LM	Overly nurturant	Kind, tender, soft-hearted, sympathetic
NO	Intrusive	Enthusiastic, extroverted, cheerful, outgoing

The non-assertive octant is located at 270 degrees. These people have a great inability to stick up for themselves and be assertive when it is needed. They feel great uneasiness when they are in authoritative roles that involve directing other people.

Finally, the exploitable octant is located at 315 degrees. This applies to a person who has exceptional difficulty in feeling and expressing anger out of fear that other people will be offended. These people have a style of being gullible and are highly susceptible to being taken advantage of by others.

Research indicates that the circumplex measures are linked meaningfully with other self-report personality scales, and the hypothesized circular structure of the circumplex is evident (e.g., Wiggins & Broughton, 1985). Perhaps the most serious criticism of circumplex measures was mounted by Jackson and Helmes (1979), who purported that the circumplex items were contaminated with social desirability response bias. These investigators showed that a measure of social desirability was indeed highly associated with the primary dimension assessing warmth. This criticism was addressed effectively by another team of Canadian researchers who showed that the interpersonal circumplex could still be identified when the variables were represented by counts of actual interpersonal behaviours (see Gifford and O'Connor, 1987). Thus, the interpersonal circumplex could be recovered and identified solely through interpersonal actions that are not influenced by response bias.

The interpersonal circumplex has many potential uses and applications. It can be used idiographically to assess the interpersonal style of a particular individual; this makes the circumplex highly useful in assessing people with clinical dysfunction. Another common use is to include circumplex measures in nomothetic research designed to examine the nature of other personality constructs when assessed in cross-sectional research with a large sample of people. For instance, use of the circumplex revealed that the attachment dimensions are "well represented in interpersonal space," with anxiety and avoidance falling in the hostile–submissiveness area of the circumplex (Gallo, Smith, & Ruiz, 2003). Pincus and Gurtman (1995) used the interpersonal circumplex to show that the content of dependency measures is quite different, even though the dependency measures are often used as if they are interchangeable. Various dependency measures were analyzed for their association with the traits of the five-factor model and the interpersonal circumplex. Three quite distinct forms of dependency were identified: (1) submissive dependency (yielding and compliant); (2) exploitable dependency (highly suggestible and gullible); and (3) love dependency (highly affiliative and needing to stay close to others). These results highlighted the great complexity of the dependency construct, in addition to the aforementioned differences in what is assessed across the various dependencies.

Research has used interpersonal circumplex analyses to gain further insight into the perfectionism dimensions assessed by the Multidimensional Perfectionism Scale (Hewitt & Flett, 1991, 2004). Hill, Zrull, and Turlington (1997) found that other-oriented perfectionism in men and women was associated with being domineering, mistrustful, and socially isolated. Socially prescribed perfectionism in men had similar correlates, but in women it was associated with a diverse array of interpersonal problems. Additional research in our laboratory has focused on distinguishing other-oriented and socially prescribed perfectionism. Evidence for the construct validity of socially prescribed perfectionism and other-oriented perfectionism was found in that socially prescribed perfectionists had an interpersonal style suggesting high dependency. In contrast, other-oriented perfectionism, particularly in men, was associated with dominance and hostility (see Habke & Flynn, 2002).

In addition to using the interpersonal circumplex to assess a specific individual or a group of people, it may also be used to evaluate situational contexts. Recently, Gallo, Smith, and Cox (2006) employed the interpersonal circumplex in a highly novel way. People with varying levels of socioeconomic status (SES) described their living environments by rating them on another circumplex measure known as the Impact Message Inventory, Circumplex Version (Kiesler, Schmidt, & Wagner, 1997). This circumplex measure is based on interpersonal messages evoked in social interactions (e.g., feeling bossed around by others, feeling that others are friendly). This study found that people with lower SES characterized their environments as high in hostility and interpersonal dominance and low in friendliness. Also, perceiving the environment as hostile accounted, in part, for the poorer health status of those with lower SES. For our purposes, though, the main point is that interpersonal circumplex can also be used to illustrate perceived social environments.

Clearly, the interpersonal circumplex has many potential applications. It has even been used to evaluate the personalities of popular rock musicians (see Dyce & O'Connor, 1994). The findings closely meshed with stereotypic descriptions of "bad boy rockers" such as the Gallagher brothers from Oasis or J. D. Fortune from the reconstituted group INXS. That is, the interpersonal circumplex results showed that the rock musicians were extroverted, arrogant, and dominant. Perhaps these characteristics are part of the interpersonal mask worn by someone who hopes to make it in a very competitive and potentially lucrative business.

KEY POINTS

- The interpersonal circumplex is a circle derived from the degree of intercorrelations among different interpersonal styles.
- Love and warmth versus hostility, and dominance versus submissiveness are the two axes at the core of the circumplex.
- Circumplex scores are represented by vector lengths. Longer vectors (lines) from the centre of the circle indicate a more rigid personality style.
- The circumplex can be used to measure individuals, samples of participants, or situations.

THE MACHIAVELLIAN PERSONALITY

Much of the early literature on the interpersonal aspects of personality focused on two personality constructs: Machiavellianism and authoritarianism.

Machiavellianism is a tough-minded orientation that it is acceptable to take advantage of others and use ingratiation for personal gain because, after all, it is a "dog eat dog world" (Christie & Geis, 1970). The concept was named after Niccolo Machiavelli, the Italian philosopher who espoused the benefits of manipulating others and competing against them for personal gain. His classic book *The Prince* outlines many of his views and how this approach can be used for benefit in the political sphere.

People high in this construct would have an interpersonal style focused on their willingness to deceive and manipulate others. Cynical attitudes are at the core of this construct. Can you think of a well-known Machiavellian? One person who comes to mind is Richard Hatch, who won on the first season of the reality TV show *Survivor*. Hatch won the contest by establishing a coalition with three other players. This coalition voted less organized players off the island. Once it was down to four players, Hatch then engaged in deceitfulness and manipulation to win the competition (only to be put in prison in 2006 for tax evasion).

Hatch was a corporate trainer who had been called many unflattering things during the game, including a liar, a villain, and a snake. Nevertheless, he always seemed one or two steps ahead of his competition (see Lance, 2000). In fact, he remarked on television to David Letterman that he started "playing the game" months before anyone else on the island. In response to one of the other players suggesting that they were a family, Hatch remarked, "This is a game of survivor... Camaraderie schmraderie." Hatch stated that:

> The first hour on the island I stepped into my strategy and thought, I'm going to focus on how to establish an alliance with four people early on. I spend a lot of time thinking about who people are and why they interact the way they do, and I didn't want to just hurt people's feelings or do this and toss that one out. I wanted this to be planned and I wanted it to be based on what I needed to do to win the game.

In short, Machiavellians keep "their eye on the prize," and they often have the skill and opportunity to make things work out according to their dictates and desires.

The ability to manipulate others is also central to Machiavellianism. When in face-to-face situations, Machiavellians "manipulate more, win more, are persuaded less, [and] persuade others more" (Christie & Geis, 1970, p. 312). Machiavellians have been described as cold, domineering, deceitful, suspicious, practical, and exploitive (McHoskey, Worzel, & Szyrato, 1998). Both men and women can be Machiavellian, but gender differences may exist in how Machiavellianism is expressed. Braginsky (1970) suggested that Machiavellian men will influence others through aggressive tactics, while Machiavellian women will influence others by altering their self-presentation. However, one of the few studies to test this prediction about self-presentation found that both women and men high in Machiavellianism were elevated in perfectionistic self-presentation (Sherry, Hewitt, Besser, Flett, & Klein, 2006).

Richard Hatch, winner of the first season of *Survivor*, exhibited Machiavellian personality constructs such as being highly competitive and manipulating others for personal gain.

Sherry et al. (2006) established that some of the cynical hostility of Machiavellians is a reflection of their perception that perfectionistic demands have been imposed on them (socially prescribed perfectionism). Thus, Machiavellianism can be regarded as an effort "to assert influence over a hostile environment" (Mudrack, 1990, p. 125) and to combat the belief that resources are controlled by hostile, powerful others who are trying to shape their lives. Machiavellians are likely to engage in perfectionistic forms of self-presentation to the extent that they perceive the presence of socially prescribed perfectionism (Sherry et al., 2006).

The standard measure of Machiavellianism is Christie's MACH-IV scale. This 20-item self-report inventory has items such as "It is safest to assume that all people have a vicious streak and it will come out when they are given a chance," "It is wise to flatter important people," and "The best way to handle people is to tell them what they want to hear." Geis and Christie (1970) tested the scale by conducting experiments that compared high and low Machiavellians (Machs). For instance, it was shown in a situation that involved bargaining over sharing resources that high Machs were able to convince other participants to let them keep more than their fair share of money made available to them. The authors suggested that high Machs are particularly effective when they can have face-to-face interactions with other people.

What do we know about Machiavellianism? This construct is indeed highly correlated with cynicism and hypercompetitiveness (Ryckman, Thornton, & Butler, 1994). It is also linked with alienation and anti-social behaviour, and it is correlated negatively with Adler's concept of social interest (McHoskey, 1999). Tests of the five-factor correlates indicate that Machiavellianism is associated primarily with low agreeableness (Lee & Ashton, 2005). Machiavellianism is also strongly negatively correlated with the HEXACO honesty–humility factor (Lee & Ashton, 2005). Circumplex analyses have also demonstrated that the constructs of Machiavellianism and low trust are related yet distinguishable. Machiavellianism is distinguished by a more extreme interpersonal style involving extreme vindictiveness and coldness. That is, Machiavellianism was linked with IAS-R adjectives such as calculating, crafty, ruthless, and unsympathetic (see Gurtman, 1992).

Paulhus and associates have studied Machiavellianism as one third of what they refer to as the **dark triad**: Machiavellianism, narcissism, and psychopathy (Paulhus & Williams, 2002). Narcissism and psychopathy are considered in more detail in Chapter 13. Paulhus and Williams (2002) reported that the three constructs are substantially intercorrelated and all are related to disagreeableness; but Machiavellianism is unique because people high in this trait seem to lack the self-enhancement and self-inflation of narcissists and psychopaths. A general characteristic that distinguished Machiavellianism from these other constructs is that Machiavellians do not suffer from maladjustment and psychiatric difficulties (see Skinner, 1982).

A study of 39 American presidents found that Machiavellianism was linked with higher ratings of charismatic leadership and presidential performance (Deluga, 2001). Machiavellianism scores were based on the pooled responses of U.S. presidents' scores on the MACH-IV as determined by three independent raters. The three presidents with the highest MACH-IV scores were Franklin Delano Roosevelt, Martin van Buren, and Richard Nixon. Roosevelt, with the highest rating, was seen as charming, engaging, and interested in people, but with a devious nature. The presidents with the lowest MACH-IV scores were William McKinley, Rutherford B. Hayes, and Zachary Taylor.

Given that Machiavellianism is believed to reflect a stable personality trait, it should be possible to detect Machiavellianism in children. Research with a measure known as the KIDDIE-MACH (Christie, 1970) has confirmed that such differences do indeed exist. A factor analysis of the KIDDIE-MACH identified three factors representing dishonesty, distrust of others, and a lack of faith in human nature. All three factors were associated with trait psychoticism (Sutton & Keogh, 2001).

Intriguing research in Greece and in Scotland has linked Machiavellianism with bullying other children (Andreou, 2004; Sutton & Keogh, 2000). This bullying is most likely for instrumental reasons (obtaining a goal) as opposed to bullying for the sake of bullying. Another investigation used self-report and teacher ratings to identify a group of early adolescents who were labelled as Machiavellians based on their strategic use of control (Hawley, 2003). These Machiavellian children were seen as having both positive and negative features. They were viewed as socially skilled and, somewhat surprisingly, they were liked and admired by their peers, perhaps because they are quite skillful and very good at what they do. In fact, they were rated as most popular, relative to four other groups of children! It is this skill that distinguished these children from another subset of participants known as the bully subgroup. Both were capable of meanness, but the Machiavellian children were also highly socially skilled.

Machiavellianism is a provocative concept. Research on this construct has been hampered by significant concerns raised about the reliability and questionable factorial validity of the MACH-IV scale. Some authors (e.g., Bloom, 1984) have even advocated abandoning this measure, yet there is no denying that the MACH-IV measure has predicted theoretically meaningful criterion variables in countless studies, and the measure has adequate test–retest reliability (for a review, see Fehr, Samson, & Paulhus, 1992). Also, it is important to recognize that Machiavellianism is a construct that has been extensively studied and has great meaning in business and organizational contexts. This research has explored such things as the ability of Machiavellianism to predict performance outcomes and to establish the leadership attributes of managers who are high versus low in Machiavellianism. Clearly, research on this construct has played a vital role in establishing an awareness of the practical applications of personality differences in real-life contexts.

KEY POINTS

- Machiavellians are cynical people who perceive the world as competitive. They feel it is justified and natural to manipulate other people for personal gain.
- Machiavellians are especially adept at manipulation in face-to-face situations.
- The MACH-IV scale is the main measure. It suffers from psychometric problems but still predicts important outcomes in real-life contexts.
- The KIDDIE-MACH shows that Machiavellianism exists in children. Machiavellian children bully other children but are still liked because they are recognized as highly skilled.
- Unlike other variables in the dark triad (narcissism and psychopathy), Machivellianism is not high in egotistical self-inflation.

THE AUTHORITARIAN PERSONALITY

Much of the general interest in theory and research on personality and interpersonal styles in the 1950s and 1960s can be attributed to work on the authoritarian personality. One of the most influential yet flawed approaches to the study of personality began in 1950 with the publication of the book *The Authoritarian Personality* by Adorno,

Frenkel-Brunswick, Levinson, and Sanford (1950). The book describes theory and research on people who are high in authoritarianism. Authoritarian individuals are domineering, anti-democratic, tough-minded individuals who are willing to follow leaders who endorse the view that some people are simply better than others and are more deserving of the opportunity to lead other people. Clearly, if a highly authoritarian person were asked to take a measure tapping the interpersonal circumplex and his or her scores were plotted, this individual would score as powerful and domineering without much interpersonal warmth. Authoritarians tend to see the world in black and white, all-or-none terms, and this includes a tendency to categorize people according to group memberships. They do not favour emotional expressions of affection and prefer situations that are clear-cut and predictable, as opposed to abstract and complex.

The work by Adorno et al. (1950) was politically charged. These researchers, based in California, were motivated by the rise of anti-Semitism and Adolf Hitler and the willingness of German people to obediently follow him. Adorno and colleagues sought to identify the personality and attitudinal factors at work and gain insights into the nature of the authoritarianism construct. In so doing, they implied that not only is it possible to study authoritarian individuals, but it is also possible to study authoritarian cultures and societies. Accordingly, a significant proportion of the research literature on authoritarianism compares certain societies and nations deemed to be particularly authoritarian at a particular point in time (e.g., South Africa) with less authoritarian nations and societies.

Adorno et al. (1950) viewed the development of authoritarianism from a psychoanalytic perspective. Specifically, they attributed authoritarianism to overcontrolling parenting, and this foreshadowed the work on authoritarian parenting described in Chapter 3. Authoritarianism was deemed to reflect a weak, irrational superego that projected its harsh evaluations onto other groups of people.

Adorno et al. (1950) developed the California F-Scale (for "fascism") to measure authoritarianism. They also developed the A-S Scale to measure anti-Semitism, the E-Scale to measure ethnocentrism, and the PEC-Scale to measure political–economic conservatism. Although authoritarianism has often been studied in the context of ultra conservative right-wing values, initially the authors tried to distinguish authoritarianism and conservatism. Table 10.3 shows subscales from the F-Scale and representative items, as well as descriptions of Altemeyer's (1981) shortened version of the F-Scale.

More than 2,000 studies on authoritarianism have been conducted since the publication of *The Authoritarian Personality*. Personality psychologists have done much of this work, but a substantial proportion of the research has been conducted by social psychologists who focus on authoritarianism as a social attitude. Other interest has come from political psychologists.

Table 10.4 is an overview of some empirically identified correlates of authoritarianism. These correlates highlight the need for judgement of others, often in a punitive manner, and the quest for domination that is inherent in extreme forms of authoritarianism. Unlike other university students, students high in authoritarianism are relatively uninterested in issues related to finding their own personal identity (Peterson & Lane, 2002).

Table 10.3 The California F-Scale of Authoritarianism

Scale	Description and Representative Item
Conventionalism	Respecting social conventions and rules (e.g., "If people would talk less and work more, everyone would be better off.")
Authoritarian Submission	Submitting to authorities (e.g., "Every person should have complete faith in some supernatural power whose decision he or she obeys without question.")
Authoritarian Aggression	Aggressive stance toward individuals/groups not liked by authorities (e.g., "Homosexuals are hardly better than criminals and ought to be punished.")
Superstition and Stereotypy	Superstitious, categorical beliefs and fatalistic view (e.g., "Wars and social troubles may some day be ended by an earthquake or flood that will destroy the whole world.")
Power and Toughness	Identification with those in power and tough-minded (e.g., "No weakness or difficulty can hold us back if we have enough willpower.")

Table 10.4 Empirically Identified Correlates of Authoritarianism

Moral elitism and a sense of a divine right to express hostility and negative views toward outgroups
Homophobic attitudes and prejudice toward gays
More negative appraisals of persons with medically controlled schizophrenia
Other-oriented perfectionism
Domineering and aggressive unwillingness to accept other's points of view
Conscientiousness, obsessionality, and rigidity
Low trait openness
Lack of interest in determining personal identity issues
Strong national identity
Intolerance of ambiguity
Greater obedience in the Milgram shock study

Some key problems have plagued research on the authoritarianism construct. First, some authors have been critical of the Freudian underpinnings of the authoritarianism construct. Adorno et al. (1950) hypothesized that authoritarianism stems from harsh and punitive parenting, and the anger, humiliation, and rage that this brings about is redirected outward in a form of displacement against non-parental targets. As with many Freudian concepts, the views are difficult to test empirically.

Another concern was articulated clearly by Martin (2001), who criticized Adorno et al. (1950) for not being objective. Martin (2001) concluded that "Political psychologists should regard *The Authoritarian Personality* as a cautionary example of bias arising from the choice of methodological assumptions" (p. 1). This is more than ironic given that authoritarianism itself is hypothesized to predict ethnocentrism.

Perhaps the biggest problem is that scale scores on measures of authoritarianism are often not reflected by differences in actual authoritarian behaviour in real-life settings. Numerous studies have failed to link authoritarianism on self-report measures with authoritarian behaviour. The primary exception is the study by Elms and Milgram (1966); they used Milgram's classic obedience paradigm to show that authoritarian people were willing to be more punitive in this experimental setting.

Another problem is that existing measures of authoritarianism have suffered from structural flaws; most notably, the California F-Scale and Ray's measure of authoritarianism did not include items worded in the non-authoritarian direction, so these measures have been shown to be susceptible to nea-saying or yea-saying (the acquiescence response bias). Past measures have also been unidimensional, and it has been argued that multi-dimensional measures are needed to fully capture the complexity of this personality construct (see Funke, 2005).

Research on the interpersonal characteristics of authoritarians indicates that whatever is being measured by authoritarianism, it does seem to leak through to their interpersonal characteristics. One study required student interviewers to assess the interpersonal features of participants varying in authoritarianism and found that those high in authoritarianism were judged to be defensive, maladjusted, and prejudiced (Lippa & Arad, 1999).

Other negative characteristics include negative and hostile attitudes toward women. Adorno et al. (1950) suggested that authoritarian men prefer to subordinate women and show general disrespect for them. This has been borne out by research showing that extreme authoritarians are high in hypermasculinity and have a higher reported likelihood of engaging in sexual harassment (Begany & Milburn, 2002). It has also been linked with sexually aggressive behaviour (Petty & Dawson, 1989; Walker, Rowe, & Quinsey, 1993).

Authoritarianism: Right-Wing versus Left-Wing

Another critical issue that is often attributed to the biases of Adorno et al. (1950) is that authoritarianism has been treated as synonymous with right-wing, conservative thinking, and the possibility that extreme left-wing thinking can also involve authoritarianism was not taken into consideration. The growth of Communism in the 1950s led authors to postulate that extreme left-wing thinking also involves authoritarianism.

Altemeyer (1996) tackled this issue by developing a measure of left-wing authoritarianism. Research with his initial sample of hundreds of students from the University of Manitoba showed that it was possible to create a measure of left-wing authoritarianism. There was only one problem: analyses of students on a case-by-case basis showed that there was not even one student in Altemeyer's sample who qualified as being a left-wing authoritarian! This discovery illustrates a potential problem that is often overlooked by personality researchers and theorists. When focusing on personality dimensions and variables from a nomothetic perspective, it is useful and potentially important to examine these variables within the context of actual people. Altemeyer (1996) addressed his version of this problem by reasoning that left-wing authoritarians are simply rare in student samples. He was able to show that people with this attribute can be identified if the sample includes people who have an established track record of political extremism.

KEY POINTS

- Research and theory on authoritarianism grew out of the atrocities of the Second World War, and the belief that people should blindly follow what they are told by authorities.
- Authoritarians show greater obedience, dominance, and willingness to judge unconventional others.
- The main measure is the California F-Scale. There is little correspondence between scale scores and actual behaviours. The scale is also vulnerable to nea-saying.
- Altemeyer identified left-wing authoritarians. He also created a briefer version of the F-Scale, and rejected the psychoanalytic roots of the construct.

Authoritarianism and Political Psychology

Although there has been continuing interest and fascination in extreme authoritarians and what makes them tick, the problems outlined above result in fewer empirical studies being conducted throughout the 1970s and 1980s as other constructs captured researchers' attention. However, there has been renewed interest in recent years, in part due to the work of political psychologists interested in applying the construct to various world situations.

One intriguing issue is whether changing political situations have had an impact on authoritarianism. Specifically, how has the fall of Communist societies affected left-wing authoritarianism? Krauss (2002) examined levels of authoritarianism and their correlates in Romania 10 years after the fall of Communism. He found initially that authoritarianism was associated with positive support for Communist principles of distributive justice and a Communist economy. These associations were still evident 10 years later, and it led Krauss to conclude that the association between Communism and authoritarianism in Eastern Europe may be more resistant to change than first thought.

Sam McFarland from Western Kentucky University and his associates analyzed levels of authoritarianism in the former Soviet Union in quota samples from Moscow in 1989 and 1991 (McFarland, Ageyev, & Abalakina-Paap, 1992). They took the position that although in the form of Communism, authoritarianism in the former Soviet Union would be compared to the Western manifestation of authoritarianism. Their results showed that the strength of the correlation between authoritarianism and endorsement of Marxist-Leninist ideology had grown weaker over two years as Communism rapidly declined. However, authoritarians were still authoritarians in that authoritarianism was still strongly associated with conventionalism and a general disdain for people who deviate from accepted conventions. The authors concluded:

> We can now only speculate about the future of Russian authoritarianism and about the personality processes that lead high authoritarians to greater conventionalism. Because authoritarianism apparently requires a strong commitment to an ideology or in-group, it appears that communism, Russian nationalism, and

> orthodoxy each may appeal to some Russian authoritarians in the near future. Procommunist demonstrations in March 1992 show that these ideals still have a following (p. 1012).

Altemeyer's Components of Right-Wing Authoritarianism

Arguably, Robert Altemeyer has been the main catalyst for renewed interest in this program of research. His first contribution was to create a measure of right-wing authoritarianism that was psychometrically superior to its predecessors (see Altemeyer, 1981, 1988, 1996). This measure avoids past problems by including positively and negatively worded items to minimize the acquiescence response set. An important aspect of this measure is that Altemeyer rejected the influence of psychodynamic factors and instead viewed the development of authoritarianism from more of a social learning perspective. He regards authoritarianism as a social attitude construct that is learned primarily through interactions with family and friends, as well as broader cultural sources (e.g., the media).

According to Altemeyer, right-wing authoritarianism has three essential features: (1) authoritarian submission; (2) authoritarian aggression; and (3) conventionalism (see Table 10.3). Authoritarian submission is a willingness to follow the dictates of established and legitimate authorities. Authoritarian aggression is willingness to direct hostile acts toward others according to the directions of established authority figures. Finally, conventionalism is the tendency to adhere to societal conventions and values that have been endorsed by authority figures.

Altemeyer's work has highlighted the tendency for extreme authoritarians to judge others in a harsh and demeaning manner. For example, his work has not only shown that authoritarians support more punitive penalties for criminals and is linked with greater prejudice, but it is even the case that right-wing authoritarians are more likely to attribute blame to a prostitute for her own murder (Altemeyer, 1988, 1996). This punitive orientation has been supported by other researchers who have linked right-wing authoritarianism with the view that homeless people are not unlucky, just lazy (Peterson, Doty, & Winter, 1993).

Altemeyer is also responsible for one of the cleverest studies conducted in the past decade. He and his son created a simulation game that could be used to study decision-making and the consequences of decisions that are made or not made. Altemeyer (1998) pre-selected an entire sample of right-wing authoritarians to find out what would happen if they were put in charge. On two successive nights, authoritarians played this game, which involved deciding how to run the world. The results from the simulation game were far from encouraging or reassuring, and suggested that authoritarians are not effective decision-makers. The world created by the authoritarians was characterized by high unemployment, famine, and disease.

Overall, Adorno et al. (1950) should probably be praised for postulating a personality construct that has generated an enormous amount of research. There is no doubt that flaws abound in their work. Martin (2001) concluded that their book is the mostly deeply flawed work of prominence in the political psychology literature. Nevertheless, some tough but important lessons have been learned along the way, including the vital importance of carefully formulating a theory and then taking the same degree of care when constructing the measure that flows from the theory.

Social Dominance Orientation

Part of the renewed interest over the past decade in authoritarianism is due to an individual difference variable that shares some general characteristics of authoritarianism yet is distinct in some key respects. **Social dominance orientation** is defined as an individual difference variable that reflects the extent to which a person needs or desires an in-group versus an out-group to be dominant and to remain in a favoured position. It is conceptualized as an attitudinal orientation that involves preferences for establishing and maintaining superiority over others in a hierarchical fashion (see Pratto, Sidanius, Stallworth, & Malle, 1994).

The measure created to assess social dominance orientation is shown in Table 10.5. Try the items and see how you might score. Note that the last half of the items are reverse-coded (i.e., they are worded in a way that reflects low social dominance orientation).

Another question is the extent to which individual differences in social dominance orientation influence how people with these attributes are perceived by others. As part of the investigation of the interpersonal factors associated with social dominance orientation, Lippa and Arad (1999) conducted interviews with 93 participants. People with elevated levels of social dominance orientation were rated as being less agreeable, less nurturant, and more prejudiced, among various unfavourable attributes.

What is the difference between social dominance orientation and authoritarianism? The key differences were illustrated in a recent study conducted in New Zealand (see Duckitt, 2006). Social dominance orientation is activated when another group is seen as highly competitive with one's own group in establishing dominance and superiority. In contrast, right-wing authoritarianism is more likely when other people are a threat to cohesion, order, and social control, as would be the case when a deviant group becomes more prominent.

Although these constructs differ in their conceptualizations and associated relevant situations, measures of social dominance orientation and authoritarianism often yield the same results, even though the two constructs are not highly correlated. A poignant example of this was provided by McFarland (2005), who surveyed the opinions of Americans one week prior to the 2003 attack by the United States on Iraq, which was supposedly motivated by the search for weapons of mass destruction. It was found that both social dominance orientation and authoritarianism were associated with support for the war, and they both increased what McFarland referred to as "blind patriotism." The main difference between the two constructs was in their cognitive correlates. While authoritarianism was associated with an increased perception that Iraq was a threat to the United States, social dominance orientation was associated with reduced concern for the human costs of the war: deaths and injuries.

Table 10.5 The Social Dominance Orientation Questionnaire

Below is a series of statements with which you may either agree or disagree. For each statement, please indicate the degree of your agreement/disagreement by circling the appropriate number from 1 to 7. Remember that first responses are usually the most accurate. Note: Items 9–16 should be reverse coded.

	Strongly Agree/ Favour						Strongly Disagree/ Disapprove
1. Some groups of people are just more worthy than others.	1	2	3	4	5	6	7
2. In getting what your group wants, it is sometimes necessary to use force against other groups.	1	2	3	4	5	6	7
3. Superior groups should dominate inferior groups.	1	2	3	4	5	6	7
4. To get ahead in life, it is sometimes necessary to step on other groups.	1	2	3	4	5	6	7
5. If certain groups of people stayed in their place, we would have fewer problems.	1	2	3	4	5	6	7
6. It's probably a good thing that certain groups are at the top and other groups are at the bottom.	1	2	3	4	5	6	7
7. Inferior groups should stay in their place.	1	2	3	4	5	6	7
8. Sometimes other groups must be kept in their place.	1	2	3	4	5	6	7
9. It would be good if all groups could be equal.	1	2	3	4	5	6	7
10. Group equality should be our ideal.	1	2	3	4	5	6	7
11. All groups should be given an equal chance in life.	1	2	3	4	5	6	7
12. We should do what we can to equalize conditions for different groups.	1	2	3	4	5	6	7
13. We should do what we can for increased social equality.	1	2	3	4	5	6	7
14. We would have fewer problems if we treated different groups more equal.	1	2	3	4	5	6	7
15. We should strive to make incomes more equal.	1	2	3	4	5	6	7
16. No one group should dominate in society.	1	2	3	4	5	6	7

Source: Adapted from Sidanius et al., 2000.

Recent research by Altemeyer (2004) has focused on those individuals who are characterized jointly by extremely high levels of social dominance orientation and right-wing authoritarianism. It is possible to find people high in both since these two personality constructs are not highly correlated. These people are referred to as "double highs" by Altemeyer (2004). One reassuring thing about double highs is that Altemeyer had to assess thousands of students and their parents to obtain enough double highs to conduct his research investigations. The bad news is that these people are among the most prejudiced people in the world. Altemeyer (2004) also cautioned that the combination of high social dominance and authoritarianism may apply to some of the most heinous figures in history. Altemeyer concluded by noting that:

> Once in control of a school prayer, or anti-homosexual, or anti-immigration, or anti-feminist, or anti-abortion, or anti-gun-control movement—not to mention a militia force—Double Highs can pose a serious threat. For they lead people who are uninclined to think for themselves, are gullible toward leaders of their "in-group," are brimming with self-righteousness and zeal, and are fain to give dictatorship a chance (p. 445).

Whereas social dominance and authoritarianism apply to only a relatively small segment of the population (fortunately), in the next section, we will shift our emphasis to an interpersonally based construct that is much more pervasive. Attachment styles play an important role in personality development and should be considered along with the myriad other factors that were described in Chapter 3. Unlike the cynical approach to others inherent in authoritarianism and Machiavellianism, the various attachment styles include some orientations that reflect a positive view of other people.

KEY POINTS

- Social dominance orientation is a need to dominate other groups when they become competitive.
- Whereas social dominance orientation prevails when there is competition, authoritarianism prevails when there is a threat to order and authority.
- Social dominance orientation and authoritarianism are not highly correlated. Double highs (people high in both) are hard to find but are among the most prejudiced people on the planet.

ATTACHMENT STYLES

Some would argue that research on attachment styles has been the most predominant theme in the personality literature over the past 15 years. The initial theory and research on attachment styles was provided by University of Toronto professor **Mary Ainsworth** and her collaborator, **John Bowlby**, a psychoanalyst from England. Eventually, Ainsworth moved to England to continue her research collaboration with Bowlby (see Ainsworth & Bowlby, 1953).

Ainsworth studied infant attachment styles by developing a paradigm known as the Strange Situation in which an infant was left in a room for a brief period of time with a stranger, while the mother left the room. Observational data indicated that there were three distinct types of infants that reflect the differences between secure attachment and anxious attachment (Ainsworth, Blehar, Waters, & Wall, 1978). A securely attached infant shows little distress and interacts quite willingly with the stranger, secure in the knowledge that his or her mother will return. This pattern of behaviour contrasts with the two attachment styles of insecurely attached infants, which both reflect an absence of secure attachment. An anxiously attached infant becomes very distressed when his or her mother leaves the room. These types of infants have been described as "clingy" and are at risk of being overly dependent, and prone to feelings of separation anxiety. When mothers of anxiously attached

The anxiously attached child is described as "clingy" and is at risk of being overly dependent and prone to feelings of separation anxiety.

infants return to the room, the babies tend to show they're upset by making a fuss as a form of protest, as if they are saying, "Don't do that to me again." In contrast, an infant with an **avoidant attachment** style displays little emotion when the mother leaves the room and shows little reaction upon her return, almost as if an attachment bond has never been formed in the first place. Avoidantly attached infants can become withdrawn and socially isolated.

Research by Ainsworth and associates established that insecure forms of attachment are likely to develop when a child is exposed to harsh parenting or inconsistent parenting (see Ainsworth, 1984). Secure attachment emerges when the parent responds to the infant's needs in a warm and predictable manner, so that the infant comes to believe that the parent will be available as a source of comfort on a regular basis.

A fourth attachment style has been identified in recent years. The **disorganized attachment style** is evident in infants who seem totally confused by their surroundings. The disorganized attachment style results from being exposed to chaotic and abusive environments (see Main & Hesse, 1990).

Research has sought to establish the early experiences and related factors that contribute to insecure attachment. A meta-analytic study conducted by researchers in Canada involved an analysis of several studies and concluded that maternal mental health variables are associated with degree of attachment security (Atkinson et al., 2000). Greater attachment security is evident when mothers report high levels of social support and marital satisfaction and low levels of stress and depression.

Insensitive, nonresponsive parenting is believed to be the main factor contributing to the development of an insecure attachment style. An earlier meta-analysis conducted by van Ijzendoorn (1995) from the University of Leiden in the Netherlands of research using the Adult Attachment Interview confirmed that nonresponsive parenting is linked with insecure attachment in young children. Van Ijzendoorn noted that according to conventional statistical criteria, the magnitude of this association is large.

KEY POINTS

- Use of the Strange Situation enabled Ainsworth and colleagues to show that infants vary in their attachment to caregivers.
- Most people have a secure attachment style. Insecure attachment can involve anxious attachment versus an avoidant attachment style.
- Insecure attachment is due, at least in part, to inconsistent, nonresponsive, or hostile parenting.

Researchers have tested the importance of sensitive, responsive parenting and child-caregiver proximity by examining the attachment styles of children who have experienced highly challenging situations. One study, for instance, tested the attachment styles of young children with incarcerated mothers (see Poehlmann, 2005). This study found that almost two thirds of these children had insecure attachment styles; those with more secure attachments had been fortunate to develop a stable caregiving situation with another adult. Older children were also less susceptible, it seemed. In general, the initial separation was seen as particularly stressful and created confusion, anger, sadness, loneliness, sleep problems, and developmental regressions. Another contemporary study examined the attachment styles of children exposed prenatally to crack cocaine (Seifer et al., 2004). Overall, these children were slightly more likely to have an anxious attachment (in the form of the anxious–ambivalent style). The most dramatic finding was the stability of attachment style over time, with the stability of attachment across an 18-month period being just slightly above what would be expected by chance. It was also found that insecure attachment at 36 months of age was closely linked with child behaviour problems.

This finding accords with numerous studies that have linked insecure attachment with personal and interpersonal adjustment problems in children and adolescents. One longitudinal study assessed children with the Strange Situation at one year of age, and then used interviews 18 years later to determine which children developed an anxiety disorder (Warren, Huston, Egeland, & Sroufe, 1997). This study found that an anxious attachment style among infants did predict subsequent anxiety disorders, while an avoidant attachment style predicted other types of psychiatric disorders. Another study conducted by researchers from Simon Fraser University found that fearful, insecure attachment in adolescents was associated with the severity of suicide ratings in a clinical sample (Lessard & Moretti, 1998).

Extensive research has examined attachment style and maladjustment among children and adults with a history of childhood maltreatment (physical, emotional, and sexual abuse). Maltreated children still form attachments to their abusive caregivers, but insecure attachment is quite common. A test of a university student sample found, for instance, that over three quarters of the students with childhood maltreatment had an insecure attachment style (Muller & Lemieux, 2000). Individuals with both an insecure attachment style and a history of maltreatment are particularly at risk for social and emotional problems. Many of their difficulties can be traced to a highly negative view of the self (McLewin & Muller, 2006).

Several important issues about attachment style have been extensively investigated. Some of these issues are now explored in some detail.

Categories or Dimensions?

Research on attachment styles in infants and children has followed the approach introduced by Ainsworth, and the focus has been on attachment style categories. According to a typological approach, you, as an infant, would either be securely attached or fall into one of the insecure attachment style categories. But is attachment style such an all-or-none thing, or are there different degrees of attachment style, as would be suggested by a dimensional approach?

Fraley and Spieker (2003) provided the clearest answer to this question. They analyzed data from more than 1,000 15-month-old children who had been studied in the Strange Situation and concluded unequivocally with sophisticated taxometric statistical techniques that the variability in attachment styles is more in keeping with a dimensional trait view of attachment styles rather than a categorical view. An earlier study of measures for adults also provided support for a dimensional interpretation (Fraley & Waller, 1998). These findings have important implications because they suggest that theoretical models of attachment style differences should also adopt this dimensional view.

How Stable Are Attachment Styles over Time?

If attachment styles represent personality variables, then regardless of whether they are dimensional or categorical, they should be relatively stable over time, as would be expected if they are indeed personality trait dimensions. Bowlby (1980) suggested that attachment styles operate "from the cradle to the grave" throughout our lifespan and that there is substantial continuity due to mental models and our associated attachment styles. However, at the same time, he also acknowledged that change is possible in response to life events. The stability of attachment styles comes from the fact that attachment styles are self-perpetuating to some degree because they are reinforced by the consequences of the behaviours that are typically related to attachment styles.

What factors predict change? Bowlby outlined a series of factors associated with change. First, attachment styles vary in stability depending on the degree of satisfaction each person derives from the pattern. Second, working models will be modified when there is a poor fit between working models and actual social exchanges. Note that this is quite similar to Kelly's notion from personal construct theory that personal constructs need to be updated when they are not working. The healthy person is able to do this without difficulty, but highly threatened people may be less willing or able to do so.

So, what does the evidence tell us about stability? Clearly, research on infants and children tends to point to stability. In general, there is high stability of .70 or greater when infants are tested at 12 months of age and 18 months of age. In addition, Main et al. (1985) found that attachment security at 12 months in the Strange Situation predicts aspects of attachment organization at six years of age. Attachment organization during infancy was measured by reunion behaviour, communication and discourse fluency in the child–parent dyad, and emotional responses to pictures of separations.

Hamilton (2000) studied changes over time in attachment classifications from infancy through adolescence. The Ainsworth Strange Situation was used in infancy, and the Adolescent Attachment Interview when participants were older. Overall, in terms of secure versus insecure attachment styles, the stability was estimated at 77%. The experience of negative events was a significant precipitating factor that contributed to attachment style changes.

Everett Waters and associates conducted a 20-year investigation of the stability of attachment style classifications of 60 white infants who were assessed in the Strange Situation at 12 months of age and then were interviewed 20 years later (Waters, Merrick, Treboux, Crowell, & Albersheim, 2000). The interviewers were "blind," meaning they were unaware of the infant attachment style results. Overall, 43 of the 60 (72%) received the same attachment style classification. Of those who did change, a disproportionate percentage of them had experienced negative life events such as loss of a parent, parental divorce, or sexual abuse.

Another longitudinal study of 155 women assessed after high school graduation also found that attachment style fluctuations could be traced back to the experience of highly aversive and sometimes traumatic early life experiences, which seemed to contribute to identifiable individual differences in susceptibility to change (Davila, Burge, & Hammen, 1997).

Fraley's (2002) meta-analysis combined the results of the various studies and found that across the first 19 years of life, there is moderate stability of attachment styles. He advanced a prototype model based on the notion that people have their usual attachment style and this can be represented by a baseline or set point. However, the experience of life events resembles a state variable that can lead to temporary fluctuations in attachment style (a separation from a loved one, for instance, makes us have a more anxious style for the time being). However, over time and across enough situations, we will see that the person has a predictable and usual attachment style.

Are Various Attachment Style Measures Equivalent?

Attachment styles are either assessed via self-report questionnaires or via an interview. The chief interview measure of attachment style in adults is the Adult Attachment Interview (AAI; George, Kaplan, & Main, 1985). This measure has often been used to test the stability of attachment style classifications based on how infants respond in the Strange Situation. The AAI is based on recollections of childhood attachment relationships. It requires respondents to retrieve autobiographical memories from their childhood. Extensive evidence attests to the validity and reliability of the AAI. It uses a semi-structured interview format and assesses secure attachment, preoccupied attachment, and dismissing attachment during childhood. It also provides information about the extent to which the person has resolved past traumatic events that may include abuse. Bakermans-Kranenburg and van Ijzendoorn (1993) found that the AII's consistency of attachment style classifications based on the interviews was quite high over time and across interviewers. Moreover, the AII classifications seemed relatively impervious to the influence of individual differences in the respondent's levels of intelligence or degree of socially desirable responding.

One vexing problem for research in this area is that several studies have found that the AII measures are not correlated with self-report measures (see Holtzworth-Munroe, Stuart, & Hutchinson, 1997). For example, a recent investigation with French-Canadian couples showed that the AII measures were not associated with two self-report measures of adult attachment style, and that secure attachment as determined by the AII predicted proactive, positive regulation strategies for dealing with emotion, but no such relationship was evident with the self-report attachment style measures (Bouthillier et al., 2002). This could reflect the difference in temporal focus (childhood versus adulthood) and the possibility that attachment styles have changed over time. Still, there ought to be some significant association given that attachment styles are supposed to be at least relatively stable.

KEY POINTS

- Although theorists describe attachment style categories, a dimensional representation is more appropriate.
- Attachment styles exist throughout the lifespan and tend to have at least moderate stability over time.
- Self-report and interview measures of attachment style are not equivalent, and ideally, both types of measures should be assessed.

Romantic Attachment Styles

A seminal paper by Hazan and Shaver (1987) accepted Bowlby's notion that attachment styles stretch from "the cradle to the grave," and they reasoned that differences in secure versus anxious attachments ought to be identifiable in the romantic attachment styles displayed by adolescents and adults. That is, just as an anxious attached baby gets distressed when the mother is not present, adults with anxious attachment style should be distressed when their partners are not present, and they will engage in behaviours designed to maintain proximity with the partner. Hazan and Shaver (1987) focused on the threefold attachment style framework outlined by Ainsworth. The three forms of relationship-based attachment were security, anxious–ambivalent, and avoidant. Paragraphs were written to represent each possibility, and participants had to select which paragraph was most accurate in describing themselves. The researchers' subsequent empirical work confirmed that adults varying in romantic attachment style could also be distinguished in their views on love and relationships, and in their memories of how they were treated by their parents. The two anxious attachment styles, relative to the secure style, are associated with relationships that are shorter in duration (Collins & Read, 1990).

Kim Bartholomew of Simon Fraser University felt that the Hazan and Shaver model was lacking because it obscures different types of avoidantly attached people (see

Bartholomew, 1990; Bartholomew & Horowitz, 1991). It was reasoned that some people avoid others but have a positive view of themselves, so avoidance takes the form of dismissing others. Others have the avoidant style more in line with what was suggested originally by Hazan and Shaver. That is, they have a negative view of themselves and other people, and they become fearfully avoidant.

The model developed by Bartholomew is outlined in Figure 10.2. It is based on Bowlby's notion that we have internal working models or cognitive representations of both the self and other people. These working models can be positive or negative in valence, so there are four possible combinations. Securely attached people have positive views of self and others. Preoccupied people have a negative view of the self but a positive view of others; their clingy desire to be with others is a way of compensating for deficiencies in the self. People with fearful attachment have negative views of self and others. Dismissing people have a positive view of self but a negative view of others.

Figure 10.2 Bartholomew's Attachment Style Model

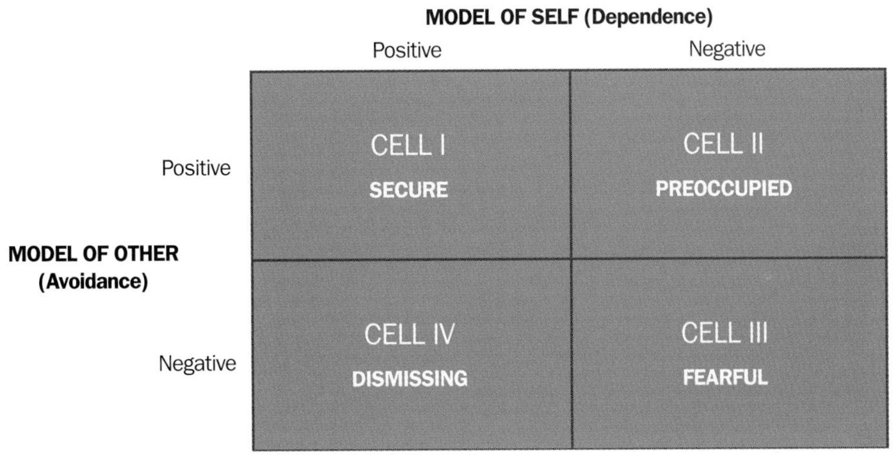

MODEL OF OTHER (Avoidance)	MODEL OF SELF (Dependence): Positive	MODEL OF SELF (Dependence): Negative
Positive	CELL I **SECURE**	CELL II **PREOCCUPIED**
Negative	CELL IV **DISMISSING**	CELL III **FEARFUL**

Source: Adapted from Bartholomew & Horowitz, 1991, p. 227.

The distinctions among different types of avoidance are necessary to make sense of someone such as the Unabomber, described in Chapter 9. Some reclusive people may have a fearful attachment style, but Ted Kaczynski would likely be found to have a dismissive attachment style. His manifesto illustrates a defensively haughty sense of the self and conveys a sense of superiority, along with a great disdain for others.

The most predominant measure in this area was created by Bartholomew and Horowitz (1991). It is labelled the Relationship Questionnaire (see Table 10.6). It consists of one paragraph for each of the four attachment styles. If attachment style is assessed as a category, participants can decide which of the four categories most applies to them. A continuous, dimensional assessment is also possible by having respondents make five-point ratings of the extent to which each of the four attachment styles described applies to them.

Try the Relationship Questionnaire and see which one of the four descriptions seems most applicable to you. Would the other people in your life also pick this category for you? Note that the original study by Bartholomew and Horowitz (1991) found that 47% of students selected the secure attachment style, 14% the preoccupied style, 18% the dismissive style, and 21% the fearful style.

Table 10.6 The Relationship Questionnaire

Measure Following are four general relationship styles that people often report. Place a checkmark next to the letter corresponding to the style that best describes you or is closest to the way you are.	
A	It is easy for me to become emotionally close to others. I am comfortable depending on them and having them depend on me. I don't worry about being alone or having others not accept me.
B	I am uncomfortable getting close to others. I want emotionally close relationships, but I find it difficult to trust others completely, or to depend on them. I worry that I will be hurt if I allow myself to become too close to others.
C	I want to be completely emotionally intimate with others, but I often find that others are reluctant to get as close as I would like. I am uncomfortable being without close relationships, but I sometimes worry that others don't value me as much as I value them.
D	I am comfortable without close emotional relationships. It is very important to me to feel independent and self-sufficient, and I prefer not to depend on others or have others depend on me.
A=secure attachment B=anxious–avoidant attachment C=preoccupied attachment D=dismissive attachment	

Source: Bartholomew & Horowitz, 1991.

Empirical work by Bartholomew and Horowitz (1991), among others, has supported the need for four attachment styles. They reported that self-reports and peer ratings confirmed that those with the dismissive orientation, relative to people in the other four groups, scored the highest on self-confidence but the lowest on the closeness of interpersonal relationships.

Research on the role of the four attachment styles in personal adjustment has focused on whether the dismissive attachment style is associated with vulnerability to psychopathology or resilience due to a tough-minded approach and less susceptibility to interpersonal loss. In general, research has established that a positive model of the self, relative to a positive model of others, is the key factor in protecting participants from the experience of psychopathology (McLewin & Muller, 2006). But what about the dismissive style, with its positive view of self and negative view of others? Some authors have suggested that the dismissive style is reactive and highly defensive orientation that is associated with vulnerability (Mikulincer, Dolev, & Shaver, 2004), while others (e.g., Fraley & Bonanno, 2004) maintain that the dismissive style makes people resilient to loss.

This issue was addressed in an important study of high exposure survivors of the September 11, 2001 attack on the World Trade Center (WTC) in New York (see Fraley, Fazzari, Bonanno, & Dekel, 2006). High exposure was defined as actually being in the WTC or within several blocks during the attack. Participants completed measures of attachment style, depression, and post-traumatic stress disorder (PTSD) at 7 months and 18 months after the attack. Informant reports were also obtained. As expected, adults with a highly secure attachment style had the best adjustment, with only modest PTSD scores at the seven month mark. Informant reports at 18 months after the attack indicated that people with the secure attachment style had psychological growth after the attack; that is, they were rated at 18 months as being more adjusted than they were before the attack. This is one of the first empirical examples of post-traumatic growth (as opposed to post-traumatic stress). Several factors likely contributed to this growth, including deriving additional meaning from existing interpersonal relationships and being inspired by the stories of heroism and dedication of others that emerged in the months following the attack.

In a study of high exposure survivors of the September 11 attacks on the World Trade Center, adults with a secure attachment style reported being more adjusted after the attack than before, while those with a dismissive attachment style had levels of maladjustment.

In contrast, the participants with the dismissive attachment style had levels of maladjustment that were comparable to the maladjustment associated with other forms of insecure attachment. A key factor here was the data collection method. The self-reports of those with a dismissive orientation indicated psychological problems, but their informants indicated that these people were actually "doing fine." In fact, informant reports indicated that the adjustment of these people was not worse or better following the WTC attack. Perhaps dismissive individuals put on a "front" and hide their emotional problems from others. The main point here, however, is that there was little evidence indicating that the dismissive orientation was protective and adaptive, at least among self-report data.

Can you identify some potential limitations involving this study? Is it possible that it was the more highly adjusted people with secure attachment who were more likely to respond to the request for volunteers? This possibility cannot be discounted. Also, ideally, it would have been better to assess attachment style prior to the attack on the WTC, but this is impossible to do when such unforeseeable, tragic events occur.

KEY POINTS

- The Bartholomew model of attachment style places positive versus negative working models of the self and other people in a 2 x 2 framework.
- This model yields four attachment styles: secure attachment (positive model of self and others), preoccupied attachment (negative model of self, positive model of others), dismissive attachment (positive model of self, negative model of others), and fearful attachment (negative model of self and of others). The dismissive attachment style is a unique addition stemming from this model.
- While dismissive attachment may be a resilient orientation, recent research indicates that it is a defensive orientation associated with distress.

Evaluation of Bartholomew's Attachment Style Model

Unfortunately, all is not rosy with the Bartholomew model. Criticisms are summarized in Fraley and Shaver (2000). Perhaps their most damning criticism of the model is that the positive model of other people that is supposed to be found in people with the preoccupied style is often lacking, and models of the self seem to have much more impact than models of other people. Also, preoccupied attachment can involve an element of anger and jealousy that, if taken to the extreme, can come in the form of rage and deep loathing of the partner. Recall the reaction of Glenn Close's character in the movie *Fatal Attraction* ("I will not be ignored") when she is rejected by the character played by Michael Douglas, who is having an extramarital affair but is in the process of returning to his wife.

In response to these concerns and other issues, other measures have emerged. The Experiences in Close Relationships Scales is composed of two 18-item scales created by Brennan, Clark, and Shaver (1998) to assess anxiety (e.g., "I worry a lot about my relationships") and avoidance (e.g., "I don't feel comfortable opening up to romantic partners"). Brennan et al. (1998) created these items by deriving a pool of 323 items that were taken from previous measures and confirming the existence of two higher order constructs representing anxiety and avoidance. They created these measures in response to a perceived need for researchers to use similar measures to facilitate comparisons across studies. The Experiences in Close Relationships Scales include general items as well as items that refer to the current romantic partner.

Attachment style differences are particularly evident when couples must be apart from each other. Fraley and Shaver (1998) conducted an *in vivo* study that analyzed couples who were separating from each other at a public airport, as one member of each couple went on a trip. Participants in this study were first asked to complete measures of attachment styles, relationship history, and degree of distress associated with the upcoming separation. The behaviours expressed during the actual separation were then observed. The authors found that the behavioural responses to the separation were similar to those expressed by young children when they experienced a separation from the caregiver. It was also found that those individuals with an anxious, preoccupied attachment style were most likely to report elevated levels of distress prior to the separation. However, they did not engage in greater proximity seeking behaviour. Other analyses focused on the women with an avoidant attachment style showed and that they were especially likely to engage in withdrawal behaviours as the separation approached.

International Focus on Discovery 10.1 Attachment Styles across Cultures

Evidence of cross-cultural differences in attachment style abounds, regardless whether the focus is on infant attachment styles or the romantic attachment styles of adults. An informative meta-analysis of the results of approximately 2,000 Strange Situation classifications involving infants from eight different countries revealed widespread differences (see van Ijzendoorn & Kroonenberg, 1988), though the overall pattern was not always found on a sample-by-sample basis. Specifically, it was found that avoidant classifications were more prevalent in Western European nations. However, putting these findings into perspective, the degree of variation in samples within cultures was 1.5 times greater than the amount of variability across cultures.

Cultures differ in what is considered an ideal form of attachment. There are indications that German mothers value avoidant attachment as the ideal, and securely attached children are regarded as spoiled and pampered (Grossmann, Grossmann, Spangler, Suess, & Unzner, 1985). The predominant form of attachment in children raised on a kibbutz was anxious–ambivalent attachment, not secure attachment (Sagi et al., 1985). Anxious–ambivalent attachment was also found to be predominant in at least one study of Japanese children (Miyake, Chen, & Campos, 1985). Moreover, very little evidence was found for the existence of the avoidant attachment style among these children. Distancing oneself from others is not culturally appropriate, and this could account for the paucity of Japanese children with the avoidant style.

The growth of the Internet has made it relatively easy to examine cross-cultural differences in adult attachment styles. Wei and associates from Iowa State University examined attachment style differences with an Internet sample (Wei, Russell, Mallinckrodt, & Zakalik, 2004). Participants completed the Experiences in Close Relationships Scales (Brennan et al., 1998) and measures of depression and anxiety. Four groups were compared: African American, Asian American, Hispanic American, and Caucasian college students. Analyses showed that African Americans and Asian Americans had greater attachment avoidance than did Caucasian students. Hispanic Americans were distinguished by higher levels of attachment anxiety.

The International Sexuality Description Project (ISDP) is a collaborative investigation with more than 100 researchers representing more than 17,000 participants from 62 cultural regions. Numerous countries are represented, including several European and Asian nations, as well as Australia, Israel, the United States, and Canada, among others. A paper from this group of investigators examines attachment style from a cross-cultural perspective (Schmitt et al., 2004). Analyses are based on the Relationship Questionnaire (RQ; Bartholomew & Horowitz, 1991). The attachment style component of the ISDP had a number of interrelated goals, including: (1) assessing the validity across cultures of the model of the self and model of others dimensions of the Relationship Questionnaire; (2) establishing whether the secure form of adult attachment is the normative style across cultures; (3) testing whether people from East Asian cultures are more prone to the preoccupied attachment style.

The validity of the self and other RQ dimensions was determined by establishing their associations across cultures with a self measure (self-esteem) and a measure focused on others (agreeableness). The RQ model of self scale was correlated with self-esteem in 92% of the cultures. The RQ model of others scale was correlated with agreeableness in 75% of the cultures.

Regarding whether secure attachment is normative across cultures, it was found that secure attachment predominated in 79% of cultures, and in several other cultures it was lower than an insecure form of attachment, but the difference was not statistically significant. Thus, the normativity hypothesis was supported. Still, the differences across cultures deserve to be noted. The dismissing attachment style prevailed in Bolivia, Belgium, Ethiopia, and Malaysia. The preoccupied attachment style was higher than the secure attachment style in Ethiopia and Japan, and fearful attachment was higher than secure attachment in Belgium, Ethiopia, and Indonesia.

The last hypothesis was confirmed. Higher levels of preoccupied attachment were found in South Asian countries, Southeast Asian countries, and East Asian countries. Figure 10.3 shows the relative levels of the model of self versus the model of others for 10 world regions. The predominance of the model of others scale, relative to the model of self scale, was clearly most evident in the region of East Asia, thus supporting views that emphasize the importance of people from these regions to feel interconnected to others.

Schmitt et al. (2004) concluded that "We feel it is reasonable to tentatively conclude that in nearly all cultures, people possess basic cognitive–emotional attitudes that constitute normative attachment Models of Self and Others" (p. 397) and internal working models were seen as "pancultural constructs." However, there was only qualified support for the normativity hypothesis, and there are clear cross-cultural variations in levels of preoccupied attachment.

Figure 10.3 Attachment Styles in World Regions

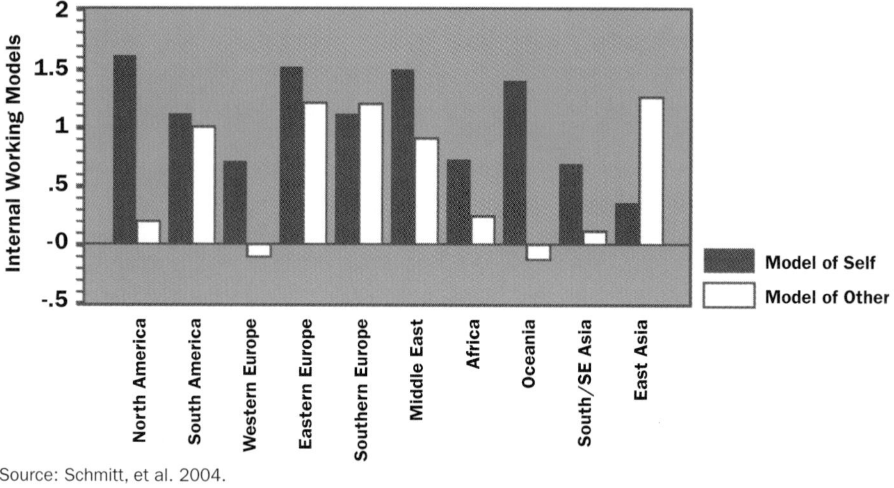

Source: Schmitt, et al. 2004.

PERSONALITY IN DATING AND MARITAL RELATIONSHIPS

Research Methods and Issues

Chapter 4 contained a review by Endler and Speers (1998) of trends in personality research methods. Recall that the prototypical study in the personality field is still a cross-sectional self-report questionnaire study. Cooper and Sheldon (2002) conducted a similar review of methods used in 70 years of research on personality and close interpersonal relationships. They found that 60% of studies were a cross-sectional investigation based on self-report methods. One important difference is that more than half of the existing studies were based on non-student participants, as opposed to the norm that about three quarters of studies are based on student samples.

Some other troubling aspects that emerged include the fact that about one third of the studies conducted on people in relationships focused on data from only one respondent (only one member of the dyad). Why is this an issue? One study found that when members of a couple were asked to keep daily diaries of the events that transpired each day, there was less than 50% agreement! Although relatively few studies have been conducted, these investigations typically show that the perceptions of both members of the couple are significant predictors of relationship adjustment scores (e.g., Gable, Reiss, & Downey, 2003).

Perceptions of the partner may be quite useful. A recent investigation conducted in Canada had both members of a couple rate their own interpersonal problems and their partner's problems (Saffrey et al., 2003). Relationship adjustment was also evaluated by each participant, as well as by an expert. This study found that perceptions of the partner's problems was a stronger predictor of relationship adjustment than were self-perceptions of personal problems. Thus, it is valuable information to have the responses of both members of the dyad, and their perceptions of their partner.

The potential difference between members of a dyad was illustrated in one of our own research studies. The research assistants brought to my attention the responses of a heterosexual couple who had completed measures of personality and relationship adjustment. The female partner rated the relationship in glowing terms. Sadly, her male partner had scrawled on one of the questionnaires, "I can't fill this questionnaire out. We don't have a relationship!" This anecdote further illustrates the need to get multiple sources of information.

Another general concern noted by Cooper and Sheldon (2002) is that only a small number of studies followed from a detailed conceptual model of personality. That is, much of the research in this area has been largely atheoretical.

Clearly, research on personality and close personal relationships poses some special challenges. It may be difficult from a pragmatic perspective to get both members of a couple to participate in a research study, especially when the relationship is "in trouble." There are also challenges from a methodological or statistical perspective. When data from a couple are being analyzed, the researcher must use more sophisticated statistical analyses that recognize the **non-independence issue**. That is, responses provided by both members of a couple cannot be treated as if they are independent; the partners are interdependent and they tend to influence each other. As a result, the usual statistical procedures cannot be used because they are based on the assumption that the participants are independent of each other. David Kenny is a statistical expert who has discussed this issue at length (see Kenny, 1996).

Regardless of these theoretical and methodological challenges, enough evidence has accumulated from personality studies to indicate that we can predict with some degree of certainty which couples are going to have extreme difficulties and which ones are going to be relatively successful. Unfortunately, personality factors are not a main focus on premarital counselling programmes, which instead tend to focus on core relationship themes such as how to improve communication in the relationship. However, it is theoretically possible to identify those couples who are more at risk and devise interventions and problem-solving programs in an attempt to improve their chances. Some personality factors relative to romantic relationships are outlined in the next section.

KEY POINTS

- Like other research in the personality field, relationship studies tend to be cross-sectional. Studies also suffer often from including only one member of the dyad.
- Relationship research has special methodological challenges due to the non-independence of data supplied when both members of the couple are included in the research.

Similarity versus Dissimilarity and Relationship Adjustment

This book stated at the outset that when it comes to mate preferences, the axiom "birds of a feather flock together" is more accurate than the axiom "opposites attract." This tendency to select someone similar to the self is known as assortative mating. If assortative mating is taking place, then people with less pleasing personalities will find each other, while people with more positive characteristics will gravitate toward each other. However, our initial example of the movie *When Harry Met Sally* is a reflection of the gradual attraction of opposites.

One illustration of assortative mating comes from research on attachment styles with the AII. A meta-analysis of AII classifications showed that autonomous, securely attached men and women were much more likely to be married to each other than would be suggested by chance. Similarly, the AII provides an unresolved category that applies to people whose issues from childhood have clearly not been resolved. There is also a greater than chance tendency for husbands in the unresolved category to have wives who are also in the unresolved category (van Ijzendoorn & Bakermans-Kranenburg, 1996).

Although assortative mating does occur, what does the evidence suggest its overall impact is? Is assortative mating good or bad for the relationship in the long term? While matching securely attached people would be adaptive, a pairing of two people with unresolved childhood issues could prove problematic. In turns out that the overall answer to this question seems to depend greatly on the research strategy used to examine this issue.

Research with a nomothetic focus using a variable-centred approach has found limited evidence that assortative mating makes a difference. For example, Neyer and Voigt (2004) found no evidence of a link between couple similarity and relationship satisfaction. The variable-centred approach to predicting marital quality has generally found weak and inconclusive evidence. Moreover, this research indicates that there is strong similarity between partners in such characteristics as age and political and religious values, and moderate similarity in education and intelligence, but relatively little similarity in personality features (for a review, see Watson et al., 2004). The similarity in values reflected pre-existing differences at the start of the relationship rather than an increasing convergence in values over the course of the relationship. It was suggested that initial differences in key values are "deal-breakers" that do not bode well for the long-term success of the relationship. The aforementioned study by Neyer and Voigt (2004) also found modest evidence of personality similarity among partners, and this was outweighed by modest to large similarities among partners in their social networks.

The above conclusion needs to be qualified by the observation that the degree of personality similarity between husband and wife will likely vary substantially according to the personality construct in question. This observation is supported by data indicating a strong association between anti-social behaviours in the husband and wife (du Fort et al., 2002). Thus, to alter the well-known axiom, it seems that "exceptionally nasty birds of a feather flock together!"

An alternative way of examining the assortative mating issue is to take a **couple-centred approach**. This is a variation of an idiographic analysis directed at a particular person. Instead, the focus is now on the couple. A couple-centred approach involves looking at the degree of similarity between the members of the dyad in their personality profiles across several traits (see Luo & Klohnen, 2005).

Previous studies have either found no evidence of a link between couple similarity and relationship adjustment (Klohnen & Mendelsohn, 1998) or there was a small but significant association (e.g., Thiessen, Young, & Delgado, 1997). However, past studies have been limited by using relatively small samples and assessing only a few personality traits. Luo and Klohnen (2005) addressed these deficiencies in their study by examining 291 sets of newlyweds across a broad range of traits, including indices representing the five-factor model and attachment style. This study was unique in establishing that *profile similarity* across the range of variables was a significant predictor of marital quality. Attachment style was one of the key elements of these profiles.

Personality Traits and Relationship Satisfaction

Several other findings point to the significance of personality factors in relationship outcomes. For instance, people who are happy or dissatisfied with their relationships tend to feel the same way across relationship partners, thus suggesting that their own personality is playing an important role across different interpersonal situations (Robins, Caspi, & Moffitt, 2002).

Personality is also valued when considering what makes for a good relationship. One recent study looked at university student perceptions of what made for great "chemistry" in a relationship (Peretti & Abplanalp, 2004). Which factors do you think are most important? Looks? Similar interests? Personality? It turned out that physical attractiveness was rated as the most important factor for both men and women. The second most important factor for men was similarity, while it was reciprocity for women. The dating partner having a warm personality was the fourth most important for women and the fifth most important factor for men. Overall, 84% of women and 59% of men rated a warm personality as important. This difference was statistically significant.

Personality factors also come up when relationships go awry. Extensive research on attributional style indicates that relationships suffer when one or more partners tend to blame negative outcomes on undesirable

A sign that a relationship may be in trouble is when one partner blames negative outcomes on undesirable aspects of the other partner's personality.

aspects of the other partner's personality, and there is an unwillingness to attribute positive outcomes to some feature of the partner's personality (see Bradbury & Fincham, 1990).

Fincham (2001) has argued that no other cognitively based variable has received more empirical attention in the relationship area than attributional style, and the link between attribution and relationship satisfaction is so robust and so often found that it is probably the most replicable and reliable phenomenon in the study of close relationships. Data suggest that negative attributions to a partner's personality may play a causal role in increasing marital distress, and the link is still evident even when controlling for other correlated factors such as depression, anger, or marital violence (see Davey, Fincham, Beach, & Brody, 2001).

The Role of Neuroticism

Neuroticism has emerged consistently as a predictor of relationship satisfaction. Karney and Bradbury's (1995) meta-analysis of personality and relationship outcomes confirmed that neuroticism is a reliable predictor of difficulties. Neuroticism is a particularly impressive predictor of long-term outcomes. Kelly and Conley (1987) reported the results of a longitudinal study that examined personality and relationship factors among 300 couples who were together in the 1930s. Twenty couples broke off their engagement in 1935. Of the remaining 278 couples who had married, 50 had divorced by the 1980s. As part of their involvement in the Kelly Longitudinal Study (KLS), the participants' personality features back in 1930s were rated by five acquaintances. Data analyses revealed that three personality factors predicted long-term relationship termination: neuroticism in the wife, neuroticism in the husband, and a low level of impulse control on the part of the husband. Previously, Bentler and Newcomb (1978) also showed in longitudinal data that poor impulse control on the husband's part was linked with marital dissolution.

Overall, there have been relatively few empirical attempts to examine how all the trait dimensions in the five-factor model (extroversion, agreeableness, openness, neuroticism, and conscientiousness) contribute to relationship difficulties. The Luo and Klohnen (2005) study suggests that similarity is important, but which elements of the five-factor model are most relevant? One of the first studies to test this issue was conducted by Buss (1991), who examined the association between personality and measures of conflict and upset in couples in their first year of marriage. Buss used an adjective measure to obtain self-ratings, spousal ratings, and observer ratings of each participant's level of surgency (extroversion), agreeableness, intellect (openness), emotional stability (low neuroticism), and conscientiousness. Each participant also reported sources of irritation and upset caused by his or her spouse over the first year of marriage. One clear finding that emerged from this study was that men with high neuroticism and low agreeableness had wives who reported being upset about many of their husband's behaviours. The same characteristics in wives were also upsetting to their husbands, but men also had a problem with high extroversion in their wives because they saw them as highly condescending.

Watson, Hubbard, and Wiese (2000) evaluated relationship satisfaction, trait affect, and the personality traits of the five-factor model in married and dating couples. Self-ratings and partner ratings were both obtained. The most salient finding from this study was that negative affectivity and trait neuroticism predicted dissatisfaction among males and females. Moreover, the partner's level of trait negative affectivity predicted dissatisfaction after taking the other partner's trait negative affectivity into account. Another intriguing finding was that ratings of the partner's personality yielded more replicable effects across the married and dating couples than did self-ratings of personality.

When considering the predictiveness of neuroticism, it is important to assess the level of neuroticism in both partners. Robins, Caspi, and Moffitt (2000) also found that low negative emotionality was the best predictor of relationship quality and satisfaction, but both personalities should be taken into account; low negative emotionality in the man and the woman both contribute additively to relationship quality. Why does trait negative emotionality play such a role? Robins et al. (2000) observed that people with high negative emotionality exhibit the four characteristics identified by Gottman (1982) as particularly destructive to relationships: criticizing the partner, showing contempt for the partner, being highly defensive, and **stonewalling** (an avoidant form of shutting down and not communicating with the partner).

The Role of Perfectionism

Given the role of neuroticism in relationship problems, it is perhaps not too surprising that neurotic perfectionists with exacting standards for others (other-oriented perfectionism) and who perceive that others demand perfection from them (socially prescribed perfectionism) are at risk with their relationships. This was illustrated by a case study from noted theorist and therapist Albert Ellis, who is best known for his work on the rational–emotive therapy. Ellis suggests that dysfunction stems from irrational beliefs such as "I must be perfect in order to be loved." Ellis (2002) related the following:

> John, a 36-year-old accountant, gave himself a perfectionistic hard time about his work and made himself exceptionally anxious if it wasn't wholly accurate. He excused his perfectionism in this respect by saying that of course it had to be perfectly accurate—since it was accounting and that meant accuracy. But John was also perfectionistic about his dress, about his tennis game, and several other aspects of his life. Because, however, he worked mightily to keep his accounting, his appearance, and his tennis game in order, he succeeded fairly well in doing so and was only temporarily anxious when things got a bit beyond his control. His compulsive striving kept things pretty much in line.
>
> John, however, was equally perfectionistic about his wife, Sally, and his two accounting partners. They, too, had to—yes, had to—perform well, dress well, and even play tennis well. And often they didn't, those laggards! John, of course, couldn't control others, as he strove for his own perfection. So he was frequently enraged against his "careless" wife and partners and much more than he was anxious about his own performances.

> I saw John for therapy because his wife and partners insisted that he go—or else. He was set for a double divorce. I had a rough time, at first, showing him the folly of his own performance-oriented perfectionism, as he was willing to strive mightily to achieve it, and suffer occasional panic attacks when he didn't. It was easier to show him that his demands on others just wouldn't work. (pp. 217–229)

Empirical research has confirmed Ellis' observation about the destructiveness of perfectionism in relationships. Hewitt, Flett, and Mikail (1995) conducted an assessment of chronic pain patients and their spouses. It was found that pain patients with high levels of socially prescribed perfectionism reported lower levels of dyadic adjustment and family adjustment. Deficits in dyadic adjustment were exacerbated among chronic pain patients with high levels of socially prescribed perfectionism if they actually lived with an other-oriented perfectionist.

More recently, Haring, Hewitt, and Flett (2003) examined the associations among perfectionism, coping, and marital adjustment in a sample of 76 married couples. Socially prescribed perfectionism was associated with reports of low marital adjustment both for the self and one's partner, and that negative marital coping strategies mediated the association between socially prescribed perfectionism and low marital adjustment.

Recent advances focus on the development of relationship-specific measures of perfectionism. The Relationship Perfectionism Scale assesses two types of perfectionism: self-directed relationship perfectionism, a relationship version of self-oriented perfectionism (e.g., "It is important that I say all the right things in a conversation"), and other-directed relationship perfectionism (e.g., "To be worthy of my friendship, others should live up to my expectation") (Wiebe & McCabe, 2002). Both types of relationship perfectionism were found to be associated with depressive symptoms (Wiebe & McCabe, 2002).

At present, perfectionism has been identified as a correlate of possible relationship problems, but its role as a causal factor has not been established thus far. Longitudinal research that examines the predictiveness of perfectionism over time is greatly needed, along with a comparison of the relative predictive ability of perfectionism versus other personality traits such as neuroticism.

KEY POINTS

- Personality factors are valued as criteria in mate selection, though there is only limited evidence from assortative mating studies about the value of being paired with someone with a similar personality.
- Neuroticism and a hostile attributional style (i.e., blaming one's partner) are long-term risk factors for poor relationship outcomes. There is greater risk if both partners are high in neuroticism and negative emotionality.
- The inability to meet perfectionistic expectations is linked with poor relationship adjustment, though the role of perfectionism in relationship problems still needs to be evaluated in prospective research.

Personality Traits and Relationship Violence

No discussion of the role of personality traits in close relationships would be complete without at least a brief discussion of the important topic involving the link between personality and relationship violence.

The five-factor model study by Buss (1991) described earlier also included a factor that assessed acts of physical and verbal abuse (e.g., "He slapped me") and another factor that was a combination of abusiveness of alcohol and emotional constriction (e.g., "He drank too much; he hid all his emotions to act tough"). Buss (1991) found that low levels of agreeableness and low levels of emotional stability in both men and women were associated with a host of complaints; but only in men did these characteristics predict both alcohol abuse and physical and verbal abuse. In addition, low intellect in men was also associated with alcohol abuse and physical and verbal abuse.

Trait hostility seems to be associated with the potential for relationship violence, and this is in keeping with the findings stated above involving low agreeableness. Leonard and Senchak (1996) formulated a mediational model of marital violence that included personality factors (hostility and gender identity), husband alcohol use, and marital conflict styles as mediators of aggression expressed by the husband to the wife. Their three-year longitudinal study of 541 couples from Buffalo, New York, confirmed that trait hostility in husbands and wives predicted violence. Moreover, the link between personality factors and marital aggression expressed by husbands was mediated by the husbands' level of alcohol use and marital conflict styles. Overall, the results suggest that personality factors may play an important role in mediational models of relationship violence. However, Leonard and Senchak (1996) observed that their model accounted for only 29% of the variance in marital aggression when premarital levels of aggression were not included in the model, and they suggested the need to explore other factors that may improve the prediction of marital aggression.

O'Leary, Malone, and Tyree (1994) conducted a prospective study that also evaluated psychological needs and levels of physical aggression and psychological aggression (e.g., verbal hostility and passive–aggressive behaviour). The personality variables included in this study were the Jackson Personality Research Form measures of defendence (defensiveness), impulsivity, and aggression. All three personality factors were predictors of psychological aggression in men and women, and trait aggression was a small but significant predictor of physical aggression in the relationship for men and for women. Thus, those people who indicate that they have a need to be aggressive actually are more aggressive!

Impulsivity is also a significant predictor according to the results of a recent study of partner violence in the United States (see Schafer, Caetano, & Cunradi, 2004). This study with a representative national sample examined a limited number of personality factors and established that impulsivity, drinking problems, and a history of childhood physical abuse by parental figures were all associated with partner violence. The link with impulsivity points to a role for general deficits in self-control in partner violence.

Magdol, Moffitt, Caspi, and Silva (1998) have also conducted a long-term developmental investigation of the antecedents of partner abuse and they found that a history of early behaviour problems in childhood was a consistent predictor of levels of partner abuse measured when at the age of 21. Collectively, the data from these studies combine to suggest that an anti-social, aggressive personality style that develops throughout childhood is a dispositional risk factor that contributes to the link between violence and substance abuse. This personality style likely develops as a function of temperament factors and negative social experiences involving the witnessing and actual experience of violence, abuse, and neglect during childhood (see Bernstein, Stein, & Handlesman, 1998; Feldman, 1997).

Unfortunately, the possible mediating role of cultural differences is seldom considered when examining the role of personality factors in couple violence. A recent meta-analysis of data from 52 nations suggested that the amount of couple violence varies according to differences in individualism versus collectivism. Archer (2006) found that higher levels of individualism and gender equality were associated with more male victimization and less female victimization. Archer's work focuses generally on incidents of aggression by females, and females are less likely to aggress and more likely to be the victims of aggression in collectivist societies. An important unanswered question is the extent to which personality factors predict relationship violence in individualistic versus collectivistic societies.

Attachment Styles and Relationship Violence

Earlier, general research on romantic attachment styles and relationship satisfaction was outlined. What is the link between attachment style and marital violence? Holtzworth-Munro and Stuart (1994) focus on attachment styles as factors that underscore the link between drinking and violence. Roberts and Noller (1998) pointed to three indicators that suggest that attachment processes play a key role in the etiology of couple violence. First, many victims of relationship violence interpret the violence as a sign of love and commitment. Second, although it is true that the earlier that violence is found in a relationship, the more likely it is to be a long-term problem, violence becomes more likely as relationships intensify and a bond, albeit a shaky one, is established. Finally, attachment is implicated because the violence exhibited by members of a couple is typically relationship-specific and is not expressed outside their union.

Dutton, Saunders, Starzomski, and Bartholomew (1994) examined the link between attachment style and abusive tendencies in abusive men and their spouses. Dutton et al. (1994) found that men with preoccupied and fearful attachment styles engaged in greater psychological and physical abuse, according to spousal reports.

Bookwala and Zdaniuk (1998) compared the attachment styles of 26 men and 59 women in reciprocally aggressive dating relationships with the attachment styles of men and women in non-aggressive relationships. Participants rated their levels of attachment style according to the four Bartholomew and Horowitz (1991) categories. They also completed a modified version of the Conflict Tactics Scale and provided reports of their interpersonal problems on the Inventory of Interpersonal Problems. They found that men and women in reciprocally aggressive relationships had higher levels of preoccupied and fearful–avoidant attachment styles and more interpersonal problems. The stronger association was with aggressive tendencies and preoccupied attachment, and this association held even after controlling for variance attributable to interpersonal problems.

Other studies have also assessed the link between attachment style and responses to conflict. Direct examinations of the experience of anger are consistent with the view that attachment styles may play a role in hostility and the expression of aggression. For instance, Mikulincer (1998) conducted studies in Israel examining attachment styles and adaptive versus maladaptive responses to anger. Individuals with an ambivalent attachment style had higher levels of anger-in and had reduced levels of anger control, relative to individuals with a secure attachment style. Individuals with an avoidant attachment style were characterized by high hostility and low awareness of the physiological indicators of anger. Roberts and Noller (1998) examined the associations between attachment style and violence in 181 couples. The sample consisted of couples recruited from the community and from psychology classes. They completed measures of attachment style, communication patterns, dyadic adjustment, and levels of physical violence. Roberts and Noller (1998) based their analyses on two attachment factors identified as discomfort with closeness and anxiety over abandonment. The results showed that both men and women reported using violence against their partner if they had an attachment style characterized by anxiety over possible abandonment (i.e., preoccupied). Partner characteristics were also important; women reported higher levels of violence against their partners if their partners were anxious about abandonment.

More recent research continues to illustrate attachment style differences in responses to conflict. A contemporary investigation of romantic attachment styles and relationship conflict by Lorne Campbell from the University of Western Ontario and his associates required dating partners to complete a daily diary for 14 days and then discuss a major problem that occurred during that period (see Campbell, Simpson, Boldry, & Kashy, 2005). The first finding that emerged was that anxiously attached participants, relative to securely attached participants, were more sensitive to conflict and perceived more conflict overall. They also reported a tendency for conflicts to escalate over time. Also, observers coded the problem-solving discussion and found that anxiously attached people were not only seen by others as more distressed, but they also seemed to act in a way that escalated the conflict.

Most studies of romantic attachment styles in adults do not include an analysis of actual behaviours, so the Campbell et al. (2005) study is somewhat unique. Also unique is a new study that used cortisol data to examine the stress responses of securely attached and insecurely attached people in dating relationships (see Powers, Pietromonaco, Gunlicks, & Sayer, 2006). This study had couples engage in a conflict negotiation task. This study used physiological measures to address two aims: (1) establish that insecurely attached people have greater stress reactions in response to interpersonal conflict; and (2) demonstrate that people with insecurely attached partners have greater stress when conflict ensues. Support was obtained for both hypotheses, but the results varied by gender. Regarding the first aim, anxious attachment predicted stress reactivity and recovery, but avoidant attachment was predictive for women, and anxious, preoccupied attachment was predictive for men. As for the second aim, being partnered with an insecure attached person was associated with greater stress reactivity for men but not for women.

Studies have linked attachment styles to relationship dissatisfaction, relationship violence, and poor responses to conflict.

Overall, the findings linking certain attachment styles not only with relationship dissatisfaction but also with relationship violence, and poor responses to conflict point to the need to focus therapeutic efforts on attachment style differences. These issues are examined in Applied Perspective 10.1.

KEY POINTS

- An anti-social, aggressive personality is a factor that predicts relationship violence, especially when substance abuse is involved.
- An insecure attachment style is linked with a greater likelihood of being the perpetrator and recipient of relationship violence.
- People with an insecure attachment style are sensitized to conflict. They tend to react poorly to conflict, may escalate conflict, and have greater physiological reactivity to conflict.

Applied Perspective 10.1 The Role of Attachment Styles in Treatment

A growing body of evidence suggests that insecure attachment styles are associated with various forms of psychological distress, such as depression, as well as with relationship dysfunction. Thus, it is not surprising from a practical perspective that there is an increasing focus on attachment styles in therapeutic contexts. As shown below, attachment styles can exert an influence in several ways.

Attachment plays a key role when the main problem in treatment is an **attachment injury**.Attachment injury is a relatively new term used to characterize specific acts of betrayal in a couple's relationship (Naaman, et al., 2005). An attachment injury causes one or both members of a couple to feel unsafe in the relationship. Treatment must focus on resolving the injury and repairing the attachment bond.

One practical consideration is the interplay of the client's attachment style and the therapist's attachment style. A more positive therapeutic alliance and subsequent outcome will come from pairing together certain attachment styles. Some data have indicated, for example, that patients with an attachment orientation identified as "deactivating" (deflecting information about attachment issues and maintaining interpersonal distance) do better with a therapist who is the opposite and is low in this tendency to deactivate (Tyrell, Dozier, Teague, & Fallot, 1999). This is in keeping with suggestions that therapists may need to learn to adapt their interventions according to the client's attachment style (Hardy et al., 1999).

Clearly, the attachment styles of both the client and the therapist are important. A recent study found that secure attachment in the therapist contributed to a good alliance with the client, and the therapist's attachment style predicted a good alliance after taking other personality factors into account (Black, Hardy, Turpin, & Parry, 2005). Therapists with an anxious attachment style respond with less empathy to clients (Rubino et al., 2000), and this is problematic because, as Carl Rogers suggested, therapist empathy is a nonspecific factor that facilitates the client's improvement. It is particularly difficult to respond with empathy to clients with a dismissing attachment style (see Rubino et al., 2000), which is understandable because dismissing attachment involves negative models of others, including the therapist.

Other research suggests that therapy is simply less effective for people with certain attachment styles. An Australian study showed that the fearful–avoidant style in depression patients has been linked with poorer response to dynamic psychotherapy (Reis & Grenyer, 2004). Another investigation found initially that different attachment styles did not predict responsiveness to interpersonal therapy for depression; however, fearful–avoidant attachment was predominant among those who recovered but then re-experienced their depression (Cyranowski et al., 2002).

Susan Johnson from the University of Ottawa is a strong advocate of incorporating an attachment style focus into therapeutic interventions. Johnson is a developer and proponent of emotion-focused couples therapy (EFT). The most recent version of EFT emphasizes adult attachment styles in relationships. Specifically, it focuses on "the innate adaptive needs for protection, security, and connectedness with significant others" (Johnson & Greenberg, 1995, p. 124). As such, relationship distress occurs when the attachment needs have not been met, and the relationship fails to provide a secure base for one or both partners. The overall goal of treatment is to develop this secure base and strengthen bonds as couples maintain emotional engagement and learn to be accessible and responsive to each other's needs. Initial indications suggest that EFT can be easily modified to incorporate a greater focus on attachment style issues. Whiffen and Johnson (1998) described how EFT from an attachment-style perspective could be used to address interpersonal conflicts that contribute to postpartum depression.

How important is attachment? Johnson (2003) observed that,

> Couple and family therapists spend their professional lives helping people change the nature of their primary attachment relationship. Our clients come to us wanting to put an end to difficult recurring conflicts, to learn how to persuade their child or their spouse to cooperate with them, to deal with the depression and anxiety that arise when the relationships they count on become ambiguous or painful, or, even worse, begin to disintegrate. This is a challenging task (p. 3).

Summary

Chapter 10 expanded on earlier descriptions of the role of interpersonal factors in personality and individual differences. The chapter began with an examination of classic work from the 1950s, beginning with the interpersonal theory of psychiatry and the contributions of Harry Stack Sullivan. Sullivan proposed that personality is derived entirely from social interactions. It is through social interactions that people form a sense of the good me, the bad me, and the not me. Sullivan's work provided the impetus for further work on interpersonal styles but aspects of his theory may be criticized because they are difficult to empirically test.

Sullivan's work and the work of others (e.g., Leary, Bakan) provided the theoretical impetus for theory and research on the interpersonal circumplex. The circumplex is a circle structure based on the intercorrelations of two primary dimensions representing dominance versus submission, and love (or warmth) versus hostility. The eight primary interpersonal styles that comprise the circumplex have been studied in various situations, including the therapeutic context.

Next, we focused on two interpersonal constructs that involve a tough-minded approach to other people: Machiavellianism and authoritarianism. Machiavellianism is a manipulative orientation that involves deceiving others in order to get ahead. Machiavellians are particularly effective in face-to-face situations. Although the MACH-IV measure suffers from psychometric problems, it does predict expected differences in real-life contexts.

Adorno et al.'s work in the 1950s on the authoritarian personality was motivated by the atrocities committed during the Second World War. Authoritarian people are tough-minded, duty-oriented people. Although authoritarianism is usually associated with right-wing conservatism, it has been shown that authoritarianism also exists among extreme left-wing supporters. Altemeyer has shown that it is possible to assess left-wing authoritarianism. He also demonstrated that right-wing authoritarianism is a multi-dimensional construct composed of three distinguishable dimensions.

Our discussion of authoritarianism was followed by an analysis of individual differences in social dominance orientation. People high in this orientation believe that some groups are better than others, and they greatly prefer to be in the dominant group. This orientation is also associated with several rather unattractive characteristics. Social dominance and authoritarianism are not highly correlated, so it is possible to identify "double highs." These people are relatively scarce in the population but they have great impact on others because they are often among the most prejudiced people in the world.

The focus then shifted to contemporary theory and research on attachment styles. Attachment styles reflecting secure versus insecure attachment can be identified in infancy, and the attachment style classifications are relatively stable over time. Attachment style itself, however, is best regarded as a dimensional personality construct rather than a categorical construct. There are differences across cultures in attachment style dimensions and the extent to which the various attachment styles are valued.

Research on romantic attachment styles in adults was then reviewed beginning with the theory introduced by Hazan and Shaver. The model outlined by Bartholomew and Horowitz was then presented, including their notion derived from Bowlby that there are positive and negative working models of the self and others, and that these combine to form four different romantic attachment styles, only one of which involves secure attachment. This model led to the identification of dismissive attachment.

Research linking insecure romantic attachment styles was then reviewed, and this provided a bridge to other research on the role of personality factors in dating and marital relationships. Methodological issues involving research on personality in dyads were first presented, followed by an overview of research linking relationship problems with such constructs as attributional style, neuroticism, and perfectionism. This segment concluded with an overview of the role of personality factors in relationship violence and the importance of attachment styles in therapeutic contexts.

Questions to Consider

1 Review research findings on personality and relationship satisfaction in couples. Do you think that having a partner with a similar personality is a key criterion for most people? If people had an unlimited number of partners that they could select from, do you think they would select someone who had similar, dissimilar, or complementary attributes?

2 According to Bowlby, attachment styles involve internal working models that guide our cognitive processing. Do you accept the notion that whether we have a secure or insecure attachment style is a key determinant of how we interpret and recall the events we experience? Sullivan would suggest that we take on different attachment styles when with one type of person versus another type of person. Do you agree? Does your current attachment style reflect your attachment style as a child?

3 Think of someone you are highly familiar with, either someone you know personally or a celebrity who has captured your interest. How do you think they would score on the interpersonal circumplex? Review the adjectives in Table 10.2 to help with your assessment.

4 Theory and research on the authoritarian personality was influenced greatly by the events before and during the Second World War. In such a politically charged atmosphere, do you think it is possible for personality theorists and researchers to remain objective when they consider the nature of personality? Do you think the initial emphasis on right-wing (versus left-wing) authoritarianism is due to bias, or is it really the case that right-wing authoritarianism is much more prevalent? Do you think that that an extreme left-wing authoritarian, when compared with a right-wing authoritarian, would be more rigid, less rigid, or as rigid?

5 The personality styles of leaders have been extensively studied. Which interpersonal personality factors do you see as important in leadership? Can you envision situations that would require a leader who is high in Machiavellianism or authoritarianism? Do you think successful entrepreneurs must be somewhat Machiavellian to be successful?

6 This chapter concluded with the assertion that courses designed for couples considering marriage would be well-advised to incorporate a focus on personality factors. Do you agree

with this assertion? Do you think that when people get married, they have anything close to a true sense of their partner's actual personality? If you were given the chance to assess your partner (current partner or future partner), which personality measures would you administer?

Key Terms

agency, p. 388
anxiously attached, p. 405
assortative mating, p. 418
attachment injury, p. 426
avoidant attachment, p. 406
circumplex, p. 389
communion, p. 388
complementarity principle, p. 388
couple-centred approach, p. 419
dark triad, p. 396
disorganized attachment style, p. 406
Machiavellianism, p. 394
non-independence issue, p. 417
personifications, p. 386
relational schemas, p. 386
securely attached, p. 405
social dominance orientation, p. 403
stonewalling, p. 421
Strange Situation, p. 405
tenderness, p. 385
theorem of escape, p. 384
theorem of reciprocal emotions, p. 384
unmitigated agency, p. 389
unmitigated communion, p. 389
vector length, p. 391

Key Theorists

Mary Ainsworth, p. 405
David Bakan, p. 388
Kim Bartholomew, p. 410
John Bowlby, p. 405
Timothy Leary, p. 388
Harry Stack Sullivan, p. 383

chapter eleven

PERSONALITY AND THE SELF-CONCEPT

- Brief History of Conceptualizing The Self-Concept
- Erik Erikson and The Psychosocial Stages of Development
- Motives and the Self-Concept
- Representations and Conceptualizations of the Self-Concept
- Self-Esteem
- The Domains of the Self-Concept
- Personality Constructs Reflecting The Self

I am always with myself, and it is I who am my tormentor.

—LEO TOLSTOY

Know thyself? If I knew myself, I'd run away.

—JOHANN WOLFGANG VAN GOETHE

What we must decide is perhaps how we are valuable, rather than how valuable we are.

—F. SCOTT FITZGERALD

No one can make you feel inferior without your consent.

—ELEANOR ROOSEVELT

WHO AM I? WHAT AM I LIKE? What will I be like in 10 years? All of these questions reflect issues involving the self-concept. Any topic that pertains to a person's self-image is relevant. And it can involve the person's current sense of self but also his or her past self and anticipated future self.

The personality literature seems enormous once it is acknowledged that the personality field also includes individual differences in the self-concept. The close link between personality and self-concept becomes particularly evident when we consider these topics from a developmental perspective. The same factors that contribute to the development of personality (see Chapter 3) also tend to operate in the development of the self-concept. This is particularly evident when we consider the role that interpersonal factors play in the shaping the self-concept.

Chapter 11 begins with a brief history of theory and research on the self-concept along with an overview of personal identity theories. Next, we examine the motives that drive the self-concept, and show that the self-concept is a complex and multi-faceted entity with both stable and permeable components. Chapter 11 concludes with an overview of key constructs including self-consciousness, self-monitoring, and self-handicapping.

A BRIEF HISTORY OF CONCEPTUALIZING THE SELF

Early psychology was largely a psychology of personal experience. The method of introspection was used to assess personal experience. As people examined and reported on their own states of consciousness, it became apparent that the conscious mind consisted largely of an individual's experience of himself or herself. This realization contributed to increased interest in the nature of the self-concept.

The early experimental psychologist Wilhelm Wundt regarded the self in terms of the person's experience of his or her own body. That is, the self was defined by such concepts as muscle tension, sensation of internal states, and so on.

The classic work of William James published during the period of 1890 to 1892 led to a radically different view of the self-concept. James accepted the view that the self is the main factor in mental life. And he made it clear that the self is one of our most basic problems or issues, and it deserves extensive consideration.

William James

In addition to his substantial influence on psychology in general, **William James** made several contributions to theory and research on the self. He is considered here because he was one of the first self-concept theorists, and because he promoted the view that the self-concept is multidimensional. In addition, he provided one of the earliest definitions of self-esteem.

James posited three components to the self-concept: (1) the material me; (2) the social me; and (3) the spiritual me. The *material me* is a very surface-level account of the self. It is the material possession of the body and the contexts that are linked with one's body, such as one's home and family environment. The *social me* is an individual's awareness of his or her identity in the eyes of others. James observed that there may be as many different social mes as there are people in our lives. That is, we will have a different social me depending on how each person perceives us. Also, other people are part of our situation, and each person in our world can represent a very different social situation. This component of James' work no doubt provided the original impetus for work by Mark Leary on the **sociometer theory**, which is the notion that our self-esteem is essentially a barometer of our relationships with others, and it goes up and down depending on the quality of our interactions and sense of positive connections with others (see Leary, 1999). Finally, the *spiritual me* is the most abstract and vague aspect of the self-concept. The spiritual me incorporates our awareness of our mental processes in terms of our subjective sense of thoughts and feelings. James likened the spiritual me to the living substance of each person's soul.

William James was one of the first self-concept theorists.

James did not examine the material me, the spiritual me, and the social me in terms of cross-cultural differences, since more basic issues involving the nature of the self-concept were paramount at the time. However, it is important for us to acknowledge that the exact nature of the spiritual me and the social me, in particular, will vary according to cultural considerations. The material in Figure 11.1 underscores this point. This figure represents the concept of selfhood in India, according to Mascolo, Misra, and Rapisardi (2004). Space limitations preclude going into all the aspects represented in Figure 11.1. However, it should be evident just how complex the self can become and how it can reflect the particular themes in a culture. The main emphasis here is on the inner spiritual self and its link with the complex relational social self. The spiritual self is represented by the concept of "atman-brahman." The atman is "the realization of one's true or essential self, and the realization that one's essential self is indistinguishable from absolute reality, which is known as *brahman*. Brahman consists of the spiritual absolute, which is not only ubiquitous but also free of form and matter" (Mascolo et al., 2004, p. 10). The material me also plays a role because the atman is fused at birth with the material aspects of self (see Mascolo et al., 2004).

The social self in India places a great emphasis on doing one's duty and respecting hierarchy, with one's father being at the top of the hierarchy. Duties must be performed according to one's extended family, one's caste (social class), and the state (the country of India). Four social values are particularly important. They are *moksa* (spiritual emancipation), *dharma* (righteous action; performing duties associated with one's station in life), *artha* (wealth), and *kama* (pleasure). The spiritual values represented by moksa take precedence.

Figure 11.1 The Indian Conception of Selfhood

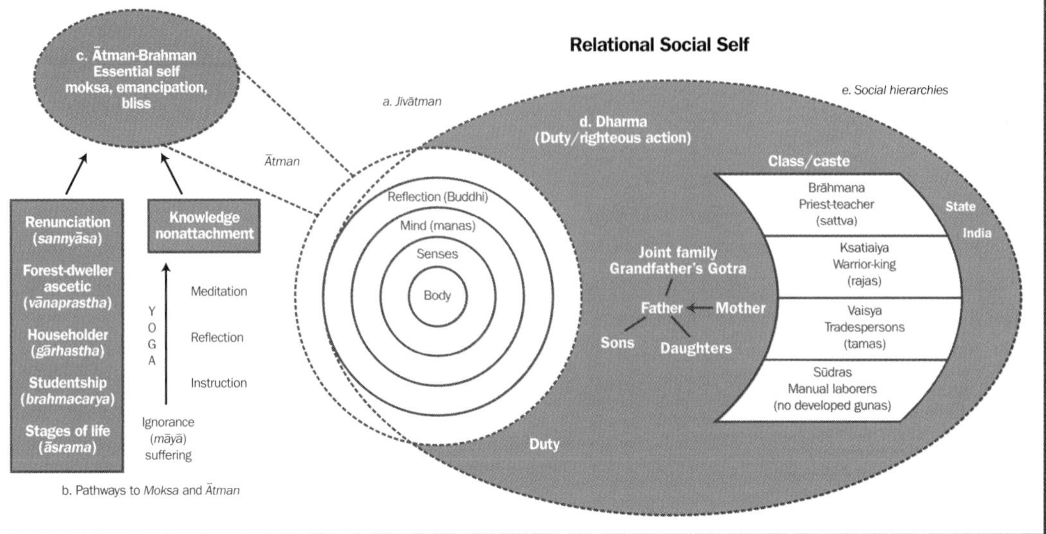

Source: Mascolo, et al. 2004.

In addition to outlining the material me, social me, and spiritual me, James also provided his thoughts on how we come to regard ourselves, including a sense of self-satisfaction versus self-dissatisfaction. He was one of the first theorists to discuss the concept of self-esteem. He defined self-esteem as the number of our successes divided by our pretensions (aims and expectations). In other words, self-esteem could be assessed as the ratio of actualities and accomplishments versus our expectations. The two ways to raise our self-esteem, according to James, are to increase our accomplishments or lower our goals and expectations.

KEY POINTS

- According to James, the self is multidimensional and consists of the material me, the social me, and the spiritual me.
- We may have a social me for each significant person in our lives.
- According to James, the self-esteem formula is our successes divided by our pretensions (our aims and expectations).

The Looking Glass Self

The views outlined by James were quite provocative, and the notion of the self continued to grow in its importance. The sociologist Charles Cooley (1912) introduced the concept of the looking glass self. That is, our sense of our self depends on the reactions of other people, and watching how other people treat us is like looking in a mirror or looking glass in order to see oneself. As you might have deduced, the looking glass self-concept was inspired by the classic Lewis Carroll book *Through the Looking Glass*. As we saw in the previous chapter, Sullivan (1947) also emphasized the effect that perceived feedback from other people had on the self.

As noted by Felson (1989), the symbolic interactionism approach has three components. In addition to our self-appraisal, there is also the actual appraisal of other people, and the person's perception of other people's appraisal. This last component is known as the **reflected appraisal**. Felson suggested that actual appraisals only operate on the self through reflected appraisals, so there should be no predictive value of actual appraisals on the self if reflected appraisals have already been taken into account.

Clearly, our sense of how others view us has a powerful influence on our affect and motivation. Research in achievement contexts indicates that the perceptions of significant others (i.e., parents and teachers) relate directly to the self-perceptions that students have of their own academic capabilities (e.g., Felson, 1989). Our perceptions of what people expect also play a vital role. Shah (2003) has shown that the perceived expectations of a significant other and the perceived value they attach to outcomes can be compelling forces that direct our goal pursuits, goal appraisals, and expectations.

The essence of the looking glass self was illustrated clearly by an experiment conducted by Gergen (1965). Participants were told that they either had to get an interviewer to like them (the ingratiation condition) or they had to get the interviewer to really get to know and understand them as a person (the accurate impression condition). For all of the participants in the ingratiation condition and in a subset of the accurate impression condition, the interviewer nodded in agreement and verbally expressed agreement whenever the participant said something positive about the self. The other participants received no reaction. It was found that those who received reinforcement in the form of a positive response from the interviewer reported significantly higher self-esteem than those who did not receive the favourable reaction from the interviewer.

Tice (1992) suggested that in certain contexts, the looking glass may become a magnifying glass. This means that behaviours that are performed in public in front of other people are much more likely to be internalized in the form of self-concept change, compared with performing the same behaviours in private.

The sociologist George Herbert Mead (1934) had earlier explored this theme with his **symbolic interactionism theory**. The essence of this theory is that we come to view the self from the standpoint of social groups. These social groups combine to provide a sense of a generalized other than is evaluating us. The self-reflection is a social construction that involves a sense of the roles that other people expect us to adopt in their presence. Symbolic interactionism involves the actual treatment we receive from others, our perception of this treatment, and how it feeds back and shapes our self-concept.

KEY POINTS

- Cooley introduced the notion of "the looking glass self;" that is, how other people treat us is like looking into a mirror and the feedback from this mirror is incorporated into our self-concept.
- Our perception of how other people regard us and view us is called the reflected appraisal. Reflected appraisals may differ from our self-appraisals or the actual way that other people see us.

- Mead's symbolic interactionism theory is an extension of the looking glass self-concept. That is, we come to view the self in terms of a generalized view of how social groups evaluate us and regard us.

An extensive literature has investigated the extent to which people are accurate in their appraisals of how they are viewed by other people. An initial review suggested there is a relatively low association between the way other people actually see a person and the person's appraisal of these social evaluations (Shrauger & Schoeneman, 1979), and this general lack of correspondence was confirmed by subsequent authors (e.g., Kenny & DePaulo, 1993). Kenny and DePaulo (1993) coined the term "meta-accuracy" to refer to the extent to which people know how others see them. Their review led to three conclusions. First, when people interact with several others, they have a generalized meta-perception that is highly consistent; that is, they perceive that there are similarities in how they are viewed by other people. In fact, people overestimate the degree of consistency.

Second, the level of meta-accuracy depends on whether the focus is on a specific dyad or on others in general. There is low accuracy in a dyad with another person, but people are "substantially correct" when they consider a more global view of how they are viewed by people in general.

Third, it was concluded that when in dyads, people do achieve a small degree of accuracy. However, to reiterate, there is greater accuracy when there is a more global focus on how the self is perceived by people in general.

This pattern of findings seems to have held across time. A new contemporary review suggests that there is at least a moderate association between how other people view us and our self-perceptions, but this association is stronger than the link between our self-perceptions and our actual level of ability as determined by objective measures (Lundgren, 2004). However, recent research also highlights the bi-directional influence of how other people's perceived appraisals influence us, and in turn, how we influence other people.

KEY POINTS

- Meta-accuracy is the term for how accurate we are in our sense of how other people view us.
- Meta-accuracy is relatively low.
- Meta-accuracy is more accurate when the data involve a global assessment of the self rather than dyadic assessment in a specific context.

James Mark Baldwin (1894), the developmental psychologist, was another noteworthy contributor who focused attention on the role of imitation in self-concept processes. Among other things, Baldwin emphasized the role of imitation in the development of self-consciousness. Baldwin also introduced the concept that how a person views himself or herself can have a substantial influence on how we perceive other people. This concept has been confirmed by extensive research.

The turn of the century saw the growing influence of Freud's theory. Freud's notion of the ego is equated with the concept of self. Horney (1932) expanded on reactions to the self by distinguishing between self-love and self-alienation. She suggested that self-love is essential for happiness, but the particular form that self-love takes is significant because there are various forms of neurotic self-love. As for self-alienation, this emerges, according to Horney, when there is an estrangement from the true or actual self.

The radical behaviourism espoused by John Watson and the emphasis on observable phenomena resulted in less interest in the self throughout much of the first half of the 20TH century. It was up to Harry Stack Sullivan, with his emphasis on the interpersonal roots of the self, as well as the self-actualization theorists (i.e., Rogers and Maslow), to renew interest in the study of the self, and this interest has continued to this day.

The Divided Self

The Rogerian notion that the actual self we manifest becomes distinct from our ideal self was elaborated by British psychiatrist R. D. Laing. In his book *The Divided Self* (1959), Laing suggested that the root of psychosis in schizophrenia is the disparity between the patient's publicly presented false self and his or her true self. The false self is the result of a long process through which the person has developed an unembodied self where there is a sense of detachment from one's own physical being. Consistent with the views of both Sullivan and Rogers, Laing suggested that the false self develops in response to the perceived expectations of significant others, but these significant others may be perceived as malevolent; hence the fear of the paranoid schizophrenic. Laing reserved the term "personality" to refer to the publicly presented self, and he saw schizophrenia as due in part to a deep divide and alienation between the true self and the presented mask.

No attempt to provide an overview of theory on the self would be complete without an examination of Erik Erikson's views of the self-concept and personal identity. His theory is outlined next.

ERIK ERIKSON AND THE PSYCHOSOCIAL STAGES OF DEVELOPMENT

Erik Erikson is a world-renowned developmental theorist. Erikson's contributions include promoting the study of development throughout the entire life span, as well as emphasizing the role of psychosocial factors and how the adult self-concept, in particular, develops within the context of our relationships with other people. Erikson also promoted the importance of personal identity and the concept of identity crisis. The concept of identity crisis is described below. Finally, Erikson was one of the earliest psychobiographers. He provided life history analyses of such famous people as Mahatma Ghandi and Martin Luther. Psychobiography is the subject of the final chapter in this book, Chapter 14.

To a large extent, Erikson's theoretical views on development and the need to establish a sense of identity are a reflection of his own experiences. Erikson became a famous scholar through a very indirect route. He was trained as a painter, but when he was 25 years old he got a job as a tutor for one of Freud's patients in Austria. He was befriended

Erik Erikson promoted the study of development throughout the entire life span, and the study of how adult self-concept developed within the context of relationships with others.

by Anna Freud, and she trained him in psychoanalytic techniques. (He also met his wife-to-be, Canadian-born teacher and dancer Joan Serson.) As a result of these Freudian influences on his theory, his work is typically found in the psychoanalytic section of personality textbooks because it is an extension and refinement of Freud's theory. It is found in this chapter because of its relevance to issues involving the self-concept and personal identity.

Erikson's theory reflects his personal experiences. He struggled with his own sense of identity throughout his adolescence and early adulthood. Part of this was uncertainty about what he wanted to do as an adult, but much of this was uncertainty about his own heritage. Erikson never knew his father because his parents separated prior to his birth in 1902 in Germany. His mother married a physician named Homburger, and Erikson was known as Erik Homburger until the age of 39, when he was living in the United States and he took Erikson as his surname.

Erikson's theory differs from Freud's in several key respects. First and foremost, whereas Freud's theories took us only to the beginning of adulthood, Erikson provided a lifespan theory that stretches from the cradle to the grave. He postulated eight different stages, and he is distinguished as being one of the very few theorists who included a focus on personality development in older people. Erikson's theory is also distinct in that he focused on psychosocial stages rather than psychosexual stages. Each stage has a task that involves a crisis and results in a positive psychological quality if successfully achieved. It is a crisis, according to Erikson (1959), because each new stage requires a radical change in perspective. Finally, he focused primarily on the ego rather than the superego, and, as such, he is often referred to as an ego psychologist.

What is meant by the term "psychosocial crisis?" Erikson (1 950) felt that the term "psychosocial" signified that development reflected the interplay of a person's biological and physical attributes as well as the impact of social factors. At the broadest level, social factors involve cultural influences. Erikson was greatly impressed by the role that culture can play, especially in contributing to a sense of identity. As a result of his visits to study various societies (such as the Sioux Indians), Erikson suggested that distress may result from developing a personal identity that is inconsistent with a person's surrounding. Thus, a key consideration is whether there is a fit between how someone sees himself or herself and the culture that they find themselves in.

The eight stages posited by Erikson are shown in Table 11.1. The stages involve core issues of trust–mistrust, autonomy–shame/doubt, initiative–guilt, industry–inferiority, identity–identity confusion, intimacy–isolation, generativity–stagnation, and integrity–despair. The stages are epigenetic, which means that it is a step-by-step model. Childhood ends after the fourth stage, and the first stage of early adulthood involves establishing a sense of identity, even though the young person in question may not be psychologically ready to do so.

Table 11.1 Erikson's Eight Stages of Psychosocial Development

Conflict	Age	Thematic Question
Trust versus Mistrust (HOPE)	Birth to 18 months	Is there a trusting relationship with the care-giver or or a sense of shame?
Autonomy versus Shame and Doubt (WILL)	1.5 to 3 years old	Does the child learn a sense of autonomy and self-control or a sense of shame?
Initiative versus Guilt (PURPOSE)	3 to 6 years old	Is the child appropriately assertive and independent or too forceful, leading to guilt?
Industry versus Inferiority (COMPETENCE)	6 to 12 years old	Can the child master new tasks and develop skills or feels incompetent?
Identity versus Role Confusion (FIDELITY)	12 to 18 years old	Can the teenager get a sense of identity and self in terms of relationship with peers and current and future life roles?
Intimacy versus Isolation (LOVE)	18 to 40 years old	Is a loving, intimate relationship formed, or is the person disconnected?
Generativity versus Stagnation (CARE)	40 to 65 years old	Does the person find ways to contribute to the next generation or lead a stagnant existence?
Ego Integrity versus Despair (WISDOM)	65 to 80 years old	Is the person able to accept his/her life or is he/she preoccupied with unfinished business marked by a fear of death?

As noted, central to each stage is the resolution of a key task or challenge in order to move on to the next stage and achieve a certain psychological characteristic. For instance, resolving the first stage provides a sense of trust, while resolving the next stage provides personal will.

The first four stages are similar to the stages identified by Freud, with Erikson implicating psychosocial challenges as the key motivating force rather than psychosexual urges. Note that Erikson believed that each new stage of the life cycle requires us to once again work through each of the stages in a way that is appropriate for the particular phase of the life cycle being experienced at the time. Also, the stages are not mutually exclusive. The attempts to resolve a new psychosocial crisis may result in the re-emergence of issues from earlier stages, and these issues may be positive or negative.

Erikson (1963) also maintained that development across these age stages contributes to greater social breadth over time. That is, as we get older, we broaden our "social radius" of family, friends, peers, and ties with the general community.

Erikson's theory becomes distinct when it accounts for personality development in adolescents. Here the focus is on the adolescent's struggle to develop a sense of personal identity. It is the time for trying to figure out what kind of person you are and what kind of person you would like to become. This is a vitally important issue that can provide a lifetime of sorrow for people who fail to develop a clear and healthy sense of identity. Attainment of identity results in the quality of fidelity, which in this context is an exactness and faithful reproduction of one's self. Failure to achieve this goal results in a sense of identity diffusion and confusion, according to Erikson. Frustrated efforts to develop a clear and adaptive identity may not only result in diffusion and confusion, because a negative identity may also develop. Negative identities reflect aimlessness and anti-social tendencies.

Erikson (1959) suggested that it is particularly important to establish a sense of identity with respect to occupational goals. Young people who are unable to form a clear sense of identity may rely on cliques that foster stereotypes and an intolerant orientation toward other people. He suggested that we need to understand the roots of this intolerance because

> ... it is difficult to be tolerant if deep down you are not quite sure that you are a man (or a woman), that you will ever grow together again and be attractive, that you will be able to master your drives, that you will really know who you are, that you will know who you want to be, that you know what you look like to others, and that you will know how to make the right decisions without, once and for all, committing yourself to the wrong friend, sexual partner, leader, or career. (Erikson, 1959, p. 205–6)

The Identity Crisis

Erikson's work gave rise to the popular term "**identity crisis**" to describe the failed search for a sense of personal identity during adolescence and early adulthood. Some people never achieve a sense of personal identity and spend the rest of their lives in search of their identity. According to Baumeister, Shapiro, and Tice (1985), there are two discernible types of identity crisis. An **identity deficit** occurs when the person is seeking to establish a desired identity (e.g., "I don't know who I am"), while an **identity conflict** is when two or more aspects of the self are in opposition with each other (e.g., "I am the type of person who wants to be with people but doesn't want to be with people"). Baumeister et al. (1985) suggested that the essence of identity conflict is finding oneself in an impossible situation due to conflict-ridden aspects of the self.

Note that according to Erikson's scheme, we must develop an intact and clear sense of our personal identity before we can establish the type of loving relationship that requires sharing our intact self with another person. This is a very contentious aspect of his model. One criticism of Erikson's model is that some people do establish an intimate relationship before they establish their sense of personal identity (see Franz, 1995).

When we consider people who have had a change in their personality identity, it seems all the more appropriate to consider personality development through the lifespan, instead of regarding personality as a fixed identity. Take, for example, the life story of Michael J.

Fox, the Canadian actor who became famous as a result of his work in the *Back to the Future* trilogy. Fox was diagnosed with Parkinson's disease in 1991. (His story was discussed earlier in Chapter 7.) He observed subsequently that:

> Before Parkinson's, when so much of my identity was tied up in my acting career, the question that burned inside me was, *How long can I keep living like this?* Then came P.D., with its slightly more pressing question, *How long will I be able to keep on living any life at all?* My sense of what really mattered had been turned upside down, and I came out of this period of self-reflection with a completely new perspective on my life and work. (Fox, 2002, p. 181)

Clearly, this dramatic change in Fox's health status was the catalyst for a distinctly different sense of identity. Changes in identity as a result of events later in one's life suggest that we do need to consider personality development from a lifespan perspective.

After being diagnosed with Parkinson's disease, actor Michael J. Fox gained a new perspective on his life and career.

The personal experience of Michael J. Fox is in keeping with empirical evidence of changes in identity status over time. That is, even among people who have attained a sense of identity achievement, fluctuations are possible, and these people may not maintain their sense of identity achievement (see Whitbourne, 1986). Longitudinal research has shown that both mature and immature forms of personal identity can vary over the life course (see Marcia, 1976; Waterman, Geary, & Waterman, 1974). For instance, a case study analysis of the writings and diary entries of British author Vera Brittain found age-related increases in generativity and intimacy themes, and an age-related decrease in overall identity themes. However, within the identity category, there was a developmental increase in identity themes related to Brittain's occupational status (see Franz, 1995).

Generativity in Older People

Michael J. Fox has dealt with his illness by becoming an activist and advocate for more research on Parkinson's disease in particular, and stem cell research in general. A strong case can be made for Fox having attained Erikson's generativity stage. Generativity (versus stagnation) is associated typically with middle adulthood. **Generativity** is the willingness to engage in acts to promote the well-being of younger generations in order to promote the long-term survival of the species. Erikson highlighted the role of generativity in his psychobiographical case analyses, including his study of Luther (Erikson, 1958) and Ghandi (Erikson, 1969).

Erikson (1950) suggested that generativity can be expressed with parents raising and taking care of their children, but there are many different forms, and generativity is obviously not limited to people who are parents. Teachers, mentors, and community activists are good candidates to be high in generativity. For instance, think of that one particular teacher who took a special interest in you and encouraged you to go on to university or college. It is likely that this teacher was high in generativity. A good way of evaluating politicians and political candidates would be to try to get a sense of their true desire for promoting the welfare of future generations. Many profess this concern, but who are the ones who actually have it?

Although generativity is primarily communal in its focus, McAdams and associates have argued that generativity can reflect the themes of both agency and communion (see McAdams & de St. Aubin, 1992). Communion is reflected by promoting the well-being of others, while agency is the need to have impact on the next generation.

McAdams and de St. Aubin (1992) made an important contribution by outlining the first complete theory of generativity following Erikson's (1950, 1963) initial theory. They argued that generativity is motivated by two key sources: (1) inner desire (including the need to be needed) and (2) cultural demand. They noted that the cultural demand can be normative and more or less expected of adults, but normativeness will vary depending on the culture people live in. Also, cultures vary in the extent to which they have constraints that mitigate against the expression of generative desires. According to these authors, once inner desire and cultural demand are in place, they contribute to a salient concern for the next generation. Other key elements include commitment to generativity, a strong belief in the species and its importance, and then engagement in specific actions to promote the well-being of others.

The ability to achieve a sense of generativity has several positive correlates. One prospective study of 86 men found, for instance, that more than half of these men had achieved generativity (Westermeyer, 2004). These men had comparatively better mental health, more successful marriages, more close friendships, and higher work achievements. Westermeyer (2004) also found that in terms of long-term predictors, generativity was more likely if the person came initially from a warm family background, had good peer group relationships, and had the benefit of a mentor. Personality traits associated with generativity include openness and extroversion (Bradley & Marcia, 1998).

Erikson's interest in promoting an understanding of the entire life cycle resulted in a compelling book titled *Vital Involvement in Old Age* (Erikson, Erikson, & Kivnick, 1986). This fascinating book is based on interviews with 50 elderly people. Erikson et al. (1986) provide illustrative case examples of how people address the eight stages of the life cycle differently as they were nearing the end of their lives. It is shown, for instance, that there are various ways of achieving a sense of generativity. Some people achieved this by taking care of their children or grandchildren, becoming teachers, and so on. However, for others, generativity is attained by avoiding certain behaviours, such as not taking one's own life because of the impact it would have on younger members of the family. Thus, not only are there many different ways to achieve the same developmental goal, but there is also great heterogeneity among people at the same developmental stage.

Erikson also made the important point that issues of personal identity continue to play great importance among the elderly, and identity issues may become quite complex. The complexities of coming to grips with identity issues later in life is illustrated by the following excerpt:

> An old woman who has long identified with being classically beautiful must somehow accept the image her mirror now reflects—perhaps faded, perhaps intensified—without retroactively invalidating the physical beauty that was hers until recently. (Erikson et al., 1986, p. 131)

According to Erikson's widow, Joan Erikson, he always intended to add a ninth stage called old age. The old age stage applies to people who are 80 years and older. This new stage is detailed in their 1997 book *The Life Cycle Completed*. The person who attains this stage is accepting of his or her death and even practises for it, but also develops a renewed sense of rebirth and hope.

KEY POINTS

- Erikson was trained in the psychoanalytic tradition, but he is an ego psychologist who postulated a series of psychosocial stages, rather than psychosexual conflicts.
- According to Erikson, development occurs across a series of eight stages that go across the lifespan. The most influential stage is the fifth stage, where the focus is on developing a sense of ego identity versus despair.
- People without an identity are said to have an identity crisis.
- Although a main focus in adolescence and early adulthood, identity concerns can persist and be found in elderly people.

Evaluation of Erikson's Model

There is much to admire about Erikson's model. It has a welcome focus on psychosocial influences and cultural factors rather than on more primitive psychosexual urges. We have already acknowledged the wisdom of focusing on personality across the lifespan, and concepts such as the identity crisis and generativity have a great deal of resonance and personal relevance for most people. The main criticism is one that has been levied at others with a psychoanalytic focus: certain concepts are difficult to empirically test and seem quite subjective. Still, it must be accepted that Erikson was an astute and keen observer of what really matters to people, and for this he deserves enormous credit. Although not a criticism per se, as we see in the next section, some authors have suggested that there is also a need to extend Erikson's theory by identifying several levels within certain stages.

Marcia's Levels of Ego Identity Status

A widely accepted extension of Erikson's identity concept was proposed by **James Marcia**, Professor Emeritus at Simon Fraser University in British Columbia. Marcia qualified Erikson's model by suggesting that ego identity is not an all-or-nothing thing. He outlined a more continuous view that entails four levels of ego identity status: (1) identity achievement; (2) moratorium; (3) foreclosure; and (4) identity diffusion. These four identity statuses reflect two variables: (1) crisis (the period of having to choose between alternatives); and (2) commitment (the amount of personal investigation or importance the person displays). Identity status is a reflection of commitment and exploration with respect to interpersonal values, ideology, and occupational pursuits (see Marcia, Waterman, Matteson, Archer, & Orlofsky, 1993).

Marcia's two endpoints (identity achievement and identity diffusion) reflect the two outcomes described by Erikson. In many ways, identity diffusion can be equated with the "worst case scenario" because people with identity diffusion have the most insecure forms of attachment and tend to distance themselves from their parents. These people are highly vulnerable and reactive to attempts by other people to manipulate their self-esteem (Marcia et al., 1993; Marcia, 2001).

In general, the term "moratorium" refers to a shutdown or freezing of activity whereby the current status quo is simply maintained. People in the moratorium identity status are in the identity crisis period and are striving to make personal commitments, but the commitments are quite vague. According to Marcia (1966), this individual often seems internally preoccupied and bewildered.

In contrast, a person with the foreclosure identity status has a clear expression of commitment but has not yet experienced a meaningful identity crisis. Marcia suggested that it is difficult with this type of person to determine where their parents' goals for them end and where their own personal goals begin. It is as if this person has overly identified with the parents' wishes and has acquiesced. Thus, foreclosure involves great overidealization of the family. According to Marcia (2001), of the four identity statuses, foreclosure involves the greatest cognitive rigidity and acceptance of authoritarian beliefs.

As might be expected, forms of identity vary in their personality correlates, so identity status and personality structure are clearly linked. Identity achievement is predicted by low neuroticism and high conscientiousness and extroversion. Identity moratorium and diffusion are associated with high neuroticism, low agreeableness, and low conscientiousness (Clancy & Dollinger, 1993).

Note that the concept of different levels or degrees of stage attainment has also been applied to the generativity stage. Bradley and Marcia (1998) distinguished five generativity status profiles along a continuum by considering variations in levels of involvement and inclusiveness in generativity-related activities. Inclusiveness refers to whether generativity is focused solely on the people with whom we already have contact, or, as is the case in full-blown generativity, an attempt is made have a more widespread impact in order to benefit people in general.

Marcia (1966) developed an open-ended interview to tap these four identity statuses. Respondents were asked questions that involved occupational and religious themes, and their responses were scored according to the descriptions of the four identity status categories. An example of sample questions from the occupational and religious areas and responses that illustrate the four different levels of identity status are shown in Table 11.2.

Table 11.2 The Identity Status Questionnaire Developed by Marcia

Sample question from the occupational area:

- How willing do you think you'd be to give up going into _______ if something better came along?

Sample responses that illustrate the four different levels of identity status:

- Identity Achievement: "Well, I might, but I doubt it. I can't see what 'something better' would be for me."
- Moratorium: "I guess if I knew for sure I could answer that better. It would have to be something in the general area—something related."
- Foreclosure: "Not very willing. It's what I've always wanted to do. The folks are happy with it and so am I."
- Identity Diffusion: "Oh, sure. If something better came along, I'd change just like that."

Sample question from the religious area:

- Have you ever had any doubts about your religious beliefs?

Sample responses that illustrate the four different levels of identity status:

- Identity Achievement: "Yeah, I even started wondering whether or not there was a god. I've pretty much resolved that now, though. The way it seems to me is ..."
- Moratorium: "Yes, I guess I'm going through that now. I just don't see how there can be a god and yet so much evil in the world or ..."
- Foreclosure: "No, not really, our family is pretty much in agreement on these things."
- Identity Diffusion: "Oh, I don't know. I guess so. Everyone goes through some sort of stage like that. But it really doesn't bother me much. I figure one's about as good as the other!"

Source: Marcia, 1996.

Marcia (2001) noted that over 35 years of research has shown that people with identity achievement have many positive features. According to Marcia, their attributes include greater resistance when exposed to laboratory manipulations designed to influence their self-esteem (less reactivity), greater resistance to stress, nonconformity to group pressure, higher levels of moral reasoning and complexity of thoughts, a capacity for intimate relationships, and a strong and autonomous sense of self.

MOTIVES AND THE SELF-CONCEPT

Most of the discussion thus far has focused on the contents of the self-concept. We now shift our emphasis to an analysis of the self-concept from a motivational concept. What needs, motives, and goals influence the self-concept and our thoughts and actions related to our self-concepts?

Five motives tend to guide the self-concept and the ways that we behave. First, some people are motivated by a drive for *accurate self-evaluation*. This motive would apply to people who are uncertain about their characteristics, opinions, and abilities compared with other people. Self-verification theory (Swann, 1983) suggests that people strive actively to confirm their sense of self, in part to foster a sense of predictability and control.

The second motive involves the desire for accurate self-evaluation. Some people are concerned primarily with maintaining a sense of *self-consistency*. Their desire is to preserve a sense of continuity and unity in their self-systems (see Swann, 1983). One implication of this is that people who have a highly negative view of themselves and are prone to depression will actually prefer negative feedback rather than positive feedback about themselves in order to maintain a consistent, stable self-view. It was found, for instance, that low self-esteem people who experienced positive life events as assessed by the Life Experiences Survey actually had poorer health functioning; in contrast, high self-esteem people who had positive life events had superior health functioning (Brown & McGill, 1989).

Other people who are feeling defensive and threatened may be motivated by a desire for self-enhancement. Their self-enhancement motives are affectively based and focused on improving how they feel about themselves. Sedikides and Gregg (2004) suggested that self-enhancement is arguably the motive that operates the most extensively.

The fourth motive is self-improvement. Heine and associates have drawn attention to this motive by detailing the highly self-critical nature of people from Japan (see Heine, Takata, & Lehman, 2000). This self-criticism motivates the Japanese to refine the self and, for some, this means striving for perfection. The self-improvement motive is comparable to the desire for self-completion that applies to most people (see Wicklund & Gollwitzer, 1982).

The final motive is self-presentation. Self-presentation became a focus with the 1959 publication of the book *The Presentation of Self in Everyday Life* by noted Canadian-born sociologist Erving Goffman. Goffman likened the act of self-presentation to being in a theatrical performance, with people acting as "performers." He argued, among other things, that performers often present an idealized self-image as a form of impression management. He coined the term "front" to refer to the fronts that we put on in order to create a particular social impression.

According to Erving Goffman, individuals put up "fronts" in order to create a particular social impression.

Contemporary research has established that some people are more preoccupied than others with projecting a certain image to others. It matters greatly to them how they are perceived, so they seek out opportunities to put positive self-aspects on display and avoid situations where negative self-aspects may be revealed. The particular impression that they are striving to convey can be quite variable. Some people simply want to make sure that other people have an accurate sense of who they are, so they accentuate their usual characteristics in order to get attention.

Clearly, two or more motives may simultaneously operate. Consider the quote below from Frank Abagnale, Jr., whose life as a con man was portrayed by Leonardo DiCaprio in the movie *Catch Me if You Can*, which was based on Abagnale's autobiography with the same title. In the movie, Abagnale was being pursued by a law enforcement character played by Tom Hanks. In real life, Abagnale often imitated an airline pilot in order to pass bad cheques. He presented himself as a pilot and found that this role and the uniform had the following effect on him:

Leonardo DiCaprio portrayed Frank Abagnale, Jr. in *Catch Me if You Can*. Abagnale often posed as a pilot to gain respect and self-worth.

> During the next five years the uniform was an alter ego. I used it in the same manner a junkie uses heroin. Whenever I felt lonely, depressed, rejected or doubtful of my own worth, I would dress up in my pilot's uniform and seek out a crowd. The uniform brought me respect and dignity. Without it on, at times, I felt useless and dejected. (Abagnale, Jr., 1980, pp. 42–43)

For Abagnale, wearing the uniform was motivated by a need for self-presentation, but it actually reflected a need for self-enhancement by alleviating negative moods.

KEY POINTS

- The self-concept, as a complex entity, can be motivated by at least five different needs. These needs reflect the desire for accurate self-assessment, but they also reflect the need for self-enhancement and self-presentation.
- Self-enhancement is improving moods and emotions related to the self, whereas self-improvement is improving the self.
- The same behaviour can simultaneously reflect two or more motives related to the self.

The example from *Catch Me if You Can* is very much in keeping with the empirical findings. Research on self-presentation has shown that playing a role that involves presenting the self in a highly positive light can actually lead to an increase in self-esteem (Jones, Rhodewalt, Berglas, & Jones, 1981). Pretending is not always positive, however. Not surprisingly, self-esteem tends to increase if a person receives praise, but the positive impact of praise on self-esteem is blunted among people who know they are pretending and playing a role (Hussain & Langer, 2003).

Finally, there are times when people present an image to others that is worse than they actually are in reality. When might this occur? Consider someone who is unemployed and seeking financial assistance from the government. It is quite possible that this person will accentuate deficiencies and shortcomings in an attempt to influence the evaluator's decisions.

The various motives outlined above can be seen in social comparison choices. As described by Festinger (1954), social comparison occurs when people are uncertain (perhaps because they have received some ambiguous feedback), so they compare themselves to other people. The most common example is when you get a test back and go and find out how a classmate did on the same test. The person whom we choose to compare with should differ depending on which self-concept motive is operating. If the goal is accurate self-evaluation, then we would prefer to compare with people who are similar to us on general characteristics (e.g., age, sex). In fact, Festinger's (1954) similarity hypothesis was based on the premise that most of the time we do seek out similar others because this provides us with the most relevant information about ourselves.

If the person's goal was self-improvement, the comparison would be with a standard setter. By comparing upward to the best available people, this may provide clues about how to become more like them.

The self-enhancement goal would best be served by comparing oneself to the worst-off others. A self-esteem boost can be provided by seeing how the historically low scorers fared. Of course, this is quite risky. It is a devastating blow to the one's self-esteem to be bested by someone who performs historically at an inferior level.

The benefits of comparing oneself to inferior others was obviously operating in a classic study by Gergen conducted with Mr. Clean versus Mr. Dirty (for a summary, see Gergen, 1972). Participants interacted with one of two stooges. Mr. Clean was dressed immaculately in "a power suit" complete with a matching briefcase and so on. Mr. Dirty had a torn sweatshirt, pants ripped at the knees, and a day's growth of beard. Gergen found that students with Mr. Clean experienced a drop in their self-esteem, but exposure to Mr. Dirty led to a sharp increase in self-esteem. Gergen (1972) concluded that the slobs of the world do us a very big favour because they make us feel better about ourselves.

The different motives that exist and the ways they are expressed represent one source of cross-cultural differences involved in the self-concept. Other cross-cultural differences are explored in International Focus on Discovery 11.1.

International Focus on Discovery 11.1 The Self-Concept across Cultures

We have already seen that the self-concepts of people from India have several unique aspects that would clearly distinguish them from North Americans. Overall, there is an extensive and growing body of research on cross-cultural differences in topics involving the self-concept. Issues addressed here include whether motives related to the self-concept vary across cultures, the content of the self-concept, and the malleability of the self-concept.

Initial research on this area focused on inherent differences in the nature of the self-concept as a function of whether a person was from an individualistic or a collectivistic culture. The concepts of individualism versus collectivism were introduced in Chapter 3. People with an individualistic orientation (e.g., most North Americans) tend to think of themselves in autonomous, independent terms, while those with a collectivistic orientation (e.g., Asian cultures) tend to think of themselves in ways that highlight their connection to other people.

Although collectivism versus individualism may be seen from an all-or-none perspective, it is important to reiterate the point made in Chapter 3 that cultures may differ in their degree of individualism or collectivism (see Hofstedt, 1980). Also, some cultures reflect a complex blend of both individualism and collectivism.

This was illustrated via an examination of individualism and collectivism in 292 people from India (see Sinha, Sinha, Verma, & Sinha, 2001). Typically, India is characterized as a country that is collectivistic. There are close ties with in-group members, and family obligations and expectations highlight a sense of interdependence. Sinha et al. (2001) showed that individualistic and collectivistic aspects are often intertwined because a person's intentions and his or her behaviours often do not match. Although there is an overall emphasis on collectivism and this is often reflected in a person's intentions, subsequent behaviours often reflect individualistic interests. One example the authors provide is a shopkeeper who is very friendly to others (and thus has a collectivistic orientation) but has an individualistic interest in increasing sales.

Sinha et al. (2001) attributed these complexities to the tendency for people from India to have a much more complex view of situational contexts, relative to Westerners. When given time to respond, they are more likely to take into account the concepts of *desh* (place or location), *kaal* (time), and *paatra* (person). This would probably contribute to a form of cognitive complexity that is both individualistic and collectivistic.

Whatever the case, clear differences exist in collectivism and individualism, and they are reflected in the self-concept. Triandis, McCusker, and Hui (1990) compared collectivists and individualists in terms of their self-definitions and perceptions of in-groups and out-groups. Comparisons were conducted of students from Illinois in the United States and students from the People's Republic of China. As expected, collectivists gave more social responses when defining the self; they made more references to family affiliations and ethnic group. Triandis et al. (1990) estimated that 30 to 50% of collectivists' self-concept statements have social references implying a connection with other people, compared with 0 to 20% for individualistic people.

Differences in the independent versus the interdependent self are also reflected in cognitive processes, memory, and information processing. This was illustrated by some clever studies conducted at the University of Waterloo (see Cohen & Gunz, 2002). Students who were originally from Canada and students who were born and raised in Asia but were now studying in Canada were compared by their autobiographical memories, as well as their judgements. The researchers found that students born in Asia were more likely to have third-person autobiographical memories in which they were less likely to be the centre of attention and instead were part of a scene or context that often involved other people. A second study identified the expected group differences in egocentric projection versus relational projection. Egocentric projection is projection in the typical sense (i.e., personal issues are projected onto other people). This was more common among the students born in Canada. Relational projection is projecting how the student would be reacted to by the generalized other (e.g., doing something that would create embarrassment for a family member). These differences point to the presence of cultural differences in the self and social information processing.

A subsequent experimental test of information processing and memory for self-descriptions also yielded explicable differences (see Wagar & Cohen, 2003). Participants were provided with adjectival words, including words referring to personal traits, and they were asked to indicate whether the word applied to themselves. This was the self-reference condition. At other times, the task was to determine whether the word applied to someone else (e.g., best friend). The typical **self-reference effect** is that the word is more quickly remembered in a subsequent memory recognition task if the participant had indicated that, yes, the word did describe them. As is usually the case, Wagar and Cohen (2003) found that the Euro-Canadians showed the standard self-reference effect and did indeed show faster recognition memory of the self-relevant words. Not so with the Asian-Canadian students, however; they were slower to recognize words encoded with reference to self, likely due to the emphasis on the collective self rather than the individual self in long-term memory.

The issue of whether motives differ across cultures has recently been a highly contentious debate. Extensive research by Stephen Heine and his colleagues points to differences in the degree to which self-enhancement takes place (see Heine, Lehman, Markus, & Kitiyama, 1999; Heine et al., 2000). They argue that self-enhancement is not universal because people from Japan are highly self-critical and they reveal their self-critical tendencies in a variety of ways. Other investigators, such as Brown (2002), have responded by suggesting that the tendency toward self-enhancement is pancultural, but the ways in which self-enhancement take place vary by culture. That is, people from countries such as Japan will self-enhance but with respect to themes that emphasize their connectedness to others. Indeed, a recent study did confirm the existence of pancultural self-enhancement, with American participants self-enhancing on individualistic traits and Japanese participants self-enhancing on collectivist traits (Sedikides, Gaertner, & Toguchi, 2003).

These apparent differences in the content and motives associated with the self-concept also seem to be accompanied by differences in the malleability (the stability versus instability) of the self-concept. Extensive evidence indicates that the self-concept can change in accordance with situational and contextual changes, leading theorists such as Markus and Kunda (1986) to discuss the dynamic self-concept. Evidence of malleability includes evidence showing that different social experiences have an impact on the cognitive accessibility and salience of certain aspects of the self-concept (Nurius & Markus, 1990).

Regarding possible cultural differences in the malleability of the self, Tafarodi and associates (Tafarodi, Lo, Yamaguchi, Lee, & Katsura, 2004) compared aspects of the inner selves of students from the University of Toronto, the University of Tokyo, and the Chinese University of Hong Kong. The general pattern that emerged was that students from China and Japan were much more likely to report differences in their inner self across situational contexts and different life activities. For instance, students were asked, "Despite variability in your actions and the views that others have of you, do you think that the beliefs that you hold about who you are (your inner self) remain the same across (different) activity domains?" Overall, 78% of women and 66% of men from the University of Toronto agreed. The respective percentages for Japanese students were 34% for women and 38% for men. The respective percentages for Chinese students were 16% for women and 40% for men.

When asked whether it would be a good thing for a person's inner self to remain constant across activity domains, 65% of the students from Canada agreed. However, only 18% of the women from China endorsed this view. These data are in keeping with reports from another investigation that showed that Japanese women, relative to American women, gave more variable responses to the prompt "Who are you?" when asked to describe themselves across four different situational contexts, including being alone versus being with other people (Kanagawa, Cross, & Markus, 2001). Thus, the self-concepts of Japanese and Chinese people are more subject to change and perhaps fluctuate as a function of the people they find themselves with, given their interdependent selves.

When considering cultural differences in the self-concept, it is important to not lose sight of the fact that there is often great heterogeneity among people within the same culture. This point was underscored in some of the relatively few studies conducted thus far on the self-concepts of people from Africa. Typically, the self-concept of African people is believed to reflect a collectivist orientation. Mpofu's (1994) study of first-year teachers in Zimbabwe showed that although collectivism prevailed, about half of the participants had individualistic aspects to their self-concepts. Greater individualism was associated with being male and being young. Degree of modernization and urbanization may also be key considerations. Ma and Schoeneman (1997) analyzed the self-concepts of young people from Kenya. Overall, more collectivistic responses were linked with less urbanization. This underscores the need to consider heterogeneity within cultures and the need to consider the potential impact of sociocultural factors (e.g., urban versus rural locations, economic factors).

REPRESENTATIONS AND CONCEPTUALIZATIONS OF THE SELF-CONCEPT

Self-Complexity and Self-Concept Clarity

Another way to consider the self-concept is in terms of individual differences in **self-complexity**. Linville (1987) has argued that some people organize self-knowledge into a few main categories involving the self, while other people organize self-knowledge into several categories that are personally meaningful and highly salient. She has suggested that the degree of self-complexity is an important buffer against stress and threat in terms of vulnerability to maladjustment. In contrast, people low in self-complexity tend to put all their "cognitive eggs in one basket" or relatively few baskets, and they are more at risk if something goes wrong in these self-concept domains. An investigation by researchers at McGill University confirmed that children low in self-complexity are indeed vulnerable to stress and depressive symptoms (Abela & Veronneau-McArdle, 2002).

People also differ in their self-concept clarity. Clarity refers to the degree of certainty and the lack of ambiguity that people have regarding their self-concepts. Someone high in the Eriksonian concept of identity diffusion would have low self-concept clarity. The concept of self-concept clarity was introduced by noted University of British Columbia researcher Jennifer Campbell (1990). Across a series of four studies, she established that people with low self-esteem have less self-concept clarity; that is, they have a less clear sense of who they are and what they are like. Their personality ratings are more variable over time, and there is less correspondence between their self-conceptions and their actual behaviour.

Campbell's research found that people with low self-esteem have less self-concept clarity and don't have a clear sense of who they are and what they are like.

Ian McGregor and his colleagues have shown that high self-esteem people actively try to increase their sense of self-certainty when they have been exposed to information or situations that make them feel uncertain about themselves (see McGregor & Marigold, 2003; McGregor, Zanna, Holmes, & Spencer, 2001). McGregor and associates have described a phenomenon they call *compensatory conviction* that is presumably linked with the motive that people have for self-consistency. Compensatory conviction is a mode of repression that serves the defensive function of keeping unwanted thoughts about the self out of conscious awareness. Compensatory conviction is the tendency to develop a more extreme view of absolute certainty about issues that are seemingly unrelated to the self almost as a form of cognitive distraction. For instance, McGregor et al. (2001) showed that being made to feel uncertain about a personal relationship resulted in more extreme views about a social issue. This process could operate for people who become highly dogmatic and authoritarian. Personal setbacks could be compensated for by becoming more extreme and more categorical about the way that things should be.

The following sections outline different ways of illustrating the multidimensionality of the self-concept. This research shows that the self is multi-faceted, with the caveat that individuals will differ in such aspects as self-complexity and self-clarity.

The Spontaneous Self-Concept

Here's an easy exercise. Take out a piece of paper and write the numbers from 1 to 20 down the left margin. Now take five minutes and write down all of the things about yourself that you can think of.

You were just asked to complete McGuire and Padawer-Singer's (1976) Tell Us about Yourself Procedure, which is a measure of the spontaneous self-concept. It is a spontaneous measure in that it is totally open-ended. It is up to each respondent to decide what to say about themselves, and how many things that they need to say in order to describe themselves. Thus, it is an unstructured measure. It is non-reactive and content-free, as opposed to structured self-report measures of the self-concept such as questionnaire measures of self-esteem (e.g., Rosenberg, 1965).

McGuire and Padawer-Singer (1976) have found that the responses provided by children can be sorted into seven different categories. These categories are activities (e.g., hobbies, sports), significant others, attitudes (e.g., likes and dislikes), school, demographic features (e.g., age, sex), physical characteristics, and self-evaluations. McGuire and associates have used this measure to make a number of very significant points. First, because seven categories are needed to fully capture the responses, there is little doubt that the spontaneous self-concept is multi-faceted and multidimensional

Second, the self-concept is much more than self-esteem. The self-evaluation category represents the self-esteem component. Typically, self-evaluative comments account for less than 10% of the total number of things that people say when describing themselves. McGuire and Padawer-Singer's (1976) analysis found that self-evaluative statements accounted for only 7% of the statements provided by children.

Finally, McGuire and associates have found that the Tell Us about Yourself Procedure is a very viable way of testing research hypotheses about the nature of the self-concept. For instance, they used this technique to test the distinctiveness hypothesis. McGuire suggested that people with a unique factor (e.g., red hair, left-handed) are disproportionately more likely to mention this characteristic when they are describing themselves. This is due in part to the fact that people are sensitive to the fact that it is more informative to describe oneself to others in a way that distinguishes them; but McGuire suggested that it is more likely that this is by-product of our need to think about ourselves in ways that highlight our uniqueness relative to other people.

KEY POINTS

- The spontaneous self-concept is derived from an open-ended, unstructured way of assessing the self-concept.
- The spontaneous self-concept is multi-faceted, with at least seven components. Self-evaluation content may comprise as little as 10% of the spontaneous self-concept.
- The distinctiveness hypothesis reflects the tendency for people to spontaneously mention personal features about themselves that make them relatively unique (e.g., being left-handed, having red hair).

Possible Selves

One finding that emerged from the McGuire and Padawer-Singer (1976) analysis of the spontaneous self-concept is that 12% of their participants listed hopes and desires, while 18% mentioned career aspirations when asked to describe themselves. Markus and Nurius (1986) built on this finding by suggesting that in addition to how we currently see ourselves, we also have a clear sense of the self that is possible for us in the future.

Markus and Nurius (1986) suggested that the possible self is a mental representation of what we could be in the future, and it is a powerful motivating force; people with a desirable possible self will be motivated to perform behaviours and conduct themselves in a manner that will hopefully help them actually achieve this goal. People encouraged to focus on a positive possible self demonstrate greater task persistence and task focus (Ruvolo & Markus, 1992).

Markus and Nurius (1986) suggested also that the possible self can take different forms. This includes the hoped-for possible self as well as the feared possible self. People who are cognitively preoccupied with the feared possible self will be highly anxious, though it is not inconceivable that the fear underscoring this possible self will motivate the person to take steps to make sure that this possible self does not actually occur.

There is every reason to expect that the specific content of the possible self will be influenced greatly by societal and cultural factors. Applied Perspective 11.1 highlights the significance that the possible self may play in the lives of young people.

Applied Perspective 11.1 Possible Selves and School Interventions

Some people seem to maintain a sense of hope and optimism even after experiencing very traumatic events, while other people feel quite hopeless about their future and act as if they have nothing to live for anyway. Hopelessness results when the anticipated negative consequences seem certain and the person feels that there is nothing that he or she can do to avoid this expected negative outcome. What seems to be missing in many of these people is a highly positive and seemingly attainable possible self. When a student has made the decision to drop out of school, or has decided to stay in school but has withdrawn effort and essentially "checked out," this suggests that a salient possible self is lacking.

A limited amount of research has examined the role of possible selves in educational outcomes, including how the development of positive possible selves serves a protective role by maintaining commitment to educational goals.

Yowell (2002) investigated the link between possible selves and school dropout in Latino students. A sample of 415 Grade 9 Latino students were evaluated on their hoped-for, expected, and feared selves. Substantial individual differences were found, with the hoped-for selves being the best predictor of educational and occupational aspirations. However, it was the feared self that was the best predictor of academic performance. The findings point to the need to create school conditions and a motivational climate that minimizes the potentially destructive impact of the feared self.

A recent chapter by Oyserman and Fryberg (in press) summarizes the results of research that examined male and female teens who differed in race and/or ethnicity. Specifically, comparisons were conducted of the possible selves of African American, Asian American, Latino, Native American, and Caucasian teenagers. The study found in general that the number of academic possible selves declined as students made the transition to high school. Group comparisons suggested that Hispanic students have fewer academic and occupational possible selves, and the possible selves that they do have are too diffuse to promote goal-directed striving.

What remains to be determined is whether interventions designed to enhance possible selves tend to increase school achievement and school involvement and, ultimately, reduce school dropout rates. An important study by Some people seem to maintain a sense of hope and optimism even after experiencing very traumatic events, while other people feel quite hopeless about their future and act as if they have nothing to live for anyway. Hopelessness results when the anticipated negative consequences seem certain and the person feels that there is nothing that he or she can do to avoid this expected negative outcome. What seems to be missing in many of these people is a highly positive and seemingly attainable possible self. When a student has made the decision to drop out of school, or has decided to stay in school but has withdrawn effort and essentially "checked out," this suggests that a salient possible self is lacking.

What remains to be determined is whether interventions designed to enhance possible selves tend to increase school achievement and school involvement and, ultimately, reduce school dropout rates. An important study by Oyserman, Terry, and Bybee (2002) examined the effects of a nine-week program that focused on fostering the images that youths had of themselves as successful adults in the future and linked these images to school participation and involvement. The intervention was called the School-to-Jobs Programme. The intervention program consisted of nine components, all of which were designed to foster the development of a positive possible self in the future. These components included (1) creating a group and a positive sense of group membership; (2) developing adult images (concrete images of possible selves in adulthood by looking at photos of adults at work, with their family, etc.); (3) making the future more concrete by developing timelines for moving from the present to a goal in the future; (4) group thinking about strategies to develop the possible self; and (5) instruction in problem-solving to address everyday problems.

The impact of this intervention was examined in 62 African American middle school students and a control group of 146 other students. Students in the intervention group reported greater bonding to the school, greater concern about doing well in school, and a more balanced possible self (the ratio of the feared self to the expected self). In addition, they were able to generate a greater number of plausible strategies to actually attain their possible selves. Finally, the boys in this program got into less trouble at school.

Self-Discrepancy Theory: The Actual, Ideal, and Ought Selves

Just as we can reflect on our possible selves, we can also reflect on the type of person we would ideally like to be, as well as the type of person we think we ought to be. This focus on the ideal self and the ought self is part of self-discrepancy theory (SDT), as outlined by **E. Tory Higgins** and his colleagues. Higgins (1987) provided a theoretical extension of the notion put forth originally by Carl Rogers that psychological distress is rooted in the awareness of the gap between ideal selves and actual selves. According to SDT, there are three basic forms of self-representation: (1) the **actual self** (the attributes that a person does indeed have); (2) the **ideal self** (the attributes that a person would ideally possess in a best-case scenario); and (3) the **ought self** (the attributes that a person should possess based on social or cultural expectations). Higgins (1987) postulated that it is possible to assess the discrepancy between the ideal self and the actual self as well as the discrepancy between the ought self and the actual self. He suggested that the actual–ideal discrepancy predicted individual differences in levels of depression. The size of the actual–ought discrepancy was hypothesized to predict individual differences in levels of anxiety.

Higgins (1987) also suggested that in addition to these three ways of representing the self, there are also two different standpoints on the self. A standpoint on the self is essentially a point of view. People can think about things from their own perspective (the personal standpoint or "own" standpoint) or from the point of view that significant others would have on the self (the external standpoint or "other standpoint"). The notion of standpoints on self combines with the actual, ideal, and ought selves to form six different self-state representations (e.g., actual–own, actual–other, ideal–own, ideal–other, ought–own, ought–other). The two self-state representations most relevant to the usual notion of the self-concept are the actual self from the standpoint of the self and from the standpoint of other people.

Empirical work has confirmed that it is possible to assess meaningful individual differences in the actual, ideal, and ought selves using either the open-ended measures created by Higgins (1987) or the structured measures developed by other investigators. Higgins and his colleagues opted for an idiographic approach that begins with participants identifying 10 traits for their actual self, as well as 10 traits each for their ideal and ought selves. Derived measures of the various selves reflect aspects that are meaningful and cognitively accessible. However, the scoring procedure used is convoluted and time-consuming. An alternative is to use a nomothetic approach that involves participants rating their selves on a predetermined set of adjectives (see Tangney, Niedenthal, Covert, & Barlow, 1998). This approach is easier to score but, relative to the idiographic approach, it may yield indices of the actual, ought, and ideal selves that are less personally meaningful, at least for some people. It is important to keep the assessment method in mind when evaluating empirical research on SDT because a new comparative study of appearance-related discrepancies that was conducted in England found clear evidence that idiographic and nomothetic measures are not equivalent and they can yield substantially different results (Halliwell & Ditmar, 2006).

Tests of SDT support many of Higgins' contentions. Strauman's (1996) longitudinal study showed that self-discrepancies are generally stable, as would be expected if a personality style is involved. He found that both the magnitude and type of self-discrepancy were stable in a sample of participants tested three years after the initial assessment. Moreover, general support has been obtained for the proposed links between self-discrepancies and depression and anxiety (e.g., Higgins, Bond, Klein, & Strauman, 1986; Strauman, 1992). One study by Alexander and Higgins (1993) tied self-discrepancies to postpartum depression and showed the importance of considering situational and life factors that may interact with self-discrepancies. They

Research indicates that a greater actual–ideal self-discrepancy in the mother prior to a child's birth is related to subsequent increases in depression after.

found that a greater actual–ideal self-discrepancy in the mother prior to the child's birth was related to subsequent increases in depression following the child's birth.

Other researchers have explored the possible role of self-discrepancies in the etiology of eating disorders. It has been found that the magnitude of the perceived discrepancy between a person's actual and ideal appearance is a significant predictor of eating disorder symptomatology, body-image dysphoria, and body-image disturbance (Forston & Stanton, 1992; Szymanski & Cash, 1995).

Strauman and his colleagues have explored other health implications of large self-discrepancies (see Strauman, Lemieux, & Coe, 1993). They found that activating self-discrepancies (particularly those related to anxiety) resulted in an objectively measured decrease in natural killer cell activity. They maintained that their work was the first experiment to show a link between negative self-evaluation and reduced immune system functioning. Subsequent research by a team of Japanese investigators has similarly established an association between decreases in natural killer cell activity and higher levels of neuroticism and lower levels of self-esteem (Hori et al., 2000).

KEY POINTS

- Higgins' self-discrepancy theory distinguishes among the actual self, the ideal self, and the ought self. It also focuses on a cognitive standpoint on the self from the point of view of the self or of other people.
- Higher levels of depression are believed to reflect the discrepancy between the actual and ideal selves. Higher levels of anxiety are believed to reflect the discrepancy between the actual and ought selves.
- Although the specificity of self-discrepancies to anxiety and depression has not been supported by empirical research, the role of self-discrepancies in health problems in general has been substantiated.

Evaluation of Self-Discrepancy Theory

The self-discrepancy theory represents an important advance because it highlighted the role of discrepancies in maladjustment, and it generated extensive theoretical and empirical interest in the actual self, ought self, and ideal self. Although the self-discrepancy theory has received extensive support, some criticisms have emerged. Tangney and her associates reported that they were unable to establish specific links between actual–ideal discrepancies and depression and between actual–ought discrepancies and anxiety. Instead, both types of discrepancy were associated with both depression and anxiety, so it may be more appropriate to suggest a general link between self-discrepancies and psychological distress rather than to posit a link between specific self-discrepancies and specific forms of distress (Tangney, Niedenthal, Covert, & Barlow, 1998).

A related problem that some researchers have found is that the empirical distinction between ought and ideal standards is quite blurry, and there is more overlap between oughts and ideals than would be expected according to Higgins' theory (see Forston & Stanton, 1992; Szymanski & Cash, 1995; Tangney et al., 1998). Our own attempt in our laboratory to evaluate self-discrepancies and perfectionism in a clinical sample had to be abandoned because we found that severely depressed patients had a very difficult time keeping the distinction in mind between the ideal self and the ought self. Some reported that it was not possible empirically to distinguish the ideal self and the ought self in their project.

A third issue involves the potential influence of other possible discrepancies. Ogilvie (1997) suggested that the feared self is a powerful determinant of motives and emotions. Subsequent research on the discrepancy between the actual self and the feared self has provided evidence suggesting that this discrepancy may actually be more important (or at least as important) as the discrepancies outlined by Higgins (see Carver, Lawrence, & Scheier, 1999).

Finally, a basic question is whether self-discrepancies have incremental validity in predicting psychological distress, above and beyond the impact of a negative self-concept. A recent study conducted in Australia found that self-discrepancy variables were unable to predict negative emotional states after controlling for a negative self-concept in general (Ozgul, Heubeck, Ward, & Wilkinson, 2003).

SELF-ESTEEM

Self-esteem is the sense of regard that we have for ourselves, with people with low self-esteem having exceeding negative views of themselves. Typically, people have a need to maintain a positive view of themselves. This need for a positive self-view becomes evident when a sample drawn from the general population (or from the student population) completes a self-report measure of self-esteem.

Our self-esteem is our regard for ourselves.

Indeed, large studies typically find that the sample as a whole tends to have a distribution of self-esteem scores that is positively skewed, and this phenomenon is not restricted to university and college student samples. That is, most people have moderate to high self-esteem, and even some people with relatively low self-esteem have an absolute score that suggests that, at worst, they have a mixed view of themselves with both positive and negative attributes recognized (see Baumeister, Tice, & Hutton, 1989; Twenge & Campbell, 2001).

Some revealing findings about self-esteem have emerged from recent studies with a broad scope. In particular, a web-based investigation of self-esteem led by Richard Robins has been quite informative (see Robins et al., 2001, 2002). This research was based on an Internet sample of 326,641 people. The nature of the sample obtained is interesting. The modal respondent was a White person from the United States. There were twice as many respondents from the United States as from elsewhere. Although the majority of participants were White (over 255,000), there were enough respondents who were Asian, Black, Latino, or Middle Eastern to conduct comparisons.

The main measure of interest was the response to one item tapping self-esteem. Consider this question yourself. The self-esteem item is "I see myself as someone who has high self-esteem." There are five response options ranging from "1" (strongly disagree) to "5" (strongly agree). How would you respond?

Robins et al. (2002) used their single-item measure to examine global self-esteem across the lifespan. The pattern that emerged is that self-esteem was high in childhood and then decreased slightly during adolescence. This decrease was only slight and not in keeping with the "storm and stress" model, which postulates dramatic decreases in self-esteem during adolescence. Levels of self-esteem increased throughout adulthood and then dropped significantly among elderly participants. Robins et al. (2002) reported that this pattern was similar across people of various ethnic backgrounds and nationalities, and it is also held for people of various incomes.

Robins et al. (2001) had earlier examined the five-factor correlates of self-esteem. Overall, it was found that the five factors accounted for approximately one third of the variance in self-esteem scores. All five factors were associated significantly with self-esteem, with the strongest correlates being emotional stability (r = .50), extroversion (r = .38), and conscientiousness (r = .24). These same three predictors were found to be most significant when Robins et al. (2001) also compiled a summary of nine earlier studies of self-esteem and the five-factor model.

Research indicates that men have higher self-esteem than women.

Who has higher self-esteem: males or females? The conventional thinking is that a variety of factors (e.g., discrimination, abuse, unrealistic body image stereotypes, a more difficult transition to adolescence) should result in lower self-esteem among females. A meta-analysis by Major, Barr, Zubek, and Babey (1999), based on various samples of data collected in Canada and in the United States from 1982 to 1992, confirmed that men have higher self-esteem than women. The overall difference was characterized as not large in magnitude, but a detectable difference was clearly evident. The obtained gender difference was greater among people of lower socio-economic status, and cultural comparisons showed that the gender difference was greatest among White North Americans and was nonexistent among people with minority status.

Similarly, the meta-analysis conducted by Twenge and Campbell (2001) showed that self-esteem tends to increase across most of the lifespan for both females and males, but that the gender difference is evident at every point. Their analysis focused primarily on age and birth cohort differences. They showed that both factors are important, but that the effect of birth cohort group is much stronger. Analyses of data across various generations of children in North America have shown a steady increase in overall levels of self-esteem, so that today's children would be expected to have even higher levels of self-esteem. Twenge and Campbell (2001) interpreted this finding as evidence for a "culture of self-worth" model. That is, they maintain that in North America at least, it is becoming increasingly acceptable to adopt an individualistic stance and attempt to promote the self-worth of each child. The authors caution that this is not "all that it is cracked up to be," however; this increase in self-esteem has not paid off in societal improvements (e.g., lower divorce rates, less crime, etc.). That is, "We as individuals may think more highly of ourselves, but we as a society apparently have little to show for it" (Twenge & Campbell, 2001, p. 341). This state of affairs requires some reflection.

KEY POINTS

- Examination of population samples indicates that most people have high self-esteem.
- Self-esteem tends to increase with age. Self-esteem cohort analyses suggest that self-esteem is increasing in a manner that fits a "culture of self-worth" model.
- Males tend to have relatively higher self-esteem, and this gender difference is even more evident among people with lower socio-economic status.

There are many different ways to conceptualize and represent individual differences in self-worth. Some additional ways of comprehending self-worth are considered here.

Self-Liking versus Self-Competence

Morris Rosenberg (1965) tends to focus on self-esteem as a global measure of general self-worth. More recently, Romin Tafarodi from the University of Toronto and William Swann from the University of Texas at Austin demonstrated that global self-esteem could be subdivided into self-liking and self-competence (see Tafarodi & Swann, 1995). Self-liking involves a perceived sense of social worth, while self-competence is similar to Bandura's concept of self-efficacy or self-capability (see Chapter 12). Self-liking is tapped by items such as "I feel great about who I am ," while self-competence is more performance-based and is tapped by items such as "I perform very well at many things."

How are self-liking and self-competence different? Self-liking reflects positive or negative evaluations of the self and related feelings of self-worth that stem from internalized social standards of appropriateness (see Tafarodi & Swann, 1995; Tafarodi & Vu, 1997). In contrast, Tafarodi and Vu (1997) suggested that self-competence resembles such concepts as effectance motivation, need for power, and Adler's concept of superiority striving, which is a form of perfectionism motivated by feelings of inferiority. The focus of this dimension is on feelings of self-efficacy and self-capability.

These two aspects of self-esteem are highly correlated among participants from North America (Tafarodi & Swann, 1995) and from Europe (Silvera, Neilands, & Perry, 2001), but two pieces of evidence attest to the differences between self-liking and self-competence. First, self-liking and self-competence can be distinguished by their correlations with other variables. For instance, research on symptoms of bulimia in undergraduate women found that both low self-liking and low self-competence were associated with bulimic symptoms, but only the self-competence variable was associated with changes in bulimic symptoms over time. That is, less change was associated with more negative views of self-competence. This suggests that boosting self-competence is an important goal when treating eating disorders. Other recent research conducted at the University of Toronto has also supported the distinction between self-liking and self-competence (see Mar, DeYoung, Higgins, & Peterson, 2006). For instance, only self-competence was associated with indices of cognitive ability and indices of academic and creative achievement.

Second, it is possible to identify individuals who are high in self-liking but low in self-competence or vice versa (Tafarodi, 1998); they are said to have **paradoxical self-esteem**. Extremely self-critical perfectionists are people who may suffer from paradoxical self-esteem. That is, they may feel very capable and sense that they can attain perfection, but this doesn't mean that they like themselves. Paradoxical self-esteem among perfectionists was demonstrated by Blatt (1995) in his seminal paper on the destructiveness of perfectionism. In this article, Blatt described three perfectionists who committed suicide. All were highly talented, ambitious, and accomplished, and they had to recognize that they were more capable than most people, yet they still lacked a basic sense of self-worth. The case of Vince Foster is illustrative. He was the American attorney who was a close personal friend of Bill and Hillary Clinton. One suggestion is that he felt disgraced by the Whitewater real estate scandal, and because he was seemingly intolerant of failure and criticism, he shot himself. In this instance, it seems that shame and a harsh form of self-scrutiny had more impact than recognizing a high level of personal capability and talent.

Explicit versus Implicit Self-Esteem

Explicit self-esteem is assessed when we circle items on a self-report self-esteem scale such as the 10-item Rosenberg Self-Esteem Scale (Rosenberg, 1965). These are conscious evaluations of the self. Explicit self-esteem is what would be assessed if you asked someone to verbally describe his or her self-esteem and personality.

Investigators studying explicit self-esteem have found many indications that it is closely tied with self-enhancement behaviours and motives. Concern has arisen that the role of self-enhancement is so strong that explicit self-esteem measures may be assessing motives related to the self-concept rather than genuine self-esteem. Farnham et al. (1999) have noted that the link between explicit self-esteem and measures of self-presentation motives creates problems for measures of explicit self-esteem in terms of their convergent, discriminant, and predictive validity because it seems that these measures tap more than self-regard. The solution is to focus on individual differences in implicit self-esteem.

Implicit self-esteem involves automatic evaluations and reactions to the self that occur outside of conscious awareness. A Freudian would suggest that people are defensive in their conscious actions because their implicit self-esteem is under attack at an unconscious level. Regardless whether you accept a Freudian perspective, it is generally accepted that there are limits to self-knowledge, and these limits stem, at least in part, from our inability to reflect consciously on the unconscious (see Wilson & Dunn, 2004).

There are various measures of implicit self-esteem. Currently, the most widely used measure is the Implicit Associations Test. This is a reaction-time measure that involves sorting words into categories across a series of trials. The categories include self-related words, positive words, and negative words. During certain segments of the task, self-related words and the right response for positive, pleasant words require the participant to hit the same computer key. In another segment of the task, the participant must hit the same computer key to identify negative, unpleasant words and self-related words. People respond quicker to words with which they have developed a stronger association. The measure of implicit self-esteem is the speed of responding when self and positive words are paired versus the speed of responding when self and negative words are paired.

Another less sophisticated measure involves what is known as the Initials Task or the Name Letter Method. This method requires people to rate how much they like each letter of the alphabet. Higher implicit self-esteem is evident to the extent that the person gives much higher ratings of likeability to his or her initials versus the other 24 letters of the alphabet. A new experiment conducted at McGill University provided a clear illustration that implicit self-esteem does indeed reflect an unconscious and seemingly automatic form of self-esteem (see Baccus, Baldwin, & Packer, 2004). This experiment used classical conditioning techniques (see Chapter 8). Specifically, after having completed a measure of explicit self-esteem (The Rosenberg Self-Esteem Scale), participants were required to click on self-relevant words and then either a smiling, frowning, or neutral face appeared very briefly (400 miliseconds.). When self-relevant words were paired with the happy face, higher levels of implicit self-esteem were detected. Supplementary analyses showed that the conditioning of implicit self-esteem was easier when there was congruence between the person's explicit and implicit self-esteem.

Explicit and implicit self-esteem are hypothesized to be orthogonal (i.e., independent). However, research has established that there are small correlations between measures of explicit and implicit self-esteem. Also, meta-analysis of studies with the Implicit Association Test (IAT), a measure of implicit self-etsteem, found that there was a significant correlation of .23 between implicit and explicit self-esteem (see Hofmann et al., 2005). Thus, implicit and explicit self-esteem are not independent. Another new investigation shows that this association is moderated by gender; the link between implicit and explicit self-esteem is higher among women than among men (Pelham et al., 2005).

Because explicit and implicit self-esteem are not strongly associated when a sample of people is examined, some people will be congruent (high in both implicit and explicit self-esteem, or low in both), but some people will be incongruent (high in one, moderate to low in the other). Researchers at the University of Waterloo have focused on people who are characterized by **defensive self-esteem**. That is, they are incongruent because they have high explicit self-esteem but low implicit self-esteem (see Jordan et al., 2003). Defensive self-esteem was linked with other indices suggesting trait defensiveness and a vulnerable self-image (e.g., narcissism). Defensive self-esteem was also associated in two separate experiments with defensiveness in the form of a prejudicial, in-group bias and a greater need to reduce cognitive dissonance (Jordan et al., 2003). Cognitive dissonance is a form of arousal that occurs when people have done something that either conflicts with their self-image, or when they must select between two equally desirable options (e.g., two attractive boyfriends) and have second thoughts about the choice they did not select. Apparently, people with defensive self-esteem are more threatened and must reduce the feelings of dissonance, as would be the case if consciously they made a choice but unconsciously they were worried about the correctness of their choice.

KEY POINTS

- According to Tafarodi and colleagues, self-worth can be partitioned into separate factors representing self-liking and perceived self-capability. Self-liking and self-capability are positively correlated, but some people are high in one component and low in another component (i.e., paradoxical self-esteem).
- Conscious judgements of self-esteem involve explicit self-esteem. Unconscious feelings of self-esteem involve implicit self-esteem.
- Although they should be independent or orthogonal, recent evidence suggests small but significant positive correlations between implicit and explicit self-esteem.

Mattering as a Form of Self-Esteem

Although most researchers have focused on individual differences in self-esteem, alternative ways of representing self-worth are equally deserving of empirical attention. *Mattering* is one concept that will have a great deal of relevance and resonance for most readers of this book. Perceived mattering is a sense of feeling significant to others, especially those who are closest to you. According to Rosenberg (1985), mattering is "the individual's feeling that he or she counts, makes a difference, 'signifies' (p. 215). Rosenberg (1985) noted that mattering can be measured by societal significance, but he stipulated that mattering to specific other people is the most essential aspect of this construct. He reported data indicating that mattering in adolescents is associated with diminished self-esteem, but after controlling for the link between low self-esteem and psychological distress, mattering still predicted significant variance in levels of psychological distress (also see Rosenberg & McCullough, 1981).

In recent years, new scales have been developed to assess perceived mattering to parents and friends (Marshall, 2001) and perceived mattering to dating partners (Mak & Marshall, 2004), as well as mattering in general (Elliott, Kao, & Grant, 2004). Clearly, mattering is a potent predictor of well-being. For instance, a recent study found that mattering predicted suicidal ideation (Elliott, Colangelo, & Gilles, 2005). A mediational model was supported; low mattering was linked with low self-esteem, and low self-esteem was associated with depression, which in turn was associated with suicidal ideation.

Collective Self-Esteem

Another way to consider self-esteem is whether positive or negative feelings about the self are derived from our group affiliations. Collective self-esteem is a particularly relevant construct for those people who derive their self-esteem, at least in part, from their connections with small and large groups and organizations. It is the sense of self-worth that a person derives from being a part of social organizations.

The predominant figures in this area are Rita Luhtanen and Jennifer Crocker. Their research team developed the 16-item Collective Self-Esteem Scale to assess four factors (see Crocker, Luhtanen, Blane, & Broadnax, 1994; Luhtanen & Crocker, 1992). These four factors are membership esteem, private collective self-esteem, public collective self-esteem, and importance to identity. Membership esteem is a person's evaluation of how worthy they are as part of an organization. Private collective and public collective self-esteem refer to an individual's own sense of the worth of his or her groups (private collective self-esteem) and a person's perception of how others regard his or her groups (public collective self-esteem). Finally, importance to identity is an evaluation of the group affiliation in terms of how relevant or central it is to a person's sense of self.

Crocker et al. (1994) developed a race-specific version of the measure by making slight alterations to the wording of the various items. Rather than responding to an item such as "I feel good about the social groups I belong to," respondents instead were given an item that read "I feel good about the race I belong to." Their study compared the mean scores for groups of White, Black, and Asian students attending university in the United States. Group differences were found on all of the subscales for both the general measure of collective self-esteem and the race-specific version. One finding that emerged is that the Asian students scored lower on the general measure of membership collective self-esteem and private collective self-esteem, but they actually scored significantly higher than the White participants on the identity factor, though they did not differ significantly on the identity factor when compared with the Black participants.

Several investigators have examined characteristics of collective self-esteem, and some interesting findings have emerged. For example, women are more likely to derive their self-esteem from their associations with groups of women, especially if these women have a strong feminine identity (Carpenter & Johnson, 2001).

THE DOMAINS OF THE SELF-CONCEPT

The Academic, Social, and Physical Self

One of the most predominant themes in the self-concept literature is the idea that the self-concept includes different self-worth domains. We all have our general sense of self-worth, but we also have specific views of our worth in specific areas. For instance, the current author is generally capable of academic and intellectual tasks but has often been reminded by family members that he is challenged when it comes to knowing which end of a hammer to use. Different domains of self-worth are often on display among students. I have often encountered students who are shy and have a very negative sense of their social self-worth, so they overcompensate for this vulnerability by becoming exceptionally accomplished in their academic achievement and attendant feelings of self-worth in the academic sphere.

These general observations about different areas or domains of the self have been confirmed by researchers who have empirically distinguished such facets as academic self-esteem, social self-esteem, physical self-esteem, athletic self-esteem, and so on (e.g., Coopersmith, 1967; Harter, 1985; Shavelson, Hubner, & Stanton, 1976). Stanley Coopersmith designed the Coopersmith Self-Esteem Inventory to assess self-esteem of children and adolescents in several domains. Coopersmith (1967) stated that it is possible to identity "Four sources of self-esteem: the ability to influence and control others (power); the acceptance, attention and affection of others (significance); adherence to moral and ethical standards (virtue); and successful performance in meeting demands for achievement (competence)" (p. 38). The scale includes a brief lie scale and subscales assessing general self, social self–peers, school–academic, and home–parents. A similar measure is the Piers–Harris Self-Concept Scale (Piers & Harris, 1969). This measure evaluates the self-concept in terms of such domains as intellectual and school status and physical appearance and attributes, but it is more a measure of general self-concept rather than self-esteem per se.

Shavelson was one of the pioneers in this area. Shavelson, Hubner, and Stanton (1976) wrote an influential article describing data in support of a hierarchical model of the self-concept. The hierarchical model is shown in Figure 11.2. They showed that an overarching general self-concept is composed of the academic self-concept and three non-academic self-concept domains: the social self-concept, the emotional self-concept, and the physical self-concept. Each of the four self-concept domains was represented by several more specific "facets." For instance, the academic self-concept reflects the self-concept across various subjects (mathematics, languages, science, etc.). The social self-concept reflects the self in relation to peers and in relation to significant others. The emotional self-concept reflects specific emotional states. Finally, the physical self-concept consists of appearance and physical ability.

Figure 11.2 Hierarchical Model of the Self-Concept

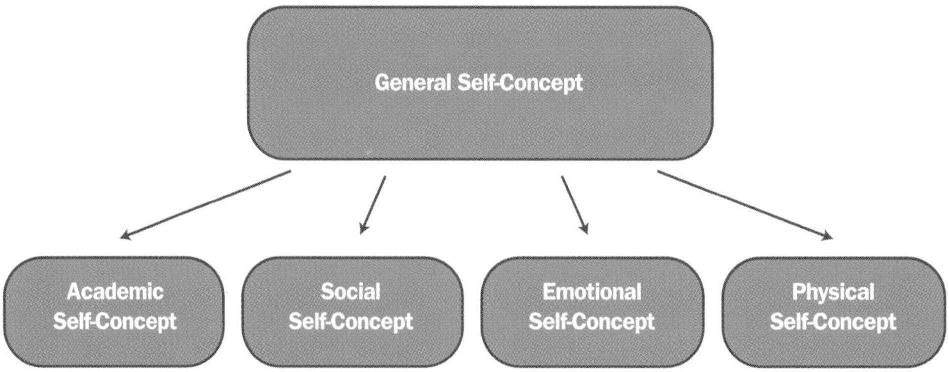

Source: Shavelson, Hubner, & Stanton, 1976.

Herbert Marsh from the University of Western Sydney in Australia has continued working on the notion that the self-concept is multi-faceted. His measure requires participants to evaluate their actual self as well as the importance they attach to each self-esteem domain. Marsh (1992) demonstrated the value of specificity in the academic sphere by showing that the specific self-concept for a particular course was a substantially better predictor of actual grade received in that course than were more general self-concept measures. Overall, people find it relatively easy to reflect on different domains of the self-concept. For instance, Pliner, Chaiken, and Flett (1990) conducted a study of visitors to the Ontario Science Centre and examined the self-rated importance of physical appearance and body weight across study participants' age range. Data analyses confirmed that concerns related to physical appearance are more central and important to the self-concepts of females, relative to males, and this gender difference held across the entire lifespan and applied to adolescents, young adults, and elderly adults.

Susan Harter has also played a prominent role in promoting the idea that self-worth can be evaluated in various domains. Her work on the Self-Perception Profile for Children (Harter, 1985) has resulted in the identification of five self-concept domains: (1) scholastic competence; (2) social acceptance; (3) athletic competence; (4) physical appearance; and (5) self-worth based on behavioural conduct.

Although most investigations of Harter's measure have confirmed the presence of all five factors, Harter and Pike's (1984) research, with a version of the measure designed for younger children, could only identify two distinguishable factors, which led Harter to conclude that a fully differentiated self-concept emerges only among older children and adolescents. Other researchers disagree with this conclusion, and a recent Belgian study showed that all five factors described by Harter (1985) could be identified among children in grades 2 and 3 (Van den Bergh & De Rycke, 2003). Clearly, this and other studies (e.g., Eccles, Wigfield, Harold, & Blumenfeld, 1993) have shown that the self-concept does become increasingly differentiated with age, but it is possible to identify self-concept domains in fairly young children (Van den Bergh & De Rycke, 2003).

What remains to be determined is whether the link between global self-worth and domains of self-worth is best represented as a "top-down model" or as a "bottom-up model." A top-down model in this instance would mean that a general, global sense of self-worth precedes the development of the specific self-worth domains. A bottom-up model would mean that we first develop a sense of self-worth in specific domains and eventually form a generalized sense of self-worth. The issue was summarized by Hattie and Marsh (1996), who observed the following:

> The place of general self-concept will remain a controversial issue. The issue relates to whether individuals somehow integrate lower-order dimensions, or whether they have a general self-concept which mediates these dimensions. The general self-concept may have a critical role in mediating the information about aspects of the self (Brown, 1993). Most current research considers the higher-order conceptions of self-concept as some kind of amalgam of the lower-order

> concepts, whereas the converse may be the case. It may be that there are critical information-processing competencies that bias, select, and retain information and affectations about the self, and these may be different depending on the level of the self-concept and on the sources of developing bias (e.g., cultural and social sources). (p. 423)

State Self-Esteem: A Multi-Domain Construct

To further underscore the complexity of the self, it is also possible to distinguish between trait self-esteem and the self-esteem that we feel immediately when in a specific situation (i.e., state self-esteem). This difference can be illustrated using the single-item measure of self-esteem described earlier.

Trait self-esteem is our usual or typical level of self-esteem. It would be assessed if you were asked to indicate your degree of agreement with the item, "In general, I usually see myself as someone who has high self-esteem."

State self-esteem is how we feel about ourselves "in the moment," at a particular time or in a particular place. It would be assessed if you were asked to indicate your degree of agreement with the item, "Right now, as I am reading this book, I see myself as someone who has high self-esteem."

The most advanced conceptualization of state self-esteem considers this construct in terms of different domains of the self so the multidimensional nature of the self is acknowledged. The State Self-Esteem Scale was developed at the University of Toronto by Heatherton and Polivy (1991). It is a 20-item scale that assesses state self-esteem in terms of academic performance (e.g., "I feel like I'm not doing well"), social evaluation (e.g., "I feel that others respect and admire me"), and physical appearance (e.g., "I feel satisfied with the way my body looks right now"). Other sample items from this scale can be found in Table 11.3.

Table 11.3 The State Self-Esteem Scale

Performance Subscale

I feel that I am having trouble understanding things that I read. *

I feel confident that I understand things.

I feel as if I have less scholastic ability right now than others. *

Social Subscale

I am worried about whether I am regarded as a success or failure. *

I am worried about what other people think of me. *

I am worried about looking foolish. *

Appearance Subscale

I am dissatisfied with my weight. *

I am pleased with my appearance right now.

I feel unattractive. *

Items are to be rated according to current, immediate feelings. Items with asterisks are worded in the low self-esteem direction (i.e., reverse-keyed).

Source: Adapted from Heatherton Polivy (1991).

The three scales tend to be positively intercorrelated, so someone who is high on the performance scale also tends to be high on the social and appearance subscales. This raises concerns about discriminant validity. However, various studies have attested to the discriminant validity of these three subscales by showing that experimental manipulations result in selective changes in the dependent variable (i.e., the mean for one subscale increases but not so with the other two subscales). For instance, a study of in-group versus out-group status by Blanton, Crocker, and Miller (2000) had Black participants complete a bogus IQ task. The researchers then examined how participants responded to positive versus negative feedback in the form of high versus low relative performance, standing compared with how others had done. The results showed the importance of distinguishing among different types of state self-esteem. Performance self-esteem varied in the expected direction depending on whether positive or negative comparative feedback was received. There were no significant differences in appearance self-esteem or social self-esteem.

Another study had participants complete laboratory stressors in the presence or absence of a social threat (Gruenewald, Kemeny, Aziz, & Fahey, 2004). The findings showed that threats to the social self contribute to feelings of shame and lower social self-esteem. Most importantly, the social threat did not contribute to lower state self-esteem in terms of reduced appearance and performance self-esteem.

PERSONALITY CONSTRUCTS REFLECTING THE SELF

The rest of this chapter focuses on personality constructs that involve individual differences in the extent to which people think about themselves (self-consciousness), the extent to which people are able to change their behaviour to fit the situation (self-monitoring), and the extent to which people defensively make excuses for themselves when they fear failure and embarrassment (self-handicapping). We begin with a discussion of self-consciousness.

Self-Consciousness

Hundreds of investigations have been conducted on individual differences in self-consciousness. To some extent, we are all self-conscious at certain times of our existence, such as when we experience the physical changes of puberty and feel that everyone is looking at us and evaluating us. However, over and above these periods of development, some people remain relatively high in self-consciousness throughout their lives.

Much of the initial research interest in self-consciousness was derived from the objective self-awareness theory by Duval and Wicklund (1972). They proposed that one's focus of attention will determine one's locus of causal attribution. If a person has focused attention inward on self-thoughts and personal feelings, when asked to make attributions, he or she will implicate the self. In contrast, if a person tends to focus his or her attention on factors in the environment, then subsequent attributions will also focus on external cues and factors outside the self.

Fenigstein, Scheier, and Buss (1975) created the Self-Consciousness Scale (SCS) to assess dispositional differences in self-focused attention. The SCS provides measures of private self-consciousness, public self-consciousness, and social anxiety. Private self-consciousness involves focusing on "thoughts and reflections that deal solely with the self" (p. 525). Fenigstein et al. regarded private self-consciousness as similar to the concept of introversion; however, they specified that whereas introverts tend to be concerned with their internal ideas and concepts, those high in private self-consciousness tend to focus on thoughts and reflections that pertain solely to the self (Fenigstein et al., 1975). Heightened levels of private self-consciousness tend to be associated with more intense experiences of positive and negative emotions.

Public self-consciousness involves a "general awareness of the self as a social object that has an effect on others" (Fenigstein, Scheier & Buss, 1975, p. 523). Fenigstein et al. (1975) likened public self-consciousness to the ideas of Mead (1934), who regarded self-consciousness as a product of one's awareness of another's perspective and hence one's awareness of oneself as a social object. Thus, public self-consciousness is primarily concerned with others' reactions to the self (Fenigstein et al., 1975). In this connection, Fenigstein and colleagues proposed that public self-consciousness may be a precursor to social anxiety.

Public self-consciousness led to the development of the Sound Princess, which is used by Japanese women to mask the sounds made in public washrooms.

Indeed, an excessive concern with public self-consciousness is often reflected by a tendency to be easily embarrassed when attention is drawn to the self in public places. Although this has not been the subject of extensive empirical work of a cross-cultural nature, anecdotal reports suggest that certain cultural groups may have heightened self-consciousness. This is illustrated by the concern that Japanese women have about what others will think of them while going to the washroom. The Sound Princess is a device that is growing in popularity in women's washrooms in Japan because it masks the usual sounds emanating from washrooms.

Subsequent psychometric analyses of private self-consciousness and public self-consciousness helped establish that the two main dimensions of the Self-Consciousness Scale actually consist of subfactors. The private self-consciousness dimension consists of one factor reflecting internal state-awareness and another factor assessing self-reflection. Similarly, private self-consciousness contains a style consciousness factor and an appearance consciousness factor (see Nystedt & Ljungberg, 2002). Although a meta-analytic quantitative review has shown that self-consciousness in general is associated with negative affect (Mor & Winquist, 2002), the specific facets of private and public self-consciousness seem to make a difference here. For example, in terms of private self-consciousness, it is the self-reflection facet that is most predictive of maladjustment (Nystedt & Ljungberg, 2002). These data suggest the need for a conceptual refinement of the self-consciousness construct.

Trapnell and Campbell (1999) distinguished rumination and reflection as motivational traits implicit in the concept of private self-consciousness. Their work was an attempt to resolve what they referred to as the **self-absorption paradox**. At times, self-focused attention seems beneficial to self-understanding, but too much attention on the self can also be highly maladaptive. Trapnell and Campbell (1999) posited that the existence of different factors could resolve this paradox. Rumination is a neurotic form of self-consciousness that seems motivated by fear and anxiety, while reflection is a cognitive form of thinking about personal characteristics and internal thoughts and feelings (Trapnell & Campbell, 1999). Relative to rumination, reflection is more adaptive and reflects a general desire to more fully understand the self. Trapnell and Campbell (1999) created the Rumination–Reflection Questionnaire (RRQ). They used it to show that rumination is correlated positively with neuroticism and correlated negatively with extroversion. In contrast, reflection was negatively correlated with neuroticism but was associated positively with openness to experience (Trapnell & Campbell, 1999).

A serious challenge to these measures has come recently from Silvia, Eichstaedt, and Phillips (2005). They argued that rumination and reflection are types of motivation and should not be considered types of self-focused attention. Across two studies, one using an Internet-based sample (n = 101) and the other a college student sample (n = 115), Silvia et al. (2004) found that neither rumination nor reflection predicted self-focused attention. Although rumination and reflection are potentially important variables in their own right, the link with self-consciousness per se remains to be established.

KEY POINTS

- The self-consciousness construct reflects aspects of private self-consciousness (an internal focus on thoughts) and public self-consciousness.
- Private self-consciousness and public self-consciousness consist of distinguishable facets.
- The self-absorption paradox is that self-focus is positive if it promotes self-understanding but is negative if it promotes rumination about distressed events and outcomes.
- According to some authors, rumination and reflection are not part of the self-consciousness construct; instead, they reflect motivational states.

Self-Monitoring

Snyder (1974) first introduced the self-monitoring construct. High self-monitors are like chameleons. They are excellent at reading situational prompts and interpersonal cues and moulding and shaping their behaviour in accordance with these cues. High self-monitors are like superb actors and actresses. Some of the most famous actors (e.g., Cate Blanchett, Johnny Depp, and Sir Anthony Hopkins) seem to have an inherent ability to seamlessly change themselves according to the demands of their latest role.

Sometimes this ability in actors is an overcompensation for perceived deficits in the self, reflecting the lack of a clear sense of personal identity. British actor Peter Sellers seemed to fit this description. His roles included playing Inspector Clouseau in the original Pink Panther movies. Despite the fact that he was masterful at changing himself like a chameleon to play a certain role, when it came to his own sense of self, he lacked a clear notion in his interior of who he was and what he was all about (see Walker, 1981). Sellers suggested that his Academy Award–nominated role as Chance, the gardener in the movie *Being There*, was probably the role that was closest to his own personality. Chance is a reclusive, passive, and aloof soul who likes to watch television to learn about his world and his place in it.

The original Self-Monitoring Scale (SMS) developed by Snyder (1974) is a 25-item true–false measure that taps several main themes. If someone is high in self-monitoring, he or she tends to (1) have a high level of concern about the appropriateness of self-presentation; (2) attend to social comparison information from other people to get indications about the appropriateness of behaviour in situations; and (3) perceive a high level of ability to control and modify self-presentation and expressive behaviour.

Extensive evidence attests to the validity of the SMS (see Snyder, 1979). For instance, peer ratings indicate that high scorers on the SMS are recognized as being good at learning what is expected in social situations. They are also seen by their peers as having excellent self-control over their emotions, and they can use this ability to create the impression they wish to convey. Also, a comparison of criterion groups shows that professional stage actors have higher SMS scores than a comparison sample of university students.

Although the SMS has adequate validity, the nature of the self-monitoring construct itself has been a very controversial topic, in part due to subfactors that seem to exist within the SMS. Rather than being unidimensional and consisting of only one factor, tests of the SMS indicate that it actually consists of two factors: an extroversion factor and a second factor identified as other-directedness (masking personal feelings in order to please others). Some research indicates that both factors are associated with outcome variables, but in opposite directions! For instance, Briggs and Cheek (1986) showed that the extroversion factor was associated with good personal adjustment and self-confidence, while the other-directedness factor was associated with poor adjustment and lower self-confidence. Snyder and Gangestad (1986) have dismissed the importance of these results. Instead, they countered by arguing that a latent class taxometric analysis showed that self-monitoring reflects a single latent factor, and that in contrast to most personality variables, self-monitoring should be regarded as a type (high versus low self-monitors) rather than as a dimensional trait.

Lennox and Wolfe (1984) hypothesized that the self-monitoring construct is even more complex than first imagined. They revised the existing measure and added two dimensions in a measure known as the Concern for Appropriateness Scale. The revised self-monitoring Scale consists of two factors that assess sensitivity to the expressions of others and the ability to modify self-presentation. The Concern for Appropriateness scale is a defensive style that involves being attentive to social comparison information and whether we behave and perform the same way as other people. It also assesses cross-situational variability (i.e., the tendency to change behaviours across settings according to situational cues).

Larkin (1991) proposed a very different way of addressing and clarifying the nature of the self-monitoring construct. Larkin evaluated the participants' implicit theories (lay beliefs) about self-monitoring. This was based on the assumption that lay beliefs have some degree of validity associated with them. She had a sample of participants use California Q-sort cards to describe the prototypical high self-monitor and low self-monitor.

Representative items that were used to describe high versus low self-monitors are shown in Table 11.4. One finding that emerged is that Larkin (1991) found no evidence of a defensive component to self-monitoring. Thus, the additional dimensions involving concern with appropriateness that were added by Lennox and Wolfe (1984) do not fit with lay conceptions, at least according to Larkin's investigation. Do you think the dimensions identified by Lennox and Wolfe should be included as part of the self-monitoring construct? Theoretically, self-monitoring can be motivated by many factors, and some people may be responding to perceived deficits in the self.

Table 11.4 Implicit Theories about High versus Low Self-Monitors

High Self-Monitors
Seem to be aware of the impression they make on others
Are talkative individuals
Initiate humour
Tend to arouse liking and acceptance in people
Are skilled in social techniques of imaginative play, pretending, and humour
Are self-dramatizing; histrionic
Are unpredictable and changeable in behaviour and attitudes
Low Self-Monitors
Do not vary roles; relate to everyone in the same way
Are moralistic
Behave in an ethically consistent manner; are consistent with own personal standards
Have a clear-cut, internally consistent personality
Value own independence and autonomy
Appear straightforward, forthright, candid in dealing with others
Are emotionally bland; have flattened affect

Source: Adapted from Larkin, 1991.

KEY POINTS

- High self-monitors are like chameleons who adapt their behaviours to fit in with situational cues and expectations.
- There is much controversy over the multidimensional nature of the self-monitoring construct. Four factors have been identified, including a defensive form that reflects concern with appropriateness.
- Snyder and Gangestad suggest that self-monitoring is among the few personality variables that is best regarded as a personality type (people are either self-monitors or not) instead of a personality trait dimension.
- The Self-Monitoring Scale appears to have criterion validity when predicting people's ability to modify their behaviours in public.

Even though the precise nature of the Self-Monitoring Scale has been highly controversial, several research findings that make a great deal of intuitive sense have emerged from the investigations conducted in this area. The ability of high self-monitors to alter their self-presentations has been evaluated in a variety of public situations. For instance, when asked to work with a group to create a comedy monologue for comedians, high self-monitors, relative to low self-monitors, were rated by themselves and others as more humorous, and they actually produced funnier monologues (Turner, 1980). This suggests that well-known comedians such as David Letterman and Chris Rock are excellent at reading situational cues and adapting themselves to others.

You might think that high self-monitors would have an advantage during job interviews. You would be correct. One study found that high self-monitors were less distressed when asked to give "the right answers" in order to get a job that did not fit with their personalities; low self-monitors were more visibly distressed when they were required to project a false self-image (Larkin & Pines, 1994).

There are also differences in the nature of personal identity. Sampson (1978) came up with a list of identity characteristics that varied in whether they included a tie to external referents (e.g., "I am a member of a rock group") or internal referents only. As might be expected, high self-monitors, when asked to provide "a sense of who I am," were more likely than low self-monitors to define themselves with externally oriented identity features.

People vary in the extent to which their private tendencies are reflected in their public behaviours. As you might expect, high self-monitors have a much lower correspondence between their private behaviours and their public behaviours than do low self-monitors (see Snyder & Campbell, 1982). Low self-monitors tend to pride themselves on being consistent and not changing to suit situational norms or cues.

Self-Handicapping

> Rachel reported that if she sat down and spent too much time studying she would get "stressed out and lose the plot." She said that procrastination was not so much used as an excuse, as it was to avoid becoming stressed. Interestingly, however, she later reported that if she did fail, she usually identified something that interfered with her success such as "going out and getting drunk every night."
>
> —*A description of a high self-handicapper based on the qualitative study conducted in Australia by Martin, Marsh, Williamson, and Debus (2003, p. 620).*

According to Berglas and Jones (1978), **self-handicapping** is any action or choice of performance setting that enhances the opportunity to externalize failure and internalize success, so that failure is seen to reflect factors outside the self, but successes reflect directly on the self. Self-handicapping is paradoxical and self-defeating in the sense that extreme attempts to protect the self from the negative implications of failure can actually increase the likelihood that failure will occur.

Leary and Shepperd (1986) argued that there are two distinct forms of self-handicapping: behavioural self-handicapping and self-reported handicapping. One form of self-handicapping involves doing something or not doing something in order to generate an excuse for the self, while self-reported handicapping is verbally making people aware of reasons why personal responsibility is not to blame for deficiencies. Self-reported handicaps are known as *claimed handicaps*. Common claimed handicaps given by students who are worried about their test performance include "I couldn't sleep. I'm tired, so I couldn't concentrate" and "Oops, I did it again. I studied the wrong material." This author recalls giving one student extra assistance aimed at improving his study skills because he was in danger of failing the course. Unfortunately, the student did not put in the required effort and instead went the claimed handicap route by arguing that he did not study because he simply did not have the time. Why? He said his car needed to be fixed because, after all, no "wheels" meant not making it to the test. He failed the test and eventually dropped out of the program. But at least he had nice "wheels."

Berglas and Jones (1978) have suggested that self-handicapping reflects a "precarious competence complex" that is due to having very uncertain self-esteem rather than simply low self-esteem per se. People with uncertain self-esteem need constant reassurance and evidence of their worthiness. The link between self-handicapping and uncertain self-esteem is supported by experimental results showing that people with uncertain self-esteem, relative to other people, practise the least when they must eventually take an intelligence test (Harris & Snyder, 1986). However, other research shows that there is a strong negative correlation between self-handicapping and self-esteem (Rhodewalt, 1989). Rhodewalt argued that this negative association is artifactual and likely a reflection of measurement error, but it is quite possible that both low self-esteem and uncertain self-esteem are involved in self-handicapping.

Rhodewalt (1990) went on to suggest that people with low self-esteem and high self-esteem may both engage in self-handicapping. Self-handicapping behaviour exhibited by people with low self-esteem is due to a need for ego protection (i.e., self-enhancement). Self-handicapping behaviour by high self-esteem individuals is a form of growth striving where they are allowed to "reach for the stars" to ultimately be successful (i.e., self-improvement).

Why do students engage in academic self-handicapping? Urdan and Midgley (2001) examined the factors associated with academic self-handicapping. The authors considered two possible factors: fear of failure and fear of looking like a fool in front of others. The authors concluded that the predominant motivating factor was fear of looking like a fool in front of others. Thus, academic self-handicapping is typically self-presentational and is designed to manipulate the impressions that other people will form if failure results. Self-handicapping is especially evident among students who feel that they must avoid showing any imperfections whatsoever to others (Hewitt et al., 2003).

A qualitative study of Australian students conducted by Martin et al. (2003) yielded information that students attributed much of their self-handicapping behaviour to being placed in highly competitive situations. This ties in with concerns about being publicly recognized as a failure. Although many students saw no advantages stemming from self-handicapping, some indicated that it helped alleviate the stress and pressures of competing.

Several personality factors have been linked with self-handicapping. Analyses of responses from students have shown that people high on trait procrastination (Ferrari, 1991) and socially prescribed perfectionism are also high on self-handicapping. High self-handicapping has also been linked with chronic underachievement, and according to Rhodewalt (1984), high self-handicappers are OK with being labelled as underachievers.

Rhodewalt et al. (1988) studied self-handicapping in various kinds of athletes, including swimmers and professional golfers. They hypothesized that high self-handicappers would engage in more excuse-generating behaviour in very important competitions, and they would be less likely to do this in less important competitions. In one study, competitive swimmers were tracked by their coaches, who recorded the amount of time and the degree of effort exerted in practice prior to an important versus a less important swim meet. Indeed, self-handicapping interacted with the importance of competition to predict practice behaviour. Low self-handicappers increased their practice prior to important swim meets, but high self-handicappers failed to do so. In a follow-up study, Rhodewalt et al. (1989) confirmed that this pattern was generalizable by showing that professional golfers high in self-handicapping reported spending less time practising when compared with low self-handicappers, and this trend was particularly evident prior to an important tournament.

Research indicates that among athletes, low self-handicappers, unlike high self-handicappers, increased their practice time prior to important meets.

The Effects of Self-Handicapping

Is self-handicapping effective? Does it blunt the impact of failure on self-esteem? And how do other people perceive the self-handicapper? People in laboratory studies who are given the chance to self-handicap tend to report that they do feel better about themselves (Rhodewalt, Morf, Hazlett, & Fairfield, 1991), but research in naturalistic contexts has shown consistently that trait self-handicapping is associated with low self-esteem (see Martin & Brawley, 2002). Thus, the issue is whether self-handicapping protects people from further blows to self-esteem. A growing number of studies suggest that self-handicapping reflects a defensiveness that is highly maladaptive. There is some evidence indicating that male self-handicappers may be able to retain a positive self-view, but this is not the case for female self-handicappers. Rhodewalt and Hill (1995) found that following academic failure feedback, high self-handicapping among men was associated with external attributions for failure and elevated self-esteem. Self-handicapping was less predictive for women, and their post-task self-esteem was unrelated to claimed handicaps. A more recent investigation of introductory psychology students found similarly that male high self-handicappers still had relatively high self-esteem and were able to maintain positive views of their capabilities in psychology despite relatively poor performance, but this pattern was not evident among female high self-handicappers (McCrea & Hart, 2001).

In general, self-handicapping seems to be associated with several costs. McCrea and Hart (2001) reported that high self-handicappers experienced more stress prior to an exam, and they had poorer exam performance. Zuckerman, Kieffer, and Knee (1998) found that high self-monitors are more likely to use ineffective coping strategies, they have poorer performance, and they have poorer adjustment over time. They concluded that there is "a vicious cycle" between self-handicapping and poor adjustment because self-handicapping and low adjustment tend to reinforce each other. Evidence of this vicious cycle was recently reported (see Zuckerman & Tsai, 2005), along with evidence linking self-handicapping with substance abuse, and a tendency for self-handicappers with jobs to report a loss of intrinsic interest in their jobs over time.

Another problem is how self-handicappers are viewed by others. Observers tend to have more negative reactions to self-handicapping actors. They not only have less regard and liking for them, but they also evaluate their performance as being poorer, even though objective ratings indicate no performance differences between high and low self-handicappers (Rhodewalt et al., 1995; Smith & Strube, 1991). Recent data highlight gender differences in reactions to self-handicappers, with women being especially likely to question the motivation of self-handicappers and be suspicious of their motives (Hirt, McCrea, & Boris, 2003).

Now that you have learned a great deal about self-handicapping, it is time for you to find out the extent to which you are a self-handicapper. Try the original Self-Handicapping Scale reproduced in Table 11.5. Although we have discussed self-handicappers versus non-self-handicappers, it is important to reiterate that self-handicapping is a dimensional construct that you will have more or less of, and it should not be regarded as an all-or-none personality type. More information about the Self-Handicapping Scale can be found in a variety of sources (see Rhodewalt, 1990; Rhodewalt & Tragakis, 2002).

KEY POINTS

- Self-handicapping is a self-defeating form of behaviour designed to protect the self by generating excuses.
- The considerable costs of self-handicapping seem to outweigh the short-term benefits.
- Observers have very negative opinions of self-handicappers.

Table 11.5 The Self-Handicapping Scale

Indicate (by writing a number in the blank each item) the degree to which you agree with each of the following statements as a description of the kind of person you think you are most of the time. Use the following scale:

0 = disagree very much
1 = disagree pretty much
2 = disagree a little
3 = agree a little
4 = agree pretty much
5 = agree very much

1. When I do something wrong, my first impulse is to blame circumstances.
2. I tend to put things off until the last moment.
3. I tend to overprepare when I have an exam or any kind of "performance."
4. I suppose I feel "under the weather" more often than most people.
5. I always try to do my best, no matter what.
6. Before I sign up for a course or engage in any important activity, I make sure I have the proper preparation or background.
7. I tend to get very anxious before an exam or "performance."
8. I am easily distracted by noises or my own creative thoughts when I try to read.
9. I try not to get too intensely involved in competitive activities so it won't hurt too much if I lose or do poorly.
10. I would rather be respected for doing my best than admired for my potential.
11. I would do a lot better if I tried harder.
12. I prefer small pleasures in the present to larger pleasures in the dim future.
13. I generally hate to be in any condition but "at my best."
14. Someday I might "get it all together."
15. I sometimes enjoy being mildly ill for a day or two because it takes off the pressure.
16. I would do much better if I did not let my emotions get in the way.
17. When I do poorly at one kind of thing, I often console myself by remembering I am good at other things.
18. I admit that I am tempted to rationalize when I don't live up to others' expectations.
19. I often think I have more than my share of bad luck in sports, card games, and other measures of talent.
20. I would rather not take any drug that interfered with my ability to think clearly and do the right thing.
21. I overindulge in food and drink more often that I should.
22. When something important is coming up, like an exam or a job interview, I try to get as much sleep as possible the night before.
23. I never let emotional problems in one part of my life interfere with other things in my life.
24. Usually, when I get anxious about doing well, I end up doing better.
25. Sometimes I get so depressed that even easy tasks become difficult.

The score is the sum of all items after first reverse scoring items 3, 5, 6, 10, 13, 20, 22, and 23. Scores range from 0 to 125. The median (50th percentile) is approximately 60.

Summary

This chapter illustrates the complex and multi-faceted nature of the self-concept. It began with an overview of key historical developments involving the self-concept, including the distinction made by one of the earliest theorists, William James, who differentiated among the material me, the social me, and the spiritual me. An analysis of self-representations of people from India was provided to demonstrate that these different types of self-representation may differ by culture. The social aspects of self were also examined with respect to the concept of the looking glass self and the impact of reflected appraisals on the self. Research on reflected appraisals indicates that our perceptions of how others view us can have a powerful impact on how we come to see ourselves. If we believe that others hold us in high regard, we incorporate these views into a more positive self-concept.

The chapter then focused on Erik Erikson's epigenetic theory and the eight proposed stages of psychosocial development. These stages stretch throughout the life cycle, and each stage involved the need to resolve a psychosocial conflict in order to move on to the next stage. One of the most important stages involves issues of identity integration versus identity diffusion. Generativity is another important part of Erikson's stage theory. Generativity is reflected in behaviours that promote the well-being and long-term existence of subsequent generations.

The discussion of Erikson's theory of identity development was supplemented by an overview of Marcia's theory and empirical research on identity statuses. Four different identity statuses were outlined: (1) identity achievement; (2) moratorium; (3) foreclosure; and (4) identity diffusion.

The nature of the self-concept in general was then examined via an analysis of the various motives associated with the self-concept. These motives include the needs for self-enhancement, self-consistency, and self-improvement. The importance of self-presentation in the self-concept was also explored, including evidence suggesting that acts of self-presentation influence levels of self-esteem.

Chapter 11 includes a lengthy description of various ways of conceptualizing and representing the self. People differ in their self-complexity (i.e., the number of components to the self) and in their self-concept clarity. Work on the spontaneous self-concept was described to show that the self-evaluative statements that are typically linked with self-esteem constitute only one of several components of the spontaneous self-concept. Other aspects of the self include likes and dislikes, demographic attributes, and so on. The spontaneous self-concept reflects the distinctiveness hypothesis, which refers to our tendencies to define ourselves in ways that make us unique (e.g., a left-hander mentioning handedness when describing the self).

It was also noted that the self can be represented in terms of possible selves, and that a positive possible self is a powerful motivator of goal-directed behaviour. Accordingly, school interventions have been devised in an attempt to improve students' learning, achievement, and general well-being.

Next, self-discrepancy theory as postulated by Higgins was outlined. This theory distinguished among the actual self, the ideal self, and the ought self. The discrepancy between the actual and the ideal self is related to depression, while the discrepancy between the actual and the ought self is related to anxiety.

Given that the self-concept is complex, it is not too surprising that there are many different ways to consider and conceptualize individual differences in self-esteem. Self-esteem was discussed in terms of perceived mattering. Explicit versus implicit self-esteem was considered in terms of our conscious sense of self-esteem (explicit self-esteem) and our unconscious aspect (implicit self-esteem). Both explicit and implicit self-esteem may be high or low, and people with paradoxical self-esteem are high in explicit self-esteem and low in implicit self-esteem. Self-esteem was also discussed in terms of collective self (self-esteem due to group memberships).

The multidimensional nature of the self was then demonstrated through a description of Shavelson's hierarchical model of the self-concept, and its differentiation of academic, physical, and social aspects of the self. The need to consider different domains of the self was also illustrated by considering the facets of state self-esteem (e.g., performance, social, physical appearance).

Chapter 11 concluded with a detailed description of three self-related constructs that have been the subject of extensive research: self-consciousness, self-monitoring, and self-handicapping. Self-consciousness can be represented as private self-consciousness versus public self-consciousness, and both forms of self-consciousness have subfacets. Elevated self-consciousness tends to be associated with more intense positive and negative emotional reactions.

Self-monitoring has been extensively studied. High self-monitors are skillful at adapting themselves to social situations. Low self-monitors pride themselves on their consistency and adherence to values without changing because of situational pressures. Problems inherent in the main measure used to assess self-monitoring have resulted in a focus on self-monitoring factors, and this has led to evidence suggesting that there are adaptive and maladaptive aspects to self-monitoring.

Self-handicapping involves generating excuses to protect the self from the negative implications of failure. Self-handicapping can come in the form of behavioural self-handicapping or claimed, self-reported handicaps. Self-handicapping is motivated by a desire to avoid shame and embarrassment. However, recent research on the negative characteristics linked with self-handicapping continue to point to the conclusion that self-handicapping is deleterious in that it is linked with poorer performance, greater anxiety and depression, and so on.

Questions to Consider

1 Research has confirmed the multidimensionality of the self-concept. Think of the various people you know and how they might see themselves in terms of their achievement goals, their interpersonal world, their physical self, and so on. Do you think that people are consciously aware of the different aspects of the self? If the self-concept is malleable as a person develops, which facet of the self is most subject to change?

2 Do you agree with James that being with different people can lead, at least momentarily, to differences in the self-concept? Do people seem different when they are with a certain person (e.g., a boyfriend or girlfriend) versus when with other people? Think of the key people in your life. Do you see yourself differently depending on who you are with?

3 Recall that reflected appraisals are the estimates we have of how other people regard us. Can you see differences among the people you know in how they are viewed by others and how much they seem to care about how they are viewed by others? In your opinion, why do some people seem to be so concerned about how they are viewed by others?

4 Consider Erikson's description of the identity crisis. Do you think that most students have a clear sense of who they are? For those who have not established a clear sense of identity, do you think they will be able to achieve a sense of identity later in life?

5 In terms of the different domains of the self-concept, which aspect or domain is most important in how you see yourself? Do you place greater importance on your academic self or your social self? Do you think this will be the same in 10 years?

6 Recall that collective self-esteem is the positive or negative sense of self that we derive from our affiliations and from being a member of a larger group. How important is this to most people's sense of self? Do you think that universities and colleges do enough to foster a positive sense of collective self-esteem among their students? What would you do if you were a university administrator and your task was to improve collective self-esteem?

7 Review the concepts of self-consciousness, self-monitoring, and self-handicapping. Which of these three specific constructs is most applicable to you?

Key terms

actual self, p. 454
collective self-esteem, p. 463
defensive self-esteem, p. 461
distinctiveness hypothesis, p. 452
explicit self-esteem, p. 460
generativity, p. 441
ideal self, p. 454
identity conflict, p. 440
identity crisis, p. 440
identity deficit, p. 440

implicit self-esteem, p. 460
looking glass self, p. 434
ought self, p. 454
paradoxical self-esteem, p. 460
private self-consciousness, p. 468
public self-consciousness, p. 468
reflected appraisal, p. 435
self-absorption paradox, p. 469
self-complepxity, p. 450
self-concept clarity, p. 451
self-enhancement, p. 446
self-esteem, p. 457
self-handicapping, p. 472
self-reference effect, p. 449
self-verification theory, p. 446
sociometer theory, p. 433
spontaneous self-concept, p. 452
symbolic interactionism theory, p. 435

Key theorists

Erik Erikson, p. 437
E. Tory Higgins, p. 452
William James, p. 432
James Marcia, p. 443
Morris Rosenberg, p. 459

chapter twelve

PERSONALITY AND HEALTH

- Coping with Sensory Deprivation and Sensation Seeking
- Personality and Coping Styles
- Theoretical Models of Personality and Health
- Methodological and Measurement Issues and Concerns
- Personality Types and Health
- Personality Traits and Health Outcomes

Even the stress caused by the same experience can produce different specific responses in different people.

—HANS SELYE (1977, P. 80)

...[it was] one of those phobias that didn't pay off.

—WARREN ZEVON, SINGER AND SONGWRITER, SUFFERING FROM TERMINAL CANCER, TELLING DAVID LETTERMAN OF HIS REFUSAL TO GET REGULAR CHECKUPS FROM HIS DOCTOR (OCTOBER 30, 2002)

I've got a question. This mental stuff can cause physical problems, right?

—TONY SOPRANO (PLAYED BY JAMES GANDOLFINI) TO HIS PSYCHIATRIST DR. MELFI, IN THE TELEVISION SHOW *THE SOPRANOS*

There is nothing alive which is not individual: our health is ours; our diseases are ours; our reactions are ours—no less than our minds or our faces.

—OLIVER SACKS, 1990

> I fell back stunned by the ghastly truth. A year? I was to live in this black coffin a year? Without light? Without bedding? Without clothing? Without toilet facilities? And without God knows what else? It was impossible, I told myself. No man could live in such a dark void, under such conditions, for a year. He would die, and his death would be slow and torturous. It would have been better had I been sentenced to the guillotine. I loved France. But what kind of country was it that countenanced such punishment for such a crime as mine? And if the government was ignorant of such prison conditions, the people unknowing, what manner of men were the French penologists, into whose hands I had been delivered? Depraved monsters, madmen, perverts, undoubtedly ... Sometimes the sounds were my own, for in my loneliness I often talked to myself just to hear the sound of a human voice. Or I would stand stooped before the door and scream at the guards to let me out or demand I be treated like a human being, with dignity and consideration if not respect. I cursed them. I cursed myself. I ranted and raved, wept and screamed, chanted and sang, laughed and bellowed, shouted and banged the bucket against the walls, splattering excrement all over my cratelike cell. I felt I was going mad. (Abagnale Jr., 1980, pp. 210, 214)

THE ABOVE EXCERPT FROM *Catch Me if You Can* by Frank Abagnale Jr. describes his reaction to being incarcerated in a French prison when he was 20 years old. He was captured in France and sentenced to one year in prison for his crimes of passing bad cheques. What he did not realize at the time of his capture is that the French penal system is based on the belief in "an eye for an eye" and, historically, the French have been very interested in punishment, but less interested in rehabilitating the prisoner. Abagnale Jr. was thrown into a cell by himself. This cell was more like a hole without light or toilet facilities. Abagnale Jr. came close to going mad, but fortunately, his time in this prison was shortened to six months. He was then transported to Sweden, where he was also convicted of passing bad cheques.

How do people cope with such situations? Are there differences between people in their ability to cope? Indeed there are. The situation described above is obviously inhumane but is similar in many respects to the classic sensory deprivation experiments conducted in the 1950s and 1960s. Participants in these experiments were isolated either in dark soundproof rooms or they were immersed in water tanks. Isolation in dark rooms could be for up to two weeks, but about one third of volunteers could last for only two days, while 10 hours was the limit for the more severe form of being immersed in a water tank (see Zuckerman, 1993). Initial research on sensory deprivation was conducted at McGill University. The general interest was to examine how people adapted and coped in general with such an adverse and challenging situation. Hallucinations and delusions were common, and most people reported an inability to concentrate, perhaps due to decreased brainwave activity. Individual differences quickly became apparent. As a result of different responses that people had to this situation (e.g., boredom, panic), the sensory deprivation situation became known as the "Walk-In Inkblot" (see Zuckerman, 1993).

COPING WITH SENSORY DEPRIVATION AND SENSATION SEEKING

As noted by Zuckerman (1969), some of the differences in responses to the sensory deprivation situation were attributable to differences in levels of anxiety, a finding that was confirmed by subsequent investigators (e.g., Forgays, 1989). Cognitive appraisal also played a clear role; that is, people who expected to have a bad reaction did indeed have a bad reaction. Research summarized by Zuckerman (1969) also shows that it matters whether a person is an introvert or extrovert. It turns out that extroverts do much better in sensory deprivation situations. Perhaps this has to do with the fact that they are physiologically under-aroused and the desire for extra stimulation keeps them going. Or perhaps even the hope of eventually re-establishing contact with other people is enough to keep them going, or it is their ability to distract themselves by recalling past events involving people they have met (note that Abagnale Jr. retained his sanity by fantasizing about past events). Whatever the case, clear individual differences exist, and these sensory deprivation experiments sparked interest in dispositional differences in coping with extreme adversity.

The sensory deprivation experiments conducted by Zuckerman also led to his seminal research on sensation seeking (for a summary, see Zuckerman, 1969). He witnessed the differences between people and posited initially that each person has an optimal level of stimulation or arousal. He and his colleagues created the Sensation Seeking Scale to distinguish high and low sensation seekers. As expected, high sensation seekers were engaged in various forms of thrill and adventure seeking, including a greater tendency to use drugs, in an attempt to combat feelings of boredom.

Sensation seeking such as skydiving has been associated with risky and dangerous behaviour.

While sensation seeking has long been associated with risky and potentially dangerous behaviours (e.g., skydiving, driving too fast), it is only within the past 15 years that the potentially deadly aspects of sensation seeking have come to light. Consider and carefully reflect on the material in Applied Perspective 12.1 before moving on to our broader discussion of personality, stress, and coping. This material on sexual sensation seeking is an early introduction to our subsequent discussion of the role of personality differences in health-related behaviours.

The sensory deprivation issue serves as an effective introduction to the notion that there are consistent individual differences in how people respond to and cope with stressful and sometimes traumatic experiences. The first segment of Chapter 12 focuses on different coping styles and the association between personality traits and coping styles.

Given that the experience of stress is inevitable, who is better at coping with this stress? What personality traits are adaptive? And what coping styles are best? These questions are addressed in the next section, which begins with an excerpt from the book *The Right Mountain: Lessons from Everest on the Real Meaning of Success.* This inspiring book by Jim Hayhurst, Sr., former chairman of Outward Bound Canada, should be required reading for every student. Hayhurst was part of a team of climbers attempting to make it to the peak of Mount Everest. Hayhurst uses *The Right Mountain* to convey some very meaningful metaphors and important points about how to navigate successfully through life. As we see below, much of it has to do with coping and identifying a personality orientation that involves effective coping.

Applied Perspective 12.1 Sensation Seeking and the Prevention of Risky Health Behaviours

Numerous studies have shown that sensation seeking and related factors such as impulsivity are strong predictors of engaging in risky sexual behaviours. This association has been found in high school students, university students, and homosexual and heterosexual adults. It has even been found among people who already have a sexually transmitted disease. Sensation seeking has predicted such variables as number of sexual partners (Fisher & Misovich, 1990).

The strength of this link has been established with Zuckerman's general measure of sensation seeking, but in recent years, researchers have supplemented this general measure with a newly created scale known as the Sexual Sensation Seeking Scale. The creators of this new scale reasoned that Zuckerman's measure contains culturally outdated items and does not tap themes involving sexuality, which is understandable since it was intended as a general measure (see Kalichman et al., 1994). Sexual sensation seeking was defined as the propensity to seek out ultimate levels of sexual experience and engage in novel sexual experiences. Items were refined and constructed based on input from five gay men described as being culturally diverse. The 10-item sexual sensation seeking measure included such items as "I like wild uninhibited sexual encounters," "I enjoy watching X-rated videos," "I feel like exploring my sexuality," and "I have said things that are not exactly true to get a person to have sex with me." It was accompanied by a 10-item measure of non-sexual sensation seeking (e.g., "I would like to try bungee jumping") and a separate subscale assessing sexual compulsivity. These subscales were included to establish the discriminant validity of the sexual sensation seeking scale.

Kalichman et al. (1994) examined the correlates of sexual sensation seeking by administering their new measure and other measures to a sample of gay men. Sexual sensation seeking, relative to the other two measures, showed stronger associations with a variety of measures, including number of sex partners, having anal intercourse without condoms, and reduced sexual self-control.

A meta-analytic review paper by Hoyle, Fejfar, and Miller (2000) examined the personality predictors of risky sexual behaviours across 53 eligible studies. This study confirmed that there is a strong link between sensation seeking and high-risk sexual behaviour. There is also a slightly less robust association between high-risk sexual behaviour and both impulsivity and low agreeableness. Hoyle et al. (2000) made another very important observation. They expressed concern about the paucity of research on high-risk sexual behaviours and traits reflecting normal personality. Other personality factors may play a role, but their impact has been largely ignored. It is possible, for example, that the personality traits associated with vulnerability to depression and hopelessness (e.g., self-criticism, dependency, and socially prescribed perfectionism) also play a role because some people may be engaging in potentially self-destructive acts due to a desire to escape unwanted pressures and other stressors.

The International Sexuality Project examined the personality predictors of more than 16,000 people

Figure 12.1 Correlations between Extroversion and Sexual Promiscuity for Men and Women across Ten World Regions

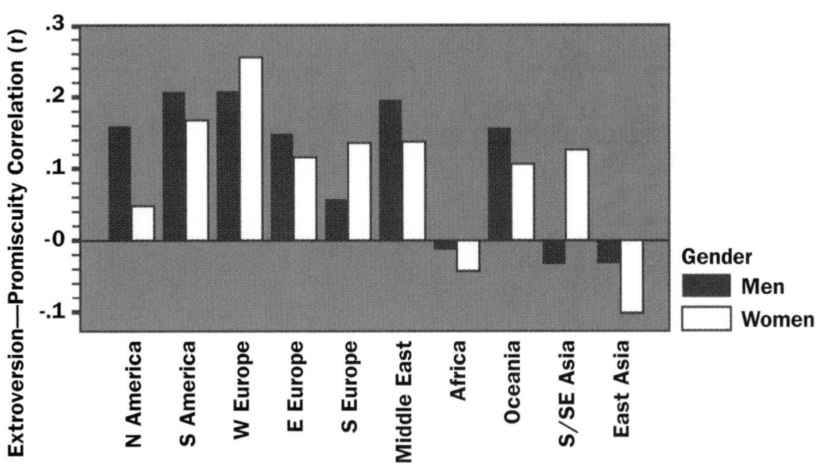

Source: Schmitt, 2004.

from 52 nations (see Schmitt, 2004). Key measures included indices of relationship infidelity and sexual promiscuity. Analyses with the five-factor model traits showed that the same factors that predicted relationship infidelity did not predict sexual promiscuity and risky sexual behaviour. For instance, neuroticism in men and women from Asia and Southeast Asia and in women from North America predicted infidelity but not risky sexual practices. Overall, the two best predictors of being unfaithful were low agreeableness and low conscientiousness. In contrast, sexual promiscuity was best predicted by extroversion. This was almost a ubiquitous finding in that it applied to most of the 10 world regions assessed in this study. However, extroversion was not associated with promiscuity in Africa, South/Southeast Asia, and East Asia. The results by world region are displayed in Figure 12.1.

Donohew and Bardo (2000) discussed how to design prevention programs for sensation seeking adolescents. Donohew and Bardo's basic message was that getting through to adolescents with high levels of sensation seeking requires interventions that are stimulating and satisfy their need for novelty and sensation (also see Donohew, Bardo, & Zimmerman, 2004). That is, messages need to be novel, complex, and emotionally intense. Higher impact is also associated with messages that are fast-paced, suspenseful, and somewhat ambiguous at first.

Another study by Trobst et al. (2000) underscored the fact that positive behaviour change is not easy, even when it is vitally important. Trobst and colleagues found that low openness to experience was associated with reduced risk for HIV infection. In addition, a four-session intervention program was implemented. This program was called the Take-Charge Program, which involved four brief sessions with peer counsellors. This program was designed to increase condom use among people with multiple sexual partners. It was found that individual differences in perceived risk were unrelated to behaviour change following the intervention. This lack of self-protective behaviour is shocking considering that even endorsing the belief that there was a "big chance" of HIV infection did not motivate people to change.

Unfortunately, the four-session intervention program resulted in only very small improvements (though enough perhaps to save some lives). It was still the case that 47% of participants did not use condoms by the end of the program, and the proportion of people who frequently used condoms increased only from 15% to 22%. Although it might be argued that more extensive interventions are required, you might think that receiving even a little bit of counselling for behaviour related to a life or death issue would result in more positive behavioural change. The lack of change is likely due to a variety of factors, including deeply ingrained behaviours that reflect personality orientations such as sensation seeking and impulsivity, a lack of desire to change, as well as superstitious, and naïve optimism about feeling and being invulnerable.

KEY POINTS

- People differ widely in their responses to sensory deprivation. Extroverts and low sensation seekers tend to have more adaptive responses to sensory deprivation.
- Initially, Zuckerman attributed individual differences in sensation seeking to levels of arousal, with high sensation seekers being below the optimal level of arousal. Low sensation seekers are already overstimulated so they do not enjoy additional stimulation.
- Sensation seeking predicts high-risk behaviour such as engaging in risky sexual activities.

PERSONALITY AND COPING STYLES

> Barry had chosen carefully. He wanted team players, guys who would sacrifice their chance at glory, at the peak of the mountain, to help others … He wanted individuals who could and would talk about issues bothering them, rather than internalizing them, and letting them come to a boil later when it was tougher to defuse them. He wanted people who could adjust to change, often dramatic change, quickly and confidently, without time-consuming cajoling. He wanted individuals who could operate under intense physical and emotional pressure, in life-and-death situations, and still be able to function at an elite level. And he wanted individuals who were entrepreneurs, quick and positive thinkers, and risk takers. (Hayhurst, 1997, p. 17)

Clearly, when it comes to coping, some people are much more effective than others, and people with certain personality styles are more capable at withstanding stress. The excerpt outlines the attributes required for coping with an extreme challenge: climbing Mount Everest.

There are various ways to examine the issue of coping and personality. A good starting point is to consider the role of personality in how stressful situations are cognitively interpreted. People differ in how they perceive or appraise stressful experiences (see Lazarus, 1966). The same stressful experience or situation may be experienced quite differently by different people.

The same stressful experience, such as taking a test or an exam, may be experienced differently by different people.

Take, for instance, a situation that all students are highly familiar with: the final exam in a course. Mere mention of this situation will send shivers down the spines of some students, while other students will ask, "What's the big deal?" One of the key differences in the cognitive appraisal of stressors is whether a stressful situation is appraised as a threat or a challenge. People who are high in neuroticism and prone to experience anxiety are probably going to perceive obvious stressors as threats, but these same people may even interpret ambiguous situations as major threats. This is the type of student who could be overwhelmed with test anxiety prior to the exam because of anticipating failure.

Primary Appraisals versus Secondary Appraisals

Richard Lazarus and **Susan Folkman** (1984) proposed one of the most influential models of stress. They made the key distinction between primary appraisal and secondary appraisal. Individual differences may exist with both types of appraisals. Primary appraisals involve assessing whether the event is a threat or a challenge. Secondary appraisals are a personal evaluation of whether the person feels that he or she has the ability to cope with the event. This distinction between primary and secondary appraisals is important because a personality factor may be associated with secondary appraisals and not primary appraisals or vice versa. For instance, Chang (1998) showed that optimists and pessimists differed in their secondary appraisals of coping responses but not in their primary appraisals of threat versus challenge. Optimists were higher in adaptive coping styles such as cognitive restructuring, and they were lower in maladaptive styles, such as engaging in wishful thinking, self-criticism, and social withdrawal.

The assumption that neuroticism is linked with stress-inducing cognitive appraisals has been supported by empirical research. For instance, a study of how students appraise exams found that neuroticism was linked with threat appraisals, while extroversion was a positive factor that was linked with challenge appraisals (Gallagher, 1990). Subsequent research by Hemenover (2001) from Kansas State University tested and confirmed that neuroticism is associated with a negative processing bias when events occur, while extroversion is associated with a positive processing bias. Bias was assessed with the Processing Bias Questionnaire that asked respondents to indicate, in general, such things as when an event occurs, to what extent they think about the positive features, and the negative features of the situation.

A traumatic event, such as the December 26, 2004 tsunami, may provide some people with an opportunity for personal growth.

Perhaps the ultimate in cognitive reappraisal is the way that some people reinterpret highly traumatic experiences after the events. Researchers studying post-traumatic stress have found that some people come to see a highly traumatic experience as beneficial because it provided an opportunity for personal growth.

The Post-Traumatic Growth Inventory by Tedeschi and Calhoun (1996) assesses perceived personal growth using five subscales: "new possibilities," relating to others, personal strength, appreciation of life, and spiritual change. Affleck and Tennen (1996) have discussed this positive approach to experiencing trauma by describing people who are benefit finding who then later reiterate the benefits by being benefit reminding. Contrast the person who takes this orientation with someone who continues to ruminate about such events in a very resentful way. An illustration of benefit finding came from a survey of Ottawa residents' reactions to the 2001 terrorist attacks in the United States. This survey found that those people who experienced greater perceived threat and more intense emotional reactions were more likely to report positive changes following the attacks, such as getting closer to family members and refocusing their personal priorities (Davis & McDonald, 2004).

Benefit finding may also play a role in recovery from illness. Recall in Chapter 7 the description of Lance Armstrong and his recovery from testicular cancer. Armstrong experienced many positive changes in his value system as a result of his illness. Part of his amazing recovery and success is a reflection of his ability to engage in benefit finding with respect to his illness. Armstrong observed that:

> The truth is that cancer was the best thing that ever happened to me. I don't know why I got the illness, but it did wonders for me, and I wouldn't want to walk away from it. Why would I want to change, even for a day, the most important and shaping event in my life? ... When I was sick, I saw more beauty and triumph and truth in a single day that I ever did in a bike race—but they were human moments, not miraculous ones. (Armstrong & Jenkins, 2000, p. 4–5)

Clearly, Armstrong engaged in a form of a process known as cognitive reframing so that he could identify the benefits of his illness. One very tangible benefit is the notable charity work done subsequently by Armstrong and his charitable foundation.

KEY POINTS

- According to Lazarus, primary appraisal involves judging whether a stressor is a threat or a challenge.
- Secondary appraisals focus on judging whether a person feels able to cope with a stressor. Feeling able or unable to cope then guides the specific coping responses.
- Neuroticism is associated with a negative processing bias that is focused on perceived threat. Extroversion is associated with a positive processing bias focused on challenges.

Cognitive appraisals are important because they determine, in part, the way that people respond to stressful situations; that is, coping differences are partly a reflection of how people appraise events cognitively. **Coping** can be defined generally as the ways in which people try to deal with a problem or handle the emotions that arise in response to the problem. Even when two people interpret a common stressor in the same way, the effects and outcome of the stress will vary as a functioning of differences in coping styles.

Problem-Focused, Emotion-Focused, and Avoidance-Focused Coping

Although the experience of stressful events is often beyond our control, the manner in which we decide to cope with these stressful events is something that is under our personal control. We can opt for various coping responses that vary in their adaptiveness and usefulness. In a sense, then, establishing that certain personality traits are linked with certain coping styles is a way of showing that personality factors guide and shape our coping responses. The good news for those individuals who have personality features that tend to be associated with poorer coping choices is that more appropriate coping and problem-solving skills can be learned.

Lazarus and Folkman (1984) identified two broad classes of coping responses. If you are a "take charge" person, you might respond to stressors with problem-focused coping. **Problem-focused coping** involves taking actions to directly solve the problem. Attempts are made to confront the problem head-on by doing such things as trying to redefine a big problem into a series of smaller, more manageable problems or by seeking information that will point to a possible solution. If a demanding final exam is looming, a problem-focused approach is to find new and more effective ways to study by yourself or set up a study group.

In *The Right Mountain*, Hayhurst outlines what it means to be a problem-focused coper. Here is his advice:

> Times change, jobs change, rules change. So what do you do? Throw up your hands? Quit? No. If you don't know what to do next, if the next step is unclear, go to the things you know. Rebuild the scenario. Look for things you might have missed. Move ahead slowly. Take small steps, and complete them one at a time. The fastest way to do it is to do it slowly. (Hayhurst, 1997, p. 110)

Problem-focused copers first try to look at a problem from various perspectives and consider a number of response alternatives. Most importantly, they confront the problem head-on rather than trying to avoid it.

The second broad class of coping responses is **emotion-focused coping**, a tendency to reflect on the emotional experiences associated with stress. This can involve rumination about the emotional feelings and the causes of these feelings, and a process of blaming the self and/or other people. An emotion-focused approach when a final examination is looming would mean focusing attention on the affective experience of test anxiety itself, including feelings of panic and dismay. Emotion-oriented coping is also at play when students have self-critical thoughts such as "Why didn't I start studying earlier?"

Lazarus and Folkman (1984) identified various forms of emotion-focused coping, including distracting oneself from the problem and seeking out comfort by affiliating with other people. Subsequent research on coping styles suggests that emotion-focused coping should be distinguished from another maladaptive form of coping: **avoidance-focused coping**. Avoidance-oriented coping includes dealing with a problem by trying to distract yourself cognitively or avoiding the problem by seeking out other people as a form of social diversion.

Table 12.1 illustrates the distinctions among these broad coping orientations with respect to the self-statements people might have and the questions they might ask as they respond to an occurrence that is all too familiar these days: a terrorist attack. How would you respond? Are you a problem-focused coper or an emotion-oriented coper?

Table 12.1 Coping Orientations in Response to a Terrorist Attack

Task-Focused Coping:
What precautions can I take to stop this from happening?
What can I do to stay out of harm's way?
What can I do to help?

Emotion-Focused Coping:
Who is to blame for this?
Could our government have done something more?
Why can't I stop thinking about this?

Avoidance-Focused Coping:
I'm going to pretend that nothing happened.
I'm going to distract myself by reading a book.

The example of a terrorist attack was selected in Table 12.1, in part, to acknowledge the increasing number of investigations into ways people respond to naturally occurring events of a highly traumatic nature. Studies have examined individual differences in coping reactions to not only terrorist attacks but also to such things as horrific accidents, natural disasters (e.g., the Asian tsunami), wars, and outbreaks of disease. For instance, Zeidner and Hammer (1992) examined how Israeli citizens coped with SCUD missile attacks during the 1991 Persian Gulf War. An emotion-oriented form of palliative coping was associated with greater anxiety and physical symptoms. Active coping was not a significant predictor, and Zeidner and Hammer (1992) suggested that the palliative coping may have been the most reasonable and adaptive way of dealing with an uncontrollable situation. The authors also noted that many people relied on spiritual resources, including prayer, and this was likely a function of "the generally religious orientation of the Israeli culture" (p. 739).

Perhaps you responded to the situation in Table 12.1 by indicating that it is difficult to say what your response would be since it would depend on the exact nature of the stressful situation being experienced. This is a reasonable response that fits with the **transactional model of stress** outlined by Lazarus (1966). The transactional model is based on the idea that coping responses depend greatly on the stressful situations themselves and how they are appraised by the individual in the stressful situation. Although the transactional model is often interpreted by scholars as a person-by-situation approach, Lazarus felt that personality factors are relatively unimportant, in part because they are too static and fixed. He tended to emphasize the problem situation as a key determinant of the coping response. The emphasis by Lazarus on coping as a fluid and ongoing process that unfolds over time is in keeping with a model of stress and coping developed by Neufeld (1999) at the University of Western Ontario. This model also reflects the premise that there is an ongoing and dynamic interplay of factors that is due, in part, to the fact that stressors and related situations change over time.

The Goodness of Fit Hypothesis

The importance of considering the specific nature of the stressor is reflected by the fact that broad statements about which type of coping is most adaptive must be qualified; whether a particular type of response is adaptive does indeed depend on the situation. Emotion-focused and avoidance-focused coping responses are generally maladaptive, and problem-focused coping responses are generally adaptive. Still, the effectiveness of attempts to cope often varies with the situation and the degree of success that results from initial attempts to address a situation. As Feather (1989) has shown, task-oriented persistence does not always work, and some people simply fail to realize when it is time to quit and adopt a more effective strategy. The **goodness of fit hypothesis** is based on the premise that whether a particular coping response is adaptive depends on the match between the coping response and what the problem situation ideally calls for. The fit between the person and environment has received extensive attention from researchers studying work and job environments. More generally, various investigators have provided at least partial support for the goodness of fit hypothesis (e.g., Endler, Speer, Johnson, & Flett, 2000; Felton & Revenson, 1984; Forsythe & Compas, 1987).

A slightly different way of framing the goodness of fit hypothesis is to examine coping and cultural fit. International Focus on Discovery 12.1 examines the personality and coping characteristics that are required when sojourners must learn to adjust to living in a new culture.

KEY POINTS

- Coping differences reflect differences in how people appraise stressful situations cognitively.
- Task-oriented coping is a problem-focused orientation that involves confronting the challenging situation. Task-oriented copers are flexible and consider various alternatives to a stressful situation.
- Emotion-oriented coping is typically maladaptive. It involves an emotional distress-oriented response to a stressor that can take the form of rumination and self-blame.
- Avoidance-oriented coping is a tendency to avoid confronting a stressful situation or problem. Common forms of this type of coping include engaging in distracting activities and seeking out social forms of diversion.
- The goodness of fit hypothesis suggests that whether a particular type of coping response is adaptive depends on the nature of the stressful situation. Thus, it is not wise to make definitive statements about the best type of coping without first considering the specific aspects of the stressor or the problem situation.

International Focus on Discovery 12.1 Personality and Coping with the Sojourner Experience

Global trends suggest that there is an increasing amount of contact between people from different cultures. This is paralleled by an ever-increasing number of people who leave their country of origin and get a job in another country. The ability to adapt to a new culture is perhaps one of the most challenging tasks for a person. Who is most suited to this situation?

The phenomenon of adjusting to a new culture has been described as **sojourner adjustment**. Not surprisingly, the five-factor model has been applied to this issue. Ones and Viswesvaran (1999) asked 96 managers of 32 expatriate employees who relocated to a new country to rate them on attributes reflecting the traits that comprise the five-factor model. Each employee was also rated on four characteristics: (1) completion of overseas assignment; (2) personal adjustment; (3) interpersonal relationships with employees from the overseas country; and (4) overall overseas job performance. Analyses of the ratings confirmed that employee conscientiousness was the strongest predictor of positive ratings across all four indicators. However, the rating of trait openness to experience was the second best predictor of completion of the overseas assignment. It is important to reiterate here that this is based on the managers' perceptions; the authors noted that the high rating given to openness to experience is at variance with the other empirical results showing that openness to experience is a weak predictor of expatriate success.

A more recent investigation compared Singaporean students and Australian students based in Australia, and Australian expatriates and Chinese Singaporeans in Singapore (Ward, Leong, & Low, 2004). Correlations examined the link between the traits of the five-factor model and psychological well-being and sociocultural adaptation. In addition, contextual factors were assessed so that the **cultural fit hypothesis** could be evaluated. This is the notion that personality will be adaptive in a new culture to the extent that it fits with existing norms in the host culture. No evidence was found in either Australia or Singapore for the cultural fit hypothesis. However, better sojourner adjustment was associated with lower neuroticism and higher levels of extroversion, agreeableness, and conscientiousness.

A team of researchers in the Netherlands has argued quite effectively for the need to create measures that are specific to the quality of interactions with people from other cultures. They have developed the Multicultural Personality Questionnaire (MPQ) to predict the ability to cope and adjust to other cultures (see van der Zee & van Oudenhoven, 2000). This questionnaire assesses not only effective performance but also the person's sense of well-being and adjustment. The MPQ was designed originally to assess seven themes: (1) cultural empathy; (2) open-mindedness; (3) emotional stability; (4) orientation to action; (5) adventurousness/curiosity; (6) flexibility; and (7) extroversion. These themes are defined in Table 12.2.

Factor analyses showed that these themes reflected four higher order factors, three of which fit with the five-factor model (openness, emotional stability, and social initiative), and one factor (flexibility) that is clearly unique. However, the first three factors have item content that stresses the multicultural context.

Van der Zee, Zaal, and Piekstra (2003) sought to establish the construct validity of the MPQ in personnel

Table 12.2 Themes Represented in the Multicultural Personality Questionnaire

Theme	Description
Cultural Empathy	The capacity to clearly project an interest in others; to obtain and to reflect a reasonably complete and accurate sense of another's thoughts, feelings, and experiences
Open-Mindedness	An open and unprejudiced attitude toward outgroup members and different cultural norms and values
Emotional Stability	Ability to deal with psychological stress in intercultural situations
Orientation to Action	The courage to take action and make things happen
Adventurousness/Curiosity	The tendency to actively search and explore new situations and to regard them as a challenge
Flexibility	The ability to switch easily from one strategy to another, to abandon familiar strategies when they are not working, and to learn from mistakes
Extroversion	A tendency to stand out in a different culture, to take the social initiative and learn new social skills

selection. A measure of the five-factor model was also included in this study, and certain scales on this measure yielded findings similar to the MPQ. However, when both sets of measures were used to predict job performance, the MPQ predicted unique variance in job performance, over and above the trait measures reflecting the five-factor model. The results of a statistical analysis known as a hierarchical regression analysis showed that emotional stability from the five-factor model predicted job performance, and then cultural empathy and openness predicted a significant degree of remaining variance in job performance. To put this in more straightforward terms, if you wanted to predict job performance, you should know about the person's levels of trait emotional stability, cultural empathy, and openness. All three factors would provide useful information.

Although this information is impressive, we're still left with the question: How does the MPQ relate to expatriate performance? A study by van Oudenhoven, Mol, and van der Zee (2003) used the MPQ to gauge the performance of expatriate employees (primarily Westerners) assigned to Taiwan. Levels of personal, professional, and social adjustment were assessed. The MPQ emotional stability factor was most predictive across all three indicators, and was seen overall as the most important factor. Social initiative was also a strong predictor of psychological well-being, and cultural empathy predicted life satisfaction. Flexibility seemed to be the most important factor in job satisfaction.

Controllable versus Uncontrollable Stressors

A key factor is whether a problem or situation is controllable or uncontrollable. Problem-focused coping is most adaptive when possible solutions exist and there is something that an individual can do to improve the situation. Emotion-focused coping is less adaptive in these situations. One of the most recent studies involved Internet data collection with a sample of students (see Park, Armeli, & Tennen, 2004). Stressors, cognitive appraisals of controllability, and positive versus negative emotions were assessed daily for 28 days. Higher control appraisals were associated positively with problem-focused coping and negatively with avoidance-oriented coping. In addition, it was found from within-person analyses that there was a much stronger link between problem-focused coping and positive emotions for events that were perceived as more controllable.

However, when a situation is uncontrollable, problem-focused coping is not adaptive; here it may be better to vent and express one's emotions as a form of tension release (Stanton, Kirk, Cameron, & Danoff-Burg, 2000). Stanton et al. (2000) have been highly critical of researchers who have focused on emotion-oriented coping as destructive but did not allow for the possible benefits of emotional expression. Follow-up research has confirmed the potential adaptiveness of coping via emotional approach and emotional expression (Austenfeld & Stanton, 2004). Indeed, we will see in the subsequent section of this chapter on the cancer-prone personality that the emotional expression of feelings of stress is believed to confer substantial benefits to expressive individuals. Some of this may be due to a tendency for emotional expression to engender social support from other people (for a review, see Mauss & Gross, 2004).

An intriguing study by Bolger (1990) illustrates why the context in which coping occurs must be given full consideration. Bolger (1990) conducted a prospective investigation in which pre-medical students were assessed several days before and after their medical school entrance examination. Although problem-focused coping is usually associated with better adjustment, Bolger found that problem-focused coping measured predicted *increases* in levels of state anxiety. Bolger suggested that in this particular context, the need to engage in active preparation for the examination may have had the effect of increasing anxiety. This study illustrates that there are no absolutes when it comes to the link between ways of coping and psychological distress, and, in certain circumstances, seemingly "adaptive" forms of coping may actually be associated with higher, not lower, distress.

Given that situational factors are important and it seems fairly obvious that different problems will require different responses, is there any role at all for personality factors when it comes to coping? Clearly, personality does make a difference, and this has been shown by various sets of investigators. In the next section, we will look at personality and dispositional differences in coping. We will also examine the related issue of what evidence indicates that coping differences reflect stable personality differences.

A Dispositional Approach to Coping

Amirkhan (1990) developed a scale called the Coping Strategy Indicator. His efforts began by amassing 161 different coping responses, including several culled from other coping measures. A series of factor analyses resulted eventually in a 33-item scale that was further reduced to 15 items with three broad factors measuring problem-solving, seeking support, and avoidance. People respont to items based on how they respond to stressors in general.

Carver, Scheier, and Weintraub (1989) sought to conduct a more differentiated assessment of facets of emotion-focused and problem-focused coping. Their COPE Inventory consists of a series of 13 scales with various subscales reflecting emotion-oriented coping (e.g., focus on venting of emotions) and other subscales reflecting problem-focused dimensions (e.g., active coping, planning) or avoidance-oriented coping (e.g., behavioural disengagement). Table 12.3 lists these scales and examples. An interesting addition to this scale was the sense of humour subscale. The COPE was completed initially as a trait measure (i.e., coping responses in general), but Carver et al. (1989) showed that the scale could also be adapted to examine coping responses to specific problems. Also, for investigators concerned about the length of the measure, Carver (1997) developed a revised measure known as the BRIEF COPE. This instrument retains the original factors but consists of only two items per subscale. Although certain COPE subscales seem to form a cluster in that they are problem-focused or emotion-focused, Carver does not advocate combining the subscales into broader factors and instead favours looking at each individual subscale.

Endler (2002) extended his interaction model of trait and state anxiety to include stress and coping components. This revised model is similar in key respects to earlier coping models (Lazarus, 1966), but it includes an emphasis on coping as an aspect of personality. In other words, people have a characteristic way to cope with stressors. Endler teamed up with Jim Parker, who is now at Trent University in Ontario, to create a new measure reflecting stable individual differences in coping styles. At the same time, in a paper subtitled "If it Changes it Might Be Unstable," criticized the measure based on the Lazarus model, the Ways of Coping Checklist, because they suggested that rather than reflecting a coping process, the measure is simply unreliable and has questionable psychometric properties.

Table 12.3 Scales and Sample Items from the COPE

Active Coping:
I've been concentrating my efforts on doing something about the situation I'm in.
Suppression of Competing Activities:
I've been putting aside other activities in order to concentrate on this.
Planning:
I've been trying to come up with a strategy about what to do.
Restraint:
I've been making sure not to make matters worse by acting too soon.
Use of Social Support:
I've been getting sympathy and understanding from someone.
Positive Reframing:
I've been looking for something good in what is happening.
Religion:
I've been putting my trust in God.
Acceptance:
I've been accepting the reality of the fact that it happened.
Denial:
I've been refusing to believe that it has happened.
Behavioural Disengagement:
I've been giving up the attempt to cope.
Use of Humour:
I've been making jokes about it.
Self-Distraction:
I've been going to movies, watching TV, or reading, to think about it less.

Source: Carver, Scheier, & Weintraub, 1989.

Norman Endler and **James Parker** (1999) created the Coping Inventory for Stressful Situations (CISS) to measure three stable, dispositional aspects of coping: (1) emotion-oriented coping; (2) task-oriented coping, and (3) avoidance-oriented coping. Avoidance-oriented coping consists of two distinguishable facets measuring diversion (e.g., watching television) and social distraction (e.g., seeing friends). Because these coping styles are regarded as components of personality structure, they are seen as relatively long-lasting and stable. In the Endler (2002) model, these stable coping styles interact with situational stressors and cognitive appraisals of these stressful situations to determine whether there is an adaptive or maladaptive response and the intensity of this response.

Avoidance-oriented coping consists of two distinguishable facets that measure diversion (e.g., watching television) and social distraction (e.g., seeing friends).

Coping with Health Problems

One impetus for this research was to examine the link between coping styles and health outcomes. Endler and Parker (2000) sought to examine coping and health more directly, so they supplemented the CISS by developing the Coping with Health Injuries and Problems (CHIP) measure. The CHIP measures individual differences in coping responses to a specific health problem rather than a generalized coping style, but the assumption here is that these coping responses are an outgrowth of the general coping styles assessed by the CISS. How do you typically respond when you have a health problem? Let's say that you want to read this book but you have a migraine headache. Do you focus on how you feel? Do you try to relax to lessen the pain? Or do you read this book (or an even more interesting book) to distract yourself and keep you from thinking about the pain?

The CHIP has four subscales that incorporate the distinctions among emotion-focused, task-focused, and avoidance coping. Emotion-oriented coping is tapped by a scale that assesses emotional preoccupation with the health problem. Emotional preoccupation may take the form of catastrophization, which is all-or-none thinking about a health problem that often involves magnifying the symptoms and their importance by "blowing them out of proportion." Emotion-oriented coping is also represented by the CHIP measure of palliative coping. Palliative coping involves attempts at soothing the distressed state by engaging in self-help and comforting activities (e.g., staying in bed, making yourself a cup of tea). The task-focused orientation is reflected by the CHIP instrumental coping subscale (specific things that can be done to overcome the illness). Finally, the avoidance orientation is reflected by the CHIP distraction subscale.

It is important to reiterate that the CHIP assesses coping responses rather than coping styles. Whereas the CISS asks respondents to complete test items based on their usual way of coping with stress in general (coping style), the CISS asks respondents to complete items regarding a particular health problem (e.g., back spasms). Not surprisingly, extensive research by Endler and his associates has shown that after taking general coping styles into account, specific measures of coping with health problems can still predict variance in outcome measures such as quality of life. Thus, general and health-specific coping styles should be considered.

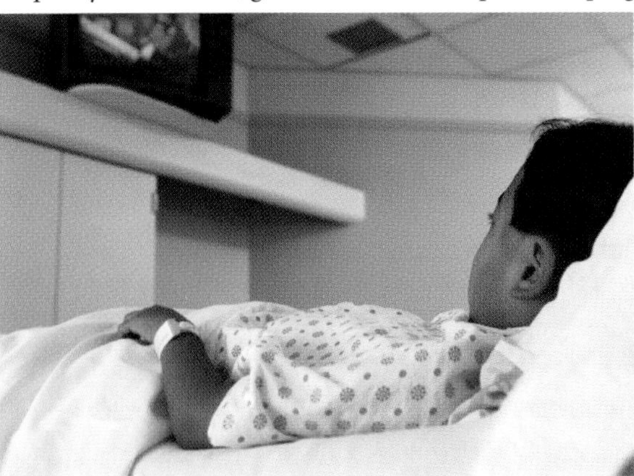

There appears to be less of an effect of stress on patients who report using high levels of distraction, such as watching T.V.

Although still a relatively new measure, the CHIP has been already used in research to investigate coping responses to a wide range of health problems, including cancer, Type II diabetes, and chronic pain. Emotional preoccupation and palliative coping have emerged as maladaptive orientation in general. For instance, comparisons of patients with acute versus chronic illnesses show that people with chronic illnesses are much more likely to be high in emotional preoccupation (Endler, Kocovski & Macrodimitris, 2001). Other research has found that quality of life in cardiac rehabilitation patients is associated negatively with emotional preoccupation and palliative coping (see Corace & Endler, 2003). Finally, Mohr et al. (2002) reported evidence suggesting that scores on the CHIP distraction scale act as a moderating factor among multiple sclerosis patients. Stress tends to exacerbate the disease and contribute to brain lesions, but there is less of an effect of stress if patients report using high levels of distraction.

Supertrait Correlates of Coping Styles

Not surprisingly, several researchers have examined how broad personality domains have been linked with coping style indices. The overall pattern of results indicates that there is an association, and it seems logical to regard broad personality domains as distal factors that contribute to more specific coping styles that in turn predict individual differences in psychological distress and physical health outcomes.

Watson and Hubbard (1996) provided both a conceptual review and an empirical study of the association between the five-factor model and coping styles. As anticipated, their research with the COPE scale showed that neuroticism was associated with emotion-focused scales such as denial, focusing on and venting of emotions, and cognitive and behavioural disengagement. Both trait conscientiousness and extroversion were linked with problem-oriented coping styles. Openness had fewer significant correlates, though it was associated positively with the positive reinterpretation and growth subscale, and it was associated negatively with the turning to religion subscale. Finally, agreeableness was associated logically with coping styles such as seeking social support. Overall, in terms of the ability of the respective coping styles to relate to individual differences in neuroticism, the strongest associations were found for neuroticism and conscientiousness (see Watson & Hubbard, 1996). This contrasted with the results of a similar study conducted by McCrae and Costa (1986), which found that the strongest coping links were with neuroticism and extroversion. Watson and Hubbard (1996) found little association between coping and extroversion when other personality traits were taken into account.

Coping Styles as Personality Traits

One of the most critical questions in research and theory on personality and coping is whether individual differences in coping responses reflect personality traits. That is, are there stable and long-lasting personality differences in coping orientations? Investigators such as Endler and Parker designed their CISS to assess stable coping dispositions. As noted earlier, a trait approach has been opposed by Lazarus (1993), who favours a process approach. His view is a reflection of results from Folkman and Lazarus (1980), who estimated that only 5% of the sample was consistent in their coping responses over time. To what extent do coping measures tap personality constructs? There are three ways to examine this issue: (1) evaluate the test–retest temporal stability of trait coping measures; (2) examine the degree of association between trait and state, situationally specific coping measures; and (3) assess how a person copes across different situations. Relevant evidence is described next.

Test–retest studies of the main coping measures tend to indicate that they have at least a moderate level of stability. For instance, Billingsley, Wachler, and Hardin (1993) administered the COPE scale (Carver, Scheier, & Weintraub, 1989) to a sample of 82 students. The one-month test–retest correlations for each coping subscale were significant, with correlations ranging from .47 to .87. Similarly, McCrae (1989) conducted a longitudinal study of elderly individuals over seven years and there were moderate test–retest correlations. The apparent degree of stability over time seems to vary according to coping measure used and the test–retest interval, with longer intervals being associated with lower test–retest correlations.

The "coping as personality trait" issue can be tested most rigorously by examining the stability of coping styles across situations. The most common way of assessing this is to compare coping responses given by the same person across two or more different stressors. Analyses indicate that scores on particular coping dimensions are correlated significantly across problem types. For instance, Causey and Dubow (1992) evaluated the coping responses of children to hypothetical achievement and interpersonal stressors. The results showed substantial consistency across problem types in coping responses. For instance, there was a .56 correlation between problem-solving coping in response to a poor test grade versus responding to an argument with a peer. Analyses of actual problems in real life also points to consistency across contexts. Stone and Neale (1984) had 120 married people complete a measure of daily coping with actual life problems for 21 consecutive days. Evidence was found for the stable use of coping mechanisms with people relying on the same coping mechanism time and again for recurring problems. Finally, Dolan and White (1988) evaluated the consistency of coping with daily events for separate samples of professional women and university students. They conducted analyses of coping responses to up to 30 different stressful episodes, and they found that while stability coefficients were significant for both the professional women and the university students, the level of consistency increased once contextual and situational differences were also considered. Analyses with one of the subsamples indicated that the consistency in coping responses was particularly evident in work and school contexts, and there was little evidence of consistency when responding to family members and friends. Perhaps the varying responses of other people make it more difficult for us to be consistent.

A unique feature of the Dolan and White (1988) study is that it also measured coping effectiveness. It found that greater coping consistency was associated with greater coping effectiveness. This issue has seldom been tested, but there is some other evidence suggesting that people high in neuroticism are less consistent in their use of coping strategies (Atkinson & Violato, 1994). This accords with the Dolan and White finding that neuroticism is associated consistently with psychological distress and an apparent inability to cope with life challenges. Overall, then, the evidence from the three different lines of investigation is pretty clear in pointing to a role for personality in the coping process. That is, measures have moderate to high test–retest reliability. There is also moderate consistency in terms of coping responses across situations.

KEY POINTS

- Analyses of the five-factor model have linked neuroticism with emotion-oriented coping, and conscientiousness and extroversion with task-oriented coping.
- Measures of test–retest reliability have found that coping style measures have moderate stability over time.
- There is also moderate consistency in coping responses across stressors and problem situations, and this argues against the notion by Lazarus that coping is a process that does not involve personality factors.

Research on coping has not been without its critics. Some authors have suggested, for instance, that coping self-report checklists are too artificial and they are of limited valued because they are too removed from naturalistic contexts and the stressors of daily existence (see Coyne & Gottlieb, 1996). Problems are exacerbated when respondents are asked to recall how they coped with an event that may have occurred months earlier. Retrospective biases could come into play. Although these points have merit, these same criticisms can be levied at many other areas of personality research that rely heavily on self-report measures. More valid are suggestions that the range of inquiry needs to be expanded to include a broader variety of coping responses and styles. It has been suggested, for instance, that it is vitally important to study proactive coping as a form of coping that may stop stress from happening at all. Proactive coping is described as multidimensional and forward-looking. Whereas most of the field takes a reactive approach and focuses on responses once an event has occurred, proactive coping takes place prior to the event and seems to have a protective role. Moreover, clear individual differences in proactive coping have been identified (see Greenglass, 2002).

Another shortcoming in the current coping literature is the limited interpersonal focus; socially based coping responses with an interpersonal flavour deserve much more attention. Monnier and Hobfoll and their associates have observed that most coping measures take an individualistic approach, and a more socially based collectivist orientation is needed to fully understand coping differences (see Monnier, Hobfoll, Dunahoo, Hulsizer, & Johnson, 1998). They underscored the need for an interpersonal approach by creating measures of pro-social coping (moving toward people) and anti-social coping (moving against people) when faced with a threatening situation.

THEORETICAL MODELS OF PERSONALITY AND HEALTH

Although the research and theory on personality and coping styles is far from perfect, it does provide extensive evidence that there are stable individual differences in coping, and these differences reflect, at least in part, broad personality traits. We now shift our focus from personality, coping, and stress to a more direct examination of the role of personality factors in health outcomes. Four models of personality and health will be described. First, however, we must state some general caveats. Extensive research has been conducted trying to link specific personality attributes with specific diseases or illnesses (e.g., Type A behaviour and heart disease, Type D personality and cancer proneness). Research on the disease-prone personality has found that there is a link between personality and health, but it is very difficult to establish a specific link between a certain personality factor and a specific disease or health problem. The available evidence is more in keeping with the claims made by Hans Selye about stress and strain having a nonspecific and general influence on the body that can be revealed in many different ways through a variety of illnesses (for a discussion, see Friedman & Booth-Kewley, 1987). That is, it is best to focus on a general disease-prone personality style and its association with health problems in general than to try to link specific personality traits with specific illnesses.

Indeed, extensive evidence suggests that stress has the general effect of lowering immune competence (see Adler & Matthews, 1994), and this can lead to a variety of health problems. In fact, a recent meta-analysis by Segerstrom and Miller (2004) of 293 studies with almost 19,000 participants provided powerful evidence that stress causes lower immunity. Accordingly, the models of personality and health are best regarded as general frameworks that tie together personality and health in general rather than specific diseases. Similarly, the personality dimensions discussed later in this chapter (e.g., optimism–pessimism, self-efficacy, health locus of control) should have an impact that cuts across a variety of health problems. This is the general premise that pervades our current work on perfectionism; we regard perfectionism as a stress-generating factor that can contribute to a variety of health problems. Indeed, perfectionism has been linked with such diverse health problems as cancer, chronic pain, chronic fatigue, and irritable bowel syndrome.

Suzanne Segerstrom from the University of Kentucky has used meta-analysis to confirm the link between stress and the immune system.

Another important caveat to keep in mind is the need to consider and weigh the importance of personality predictors of health problems, relative to other predictors. Numerous authors have suggested that, at best, personality factors will be one of several factors that can predict health problems and the overall amount of variance in health problems that is attributable to personality factors will not be great in magnitude and will not be greater than other predictive factors (Holroyd & Coyne, 1987). Authors such as Robbins, Spence, and Clark (1991) have argued that we need to assess personality factors within the context of other factors of potential importance. This is best done by administering multiple personality measures as well as assessing a range of other measures (e.g., stress, psychosocial factors, demographic factors) in order to empirically determine the relative predictiveness of personality factors.

Three models linking personality and health have been identified and extensively researched. A fourth model, the stress generation model, is one that has emerged from research on personality and depression but merits broader consideration in the health field. Each model is described below.

The Constitutional Risk Factor Model

The constitutional risk factor model has also been referred to as the etiologic trait model (see Ranchor & Sanderman, 1997). This model is based on the premise that personality is an independent risk factor for health and illness. That is, both personality and health are influenced by early biological responses of the organism. This model would encompass personality differences occurring due to genetic factors. Another factor considered here would be the impact of early trauma on physiological reactivity (see Ranchor & Sanderman, 1997).

The sensation seeking construct by Zuckerman that was described at the beginning of this chapter is an obvious example of a constitutional risk factor. In his initial theorizing, Zuckerman attributed differences in sensation seeking to underlying differences in levels of arousal, with high sensation seekers looking for stimulation because they are below the optimal level of arousal. However, Zuckerman (1994) refined his theory over time by emphasizing more precise biological factors and processes based on psychophysiological and psychobiological methods. For instance, he has established that sensation seekers have a stronger reaction to the initial presentation of novel stimuli, as determined by skin conductance and heart rate measures. Research on a direct measure of brain reactivity known as the cortical evoked potential, shows that in response to increasing stimulus intensity, sensation seekers show augmentation (an increased cortical response). Low sensation seekers show a reduced cortical response to high intensity stimuli, and this suggests that low sensation seekers are born with a physiological intolerance for high intensity stimuli. Other biochemical research found an inverse association between sensation seeking and the enzyme monoamine oxidase (MAO). Because MAO is linked with neurotransmitters, Zuckerman could then link sensation seeking with the neurotransmitters dopamine and serotonin; impulsive sensation seeking was attributed to high dopamine and low serotonin. Currently, Zuckerman attributes sensation seeking to a host of biological factors, including the D4 dopamine receptor gene, the MAO enzyme, and the augmention or reduction of cortical evoked potential (see Zuckerman, 2005; Zuckerman & Kuhlman, 2000).

In line with the constitutional risk factor model and research on the role of genetic factors in personality development (see Chapter 3), research has confirmed that there is indeed a genetic component in sensation seeking. One of the most comprehensive studies of this issue has been conducted with adolescent twins from the Netherlands (see Koopmans et al., 1995; Stoel, De Geus, & Boosma, 2006). The most recent study by Stoel et al. (2006) supports the conclusion that sensation seeking is "highly heritable." The highest heritability was found for experience seeking and disinhibition in males.

This work is important because it underscores the need to consider the biological roots of personality constructs that serve as constitutional risk factors. It is not enough to simply identify constitutional risk factors; we must also seek to identify developmental factors that have shaped these personality differences.

The Illness Behaviour Model

The illness behaviour model is based on the premise that people differ in terms of the specific behaviours they engage in, and this is associated with personality factors. The health process model outlined by Adler and Matthews (1994) is a similar model that focuses on health behaviours as mediators of the personality–disease link. Some behaviours are clearly adaptive and associated with good long-term outcomes (e.g., going to the doctor for regular checkups, watching what you eat), while other behaviours are highly destructive and likely to cut short a person's life. This can include risky sexual practices, inappropriate driving behaviours, various forms of sensation seeking behaviour, and substance abuse. Some people are willing to assume a level of risk or, for whatever reason, they simply cannot stop themselves and lack self-control. Of course, among famous contributors to the personality field, Sigmund Freud, with his cocaine addiction, is perhaps the most prominent example of someone engaging in a risky behaviour.

The beginning of this chapter included a quote by the late singer–songwriter Warren Zevon. He clearly implicated his phobia of doctors as responsible for not getting regular checkups, which may have detected his cancer in its early stages. This suggests a particular manifestation of neuroticism that had lethal consequences in this case.

So why are some people particularly willing to expose themselves to risk? This usually involves a series of choice points where decisions are made or not made. Why is it that one person who suffers a heart attack resumes smoking, while another person takes it as a sign and never smokes again? Why do some people who find out they are in the initial stages of diabetes continue to avoid exercise and eat sugary foods that can only hasten their demise, while other people go on a strict regimen and will only eat the most healthful foods possible? Clearly, personality has something to do with it.

Recognizing that health behaviours play a vital role in health outcomes is important because it allows an element of personal choice and responsibility that supplements the notion that health outcomes are biologically determined. People can choose whether to exercise, and they can choose whether to smoke (or to avoid peers who encourage them to smoke). Nevertheless, the links between personality traits and specific health behaviours indicate that there are predictable associations between them.

A full review of the link between personality and risky versus protective behaviours is beyond the scope of this book. However, Table 12.4 is a summary of the existing literature that was compiled by Jose Bermudez from Madrid, Spain, who presented these data in 1998 as part of the Presidential Address for the European Association of Personality Psychology (see Bermudez, 1999). Some of the personality factors represented in Table 12.4 are discussed at length in subsequent sections of this chapter. In this table, the "+" sign indicates a positive association has been established. Thus, extroversion has been linked with both negative and positive behaviours. The "–" sign indicates a negative association has been established. For example, high levels of substance abuse are linked with low levels of agreeableness.

Table 12.4 Personality and Risky versus Healthy Behaviours

Personality Factor	Substance Abuse	Unsafe Driving	Risky Sex	Healthy Behaviour
Extroversion	+	+	+	+
Neuroticism	+	+	–	–
Agreeableness	–	–		+
Conscientiousness	–	–		+
Openness	+	+		+
Impulsivity	+	+	+	
Psychoticism	+		+	
Sensation seeking	+			
Thrill seeking		+		
Boredom susceptibility		+		
Venturesomeness			+	
Anxiety	+	+		–
Hostility	+	+		–
Impatience	+	+		–
Cynicism	+	+		–
Hardiness	–			+
Self-esteem	–			
Optimism				+
Self-efficacy				+
Internal LOC				+
Sense of coherence				+

A minus sign (–) signifies that there is a negative association between the personality factor and the unhealthy/healthy behaviour, while a plus sign (+) indicates a positive association, and a blank space indicates either no association or not enough research conducted to make a determination.

Sorce: Bermudez, 1999.

Research reported after the review by Bermudez continues to generate findings that are in keeping with the results of his review. For instance, an investigation conducted in Switzerland examined the associations among personality factors, risky health behaviours, and perceptions of health risks in a sample of 683 university students (Vollrath, Knoch, & Cassano, 1999). Risky activities assessed in this study included smoking, being drunk, drunk driving, and risky sexual behaviour. This study found that agreeableness and conscientiousness were protective both in terms of being associated negatively with risky activities as well as in terms of perceived susceptibility to health risks. That is, students high in agreeableness and conscientiousness were more optimistic about their perceived health risks (perhaps with good reason). In contrast, neuroticism was linked with more negative perceptions of susceptibility to risk; it was associated with perceived risk on three of the four indicators assessed. Moreover, this was not simply because students were already engaging in risky practices; this link with negative perceptions held after controlling for actual behaviours. This is in keeping with the tendency for people high in neuroticism to be highly concerned and worried about their health status, both at the current time and in the future.

Zuckerman and Kuhlman (2000) examined personality and risk-taking behaviour in 260 college students. Six types of risks were assessed: gambling, smoking, drinking, sex, drugs, and driving behaviour. Participants completed Zuckerman et al.'s (1993) five-factor measure, which includes a measure of impulsive sensation seeking. The study sought to replicate past findings linking high sensation seeking with involvement in risky activities (Zuckerman, 1979, 1994). Table 12.4 lists the results for the four sensation seeking factors (sensation seeking, thrill seeking, boredom susceptibility, and venturesomeness) on various versions of Zuckerman's Sensation Seeking Scale. Each one of the four factors has an established link with either unsafe sex, risky driving, or substance abuse. Some of this behaviour is cognitively mediated because sensation seekers, relative to non-sensation seekers, give lower appraisals of risk even when it involves an activity they have never attempted (Horvath & Zuckerman, 1993; Zuckerman, 1979).

KEY POINTS

- The focus on a general disease-prone personality is based on the non-specific and pervasive role that stress has on health status. A meta-analysis has confirmed that stress causes reduced immunity.
- One model of personality and health regards personality as a constitutional risk factor that reflects genetic factors and psychobiological influences. Sensation seeking is an example of a constitutional risk factor that reflects a range of biological influences, including neurotransmitters, with high sensation seeking linked with high dopamine and low serotonin.
- The illness behaviour model is based on the premise that personality is linked with health outcomes through its association with adaptive or maladaptive health-related actions (e.g., exercising or not exercising). The link with specific behaviours allows for the role of personal choice and personal ability to determine your own health outcomes.
- Neuroticism is an example of a personality trait that is linked with frequent negative health behaviours (substance abuse, unsafe driving) and infrequent positive health behaviours. Extroversion is linked with frequent positive and negative behaviours. Thus, the link between personality and health behaviours varies across personality traits.

The Stress Moderation–Mediation Model

According to the stress moderation–mediation model, personality can play a role in health outcomes by mediating or moderating the impact of stress. Recall that a moderating variable is one that interacts with or combines with another factor so that their joint combination predicts a particular outcome. Consider, for instance, individual differences in procrastination. Research on procrastination, daily stress, and depression (see Flett, Blankstein, & Martin, 1995) shows that procrastination combines with the persistent experience of daily hassles to predict elevated levels of depression. These data suggest that procrastination may exacerbate the link between stressful events and illness; that is, people may be especially prone to health problems if they experience stress yet are the type of person who characteristically delays and avoids dealing with issues that must be addressed. In this instance, it is the joint combination of procrastination and stress that is predictive. This type of research is in keeping with the need to study personality–environment interactions in health (for a discussion, see van Heck, 1997).

However, when a variable acts as a mediating variable, it comes between two variables in a sequence. That is, one variable predicts the mediator, which, in turn, predicts the outcome variable. Going back to our original example, a mediational sequence could occur if the link between stress and illness is due, at least in part, to the tendency for highly stressed people to procrastinate and rely on avoidant coping, which in turn leads to health problems. Mediational models are best tested with longitudinal research since a temporal sequence is posited among the variables.

Although models with stress as a mediator or a moderator have been suggested, a current review of research on personality and health led to the conclusion that formal mediational tests of the role of stress in personality and health are relatively lacking and that more research is required (Smith & MacKenzie, 2006). Such research can focus on stress in general, or particular forms of stress such as negative social interaction and chronic stressors. Note as well that there are many other possible mediating and moderating factors that merit consideration in addition to stress, including individual differences in social support and coping efficacy.

The Stress Generation Model

The essence of the stress generation model is that certain people find ways to make things more stressful for themselves. This is, at least in part, an outgrowth of related differences in personality.

The astute and famous scientist **Hans Selye** discussed the role of individual differences in stress generation (see Selye, 1977). Selye is regarded as the father of the concept of "stress." Selye moved to Canada and became a Canadian citizen, with most of his world-famous research being conducted at McGill University in Montreal. Regarding stress generation, Selye (1977) observed:

> It is not usually enough to say, "Relax and refrain from strenuous activities." Some people find sufficient diversion in leisure activities to keep their own stress level at a desirable point. But many of us have an irresistible drive to seek stress, in the form of challenge, competition, and the like, even when we are supposed to be playing. It is a common experience for a person under pressure to get the feeling of merely wasting time when engaging in leisure activities. Not everyone knows how to play or how to enjoy the passive experiences of music, spectator sports, or reading. (p. 104)

Hans Selye is considered the father of the concept of "stress."

Empirical investigations of the stress generation concept have been performed by Hammen and her colleagues within the context of examining the link between stress and depression (see Hammen, 1991). The essence of this work is that certain people are vulnerable to depression, at least in part, because they create problems for themselves in terms of the choices they make, such as the people they choose as potential life partners.

Research on Type A behaviour is also in keeping with the concept of stress generation. The notion here is that people with Type A features make things more stressful for themselves by pursuing extremely high goals and by expressing hostility that elicits increasingly negative reactions from other people (see Smith & Rhodewalt, 1986).

We now turn our attention to research and theory on specific personality types involved in health and illness. First, however, some issues that complicate the study of personality and health are outlined next.

METHODOLOGICAL AND MEASUREMENT ISSUES AND CONCERNS

Specific personality traits associated with health problems are described below. First, however, it is important to emphasize measurement and methodological issues that have direct bearing on the research conducted with these personality traits. Four relevant issues are described below.

Health Status as a Categorical versus a Continuous Variable

One important distinction to keep in mind when evaluating the role of personality in health outcomes is that studies vary widely in terms of how the health outcome is defined. Some studies focus solely on categorical and discrete outcome measures. This would include measures of mortality status, which is often the variable being examined in longitudinal research. Another categorical variable is the presence versus absence of certain diseases or other illnesses as determined by medical diagnoses. Note that if assessed in a cross-sectional study, some people in the non-illness group may be categorized inappropriately because they will develop the illness later in life. Also, as noted by Holroyd and Coyne (1987), when data are categorical, we should not lose sight of the qualitative differences between specific illnesses, and there is little reason for assuming that variables associated with one type of diagnosed illness will necessarily generalize to other types of illness.

The alternative is to use continuous indices, which may include continuous measures of health functioning and symptom counts. Some studies also use dimensional ratings from informants. For instance, a common measure is the physician's rating of an individual's health status and level of functioning. Continuous measures may involve composites of various health problems and health symptoms, and this is more suited to general tests of the disease-prone personality.

Problems with Self-Report Symptom Measures

Unfortunately, a common limitation is that many studies simply reply on the participant's self-reported health status. Here, several different measures are available. Possible measures include Pennebaker's Inventory of Limbid Languidness, and the SUNYA Symptom Checklist. These measures can tap a variety of response dimensions, including the frequency of symptoms, the intensity or magnitude of symptoms, and the duration that symptoms are experienced when they occur.

There are two obvious problems associated with these self-report measures. First, if you were to compare measures side-by-side it would become immediately obvious that the existing measures differ substantially in their breadth of item content. They may also differ in their response keys. Does a scale measure the frequency of symptoms, the intensity of symptoms, or both? We cannot assume that the existing self-report health symptom measures are comparable, and this may make it difficult to compare across studies. This problem becomes magnified if the researchers, as is sometimes the case, create their own symptom measure or abbreviate existing measures because of practical considerations involving the demands being placed on people who may be quite ill.

A more significant problem with relying on self-reports is that we know that personality traits such as neuroticism and associated levels of negative affect are linked consistently with higher somatic complaints (see Watson & Pennebaker, 1989). To what extent do personality factors such as neuroticism represent a source of bias? We have already seen that there are negative processing biases when people high in neuroticism react to stressful events (see Hemenover, 2001). Do personality factors create concerns about hypochondriacal reports?

Three hypotheses have been advanced to account for the link between higher symptoms reporting and elevated neuroticism and negative affect (see Watson & Pennebaker, 1989). The **psychosomatic hypothesis** is that negative affect and neuroticism cause health problems, and this accounts for the association. The **disability hypothesis** is that illness leads to higher levels of negative affect. Finally, the hypothesis that has received the most support, the **symptom perception hypothesis**, is that neuroticism and negative affect are accompanied by greater attentiveness to somatic cues, and it is this greater attentiveness that accounts for the link between neuroticism and physical symptoms. If viewed from this perspective, neuroticism is a nuisance factor that biases reports of physical symptoms.

Costa and McCrae (1985) have discussed the link between neuroticism and hypochondriasis, and they used the term "naïve realism" to refer to the mistaken belief that health self-reports are an accurate reflection of objectively determined health status. In a follow-up paper, Costa and McCrae (1987) analyzed data and concluded that neuroticism is indeed associated with somatic complaints, but there is only weak evidence for its role in disease as determined by objective indicators.

Nevertheless, Costa and McCrae (1987) cautioned that it would be a mistake to underestimate the potential importance of neuroticism in health problems, stating:

> It would, however, be extremely short-sighted to conclude that Neuroticism has nothing to do with health. On the contrary, it is intimately linked to health perceptions and behaviors, and thus to every interaction of the individual with the health care system. Further, Neuroticism is indirectly related to health through a variety of maladaptive behaviors. This is most dramatically seen in the case of suicide and accidental death. (p. 312)

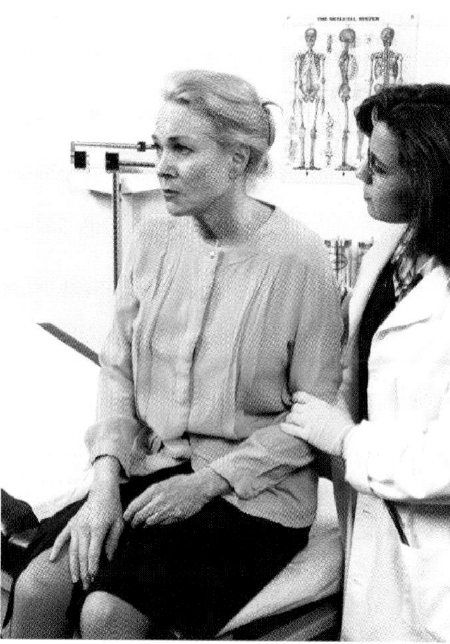
Neuroticism has been linked with over-reporting of health problems, and people with this personality trait are more likely to visit their physicians.

They further noted that people high in this personality trait are more likely to visit physicians. As a result, Costa and McCrae (1987) recommended that researchers measure and control for neuroticism on a routine basis when seeking to predict health outcomes and related behaviours.

More recent evidence continues to indicate that neuroticism is linked with over-reporting of health problems. A well-designed study by Feldman et al. (1999) involved inoculating student volunteers with a common cold virus and assessing their objective and self-reported symptoms over the next five days. The study showed that neuroticism was associated with the false report of health problems. Neuroticism was not the only personality factor associated with false reports. Conscientiousness also predicted false reports; in this instance, however, it was suggested that conscientious people may use lower criteria to determine whether illness exists, and this is adaptive in the long run because it may contribute to more contact with the medical system. Whatever the case, it is clear from this and other studies that personality factors are associated with biases in the self-reporting of illnesses.

Limitations of Cross-Sectional Research

Another significant limitation is that just as many personality studies in general are one-shot cross-sectional investigations; many personality and health studies also assess participants at only one point in time. Once it is established that a personality factor is associated with health status, it is still not possible to claim that personality played a causal role. Why?

Although personality factors may lead to illness, it is equally plausible that the illness itself has shaped the personality factors. Alternatively, some third factor could be responsible for the association between the two variables in question. Another problem common to cross-sectional studies is outlined below.

Longitudinal Changes in the Association between Personality and Health

It is particularly important to assess the association between personality and health over time in a longitudinal research design. Why? Several studies indicate that the initial association between personality and health may change over time. Some longitudinal investigations with university students underscore the need to examine personality and health over a longer time.

Tice and Baumeister (1997) examined the associations among procrastination, performance, stress, and health in students. One finding that emerged from this study is that student procrastinators reported less stress and illness than non-procrastinators during the early part of the semester. There was no initial link between procrastination and the number of health centre visits. However, an opposite pattern of results was detected late in the semester. Procrastinators reported more stress and illness, and procrastination was correlated positively with the number of health centre visits.

Contemporary research on optimism versus pessimism has also yielded data that demonstrate the need to examine adaptiveness over a long time frame. Segerstrom (2001) found that when faced with conflicting goals, optimists, relative to pessimists, experienced more stress. Another recent experiment also confirmed that optimists suffer short-term physiological costs (see Nes, Segerstrom, & Sephton, 2005). Why? Optimists stayed engaged in the task of resolving the goal, and their persistence can be stressful. Segerstrom (2001) concluded that optimists may not do so well in the short-term but they do much better than pessimists in the long-term once conflict is no longer evident. The nature of the stressor also makes a difference. Segerstrom (2005) found inconsistent evidence when reviewing the association between trait optimism and immunity, and she attributed this to the fact that optimists will not disengage when faced with an extremely challenging goal. Optimism is favoured, however, when confronted with less difficult and challenging situations. Optimism is discussed in more detail later in this chapter.

Finally, the health impact of **defensive pessimism** also seems to vary over time. Defensive pessimists are people who motivate themselves by making them themselves feel anxious about possible negative outcomes (see Cantor & Norem, 1989; Norem, 2002). In the student context, this is represented by the student who says, "I just know that I am going to bomb the test and fail." While this type of negative expectancy is accurate for some students, many defensive pessimists scare themselves into overpreparing so they actually end up doing much better than predicted, even sometimes scoring among the highest performers (and then incurring the wrath of fellow students who believed their dire predictions about failure!). Defensive pessimism is adaptive in that it provides motivation, and it also seems to provide a psychological cushion when disappointing results are experienced (Martin,

Marsh, Williamson, & DeBus, 2003). Cantor and Norem's (1989) longitudinal research showed that in the initial phases of their investigation, it seemed that defensive pessimism had several advantages in terms of performance and life satisfaction outcomes. However, by the time these students reached their senior years of study, defensive pessimism had the exact opposite effect: it was associated with greater stress and depression, less satisfaction, and poorer grades! There are several possible explanations. Perhaps the stress of being a defensive pessimist wore them down.

KEY POINTS

- Research on personality and health needs to be longitudinal. Factors that are associated with better health in the short-term may be associated with poorer health in the long-term and vice versa.
- Studies that rely on self-report checklists of health symptoms may have biased indices of health. The bias could involve inflated illness reports due to neuroticism and negative affect.
- Although neuroticism may involve a reporting bias, it is still likely to play a role in health problems.

Are you a defensive pessimist? Table 12.5 contains four items selected from the revised 17-item Defensive Pessimism Questionnaire (see Norem, 2002). If you find yourself agreeing with many of these statements, perhaps you do tend to rely on pessimistic beliefs as a way of motivating yourself. If so, you should consider ways of maintaining a high level of motivation without scaring yourself and creating a very stressful existence in the long run. When reviewing the statements, think about how you prepare for and think about academic situations. Each statement describes how people sometimes think or feel about these kinds of situations. For each item, consider how true it is of you, in academic situations, according to the response key.

Table 12.5 The Revised Defensive Pessimism Questionnaire

1	2	3	4	5	6	7
Not at all true of me						Very true of me

1. I go into these situations expecting the worst, even though I know I will probably do OK.
2. I often worry in these situations that I won't be able to carry through my intentions.
3. I often think about how I will feel if I do poorly in these situations.
4. In these situations, sometimes I worry more about looking like a fool than doing really well.

Source: Adapted from Norem, 2002.

The final segments of this chapter focus on specific personality styles linked with predisposition to illness. Personality has been explored as a constellation or cluster of attributes that combine to form a particular personality type, and the personality type is believed to play a role in either the onset of a health problem or the course of recovering from a health problem. The personality types discussed are the Type A personality, the Type C personality, the Type D personality, and the hardy personality. Personality has also been investigated, as specific trait dimensions play a role in vulnerability to and recovery from health problems. The chapter concludes with an examination of health problems and several traits, including the traits of the five-factor model, optimism–pessimism, self-efficacy, and health locus of control.

PERSONALITY TYPES AND HEALTH

Theory and research on personality and susceptibility to health problems has emphasized individual differences in terms of how people experience emotion and how they express emotion. The Type A construct was described in Chapter 3 as part of our analysis of personality development, so it is discussed only briefly below. The destructive element of Type A seems to be the experience of hostility. Another personality constellation known as the Type D construct involves risk due to the restricted expression of emotion.

The Type A Personality

Friedman and Rosenman (1959) were two physicians who introduced the concept of the Type A Behavior Pattern, or the coronary prone behaviour pattern. As described by Friedman and Rosenman, **Type A personality** attributes included six distinguishable attributes: (1) a strong competitive drive; (2) an intense desire to meet goals that are sometimes ambiguous and poorly defined; (3) a strong need for public recognition and advancement; (4) speed and impatience, especially with respect to deadlines; (5) persistent and vigorous physical and mental activity; and (6) a high level of mental and physical alertness. Thus, it is a pattern of high activation, achievement striving, competitiveness, and proneness to hostility, and it was linked with heart attack risk. An opposite pattern of behaviour known as the Type B style was seen as much more adaptive from a health perspective. In subsequent research, independent raters evaluated the presence of Type A versus Type B characteristics and found that Type A behaviour was linked with higher serum cholesterol and incidence of heart disease (Rosenman & Friedman, 1961). Subsequent longitudinal studies confirmed the link between Type A characteristics and susceptibility to heart problems (Rosenman et al., 1978).

The initial findings with the Type A construct led to a proliferation of various psychologically based explanatory models that were designed to understand the nature of individual differences in Type A behaviour. For instance, the **uncontrollability model** (Glass, 1977) interpreted Type A behaviour as an excessive need to assert and maintain control over the environment. The sense of uncontrollability is heightened when stressors threaten personal control, and Type A behaviour is an attempt to reassert a sense of control over the environment. The uncontrollability model has two elements: environmental control and self-control. Environment control reflects excessive striving in order to overcome uncontrollable situations (e.g., Krantz, Glass, & Snyder, 1974), while self-control involves the suppression of internal stages (feelings of fatigue and hunger, for instance) that could interfere with attempts to overcome and master stressful circumstances (see Carver, Coleman, & Glass, 1976).

The self-evaluation model (Matthews, 1982) is based on the premise that the Type A person has high and diffuse standards, and this is accompanied by excessive self-focused attention and self-consciousness. The self-awareness is aversive to the extent that it highlights a gap between performance and perfectionistic standards. The relentless activity of Type A people is an attempt to satisfy these standards and associated self-worth contingencies.

Finally, the social learning model of Type A behaviour (Price, 1982) regards Type A behaviour as being driven by a particular cognitive belief system. This belief system has three primary themes: (1) a person must constantly prove himself or herself through his or her achievements; (2) there is no universally applicable moral principle, and the lack of this moral principle accounts for immoral behaviours displayed by others (it is this component that likely contributes to hostility); and (3) there is low availability of resources, so it is important to be highly competitive.

In recent years, research on the Type A construct has waned, partly due to the fact that several studies yielded contradictory findings showing that Type A behaviour did not predict susceptibility to heart problems (for a review, see Dembrowski & Costa, 1987). However, research on the Type A components has still managed to find fairly consistent evidence showing that extreme anger and hostility is a risk factor that predicts the incidence and course of hypertension and cardiovascular heart disease (see Gallo & Matthews, 2003; Kubzansky & Kawachi, 2000).

Findings over the past five years have indicated that the role of hostility in health problems may have been overstated. Some prospective studies have found no link between hostility and heart problems. For example, a contemporary prospective study by Surtees et al. (2005) from the University of Cambridge examined hostility and cardiovascular mortality in a sample of more than 20,000 men and women. Hostility was not associated with cardiovascular disease mortality, though there was some evidence indicating that extremely high hostility was a risk factor, and hostility in general predicted cardiovascular mortality in people who died under the age of 60.

There have been contradictory findings regarding health problems and hostility, a Type A personality component.

Why is hostility only sometimes associated with cardiovascular deaths? It seems quite reasonable to suggest that the increased blood pressure and general stress reaction that would accompany high trait hostility will still play a role if combined with other vulnerability factors, such as other deleterious personality traits and a lack of available coping resources in the form of low social support. Possible mediators or moderators of the link between hostility and health include the need for control and the experience of interpersonal stressors. Lawler, Schmied, Armstead, and Lacy (1991) showed in a sample of women that Type A behaviour interacted with desire for control to predict elevated heart rates and blood pressure reactivity during a challenging task. This suggests that a particular subset of individuals with Type A features such as high hostility might be at risk. As for interpersonal stressors, Williams, Barefoot, and Shekelle (1985) have postulated a person-by-situation stress moderation model. Smith and Spiro (2002) proclaimed that this is the most influential model of hostility and health. Smith and Gallo (2001) have reviewed evidence from laboratory investigations and ambulatory studies in which measures are obtained in naturalistic environments, and it has been found consistently that people high in hostility who experienced interpersonal stressors (frustrations and conflicts) respond with higher blood pressure and heart rate and greater neuroendocrine activation. People high in trait hostile, relative to non-hostile people, tend to receive less social support (Smith et al., 1988), perhaps because they antagonize other people; and when social support is received, they have less reduction in physiological reactivity (Lepore, 1995; Smith, Uno, Uchino, & Ruiz, 2000), suggesting that they derive less comfort for the support received.

Although interest in Type A behaviour has decreased in recent years, perhaps a greater appreciation of the need to examine features of Type A and stressors will result in renewed interest. Hopefully, this interest will result in greater work on the efficacy of interventions designed to reduce Type A behaviour. Two such interventions conducted in the 1980s are described in Applied Perspective 12.2.

Applied Perspective 12.2 Reducing Type A Behaviours Via Treatment Interventions

Eysenck argued that the success of treatment interventions represents one of the most impressive illustrations of the role of personality factors in health outcomes. Several such interventions have been attempted with Type A behaviour, but two deserve particular mention because other interventions had outcome measures of dubious merit. Friedman et al. (1984) conducted an investigation of a treatment program designed to change Type A behaviour and reduce subsequent heart attacks in a sample of men with a prior heart attack. The participants were 800 men who were assigned randomly to the intervention or no intervention condition. It was found over a three-year period that those who received the intervention had a significantly lower rate of suffering another myocardial infarction. What were the features of the intervention program? It included training in muscle relaxation, learning to foster a greater sense of emotional self-control, along with a re-examination of personal values and learning to set less demanding goals. Thus, it had features that made it similar to a cognitive behavioural intervention and emotion-focused therapy.

The other intervention program was led by Ethel Roskies from the University of Montreal and was known as The Montreal Type A Intervention Project (see Roskies et al., 1986). This project had several different phases over several years. Roskies et al. (1986) described a component in which healthy Type A men were assigned to one of three intervention groups. Note that this is quite different than the Friedman et al. (1985) study, which focused on cardiac patients. One group in the Roskies et al. study received aerobic exercise training, another received cognitive–behavioural stress management training, and the third received weight training. The stress management group, relative to the two exercise groups, had improved behavioural reactivity and the authors concluded that this finding could have substantial clinical significance.

In a review paper in which she reflected on the program after it was over, Roskies (1990) seemed to express substantial disillusionment with the end result. She noted in the abstract of this paper that:

> Two years ago I reluctantly called a halt to these intervention studies, not because I had found the magical cure, or even because my treatments had shown themselves to be clearly ineffective but, rather, because I was increasingly

> uncertain about the purposes of the treatment and the methods of evaluating its effectiveness. I stopped because I strongly felt that if Type A intervention were to be anything more than another passing fad, it had to demonstrate both conceptual and methodological rigor (Roskies, 1980), but I personally could not overcome some of the conceptual and methodological problems that surfaced during my research efforts. (p. 419)

Roskies (1990) indicated that she was particularly troubled by the fact that the intervention led to improvements in behavioural reactivity, as noted above, but did not lead to improvements in key elements of Type A physiological reactivity, as determined by physiological measures (see Roskies et al., 1986). Roskies (1990) also noted that it is difficult to determine what the proper measures of treatment outcome should be when conducting this type of research, and other researchers seemed unaware of the limitations of the inadequacy of the outcomes that they used to assess treatment change. Roskies (1990) suggested that the key is to evaluate how Type A people respond when in highly challenging, energizing situations. This was assessed in her research by six stress tests conducted in the laboratory, and no differences were found. She also noted that the success reported in the other intervention program conducted by Friedman et al. (1984) might not have been due to changes in Type A behaviour per se; instead it could have been due to a process that resulted in increased social support.

Although Roskies (1990) was frustrated by her "failure" (as she described it), the participants in her intervention studies almost without exception found the interventions to be very useful. Also, because long-term assessment of health status was not conducted, it is still possible that the intervention was successful, unbeknownst to Roskies and her associates. Finally, it can be argued that the treatment protocol (10 sessions representing seven specific modules) needed to be longer in duration given that the goal is to modify a personality style that has developed and been reinforced since early childhood. In short, it may be premature to conclude that these types of interventions do not work! Hopefully, future investigators will revisit this issue.

KEY POINTS

- The Type A style is an intense and competitive achievement-oriented approach. Type A people like to do things quickly and can be quite impatient. Although Type A has many features, it is the hostility component that is linked with susceptibility to heart attacks.
- The social learning model suggests that Type A individuals are distressed by their belief systems (that people must constantly prove themselves and be competitive in a world of diminishing resources).
- The self-evaluation model of Type A behaviour attributes behaviour to the pursuit of exceptionally high standards and elevated levels of self-consciousness and self-awareness.

The Type C Personality

One line of investigation in the personality and health field is the identification of personality factors associated with proneness to cancer. The various models linking personality and illness that were described earlier have also been proposed with respect to the cancer-prone personality. Figure 12.2 is adapted from a paper by Schapiro et al. (2002) on personality factors in cancer. Their diagram provides an illustration of the key differences among the cancer-prone personality model, the personality health behaviour model, and the constitutional risk factor model.

The **Type C personality** was postulated by Greer and Morris. It was described as a personality style applying to people who were "emotionally contained," and it was linked with cancer proneness and faster disease progression (Greer & Morris, 1975; Morris & Greer, 1980).

The key elements of the Type C personality were an increased tendency to experience stress, an inability or unwillingness to express emotions, a sense of helplessness and hopelessness, and disrupted social support, including a history of early loss and lack of parental closeness. Although mentioned with specific reference to cancer, it should be immediately evident to readers that the hypothesized Type C personality contains a number of elements that could play a role in a host of health problems. A series of experiments by Temoshok (1987) found that those with a Type C personality were less likely to survive cancer.

Figure 12.2 Hypothesis for an Association Between Personality and Risk for Cancer

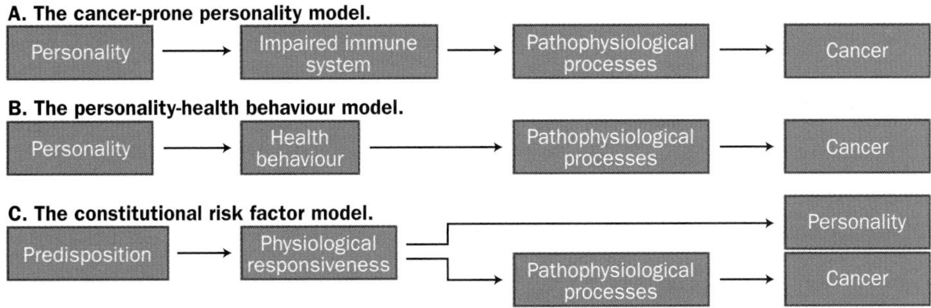

The figure illustrates three hypothesis for an association between personality and cancer. Model A was originally described by Ader et al. (1991), and model B and C were described by Smith and Gallo (2002).

Source: Schapiro et al., 2002.

Unfortunately, subsequent studies found little evidence for a link between personality factors and cancer proneness (Kreitler, Chaitchik, & Kreitler, 1993; Schwarz, 1993). Negative results also emerged from a prospective study conducted in the Netherlands by Bleiker and colleagues, who compared the characteristics of women who did or did not develop breast cancer (Bleiker, van der Ploeg, Hendriks, & Ader, 1996). Most predictors were not significant, except for a weak effect involving a factor labelled as anti-emotionality (a lack of emotional expression). Much more predictive were demographic factors (having a relative with breast cancer and not having any children). Thus, there was little evidence for the role of personality factors in cancer onset. Another study conducted on more than 2,000 women from Australia undertaking routine mammography screening also compared those without and without breast cancer (Price et al., 2001). This study included a host of personality measures, including indices of defence style, locus of control, depression, and emotional expression. No evidence was found to indicate the presence of a cancer-prone personality study. One limitation of this study is that the helplessness–hopelessness component of the Type C personality was not adequately measured because general measures of depression and anxiety and even the Rosenberg Self-Esteem Inventory were relied on rather than measures that explicitly tap helplessness and hopelessness. The failure to directly measure hopelessness is worth noting because some studies have found clear evidence linking hopelessness with cancer risk (Everson, Goldberg, & Kaplan, 1996).

Measurement problems aside, another longitudinal study of twins in the Swedish twin registry also failed to establish a link between personality and the development of cancer (Hansen, Floderus, Frederiksen, & Johansen, 2005). This study tested the predictive role of neuroticism, extroversion, and psychoticism, as assessed by the Eysenck Personality Questionnaire, and no evidence was found between these traits and cancer. Another new longitudinal reported by Japanese researchers also failed to establish a link between these personality traits and death due to cancer (see Nakaya et al., 2005).

In general, recent reviews of the possible role of personality and other psychological factors in cancer proneness have concluded that there is very little evidence linking personality factors with cancer proneness (see Pettigrew, Bell, & Hunter, 1992). However, in a new development, Solano, Temoshok, and their colleagues have found evidence that the presence of the Type C personality predicts a faster HIV disease progression when measured 12 months later (Solano et al., 2002). Subsequent research by Temoshok, Wald, Garzino-Demo, and Sun (2005) established that the Type C personality is linked with lower production of the two main beta-chemokines associated with HIV disease status. Thus, although seemingly not involved in cancer proneness, the characteristics of the Type C personality may play a role in other illnesses.

The Type D Personality

The Type D personality was described by **Johan Denollet** from Tilburg University in the Netherlands. Type D refers to the distressed personality. It consists of two components: negative affectivity and social inhibition (inhibiting the expression of negative emotions in social situations). Social inhibition also involves fewer affiliative ties with others and greater fear of strangers. Type D is considered a chronic psychological risk factor that is associated with risk of coronary heart disease. Importantly, Type D involves *the joint effects* of both components.

Pederson and Denollet (2003) also stipulated that Type D is different from repression. Repression occurs at an unconscious level, but people of Type D have high levels of interpersonal distress and are consciously trying to suppress their emotional expression.

Existing research has thus far supported the role played by the Type D personality in cardiac outcomes. The first study conducted by Denollet, Sys, and Brutsaert (1995) showed that among those Belgian patients who died of a heart attack, the presence of the Type D personality was associated with a six-fold increase in risk. Comparable findings have emerged from subsequent studies (for a review, see Pederson & Denollet, 2003).

Denollet (1998) has created a self-report measure known as the Type D Scale-16 (DS16) with 16 items that tap the two components. Denollet, Vaes, and Brutsaert (2000) confirmed with prospective data that the DS16 predicts subsequent cardiac events in patients with a history of heart disease, after controlling for levels of depression and other risk factors. Contemporary research indicates that over a five-year period, the DS16 predicts cardiac events after taking stress into account. The Type D variable, relative to stress, was a much stronger predictor.

The association between the DS16 and other personality constructs has also been evaluated. An investigation of Flemish police officers and nurses investigated the associations with the traits of the five-factor model. The negative affectivity factor was associated with higher neuroticism and lower levels of extroversion, agreeableness, and conscientiousness. The social inhibition factor was linked primarily with low extroversion and high neuroticism (see DeFruyt & Denollet, 2002).

KEY POINTS

- The Type C personality reflects cancer-proneness. Although initial work suggested a link between personality and cancer, more recent research has not supported this association.
- Type C personality features may have a more non-specific link with illness.
- Type D personality studies by Denollet refers to the distress-prone personality. Type D factors are distress and social inhibition.
- Type D personality has been linked with cardiac problems after controlling for other risk factors (such as stress).

The Hardy Personality

The **hardy personality** is included as a contrast to the Type A, Type C, and Type D personalities because it represents a construct of unique importance. In addition, whereas the other personality types represent sources of vulnerability, hardiness is a protective, resiliency factor that is in keeping with the recent emphasis in psychology on **positive psychology** (factors that promote well-being). The mountain climbers described by Hayhurst (1997) in the introduction to the section Personality and Coping Styles would be high in hardiness.

The history of the hardiness construct is much like the history of the authoritarianism construct described in Chapter 10. Once again, we have a construct that has generated great interest, but one that is fraught with conceptual and measurement problems almost to the extent that we have probably learned more by the critical challenges to the construct rather from the construct itself.

What is hardiness? Hardiness was first described by Suzanne Kobasa (who later changed her last name to Ouellette). Hardiness as defined by Kobasa (1979) is composed of three integrated orientations toward the self and the world: a sense of control, commitment, and challenge. These variables have been referred to as the three C's by Kobasa and Salvatore Maddi, another prominent researcher in this area. If all three components exist in an individual, then that person should be relatively resistant to stress and less likely to develop an illness, relative to the person who is low in one or more of these components. The control component is akin to the type of self-control perceived by someone with an internal locus of control. Commitment exists when people are highly involved in their lives and feel a sense of purpose and meaningfulness. People who are committed typically are quite focused on goal attainment and have a sense that their goals are attainable. Finally, people with a sense of challenge recognize that obstacles will arise and changes will occur, and confronting them head-on will lead to positive developments. This ability to respond to challenge is important because several studies suggest that people high in hardiness, when compared with people low in hardiness, tend to respond to stressful and challenging situations with higher performance (for a review, see Maddi et al., 2002).

An important aspect of hardiness is that it is postulated that all three components must be present in order for hardy people to experience the protective health benefits of hardiness. Ouellette (1993) argued that having two of the three components is not sufficient. Consider, for instance, the person who has high commitment and a sense of challenge, but who is moderate to low in control. This lack of control would likely be a source of distress that would undermine overall coping efforts.

Hardiness could play a role in the initial onset of illness by contributing to a health problem, but it can also play a vital role in contributing to positive coping responses when threatened by a potentially fatal disease. Hardiness is reflected by Hans Selye in his autobiography *The Stress of My Life*. Selye disclosed that he contracted a form of cancer that is typically lethal and one of the most aggressive forms of cancer ever identified. This type of cancer usually kills the person within a year. Selye did not succumb to this cancer and lived for many additional years, in part because his reaction, in many ways, was the embodiment of the control, commitment, and challenge aspects of hardiness. Selye (1977) recounted the following:

> I refused to retreat from life in desperation and, although I knew it would take tremendous self-discipline, I was determined to continue living and working without worrying about the end. It's difficult to live normally when you are treated like a man condemned to die, so I told no one outside my immediate family about my predicament. In a sense, I refused to believe my fate; I suppressed any thoughts of my presumably imminent death, and apparently, even my closest friends and associates failed to notice any difference in my behavior. I rewrote my will, including several suggestions for the continuation of my work by my colleagues; and having taken care of that business, I promptly forced myself to disregard the whole calamity. I immersed myself in my work, summoning all of my strength to get on with living and avoid brooding. (p. 126)

Selye went on to note two years went by and he discovered that he was "the fortunate exception" because he survived his bout with cancer.

Kobasa's (1979) initial research on hardiness and health explored how hardiness influenced the outcomes of male business executives under a high degree of stress. She confirmed that executives with high hardiness had fewer illnesses. Subsequent research showed that hardiness has an important **buffering effect**. That is, hardiness moderates the link between stress and illness so that people with high hardiness have a resource that lessens the impact of stress on them (Kobasa, Maddi, & Kahn, 1982). Although other researchers have identified this buffering effect the results have not been universal. Hull, Van Treuren, and Virnelli (1987) found no evidence of a buffering effect. Instead, they found that lack of control and lack of commitment were linked directly with health

Kobasa researched how hardiness influenced the outcomes of male business executives under a high degree of stress and found that executives with high hardiness had fewer illnesses.

problems, and they suggested that this is because deficits in both areas are highly stressful in and of themselves. They suggested that any buffering effects are probably situationally specific, so buffering will depend on the circumstances.

Differences in cognitive appraisal seem to play an important role in hardiness. Rhodewalt and Zone (1989) compared life event appraisals of people high versus low in hardiness. People described as "non-hardy" evaluated a greater proportion of their life events as undesirable and viewed negative events as needing a bigger response in order to maintain adjustment. There were also indications that controlling for differences in cognitive appraisal eliminated the adaptive advantage of hardiness in terms of the link between hardiness and reduced depression. Cognitive appraisal differences also played a central role in recent research showing that women high in hardiness, relative to those low in hardiness, were less upset after being exposed to gender discrimination (Foster & Dion, 2003). Women high in hardiness were less upset, in part, because they attributed the discrimination to specific causes that minimized the perceived pervasiveness of gender discrimination. The original impetus for this study came from earlier research with Toronto's Chinese community showing that the link between perceived discrimination and psychological distress was greater among those low in hardiness (Dion, Dion, & Pak, 1992).

The ability of hardiness to predict important outcomes must be interpreted within the context of measurement and methodological problems that have plagued the construct. So what are some of the problems that have emerged with the hardiness construct over the years? The first issue is that the predictive usefulness of the challenge component is quite weak relative to the control and commitment components, and challenge shows relatively little association with health problems (see Funk, 1992). Hull, Van Treuren, and Vinelli (1987) attributed this to the weaker psychometric properties of the original commitment scale.

A third problem for measurement and interpretation is not specific to only hardiness research, but it is a pervasive problem that clearly applies to this area as well. That is, the items used to assess hardiness also seem to tap levels of negative affectivity, so the empirical link between hardiness and personal adjustment has probably been overestimated (Funk, 1992; Hull et al., 1987).

A final issue that needs to be understood is why it is the case that hardiness seems to have a stronger buffering effect for men than for women (Klag & Bradley, 2004). In general, not enough attention is paid to possible gender differences in the association between personality factors and health outcomes, and this seems to make a difference in the role of hardiness.

Although hardiness per se was not assessed directly in his initial investigation, Maddi became convinced of the benefits of hardiness as a result of his research with Illinois Bell Telephone employees who were laid off due to downsizing (see Maddi, 1987). Approximately one third of the employees actually seemed to thrive as a result of the changes, and it was these people who seemed to have the characteristics of hardiness. As a result of his investigations, Maddi and his colleagues developed and implemented an intervention (known as Hardi-Training) designed to increase the hardiness level of employees (see Khoshaba & Maddi, 2001; Maddi, 1987, 2002). Research suggests that hardiness training decreases anxiety and depression and increases self-confidence, so the American Psychological Association has developed programs designed to increase resiliency in children, adolescents, and adults who are faced with challenging life situations.

KEY POINTS

- Hardiness is a resilience factor. Empirical research on hardiness has been limited somewhat by psychometric issues involving questionnaire measures of hardiness.
- The three C's of hardiness are control, commitment, and challenge.
- Hardiness is a buffer of the association between stress and illness, and this is the case particularly for men.
- Hardiness training results in increased self-confidence and lower levels of anxiety and depression.

PERSONALITY TRAITS AND HEALTH OUTCOMES

The final section of this chapter explores the association between particular personality trait dimensions and health. The various constructs that are explored include those that comprise the five-factor model (with a particular emphasis on conscientiousness) as well as optimism–pessimism, self-efficacy, and health locus of control.

As a preview to this section, review Table 12.4. It can be seen that optimism, self-efficacy, and an internal locus of control are all associated with positive health behaviours. In contrast, links with the traits from the five-factor model tend to vary as a function of the supertrait being considered.

The Five-Factor Model

Investigations of the associations between the traits in the five-factor model and health symptoms and health problems continue to emerge. One recent investigation examined the levels of the five personality traits in a sample of elderly Americans who have never smoked and those who have quit smoking or continued to smoke (Terracciano & Costa, 2004). The three groups differed in levels of conscientiousness, neuroticism, and agreeableness. People who had never been smokers had substantially higher levels of conscientiousness and agreeableness and lower levels of neuroticism. These data accord with other findings linking smoking with higher neuroticism and lower conscientiousness (Vollrath & Torgersen, 2002).

A facet analysis of the NEO-PI-R factors by Terracciano and Costa (2004) showed that all facets of neuroticism were elevated in current smokers with the exception of self-consciousness. The conscientiousness facets that best distinguished non-smokers and smokers were higher levels of achievement striving, deliberation, and dutifulness among non-smokers.

Booth-Kewley and Vickers (1994) investigated the five-factor model and health behaviours in two large samples of military personnel. They established that each element of the five-factor model was linked with health behaviours, but findings were particularly robust for conscientiousness. Conscientiousness was linked with wellness behaviour, accident control, and less risk-taking in traffic.

Friedman et al. (1993, 1995) conducted analyses of the longitudinal Terman Life Cycle Study that followed gifted children throughout their entire lives. It was possible to analyze the ratings of "the Termites" provided by teachers and parents and derive indicators of the personality traits assessed by the five-factor model. Friedman et al. (1993) reported that two personality factors predicted longevity: the number of years lived was associated positively with conscientiousness, and it was associated negatively with a factor measuring cheerfulness/humour. The latter finding seems peculiar. Why were cheerfulness and a sense of humour risk factors rather than protective factors? Supplementary analyses reported by Friedman et al. (1995) indicated that part of the problem is that cheerful people were more likely to engage in risky behaviours and less likely to engage in protective behaviours that safeguard their health. Also, perhaps cheerful people are less able to mobilize appropriate coping responses and resources when health challenges are experienced. Finally, further analyses established that among other risk factors, low conscientiousness and elevated cheerfulness/humour were comparable in the magnitude of their predictive validity versus other known risk factors for all cause mortality, including high cholesterol and blood pressure.

Recently, a related study of great interest was conducted by Stewart McCann from Cape Breton University in Nova Scotia. McCann (2005) used archival measures to examine the link between personality and health in 32 American presidents stretching from George Washington to Richard Nixon. McCann made clever use of assessments of the traits from the five-factor model gathered in previous research by Rubenzer, Faschingbauer, and Ones (2000) and related these personality factors with presidential death ages. Indices of smoking, drinking, and exercise were also used. Once again, a relatively strong correlation was found between conscientiousness and death age ($r = .41$). The other four personality traits were not correlated with death age. As expected, death age was also predicted by smoking, drinking, and exercise. Trait conscientiousness was correlated negatively with smoking and drinking.

The lack of an association between neuroticism and age of death in these studies may be due to the specific samples being studied. Although Costa and McCrae (1987) have cautioned that neuroticism is not linked strongly with objective indices such as mortality, a recent study of Catholic clergymen suggests otherwise. Wilson et al. (2004) studied a sample of 883 older Catholic clergymen over a five-year period. Each participant completed the NEO-FFI. The protective effects of high conscientiousness were found once again, but it was found that those with high neuroticism had a rate of death that was double the norm. Thus, the possible influence of neuroticism in at least certain segments of the population should not be discounted.

The authors posited that health behaviour is the likely mediator in this relationship. Indeed, a recent meta-analysis of data from 194 studies confirmed that the benefits of trait conscientiousness are due to its links with positive health-related behaviours such as exercise and healthy eating. Also, conscientiousness is associated negatively with negative health-related behaviours such as tobacco consumption, risky sexual behaviour, illicit drug use, and involvement in car accidents (Bogg & Roberts, 2004). Bogg and Roberts found that conscientiousness was related to all of the most important behaviours in terms of established predictors of mortality. This meta-analysis also found that there were significant benefits in predictive validity if conscientiousness was assessed by specific facets rather than by one overall score. The three conscientiousness facets most predictive of health behaviours were responsibility, self-control, and traditionalism.

Optimism versus Pessimism

Numerous authors have suggested that having an optimistic orientation is one factor that protects people from health problems. However, this general premise is qualified by the fact that the optimism–pessimism construct is very complex, and the link that optimism has with health depends greatly on how optimism is conceptualized. The reasons for including this caveat are outlined below.

Although optimism can be adaptive, we have already seen with Segerstrom's work that optimism can be linked with stress in the short term at least, due to the challenges pursued by optimistic people. Optimism is also not adaptive when it provides a false sense of security. Individual differences in optimism have been identified as one factor that promotes a delay in seeking help for medical problems, despite evidence that a medical problem exists (Jones, 1990). A pervasiveness sense of unrealistic optimism about one's health appears to apply to most people. Weinstein (1984) has described this as **naïve optimism**. Weinstein (1984) provided a list of significant health problems and asked students to rate their chances of contracting these diseases versus the chances that other people had of contracting these diseases. Weinstein (1984) found that most people rated themselves as being at a comparatively lower level of risk than statistically should be the case. Naïve optimism can come in two forms: undermining the likelihood of negative events and overestimating the likelihood of positive events. A follow-up investigation by Weinstein (1987) of unrealistic optimism about health problems in a community sample yielded comparable findings. Unrealistic optimism was assessed in terms of seeing one's own risk as less than average. The health problems associated with the greatest degree of unrealistic optimism were developing a drug addiction, having a drinking problem, attempting suicide, becoming asthmatic, and getting food poisoning. Cancer and high blood pressure were among the very few health problems not associated with unrealistic optimism. Unrealistic optimism was found to be most evident when health problems were perceived as infrequent and preventable and the respondent had not had personal experience with the health problem.

A recent study examined the level of naïve optimism shown by Canadian students and Chinese students about the possibility of contracting severe acute respiratory syndrome (SARS) (Ji, Zhang, Usborne, & Guan, 2004). It was found that both groups were high in unrealistic optimism as reflected by the belief that the self was much less likely than the average person to contact SARS. However, group differences were also evident: in this case, the optimism bias was stronger among the Chinese students. Ji et al. (2004) suggested that the greater optimism of Chinese students stemmed, in part, from their greater awareness of the positive changes that were implemented as a result of the SARS outbreak.

KEY POINTS

- Unrealistic optimism is known as naïve optimism, which most likely occurs when people are asked to rate the likelihood of low frequency events that they have not experienced.
- Naïve optimism is linked with higher levels of extroversion and lower levels of neuroticism.

Schwarzer (1999) has coined different terms to help distinguish the general benefits of a positive outlook from the naïve optimism that can lead to greater risk. **Functional optimism** refers to the benefits of optimism when a threat is actually experienced. Defensive optimism is the term used to refer to the optimistic bias that seems to characterize the vast majority of people.

Functional optimism is assessed most commonly by the Life Orientation Test (LOT; Scheier & Carver, 1985). The LOT was designed solely to measure generalized expectancies. It consists of four items worded in the optimism direction, four items worded in the pessimism direction, and four filler items.

To what extent is trait pessimism distinguishable from trait neuroticism? Smith et al. (1989) have criticized the LOT for having restricted discriminant validity relative to general measures of neuroticism. They showed that correlations between optimism and measures of health symptoms and coping tendencies were no longer significant after removing variance due to trait anxiety. In related research, Smith, O'Keeffe, and Allred (1989) found in two studies that significant associations between optimism and measures of coping tendencies and physical symptoms disappeared after removing variance due to neuroticism. Previously, Scheier et al. (1989) responded to similar findings by suggesting that there is a link between pessimism and neuroticism, that pessimism may be one of the facets that comprises the broader construct of neuroticism, and that pessimism may be related to maladaptive coping independent of other facets of neuroticism.

Findings from the health field suggest that general optimism–pessimism is very effective in predicting health outcomes, especially the course of illness. A recent study of the progress of HIV infection, for instance, showed that trait optimism predicted slower disease progression (Ironson et al., 2005). People low on optimism (the 25th percentile), relative to those high on optimism (the 75th percentile), lost cells at a rate that was 1.55 times faster.

Although dispositional optimism seems to be a key factor, there is also a role to be played by illness-specific versions of optimism. The need to consider both general measures of expectancy and domain-specific measures was demonstrated recently by Taylor et al. (1992). These researchers investigated optimism, coping, psychological adjustment, and risk-taking behaviour in a sample of gay men. The measures in this study included a general measure of optimism (the Life Orientation Test), as well as event-specific measures, including indices of AIDS-specific optimism (a belief in invulnerability to AIDS) and fatalistic vulnerability (a belief that the outcome of AIDS is inevitable and almost impossible to prevent). One of the primary findings of this study was that the measure of optimism, the LOT, did not predict risk-related sexual behaviour. Further analyses showed that only the domain-specific measure predicted coping avoidance of AIDS and that HIV-seropositive men differed from HIV-seronegative men in levels of AIDS-specific optimism but not in generalized optimism.

In general, it seems that coping is a potential mediator of the link between optimism and illness. For instance, in the study predicting HIV progression, Ironson et al. (2005) found that less avoidant coping and greater proactive coping efforts mediated the association between optimism and reduced HIV progression.

KEY POINTS

- Dispositional optimism is assessed by the LOT (Life Orientation Test). Scores on the LOT are relatively stable over time and not unduly influenced by traumatic events, such as experiencing a severe illness.
- Dispositional optimism is a consistent predictor of health outcomes. Illness-specific measures of optimism (e.g., optimism about coping with cancer) are also significant and unique predictors.

Self-Efficacy

The **self-efficacy** construct also plays an important role in health outcomes. Given the link between self-efficacy and health, the decision was made to discuss self-efficacy in this chapter rather than in Chapter 11, but readers should not lose sight of the fact that self-efficacy is obviously a self-concept variable, and it is a vital part of how people see themselves. In fact, self-efficacy is a construct that depends greatly on judgements of personal capability, and it is quite similar to the self-competence aspect of self-esteem that was described in Chapter 11.

Albert Bandura has provided us with much of what we know about the self-efficacy construct. Self-efficacy has been defined generally by Bandura (1997) as the belief in one's ability to perform a task or successfully perform a specified behaviour. According to Bandura (1997), self-efficacy has three components components: (1) magnitude (belief about performance in increasingly difficult aspects of the task); (2) strength (the amount of effort exerted to maintain the behaviour in the face of obstacles); and (3) generality (the breadth of applying the construct).

Bandura has maintained that self-efficacy beliefs exist and can be measured in various domains (e.g., academic self-efficacy is the sense of efficacy in school-related matters), but ultimately, specific efficacy beliefs contribute to a generalized sense of self-efficacy that may operate across various situations and tasks. Bandura and associates have conducted research on the generality of self-efficacy beliefs. Their research showed that coping behaviours learned in one situation were also displayed in other community settings, and it was suggested that this reflected a generalized sense of self-efficacy (Bandura, Adams, Hardy, & Howells, 1980). Smith (1980) investigated how cognitive–behavioural training designed to enhance the coping skills of test-anxious students not only increased their test-taking self-efficacy but also led to increases in generalized self-efficacy. Importantly, Smith (1980) also found that the coping skills trained increased self-efficacy but not internal locus of control, and this is noteworthy because concerns have been raised about whether self-efficacy can be distinguished from locus of control. Other research indicates that general self-efficacy is associated with low anxiety in high and low controllability situations (Endler, Speer, Johnson, & Flett, 2001).These data combine to suggest that learning to cope with specific problems contributes to a more general sense of personal capability that applies to various types of situations.

One factor that contributes to a sense of self-efficacy is encouragement from others that motivates and leads to success.

According to Bandura (1994), four different sets of factors contribute to a sense of self-efficacy. First, self-efficacy develops following mastery experiences. If tasks and challenges are mastered, this enhances a sense of personal capability. Second, social learning plays a role. Greater self-efficacy is likely if a person is exposed to models with high self-efficacy. Third, other people may persuade us that we are capable, and their persuasive efforts may motivate us to behave in a way that leads to success and increased feelings of self-efficacy. So, telling someone "I believe you can do it!" might actually increase that person's self-efficacy. This can be taken to the extreme, however. Children with parents who tell them at an early age that they are capable of greatness may foster a grandiose sense of self-importance and self-efficacy. Likewise, repeatedly telling someone that they can't do something is bound to undermine their sense of self-efficacy. Finally, self-efficacy may be influenced by an individual's somatic and emotional cues. Bandura (1994) suggested that feelings of stress may undermine self-efficacy beliefs. Perhaps it is not surprising then that people who are chronically high in stress, such as socially prescribed perfectionists, also tend to have low general self-efficacy (see Martin, Flett, Hewitt, Krames, & Szanto, 1996).

What about the health benefits of self-efficacy? Bandura (1986) has argued that perceived self-efficacy is a critical determinant of health-related stress reactions and extensive empirical evidence supports this association (see also O'Leary, 1992; Wiedenfeld et al.,

1990). In a meta-analysis of 56 samples, Holden (1991) examined self-efficacy as a predictor of health outcome measures. Overall results across studies indicated a moderate effect size ($r = .30$). Moreover, people with high self-efficacy respond with more adaptive forms of coping when an illness is experienced. For instance, higher self-efficacy is associated with greater ability to withstand pain (Litt, 1988). Contemporary research with cancer patients suggests that self-efficacy is effective, in part, because it promotes positive appraisals of benefit finding. This study found that self-efficacy was associated directly with cognitive appraisals of personal growth and acceptance of life imperfections (Luszczynska, Mohamed, & Schwarzer, 2005).

Bandura's work on self-efficacy and health is particularly intriguing because he is one of a team of researchers who have shown with objective physiological measures that the level of self-efficacy predicts the response of the immune system to stress (see Wiedenfeld et al., 1990). That is, believing that you are capable of rising to the challenge actually seems to confer a benefit by bolstering your immune system (also see Bandura, 1997).

Another important question is just how general is general self-efficacy in terms of being a universal construct that applies across cultures? Evidence gathered by Ralf Schwarzer from Germany and his associates has attested to the seeming universality of self-efficacy. Participants in this research completed a 10-item measure of general self-efficacy created by Schwarzer and Jerusalem (1995). The English language version of the scale is replicated in Table 12.6. Consider how you would respond to these items. Are you high, moderate, or low in general self-efficacy? If you are high in self-efficacy, to what extent does this make you feel that you are able to withstand stress?

Table 12.6 Schwarzer and Jerusalem's General Self-Efficacy Scale

1. I can always manage to solve difficult problems if I try hard enough.
2. If someone opposes me, I can find the means and ways to get what I want.
3. It is easy for me to stick to my aims and accomplish my goals.
4. I am confident that I could deal efficiently with unexpected events.
5. Thanks to my resourcefulness, I know how to handle unforeseen situations.
6. I can solve most problems if I invest the necessary effort.
7. I can remain calm when facing difficulties because I can rely on my coping abilities.
8. When I am confronted with a problem, I can usually find several solutions.
9. If I am in trouble, I can usually think of a solution.
10. I can usually handle whatever comes my way.

Source: Schwarzer & Jerusalem, 1995.

KEY POINTS

- Self-efficacy appears to be a general construct that is applicable and generalizable across many cultures, and has been shown to be a consistent predictor of health outcomes.
- According to Bandura, self-efficacy develops as a result of several influences. These include mastery experiences that foster a sense of capability, social learning (imitation and reward), social feedback from others about how capable we are, and physiological sensations and cues that make us feel more or less confident.

Luszczynska, Gutiérrez-Doña, and Schwarzer (2004) investigated self-efficacy in 8,796 participants from five countries (Costa Rica, Germany, Poland, Turkey, and the United States). Participants also completed measures of cognitive appraisals of stress, social relationships, well-being, distress, and attainment of achievement goals. Comparable results were obtained across countries. General self-efficacy was associated with higher levels of optimism and self-esteem and lower levels of anxiety and depression. Greater self-efficacy was also associated with greater academic achievement and higher job satisfaction. Finally, general self-efficacy was linked with a tendency to appraise stressful situations as a challenge (as opposed to a personal threat). Thus, there is substantial universality (in these five countries at least) in the correlates of general self-efficacy.

Scholz, Gutiérrez-Doña, Sud, and Schwarzer (2002) examined the psychometric properties of the General Self-Efficacy Scale when administered to 19,120 participants from 25 countries. Results confirmed that the scale is unidimensional, with comparable psychometric properties across all 25 countries. Meta-analyses continue to indicate that the correlates of general self-efficacy are quite similar across various countries (Lusz-czynska, Scholtz, & Schwarzer, 2005).

Schwarzer (1999) has noted that it is important to distinguish among four phase-specific forms of self-efficacy. That is, there are individual differences in goal-setting self-efficacy (the perceived capability to develop realistic, meaningful, and challenging goals), action self-efficacy (the perceived ability to develop effective plans), coping self-efficacy (different levels of confidence in the perceived ability to deal with stressors), and recovery self-efficacy (the sense of conviction that the health problem will be overcome). Effective coping follows from having high self-efficacy in all of these specific forms of self-efficacy.

Health Locus of Control

Consider the following case: A man knows that he must go into the hospital for surgery on a suspected heart aneurysm. Rather than go to the hospital, he feels he has little control over what will happen, and going into the hospital will only hasten his demise. He resists attempts from others to get the necessary surgery.

Clearly, the beliefs we have about our control over health outcome can be a powerful determinant of the behaviours we engage in (or fail to engage in as the case may be). In the case of the person described above, the lack of action due to feeling out of control ultimately had fatal consequences, as he later suffered a heart attack.

We will never know whether earlier intervention would have made a difference in the above case. However, we do know that there are widespread differences in people's beliefs about whether they have personal control over health outcomes. To some extent, an internal locus of control with respect to health issues is very similar to a sense of self-efficacy and a sense of optimism. As is the case with these constructs, there are clear benefits associated with an internal health locus of control (see Wallston, 1989).

Systematic research on the health locus of control construct began when Wallston, Wallston, and DeVellis (1978) observed the progress made by some women with breast cancer and reached the conclusion that this progress was a reflection of individual differences in locus of control but not locus of control in general. They suggested that there are domain-specific beliefs about locus of control, and one of the most salient domains is locus of control with respect to health outcomes and health behaviours. The Health Locus of Control Scale comes in various forms. Form A and Form B are parallel forms of health locus of control in general. Form C is an 18-item measure that assesses internal beliefs, chance, and powerful others with respect to a specific illness (Wallston, Stein, & Smith, 1994). Internal beliefs are reflected by such test items as "I am directly responsible for my condition getting better or worse." Change is reflected by items such as "If my condition worsens, it is a matter of fate." The powerful others factor is reflected by items such as "The type of help I receive from other people determines how soon my condition improves."

Although most of the research conducted on health locus of control has involved people from Western cultures (see Wallston & Wallston, 1981; Wallston, 1989), there is some evidence of generalizability. Kuwahara et al. (2004) examined health locus of control in Japanese people from a rural setting and confirmed that the subscales have comparable psychometric properties, and a more internal health locus of control was associated with more healthy, adaptive behaviours.

Individual differences in health locus of control have been linked with health problems and associated behaviours. For example, research has indicated that there is a negative association between smoking and an internal health locus of control (Winefield, Winefield, Tiggeman, & Goldney, 1989). Other research indicates that smokers who place low value on their health are especially likely to endorse chance instead of self-control (Bennett et al., 1997).

Wallston et al. (1999) supplemented these three scales with another health locus of control dimension assessing "God Locus of Control." This was very insightful because for some people, positive or negative beliefs about the role played by spiritual beings can be a powerful determinant of adjustment and coping.

The God Locus of Control Scale was designed in recognition of the number of people who cope primarily by saying that their fate "is in God's hands" (regardless of the type of God that is believed in). It was also designed out of an interest in measuring beliefs in specific powerful others. A representative item is "God is directly responsible for my condition getting better or worse." Wallston et al. (1999) examined God Locus of Control in patients with rheumatoid arthritis or systematic sclerosis and found that God Locus of Control was not associated with disability status, level of functioning, and other objective indicators of health status, but it was associated with more passive pain coping, more negative affect, and less positive affect.

Is the belief that your fate is in the hands of a higher entity a good thing or a bad thing? This is a very complicated issue. This belief could provide you with a sense of hope and optimism, but it could also preclude you from seeking other forms of tangible assistance, including medical interventions.

Integrating Personality Constructs into Larger Models

While it is important to establish a role for personality factors such as self-efficacy and locus of control in health outcomes, it is important to reiterate that these personality variables are best considered within a broader conceptual framework that includes numerous other factors of likely importance (e.g., stress, coping, social support). We should also not lose sight of the possibility that certain personality vulnerability factors interact and combine with each other to produce elevated risk. Finally, it is not enough to simply describe and detail an association between personality factors and poor health outcomes. It is best to regard personality factors from a theoretical perspective that includes explanation.

It should be evident from this chapter that there is a great deal of complexity involved in the link between personality and health, and the personality-health association can be looked at from a variety of different perspectives that involve a variety of personality constructs. Chapter 12 began with an illustration of differences in coping responses to a traumatic situation (in this case, sensory deprivation) and then progressed to an analysis of differences in cognitive appraisal and related differences in coping styles. It is important to examine individual differences in coping because there are differences in the ways people cope with stress, and these differences relate to health outcomes. The key distinction between primary appraisals (perceptions of threat and challenge) versus secondary appraisal (an evaluation of whether coping responses will be adequate) was made apparent. Different coping styles were then identified (task-focused, emotion-focused, and avoidance-focused), and it was also noted that there are illness-specific coping styles that are associated with adjustment to the illness. Poorer adjustment was linked with emotional preoccupation and palliative coping. Next, the goodness of fit model was used to indicate that the adaptiveness of a particular coping orientation depends, in part, on situational demands and task parameters. The notion of cultural fit was also explored in terms of sojourner experiences.

The emphasis of this chapter then shifted to various models of the association between personality and health. The models outlined in this chapter were the constitutional risk factor model, the illness behaviour model, the stress moderation–mediation model, and the stress generation model. While the constitutional risk factor model (also known as the etiologic model) is based on the notion of an inherited vulnerability or biological weakness that is attributable to personality orientations, the illness behaviour model is based on the premise that personality confers risk through its association with adaptive or maladaptive behaviours. Stress moderation and mediation views stress as a variable that combines with personality to create health problems (moderation model) or that stress is a result of personality (mediation model). The stress generation model is a form of the mediation model that is based on the notion that people with certain personality styles act in ways that create stress for themselves.

The next primary focus was on various personality types believed to be associated with illness (Type A, Type C, and Type D personalities) and resilience to illness (the hardy personality). Although the validity of the personality types as a whole in terms of vulnerability is currently at issue, certain elements of the personality styles (hostility, depression, and emotional inexpressiveness) do indeed seem to be associated with risk of health problems.

Chapter 12 concluded with an examination of specific personality trait dimensions associated with health problems. The five-factor model was explored with a particular emphasis on the protective effects of high trait conscientiousness. Next, we examined the role of trait optimism in the onset of illness and the persistence and long-term course of illness. Self-efficacy was also discussed, not only in terms of general self-efficacy, but also in terms of phase-specific forms of self-efficacy (e.g., planning self-efficacy and recovery self-efficacy). Finally, as a supplement to earlier discussions in this book on locus of control in general, the predictive utility of a domain-specific version (health locus of control) was explored.

Questions to Consider

1 Theorists such as Zuckerman place great emphasis on the biological roots of personality. To what extent do you think that personality is biological? If biology plays a key role, do you still see a role for interventions designed to promote a healthy lifestyle?

2 Do you think that people really differ in how they cognitively appraise and evaluate stressful events? Think of the key people in your life. Would they differ in how they perceive and respond to the same stressful event (such as taking a driving test)?

3 Do you cope differently or the same with stressful situations that are controllable or uncontrollable? Do you see some benefit in at least initially denying the existence of overwhelming, uncontrollable events? Or is denial just part of the procrastination process?

4 Do you agree with Lazarus that personality plays little role in the coping process, or do you think that it plays a vital role? Why?

5 List some of the components of the Type A construct. Do you think that it is essential for students who want to succeed to have some aspects of Type A behaviour? Do you think that modern society is becoming more or less Type A? If given the choice, would you choose to live in a Type A or Type B society? When you think of Type A societies, what nations do you think of?

6 Do you accept the possibility that there is a cancer-prone personality style? Do you see a role for personality factors in the onset of an illness such as cancer that is usually thought of in purely biological terms? What about recovery? Do you see a role for personality in recovery from cancer?

7 It was suggested earlier that personality variables are unlikely to be more predictive of health problems than other variables. Do you think this is the case? A recent review of past findings identified neuroticism, hostility, and low optimism as the personality factors with the strongest associations with health problems (Smith & MacKenzie, 2006). Which personality traits do you think have the most promise in being able to predict the onset or persistence of health problems? Why did you choose these particular traits?

Key Terms

avoidance-focused coping, p. 489
buffering effect, p. 518
catastrophization, p. 496
coping, p. 488
cultural fit hypothesis, p. 492
defensive pessimism, p. 509
disability hypothesis, p. 507
emotion-focused coping, p. 589
functional optimism, p. 523
goodness of fit hypothesis, p. 491
hardy personality, p. 517
naïve optimism, p. 522
palliative coping, p. 496
positive psychology, p. 517
primary appraisals, p. 487
problem-focused coping, p. 489
psychosomatic hypothesis, p. 507
secondary appraisals, p. 487
self-efficacy, p. 524
sojourner adjustment, p. 491
symptom perception hypothesis, p. 507
transactional model of stress, p. 490
Type A personality, p. 511
Type C personality, p. 514
Type D personality, p. 516
uncontrollability model, p. 511

Key Theorists

Albert Bandura, p. 524
John Denollet, p. 516
Norman Endler, p. 495
Susan Folkman, p. 487
Richard Lazarus, p. 487
James Parker, p. 495
Hans Selye, p. 505

chapter thirteen

PERSONALITY, MENTAL HEALTH, AND PSYCHOPATHOLOGY

- Abnormality Defined
- Personality Disorder Clusters
- Dimensional Models and Personality Dysfunction
- Personality, Binge Drinking, and Alcoholism
- The Role of Personality Factors in Depression

My chronic feelings of emptiness and boredom came from the fact that I was living a life based on my incapacities, which were numerous.... My self-image was not unstable. I saw myself, quite correctly, as unfit for the educational and social systems.

—SUSANNA KAYSEN, FROM HER AUTOBIOGRAPHY *GIRL, INTERRUPTED*, ANALYZING HER SYMPTOMS IN RESPONSE TO THE DIAGNOSIS GIVEN TO HER OF BORDERLINE PERSONALITY DISORDER

You got to watch out for that rigidness Edith. It will warp your personality!

—ARCHIE BUNKER, PLAYED BY CARROLL O'CONNER, ON THE TELEVISION SHOW *ALL IN THE FAMILY*

Case Study 13.1 Arlene

A polished and attractive woman of 47, Arlene entered therapy because "I'm just not feeling up to par, and never have." Feelings of depression and despair increased substantially after her third marriage began to dissolve. Not yet divorced, but living apart from her husband, she reports extreme anger and feelings of worthlessness at being left helplessly alone. She states that she cannot deal with the situation, and instead spends her time shopping, buying what she cannot afford, drinking too much, and looking for someone to take the place of her husband. "Marital therapy failed," she states, and "after I began phoning him four or five times a day, he has changed his number and moved away. I have no idea where he is."

Arlene seems to have two sides to her. In some ways, she is immersed in the existential angst appropriate to a teenager, still trying to discover who she really is. In other ways, she seems hard, calculating, and embittered. Though admittedly not a particularly good relationship, the marriage nevertheless gave Arlene "someone to be." Sometimes her husband is described as "the most loving person" and sometimes as "the asshole."

Instability runs through Arlene's history. She has lost contact with her oldest brother. Her mother's numerous marriages have left her with a combination of half-sisters, half-brothers, and ex-stepsiblings. Family infighting has taken the place of genuine communication. Arlene states that she always received the "short end of the stick" when her mother remarried. Because each marriage required a move, Arlene was unable to make lasting friends as a child, and her schoolwork suffered. Her mother didn't care about her grades, and Arlene found it convenient to adopt this apathetic attitude rather than make a real effort in her studies.

Arlene states that although she never really loved any of her husbands, she "completely lost it" when each marriage failed. Further, she discloses that she has been hospitalized three times, twice following suicide attempts, once for substance abuse. She received follow-up therapy after each hospitalization and is being seen by a different therapist at the current time. Initially, she thought very highly of her latest therapist, feeling sure that he would finally get to the root of the problem. More recently, she is disappointed and angry that he is not more readily accessible to her and is unable to see her more than twice a week. Her visit today seems designed to secure additional nurturance. Arlene will be referred back to the therapist she is currently seeing.

Source: Millon & Davis, 2000.

ARLENE IS A CASE of a person who has been diagnosed with borderline personality disorder—one of the most commonly diagnosed personality disorders. Its symptoms include a negative and unstable self-image, a history of fluctuating and unstable social relationships, and intense emotional feelings, often in the form of anger and rage. It is a personality disorder in that it appears to reflect long-lasting and stable yet maladaptive aspects of a person's character. Unfortunately, most people with personality disorders are unaware of the negative aspects of their personality and how it causes distresses, not only for themselves but also for the people around them.

Chapter 13 examines the role of personality factors in mental health and psychopathology. Much of this chapter focuses on a description of personality disorders and the personality frameworks that have been developed to describe and understand them. Personality factors also play a role in other types of disorders beyond the link with personality disorders. Accordingly, as a supplement to this focus on personality disorders, Chapter 13 also includes an overview of the role of personality factors in such disorders as alcohol abuse and depression.

There are several ways that personality variables may be important to mental health and psychopathology. First, personality factors may serve as vulnerability factors that are involved in the etiology of psychopathology. Personality can operate solely but is more likely to combine with other factors (e.g., life stress) to produce psychopathology.

Even if they are not involved in the development of a disorder, personality factors can contribute to the persistence of a disorder. Certain disorders (e.g., depression) are intermittent and episodic but a subset of people have a persistent form of disorder. Perhaps personality is responsible for this chronicity.

In addition, personality factors may differentially predict different symptom profiles (e.g., Robins, Block, & Peselow, 1989). Here is it important to realize that among people who share the same disorder, there is a great deal of heterogeneity in how the disorder came about and the primary symptoms that people display, even when they have the exact same diagnosis. Perhaps personality factors account for these differences. Or perhaps personality factors combine with cultural factors to influence symptom expression. We know from the depression literature, for instance, that people from Eastern cultures are more likely to express somatic symptoms of depression, while people from Western cultures are more likely to express psychological symptoms reflecting the self-concept. There are also many culture-bound syndromes that go by such names as *amok*, *dhat*, and ghost sickness (see Mezzich, Lewis-Fernandez, & Ruiperez, 2003). Perhaps the phenomenological expression of disorder is a joint focus of personality and culture. Personality likely interacts with immediate situational factors as well; we know, for instance, that people being treated in a biomedical setting are much more likely to focus on the physical symptoms they have experienced (Kirmayer, Rousseau, Jarvis, & Guzder, 2003).

Personality factors also play a role in how people respond to their mental illness. We have already examined in Chapter 12 how personality can be associated with coping responses. This can be taken a step further by acknowledging that personality also predicts whether a person will seek professional help for their distress and dysfunction. Personality can also become vitally important in determining a client's responsiveness (or lack of responsiveness) to treatment. Recall that this issue was already discussed in Chapter 10 in our analysis of the role of insecure attachment styles and therapy outcomes (see Applied Perspective 10.1).

This last point can be illustrated further by a description provided by Albert Ellis about someone he identified as his most difficult case. This excerpt is from an intriguing case titled The Woman Who Hated Everyone and Everything. It describes a woman named Dorothy who suffered from apparent borderline personality disorder, and illustrates the affectivity instability and rage of people with borderline personality disorder. This is a personality style that not only alienates other people it also tends to alienate therapists, who may become quite unwilling or unable to fully assist patients with borderline disorder.

Case Study 13.2 Dorothy

"Dorothy had practically everything under the sun that I aim to change in therapy. First of all, she was low in USA—that's unconditional self-acceptance. She put herself down immensely and beat herself up continuously. Second, she was very hostile to many other people and had practically no UOA (unconditional other acceptance)."

What Ellis is telling us is that Dorothy was not only critical of herself but also especially critical of others. She made life extremely difficult for others in her therapy group and in her outside life, because she was so accusatory and consistently blamed everyone and everything for not meeting her expectations. She reserved some of her most angry outbursts for Ellis.

As if that were not challenging enough, Dorothy also had an almost complete absence of what Ellis calls ULA: unconditional life acceptance. Rather than taking things in stride, she was easily frustrated by almost everything that happened in her life. By showing steady rage and low tolerance of frustration, she managed to chase away everyone with whom she came into contact.

"Most of her hostility," Ellis said "was reserved for her mother. She called her the worst bitch under the sun! At work, everybody was 'thoroughly reprehensible.' In the therapy group, she was constantly fighting with others. She often bawled me out personally and accused me of all kinds of skulduggery."

Ellis saw Dorothy for two years, in both group and individual therapy. Even so, she didn't have enough outlets for her wrath, so she began seeing another therapist at the same time just so she could lash out at two targets at once.

"I've never seen anybody so consistently hostile all over the place to various kinds of people. You name it and she could easily—very easily!—make herself enraged at them. You could say she was a genius in this respect!"

During one group session, Ellis said something to set Dorothy off. He pointed out to her that by being so angry and ornery all the time, she was not getting what she wanted. Quite the reverse!

"I have never seen anything like the tirade that followed," Ellis recalled. "She went off against me, against our institute, against the world, against everything she could possibly think of. She just bawled me out and said she was going to prosecute me and persecute me. She told me I was no damn good and I wasn't helping her at all."

Source: Kottler & Carlson, 2003, pp. 127–128.

The case of Dorothy provided an illustration of an extreme personality disorder. We now continue our discussion of personality disorders with a brief overview of the nature of mental disorder and how personality disorders are defined in general. Next, we review the evidence on whether it is best to regard personality dysfunction from a categorical perspective (types) or from a continuous perspective (dimensions). Implicit in the descriptions of Arlene and Dorothy is the assumption that it is valid to identify discrete all-or-none categories that represent various personality disorders (similar to personality types). This is the prevailing assumption in the psychiatric community about personality dysfunction. However, perhaps a dimensional approach is more valid.

The next part of this chapter focuses on a description of different types of personality disorders. This is followed by a presentation of the different conceptual schemes that have emerged to understand personality dysfunction from a dimensional perspective.

The chapter concludes with a broader analysis of personality factors in distress and dysfunction. Personality is examined in terms of its link with addiction in the form of drinking problems. This chapter concludes with a discussion of personality factors in depression, followed by a description of the role of personality factors in treatment response.

KEY POINTS

- Personality has several potential roles in psychopathology. It may, for instance, have etiological significance as a vulnerability factor for the development of psychopathology.
- Personality also plays a role in the persistence or long-term stability of psychopathology.
- Personality factors may predict symptom profile differences and help explain some of the heterogeneity among people who share the same diagnosis yet differ in the symptoms they express.
- Personality may have a direct role in determining how a person responds to their dysfunction by influencing such things as the willingness to seek help.

ABNORMALITY DEFINED

When it comes to defining abnormal behaviour, the criterion of statistical infrequency is only one of several criteria that can be used (see Davison, Neale, Blankstein, & Flett, 2005). Behaviours that are highly atypical in the statistical sense may reflect abnormal behaviour, but this is not always the case. If so, uncommon yet highly desirable characteristics (e.g., extremely high intelligence) would be interpreted as a reflection of abnormality. Other characteristics that are typically considered include whether the behaviour causes significant distress to the self or to other people, and whether the pattern of behaviour is associated with significant impairment or disability. That is, does the behaviour impair the person's ability to meet his or her life demands? Is it self-defeating in that it detracts from the attainment of personal goals?

There is also a cultural component to definitions of abnormality. Before abnormality can be confirmed, it is important to consider whether the person is engaging in behaviour that is in keeping with his or her cultural background. Actions that are deemed inappropriate for one culture may, in fact, simply be a reflection of a different way of life and different orientation.

Simonsen (2005) made an intriguing observation as part of his discussion about the need to consider possible cultural biases. He observed that failure to consider cultural factors would mean that Buddhist monks in Asian countries would likely fit the diagnostic criteria for schizoid personality disorder! Traits of the monks that could be misinterpreted as symptoms include engaging in solitary activities, lack of emotional expression, lack of sexual desire, constricted affect (low emotional expression), and a seeming indifference to praise and criticism. Similarly, he suggested that shamans from different cultures could be mistakenly labelled with a schizotypal personality disorder due to their magical thinking and unusual perceptual experiences.

Cultural factors must be considered when defining abnormal behaviour because cultural traits, such as those of Buddhist monks, could be misinterpreted.

Conceptualizations of Personality Disorders

Although diagnostic systems use disorder categories to describe people, evidence is reviewed below that favours a dimensional approach to personality disorders. Given the apparent importance of dimensions, there is a temptation to define personality disorders as the extreme ends or variants of the dimensions that predict the presence or absence of characteristics associated with adjustment. However, the other criteria described should also be considered. In particular, to what extent does the individual experience distress? Many personality disorders involve very little personal distress but involve great discomfort for other people. And is maladaptive personality functioning associated with significant levels of impairment? The degree of impairment cannot be easily evaluated by self-reports; it typically requires a clinician to make this kind of determination. Beck and Freeman (1990) noted that patients with personality disorders will often see the problems they encounter as external to themselves and originating in the bizarre behaviour of other people. Other patients may realize that they have a problem but be at a total loss to explain how their problems developed.

Beck and Freeman (1990) further stated that personality disorders are among the most difficult disorders to change. They attributed this to a variety of factors including the patients' desire to avoid psychotherapy, their reluctance or inability to change, and the fact that change is often at the request of family members or the legal system. Their lack of self-awareness also hampers change efforts.

KEY POINTS

- The definition of abnormal behaviour takes into account several criteria in addition to the low statistical frequency of the abnormal behaviour.
- Self-reports of personality disorder should be supplemented by observer ratings because people with personality disorders often lack self-insight and may be unaware of their problems and impact on other people.
- Personality disorders are difficult to treat, and people with personality disorders often do not respond well to psychologically based interventions.

How should personality disorders be conceptualized? One approach is to regard personality disorder as a failure or inability to formulate adaptive solutions to life tasks (see Livesley, Schroeder, Jackson, & Jang, 1994). Livesley (1998) focused on three life tasks that are particularly significant, and failure to meet the requirements of any of these characteristics could be enough to warrant a personality disorder diagnosis. The three tasks or goals are (1) to form stable, integrated, and coherent representations of self and others; (2) to form intimate and positive affiliations with other people; and (3) to be a useful member of society in that the person can engage in pro-social and co-operative activities.

The ability to form intimate and positive affiliations is especially important because personality disorders are often identified based on extreme, aberrant interpersonal behaviour. The fundamental importance of interpersonal functioning in personality disorders has provided great impetus to the interpersonal study of personality. Researchers who study the interpersonal circumplex have shown that the various interpersonal styles represent a very viable way of highlighting the extreme and intense interpersonal difficulties of some people, and it is also a very useful way of distinguishing among the various personality disorders. Much of this research and conceptualization was conducted in Wiggins' lab at the University of British Columbia (see Pincus & Wiggins, 1990; Wiggins & Pincus,

1989; Wiggins, Trapnell, & Phillips, 1988). The interpersonal circumplex was described in Chapter 10. Anti-social and narcissistic personality disorder reflects extreme dominance, while avoidant personality disorder reflects submissiveness.

Theodore Millon is one of the most prominent theorists in the personality disorders field. Millon (1986) identified three key criteria that help distinguish normal versus disordered personality. First, disordered personality is indicated by rigid and inflexible behaviour. This is an important factor because it means that the afflicted person has difficulty altering his or her behaviour according to changes in the situation. Second, the person engages in self-defeating behaviour that fosters vicious cycles. That is, behaviours and cognitions simply perpetuate and exacerbate existing conditions. Self-defeating behaviour gets us further away from our goals rather than closer to them. Acting in ways that only make things worse was clearly displayed in the case example described by Ellis. Recall that in this instance, extreme hostility only made things worse for Dorothy. Finally, there is structural instability. This is the term Millon uses to refer to a fragility to the self that "cracks" under conditions of stress. This would pertain to a student who functions at a reasonably high level during the early part of a term but loses the ability to cope due to the mounting pressure of multiple deadlines.

KEY POINTS

- Millon posited three useful criteria for establishing personality disorder. First, the person is being rigid and inflexible in his or her tendencies.
- Second, the person is habitually engaging in self-defeating behaviours. Self-defeating behaviour moves us further from our goals rather than closer to them.
- Third, the person has a structural instability to the self so that he or she find it hard to withstand stress and novel situations.

The Psychiatric Approach to Personality Disorders

The attributes outlined above are consistent with the official definitions of personality disorder used in prevailing diagnostic systems. The American Psychiatric Association defines personality disorder as "an enduring pattern of inner experience and behavior that deviates markedly from the expectations of the individual's culture, is pervasive and inflexible" (APA, 1994, p. 629). The deviation is reflected in two or more of the following areas: (1) cognition (ways of interpreting and perceiving the self, others, and the world); (2) affect (the range, intensity, lability, and appropriateness of the emotional response); (3) interpersonal functioning; and (4) impulse control. Thus, personality disorders typically involve aberrations and dysfunctions in terms of the self, interpersonal relationships, affective responses, and thinking patterns. In addition, the pattern is inflexible and generalizes across situational contexts, and it is a stable and long-standing pattern that can be distressed back to adolescence. Finally, as mentioned earlier, the pattern involves significant distress or impairment.

A similar definition of personality disorder guides the criteria developed by the World Health Organization. These criteria form the ICD-10 (International Classification of Diseases, 10th edition) Classification of Mental and Behavioural Disorders. A personality disorder is a severe disturbance in the characterological constitution and behavioural tendencies of the individual, usually involving several areas of the personality, and nearly always associated with considerable personal and social disruption.

There are 10 personality disorders in the Diagnostic and Statistical Manual of Mental Disorders, fourth edition (DSM-IV; APA, 1994). These personality disorders are grouped into three personality disorder clusters: odd–eccentric, dramatic–emotional, and anxious–fearful. These clusters are described in more detail later in this chapter.

The prevailing system used in psychiatry to diagnose and classify people with suspected mental illness is flawed in several respects. One problem is the issue of **comorbidity**. The ultimate goal of the diagnostician is to identify the one diagnosis that pertains to someone, yet most people with a diagnosable disorder rarely qualify for just one disorder, and they typically have two or more disorders. People are often diagnosed with two or more disorders in part because the categories are imprecisely defined and they have overlap. In most instances, it is simply the case that severely disordered individuals have enough characteristics to fulfill the criteria for multiple categories. This inability to arrive at a single diagnosis undermines the categorical approach and suggests that it might make more sense instead to characterize people based on their scores on several personality dimensions.

Howard Hughes had characteristics and symptoms of several disorders (i.e., co-morbidity).

If two or more disorders exist, then the person is said to have comorbid diagnoses, with greater dysfunction being associated with a greater number of disorders. An example would be Howard Hughes, whose life story provided the basis for the movie *The Aviator*. Hughes, as portrayed by Leonardo DiCaprio, suffered from many problems throughout his life, and he probably could have been diagnosed with several psychological disorders (e.g., narcissistic personality disorder) in addition to his primary diagnosis of obsessive–compulsive disorder.

Comedian Roseanne Barr is another celebrity with comorbid disorders. In 2006, she stated on *Larry King Live* that "I was diagnosed with 15... disorders." Barr alleged that as a child she experienced physical and sexual abuse from both her father and mother.

Empirical research indicates that comorbidity is normative when personality disorder is involved. Studies have shown that if a patient meets criteria for one personality disorder, then there is an 80% probability that the patient will meet criteria for a second personality disorder (Livesley, 1998).

Perhaps the biggest problem is that the personality disorder categories were not theoretically or empirically derived; rather, they mostly reflect the subjective views of the American psychiatric community. Although we will discuss three clusters, this is primarily a useful heuristic device for descriptive purposes because empirical research shows that the personality disorders do not break neatly and tidily into the three clusters that are described below (see Livesley, 1998). The clusters were formed to group together disorders that seem to share a common theme, but the use of clusters obscures some of the important differences among the various personality disorders.

Personality Disorder Dimensions

Empirical tests of the categorical versus dimensional view have provided extensive support for a dimensional conceptualization of personality disorders (e.g., Livesley et al., 1994), and this has been shown with a variety of methodologies. For example, personality traits (e.g., social apprehensiveness, oppositionality) have been shown to be continuous for both general population and clinical samples (Livesley, Jackson, & Schroeder, 1992). The basic premise is that disordered personality represents one extreme end of a continuum and normal personality lies along the same continuum (Widiger & Frances, 1985). This conclusion has been supported by a recent comprehensive review of the available evidence (see Trull & Durrett, 2005). This conclusion was based on studies such as the one conducted by Morey et al. (2000). The participants were 144 patients with various diagnosed Axis II disorders with the most common ones being avoidant, borderline, paranoid, dependent, and obsessive–compulsive personality disorders. They completed self-report measures tapping the five-factor model and personality disorder symptoms. Morey et al. (2000) concluded that the differences among the personality disorders reflected "subtle shadings rather than extremes of orthogonal dimensions" (p. 212) and, overall, there was "a remarkable configural similarity ... of the dimensional profiles for the 11 DSM-III-R personality disorders when compared to the general population at large" (p. 214).

O'Connor and Dyce at Lakehead University in Ontario have shown similarly that dimensional differences exist when characterizing normal versus abnormal personality; personality disorders reflect extreme and rigid response tendencies that differ in degree, not in kind, from the responses of people without disorders (O'Connor, 2002; O'Connor & Dyce, 2001). Thus, the personality disorders can be construed as the extremes of characteristics we all possess.

The one exception seems to be personality disorder in the form of psychopathy. Psychopathy is the psychological component of anti-social personality disorder. Canadian researchers have provided some evidence to suggest that the psychopathy may represent a discrete category (Skilling, Harris, Rice, & Quinsey, 2002). This means that a person cannot be a little high or moderately high on psychopathy; the person either is a psychopath or is not a psychopath. Overall, however, a dimensional approach seems to apply to most other personality characteristics.

If a dimensional approach is valid and normal, and disordered personality is continuous, then it is not surprising that behavioural genetics research has shown comparable heritability rates for both normal and disordered personality traits (Livesley, Jang, Jackson, & Vernon, 1993; Plomin, Chuiper, & Loehlin, 1990). Livesley et al. (1993) investigated heritability rates for personality disorders. Studies of twins have demonstrated heritability rates for normal personality traits to be in the range of 40 to 60% (Plomin et al., 1990). Livesley et al. (1993) have shown that heritability rates for most personality disorder dimensions are in the range of 40 to 60% (i.e., for 12 of 18 personality disorder dimensions, such as suspiciousness and narcissism). Livesley et al. (1993) also found higher correlations for monozygotic twins compared with dizygotic twins. These results, with respect to heritability, have also been found to be similar in a German twin sample (Jang, McCrae, Angleitner, Riemann, & Livesley, 1998).

Is it possible to somehow combine a dimensional and categorical approach? Livesley and Jang (2000) have proposed a two-phase approach in which clinicians first determine whether a personality disorder exists in general terms and then establish the specific nature of the disorder via dimensional ratings on a series of personality trait dimensions.

If there is continuity and a dimensional approach is appropriate, then there should not be extensive evidence of cross-cultural differences in personality disorders. What does the evidence indicate? International Focus on Discovery 13.1 examines personality disorders and personality dysfunction from a cross-cultural perspective.

KEY POINTS

- The categorical approach reflects the psychiatric approach to classification and diagnosis. Several pieces of evidence argue against the categorical approach including the great comorbidity that exists with more severe dysfunction involving multiple diagnoses.
- One possibility is that the categorical approach is marred by subjective and ill-defined personality disorder categories.
- The empirical evidence strongly favours the dimensional approach. The main exception is psychopathy, which seems to reflect a category variable.

International Focus on Discovery 13.1 Personality Disorders across Cultures

Given that frameworks such as the five-factor model are supposed to be universally applicable, and there is strong evidence for a dimensional approach to personality disorders, it follows that there should be substantial similarities across cultures in the symptoms and prevalence of personality disorders. However, Joel Paris, a psychiatrist based in Montreal, suggests that there should be widespread differences (see Paris, 1998). His view emphasizes the sociocultural roots of personality disorders. He has maintained that personality disorders that emphasize the contents and fragility of the self-concept should be more evident in individualistic cultures than in collectivist cultures. Also, the social structure in collectivistic nations provides a source of social support that protects individuals from experiencing personality disorders.

What does the empirical evidence indicate? It seems that the answer to this issue depends greatly on how the issue is evaluated. Cross-cultural analyses of the structure of personality disorder symptoms tend to support the cross-cultural generalizability issue. For instance, a study of the structure of personality disorders in China tested large samples of psychiatric patients and obtained substantial evidence of cross-cultural generalizability (Yang, Bagby, Costa, Ryder, & Herbst, 2002). The authors concluded that factor analyses with self-report and interview data replicated the four-factor structure that was obtained with North American samples (see O'Connor & Dyce, 1998). The authors concluded that the dimensions underlying personality disorders are cross-culturally generalizable to Chinese people.

Another study of personality disorders in a sample of depressed Japanese patients found that the prevalence rates of most personality disorders was comparable to the rates found in North American samples (Sato et al., 1997). Surprisingly, narcissistic personality disorder and schizoid personality disorder were more evident than expected in the Japanese sample. Another comparative test of the symptoms of borderline personality disorder in Japanese versus American patients found that the symptoms were virtually identical across the two groups (Ikuta et al., 1994). Other research with Dutch psychiatric samples used the NEO-PI-R (NEO Personality Inventory-Revised) and the PSY-5 (Psychopathy-Five) to confirm the structure of the five-factor model (Egger, DeMey, Derksen, & van der Staak, 2003). Also, the pattern of correlations between the NEO-PI-R and PSY-5 factors were very similar to the results obtained with North American samples.

A test of a German version of Livesley's DAPP-BQ (Dimensional Assessment of Personality Pathology Basic Questionnaire) in a mixed German sample composed of patients and control participants provided strong support for the four higher-order factors of the DAPP-BQ (emotional dysregulation, dissocial behaviour, inhibitedness, and compulsivity). Also, the measure's validity was shown by linking these factors with dimensions ratings of personality disorder symptoms (Pukrop, Gentil, Steinbring, & Steinmeyer, 2001). Another study of the DAPP-BQ in a Chinese sample yielded findings that were quite comparable to those found with North American samples. The only exception was the lack of a clear intimacy factor. Overall, the authors concluded that the DAPP-BQ seems be culturally invariant (see Zheng et al., 2002).

Another line of investigation has focused on the cross-cultural application of the Hare's PCL-R (Psychopathology Checklist-Revised), and strong support has been found for the psychometric properties and comparability of this measure of psychopathy across cultures (Hare, Clark, Grann, & Thornton, 2000). Although the nature of the psychopathy construct seems to be similar across cultures, Hare (1998) has raised the possibility that there are cross-national differences in the overt expression of psychopathy. This observation is supported by comparative research on the PCL-R in Scotland versus the United States. A study conducted in Glasgow by Cooke and Michie (1999) found that the nature of the construct when evaluated in 246 Scottish prisoners was very similar to the results found in North American samples. However, there was a dramatic difference in the level of psychopathy, with the level being much lower in Scotland. Sophisticated item analyses also showed that extremely high levels of individual items had to be present in the Scottish sample before the symptoms representing psychopathy (superficial charm, lack of empathy, and irresponsibility) were clearly evident.

This study is remarkable in that it has yielded one of the few cross-cultural differences so far! In their discussion of their results, Cooke and Michie (1999) considered other factors that serve as alternative explanations that could have influenced their results. This discussion underscores the complex concerns facing personality researchers conducting cross-cultural research when differences are found across cultures. In this instance, Cooke and Michie speculated that perhaps there were different tendencies among interviewers with different nationalities, and this factor needs to be controlled. They also noted that psychopaths tend to migrate to urban centres because they have more opportunity to take advantage of their glib charm and manipulate others. They speculated that rates of psychopathy in Scotland were lower because many of the psychopaths had migrated to cities in other countries. Thus, even when differences are found, interpreting these differences can be a difficult matter.

A final study by Oishi and Diener (2001) points to the possibility that perhaps the main difference across cultures is not in the expression and nature of personality disorders and other forms of psychopathology. Rather, perhaps the key difference lies in the goals we pursue and how we evaluate and value our goal progress. These authors found that independent goal pursuit (for personal enjoyment) had a much stronger impact on subjective well-being and happiness following goal attainment for European Americans than it did for Asian Americans. In contrast, Asian American students and Japanese college students derived their happiness and well-being from the pursuit and attainment of interdependent goals (to please friends and parents). Thus, there may be key differences in the self-evaluative cues and motives we used to judge ourselves.

PERSONALITY DISORDER CLUSTERS

When a categorical approach is used, and DSM-IV criteria are involved, personality disorders are grouped into three clusters. Each cluster is described below, and one or more personality disorders within the cluster is examined in more detail.

Cluster A

The first cluster is referred to as Cluster A. The three personality disorders in this category are paranoid personality disorder, schizoid personality disorder, and schizotypal personality disorder. The personality disorders within a cluster tend to share a similar theme. In this instance, Cluster A personality disorders reflect a tendency to be odd or eccentric. The oddness here is most marked with respect to a lack of or avoidance of social contact.

The schizoid and schizotypal personality disorders are regarded as components of what is referred to as schizophrenia spectrum disorders. They involve a lack of meaningful connectedness and interaction with others. Schizophrenia was described initially as "the shut-in personality," referring to the fact that people with schizophrenic and schizotypal characteristics suffer from a deterioration and disintegration of the self that makes it very difficult for them to relate to others and express themselves in the ways that more sociable individuals relate to others. The personality features here include a schizoid form of introversion that involves being cold and distant to others, with low positive emotions and a desire to be alone (see Widiger et al., 1994).

Whereas people with the schizoid or schizotypal personality disorder may maintain a distance from others due to a lack of social skill or a general state of confusion, the person with the paranoid personality disorder remains distant from others because of a highly negative cognitive orientation that involves great suspiciousness of others. People with this diagnosis are continually on the lookout for trouble because they expect to be mistreated or exploited by others. They are wary and vigilantly scan for possible signs of trickery and abuse. Such individuals are reluctant to confide in others and tend to blame others even when they themselves are at fault.

Recall the case of the "Unabomber," Ted Kaczynski, described in Chapter 9. He was diagnosed by psychiatrist Dr. Sally Johnson as having paranoid personality disorder with anti-social features. Kaczynski had a deep conviction that technology and corporate influences had evolved to take control over the individual person. He expressed his frustration by engaging in violent acts.

The Unabomber's beliefs fit with the results of a study conducted in Israel by Kreitler and Kreitler (1997). Their analysis of cognitive beliefs found that a paranoid view of the self and the world was associated with admiring the strength and authority of others, as well as a desire for freedom from control. The paranoid view of the self also emphasized personal weakness and fears of being controlled by forces outside the self.

The cognitive theory of personality disorders outlined by Beck and Freeman and their associates is a very viable and interesting way of conceptualizing the different personality disorders. The cognitive approach illustrates the beliefs of people with various personality disorders and how they perceive themselves and other people. Table 13.1 outlines the main beliefs and cognitive views of the self and others that are associated not only with the Cluster A disorders but also with the Cluster B and Cluster C disorders that will be discussed later. Table 13.1 also outlines the main behavioural strategies associated with each personality disorder. Paranoid personality disorder includes a self model emphasizing vulnerability and innocence, along with a cynical model of other people as interfering, malicious, and possibly abusive. The main cognitive set of these people involves beliefs that others are to be mistrusted, and it is important to be hypervigilant and on guard for imminent mistreatment of the self. Indeed, an analysis of facets of disagreeableness (antagonistic traits) confirmed that there is a strong association between the facet measuring lack of trust and the symptoms of paranoid personality disorder (Axelrod, Widiger, Trull, & Corbitt, 1997).

Table 13.1 Personality Disorders from a Cognitive Perspective

Personality Disorder	View of Self	View of Others	Main Beliefs	Main Strategy
Avoidant	Vulnerable to depreciation, rejection Socially inept Incompetent	Critical Demeaning Superior	It's terrible to be rejected, put down If people know the real me, they will reject me I can't tolerate unpleasant feelings	Avoid evaluative situations Avoid unpleasant feelings or thoughts
Dependent	Needy Weak Helpless Incompetent	(Idealized) Nurturant Supportive Competent	Need people to survive, be happy Need for steady flow of support and encouragement	Cultivate dependent relationships
Passive-Aggressive	Self-sufficient Vulnerable to control, interference	Intrusive Demanding Interfering Controlling Dominating	Others interfere with my freedom of action Control by others is intolerable Have to do things my own way	Passive resistance Surface submissiveness Evade, circumvent rules
Obsessive-Compulsive	Responsible Accountable Fastidious Competent	Irresponsible Casual Incompetent Self-indulgent	I know what's best Details are crucial People should be better, try harder	Apply rules Perfectionism Evaluate, control Shoulds, criticize, punish
Paranoid	Righteous Innocent, noble Vulnerable	Interfering Malicious Discriminatory Abusive motives	Motives are suspect Be on guard Don't trust	Wary Look for hidden motives Accuse Counterattack

Anti-social	Loner Autonomous Strong	Vulnerable Exploitative	Entitled to break rules Others are patsies, wimps Others are exploitative	Attack, rob Deceive Manipulate
Narcissistic	Special, unique Deserves special rules; superior Above the rules	Inferior Admirers	Since I'm special, I deserve special rules I'm above the rules I'm better than others	Use others Transcend rules Manipulative Competitive
Histrionic	Glamorous Impressive	Seducible Receptive Admirers	People are there to serve or admire me They have no right to deny me my just desserts	Use dramatics, charm; temper tantrums, crying; suicide gestures
Schizoid	Self-sufficient Loner	Intrusive	Others are unrewarding Relationships are messy, undesirable	Stay away

Source: Leahy, Beck, & Beck, 2004.

Behavioural responses as a strategy include looking for signs of the hidden motives of others, provoking others by accusing them of acting in a hostile manner or intending to do so, and revenge because of the need to pay back others. Treatment according to the cognitive perspective involves replacing maladaptive beliefs and views of the self and others with more adaptive and healthy beliefs and views.

The cognitive beliefs of paranoid individuals may be fuelled to some extent by public self-consciousness (see Chapter 11). Fenigstein and Vanable (1992) created a self-report measure called the Paranoia Scale and showed that paranoia was linked with elevated public self-consciousness. Various authors have noted that the inner self of those with paranoid personality disorder may be quite fragile and markedly different from the personality displayed in public (see Akhtar, 1990; Shapiro, 1965). That is, they may outwardly seem to be strong people who are demanding, arrogant, and mistrustful, yet inwardly they are frightened and timid and very sensitive to criticism and mistreatment.

Cluster B

Cluster B personality disorders include the anti-social personality disorder, the borderline personality disorder, the histrionic personality disorder, and the narcissistic personality disorder. The shared theme among disorders is that they all reflect *dramatic and erratic* behaviours. These behaviours can be very extrapunitive and hostile. As seen in Table 13.1, these disorders reflect hostile interpersonal beliefs; that is, other people exist primarily to be used and taken advantage of (anti-social personality disorder) or to give attention and adoration to the self (narcissistic and histrionic personality disorders).

An extreme example of hostile behaviour that seems to fit this description was related to this author by a student. The student wanted to study histrionic personality disorder because of an incident involving a friend. The student was always concerned about her friend's extreme attention-seeking behaviours, but things seem to boil over at the friend's wedding. At one point in the ceremony, the bride (who had arranged the room so that it was perfectly symmetrical around her location) became upset because she was not receiving enough attention. (How many brides don't get enough attention?) She finally lost her temper and jumped up on the head table and starting flinging dinner plates at the guests! This extreme example of dramatic, erratic, and hostile behaviour should give pause to those who are considering the joys of matrimony!

Three of the four Cluster B disorders (anti-social, borderline, and narcissistic personality disorders) have been the subject of extensive theoretical and empirical attention. The anti-social personality disorder is diagnosed if highly anti-social behaviour resulted in the diagnosis of a conduct disorder prior to the age of 15 and the symptoms persist in adulthood. Signs and symptoms of conduct disorder include frequent lying, theft, arson, and property destruction. Anti-social personality disorder is fairly common, with one community study conducted in Edmonton, Alberta finding that 3% of respondents met diagnostic criteria for anti-social personality disorder (Swanson, Bland, & Newman, 1994).

Anti-Social Personality Disorder and Psychopathy

A subset of people with anti-social personality disorder have a more extreme condition known as **psychopathy**. People with psychopathy have no sense of shame or remorse when they engage in extremely anti-social acts (Cleckley, 1976). They often have a glib sense of charm and a superior ability to manipulate people, who often become the target of violent behaviour. Psychopaths can engage in extreme acts of violence, including homicides. Comparisons of homicides committed by psychopaths versus non-psychopaths indicates that psychopaths are more likely to commit cold-blooded murder for instrumental reasons (i.e., premeditated acts for personal gains such as getting money) (see Woodsworth & Porter, 2002). However, when asked to describe their violence, psychopaths portray their murderous acts as more reactive than indicated by official crime reports, and they minimize the instrumental and premeditated aspects (Porter & Woodsworth, 2006). This could reflect their attempts to charm, mislead, and manipulate people.

Psychopathy is commonly assessed with the Psychopathy Checklist–Revised (PCL-R), which was developed by **Robert Hare** and his associates at the University of British Columbia (Hare, 1991). The PCL-R consists of 20 items rated by the assessor on a three-point scale. It has two factors. Factor 1 measures emotional detachment, while Factor 2 measures an unstable, anti-social, and impulsive lifestyle. Psychopathy, as assessed by the PCL-R, is often comorbid with abuse of alcohol and other drugs (Smith & Newman, 1990).

Aileen Wuornos is an example of a person who was diagnosed with psychopathy. Wuornos is the woman who was executed in Florida for the serial murders of seven men. Her story was depicted in the movie *Monster*, with Wuornos portrayed by Charlize Theron. Wuornos was assessed as part of her incarceration. She was diagnosed with anti-social personality disorder, borderline personality disorder, and psychopathy (see Myers, Grooch, & Meloy, 2005). Her psychopathy was revealed by a score of 32 on the PCL-R. A score of

Serial killer Aileen Wuornos was diagnosed with psychopathy and anti-social personality disorder prior to her execution in Florida.

30 or more in North America is the cut-off for psychopathy (Hare, 2003). Her dysfunction was attributed to childhood attachment disruptions and a traumatic history of abuse.

Experts are quite negative about the prospects of using psychologically based treatment interventions to change people characterized as psychopaths or as having extreme forms of anti-social personality disorder. It is believed that psychopathy involves a level of dysfunction that is so extreme, little can be done to improve the mindset and tendencies of psychopathic individuals (Rice, 1997), and there is evidence that psychopaths are quite likely to reoffend in a violent manner (Rice, 1997). This stands in stark contrast to the belief that matching personality features to a particular therapy can result in substantial improvements for people with other disorders (see Applied Perspective 13.1 later in the chapter).

Narcissistic Personality Disorder

Narcissistic personality disorder (NPD) is included along with anti-social personality disorder as a Cluster B disorder, but it is quite different from anti-social personality disorder. NPD is based on the ancient Greek myth about Narcissus, who fell in love with his own reflection in a pool of water and remains transfixed forever as he is fascinated by his own beauty. By extension, people with NPD have a grandiose view of their specialness; they are preoccupied with their possible greatness, and they have a level of self-focus that is unparalleled compared with most other personality disorders. They have a desire to be with equally special people but often respond with jealousy and anger when in the presence of these people because others might get the attention that they feel they deserve and absolutely must have. The self-focus means that they are exceptionally arrogant and have very little empathy or concern for others.

The person with NPD projects an image of their own personal importance, and this often takes the form of a profound sense of entitlement; they feel that they deserve special favours. Anyone who does not pay them adequate attention or grant them the favours that they feel entitled to is likely to experience the scorn of the seemingly superior narcissist. Constantly seeking attention and adulation, narcissistic personalities are very sensitive to criticism and deeply fearful of failure. Sometimes they seek out others whom they can idealize because they are disappointed in themselves, but others are not allowed to become genuinely close. Their relationships are few and shallow; people with NPD become angry and rejecting when people fall short of their unrealistic expectations. Their inner lives are impoverished, because despite their self-aggrandizement, they have a very fragile self-image and, at some implicit, unconscious level, they have a negative sense of themselves.

Consider the following example. At the break in the introductory class of a new course, a student bounds down the steps to inform the professor that he has stepped on his shoelace (something the professor is well aware of). Sensing that great difficulties lie ahead with this student, in response to a question about the reading, the professor suggests that the course has an exceptionally heavy reading load (since it is an abbreviated summer course) and it might be better to take the course in the regular term. The student, without batting an eye, tells the professor that the reading is no problem. Also, the student, in all seriousness, says, "Why not just give me an A+ now, since I am going to get an A+ anyway? This will save everyone's time and effort!" Similar narcissistic characteristics are revealed during the student's interactions with the teaching assistant. The exasperated TA finally reaches the point where he asks the professor to give a lecture on narcissistic personality disorder while looking directly at the offending student the entire time. Just as the professor refused to grant the automatic A+, he also declined the TA's request.

Years of inquiry have confirmed that the narcissism construct is complex and multidimensional. The Narcissistic Personality Inventory (NPI; Raskin & Hall, 1981) is the most widely used and studied self-report measure of the construct. Analyses have established that the NPI has four factors: (1) leadership/authority; (2) superiority/arrogance; (3) self-absorption/self-admiration; and (4) exploitativeness/entitlement. Extensive research on these four NPI dimensions suggests that the first three factors are relatively adaptive, while the fourth factor of exploitativeness/entitlement is consistently maladaptive (see Emmons, 1987). For instance, the leadership/authority factor has been linked with characteristics such as optimism, high self-esteem, and low social anxiety (for a review, see Sturman, 2000). Evidence that certain elements of narcissism may be adaptive are in keeping with observations that it is normal for most people to have some element of narcissism, and a smaller subset of narcissists have the more pathological forms of the disorder.

One problem with the notion of "adaptive narcissism" is that research findings that constitute evidence of adaptive narcissism are often based exclusively on self-report measures. Do narcissists have enough self-awareness to know that other people do not tend to like narcissists, and that narcissism may cause social problems? The need to supplement self-reports with informative ratings and perhaps observations from a clinician was discussed in Chapter 4, and this point is particularly important when it comes to evaluating the research literature on disorders such as narcissistic personality disorder. Research in general has illustrated that it is vitally important to supplement self-assessments of personality disorder with informant ratings. For example, Klein's (2003) seven-year investigation of personality disorders in patients with a diagnosis of depression showed that reports from both the patients and the informants uniquely predicted follow-up measures of global functioning and depression, but only the informant ratings predicted the patients' level of social functioning. Westen's (1997) survey of clinicians showed that they felt almost uniformly that the opportunity for them to observe a person's behaviour during a clinical interview and to observe their interactions with significant others were both essential and central to any personality disorder diagnosis. That is, they emphasized **signs** (cues spotted by the clinician) expressed by often oblivious patients. Westen and Shedler developed the Shedler-Westen Assessment Procedure (or SWAP-200) to assess personality disorders. The SWAP is a Q-sort technique that requires the clinician to sort 200 personality statements into piles varying in relevance as a way of describing the patient. The personality dimensions evaluated in the SWAP are shown later in this chapter in a comparative summary table (see Table 13.2).

As for narcissism, several authors have evaluated the association between self-reported narcissism and informant ratings, and the results generally indicate that there is often a great divergence between how narcissistic people see themselves and how other people see them. Klonsky et al. (2002) conducted a quantitative review of past studies on the agreement between self-reports and informant reports of various personality disorders. The levels of agreement across 10 personality disorders ranged from correlations of .29 to .56, but the lowest level of agreement was found for narcissistic personality disorder! The highest levels of agreement were found for disorders such as anti-social and borderline personality disorder, perhaps because these disorders involve more dramatic, erratic, and visible forms of behaviour. The visibility factor is quite important. A study of self-reports and peer ratings with Clark's (1993) Schedule for Nonadaptive and Adaptive Personality (SNAP) found that agreement was substantially lower on "difficult-to-judge" traits (Ready, Clark, Watson, & Westerhouse, 2000). The dimensions tapped by the SNAP are shown also in Table 13.2. When a trait domain proved difficult to rate, a phenomenon the authors referred to as the **self-based heuristic** came into play; that is, the ratings of difficult-to-rate traits became more reflective of the rater's personality features.

We are left to reconcile the adaptive self-reports of certain narcissists with the highly negative accounts of people suffering from NPD. Part of the answer here may involve the distinction between explicit and implicit self-esteem (see Chapter 11). Jordan et al. (2003) have shown that narcissists are defensive externals in that they report high levels of self-esteem, yet implicit self-esteem measures suggest that they are actually quite defensive, albeit at an unconscious level. This is in keeping with the view that narcissistic people have a very fragile sense of self. Their defensiveness may also blind them to the social consequences of the narcissistic personality style.

An Internet-based study investigated whether scores on the NPI vary according to the respondent's age, sex, and world region (see Foster, Campbell, & Twenge, 2003). This study of almost 3,500 participants found that narcissism declines in successive age groups from 15 years of age to 54 years of age, and then there is a slight increase in participants aged 55 years and older. Also, males have higher scores than females. Finally, as might be expected, narcissism is higher in individualistic societies than in collectivistic societies. The highest levels of narcissism were found in the United States and in European countries. The lowest NPI scores were found among respondents from the Middle East.

Cluster C personality disorders are described below. First, however, one final point about informant ratings needs to be expressed. Contemporary research by Achenbach has surveyed the adult psychopathology literature and he concluded that relatively few studies involve informant reports. Achenbach has suggested that two or more informants are needed, since any one rater can be biased or inaccurate. Overall, it was found that only 108 of 51,000 studies (0.2%) included cross-informant correlations (see Achenbach, 2006). It was concluded that cross-informant issues are being neglected for the most part when it comes to the study of adult psychopathology. Thus, once again, there is far too much reliance on self-reports, and this is a problem when constructs such as narcissism are involved.

KEY POINTS

- Narcissism is a multidimensional construct with maladaptive and adaptive components (e.g., leadership).
- People with high levels of narcissism are especially likely to lack self-awareness. Their self-reports should be supplemented with observer/informant reports.
- Narcissism scores tend to be lower among older people, females, and people from collectivistic cultures.

Cluster C

Cluster C personality disorders include avoidant personality disorder, dependent personality disorder, and the obsessive–compulsive personality disorder. The shared theme that applies here is a high level of fearfulness. The beliefs outlined in Table 13.1 indicated that the reasons for this fearfulness vary across the disorders. The reason could be agitation because other people are unrewarding (schizoid personality disorder) and rejecting (avoidant personality disorder) or because the self is weak and requires protection and comfort from other people (dependent personality disorder).

Given the common theme of fearfulness, it is not surprising that personality disorder symptoms reflecting all three disorders in this category are linked with an anxious, fearful attachment style and a preoccupied attached style (Brennan & Shaver, 1998). However, dependent personality disorder was unique in its much stronger link with the preoccupied attachment style.

The dependent personality disorder and the dependency construct have received the most attention in the literature thus far. Accordingly, we will discuss this disorder in greater detail.

Dependent Personality Disorder

People with symptoms of dependent personality disorder tend to rely excessively on other people, perhaps as a way of compensating for a weak self-image (while they see other people as powerful). Not surprisingly, an insecure and preoccupied form of attachment style is at the root of dependent personality disorder (Brennan & Shaver, 1998). They also have an intense need to be taken care of, which makes them feel uncomfortable when alone; they may be preoccupied with fears of being left alone to take care of themselves. Thus, they may be prone to feelings of separation anxiety.

Because of the need to maintain interpersonal relationships, people with dependent personality disorder will be most forgiving and willing to overlook the shortcomings and behavioural excesses of the people they wish to be with. They will make sacrifices and neglect their own personal wishes if it will help them maintain proximity with significant others.

In contrast to people with other personality vulnerability factors that decrease the likelihood of seeking help, people high in dependency are particularly likely to seek out treatment, and it is important to them to foster an alliance with their doctors or therapists. This was shown most recently by O'Neill and Bornstein (2001). They compared patients with high versus low dependency and showed that higher dependency was associated with more medical consultations and receiving a greater number of medications.

Robert Bornstein is one of the most prominent theorists and researchers studying dependency and dependent personality disorder. A unifying theme of his work is the desire to understand more about the nature of the dependency construct and its antecedents. For instance, he suggested that dependency is best regarded as four distinguishable components: the cognitive, motivational, emotional, and behavioural aspects of dependency (see Bornstein, 1993). The cognitive component involves mentally representing the self as powerless and others as powerful. The motivational component is the constant need for support from others. The emotional component is the anxiety-based reaction when isolated from significant others. Finally, the behavioural component is the acts of help-seeking and reassurance-seeking that are designed to increase proximity to others.

What would you expect to find if looking at the link between dependency and the five-factor model? A meta-analysis reported by Bornstein and Cecero (2000) confirmed that there were small to moderate significant correlations between dependency and all five factors. Specifically, high dependency was associated with elevated levels of neuroticism and agreeableness and low levels of extroversion, openness, and conscientiousness. The low to moderate correlations led Bornstein and Cecero (2000) to conclude that the five-factor model captured a "relatively modest" proportion of the variance in dependency scores.

Other research by Bornstein has suggested that there are both adaptive and maladaptive forms of dependency (see Bornstein, 1998). At milder levels, dependency may foster a sense of connectedness and enhance social relations. In contrast, maladaptive dependency involves too much connectedness with others and excessive need to seek reassurance. Bornstein has also raised the issue that the adaptiveness or maladaptiveness of dependency may vary by culture; clearly, dependency may be normative and expected in cultures with a collectivist orientation and an emphasis on the interconnectedness of people.

A comprehensive study by Pincus and Gurtman (1995) illustrates the various ways that dependency can be expressed. Interpersonal circumplex analyses revealed that the dependency construct consisted of three types: (1) love dependency (e.g., being isolated from others is bound to lead to unhappiness); (2) exploitable dependency (e.g., "I am afraid of hurting other people's feelings"); and (3) submissive dependency (e.g.,

"I would rather be a follower than a leader"). All three forms of dependency were associated with neuroticism. Pincus and Gurtman (1995) suggested that all three factors may be associated with vulnerability to depression as a result of loss, but the type of loss needs to be closely examined. They observed that submissive dependents may become depressed after the loss of a relationship with an influential mentor or guide, while love dependents may become depressed after the loss of a nurturing relationship with an attachment figure.

We will return to the role of dependency in psychological distress in our subsequent discussion of the role of personality factors in depression. Clearly, people are prone to distress if they have extreme dependency needs that are not being satisfied by their interpersonal relationships.

Psychotherapy and Personality Disorder Clusters

Paris (2004) has summarized the differences in psychotherapy issues for patients with disorders from the three clusters. Patients with a disorder from Cluster A do not tend to seek psychotherapy, and there has been relatively little empirical investigation of their treatment responses. Their main problem is a difficulty in sustaining interpersonal relationships. Patients with a disorder from Cluster B are difficult to treat, and psychotherapy, according to Paris, must be quite pragmatic. A unifying theme is that these patients need structure in their lives, and they can benefit from social structures to increase attachment security or facilitate their competence, achievement, and persistence in work. A central goal is to make them less dependent and responsive to external reinforcers such as power and sexual attraction. Finally, patients with Cluster C personality disorders have self-sustaining anxieties, and the goal is to prevent them from engaging in the usual avoidance behaviours. Care must be taken to not encourage dependency in the therapy session or permit them to procrastinate about therapy.

KEY POINTS

- The personality disorder clusters are best regarded as heuristic categories. In reality, a dimensional approach is probably more valid.
- The personality disorders in a cluster all reflect a common, shared theme.
- There are three clusters in total. Cluster A reflects odd, eccentric behaviour. Cluster B reflects dramatic and erratic behaviour. Cluster C reflects fearful behaviour.

DIMENSIONAL MODELS AND PERSONALITY DYSFUNCTION

We now turn our attention to dimensional models that have been applied to personality dysfunction. Various models have been suggested, and all seem relevant for different reasons. The fact that numerous frameworks have been outlined is a reflection of the heterogeneity and the numerous forms that personality dysfunction has taken.

Cloninger's Tridimensional Model

C. Robert Cloninger's tridimensional model is one of the most influential models of personality and psychopathology. This model combines temperament-based factors with three character factors. Temperament accounts for the initial development of disorder, and the character factors help determine the specific type of disorder expressed.

A unique feature of this model is its biological roots. Cloninger (1987a, 1987b) suggested that brain systems associated with behavioural activation and behavioural inhibition are associated with three genetically inherited dimensions of personality: novelty seeking, harm avoidance, and reward dependence. These dimensions are assessed by Cloninger's Temperament and Character Inventory. Cloninger conceptualized temperament as biological biases in automatic responses to emotional stimuli. According to Cloninger, temperament is moderately heritable and is stable throughout life, regardless of culture or social experiences.

The harm avoidance concept is similar to the harm avoidance concept espoused by Murray (1938). Harm avoidance has four facets: anticipatory worry, fear of uncertainty, shyness, and fatigability, which reflects the strain of constantly being on alert for possible threats. Harm avoidance has been linked with depression, anxiety, and anxiety sensitivity (Ongur, Farabaugh, Iosifescu, Perlis, & Fava, 2005). Harm avoidance is associated with levels of serotonin. Serotonin is also a neurotransmitter believed to be involved in affective disorders, such as anxiety and depression.

Novelty seeking is highly relevant to various behavioural disorders, including problems related to addiction. Novelty seeking also has four facets: explanatory excitability, impulsiveness, extravagance, and disorderliness. Novelty seeking is associated with levels of dopamine. Dopamine acts as a neurotransmitter or chemical produced in the body and is actually a neurohormone released by the hypothalamus in the brain.

Reward dependence reflects a sensitivity to punishment and reinforcement. Reward dependence, as conceptualized by Cloninger, has interpersonal aspects. It involves the three elements of dependence, attachment, and sentimentality. Reward dependence is associated with norepinephrine, which is also a neurotransmitter involved in chemical communication in the sympathetic nervous system.

Cloninger et al. (1993) found that the three personality disorder clusters lined up with the three temperament dimensions. Cluster A disorders (e.g., paranoid personality disorder) were linked with low reward dependence. Cluster B disorders were associated with high novelty seeking. Finally, Cluster C disorders were associated with high harm avoidance.

Recently, the tridimensional model has become a bit of a misnomer because the three main dimensions of temperament suggested above (harm avoidance, novelty seeking, reward dependence) have been supplemented by a fourth dimension known as persistence. All four dimensions and their facets are shown in Table 13.2. Persistence is the tenacious goal-directed behaviour that reflects a high activity level. Inclusion of the persistence dimension adds a motivational temperament component. Persistence was likely included, at least in part, to add an element that would reflect individual differences.

Table 13.2 Some Dimensional Models of Personality Disorder

TCI[1]	FFM[2]	DAPP-BQ[3]	SNAP[4]	SWAP-200[5]
Novelty seeking	Neuroticism	Compulsivity	Mistrust	Psychological health
Exploratory excitability	Anxiousness	Conduct problems	Manipulation	Psychopathy
Impulsiveness	Angry hostility	Diffidence	Aggression	Hostility
Extravagance	Depressiveness	Identity problems	Self-harm	Narcissism
Disorderliness	Self-consciousness	Insecure attachment	Eccentric perceptions	Emotional dysregulation
Harm avoidance	Impulsiveness	Intimacy problems	Dependency	Dysphoria
Anticipatory worry	Vulnerability	Narcissism	Exhibitionism	Schizoid orientation
Fear of uncertainty	Extroversion	Suspiciousness	Entitlement	Obsessionality
Shyness	Warmth	Affective lability	Detachment	Thought disorder
Fatigability	Gregariousness	Passive opposition	Impulsivity	Oedipal conflict
Reward dependence	Assertiveness	Cognitive distortion	Propriety	Dissociated
Sentimentality	Activity	Rejection	Workaholism	Sexual conflict
Attachment	Excitement seeking	Self-harm behaviours		
Dependence	Positive emotion	Restricted expression		
Persistence	Openness	Social avoidance		
Self directedness	Fantasy	Stimulus seeking		
Responsibility	Aesthetics	Interpersonal dis-esteem		
Purposefulness	Feelings	Anxiousness		
Resourcefulness	Actions			
Self-acceptance	Consciousness			
Congruency	Ideas			
Co-operativeness	Values			
Social acceptance	Agreeableness			
Empathy	Trust			
Helpfulness	Straightforwardness			
Compassion	Altruism			
Pure-heartedness	Compliance			
Self-transcendence	Modesty			
Self-forgetfulness	Tendermindedness			
Trans-identification	Conscientiousness			
Spiritual acceptance	Competence			
	Order			
	Dutifulness			
	Achievement striving			
	Self-discipline			
	Deliberation			

[1]Temperament and Character Inventory (Cloninger et al., 1993)
[2]Five-Factor Model (Costa & McCrae, 1992c)
[3]Dimensional Assessment of Personality Pathology–Basic Questionnaire (Livesley et al., 1998)
[4]Schedule for Nonadaptive and Adaptive Personality (Clark, 1993)
[5]Shedler-Westen Assessment Procedure (Westen & Shedler, 1999a)

The tridimensional model became even more of a misnomer when Cloninger, Svrakic, and Przybeck (1993) extended Cloninger's (1987) original psychobiological model by supplementing the four temperament factors with three dimensions assessing individual differences in character. According to Cloninger et al. (1993), the model was extended to be more comprehensive and to improve the ability of the measure representing the model, the Tridimensional Personality Questionnaire (TPQ), to assist in the differential diagnosis of personality disorders. They suggested that the temperament dimensions are very useful in identifying neurotic and somatoform disorders, and they are somewhat useful in distinguishing among various personality disorders, but the character dimensions are helpful in first establishing whether a personality disorder exists. This arose from a concern that some people without a personality disorder nevertheless had a temperament pattern that resembled people with a personality disorder, and something more was needed to distinguish the adjusted and the maladjusted.

The three character dimensions were selected, in part, because an interview assessment of people with personality disorders showed that these dimensions were highly relevant and useful. In addition, empirical analyses showed that the character dimensions were uncorrelated with the temperament factors. Cloninger et al. (1993) noted that the three character dimensions were included to tap acceptance of the self, acceptance of other people, and acceptance of nature in general. The three dimensions added were self-directedness, co-operativeness, and self-transcendence. The facets of each of these dimensions are shown in Table 13.2.

The self-directedness scale is the most clinically important dimension in terms of determining the presence or absence of personality disorder. It involves identifying the self as autonomous. High self-directedness is reflected by being responsible and goal-directed. Low self-directedness involves being insecure and inept.

The co-operative dimension is comparable to the five-factor dimension reflecting agreeableness versus disagreeableness. Cloninger et al. (1993) focused on co-operative people as key elements of human society. One end of the dimension is reflected by traits such as being helpful and empathic, and hostile and aggressive are at the other end.

The self-transcendence factor is derived from self-actualization models and religions that emphasize establishing a sense of unity and connection with the broader universe and freeing the self from personal concerns. It involves becoming one with the universe. Those who are able to attain self-transcendence are imaginative and unconventional, while those who are low in this dimension have an egocentric self-focus reflected by a very controlling and materialistic nature.

Empirical research by Cloninger et al. (1993) confirmed via factor analyses that the seven factors could be identified. Moreover, specific patterns reflecting various factors have been associated reliably with specific disorders. For instance, the dependent personality disorder is linked with low self-directedness, low self-transcendence, and high co-operativeness. Depression has been associated with high harm avoidance, low self-directedness, and low co-operativeness.

An examination of Cloninger's model in a sample of 136 psychiatric patients confirmed that the defining feature of Cluster A was reward dependence, while the defining features of Clusters B and C, respectively, were high novelty seeking and high harm avoidance (Svrakic, Whitehead, Przybeck, & Cloninger, 1993). This study also confirmed that low self-directedness and co-operativeness were "core features of all personality disorders" (p. 991).

O'Connor and Dyce (1998) evaluated the validity of various personality disorder models by obtaining data from previous investigators who had studied personality disorders in community and clinical samples. Models that were evaluated included an interpersonal circumplex model and Millon's (1996) biosocial learning theory. The results showed that the expanded seven-factor model postulated by Cloninger (1987) was among the models that provided the best fit to the data. The seven-factor model was superior to Cloninger's three-factor model. The five-factor model was the only model that rivalled it in terms of adequately representing the configuration of personality disorders, though the authors noted that a four-factor model that did not include openness seemed more appropriate than the full five-factor model.

One concern about Cloninger's conceptual scheme has emerged from a new study on the treatment of social anxiety (see Hoffman & Loh, 2005). As dimensions of temperament, harm avoidance, reward dependence, and novelty seeking should remain relatively stable. This new study found that levels of harm avoidance fluctuated over the course of treatment for people with social phobia, with recovery being associated with less harm avoidance. Thus, there appears to be a state-dependent component of harm avoidance, and this impermanence is not in keeping with the presumed stability of temperament.

Another critical issue is whether there is evidence to support the presumed neurobiological basis of the temperament dimensions. Unfortunately, supportive evidence is limited. A recent review by Paris (2005) led him to conclude that the extant research findings are "highly inconsistent" and "often yield negative findings." In general, Paris (2005) concluded that we still have a limited understanding of neurobiology, and it is not advisable to base personality models on neurobiological models at present.

Cloninger's model is not the only one that incorporates a biological focus. Recall from the previous chapter how biological factors also play a role in a framework suggested by Zuckerman and associates. Additional aspects of Zuckerman's framework are discussed later in this chapter. First, however, we discuss the relevance and applicability of the five-factor model.

KEY POINTS

- The dimensions of Cloninger's tridimensional model have their roots in biology.
- The tridimensional model is a misnomer because the original three dimensions had to be supplemented by four additional dimensions.
- The tridimensional model has limited support for its biological bases, and evidence suggests that changes in emotional states contribute to related changes in the harm avoidance dimension.

The Five-Factor Model in Personality Dysfunction

Costa and McCrae (1992a) have suggested that their five-factor model is highly relevant to the assessment and conceptualization of personality disorders. They added six specific facets to each superfactor because these can be useful in distinguishing among the various personality disorders. The facets associated with each of the five factors are displayed in Table 13.2.

Costa and McCrae (1992d) have argued in general that there are several benefits associated with the clinical assessment of the traits that comprise the five-factor model.

Assessment provides a comprehensive overview of personality structure and points to possible avenues for treatment. They also reported data on the association between the NEO Personality Inventory domains and the clinical scales assessed by Morey's Personality Assessment Inventory. Neuroticism was linked with numerous adjustment problems, including depression and anxiety-related disorders, as well as paranoia and borderline personality disorder symptoms. Low agreeableness was also associated with paranoia, schizophrenia, borderline features, and anti-social features.

Widiger and Mullins (2003) compiled a summary table that lists the personality trait facets of each DSM-IV-TR personality disorders. Their summary (see Table 13.3) is descriptive and is based on their conceptual analysis. It can be seen that one or more facets of neuroticism is found in 9 of the 10 disorders. Next is agreeableness, which has one or more facets involved in 8 disorders, and this is followed by extroversion (7 disorders).

One thing evident from Table 13.3 is that each personality disorder has a unique pattern of correlated personality facets. The clearest differences exist among the Cluster A disorders. The paranoid personality is associated with high angry hostility and low levels of trust, straightforwardness, and compliance. The schizoid personality disorder is associated with low warmth, low gregariousness, low feelings, and low positive emotionality. It is the only personality disorder that is conceptualized entirely based on the *relative absence* of personality facets. The schizotypal personality disorder is quite different. It is characterized by high anxiousness, high self-consciousness, low warmth, low gregariousness, low positive emotionality, low levels of trust, and high scores on the openness facets of fantasy, actions, and ideas.

Comparisons of the disorders with clusters also show that in Cluster C (disorders characterized by fearfulness) there are striking differences between obsessive–compulsive personality disorder and both avoidant personality disorder and dependent personality disorder. Obsessive–compulsive personality disorder is characterized uniquely by high assertiveness, high levels of four conscientiousness facets (competence, order, dutifulness, and achievement striving), and low levels of compliance and values. The avoidant and dependent personality disorders involve elevations on several neuroticism facets, with dependent personality disorder also involving elevations on several agreeableness facets.

A meta-analysis conducted on data from 15 independent samples has confirmed that neuroticism, extroversion, and agreeableness are the three broad factors from the five-factor model that have the broadest associations with personality disorders. This study by a team of Australian researchers showed that extroversion is unique, because some disorders involve high extroversion and others low extroversion (Saulsman & Page, 2004). In contrast, neuroticism and agreeableness play a similar role across personality disorders (high neuroticism and low agreeableness). This meta-analysis also found empirically that the five-factor model was much more relevant to some disorders (e.g., avoidant and borderline personality disorders) than it was to others (e.g., obsessive–compulsive and schizoid personality disorders).

Table 13.3 DSM-IV-TR Personality Disorders from the Perspective of the Five-Factor Model

	PRN	SZD	SZT	ATS	BDL	HST	NCS	AVD	DPD	OCP
Neuroticism										
Anxiousness			High		High			High	High	
Angry hostility	High			High	High		High			
Depressiveness					High	High		High		
Self-consciousness			High			High	High	High	High	
Impulsivity					High					
Vulnerability					High			High	High	
Extroversion										
Warmth		Low	Low			High			High	
Gregariousness		Low	Low			High		Low		
Assertiveness								Low	Low	High
Activity										
Excitement seeking				High		High		Low		
Positive emotionally		Low	Low			High				
Openness										
Fantasy			High			High	High			
Aesthetics										
Feelings		Low				High				
Actions			High							
Ideas			High							
Values										Low
Agreeableness										
Trust	Low		Low		Low	High			High	
Straightforwardness	Low			Low						
Altruism				Low			Low		High	
Compliance	Low			Low	Low				High	Low
Modesty							Low		High	
Tender-mindedness				Low			Low			
Conscientiousness										
Competence					Low					High
Order										High
Dutifulness				Low						High
Achievement-striving							High			High
Self-discipline				Low						
Deliberation				Low						

PRN = paranoid pd, SZD = schizoid pd, SZT = schizotypal pd, ATS = anti-social pd, BDL = borderline pd, HST = histrionic pd, NCS = narcissistic pd, AVD = avoidant pd, DPD = dependent pd, OCP = obsessive-compulsive pd

Source: Adapted from Widiger & Mullins, 2003, p. 1608.

Research indicates that it is important to examine specific facets and go beyond the five broad supertrait dimensions. Investigations indicate that the 30 NEO-PI-R facet scales are much better than the five broad factors at predicting specific forms of psychopathology (Miller, Lynam, Widiger, & Leukefeld, 2001). For instance, a study of psychopathy by Miller et al. (2001) showed that the overall measure of neuroticism was not useful, because four facets of neuroticism (anxiety, depression, self-consciousness, and vulnerability) were associated negatively with psychopathy, while two facets of neuroticism (angry hostility and impulsiveness) were associated *positively* with psychopathy. Another recent study was conducted with a Dutch sample, comparing the NEO-PI-R and Cloninger's TCI in terms of their respective ability to predict personality disorders (De Fruyt et al., 2006). The two measures were comparable when the predictors were the broad superfactors from these instruments. However, when analyses were conducted with the 30 facets of the NEO-PI-R, these facets proved to be the superior predictors.

These data notwithstanding, other investigations suggest that it is important to go beyond the five-factor model to more fully account for the link between personality and psychopathology. This theme is explored further in the discussion of the PSY-5 model.

KEY POINTS

- The five-factor model is linked with personality disorders. The traits linked most consistently are neuroticism, low agreeableness, and either low or high extroversion.
- The traits of the five-factor model vary across disorders in terms of their relevance. The traits are especially applicable to borderline and avoidant personality disorder.
- The 30 specific facets of the NEO-PI-R are typically more predictive of personality dysfunction than are the five broad supertraits.

The Psychopathology-5 (PSY-5)

Butcher and Rouse (1996) attributed the predictive difficulties of the NEO-PI-R to the fact that it reflects the lexical approach and the decision made several decades earlier by Allport and Odbert to remove personality items with evaluative content and only retain adjectives with non-evaluative content. Butcher and Rouse (1996) observed that several different forms of psychopathology do indeed involve evaluation-based individual differences, and personality measures need to capture these differences.

Butcher and Rouse (1996) have seemingly mocked the strong position taken by those who espouse five-factor assessment. For instance, they observed that:

> Proponents of the five-factor approach have made dramatic claims about its usefulness for the study and assessment of personality structure. Some believe the existence of five, and only five, factors to be an empirical fact as undeniable as the existence of seven continents on the earth (McCrae & John, 1992) and as valuable as the cartographic convention of using four directional poles (i.e. north, south, east, and west) in geography and navigation (Goldberg, 1993). (p. 97)

An intense debate occurred over the suitability of the five-factor model to distinguish among personality disorders (see Ben-Porath & Waller, 1992; Costa & McCrae, 1992d). Critics of the five-factor model have raised some important points. Ben-Porath and Waller (1992) suggested that the broad factors tapped by the NEO-PI-R are too general to be useful for clinical diagnoses. This general concern led to the formation of the six facet scales developed for each of the five factors. Another concern about the NEO-PI-R is the lack of validity scales to evaluate invalid responses (Ben-Porath & Waller, 1992).

Costa and McCrae (2005) have countered by stating that other frameworks do not adequately assess individual differences in openness. Indeed, we know from the phenomenological–humanistic theorists that openness to experience is of central importance to reactions to and understanding of the therapy process.

An alternative framework stems from one of the most well-known personality measures used in clinical settings: the Minnesota Multiphasic Personality Inventory (MMPI). Scoring schemes using MMPI items have been created to assess the symptoms of specific personality disorders. Harkness, McNulty, and Ben-Porath (1995) described a set of MMPI-2 scales they developed to assess five dimensional personality constructs to reflect psychopathology. This framework consists of dimensions assessing negative emotionality/neuroticism, lack of positive emotionality, aggressiveness, lack of constraint, and psychoticism. The resultant scale is called the Psychopathology-Five (PSY-5). The five dimensions are shown in Table 13.4. Recently, facets have also been found for four of the five factors, and these are also shown in Table 13.4.

Table 13.4 Broad Domains and Facets of the PSY-5

Broad Psy-5 Domain	Facets	NEO-PI-R Equivalent
Aggression	Hostility Grandiosity/indignation	Low agreeableness
Disconstraint	Delinquent behaviours and actions Norm violation	None
Introversion	Low drive/expectations Low sociability	Introversion
Psychoticism	Psychotic beliefs/experiences Odd mentation	None
Neuroticism/negative emotionality	No facets	Neuroticism

It can be seen that the five-factor model and the PSY-5 have similar item content for three of the five dimensions. However, with the aggressive factor, the PSY-5 assesses more extreme behaviour that goes well beyond low agreeableness. This could make a difference when seeking to identify a psychopath who engages in violent acts. The heinous acts of psychopaths are more extreme than "disagreeableness."

Research has confirmed that the PSY-5 dimensions can be identified via confirmatory factor analyses (Bagby et al., 2002), and other research has shown that these dimensions are associated in the expected manner with personality disorder symptom counts (Trull, Useda, Costa, & McCrae, 1995). As Trull et al. (1995) noted, a measure such as the PSY-5 constraint scale should be associated with anti-social personality disorder symptoms, given that the constraint scale has items that assess lying, stealing, and getting into trouble with the law.

Most important is recent evidence from a study of 647 clients in a private practice setting, which showed that the PSY-5 predicted personality disorder outcome measures over and above the predictive ability of the MMPI-2 clinical scales (Wygart, Sellbom, Graham, & Schenk, 2006). This indicates that the PSY-5 scales have incremental validity in predicting personality dysfunction.

A study of combat veterans with post-traumatic stress disorder has shown that the constraint and emotionality factors of the PSY-5 are linked with psychological distress. A PSY-5 pattern of high negative emotionality and low positive emotionality was associated with internalizing symptoms and high rates of panic disorder and major depressive disorder (Miller, Kaloupek, Dillon, & Keane, 2004). In contrast, a PSY-5 pattern of high negative emotionality and low constraint was associated with externalizing symptoms, anti-social personality disorder, and alcohol-related disorders.

A study of combat veterans with post-traumatic stress disorder indicates a link between the constraint and emotionality factors of the PSY-5 and psychological distress.

The PSY-5 is derived from the MMPI, and the MMPI itself was modified to create a version for adolescents known as the MMPI-A (Butcher et al., 1992). Similarly, an adolescent version of the PSY-5 has been created to assess personality dysfunction in adolescents. Existing research suggests that the adolescent version is quite comparable to the original PSY-5 (Bolinskey, Arnau, Archer, & Handel, 2004). What is perhaps more important is that the existence of these dimensions is in keeping with the general view that personality dysfunction has its roots in childhood and adolescence; when personality dysfunction is detected in adults, it is likely a reflection of a long-standing problem.

KEY POINTS

- PSY-5 refers to the psychopathology five, derived from the MMPI. The PSY-5 scales predict personality dysfunction above and beyond the variance predicted by the standard MMPI clinical scales.
- The PSY-5 is better than the NEO-PI-R at predicting extreme violence and impulse control disorders.
- The PSY-5 can be assessed in adolescence. This is a reminder that personality disorders reflect long-standing disorders that should be detectable in adolescents.

Livesley's Dimensional Assessment of Personality

Research originating in British Columbia by **John Livesley** and colleagues has provided much insight into the personality disorder dimensions. Livesley and Jackson's (2002) self-report scale known as the Dimensional Assessment of Personality Pathology–Basic Questionnaire (DAPP-BQ) has 22 scales that assess 18 personality trait dimensions (e.g., anxiousness, affective lability, callousness, insecure attachment, narcissism) and various response styles. Statistical tests show that DAPP-BQ trait scales reflect the higher-order factors of emotional dysregulation (affective lability and impulsivity), dissocial behaviour (callousness, conduct problems, and narcissism), inhibitedness (avoidance of intimacy and restricted expression of emotions), and compulsivity (Livesley, Jang, & Vernon, 1998).

The first factor was named "emotional dysregulation," since it describes unstable and reactive tendencies, dissatisfaction with the self and life experiences, and interpersonal problems. This factor subsumes the personality trait of neuroticism and broadly resembles the DSM-IV Cluster B diagnosis of borderline personality disorder. The second factor was named "dissocial behaviour." It describes anti-social personality characteristics and clearly resembles the DSM-IV Cluster B anti-social personality diagnosis or psychopathy. The third factor is "inhibition," defined by DAPP-DQ intimacy problems and restricted expression, which resembles the DSM-IV avoidant and schizotypal personality disorders. The fourth factor was named "compulsivity" because it clearly resembles DSM-IV Cluster C obsessive–compulsive personality disorder.

Livesley et al. (1998) investigated this higher-order structure of personality disorder dimensions with various samples of personality disordered patients, twins, and general population participants. Evidence that the statistical analyses yielded the same four factors regardless whether the sample was of personality disordered participants or general population participants lends support for the continuity hypothesis of personality.

Other research relating the DAPP-BQ to the five-factor model and Eysenck's dimensions of psychoticism, extroversion, and neuroticism shows that neuroticism is linked with emotional dysregulation, dissocial behaviour is linked with high psychoticism, inhibitedness is linked with low extroversion, and compulsivity is linked with high conscientiousness (Larstone, Jang, Livesley, Vernon, & Wolf, 2002).

Zuckerman's Alternative Five

Certain trait frameworks have emerged from a psychobiological perspective. Eysenck's three-factor model of extroversion, neuroticism, and psychoticism has its roots in biological differences. The "Alternative Five" identified by **Marvin Zuckerman** and his associates (see Zuckerman, Kuhlman, Joireman, Teta, & Kraft, 1993) is in keeping with his interest in biological factors as described in Chapter 12. The Alternative Five includes some of the broad supertraits found in other models, but also reflects Zuckerman's theoretical interests in temperament factors as reflected by impulsivity and sensation seeking. Eysenck (1992) felt that factors such as impulsivity and sensation seeking were subcomponents of his three supertraits or a reflection of some combination of extroversion, neuroticism, and psychoticism. Zuckerman and associates differ by suggesting that factors such as impulsivity and sensation seeking are related to but distinguishable from Eysenck's supertraits.

The first factor in the Alternative Five is neuroticism–anxiety. It is reflected by worry, fearfulness, obsessive indecision, lack of self-confidence, and sensitivity to criticism. The second factor is sociability. It is highly similar to extroversion and is reflected by outgoingness and spending time with others. The third factor is aggression–hostility. Indicators of aggression–hostility include a readiness to express verbal aggression, a quick-temperedness, impatience with others, rudeness, and thoughtlessness. The fourth and fifth factors are the ones that most reflect the body of Zuckerman's work. The fourth factor is impulsive sensation seeking. It consists of lack of planning and acting without thinking. It also involves experience seeking and a willingness to take risks just for the sake of risk. Impulsivity can be reflected by excitement seeking or novelty seeking. Finally, the fifth factor is activity. People high in activity are very similar to Type A individuals in that they have such a need for activity they find it difficult to relax. They are high-energy people who lead an active and busy lifestyle, and when they can choose, they opt for hard, challenging tasks rather than easier tasks.

Zuckerman's Alternative Five was identified on the basis of a factor analysis of his measure as well as the Eysenck Personality Questionnaire (EPQ). Zuckerman et al. (1993) conducted a comparative analysis of the Alternative Five, the five-factor model, and Eysenck's EPQ model. Factor analyses confirmed that three factors were not sufficient in order to accurately represent the data. Four factors emerged in the factor analyses. The first factor was an extroversion dimension that included Zuckerman et al.'s sociability and activity subscales. The second factor was a neuroticism factor that included all of the neuroticism subscales. The third factor was a psychoticism factor that included the sensation seeking subscale. Conscientiousness also had a strong negative loading on this factor. The final factor included a strong negative loading on Zuckerman et al.'s aggression–hostility factor, as well as positive loadings for the NEO-PI agreeableness and openness scale. The inclusion of openness on this factor calls into question whether openness represents a distinct fifth factor.

Overall, several different conceptual frameworks have been presented. Which one do you think is most relevant? This will continue to be a hot topic in the years to come. It is likely that some new model will emerge that will combine some of the factors from the various conceptual frameworks.

The final portion of this chapter focuses on the link between personality and binge drinking, and the association between personality and depression. The role of personality factors in drinking problems is discussed for two reasons. First, many students suffer from drinking problems in the form of binge drinking, and it is important to examine the personality factors that might play a role. Second, it is important to illustrate that personality factors may play a role in a variety of behavioural disorders, and binge drinking and alcoholism represent but one of them.

PERSONALITY, BINGE DRINKING, AND ALCOHOLISM

Researchers are increasingly turning their attention to the factors that are associated with alcoholism and other problems of substance abuse because of epidemiological studies indicating that addiction is sadly a very common problem that might be growing in incidence and prevalence. Researchers have focused on college and university students due to the exceptionally high levels of binge drinking detected on campuses. Binge drinking is defined as having five or more drinks in a row for females, and six or more for males.

Alarmingly, a 1993 American survey found that on campuses, 50% of men and 40% of women engaged in binge drinking (Wechsler et al., 1994). This might seem like an overestimate, but the survey was repeated in 1999 and similar findings emerged (see Wechsler, Lee, Kwo, & Lee, 2000). Research on more than 14,000 students found that 44% engaged in binge drinking and 23% fulfilled the criteria for frequent binge drinking. Equally alarming were the associated consequences of binge drinking. Students who binge drink are more likely to get into legal trouble, experience personal injuries, and engage in unsafe sexual practices. The Canadian Campus Survey by Gliksman and Adlaf and their colleagues has yielded similar findings. This survey is conducted every two years and involves almost 8,000 students at 16 universities across Canada (see Gliksman, Demers, Adlaf, Newton-Taylor, & Schmidt, 2000). Overall, almost two thirds of students reported at least one episode of binge drinking since the start of the school year (Gliksman, Adlaf, Demers, & Newton-Taylor, 2003). Men were much more likely to engage in an excessive level of drinking. About twice as many men report binge drinking two to four or more times a week. Clearly, for many North American students, drinking is out of control. Another recent investigation found that 18% of U.S. college students (24% for men and 13% for women) were characterized by clinically significant alcohol-related problems, and college students were significantly more likely to be diagnosed with alcohol abuse than were their non-college attending peers (Slutske, 2005).

One explaination of binge drinking is that people are at risk because they have an **addiction-prone personality**. What evidence exists for an addiction-prone personality? Prospective research has shown clearly that personality factors are risk factors for excessive drinking and substance abuse. Shedler and Block (1990) studied 101 participants who were first evaluated when they were three years old and were re-evaluated when they were 18 years old. They found that substance abuse was predicted by three factors: (1) poor impulse control (impulsivity); (2) interpersonal alienation (insecurity and inability to form healthy relationships); and (3) emotional distress (anxiety, depression, anger).

Personality factors such as poor impulse control, interpersonal alienation, and emotional distress have been linked to binge drinking and other substance abuse.

In another study, Sher, Bartholow, and Wood (2000) had 489 university students participate in a diagnostic interview and complete measures reflecting the models outlined by Cloninger and Eysenck. These students also had the diagnostic interview a second time six years later. This research design enabled Sher et al. (2000) to examine the role of personality factors in predicting the development of substance use disorders in students who did not already have a history of substance abuse or other disorders. This study revealed that students who were characterized by novelty seeking or psychoticism were more likely to develop substance use disorders. Traits related to negative emotionality (neuroticism) were correlated with substance use disorders, but prospective analyses could not determine whether negative emotionality was a cause or a result of substance abuse. However, a more recent longitudinal study by Jackson and Sher (2003) that considered neuroticism over an 11-year period found that it was a significant predictor of subsequent alcohol use disorders.

Elkins and associates have concluded that both neuroticism and low constraint are predictors of alcohol use disorders, but low constraint is a substantially more robust predictor (Elkins, King, McGue, & Iacono, 2006). Their own investigation found that both trait negative emotionality and low constraint did indeed predict the onset of alcoholism. However, a similar pattern emerged for predicting nicotine disorders and illicit drug disorders. Thus, personality factors may have a more general impact that is not limited to alcohol use disorders.

In light of this accumulating evidence of the role of personality in substance abuse, researchers have turned their attention to the search for developmental factors that can help explain the association between personality and substance abuse. Twin research has implicated genetic factors as contributors to the link between personality and alcohol abuse (e.g., Slutske et al., 2002). Slutske and associates, for instance, formed three higher-order factors (positive emotionality, negative emotionality, and behavioural undercontrol) based on responses to Cloninger's TPQ and the Eysenck Personality Questionnaire. They found that genetic factors were modest when examining the link between individual differences in both positive and negative emotionality and alcohol dependence. However, genetic factors had a substantial impact on the association between behavioural undercontrol and alcohol dependence. Another investigation by Krueger et al. (2002) also found a highly heritable factor labelled "externalizing" that included substance use disorders, anti-social personality disorder, and low constraint as a personality construct.

KEY POINTS

- Binge drinking occurs at exceptionally high rates among North American college and university students, and it has many documented negative consequences.
- Binge drinking is linked with novelty seeking and high levels of psychoticism and neuroticism.

Personality and Varying Motives for Drinking

Overall, theoretical and empirical attempts to link personality factors with various forms of substance abuse have focused on two main classes of variables. First, theorists have focused on a class of personality variables involved in behavioural disinhibition. Sensation seeking is one of these factors. Recall that sensation seekers are thrill seekers who enjoy heightened levels of arousal. One way to increase arousal is to ingest certain drugs. The role of sensation seeking in drinking is even reflected by item content on the disinhibition subscale of Zuckerman's Sensation Seeking Scale. It contains two items that refer directly to drinking (e.g., "I feel best after taking a couple of drinks"). Some authors have noted correctly that this item content creates a problem in item overlap that could artificially inflate the degree of correlation between sensation seeking and drinking (see Sher, Trull, Bartholomew, & Vieth, 1999).

Cloninger and Eysenck are other theorists who have attempted to link alcohol and drug use with personality factors that are believed to be associated with behavioural disinhibition. Cloninger (1987a, 1987b) suggested that novelty seeking is the dimension that is most relevant to alcohol dependence (Cloninger, 1987a). According to Eysenck's three-factor model, substance use and abuse are likely among individuals characterized by high levels of neuroticism and psychoticism (Eysenck & Eysenck, 1977). Eysenck's suggested link between psychoticism and drug use is in keeping with several studies that link anti-social tendencies with drug use. An association has also been found between drug use in general and anti-social personality disorder (Ball et al., 1994). Similarly, research conducted with adolescents from Montreal found that trait rebelliousness and a high level of aggression are also related to substance abuse (Masse & Tremblay, 1997).

The second class of variables focuses on drinking as a form of tension release. This is one reason why factors such as neuroticism are associated with substance use and abuse. Thus, any personality trait linked with susceptibility to anxiety and depression could conceivably be associated with substance abuse. This is the primary motivation for depression-prone people who have suffered from alcoholism, such as the famous actor Sir Anthony Hopkins, who has acknowledged that earlier in his career, he drank as a way of "killing" his discomfort and self-contempt. Drinking for Hopkins was a form of self-destruction that was driven by suicidal urges.

Actor Anthony Hopkins admitted that he drank to excess to relieve distress.

Drinking as a form of tension and distress relief is clearly implicated in the following account from Terri, a female student who took part in the College Alcohol Study conducted at Harvard by Wechsler and associates:

> At the beginning of the school year, I drank way too much at a sorority/fraternity football tailgate. I blacked out on my way home (by myself). I don't remember my walk home or anything occurring afterwards. I have dysthymia and alcohol is a depressant. I tried to kill myself by overdosing on Tylenol and Wellbutrin, apparently without any real cause. This is a decision I never would have made

> had I been sober. I ended up in the hospital for three days. I am an A/B student, so to speak, but because of the basically inherent complexity regarding the aforementioned event, I began failing most of my classes and withdrew my semester. (Wechsler & Wuethrich, 2002, p. 191)

An example of binge drinking by a young woman was selected to highlight the need to consider whether the personality correlates of binge drinking are comparable for women and men. Possible gender differences are not always explored, but we cannot assume that the findings will be similar for women and men. A recent study of college-aged social drinkers found, for instance, that conscientiousness was associated with less drinking for women but not for men. Neuroticism was not associated with drinking by women or men in this study. However, neuroticism was linked with greater use of illicit substances for men but not women (Kashdan, Vetter, & Collins, 2005). In general, it is believed that females are more likely than males to drink in response to stress, while males are more likely to drink as a form of excitement seeking and affiliation with others.

Cloninger (1987) postulated that this distinction between drinking for tension release versus drinking for maximizing sensations and pleasures is reflected by two different types of alcoholics. Type 1 alcoholics are quiet and dependent people who are more likely to drink in response to stress. Drinking is a reaction to stress. The onset of drinking problems occurs later in life and may not appear until adulthood. Type 2 alcoholics are described as impulsive sensation seekers who may be quite aggressive. This pattern emerges in adolescence and would most likely apply to underage drinkers.

According to Cloninger, Type 1 alcoholics drink to relieve stress while Type 2 alcoholics drink for excitement and sensation seeking.

As might be expected, these two different personality styles are paralleled by related differences in the motives for drinking. Cooper (1994) identified four motives: (1) social reasons (drinking to be sociable); (2) enhancement (drinking to get high); (3) coping (drinking to forget worries); and (4) conformity (drinking so that others do not tease the person about not drinking). Cooper, Frone, Russell, and Mudar (1995) linked impulsivity with drinking for enhancement (maximizing positive moods), while neuroticism is associated with drinking to cope. This framework treats personality factors as distal predictors while drinking motives are more proximal predictors of excessive drinking. That is, personality predicts drinking motives, which, in turn, predict drinking behaviours.

Contemporary research has explored how other personality traits relate to drinking motives. For instance, an investigation of drinking motives conducted with university students found that there was a strong negative association between conscientiousness and enhancement (Stewart, Loughlin, & Rhyno, 2001). Drinking to cope was associated with high neuroticism, low extroversion, and low agreeableness. This pattern is very much in keeping with more general research on personality and alcohol use. Walton and Roberts (2004) identified heavy alcohol users among a sample of university students and found that they were significantly lower in conscientiousness and agreeableness and significantly higher in impulsivity. Heavy users, moderate users, and abstainers did not differ in perfectionism as assessed by the Frost Multidimensional Perfectionism Scale.

Although it seems evident that different personality styles are associated with differences in why people drink, this research has to be qualified for at least two reasons. First, as noted by Sher et al. (1999), even when drinking motives are taken into account and controlled statistically, personality factors are still robust enough to predict drinking behaviour. Second, research on personality and motives for drinking assumes that people have accurate insights into why they drink. People who drink to excess may have a form of self-deception that helps justify why they drink and we cannot assume that problem drinkers are accurate and veridical in their assessments of why they drink. Thus, we need to distinguish between stated motives and actual motives.

KEY POINTS

- People engage in excessive drinking as a form of tension release or as a form of excitement seeking.
- Cloninger distinguished the Type 1 alcoholic (drinks to relieve stress) and the Type 2 alcoholic (drinks for excitement and sensation seeking). Type 2 alcoholism develops earlier in life.
- Personality is related to the motives for drinking. Both personality and motives for drinking predict drinking and related outcomes.

Models of Drinking Behaviour

Current theories seeking to account for vulnerability to alcoholism have focused on cognitively based explanations. Three primary models will be described briefly in order to illustrate the various ways that different personality factors may play in the etiology of alcoholism and binge drinking.

The Social Learning Theory of Alcoholism

The **social learning theory of alcoholism** is based on the premise that alcohol outcome expectancies are key mediators of drinking behaviour, and that these expectancies are influenced by a person's social learning experiences (see Goldman, Brown, & Christiansen, 1986). The issue of whether excessive drinking takes place is based on whether the individual holds positive or negative expectancies about alcohol. Six positive beliefs have been identified: (1) alcohol as a global positive force in change; (2) alcohol as a social and physical enhancer of pleasure; (3) alcohol as a sexual enhancer; (4) alcohol increasing a feeling of power; (5) alcohol increasing social assertiveness; and (6) alcohol as a tension reducer (Goldman et al., 1986). Negative expectancies include the notion that alcohol impairs performance and encourages irresponsibility and a loss of self-control that can only lead to trouble.

This is a social learning model because children develop alcohol expectancies as a result of observing models. They are influenced by parents, peers, and people on television and in movies. Their expectancies are later incorporated and solidified in an alcohol expectancy schema. Drinking is more likely if this alcohol expectancy schema has a preponderance of positive expectancies relative to negative expectancies. General support for this model comes from research showing that the expectancies of young adolescents are able to predict when they will begin drinking, even when other well-known predictors of drinking onset (e.g., age, religious background, parental drinking patterns) are already taken into account and statistically controlled. Also, as might be expected, heavy drinkers have stronger positive expectancies than do lighter drinkers (Southwick, Steele, Marlatt, & Lindell, 1981).

Personality factors are not independent of these alcohol expectancies. People who are self-critical or socially inhibited and fear negative evaluation tend to endorse the beliefs that alcohol is a positive transforming force and that alcohol increases social assertiveness. Also, people high in hostility endorse the view that alcohol increases power (Leonard & Blane, 1988). Sensation seeking is associated with positive expectancies for heavy drinking and engaging in risky sex, and it is also associated with fewer negative expectancies (Katz, Fromme, & D'Amico, 2000). Although personality and expectancies are associated, they still are able to account for significant differences in risky behaviour, so both factors are important (Katz et al., 2000).

Self-Awareness Model of Drinking

The self-awareness model of drinking incorporates individual differences in self-consciousness (Hull, 1987). Hull's model is based on the premise that the reinforcing power of alcohol is its ability to disrupt cognitive processes and information processes. Drinking results in reduced self-awareness and decreases the cognitive ability to focus on personal shortcomings and deficiencies. According to this model, alcohol is reinforcing in two ways. Drinking provides a heightened sense of personal power and efficacy, and it also acts as a form of negative reinforcement by reducing painful feelings of guilt and inadequacy. This model would apply to the person who drinks to avoid tension and, as "The Piano Man" Billy Joel told us in song, it applies to those who come to bars to "forget about life for a while."

The distracting ability of alcohol was illustrated in an experiment conducted by Banaji and Steele (1989). Students were asked to rate their actual selves and their ideal selves on a number of attributes. One subset of students then had some drinks, while another subset of students were given drinks that were portrayed as alcoholic beverages but in fact did not contain alcohol. This was known as the placebo experimental condition. Placebos test the expectancy component (drinking will make me happy) without providing the actual substance. Banaji and Steele (1989) found that drinking alcohol caused people to elevate their self-ratings when retested, so that there was little gap between the actual self and the ideal self. No such elevation resulted from ingestion of the placebo cocktails. Presumably, participants who drank the actual drink became less able to cognitively attend to the ways in which they were less than ideal.

Another way to interpret this model is that people will drink to excess when they are made to feel threatened and self-conscious. Hull and Young (1983) compared students who were high versus low in self-consciousness after they had either succeeded or failed on an intellectual task. They were then asked to participate in a "wine-tasting" experiment. Self-conscious people who had experienced failure feedback drank significantly more wine during the wine-tasting component.

The predictions from this model also have long-term treatment implications. Hull, Young, and Jouriles (1986) found that alcoholics with high levels of self-consciousness were especially likely to relapse after treatment following the experience of negative life events. Thus, life stress may combine with self-awareness to produce a tendency toward alcohol abuse.

The Self-Handicapping Theory of Drinking

Finally, the **self-handicapping theory of drinking** is based on the notion that excessive drinking provides a person with an excuse as a form of self-protection. Here drinking to excess is regarded as an unconsciously motivated way of shifting blame away from the self and attributing it to the effects of alcohol instead. For instance, consider the student who has a big exam on Friday but still goes to pub night and gets drunk on the preceding Thursday night. When he or she does not do well on the Friday exam, instead of being forced to consider a lack of ability, the student can point to the inappropriate choices made the night before and still try to maintain the image of being a highly capable and talented student. Although this phenomenon certainly occurs a great deal, empirical research has yet to show that chronic self-handicapping actually *causes* drinking problems.

This segment will conclude by outlining some cogent observations made in a review of personality and alcoholism by Sher, Trull, Bartholomew, and Vieth (1999). Although they raised many important points, we will focus on three. First and foremost, they noted that the significance of personality as an explanatory has waxed and waned over the years, but we are in a period where recognition of the potential etiological significance of personality factors has perhaps never been greater. Second, the evidence as a whole provides greater support for some factors more than others. Sher et al. (1999) concluded that evidence is strongest for impulsivity–disinhibition and is less clear-cut for factors such as neuroticism and extroversion–sociability. Finally, they suggested that personality variables are best regarded as distal factors of etiological importance. More proximal factors such as alcohol expectancies will likely be more amenable to treatment via psychological interventions than will personality traits; however, we should not lose sight of the long-term role that personality factors play in vulnerability to alcoholism and related forms of alcohol abuse.

THE ROLE OF PERSONALITY FACTORS IN DEPRESSION

Depression is a highly debilitating mood disorder that can have a profound impact on the depressed person and his or her loved ones. Depression is also very common. It is among the two or three most frequent disorders identified in epidemiological disorders. Estimates of the proportion of the population who will suffer from depression at least once in their lives have ranged from 5 to 17% (Kessler et al., 1994; Weissman et al., 1996).

The chief symptoms of depression are a sad mood for most of the day and a loss of interest in pleasurable activities. A very negative self-concept and suicidal thoughts are also common. Depression can also include a host of physical symptoms, including sleep loss, fatigue, and demonstrable changes in appetite and weight. Typically, symptoms must persist for at least two weeks in order to warrant a diagnosis of depression.

The notion that personality factors play a role in vulnerability to depression was first explored in Chapter 9 when individual differences in attributional style were considered. Recall that it was indicated that depression-prone people have a self-blaming, stable, and global attributional style when they make attributions for the causes of negative events. Although attributional style has been the subject of extensive theoretical and empirical attention, in recent years, other constructs have received just as much attention. In the sections that follow, research on depression is summarized by its link with the five-factor model: self-criticism, dependency, sociotropy, autonomy, and perfectionism.

First, however, it is important to reiterate a key point made by attributional style theorists such as Abramson et al. (1978). They argued that attributional style is a diathesis–stress factor that interacts with the experience of negative life events to produce elevated levels of depression. That is, stress is a moderator in the personality and depression link. The need to consider a diathesis–stress model is implicit or explicit in research testing each of the personality vulnerability factors described below.

Why is there interest in identifying personality factors associated with depression? Part of this is simply because depression is widely recognized as a prevalent and serious mental health problem with severe consequences. In addition, a number of personality constructs that seem highly relevant to depression have been identified. Some of these personality constructs are outlined below. Note that due to space limitations, other personality traits linked with depression are not discussed here. This includes such attributes as low trait optimism, low self-efficacy, and self-consciousness. All of these factors have been linked with depression.

The Five-Factor Model and Depression

Neuroticism has been a focus of interest for many years. Following work by Eysenck and Eysenck (1969), it is accepted generally that individuals with higher levels of neuroticism tend to experience higher levels of depression (see Barnett & Gotlib, 1988). Moreover, there are some indications that levels of neuroticism remain elevated in remitted depressives (Roy, 1990). Some researchers have analyzed the link between neuroticism and depression by focusing on the role of information processing variables (Teasdale & Dent, 1987).

In general, however, several questions about neuroticism and depression remain unanswered at both the empirical and theoretical levels. There are some critical questions that need to be addressed conceptually. (1) To what extent should or should not neuroticism be associated with other personality variables (e.g., anxiety, self-concept) in depression? (2) What are the implications of including depression at a dispositional level as a facet of neuroticism? A measure such as the NEO-PI includes trait depression as one of the trait facets of neuroticism (see Costa & McCrae, 1985). It is not too surprising to then discover that trait neuroticism is linked with a self-report measure of depressive symptoms. Clearly, there is overlap between the predictor and criterion variables. (3) What is the role of neuroticism in the persistence of depression? Initial work suggests a link between neuroticism and persistent depression (Scott, Williams, Brittlebank, & Ferrier, 1995), but more research is needed.

Over the past decade, research on personality traits and depression has expanded to include an assessment of depression and the entire the five-factor model. Collectively, this research indicates that high neuroticism and low conscientiousness are consistent correlates of depression. In addition, low extroversion and low agreeableness have been also linked with depression (e.g., Trull & Sher, 1994).

There are four key limitations to existing research on depression and the five-factor model. First, there has been only a limited attempt thus far to consider the possibility that personality traits interact with each other or combine with other individual difference factors (e.g., social support) to produce elevated levels of depression. Some research has found that neuroticism combines with low extroversion to produce elevated distress in college students (Gershuny & Sher, 1998), but this interaction effect has not been detected when tested in community samples (see Jorm et al., 2000).

A second limitation that must be recognized is that the five-factor model seems to have limited relevance in its specific applicability to depression versus other types of psychopathology. The same personality traits linked with depression also tend to be linked with a host of other forms of maladjustment (Trull & Sher, 1994).

Third, almost without exception, research on the five-factor model and depression has been cross-sectional. The ability of the five-factor model to predict long-term susceptibility to depression has not been fully evaluated.

Finally, a fourth limitation pertains to concerns that the experience of depression inflates self-reported maladaptive traits. A recent investigation conducted in Toronto by Costa and associates assessed the five-factor model by comparing NEO-PI-R scores in patients before and after drug treatment (see Costa, Bagby, Herbst, & McCrae, 2005). This study found that non-responders to treatment showed little change in NEO-PI-R scores over time, so their scores were quite stable. However, those patients who improved due to treatment had decreases in neuroticism and increases in extroversion, openness, and conscientiousness. But shouldn't personality traits remain relatively stable and not change? The authors argued that these changes were not response distortions and represented veridical changes that accurately reflected the patients' current condition. However, why should personality change as a result of drug treatment? Psychotherapy focused on issues involving the self would make more sense. The only way to reconcile these findings is to allow for the effects of personality states, and it is still quite possible that personality self-reports are biased by negative mood states.

Given that there is a consistent correlation between trait neuroticism and depressive symptoms, a stringent test for other personality traits is to determine whether they can predict depressive symptoms after considering related individual differences in neuroticism. If a personality variable is a significant predictor of depression, after taking the predictiveness of neuroticism into account, then this points to the need to consider broad personality factors (the five-factor model) and more specific personality factors that might also play a role. Some of these more specific personality factors are outlined below.

KEY POINTS

- Personality factors are hypothesized to be associated with vulnerability to depression following the experience of stressful life events.
- More longitudinal research is needed on the role of certain personality factors (e.g., the five-factor model) in the long development of and susceptibility to depression.
- One methodological issue is whether changes in mood states lead to changes in self-reported personality traits (people score as less neurotic and less self-critical as their mood improves).

Self-Criticism and Dependency

Sidney Blatt from Yale University is arguably the leading theorist in the study of personality and depression. Blatt (1974, 1995) detailed the introjective and anaclitic personality styles and their role in depression. The introjective orientation involves excessive levels of self-criticism and self-punitiveness. The anaclitic orientation involves excessive levels of dependency on others. Dependency was discussed in detail earlier in this chapter.

Table 13.5 contains sample items from the self-criticism and dependency subscales of the McGill revision of the Depressive Experiences Questionnaire. You can assess your own levels of self-criticism and dependency by thinking about the extent to which you would agree with each statement on a 1 to 7 scale.

Table 13.5 Sample Items on the McGill Revision of the Depressive Experiences Questionnaire

Self-Criticism
If I fail to live up to my expectations, I feel unworthy.
I tend to be very critical of myself.
I often feel guilty.
Dependency
I become frightened when I feel alone.
I would feel as if I'd be losing an important part of myself if I lost a very close friend.
After a fight with a friend, I must make amends as soon as possible.

Although research tends to focus on self-criticism and dependency as separate, independent constructs, it is important to keep in mind from an idiographic, person-centred focus that people who are characterized jointly by high self-criticism and high dependency should be especially vulnerable to depression. Writer and poet Sylvia Plath was characterized by high levels of both self-criticism and dependency. Her case will be discussed further in Chapter 14 as part of a psychobiographical sketch.

How do people develop high levels of self-criticism and dependency? Blatt is a psychoanalytic theorist who places importance on early experience in the family. He focuses on the role of attachment styles (see Chapter 10 for a review). He attributes the self-critical style to exposure to intrusive, controlling, and punitive parents who foster an anxious avoidant attachment style in their child. The dependent style is attributed to parental behaviour that is inconsistent, neglectful, and abandoning. This type of parental behaviour creates an anxious, insecure attachment style (see Blatt & Zuroff, 1992).

Extensive research has shown a consistently strong association between self-criticism and depression. The association between dependency and depression is less robust but still evident across many studies (e.g., Mongrain & Zuroff, 1994). Dependency has a weaker association with depression because research with the primary measure of self-criticism and dependency, the Depressive Experiences Questionnaire (DEQ), has found that the DEQ actually measures both a needy, maladaptive form of dependency and a healthy, adaptive form of dependency that highlights positive affiliations and connections with other people (Blatt, Zohar, Quinlan, Zuroff, & Mongrain, 1995). This accords with Bornstein's claim, cited earlier, that there are adaptive aspects to dependency. Another complicating factor is that whether dependency is seen as negative or positive appears to depend on cultural factors. Programmatic research in Israel by Besser and Priel has often found that dependency, as assessed by the DEQ, is associated with *less depression* (Besser & Priel, 2003; Priel & Besser, 1999) and Besser has suggested that this reflects the cultural value and importance attached to establishing close connections with others. It is logical to suggest that dependency will have a much more negative connotation in a highly individualistic culture but will be favoured in a more collectivistic society.

Blatt has contributed extensively to therapy and research on the role of personality factors in treatment outcomes. Applied Perspective 13.1 addresses the issue of whether it is useful to match certain treatments to certain personality styles.

Applied Perspective 13.1 Personality, Treatment Matching, and Schema Therapy

We know that people who have the same adjustment problem may vary substantially in their personality characteristics, and these differences have implications for treatment success. This was illustrated by the results of a recent study of eating disorder patients with bulimic symptoms. This study confirmed that there is substantial heterogeneity among patients, and this has important treatment implications (see Thompson-Brenner & Westen, 2005). Clinicians distinguished three different personality types: (1) a high functioning perfectionistic group (which, coincidentally, was the largest group); (2) an emotionally constricted group; and (3) a dysregulated group. The dysregulated group had the poorest functioning and had problems with impulsivity, self-esteem, and feeling neglected. Group comparisons showed that the conscripted and dysregulated groups had the poorest treatment outcomes, with recovery occurring 5 to 10 months later than the recovery time for the perfectionistic group.

Several authors have attested to the importance of matching treatments to the clients' personality characteristics. Blatt and Felsen (1993) have noted that depression-prone individuals who vary in their personality features also tend to differ in the types of issues that surface during the treatment process and in their responses to specific clinical interventions (Blatt & Felsen, 1993). An interactionistic approach is relevant here because some evidence suggests that improvement occurs when there is a match between the client's personality structure and the particular therapeutic context that they encounter (Blatt & Felsen, 1993). Blatt and his colleagues have explored the matching of treatments to personality characteristics as part of their Menninger Psychotherapy Research Project (see Blatt, 1992; Blatt & Shahar, 2004). Blatt (1992) compared traditional psychotherapy with supportive expressive therapy as delivered to patients high in self-criticism (the introjective style) or high in dependency (the anaclitic style). It was found that psychoanalysis was generally more effective than supportive expressive therapy but especially for the people who were high in self-criticism. Blatt and Shahar (2004) conducted a follow-up study that further evaluated the treatment effects. They found that psychoanalysis with self-critical patients resulted in a significant reduction in malevolent hostile imagery, while the same reduction in malevolent hostile imagery was found for dependent patients who received supportive expressive therapy. The authors argued that the supportive therapy offers a form of emotional support that satisfied the yearning for intimacy and connectedness of those patients high in dependency. These findings emerged even though the results were based on a small sample of participants.

Other research by Blatt and Zuroff and their colleagues has found that depression patients who are high in perfectionism tend to be treatment-resistant and seem to require longer treatment interventions (see Blatt & Zuroff, 2002). Part of the problem may be an unwillingness for perfectionists to relinquish their impossibly high standards. These standards may have become a central part of their personal identities.

Costa and McCrae (1992a) noted that people with high levels of neuroticism are less likely to benefit from treatment, even though scores from the treatment rejection subscale of the Morey's Personality Assessment Inventory showed that people with high neuroticism were much less likely to reject treatment. They also noted in general that attempts should be made to match treatments with broad personality characteristics. Specifically, they suggested that extroverts will benefit from treatments that require social interaction, while introverts should prefer therapies such as a behavioural or Gestalt intervention, where the therapist has a greater and more directive role. People high in openness should be open to novel ideas and approaches, while people low in openness will have conventional beliefs and should be more responsive to directive psychotherapies.

Schema therapy is a newly emerging technique that clearly has its roots in individualized personality assessment. Schema therapy has evolved from the pioneering efforts of cognitive theorists such as Aaron Beck. Schema therapy was developed by Geoffrey Young and his colleagues (see Young, Klosko, & Weishaar, 2003). Recall that schemas are cognitive categories that guide our attention to and retention of information, both past and present. Young has attributed vulnerability to psychological disorders to the early maladaptive schemas (EMSs) that we have formed. EMSs are broad, pervasive, and dysfunctional patterns involving the self and the self in relation to others. It includes memories, bodily sensations, emotions, and, of course, cognitions. The EMSs reflect enduring patterns that may be latent but activated following the occurrence of life events relevant to specific EMSs. The links with models such as those proposed by Murray and Erikson are readily apparent because it is hypothesized that EMSs develop when needs are frustrated and not met. The key needs are the needs for (1) safety; (2) predictability; (3) love, nurturance, and attention; (4) acceptance and praise; (5) empathy; (6) guidance and protection; and (7) validation of feelings of need.

A total of 18 EMSs have been identified thus far. Some representative EMSs are abandonment, abuse and mistrust, failure, emotional deprivation, entitlement, overcontrol, and unrelenting standards. The first goal in schema therapy is to assess each unique personality and identify its particular EMS. Therapy can be directed to changing and perhaps removing each EMS. Several studies have associated particular EMSs with personality dysfunction. For instance, patients with borderline personality disorder tend to have EMSs reflecting themes of abandonment, defectiveness/shame, and dependence/incompetence (Jovev & Jackson, 2002). The same investigation found that obsessive–compulsive personality disorder was associated with unrelenting standards, while avoidant personality disorder was associated with emotional inhibition.

Initial evidence indicates that schema therapy may be quite effective. For instance, Bamber (2004) recounted the case study analysis of Jimmy, a man who had suffered from chronic agoraphobia for over 30 years. Agoraphobia is a fear of open spaces, and people with agoraphobia have been known to stay inside their houses for several years. Bamber reported that schema therapy was highly successful with Jimmy, even though other therapies had failed. Another recent intervention study conducted in Norway confirmed that EMSs were linked meaningfully with personality disorder functions, and removal of the EMS predicted relief from the symptoms of personality disorder (Nordahl, Holthe, & Haugum, 2005).

It seems rather obvious that treatment interventions should take core personality factors into account, and if this is done, there is the promise of improvement. However, it must also be acknowledged that personality change can be quite difficult, in part because attempts to modify personality can be very threatening for the patient. The patient must be highly motivated and realize that an intervention that takes place over a considerable period of time may be what is needed.

Sociotropy and Autonomy

Beck (1983) proposed that depression is associated with two personality styles known as **sociotropy** and **autonomy**. Sociotropic individuals are dependent on others. They are especially concerned with pleasing others, avoiding disapproval, and avoiding separation. Autonomy is an achievement-related construct that focuses on self-critical goal striving, along with a desire for solitude and an individualistic form of freedom from control. The Sociotropy–Autonomy Scale (SAS; Beck, Epstein, Harrison, & Emery, 1983) is the primary measure used to assess these dimensions. The scale consists of two 30-item subscales representing sociotropy and autonomy.

At present, research with the SAS has indicated a fairly consistent positive association between sociotropy and depression, but it has often been found that autonomy and depression are unrelated (Nietzel & Harris, 1990). Psychometric investigations have provided some insight into these data. Research has shown that the autonomy subscale suffers from comparatively low internal consistency and test–retest reliability (Robins, 1985). Moreover, the items comprising the SAS autonomy scale have been questioned on whether they have adequate content validity. For example, Blaney and Kutcher (1991) concluded that the SAS autonomy scale may be more suitable as an inverse measure of dependency, rather than as a measure of self-critical, autonomous tendencies.

The problems inherent in the SAS led to the development of alternative measures of sociotropy and autonomy. The revised Sociotropy–Autonomy Scale by Clark and Beck (1991) assesses sociotropy and two aspects of autonomy known as solitude and independence. Currently, the most extensively used measure of sociotropy and autonomy is the Personal Style Inventory (PSI; Robins et al., 1994). Sociotropy is tapped by three subscales that assess dependency, an excessive concern about what other people think of the self, and an excessive need to please others. Autonomy is tapped by three subscales measuring need for control, defensive separation from others, and self-critical perfectionistic strivings. Interestingly, a new study with the PSI found that autonomy was a prospective predictor of the recurrence of depression among those with a history of depression (Mongrain & Blackburn, 2006).

Thus, past indications of the limited predictiveness of autonomy probably reflected, at least to some degree, the psychometric limitations of the initial autonomy measure.

Perfectionism

In Chapter 12, we discussed Blatt's (1995) seminal paper on the destructiveness of perfectionism and the case histories he outlined. Unfortunately, history is replete with well-known perfectionists who suffered from depression and who seemed to evaluate themselves according to very exacting standards (e.g., Winston Churchill, Virginia Woolf).

Perfectionism has been discussed already in various chapters of this book, so an extensive definition of perfectionism will not be provided here. Over the past 15 years, extensive research on depression has explored the role of individual differences in perfectionism (Hewitt & Flett, 1991, 1993). This research indicates that certain dimensions of perfectionism may be associated not only with concurrent levels of depressive symptomatology but also with the chronicity and persistence of depressive symptoms (Hewitt, Flett, Ediger, Norton, & Flynn, 1999).

Research with the Multidimensional Perfectionism Scale (Hewitt & Flett, 1991) has focused on three perfectionism dimensions: self-oriented perfectionism (exceeding high personal standards), other-oriented perfectionism (demanding perfection from others), and socially prescribed perfectionism (a pressure to be perfect imposed on the self). This research has shown that self-oriented perfectionism has an inconsistent link with depression in student samples, but it tends to be associated consistently with elevated depression in patient samples (see Hewitt & Flett, 1993). Socially prescribed perfectionism is associated consistently with depression in student samples and in clinical samples (e.g., Hewitt & Flett, 1993). However, one concern is the specificity issue. Research has established that not only is socially prescribed perfectionism linked with depression, but it is also associated with other forms of maladjustment, including anxiety (Hewitt & Flett, 1991). Thus, association with depression is said to be non-specific.

Another concern is that perhaps the consistent link between socially prescribed perfectionism and depression reflects a mood congruent with self-reporting bias. That is, perhaps the association with socially prescribed perfectionism reflects a tendency for people in a depressed state to complain about unpleasant things (e.g., "People expect too much from me"). However, a recent study conducted in Israel found that peers rated their friends as elevated in both socially prescribed perfectionism and depression (Flett, Besser, & Hewitt, 2005). Thus, the association between socially prescribed perfectionism and depression is detectable with various forms of assessment.

It was suggested above that self-oriented perfectionism has sometimes been linked with depression, but not always; in fact, some data from student samples indicate that self-oriented perfectionism is a protective factor that is associated negatively with depression. These results underscore the need to consider self-oriented perfectionism and other perfectionism dimensions within the context of ego-involving life stressors. Self-oriented perfectionists are especially likely to be depressed following failure experiences (Besser, Flett, & Hewitt, 2005).

In addition to considering stress as a moderating factor, it is important to evaluate other possible mediating and moderating factors as well. For instance, Martin et al. (1996) showed that low self-efficacy moderated the link between socially prescribed perfectionism and depression. Other research has focused on coping styles and social support in terms of their role as moderators and mediators (see Blankstein & Dunkley, 2002; Hewitt & Flett, 2002).

It is not enough to suggest at the theoretical level that perfectionism is associated with depression, and various mechanisms may contribute to this association. The overarching question is: How do people become perfectionistic in the first place to the point that it may put them in personal jeopardy? Flett and Hewitt (2002) outlined three models, which are described next.

The Social Expectations Model

Both Hamachek (1978) and Missildine (1963) discussed the development of perfectionism in response to contingent parental approval. That is, the child learns that parental approval is forthcoming if the child is perfect. This idea is derived from Rogers' (1951) work on conditions of worth. Rogers maintained that children are prone to low self-esteem when parental approval is contingent on meeting parental expectations. In the case of perfectionism, it is believed that the parental standards are quite high, and this emphasis is reflected in the content of perfectionism instruments, such as the Frost Multidimensional Perfectionism Scale, which has a high parental expectations subscale (Frost, Marten, Lahart, & Rosenblate, 1990).

The Social Learning Model

The social learning model focuses on the role of imitation of perfectionism that presumably resides in parents. Children with perfectionistic parents will have a tendency to imitate their parents. Social learning will also take place as a result of the developmental tendency for young children to have a very idealized notion of their parents; many children will want to be like their "perfect" parents.

The possible role of social learning in the acquisition of perfectionistic tendencies was demonstrated in the classic research conducted by Bandura and his colleagues (for a summary, see Bandura, Grusec, & Menlove, 1967; Bandura & Kupers, 1964, 1986). This research demonstrates that children tend to imitate and embrace the evaluative standards modelled by others, and this extends to imitating the self-evaluative tendencies of adults. For example, in the Bandura and Kupers (1964) experiment, children were exposed to an adult model who had high or low standards that had to be met in order to engage in self-reward. Bandura and Kupers found that children exposed to models who rewarded themselves only after meeting high standards were unlikely to reward themselves unless they met high standards as well. In contrast, children exposed to models who rewarded themselves for meeting lower standards imitated this pattern of self-reinforcement.

The Social Reaction Model

The social reaction model is based on the premise that children who become perfectionists have been exposed to a harsh environment. Harshness can come in many forms; it can involve exposure to physical abuse and psychological maltreatment, including love withdrawal and exposure to shame, or it can involve a chaotic family environment. The child reacts or responds to this environment by becoming perfectionistic, almost as a coping mechanism. Perfectionism as a social reaction or response to adversity can involve several interrelated goals. The child can become perfectionistic in an attempt to escape from or to minimize further abuse and to reduce exposure to shame and humiliation (e.g., "If I am perfect, no one will hurt me"). Alternatively, the child may become perfectionistic as a way of trying to establish a sense of control and predictability in a highly unpredictable environment. One aspect of this is a lack of consistency on the part of parents and other caregivers.

In 2006, Ashley Judd revealed that she received treatment for perfectionism and depression. Extreme perfectionism was her response to chaos in her childhood.

The social reaction model of perfectionism can be applied to actress Ashley Judd. In 2006, she revealed that she received treatment for depression for 47 days. Judd attributed her illness to extreme perfectionism. She indicated that her perfectionism stemmed from a chaotic upbringing that saw her move 12 times in 11 years during her childhood. In an interview in a magazine, Judd described perfectionism as the highest form of self-abuse.

Chapter 13 presented a comprehensive overview of the role of personality factors in psychopathology. Not only may personality traits and temperaments be associated with vulnerability to psychological problems, but they may also influence the persistence and course of symptoms, and the individual's willingness to seek and their responsiveness to treatment.

Abnormality in general and personality dysfunction in particular were discussed in terms of the need to go beyond the criterion of unusual or atypical behaviour in a statistical sense. Several criteria must be considered, including the situational appropriateness of the behaviour and the person's cultural background, along with the issues of whether the abnormal behaviour is associated with role impairment and is causing significant distress for the afflicted person as well as the people in their lives. Conceptualizations of personality disorder consider such issues as the rigidity of the behaviour and whether it reflects a fragile sense of self. Aberrant interpersonal relationships are strongly considered as well.

This general discussion of personality dysfunction then was supplemented by an analysis of personality dysfunction from both a categorical and a dimensional perspective, with the caveat that existing evidence is mostly consistent with a dimension view. The categorical approach was outlined with respect to Cluster A, Cluster B, and Cluster C personality disorders. Cluster A disorders reflect odd and eccentric tendencies, Cluster B disorders reflect hostile and extrapunitive tendencies, and Cluster C disorders reflect anxious and fearful tendencies. With Cluster B, extreme forms of anti-social personality disorder get reflected in psychopathy, which often involves a great propensity for violence without any remorse for the victim.

The discussion of personality disorder categories was followed by descriptions of dimensional models. Particular attention was given to Cloninger's tridimensional model, consisting initially of reward dependence, novelty seeking, and harm avoidance temperament dimensions. These dimensions were related to individual differences in biological functioning. Subsequent extensions of Cloninger's model added the temperament dimension of persistence as well as three character orientations (self-transcendence, co-operativeness, and self-directedness). Self-directedness and co-operativeness were found to have associations with most personality disorders.

The five-factor model was also examined in terms of its relevance to personality disorders. Some scholars have suggested that the five-factor model is not adequate from a clinical perspective, so it has been supplemented with other dimensional frameworks, including the PSY-5 model from the MMPI and the Alternative Five posited by Zuckerman and his associates. These models are particularly useful in accounting for behavioural disorders that reflect a lack of constraint and anti-social and aggressive behaviours. The dimensional framework advocated by Livesley and his associates is also receiving a great deal of attention. It consists of several dimensions that reflect the factors of emotional dysregulation (similar to neuroticism), dissocial behaviour, inhibition, and compulsivity.

The chapter concluded with a discussion of the role of personality factors in alcoholism and binge drinking and the role of personality in depression. There have been long stretches where the importance of personality factors has been discounted, and the concept of "the addictive personality" has fallen out of favour. Contemporary research suggests that personality factors that reflect either disinhibition (e.g., sensation seeking) and the need to relieve stress and tension do indeed play a role in vulnerability to addiction. These issues were explored further within the context of explanatory theories that focus on the principles of social learning theory and on personality constructs such as self-handicapping and self-consciousness.

Depression was explored in terms of its association with numerous personality constructs. In addition to the five-factor model, depression was examined with respect to Blatt's model of self-criticism and autonomy, and Beck's model of sociotropy and autonomy. Perfectionism was also explored as a multidimensional entity. The development of individual differences in perfectionism was explored with respect to the social learning model (imitating the standards of models), the social expectations model, and the social reaction model (a response to abuse or chaos).

Questions to Consider

1 Most evidence indicates that personality disorder symptoms are generalizable and fairly similar across cultures, yet recall that Paris disagrees with this set of findings. He believes that there will be culture-specific differences in the phenomenology and antecedents of personality disorders. What do you believe? Do you think that future research will identify differences in personality disorders between collectivistic and individualistic cultures?

2 Do you believe in the concept of depressive personality disorder? Have you encountered some people who seem persistently gloomy and depressed in their outlook? If so, what developmental factors do you think contributed to this outlook? Is the family of origin a key factor in terms of early life experiences? Or do you emphasize the role of biologically inherited differences?

3 Why do you think a categorical approach to diagnosis has persisted despite overwhelming evidence suggesting that a dimensional view is more appropriate? Do you think it has anything to do with it being easier to think of other people as being in a category or not being in a category? Do you think it is reasonable to suggest that the best approach could be to establish whether a person is or is not suffering from a disorder (categorical) and then look for dimensional differences within the category?

4 It was noted that people with personality disorders are often unaware of their symptoms and that self-reports need to be supplemented with observer ratings. Do you think those with personality disorders really are unaware? Can you think of people in your life who seem oblivious to how other people regard them?

5 Comorbidity is a major challenge to a categorical diagnostic approach to abnormality. Do you think that comorbidity exists because diagnostic categories simply need to be refined and described more clearly? Or do you think that extreme dysfunction comes in many forms, and deeply disturbed people simply do have a wide range of symptoms?
Do you think it is possible for narcissism to have an adaptive component? Do you think that narcissism is expressed similarly in how it is displayed and developed in collectivistic versus individualistic cultures?

6 Do you think it is possible for narcissism to have an adaptive component? Do you think that narcissism is expressed similarly in how it is displayed and developed collectivistic versus individualistic cultures?

7 Review the characteristics of psychopaths. When it comes to responding to treatment, do you think that psychopaths are beyond hope? Could it be that sufficient resources have simply not been available so most psychopaths never receive the level of treatment they require? What would Carl Rogers say about the possibility of treating psychopaths? What would he do?

8 Do you think that binge drinking is a problem on your campus? Are male and female binge drinkers very different, or are they basically the same in terms of their behaviours, motives, and personality features? If you were hired to put a preventive program into place on your campus, what things would you do? How would you incorporate a focus on personality factors?

Key Terms

addiction-prone personality, p. 565
autonomy, p. 577
comorbidity, p. 540
culture-bound syndromes, p. 535
narcissistic personality disorder, p. 548
psychopathy, p. 547
schema therapy, p. 576
self-awareness model of drinking, p. 570
self-based heuristic, p. 550
self-handicapping theory of drinking, p. 571
signs, p. 550
social learning theory of alcoholism, p. 569
sociotropy, p. 577

Key Theorists

Sidney Blatt, p. 574
Robert Bornstein , p. 552
C. Robert Cloninger, p. 554
Robert Hare, p. 547
John Livesley, p. 563
Theodore Millon, p. 539
Marvin Zuckerman, p. 563

chapter fourteen

PSYCHOBIOGRAPHY AND PERSONOLOGY: SUMMING UP THE WHOLE PERSON

- What Psychobiography Tells Us about Personality
- Methodological Issues and Concerns
- Psychobiographical Sketches
    - Salvador Dali
    - Sylvia Plath
    - Anne Sexton
    - Ozzy Osbourne

Lives are not lived in the laboratory. In the real world, personalities are not divided into statistically analyzable components. Experiments and correlational studies, and statistical analyses of the data they generate, may identify significant variables in the lives of people-in-general. But I haven't encountered a psychologist yet who could put together a whole person from those statistical body-parts and honestly cry out, "It's Alive!"

—ALAN ELMS (1994, P. 12–13)

Trying to understand someone by giving them a diagnosis is virtually worthless.

—WILLIAM TODD SCHULTZ (2005)

It is our one-sided preoccupation with the general that renders our encounters with concrete personalities often inept and sometimes clownish.

—GORDON ALLPORT (1962)

CONSIDER THE FOLLOWING SCENARIO and how you might react. Suppose you came into a personality lab with several other students and the researcher had everyone complete some self-report scales and some questions tapping whether you are a night person or a day person. Years later, you are reading the work of this researcher and you come across a published description of the study you participated in. For argument's sake, let's say that the study found that morning people, relative to night people, do better at university. Yet you know that you are a night person and you graduated at the top of your class. If you could contact the researcher with your comments, what would you say? You would probably tell the researcher that things are not so simple; and in order to know you and the other students in this study, they need to spend more time and really get to know each person in the study. It is through this approach that the researcher would discover that heterogeneity exists among the night people, and generalizations simply do not capture the uniqueness of these people.

Chapter 14 fits with this line of thinking because it adopts an idiographic focus and examines the role of personality factors in psychobiographies. This chapter presents an opportunity to reiterate the message first espoused by Allport and Murray that we must retain a focus on the whole person, as a supplement to variable-centred approaches. In addition, Chapter 14 illustrates the relevance of personality traits and personality theories mentioned earlier in this book and shows how they pertain to the study of actual people and their actual lives. The chapter begins with an overview of the strengths and limitations of psychobiography and the various purposes that are served through psychobiographies. This discussion includes an overview of methodological factors and issues that must be considered when seeking to provide an accurate psychobiography. This more general discussion of psychobiography is followed by a series of brief psychobiographical sketches that illustrate how personality factors and theories can be applied to the lives of some well-known personalities.

Many psychobiographies can be found in the published literature. **Psychobiographies** are case studies that are conducted from a psychological perspective, identifying and explaining issues and themes throughout a person's life. Because they are case studies, psychobiographies have inherent methodological limitations, including limited generalizability and concerns about interpretive biases. These issues are discussed in more detail below. However, a huge plus for psychobiographies is that in a study of an actual person, there is little doubt that the personality themes reflect what is personally significant for that person. As noted by **Alan Elms** (1994), cross-sectional nomothetic investigations establish statistical significance; but are the variables being investigated personally significant for the participants? Idiographic investigations tend to focus on what matters to a particular person.

In Chapter 6, a psychobiography of Adolf Hitler was mentioned. The Office of Strategic Services (OSS), the wartime U.S. intelligence agency, conducted it in 1943 to gain military advantages. (This analysis is available online at www.lawschool.cornell.edu/library/donovan/hitler/).

As one of the leading advocates of studying the whole person, Murray contributed to that analysis of Hitler. He also conducted a lifelong study of Herman Melville (the author of *Moby Dick*). Murray never published his complete analysis of Melville, though he did publish papers with segments of his analysis. Recall that Murray believed in using multiple methods (methodological pluralism) as shown by the initial work reported in his 1938 book *Explorations in Personality*.

Freud published many psychobiographies. His analysis of Leonard da Vinci, published in 1910, is regarded as the most well-known of the early psychobiographies. It is also noteworthy because it is seen as a highly erroneous interpretation (see Elms, 2005). The chief limitation is that Freud based his analysis on just one childhood memory recounted by da Vinci: that of a vulture coming down to him when he was an infant. The vulture then used its tail feathers to beat da Vinci around the mouth! Elms (2003) felt that Freud's singular analysis of da Vinci was somewhat surprising in that Freud (1910) outlined a series of "proscriptive guidelines" that explicitly cautioned other scholars not to base an analysis on a single clue. Other guidelines advanced by Freud (1910) included examining the **external probability** and **internal probability** of data. External probability is a form of external validity, which requires establishing whether new information fits with accepted old information. Internal probability is a form of internal validity, which requires judging how new information about someone's internal psychological processes and internal structure fits with existing information about these processes.

Freud's analysis of Leonardo da Vinci is one of the most influential early psychobiographies, yet it was highly flawed.

KEY POINTS

- Psychobiographies are designed to inform us about the whole person. They illustrate the uniqueness and complexity of individuals.
- The conclusions drawn in psychobiographies cannot be generalized to other people. The lack of focus on general laws and scientific principles have led some to argue that psychobiographies are not scientific.

Other noteworthy contributions to the literature include the remarkable work of Erik Erikson. He is acknowledged primarily for his psychobiographies of Luther and Gandhi, which won the Pulitzer Prize. Erikson's psychobiographies as well as his work with people in particular societies (e.g., the Sioux Indians and Yurok Indians) helped demonstrate that one's cultural upbringing can have a profound impact on personal identity. Erikson has also been praised for removing "the handicap of orthodox psychology" (classic psychoanalytic theory) by providing a simple stage theory incorporating realistic life challenges to explain why people differ (Alexander, 2005). Whereas past authors had relied on classic Freudian theory, Erikson's analyses of Gandhi and Luther focused on his own theoretical views.

Other key developments in the history of psychobiography include **William Runyan's** widely cited paper in which he illustrated how different psychobiographical methods point to different explanations for why Vincent van Gogh cut off part of his ear (Runyan, 1981). Also worth noting is the insightful and detailed analysis of the psychological needs of disgraced U.S. president Richard Nixon. This analysis illustrated the utility of needs theory and concluded that Nixon was only moderate in the need for power, but he was quite high in the needs for affiliation and achievement (Winter & Carlson, 1988).

More recent psychobiographies can be found in the *Journal of Personality*. For instance, Simonton (1998) conducted a fine-grained analysis of British monarch King George III, whose trials and tribulations were summarized in the film *The Madness of King George*. King George III had at least five acknowledged bouts of mental illness and was often restrained against his wishes in a straightjacket. Simonton's study was unique because it included a measure of stress that was completed by raters to assess the stress experienced by King George during certain times in his life. This kind of analysis is known as a **time series analysis**: a statistical procedure applied to a single unit (person) with the unit being measured at several points in time with equal time intervals between assessments (Velicer & Plummer, 1998). It permits a prospective assessment of change over time in an individual. Simonton found some evidence that life stress played a role in the symptoms experienced by King George III, and this qualified past accounts that minimized the role of psychological factors. The correlations obtained were statistically significant but not large in magnitude. Note that a previous analysis of Beethoven found a stronger correlation ($r = .53$) between physical illness and biographical accounts of stress (Simonton, 1987). More important, the time series analysis of the King George III data established that the onset of stress preceded the onset of symptoms, and not vice versa. Thus, it is possible that his mental illness was, at least in part, a psychological response to stress. What stands out about this study in particular is that whereas most case histories focus solely on qualitative, subjective data analyses, Simonton demonstrated a way for psychobiographers to use quantitative data to evaluate a particular person. Simonton (2003) described at length ways in which qualitative research can become more scientific and can incorporate quantitative measures.

Perhaps the most compelling psychobiography was an analysis by Nasby and Read (1997) of the solo circumnavigator Dodge Morgan. Morgan, at the age of 54, sold his business and sailed around the world in just 150 days in 1986. What is particularly remarkable about this psychobiographical analysis is that Morgan completed personality tests both before and after his voyage. The tests included the Thematic Apperception Test and Jackson's Personality Research Form, which, as noted earlier, is based on Murray's theory of psychological needs. Morgan also provided an ongoing detailed account of his thoughts, feelings, and behaviours on the voyage and how these varied as a function of the events throughout the voyage. Life history data were also obtained. Thus, the psychobiography of Morgan is unique for its use of multiple methods (methodological pluralism).

Nasby and Read (1997) concluded that Morgan's predominant personality trait was autonomy. He was deemed to be highly independent and overly agentic in his orientation toward life, and this included an extremely high level of conscientiousness. He also had exhibitionistic needs and a strong need for control. Additional analyses of data gathered at the end of the voyage demonstrated how personality can shift over time, as the authors discovered that Morgan had increased significantly in his communal orientation after spending so much time by himself at sea.

KEY POINTS

- The psychobiography of circumnavigator Dodge Morgan stands as probably the most complete such analysis done thus far.
- It is a model example of the use of multiple methods (methodological pluralism) and multiple time frames (before, during, and after his voyage).
- The analysis concluded that Morgan was overly agentic, autonomous, and independent. He became more communal in his responses as he spent more time isolated at sea.

My own interest in psychobiography stemmed originally from two sources. First, I became interested in determining whether existing conceptualizations of perfectionism as a multidimensional construct could actually be applied and seem meaningful and useful when examining famous perfectionists. That is, when there is a focus on perfectionists rather than the perfectionism construct, does it make sense to distinguish among such dimensions as self-oriented, other-oriented, and socially prescribed perfectionism? The short answer is "Yes." My subsequent information search yielded many cases of perfectionists, some famous and some unknown, who had apparent elevations of various dimensions of perfectionism in a way that is in keeping with a multidimensional approach to the construct. Parenthetically, many of these perfectionists also suffered from health problems or diminished psychological well-being (for a summary, see Flett & Hewitt, 2002).

My interest also stemmed from teaching a fourth year senior undergraduate seminar course at York University on personality theory and behavioural disorders. This course had a psychobiographical component. Students were given the task of selecting a person, either living or dead, who had a behavioural disorder, and conducting a psychobiography of this person. Students enjoyed the opportunity to examine personality issues within the context of actual people and their life events. The emphasis on behavioural disorders meant that students had the opportunity to play the role of psychologist or psychiatrist, because the initial task was to identify someone with a diagnosable behavioural problem and be able to convince others that a problem could be detected. Over the years, students in my course have provided some amazing accounts of a wide range of characters. Favourite choices include authors (Virginia Wolfe, Ernest Hemingway, Edgar Allan Poe, Tennessee Williams), performers (Judy Garland, Billie Holiday), and anti-social and sadistic killers (Ted Bundy, Jeffrey Dahmer, Charles Manson, the Boston Strangler). More contemporary figures such as Syd Barrett from Pink Floyd, Kurt Cobain from Nirvana, Eminem, and Brian Warner (aka Marilyn Manson) have also been of interest. Fictional characters have even been analyzed (including such TV notables as Marge Simpson and Tony Soprano), as have people with unknown identities (Jack the Ripper).

This type of assignment requires students to review existing theories and select the ones that best fit the people under consideration. Students have used a wide range of theories in attempt to provide completed and rounded analyses. This is in keeping with sound advice from Elms (1994), who suggested that a key criterion in good versus bad psychobiography is the psychobiographer's eclecticism. Rather than being locked into one particular theoretical orientation, it makes sense to match the complexity of the person being studied with a complex approach using many theoretical orientations. Some aspects of a person are best explained by one theoretical approach, while other aspects of the same person fit better with other theories.

Developmental theories have often been cited, including the theoretical accounts provided by Freud, Erikson, and Maslow. This accords with Elms (2005) who examined the theories he has used most often in psychobiographies. Elms concluded that the top choices include Freudian theory, Erikson's developmental stages, clinical theory, and **Silvan Tomkin's** script theory. Script theory has not been discussed previously in this text. It is discussed in more detail below in the section on life stories.

Other theories that have been used to great effect by students include Murray's theory of psychological needs, and Horney's conceptualization of neurotic needs and the tendencies to move toward, away from, and against people. That Horney's views have proved useful should come as no surprise. Paris (2002) provided a lengthy list of famous people who have been analyzed according to Horney's conceptualizations.

When it comes to using the work of other theorists from the psychoanalytic orientation, not surprisingly, students often interpreted evil characteristics in terms of Jung's concept of the shadow, while self-esteem issues were traced back to Adler's concept of the inferiority complex and the role of birth order in personality development. Self-esteem deficits were occasionally interpreted through reference to Sullivan's concepts of the good me and the bad me. The concepts of reward, punishment, and imitation are also highly relevant, so social learning theory and operant conditioning were often cited. Finally, attachment style theory was often employed to account for neurotic tendencies involving high levels of anxiety or extreme detachment from other people, while the interpersonal circumplex has been applied to dominant and hostile individuals.

WHAT PSYCHOBIOGRAPHY TELLS US ABOUT PERSONALITY

The seminar course described above has retained a psychobiographical component over the years because of the many lessons that have been learned. First and foremost, this psychobiography assignment taught students that an individual's personality is exceedingly complex. If the goal of these budding personologists is to obtain a complete analysis of a person, they must consider multiple traits and the overall structure of personality. The complexity of individual personalities can be illustrated in many ways. Consider, for instance, notorious serial killers such as Ted Bundy. How can students come to grips with both his heinous acts and his pro-social acts (e.g., working on a suicide hotline and saving an elderly woman who was being mugged)? Bundy is an example of someone who was exceedingly extroverted (highly oriented toward other people), but this extroversion often veered into extreme anti-social, murderous behaviour.

Allport (1962) reminded us that when seeking to understand a person, we need to focus both on personality content (the cardinal traits) and on personality structure (the various components of the self and how they might be interrelated). He advocated a return to Baldwin's (1942) concept of **personal structure analysis** as one way to obtain insight into structural issues. Personal structure analysis involves an if-then contingency analysis that can be used when people describe themselves and their life stories. Once a person mentions some aspect of his or her self, that statement's context is analyzed. For instance, if a person describes his or her occupation, is the accompanying affective tone positive, negative, or neutral? When this person describes a personally relevant trait, is it closely followed by references to other people (the self in relation to others)? And is the description of these other people done in a way that is positive, negative, neutral, or seemingly indifferent? This type of analysis provides a sense of what concepts and themes are linked within a person.

Psychobiography and the study of individual lives also reinforce that it is absolutely necessary to take situational factors into account when seeking to describe and explain someone. Any attempt to study someone in detail must allow for the influence of situational factors (the concept of "press" to which Murray referred; see Chapter 6). Situational factors may lead to positive development (positive press) or they can lead to negative development (negative press). When conducting a psychobiography, situational factors often involve negative life events that are interpreted within the framework of diathesis–stress models, with personality serving as the diathesis or vulnerability component that is activated or triggered by a life event that is a reflection of this personality vulnerability.

Psychobiographical analyses also illustrate just how unsatisfying it is to restrict a personal analysis to a descriptive account without also including an explanatory component. Many scholars have observed that the ultimate goals of personality (indeed psychology) are explanation and prediction rather than mere description. Accordingly, students in my course were required to first describe an individual's personality traits (the "what" of personality—what traits are evident) and then explain how these traits came about. Here the classic personality theories proved to be very useful. Although psychoanalytic theorists are often criticized because many psychoanalytic concepts are untestable, psychoanalytic theories seem quite applicable when conducting a psychobiographical analysis. Clearly, theorists such as Freud, Adler, and Horney had their own biases, but they also seemed to have an inherent capacity to understand people and the underlying dynamics of personality processes. Of course, students also made use of other classic theories including the phenomenological and humanistic theories and the learning theories.

Psychobiographies can also be a very useful way of testing theories and frameworks that stem originally from a variable-centred approach but have seldom been applied to an individual case study. Important insights can be obtained about personality constructs by examining them with respect to actual people. One example is the desire for control construct, which is assessed by Burger and Cooper's (1979) Desire for Control Scale. Much of the item content on this 20-item inventory has positive connotations. Burger's (1992) book contains extensive descriptions of the positive aspects of desire for control. The negative aspects of the desire for control may have been masked by a research strategy that relied heavily on self-report data. History is replete with famous and infamous people who have been described uncharitably as "control freaks," and with these people, the desire for control has very negative features. Examining the need for control in specific individuals would enable personologists to determine whether it is possible to distinguish an adaptive versus maladaptive need for control, and it would help pinpoint when functional forms of the need for control become dysfunctional.

As well, psychobiographies that include personality factors can help identify constructs or frameworks that deserve more theoretical and empirical attention. One clear example is the relevance of personality capabilities as opposed to personality traits. The detailed study of an individual across his or her lifespan can help distinguish usual and typical personality features (traits) from capabilities that are revealed during isolated incidents or only in certain contexts. The significance of distinguishing how someone usually is versus what they are capable of is particularly evident when examining a person who has little history of anti-social activity (someone who is low on the trait PSY-5 aggressiveness scale) yet at isolated times demonstrates the capacity of acting in a very anti-social way.

Finally, psychobiographies remind us of the need to always keep in mind the limitations of the data and the methods used to collect them. There is no way to get around the fact that psychobiographies are constructed from inherently subjective analyses that may reflect the psychobiographer's biases and perspectives. What are we referring to when we discuss the concepts of validity and reliability in the context of psychobiography? Validity is almost impossible to establish, because what criterion can be used to determine the validity of a psychobiographical analysis? However, as noted by Elms (1994), one of psychobiography's virtues is that it is based on publicly available data. One general way to evaluate validity is to see whether the inferences and conclusions reached by one psychobiographer can be evaluated and accepted by subsequent scholars. Of course, these subsequent scholars may be bringing their own biases to the re-analysis of data. Still, as noted by Allport (1962), for the study of the individual to be regarded as scientific or even an approximate science, established observer reliability is an absolute must.

Reliability can be evaluated in different ways. As noted by **Irving Alexander** (1988), reliability can be assessed based on whether different pieces of information about a particular person from different periods of the person's life all converge consistently on the same theme. That is, reliability can be evaluated by what Alexander refers to as the **consistency criterion**. Reliability can also be investigated in terms of whether different analysts with access to the same information tend to reach the same conclusions about a person. Even here however, it is complicated because in order to conduct a fair test, it is essential to begin with two or more psychobiographers who have an equal level of insight into people and equivalent backgrounds in core psychological theories, including personality theories. All of this underscores that a more qualitative approach is going to be subjective to some degree, but measures such as inter-rater agreement can still lend a quantitative aspect to qualitative approaches.

Regarding the subjective nature of psychobiographies, a reasonable approach was suggested by **William Runyan** (2005) in his chapter in the *Handbook of Psychobiography* (see Schultz, 2005). In addition to coining the term **historical–interpretive psychology** to describe this area, Runyan (2005) suggested that psychobiography should not be a "one-shot affair," but instead should use "quasi-judicial" procedures, analogous to procedures in courts of law, where people with different interests and different evidence argue for different conclusions (p. 21). If viewed from this perspective, differences in opinion among scholars engaged in psychobiography may lead ultimately to new insights. Thus, the subjective aspect of psychobiography is recognized, but it is also valued to the extent that different viewpoints have merit.

The Functions of Psychobiography

What purposes are served by psychobiography? A psychobiography can be conducted for several different reasons. The McAdams and West (1997) review paper summarizes the various types of case studies that have been conducted and the forms they have taken. They identified three functions that also apply to psychobiographies. The first function is **exemplification**, with the goal to illustrate or display how a personality concept or theory is relevant to a specific person. For instance, regarding Sylvia Plath, who is discussed later in this chapter, a scholar wishing to exemplify the Electra complex could point to Plath's affection for her father and the impact that his death had on her psyche. As noted by Simonton (1989), exemplification reflects a nomothetic goal because the emphasis is on using data from an individual to support a general psychological principle.

The second function is discovery. McAdams and West (1997) cited Allport (1942) for his contention that case studies are a very viable way of taking the information from a particular person and coming up with a new insight or theory that advances understanding. It is probably no coincidence that many major personality theorists (e.g., Freud, Rogers, Horney, Sullivan) provided treatment to clients, and the insights learned from specific individuals were subsequently incorporated into comprehensive theories. We know that this is certainly the case with Freud because of the well-known case studies he provided.

The third function is comparison. McAdams and West (1997) observed that comparison "is at the heart of science" (p. 765), and comparisons can occur at many different levels. First, it is possible to compare how the characteristics of an individual fit with a theory of personality (see McAdams & West, 1997). It is also possible to compare the psychobiographies of different people with different lives but who share some attribute (e.g., comparisons among perfectionists). This kind of comparative analysis underscores that just like snowflakes, no two people are exactly alike, even though they may share some general characteristics. In the case of perfectionists, for example, it is possible and important to distinguish neurotic perfectionists (people who despair over their imperfections) and narcissistic perfectionists (people who think they are capable of being perfect or at least much more capable than other people). Any comparison of perfectionists would likely identify differences but it would also identify some similarities and commonalities that pertain to most perfectionists. A final type of comparison is a case study that compares the usefulness and comprehensiveness of various personality theories and personality frameworks. A challenging test for existing frameworks is to see the extent to which they are actually used when a student is given the task of conducting his or her own psychobiography. For instance, regarding the clinical usefulness of the five-factor model versus the PSY-5 (see Chapter 13), numerous students have related to me that they found the PSY-5 to be much more relevant. Highly anti-social people with little constraint were more easily understood and better interpreted by referring to the PSY-5. Other students reported that the interpersonal circumplex was particularly helpful, especially when the person under consideration seemed to have a personality disorder with clear interpersonal manifestations.

A fourth function that should be noted is that psychobiographies can also be conducted for very practical, applied purposes. We noted earlier that the United States OSS conducted a psychobiography of Hitler to try to predict what he would do depending on how the Second World War progressed. What are some of the other practical uses of psychobiography? Applied Perspective 14.1 examines this issue with reference to a very different form of psychobiography as case study analysis.

KEY POINTS

- Psychobiographers have been used for important practical purposes, including predicting the actions of political figures (e.g., Hitler) and trying to identify criminals (e.g., Jack the Ripper).
- Psychobiographies are used for the purposes of discovery, exemplification, and comparison. Exemplification represents using an individual case to confirm general principles derived from the nomothetic approach.

Applied Perspective 14.1 The Limitations of Using Psychobiographical Information to Identify Criminals

Personality profiles invariably include an element of psychobiography. Personality profiles examine an individual's motives and behaviours, personality traits, life history, and environmental contexts. Profiling of this sort is often for applied purposes such as establishing an unknown person's identity. For instance, a recent development is that companies and individuals are hiring psychologists to perform psychological profiles using psychobiographical information. This was illustrated in an interview conducted in 2003 with Richard Pomerance for *The New England Psychologist* (see Pomerance, 2003). It was noted in this article that Pomerance conducted one profile analysis of a company and its employees to help a group of executives decide whether they were going to join a competing firm. Another profiling analysis was done to help a woman cope with the knowledgethat her dead boyfriend had deceived her. Presumably, she was seeking to understand how and why the deception occurred through an analysis of his characteristics and behaviours. Other psychologists have reported doing profilesfor people who wanted to get a better understanding into the nature and character of their partners.

The one practical use of profiling that has garnered the most attention by far is the use of psychobiographical information by the police and related agencies to identify criminals. This is a very different kind of psychobiographical analysis, because in most instances, the person being profiled is unknown and remains to be identified. Thus, it goes against Allport's (1938) advice for personologists to conduct case studies only on people they have known for a long time.

To what extent is this offender profiling actually representing "personality profiling?" Douglas et al.

(1986) described offender profiling as "identifying the major personality and behavioral characteristics of an individual" (p. 405). Turvey (1999) stated that "Personality is perhaps the most frequently cited offender characteristic in the profiling literature" (p. 164). Personality is also implicated if, as Turco (1990) has suggested, the crime scene is, in essence, a personality projection (Turco, 1990).

Profiling is a general investigative tool that supplements but does not replace other investigation techniques and is most likely to be used with unusual crimes that are not solved easily through other methods (see Geberth, 1983, 1996; Hazelwood, Ressler, Depue, & Douglas, 1995). The use of profiling to identify unknown offenders accounts for only some instances when profiling is used. The original and most common use of profiling is to eliminate suspects (see Hazelwood et al., 1995; Petherick, 2006). It is also used to suggest effective lines of questioning when interviewing and interrogating suspected offenders. Compare, for instance, how you would frame questions for an introverted and reserved person versus a narcissistic suspect you hope to trip up because of their need to show how "smart" and "superior" they are.

When used for identifying unknown offenders, profiling may be defined as "an educated attempt to provide investigative agencies with specific information as to the type of individual who would have committed a certain crime" (Geberth, 1996, p. 492). Information will include conclusions drawn about demographic characteristics, motivational orientation, and related personality traits.

Norris (2006) noted that one of the earliest uses of profiling was an attempt to identify the nortorious serial killer Jack the Ripper, who murdered five prostitutes in London in the 1880s. More recently, the practice of offender profiling has been sensationalized as a result of movies such as *The Silence of the Lambs* and television shows such as *Profiler.* Offender profiling has also received attention from the media and the general public due to the published exploits of crime detection superstars such as John Douglas, who worked for the Federal Bureau of Investigation (FBI) in the United States, as well as instances when British psychologists and psychiatrists have put together accurate profiles that lead to the arrest and conviction of unknown offenders (see Bekerian & Jackson, 1997; Stevens, 1997; Turvey, 1999).

Criminal profiling has provided the prototype for movies such as *The Silence of the Lambs.*

Two models of criminal profiling have been identified (see Turvey, 1999). One model uses **deductive profiling**. The profile is based on deductive logic and inference after taking into account the information for a specific case.

The alternative model is known as **inductive profiling**, which uses general principles and patterns that have been gleaned from analyses of a relatively large database. This is a statistically based, actuarial form of prediction that tries to apply general principles to specific cases. The problem, of course, is that there is no assurance that general tendencies will apply to specific and unique cases.

According to Douglas and Olshaker (1997), profilers using the FBI-based approach believe that behaviour reflects personality, and they proceed in seven stages:

(1) Evaluation of the criminal act.
(2) Evaluation of the crime scene.
(3) Comprehensive analysis of the victim(s).
(4) Evaluation of initial police reports.
(5) Evaluation of the autopsy procedure and results.
(6) Development of a profile based on critical offender characteristics.
(7) Offering investigative suggestions.

Crime scenes are analyzed based on the FBI distinction between organized and disorganized offenders. Disorganized offenders tend to be younger and impulsive, while organized offenders are more systematic and methodical. This distinction was derived from the **Criminal Personality Research Project** conducted by the FBI (see Douglas, Ressler, Burgess, & Hartman,

1986). Douglas and associates conducted detailed interviews with incarcerated sex offenders about their behaviours, motives, and life history variables so the researchers could then distinguish disorganized and organized offenders and their associated characteristics. Douglas and associates found that for many, the violent act is a byproduct of a homicidal rage due to years of maltreatment, while for others, such as serial killer Charles Manson, sensational, planned acts of murder reflect a narcissistic need for recognition and attention (see Douglas & Olshaker, 1997). Violent acts that are not planned are commited by disorganized offenders.

How useful are criminal personality profiles? It depends on the criteria for success (see Petherick, 2006). By and large, user satisfaction surveys indicate that the police regard profiling as one of many valuable investigative tools. According to stricter criteria, offender profiles have much less usefulness. Profiles are incorrect at least as often as they are correct, as illustrated dramatically by the many incorrect aspects of the FBI profile formulated to identify the Unabomber. Of course, subjectivity is ever present and can undermine a profile's usefulness. Douglas alluded to this when he recounted that:

> One of the defense attorneys asked me if there was an objective numerical scale I used for measuring uniqueness. In other words, could I assign a number value to everything we did? The answer, of course, is no. Many, many factors come together in our evaluations, and, ultimately, it comes down to the individual analyst's judgment rather than any objective scale or test. (Douglas & Olshaker, 1997 p. 31)

Given this subjectivity, how accurate are criminal personality profiles? Unfortunately, the weight of existing evidence indicates that they are not very accurate (for current reviews, see Hicks & Sales, 2006; Petherick, 2006). Empirical research has also failed to support one of the key assumptions of the data-driven inductive approach: that there is no demonstrable association between one type of defence behaviour and presumed correlates in other domains (e.g., sociodemographic characteristics and offence history) (Mokros & Alison, 2002). These findings have led many reviewers to conclude that at present, criminal profiling is more of an art than a science (Turvey, 1999).

What problems limit the usefulness of profiling? One concern is that personality is often conceptualized and considered in a cursory way in personality profiles and these profiles simply do not reflect contemporary research and the broad range of theoretical approaches from the personality field that could be used. Other issues are that the profile's accuracy depends heavily on the skills of the individual profiler, and that two profilers may not produce the same profile due to different skills and perspectives (Bekerian & Jackson, 1997). However, to be fair, it is a very difficult task to identify offenders when the available information is limited and it is applied to the most challenging and unique cases. Also, there have been numerous cases where the profile has been accurate, or, as is more commonly the case, it was not possible to identify the offender but the profile did help eliminate innocent suspects (Rogers, 2003).

How can offender profiling be made more scientific? One recommendation is to simply adopt a more sophisticated approach to studying personality and to make greater use of contemporary research and theory. In addition, some authors have outlined the need for a dynamic interactionism approach that considers personality factors and situational factors (Allison, Bennell, & Mokros, 2002). Along similar lines, Stevens (1997) suggested that cultural differences need to be considered; to this end, methods developed primarily in North America and Britain may need to be tailored and altered for other jurisdictions.

In retrospect, it would probably be very useful to conduct a mega-project using the interview assessments that occurred as part of the Criminal Personality Research Project. It would be very useful to have unlimited resources and return to a more typical approach to psychobiography by conducting detailed psychobiographical analyses of a large number of incarcerated offenders. Ideally, psychobiographies would be conducted by multiple personologists trained in psychobiography to establish common personality themes across assessors. Offenders from around the world could be evaluated according to established and newer personality models. This information could then be incorporated into the personality profiles in the hopes of identifying unknown offenders.

METHODOLOGICAL ISSUES AND CONCERNS

Psychobiographies use a case study methodology and, as a result, will always have certain limitations. Clearly, it is not warranted to make generalizations from case studies to other individuals. Also, as noted earlier, the inherent subjectivity raises concerns about the possible role of bias in the issues that are focused on and the way they are selected. Various biases may exist, such as the **actor–observer bias**. People have an unfortunate tendency to ignore situational factors and instead focus on the dispositional personality features of the actor when asked to account for someone else's behaviour. A **confirmatory bias** also exists: people tend to disproportionately focus on information that is consistent with their initial beliefs about why specific events have occurred and why people have acted in particular ways. Other sources of bias include sexism: concerns have been raised that interpretations may be based on preconceived beliefs about differences between men and women (see Reinharz, 1994). Finally, cultural bias is also quite possible. These various biases remind us that psychobiographies have a subjective element, and this subjectivity can be repulsive to empiricists who wish to restrict the focus to observable and replicable phenomena.

These types of criticisms will always apply to psychobiographies no matter how well they are done. It is important to acknowledge these limitations from the outset and then use sound methodological principles and guidelines as much as possible to enhance the level of interpretation. What guidelines should be followed? The subsequent discussion of problems that limit psychobiographies includes a list of several criteria to keep in mind.

Criticisms of Psychobiography

Several criticisms of psychobiography are outlined below. More complete discussions can be found in Alexander (1988, 1990, 1992) and in the recently published *Handbook of Psychobiography* (see Schultz, 2005). Alexander (1990) compiled the problems outlined below.

One problem is referred to as the **critical period fallacy**. This is a tendency to place undue emphasis on one period of an individual's life without fully considering other periods. Too much may be made of a particular point in time. It is quite common, for instance, for psychobiographers to become quite Freudian in their approach and place great importance on early life experiences, which is known as **originology**. Erikson introduced the concept of originology to remind personologists to take a lifespan approach. Freud has been described as one of the chief "originologists" because of the psychobiographies he compiled. Elms (1994) noted that placing too much emphasis on originology undermines even many of the psychobiographies conducted on Freud himself and his life experiences.

One criticism of psychobiographies is referred to as critical period fallacy, where undue emphasis is placed on one period of an individual's life, such as early childhood.

Eventism is a problem related to the critical period fallacy and originism. This is the tendency to trace most of the characteristics and interpretation of an individual back to only one or two key events. There can be no denying that some people do experience an event that is so spectacular or traumatic that it has had a lasting and overarching influence on them. However, as documented by Howe (1997), most of us are influenced by a protracted series of events over a protracted time, which requires a broader focus.

Another problem in psychobiography occurs when there is simply a lack of adequate evidence. In general, psychobiographers should attempt to obtain as many different sources of relevant evidence as possible. Evidence can come in many forms, including letters, work products (paintings, books, songs), diaries and journals, and biographies and autobiographies. Unfortunately, some scholars engage in a very limited information search, or there simply is not enough evidence to fill in the gaps. This appears to be the case with a new book on the identity of Jack the Ripper, the notorious nineteenth-century serial killer in London. In the book, entitled *Uncle Jack*, author Tony Williams (Williams & Price, 2005) suggests that his ancestor Dr. John Williams, a Welsh physician, was actually Jack the Ripper. This doctor has not previously been identified as a possible suspect, even though he had contact in his physician's role with several of the victims. This book makes a highly readable case that the doctor was, in fact, Jack the Ripper, but the case is undermined by the need for additional evidence of a more definitive nature.

Yet another problem is the common tendency for attributors to ignore situational factors when trying to understand another person. A good starting point for novice psychobiographers is to begin by listing possible social, historical, and cultural factors that may have contributed to a person's behaviours and apparent characteristics. A related question is whether the individual's behaviour is a true reflection of the self or whether it is a public mask put on for self-presentation.

A final problem with psychobiography also applies to the psychology field in general: the tendency to over-pathologize. When listing and focusing on a person's negative attributes, it is essential to consider their positive attributes as well to create a balanced and even-handed representation.

KEY POINTS

- Psychobiographies cannot be generalized, in part because of subjective biases that may limit the accuracy of the analysis.
- The confirmatory bias exists when a person focuses on what he or she expects or wants to see (preconceived notions). The actor–observer bias reflects a tendency to discount or ignore situational factors and instead attribute outcomes to an individual's personality or character.
- Limitations occur when the psychobiographer focuses too much on a particular event or critical period. Like much of psychology, there is also a tendency to focus on negative characteristics (over-pathologize) and not focus on positive characteristics to a similar degree.

Guidelines for Extracting Data

With these limitations of psychobiography in mind, what are some ways to approach the potential importance of data? Irving Alexander is one of the most influential psychobiographers in the field. He has outlined guidelines for gathering data, which are described below. (More information on these guidelines can be found in Alexander, 1988.)

The **primacy guideline** is the premise that the theme that emerges first is the most important; that is, the first thing that is evident is the most significant. A related guideline is the frequency of theme: the themes that appear most often may be the most salient and relevant cues for interpreting an individual.

Another guideline is the theme's apparent uniqueness. This guideline is relevant to the discussion in Chapter 13 of defining abnormality in a purely statistical sense. Of course, from a personality perspective, it makes a great deal of sense to place special emphasis on highly distinctive themes.

The fourth guideline is **negation**. This is the tendency to deny an attribute or represent it in a way that is opposite to the theme. This guideline suggests in general that psychobiographers should be on the lookout for defence mechanisms and defence styles that might undermine the veridicality of someone's claims. A related guideline is **omission**. If a key aspect of a person's life does not get the attention that it deserves, then perhaps this is significant. The tendency for a person to skip a particular period of their life may not be because it is not pertinent; perhaps something of great importance occurred but the person is unwilling or unable to discuss it.

A similar consideration is whether a person has seemingly underestimated or overestimated the importance of some life event or life role. This, too, may be a useful indicator of an important theme.

Erikson's Triple Bookkeeping Concept

The guidelines outlined above are quite general and still leave room for subjective interpretation. Noted theorist Erik Erikson suggested some specific considerations as part of what he described as the **triple bookkeeping approach**. Erikson suggested that anybody's life could be understood and evaluated on three complementary levels. The first level is the level of the body and all of the constitutional givens with which the person is endowed, including sexual urges. Psychological attributes that can be traced to physical characteristics would be highly relevant here.

The second level is the ego, reflecting the fact that Erikson was an ego psychologist. The ego involves how a person makes sense of the world and copes with realistic conflicts and sources of anxiety. The concept of ego identity has been used extensively in psychobiographies after McAdams conceptualized differences in ego identity as **life stories** (see McAdams, 1988). The essence of this approach is that everybody has their own story and much can be learned about a person's sense of ego identity by analyzing the psychosocial themes that emerge when they describe their life and the events that have occurred. Life stories reflect the **narrative approach** to psychobiography, using an individual's personal story and sense of identity. The foundations of the narrative approach were outlined in Runyan's (1982) highly influential book *Life Histories and Psychobiography*.

Barressi and Juckes (1997) endorsed the narrative approach and the view that people's lives are structured and experienced in "a storylike manner." They outlined various forms that narratives may take. First, narratives can be in the form of autobiographical first-person accounts or they may be evaluated indirectly via the Thematic Apperception Test, which, as was noted earlier, involves telling stories to account for depicted scenes. If the analysis is of someone from the past, that person's creative output and expression (books, letters, diaries) can be examined from a narrative perspective. Also, at a more global level, a person's entire life can be represented and interpreted as an integrative narrative.

Because they are narratives, life stories are not necessarily veridical and accurate renderings of what has happened in a person's life. For this, we need to obtain descriptions of a person's life story from key informants. However, it is important to note that it is highly instructive and informative when it can be confirmed that the narrative provided is a gross fabrication. This was the case with well-known novelist Anaïs Nin who sensationalized events in her personal diaries and was accused of including events that did not happen.

McAdams (1996) has suggested that one of the main functions of the life story is that it is integrative; that is, it provides an overall sense of coherence and unity to the self by integrating diverse aspects and occurrences into one overall narrative. People who are unable or unwilling to do this likely suffer from distress due to a fragmented sense of self. Pals (2006) referred to this as low "coherent positive resolution" of a narrative construction of identity. She showed that low coherent positive resolution contributed to low ego resiliency, which, in turn, predicted reduced life satisfaction.

A complementary approach to psychobiography via life stories is to consider the scripts that apply to an individual's life. Tomkins outlined **script theory** as an extension of his earlier work based on the premise that emotion is the key motivating force in our lives (see Tomkins, 1979, 1987). According to Tomkins, people are analogous to playwrights in how they chronicle and represent their lives. The experience of intense emotions in certain situations and scenes is compiled into a script that helps organize what happens in our lives, when it happens, and who is present when it happens. Carlson (1988) has been particularly influential in applying a script analysis in psychobiography.

The final level of triple bookkeeping, the level of the family and society, underscores that Erikson was, first and foremost, a psychosocial theorist. This addresses one of the possible problems outlined above, because Erikson advocated for a full analysis of the societal, cultural, and historical factors that affect an individual. Erikson is arguably the scholar most responsible for injecting a cultural focus into psychobiographical analysis. The need to consider cultural factors is explored further in International Focus on Discovery 14.1.

International Focus on Discovery 14.1 Psychobiography and Psychohistory from a Cultural Perspective

Historically, psychobiographers have varied substantially in being cognizant of cultural factors and incorporating these into their analysis. Runyan (1982) observed that there have been times when psychobiographers have been seemingly unaware of or unconcerned with cultural differences, and this has substantially biased their interpretations.

Cultural factors are most likely to be recognized when performing a specific type of psychobiographical analysis known as psychohistory. Whereas psychobiography is the study of a person in general from a psychological perspective, a **psychohistory** is an analysis of a person's psychological features at a particular point in history and how the era influenced the individual (and perhaps how the individual influenced the era). According to Alexander (2005), Erikson was eager to see an end to the term "psychohistory" because he hoped that the study of psychological factors had become accepted and incorporated by all historians conducting case analyses.

Just as historical factors should always be taken into account, cultural factors should also be given strong consideration as well. Cultural factors go back to Allport's (1962) statement that personologists need to focus not only on what makes a person unique, but also on what they share with other people. Psychobiographies should openly discuss the characteristics and factors that influence everyone in a particular culture, and they should highlight unique features that make a person distinct from others in the same culture.

Runyan (1982) outlined various ways of incorporating a greater appreciation of cultural factors into psychobiographies. First, he suggested that the psychobiographer must learn enough about the cultural context to have an accurate frame of reference. This could require an indirect analysis or direct contact with experts who are familiar with a particular culture.

Second, Runyan (1982) suggested that a comparative analysis be conducted of relevant comparison groups. Specifically, he stated that "study of relevant comparison groups and of local contexts with the subject's social and historical world may help in developing understandings of the individual" (p. 216). The key is to identify aspects that differentiate the person from others in the same context. Elms (2003) also emphasized the need for a comparative analysis involving other people living in the same era and culture. He cited the need to compare da Vinci's inability to complete his paintings and how this was first interpreted as a general attribute of artists from this era. However, further comparison and probing established that this tendency to leave unfinished work went beyond the prevailing norm.

Finally, Runyan (1982) advocated an ongoing review of personality theories to establish their degree of applicability across cultures. That is, to what extent do the theories themselves reflect an ethnocentric bias that limits their applicability?

Fortunately, in recent years, it seems that there is growing interest in studying psychobiography from a cross-cultural perspective. This interest is reflected by a book by Feldman and Valenti (2001) that consists of psychobiographies of political leaders across cultures. Case study analyses are provided for several prominent leaders, including Mao Zedong of China, Nobusuke Kishi of Japan, Tony Blair from the United Kingdom, Helmut Kohl from Germany, Benjamin Netanyahu of Israel, and David Lange of New Zealand, among others. This book represents an important development; unfortunately, different authors wrote different chapters. Since each author tends to focus on a particular person, there is only a limited attempt to use a **cross-cultural comparative approach** that compares and contrasts the attributes of two or more political leaders.

Glad (2005) showed how the cross-cultural comparative approach can be used to illustrate the role of contextual, cultural factors in psychobiography. She was interested in examining the attributes of people from different cultures who were all deemed to be tyrants. She conducted a psychobiographical analysis of three well-known tyrants (Adolf Hitler, Joseph Stalin, and Mao Zedong) and reported on their similarities and differences. She then compared these figures with other tyrants deemed to have had less political influence. More effective tyrants were said to have "instrumental rationality"; that is, they were able to recognize external constraints and modify their behaviours when it was in their best interests. Of course, the particular ways that instrumental rationality was expressed was influenced, in part, by the historical and cultural context each leader experienced.

Although a comparative approach is preferable, much can be learned from analyses that restrict their focus to a particular individual. This is best illustrated by recent work on Mao Zedong of China. Sheng (2001) is a historian who conducted a psychobiographical analysis of Mao. He concluded that Mao suffered from a pathological form of narcissistic personality disorder. More recently, Chang and Halliday (2005) published an extremely unfavourable account of Mao's behaviours, life history, and personality that highlight his narcissistic ambitions and paranoia.

Psychobiographies of Mao Zedong illustrate two potential pitfalls: psychobiographers may fail to consider all valid disorders, or their own biases may affect their analysis.

The works by Sheng (2001) and Chang and Halliday (2005) are illuminating and fascinating, but they also highlight the potential pitfalls when conducting a psychobiography. Sheng (2001) was so focused on illustrating that Mao fits the diagnostic criteria for narcissistic personality disorder that he failed to address the issue of whether other types of disorder (e.g., paranoid personality disorder, anti-social personality disorder) are equally valid. Sheng (2001) also based his explanations on psychoanalytic theories of narcissism outlined by Kohut and Kernberg. While these theories seem quite relevant, other theoretical orientations should have been considered. In particular, Kelly's personal construct theory would have been highly effective in outlining Mao's psychological constructs. As for Chang and Halliday (2005), they have been criticized on two grounds (see Hamstra, 2006). First, their evidence for certain claims was deemed scant and unconvincing. Second, they have been accused of letting their sense of moral outrage bias their overall analysis and interpretation. In fact, it was suggested that their "accumulation of Mao's calculated misdeeds is so relentless as to be ultimately unbelievable" (Hamstra, 2006, p. 232).

Still, these accounts of Mao are valuable for at least two reasons. First, they draw renewed attention to the claim that Mao's decisions and actions contributed to the deaths of an estimated 70 million Chinese people (Hamstra, 2006). For instance, millions of people died alleged as a result of Mao's unrealistic attempt to industrialize China (known as The Great Leap Forward) and use of workers who were impoverished and undernourished.

Second, these accounts of Mao reiterate and underscore the link between psychobiography and culture. In contrast to prevailing norms, Mao Zedong rejected the authority of his father and the tenets of the prevailing Chinese culture. One of his ultimate goals was to create a new society (The Cultural Revolution). This quest cost the lives of millions of people, and it reminds us that culture influences people, but certain people in particular can also shape and influence culture, for better or for worse.

KEY POINTS

- Erikson is among those with the greatest contributions to psychobiography. He helped to establish a role for culture in the development of personal identity. He also provided more balance because, unlike many others, he did not rely on Freudian concepts for his analysis.
- Erikson's triple bookkeeping approach is a framework for evaluating a person by the levels of the body, the ego, and family and society.
- The focus on the ego and a person's whole life has facilitated a narrative approach to psychobiography that emphasizes life stories.

PSYCHOBIOGRAPHICAL SKETCHES

With these potential problems of psychobiography and general guidelines for extracting data in mind, we now turn to psychobiographical accounts of some famous individuals. I have included such noteworthy people as Salvador Dali, Sylvia Plath, and Anne Sexton. The final person considered is rock star Ozzy Osbourne.

The final segment of this chapter contains some psychobiographical "sketches" of some famous people who suffered from mental illness. Each person identified in a sketch could be the subject of a separate volume of work and the analyses represent just a snapshot of each person from a psychobiographical perspective. Even this brief treatment should be enough to convince readers of the potential usefulness of personality factors and concepts in psychobiography and may even spur some readers to conduct their own psychobiographical analysis of a famous or infamous person, or at least consider these issues in the future when reading biographies and autobiographies. Students wishing more information on psychobiography can check out the very useful website www.psychobiography.com.

Each of the following sketches includes a concise life history, followed by an overview of relevant personality traits and theories that attempt to explain the unique features of each person. In light of the advice of Elms (1994), we use an eclectic approach that incorporates several theories. We begin with Salvador Dali.

Salvador Dali

> Painting is an infinitely minute part of my personality.
>
> —*Salvador Dali*

There can be little doubt that Salvador Dali was one of the most famous and provocative artists of the twentieth century. Dali is known primarily for two things: his important contributions to the art world with surrealist paintings and his unsurpassed ability to draw attention to himself, both through his work and his antics.

Life History

Dali was born on May 11, 1904 in Figueras in the district of Catalonia in Spain, near the border of France. He died on January 23, 1989. He had been one of the most prolific and controversial artists in history, producing almost 2,000 works, including some of the most widely recognized surrealist masterpieces.

At the risk of engaging in eventism and originology, one of the keys in understanding Dali's need for attention can be traced to his birth order status. Dali had an older brother who died when he was two years old and before Salvador Dali was born. This brother's name was also Salvador! Dali was named after his dead brother and was treated as the replacement child; in fact, he was openly told that he was the reincarnation of his dead brother. Perhaps this accounts in large part for his great efforts to forge an exceedingly unique persona throughout his remarkable life.

Much of Dali's childhood is recounted in his autobiography *The Secret Life of Salvador Dali*. He was a solitary child who was allowed to do whatever he pleased. His narcissistic ways (such as wearing a king's robe and crown) were often encouraged, as were his emerging artistic talents. He was enrolled in art schools as an adolescent and young adult.

After becoming an established artist, Dali moved to the United States. In 1929, Dali met Gala, the wife of his friend Paul Eluard, and became obsessed with her. Dali decided he had to have Gala for his own; she divorced Eluard and married Dali in 1934. The two were exceptionally close, but it was far from the ideal relationship. They had little sexual relations, and Gala often mistreated and mocked Dali while hosting a bevy of younger men she took as lovers. There were also times when Gala locked him in a room and refused to let him come out until he had completed artwork that could be sold.

Not surprisingly, given his great dependency on his wife, Dali had an exceptionally bad reaction to her death in 1982. He tried to kill himself by not eating and drinking.

Sigmund Freud was another vitally important person in Dali's life. Surrealist artists such as Dali idolized Freud. As a result, surrealism can be regarded as the visual depiction of the internal conflicts that operate at an unconscious level. For surrealists, bold and irrational images that reflect the subconscious are the basis of masterpieces. Dali saw dreams and dream analysis as a great source of imagery, and there are reports that Dali decided to eat Camembert cheese before bed because he believed that the cheese would enhance the vividness and absurdity of his own dreams. Dali also created what he referred to as the method of paranoid criticism, using his own analysis of his subconscious, irrational images.

Dali met with Freud in 1938 in London. Freud had no positive regard for surrealist art, and he regarded the artists as fools, though he seemed to develop a fascination with Dali. One can only imagine how Freud would have interpreted Dali's personal attributes if he had conducted a complete analysis of the artist.

Problems in Adjustment

> The only difference between myself and a madman is that I am not mad.
>
> —*Salvador Dali*

Dali is perhaps the closest that one can come to a textbook case of narcissistic personality disorder (discussed in Chapter 13). He was entirely self-absorbed and preoccupied, with the exception of his attentiveness to his wife Gala, whom he adored. This tendency to overidealize someone is also a characteristic of narcissism. How extreme was Dali's narcissism? Dali proclaimed himself as a genius without a contemporary peer, so he openly compared himself to past masters. He was so confident of his abilities that, as a student, he considered it a slight to have his work judged by "inferior" professors, so he would not permit them to evaluate his work. As a result, Dali was expelled in 1926 from the Academy of Arts in Madrid before his final exams because of his refusal to be tested.

Dali was also on record as saying that he could repeat his own name tirelessly. Unlike many narcissists, Dali seemed aware of his own narcissism, at least to some extent. Later, one of his most famous works would be *The Metamorphis of Narcissus*. This tribute to Narcissus has been interpreted as a self-portrait, but Dali suggested that it was actually based on Gala.

While some narcissistic people are actively engaged in self-presentation, others accept their unique ability as a matter of fact and simply assume that their talents are evident to everyone. Dali was just this type. This is perhaps best revealed by his comment "Each morning, on awakening, I experience a supreme joy which, for the first time today, I discover is the joy of being Salvador Dali...And each day I find it more difficult to understand how other people can live without being Gala or Salvador Dali." (Dali, 1965, p. 97).

He was also prone to a condition known as narcissistic injury. Narcissistic people respond strongly to perceived slights. In 1949, Dali's sister wrote a book about him and suggested he had a childhood that was quite normal and happy. Dali was furious with his sister's portrayal of him as normal and typical, likely because this clashed with his extreme need to be unique and special. He responded by creating a highly unflattering painting that depicted his sister.

Personality Traits

As might be expected when narcissism is present, there is clear evidence of Dali's disagreeable personality traits and lack of empathy for others, which is in keeping with Cluster B disorders that reflect hostility and extrapunitiveness. In his autobiographical accounts of his childhood, Dali recounts an episode when he was five and tossed another child from a bridge, just to see what would happen. He recounted how the commotion that he caused, as adults attended to the injured boy's bleeding head, put him into "a delightful hallucinatory mood" (Dali, 1965, p. 11). He also acknowledged kicking his younger sister in the head for entertainment. Later, as an adolescent, he recounted his great pleasure in mistreating and humiliating his first girlfriend.

Dali's hostile acts toward others and his subsequent attention-getting behaviour seem to reflect a personality construct known as *effectance*. Effectance is a need to have an impact on people or things. Dali seemed overly invested in eliciting a reaction from others and would go to increasingly greater lengths to elicit these reactions.

The list of psychological needs described by Murray seems to be particularly well-suited to Dali. He openly acknowledged that he had limited sexual activity with Gala and had one homosexual encounter prior to meeting her. Sexual gratification was not high among his needs, in part because he had an acknowledged fear of sex (that he claimed was cured by Gala). McGirk (1989) suggested that there is clear evidence that Dali abhorred physical contact and that accounts of his sexual activity are overstated; instead, there were allegations that Dali preferred to be a voyeur.

His predominant need was the need for exhibition, either of his work or of bizarre tendencies on display for others to see. As a child, he set up a booth and for each five centimos coin he received, he gave a ten centimos coin in return. Clearly, his need for attention outweighed his need for money. As an adult, he regularly drew attention to himself through his physical appearance (including his moustache and some of his non-verbal expressions) and by wearing unusual clothes. One of his most famous acts of exhibition was appearing in a diving suit at the opening of an art display in 1936. The need for attention led Dali to take things too far on several occasions. One of the clearest examples of this was including a donkey in one of his art exhibits, which he killed to elicit reaction from onlookers.

He also had a need for dominance, as reflected by the mistreatment of others during childhood. The need for dominance could have been a compensation for the intense shyness he experienced during childhood. In many respects, it seems that Dali had an anxious temperament and the shyness signifies a high level of social inhibition.

Given the images in his surrealistic art, it is also quite likely that Dali would have scored exceptionally high on psychoticism. Dali generated bizarre images that deviated markedly from reality. Eysenck (1993) suggested that there is a strong link between creativity and psychoticism, and psychoticism underscores the established link between creativity and madness. Even a brief inspection of Dali's surrealistic art would suggest that he would be high in psychoticism.

Finally, Dali was an acknowledged workaholic who no doubt would have scored exceptionally high on the workaholism scale of Clark's SNAP inventory, which was described in Chapter 13. Dali was proud of his work ethic and noted that "I worked a hundred times harder than any mediocre painter, preparing new exhibits" (Dali, 1965, p. 69). Some of his drive and energy came from the fact that Dali and Gala found themselves running out of money at various times, and they needed to sell his paintings to survive.

As noted earlier, it is important to consider situational factors when piecing together a psychobiographical analysis. In this instance, it cannot be denied that the overwhelming presence of Gala reflected a chronic and profound interpersonal situation that not only influenced Dali's personality, but also interacted with it to produce his behavioural responses. Gala became the dominant force in Dali's life and he assumed a submissive, subordinate interpersonal style. His submissiveness would have been clearly evident if he had been assessed on the interpersonal circumplex. How domineering was Gala? One biographer described her as "a personality of such relentless self-will, such monumental self-regard, such icy disregard for the feelings of almost anything except herself, that she sent shivers down the spine of almost everyone she met" (Etherington-Smith, 1992, p. 296).

Explanatory Theories

Any attempt to account for Dali's uniqueness must come back to his start in the world as the "reincarnated" replacement of his brother. This led to Dali being treated as special and cherished from the beginning. However, the ultimate challenge for Dali would be to establish his own unique sense of identity, so Erikson's developmental theory is particularly useful in accounting for Dali's search for identity. It is likely that Dali was unable to ever resolve this issue, as witnessed by his bizarre and atypical relationship with Gala. There is little evidence that he was able to have a healthy resolution of the stage of intimacy versus isolation. The identity diffusion was probably exacerbated by problems with the stage of industry versus inferiority because Dali was, by all accounts, a poor student. Even when he excelled in an area (art), he was expelled for insubordination.

Adler's theory can also be applied to Dali. There are videotaped interviews with Dali in which he acknowledges that he felt great inferiority compared with the idealized image of his dead brother. He felt that his brother was the yardstick against which his accomplishments were measured. Adler suggested that a sense of inferiority and fear of failure leads to strivings for superiority, and it seems that Dali suffered enormously from this superiority complex. At best, he could be similar and on a par with but never better than his dead brother.

Dali's narcissism could have stemmed from the fact that his family regarded him as a special reincarnation as a boy. However, over time, his parents tired of his antics and eventually disowned him because of his obsession to have Gala, another man's wife. Also, one incident in particular was especially damaging. Dali, in an attempt to get publicity, joked that he would spit on his mother's photograph. The family did not respond well to this "joke," and he was banished by his family and cursed by his father (McGirk, 1989). This must have been very disquieting to someone who felt he was being compared with the ideal, dead brother he was supposed to replace. In fact, Dali reported that he was very distressed when he found out about being disowned, so he went to a mountain top and sheared off all of his hair.

Finally, the worldwide attention Dali received is important to consider from an operant conditioning perspective. The tendency to be rewarded with attention for dramatic works of art and dramatic behavioural displays would only further increase narcissism and the likelihood of attention-seeking behaviour. Whether something has reward value depends, in part, on the individual's needs and values. Dali's grandmother noted that as a child, he did not respond to the usual rewards (e.g., food treats); however, he did respond if the reward was the opportunity to dress up as Napoleon and become the emperor.

We now turn to two other creative people. Both of these women suffered from a form of self-criticism that is far removed from Dali's blatant narcissism.

Sylvia Plath

Sylvia Plath and Anne Sexton (whose sketch follows separately) are two authors with much in common, in addition to being good friends. Both women were poets and professors in the eastern United States. And, sadly, both women killed themselves even though their accomplishments were widely recognized.

Much has been written about the life and psychological problems of Sylvia Plath, but less has been written about Anne Sexton. Other similarities and differences between these two women will become apparent in the psychobiographical sketches that follow.

Life History and Adjustment Problems

Sylvia Plath was born in 1932 in Boston, Massachusetts. Her father had emigrated to the United States from Germany. Otto Plath mastered several languages and was hired as a university professor to teach languages. He met and married Aurelia Schober, who served as his assistant. The family environment was generally happy, and great emphasis was placed on reading, learning, and language (see Wagner-Martin, 1999). The happiness came to an abrupt end in 1940 when Otto Plath died unexpectedly from complications stemming from his undiagnosed diabetes. Aurelia then had to spend long hours away from her children as she worked to support the family. She eventually took a teaching post at Boston University.

Sylvia Plath's superb ability to write and read was evident at a fairly early age, and she was relatively successful throughout her high school years. She was awarded a scholarship to attend Smith College in Massachusetts. Plath was an accomplished but troubled undergraduate. She suffered from bouts of extreme depression and was hospitalized, where she received electroconvulsive shock therapy and she attempted suicide.

Plath graduated in 1955. The next year, she met and married the poet Ted Hughes. They had two children over the next seven years but, experienced severe marital troubles as it became evident that Hughes was having an extramarital affair.

In 1963, Plath published the widely acclaimed book *The Bell Jar*, a work of fiction that is quite autobiographical. Later that year, Plath committed suicide, at age 30, by gassing herself in the kitchen oven. Much of her depression and distress is attributed to the shame and despair she experienced because of marital problems.

Personality Traits

There is a wealth of information to provide clues about Plath's personality traits. Numerous books have been written about her, and people who knew her have been interviewed. Other sources that have been examined include her poems and book, as well as her letters and journals.

Plath's perfectionistic tendencies have been often described. What has not been identified is how her characteristics fit with a multidimensional view of perfectionism. Accounts indicate that she had exacting standards for herself (self-oriented perfectionism) but she also had exacting standards for others (other-oriented perfectionism), and she became very frustrated when other people did not meet her expectations. It is difficult to tell whether her other-oriented perfectionism created interpersonal conflict, but this is quite possible given the known correlates of this perfectionism dimension.

Plath's perfectionism was combined with a highly destructive form of self-criticism. In many respects, Plath fit the description provided by Blatt (1995) of self-critical perfectionists. Unfortunately for Plath, her self-criticism was so extreme that it was more akin to self-hatred. Her level of self-loathing was particularly evident in her letters and journals:

> I cannot ignore this murderous self: it is there. I smell it and feel it, but I will not give it my name. I shall shame it. When it says: you shall not sleep, you cannot

> teach, I shall go on anyway, knocking its nose in. Its biggest weapon is and has been the image of itself as a perfect success: in writing, teaching, and living. As soon as I sniff non-success in the form of rejection, puzzled faces in class when I'm blurring a point, or a cold horror in personal relationships, I accuse myself of being a hypocrite, posing as better than I am, and being, at bottom, lousy. (Plath, in Kukil, 2000, p. 618)

This excerpt not only highlights her extremely negative self-view, but also how external feedback in the social world can serve as a cue that activates this highly negative self-concept.

This self-hatred is important to acknowledge because a recent development in the field of personality and depression is the development of a new scale by Gilbert that includes an assessment of individual differences in self-hatred (Gilbert et al., 2005). This exceptionally negative orientation toward the self most definitely characterized Plath.

Plath also seemed to be acutely aware of the differences between the sexes. Perhaps she became sensitive to this while growing up and seeing her mother put her own career ambitions on hold to assist her husband. A theorist such as George Kelly would no doubt conclude that one of Sylvia Plath's personal constructs was masculinity versus femininity. Plath felt guilty because of mixed feelings about motherhood; clearly, she resented the constraints put on her as a result of becoming a mother. In an earlier letter, she stated that "my tragedy is to have been born a woman" (Plath, 1982, p. 214). She seemed to long for greater autonomy, perhaps so she could have more freedom to try to fulfill her aspirations.

Explanatory Theories

Plath's low self-worth can be readily explained by Carl Rogers' theory of conditions of worth. According to some authors (e.g., Wagner-Martin, 1999), Plath's parents valued quiet, achievement-focused behaviour from their children. Much of the parents' attention was focused on Otto's academic work, and Sylvia and her brother were given the clear message that parental approval was contingent on them meeting parental expectations of appropriate behaviour. This would foster a highly conditional sense of self-worth and a heightened awareness of the actual self and how it varied from the self prescribed by Plath's parents.

The early loss of a parent is often implicated as a risk factor in depression. This is especially the case among children who come to perceive that they are somehow responsible for their parent's death. It has been suggested that both Sylvia Plath and her brother felt guilty about their father's death, as if it had to do with their misdeeds and shortcomings. This tendency for children to blame themselves can be seen as a reflection of an overly rigid superego, or it can be interpreted within the context of the attributional theory of depression. Abramson, et al. (1978) suggested that people are prone to depression to the extent that they blame themselves for negative outcomes (an internal attribution) and the cause is seen as stable and global. Blaming the self for a parent's death is natural if the person has developed a tendency to see themselves as responsible for outcomes.

Harry Stack Sullivan's interpersonal theory could be applied to Sylvia Plath because it was evident that she had a clear and well-articulated sense of the good me, the bad me, and the not me. In fact, she observed that

> I have a good self, that loves skies, hills, ideas, tasty meals, bright colors. My demon would murder this self by demanding that it be a paragon, and saying it should run away if it is anything less. … I have this demon who wants me to run away screaming if I am going to be flawed, fallible. It wants me to think I'm so good I must be perfect. Or nothing. (Plath, 1982, p. 176)

Erikson's theory also applies to Plath because she had a longstanding struggle with issues of personal identity. Here again Plath showed a remarkable yet painful self-awareness. She concluded that, "As for the Who Am I? What Am I? … that will preoccupy me until the day I die" (Plath, 1982, p. 59). Perhaps her negative sense of identity reflected the excessive focus on achievement in her family; given the high standards, it would have been difficult for Plath to resolve the preceding stage of industry versus inferiority. Her subsequent marital difficulties and lack of intimacy would have blunted further development along the stages outlined by Erikson.

One final point that deserves mention is how Plath's ultimate death by suicide accords with the diathesis–stress model of perfectionism and depression (see Hewitt & Flett, 1993, 2002). This model is based on the premise that perfectionists are especially vulnerable following the experience of negative life events. Plath acknowledged that she felt a deep sense of shame and humiliation as a result of her husband's affair. The shame signifies that she attributed the affair, at least in part, to her own inadequacies; people typically feel shame when they perceive undesirable aspects of themselves. This would be an extremely threatening and high impact stressor for perfectionists, who would find it difficult to reconcile their desire for perfection and their shortcomings. For such perfectionists, it is vitally important that they develop positive coping styles as a way of buffering the impact of stressors.

While perfectionism is central to an understanding of Sylvia Plath, other personality factors seem more relevant when evaluating Anne Sexton, as we will see in the following psychobiographical sketch.

Anne Sexton

Anne Sexton is famous partly for having won a Pulitzer Prize. She was a confessional poet who became known largely for the images she evoked during her self-revelations. Like Sylvia Plath, she suffered from mental illness and killed herself at an early age.

Life History

Anne Sexton was born Anne Gray Harvey in 1928, the youngest of three sisters. The family owned a wool business, and her parents were educated and financially stable.

According to Middlebrook (1991), Sexton wrote poems as a teenager but stopped when her mother accused her of plagiarism. At the age of 19, she was sent to a finishing school in Boston. Just one year later, she met and married Alfred Muller Sexton II. The catalyst for their marriage was Sexton's conviction that she was pregnant, but she was not.

Their first daughter was born in 1953 (Linda Gray Sexton), and their second daughter was born in 1955. The birth of Sexton's second daughter was the catalyst for her problems with mental illness, as described in more detail below. As part of her treatment, she was encouraged to write poetry, and this culminated in the 1960 publication of her autobiographical book of poems *To Bedlam and Back*. She continued to write poetry and short stories for the next 14 years, and her work received great acclaim. She also taught courses at Boston University.

Problems in Adjustment

As noted above, the birth of her second child was a critical event for Anne Sexton. Just after giving birth, she began a year-long slide into depression, which persisted in various forms throughout the rest of her life. Unfortunately, she experienced one of the most severe forms of postpartum depression: postpartum depression with psychotic features (also known as postpartum psychosis). One of her primary symptoms was a great fear of being alone with her children because of the anger and rage that built up inside of her. Middlebrook (1991) described the mistreatment that was experienced by Linda, the oldest daughter, while still a toddler:

> Increasingly, Sexton became prone to episodes of blinding rage in which she would seize Linda and begin choking or slapping her. In later life she recalled with great shame a day she found Linda stuffing her excrement in a toy truck and as punishment picked her up and threw her across the room. She felt she could not control these outbursts, and she began to be afraid that she would kill her children. (p. 32–33)

Sexton's adjustment problems continued, so she sought treatment at a facility in 1956, and it was there that she met Dr. Martin Orne, who would become her psychiatrist for the next eight years. Recall that Orne is the psychiatrist who also made several research contributions, including focusing attention on the role of demand characteristics in experimental research.

Sexton was treated both for her depression and for alcoholism. She also received treatment earlier from Orne's mother, Dr. Martha Brunner-Orne, who detailed the symptoms of Sexton's postpartum depression. She described:

> Wildly alternating moods, anorexia, insomnia, waves of suicidal and other impulses, rage, rapid heartbeat. It is possible that biochemical imbalances throughout her life intensified the underlying psychological vulnerabilities that were the primary focus of her psychotherapy. (Middlebrook, 1991, p. 334)

Sexton was institutionalized and tried to kill herself with a drug overdose when she ingested what she referred to as her "kill-me pills." It was Orne who encouraged her to write down her thoughts in poems as a form of therapy.

Sexton displayed symptoms of mental disorder at various times. One shocking account provided by Linda Sexton underscores how disturbing it must have been to see one's mother in such a state. Linda Sexton recounted that:

> The evening meal became a pivotal point, rimmed and edged with tension. At the table, Mother was often so crazed, we had to contain it somehow. She'd talk gibberish, she'd stare at the wall, her eyes traveling mechanically up then down in a way my father called "headlighting"—it drove him wild. We'd have to put her to bed. One night she fell straight forward and her face landed in the mash potatoes! My father would say, "Anne, stop it, you're frightening the children." (Middlebrook, 1991, p. 334–335)

Sexton eventually recovered enough to be released, and as her work became known, accolades and awards followed, most notably the Pulitzer Prize in 1966. She continued to struggle with her mental illness, and exacerbated the problem when she decided to divorce her husband in 1973 because she assumed, perhaps incorrectly, that he had been unfaithful. She was quite promiscuous herself and had a need for constant companionship.

Sexton experienced profound loneliness and depression after her divorce. Even the attention and accolades of her students were not enough to carry her through the dark days. She killed herself at the age of 45 in 1974, just one day after returning from a trip and being met at the airport by one of her adoring students. Sexton died of carbon monoxide poisoning in her car in the garage (Middlebrook, 1991).

Orne created controversy because after Sexton's death he released transcripts of his sessions with her to the biographer Diane Middlebrook. This met with scorn and ridicule as many people believed that even though Sexton was no longer alive, Orne had breached her right to confidentiality. Orne responded with the claim that Sexton's daughter Linda wanted these transcripts to be released, and Sexton herself would have approved. The tapes included some shocking information, including Sexton's revelation of engaging in sexual relations with Linda.

Personality Traits

Anne Sexton's core personality traits included impulsivity, dependency, a preoccupied and insecure attachment style, self-criticism, neuroticism, interpersonal sensitivity, and the need for approval and attention. Impulsivity is revealed through her suicidal acts and general lack of self-control, including engaging in many sexual liaisons with numerous partners and perpetrating incest.

Perhaps her extreme dependency is the most certain part of her personality, however. Her dependency on others was well-known and may have been extreme enough to warrant the diagnosis of dependent personality disorder. One of her closest friends and neighbours, Sandy Robart, recalled that Sexton was especially likely to play the dependent role in the presence of her mother. She stated that Sexton was "a passive, helpless, dependent goody-goody! I think she just got to a stage where her whole feeling was of terrible inadequacy. If she had been a healthier person in general, she would have been able to defend her own turf" (Middlebrook, 1991, p. 30).

This dependency often reflects a highly insecure form of attachment. According to Middlebrook (1991), Orne stated that even at the age of 28, Sexton was "agonizingly attached" to her own mother, Mary Gray, who often neglected her when she was a young child because of her own problems with alcoholism, self-absorption, and demands for attention. This dependency was also accompanied by high self-criticism. This is best reflected by one autobiographical poem ("Her Kind") that Sexton wrote about a middle-aged witch.

Close inspection revealed that Sexton was very high in neuroticism and seemed to have all the facets of neuroticism described by Costa and McCrae. That is, in addition to the impulsivity described earlier, she was also high in anxiety, anger, hostility (recall the earlier reference to blinding rage), depression, and self-consciousness that took the form of neurotic self-absorption. She was also very vulnerable, and this vulnerability took the form of very high interpersonal sensitivity. She reacted strongly to criticisms of herself or her family (she was often humiliated by her father's mistreatment of her husband), and to the criticisms she received from her own mother and her mother-in-law.

Any five-factor analysis of Sexton would have to reflect a high level of openness due to her creativity and her willingness to put her private thoughts and feelings on display for others to see. Although she was very accomplished, her level of conscientiousness was often influenced by her mood states, and thus would be characterized as moderate at best. She often had periods of being incapacitated and was not capable of achievement striving.

Explanatory Theories

A multitude of theories and models could be used to account for Sexton's tendencies, but we will focus on four of them: (1) attachment theory; (2) Blatt's model of anaclitic and introjective depression; (3) Erikson's developmental theory; and (4) social learning theory.

Attachment theory is highly relevant because Sexton appeared to have an extreme form of the anxious–ambivalent attachment style, as described by Bowlby. In this instance, this style involved a preoccupation and overidealization of the parents, despite the fact that, in reality, both parents were far from ideal. Sexton's mother was self-absorbed and her father was a harsh alcoholic with rigid rules about proper attire, and who banished young children who were messy from the dinner table. Clearly, there is little evidence that Sexton received the sensitive and responsive behaviour from caretakers that facilitates secure attachment. Her unsatisfied needs for attachment and nurturance led Sexton to acknowledge that when she became a mother, she had mixed feelings because "I want to be a child and not a mother, and I feel guilty about this" (Middlebrook, 1991, p. 39). Her working model of self and others reflected an overreliance on maintaining close proximity with significant others. One byproduct of this working model is that Sexton had a poor reaction to her own daughters' striving for independence and autonomy because it did not feed her "hunger for acceptance" (Middlebrook, 1991, p. 39).

Blatt's (2004) model is implicated here as well not only because of Sexton's high levels of anaclitic depression, but also because Blatt traced dependency to the inability to develop a secure attachment style. Although not as self-critical as Plath, Sexton also experienced bouts of self-criticism (along with the guilt mentioned earlier). The notion of the looking glass self also came into play here. Sexton recalled vivid memories of the emotional abuse she received from her father. Much of this came during his drinking binges. Middlebrook (1991) summarized these episodes as follows:

> "He would just suddenly become very mean, as if he hated the world," she later told her psychiatrist. "He would sit and look at you as though you had committed some terrible crime. He hated everyone! Mostly I remember the expression on his face." It seemed that he singled her out for verbal abuse when he was drinking, complaining that her acne disgusted him and that he could not eat at the same table with her. She felt invaded by his expressions of revulsion, and it seemed that no one tried to shield her from these attacks. His drinking permanently destroyed her trust in his love. (p. 14)

This kind of emotional abuse would have fostered a very negative and insecure sense of self. Theory and research has shown that a history of emotional abuse contributes to cognitive vulnerabilities such as blaming negative events on the self (Gibb, Alloy, & Abramson, 2003; Rose & Abramson, 1994).

Some of Sexton's negative self would also have come from failing to please her mother. As one illustration of maternal harshness, when Mary Gray was diagnosed with breast cancer in 1956, she openly stated that the cause was the stress of Sexton's nervous breakdown. Gray died two years later, which would have exacerbated any of Sexton's guilty feelings.

Erikson's developmental theory is implicated in the excerpt about Sexton's father and his abusiveness in that the early stage of trust versus mistrust would not have been adequately resolved and would have resurfaced continually throughout Sexton's life. According to Erikson (1968), failure to achieve a sense of trust can contribute to feelings of abandonment, a poorly integrated self, lifelong problems, and schizoid and depressive states. Recall that Sexton divorced her husband because of suspected but not confirmed infidelities. This inability to trust would set the stage for difficulties in later developmental stages. Most notably, Sexton suffered profound confusion from issues surrounding her sense of personal identity in a way that might have been the psychological "straw that breaks the camel's back." Accounts indicate that in late 1970, less than four years prior to Sexton's suicide, Azel Mack, a family friend of her parents, confessed to her that he was her real father and she was the product of one of his many liaisons with Mary Gray. This revelation, true or not, could only have a profound impact on a person with an already unstable self-image and an inability to trust others. Not surprisingly, this revelation prompted another suicide attempt.

Finally, social learning theory also seems relevant here in many respects. Most notably, Sexton could have learned to imitate the inappropriate drinking behaviours and impulsive ways of both her mother and her father. Imitation may also have been relevant since her peer, Sylvia Plath, had committed suicide and Sexton was to follow in her footsteps.

Ozzy Osbourne

Ozzy Osbourne made a name for himself throughout the 1970s as the colourful singer of the rock group Black Sabbath. This controversial band was linked with satanic worship and is regarded as one of the pre-eminent heavy metal bands. Osbourne was ultimately fired from the group and became even more prominent as a solo artist in the 1980s. This also came with great controversy because bereaved parents have unsuccessfully sued him because his song *Suicide Solution* was played by some teenagers who then took their own lives. The song was not written for this purpose, of course.

Osbourne's fame has been perpetuated in recent years by the annual Ozzfest concerts and the MTV hit reality show *The Osbournes*, which ran for three seasons and followed the exploits and profanity-laced interactions of Osbourne and his wife Sharon and two of their children (Kelly and Jack).

Ozzy Osbourne has sold more than 75 million records, and he has been given a star on Hollywood's Walk of Fame. Clearly, he is a very successful and creative performer. However, he has often lamented that he may be remembered most for some of his outrageous behaviours. The unauthorized biography *Ozzy Knows Best* contains a list of his five most outrageous stunts: being arrested twice for burglary as a teenager (and subsequently being incarcerated), biting the head off a dove at a meeting with record company executives, biting the head off a bat during a live performance, urinating on the wall of the Alamo (the historical landmark in Texas), and snorting a line of ants as if they were cocaine. The Alamo incident resulted in Osbourne being arrested and charged with defiling a national monument. Even worse was the fact that he engaged in this behaviour in public while wearing one of Sharon's evening dresses! She had confiscated his clothes for fear of what he would do if he went outside in his drugged condition; he went out anyway in her clothes.

Life History and Adjustment Problems

Ozzy Osbourne was born and raised in Birmingham, England. He was raised in relative poverty. He did not do well in school, at least in part due to his dyslexia. Some authors have interpreted his criminal past as a reflection of his desire to escape his impoverished circumstances.

Osbourne worked a series of jobs before becoming a singer in a rock band. He spent time as a plumber's apprentice. He also worked in a mortuary, which is interesting given his subsequent role as lead in Black Sabbath, a group that evoked images of devilry and satanic worship.

Osbourne has been married twice and has children from both marriages. He first married in 1971 to Thelma Mayfair. They had two children together but were divorced in 1981, perhaps due to Osbourne's numerous flings with groupies. Osbourne married his manager, Sharon Arden, in 1982, and they have had three children. They have both acknowledged that their initial years of marriage were marked by legendary fights and disputes.

Osbourne's history is influenced heavily by his substance abuse and addiction and a lack of self-control. The "stunts" described earlier were often a by-product of the impulsivity that is often displayed by someone who is drunk or stoned and who is unconcerned about the possible consequences of such behaviour. Osbourne has noted that every extreme thing he has done has been under the influence of a substance. Osbourne was treated several times at the Betty Ford Clinic before seemingly overcoming his addictions, and his extreme behaviour was no longer evident after he became sober.

Personality Traits

Ozzy Osbourne has cultivated his stage persona and has referred to himself as "The Prince of Darkness." Any attempt to analyze Osbourne in a psychobiography must allow for the difference between his stage persona or mask and the more reserved family-loving man that he seems to be at home (as seen in *The Osbournes* television show). In his personal life, Osbourne is a quiet, introverted person who would rather stay at home with his family than interact with other people.

The PSY-5 model is a particularly useful model for examining Osbourne's characteristics because his outrageous acts and excessive drinking can be seen as a reflection of a very low level of constraint. Clearly, he has a very impulsive nature and would be high in sensation seeking, especially in the disinhibition component. This lack of constraint manifests itself in all-or-none behaviour. Osbourne once noted that "There's not enough alcohol in the world for me. There's no such thing as moderation in Ozzy Osbourne's vocabulary. I've never had a pint in my life. It's all or nothing—whether it's drugs, sex, drinking, falling in love, anything" (Nickson, 2002, p. 83).

It might be tempting to conclude that Osbourne also has a high level of aggressiveness, since it is documented that he tried to strangle Sharon in 1984 with the intent of killing her. He did this after consuming four bottles of vodka. Here it is important to distinguish what a person is capable of versus how they usually are because this act notwithstanding, there is very little to indicate that Osbourne is an aggressive and potentially anti-social character, despite his stage persona.

The five-factor model is also potentially useful here because Osbourne does indeed have a very loving nature and he seems to be, on the whole, fairly high in agreeableness. His agreeableness extends beyond his family as shown by his work for charitable causes (including performing a benefit concert for the families who lost relatives in the attack on the World Trade Center). Another illustration of this side of Osbourne was his willingness to cheer up the employees who work on the Conan O'Brien television show in 2001 after the terrorist attacks in New York. In terms of facets of agreeableness, Osbourne seems exceptionally high in straightforwardness. He tends to say what is on his mind without attempts to cover up his behaviour or be something he is not.

Any attempt to analyze Osbourne's psychological needs would examine his need for exhibitionism and showmanship, but the main focus would be on his low level of dominance. It is clear from his relationship with his wife that he is submissive and exceptionally dependent on her. This would be reflected by an extreme score on the submissive axis of the interpersonal circumplex. Sharon took over as his manager in 1982 and runs both their house and his career. When she was diagnosed with cancer, Ozzy Osbourne indicated that his life would simply be over if his wife succumbed to the disease.

Explanatory Theories

Many of the theories that apply generally to addictive personalities can be invoked to account for Ozzy Osbourne's extreme level of alcohol and drug addiction over the years. Given that his own father had a drinking problem, and two of his children (Jack and Kelly) subsequently developed their own problems with addiction, we cannot rule out the role of temperament factors that may have a genetic basis (see Chapter 3). Propensity to addiction could reflect an inactive behavioural inhibition system and an overly involved behavioural activation system.

As for psychological explanations, if viewed from a Freudian perspective, Osbourne's addiction could reflect the handiwork of an overactive id that operates according to the pleasure principle, and a lack of superego functioning when not sober. Osbourne sought pleasure in various forms, including sexual gratification from groupies. The overactive id and Osbourne's subsequent alcoholism and smoking addiction could possibly be traced to an oral fixation and his lack of closeness with his mother. Oral fixations are also linked with high levels of dependency, and this fits with Osbourne's reliance on his wife to take care of things for him.

Social learning theory and imitative processes also seem relevant here. Osbourne was exposed to his own father's drinking problems. He is quoted as saying, "My mother was an amateur singer, my father was an amateur drunk" (Nickson, 2002, p. 141). Although he was not close to either parent, according to Nickson (2002), Osbourne idolized his father, and this makes it all the more likely that he would imitate his father.

Theories of substance abuse that emphasize using alcohol and drugs to overcome a sense of inferiority are also relevant here. Was Osbourne alluding to the sense of power and disinhibition that comes when he stated that "When I hit the bottle for the first time, I hated the taste, but the feeling was what I'd been looking for all of my life" (Nickson, 2002, p. 91).

Just as it was the case that Dali's outrageous behaviour was likely reinforced by the attention it received, the same can likely be said of Osbourne. With attention comes greater sales and greater attendance at concerts, and this means more money. Having come from a background of poverty, the chance to make more money by acting in an extreme way was probably a very salient reinforcer for Osbourne.

Finally, can personalities change? Ozzy Osbourne deserves credit for overcoming his addictions. Also, he has developed an Eriksonian sense of generativity because he openly warns young people about the dangers of drugs and drinking, as well as engaging in unprotected sex. While you are reflecting on the broader issues of whether personality can change, imagine how this psychobiographical sketch would have looked if it had been written in 1985, prior to Osbourne's transformation.

Common Themes across the Psychobiographical Sketches

While each person described above has many unique attributes, some common themes emerge if these four psychobiographical sketches are examined as a whole. First, the analyses demonstrated that descriptive accounts must go beyond the five-factor model to account for key personality differences. Specific and narrowly defined personality traits such as dependency and perfectionism are not highly correlated with the traits of the five-factor model, and failing to mention these specific traits would have missed some key features of these individuals.

Second, Allport was correct in suggesting that there are core cardinal traits that apply to the specific individual. If we had restricted the analysis of each person to their three main personality traits, albeit subjectively determined, we still would have had a fairly accurate sense of each individual's main personality features.

Third, when it comes to describing a person as accurately as possible, any descriptive analysis of personality traits needs to be supplemented with some discussion of the individual's self-concept and sense of personal identity. Both Sylvia Plath and Anne Sexton suffered from extreme self-criticism, with Plath's self-criticism crossing the boundary and resembling self-hatred. In contrast, Salvador Dali had a highly inflated self-view, consistent with his narcissistic orientation. Finally, Ozzy Osbourne illustrates the difference between the flamboyant person that is his public self and the more reserved and humble family man that is his private self.

A fourth theme that also pertains to the self-concept is that each person could be analyzed by his or her sense of self in relation to others and to his or her communal needs. Although each individual assessed had established a remarkable level of accomplishment and creativity (high agency), it was still the case that their communal needs played a vital role. Both the women and men studied demonstrated a heavy reliance and dependency on other people, and in the cases of Dali, Plath, and Sexton, the loss of key people in their lives had devastating effects.

Finally, the psychobiographical sketches illustrated the role of theory as a form of explanation. The analyses demonstrated how multiple theories can and should be applied to each person. An eclectic theoretical approach seems reasonable given the extremely complex aspects of each individual.

Summary

Chapter 14 served as a reminder that personologists should focus on the whole person by taking a person-centred approach. This chapter also reviewed and illustrated the potential usefulness of certain concepts (such as social learning, psychological needs, and the superiority complex) discussed in earlier chapters. But most importantly, Chapter 14 described psychobiographies and the methods used in good versus poor ones.

The chapter included a brief overview of some well-known psychobiographies, including recent analyses of King George III and Dodge Morgan. It was then argued that students who conduct a psychobiography can learn many valuable lessons. These lessons include the inherent complexity of the individual person, the critical importance of examining the interplay of the personal and situational and cultural factors, and the need to move beyond a descriptive analysis to understand and explain a person's unique characteristics.

Methodological issues that influence the quality of psychobiographies were then reviewed. Problems include the critical period fallacy and eventism. Alexander's suggestions for analyzing psychobiographical data were then presented, including the guidelines of primacy, frequency, and uniqueness, as well as negation and omission. Erikson's concept of triple bookkeeping was also presented. This approach analyzes people with the three levels of the body, the ego, and family and society.

The chapter concluded with psychobiographical sketches of four famous people (Salvador Dali, Sylvia Plath, Anne Sexton, and Ozzy Osbourne). These psychobiographical analyses underscored that famous people may nevertheless suffer from adjustment difficulties. The sketches described each person's life history, reviewed their central personality traits, and provided some theories that help explain how they became the people that we have known. It was suggested that an eclectic approach that includes numerous theories is the best way to capture the complexities of an individual.

Questions to Consider

1 Imagine that you are a hard-core behaviourist. Do you see psychobiography as having scientific merit? Could you perform an effective psychobiography by focusing solely on a person's externally displayed behaviours and learning history?

2 According to McAdams and West (1997), psychobiographies exist for the purposes of exemplification, discovery, and comparison. Which of these purposes is most important? Why?

3 It was suggested that personality profiling of offenders is limited by several problems. It was also mentioned that this form of psychobiography must better use the broader range

of personality concepts and theories. What personality traits, needs, and theories do you see as potentially useful when seeking to identify or understand criminals?

4 What would be included in a psychobiographical analysis of yourself? How are you different from and how are you similar to other people? What are your defining attributes? Would you adopt a psychoanalytic, humanistic, cognitive, or learning perspective in trying to explain your personality?

5 Were you familiar with Salvador Dali, Sylvia Plath, Anne Sexton, or Ozzy Osbourne prior to reading this chapter? Did you get a better sense of how complex any one person can actually be? Did the brief psychobiographical sketches enhance your understanding of the people you had heard of before? Because the analysis of each person had to be brief, it was merely an overview. Which theories would you like to add to these psychobiographies to get a more complete picture of these individuals' personalities?

6 Do you think it is ever possible for a psychobiographer to keep her or his biases out of the analysis? What steps would you take to assess the reliability and validity of a psychobiography?

Key Terms

actor–observer bias, p. 597
confirmatory bias, p. 597
consistency criterion, p. 592
Criminal Personality Research Project, p. 595
critical period fallacy, p. 597
cross-cultural comparative approach, p. 601
deductive profiling, p. 595
eventism, p. 598
exemplification, p. 593
external probability, p. 587
historical–interpretive psychology, p. 593
inductive profiling, p. 595
internal probability, p. 587
life stories, p. 599
omission, p. 599
originology, p. 597
narrative approach, p. 599
negation, p. 599
personal structure analysis, p. 591
primacy guideline, p. 599
psychobiographies, p. 586
psychohistory, p. 601
script theory, p. 600
time series analysis, p. 588
triple bookkeeping approach, p. 599

Key Theorists

Irving Alexander, p. 592
Alan Elms, p. 586
William Runyan, p. 593
Silvan Tomkin, p. 590

GLOSSARY

accentuation principle: The concept that life stressors increase the stability of personality traits over time by magnifying existing psychological features during transitions.

acquiescence response bias: Yea-saying by agreeing with test items.

actor–observer bias: The tendency to ignore situational factors and instead focus on the dispositional personality features of the actor when making attributions.

actualizing tendency: A drive that reflects the need for self-actualization and the need to become one's best possible self. This need reflects the basic motive to change and grow.

actual self: The attributes that a person does indeed have, as opposed to the ideal or ought self.

addiction-prone personality: A personality style associated with vulnerability to a wide array of addictions (e.g., drinking, gambling). It can involve addiction due to the enjoyment of thrill seeking or a need to avoid feelings of distress.

additive model: The model that two factors make independent contributions to the prediction of the outcome variable (i.e., maladjustment). Also known as **main effects model**.

adoptees method: Comparing children who have no genes in common but who were adopted by the same parents. It is used to test the heritability of individual differences.

agency: A need to have an instrumental impact on outcomes. High agency reflects the drive to be dominant and establish status, while low agency reflects passivity, weakness, and submission.

aggregation: The practice of collecting repeated measures, which has the effect of decreasing measurement errors and producing more reliable assessments.

alpha: One of Digman's two super super-factors that incorporate agreeableness, conscientiousness, and emotional stability (i.e., elements of the five-factor model).

alpha coefficient: A statistic proposed by Cronbach, used to characterize the internal consistency of a measure. It is based on the average intercorrelation among scale items and the total number of scale items involved.

alpha press: An actual situation as it objectively exists.

ambiverts: People who are both introverted and extroverted and have moderate scores on this dimension. They are comfortable with being with others or being by themselves.

anaclitic orientation: Personality style involving excessive dependency on others.

anal stage: Freud's second stage of psychosexual development. It stretches from approximately 18 months to 3 to 4 years of age. Pleasure is centred around the anus. Too much or too little gratification at this stage results in an anal retentive or anal expressive personality.

analogue situations: Manufactured scenarios designed to test response to certain environments.

androgyny: A reflection of both high masculinity and femininity. Androgyny is believed to be highly adaptive because the person with this attribute is capable of acting masculine or feminine when required.

anima/animus archetype: An archetype posited by Jung that applies to both males and females. We all have a feminine side (anima) and a masculine side (animus).

anxiously attached infant: Infants who becomes very distressed when their mother leaves the room. These types of infants are at risk of being overly dependent and prone to feelings of separation anxiety.

Apollonian type: One of Benedict's categorizations of the personalities of cultures. Applies to passive and calm cultures.

approach gradient: The significance of the proximity to a goal. There is a stronger pull toward the goal as we get closer to it.

approach–approach conflict: A situation in which one is presented with two equally desirable options; a motivational element suggested by Dollard and Miller.

archetypes: Inherited universal symbols that reflect our instincts and how they are expressed. Jung suggested that archetypes are primordial images that reflect themes stretching back to our early ancestors.

assortative mating: The tendency to select a mate who is similar to the self.

attribution: The causal explanations we come up with when seeking to understand why an event occurred. Attributions are reflected when blame or responsibility is allocated.

attributional complexity: The tendency to make complex attributions to two or more causes (internal and external) when explaining the cause of an event.

attributional style: The typical way that people explain events. For instance, events may be usually attributed to internal factors reflecting the self or external factors outside the self (i.e., environment).

authoritarian personality: One who is dogmatic and domineering, as described originally by Adorno and colleagues.

autobiographical memories: Memories of your own past.

autonomy: An achievement-related personality orientation that is focused on goal striving, a desire for solitude, and freedom from control and external influence.

aversion therapy: An attempt to reduce a behaviour by pairing it with a highly noxious stimulus.

avoidance–avoidance conflict: A situation in which one is presented with two equally undesirable alternatives.

avoidance-focused coping: A characteristic coping style that involves failing to address or confront stressful situations. Avoidance-oriented copers distract themselves or seek out others as a form of social diversion.

avoidance gradient: The significance of the proximity to a goal. There is a stronger need to avoid the goal as we get closer to it.

avoidant attachment style: A trait of an infant who displays little reaction when the mother leaves or re-enters the room, almost as if an attachment bond has never been formed. Avoidantly attached infants can become withdrawn and socially isolated.

avoiding type: People who are regarded as socially avoidant and isolated and who do not mix well with others.

back translation: The translation of a scale into another language and then back into its original language, to ensure that no meaning was lost in the translation.

Barnum effect: The widespread tendency for people to accept personality feedback provided to them as accurate even though the feedback itself is quite general and vague. Named after the circus owner P.T. Barnum.

basic anxiety: An element of Horney's theory that involves anxious concerns and feelings of helplessness and worries about possible abandonment. It occurs when our basic needs are not met.

basic hostility: A reaction to parental indifference and neglect as postulated by Horney. This child does not express basic hostility because he or she is fearful about the consequences of expressing hostility to parental figures.

basic needs: Lower level needs that are instinctual, or instinctoid needs that must be satisfied in order to survive (e.g., need for food and water), as suggested by Maslow.

behavioural approach system: The system proposed by Gray that accounts for individual differences in impulsivity. It is linked with an appetitive orientation and involves a sensitivity to reward (and situations involving non-punishment).

behavioural inhibition: A trait often expressed in social situations that is closely linked with shyness.

behavioural inhibition system: The system proposed by Gray that accounts for individual differences in anxiety. It is linked with a defensive orientation and elevated sensitivity to punishment and non-reward.

behaviourism: An approach that focuses on the study of observable actions rather than cognitions and internal stimuli.

belonging and love needs: Needs for sustained intimacy with others, either in the form of knowing that we fit in with significant others, or establishing a mutual loving relationship.

benefit finding: A form of coping that involves cognitive re-appraisals that focus on the positive things that result from traumatic experiences.

benefit reminding: Recalling re-appraisals of positive things resulting from traumatic experiences.

beta press: An individual's perception or appraisal of the situation, as proposed by Murray.

beta: The second of Digman's super super-traits that incorporated extroversion and intellect components of the five-factor model.

between-subjects variable: When one level of an independent variable is applied to some participants in an experiment but not others.

bicultural identity: Two or more cultural identities. People with bicultural identities are called "biculturals."

bidirectional: When two people influence each other in an ongoing sequence. The effects of the parent and child on each other are bidirectional.

blocking effect: In classical conditioning, the introduction of a second unconditioned stimulus once another unconditioned stimulus has already been used to create a conditioned response. The response to the second unconditioned stimulus is suppressed (blocked) by the already established conditioning link.

buffering effect: The tendency for a factor to moderate and lessen the impact of a previous factor. Research on hardiness showed that it buffered the link between stress and illness.

b-values: The meta-motivations postulated by Maslow. Meta-motivations must be realized to avoid illness and realize one's full potential. Failure to realize and attain these values results in "metapathologies" or illnesses.

cardinal disposition: A trait or drive that defines a personality, according to Allport.

castration anxiety: According to Freud, what a boy feels when he fears that his father will remove his penis as punishment for desiring his mother.

catastrophization: All-or-none thinking about a health problem that often involves magnifying the symptoms and their importance by blowing them out of proportion.

catharsis: The reduction of tension by engaging in processes (e.g., primary process thinking, wish fulfillment) that provides some temporary relief.

central disposition: As suggested by Allport, these are less generalized traits than cardinal ones but are sufficiently strong that they manifest and influence behaviour.

cerebrotonia: A category of people who are socially restrained and high in the need for privacy. Associated with ectomorphs. Part of Sheldon's theory of somatotypes.

choice corollary: When a person selects the option in a dichotomized corollary that is anticipated to provide the best possibility for extending and defining the construct system. The poles of a construct may have very different properties and associated characteristics.

circumplex: When variables are organized in a circle, or perhaps a diamond shape.

class variable: An independent variable in an experiment that differs between participants but is not manipulated (e.g., comparing males and females).

classical conditioning: A type of associative learning in which there repetitively occurs a stimuli-condition pairing. When the stimuli is presented, a conditioned response is involuntarily or reflexively displayed. A form of conditioning illustrated by Pavlov.

client-centred therapy: A form of humanistic therapy proposed by Rogers. The client is the agent of change and is personally responsible for personal change.

cognitive complexity: The structure and interrelation of cognitions rather than the actual content or theme of the cognitions.

cohort effect: Differences that are attributable to living in a particular epoch or era. Cohort effects usually involve differences among people that reflect their year of birth.

collective self-esteem: When people derive their self-esteem, at least in part, from their connections to small and large groups and organizations.

collective unconscious: A shared form of unconscious postulated by Jung. It consists of universal symbols known as archetypes.

collectivism: A group emphasis and fostering of the connection between the self and other people. People are integrated, interdependent, and cohesive in a collectivist society. The self is viewed and conceptualized in relation to the connections with others.

common trait: Certain personality traits that are shared by other people.

commonality corollary: The theory that accounts for similarities between people, according to Kelly. People will have similar psychological processes and perceptions to the extent that they rely on similar constructions of experience.

communion: A need to connect with and relate to other people.

comorbidity: When two or more diagnoses apply to an individual.

competencies: Skills or capabilities that distinguish people. A central component of the theoretical framework proposed by Mischel & Shoda.

complementarity principle: The notion that the specific type of interpersonal behaviour expressed by one person will elicit a corresponding or supplementary behaviour from another person (e.g., dominance elicits submissiveness).

complexes: The personal unconscious, as described by Jung, is composed of feeling-toned sources of energy that reflect personal conflicts and tensions.

conceptual equivalence: The issue of whether a personality concept or construct has the exact same meaning and significance across cultures.

concordance: A statistical term for the amount of shared presence of a genetically based trait. It is usually expressed in terms of whether twins have the same attribute.

concurrent validity: The significant association between the personality measure and a criterion variable that it should be associated with. Both measures are assessed at the same time.

conditionability: The ability in people to learn from mistakes by linking behaviours with the consequences that follow.

conditioned response: The previously unconditioned response brought on by a conditioned stimulus. For instance, the salivation in Pavlov's dogs was originally brought on by the presentation of the meat powder. After enough powder-bell pairings the dogs would salivate at the sound of the bell even without the presentation of the powder. This behaviour is the conditioned response.

conditioned stimulus: A neutral stimulus that initially has no effect on the subject (in Pavlov's case the bell) and that, when paired with an unconditioned stimulus (presentation of the meat powder) produces an unconditioned response (salivation). The neutral stimulus (bell) becomes the conditioned stimulus when unconditioned response (salivation) occurs without the presence of the unconditioned stimulus (meat powder).

conditions of worth: A source of primary threat to self-regard, according to Rogers. Children act to meet parental expectations rather than according to their true self, and self-worth depends on meeting parental approval. Conditions of worth contribute to an alienation from the true self.

confirmatory bias: Tendency to disproportionately focus on information that is consistent with one's initial beliefs.

confirmatory factor analyses: Analyses in multivariate statistics in which the researcher stipulates that the proposed factor structure to emerge from a factor analysis will fit the theoretical model that was originally postulated.

constitutional psychology: The link between personality and physical attributes, as coined by Sheldon.

construct validity: An abstract concept that reflects the need for personality measures to stem from a theory. Construct validity involves a theory of a set of hypotheses about a psychological construct.

construction corollary: The notion that a person anticipates events by construing their replications, according to Kelly.

constructive alternativism: When two people have different interpretations of the same event.

constructs: Psychologically meaningful cognitive categories. Kelly's theory is based on the premise that people differ in their personal constructs.

content validity: Whether test items and representative samples of the universe that make up a particular construct are adequate.

convergent validity: When a measure is highly correlated with another measure that purports to be measuring the same construct (i.e., it is related to things it should be related to).

coping: The ways in which people try to deal with a problem or handle the emotions that arise in response to the problem. Even when two people interpret a common stressor in the same way, the effects and outcome of the stress will vary as a functioning of differences in coping styles.

couple-centred approach: A method of looking at the degree of similarity between the members of the dyad in their personality profiles across several traits.

covert sensitization: A psychosomatic manifestation of aversion therapy.

A person feels unwell or unpleasant merely by thinking about the undesired behaviour.

critical period fallacy: A tendency when conducting a psychobiography to place undue emphasis on one period of an individual's life and exclude other periods.

cross-cultural comparative approach: An approach designed to estimate whether factors apply across two or more cultures to specific people or to specific constructs.

cultural fit hypothesis: The notion that personality will be adaptive in a new culture to the extent that it fits with existing norms in the host culture.

culture-bound syndromes: Syndromes that are tied to certain cultures, such as *amok*, *dhat*, and ghost sickness.

cynical hostility: Pessimistic beliefs about the world and other people. The key element of hostility associated with health problems.

dark triad: Three interrelated constructs that reflect mistreatment of others (Machiavellianism, narcissism, and psychopathy), as proposed by Paulhus.

deductive profiling: Basing a psychological profile on deductive logic and inference after taking into account the information for a specific case.

defence mechanism: An unconscious strategy that helps the ego by warding off anxiety; often referred to as ego defence mechanisms.

defence styles: Typical ways that people respond when feeling anxious and challenged, although most defence styles are unconscious.

defensive pessimism: When people motivate themselves by feeling anxious about possible negative outcomes.

defensive self-esteem: People who are incongruent because they have high explicit self-esteem, but low implicit self-esteem.

demand characteristics: Clues in the experimental setting or procedure that enable the participant to figure out the hypothesis and act in a manner to support the hypothesis.

denial: A defence mechanism that involves refusing to acknowledge past traumas.

dependent variable: The outcome variable that is measured in an experiment. The dependent variable represents the effect in a cause–effect relationship, and it responds to changes in the independent variable.

depressive predictive certainty: When a person believes that negative events are absolutely certain to occur and there is nothing he or she can do to avoid them.

desacralizing: A defensive way of minimizing and ignoring the sacred value of being needs.

developmental trajectory: The levels of a particular behaviour over time. Does the behaviour increase, decrease, or stay at about the same level over time?

diathesis: A vulnerability factor that is expressed following certain life experiences.

dichotomy corollary: Kelly's notion that each theme or construct is represented by endpoints of a dichotomy, and sometimes the endpoints are polar opposites.

differential reliability index: Statistical test used to evaluate whether a particular test item has too high a correlation with a measure of social desirability.

differential stability: The chances that upon subsequent retesting, people will end up with the same answers or the same score as the first test.

differentiation: Occurs when the organism learns to respond specifically to the exact conditioned stimulus and does not respond to a highly similar stimulus.

Dionysian type: One of Benedict's cultural personality categorizations. Cultures that typify this classification are impulsive and expressive cultures that engage in excess.

directionality issue: The issue that if two variables are related, all that can be stated is that they are associated with each other; it cannot be assumed that the variability associated with one variable caused or contributed to the variability of the other variable.

disability hypothesis: Hypotheses advanced to account for the link between higher symptoms reporting and elevated neuroticism and negative affect. The disability hypothesis is that illness leads to higher levels of negative affect.

discriminant validity: The trait of a personality scale when it is unrelated to a measure with which it theoretically should not be associated.

discriminative stimulus: The ability that develops over repeated stimulus–response outcomes to identify a specific stimulus and its associated response to lead to rewards or punishments.

disorganized attachment style: A style found in infants who seem totally confused by their surroundings. The disorganized attachment style is highly maladaptive and results from being exposed to chaotic and abusive environments.

displacement: A defence that involves channelling a negative emotional reaction away from the true source of the negative emotion and instead directing it toward a less threatening target.

display rules: Learned rules that indicate when it is appropriate to express emotions in social situations, with appropriate emotions being reinforced.

distinctiveness hypothesis: McGuire's notion that the self-concept is composed of attributes that make us highly unique from others (e.g., having red hair).

dizygotic twins: Fraternal or non-identical twins who share only 50% of genetic material.

dream analysis: A projective technique. It is believed that our defences are relaxed during sleep so unconscious conflicts can be expressed through the themes inherent in our dreams.

dream symbolism theory: The theory that certain objects in dreams are supposed to represent male and female forms of sexuality. Although the dream symbolism theory per se has not met with much empirical support, research does show that people who are anxious tend to be more likely to have dreams with sexual content.

dream work: The process of transforming latent dream content into manifest content.

dynamic constructivist approach: The view that cognitive categories experience ongoing change as a function of life and a function of situational differences that influence the content of constructs and the degree to which constructs can be cognitively accessed.

dynamic stability: A characteristic or predictable pattern of variability in a person's responses over time.

ecological validity: A probabilistic notion that involves the degree to which the research reflects the actual phenomenon in nature.

ectomorphy: A body shape that is thin or slender.

effectance: A need to have an impact on people, places, and objects.

effortful control: A voluntary attempt to control inhibitions and impulses.

ego: Develops out of the id, and this process starts to occur in the second half of a baby's first year. The ego is mostly but not entirely conscious. The ego's main purpose is to address the demands of the environment and reality.

ego control: A person's degree of impulse control, including control of emotional and motivational tendencies.

ego resiliency: The ability to alter behaviours according to situational demands.

Electra complex: According to Freud, a girl's desire for her father during the phallic period of development.

emic approach: An indigenous approach in cross-cultural psychology that looks to establish and identify culture-specific factors and processes.

emotion-focused coping: A tendency to reflect on the emotional experiences associated with stress. This can involve rumination about emotional states and a sense of blame.

endomorphy: A body shape that can be classified as overweight.

episodic memory: The ability to remember events from one's past.

equal environment assumption: The assumption that children are treated the same by their caregivers.

eros: The sexual energy and life instinct postulated by Freud, reflected in the libido. One of two instincts, the other being **thanatos** (the death instinct).

esteem needs: The need for people to perceive themselves as competent and achieving; the fourth level of Maslow's hierarchy.

etic approach: An approach in cross-cultural psychology that looks at exporting supposed universal findings and models and applying them to specific cultures.

eventism: A criticism of psychobiographies that involves a tendency to trace most of the characteristics and interpretation of a person back to one or two key events.

evoked culture: Culturally inclined cognitive tendencies that develop in response to one's environment.

excitation: Active and excitable behaviour, such as that shown by dogs in Pavlov's experiments when confronted with two or more conditioned responses of equal strength and magnitude.

exemplification: A function or purpose of psychobiographies that involves illustrating how a personality concept or theory is relevant to a specific person.

experience corollary: The notion that the change in the construction system as a person successively construes the replication of events.

experience sampling: An emerging technique designed to increase the ecological validity of psychological research. In experience sampling, participants are required to record their behaviours, cognitions, and emotions at various points throughout their day.

experimental condition: One of two or more levels of an independent variable that a participant receives in an experiment.

experimental neuroses: The stress and confusion displayed by the respondent when presented with two or more conditioned responses of equal strength and magnitude.

explanatory style: How people go about explaining events; related to attributional style.

explicit culture: Objectively defined culture.

explicit measures: Structured self-report measures.

explicit self-esteem: Positive or negative conscious evaluations of the self as measured by self-report measures such as the Rosenberg Self-Esteem Scale. Explicit self-esteem is what would be assessed if you asked someone to verbally describe their self-esteem and personality.

exposure therapy: One of the most common techniques for treating anxiety disorders in the form of phobias. The patient is exposed to the object or situation associated with the phobia (e.g., making a snake-phobic patient touch a snake) while being put into a relaxed state. The fear is extinguished via exposure.

external validity: The notion that differences in behaviours that are obtained in the laboratory setting may be quite artificial and not reflect what happens in real-world settings.

extinction phase: The process by which a conditioned stimulus reverts back to neutral status.

extinction: When a conditioned response eventually disappears because the pleasurable stimulus is no longer evident. Eventually the organism adapts to this new reality.

face validity: A form of visual inspection (i.e., eyeball test) that involves the question, "On the surface or face of the test itself, do the items seem to measure the construct?" There is no established statistical test to evaluate face validity.

factor analysis: A statistical technique used to discover the relationships between variables. The aim is to discover if the observed variables can be explained primarily or entirely in terms of a much smaller number of variables.

factorial validity: When an assessment measure based on a construct that is conceptualized as having several different factors does indeed seem to have these factors when factor analyses are conducted.

familiarity hypothesis: The hypothesis that constructs will be more complex when they involve people we are highly familiar with.

field dependence vs. field independence: The difference between field-dependent people, who are described as being global in their perceptual and cognitive functioning, and field-independent people, who tend focus on specific details and are relatively uninfluenced by the surrounding context.

fields: Items that reflect how the person has come to cognitively organize his world and experiences; similar to constructs.

fixation: What results from getting too much or too little gratification in a psychosexual stage, according to Freud. This involves becoming stuck or fixated at a particular stage, and the adult personality is a reflection of when and if fixation has occurred.

fixed interval schedule: A schedule of reinforcement where the key factor is the amount of time involved; the amount of time between reinforced responses is held constant.

fixed ratio schedule: A schedule of reinforcement where the number of responses occurring between two reinforced responses is held constant.

fixed role therapy: A therapy arising from Kelly's theory that allows the client to play various roles in order to identify and explore the constructs of self and others, and try out these constructs as a different way of construing and interpreting reality.

flashbulb memories: The tendency for people to remember exact details with great accuracy because the original events were emotionally intense.

flooding: A behaviour modification technique used to treat extreme phobias of specific objects. The person is exposed to the feared object and is not permitted to escape.

flux: The amount of variability that a person has around his or her mean score. If someone were high in interpersonal sensitivity and quite reactive to feedback (i.e., if criticized they returned the criticism), this person would probably be high in flux. Another person might be relatively indifferent to feedback and would be low in flux.

force: An inner drive caused by tension.

fragmentation corollary: The concept that a person can simultaneously use two or more construction subsystems even though these subsystems may seem logically incompatible.

free association: A psychoanalytic technique that involves telling whatever thoughts come into mind while in a state of relaxation. Relaxation lowers one's defences so that unconscious conflicts can come into conscious awareness.

frustration–aggression hypothesis: Dollard et al.'s theory that all acts of aggression are the result of frustration, and all frustration leads to aggression. Frustration is said to occur when the organism is blocked from acquiring a goal or source of gratification and must delay attaining the gratification.

functional optimism: A term coined by Schwarzer to distinguish the general benefits of a positive outlook when a threat actually exists (functional optimism) from the naïve optimism that can lead to greater risk.

fusion of needs: A phenomenon that occurs when one action can satisfy two or more needs at the same time.

gender schemas: Cognitive categories that people have as a means of thinking about themselves and others in terms of gender and gender-related characteristics.

gender similarities hypothesis: Hyde's concept that there are far more similarities than differences between the sexes.

generalizability: Generalizing beyond the laboratory setting to more naturalistic contexts.

generalization: A conditioned response that occurs in response to stimuli that resembles the original conditioned stimulus.

generativity: The willingness to engage in acts to promote the well-being of younger generations in order to promote the long-term survival of the species. A key stage of Erikson's theory that is associated with aging to maturity.

genetic variation: The controversial notion that psychological differences between cultures reflect genetic differences.

genital stage: Freudian stage that coincides closely with adolescence and the physical changes that accompany puberty. Here psychosexual pleasure is refocused on the genital area with the goal of establishing healthy heterosexual relationships (as opposed to unconsciously lusting after the opposite-sexed parent as a young child).

genotype: A person's unobservable genetic constitution in the form of inherited genes; it is someone's potential according to genetic background.

genotypical disposition: An explanatory account of a more fundamental and deeper disposition (i.e., a person's core).

getting type: A type of person described by Adler. This type of person is very dependent on others and lets other people take the lead with various things. The getting type is the end result of being a pampered child.

goodness of fit hypothesis: The premise that whether a particular coping response is adaptive depends on the match between the coping response and what is called for in the problem situation. Thus, problem-focused coping is adaptive in controllable situations.

guan: A mode of parenting among Chinese parents that is focused on training, as suggested by Chao.

Guttman scale analysis: A statistical technique that tests whether hypothesized stages can be detected in empirical data.

habit system: Customary modes of behaviour that have become almost automatic and occur repeatedly without conscious thought. The habit system accounts for overly rigid behaviours that persist over time.

hardy personality: A resilient personality style studied by Maddi and Kobasa. Hardy people must have high levels of control, commitment, and challenge.

heritability: The proportion of phenotypic variation in a sample or population that is attributable to genetic factors. If something is said to be 100% heritable, then the variability would be entirely due to genetic factors.

historical-interpretive psychology: Psychobiographical analysis that interprets a person in a historical context. The term was coined originally by Runyan, who advocated assessing people across various time periods.

holistic theories: Theories that focus on the development of the entire organism. Also known as **organistic theories.**

id: A structure that is present at birth and is the primitive and least rational part of our selves. The id is unconscious and operates according to the pleasure principle.

ideal self: The attributes that a person would ideally possess in a best-case scenario.

identity conflict: When two or more aspects of the self are in opposition with each other (e.g., "I am the type of person who wants to be with people but doesn't want to be with people").

identity crisis: The failed search for a sense of personal identity during adolescence and early adulthood. An identity deficit described by Erikson.

identity deficit: Occurs when the person is seeking but has failed thus far to establish a desired identity (e.g., "I don't know who I am").

idiographic: An approach that involves gathering a large amount of data from one person or only a few people (i.e., a case study method). The idiographic approach can be regarded as a person-centred approach focused on understanding the entire person.

immature defences: Highly maladaptive defence mechanisms.

implicit culture: Subjectively defined culture.

implicit measures: The means by which a person derives motives that are not consciously reflected upon.

implicit personality theories: The tendency to link together certain personality characteristics in our minds, perhaps without basis.

implicit self-esteem: Automatic evaluations and reactions to the self that occur outside of conscious awareness.

impostor phenomenon: A condition based on the notion that one is faking one's way through something and the impostor status is about to be discovered.

incongruence between the self and experience: What occurs when, according to Rogers, a person exposed to conditions of worth will increasingly fail to act in accordance with their true nature and will instead act in a non-authentic way to satisfy the conditions of worth.

incremental validity: Showing that a new measure accounts for meaningful unique variability not accounted for by already existing measures.

independent variable: The variable that is manipulated in an experiment. It is regarded as the causal variable as it is the one that creates change.

individual psychology: Adler's theory that each person is unique and no previous theory adequately reflects this individuality.

individual trait: A trait that is particular to a specific person.

individualism: An extensive self-focus on the individual and his or her immediate family. The emphasis is on the self in relation to the self, and the emphasis is on personal goals and achievements.

individuality corollary: A theory that accounts for the differences between people; that is, persons differ from each other in their construction of events.

individuation: Occurs when a person becomes a psychological individual by achieving a separate unity or whole.

inductive profiling: A statistically based, actuarial form of prediction that tries to apply general principles to specific cases. Based on the use of general principles and patterns that have been gleaned from analyses of a relatively large database.

inferiority complex: A sense of not measuring up to expectations and not being on par with other people. Originally proposed by Adler.

inhibition: Anxiety and distress when confronted with two or more conditioned responses of equal strength and magnitude.

inner-directedness: A higher level of self-actualization. Inner-directed people are guided by their own motives and goals.

instrumental conditioning: A pattern of learning through experience, first thoroughly examined by Thorndike. A subject will be more disposed toward a behaviour if the consequence is positive or satisfying. Later to become known as **operant conditioning** under Skinner's investigation.

interaction effect: When the effect of an independent variable is moderated or influenced by the level of another independent variable. Also called **moderator effect**.

interactionism: The view that differences in behaviour often reflect the joint influence and interplay of personality traits and situational factors.

interdependent self-construal: A trait found in people who are high in affiliation and nurturance needs and are more likely to think of themselves in terms of their relationships with other people.

internal consistency: The degree of homogeneity of test items; a kind of reliability.

introjection: The process of identification where a person comes to internalize another's values; implicated during superego development.

introjective orientation: The personality style proposed by Blatt that involves excessive levels of self-criticism and self-punitiveness.

introspective method: An analysis of internal thoughts and images, including dreams.

ipsative scoring: A form of scoring that results in two scores not being independent. A higher score on one variable decreases or limits the possible value of another variable.

ipsative stability: A form of test–retest reliability that reflects whether a profile of scores is consistent over time.

Jonah complex: A fear of greatness and a fear of our own destiny, as defined by Maslow.

Kelly's fundamental postulate: The idea by Kelly that "a person's processes are psychologically channelized by the ways in which he anticipates events."

language equivalence: The degree to which the translation of a scale conveys the same meaning as the original scale.

latency period: A period from 6 to 12 years when psychosexual urges seem relatively dormant and are sublimated into a focus on school activities and achievements and developing and maintaining friendships.

latency-based validity indices: Measures tapping the speed of responses to inventories, based on the fact that it takes time to lie when completing inventories.

latent content: The deeper meaning or significance of a dream.

law of effect: Thorndike's belief that a behaviour followed by positive outcomes is repeated and behaviours followed by negative outcomes are less likely to be repeated.

leniency effect: See *positivity bias.*

lexical approach: The tendency to identify the personality differences represented in language.

libido: The individual's psychic energy that demands expression, contained in the id. Freud believed that much of our behaviour is fuelled by this psychosexual energy.

life space: All of the factors that have an impact on a person, according to Lewin. Refers to the whole psychological field. A person's behaviour must be interpreted within the context of their entire life space. Includes all possible events that someone experiences.

life stories: The use of an individual's personal story and sense of identity with the narrative approach to psychobiography.

linear: Datapoints arranged in a straight line. As a statistical concept, one variable increases in a fairly constant manner as a function of increases in another variable.

linguistic equivalence: The need to have measures in different languages to tap the diversity found within countries.

little emperor phenomenon: A stereotyped view of the negative attributes of only children arising from the one-child policy in China.

little five: The test of the five-factor model in young people.

locus of control: Individual differences in internal vs. external control of reinforcement.

looking glass self: Our sense of our self that depends on the reactions of other people, as if reflected back to us in a mirror or looking glass.

Machiavellianism: A tough-minded orientation with the general belief that it is acceptable to take advantage of others and use ingratiation for personal gain.

main effects model: See *additive model.*

malingering: The tendency to "fake bad," perhaps by trying to seem mentally ill in order to not be criminally responsible for misdeeds.

mandala: The most central archetype, which is represented by images of circles.

manifest content: The symbols or images in a dream.

manipulated variable: In an experiment, when one level or form of the variable is applied by the experimenter to a subset of the experiment participants, but a different level or form of the independent variable is applied to another subset of participants.

masking: The hiding of one's response to a stimulus based on social expectation.

mastery goals: An intrinsic desire to master the material rather than to achieve a particular performance goal. It is learning for the sake of learning.

matched-dependent behaviour: A type of imitation that requires two people to be together, and the second person imitates the behaviour of the first person. The cues for these two people are different. The first person is responding to some cue, but the cue for the second person is the behaviour of the first person.

mature defences: Adaptive defence mechanisms such as sublimation.

maximal approach: The range in behaviours or responses that a person is capable of expressing. This differs from the tendency for personality to focus on what a person typically or usually does.

mean-level stability: A test of the long-term consistency of personality that involves following the same sample of participants over time and comparing means across time.

measurement error: What is present when a number that has been measured and counted is not an accurate reflection of the true value.

median split: What a researcher performs when interested in creating only two groups. The researcher establishes a midpoint in the range of scores on the variable in question; people above this midpoint would be in one group and those below the midpoint would be in the other.

mediator effect: A link between two variables, which exists as a result of their mutual link with an intervening variable. This intervening variable influences both of these variables.

megalomaniac type: One of Benedict's cultural personality classifications, which reflects behaviours that overemphasize wealth, social prestige, personal glory, and superiority.

mesomorphy: A body type classified as medium or somewhat muscular.

meta-analysis: A quantitative review that involves tabulating the average effect sizes across all of the available studies that have examined a particular topic.

metatraits: Traits that are highly relevant to an individual. Another term for the metatrait concept is **traitedness**. If a concept is "traited," it is high in trait relevance.

method variance: Variability in responding that is due to the specific properties of the assessment method used (e.g., gathering self-reports vs. informant ratings).

methodological pluralism: The principle that a phenomenon should be assessed with many different methods in order to obtain a more reliable and valid assessment.

mindfulness: Awareness of the moment as it emerges.

minimization: The tendency to portray oneself in a way that minimizes psychopathology to influence treatment and placement decisions.

modal personality: The characteristics that are most predominant in a society or culture and how often a trait is manifested in a group of people.

mode: In statistics, the number that occurs the most times.

moderation norm: A dispositional tendency to overuse the midpoint of possible responses on a response scale. It may reflect normative pressures toward modesty and not drawing attention to the self.

moderator effect: See *interaction effect*.

modulation corollary: The notion that variation in the construction system is limited by the permeability of the constructs in the construction system; that is, to what extent new elements are assimilated (permeable) or not assimilated (impermeable).

monozygotic twins: Identical twins. They share 100% of their genes.

moral anxiety: Anxiety that reflects fear that the superego will overwhelm the ego.

morphogenic: Replacement term for "idiographic." The aim is to reflect a greater focus on the pattern or structure that exists within the individual.

moving against people: A sense of detachment and alienation from others.

moving away from people: A sense of isolation inherent in basic anxiety.

moving toward people: An excessive tendency to move toward people reflects the compliant type personality, which is characterized by a sense of helplessness.

multiform method: The practice of gathering data periodically over time and in naturalistic settings by different people.

multitrait–multimethod matrix: An essential aspect of test construction and refinement that is used to evaluate concurrent and discriminant validity.

naïve optimism: A pervasive sense of unrealistic optimism about one's health, which appears to apply to most people, as described by Weinstein.

Narcissistic personality disorder (NPD): A grandiose view of one's specialness, based on the ancient Greek myth about Narcissus, who falls in love with his own reflection. People with NPD are also preoccupied with their possible greatness.

narrative approach: An analytical strategy that is a case study analysis of a person's life story.

national character study: Sweeping evaluations of all the people in a particular country that has been criticized for fostering stereotypes. Benedict suggested that this is the study of learned cultural behaviour.

negation: A criterion used by psychobiographers to gain insights by focusing on a tendency to deny an attribute or represent it in a way that is opposite to the theme.

negative correlation: Exists when there is a linear association between variables, such that as one variable increases, the other variable decreases to a corresponding degree.

negative identity: The lack of a clear and adaptive identity, reflecting aimlessness and anti-social tendencies, which may result in diffusion and confusion.

negative reinforcement: A form of reward that involves a response that is followed by the removal or termination of a noxious, unpleasant stimulus. Negative reinforcement increases the likelihood that a response will be repeated.

neurotic anxiety: A form of anxiety suggested by Freud that reflects the id's predominance in the conflict among the id, ego, and superego.

niche model of birth order: The theory that secondborns are rebellious because this is one way of gaining parental attention and distinguishing them from firstborns who are higher in achievement orientation and more accepting of parental dictates.

nomological network: The factors and variables that are theoretically related to the construct in question. The nomological network needs to be defined fully with respect to the hypothesized interrelations among variables.

nomothetic: A variable-centred approach that involves gathering a small amount of data from a relatively large sample in the hopes of identifying general laws or principles.

nonadditive genetic effects: The idea that personality does not depend on single genes in isolation, but on clusters or combinations of genes that coexist in the same person.

non-independence issue: The issue that responses provided by both members of a couple cannot be treated as if they are independent; the partners are interdependent and they tend to influence each other. As a result, the usual statistical procedures cannot be used because they are based on the assumption that the participants are independent of each other.

nonshared environment: Unique situational influences specific to one individual.

normative equivalence: The comparability of a measure across cultural groups. The issue is whether the similar norms (i.e., group means and the variability of the distribution of scores) are found across cultures for a specific measure.

object relations theory: How people come to view relationships with other people, including such things as our interpersonal wishes and our emotional responses to other people. This stems from the psychoanalytic perspective.

objective self-awareness theory: Duval and Wicklund's theory that one's focus of attention will determine one's locus of causal attribution. If a person has focused attention inward on self-thoughts and personal feelings, when asked to make attributions, the self will be implicated.

Oedipus complex: Freud's concept that a boy in the phallic stage of development desires his mother. Identification with the father out of fear of his response contributes to superego development.

old remembrances: Childhood memories, as proposed by Adler. They contribute to the cognitive prototypes that underscore styles of life as an adult.

omission: A guideline for interpreting psychobiographical information. The tendency for a person to skip or omit a personal detail may signify something of importance.

operant conditioning: The use of positive or negative consequences to modify voluntary behaviour.

oral stage: Freudian stage that stretches from birth to 18 months of age. Pleasure is centred around the mouth. Too little or too much gratification results in a fixation and the development of an oral dependent or aggressive personality.

order effect: When the same person is used repeatedly across different experimental conditions, the order that the conditions are experienced in may create a source of bias.

ordination: The process of planning and implementing schedules in order to reduce conflict among two or more goals that are seeking expression at the same time.

organ inferiority: Biological weaknesses that provided the basis for Adler's concept of the inferiority complex.

organismic valuing process: Our intuitive knack for intrinsically knowing the things that are good for us and the things that are bad for us, as proposed by Rogers.

organistic theories: See *holistic theories.*

organization corollary: The concept that each person characteristically evolves a construction system that includes ordinal relationships between constructs. This system is created due to the person's desire to easily anticipate and understand future events.

originology: An error in psychobiographical analysis that places too much emphasis on the role of early life experiences as an influence on development. Erikson introduced this concept to remind personologists to take a lifespan approach.

other-oriented perfectionism: A trait dimension of perfectionism that centres on the belief that others are imposing unrealistic demands on the self.

ought self: The attributes that a person should possess based on social or cultural expectations, obligations, and duties.

outer-directedness: Being highly sensitive to external cues and dictates. Outer-directed people respond to external pressures.

overcontrolling type: A personality type described as highly constricted, tense, uneasy, introverted, and passive.

palliative coping: Attempts at soothing one's distressed state by engaging in self-help and comforting activities (e.g., making yourself a cup of tea).

paradoxical self-esteem: A contradictory form of self-worth whereby individuals are high in self-liking but low in self-competence or vice versa.

paranoid type: One of Benedict's cultural personality classifications. Typified by preoccupation with possible betrayals and attacks.

partial mediation: When the link between a variable and another variable depends partly on an intervening variable.

partial reinforcement: When rewards are provided on only certain trials following certain responses. Behaviours learned via a partial reinforcement schedule are quite resistant to extinction because it is difficult to ascertain that reinforcement is no longer available.

peak experiences: Moments when a person feels heavenly, where time and space and the self have been transcended. People having these experiences are free, at least for the moment, from feelings of fear and self-doubt.

PEN model: Eysenck's theory that the criminal personality is characterized by high levels of psychoticism, extroversion, and neuroticism.

penis envy: Envy of boys felt by girls, who can compensate for their own lack of a penis by developing a relationship with the father. A part of the Electra complex.

perfection principle: The principle that drives the functioning of the superego (i.e., we must act perfectly by meeting societal dictates, which often come in the form of endorsing and internalizing our parents' values).

persona: The face we show the world, stemming from the masks that Greek actors would wear according to which character they were portraying.

personal growth: The growth process resulting from a motivation to continually better ourselves. According to self-actualization theorists, we rarely cease striving when our immediate needs have been met.

personal responsibility: Personal culpability for our actions. According to a humanistic approach, we should reject a person's mechanistic views that promote the idea that we are unable to exercise self-determination.

personal unconscious: The part of ourselves that reflects our own experiences and conflicts, which distinguishes us and makes us unique.

personality capabilities: Individual ability. Refers to maximal tendencies in the range of behaviours a person can exhibit.

personality coefficient: Mischel's theory that 0.30 is the maximum correlation between personality traits and behaviours. This term was used to suggest that most of the variability in behaviour is not attributable to stable personality attributes.

personality sphere: The totality of human behaviour.

personality type: Discrete categories that differ qualitatively in kind rather than in degree. Personality types are categories that can involve a constellation of personality characteristics that are present in an all-or-none fashion.

personifications: Mental prototypes (cognitive categories). These prototypes are similar to the concept of schemas. These mental prototypes are formed early in life and are used as a guide that assists us in our perceptions of events.

personologist: One who studies personality.

personology: The study of human lives and the factors that influence their development, with a particular emphasis on differences among individuals and their personality types.

phallic stage: The psychosexual stage where libidinal pleasure is focused on the genital area. It occurs normally during the ages of four to six years, and is the most controversial of Freud's stages because it includes the Oedipus and Electra complexes.

phenomenal field: The perceptual field of awareness and cognition.

phenotype: A person's behavioural expression of genetic potential. Phenotype can be and usually is influenced by experience.

pilot study: A preliminary investigation that typically leads to a more complicated follow-up study.

plaster hypothesis: James' theory that personality is mostly set for most people after a certain age and that changes are difficult to make.

plasticity hypothesis: The idea that personality is flexible. James felt that plasticity in personality is reflected by gradual, evolving change.

pleasure principle: The concept that the id is a demanding structure that seeks pleasure and immediate gratification without concern for the possible consequences of inappropriate thoughts and actions.

positive correlation: A linear association between variables, such that as one variable tends to increase, the other variable tends to increase to a corresponding degree.

positive psychology: A school of thought that studies optimal human function or the conditions under which people thrive.

positive reinforcement: Reinforcement that increases the likelihood of a behaviour being repeated due to the occurrence of positive, pleasurable outcomes after the behaviour has been expressed.

positivity bias: A greater tendency to ascribe more desirable traits to the target person who is being evaluated; also called the **leniency effect**.

postulate of individual differences: One of Eysenck's two postulates on personality and conditioning. Posits that the speed, strength, and dissipation of inhibition or excitation are properties of physical structures involved in stimulus connections.

predictive validity: The issue of whether a personality measure can predict measures that it should be related to when assessed in the future.

preferences: How we interact with and engage our worlds.

prepared learning: The theory that we are biologically prepared to fear only certain stimuli and not others.

press: The role of situational factors that operate like a pressure on the individual and contribute to his or her behaviour.

preverbal constructs: Subconscious cognitive categories that are likely involved in the tip-of-the-tongue phenomenon that occurs when you can almost but not quite put something into words; also known as **construing**.

primacy guideline: The premise in psychobiography that the theme that emerges first is the most important; that is, the first thing that is evident is the most significant.

primary appraisals: Appraisals that assess whether an event is a threat or a challenge.

primary needs: Physiological needs in Maslow's hierarchy of needs. These are primary because they are essential for survival and relate to internal bodily processes.

primary process thinking: The tendency for a person to generate cognitive images of pleasurable stimuli. This would occur, for instance, when fantasizing about sexual activities with someone who is appealing yet unavailable.

primary reinforcer: Something that has inherently rewarding properties in its ability to reduce a drive state. For instance, water is a primary reinforcer because it reduces thirst and water is needed for survival.

private self-consciousness: An internal focus of attention on thoughts and feelings. Heightened levels of private self-consciousness tend to be associated with more intense experiences of positive and negative emotions.

Problem-focused coping: Taking actions to directly solve the problem in a task-focused manner. This approach is most adaptive when the problem situation is controllable.

projection: A defence mechanism that involves displacing unacceptable aspects of the self on other people or other things. Projection occurs because it is too threatening to admit unacceptable aspects of the self to oneself at a conscious level.

projective hypothesis: The notion that unconscious themes that reveal the self will be projected on to ambiguous stimuli and differences in responses reflect meaningful individual differences among people.

prospective memory: Remembering that you will have to do something in the future (e.g., recalling that you have to phone your bank next week).

pseudotrait: The erroneous belief about a person's personality brought about when we fail to discern that a person has acted in a false way in order to create a particular impression or appearance to others.

psychobiographies: Case studies that are conducted from a psychological perspective, identifying and explaining issues and themes throughout a person's life. Because they are case studies, psychobiographies have limited generalizability.

psychodrama: A test to determine how people respond when placed in lifelike situations.

psychohistory: An analysis of a person's psychological features at a particular point in time and how the era influenced the individual (and perhaps how the individual influenced the era).

psychopathy: A highly anti-social personality style that involves no sense of shame or remorse when someone engages in extremely anti-social acts. Psychopaths often have a glib sense of charm and a superior ability to manipulate people.

psychosexual stages: Stages in Freud's theory that at different ages, a particular area of the body is the main source of pleasure and sexual gratification for the id and its impulses.

psychosomatic hypothesis: The hypothesis that negative affect and neuroticism cause health problems, and this accounts for the association.

public self-consciousness: A general awareness of the self as a social object being evaluated and scrutinized by others.

pulse: The regular variability of a person's interpersonal behaviours across time.

Q-sort technique: A technique that requires sorting a pile of 100 cards into 9 categories. It can be used to tap the actual vs. ideal self because a person can be asked to derive categories that reflect the current self and then the ideal self.

radical behaviourism: A subset of behaviourism that holds that subjective factors (thoughts, feelings) are unobservable and therefore have no place in the psychological spectrum. Only overt behaviours should be assessed.

radical environmentalism: A tenet in Watson's theory that states that the environment is a more important determinant of behaviour than heredity or temperament.

random assignment: A key part of those experiments that are designed to make inferences about cause and effect relations. That is, participants should be allocated randomly to one of the experimental conditions so that additional variables that might influence behaviour (e.g., age differences) are spread out evenly across the groups.

range corollary: A construct that is convenient for anticipating a finite range of events.

range of convenience: All of the things that the person with a particular construct feels would apply to the construct. The range of convenience is one source of individual difference because the range for a specific construct ought to vary from person to person.

rank-order stability: A form of test–retest reliability that assesses the extent to which, when repeatedly measured, scores in a distribution of scores have the same relative rank or order.

rationalization: A more adaptive form of defence. It involves coming up with a cognitive explanation to counter unacceptable thoughts, impulses, and behaviours.

reaction formation: A defence mechanism that converts an unacceptable impulse, image, or thought into its exact opposite.

realistic anxiety: What is experienced if the ego is in control; also known as **objective anxiety**.

reality principle: Principle by which the ego tries to balance the primitive urges of the id with the reality of the situation.

reciprocal determinism: Bandura's theory that there is constant interaction among a person's characteristics, behaviours, and the environment.

reciprocal interactionism model: A model that allows for the possibility that the situation not only has an influence on the person, but the person can also have an influence on the situation.

reflected appraisal: A person's perception of how he or she is being evaluated by other people. It is a concept that stems from the idea of the looking glass self.

regnancy: The concept of a need that is prepotent and thus reigns or rules (is dominant). Regnate needs must be satisfied with some degree of urgency because there is some overarching physiological requirement involved.

regression to the mean: When extreme scores are pulled— either by decreasing or increasing—toward the mean or middle.

regression: A psychoanalytic concept that refers to retreating unconsciously to an earlier stage of development that was presumably not as threatening as the current age.

relational schemas: Hypothesized cognitive structures that guide perception of our associations with other people.

repeated measures: When the same person is being studied across experimental conditions, variability reflecting the person's characteristics is not an issue.

repression: The submergence of distressing impulses and past experiences into the unconscious, where they continue to operate. One of the most significant defence mechanisms, repression resembles the act of forgetting.

repressors: People who tend to deny and distort situations in a way to make them seem less problematic.

resilient type: People who have respect for themselves and others and accept personal responsibility for their actions. They have a well-integrated ego structure, high adjustment, and are open to new experiences.

response hierarchy: The concept that the same cue for a particular person can have multiple responses associated with it, with one response being more dominant than another.

right stuff personality: Adaptive personality style for astronauts that includes high levels of task focus, positive interpersonal orientation, and achievement motivation, and low levels of hostility, aggressiveness, and competitiveness.

Rorschach inkblot test: A projective test that involves presenting respondents with 10 inkblots and having them list as many things as they can see in these ambiguous stimuli.

ruling type: An individual who needs to control others. If one seeks to dominate and rule over others, it is important to be competitive, so the ruling type tends to apply to higher achievers with a great desire for control.

same behaviour: This occurs when two people independently experience the same cue and end up making the same response.

schedule: A plan for reducing the conflict among different goals that are seeking expression at the same time; it enables different needs to be satisfied at different times.

schema: Hypothesized, internal cognitive structure that contains knowledge about concepts, objects, events, and people, both other people and ourselves.

schema therapy: A cognitive intervention that focuses on changing a person's cognitive categories by replacing maladaptive schemas with adaptive schemas.

script theory: Tomkins' notion that people are analogous to playwrights in how they chronicle and represent their lives. The experience of intense effects in certain situations and scenes is compiled into a script that helps organize what happens in our lives, when it happens, and who is present when it happens.

secondary appraisals: A personal evaluation of whether the person feels that he or she has the ability to cope with the event.

secondary disposition: Behavioural traits that are peripheral and more akin to habits or smaller regularities in behaviour that a person exhibits, but some sparingly (e.g., a student who tends to chew on a pencil while pondering the answers to multiple choice questions).

self-absorption paradox: The paradox that at times, self-focused attention seems beneficial to self-understanding, but too much attention on the self can also be highly maladaptive.

self-monitoring: A tendency to be very attentive to situational cues and adjust behaviour in a chameleon-like way according to changes in the situation.

secondary needs: Psychological needs that reflect emotional and psychological concerns.

similarity hypothesis: Festinger's belief that we prefer to compare with similar others based on general characteristics such as gender.

secondary process thinking: Planful thoughts and decisions that consider environmental contingencies and challenges.

secondary reinforcer: A reinforcer that has acquired rewarding properties through its association with primary reinforcers. For instance, money is a secondary reinforcer because students have learned that money can buy food, which satisfies a basic need.

securely attached infant: An infant who shows little distress and interacts quite willingly with people, secure in the knowledge that his or her mother will return.

self-actualization: A humanistic concept that involves maximizing one's full potential. One of the key motivating drives according to humanistic theorists.

self-awareness model of drinking: Hull's premise that the reinforcing power of alcohol is in its ability to disrupt cognitive processes and distract us from focusing our attention on the self.

self-based heuristic: The ratings of difficult-to-rate traits become more reflective of the rater's personality features.

self-complexity: The aspect of the self-concept, introduced by Linville, in which an individual sees himself or herself in terms of only a few categories or many categories.

self-concept clarity: The degree of certainty and the lack of ambiguity that people have regarding their self-concepts.

self-deception: An intrapsychic phenomenon that involves overly positive self-evaluations that the person actually believes. Self-deception is seen as a trait form of self-enhancement.

self-effacing solution: This "solution" requires people to forestall their own desires to satisfy the desires of others, mainly because of the appeal of love.

self-efficacy: The individual's sense that she or he is capable of something (high self-efficacy) or incapable of something (low self-efficacy).

self-enhancement: A need to improve the self and feelings about the self.

self-esteem: The sense of regard that one has for oneself.

self-evaluation model: The premise that the Type A person has high standards, accompanied by excessive self-focused attention and self-consciousness. The relentless activity of Type A people is an attempt to satisfy these standards and associated self-worth contingencies.

self-handicapping: Any action or choice of performance setting that enhances the opportunity to externalize failure and internalize success so that failure is seen to reflect factors outside the self.

self-handicapping theory of drinking: Excessive drinking in order to provide a person with an excuse as a form of self-protection.

self-oriented perfectionism: Perfectionism that reflects exceedingly high personal standards and tenacious striving to achieve these standards.

self-reference effect: An effect where a participant more quickly remembers a word in a subsequent memory recognition task if they had indicated that, yes, the word applies to himself or herself.

self-regard: A positive orientation toward the self that is experienced independently of a person's interactions with other people.

self-regulation: The process of taking personal control over thoughts and actions through various means, including self-rewards and self-punishments.

self-reinforcement: A form of self-talk by which a person praises himself or herself.

self-serving attribution bias: The attribution of positive events to internal causes reflecting the self and negative events to external causes outside the self.

self-socialization: A developmental process based on the realization that we can make choices and act in such a manner as to influence the feedback received from others and the situations experienced; people are active participants in their own development.

self-verification theory: A theory that people strive actively to confirm their sense of self in part to foster a sense of predictability and control.

sensitizers: People who are oriented toward threatening situations. They tend to ruminate and obsess over a situation and will analyze it thoroughly.

sex role development: The process of acquiring the attributes and behaviours that are defined culturally as appropriate for one's biological sex.

shadow archetype: A Jungian archetype referring to a dark side of personality in all of us.

shaping: Providing rewards in a gradual sequence to responses that are successive approximations.

shared environment: Common environmental influences.

signs: Cues spotted by the clinician that are expressed by often oblivious patients.

situation coefficient: The degree of variability in behaviours that is attributable to the situation.

situationism: An approach that emphasizes the impact of situational factors and their role in contributing to differences in behaviour.

social desirability response bias: The tendency to answer personality items in a way that makes one appear desirable and important and create a positive impression in the eyes of other people.

social dominance: A sense of power or authority over other people.

social dominance orientation: A need to dominate other groups when they become competitive. Social dominance orientation prevails when there is competition.

social interest: A key to personal adjustment according to Adler. It grows out of a person's ability to master three basic tasks of life: work, love, and social interaction.

social learning theory (also known as social cognitive theory): The theory that behaviours that make up our personality are obtained by operant conditioning and by observational learning.

social learning model of Type A behaviour: A model that regards Type A behaviour as being driven by a particular cognitive belief system emphasizing three themes: (1) a person must constantly prove himself or herself; (2) there is no universally applicable moral principle; and (3) there is low availability of resources, so it is important to be highly competitive.

social learning theory of alcoholism: The premise that alcohol outcome expectancies are key mediators of drinking behaviour, and these expectancies are influenced by a person's social learning experiences. Excessive drinking takes place based on whether the individual holds positive or negative expectancies about alcohol.

social vitality: The degree of one's social contact and outgoingness.

sociality corollary: The idea that a person may play a role in a social process involving one or more other people to the extent that he or she is able to accurately construe the construction processes of other people.

socially prescribed perfectionism: The belief or perception that specific others or society demands perfection from the self.

socio-instrumental control: The notion that we can develop a sense of control via our interpersonal relationships at work, and socio-instrumental control should be elevated in cultures that emphasize the connection between self and other people.

sociometer theory: The theory that our self-esteem is essentially a barometer of our relationships with others, and it goes up and down depending on the quality of our interactions and sense of positive connections with others.

sociotropy: A personality style proposed by Beck that involves dependency, concern with pleasing others, and avoiding disapproval.

sojourner adjustment: The phenomenon of adjusting to a new culture.

somatotonia: An emphasis on physical assertion and high activity level. Associated with mesomorphy.

somatotype: Body types that involve endomorphy, ectomorphy, and memomorphy.

spin: Individual differences in the use of different interpersonal styles (e.g., hostile toward one person vs. warm and agreeable to another person).

spontaneous self-concept: An unstructured way of assessing how people see themselves by asking someone to tell you about himself or herself.

squeaky wheel hypothesis: The tendency to allocate more resources to those who are more likely to fuss and make their needs known to caregivers.

S–R learning: Stimulus–response paired learning. A particular stimulus becomes associated with a particular response as a function of whether positive consequences follow the response.

state anxiety: Current momentary feelings of anxiety experienced at a specific time.

stimulus generalization: A phenomenon that is present when any stimulus that is similar to the originally conditioned stimulus will evoke the same response.

stonewalling: An avoidant form of shutting down and not communicating with the partner.

strange situation: Paradigm used to test attachment styles in which an infant is left in a room for a brief period of time with a stranger, while the mother leaves the room.

structural instability: A fragility to the self that "cracks" under conditions of stress, as proposed by Millon.

structured assessments: Close-ended scales in which the scale content has already been determined by the people who have constructed the measure. Respondents select from options provided to them.

styles of life: Forms of individual expression that derive from early life difficulties and the ways in which an individual strives to achieve goals.

subception: A perceptual defence described by Rogers that involves using unconscious tendencies to prevent a threatening stimulus from entering consciousness.

subject variables: Differences between people (e.g., demographic factors such as gender) that can be used to classify participants into discrete groups when conducting an experiment.

sublimation: A defence that occurs at an unconscious level by channelling unacceptable tendencies and urges into socially acceptable behaviours and outlets of expression, such as works of art.

submerged constructs: One or both ends of a construct that are not available for conscious reflection and verbalization.

subsidation of needs: Occurs when other needs are recruited to promote another need that is more powerful (at least for the time being). The recruited need is known as the **subsidiary need** and the more powerful one is the **determinant need**.

successive approximation: The process of requiring the respondent to display responses that get closer and closer to ultimately desired behaviour in order to be reinforced.

superego: The moralistic part of personality that forms between the ages of three or four, according to Freud. The superego requires us to act according to accepted societal standards, rules, and principles. An overly strong superego contributes to moral anxiety.

superiority complex: Adler's concept that people overcompensate for feelings of inferiority by conveying superiority. It involves a conscious sense of possessing superhuman tendencies.

supertraits: The very broad traits that are universal and that capture the major proportion of variance in behaviour.

suspended construct: A previously accessible construct now forgotten because of current events; similar to repression.

symbolic interactionism theory: The theory that we come to view the self from the standpoint of social groups. These social groups combine to provide a sense of a generalized other that is evaluating us.

symptom perception hypothesis: The notion that neuroticism and negative affect are accompanied by greater attentiveness to somatic cues. Hypothesis to account for the link between higher symptoms reporting and elevated neuroticism and negative affect.

synchronicity: The coincidental co-occurrence of two things that are actually paired randomly but seem to go together, as proposed by Jung.

synergy: A societal trait where the focus is on mutual rewards and well-being; a society with low **synergy** is composed of people and cultures where one person's advancement and wealth occurs at the expense of many other people. Concept proposed by Benedict.

systematic desensitization: A form of **exposure therapy** by Wolpe that requires confronting increasingly frightening events in a fear hierarchy while being relaxed.

taxometrics: The complex statistical approach used to test for personality types or discrete categories in general. **taxon:** An identified category in taxometrics.

temperament: General and stable traits and behavioural patterns developed in early childhood that tend to persist through life and have an inherited, biological component.

Terman study: A longitudinal study of gifted children started in 1921 by famous Stanford psychologist Lewis Terman. His participants came to be known as "Termites." There were substantial personality and life circumstance differences among the Termites even though they were all intellectually gifted.

tertial split: The division of a sample into thirds based on the distribution of scores.

test–retest correlation: A form of reliability that involves assessing **rank-order stability** or **differential stability**. That is, when a sample of people is retested, in the overall distribution of scores, do people tend to maintain their rank in personality dimension scores relative to other people also evaluated on this personality dimension?

test–retest reliability: The stability of test scores over time. This type of reliability is important, given that individual differences are supposed to be relatively stable over time.

thanatos: The death instinct, as proposed by Freud. One of two instincts, the other being **eros** (the life instinct).

the here and now: The importance of living in the moment as opposed to being preoccupied with the past or future. People focused on the here and now have a life process approach that allows them to experience daily events as they happen.

Thematic Apperception Test: A projective test developed by Murray and Morgan that requires the respondent to tell stories when presented with black-and-white photographs that depict various scenes. Each photograph taps a psychological need.

theorem of escape: The notion that we resist experiences that evoke feelings of anxiety.

theorem of reciprocal emotions: The notion that other people influence our emotions, and we, in turn, influence their emotions.

third-variable problem: The problem that a possible influence of a third variable limits the ability to conclude that one variable or factor is the cause of another variable or factor. Both factors could be influenced mutually by another variable.

time series analysis: A statistical procedure applied to a single unit (person) with the unit being measured at several points in time with equal time intervals between assessments.

tolerance of ambiguity: A personality construct that reflects whether a person perceives an ambiguous situation as upsetting and threatening or energizing and interesting.

trait anxiety: A person's usual or typical level of anxiety.

trait relevance: The degree to which a trait is *consequential* in influencing an individual's thoughts, affects, and behaviours.

trait relevance validity: The degree to which the construct being assessed is pertinent and relevant to the target population being studied.

traitedness: See *metatrait.*

transactional model: A model that allows for the various individuals to have an impact on each other in an ongoing sequence of behaviours.

transactional model of stress: A model based on the idea that coping responses depend greatly on the stressful situations themselves and how they are appraised by the individual in the stressful situation.

transmitted culture: Differences that are transmitted from one generation to the next via processes such as social learning and imitation.

transpersonal psychology: The psychological study of spirituality and mystical, spiritual experiences.

triadic reciprocal causation: See *reciprocal determinism.*

triple bookkeeping approach: The approach suggested by Erikson when conducting a psychobiography that a person's life could be understood and evaluated in terms of issues involving the body, the ego, and family and society.

twin registries: Databases containing information on twin studies.

Type A personality: The coronary-prone behaviour pattern that includes intense competitive drive, impatience, and hostility. The hostility component is linked empirically with susceptibility to heart attacks.

type approach: A method of categorization into discrete groups.

Type C personality: The personality style postulated by Greer and Morris applying to people who are "emotionally contained." It is linked with cancer proneness and faster disease progression.

Type D personality: The distress-prone personality proposed by Denollet as a risk factor for cardiac problems. Type Ds have high negative affectivity and high social inhibition.

typological postulate: The premise proposed by Eysenck that people who are predisposed to experience-elevated physiological arousal are prone to introversion and do not react well to stress.

uncertainty orientation: A motivational orientation that reflects the fact that some people simply cannot tolerate ambiguity and uncertainty, while others seem to thrive on it because it affords an opportunity for stimulation and creativity.

unconditional positive regard: The receipt of positive feedback and love from other people regardless of one's behaviour. A key to well-being according to Rogers.

unconditioned response: The behaviour elicited by an unconditioned stimulus.

unconditioned stimulus: A neutral stimulus that elicits an unconditioned response.

uncontrollability model: A model of Type A behaviour that focuses on Type A as a reaction to feelings of uncontrollability.

undercontrolling type: A personality type that involves impulsive expression of desires and deficits in self-control. This type is linked with low levels of academic, behavioural, and emotional functioning and is high in both internalizing and externalizing symptoms.

undoing: A cognitive attempt to reconstruct the past so it appears that an event did not actually take place.

unmitigated agency: Excessive agency that is associated with undesirable forms of instrumental, masculine traits.

unmitigated communion: An extreme focus on connecting with others and fostering relationships.

unstructured assessments: Open-ended assessments where people generate their responses. Unstructured assessments can be in the form of verbal responses in an interview.

variable ratio schedule: A schedule of reinforcement that occurs based on a set number of responses, on average.

vector length: A line assessing each interpersonal style. The length of the line represents the intensity with which the prototypical octant is expressed.

Vipassana meditation: Focused concentration.

viscerogenic: How primary needs are described. These are needs that can be grouped into things that we lack that we need (e.g., food), distensions that lead to outputs (e.g., urination), and possible harms (e.g., noxavoidance).

wish fulfillment: Satisfying a wish or desire through primary process thinking.

within-subject variable: A repeated measure in an experiment. The participant is exposed to two or more levels of the independent variable. The unique characteristics of the person are controlled because they are common to all levels of the independent variable.

womb envy: The type of envy experienced by males because of their inability to bear a child, according to Horney. It was proposed as an alternative to Freud's concept of penis envy among females.

Word Association Test: A projective test that requires people to respond as quickly as possible to 100 stimulus words and to report whatever comes to mind for each word.

PERMISSION CREDITS

Care has been taken to trace ownership of copyright material contained in this text. The publisher will gladly take any information that will enable it to rectify any reference or credit in subsequent printings.

Chapter 1: Page 3, Table 1.1 Copyright Senior Product Manager, CNET Networks Inc. (Parent Company of Metacritic), 235 Second Street, San Francisco, CA 94105. Page 16 excerpt reprinted from *Journal of Research in Personality*, 36, Diener, E., & Scollon, C.N., Our desired future for personality psychology, 633–634, 2002 with permission from Elsevier. Page 26 exerpt copyright 2002 from Using the P.T. Barnum effect to teach critical thinking: Applications for a course in psychological research methods. *Teaching of Psychology*, 29. Boyce, T.E., & Geller, E.S. Reproduced by permission of Taylor & Francis Group, LLC., http://taylorandfrancis.com

Chapter 2: Page 32 excerpt reprinted from "Culture and Personality" (S. Stansfeld Sargent and Marian W. Smith, eds., The Wenner-Gren Foundation for Anthropological Research, Inc., New York, New York, 1949), by permission of the Wenner-Gren Foundation. Page 35, Table 2.2 Patterns of self-regulation and the Big Five, *European Journal of Personality*, 18. Gramzow, R., Sedikides, C., Panter, A.T., Sathy, V., Harris, J., & Insko, C.A. (2004). Copyright John Wiley & Sons Limited. Reproduced with permission. Page 54, Table 2.3 reproduced by special permission of the Publisher, Psychological Assessment Resources, Inc., 16204 North Florida Avenue, Lutz, Florida 33549, from NEO Personality Inventory-Revised by Paul T. Costa Jr., PhD and Robert R. McCrae, PhD, copyright 1978, 1985, 1989, 1991, 1992, by Psychological Assessment Resources, Inc. (PAR). Further reproduction is prohibited without permission of PAR. Page 65, Table 2.7 copyright 1966 by the American Psychological Association. Reprinted with permission.

Chapter 3: Page 93, Case Study 3.1 and Page 98, Applied Perspective 3.1 from Applications of temperament concepts. In G.A. Kohnstamm, J.E. Bates, & M.K. Rothbart (Eds.) Temperament in childhood. Bates, J.E. (1989). Reprinted with permission of John Wiley & Sons, Inc. Page 99 excerpt and Page 100, Figure 3.1 from The complex interplay of temperament factors with other factors. *European Journal of Personality*, 15. Strelau, J. (2001). Copyright John Wiley & Sons Limited. Reproduced with permission. Page 103, Figure 3.2 Personality Traits and Parenting: Neuroticism, Extraversion, and Openness to Experience as Discriminative Factors. *European Journal of Personality*, 17. Riitta-Leena Metsapelto & Lea Pulkkinen, (2003). Copyright John Wiley & Sons Limited. Reproduced with permission. Page 109 excerpt from Parenting self-efficacy among Japanese mothers: Qualitative and quantitative perspectives on its associations with childhood memories of family relations. *New Directions for Child and Adolescent Development*, 96, Holloway, S.D., & Behrens, K.Y. (2002). Copyright John Wiley & Sons Limited. Reproduced with permission.

Chapter 4: Page 123, Figure 4.1 Personality and the experimental study of education. *European Journal of Personality*, 10, Eysenck, H.J. (1996). Copyright John Wiley & Sons Limited. Reproduced with permission. Page 131, Figure 4.3 *Research in psychology: Method and design*. Goodwin, J. F. (2005). Reprinted with permission of John Wiley & Sons, Inc.

Chapter 6: Page 216 excerpt from My role in the assessment program of the Office of Strategic Services. *Behavioral Science*, 41, issue 4, Miller, J.G. (1996). Copyright John Wiley & Sons Limited. Reproduced with Permission. Page 221 excerpt from *Let Me Take You Down* by Jack Jones, copyright 1992 by Jack Jones, used by permission of Villard Books, a division of Random House, Inc. Page 230 excerpt from De Vos, G. Heritage of exploitation: A brief TAT report of South Brazilian youth. *Political Psychology*, 18, Blackwell Publishing. Page 239, Table 6.3 Emmons, R.A., & McAdams, D.P. Personal strivings and motive dispositions: Exploring the links. *Personality and Social Psychology Bulletin*, 17, 648-654. Copyright 2000 by Sage Publications. Reprinted by Permission of Sage Publications Inc.

Chapter 7: Page 246 excerpt from *The Carl Rogers Reader*, edited by Howard Kirschenbaum and Valerie Land Henderson. Copyright 1989 by Howard Kirschenbaum and the Estate of Carl Rogers. Reprinted by Permission of Houghton Mifflin Company. All rights reserved.

Chapter 8: Page 288 excerpt from *Behaviourism* by John B. Watson. Copyright 1924, 1925 by the People's Institute Publishing Company. Copyright 1930 by W.W. Norton & Company, Inc., renewed 1952, 1953, ©1958 by John B. Watson. Used by permission of W.W. Norton & Company, Inc. Page 290, Figure 8.1 *Abnormal Psychology*, Kring et al (2007). Reprinted with permission of John Wiley & Sons, Inc. Page 320, Figure 8.2 *Research in psychology: Method and design*. Goodwin, J. F. (2005). Reprinted with permission of John Wiley & Sons, Inc.

Chapter 9: Page 345 excerpt from *The Mummy At The Dining Room Table: Eminent Therapists Reveal Their Most Unusual Cases*. Kottler & Carlson. (2003). Reprinted with permission of John Wiley & Sons, Inc. Page 349, Table 9.1 and Page 350, Figure 9.2 Culture-shocked marriages. In A.W. Landfield & L.M. Lietner (Eds.), *Personal Construct Psychology: Psychotherapy and Personality*. McCoy (1980). Reprinted with permission of John Wiley & Sons, Inc. Page 367, Table 9.3 copyright 2002 from The efficient assessment of need for cognition. *Journal of Personality Assessment, 48*. Cacioppo, J.T., Petty, R.E., & Kao, C.F. Reproduced by permission of Taylor & Francis Group, LLC., http://taylorandfrancis.com. Page 372, Figure 9.5 Pessimism and behavioural signs of depression in East versus West Berlin. *European Journal of Social Psychology*, 20. Oettingen, G., & Seligman, M. E. P. (1990). Copyright John Wiley & Sons Limited. Reproduced with permission. Page 373, Table 9.4 copyright 1986 by the American Psychological Association. Reprinted with permission.

Chapter 10: Page 391, Table 10.1 copyright 1990 from Construction of circumplex scales for the Inventory of Interpersonal Problems. *Journal of Personality Assessment*, 55, Alden, L.E. Wiggins, J.S., & Pincus, A.L. Reproduced by permission of Taylor & Francis Group, LLC., http://taylorandfrancis.com. Page 416, Figure 10.3 Schmitt, D.P., et al. Patterns and universals of adult romantic attachment across 62 cultural regions. *Journal of Cross-Cultural Psychology*, 35. Copyright 2004 by Sage Publications. Reprinted by Permission of Sage Publications Inc.

Chapter 11: Page 434, Figure 11.1 Culture and Developing Selves: Beyond Dichotomization. *New Directions for Child and Adolescent Development*, No. 104. Michael F. Mascolo, Jin Li, Eds. (1966). Reprinted with permission of John Wiley & Sons, Inc.

Chapter 12: Page 485, Figure 12.1 The big five related to risky sexual behaviour across 10 world regions: Differential personality associations of sexual promiscuity and relationship infidelity. *European Journal of Personality*, 18, Schmitt, D.P. (2004). Copyright John Wiley & Sons Limited. Reproduced with permission. Page 486 excerpt from *The Right Mountain: Lessons from Everest on the Real Meaning of Success*, Hayhurst, 1997. Reprinted with permission of John Wiley & Sons, Inc. Page 488 excerpt from *It's Not about the Bike* by Lance Armstrong, copyright 2000 by Lance Armstrong. Used by permission of G.P. Putnam's Sons, a division of Penguin Group (USA) Inc. Page 495, Table 12.3 Copyright 1989 by the American Psychological Association. Reprinted with permission. Page 515, Figure 12.2 Hypothesis for an Association Between Personality and Risk for Cancer. *Cancer* Volume 94/ Number 12. Schapiro et al. Copyright 2002 Wiley-Liss. Reprinted with permission of Wiley-Liss, Inc, a subsidiary of John Wiley & Sons, Inc.

Chapter 13: Page 535, Case Study 13.2 from *The Mummy At The Dining Room Table: Eminent Therapists Reveal Their Most Unusual Cases*. Kottler & Carlson. (2003). Reprinted with permission of John Wiley & Sons, Inc. Page 545, Table 13.1 Cognitive therapy for the personality disorders. In S. Strack (Ed.), *Handbook of Personality and Psychopathology*. Leahy, R.L., Beck, J., & Beck, A.T. (2005). Copyright John Wiley & Sons Limited. Reproduced with permission. Page 559, Table 13.3 Personality disorders. In A. Tasman, J. Kay, & J.A. Lieberman (Eds.), Psychiatry, 2nd Edition. Widiger, T.A., & Mullins, S. (2003). Copyright John Wiley & Sons Limited. Reproduced with permission. Page 560 excerpt from *Annual Review of Psychology*, Vol. 47: 87-111 (1996).

Chapter 14: Page 611 to 614 excerpts from *Anne Sexton: A biography*, by Daine Wood Middlebrook. Copyright 1991 by Diane Wood Middlebrook. Reprinted by permission of Houghton Mifflin Company. All rights reserved.

PHOTO CREDITS

Chapter 1: Page 4: PhotoDisc, Inc./Getty Images. Page 8: Paul J. Sutton/Duomo/Corbis. Page 15: Digital Vision. Page 21: Chris O'Meara/Associated Press.

Chapter 2: Page 32: Bettmann/Corbis. Page 35: Digital Vision. Page 40: John Springer Collection/Corbis. Page 41: Tim Graham Photo Library. Page 45: Courtesy of York University. Page 51: Purestock. Page 53: Corbis Digital Stock. Page 60: Courtesy of Dr. Fanny Mui-ching Cheung.

Chapter 3: Page 75: Purestock. Page 83: Purestock. Page 90: Petre Buzoianu/Corbis. Page 92: IT Stock. Page 97: IT Stock. Page 102: Purestock. Page 111: PhotoDisc, Inc./Getty Images. Page 113: Courtesy of Karen Matthews.

Chapter 4: Page 125: PhotoDisc, Inc./Getty Images. Page 133: PhotoDisc, Inc./Getty Images. Page 135: IT Stock. Page 137: Courtesy of Delroy Paulus. Page 140: Digital Vision. Page 141: David Hume Kennerly/Getty Images. Page 145: PhotoDisc, Inc./Getty Images.

Chapter 5: Page 161: Bettmann/Corbis. Page 167: Paul Drinkwater/© NBC/Courtesy: Everett Collection. Page 174: Bettmann/Corbis. Page 177: Lynn Goldsmith/Corbis. Page 178: CP/RNS(New Line Productions/ Pierre Vinet). Page 182: Courtesy of the Alfred Adler Institute. Page 187: Courtesy of Toni Falbo. Page 190: Bettmann/Corbis. Page 198: Purestock. Page 201: John Wiley & Sons, Inc.

Chapter 6: Page 207: Courtesy of Harvard University. Page 215: Heinrich Hoffmann/Corbis. Page 218: Seanna O'Sullivan/Corbis Sygma. Page 221: ©Associated Press. Page 233: Digital Vision. Page 236: (left) Reuters/ Corbis; (right) Wally McNamamee/Corbis. Page 238: Purestock.

Chapter 7: Page 249: Ann Kaplan/Corbis. Page 257: Jacky Naegelen/Reuters/Corbis. Page 258: (left/right) Purestock. Page 266: Roger Ressmeyer/Corbis. Page 273: PhotoDisc, Inc./Getty Images. Page 282: Courtesy of Carol Ryff.

Chapter 8: Page 289: Bettmann/Corbis. Page 295: PhotoDisc, Inc. Page 300: PhotoDisc, Inc. Page 304: Kathy Bendo/John Wiley & Sons, Inc. Page 313: IT Stock. Page 314: Nicola Goode/Universal Pictures/ZUMA/ Corbis. Page 319: Courtesy of Frank Pajares. Page 322: Purestock.

Chapter 9: Page 336: Courtesy of Hemant Desai/University of Nebraska. Page 339: Robert Galbraith/Reuters/ Corbis. Page 343: Courtesy of Jack Adams-Webber. Page 351: Digital Vision. Page 354: Courtesy of Thomas Lewin. Page 363: Purestock. Page 368: Purestock. Page 374: Purestock.

Chapter 10: Page 382: Castle Rock/MPTV.net. Page 383: Purestock. Page 395: Zack Seckler/Corbis. Page 406: Purestock. Page 413: Reuters/Corbis. Page 419: PhotoDisc, Inc./Getty Images. Page 426: PhotoDisc, Inc./Getty Images.

Chapter 11: Page 433: Bettmann/Corbis. Page 438: Ted Streshinsky/Corbis. Page 441: Rufus F. Folkks/Corbis. Page 446: Digital Vision. Page 447: DreamWorks/Courtesy Everett Collection. Page 451: Digital Vision. Page 455: Purestock. Page 457: Purestock. Page 458: Digital Vision. Page 468: Linda Ebersold/Associated Press. Page 474: Corbis Digital Stock.

Chapter 12: Page 483: PhotoDisc, Inc./Getty Images. Page 486: PhotoDisc, Inc./Getty Images. Page 487: Canadian Press Images. Page 495: Purestock. Page 496: PhotoDisc, Inc. Page 500: Courtesy of Suzanne Segerstrom. Page 506: Bettmann/Corbis. Page 508: PhotoDisc, Inc./Getty Images. Page 512: Purestock. Page 519: PhotoDisc, Inc./Getty Images. Page 525: ©IT Stock.

Chapter 13: Page 537: Flat Earth. Page 540: Bettmann/Corbis. Page 548: Corbis/Daytona Beach News JRNL. Page 562: Photo from Canadian Forces Image Gallery, http://www.combatcamera.forces.gc.ca, 2006. Department of National Defence. Reproduced with the permission of the Minister of Public Works and Government Services Canada, 2006. Page 565: PhotoDisc, Inc./Getty Images. Page 567: Gregory Pace/Corbis. Page 568: (left) Corbis Digital Stock; (right) Purestock. Page 580: Frank Trapper/Corbis.

Chapter 14: Page 587: Bettmann/Corbis. Page 595: CP Images/Copyright ©Orion Pictures Corp./Courtesy Everett Co./Everett Collection. Page 597: PhotoDisc, Inc./Getty Images. Page 602: Flat Earth. Page 603: Bettmann/Corbis. Page 607: CP Images/CSU Archives/Everett Collection. Page 611: Bettmann/Corbis. Page 615: Neal Preston/Corbis.

REFERENCES

Abagnale, F.W., Jr. (1980). *Catch me if you can*. New York: Pocket Books.

Abramson, L.Y., Metalsky, G.I., & Alloy, L.B. (1989). Hopelessness depression: A theory-based subtype of depression. *Psychological Review, 96*, 358–372.

Abramson, L.Y., Seligman, M.E.P., & Teasdale, J.D. (1978). Learned helplessness in humans: Critique and reformulation. *Journal of Abnormal Psychology, 87*, 49–74.

Achenbach, T. (2006). Clinical and research implications of cross-informant correlations for psychopathology. *Current Directions in Psychological Science, 15*, 94–98.

Adams-Webber, J.R. (1998). Differentiation and sociality in terms of elicited and provided constructs. *Psychological Science, 9*, 499–501.

Adams-Webber, J.R. (2001). Cognitive complexity and role relationships. *Journal of Constructivist Psychology, 14*, 43–50.

Adams-Webber, J.R. (2003). Prototypicality of self and differentiating among others in terms of personal constructs. *Journal of Constructivist Psychology, 16*, 341–347.

Adler, A. (1931/1958). *What life should mean to you*. New York: Capricorn Books.

Adler, A. (1938/1998). *Social interest: Adler's key to the meaning of life*. Oxford, England: Oneworld Publications.

Adler, N., & Matthews, K. (1994). Health psychology: Why do some people get sick and some stay well? *Annual Review of Psychology, 45*, 229–259.

Adorno, T.W., Frenkel-Brunswik, E., Levinson, D.J., & Sanford, R.N. (1950). *The authoritarian personality*. New York: Harper & Row.

Andreou, E. (2004). Bully/victim problems and their association with Machiavellianism and self-efficacy in Greek primary school children. *British Journal of Educational Psychology, 74*, 297–309.

Ainsworth, M.D. (1984). Attachment. In N.S. Endler & J.M. Hunt (Eds.), *Personality and the behavioral disorders* (Vol. 1, 2nd ed., pp. 559–602). New York: John Wiley & Sons Inc.

Ainsworth, M.D., Blehar, M.C., Waters, E., & Wall, S. (1978). *Patterns of attachment: A psychological study of the strange situation*. Hillsdale, NJ: Erlbaum.

Ainsworth, M.D., & Bowlby, J. (1953). *Research strategy in the study of mother-child separation*. Paris: Courrier de la Centre International de l'Enfance.

Akse, J., Hale, W.W. III., Engels, R.C.M.E., Raaijmakers, Q.A.W., & Meeus, W.H.J. (2004). Personality, perceived parental rejection, and problem behavior in adolescence. *Social Psychiatry and Psychiatric Epidemiology, 39*, 980–988.

Alden, L.E., Wiggins, J.S., & Pincus, A.L. (1990). Construction of circumplex scales for the Inventory of Interpersonal Problems. *Journal of Personality Assessment, 55*, 521–536.

Alexander, C.N., Rainforth, M.V., & Gelderloos, P. (1991). Transcendental meditation, self-actualization, and psychological health: A conceptual overview and statistical meta-analysis. *Journal of Social Behavior and Personality, 6*, 189–247.

Alexander, I. (1988). Personality, psychological assessment, and psychobiography. *Journal of Personality, 56*, 265–294.

Alexander, I. (2005). Erikson and psychobiography, psychobiography and Erikson. In W.T. Schultz (Ed.), *Handbook of psychobiography* (pp. 265–284). New York: Oxford University Press.

Alexander, M.J., & Higgins, E.T. (1993). Emotional trade-offs of becoming a parent: How social roles influence self-discrepancy effects. *Journal of Personality & Social Psychology, 65*, 1259–1269.

Allison, L., Bennell, C., Mokros, A., & Ormerod, D. (2002). The personality paradox in offender profiling: A theoretical review of the processes involved in deriving background characteristics from crime scene actions. *Psychology, Public Policy, and Law, 8*, 115–135.

Allport, G.W. (1937). *Personality: A psychological interpretation*. New York: Holt, Rinehart, & Winston.

Allport, G.W. (1938). William Stern: 1871–1938. *American Journal of Psychology, 51*, 770–773.

Allport, G.W. (1961). *Pattern and growth in personality*. New York: Holt, Rinehart, & Winston.

Allport, G.W. (1962). The general and the unique in psychological science. *Journal of Personality, 30*, 405–422.

Allport, G.W. (1968). *The person in psychology: Selected essays by Gordon W. Allport*. Boston: Beacon.

Allport, G.W., & Odbert, H.S. (1936). Trait names: A psycho-lexical study. *Psychological Monographs, 47*, (1 Whole No. 211).

Almagor, M., Tellegen, A., & Waller, N.G. (1995). The Big Seven model: A cross-cultural replication and further exploration of the basic dimensions of natural language trait descriptors. *Journal of Personality and Social Psychology, 69*, 300–307.

Altemeyer, B. (1981). *Right-wing authoritarianism*. Winnipeg, MB: University of Manitoba Press.

Altemeyer, B. (1996). *The authoritarian specter*. Cambridge, MA: Harvard University Press.

Altemeyer, B. (2003). What happens when authoritarians inherit the earth: A simulation. *Analyses of Social Issues and Public Policy, 3*, 161–169.

Altemeyer, B. (2004). Highly dominating, highly authoritarian personalities. *The Journal of Social Psychology, 144*, 421–447.

Amirkhan, J.H. (1990). A factor analytically derived measure of coping: The Coping Strategy Indicator. *Journal of Personality and Social Psychology, 59*, 1066–1074.

Anderson, C.A. (1995). Implicit personality theories and empirical data: Biased assimilation, belief perseverance and change, and covariation detection sensitivity. *Social Cognition, 13*, 25–48.

Anderson, C.A. (1999). Attributional style, depression, and loneliness: A cross-cultural comparison of American and Chinese students. *Personality and Social Psychology Bulletin, 25*, 482–499.

Anderson, C.A., Berkowitz, L., Donnerstein, E., Huesmann, L.R., Johnson, J.D., Linz, D., Malamuth, N.M., & Wartella, E. (2003). The influence of media violence on youth. *Psychological Science in the Public Interest, 4*, 81–110.

Anderson, K.B., Anderson, C.A., Dill, K.E., & Deuser, W.E. (1998). The interactive relations between trait hostility, pain, and aggressive thoughts. *Aggressive Behavior, 24*, 161–171.

Ando, K. (1995). "Blood-typing is still popular in Japan." *Japan Labor Bulletin, 34* (http://www.jil.go.jp/bulletin/year/1995/vol34-06/05.htm).

Appignanesi, L., & Forrester, J. (2005). *Freud's women*. London: Phoenix (an imprint of Orion Books Limited).

Archer, J. (2006). Cross-cultural differences in physical aggression between partners: A social role analysis. *Personality and Social Psychology Review, 10*, 133–153.

Armstrong, L. (2001). *It's not about the bike: My journey back to life*. New York: Putnam.

Arnau, R.C., Green, B.A., Rosen, D.H., Gleaves, D.H., & Melancon, J.G. (2003). Are Jungian preferences really categorical? An empirical investigation using taxometric analysis. *Personality and Individual Differences, 34*, 233–251.

Arnett, J. (1991). Winston Churchill, the quintessential sensation seeker. *Political Psychology, 12*, 609–621.

Asendorpf, J.B., Borkenau, P., Ostendorf, F., & Van Aken, M.A.G. (2001). Carving personality description at its joints: Confirmation of three replicable personality prototypes for both children and adults. *European Journal of Personality, 15*, 169–198.

Asendorpf, J.B. & van Aken, M.A.G. (1999). Resilient, overcontrolled, and undercontrolled personality prototypes in childhood: Replicability, predictive power, and trait-type issue. *Journal of Personality and Social Psychology, 77*, 815–832.

Asendorpf, J.B. & van Aken, M.A.G. (2003). Validity of Big Five personality judgments in childhood. *European Journal of Personality, 17*, 1–17.

Ashton, M.C., Jackson, D.N., Paunonen, S.V., Helmes, E., & Rothstein, M.G. (1995). The criterion validity of broad factor scales versus specific facet scales. *Journal of Research in Personality, 29*, 432–442.

Ashton, M.C., Lee, K., & Son, C. (2000). Honesty as the sixth factor of personality: Correlations with Machiavellianism, primary psychopathy, and social adroitness. *European Journal of Personality, 14*, 359–368.

Assor, A., Roth, G., & Deci, E.L. (2004). The emotional costs of parents' conditional regard: A self-determination theory analysis. *Journal of Personality, 72*, 47–89.

Atkinson, J.W. (1957). Motivational determinants of risk-taking behavior. *Psychological Review, 64*, 359–372.

Atkinson, L., et al. (2000). Attachment security: A meta-analysis of maternal mental health correlates. *Clinical Psychology Review, 20*, 1019–1040.

Atkinson, M., & Violato, C. (1994). Neuroticism and coping with anger: Transituational consistency of coping responses. *Personality and Individual Differences, 17*, 769–782.

Austenfeld, J.L., & Stanton, A.L. (2004). Coping through emotional approach: A new look at emotion, coping, and health related outcomes. *Journal of Personality, 72*, 1335–1363.

Avila, C., & Parcet, M.A. (2000). The role of Gray's impulsivity in anxiety-mediated differences in resistance to extinction. *European Journal of Personality, 14*, 185–198.

Axelrod, S.R., Widiger, T.A., Trull, T.J., & Corbitt, E.M. (1997). Relationship of five factor model antagonism facets with personality disorder symptomatology. *Journal of Personality Assessment, 67*, 297–313.

Aydin, G., & Aydin, O. (1990). Learned helplessness and explanatory style in Turkish samples. *The Journal of Social Psychology, 132*, 117–119.

Baccus, J.R., Baldwin, M.W., & Packer, D.J. (2004). Increasing implicit self-esteem through classical conditioning. *Psychological Science, 15*, 498–502.

Bae, H., & Crittenden, K.S. (1988). From attributions to dispositional inferences: Patterns of Korean students. *The Journal of Social Psychology, 129*, 481–489.

Bailey, M., & McLaren, S. (2005). Physical activity alone and with others as predictors of sense of belonging and mental health in retirees. *Aging and Mental Health, 9*, 82–90.

Bakan, D. (1966). *The duality of human existence: Isolation and communion in Western man.* Boston: Beacon.

Baker, S.R., Victor, J.B., Chambers, A.L., & Halverson, C.F., Jr. (2004). Adolescent personality: A five-factor model construct validation. *Assessment, 11*, 303–315.

Bakersmann-Kranenburg, M.J., & van Ijzendoorn, M.H. (1993). A psychometric study of the Adult Attachment Interview: Reliability and discriminant validity. *Developmental Psychology, 29*, 870–880.

Baldwin, A.L. (1942). Personal structure analysis: A statistical method for investigation of the single personality. *Journal of Abnormal and Social Psychology, 37*, 163–183.

Baldwin, J.M. (1894). Imitation: A chapter in the natural history of consciousness. *Mind, 3*, 25–55.

Baldwin, M.W. (1992). Relational schemas and the processing of social information. *Psychological Bulletin, 112*, 461–484.

Baldwin, M.W., Carrell, S.E., & Lopez, D.F. (1990). Priming relationship schemas: My advisor and the Pope are watching me from the back of my mind. *Journal of Experimental Social Psychology, 26*, 435–454.

Ball, S. A., Poling, J. C., Tennen, H., & Kranzler, H. R. (1997). Personality, temperament, and character dimensions and the DSM-IV personality disorders in substance abusers. *Journal of Abnormal Psychology, 106*, 545–553.

Bamber, M. (2004). "The good the bad and the defenceless Jimmy": A single case study of schema mode therapy. *Clinical Psychology and Psychotherapy, 11*, 425–438.

Banaji, M., & Steele, C.M. (1989). Alcohol and self-evaluation: Is a social cognition approach beneficial? *Social Cognition, 7*, 137–151.

Bandura, A. (1977). Self-efficacy: Toward a unifying theory of behavioral change. *Psychological Review, 84*, 191–215.

Bandura, A. (1986). *Social foundations of thought and action: A social cognitive theory.* Englewood Cliffs, NJ: Prentice-Hall.

Bandura, A. (1997). *Self-efficacy: The exercise of control.* New York: Freeman.

Bandura, A. (2006). Toward a psychology of human agency. *Perspectives on Psychological Science, 1*, 164–180.

Bandura, A., Grusec, J.E., & Menlove, F.L. (1966). Observational learning as a function of symbolization and incentive set. *Child Development, 37*, 499–506.

Bandura, A., & Kupers, C.J. (1964). Transmission of patterns of self-reinforcement through modeling. *Journal of Abnormal and Social Psychology, 69*, 1–9.

Bandura, A., & Rosenthal, T.L. (1966). Vicarious classical conditioning as a function of arousal level. *Journal of Personality and Social Psychology, 3*, 54–62.

Bandura, A., Ross, D., & Ross, S.A. (1963). Imitation of film-mediated aggressive models. *Journal of Abnormal and Social Psychology, 66*, 3–11.

Bandura, A., & Walters, R.H. (1963). *Social learning and personality development.* New York: Holt, Rinehart & Winston.

Barbaranelli, C. (2002). Evaluating cluster analysis solutions: An application to the Italian NEO Personality Inventory: The replicability and utility of three personality types. *European Journal of Personality, 16*, 43–55.

Barnett, P.A., & Gotlib, I.H. (1988). Psychosocial functioning and depression: Distinguishing among antecedents, concomitants, and consequences. *Psychological Bulletin, 104*, 97–126.

Baron, R.M., & Kenny, D.A. (1986). The moderator-mediator variable distinction in social psychological research: Conceptual, strategic and statistical considerations. *Journal of Personality and Social Psychology, 51*, 1173–1182.

Barressi, J., & Juckes, T.J. (1997). Personology and the narrative interpretation of lives. *Journal of Personality, 65*, 693–719.

Barrett, G.V., et al. (2003). Practical issues in the use of personality tests in police selection. *Public Personnel Management, 32*, 497–518.

Barrett, P., & Eysenck, S. (1984). The assessment of personality across 25 countries. *Personality and Individual Differences, 66*, 615–632.

Barrick, M.R. & Mount, M.K. (1991). The Big Five personality dimensions and job performance: A meta-analysis. *Personnel Psychology, 44*, 1–26.

Barrick, M.R., & Mount, M.K. (1996). Effects of impression management and self-deception on the predictive validity of personality constructs. *Journal of Applied Psychology, 81*, 261–272.

Bartholomew, K. (1990). Avoidance of intimacy: An attachment perspective. *Journal of Social and Personal Relationships, 7*, 147–178.

Bartholomew, K., & Horowitz, L.M. (1991). Attachment styles among young adults: A test of a four-category model. *Journal of Personality and Social Psychology, 61*, 226–244.

Bates, J.E. (1989). Applications of temperament concepts. In G.A. Kohnstamm, J.E. Bates, & M.K. Rothbart (Eds.), *Temperament in childhood* (pp. 321–355). New York: John Wiley & Sons Inc.

Bates, J.E., Wachs, T.D., & Emde, R.N. (1994). Toward practical uses of biological concepts of temperament. In J.E. Bates & T.D. Wachs (Eds.), *Temperament: Individual differences in the interface of biology and behavior* (pp. 275–306). Washington, DC: American Psychological Association.

Baumeister, R.F., Dale, K., & Sommer, K.L. (1998). Freudian defense mechanisms and empirical findings in modern social psychology: Reaction formation, projection, displacement, undoing, isolation, sublimation, and denial. *Journal of Personality, 66,* 1081–1124.

Baumeister, R.F., & Leary, M.R. (1995). The need to belong: Desire for interpersonal attachments as a fundamental human motivation. *Psychological Bulletin, 117,* 497–529.

Baumeister, R.F., Shapiro, J.J., & Tice, D.M. (1985). Two kinds of identity crisis. *Journal of Personality, 53,* 407–424.

Baumeister, R.F., & Tice, D.M. (1988). Metatraits. *Journal of Personality, 56,* 571–598.

Baumeister, R.F., Tice, D.M., & Hutton, D.G. (1989). Self-presentational motivations and personality differences in self-esteem. *Journal of Personality, 57,* 547–579.

Baumrind, D.H. (1971). Current patterns of parental authority. *Developmental Psychology Monographs, 4,* (1, Part 2).

Baumrind, D. (1989). Rearing competent children. In W. Damon (Ed.), *Child development today and tomorrow* (pp. 349–378). San Francisco: Jossey-Bass.

Beck, A.T. (1967). *Depression: Clinical, experimental and theoretical aspects.* New York: Harper & Row.

Beck, A.T. (1983). Cognitive therapy of depression: New perspectives. In P.J. Clayton & J.E. Barrett (Eds.), *Treatment of depression: Old controversies and new approaches* (pp. 265–290). New York: Raven Press.

Beck, A.T., Epstein, N., Harrison, R.P., & Emery, G. (1983). *Development of the Sociotropy-Autonomy Scale: A measure of personality factors in psychopathology.* Unpublished manuscript, University of Pennsylvania, Philadelphia.

Bedell Smith, S. (1999). Diana in search of herself: Portrait of a troubled princess. New York: Times Books.

Beer, J.M., & Horn, J.M. (2000). The influence of reading order on personality development within two adoption cohorts. *Journal of Personality, 68,* 789–819.

Begany, J.J., & Milburn, M.A. (2002). Psychological predictors of sexual harassment: Authoritarianism, hostile sexism, and rape myths. *Psychology of Men and Masculinity, 3,* 119–126.

Bekerian, D.A., & Jackson, J.L. (1997). Critical issues in offender profiling. In J.L. Jackson & D.A. Bekerian (Eds.) *Offender profiling: Theory, research, and practice* (pp. 209–220). Chichester, UK: John Wiley & Sons.

Bell, R.Q., & Chapman, M. (1986). Child effects in studies using experimental or brief longitudinal approaches to socialization. *Developmental Psychology, 22,* 595–603.

Belsky, J. (1984). The determinants of parenting: A process model. *Child Development, 55,* 83–96.

Benedict, R. (1934). *Patterns of culture.* Boston: Houghton-Mifflin.

Benedict, R. (1946). The study of cultural patterns in European nations. *Trans. New York Academy of Science,* Ser. II, *8,* 274–279.

Benet-Martínez, V., & Waller, N.G. (1997). Further evidence for the cross-cultural generality of the 'Big Seven' model: Imported and indigenous Spanish personality constructs. *Journal of Personality,* 65, 567–598.

Ben-Porath, Y.S. & Waller, N.G. (1992). "Normal" personality inventories in clinical assessment: General requirements and the potential for using the NEO Personality Inventory. *Psychological Assessment, 4,* 14–19.

Bentler, P., & Newcomb, M.D. (1978). Longitudinal study of marital success and failure. *Journal of Consulting and Clinical Psychology, 46,* 1053–1070.

Berglas, S., & Jones, E.E. (1978). Drug choice as a self-handicapping strategy in response to noncontingent success. *Journal of Personality and Social Psychology, 36,* 405–417.

Berkowitz, L., & Donnerstein, E. (1982). External validity is more than skin deep: Some answers to criticisms of laboratory experiments. *American Psychologist, 37,* 245–257.

Bermudez, J. (1999). Personality and health-protective behavior. *European Journal of Personality, 13,* 83–103.

Bernstein, D.P., Stein, J.A., & Handlesman, L. (1998). Predicting personality pathology among adult patients with substance use disorders: Effects of childhood maltreatment. *Addictive Behaviors, 23,* 855–868.

Besser, A., Flett, G.L., & Hewitt, P.L. (2004). Perfectionism, cognition, and affect in response to performance failure versus success. *Journal of Rational-Emotive and Cognitive-Behavior Therapy, 22,* 301–328.

Biederman, J., et al. (2001). Further evidence of association between behavioral inhibition and social anxiety in children. *American Journal of Psychiatry, 158,* 1673–1679.

Bieri, J., Bradburn, W.M., & Galinsky, M.D. (1958). Sex differences in perceptual behavior. *Journal of Personality, 26,* 1–12.

Biesanz, J.C., & West, S.G. (2004). Towards understanding assessments of the big five: Multitrait-multimethod analyses of convergent and discriminant validity across measurement occasion and type of observer. *Journal of Personality, 72,* 845–876.

Billingsley, K.D., Waehler, C.A., & Hardin, S.I. (1993). Stability of optimism and choice of coping strategy. *Perceptual and Motor Skills, 76,* 91–97.

Bishop, S.L., & Primeau, L. (2002, October). *Through the long night: Stress and group dynamics in Antartica.* Presented at the 53rd International Astronautical Congress (IAC) of the International Astronautical Federation (IAF), International Academy of Astronautics (IAA), and the International Institute of Space Law (IISL), Human Factors for Long Duration Spaceflight, World Space Congress.

Bissonnette, V., Ickes, W., Bernstein, I., & Knowles, E. (1990). Personality moderating variables: A warning about statistical artifact and a comparison of analytic techniques. *Journal of Personality, 58,* 567–587.

Black, S., Hardy, G., Turpin, G. & Parry, G. (2005). Self-reported attachment styles and therapeutic orientation of therapists and their relationship with reported general alliance quality and problems in therapy. *Psychology and Psychotherapy: Therapy, Research, and Practice, 78,* 363–377.

Blaney, P.H., & Kutcher, G.S. (1991). Measures of depressive dimensions: Are they interchangeable? *Journal of Personality Assessment, 56,* 502–512.

Blanton, H., Crocker, J., & Miller, D.T. (2000). The effects of in-group versus out-group social comparison on self-esteem in the context of a negative stereotype. *Journal of Experimental Social Psychology, 36,* 519–530.

Blankstein, K.R., & Dunkley, D.M. (2002). Evaluative concerns, self-critical, and personal standards perfectionism: A structural equation modeling strategy. In G.L. Flett & P.L. Hewitt (Eds.), *Perfectionism: Theory, research, and treatment* (pp. 285–315). Washington, DC: American Psychological Association.

Blass, T. (1991). Understanding behavior in the Milgram obedience experiment: The role of personality, situations, and their interactions. *Journal of Personality and Social Psychology, 60,* 398–413.

Blatt, S.J. (1974). Levels of object representation in anaclitic and introjective depression. *Psychoanalytic Study of the Child, 29,* 107–157.

Blatt, S.J. (1992). The differential effect of psychotherapy and psychoanalysis with anaclitic and introjective patients: The Menninger Psychotherapy Research Project revisited. *Journal of the American Psychoanalytic Association, 40,* 691–724.

Blatt, S.J. (1995). The destructiveness of perfectionism: Implications for the treatment of depression. *American Psychologist, 50,* 1003–1020.

Blatt, S.J., & Felsen, I. (1993). Different kinds of folks may need different kinds of strokes: The effect of patients' characteristics on therapeutic process and outcome. *Psychotherapy Research, 3*, 245–259.

Blatt, S.J., Quinlan, D.M., Pilkonis, P.A., & Shea, M.T. (1995). Impact of perfectionism and need for approval on the brief treatment of depression: The National Institute of Mental Health Treatment of Depression Collaborative Research Program revisited. *Journal of Consulting and Clinical Psychology, 63*, 125–132.

Blatt, S.J., & Shahar, G. (2004). Stability of the patient-by-treatment interaction in the Menninger Psychotherapy Research Project. *Bulletin of the Menninger Clinic, 68*, 23–38.

Blatt, S.J., Zohar, A.H., Quinlan, D.M., Zuroff, D.C., & Mongrain, M. (1995). Subscales within the dependency factor of The Depressive Experiences Questionnaire. *Journal of Personality Assessment*, *64*, 319–339.

Blatt, S.J., & Zuroff, D.C. (1992). Interpersonal relatedness and self-definition: Two prototypes for depression. *Clinical Psychology Review, 12*, 527–562.

Blatt, S.J., & Zuroff, D.C. (2002). Perfectionism and the therapeutic context. In G.L. Flett, & P.L. Hewitt (Eds.), *Perfectionism: Theory, research, and treatment* (pp. 393–406). Washington, DC: American Psychological Association.

Block, J. (1971). *Lives through time*. Berkeley, CA: Bancroft Books.

Block, J. (1977). Advancing the psychology of personality: Paradigmatic shift or improving the quality of research? In D. Magnusson & N.S. Endler (Eds.), *Psychology at the Crossroads: Current Issues in Interactional Psychology* (pp. 37–63). Hillsdale, NJ: Erlbaum.

Block, J. (1978). *The Q-sort method in personality assessment and psychiatric research*. Palo Alto, CA: Consulting Psychologists Press.

Block, J. (1995). A contrarian view of the five-factor approach to personality description. *Psychological Bulletin, 117*, 187–215.

Block, J. (2002). *Personality as an affect-processing system: Toward an integrative theory*. Mahwah, NJ: Erlbaum.

Block, J.H., & Block, J. (1980). *The California Child Q-Set*. Palo Alto, CA: Consulting Psychologists Press.

Bloom, R.W. (1984). Comment on measuring Machiavellianism with Mach V: A psychometric investigation. *Journal of Personality Assessment, 48*, 26–27.

Blunt, A., & Pychyl, T.A. (2000). Task aversiveness and procrastination: A multi-dimensional approach to task aversiveness across stages of personal projects. *Personality and Individual Differences, 28*, 153–167.

Boden, J.M., & Baumeister, R.F. (1997). Repressive coping: Distraction using pleasant thoughts and memories. *Journal of Personality and Social Psychology, 73*, 45–62.

Bogg, T., & Roberts, B.W. (2004). Conscientiousness and health behaviors: A meta-analysis. *Psychological Bulletin, 130*, 887—919.

Boies, K., Lee, K., Ashton, M.C., Pascal, S. and Nicol, A.M. (2001). The structure of the French personality lexicon. *European Journal of Personality, 15*, 277–295.

Bolger, N. (1990). Coping as a personality process: A prospective study. *Journal of Personality and Social Psychology, 59*, 355–386.

Bond, M.H. (1979). Dimensions used in perceiving peers: Cross-cultural comparisons of Hong Kong, Japanese, American, and Philipino university students. *International Journal of Psychology, 14*, 47–56.

Bono, J.E., & Judge, T.A. (2003). Core self-evaluations: A review of the trait and its role in job satisfaction and job performance. *European Journal of Personality, 17*, 5–18.

Bookwala, J., & Zdaniuk, B. (1998). Adult attachment styles and aggressive behavior within dating relationships. *Journal of Social and Personal Relationships, 15*, 175–190.

Booth-Kewley, S., & Vickers, R.R. (1994). Associations between major domains of personality and health behavior. *Journal of Personality, 62*, 282–298.

Borkenau, P., & Ostendorf, F. (1989). Descriptive consistency and social desirability in self- and peer reports. *European Journal of Personality, 3*, 31–45.

Bornstein, R.F. (1993). *The dependent personality*. New York: Guilford Press

Bornstein, R.F. (1998). Depathologizing dependency. *Journal of Nervous and Mental Disease, 186*, 67–73.

Bornstein, R.F., & Cecero, J.J. (2000). Deconstructing dependency in a five-factor world: A meta-analytic review. *Journal of Personality Assessment, 74*, 324–343.

Bouchard, T.J., Jr. (1997). The genetics of personality. In K. Blum & E.P. Noble (Eds.), *Handbook of psychiatric genetics* (pp. 273–296). Boca Raton, FL: CRC Press.

Bouchard, T.J., Jr., (2004). Genetic Influence on Human Psychological Traits. *Current Directions in Psychological Science, 13*, 148–151.

Bouchard, T.J., & Loehlin, J.C. (2001). Genes, evolution, and personality. *Behavior Genetics, 31*, 243–273.

Bouchard, T.J., Jr., & McGue, M. (2003). Genetic and environmental influences on human psychological differences. *Journal of Neurobiology, 54*, 4–45.

Bouthillier, D., Julien, D., Dube, M., Belanger, I., & Hamelin, M. (2002). Predictive validity of adult attachment measures in relation to emotion regulation behaviors in marital interactions. *Journal of Adult Development, 9*, 291–305.

Bowers, K.S. (1973). Situationism in psychology: An analysis and a critique. *Psychological Review, 80*, 307–336.

Bowlby, J. (1980). Attachment and loss: Vol. 3: Sadness and depression. New York: Basic Books.

Boyce, T.E., & Geller, E.S. (2002). Using the P.T. Barnum effect to teach critical thinking: Applications for a course in psychological research methods. *Teaching of Psychology, 29*, 316–318.

Bradbury, T.N., & Fincham, F.D. (1990). Attributions in marriage: Review and critique. *Psychological Bulletin, 107*, 3–33.

Braginsky, D.D. (1970). Machiavellianism and manipulative interpersonal behaviour in children. Journal of Experimental Social Psychology, 6, 77–99.

Brennan, K.A., Clark, C.L., & Shaver, P.R. (1998). Self-report measurement of adult attachment: An integrative overview. In J.A. Simpson & W.S. Rholes (Eds.), *Attachment theory and close relationships* (pp. 46–76). New York: Guilford Press.

Briggs, S.R., & Cheek, J.M. (1986). The role of factor analysis in the development and evaluation of personality scales. *Journal of Personality, 54*, 107–148.

Britt, T.W. (1993). Metatraits: Evidence relevant to the validity of the construct and its implications. *Journal of Personality and Social Psychology, 65*, 554–562.

Britt, T.W., & Shepperd, J.A. (1999). Trait relevance and trait assessment. *Personality and Social Psychology Review, 3*, 108–122.

Brown, J.D., and McGill, K.L. (1989). The cost of good fortune: When positive life events produce negative health consequences. *Journal of Personality and Social Psychology, 57*, 1103–1110.

Brown, K.W., & Moskowitz, D.S. (1998). Dynamic stability of behavior: The rhythms of our interpersonal lives. *Journal of Personality, 66*, 105–134.

Brown, L.L., Tomarken, A.J., Orth, D.N., Loosen, P.T., Kalin, N.H., & Davidson, R.J. (1996). Individual differences in repressiveness-defensiveness predict basal salivary cortisol levels. *Journal of Personality and Social Psychology, 70*, 362–371.

Brunswick, E. (1955). Representative design and probabilistic theory in a functional psychology. *Psychological Review, 62*, 193–217.

Buchanan, T. (2000). Internet Research: Self-monitoring and judgments of attractiveness. *Behavior Research Methods, Instruments & Computers, 32*, 521–527.

Buchanan, T., Johnson, J.A., & Goldberg, L.R. (2005). Implementing a five-factor personality inventory for use on the Internet. *European Journal of*

Psychological Assessment, 21, 115–127.

Buchanan, T., & Smith, J.L. (1999). Using the internet for psychological research: Personality testing on the World Wide Web. *British Journal of Psychology, 90*, 125–144.

Burger, J.M. (1984). Desire for control, locus of control, and proneness to depression. *Journal of Personality, 52*, 71–89.

Burger, J.M. (1990). Desire for control and interpersonal interaction style. *Journal of Research in Personality, 24*, 32–44.

Burger, J.M. (1992). *Desire for control: Personality, social, and clinical perspectives*. New York: Plenum.

Burger, J.M., & Cooper, H.M. (1979). The desirability of control. *Motivation and Emotion, 3*, 381–393.

Burger, J.M., & Lynn, A.L. (2005). Superstitious behavior among American and Japanese professional baseball players. *Basic and Applied Social Psychology, 27*, 71–76.

Buri, J.R. (1991). Parental authority questionnaire. *Journal of Personality Assessment, 57*, 110–119.

Burisch, M. (1984). Approaches to personality inventory construction: A comparison of merits. *American Psychologist, 39*, 214–227.

Buss, A.H., & Plomin, R. (1984). *Temperament: Early developing personality traits.* Mahwah, NJ: Erlbaum.

Buss, D.M. (1991). Conflict in married couples: Personality predictors of anger and upset. *Journal of Personality, 59*, 663–688.

Butcher, J.N., & Rouse, S.V. (1996). Personality: Individual differences and clinical assessment. *Annual Review of Psychology, 47*, 87–111.

Byrne, D. (1961). The Repression-Sensitization Scale: Rationale, reliability, and validity. *Journal of Personality, 29*, 463–468.

Byrne, D., McDonald, R.D., & Mikawa, J. (1961). Approach and avoidance affiliation motives. *Journal of Personality, 31*, 21–37.

Cacioppo, J.T. (2004). Common sense, intuition, and theory in personality and social psychology. *Personality and Social Psychology Review, 8*, 114–122.

Cacioppo, J.T., & Petty, R.E. (1982). The need for cognition. *Journal of Personality and Social Psychology, 42*, 116–131.

Cacioppo, J.T., Petty, R.E., & Kao, C.F. (1984). The efficient assessment of need for cognition. *Journal of Personality Assessment, 48*, 306–307.

Cacioppo, J.T., Petty, R.E., & Morris, K.J. (1983). Effects of need for cognition on message evaluation, recall, and persuasion. *Journal of Personality and Social Psychology, 45*, 805–818.

Campbell, D.T. (1986). Science's social system of validity-enhancing collective belief change and the problems of the social sciences. In D.W. Fiske & R.A. Shweder (Eds.), *Metatheory in social science: Pluralisms and subjectivities* (pp. 108–135). Chicago, IL: University of Chicago Press.

Campbell, D.T., & Fiske, D.W. (1959). Convergent and discriminant validation by the multitrait-multimethod matrix. *Psychological Bulletin, 56*, 81–105.

Campbell, L., Simpson, J.A., Boldry, J., & Kashy, D.A. (2005). Perceptions of conflict and support in romantic relationships: The role of attachment anxiety. *Journal of Personality and Social Psychology, 88*, 510–531.

Campbell, L., White, J., & Stewart, A. (1991). The relationship of psychological birth order to actual birth order. *Individual Psychology, 47*, 380–391.

Campbell, W.K., Bonacci, A.M., Shelton, J., Exline, J.J., & Bushman, B.J. (2004). Psychological entitlement: Interpersonal consequences and validation of a self-report measure. *Journal of Personality Assessment, 83*, 29–45.

Canli, T. & Amin, Z. (2002). Neuroimaging of emotion and personality: Scientific evidence and ethical considerations. *Brain and Cognition, 50*, 414–431.

Cannon, W.B. (1932). *The wisdom of the body.* New York: Norton.

Cantor, N. (1990). From thought to behavior: "Having" and "Doing" in the study of personality and cognition. *American Psychologist, 45*, 735–750.

Cantor, N., & Norem, J.K. (1989). Defensive pessimism and stress coping. *Social Cognition, 7*, 92–112.

Cantor, N., Norem, J.K., Niedenthal, P.M., Langston, C.A., & Brower, A.M. (1987). Life tasks, self-concept ideals, and cognitive strategies in a life transition. *Journal of Personality and Social Psychology, 53*, 1178–1191.

Carlson, R. (1971). Where is the person in personality research? *Psychological Bulletin, 75*, 203–219.

Carlson, R. (1988). Exemplary lives: The uses of psychobiography for theory development. *Journal of Personality, 56*, 105–138.

Carver, C.S. (1989). How should multifaceted personality constructs be tested? Issues illustrated by self-monitoring, attributional style, and hardiness. *Journal of Personality and Social Psychology, 56*, 577–585.

Carver, C.S. (1997). You want to measure coping but your protocol's too long: Consider the Brief COPE. *International Journal of Behavioral Medicine, 4*, 92–100.

Carver, C.S., & Baird, E. (1998). The American dream revisited: Is it what you want or why you want it that matters? *Psychological Science, 9*, 289–292.

Carver, C.S., Coleman, A.E., & Glass, D.C. (1976). The coronary-prone behavior pattern and the suppression of fatigue on a treadmill test. *Journal of Personality and Social Psychology, 4*, 460–466.

Carver, C.S., Lawrence, J.W., & Scheier, M.F. (1999). Self-discrepancies and affect: Incorporating the role of feared selves. *Personality and Social Psychology Bulletin, 25*, 783–792.

Carver, C.S., Scheier, M.F., & Weintraub, J.K. (1989). Assessing coping strategies: A theoretically-based approach. *Journal of Personality and Social Psychology, 56*, 267–283.

Carver, C.S., & White, T.L. (1994). Behavioral inhibition, behavioral activation, and affective responses to impending reward and punishment: The BIS/BAS Scales. *Journal of Personality and Social Psychology, 67*, 319–333.

Caspi, A., & Bem, D.J. (1990). Personality continuity and change across the life course. In L. Pervin (Ed.), *Handbook of personality: Theory and research* (1st ed., pp. 549–575). New York: Guilford Press.

Caspi, A., Elder, G.H., & Bem, D.J. (1987). Moving against the world: Life-course patterns of explosive children. *Developmental Psychology, 23*, 308–313.

Caspi, A., Elder, G.H., & Bem, D.J. (1988). Moving away from the world: Life-course patterns of shy children. *Developmental Psychology, 24*, 824–831.

Caspi, A., Roberts, B.W., & Shiner, R. (2005). Personality development. *Annual Review of Psychology, 56*, 453–484.

Caspi, A., & Silva, P.A. (1995). Temperamental qualities at age three predict personality traits in young adulthood: Longitudinal evidence from a birth cohort. *Child Development, 66*, 486–498.

Cattell, R.B. (1943). The description of personality: Basic traits resolved into clusters. *Journal of Abnormal and Social Psychology, 38*, 476–506.

Cattell, R.B. (1946). *The description and measurement of personality*. Yonkers, NY: World Book.

Cattell, R.B. (1965). Factor analysis: An introduction to essentials. I. The purpose and underlying models. *Biometrics, 21*, 190–215.

Cattell, R.B., Eber, H.W., & Tatsuoka, M.M. (1970). *The handbook for the Sixteen Personality Factor Questionnaire.* Champaign, IL: Institute for Personality and Ability Testing.

Center, D.B., & Kemp, D.E. (2002). Antisocial behaviour in children and Eysenck's theory of personality: An evaluation. *International Journal of Disability, Development, and Education, 49*, 353–357.

Chabot, J. (1973). Repression-sensitization: A critique of some neglected variables in the literature. *Psychological Bulletin, 80*, 122–129.

Chang, E.C. (1998). Dispositional optimism and primary and secondary appraisal of a stressor: Controlling for confounding influences and relations to coping and psychological and physical adjustment. *Journal of Personality and Social Psychology, 74*, 1109–1120.

Chang, J., & Halliday, J. (2005). *Mao: The unknown story*. New York: Alfred A. Knopf.

Chao, R.K. (1994). Beyond parental control and authoritarian parenting style: Understanding Chinese parenting through the cultural notion of training. *Child Development, 65*, 1111–1119.

Chaplin, W.F. (1991). The next generation of moderator research in personality psychology. *Journal of Personality, 59*, 143–173.

Chase, A. (2003). *Harvard and the Unabomber: The education of an American terrorist*. London: W.W. Norton & Company.

Chen, X., et al. (1998). Childrearing attitudes and behavioral inhibition in Chinese and Canadian toddlers: A cross-cultural study. *Developmental Psychology, 34*, 677–686.

Chen X., Rubin, K.H., Li, B., & Li, D. (1999). Adolescent outcomes of social functioning in Chinese children. *International Journal of Behavioral Development, 23*, 199–223.

Chen, X., Wang, L., Chen, H., & Liu, M. (2002). Noncompliance and childrearing attitudes as predictors of aggressive behavior: A longitudinal study in Chinese children. *International Journal of Behavioral Development, 26*, 225–233.

Cheung, F.M., & Cheung S.F. (2003). Measuring personality and values across cultures: Imported versus indigenous measures. In W.J. Lonner, D.L. Dinnel, S.A. Hayes, & D.N. Sattler (Eds.), Online readings in psychology and culture (Unit 6, Chapter 5). (http://www.ac.wwu.edu/aculture/Cheung.htm). Center for Cross-Cultural Research, Western Washington University, Bellingham, Washington, USA.

Cheung, F.M., Cheung, S.F., Leung, I.C., Ward, C., & Leong, F. (2003). The English version of the Chinese Personality Assessment Inventory, *Journal of Cross-Cultural Psychology, 34*, 433–452.

Cheung, F.M., Cheung, S-F., Zhang, J., & Wada, S. (2003). Indigenous measures of personality assessment in Asian countries: A review. *Psychological Assessment, 15*, 280–289.

Cheung, F.M., Leung, K., Song, W.Z., & Zhang, J.X. (2001). The Chinese Personality Assessment Inventory – 2 (CPAI-2). (http://www.psy.cuhk.edubk/2cpaiweb/publicdocument/PublicFiles.htm).

Child, I.L. (1950). The relation of somatotype to self-rating on Sheldon's temperamental traits. *Journal of Personality, 18*, 440–453.

Christie, R. (1970). Scale construction. In R. Christie & F.L. Geis (Eds.), *Studies in Machiavellianism* (pp. 10–34). New York: Academic Press.

Christie, R., & Geis, F.L. (1970). *Studies in Machiavellianism*. New York: Academic Press.

Church, A.T., Reyes, J.A., Katigbak, M.S., & Grimm, S.D. (1997). Filipino personality structure and the big five model: A lexical approach. *Journal of Personality, 65*, 477–528.

Clance, P.R., & Imes, S., (1978). The imposter phenomenon in high achieving women: Dynamics and therapeutic intervention. *Psychotherapy Theory, Research, and Practice, 15*, 1–8.

Claridge, G. (1993). When is psychoticism psychoticism? And how does it really relate to creativity? *Psychological Inquiry, 4*, 184–188.

Clark, D.A., & Beck, A.T. (1991). Personality factors in dysphoria: A psychometric refinement of Beck's Sociotropy-Autonomy Scale. *Journal of Psychopathology and Behavioral Assessment, 13*, 369–388.

Clarke, I., III. (2000). Extreme response style in cross-cultural research: An empirical investigation. *Journal of Social Behavior and Personality, 15*, 137–152.

Clark, L.A. (1993). *Schedule for Nonadaptive and Adaptive Personality: Manual for Administration, Scoring, and Interpretation*. Minneapolis, MN: University of Minnesota Press.

Clark, L.A., Kochanska, G., & Ready, R. (2000). Mothers' personality and its interaction with child temperament as predictors of parenting. *Journal of Personality and Social Psychology, 79*, 274–285.

Cloninger, C.R. (1987a). Neurogenetic adaptive mechanisms in alcoholism. *Science, 236*, 410–416.

Cloninger, C.R. (1987b). A systematic method for clinical description and classification of personality variants. *Archives of General Psychiatry, 44*, 573–588.

Cloninger, C.R., Svrakic, D.M., & Przybeck, T.R. (1993). A psychobiological model of temperament and character. *Archives of General Psychiatry, 50*, 975–990.

Cohen, A.R., Stotland, E., & Wolfe, D.M. (1955). An experimental investigation of need for cognition. *Journal of Abnormal and Social Psychology, 51*, 291–294.

Cohen, D. & Gunz, A. (2002). As seen by the other…: Perspectives on the self in the memories and emotional perceptions of Easterners and Westerners. *Psychological Science, 13*, 55–59.

Cohen, J. (1988). *Statistical power analysis for the behavioral sciences* (2nd edition). Hillsdale, NJ: Erlbaum.

Cohen, J. (1990). Things I have learned (so far). *American Psychologist, 45*, 1304–1312.

Colder, C.R., & O'Connor, R.M. (2004). Gray's reinforcement sensitivity model and child psychopathology: Laboratory and questionnaire assessment of the BAS and BIS. *Journal of Abnormal Child Psychology, 32*, 435–351.

Collins, J.M., & Gleaves, D.H. (1998). Race, job applicants, and the five-factor model of personality: Implications for black psychology, I/O psychology, and the five-factor model. *Journal of Applied Psychology, 83*, 531–544.

Collins, N.L., & Read, S. (1990). Adult attachment, working models, and relationship quality in dating couples. *Journal of Personality and Social Psychology, 58*, 644–663.

Conrod, P.J., Stewart, S.H., Pihl, R.O., Cote, S., Fontaine, V., & Dongier, M. (2000). Efficacy of brief coping skills interventions that match different personality profiles of female substance abusers. *Psychology of Addictive Behaviors, 14*, 231–242.

Cooke, D.J., & Michie, C. (1999). Psychopathy across cultures: North America and Scotland compared. *Journal of Abnormal Psychology, 108*, 58–68.

Cooley, C. (1912) *Human nature and social order*. New York: Scribers.

Cooper, M.L. (1994). Motivations for alcohol use among adolescents: Development and validation of a four-factor model. *Psychological Assessment, 6*, 117–128.

Cooper, M.L., Frone, M.R., Russell, M., & Mudar, P. (1995). Drinking to regulate positive and negative emotions: A motivational model of alcohol use. *Journal of Personality and Social Psychology, 69*, 990–1005.

Cooper, M.L., & Sheldon, M.S. (2002). Seventy years of research on personality and close relationships: Substantive and methodological trends over time. *Journal of Personality, 70*, 783–812.

Coopersmith, S. (1967). *The antecedents of self-esteem*. Palo Alto, CA: Consulting Psychologists Press.

Corrigan, S.A., & Moskowitz, D.S. (1983). Type A behavior in preschool children: Construct validation evidence for the MYTH. *Child Development, 54*, 1513–1521.

Costa, P.T., Jr., Bagby, R.M., Herbst, J.H., & McCrae, R.R. (2005). Personality self-reports are concurrently reliable and valid during acute depressive episodes. *Journal of Affective Disorders, 89*, 45–55.

Costa, P.T., Jr., & McCrae, R.R. (1985). *The NEO-Personality Inventory Manual*. Odessa, FL: Psychological Assessment Resources.

Costa, P.T., Jr., & McCrae, R.R. (1987). Neuroticism, somatic complaints, and disease: Is the bark worse than the bite? *Journal of Personality, 55*, 299–316.

Costa, P.T., Jr., & McCrae, R.R. (1988). From catalog to classification: Murray's needs and the Five-Factor model. *Journal of Personality and Social Psychology, 55*, 258–265.

Costa, P.T., & McCrae, R.R. (1992a). Normal personality assessment in clinical practice: The NEO Personality Inventory. *Psychological Assessment, 4*, 5–13.

Costa, P.T., Jr., & McCrae, R.R. (1992b). Four ways five factors are basic. *Personality and Individual Differences, 13*, 653–665.

Costa, P.T., Jr., & McCrae, R.R. (1992c). *NEO-PI-R*. Odessa, FL: Psychological Assessment Resources.

Costa, P.T., Jr., & McCrae, R.R. (1992d). The five-factor model of personality and its relevance to personality disorders. *Journal of Personality Disorders, 6,* 343–359.

Costa, P.T., Jr., & McCrae, R.R. (1994). Set like plaster? Evidence for the stability of adult personality. In T. Heatherton & J.L. Weinberger (Eds.), *Can personality change?* (pp. 21–40). Washington, DC: American Psychological Association.

Coutinho, S.A., & Woolery, L.M. (2004). The need for cognition and life satisfaction among college students. *College Student Journal, 38,* 203–206.

Covington, M.V. (2000). Goal theory, motivation, and school achievement: An integrative review. *Annual Review of Psychology, 51,* 171–200.

Covington, M.V., & Mueller, K.J. (2001). Intrinsic versus extrinsic motivation: an approach/avoidance reformulation. *Educational Psychology Review, 13,* 157–176.

Coyne, J.C., & Gottlieb, B.H. (1986). The mismeasure of coping by checklist. *Journal of Personality, 64,* 959–991.

Craik, K.H. (1986). Personality research methods: An historical perspective. *Journal of Personality, 54,* 18–51.

Cramer, P. (1987). The development of defense mechanisms. *Journal of Personality, 55,* 597–614.

Cramer, P. (1991). Anger and the use of defense mechanisms in college students. *Journal of Personality, 59,* 39–55.

Cramer, P. (1998). Coping and defense mechanisms: What's the difference? *Journal of Personality, 66,* 919–944.

Crandall, R., McCown, D.A., & Robb, Z. (1988). The effects of assertiveness training on self-actualization. *Small Group Behavior, 19,* 134–145.

Crawford, I., Hammack, P.L., McKirnan, D.J., Ostrow, D., Zamboni, B.D., Robinson, B., & Hope, B. (2003). Sexual sensation seeking, reduced concern about HIV and sexual risk behaviour among gay men in primary relationships. *AIDS Care, 15,* 513–524.

Crocker, J., & Luhtanen, R.K. (2003). Level of self-esteem and contingencies of self-worth: Unique effects on academic, social, and financial problems in college freshmen. *Personality and Social Psychology Bulletin. 29,* 701–712.

Crocker, J., Luhtanen, R., Blaine, B., & Broadnax, S. (1994). Collective self-esteem and physiological well-being among White, Black, and Asian college students. *Personality and Social Psychology Bulletin, 20,* 503–513.

Crocker, J., McGraw, K.M., Thompson, L.L., & Ingerman, C. (1987). Downward comparison, prejudice, and evaluations of others: Effects of self-esteem and threat. *Journal of Personality and Social Psychology, 52,* 907–916.

Crocker, J., Sommers, S., & Luhtanen, R.K. (2002). Hopes dashed and dreams fulfilled: Contingencies of self-worth in the graduate school admissions process. *Personality and Social Psychology Bulletin, 28,* 1275–1286.

Cronbach, L.J. (1951). Coefficient alpha and the internal structure of tests. *Psychometrika, 16,* 297–334.

Cronbach, L.J. (1957). The two disciplines of scientific psychology. *American Psychologist, 12,* 671–684.

Cronbach, L.J., & Meehl, P.E. (1955). Construct validity in psychological tests. *Psychological Bulletin, 52,* 281–302.

Crowne, D. P., & Marlowe, D. (1960). A new scale of social desirability independent of psychopathology. *Journal of Consulting Psychology, 24,* 349–354.

Crowne, D. P., & Marlowe, D. (1964). *The approval motive: Studies in evaluative dependence.* New York: John Wiley & Sons Inc..

Cyranowski, J.M. et al. (2002). Adult attachment profiles, interpersonal difficulties, and response to interpersonal psychotherapy in women with recurrent major depression. *Journal of Social and Clinical Psychology, 21,* 191–217.

Dali, S. (1965). *Diary of a genius* (translated by Richard Howard). Garden City, NY: Doubleday & Company, Inc.

Danoff-Burg, S., Revenson, T.A., Trudeau, K.J., & Paget, S.A. (2004). Unmitigated communion, social constraints, and psychological distress among women with rheumatoid arthritis. *Journal of Personality, 72,* 29–46.

Darling, N., & Steinberg, L. (1993). Parenting style as context: An integrative model. *Psychological Bulletin, 113,* 487–496.

Davey, A., Fincham, F.D., Beach, S.R.H., & Brody, G.H. (2001). Attributions in marriage: Examining the entailment model in dyadic context. *Journal of Family Psychology, 15,* 721–734.

Davila, J., Burge, D., & Hammen, C. (1997). Why does attachment style change? *Journal of Personality and Social Psychology, 73,* 826–838.

Davis, R.A., Flett, G.L., & Besser, A. (2002). Validation of a new scale for measuring problematic Internet use: Implications for pre-employment screening. *CyberPsychology and Behavior, 5,* 331–345.

Davison, G.C., Neale, J.M., Blankstein, K.R., & Flett, G.L. (2005). *Abnormal psychology (2nd Canadian edition).* Toronto: John Wiley & Sons Canada, Ltd.

De Fruyt, F., & Denollet, J. (2002). Type D personality: A five-factor model perspective. *Psychology and Health, 17,* 671–683.

Deluga, R.J. (2001). American presidential Machiavellianism: Implications for charismatic leadership and rated performance. *The Leadership Quarterly, 12,* 339–363.

Dembroski, T.M., & Costa, P.T., Jr. (1987). Coronary prone behavior: Components of the Type As pattern and hostility. *Journal of Personality, 55,* 211–235.

Denollet, J. (1998). Personality and coronary heart disease: The Type-D Scale-16 (DS16). *Annals of Behavioral Medicine, 20,* 209–215.

Denollet, J., Sys, S.U., & Brutsaert, D.L. (1995). Personality and mortality after myocardial infarction. *Psychosomatic Medicine, 57,* 582–591.

Denollet, J., Vaes, J., & Brutsaert, D.L. (2000). Inadequate response to treatment in coronary heart disease: Adverse effects of Type-D personality and younger age on 5-year prognosis and quality of life. *Circulation, 102,* 630–635.

De Vos, G. (1997). Heritage of exploitation: A brief TAT report of South Brazilian youth. *Political Psychology, 18,* 439–481.

de Vries, M.W. (1987). Cry babies, cultures, and catastrophes: Infant temperament among the Masai. In N. Sheper-Hughes (Ed.), *Child survival* (pp. 165–185). Dordrecht, Holland: D. Reidel.

DeYoung, C.G., Peterson, J.B., & Higgins, D.M. (2002). Higher-order factors of the Big Five predict conformity: Are there neuroses of health? *Personality and Individual Differences, 33,* 533–552.

DiBartolo, P.M., Frost, R.O., Chang, P., LaSota, M., & Grills, A. E. (2004). Shedding light on the relationship between personal standards and psychopathology: The case for contingent self-worth. *Journal of Rational-Emotive and Cognitive-Behavior Therapy, 22,* 241–254.

Dickson, D.H., & Kelly, I.W. (1985). The "Barnum effect" in personality assessment: A review of the literature. *Psychological Reports, 57,* 367–382.

Diener, E., Horwitz, J., & Emmons, R.A. (1985). Happiness of the very wealthy. *Social Indicators Research, 16,* 263–274.

Diener, E., & Scollon, C.N. (2002). Our desired future for personality psychology. *Journal of Research in Personality, 36,* 629–637.

Dietch, J. (1978). Love, sex roles, and psychological health. *Journal of Personality Assessment, 42,* 626–634.

Digman, J.M. (1997). Higher-order factors of the Big Five. *Journal of Personality and Social Psychology, 73,* 1246–1256.

Digman, J.M., & Takemoto-Chock, N.K. (1981). Factors in the natural language of personality: Reanalysis, comparison, and interpretation of six major studies. *Multivariate Behavioral Research, 16,* 149–170.

Dill, K.E., Anderson, C.A., Anderson, K.B., & Deuser, W.E. (1997). Effects of aggressive personality on social expectations and social perceptions. *Journal of Research in Personality, 31,* 272–292.

Dion, K.L., Dion, K.K., & Pak, A. (1992). Personality-based hardiness as a buffer for discrimination-related stress in members of Toronto's Chinese community. *Canadian Journal of Behavioural Science, 24,* 517–536.

Dion, K.L., & Yee, P.H. (1987). Ethnicity and personality in a Canadian context. *Journal of Social Psychology, 127,* 175–182.

Dixon, W.E., Jr., & Hull Smith, P. (2003). Who's controlling whom? Infant contributions to maternal play behavior. *Infant and Child Development,* 12, 177–195.

Doherty, W.J., & Baldwin, C. (1985). Shifts and stability in locus of control during the 1970s: Divergence of the sexes. *Journal of Personality and Social Psychology, 48,* 1048–1053.

Dolan, C.A., & White, J.W. (1988). Issues of consistency and effectiveness in coping with daily stressors. *Journal of Research in Personality, 22,* 395–407.

Dollard, J., Doob, L.W., Miller, N.E., Maurer, O.H., & Sears, R.R. (1939). *Frustration and aggression.* New Haven, CT: Yale University Press,

Dollard, J., & Miller, N.E. (1950). *Personality and psychotherapy.* New York: McGraw-Hill.

Dominguez, M.M., & Carton, J.S. (1997). The relation between self-actualization and parenting style. *Journal of Social Behavior and Personality, 12,* 1093–1100.

Donohew, L., & Bardo, M. (2000). Designing prevention programs for sensation seeking adolescents. In W.B. Hansen, S.M. Giles, & M.D. Fearnow-Kenney (Eds.), *Improving prevention effectiveness* (pp. 195–203). Greensboro, NC: Tanglewood Research.

Donohew, L., Bardo, M., & Zimmerman, R. (2004). Personality and risky behavior: Communication and prevention. In R.M. Stelmack (Ed.), *On the psychobiology of personality: Essays in honor of Marvin Zuckerman* (pp. 223–245). Oxford, UK: Elsevier.

Donohew, L., Zimmerman, R., Cupp, P.S., Novak, S., Colon, S., & Abell, R. (2000). Sensation seeking, impulsive decision-making, and risky sex: Implications for risk-taking and design of interventions. *Personality and Individual Differences, 28,* 1079–1091.

Douglas, J.E., & Olshaker, M. (1997). *Journey into darkness.* New York: Simon & Schuster, Inc.

Douglas, J.E., Ressler, R.K., Burgess, A.W., & Hartman, C.R. (1986). Criminal profiling from crime scene analysis. *Behavioral Sciences and the Law, 4,* 401–421.

Du Bois, C. (1944). *The people of Alor.* Minneapolis, MN: University of Minnesota Press.

Duckitt, J. (2006). Differential effects of right wing authoritarianism and social dominance orientation on outgroup attitudes and their mediation by threat from and competitiveness to outgroups. *Personality and Social Psychology Bulletin, 32,* 684–696.

Dutton, D.G., Saunders, K., Starzomski, A., & Bartholomew, K. (1994). Intimacy-anger and insecure attachment as precursors of abuse in intimate relationships. *Journal of Applied Social Psychology, 24,* 1367–1386.

Duval, S., & Wicklund, R.A. (1972). *A theory of objective self awareness.* New York: Academic Press.

Dyce, J.A., & O'Connor, B.P. (1994). The personalities of popular musicians. *Psychology of Music, 22,* 168–173.

Eaves, L., et al. (1999). Comparing the biological and cultural inheritance of personality and social attitudes in the Virginia 30,000 study of twins and their relatives. *Twin Research, 2,* 62–80.

Ebersole, P., & Persi, R. (1993). The Short Index of Self-Actualization and death anxiety. *Journal of Psychology, 127,* 359–360.

Edwards, A.L. (1957). *The social desirability variable in personality assessment and research.* New York: Dryden Press.

Edwards, A.L. (1964). Social desirability and performance on the MMPI. *Psychometrica, 29,* 295–308.

Edwards, A.L., Abbott, R.D., & Klockars, A.J. (1972). A factor analysis of the EPPS and PRF personality inventories. *Educational and Psychological Measurement,* 32, 23-29.

Edwards, J.A., Lanning, K., & Hooker, K. (2002). The MBTI and social information processing: An incremental validity study. *Journal of Personality Assessment, 78,* 432–450.

Egger, J.I.M., et al. (2003). Cross-cultural replication of the five-factor model and comparison of the NEO-PI-R and MMPI-2 PSY-5 scales in a Dutch psychiatric sample. *Psychological Assessment, 15,* 81–88.

Eisenberg, N., et al. (2000). Dispositional empathy and regulation: Their role in predicting quality of social functioning. *Journal of Personality and Social Psychology, 78,* 136–157.

Ekehammar, B., Akrami, N., Gylje, M., & Zakrisson, I. (2004). What matters most to prejudice: Big five personality, social dominance orientation, or right-wing authoritarianism? *European Journal of Personality, 18,* 463–482.

Ekman, P. (1997). What we have learned by measuring facial behavior. In P. Ekman & E.L. Rosenberg (Eds.), *What the face reveals: Basic and applied studies of spontaneous expression using the Facial Action Coding System (FACS)* (pp. 469–485). New York: Oxford University Press.

Ekman, P. & Friesen, W.V. (1969). A tool for the analysis of motion picture film or videotape. *American Psychologist, 24,* 240–243.

Ellingson, J.E., Sackett, P.R., & Hough, L.M. (1999). Social desirability corrections in personality measurement: Issues of applicant comparison and construct validity. *Journal of Applied Psychology, 84,* 155–166.

Ellis, A. (2002). The role of irrational beliefs in perfectionism. In G.L. Flett & P.L. Hewitt (Eds.), *Perfectionism: Theory, research, and treatment* (pp. 217–229). Washington, DC: American Psychological Association.

Ellis, A. (2003). The woman who hated everyone and everything. In J.A. Kottler & J. Carlson (Eds.), *The mummy at the dining room table: Eminent therapists reveal their most unusual cases* (pp. 126–135). San Francisco: Jossey-Bass.

Elms, A.C. (1972). *Social psychology and social relevance.* Boston: Little, Brown.

Elms, A.C. (1988). Freud as Leonardo: Why the first psychobiography went wrong. *Journal of Personality, 56,* 19–40.

Elms, A.C. (1994). *Uncovering lives: The uneasy alliance of biography and psychology.* New York: Oxford University Press.

Elms, A.C. (2003). "Sigmund Freud, Psychohistorian." *Annual of Psychoanalysis,* Volume XXXI: Psychoanalysis and History (pp. 65–78). Hillsdale, NJ: Analytic Press.

Elms, A.C. (2005). If the glove fits: The art of theoretical choice in psychobiography. In W.T. Schultz (Ed.), *Handbook of psychobiography* (pp. 84–95). New York: Oxford University Press.

Emavardhana, T., & Tori, C.D. (1997). Changes in self-concept, ego defense mechanisms, and religiosity following seven-day Vipassana meditation retreats. *Journal for the Scientific Study of Religion, 36,* 194–206.

Emmons, R.A. (1986). Personal strivings: An approach to personality and subjective well-being. *Journal of Personality and Social Psychology, 51,* 1058–1068.

Emmons, R.A. (1987). Narcissism: Theory and measurement. *Journal of Personality and Social Psychology, 52,* 11–17.

Emmons, R.A. (1991). Personal strivings, daily life events, and physical and psychological well-being. *Journal of Personality, 59,* 453–472.

Emmons, R.A., Diener, E., & Larsen, R.J. (1985). Choice of situations and congruence models of interactionism. *Personality and Individual Differences, 6,* 693–702.

Emmons, R.A., & King, L.A. (1988). Conflict among personal strivings: Immediate and long-term implications for psychological and physical well-being. *Journal of Personality and Social Psychology, 54,* 1040–1048.

Emmons, R.A., & McAdams, D.P. (1991). Personal strivings and motive dispositions: Exploring the links. *Personality and Social Psychology Bulletin, 17,* 648–654.

Endler, N.S. (1982). Interactionism comes of age. In M.P. Zanna, E.T. Higgins, & C.P. Herman (Eds.), *Consistency in social behavior* (pp. 209–249). Hillsdale, NJ: Erlbaum.

Endler, N.S. (1983). Interactionism: A personality model, but not yet a theory. In M.M. Page (Ed.), *Nebraska symposium on motivation 1982: Personality: Current theory and research* (pp. 155–200).

Lincoln, NE: University of Nebraska Press.

Endler, N.S. (2002). Multidimensional interactionism: Stress, anxiety, and coping. In L. Backman & R.C. von Hofsen (Eds.), *Psychological science 2000: Social, personality, and health perspectives* (Volume 2, pp. 281–304). Brighton, UK: Taylor & Francis, Psychology Press.

Endler, N.S. (2004). The joint effects of person and situation factors on stress in spaceflight. *Aviation, Space, and Environmental Medicine, 75,* C22–C27.

Endler, N.S., Corace, K.M., Summerfeldt, L.J., Johnson, J.M., & Rothbart, P. (2003). Coping with chronic pain. *Personality and Individual Differences, 34,* 323–346.

Endler, N.S., Crooks, D.S., & Parker, J.D.A. (1992). The interaction model of anxiety: An empirical test in a parachute jumping situation. *Anxiety, Stress and Coping, 5,* 301–311.

Endler, N.S., Kocovski, N.L., & Macrodimitris, S.D. (2001). Coping, efficacy, and perceived control in acute vs chronic illnesses. *Personality and Individual Differences, 30,* 617–625.

Endler, N.S., & Magnusson, D. (1976). Toward an interactional psychology of personality. *Psychological Bulletin, 83,* 956–974.

Endler, N.S. & Magnusson, D. (1977). The interaction model of anxiety: An empirical test in an examination situation. *Canadian Journal of Behavioural Science, 9,* 101–107.

Endler, N.S., & Parker, J.D.A. (1991). Personality research: Theories, issues, and methods. In M. Hersen, A.E. Kazdin, & A.S. Bellack (Eds.), *The clinical psychology handbook* (2nd ed., pp. 258–275). New York: Pergamon Press.

Endler, N.S., & Parker, J.D.A. (1992). Interactionism revisited: Reflections on the continuing crisis in the personality area. *European Journal of Personality, 6,* 177–198.

Endler, N.S., & Parker, J.D.A. (1999). *The Coping Inventory for Stressful Situations (CISS): Manual* (2nd ed.). Toronto: Multi-Health Systems, Inc.

Endler, N.S., & Parker, J.D.A. (2000). *Coping With Health, Injuries and Problems (CHIP): Manual.* Toronto: Multi-Health Systems, Inc.

Endler, N.S., Parker, J.D.A., & Summerfeldt, L.J. (1993). Coping with health problems: Conceptual and methodological issues. *Canadian Journal of Behavioural Science, 25,* 384–399.

Endler, N.S., & Speer, R.L. (1998). Personality psychology: Research trends for 1993–1995. *Journal of Personality, 66,* 621–669.

Endler, N.S., Speer, R.L., Johnson, J.M., & Flett, G.L. (2000). Controllability, coping, efficacy, and distress. *European Journal of Personality, 14,* 245–264.

Enns, M.W., Cox, B.J., & Pidlubny, S.R. (2002). Group cognitive behavior therapy for residual depression: Effectiveness and predictors of response. *Cognitive Behavior Therapy, 31,* 1–10.

Erikson, E.H. (1950). *Childhood and society.* New York: Norton.

Erikson, E.H. (1958). *Young man Luther.* New York: Norton.

Erikson, E.H. (1959). *Identity and the life cycle.* Selected papers. New York: International Universities Press.

Erikson, E.H. (1963). *Childhood and society* (2nd ed.) New York: Norton.

Erikson, E.H. (1968). *Identity: Youth and crisis.* New York: Norton.

Erikson, E.H. (1969). *Ghandi's truth.* New York: Norton.

Erikson, E.H., Erikson, J.M., & Kivnick, H.Q. (1986). *Vital involvement in old age.* New York: Norton.

Ernst, C., & Angst, J. (1983). *Birth order.* New York: Springer-Verlag.

Eron, L.D. (1987). The development of aggressive behavior from the perspective of a developing behaviorism. *American Psychologist, 42,* 435–442.

Etherington-Smith, M. (1992). *The persistence of memory.* New York: Random House.

Evans, A.W., Leeson, R.M.A., & Newton-John, T.R.O. (2002). The influence of self-deception and impression management on surgeons' self-assessment scores. *Medical Education, 36,* 1084–1110.

Evans, C.J., Kirby, J.R., & Fabrigar, L.R. (2003). Approaches to learning, need for cognition, and strategic flexibility among university students. *British Journal of Educational Psychology, 73,* 507–528.

Evans, G.W., Palsane, M.N., & Carrere, S. (1987). Type A behavior and occupational stress: A cross-cultural study of blue-collar workers. *Journal of Personality and Social Psychology, 52,* 1002–1007.

Everson, S.A., Goldberg, D.E., & Kaplan, G.A. (1996). Hopelessness and risk of mortality and incidence of myocardial infarction and cancer. *Psychosomatic Medicine, 58,* 113–121.

Exner, J.E. (1991). *The Rorschach: A comprehensive system. Vol. 2 Interpretation* (2nd ed.). New York: John Wiley & Sons Inc..

Eysenck, H.J. (1947). *Dimensions of personality.* London: Routledge & Kegan Paul.

Eysenck, H.J. (1957). *The dynamics of anxiety and hysteria: An experimental application of modern learning theory to psychiatry.* London: Routledge & Kegan Paul.

Eysenck, H.J. (1959). *Uses and abuses of psychology.* Harmondworth, England: Penguin Books.

Eysenck, H.J. (1967). *The biological basis of personality.* Springfield, IL: Charles C. Thomas.

Eysenck, H.J. (1970). *The structure of human personality* (3rd ed.). London: Methuen.

Eysenck, H.J. (1977). *Crime and personality* (3rd ed., rev.). London: Routledge & Kegan.

Eysenck, H.J. (1992). Four ways five factors are not basic. *Personality and Individual Differences, 13,* 667–673.

Eysenck, H.J. (1993). Creativity and personality: Suggestions for a theory. *Psychological Inquiry, 4,* 147–178.

Eysenck, H.J., & Cookson, D. (1969). Personality in primary school-children: I. Ability and achievement. *British Journal of Educational Psychology, 39,* 109–122.

Eysenck, H.J., & Eysenck, M.W. (1985). *Personality and individual differences: A natural science approach.* New York: Plenum.

Eysenck, H.J., & Eysenck, S.B.G. (1969). *Personality structure and measurement.* San Diego, CA: Knapp.

Eysenck, H.J., & Wakefield, J.A. (1981). Psychological factors as predictors of marital satisfaction. *Advances in Behavior Research and Therapy, 3,* 151–192.

Eysenck, M.W., & Eysenck, M.C. (1979). Memory scanning, introversion-extraversion, and levels of processing. *Journal of Research in Personality, 13,* 305–315.

Eysenck, S.B.G., & Eysenck, H.J. (1968). The measurement of psychoticism: A study of factor stability and reliability. *British Journal of Social and Clinical Psychology, 7,* 286–294.

Falbo, T. & Polit, D. (1986). Quantitative review of the only child literature: Research evidence and theory development. *Psychological Bulletin, 100,* 176–189.

Falbo, T., & Poston, D.L. (1993). The academic, personality, and physical outcomes of only children in China. *Child Development, 64,* 18–35.

Fancher, R.E. (1990). *Pioneers of psychology* (2nd ed.). London: Norton.

Farber, M.L. (1953). Time-perspective and feeling-tone: A study in the perception of the days. *The Journal of Psychology, 35,* 253–257.

Fehr, B., Samson, D., & Paulhus, D.L. (1992). The construct of Machiavellianism: 20 years later. In C.D. Spielberger & J.N. Butcher (Eds.), *Advances in personality assessment* (Vol. 9, pp. 77–116). Hillsdale, NJ: Erlbaum.

Fekken, G.C., & Holden, R.R. (1992). Response latency evidence for viewing personality traits as schema indicators. *Journal of Research in Personality, 26,* 103–120.

Fekken, G.C., Holden, R.R., Jackson, D.N., & Guthrie, G.M. (1987). An evaluation of the validity of the Personality Research Form with Filipino university students. *International Journal of Psychology, 22,* 399–407.

Feldman, C.M. (1997). Childhood precursors of adult interpartner violence. *Clinical Psychology: Science and Practice, 4,* 307–334.

Feldman, O., & Valenty, L.O. (2001). *Profiling political leaders: Cross-cultural studies of personality and behavior.* Westport, CT: Praeger.

Feldman, P.J., et al. (1999). The impact of personality on the reporting of unfounded symptoms and illnesses. *Journal of Personality and Social Psychology, 77,* 370–378.

Feldman, R., Greenbaum, C.W., Mayes, L.C., & Erlich, S.H. (1997). Change in mother-infant interactive behavior: Relations to change in the mother, the infant, and the social context. *Infant Behaviour and Development, 20,* 151–163.

Felson, R.B. (1989). Parents and the reflected appraisal process: A longitudinal analysis. *Journal of Personality and Social Psychology, 56,* 965–971.

Felson, R.B. (1993). The (somewhat) social self: How others affect self-appraisals. In J. Suls (Ed.), *Psychological perspectives on the self* (Vol. 4, pp. 1–26). Hillsdale, NJ: Erlbaum.

Felton, B.J., & Revenson, T.A. (1984). Coping with chronic illness: A study of illness controllability and the influence of coping strategies on psychological adjustment. *Journal of Consulting and Clinical Psychology, 12,* 343–353.

Fenigstein, A., Scheier, M.F., & Buss, A.H. (1975). Public and private self-consciousness: Assessment and theory. *Journal of Consulting and Clinical Psychology, 43,* 522–527.

Ferrari, J.R. (1991). Self-handicapping by procrastinators: Protecting self-esteem, social-esteem, or both? *Journal of Research in Personality, 25,* 245–261.

Festinger, L. (1954). A theory of social comparison processes. *Human Relations, 7,* 114–140.

Fincham, F.D. (2001). Attributions and close relationships: From balkanization to integration. In G.J. Fletcher & M. Clark (Eds.), *Blackwell handbook of social psychology* (pp. 3–31). Oxford: Blackwell.

Fisher, J.D., & Misovich, S.J. (1990). Evolution of college students' AIDS-related behavioral responses, attitudes, knowledge, and fear. *AIDS Education and Prevention: An Interdisciplinary Journal, 2,* 322–337.

Fiske, D.W. (1973). Can a personality construct be empirically validated? *Psychological Bulletin, 80,* 89–92.

Fitzgerald, T.E., Tennen, H., Affleck, G., & Pranksy, G.S. (1993). The relative importance of dispositional optimism and control appraisals in quality of life after coronary artery bypass surgery. *Journal of Behavioral Medicine, 16,* 25–43.

Fletcher, G.J.O., Danilovics, P., Fernandez, G., Peterson, D., & Reeder, G.D. (1986). Attributional complexity: An individual differences measure. *Journal of Personality and Social Psychology,* 51, 875–884.

Flett, G.L., Besser, A., & Hewitt, P.L. (2005). Perfectionism, ego defense styles, and depression: A comparison of self-reports versus informant ratings. *Journal of Personality, 73,* 1355–1396.

Flett, G. L., Blankstein, K. R., & Hewitt, P. L. (1991). Factor structure of the Short Index of Self-Actualization. *Journal of Social Behavior and Personality, 6,* 321-329.

Flett, G.L., Blankstein, K.R., & Martin, T.R. (1995). Procrastination, negative self-judgments, and stress in depression and anxiety: A review and preliminary model. In J.R. Ferrari, J.L. Johnson, & W.G. McCown (Eds.), *Procrastination and task avoidance: Theory, research, and treatment* (pp. 137–167). New York: Plenum.

Flett, G.L., Endler, N.S., & Fairlie, P. (1999). The interactional model of anxiety and the threat of Quebec's separation from Canada. *Journal of Personality and Social Psychology, 76,* 58–65.

Flett, G.L., & Hewitt, P.L. (2002). Perfectionism and maladjustment: Theoretical, definitional, and treatment issues. In G.L. Flett & P.L. Hewitt (Eds.), *Perfectionism: Theory, research, and treatment* (pp. 5–31). Washington, DC: American Psychological Association Press.

Flett, G.L., Hewitt, P.L., Blankstein, K.R., & Gray, L. (1998). Psychological distress and the frequency of perfectionistic thinking. *Journal of Personality and Social Psychology, 75,* 1363–1381.

Flett, G.L., Hewitt, P.L., Endler, N.S., & Bagby, R.M. (1995). Conceptualization and assessment of personality factors in depression. *European Journal of Personality, 9,* 309–350.

Flett, G.L., Vredenburg, K., & Krames, L. (1995). The stability of depressive symptoms in college students: An empirical demonstration of regression to the mean. *Journal of Psychopathology and Behavioral Assessment, 17,* 403–415.

Flett, G.L., Vredenburg, K., & Krames, L. (1997). The continuity of depression in clinical and nonclinical samples. *Psychological Bulletin, 121,* 395–416.

Flett, G.L., Vredenburg, K., Pliner, P., & Krames, L. (1985). Sex roles and depression: A preliminary investigation of the direction of causality. *Journal of Research in Personality, 19,* 429–435.

Folkman, S., & Lazarus, R.S. (1980). An analysis of coping in a middle-aged community sample. *Journal of Health and Social Behavior, 21,* 219–239.

Fontaine, K.R., Manstead, A.S.R., & Wagner, H. (1993). Optimism, perceived control over stress, and coping. *European Journal of Personality, 7,* 267–281.

Forgays, D.G. (1989). Behavioral and physiological responses of stayers and quitters in underwater isolation. *Aviation Space and Environmental Medicine, 60,* 937–942.

Forrest, R. (1977). Personality and delinquency: A multivariate examination of Eysenck's theory with Scottish delinquent and non-delinquent boys. *Social Behavior and Personality, 5,* 157–167.

Forston, M.T., & Stanton, A.L. (1992). Self-discrepancy theory as a framework for understanding bulimic symptomatology and associated distress. *Journal of Social and Clinical Psychology, 11,* 103–118.

Forsythe, C.J., & Compas, B.E. (1987). Interaction of cognitive appraisals of stressful events and coping: Testing the goodness of fit hypothesis. *Cognitive Therapy and Research, 11,* 473–485.

Foster, M.D., & Dion, K.L. (2003). Dispositional hardiness and women's well-being relating to gender discrimination: The role of minimization. *Psychology of Women Quarterly, 27,* 197–208.

Fox, M.J. (2002). *Lucky man: A memoir.* New York: Hyperion.

Fox, N.A., et al. (2001). Continuity and discontinuity of behavioral inhibition and exuberance: Psychophysiological and behavioral influences across the first four years of life. *Child Development, 72,* 1–21.

Fraley, R.C. (2002). Attachment stability from infancy to adulthood: Meta-analysis and dynamic modeling of developmental mechanisms. *Personality and Social Psychology Review, 6,* 123–151.

Fraley, R.C. (2007). Using the Internet for personality research: What can be done; how to do it, and some concerns. In R.W. Robins, R.C. Fraley, & R.F. Krueger (Eds.), *Handbook of research methods in personality psychology.* New York: Guilford.

Fraley, R.C., Fazzari, D.A., Bonanno, G.A., & Dekel, S. (2006). Attachment and psychological adaptation in high exposure World Trade Center survivors. *Personality and Social Psychology Bulletin, 32,* 538–551.

Fraley, R.C., & Roberts, B.W. (2005). Patterns of continuity: A dynamic model for conceptualizing the stability of individual differences in psychological constructs across the lifespan. *Psychological Review, 112,* 60–74.

Fraley, R.C., & Shaver, P.R. (2000). Adult romantic attachment: Theoretical developments, emerging controversies, and unanswered questions. *Review of General Psychology, 4,* 132–154.

Fraley, R.C., & Spieker, S.J. (2003). Are infant attachment patterns continuously or categorically distributed? A taxometric analysis of strange situation behavior. *Developmental Psychology, 39,* 387–404.

Fraley, R.C., & Waller, N.G. (1998). Adult attachment patterns: A test of the typological model. In J.A. Simpson & W.S. Rholes (Eds.), *Attachment theory and close relationships* (pp. 77–114). New York: Guilford Press.

Fransella, F. (2003). *International handbook*

of personal construct psychology. London: John Wiley & Sons.

Fransella, F., & Neimeyer, R.A. (2005). George Alexander Kelly: The man and his theory. In F. Fransella (Ed.), *The essential practitioner's handbook of personal construct psychology* (pp. 1–13). London: John Wiley & Sons.

Franz, C.E. (1995). A quantitative case study of longitudinal changes in identity, intimacy, and generativity. *Journal of Personality, 63*, 27–46.

Freese, J., Powell, B., & Steelman, L.C. (1999). Rebel without a cause or effect: Birth order and social attitudes. *American Sociological Review, 64*, 207–231.

Freud, A. (1946). *The ego and mechanisms of defense*. New York: International Universities Press.

Freud, A. (1966). *The ego and the mechanisms of defense*. New York: International Universities Press.

Freud, S. (1910). Leonardo da Vinci and a memory of his childhood. In S. Freud (1985) *The Penguin Freud Library Vol. 14 Art and Literature* (pp. 143–232). London: Penguin.

Freud, S. (1917). Mourning and melancholia. In *Collected papers* (Vol. 4). London: Hogarth and the Institute of Psychoanalysis, 1950.

Freud, S. (1930). *Civilization and its discontents*. New York: Norton.

Friedman, H.S. et al. (1995). Childhood conscientiousness and longevity: Health behaviors and cause of death. *Journal of Personality and Social Psychology, 68*, 696–703.

Friedman, H.S. et al. (1993). Does childhood personality predict longevity? *Journal of Personality and Social Psychology, 65*, 176–185.

Friedman, M., & Rosenman, R.H. (1959). Association of specific overt behavior pattern with blood and cardiovascular findings. *Journal of the American Medical Association, 169*, 1286–1296.

Friedman, S., & Rosenman, R.H. (1957). Comparison of fat intake of American men and women: Possible relationship to incidence of clinical coronary artery disease. *Circulation, 16*, 339–347.

Frost, R.O., Marten, P.A., Lahart, C., & Rosenblate, R. (1990). The dimensions of perfectionism. *Cognitive Therapy and Research, 14*, 449–468.

Fry, P.S., & Ghosh, R. (1980). Attributions of success and failure: Comparison of cultural differences between Asian and Caucasian children. *Journal of Cross-Cultural Psychology, 11*, 343–363.

Funder, D.C. (1980). On seeing ourselves as others see us: Self-other agreement and discrepancy in personality ratings. *Journal of Personality, 48*, 473–493.

Funder, D.C., Kolar, D.W., & Blackman, M.C. (1995). Agreement among judges of personality: Interpersonal relations, similarity, and acquaintanceship. *Journal of Personality and Social Psychology, 69*, 656–672.

Funder, D.C., & Ozer, D.J. (1983). Behavior as a function of the situation. *Journal of Personality and Social Psychology, 44*, 107–112.

Funk, S.C. (1992). Hardiness: A review of theory and research. *Health Psychology, 11*, 335–345.

Funke, F. (2005). The dimensionality of right-wing authoritarianism: Lessons from the dilemma between theory and measurement. *Political Psychology, 26*, 195–218.

Gable, S.L., Reis, H.T., & Downey, G. (2003). He said, she said: A quasi-signal detection analysis of spouses' perceptions of everyday interactions. *Psychological Science, 14*, 100–105.

Gaines, B.R., & Shaw, M.L.G. (2003). Personal construct psychology and the cognitive revolution. In J.D. Raskin & S.K. Bridges (Eds.), *Studies in meaning* New York: Pace University Press.

Gallagher, D.J. (1990). Extraversion, neuroticism, and appraisal of stressful academic events. *Personality and Individual Differences, 11*, 1053–1057.

Gallo, L.C., & Matthews, K.A. (2003). Understanding the association between socioeconomic status and physical health: Do negative emotions play a role? *Psychological Bulletin, 129*, 10–51.

Gallo, L.C., Smith, T.W., & Cox, C. (2006). Socioeconomic status, psychosocial processes, and perceived health: An interpersonal perspective. *Annals of Behavioral Medicine, 31*, 109–119.

Gallo, L.C., Smith, T.W., & Ruiz, J. (2003). An interpersonal analysis of adult attachment style: Circumplex descriptions, recalled developmental experiences, self-representations, and interpersonal functioning in adulthood. *Journal of Personality, 71*, 141–181.

Gangestad, M., & Snyder, M. (1985). To carve nature at its joints: On the existence of discrete classes in personality. *Psychological Review, 33*, 317–348.

Garcia-Coll, C., Kagan, J., & Reznick, J.S. (1984). Behavioral inhibition in young children. *Child Development, 55*, 1005–1019.

Gauvin, M., & Fagot, B. (1995). Child temperament as a mediator of mother-toddler problem solving. *Social Development, 4*, 257–276.

Geberth, V.J. (1986). Mass, serial, and sensational homicides: The investigative perspective. *Bulletin of the New York Academy of Medicine, 62*, 492–496.

Geberth, V. (1996). *Practical homicide investigation*. Boca Raton, FL: CRC Press.

Gebhardt, W.A., & Brosschot, J.F. (2002). Desirability of control: Psychometric properties and relationships with locus of control, personality, coping, mental and somatic complaints in three Dutch samples. *European Journal of Personality, 16*, 423–438.

George, C., Kaplan, N., & Main, M. (1985). The Adult Attachment Interview. Unpublished manuscript, University of California at Berkeley.

Geraerts, E., Merckelbach, H., Jelicic, M., & Smeets, E. (in press). Long term consequences of suppression of intrusive anxious thoughts and repressive coping. *Behaviour Research and Therapy*.

Gergen, K.J. (l965). Interactions goals and personalistic feedback as factors affecting the presentations of self. *Journal of Personality and Social Psychology, 1*, 413–424.

Gibb, B.E., Alloy, L.B., & Abramson, L.Y. (2003). Global reports of childhood maltreatment versus recall of specific maltreatment experiences: Relationships with dysfunctional attitudes and depressive symptoms. *Cognition and Emotion, 17*, 903–915.

Gibb, B.E., Lin Zhu, B.E., Alloy, L.B., & Abramson, L.Y. (2002). Attributional styles and academic achievement in university students: A longitudinal investigation. *Cognitive Therapy and Research, 26*, 309–316.

Gifford, R., & O'Connor, B. (1987). The interpersonal circumplex as a behavioral map. *Journal of Personality and Social Psychology, 52*, 1019–1026.

Gilbert, P., & Reynolds, S. (1990). The relationship between the Eysenck Personality Questionnaire and Beck's concepts of sociotropy and autonomy. *British Journal of Clinical Psychology, 29*, 319–325.

Gjerde, P.F., Block, J. & Block, J.H. (1988). Depressive symptoms and personality during late adolescence: Gender differences in the externalization-internalization of symptom expression. *Journal of Abnormal Psychology, 97*, 475–486.

Glad, B. (2005). Psychobiography in context: Predicting the behavior of tyrants. In W.T. Schultz (Ed.), *Handbook of psychobiography* (pp. 357–368). New York: Oxford University Press.

Gliksman, L., Adlaf, E., Demers, A., & Newton-Taylor, B. (2003). Heavy drinking on Canadian campuses. *Canadian Journal of Public Health, 94*, 17–21.

Gliksman, L., Demers, A., Adlaf, E., Newton-Taylor, B., & Schmidt, K. (2000). *Canadian Campus Survey 1998*. Toronto: Centre For Addiction and Mental Health.

Goffman, E. (1959). *The presentation of self in everyday life*. New York: Anchor.

Goldberg, L.R. (1981). Developing a taxonomy of trait-descriptive terms. In D.W. Fiske (Ed.), *Problems with language imprecision: New directions for methodology of social and behavioral science, No. 9* (pp. 43–65). San Francisco: Jossey-Bass.

Goldberg, L.R. (1992). The development of markers for the Big-Five factor structure. *Psychological Assessment, 4*, 26–42.

Goldberg, L.R. (1993). The structure of

phenotypic personality traits. *American Psychologist, 48*, 26–34.

Goldsmith, H.H., et al. (1987). What is temperament? Four approaches. *Child Development, 58*, 505–529.

Gomez, R., & Gomez, A. (2005). Convergent, discriminant, and concurrent validities of measures of the behavioral approach and behavioral inhibition systems: Confirmatory factor analytic approach. *Personality and Individual Differences, 38*, 87–102.

Goodwin, J.F. (2005). *Research in psychology: Method and design*. New York: John Wiley & Sons Inc.

Gosling, S.D., Vazire, S., Srivastava, S., & John, O.P. (2004). Should we trust web-based studies? A comparative analysis of six preconceptions about Internet questionnaires. *American Psychologist, 59*, 93–104.

Gottman, J.M. (1982). Emotional responsiveness in marital conversations. *Journal of Communication, 32*, 108–120.

Gough, H.G., & Heilbrun, A.B. (1965). *The Adjective Checklist Manual*. Palo Alto, CA: Consulting Psychologists Press.

Gramzow, R., Sedikides, C., Panter, A.T., Sathy, V., Harris, J., & Insko, C.A. (2004). Patterns of self-regulation and the Big Five. *European Journal of Personality, 18*, 367–386.

Grauer, N.A. (1999). Remembering Papa. *Cigar Aficionado*, July/August.

Gray, J.A. (1972). The psychophysiological basis of introversion-extraversion: A modification of Eysenck's theory. In V.D. Nebylitsyn & J.A. Gray (Eds.), *Biological bases of individual behavior* (pp. 182–205). New York: Academic.

Gray, J.A. (1981). A critique of Eysenck's theory of personality. In H.J. Eysenck (Ed.), *A model of personality* (pp. 246–276). Berlin: Springer.

Gray, J.A. (1982). *The neuropsychology of anxiety: An inquiry into the functions of the septo-hippocampal system*. New York: Oxford University Press.

Green, B. (2004). Personal construct psychology and content analysis. *Personal Construct Theory and Analysis, 1*, 82–91.

Greenberg, L., Elliot, R., & Lietaen, G. (1994). Research on experiential therapies. In A.E. Bergin & S.L. Garfield (Eds.), *Handbook of psychotherapy and behavioral change* (4th ed., pp. 505–539). New York: John Wiley & Sons Inc.

Greenberg, L.S., Elliot, R., Watson, J.C., & Bohart, A.C. (2001). Empathy. *Psychotherapy, 38*, 380–384.

Gretton, H., Hare, R.D., & Catchpole, R. (2004). Psychopathy and offending from adolescence to adulthood: A Ten-Year Follow-Up. *Journal of Consulting and Clinical Psychology, 72*, 636–645.

Griffin, D.W., & Bartholomew, K. (1994). The metaphysics of measurement: The case of adult attachment. *Advances in Personal Relationships, 5*, 17–52.

Griffith, R. (1997). *Faking of non-cognitive selection devices: Red herring is hard to swallow*. Unpublished doctoral dissertation, University of Akron, Akron, OH.

Grossman, K., Grossman, K.E., Spangler, G., Suess, G., & Unzner, L. (1985). Maternal sensitivity and newborns' orientation responses as related to quality of attachment in Northern Germany. *Monographs of the Society for Research in Child Development, 50*(1-2), 233–256.

Grossman, L.S., Wasyliw, O.E., Benn, A.F., & Gyoerkoe, K.L. (2002). Can sex offenders who minimize on the MMPI conceal psychopathology on the Rorschach? *Journal of Personality Assessment, 78*, 484–501.

Gudjonsson, G.H., Sigurdsson, J.F., Bragason, O.O., Einarsson, E., & Valdimarsdottir, E.B. (2004). Compliance and personality: The vulnerability of the unstable introvert. *European Journal of Personality, 18*, 435–444.

Guo, H. (2000). The 'Little Emperors' Grow Up: Psychology of only children. *Psychology Today*, 33, 10.

Gurtman, M.B. (1992). Construct validity of interpersonal personality measures: The interpersonal circumplex as a nomological net. *Journal of Personality and Social Psychology, 63*, 105–118.

Gurtman, M.B. (1992). Trust, distrust, and interpersonal problems: A circumplex analysis. *Journal of Personality and Social Psychology, 62*, 989–1002.

Hahn, D.W., Lee, K., & Ashton, M.C. (1999). A factor analysis of the most frequently used Korean personality trait adjectives. *European Journal of Personality, 13*, 261–282.

Halliwell, E. & Dittmar, H. (2006). Associations between appearance-related self-discrepancies and young women's and men's affect, body satisfaction, and emotional eating: a comparison of fixed-item and participant-generated self-discrepancies. *Personality and Social Psychology Bulletin, 32*, 447–458.

Halverson, C.F., et al. (2003). Personality structure as derived from parental ratings of free descriptions of children: The Inventory of Child Individual Differences. *Journal of Personality, 71*, 995–1018.

Hamachek, D.E. (1978). Psychodynamics of normal and neurotic perfectionism. *Psychology, 15*, 27–33.

Hamid, P.N., Lai, J.C.L., & Cheng, S.T. (2000). Response bias and public and private self-consciousness in Chinese. *Journal of Social Behavior and Personality, 15*, 431–440.

Hamilton, C.E. (2000). Continuity and discontinuity of attachment from infancy through adolescence. *Child Development, 71*, 690–694.

Hamstra, J.W. (2006). "Half of China may well have to die." *The Fletcher Forum of World Affairs, 30*, 229–233.

Handler, L. (2001). Assessment of Men: Personality assessment goes to war by the office of strategic services assessment staff. *Journal of Personality Assessment, 76*, 558–578.

Hanley, S.J., & Abell, S.C. (2002). Maslow and relatedness: Creating an interpersonal model of self-actualization. *Journal of Humanistic Psychology, 42*, 37–56.

Hardy, G.E., et al. (1999). Therapist responsiveness to client attachment styles and issues observed in client-identified significant events in psychodynamic-interpersonal psychotherapy. *Psychotherapy Research, 9*, 36–53.

Hare, R.D. (1998). The Hare PCL-R: Some issues concerning its use and misuse. *Legal and Criminological Psychology, 3*, 101–122.

Hare, R.D. (1991). *The Hare Psychopathy Checklist-Revised*. Toronto: Multi-Health Systems.

Hare, R.D., Clark, D., Grann, M., & Thornton, D. (2000). Psychopathy and the predictive utility of the PCL-R: An international perspective. *Behavioral Sciences and the Law, 18*, 623–645.

Haring, M., Hewitt, P.L., & Flett, G.L. (2003). Perfectionism, coping, and quality of intimate relationships. *Journal of Marriage and the Family, 65*, 143–158.

Harkness, A.R., McNulty, J.L., & Ben-Porath, Y.S. (1995). The Personality Psychpathology Five (PSY-5): Constructs and MMPI-2 scales. *Psychological Assessment, 7*, 104–114.

Harmon-Jones, E., & Allen, J.B. (1997). Behavioral activation and resting frontal EEG asymmetry: Covariation of putative indicators related to risk for mood disorders. *Journal of Abnormal Psychology, 106*, 159–163.

Harris, J.R. (1998). *The nurture assumption: Why children turn out the way they do*. London: The Free Press.

Harris, R.N., & Snyder, C.R. (1986). The role of uncertain self-esteem in self-handicapping. *Journal of Personality and Social Psychology, 51*, 451–458.

Harrist, K.A., Zaia, A.F., Bates, J.E., Dodge, K.A., & Pettit, G.S. (1997). Subtypes of social withdrawal in early childhood: Sociometric status and social-cognitive differences across four years. *Child Development, 68*, 332–348.

Hart, D., Atkins, R., & Fegley, S. (2003). Personality and development in childhood: A person-centered approach. *Monographs of the Society for Research in Child Development, 68*(1, Serial No. 272).

Harter, S. (1985). *The Self-Perception Profile for Children: Revision of the Perceived Competence Scale for Children: Manual*. University of Denver.

Harter, S., & Pike, R. (1984). The Pictorial Scale of Perceived Competence and Social Acceptance for Young Children. *Child Development, 55*, 1969–1982.

Harter, S.L., Erbes, C.R., & Hart, C.C. (2004). Content analysis of the personal constructs of female sexual abuse survivors elecited through Repertory Grid technique. *Journal of Constructivist Psychology*, *17*, 27–43.

Hartley, M., & Commire, A., (1990). *Breaking the Silence*, New York: G. P. Putnam's Sons.

Harvey, J.H., & Katz, C. (1985). *If I'm so successful why do I feel like a fake? The impostor phenomenon*. New York: St. Martin's Press.

Hassenzahl, M., & Trautman, T. (2001). Analysis of websites with the Repertory Grid Technique. *CHI 2001 Conference Proceedings on Human Factors in Computing Systems*, 167–168.

Hattie, J.A., & Marsh, H.W. (1996). Future research in self-concepts. In B. Bracken (Ed.), *Handbook on self-concept* (pp. 421–462). Hillsdale, NJ: Erlbaum.

Hawley, P.H. (2003). Prosocial and coercive configurations of resource control in early adolescence: A case for the well-adapted Machiavellian. *Merrill-Palmer Quarterly*, *49*, 279–309.

Hayhurst, J. (1997). *The right mountain: Lessons from Everest on the real meaning of success*. Toronto: John Wiley & Sons Canada, Ltd.

Haynes, S.N., & Lench, H.C. (2003). Incremental validity of new clinical assessment measures. *Psychological Assessment*, *15*, 456–466.

Hazan, C., & Shaver, P.R. (1987). Romantic love conceptualized as an attachment process. *Journal of Personality and Social Psychology*, *52*, 511–524.

Hazelwood, R.R., Ressler, R.K., Depue, R.L., & Douglas, J.E. (1995). Criminal investigative analysis: An overview. In R.R. Hazelwood & A.W. Burgess (Eds.), *Practical aspects of rape investigation: A multidisciplinary approach* (2nd ed.). Boca Raton, FL: CRC Press.

Heatherton, T.F., & Polivy, J. (1991). Development and validation of a scale for measuring state self-esteem. *Journal of Personality and Social Psychology*, *60*, 895–910.

Heft, L., et al. (1988). Emotional and temperamental correlates of Type A in children and adolescents. *Journal of Youth and Adolescence*, *17*, 461–475.

Heine, S.J., Lehman, D.R., Markus, H.R., & Kitayama, S. (1999). Is there a universal need for positive self-regard? *Psychological Review*, *106*, 766–794.

Heine, S.J., & Norenzayan, A. (2006). Toward a psychological science for a cultural species. *Psychological Science*, *1*, 251–269.

Heine, S.J., Takata, T., & Lehman, D.R. (2000). Beyond self-presentation: Evidence for Japanese self-criticism. *Personality and Social Psychology Bulletin*, *26*, 71–s78.

Helgeson, V.S., & Fritz, H.L. (1999). Unmitigated agency and unmitigated communion: Distinctions from agency and communion. *Journal of Research in Personality*, *33*, 131–158.

Helgeson, V.S., & Fritz, H.L. (2000). The implications of unmitigated agency and unmitigated communion for domains of problem behavior. *Journal of Personality*, *68*, 1031–1057.

Helmes, E., & Holden, R.R. (2003). The construct of social desirability: One or two dimensions? *Personality and Individual Differences*, *34*, 1015–1023.

Helmreich, R.L. (2001). Culture and error in space: Implications for analog environments. *Aviation, Space and Environmental Medicine*, *71*, 133–139.

Hemenover, S. H. (2001). Self-reported processing bias and naturally occurring mood: Mediators between personality and stress appraisals. *Personality and Social Psychology Bulletin*, *27*, 387–394.

Hemphill, J.F. (2003). Interpreting the magnitudes of correlation coefficients. *American Psychologist*, *58*, 78–80.

Hendriks, A.A.J., Hofstee, W.K.B., & De Raad, B. (1999). *The Five-Factor Personality Inventory (FFPI), Professional Manual*. Lisse: Swets Test Publishers.

Hendriks, A.A.J., et al. (2003). The five-factor personality inventory: Cross-cultural generalizability across 13 countries. *European Journal of Personality*, *17*, 347–373.

Herrera, N.C., Zajonc, R.B., Wieczorkowska, G., & Cichomski, B. (2003). Beliefs about birth order and their reflections in reality. *Journal of Personality and Social Psychology*, *85*, 142–150.

Hewitt, P.L., & Flett, G.L. (1991). Perfectionism in the self and social contexts: Conceptualization, assessment, and association with psychopathology. *Journal of Personality and Social Psychology*, *60*, 456–470.

Hewitt, P.L., & Flett, G.L. (1993). Dimensions of perfectionism, daily stress, and depression: A test of the specific vulnerability hypothesis. *Journal of Abnormal Psychology*, *102*, 58–65.

Hewitt, P.L., & Flett, G.L. (1996). Personality traits and the coping process. In M. Zeidner & N.S. Endler (Eds.), *Handbook of coping* (pp. 410–433). London: John Wiley & Sons Inc.

Hewitt, P.L., & Flett, G.L. (2002). Perfectionism and stress in psychopathology. In G.L. Flett & P.L. Hewitt (Eds.), *Perfectionism: Theory, research, and treatment* (pp. 255–284). Washington, DC: American Psychological Association Press.

Hewitt, P.L., Flett, G.L., Ediger, E., Norton, G.R., & Flynn, C. (1998). Dimensions of perfectionism and chronic symptoms of unipolar and bipolar depression. *Canadian Journal of Behavioural Science*, *30*, 234–242.

Hewitt, P.L., Flett, G.L., & Mikail, S. (1995). Perfectionism and family adjustment in pain patients and their spouses. *Journal of Family Psychology*, *9*, 335–347.

Heylighen, F. (1992). A cognitive-systemic reconstruction of Maslow's theory of self-actualization. *Behavioral Science*, *37*, 39–58.

Hicks, S.J., & Sales, B.D. (2006). *Criminal profiling: Developing an effective science and practice*. Washington, DC: American Psychological Association.

Higgins, E.T. (1987). Self-discrepancy: A theory relating self and affect. *Psychological Review*, *94*, 319–340.

Higgins, E.T., Bond, R.N., Klein, R. and Strauman, T. (1986). Self-discrepancies and emotional vulnerability: How magnitude, accessibility, and type of discrepancy influence affect. *Journal of Personality and Social Psychology*, *351*, 5–15.

Hill, C.A. (1987). Affiliation motivation: people who need people... but in different ways. *Journal of Personality and Social Psychology*, *52*, 1008–1018.

Hill, C.A. (1991). Seeking emotional support: the influence of affiliative need and partner warmth. *Journal of Personality and Social Psychology*, *60*, 112–121.

Hill, R.W., Zrull, M.C. & Turlington, S. (1997). Perfectionism and interpersonal problems. *Journal of Personality Assessment*, *69*, 81–103.

Hirschfeld, R.M.A., & Cross, C.K. (1987). The measurement of personality in depression. In A.J. Marsella, R.M.A. Hirschfeld, & M.M. Katz (Eds.), *The measurement of depression* (pp. 319–343). New York: Guilford.

Hirt, E.R., McCrea, S.M., & Boris, H.I. (2003). "I know you self-handicapped last exam": Gender differences in reactions to self-handicapping. *Journal of Personality and Social Psychology*, *84*, 177–193.

Hofstede, G. (1980). *Culture's consequences*. Beverly Hills, CA: Sage.

Hoffman, E. (1992, January-February). The last interview of Abraham Maslow—conducted in 1968. *Psychology Today*, *25*, 68–69.

Hogan, R., Hogan, J., & Roberts, B. (1996). Personality measurement and employment decisions: Questions and answers. *American Psychologist*, *51*, 469–477.

Holden, R.R. (1998). Detecting fakers on a personnel test: Response latencies versus a standard validity scale. *Journal of Social Behavior and Personality*, *13*, 387–398.

Holden, R.R., & Hibbs, N. (1995). Incremental validity of response latencies for detecting fakers on a personality test. *Journal of Research in Personality*, *29*, 362–372.

Holden, R.R., & Kroner, D.G. (1992). The relative efficacy of differential response latencies for detecting faking on a self-report measure of psychopathology. *Psychological Assessment*, *4*, 170–173.

Holloway, S.D., & Behrens, K.Y. (2002). Parenting self-efficacy among Japanese mothers: Qualitative and quantitative perspectives on its associations with childhood memories of family relations. *New Directions for Child and Adolescent Development*, *96*, 27–43.

Hollon, S.D., & Kendall, P.C. (1980). Cognitive self-statements in depression: Development of an automatic thoughts questionnaire. *Cognitive Therapy and Research, 4,* 383–395.

Holroyd, K.A., & Coyne, J.C. (1987). Personality and health in the 1980s: Psychosomatic medicine revisited? *Journal of Personality, 55,* 359–375.

Holtgraves, T. (2004). Social desirability and self-reports: Testing models of socially desirable responding. *Personality and Social Psychology Bulletin, 30,* 161–172.

Holtzworth-Munroe, A., & Stuart, G. L. (1994). Typologies of male batterers: Three subtypes and the differences among them. *Psychological Bulletin, 116,* 476–497.

Holtzworth-Munroe, A., Stuart, G.L, & Hutchinson, G. (1997). Violent versus nonviolent husbands: Differences in attachment patterns, dependency, and jealousy. *Journal of Family Psychology, 11,* 314–331.

Hori, S., et al. (2000). Psychosocial factors regulating natural killer-cell activity in recurrent spontaneous abortions. *American Journal of Reproductive Immunology, 44,* 299–302.

Horney, K. (1937). *The neurotic personality of our time.* New York: Norton.

Horney, K. (1945). *Our inner conflicts: a constructive theory of neurosis.* New York: Norton.

Horney, K. (1950). *Neurosis and human growth: The struggle toward self-realization.* New York: Norton.

Horowitz, L.M., Rosenberg, S.E., Baer, B.A., Ureno, G., & Villasenor, V.S. (1988). Inventory of Interpersonal Problems: Psychometric properties and clinical applications. *Journal of Consulting and Clinical Psychology, 56,* 885–892.

Horvath, A.O. (2000). The therapeutic relationship: From transference to alliance. *Journal of Clinical Psychology, 56,* 163–173.

Hosaka, T., &Tagawa, R. (1987). The Japanese characteristic of Type A behavior pattern. *Tokai Journal of Experimental, Clinical, and Medicine, 12,* 287–303.

Hough, L.M., & Oswald, F.L. (2000). Personnel selection: Looking toward the future—remembering the past. *Annual Review of Psychology, 51,* 631–664.

Howarth, E., & Eysenck, H.J. (1968). Extraversion, arousal, and paired associate results. *Journal of Experimental Research in Personality, 3,* 114–116.

Howe, M.J.A. (1997). Beyond psychobiography: Towards more effective syntheses of psychology and biography. *British Journal of Psychology, 88,* 235–248.

Howell, S. H. (2004). Students' perceptions of Jesus' personality as assessed by Jungian-type inventories. *Journal of Psychology and Theology, 32,* 50–58.

Hoyle, R.H., Fejfar, M.C., & Miller, J.D. (2000). Personality and sexual risk-taking: A quantitative review. *Journal of Personality, 68,* 1203–1231.

Hull, J.G. (1987). Self-awareness model. In H.T. Blane & K.E. Leonard (Eds.), *Psychological theories of drinking and alcoholism* (pp. 272–304). New York: Guilford.

Hull, J.G., Jouriles, E., & Young, R.D. (1986). Applications of the self-awareness model of alcohol consumption: Predicting patterns of use and abuse. *Journal of Personality and Social Psychology, 51,* 790–796.

Hull, J.G., Van Treuren, R.R., & Virnelli, S. (1987). Hardiness and health: A critique and alternative approach. *Journal of Personality and Social Psychology, 53,* 518–530.

Hull, J.G., & Young, R.D. (1983). Self-consciousness, self-esteem, and success-failure as determinants of alcohol consumption in male social drinkers. *Journal of Personality and Social Psychology, 44,* 1097–1109.

Hunsley, J., & Bailey, J.M. (1999). The clinical utility of the Rorschach: Unfulfilled promises and an uncertain future. *Psychological Assessment, 11,* 266–277.

Hunsley, J., & Lee, C.M. (2006). *Introduction to clinical psychology.* Toronto: John Wiley & Sons Canada, Ltd.

Hyde, J.S. (2005). The gender similarities hypothesis. *American Psychologist, 60,* 581–592.

Hyde, J.S., Else-Quest, N.M., Goldsmith, H.H., & Biesanz, J.C. (2004). Children's temperament and behavior problems predict their employed mothers' work functioning. *Child Development, 75,* 580–594.

Ikuta, N., et al. (1994). Comparison of American and Japanese outpatients with borderline personality disorder. *Comprehensive Psychiatry, 35,* 382–385.

Ingledew, D.K., & Brunning, S. (1999). Personality, preventive health behaviour and comparative optimism about health problems. *Journal of Health Psychology, 4,* 193–208.

Ingraham, L.J., & Wright, T.L. (1987). A social relations model test of Sullivan's anxiety hypothesis. *Journal of Personality and Social Psychology, 52,* 1212–1218.

Inkeles, A., & Levinson, D.J. (1954). National character: The study of modal personality and sociocultural systems. In G. Lindzey (Ed.), *Handbook of social psychology: Vol. II Special fields and applications* (pp. 977–1020). London: Addison-Wesley.

Irronson, G., et al. (2005). Dispositional optimism and the mechanisms by which it predicts slower disease progression in HIV: Proactive behavior, avoidant coping, and depression. *International Journal of Behavioral Medicine, 12,* 86–97.

Jackson, D.N. (1970). A sequential system for personality scale development. In C.D. Spielberger (Ed.), *Current topics in clinical and community psychology* (pp. 61–96). New York: Academic Press.

Jackson, D.N. (1971). The dynamics of structured personality tests. *Psychological Review, 78,* 229–248.

Jackson, D.N. (1974). *Personality Research Form Manual.* Goshen, NY: Research Psychologists Press.

Jackson, D.N., & Helmes, E. (1979). Personality structure and the circumplex. *Journal of Personality and Social Psychology, 37,* 2278–2285.

Jackson, D.N., Wroblewski, V.R., & Ashton, M.C. (2000). The impact of faking on employment tests: Does forced choice offer a solution? *Human Performance, 13,* 371–388.

Jackson, T., Weiss, K.E., Lundquist, J.J., & Sonderlind, A. (2002). Perceptions of goal-directed activities of optimists and pessimists: A personal projects analysis. *Journal of Psychology, 136,* 521–532.

Jamner, L.D., & Leigh, H. (1999). Repressive/defensive coping, endogenous opioids and health: How a life so perfect can make you sick. *Psychiatry Research, 85,* 17–31.

Jang, K.L., Livesley, W.J., & Vernon, P.A. (1996). Heritability of the big five personality dimensions and their facets: A twin study. *Journal of Personality, 64,* 577–591.

Jang, K.L., Livesley, W.J., & Vernon, P.A. (1999). The relationship between Eysenck's P-E-N model of personality and traits delineating personality disorder. *Personality and Individual Differences, 26,* 121–128.

Jankowicz, A.D. (1987). Whatever became of George Kelly? *American Psychologist, 42,* 481–487.

Jaques, E. (1955). The clinical use of the Thematic Apperception Test with soldiers. In D. C. McClelland, (Ed.), *Studies in motivation* (pp. 71-82). New York: Appleton-Century-Crofts Inc.

Jefferson, T.J., Herbst, J.H., & McCrae, R.R. (1998). Associations between birth order and personality traits: Evidence from self-reports and observer ratings. *Journal of Research in Personality, 32,* 498–509.

Jerusalem, M., & Schwarzer, R. (1992). Self-efficacy as a resource factor in stress appraisal processes. In R. Schwarzer (Ed.), *Self-efficacy: Thought control of action* (pp. 195–213). Washington, DC: Hemisphere.

Ji., L-J., Zhang, Z., Usborne, E., & Guan, Y. (2004). Optimism across cultures: In response to the severe acute respiratory syndrome outbreak. *Asian Journal of Social Psychology, 7,* 25–34.

Jiao, S., Ji, G.P., & Jing, Q.H. (1986). Comparative study of behavioral qualities of only children and sibling children. *Child Development, 57,* 357–361.

John, O.P., Caspi, A., Robins, R.W., Moffitt, T.E., & S-L, M. (1994). The "little five": Exploring the nomological network of the five-factor model of personality in adolescent boys. *Child Development, 65*, 160–178.

Johnson, E.A. (1995). Self-deceptive responses to threat: Adaptive only in ambiguous contexts. *Journal of Personality, 63*, 759–791.

Johnson, E.A., Vincent, N., & Ross, L. (1997). Self-deception versus self-esteem in buffering the negative effects of failure. *Journal of Research in Personality, 31*, 385–405.

Johnson, S.M. (2003). Introduction to attachment: A therapist's guide to primary relationships and their renewal. In S.M. Johnson & V. Whiffen (Eds.), *Attachment processes in couple and family therapy* (pp. 3–17). New York: Guilford.

Johnson, S.M., & Greenberg, L.S. (1995). The emotionally focused approach to problems in adult attachment. In N.S. Jacobson & A.S. Gurman (Eds.), *Clinical handbook of couples therapy* (pp. 121–141). New York: Guilford.

Johnson, T.P., & van de Vijver, F. (2003). Social desirability in cross-cultural surveys. In J. Harkness, F.J.R. van de Vijver, & P. Ph. Mohler (Eds.), *Cross-cultural survey methods* (pp. 195–204). New York: John Wiley & Sons Inc.

Jones, A., & Crandall, R. (1986). Validation of a short index of self-actualization. *Personality and Social Psychology Bulletin, 12*, 63–73.

Jones, J., (1992). *Let Me Take You Down: Inside the Mind of Mark David Chapman,the Man Who Killed John Lennon.* New York:Villard, a Division of Random House.

Jordan, C.H., Spencer, S.J., Zanna, M.P., Hoshino-Brown, E., & Correll, J. (2003). Secure and defensive high self-esteem. *Journal of Personality and Social Psychology, 85*, 969–978.

Jorgensen, M.M., & Zachariae, R. (2006). Repressive coping style and autonomic reactions to two experimental stressors in healthy men and women. *Scandinavian Journal of Psychology, 47*, 137–148.

Jorm, A.F., et al. (1999). Using the BIS/BAS scales to measure behavioral inhibition and behavioral activation: Factor structure, validity, and norms in a large community sample. *Personality and Individual Differences, 26*, 49–58.

Jovev, M., & Jackson, H.J. (2002). Early maladaptive schemas in personality disordered individuals. *Journal of Personality Disorders, 18*, 467–478.

Judge, T.A., Erez, A., Bono, J.E. & Thoreson, C.J. (2002). Are measures of self-esteem, neuroticism, locus of control, and generalized self-efficacy indicators of a common core construct? *Journal of Personality and Social Psychology, 83*, 693–710.

Jung, C.G. (with H.G. Baynes) (1921). *Psychological types*. London: Kegan Paul.

Jung, C.G. (1961). *Memories, dreams, reflections*. (R. & C. Winston, Trans.). New York: Pantheon Books.

Kabat-Zinn, J. (1994). *Wherever you go, there you are—Mindfulness meditation in everyday life*. New York: Hyperion.

Kagan, J. (1988). The meanings of personality predicates. *American Psychologist, 43*, 614–620.

Kagan, J., & Snidman, N. (1991). Infant predictors of inhibited and uninhibited profiles. *Psychological Science, 2*, 40–44.

Kalichman, S.C., Cain, D., Knetch, J., & Hill, J. (2005). Patterns of sexual risk behavior change among sexually transmitted infection clinic patients. *Archives of Sex Behaviour, 34*, 307–319.

Kalichman, S., et al. (1994). Sexual sensation seeking: Scale development and predicting AIDS-risk behaviour among homosexually active men. *Journal of Personality Assessment, 62*, 385–397.

Kalichman, S.C., Tannenbaum, L., & Nachimson, D. (1998). Personality and cognitive factors influencing substance use and sexual risk for HIV infection among gay and bisexual men. *Psychology of Addictive Behaviors, 12*, 262–271.

Kanagawa, C., Cross, S., & Markus, H. (2001). "Who am I?" The cultural psychology of the conceptual self. *Personality & Social Psychology Bulletin, 27*, 90–103.

Kao, E.M., Nagata, D.K., & Peterson, C. (1997). Explanatory style, family expressiveness, and self-esteem among Asian American and European American college students. *The Journal of Social Psychology, 137*, 435–444.

Karney, B.R. & Bradbury, T.N. (1995). The longitudinal course of marital quality and stability: A review of theory, method, and research. *Psychological Bulletin, 118*, 3–34.

Karp, J., Serbin, L.A., Stack, D.M., & Schwartzman, A.E. (2004). An observational measure of children's behavioral style: Evidence supporting a multi-method approach to studying temperament. *Infant and Child Development, 13*, 135–158.

Kasser, T., & Ryan, R.M. (1993). A dark side of the American dream: Correlates of financial success as a central life aspiration. *Journal of Personality and Social Psychology, 65*, 410–422.

Kasser, T., & Ryan, R.M. (1996). Further examining the American dream: Diferential correlates of intrinsic and extrinsic goals. *Personality and Social Psychology Bulletin, 22*, 280–287.

Katz, E., Fromme, K., & D'Amico, E. (2000). Effects of outcome expectancies and personality on young adults' illicit drug use, heavy drinking, and risky sexual behavior. *Cognitive Therapy and Research, 24*, 1–22.

Kelly, E.L., & Conley, J.J. (1987). Personality and compatibility: A prospective analysis of marital stability and marital satisfaction. *Journal of Personality and Social Psychology, 52*, 27–40.

Kelly, G.A. (1955). *The psychology of personal constructs*. New York: Norton (reprinted in 1991 by Routledge, London).

Kenny, D.A. (1994). *Interpersonal perception: A social relations analysis*. New York: Guilford.

Kenny, D.A. (1996). Models of non-independence in dyadic research. *Journal of Social and Personal Relationships, 13*, 279–294.

Kenny, D.A., & DePaulo, B.M. (1993). Do people know how others view them? An empirical and theoretical account. *Psychological Bulletin, 114*, 145–161.

Kring, A. M., Davison, G. C., Neale, J. M., & Johnson, S. L. (2007). Abnormal Psychology, (10th ed.). Hoboken, New Jersey: John Wiley & Sons, Inc.

Keogh, B.K. (1989). Applying temperament research in school. In G.A. Kohnstamm, J.E. Bates, & M.K. Rothbart (Eds.), *Temperament in childhood* (pp. 437–450). New York: John Wiley & Sons Inc.

Kerr, M. (2001). Culture as a context for temperament: Suggestions from the life courses of shy Swedes and Americans. In T.D. Wachs & G.A. Kohnstamm (Eds.), *Temperament in context* (pp. 139–153). Mahwah, NJ: Erlbaum.

Kerr, M., Lambert, W.W., & Bem, D.J. (1996). Life course sequelae of childhood shyness in Sweden: Comparison with the United States. *Developmental Psychology, 32*, 1100–1105.

Kesner, J.E., & McKenry, P.C. (1998). The role of childhood attachment factors in predicting male violence toward female intimates. *Journal of Family Violence, 13*, 417–432.

Keyes, C.L.M., Shmotkin, D., & Ryff, C.D. (2002). Optimizing well-being: The empirical encounter of two traditions. *Journal of Personality and Social Psychology, 82*, 1007–1022.

Khoshaba, D.M., & Maddi, S.R. (2001). *HardiTraining*. Newport Beach, CA: Hardiness Institute.

Kiesler, D.J. (1983). The 1982 interpersonal transaction circle: A taxonomy for complementarity in human processes. *Psychological Review, 77*, 421–430.

Kiesler, D.J., Schmidt, J.A., & Wagner, C.C. (1997). A circumplex inventory of impact messages: An operational bridge between emotion and interpersonal behavior. In R. Plutchik and H.R. Conte (Eds.), *Circumplex models of personality and emotions* (pp. 221–244). Washington, DC: American Psychological Association.

King, P.R., & Endler, N.S. (1990). Interactional anxiety and the evaluation of driving skills: An empirical examination of a composite predictor for state anxiety. *Canadian Journal of Behavioural Science, 22*, 13–19.

King, P.R., & Endler, N.S. (1992). Interactional anxiety and dental treatment: An empirical test of a composite predictor for state anxiety. *Personality and Individual Differences, 13*, 85–89.

Klag, S., & Bradley G. (2004). The role of hardiness in stress and illness: An exploration of the effect of negative affectivity and gender. *British Journal of Health Psychology, 9*, 137–161.

Klein, D.N. (2003). Patients' versus informants' reports of personality disorders in predicting 7½-year outcome in outpatients with depressive disorders. *Psychological Assessment, 15*, 216–222.

Kleinsmith, L., & Kaplan, S. (1963). Paired associate learning as a function of arousal and interpolated interval. *Journal of Experimental Psychology, 65*, 190–193.

Klineberg, O. (1949). Recent studies of national character. In S.S. Sargent & M.W. Smith (Eds.), *Culture and personality* (pp. 127–138). New York: The Viking Fund.

Klinger, E. (1989). Goal orientation as psychological linchpin: A commentary on Cantor and Kihlstrom's social intelligence and cognitive assessments of personality. In R.S. Wyer, Jr., & T.K. Srull, *Advances in social cognition, Vol. 2* (pp. 123–130). Hillsdale, NJ: Erlbaum.

Klohnen, E.C., & Mendelsohn, G. (1998). Partner selection for personality characteristics: A couple-centered approach. *Personality and Social Psychology Bulletin, 24*, 268–278.

Klonsky, E.D., Oltmanns, T.F., & Turkheimer, E. (2002). Informant-reports of personality disorder: Relation to self-reports and future research directions. *Clinical Psychology Science and Practice, 9*, 300–311.

Kluckhohn, C. (1954). Culture and behavior. In G. Lindzey (Ed.), *Handbook of social psychology: Vol. II Special fields and applications* (pp. 921–976). London: Addison-Wesley.

Kluckhohn, C., & Murray, H.A. (1953). Personality formation: The determinants. In C. Kluckhohn, H.A. Murray, & D. Schneider (Eds.), *Personality in nature, society, and culture* (pp. 53–67). New York: Knopf.

Kobasa, S.C. (1979). Stressful life events, personality, and health: An inquiry into hardiness. *Journal of Personality and Social Psychology, 37*, 1–11.

Kobasa, S.C., Maddi, S.R., & Kahn, S. (1982). Hardiness and health: A prospective study. *Journal of Personality and Social Psychology, 42*, 168–177.

Kochanska, G. (1992). Children's interpersonal influence with mothers and peers. *Developmental Psychology, 28*, 491–499.

Kochanska, G., Friesenborg, A.E., Lange, L.A., & Martel, M.M. (2004). The parents' personality and the infants' temperament as contributors to their emerging relationship. *Journal of Personality and Social Psychology, 86*, 744–759.

Koestner, R., Weinberger, J., & McClelland, D.C. (1991). Task-intrinsic and social-extrinsic sources of arousal for motives assessed in fantasy and self-report. *Journal of Personality, 59*, 57–82.

Koopmans, J.R., Boomsma, D.I., Heath, A.C., & Doorner, L.J.P. (1995). A multivariate genetic analysis of sensation seeking. *Behavior Genetics, 25*, 349–356.

Krantz, D.S., & Hedges, S.M. (1987). Some cautions for research on personality and health. *Journal of Personality, 55*, 351–357.

Krauss, S.W. (2002). Romanian authoritarianism 10 years after communism. *Personality and Social Psychology Bulletin, 28*, 1255–1264.

Kring, A. M., Davison, G. C., Neale, J. M., & Johnson, S. L. (2007). *Abnormal Psychology*, (10th ed.). Hoboken, New Jersey: John Wiley & Sons, Inc.

Kroes, G., Veerman, J.W., & De Bruyn, E.E. (2005). The impact of the big five personality traits on reports of child behavior problems by different informants. *Journal of Abnormal Child Psychology, 33*, 231–240.

Kruger, J., & Dunning, D. (1999). Unskilled and unaware of it: How difficulties in recognizing one's own incompetence lead to inflated self-assessments. *Journal of Personality and Social Psychology, 77*, 1121–1134.

Kuiper, N.A., Olinger, L.J., & Macdonald, M.R. (1988). Vulnerability and episodic cognitions in a self-worth contingency model of depression. In L. Alloy (Ed.), *Cognitive processes in depression* (pp. 289–309). New York: Guilford.

Kukil, K.V. (2000). (Ed.), *The unabridged journal of Sylvia Plath*. New York: Anchor Books.

Kumari, V., ffytche, D.H., Williams, S.C.R., & Gray, J.A. (2004). Personality predicts brain responses to cognitive demands. *Journal of Neuroscience, 24*, 10636–10341.

Kusyszyn, I. (1990). Existence, effectance, esteem: From gambling to a new theory of human motivation. *The International Journal of the Addictions, 25*, 159–177.

Kwong, J., & Cheung, F.M. (2003). Prediction of performance facets using specific personality traits in the Chinese context. *Journal of Vocational Behavior, 63*, 99–110.

Lafferty, P., Beutler, L.E., & Crago, M. (1989). Differences between more and less effective psychotherapists: A study of select therapist variables. *Journal of Consulting and Clinical Psychology, 57*, 76–80.

LaForge, R. (1985). The early development of the Freedman-Leary-Coffee interpersonal system. *Journal of Personality Assessment, 49*, 613–621.

Laing, R.D. (1959). *The divided self: An existential study in sanity and madness*. New York: Pelican Books.

Lakey, B., Lutz, C.J., & Scoboria, A. (2004). The information used to judge supportiveness depends on whether the judgment reflects the personality of perceivers, the objective characteristics of targets, or their unique relationships. *Journal of Social and Clinical Psychology, 23*, 817–835.

Lance, P. (2000). *Stingray: The lethal tactics of the soul survivor*. Berryville, VA: Berryville Graphics.

Larkin, J. E. (1991). The implicit theories approach to the self-monitoring controversy. *European Journal of Personality, 5*, 15–34.

Larsen, R.J., & Diener, E. (1987). Affect intensity as an individual difference characteristic: A review. *Journal of Research in Personality, 21*, 1–39.

Larstone, R.M., Jang, K.L., Livesley, W.J., Vernon, P.A., & Wolf, H. (2002). The relationship between Eysenck's P-E-N model of personality, the five-factor model of personality, and traits delineating personality dysfunction. *Personality and Individual Differences, 33*, 25–37.

Lavoie, J.A.A., & Pychyl, T.A. (2001). Cyberslacking and the procrastination superhighway: A web-based survey of online procrastination, attitudes, and emotion. *Social Science Computer Review, 19*, 431–444.

Lay, C.H. (1986). At last, my research article on procrastination. *Journal of Research in Personality, 20*, 474–495.

Lay, C.H. (1987). A modal profile analysis of procrastinators: A search for types. *Personality and Individual Differences, 8*, 705–714.

Lay, C.H. (1988). The relationship of procrastination and optimism to judgments of time to complete an essay and anticipation of setbacks. *Journal of Social Behavior and Personality, 3*, 201–214.

Lay, C.H. (1990). Working to schedule on personal projects: An assessment of person-object characteristics and trait procrastination. *Journal of Social Behavior and Personality, 5*, 91–103.

Lay, C.H. (1997). Explaining lower-order traits through higher-order factors: The case of trait procrastination, conscientiousness, and the specificity dilemma. *European Journal of Personality, 11*, 267–278.

Lazarus, R.S., & Folkman, S. (1984). *Stress, appraisal, and coping*. New York: Springer.

Leahy, R.L., Beck, J., & Beck, A.T. (2005). Cognitive therapy for the personality disorders. In S. Strack (Ed.), Handbook of personality and psychopathology (pp. 442-461). New York: John Wiley & Sons Inc.

Leahy, R.L., Beck, J., & Beck, A.T. (2005). Cognitive therapy for the personality disorders. In S. Strack (Ed.), *Handbook of personality and psychopathology* (pp. 442–461). New York: John Wiley & Sons Inc.

Leary, M.R. (1999). Making sense of self-esteem. *Current Directions in Psychological Science, 8*, 32–35.

Leary, M.R., & Shepperd, J.A. (1986). Behavioral self-handicaps versus self-reported handicaps: A conceptual note. *Journal of Personality and Social Psychology, 51,* 1265–1268.

Leary, T. (1957). *Interpersonal diagnosis of personality.* New York: Ronald Press.

Lecci, L., Karoly, P., Briggs, C., & Kuhn, K. (1994). Specificity and generality of motivational components in depression: A personal projects analysis. *Journal of Abnormal Psychology, 103,* 404–408.

Leclerc, G., Lefrancois, M., Dube, M., Hebert, R., & Gaulin, P. (1998). The self- actualization concept: A content validation. *Journal of Social Behavior and Personality, 13,* 69–84.

Lefrancois, R., Leclerc, G., Dube, M., Hebert, R., & Gaulin, P. (1997). The development and validation of a self-report measure of self-actualization. *Social Behavior and Personality, 25,* 353–366.

Lee, F., et al. (1996). Explaining real-life events: How culture and domain shape attributions. *Personality and Social Psychology Bulletin, 22,* 732–741.

Lee, K., & Ashton, M.C. (2005). Psychopathy, machiavellianism, and narcissism in the Five-Factor model and the HEXACO model of personality structure. *Personality and Individual Differences, 38,* 1571–1582.

Lee, S., & Klein, H.J. (2002). Relationships between conscientiousness, self-efficacy, self-deception, and learning over time. *Journal of Applied Psychology, 87,* 1175–1182.

Leeper, A., Carwile, S., & Huber, J.R. (2002). An Adlerian analysis of the Unabomber. *Journal of Individual Psychology, 58,* 169–176.

Lefcourt, H.M. (1966). Internal versus external control of reinforcement: A review. *Psychological Bulletin, 65,* 206–220.

Lennox, R.D., & Wolfe, R.N. (1984). Revision of the self-monitoring scale. *Journal of Personality and Social Psychology, 46,* 1349–1364.

Leonard, K.E., & Blane, H.T. (1988). Alcohol expectancies and personality characteristics in young men. *Addictive Behaviors, 13,* 353–357.

Leonard, K.E., & Senchak, M. (1996). Prospective prediction of husband marital aggression within newlywed couples. *Journal of Abnormal Psychology, 105,* 369–380.

Lessard, J.C., & Moretti, M.M. (1998). Suicidal ideation in an adolescent clinical sample: Attachment patterns and clinical implications. *Journal of Adolescence,* 21, 383–395.

Levenson, D. (1978). *The seasons of a man's life.* New York: Ballantine.

Levenson, H. (1981). Differentiating among internality, powerful others, and chance. In H.M. Lefcourt (Ed.), *Research with the locus of control construct. Volume 1: Assessment Methods* (pp. 15–63). New York: Academic Press.

LeVine, R.A. (2002). Contexts and culture in psychological research. *New Directions for Child and Adolescent Development, 96,* 101–106.

Lewin, K. (1935). *A dynamic theory of personality.* New York: McGraw-Hill.

Lewin, K. (1936). *Principles of topological psychology.* New York: McGraw-Hill.

Lewin, K. (1951). *Field theory in social science; selected theoretical papers* (Edited by D. Cartwright). New York: Harper & Row.

Lewinsohn, P.M., Solomon, A., Seeley, J.R., & Zeiss, A. (2000). Clinical implications of "subthreshold" depressive symptoms. *Journal of Abnormal Psychology, 109,* 345–351.

Lin, E. J-L., & Church, A.T. (2004). Are indigenous Chinese personality dimensions culture-specific? *Journal of Cross-Cultured Psychology, 35,* 585–605.

Lindsay, J.L., & Anderson, C.A. (2000). From antecedent conditions to violent actions: A general affective aggression model. *Personality and Social Psychology Bulletin, 26,* 533–547.

Lindsley, O.R. (2001). Studies in Behavior Therapy and Behavior Research Laboratory: June 1953–1965. In W.T. O'Donohue, D.A. Henderson, S.C. Hayes, J.E. Fisher, & L.J. Hayes (Eds.), *A history of the behavioral therapies: Founders' personal histories* (pp. 125–153). Reno, NV: Context Press.

Linehan, M.M. (1987). Dialectical behavior therapy for borderline personality disorder. *Bulletin of the Menninger Clinic, 51,* 261–276.

Linville, P.W. (1987). Self-complexity as a cognitive buffer against stress-related illness and depression. *Journal of Personality and Social Psychology, 52,* 663–676.

Lippa, R., & Arad, S. (1999). Gender, personality, and prejudice: The display of authoritarianism and social dominance in interviews with college men and college women. *Journal of Research in Personality, 33,* 463–493.

Little, B.R. (1983). Personal projects: A rationale and method for investigation. *Environment and Behavior, 15,* 273–309.

Little, B.R. (2005). Personality science and personal projects: Six impossible things before breakfast. *Journal of Research in Personality, 39,* 4–21.

Little, B.R., Lecci, L., & Watkinson, B. (1992). Personality and personal projects: Linking Big Five and PAC units of analysis. *Journal of Personality, 60,* 501–525.

Livesley, W.J. (1998). Suggestions for a framework for an empirically based classification of personality disorder. *Canadian Journal of Psychiatry, 43,* 137–147.

Livesley, W.J., & Jackson, D.N. (2002). *Manual for the Dimensional Assessment of Personality Problems-Basic Questionnaire.* Port Huron, MI: Sigma.

Livesley, W.J., Jackson, D.N., & Schroeder, M.L. (1992). Factorial structure of traits delineating personality disorders in clinical and general population samples. *Journal of Abnormal Psychology, 101,* 432–440.

Livesley, W.J., & Jang, K.L. (2000). Toward an empirically based classification of personality disorder. *Journal of Personality Disorders, 14,* 137–151.

Livesley, W.J., Jang, K.L., Jackson, D.N., & Vernon, P.A. (1993). Genetic and environmental contributions of dimensions of personality disorder. *American Journal of Psychiatry, 150,* 1826–1831.

Livesley, W.J., Jang, K.L., & Vernon, P.A. (1998). Phenotypic and genetic structure of traits in delineating personality disorder. *Archives of General Psychiatry, 55,* 941–948.

Livesley, W.J., Schroeder, M.L., Jackson, D.N., & Jang, K.L. (1994). Categorical distinctions in the study of personality disorder: Implications for classification. *Journal of Abnormal Psychology, 103,* 6–17.

Lobel, T.E., Gilat, I., & Endler, N.S. (1993). The Gulf War: Distressful reactions to scud missiles attacks. *Anxiety, Stress, and Coping, 6,* 9–23.

Loehlin, J.C. (1992). *Genes and environment in personality development.* Newbury Park, CA: Sage Publications.

Loehlin, J.C., McCrae, R.R., Costa, P.T., Jr., & John, O.P. (1998). Heritabilities of common and measure-specific components of the big five personality factors. *Journal of Research in Personality, 32,* 431–453.

Loehlin, J.C., & Nichols, R.C. (1976). *Heredity, environment, and personality: A study of 850 sets of twins.* Austin, TX: University of Texas Press.

Loehlin, J.C., Willerman, L., & Horn, J.M. (1985). Personality resemblances in adoptive families when the children are late-adolescent or adult. *Journal of Personality and Social Psychology, 48,* 376–392.

Loftus, E.F., Miller, D.G., & Burns, H.J. (1978). Semantic integration of verbal information into a visual memory. *Human Learning and Memory, 4,* 19–31.

Luciano, M., Leisser, R., Wright, M.J., & Martin, N.G. (2004). Personality, arousal theory, and the relationship to cognitive ability as measured by inspection time and IQ. *Personality and Individual Differences, 37,* 1081–1089.

Luhtanen, R., & Crocker, J. (1992). A collective self-esteem scale: Self-evaluation of one's social identity. *Personality and Social Psychology Bulletin, 18,* 302–318.

Lundberg, U., Rasch, B., & Westermark, O. (1990). Familial similarity in Type A behavior and physiological measurements as related to sex. *Scandinavian Journal of Psychology, 31,* 34–41.

Lundy, A. (1985). The reliability of the Thematic Apperception Test. *Journal of*

Personality Assessment, 49, 141–145.
Luo, S., & Klohnen, E.C. (2005). Assortative mating and marital quality in newlyweds: A couple-centered approach. *Journal of Personality and Social Psychology, 88*, 304–326.
Luszczynska, A., Guiterrez-Dona, B., & Schwarzer, R. (2004). General self-efficacy in various domains of human functioning: Evidence from five countries. *International Journal of Psychology, 40*, 80–89.
Luszczynska, A., Mohammed, N.E., & Schwarzer, R. (2005). Self-efficacy and social support predict human benefit finding 12 months after cancer surgery: The mediating role of coping strategies. *Psychology, Health, and Medicine, 10*, 365–375.
Lynn, R., & Martin, T. (1995). National differences for thirty-seven nations in extraversion, neuroticism, psychoticism, and economic, demographic, and other correlates. *Personality and Individual Differences, 19*, 403–406.
Lynn, R., & Martin, T. (1997). Gender differences in extraversion, neuroticism, and psychoticism in 37 nations. *Journal of Social Psychology, 137*, 369–373.
Lyons, A., & Chamberlain, K. (1994). The effects nor events, optimism and self-esteem on health. *British Journal of Clinical Psychology, 33*, 559–570.
Ma, V., & Schoeneman, T.J. (1997). Individualism versus collectivism: A comparison of Kenyan and American self-concepts. *Basic and Applied Social Psychology, 19*, 261–273.
Maddi, S.R. (1987). Hardiness training at Illinois Bell Telephone. In J.P. Opatz (Ed.), *Health promotion evaluation* (pp. 101–115). Stevens Point, WI: National Wellness Institute.
Maddi, S.R. (2002). The story of hardiness: Twenty years of theorizing, research and practice. *Consulting Psychology Journal, 54*, 173–185.
Maddi, S.R., Khoshaba, D.M., Persico, M., Lu, J., Harvey, R., & Bleecker, F. (2002). The personality construct of hardiness: II. Relationships with comprehensive tests of personality and psychopathology. *Journal of Research in Personality, 36*, 72–85.
Magdol, L., Moffitt, T.E., Caspi, A., & Silva, P.A. (1998). Developmental antecedents of partner abuse: A prospective-longitudinal study. *Journal of Abnormal Psychology, 107*, 375–389.
Magnusson, D. (1999). Holistic interactionism: A perspective for research on personality development. In L.A Pervin & O.P. John (Eds.), *Handbook of personality: Theory and research* (2nd ed., pp. 219–247). New York: Guilford Press.
Magnusson, D., & Stattin, H. (1998). Person-context interaction theories. In W. Damon & R.M. Lerner (Eds.), *Handbook of child psychology: Vol. 1: Theoretical models of human development* (5th ed., pp. 685–759). New York: John Wiley & Sons Inc.
Maiden, R.J., Peterson, S.A., Caya, M., & Hayslip, B., Jr. (2003). Personality changes in the old-old: A longitudinal study. *Journal of Adult Development, 10*, 31–39.
Main, M., & Hesse, E. (1990). Parents' unresolved traumatic experiences are related to infant disorganized attachment status: Is frightened and/or frightening parental behavior the linking mechanism? In M.T. Greenberg, D. Cicchetti, & E.M. Cummings (Eds.), *Attachment during the preschool years: Theory, research, and intervention* (pp. 161–182). Chicago: University of Chicago Press.
Main, M., Kaplan, N., & Cassidy, J. (1985). Security in infancy, childhood, and adulthood: A move to the level of representation. In I. Bretherton & E. Waters (Eds.), *Monographs of the Society for Research in Child Development, 50*, (1-2, Serial No. 209, 66–106).
Mallon, S.D., Kingsley, D., Affleck, G., & Tennen, H. (1998). Methodological trends in *Journal of Personality*: 1970–1995. *Journal of Personality, 66*, 671–685.
Mandel, H.P. (2004). Constructive confrontation: Cognitive-behavioral therapy with one type of procrastinating underachiever. In H. Schouwenberg, C. Lay, J.R. Ferrari, and T. Pychyl (Eds.), *Counseling the procrastinator in academic contexts*. Washington, DC: American Psychological Association.
Mar, R., DeYoung, C.G., Peterson, J.B., & Higgins, D.M. (2006). Self-liking and self-competence separate self-esteem from self-deception in self-report and actual achievement. *Journal of Personality, 74*, 1047–1078.
Marcia, J.E. (1966). Development and validation of ego-identity status. *Journal of Personality and Social Psychology, 3*, 551–558.
Marcia, J.E. (1976). Identity six years after: A follow-up study. *Journal of Youth and Adolescence, 5*, 145–160.
Markus, H.R. (2004). Culture and personality: Brief for an arranged marriage. *Journal of Research in Personality, 38*, 75–83.
Markus, H., & Kitayama, S. (1991). Culture and the self: Implications for cognition, emotion, and motivation. *Psychological Review, 98*, 224–253.
Markus, H., & Kunda, Z. (1986). Stability and malleability of the self-concept. *Journal of Personality and Social Psychology, 51*, 858–866.
Markus, H., & Nurius, P. (1986). Possible selves. *American Psychologist, 41*, 954–969.
Marsella, A.J., Dubanoski, J., Hamada, W.C., & Morse, H. (2000). The measurement of personality across cultures. *American Behavioral Scientist, 44*, 41–62.
Marshall, G.N., Wortman, C.B., Kusulas, J.W., Hervig, L.K., & Vickers, R.R., Jr. (1992). Distinguishing optimism from pessimism: Relations to fundamental dimensions of mood and personality. *Journal of Personality and Social Psychology, 62*, 1067–1074.
Marshall, W.L. (2005). Therapist style in sexual offender treatment: Influence on indices of change. *Sexual Abuse, 17*, 109–116.
Marshall, W.L., Ward, R.E., Moulden, H., et al. (2005). Working positively with sexual offenders: Maximizing the effectiveness of treatment. *Journal of Interpersonal Violence, 20*, 1096–1104.
Martin, A.J., Marsh, H.W., Williamson, A., & Debus, R.L. (2003). Self-handicapping, defensive pessimism, and goal orientation: A qualitative study of university students. *Journal of Educational Psychology, 95*, 617–628.
Martin, J.L. (2001). The authoritarian personality, 50 years later: What questions are there for political psychology? *Political Psychology, 22*, 1–26.
Martin, K.A., & Brawley, L.R. (2002). Self-esteem, self-efficacy, and self-handicapping: The relationship between stable and situational forms of self-doubt and self-handicapping in physical achievement settings. *Self and Identity, 1*, 337–351.
Martin, M.M., Anderson, C.M., & Thweatt, K.S. (1998). Individuals' perceptions of their communication behaviors: A validity study of the relationship between the Communication Flexibility Scale and the Cognitive Flexibility Scale with aggressive communication traits. *Journal of Social Behavior and Personality, 13*, 531–540.
Martin, R.P. (1989). Temperament and education: Implications for underachievement and learning disabilities. In W.B. Carey & S.C. McDevitt (Eds.), *Clinical and educational applications of temperament research* (pp. 37–51). Berwyn, PA: Swets North America.
Martin, T.R., Flett, G.L., Hewitt, P.L., Krames, L., & Szanto, G. (1996). Personality correlates of depression and health symptoms: A test of a self-regulation model. *Journal of Research in Personality, 31*, 264–277.
Maruko, M. (2001, September 16). Can blood type determine character? *The Japan Times Online*.
Mascolo, M.F., Misra, G., & Rapisardi, C. (2004). Individual and relational conceptions of self in India and the United States. *New Directions for Child and Adolescent Development, 104*, 9–26.
Maslow, A.H. (1962). *Toward a psychology of being*. New York: Van Nostrand-Reinhold.
Maslow, A.H. (1970). *Motivation and personality* (2nd ed.) New York: Harper.
Maslow, A.H. (1971). *The farther reaches of human nature*. New York: Viking.
Maslow, A.H. (1987). *Motivation and*

Personality, $3^{rd\ ed.}$ New York: Harper & Row.

Maslow, A.H. (1992, January-February). The last interview of Abraham Maslow—conducted in 1968 (by Edward Hoffman). *Psychology Today, 25*, 68–69.

Masse, L.C., & Tremblay, R.E. (1997). Behavior of boys in kindergarten and the course of substance use during adolescence. *Archives of General Psychiatry, 54*, 62–68.

Matsumoto, D. (2006). Are cultural differences in emotion regulation mediated by personality traits? *Journal of Cross-Cultural Psychology, 37*, 421–437.

Matsumoto, D., Takeuchi, S., Kudoh, T., Andayani, S., Kouznetsouva, N., & Krupp, D. (1998). The contribution of individualism-collectivism to cross-national differences in display rules. *Asian Journal of Social Psychology, 1*, 147–165.

Matsumoto, D., Yoo, S., H., Hirayama, S., & Petrova, G. (2005). Development and validation of a measure of display rule knowledge: The Display Rule Assessment Inventory. *Emotion*, 5, 23–40.

Matthews, K.A. (1978). Assessment and developmental antecedents of the coronary-prone behavior pattern in children. In T. Dembroski, S. Weiss, J. Shields, S. Haynes, & M. Feinleib (Eds.), *Coronary-prone behavior*. New York: Springer-Verlag.

Matthews, K.A. (1982). Psychological perspectives on the Type A behavior pattern. *Psychological Bulletin, 91*, 293–323.

Mauss, I.B., Evers, C., Wilhelm, F.H., & Gross, J.J. (2006). How to bite your tongue without blowing your top: Implicit evaluation of emotion regulation predicts affective responding to anger provocation. *Personality and Social Psychology Bulletin*, *32*, 589–602.

Mauss, I.B., & Gross, J.J. (2004). Emotion suppression and cardiovascular disease: Is hiding feelings bad for your heart? In I. Nyklíček, L. Temoshok, & A. Vingerhoets (Eds.), *Emotional Expression and Health: Advances in theory, assessment and clinical applications* (pp. 61–81). New York: Brunner-Routledge.

Maziade, M., Cote, R., & Bourderault, M. (1984). The NYLS model of temperament: Sex differences and demographic correlates in a French-speaking population. *Journal of the American Academy of Child Psychiatry, 23*, 213–226.

McAdams, D.P. (1982). Experiences of intimacy and power: Relationships between social motives and autobiographical memory. *Journal of Personality and Social Psychology, 42*, 292–302.

McAdams, D.P. (1988). *Power, intimacy, and the life story: Personological inquiries into identity*. New York: Guilford.

McAdams, D.P. (1992). The five-factor model in personality: A critical appraisal. *Journal of Personality, 60*, 329–361.

McAdams, D.P. (1996). Personality, modernity, and the storied self: A contemporary framework for studying persons. *Psychological Inquiry, 7*, 295–321.

McAdams, D.P., & de St. Aubin, E. (1992). A theory of generativity and its assessment through self-report, behavioral acts, and narrative themes in autobiography. *Journal of Personality and Social Psychology, 62*, 1003–1015.

McAdams, D.P., & West, S.G. (1997). Introduction: Personality psychology and the case study. *Journal of Personality, 65*, 757–783.

McCann, J.T. (1998). Defending the Rorschach in court: An analysis of admissibility using legal and professional standards. *Journal of Personality Assessment*, *70*, 125–144.

McCann, S.J.H. (2005). Longevity, big five personality factors, and health behaviors: Presidents from Washington to Nixon. *The Journal of Psychology*, *139*, 273–286.

McClelland, D.C. (1955). Some social consequences of achievement motivation. In M.R. Jones (Ed.), *Nebraska Symposium on Motivation* (pp. 41–65). Lincoln, NE: University of Nebraska Press.

McClelland, D.C. (1961). *The achieving society*. New York: The Free Press.

McClelland, D.C. (1985). How motives, skills, and values determine what people do. *American Psychologist, 40*, 812–825.

McClelland, D.C., Davis, W.N., Kalin, R., & Warner, E. (1972). *The drinking man*. New York: Free Press.

McClelland, D.C., & Friedman, G.A. (1952). A cross-cultural study of the relationship between child-training practices and achievement motivation appearing in folk tales. In G.E. Swanson, T.M. Newcomb, & E.L. Hartley (Eds.), *Readings in social psychology*, (pp. 243–249). New York: Holt.

McCoy, M. (1980). Culture-shocked marriages. In A.W. Landfield & L.M. Lietner (Eds.), *Personal construct psychology: Psychotherapy and personality* (pp. 141–165). New York: John Wiley & Sons Inc.

McCown, W.G., Johnson, J.L., & Shure, M.B. (Eds.) (1993) *The impulsive client: Theory, research, and treatment* (pp. 247–263). Arlington, VA: American Psychological Association Press.

McCrae, R.R. (1993). Moderated analyses of longitudinal personality stability. *Journal of Personality and Social Psychology, 65*, 577–585.

McCrae, R.R. (2004). Human nature and culture: A trait perspective. *Journal of Research in Personality, 38*, 3–14.

McCrae, R.R., & Costa, P.T., Jr. (1983). Social desirability scales: More substance than style. *Journal of Consulting and Clinical Psychology*, *51*, 882–888.

McCrae, R.R., & Costa, P.T., Jr. (1986). Personality, coping, and coping effectiveness in an adult sample. *Journal of Personality*, *54*, 385–405.

McCrae, R.R., Costa, P.T., Jr., Hrebickova, M., Urbanek, T., Martin, T.A., Oryol, V.E., Rukavishnikov, A.A., & Senin, I.G. (2004). Age differences in personality traits across cultures: Self-report and observer perspectives. *European Journal of Personality, 18*, 143–157.

McCrae, R.R., Stone, S.V., Fagan, P.J., & Costa, P.T., Jr. (1998). Identifying causes of disagreement between self-reports and spouse ratings of personality. *Journal of Personality*, *66*, 285–313.

McCrae, R.R., & Terracciano, A. (2006). National character and personality. *Current Directions in Psychological Science, 15*, 156–161.

McCrea, S.M., & Hirt, E.R. (2001). The role of ability judgments in self-handicapping. *Personality and Social Psychology Bulletin*, *27*, 1378–1389.

McFadden, T.J., Helmreich, R.L., Rose, R.M., & Fogg, L.F. (1994). Predicting astronauts' effectiveness: A multivariate approach. *Aviation, Space, and Environmental Medicine*, *65*, 904–909.

McFarland, S.G. (2005). On the eve of war: Authoritarianism, social dominance, and American students' attitudes toward attacking Iraq. *Personality and Social Psychology Bulletin*, *31*, 360–367.

McFarland, S.G., Ageyev, V.S., & Abalakina-Paap, M. (1992). Authoritarianism in the former Soviet Union. *Journal of Personality and Social Psychology, 63*, 1004–1010.

McGirk, T. (1989). *Wicked lady: Salvador Dali's muse*. New York: Hutchinson.

McGregor, I., & Little, B.R. (1998). Personal projects, happiness, and meaning: On doing well and being yourself. *Journal of Personality and Social Psychology*, *74*, 494–512.

McGregor, I., & Marigold, D.C. (2003). Defensive zeal and the uncertain self: What makes you so sure? *Journal of Personality and Social Psychology, 85*, 838–852.

McGuire, W.J. & Padawer-Singer, A. (1976). Trait salience in the spontaneous self-concept. *Journal of Personality and Social Psychology*, *33*, 743–754.

McHoskey, J.W., Worzel, W., & Szyarto, C. (1998). Machiavellianism and psychopathy. *Journal of Personality and Social Psychology*, *74*, 192–210.

McLewin, L.A., & Muller, R.T. (2006). Childhood trauma, imaginary companions, and the development of pathological dissociation. *Aggression and Violent Behaviour: A Review Journal*, *11*, 531–545.

Mead, G.H. (1934). *Mind, self, and society*. Chicago: University of Chicago Press.

Meehl, P.E. (1992). Factors and taxa, traits and types, differences of degree and differences in kind. *Journal of Personality, 60*, 117–174.

Megargee, E.I. (1966). Undercontrolled

and overcontrolled personality types in extreme antisocial aggression. *Psychological Monographs, 80*(3) (Whole).

Mehl, M.R., Gosling, S.D., & Pennebaker, J.W. (2006). Personality in the natural habitat: Manifestations and implicit folk theories of personality in daily life. *Journal of Personality and Social Psychology, 90*, 862–867.

Meloy, J.R., Hansen, T.L., & Weiner, I.B. (1997). Authority of the Rorschach: Legal citations during the past 50 years. *Journal of Personality Asssessment, 69*, 53–62.

Meston, C.M., Heiman, J.R., Trapnell, P.D., & Paulhus, D.L. (1998). Socially desirable responding and sexuality self-reports. *Journal of Sex Research, 35*, 148–157.

Metsäpelto, R-L., & Pulkkinen, L., (2003). Personality Traits and Parenting: Neuroticism, Extraversion, and Openness to Experience as Discriminative Factors. *European Journal of Personality, 17*, 59-78.

Meyer, B., Olivier, L., & Roth, D.A. (2005). Please don't leave me! BIS/BAS, attachment styles, and responses to relationship threat. *Personality and Individual Differences, 38*, 151–162.

Meyer, F.P., et al. (1998). 'Dominance' personality trait and immune system in healthy volunteers. *Human Psychopharmacology, 13*, 183–189.

Michalon, M. (2001). "Selflessness" in the service of the ego: Contributions, limitations and dangers of Buddhist psychology for Western psychology. *American Journal of Psychotherapy, 55*, 202–218.

Michalski, M. R. L., & Shackelford, T.K. (2002). An attempted replication of the relationships between birth order and personality. *Journal of Research in Personality*, 36, 182–188.

Middlebrook, D. (1991). *Anne Sexton: A biography*. New York: Random House.

Mikulincer, M. (1998). Adult attachment style and individual differences in functional versus dysfunctional experiences of anger. *Journal of Personality and Social Psychology, 74*, 513–524.

Mikulincer, M., Dolev, T., & Shaver, P.R. (2004). Attachment-related strategies during thought-suppression: Ironic rebounds and vulnerable self-representations. *Journal of Personality and Social Psychology, 87*, 940–956.

Milgram, S. (1975). *Obedience to authority*. New York: Harper & Row.

Milgram, N.A., Sroloff, B., & Rosenbaum, M. (1988).The procrastination of everyday life. *Journal of Research in Personality*, 22, 197–212.

Miller, J.G.(1996). My role in the assessment program of the Office of Strategic Services. *Behavioral Science*, 41, 245-261.

Miller, L.M., & Thayer, F.J. (1988). On the nature of self-monitoring: Relationships with adjustment and identity. *Personality and Social Psychology Bulletin, 29*, 544–553.

Miller, N.E. (1941). The frustratrion-aggression hypothesis. *Psychological Review, 48*, 337–342.

Miller, N.E. (1944). Experimental studies of conflict. In J.M. Hunt (Ed.), *Personality and the behavior disorders* (Vol. 1), New York: Ronald.

Miller, N.E. & Dollard, J. (1941). *Social learning and imitation.* New Haven, CT: Yale University Press.

Miller, S. (2003). The Terminator Finds Himself on a Mental Ward. In J.A. Kottler & J. Carlson (Eds.), *The mummy at the dining room table: Eminent therapists reveal their most unusual cases* (pp. 100). San Francisco: Jossey-Bass.

Millon, T. (1996). *Disorders of personality: DSM-IV and beyond.* New York: John Wiley & Sons Inc.

Millon, T., & Davis, R. (2000). *Personality disorders in modern life*. Singapore: John Wiley & Sons.

Miovic, M. (2004). An introduction to spiritual psychology: Overview of the literature, East and West. *Harvard Review of Psychiatry, 12*, 105–115.

Mirsky, A.F., et al. (2000). A 38-year followup of the Genain quadruplets. *Schizophrenia_Bulletin, 14*, 595–612.

Mischel, W. (1968). *Personality and assessment*. New York: John Wiley & Sons Inc.

Mischel, W. (1969). Continuity and change in personality. *American Psychologist, 24*, 1012–1018.

Mischel, W., & Shoda, Y. (1995). A cognitive-affective system theory of personality: Reconceptualizing situations, dispositions, dynamics and invariance in personality structure. *Psychological Review, 102*, 246–268.

Missildine, W.H. (1963). Perfectionism: If you must strive to "do better." In W.H. Missildine (Ed.), *Your inner child of the past* (pp. 75–90). New York: Pocket Books.

Mitterer, J., & Adams-Webber, J. (1988). OMNIGRID: A general repertory grid design, administration and analysis program. *Behavior Research Methods, Instruments & Computers, 20*, 359–360.

Miyake, K., Chen, S., & Campos, J.J. (1985). Infant temperament, mother's mode of interaction, and attachment in Japan: An interim report. *Monographs of the Society for Research in Child Development, 50* (1–2), 276–297.

Mokros, A., & Alison, L.J. (2002). Is profiling possible? Testing the predicted homology of crime scene actions and background characteristics in a sample of rapists. *Legal and Criminological Psychology, 7*, 25–43.

Moneta, G.B., & Wong, F.H.Y. (2001). Construct validity of the Chinese adaptation of four thematic scales of the Personality Research Form. *Social Behavior and Personality, 29*, 459–475.

Mongrain, M., & Blackburn, S. (2005). Cognitive vulnerability, lifetime risk, and the recurrence of major depression in graduate students. *Cognitive Therapy and Research, 29*, 747–768.

Mongrain, M., & Zuroff, D.C. (1994). Ambivalence over emotional expression and negative life events: Mediators of depressive symptoms in dependent and self-critical individuals. *Personality and Individual Differences, 16*, 447–458.

Monnier, J., Hobfoll, S.E., Dunahoo, C.L., Hulzier, M., & Johnson, R. (1998). There's more than rugged individualism in coping: Construct validity and further model testing, Part II. *Anxiety, Stress, and Coping, 11*, 247–272.

Mor, N., & Winquist, J. (2002). Self-focused attention and negative affect: A meta-analysis. *Psychological Bulletin, 128*, 638–662.

Morey, L.C., Quigley, B.D., et al. (2002). Substance or style? An investigation of the NEO-PI-R validity scales. *Journal of Personality Assessment, 79*, 583–599.

Morey, L.C., & Zanarini, M.C. (2000). Borderline personality: Traits and disorder. *Journal of Abnormal Psychology, 109*, 733–737.

Morris, T., & Greer, S. (1980). A "Type C" for cancer? *Cancer Detection and Prevention, 3*, Abstract No. 102.

Moskowitz, D.S., & Zuroff, D.C. (2004). Flux, pulse, and spin: Dynamic additions to the personality lexicon. *Journal of Personality and Social Psychology, 86*, 880–893.

Mowrer, O.H. (1947). On the dual nature of learning: A reinterpretation of "conditioning" and "problem-solving." *Harvard Educational Review, 17*, 102–148.

Mpofu, E. (1994). Exploring the self-concept in African culture. *Journal of Genetic Psychology, 155*, 341–354.

Mudrack, P.E. (1990). Machiavellianism and locus of control: A meta-analytic review. *Journal of Social Psychology, 130*, 125–126.

Muller, R.T., & Lemieux, K. (2000). Social support, attachment, and psychopathology in high risk formerly maltreated adults. *Child Abuse and Neglect, 24*, 883–900.

Murphy, E.E., Gordon, G.D., & Mullen, A. (2004). A preliminary study exploring the value changes taking place in the United States since the September 11, 2001 terrorist attack on the World Trade Center in New York. *Journal of Business Ethics, 50*, 81–96.

Murphy, M., & Neimeyer, R.A. (1986). *AUTOREP: Software reference manual.* Memphis, TN: Memphis State University.

Murray, H.A. (1938). *Explorations in personality.* New York: Oxford University Press.

Murray, H.A. (1943). *The Thematic Apperception Test: Manual.* Cambridge, MA: Harvard University Press.

Murray, H.A. (1943). *Analysis of the*

personality of Adolf Hitler with predictions of his future behavior and suggestions for dealing with him now and after Germany's surrender. OSS Archives, DD 247. H5 M87 1943.

Murray, H.A. (1951). Some basic psychological assumptions and conceptions. *Dialectica, 5*, 266–292.

Musson, D.M., Sandal, S.M., & Helmreich, R.L. (2004). Personality characteristics and trait clusters in final stage astronaut selection. *Aviation, Space, and Environmental Medicine, 75*, 342–349.

Myers, P.E., & Perkins, G.H. (2001). A common denominator. *The Western Scholar, 2*, 8–11.

Naaman, S., et al. (2005). Treating attachment injured couples with emotionally focused therapy: A case study approach. *Psychiatry: Interpersonal and Biological Processes, 68*, 55–78.

Nabi, H., Consoll, S.M., et al. (2005). Type A behavior pattern, risky driving behaviors, and serious road traffic accidents: A prospective study of the GAZEL cohort. *American Journal of Epidemiology, 161*, 864–870.

Nagin, D.S., & Tremblay, R.E. (2001). Parental and early childhood predictors of persistent physical aggression in boys from kindergarten to high school. *Archives of General Psychiatry, 58*, 389–394.

Najstrom, M., & Jansson, B. (2006). Unconscious responses to threatening pictures: Interactive effect of trait anxiety and social desirability on skin conductance responses. *Cognitive Behaviour Therapy, 35*, 11–18.

Nakaya, N., Tsubono, Y., Nishino, Y., Hosokawa, T., et al. (2005). Personality and cancer survival: The Miyagi cohort study. *British Journal of Cancer, 92*, 2089–2094.

Nasby, W., & Read, N.W. (1997). The life voyage of a solo circumnavigator: Integrating theoretical and methodological perspectives. *Journal of Personality, 65*, 785–1068.

Nay, R.E., & Wagner, M.K. (1990). Behavioral and psychological correlates of Type A behavior in children and adolescents: An overview. *Psychology and Health, 4*, 147–157.

Neimeyer, R. A., Fontana, D.J., & Gold, K. (1984). A manual for content analysis of death constructs. In F.R. Epting & R.A. Neimeyer (Eds.), *Personal meanings of death: Applications of personal construct theory to clinical practice* (pp. 213–234). Washington: Hemisphere Publishing.

Nes, S.L., Segerstrom, S.C., & Sephton, S.E. (2005). Engagement and arousal: Optimism's effects during a brief stressor. *Personality and Social Psychology Bulletin, 31*, 111–120.

Nevis, E.C. (1983). Using an American perspective in understanding another culture: Toward a hierarchy of needs for the People's Republic of China. *The Journal of Applied Behavioral Science, 19*, 249–264.

Neyer, F.J., & Voigt, D. (2004). Personality and social network effects on romantic relationships: A dyadic approach. *European Journal of Personality, 18*, 279–299.

Nicholls, J.G., Licht, B.G., & Pearl, R.A. (1982). Some dangers of using personality questionnaires to study personality. *Psychological Bulletin, 92*, 572–580.

Nicholson, I.A.M. (2003). *Inventing personality: Gordon Allport and the science of selfhood*. Washington, DC: American Psychological Association.

Nickson, C. (2002). *Ozzy knows best: An unauthorized biography*. New York: Thomas Dunne Books.

Nietzel, M.T., & Harris, M.J. (1990). Relationship of dependency and achievement/autonomy to depression. *Clinical Psychology Review, 10*, 279–297.

Nisbett, R.E. (1980). The trait construct in lay and professional psychology. In L. Festinger (Ed.), *Retrospections on social psychology* (pp. 109–130). New York: Oxford University Press.

Nordahl, H.M., Holthe, H., & Haugum, J.A. (2005). Early maladaptive schemas in patients with or without personality disorders: Does schema modification predict symptomatic relief? *Clinical Psychology and Psychotherapy, 12*, 142–149.

Norem, J.K. (2002). Defensive pessimism, optimism, and pessimism. In E.C. Chang (Ed.), *Optimism and pessimism: Implications for theory, research, and practice* (pp. 77–100). Washington, DC: American Psychological Association.

Norenzayan, A., & Heine, S. J. (2005). Psychological universals: What are they and how can we know? *Psychological Bulletin, 131*, 763–784.

Norman, W.T. (1963). Toward an adequate taxonomy of personality attributes: Replicated factor structure in peer nomination personality ratings. *Journal of Abnormal Psychology, 66*, 574–583.

Norman, W.T., & Goldberg, L.R. (1966). Raters, ratees, and randomness in personality structure. *Journal of Personality and Social Psychology, 4*, 681–691.

Norris, G. (2006). Criminal profiling: A continuing history. In K. Burgess & W. Petherick (Eds.), *Criminal profiling: A continuing history* (pp. 1–14). New York: Academic Press.

Nurmi, J-E. (1992). Cross-cultural differences in self-serving bias: Responses to the attributional style questionnaire by American and Finnish students. *The Journal of Social Psychology, 132*, 69–76.

Nurius, P.S., & Markus, H. (1990). Situational variability in the self-concept: Appraisals, expectancies, and asymmetries. *Journal of Social and Clinical Psychology, 9*, 316–333.

Nystedt, L., & Ljungberg, A. (2002). Facets of private and public self-consciousness: Construct and discriminant validity. *European Journal of Personality, 16*, 143–159.

O'Brien, T.B., & DeLongis, A. (1996). The interactional context of problem-, emotion-, and relationship-focused coping: The role of the big five personality factors. *Journal of Personality, 64*, 775–813.

O'Connor, B.P. (2002). The search for dimensional structure differences between normality and abnormality: A statistical review of published data on personality and psychopathology. *Journal of Personality and Social Psychology, 83*, 962–982.

O'Connor, B.P., & Dyce, J.A. (1998). A test of models of personality disorder configuration. *Journal of Abnormal Psychology, 107*, 3–16.

Oettingen, G. (1995). Explanatory style in the context of culture. In G.M. Buchanan & M.E.P. Seligman (Eds.), Explanatory styles (pp. 209–224). Hillsdale, NJ: Erlbaum.

Oettingen, G., & Seligman, M.E.P. (1990). Pessimism and behavioural signs of depression in East versus West Berlin. *European Journal of Social Psychology, 20*, 207–220.

O'Leary, K.D., Malone, J., & Tyree, A. (1994). Physical aggression in early marriage: Pre-relationship and relationship effects. *Journal of Consulting and Clinical Psychology, 62*, 594–602.

Ouellette, S.C. (1993). Inquiries into hardiness. In L. Goldberger & S. Breznitz (Eds), *Handbook of stress: Theoretical and clinical aspects* (2nd ed., pp. 77–100). New York: Free Press.

Ohaeri, J.U., & Lewis, C.A. (2004). Profile of the personality of educated Urban Nigerians. *International Journal of Mental Health & Addiction, 2*, 35–43.

Ohtani, Y., & Sakurai, S. (1995). Relationship of perfectionism to depression and hopelessness in college students. *Shinrigaku Kenkyu, 66*, 41–47.

Oishi, S. (2004). Personality in culture: A neo-Allportian view. *Journal of Research in Personality, 38*, 68–74.

Oishi, S., & Diener, E. (2001). Goals, culture, and subjective well-being. *Personality and Social Psychology Bulletin, 27*, 1674–1682.

Omodei, M.M., & Wearing, A. J. (1990). Need satisfaction and involvement in personal projects: Toward an integrative model of subjective well-being. *Journal of Personality and Social Psychology, 59*, 762–769.

O'Neill, T.R. (1979). *The individual hobbit: Jung, Tolkien, and the archetypes of Middle-Earth*. Boston: Houghton Mifflin.

Ones, D.S., & Viswesvaran, C. (1999). Relative importance of personality dimensions for expatriate selection: A policy capturing study. *Human Performance, 12*, 275–294.

Ongur, D., Farabaugh, A., Iosifescu,

D.V., Perlis, R., & Fava, M. (2005). Tridimensional personality questionnaire factors in major depressive disorder: Relationship to anxiety disorder comorbidity and age of onset. *Psychotherapy and Psychosomatics, 74,* 173–178.

Orne, M.T. (1962). On the social psychology of the psychological experiment: With particular reference to demand characteristics and their implications. *American Psychologist, 17,* 776–783.

Osberg, T.M. (1987). The convergent and discriminant validity of the need for cognition scale. *Journal of Personality Assessment, 51,* 441–450.

OSS Assessment Staff. (1948). *Assessment of men: Selection of personnel for the Office of Strategic Services.* New York: Rinehart.

Oyserman, D. (in press). Working with culturally/racially diverse to improve connection to school and academic performance. In C. Franklin, M. Harris, & P. Allen-Meares (Eds.), *The school services sourcebook: A guide for social workers, counselors, and mental health professionals* (p. 753–764). New York: Oxford University Press.

Oyserman, D., Terry, K., & Bybee, D. (2002). A possible selves intervention to enhance school involvement. *Journal of Adolescence, 25,* 313–326.

Ozer, D.J., & Benet-Martinez, V. (2006). Personality and the prediction of consequential outcomes. *Annual Review of Psychology, 57,* 401–421.

Ozgul, S., Heubeck, B., Ward, J., & Wilkinson, R. (2003). Self-discrepancies: Measurement and relation to various negative affective states. *The Australian Journal of Psychology, 55,* 56–62.

Palinkas, L.A. (2001). Psychosocial issues in long-term space flight: Overview. *Gravitational and Space Biological Bulletin, 14,* 25–33.

Pals, J. (2006). Narrative identity processing of difficult life experiences: Pathways of personality development and positive self-transformation in adulthood. *Journal of Personality, 74,* 1079–1110.

Palyo, S.A., & Beck, J.G. (2005). Is the concept of "repression" useful for understanding chronic PTSD? *Behaviour Research and Therapy, 43,* 55–68.

Palys, T.S., & Little, B.R. (1983). Perceived life satisfaction and the organization of personal project systems. *Journal of Personality and Social Psychology, 46,* 1221–1230.

Pang, J.S., & Schultheiss, O.C. (2005). Assessing implicit motives in U.S. college students: Effects of picture type and position, gender and ethnicity, and cross-cultural comparisons. *Journal of Personality Assessment, 85,* 280–294.

Paris, B.J. (2002). *The unknown Karen Horney: Essays on gender, culture, and psychoanalysis.* New Haven, CT: Yale University Press.

Paris, J. (1993). Personality disorders: A biopsychosocial model. *Journal of Personality Disorders, 7,* 255–264.

Paris, J. (1998). Personality disorders in sociocultural perspective. *Journal of Personality Disorders, 12,* 289–301.

Parker, S.J., & Barrett, D.E. (1992). Maternal Type A behavior during pregnancy, neonatal crying, and early infant temperament: Do Type A women have Type A babies? *Pediatrics, 89,* 474–479.

Parker, W.D. (1998). Birth-order effects in the academically talented. *Gifted Child Quarterly, 42,* 29–38.

Passini, F.T., & Norman, W.T. (1966). A universal description of personality structure? *Journal of Personality and Social Psychology, 46,* 384–403.

Patrick, H., Neighbors, C., & Knee, C.R. (2004). Appearance -related social comparisons: The role of contingent self-esteem and perceptions of attractiveness. *Personality and Social Psychology Bulletin, 30,* 501–514.

Paulhus, D.L. (1994). *Balanced Inventory of Desirable Responding: Reference manual for BIDR Version 6.* Unpublished manuscript, University of British Columbia, Vancouver, B.C.

Paulhus, D.L. (1998a). Interpersonal and intrapsychic adaptiveness of trait self-enhancement: A mixed blessing? *Journal of Personality and Social Psychology, 74,* 1197–1208.

Paulhus, D.L. (1998b). *The Balanced Inventory of Desirable Responding.* Toronto: Multi-Health Systems.

Paulhus, D.L. (2002). Socially desirable responding: The evolution of a construct. In H. I. Braun, D.N. Jackson, & D. E. Wiley (Eds.), *The role of constructs in psychological and educational measurement* (pp. 49–69). Mahwah, NJ: Erlbaum.

Paulhus, D.L., & Martin, C.L. (1987). The structure of personality capabilities. *Journal of Personality and Social Psychology, 52,* 354–365.

Paulhus, D.L., & Martin, C.L. (1988). Functional flexibility: A new conception of interpersonal flexibility. *Journal of Personality and Social Psychology, 55,* 88–101.

Paulhus, D.L., & Reid, D.B. (1991). Enhancement and denial in socially desirable responding. *Journal of Personality and Social Psychology, 60,* 307–317.

Paulhus, D.L., Trapnell, P.D., & Chen, D. (1999). Birth order effects on personality and achievement within families. *Psychological Science, 10,* 482–488.

Paulhus, D.L., & Williams, K.M. (2002). The dark triad of personality: Narcissism, Machiavellianism, and psychopathy. *Journal of Research in Personality, 36,* 556–563.

Paunonen, S.V. (2003). Big five factors of personality and replicated predictions of behavior. *Journal of Personality and Social Psychology, 84,* 411–424.

Paunonen, S.V., Haddock, G., Forsterling, F., & Keinonen, M. (2003). Broad versus narrow personality measures and the prediction of behaviour across cultures. *European Journal of Personality, 17,* 413–433.

Paunonen, S.V., & Jackson, D.N. (2000). What is beyond the Big Five? Plenty! *Journal of Personality, 68,* 821–835.

Pavlov, I.P. (1927). *Conditioned reflexes: An investigation of the physiological activity of the cerebral cortex* (translated by G.V. Anrep). London: Oxford University Press.

Pavlov, I.P. (1928). *Lectures on conditioned reflexes* (Vol. 1). New York: International.

Peabody, D. (1985). *National characteristics.* New York: Cambridge University Press.

Peabody, D., & Shmelyov, A.G. (1987). Psychological characteristics of Russians. *European Journal of Social Psychology, 26,* 507–512.

Pedersen, S.S., & Denollet, J. (2003). Type D personality, cardiac events, and impaired quality of life: A review. *European Journal of Carviovascular Prevention and Rehabilitation, 10,* 241–248.

Peretti, P.O., & Abplanalp, R.R., Jr. (2004). Chemistry in the college dating process: Structure and function. *Social Behavior and Personality, 32,* 147–154.

Perry, H.S. (1982). *Psychiatrist of America: The life of Harry Stack Sullivan.* Harvard: Belknap.

Peterson, B.E., & Lane, M.D. (2001). Implications of authoritarianism for young adulthood: Longitudinal analysis of college experiences and future goals. *Personality and Social Psychology Bulletin, 27,* 678–690.

Peterson, C., Luborsky, L., & Seligman, M.E.P. (1983). Attributions and depressive mood shifts: A case study using the symptom-context method. *Journal of Abnormal Psychology, 92,* 96–103.

Peterson, C., Seligman, M.E.P., & Vaillant, G.E. (1988). Pessimistic explanatory style is a risk factor for physical illness: A thirty-five year longitudinal study. *Journal of Personality and Social Psychology, 55,* 23–27.

Peterson, J.B., et al. (2003). Self-deception and failure to modulate responses despite accruing evidence of error. *Journal of Research in Personality, 37,* 205–223.

Petherick, W.A. (2006). The fallacy of accuracy in criminal profiling. In W. Petherick (Ed.), *Serial crime: Theoretical and practical issues in behavioral profiling* (pp. 53–67). Sydney: Academic Press.

Petty, G.M., & Dawson, B. (1989). Sexual aggression in normal men: Incidence, beliefs, and personality characteristics. *Personality and Individual Differences, 10,* 355–362.

Phipps, M. (1983). *The myth and magic of "star wars": A Jungian interpretation.* ERIC Document No. 315833.

Pickenhain, L. (1999). The importance of I.P. Pavlov for the development of a neuroscience. *Integrative Physiological and Behavioural Science, 34*, 85–89.

Pickett, C.L., Gardner, W.L., & Knowles, M. (2004). Getting a cue: The need to belong and enhanced sensitivity to social cues. *Personality and Social Psychology Bulletin, 30*, 1095–1107.

Pincus, A.L., & Gurtman, M.B. (1995). The three faces of interpersonal dependency: Structural analyses of self-report dependency measures. *Journal of Personality and Social Psychology, 69*, 744–758.

Pistole, M.C., & Tarrant, N. (1993). Attachment style and aggression in male batterers. *Family Therapy, 20*, 165–173.

Pliner, P., Chaiken, S., & Flett, G.L. (1990). Gender differences in concern with body-weight and physical appearance over the life-span. *Personality and Social Psychology Bulletin, 16*, 263–273.

Plomin, R., & Asbury, K. (2005). Nature and nurture: Genetic and environmental influences on behavior. *Annals of the American Academy of Political and Social Science, 600*, 86–98.

Plomin, R., Asbury, K., & Dunn, J. (2001). Why are children in the same family so different? Nonshared environment a decade later. *Canadian Journal of Psychiatry, 46*, 225–233.

Plomin, R., Chipuer, H.M., & Loehlin, J.C. (1990). Behavioral genetics and personality. In L.A. Pervin (Ed.), *Handbook of personality theory and research* (pp. 225–243). New York: Guilford.

Poehlmann, J. (2005). Narrative representations of attachment in children of incarcerated mothers. *Child Development, 76*, 679–696.

Pomerance, R. (2003). Personality profiling helps business people find out who they are dealing with. *New England Psychologist* (nePsy.com; http://www.masspsy.com/leading/0307_ne_qa.html)

Pope, M.K., Smith, T.W., & Rhodewalt, F. (1990). Cognitive, behavioral, and affective correlates of the Cook and Medley HO Scale. *Journal of Personality Assessment, 54*, 501–514.

Porat, B. (1977). Guttman scale test for Maslow need hierarchy. *Journal of Psychology, 97*, 85–92.

Poston, D.L., & Falbo, T. (1990). Scholastic and personality characteristics of only children and children with siblings in China. *International Family Planning Perspectives, 16*, 45–48.

Powers, S. I., Pietromonaco, P., Gunlicks, M., & Sayer, A. (2006). Dating couples' attachment styles and patterns of cortisol reactivity and recovery in response to a relationship conflict. *Journal of Personality and Social Psychology, 90*, 613–628.

Pratto, F., Sidanius, J., Stallworth, L.M., & Malle, B.F. (1994). Social dominance orientation: A personality variable predicting social and political attitudes. *Journal of Personality and Social Psychology, 67*, 741–763.

Price, V.A. (1982). *The Type A behavior pattern: A model for research and practice*. Orlando, FL: Academic Press.

Priel, B., & Besser, A. (1999). Vulnerability to postpartum depressive symptomatology: Dependency, self-criticism and the moderating role of antenatal attachment. *Journal of Social and Clinical Psychology, 18*, 240–253.

Priel, B., & Besser, A. (2000). Dependency and self-criticism among first-time mothers: The roles of global and specific support. *Journal of Social and Clinical Psychology, 19*, 437–450.

Prinzie, P., Onghena, P., & Hellinckx, W. (2005). The effect of parent and child personality characteristics on children's externalizing problem behavior from age 4 to 9 years: A cohort-sequential latent growth curve analysis. *Merrill-Palmer Quarterly, 51*, 335–366.

Pufal-Struzik, I. (1999). Self-actualization and other personality dimensions as predictors of mental health of intellectually gifted students. *Roeper Review, 22*, P44–P51.

Pukrop, R., Gentil, I., Steinbring, I., & Steinmeyer, E. (2001). Factorial structure of the German version of the Dimensional Assessment of Personality Pathology-Basic Questionnaire in clinical and nonclinical samples. *Journal of Personality Disorders, 15*, 450–456.

Pulkkinen, L. (1996). Female and male personality types: A typological and developmental analysis. *Journal of Personality and Social Psychology, 70*, 1288–1306.

Punamaki, R-L., Kanninen, K., Qouta, S., & El-Sarraj, E. (2002). The role of psychological defenses in moderating between trauma and post-traumatic symptoms among Palestinian men. *International Journal of Psychology, 37*, 286–296.

Raikkonen, K., & Keltikangas-Jarvinen, L. (1992). Childhood hyperactivity and the mother-child relationship as predictors of Type A behavior in adolescence: A six year follow-up. *Personality and Individual Differences, 13*, 321–327.

Raskin, R., & Hall, C.S. (1981). The Narcissistic Personality Inventory: Alternate form reliability and further evidence of construct validity. *Journal of Personality Assessment, 45*, 159–162.

Read, J.D., Connolly, D., & Turtle, J.W. (2001). Eyewitness testimony: Remembering events, circumstances, and people. In J. Ogloff & R. Schuller (Eds.), *An introduction to law and psychology: Canadian perspectives* (pp. 95–125). Toronto: University of Toronto Press.

Ready, R.E., Clark, L.A., Watson, D., & Westerhouse, K. (2000). Self- and peer-reported personality: Agreement, trait ratability, and the "self-based heuristic". *Journal of Research in Personality, 34*, 208–224.

Reis, S., & Grenyer, B.F.S. (2004). Fearful attachment, working alliance and treatment response for individuals with major depression. *Clinical Psychology and Psychotherapy, 11*, 414–424.

Reiss, S. (2004). Multifaceted nature of intrinsic motivation: The theory of 16 basic drives. *Review of General Psychology, 8*, 179–193.

Reiss, S., & Havercamp, S.M. (1998). Toward a comprehensive assessment of fundamental motivation: Factor structure of the Reiss Profile. *Psychological Assessment, 10*, 97–106.

Renshon, S.A. (1994). A preliminary assessment of the Clinton presidency: Character, leadership, and performance. *Political Psychology, 15*, 375–394.

Rescorla, R.A. (1987). A Pavlovian analysis of goal-directed behavior. *American Psychologist, 42*, 119–129.

Revelle, W. (1989). Personality, motivation, and cognitive performance. In P.L. Ackerman, R. Cudeck, & R. Kanfer (Eds.), *Learning and individual differences: Abilities, motivation, and methodology* (pp. 297–341). Hillsdale, NJ: Erlbaum.

Revelle, W. (1995). Personality processes. *Annual Review of Psychology, 46*, 295–328.

Revelle, W., Amaral, P., & Turriff, S. (1976). Introversion/extroversion, time stress, and caffeine: Effect on verbal performance. *Science, 192*, 149–150.

Rhodewalt, F. (1984). Self-involvement, self-attribution, and the Type A coronary-prone behavior pattern. *Journal of Personality and Social Psychology, 47*, 662–670.

Rhodewalt, F. (1990). Self-handicappers: Individual differences in the preference for anticipatory self-protective acts. In R. Higgins, C.R. Snyder, and S. Berglas, (Eds.), *Self-Handicapping: The paradox that isn't* (pp. 69–106). New York: Guilford Press.

Rhodewalt, F., & Hill, S.K. (1995). Self-handicapping in the classroom: The effects of claimed self-handicaps on responses to academic failure. *Basic and Applied Social Psychology, 16*, 397–416.

Rhodewalt, F., Morf, C., Hazlett, S., & Fairfield, M. (1991). Self-handicapping: The role of discounting and augmentation in the preservation of self-esteem. *Journal of Personality and Social Psychology, 61*, 122–131.

Rhodewalt, F., Strube, M.J., Hill, C.A., & Sansone, C. (1988). Strategic self-attribution and Type A behavior. *Journal of Research in Personality, 22*, 60–74.

Rhodewalt, F., & Tragakis, M. (2002). Self-handicapping and the social self: The costs and rewards of interpersonal self-construction. In J. Forgas & K. Williams (Eds.), *The social self: Cognitive, interpersonal, and intergroup perspectives* (pp. 121–143). Philadelphia, PA: Psychology Press.

Rhodewalt, F., & Zone, J.B. (1989). Appraisal of life change, depression, and illness in hardy and nonhardy women. *Journal of Personality and Social Psychology, 56,* 81–88.

Rice, M. (1997). Violent offender research and implications for the criminal justice system. *American Psychologist, 52,* 414–423.

Riemann, R., Angleitner, A., & Strelau, J. (1997). Genetic and environmental influences on personality: A study of twins reared together using the self- and peer report NEO-FFI scales. *Journal of Personality, 65,* 449–475.

Robbins, A.S., Spence, J.T., & Clark, H. (1991). Psychological determinants of health and performance: The tangled web of desirable and undesirable characteristics. *Journal of Personality and Social Psychology, 61,* 755–765.

Roberts, B.W., & Bogg, T. (2004). A 30-year longitudinal study of the relationships between conscientiousness-related traits, and the family structure and health-behavior factors that affect health. *Journal of Personality, 72,* 325–354.

Roberts, B.W., Chernyshenko, O., Stark, S., & Goldberg, L. (2005). The structure of conscientiousness: An empirical investigation based on seven major personality questionnaires. *Personnel Psychology, 58,* 103–139.

Roberts, B.W., & DelVecchio, W.F. (2000). The rank order consistency of personality from childhood to old age: A quantitative review of longitudinal studies. *Psychological Bulletin, 126,* 3–25.

Roberts, B.W., Robins, R.W., Trzesniewski, K.H., & Caspi, A. (2003). Personality trait development in adulthood. In J.T. Mortimer & M.J. Shanahan (Ed.), *Handbook of the life course* (pp. 579–595). New York: Kleuwer Academic/Plenum Publishers.

Roberts, B.W., Walton, K., & Viechtbauer, W. (2006a). Patterns of mean-level change in personality traits across the life course: A meta-analysis of longitudinal studies. *Psychological Bulletin, 132,* 1–25.

Roberts, B.W., Walton, K., & Viechtbauer, W. (2006b). Personality changes in adulthood: Reply to Costa & McCrae (2006). *Psychological Bulletin, 132,* 29–32.

Roberts, N., & Noller, P. (1998). The associations between adult attachment and couple violence: The role of communication patterns and relationship satisfaction. In J.A. Simpson & W.S. Rholes (Eds.), *Attachment theory and close relationships* (pp. 317–350). New York: Guilford.

Robins, C.J., et al. (1994). The Personal Style Inventory: Preliminary validation studies of new measures of sociotropy and autonomy. *Journal of Psychopathology and Behavioral Assessment, 16,* 277–300.

Robins, R.W., Caspi, A., Moffitt, T.E. (2000). Two personalities, one relationship: Both partners' personality traits shape the quality of their relationship. *Journal of Personality and Social Psychology, 79,* 251–259.

Robins, R.W., Caspi, A., & Moffitt, T.E. (2002). It's not just who you're with, it's who you are: Personality and relationship experiences across multiple relationships. *Journal of Personality, 70,* 925–964.

Robins, R.W., Fraley, R.C., Roberts, B.W., & Trzesniewski, K.H. (2001). A longitudinal study of personality change in young adulthood. *Journal of Personality, 69,* 618–640.

Robins, R., John, O., Caspi, A., Moffitt, T., & Stouthamer-Loeber, M. (1996). Resilient, overcontrolled, and undercontrolled boys: Three replicable personality types. *Journal of Personality and Social Psychology, 70,* 157–171.

Robins, R.W., Noftle, E.E., Trzesniewski, K.H., & Roberts, B.W. (2005). Do people know how their personality has changed? Correlates of perceived and actual personality change in young adulthood. *Journal of Personality, 73,* 489–521.

Robins, R.W., Tracy, J.L., & Trzesniewski, K. (2001). Personality correlates of self-esteem. *Journal of Research in Personality, 35,* 463–482.

Robins, R.W., Tracy, J.L., Trzesniewski, K., Gosling, S.D., & Potter, J. (2002). Global self-esteem across the life span. *Psychology and Aging, 17,* 423–434.

Robinson, D.L. (1989). The neurophysiological basis of high IQ. *International Journal of Neuroscience, 46,* 209–234.

Robinson-Whelan, S., et al. (1997). Distinguishing optimism from pessimism in older adults: Is it more important to be optimistic or not to be pessimistic? *Journal of Personality and Social Psychology, 73,* 1345–1353.

Rogers, C.R. (1947). Some observations on the organization of personality. *American Psychologist, 2,* 358–368.

Rogers, C.R. (1951). *Client-centered therapy: Its current practice, implications and theory.* Boston: Houghton Mifflin.

Rogers, C.R. (1959). A theory of therapy, personality, and interpersonal relationship, as developed in the client-centered framework. In S. Koch (Ed.), *Psychology: A study of a science, Vol. 3. Formulations of the person and the social context* (pp. 184–256). New York: McGraw-Hill.

Rogers, C.R. (1961). *On becoming a person: A therapist's view of psychotherapy.* Boston: Houghton Mifflin.

Rogers, C.R. (1980). *A way of being.* Boston: Houghton Mifflin.

Rogers, M. (2003). The role of criminal profiling in computer forensic investigations. *Computers & Security, 22,* 292–298.

Rorer, L.G. (1965). The great response-style myth. *Psychological Bulletin, 63,* 129–156.

Rose, R.M., Fogg, L.F., Helmreich, R.L., & McFadden, T.J. (1994). Psychological predictors of astronaut effectiveness. *Aviation, Space, and Environmental Medicine, 65,* 910–915.

Rosenberg, M. (1965). *Society and the adolescent self-image.* Princeton, NJ: Princeton University Press.

Rosenberg, M. (1986). *Conceiving the self.* Malabar, FL: Krieger.

Rosenthal, D. (1963). *The Genain Quadruplets: A case study and theoretical analysis of heredity and environment in schizophrenia.* New York: Basic Books.

Rosenthal, R. (1966). *Experimenter bias in behavioral research.* New York: Appleton-Century-Crofts.

Roskies, E. (1990). Type A intervention: Where do we go from here? *Journal of Social Behavior and Personality, 5,* 419–438.

Roskies, E., et al. (1986). The Montreal Type A intervention project: Major findings. *Health Psychology, 5,* 45–69.

Rothbaum, F. et al. (2000). The development of close relationships in Japan and the United States: Paths of symbiotic harmony and generative tension. *Child Development, 71,* 1121–1142.

Rothbart, M.I.C. (1981). Measurement of temperament in infancy. *Child Development, 52,* 569–578.

Rothbart, M.K., Ahadi, S.A., Hershey, K.L., & Fisher, P. (2001). Investigations of temperament at three to seven years: The children's behavior questionnaire. *Child Development, 72,* 1394–1408.

Rothbart, M.K., & Putnam, S.P. (2002). Temperament and socialization. In L. Pulkkinen & A. Caspi (Eds.), *Personality in the life course: Paths to successful development* (pp. 19–45). Mahwah, NJ: Erlbaum.

Rottenberg, J., & Gotlib, I.H. (2004). Socioemotional functioning in depression. In M. Power (Ed.), *Mood disorders: A handbook of science and practice* (pp. 61–77). New York: John Wiley & Sons, Inc.

Rotter, J.B. (1960). Some implications of a social learning theory for the prediction of goal-directed behavior from testing procedures. *Psychological Review, 67,* 301-316.

Rotter, J.B. (1966). Generalized expectancies for internal versus external control over reinforcement. *Psychological Monographs, 80,* 1–28.

Roy, A. (1990). Personality variables in depressed and normal controls. *Neuropsychobiology, 23,* 119–123.

Rubin, D.C., & Siegler, I.C. (2004). Facets of personality and the phenomenology of autobiographical memory. *Applied Cognitive Psychology, 18,* 913–930.

Rubino, G., et al. (2000). Therapist empathy and depth of interpretation in response to potential alliance ruptures: The role of therapist and patient attachment styles. *Psychotherapy Research, 10,* 408–420.

Ruehlman, L.S., & Wolchik, S.A. (1988). Personal goals and interpersonal support and hindrance as factors in psychological distress and well-being. *Journal of Personality and Social Psychology, 55,* 293–301.

Rundquist, E.A. (1966). Item and response characteristics in attitude and personality measurement: A reaction to L.G. Rorer's "The great response style myth." *Psychological Bulletin, 66,* 166–177.

Runyan, W.M. (1982). *Life histories and psychobiography: Explorations in theory and method.* New York: Oxford University Press.

Runyan, W.M. (2005). Evolving conceptions of psychobiographers and the study of lives: Encounters with psychoanalysis, personality psychology, and historical science. In W.T. Schultz (Ed.), *Handbook of psychobiography* (pp. 19–41). New York: Oxford University Press.

Ruscio, J., & Ruscio, A.M. (2000). Informing the continuity controversy: A taxometric analysis of depression. *Journal of Abnormal Psychology, 109,* 473–489.

Rutherford, A. (2003). Skinner boxes for psychotics: Operant conditioning at Metropolitan State Hospital. *The Behavior Analyst, 26,* 267–279.

Ruvolo, A., & Markus, H. (1992). Possible selves and performance: The power of self-relevant imagery. *Social Cognition, 10,* 95–125.

Ryckman, R.M., Thornton, B., & Butler, J.C. (1994). Personality correlates of the Hypercompetitive Attitude Scale: Validity tests of Horney's theory of neurosis. *Journal of Personality Assessment, 62,* 84–94.

Ryff, C.D. (1989). Happiness is everything, or is it? Explorations on the meaning of psychological well-being. *Journal of Personality and Social Psychology, 57,* 1069–1081.

Ryff, C.D. (1995). Psychological well-being in adult life. *Current Directions in Psychological Science, 4,* 99.

Ryff, C., & Keyes, C. (1995). The structure of psychological well-being revisited. *Journal of Personality and Social Psychology, 69,* 719–727.

Ryff, C.D., Keyes, C.L.M., & Hughes, D.L. (2003). Status inequalities, perceived discrimination, and eudaimonic well-being: Do the challenges of minority life hone purpose and growth? *Journal of Health and Social Behavior, 44,* 275–291.

Ryff, C.D., & Singer, B. (1998). The contours of positive human health. *Psychological Inquiry, 9,* 1–28.

Ryff, C.D., Singer, B.H., & Love, G.D. (2004). Positive health: Connecting well-being with biology. *Philosophical Transactions of the Royal Society of London, 359,* 1383–1394.

Sachs-Ericsson, N., Verona, E., Joiner, T., & Preacher, K.J. (2006). Parental verbal abuse and the mediating role of self-criticism in adult internalizing disorders. *Journal of Affective Disorders, 93,* 71–78.

Sackeim, H. A., & Gur, R. C. (1979). Self-deception, other-deception, and self-reported psychopathology. *Journal of Consulting and Clinical Psychology, 47,* 213–215.

Sadowski, C.J., & Cogburn, H.E. (1997). Need for cognition in the big-five factor structure. *The Journal of Psychology, 131,* 307–312.

Saffrey, C., et al. (2003). Self- and partner-perceptions of interpersonal problems and relationship functioning. *Journal of Social and Personal Relationships, 20,* 117–139.

Sakamoto, S., & Kambara, M. (1998). A longitudinal study of relationship between attributional style, life events, and depression in Japanese undergraduates. *The Journal of Social Psychology, 138,* 229–240.

Saklofske, D.H. (1985). The relationship between Eysenck's major personality dimensions and simultaneous and sequential processing in children. *Personality and Individual Differences, 6,* 429–433.

Salgado, J.F. (1998). Big five personality dimensions and job performance in army and civilian occupations: A European perspective. *Human Performance, 11,* 271–288.

Salgado, J.F. (2003). Predicting job performance using FFM and non-FFM personality measures. *Journal of Occupational and Organizational Psychology, 76,* 323–346.

Salmela-Aro, K. (1992). Struggling with self: The personal projects of students seeking psychological counseling. *Scandinavian Journal of Psychology, 33,* 330–338.

Sandal, G.M. (1998). The effects of personality and interpersonal relations on crew performance during space simulation studies. *Life Support and Biosphere Science, 5,* 461–470.

Santor, D.A., & Zuroff, D.C. (1994). Depressive symptoms: Effects of negative affectivity and failing to accept the past. *Journal of Personality Assessment, 63,* 294–312.

Santy, P.A. (1994). *Choosing the right stuff: The psychological selection of astronauts and cosmonauts.* Westport, CT: Praeger Publications.

Sato, T., et al. (1997). Personality disorder diagnoses using DSM-III-R in a Japanese clinical sample with major depression. *Acta Psychiatrica Scandinavica, 95,* 451–453.

Saucier, G. (2002). Gone too far, or not far enough? Comments on the article by Ashton and Lee (2001). *European Journal of Personality, 16,* 55–62.

Saucier, G., & Goldberg, L.R. (1998). What is beyond the Big Five? *Journal of Personality, 66,* 495–524.

Saucier, G., & Goldberg, L.R. (2001). Lexical studies of indigenous personality factors: Premises, products, and prospects. *Journal of Personality, 69,* 847–880.

Scaramella, L.V., Conger, R.D., Spoth, R., & Simons, R.L. (2002). Evaluation of a social contextual model of delinquency: A cross-study replication. *Child Development, 73,* 175–195.

Schafer, J., Caetano, R., & Cunradi, C. (2004) A path model of risk factors for intimate partner violence among couples in the United States. *Journal of Interpersonal Violence, 19,* 127–142.

Schaie, K.W., Dutta, R., & Willis, S.L. (1991). The relationship between rigidity-flexibility and cognitive abilities in adulthood. *Psychology and Aging, 6,* 371–383.

Schapiro, I.R., Nielsen, L.F., et al. (2002). Psychic vulnerability and associated risk for cancer. *Cancer, 94,* 3299–3306.

Scheier, M.F., & Carver, C.S. (1985). Optimism, coping, and health: Assessment and implications of generalized outcome expectancies. *Health Psychology, 4,* 219–247.

Scheier, M.F., & Carver, C.S. (1987). Dispositional optimism and physical well-being: The influence of generalized outcome expectancies on health. *Journal of Personality, 55,* 169–204.

Scheier, M.F., Carver, C.S., & Bridges, M.W. (1994). Distinguishing optimism from neuroticism (and trait anxiety, self-mastery, and self-esteem): A reevaluation of the life orientation test. *Journal of Personality and Social Psychology, 67,* 1063–1078.

Scheier, M.F., et al. (1989). Dispositional optimism and recovery from coronary artery bypass surgery: The beneficial effects of physical and psychological well-being. *Journal of Personality and Social Psychology, 57,* 1024–1040.

Schmidt, L.A. (1999). Frontal brain electrical activity in shyness and sociability. *Psychological Science, 10,* 316–320.

Schmidt, L.A., & Fox, N.A. (1994). Patterns of cortical electrophysiology and autonomic activity in adults' shyness and sociability. *Biological Psychology, 38,* 183–198.

Schmidt, L.A., Fox, N.A., & Schulkin, J. (1999). Behavioral and psychophysiological correlates of self-presentation in temperamentally shy children. *Developmental Psychobiology, 35,* 119–135.

Schmitt, D.P. (2004). The big five related to risky sexual behaviour across 10 world regions: Differential personality associations of sexual promiscuity and relationship infidelity. *European Journal of Personality, 18,* 301–319.

Schmitt, D.P., et al. (2004). Patterns and universals of adult romantic attachment across 62 cultural regions. *Journal of Cross-Cultural Psychology, 35,* 367–402.

Schouwenburg, H., Lay, C. H., Pychyl, T. A., & Ferrari, J. R. (2004). Counseling the procrastinator in academic settings. Washington, D.C.: American Psychological Association.

Schultheiss, O.C., & Brunstein, J.C. (1999). Goal imagery: Bridging the gap between implicit motives and explicit goals. *Journal of Personality, 67,* 1–38.

Schultheiss, O.C., Dargel, A., & Rohde, W. (2003). Implicit motives and sexual motivation and behavior. *Journal of Research in Personality, 37*, 224–230.

Schultheiss, O.C., Wirth, M.M., Torges, C.M., Pang, J.S., Villacorta, M.A., & Welsh, K.M. (2005). Effects of implicit power motivation on men's and women's implicit learning and testosterone changes after social victory or defeat. *Journal of Personality and Social Psychology, 88*, 174–188.

Schultz, W.T. (1995). *Handbook of psychobiography*. New York: Oxford University Press.

Schultz, W.T. (2005). Introducing psychobiography. In W.T. Schultz (Ed.), *Handbook of psychobiography* (pp. 3–18). New York: Oxford University Press.

Schultz, P.W., & Searleman, A. (2002). Rigidity of thought and behavior: 100 years of research. *Genetic, Social, and General Psychology Monographs*, 128, 165–207.

Schwarzer, R. (1999). Self-regulatory processes in the adoption and maintenance of health behaviors. *Journal of Health Psychology, 4*, 115–127.

Scollon, C.N., Diener, E., Oishi, S, & Biswas-Diener, R. (2004). Emotions across cultures and methods. *Journal of Cross-Cultural Psychology, 35*, 304–326.

Sears, D.O. (1986). College sophomores and the laboratory: Influences of a narrow database on social psychology's view of human nature. *Journal of Personality and Social Psychology, 51*, 515–530.

Sedikides, C., Gaertner, L., & Toguchi, Y. (2003). Pancultural self-enhancement. *Journal of Personality and Social Psychology, 84*, 60–70.

Sedikides, C., & Gregg, A.P. (2003). Portraits of the self. In M.A. Hogg & J. Cooper (Eds.), *Sage handbook of social psychology* (pp. 110–138). London: Sage Publications.

Seeman, W., Nidich, S., & Banta, T. (1972). Influence of transcendental meditation on a measure of self-actualization. *Journal of Counseling Psychology, 19*, 184–187.

Segal, N.L. (1999). *Entwined lives: Twins and what they tell us about human behavior*. New York: Plume.

Segerstrom, S.C. (2005). Optimism and immunity: Do positive thoughts always lead to positive effects? *Brain, Behavior, and Immunity, 19*, 195–200.

Segerstrom, S.C., & Miller, G.E. (2004). Psychological stress and the human immune system: A meta-analytic study of 30 years of inquiry. *Psychological Bulletin, 104*, 601–630.

Seifer, R., LaGasse, L.L., Lester, B., et al. (2004). Attachment status in children prenatally exposed to cocaine and other substances. *Child Development, 75*, 850–868.

Sekiguchi, C., Umikura, S., Sone, K., & Kume, M. (1994). Psychological evaluation of Japanese astronaut applicants. *Aviation, Space, and Environmental Medicine, 65*, 920–924.

Selye, H. (1974). *Stress without distress*. Philadelphia: J.B. Lippincott Company.

Sewell, K.W., & Cruise, K.R. (2004). Adolescent psychopathy and repertory grids: Preliminary data and focused case study. *Personal Construct Theory and Practice, 1*, 92–104.

Shah, J. (2003). The motivational looking glass: How significant others implicitly affect goal appraisals. *Journal of Personality and Social Psychology, 85*, 424–439.

Shedler, J., & Westen, D. (2004). Dimensions of personality pathology: An alternative to the five-factor model. *American Journal of Psychiatry, 161*, 1743–1754.

Sheehy, N. (2004). *Fifty key thinkers in psychology*. London: Routledge.

Sheldon, W. (1942). *The varieties of temperament*. New York: Harper & Brothers.

Sheng, M.M. (2001). Mao Zedong's narcissistic personality disorder and China's road to disaster. In O. Feldman & L.O. Valenty (Eds.), *Profiling political leaders: Cross-cultural studies of personality and behavior* (pp. 111–127). Westport, CT: Praeger.

Sher, K.J., Trull, T.J., Bartholow, B., & Vieth, A. (1999). Personality and alcoholism: Issues, methods, and etiological processes. In H. Blane and K. Leonard (Eds.), *Psychological theories of drinking and alcoholism* (2nd ed., pp. 55–105). New York: Plenum.

Sherry, S.B., Hewitt, P.L., Besser, A., Flett, G.L., & Klein, C. (2006). Machiavellianism, trait perfectionism, and perfectionistic self-presentation. *Personality and Individual Differences, 40*, 829–839.

Sherry, S.B., Hewitt, P.L., Flett, G.L., Lee-Baggley, D.L., & Hall, P.A. (in press). Trait perfectionism and perfectionistic self-presentation in personality pathology. Personality and Individual Differences.

Shiner, R., & Caspi, A. (2003). Personality differences in childhood and adolescence: Measurement, development, and consequences. *Journal of Child Psychology and Psychiatry, 44*, 2–32.

Shrauger, J.S., & Schoeneman, T.J. (1979). Symbolic interactionist view of self-concept: Through the looking glass darkly. *Psychological Bulletin, 86*, 549–573.

Shrauger, J.S., & Schohn, M. (1995). Self-confidence in college students: Conceptualization, measurement, and behavioral implications. *Assessment, 2*, 255–278.

Sidanius, J., Levin, S., Liu, J.H., & Pratto, F. (2000). Social dominance orientation and the political psychology of gender: An extension and cross-cultural replication. *European Journal of Social Psychology, 30*, 41–67.

Siddle, D.A.T., & Bond, N.W. (1988). Avoidance learning, Pavlovian conditioning, and the development of phobias. *Biological Psychology, 27*, 167–183.

Silvera, D.H., Neilands, T.B., & Perry, J.A. (2001). A Norwegian translation of the Self-Liking and Competence Scale. *Scandinavian Journal of Psychology, 42*, 417–427.

Silvia, P.J., Eichstaedt, J., & Phillips, A.G. (2005). Are rumination and reflection types of self-focused attention? *Personality and Individual Differences, 38*, 871–881.

Simons, J.S., Christopher, M.S., & McLaury, A.E. (2004). Personal strivings, binge drinking, and alcohol-related problems. *Addictive Behaviors, 29*, 773–779.

Simonton, D.K. (1987). Musical aesthetics and creativity in Beethoven: A computer analysis of 105 compositions. *Empirical Studies of the Arts, 5*, 87–104.

Simonton, D.K. (1998). Mad King George: The impact of personal and political stress on mental and physical health. *Journal of Personality, 66*, 443–466.

Simonton, D.K. (2003). Qualitative and quantitative analyses of historical data. *Annual Review of Psychology, 54*, 617–640.

Singer, J.L., & Kolligian, J., Jr. (1987). Personality: Developments in the study of private experience. *Annual Review of Psychology, 38*, 533–574.

Sinha, J.B.P., Sinha, T.N., Verma, J., & Sinha, R.B.N. (2001). Collectivism coexisting with individualism: An Indian scenario. *Asian Journal of Social Psychology, 4*, 133–145.

Skilling, T.A., Harris, G.T., Rice, M.E., & Quinsey, V.L. (2002). Identifying persistently antisocial offenders using the Hare Psychopathy Checklist and the DSM Antisocial personality disorder criteria. *Psychological Assessment, 14*, 27–38.

Skinner, B.F. (1957). The experimental analysis of behavior. *American Scientist, 45*, 343–371.

Skinner, B.F. (1971) *Beyond freedom and dignity*. Toronto: Bantam Books.

Skinner, B.F. (1980). *Notebooks* (edited by R. Epstein). Englewood Cliffs, NJ: Prentice-Hall.

Skinner, B.F. (1989). The origins of cognitive thought. *American Psychologist, 44*, 13–18.

Skinner, B.F. (1990). Can psychology be a science of mind? *American Psychologist, 45*, 1206–1210.

Skinner, B.F. (1971). Beyond freedom and dignity. Toronto: Bantam Books.

Skinner, B.F., Solomon, H. & Lindsley, O.R. (1954). A new method for the experimental analysis of the behavior of psychotic patients. *Journal of Nervous and Mental Disease, 120*, 403–406.

Skinner, H.A., Jackson, D.N., & Rampton, G.M. (1976). The Personality Research Form in a Canadian context: Does language make a difference? *Canadian Journal of Behavioural Science, 8*, 156–168.

Slutske, W.S. (2005). Alcohol use disorders among US college students and their non-college-attending peers. *Archives of General Psychiatry, 62*, 321–327.

Smith, D.B., & Ellingson, J.E. (2002). Substance versus style: A new look at social desirability in motivating contexts. *Journal of Applied Psychology, 87*, 211–219.

Smith, D.S., & Strube, M.J. (1991). Self-protective tendencies as moderators of self-handicapping impressions. *Basic and Applied Social Psychology, 12*, 63–80.

Smith, T.W. (1992). Hostility and health: Current status of a psychosomatic hypothesis. *Health Psychology, 11*, 139–150.

Smith, T.W., & Gallo, L.C. (2001). Personality traits as risk factors for physical illness. In A. Baum, T. Revenson, & J. Singer (Eds.), *Handbook of health psychology* (pp. 139–172). Hillsdale, NJ: Erlbaum.

Smith, T.W., McGonagle, M.A., & Benjamin, L.S. (1998). Sibling interactions, self-regulation, and cynical hostility in adult male twins. *Journal of Behavioral Medicine, 21*, 337–349.

Smith, T.W., O'Keeffe, J.L., & Allred, K.D. (1989). Neuroticism, symptom reports, and Type A behavior: Interpretive cautions for the Framingham Scale. *Journal of Behavioral Medicine, 12*, 1–11.

Smith, T.W., Pope, M.K., Rhodewalt, R., & Poulton, J.L. (1989). Optimism, neuroticism, coping, and symptom reports: an alternative interpretation of the Life Orientation Test. *Journal of Personality and Social Psychology, 56*, 640–648.

Smith, T.W., & Spiro, A. (2002). Personality, health, and aging: Prolegomenon for the next generation. *Journal of Research in Personality, 36*, 363–394.

Snyder, C.R., Crowson, J.J., & Poirer, J. (1997) Assessing hostile automatic thoughts: Development and validation of the HAT Scale. *Cognitive Therapy and Research, 21*, 477–492.

Snyder, M. (1974). The self-monitoring of expressive behavior. *Journal of Personality and Social Psychology, 30*, 526–537.

Snyder, M. (1983). The influence of individuals on situations: Implications for understanding the links between personality and social behavior. *Journal of Personality, 51*, 497–516.

Snyder, M., & Gangestad, S. (1986). On the nature of self-monitoring: Matters of assessment, matters of validity. *Journal of Personality and Social Psychology, 51*, 125–139.

Soldz, S., & Vaillant, G.E. (1999). The big five personality traits and the life course: A 45-year longitudinal study. *Journal of Research in Personality, 33*, 208–232.

Solomon, L.J., & Rothblum, E.D. (1984). Procrastination in academic settings: Frequency and cognitive-behavioral correlates. *Journal of Counseling Psychology, 31*, 503–509.

Sommers, S.R., & Kassin, S.M. (2001). On the many impacts of inadmissible testimony: Selective compliance, need for cognition, and the overcorrection bias. *Personality and Social Psychology Bulletin, 27*, 1368–1377.

Souter, C.R. (2003). Psychological profiler explains unique niche. *New England Psychologist, 10*, July issue (http://www.nepsy.com/leading/0307_ne_qa.html).

Southwick, L., Steele, C., Marlatt, A., & Lindell, M. (1981). Alcohol-related expectancies: Defined by phase of intoxication and drinking experience. *Journal of Consulting and Clinical Psychology, 49*, 713–721.

Spector, P.E., Cooper, C.L., Sanchez, J.I., O'Driscoll, M., Sparks, K., Bernin, P., et al. (2002). Locus of control and well-being at work: How generalizable are western findings? *Academy of Management Journal, 45*, 453–466.

Spector, P.E., et al. (2004). Eastern versus western control beliefs at work: An investigation of secondary control, socioinstrumental control, and work locus of control in China and the US. *Applied Psychology: An International Review, 53*, 38–60.

Spielberger, C.D. (1972). Anxiety as an emotional state. In C.D. Spielberger (Ed.), *Anxiety: Current trends in theory and research* (Vol. 1, pp. 23–49). Orlando, FL: Academic Press.

Srivastava, S., John, O.P., Potter, J., & Gosling, S.D. (2003). Development of personality in early and middle adulthood: Set like plaster or persistent change?. *Journal of Personality and Social Psychology, 84*, 1041–1053.

Stainton, M., Lay, C.H., & Flett, G.L. (2000). Trait procrastinators and behavior/trait-specific cognitions. *Journal of Social Behavior and Personality, 15*, 297–312.

Standing, L.G., & Huber, H. (2003). Do psychology courses reduce beliefs in psychological myths? *Social Behavior and Personality, 31*, 585–592.

Steinberg, L. (1985). Early temperamental antecedents of adult Type A behaviors. *Developmental Psychology, 21*, 1171–1180.

Stevens, A. (1995). Jungian approach to human aggression with special emphasis on war. *Aggressive Behavior, 21*, 3–11.

Stevens, J. (1997). Standard investigatory tools and offender profiling. In J. Jackson & D. Bekerian (Eds.), *Offender profiling: Theory, research and practice* (pp. 77–91). New York: John Wiley & Sons Inc.

Stewart, A.J., & Winter, D.G. (1976). Arousal of the power motive in women. *Journal of Consulting and Clinical Psychology, 44*, 495–496.

Stewart, S.H., Loughlin, H.L., & Rhyno, E. (2001). Internal drinking motives mediate personality domain-drinking relations in young adults. *Personality and Individual Differences, 30*, 271–286.

Stewart, S.M., & Bond, M.H. (2002). A critical look at parenting research from the mainstream: Problems uncovered while adapting Western research to non-Western cultures. *British Journal of Developmental Psychology, 20*, 379–392.

Stewart, S.M., Bond, M.H., Kennard, B.D., Ho, L.M., & Zaman, R.M. (2002). Does the Chinese construct of guan export to the west? *International Journal of Psychology, 37*, 74–82.

Stewart V., & Stewart, A. (1981). *Business applications of repertory grid technique.* New York: McGraw-Hill.

Stober, J. (2001). The Social Desirability Scale-17 (SDS-17): Convergent validity, discriminant validity, and relationship with age. *European Journal of Psychological Assessment, 17*, 222–232.

Stoeckli, G. (2002). Shyness in cultural context. *Zeitschrift "Psychologie in Erziehung und Unterricht", 49*, 151–159.

Stoel, R.D., De-Geus, E.J.C., & Boomsma, I. (2006). Genetic analysis of sensation seeking with an extended twin design. *Behavior Genetics, 36*, 229–237.

Stone, A.A., Hedges, S.M., Neale, J.M., & Satin, M.S. (1985). Prospective and cross-sectional mood reports offer no evidence of a "blue Monday" phenomenon. *Journal of Personality and Social Psychology, 49*, 129–134.

Strauman, T.J. (1992). Self-guides, autobiographical memory, and anxiety and dysphoria: Toward a cognitive model of vulnerability to emotional distress. *Journal of Abnormal Psychology, 101*, 87–95.

Strauman, T.J. (1996). Stability within the self: A longitudinal study of the structural implications of self-discrepancy theory. *Journal of Personality and Social Psychology, 71*, 1142–1153.

Strauman, T.J., Lemieux, A., & Coe, C. (1993). Self-discrepancies and natural killer cell activity: The influence of individual differences in self-regulation on stress physiology. *Journal of Personality and Social Psychology, 64*, 1042–1052.

Strelau, J. (1998). *Temperament: A psychological perspective.* New York: Putnam.

Strelau, J. (2001). The complex interplay of temperament factors with other factors. *European Journal of Personality, 15*, 311–325.

Strube, M.J. (1989). Evidence for the "type" in Type A behavior: A taxometric analysis. *Journal of Personality and Social Psychology, 56*, 972–987.

Stumpf, H. (1993). The factor structure of the Personality Research Form: A cross-national investigation. *Journal of Personality, 61*, 27–48.

Suedfeld, P. (2003). Canadian space psychology: The future may almost be here. *Canadian Psychology, 44*, 85–92.

Suedfeld, P., Soriano, E., McMurtry, D.L.,

Paterson, H., Weiszbeck, T.L., & Krell, R. (2005). Erikson's "components of a healthy personality" among holocaust survivors immediately and 40 years after the war. *International Journal of Aging & Human Development, 60,* 229–249.

Suedfeld, P., & Steel, G.D. (2000). The environmental psychology of capsule habitats. *Annual Review of Psychology, 51,* 227–253.

Sullivan, G. (2004). A four-fold humanity: Margaret Mead and psychological types. *Journal of the History of the Behavioral Sciences, 40,* 183–206.

Sullivan, H.S. (1953). *The interpersonal theory of psychiatry.* New York: W.W. Norton & Company.

Sulloway, F.J. (1996). *Born to rebel.* New York: Pantheon.

Surtees, P., et al. (2005). Prospective cohort study of hostility and the risk of cardiovascular disease mortality. *International Journal of Cardiology, 100,* 155–161.

Sutton, J., & Keogh, E. (2000). Social competition in school: Relationships with bullying, Machiavellianism, and personality. *British Journal of Educational Psychology, 70,* 44–456.

Sutton, J., & Keogh, E. (2001). Components of Machiavellian beliefs in children: Relationships with personality. *Personality and Individual Differences, 30,* 137–148.

Svrakic, D.M., Whitehead, C., Przybeck, T.R., & Cloninger, C.R. (1993). Differential diagnosis of personality disorders by the seven factor model of temperament and character. *Archives of General Psychiatry, 50,* 991–999.

Swann, W.B., Jr. (1983). Self-verification: Bringing social reality into harmony with the self. In J. Suls & A.G. Greenwald (Eds.), *Social psychological perspectives on the self* (Vol. 2, pp. 33–66). Hillsdale, NJ: Erlbaum.

Swann, W.B., Jr. & Seyle, C. (2005). Personality psychology's comeback and its emerging symbiosis with social psychology. *Personality and Social Psychology Bulletin, 31,* 155–165.

Szymanski, M.L., & Cash, T.F. (1995). Body-image disturbances and self-discrepancy theory: Expansion of the Body-Image Ideals Questionnaire. *Journal of Social and Clinical Psychology, 14,* 134–146.

Tafarodi, R.W. (1998). Paradoxical self-esteem and selectivity in the processing of social information. *Journal of Personality and Social Psychology, 74,* 1181–1196.

Tafarodi, R.W., & Ho, C. (2006). Implicit and explicit self-esteem: What are we measuring? *Canadian Psychology, 47,* 195–202.

Tafarodi, R.W., Lo, C., Yamaguchi, S., Lee, W. W.-S., & Katsura, H. (2004). The inner self in three countries. *Journal of Cross-Cultural Psychology, 35,* 97–117.

Tafarodi, R.W., Marshall, T.C., & Katsura, H. (2004). Standing out in Canada and Japan. *Journal of Personality, 72,* 785–814.

Tafarodi, R.W., & Milne, A.B. (2002). Decomposing global self-esteem. *Journal of Personality, 70,* 443–483.

Tafarodi, R.W., & Swann, W.B., Jr. (1995). Self-liking and self-competence as dimensions of global self-esteem: Initial validation of a measure. *Journal of Personality Assessment, 65,* 322–342.

Tafarodi, R.W., & Vu, C. (1997). Two-dimensional self-esteem and reactions to success and failure. *Personality and Social Psychology Bulletin, 23,* 626–635.

Tan, F.B. (1999). Exploring business IT-alignment using the Repertory Grid. *Proceedings of the 10th Australasian Conference on Information Systems,* 931–943.

Tangney, J.P., Niedenthal, P.M., Covert, M.V., & Barlow, D.H. (1998). Are shame and guilt related to distinct self-discrepancies? A test of Higgins's (1987) hypothesis. *Journal of Personality and Social Psychology, 75,* 256–268.

Taylor, G.J. (1984). Alexithymia: Concept, measurement, and implications for treatment. *The American Journal of Psychiatry, 141,* 725–732.

Taylor, G.J., Ryan, D., & Bagby, R.M. (1985). Toward the development of a new self-report alexithymia scale. *Psychotherapy and Psychosomatics, 44,* 191–199.

Taylor, G.J., Bagby, R.M., & Parker, J.D.A. (1991). The alexithymia construct: A potential paradigm for psychosomatic medicine. *Psychosomatics, 32,* 153–164.

Taylor, S.E., & Brown, J.D. (1988). Illusion and well-being: A social psychological perspective on mental health. *Psychological Bulletin, 103,* 193–210.

Taylor, S.E., Kemeny, M.E., et al. (1992). Optimism, coping, psychological distress, and high-risk sexual behavior among men at risk for Acquired Immunodeficiency Syndrome (AIDS). *Journal of Personality and Social Psychology, 63,* 460–473.

Taylor, S.E., Klein, L.C., Lewis, B.P., Gruenewald, T.L., Gurung, R.A.R., & Updegraff, J.A. (2000). Biobehavioral responses to stress in females: Tend-and-befriend, not fight-or-flight. *Psychological Review, 107,* 411–429.

Teasdale, J.D., & Dent, J. (1987). Cognitive vulnerability to depression: An investigation of two hypotheses. *British Journal of Clinical Psychology, 26,* 113–126.

Terracciano, A., & Costa, Jr., P.T. (2004). Smoking and the Five-Factor Model of personality. *Addiction, 99,* 472–481.

Terracciano, A., McCrae, R.R., et al. (2005). National character does not reflect mean personality trait levels in 49 cultures. *Science, 310,* 96–100.

Thiessen, D., Young, R.K., & Delgado, M. (1997). Social pressures for assortative mating. *Personality and Individual Differences, 22,* 157–164.

Thomas, A., & Chess, S. (1977). *Temperament and development.* New York: Brunner/Mazel.

Thomas, A., & Chess, S. (1989). Temperament and personality. In G.A. Kohnstamm, J.E. Bates, & M.K. Rothbart (Eds.), *Temperament in childhood* (pp. 254–261). New York: John Wiley & Sons Inc.

Thomas, A.; Chess, S.; Birch, H. G.; Hertzig, M. E.; & Korn, S. (1963). *Behavioral individuality in early childhood.* New York: New York University Press.

Thompson, M.M., & Zanna, M.P. (1995). The conflicted individual: Personality-based and domain-specific antecedents of ambivalent social attitudes. *Journal of Personality, 63,* 259–288.

Thompson, R.A., & Goodvin, R. (2005). The individual child: Temperament, emotion, self, and. personality. In M.H. Bornstein & M.E. Lamb (Eds.), *Developmental science: An advanced textbook* (pp. 391–428). Mahwah, NJ: Erlbaum.

Thompson-Brenner, & Westen, D. (2005). Personality subtypes in eating disorders: Validation of a classification in a naturalistic sample. *The British Journal of Psychiatry, 186,* 516–524.

Tice, D.M. (1992). Self-presentation and self-concept change: The looking-glass self is also a magnifying glass. *Journal of Personality and Social Psychology, 63,* 435–451.

Tice, D.M., & Baumeister, R.F. (1997). Longitudinal study of procrastination, performance, stress, and health: The costs and benefits of dawdling. *Psychological Science, 8,* 454–458.

Tomaka, J., Blascovich, J., & Kelsey, R.M. (1992). Effects of self-deception, social desirability, and repressive coping on psychophysiological reactivity to stress. *Personality and Social Psychology Bulletin, 18,* 616–624.

Tomi, L.M., Rossokha, K., & Hosein J. (2002). The role of cross-cultural factors in long-duration international space missions: Lessons from the SFINCSS-99 study. *Space Technology, 22,* 137–144.

Tomkins, S.S. (1979). Script theory: Differential magnification of affects. In H.E. Howe & R.A. Dienstbier (Eds.), *Nebraska Symposium on Motivation,* 26, 201–236.

Tomkins, S.S. (1987). Script theory. In J. Aronoff, A.I. Rabin, et al. (Eds.), The emergence of personality: Michigan State University-Henry A. Murray lectures in personality (pp. 147–216). New York: Springer.

Torquati, J.C., & Raffaelli, M. (2004). Daily experiences of emotions and social contexts of securely and insecurely attached young adults. *Journal of Adolescent Research, 19,* 740–758.

Torrubia, R., & Tobena, A. (1984). A scale for the assessment of susceptibility to punishment as a measure of anxiety: Preliminary results. *Personality and Individual Differences, 5,* 371–375.

Torrubia, R., Avila, C., Molto, J., &

Grande, I. (1995). Testing for stress and happiness: The role of the behavioral inhibition system. In C.D. Spielberger, I.G. Sarason, J.B. Brebner, E. Greenglass, P. Laingani, & A.M. O'Roark (Eds.), *Stress and emotion: Anxiety, anger, and curiosity* (Vol. 15, pp. 18–211). Washington, DC: Taylor.

Torrubia, R., Avila, C., Molto, J., & Caseras, X. (2001). The sensitivity to punishment and sensitivity to reward questionnaire (SPSRQ) as a measure of Gray's anxiety and impulsivity dimensions. *Personality and Individual Differences, 31*, 837–862.

Trapnell, P.D., & Campbell, J.D. (1999). Private self-consciousness and the five-factor model of personality: Distinguishing rumination from reflection. *Journal of Personality and Social Psychology, 76*, 284–304.

Triandis, H.C., & Suh, E.M. (2002). Cultural influences on personality. *Annual Review of Psychology, 53*, 133–160.

Trobst, K.K., Wiggins, J.S., et al. (2000). Personality psychology and problem behaviors: HIV risk and the five-factor model. *Journal of Personality, 68*, 1233–1253.

Trull, T.J., & Durrett, C. (2005). Categorical and dimensional models of personality disorders. *Annual Review of Clinical Psychology, 1*, 355–380.

Trull, T.J., & Sher, K.J. (1994). Relationship between the five-factor model of personality and Axis I disorders in a nonclinical sample. *Journal of Abnormal Psychology, 103*, 350–360.

Trull, T.J., Useda, J.D., Costa, P.T., Jr., & McCrae, R.R. (1995). Comparison of the MMPI-2 personality psychopathology five (PSY-5), the NEO-PI, and the NEO-PI-R. *Psychological Assessment, 7*, 508–516.

Tsai, J.L. (1999). Culture. In D. Levinson, J. Ponzetti, & P. Jorgensen (Eds.), *Encyclopedia of human emotion* (pp. 159–166). New York: Macmillan Press.

Tuckman, B.W., & Schouwenburg, H.C. (2004). Behavioral interventions for conquering procrastination among university students. In H. Schouwenberg, C. Lay, J.R. Ferrari, and T. Pychyl (Eds.), *Counseling the procrastinator in academic contexts*. Washington, DC: American Psychological Association.

Tupes, E.C., & Christal, R.C. (1961). *Recurrent personality factors based on trait ratings*. USAF ASD Technical Report, No. 61-97, U.S. Air Force.

Turco, R.N. (1990). Psychological profiling. *International Journal of Offender Therapy and Comparative Criminology, 34*, 147–154.

Turvey, B.E. (1999). *Criminal profiling: An introduction to behavioural evidence analysis*. San Diego, CA: Academic.

Twenge, J.M., & Campbell, W.K. (2001). Age and birth cohort differences in self-esteem: A cross-temporal meta-analysis. *Personality and Social Psychology Review, 5*, 321–344.

Twenge, J.M., Zhang, L., & Im, C. (2004). It's beyond my control: A cross-temporal meta-analysis of increasing externality in locus of control, 1960–2002. *Personality and Social Psychology Review, 8*, 308–319.

Tyrrell, C., Dozier, M., Teague, G.B., & Fallot, R.D. (1999). Effective treatment relationships for persons with serious psychiatric disorders: The importance of attachment states of mind. *Journal of Consulting and Clinical Psychology, 67*, 725–733.

Urdan, T., & Midgley, C. (2001). Academic self-handicapping: What we know, what more there is to learn. *Educational Psychology Review, 13*, 115–138.

Urry, H.L., et al. (2004). Making a life worth living: Neural correlates of well-being. *Psychological Science, 15*, 367–372.

Vaillant, G.E. (1977). *Adaptation to life*. Boston: Little & Brown.

Vaillant, G.E. (1992). *Ego mechanisms of defense: A guide for clinicians and researchers*. Washington, DC: American Psychiatric Press.

Vaillant, G.E. (1994). Ego mechanisms of defense and personality psychopathology. *Journal of Abnormal Psychology, 103*, 44–50.

Vaillant, G.E. (2002). *Aging well: Surprising guideposts to a happier life from the landmark Harvard Study of Adult Development*. London: Little, Brown, and Company.

Vaillant, G.E., & Vaillant, C.O. (1992). A cross-validation of two methods of investigating defenses. In G.E. Vaillant (Ed.), *Ego mechanisms of defense: A guide for clinicians and researchers* (pp. 159–170). Washington, DC: American Psychiatric Press.

van Aken, M.A.G., & Dubas, J.S. (2005). Personality type, social relationships, and problem behaviour in adolescence. *European Journal of Developmental Psychology, 1*, 331–348.

van der Zee, K.I., & van Oudenhoven, J.P. (2000). The multicultural personality questionnaire: A multidimensional instrument of multicultural effectiveness. *European Journal of Personality, 14*, 291–309.

van der Zee, K.I., & van Oudenhoven, J.P. (2001). The multicultural personality questionnaire: Reliability and validity of self- and other ratings of multicultural effectiveness. *Journal of Research in Personality, 35*, 278–288.

van der Zee, K.I., Zaal, J.N., & Piekstra, J. (2003). Validation of the multicultural personality questionnaire in the context of personnel selection. *European Journal of Personality, 17*, 77–100.

van Eerde, W. (2004). Procrastination in academic settings and the big five model of personality: A meta-analysis. In H. Schouwenberg, C. Lay, J.R. Ferrari, and T. Pychyl (Eds.), *Counseling the procrastinator in academic contexts*. Washington, DC: American Psychological Association.

van Essen, T., van de Heuvel, S., & Ossebaard, M. (2004). A student course on self-management for procrastination. In H. Schouwenberg, C. Lay, J.R. Ferrari, and T. Pychyl (Eds.), *Counseling the procrastinator in academic contexts*. Washington, DC: American Psychological Association.

van Herk, H., Poortinga, Y.H., & Verhallen, T.M. (2004). Response styles in rating scales: Evidence of method bias in data from six EU countries. *Journal of Cross-Cultural Psychology, 35*, 346–360.

van Ijzendoorn, M.H. (1995). Adult attachment representations, parental responsiveness, and infant attachment: A meta-analysis on the predictive validity of the Adult Attachment Interview. *Psychological Bulletin, 117*, 387–403.

van Ijzendoorn, M.H., & Kroonenberg, P.M. (1988). Cross-cultural patterns of attachment: A meta-analysis of the Strange Situation. *Child Development, 59*, 147–156.

van Oudenhoven, J.P., Mol, S., & van der Zee, K.I. (2003). Study of the adjustment of western expatriates in Taiwan ROC with the Multicultural Personality Questionnaire. *Asian Journal of Social Psychology, 6*, 159–170.

van Oudenhoven, J.P., Mol, S., & van der Zee, K.I. (in press). A new approach to the study of expatriate effectiveness: Validation of the Multicultural Personality Questionnaire (MPQ) amongst a sample of expatriates in Taiwan. *Asian Journal of Social Psychology*.

Vega-Lahr, N., & Field, T.M. (1986). Type A behavior in preschool children. *Child Development, 57*, 1333–1348.

Vollrath, M., Knoch, D., & Cassano, L. (1999). Personality, risky health behavior, and perceived susceptibility to health risks. *European Journal of Personality, 13*, 39–50.

Vollrath, M., & Torgersen, S. (2002). Who takes health risks? A probe into eight personality types. *Personality and Individual Differences, 32*, 1185–1197.

Von Davier, M., & Rost, J. (1997). Self-monitoring: A class variable? In J. Rost & R. Langeheine (Eds.), *Applications of latent trait and latent class models in the social sciences* (pp. 286–295). Munich, Germany: Waxmann.

Wagar, B.M., and Cohen, D. (2003). Culture and the self: An analysis of the personal and collective self in long-term memory. *Journal of Experimental Social Psychology, 39*, 468–475.

Wagner-Martin, L. (1999). *Sylvia Plath: A literary life*. New York: Palgrave MacMillan.

Walker, B.M., Ramsey, F.L. & Bell, R.C. (1988). Dispersed and undispersed dependency, *International Journal of Personal Construct Psychology, 1*, 63–80.

Westen, D. (1991). Clinical assessment of object relations using the TAT. Journal of

Personality Assessment, 56, 56-74.

Walker, W.D., Rowe, R.C., & Quinsey, V.L. (1993). Authoritarianism and sexual harassment. *Journal of Personality and Social Psychology, 65*, 1036–1045.

Wallace, A.F.C. (1961). *Culture and personality*. New York: Random House.

Wallace, A.F.C. (1985). Comments on this week's Citation Classic: *Culture and personality. Current Contents, 21*, 84.

Wallace, J. (1966). An abilities conception of personality: Some implications for personality measurement. *American Psychologist, 21*, 132–138.

Waller, N.G. (1999). Evaluating the structure of personality. In C.R. Cloninger (Ed.), *Personality and psychopathology* (pp. 155–197). Washington, DC: American Psychiatric Association.

Walters, G.D. (2004). The trouble with psychopathy as a general theory of crime. *International Journal of Offender Therapy and Comparative Criminology*, 48, 133–148.

Walton, K.E., & Roberts, B.W. (2004). On the relationship between substance use and personality traits: Abstainers are not maladjusted. *Journal of Research in Personality, 38*, 515–535.

Ward, C., Leong, C.-H., & Low, M. (2004). Personality and sojourner adjustment: An exploration of the "Big Five" and the "Cultural Fit" proposition. *Journal of Cross-Cultural Psychology, 35*, 137–151.

Warren, S.L, Huston, L., Egeland, B., & Sroufe, L.A. (1997). Child and adolescent anxiety disorders and early attachment. *Journal of the American Academy of Child and Adolescent Psychiatry, 36*, 637–644.

Waterman, G., Geary, P., & Waterman, C. (1974). Longitudinal study of changes in ego identity status from the freshman to the senior year at college. *Developmental Psychology, 10*, 387–392.

Waters, E., Merrick, S., Treboux, D., Crowell, J., & Albersheim, L. (2000). Attachment security in infancy and early adulthood: A twenty-year longitudinal study. *Child Development, 71*, 684–689.

Watson, D., & Clark, L.A. (1991). Self- versus peer ratings of specific emotional traits: Evidence of convergent and discriminant validity. *Journal of Personality and Social Psychology, 60*, 927–940.

Watson, D., & Hubbard, B. (1996). Adaptational style and dispositional structure: Coping in the context of the five-factor model. *Journal of Personality, 64*, 737–774.

Watson, D., Hubbard, B., & Wiese, D. (2000). Self-other agreement in personality and affectivity: Effects of acquaintanceship, trait visibility, and assumed similarity. *Journal of Personality and Social Psychology, 78*, 546–558.

Watson, D., et al. (2004). Match makers and deal breakers: Analyses of assortative mating in newlywed couples. *Journal of Personality, 72*, 1029–1068.

Watson, D.C. (2001). Procrastination and the five-factor model: A facet level analysis. *Personality and Individual Differences, 30*, 149–158.

Watson, J.B. (1913). Psychology as the behaviorist views it. *Psychological Review, 20*, 158–177.

Watson, J.B. (1924/1970). *Behaviorism*. New York: Norton.

Watson, J.B., & Rayner, R. (1920). Conditioned emotional reactions. *Journal of Experimental Psychology, 3*, 1–14.

Watson, M., Haviland, J.S., Greer, S., Davidson, J., & Bliss, J.M. (1999). Influence of psychological response on survival in breast cancer: A population-based cohort study. *The Lancet, 354*, 1331–1336.

Watts, R.E. (1998). The remarkable parallel between Rogers' core conditions and Adler's social interest. *Journal of Individual Psychology, 54*, 4–9.

Webb, B. (1990). Type-casting life with Myers-Briggs. *Library Journal, 115*, 32–37.

Webster, D.M., & Kruglanski, A.W. (1994). Individual differences in need for cognitive closure. *Journal of Personality and Social Psychology, 67*, 1049–1062.

Wechsler, H., Davenport, A., Dowdell, G., Moeykens, B., & Castillo, S. (1994). Health and behavioral consequences of binge drinking in college: A national survey of students at 140 campuses. *Journal of the American Medical Association, 272*, 1672–1677.

Wechsler, H., Lee, J.E., Kuo, M., & Lee, H. (2000). College binge drinking in the 1990s: a continuing problem. Results of the Harvard School of Public Health 1999 College Alcohol Study. *Journal of American College Health, 48*, 199–210.

Wei, M., Russell, D.W., Mallinckrodt, B., & Zakalik, R.A. (2004). Cultural equivalence of adult attachment across four ethnic groups: Factor structure, structured means, and associations with negative mood. *Journal of Counseling Psychology, 51*, 408–417.

Weiner, I.B., Exner, J.E., Jr., & Sciara, A. (1996). Is the Rorschach welcome in the courtroom? *Journal of Personality Assessment, 67*, 422–424.

Weinstein, N.D. (1984). Why it won't happen to me: Perceptions of risk factors and susceptibility. *Health Psychology, 3*, 431–457.

Weinstein, N.D. (1987). Unrealistic optimism about susceptibility to health problems: Conclusions from a community-wide sample. *Journal of Behavioral Medicine, 10*, 481–500.

Weir, R.C., & Gjerde, P.F. (2002). Preschool personality prototypes: Internal coherence, cross-study replicability, and developmental outcomes in adolescence. *Personality and Social Psychology Bulletin, 28*, 1229–1241.

Weissman, M.M., Bland, R.C., Canino, G.J., et al. (1996). Cross-national epidemiology of major depression and bipolar disorder. *Journal of the American Medical Association, 276*, 293–299.

Wentzel, K.R. (2002). Are effective teachers like good parents? Teaching styles and student adjustment in early adolescence. *Child Development, 73*, 287–301.

West, S.G., Newsom, J.T., & Fenaughty, A.M. (1992). Publication trends in *JPSP*: Stability and change in topics, methods, and theories across two decades. *Personality and Social Psychology Bulletin, 18*, 473–484.

Westen, D. (1991). Clinical assessment of object relations using the TAT. *Journal of Personality Assessment, 56*, 56–74.

Westen, D. (1998). The scientific legacy of Sigmund Freud: Toward a psychodynamically informed psychological science. *Psychological Bulletin, 124*, 333–371.

Westermeyer, J.F. (2004). Predictors and characteristics of Erikson's life cycle model among men: A 32-year longitudinal study. *International Journal of Aging and Human Development, 58*, 29–48.

Whalen, C.K., & Henker, B. (1986). Type A behavior in normal and hyperactive children: Multisource evidence of overlapping constructs. *Child Development, 57*, 688–699.

Whiffen, V.E., & Johnson, S.M. (1998). An attachment theory framework for the treatment of childbearing depression. *Clinical Psychology: Science and Practice, 5*, 478–493.

Whitbeck, L.B., Hoyt, D.R., Simons, R.L., Conger, R.D., Elder, G.H., Jr., Lorenz, F.O., & Huck, S. (1992). Intergenerational continuity of parental rejection and depressed affect. *Journal of Personality and Social Psychology, 63*, 1036–1045.

Whitbourne, S.K. (1986). *The me I know: A study of adult identity*. New York: Springer-Verlag.

White, R.W. (1959). Motivation reconsidered: The question of competence. *Psychological Review, 66*, 297–333.

Wicker, F.W., Brown, G.S., Wiehe, J.A., Hagen, A.S., & Reed, J.H. (1993). On reconsidering Maslow: An examination of the deprivation/domination proposition. *Journal of Research and Personality, 27*, 118–133.

Wicklund, R.A., & Gollwitzer, P.M. (1982). *Symbolic self-completion*. Hillsdale, N.J.: Lawrence Erlbaum.

Widiger, T.A., & Frances, A. (1985). The DSM-III personality disorders: perspectives from psychology. *Archives of General Psychiatry, 42*, 615–623.

Widiger, T.A., & Mullins, S. (2003). Personality disorders. In A. Tasman, J. Kay, & J.A. Lieberman (Eds.), *Psychiatry, 2nd Edition* (pp. 1603–1637). Chichester, England: John Wiley & Sons.

Widom, C.S. (1989). Does violence beget

violence? A critical examination of the literature. *Psychological Bulletin, 106*, 3–28.

Wiebe, R. & McCabe, S.B. (2002). Social perfectionism, dysphoria and aversive interpersonal behaviours. *Journal of Social and Clinical Psychology, 21*, 67–90.

Wiggins, J.S. (1973). *Personality and prediction: Principles of personality assessment*. Reading, MA: Addison Wesley Publishing Company.

Wiggins, J.S. (1991). Agency and communion as conceptual coordinates for the understanding and measurement of interpersonal behavior. In W.M. Grove & D.C. Ciccetti (Eds.), *Thinking clearly about psychology: Volume 2, Personality and psychopathology* (pp. 89–113). Minneapolis, MN: University of Minnesota Press.

Wiggins, J.S. (1996). An informal history of the interpersonal circumplex tradition. *Journal of Personality Assessment, 66*, 217–233.

Wiggins, J.S., & Broughton, R. (1985). The interpersonal circle: A structural model for the integration of personality research. In R. Hogan & W. H. Jones (Eds.), *Perspectives in personality* (Vol. 1, pp. 1–47). Greenwich, CT: JAI Press.

Wiggins, J.S., & Pincus, A.L. (1992). Personality: Structure and assessment. *Annual Review of Psychology, 43*, 473–504.

Wilson, D.J., Doolabh, A., Cooney, J., Khalpey, M., et al. (1990). A cross-cultural validation of the Personality Research Form in Zimbabwe. *International Journal of Psychology, 25*, 1–12.

Wilson, G.D., Barrett, P.T., & Gray, J.A. (1989). Human reactions to rewards and punishment: A questionnaire examination of Gray's personality theory. *British Journal of Psychology, 80*, 509–515.

Winefield, H.R., Winefield, A.H., Tiggeman, M., & Goldney, R.D. (1989). Psychological concomitants of tobacco and alcohol use in young Australian adults. *British Journal of Addiction, 84*, 1067–1073.

Wink, P. (1991). The two faces of narcissism. *Journal of Personality and Social Psychology, 61*, 590–597.

Winter, D.G. (1994). *Manual for scoring motive imagery in running text* (4th ed.). Department of Psychology, University of Michigan, Ann Arbor: Unpublished manuscript.

Winter, D.G. (2005). Things I have learned about personality from studying political leaders at a distance. *Journal of Personality, 73*, 557–584.

Winter, D.G., & Carlson, R.D. (1988). Using motive scores in the psychobiographical study of an individual: The case of Richard Nixon. *Journal of Personality, 56*, 75–103.

Winter, D.G., Hermann, M.G., Weintraub, W., & Walker, S.G. (1991a). The personalities of Bush and Gorbachev measured at a distance: Procedures, portraits, and policy. *Political Psychology, 12*, 215–245.

Winter, D.G., Hermann, M.G., Weintraub, W., & Walker, S.G. (1991b). The personalities of Bush and Gorbachev at a distance: Follow-up on predictions. *Political Psychology, 12*, 457–464.

Winter, D.G., John, O.P., Stewart, A.J., Klohnen, E.C., & Duncan, L.E. (1998). Traits and motives: Toward an integration of two traditions in personality research. *Psychological Bulletin, 105*, 230–250.

Woike, B.A. (1995). Most memorable experiences: Evidence for a link between implicit and explicit motives and social cognitive processes in everyday life. *Journal of Personality and Social Psychology, 68*, 1081–1091.

Woike, B.A., Gershkovich, I., Piorkowski, R., & Polo, M. (1999). The role of personality motives in the content and structure of autobiographical memories. *Journal of Personality and Social Psychology, 76*, 600–612.

Woike, B.A., & McAdams, D.P. (2001). TAT-based personality measures have considerable validity: A response to Lilienfeld, Woods, and Garb. *APS Observer, 14*, 10.

Woodall, K.L., & Matthews, K.A. (1989). Familial environment associated with type A behaviors and psychophysiological responses to stress in children. *Health Psychology, 8*, 403–426.

Yang, J., Bagby, R.M., Costa, P.T., Jr., Ryder, A.G., & Herbst, J.H. (2002). Assessing the DSM-IV structure of personality disorder with a sample of Chinese psychiatric patients. *Journal of Personality Disorders, 16*, 317–331.

Yang, K.S. (2003). Beyond Maslow's culture-bound linear theory: a preliminary statement of the double-Y model of basic human needs. *Nebraska Symposium on Motivation, 49*, 175–255.

Yang, K.S., & Bond, M.H. (1990). Exploring implicit theories with indigenous or imported constructs: The Chinese case. *Journal of Personality and Social Psychology, 58*, 1087–1095.

York, K.L., & John, O.P. (1992). The four faces of Eve: A typological analysis of women's personality at midlife. *Journal of Personality and Social Psychology, 63*, 494–508.

Yorke, M. (1989). The intolerable wrestle: Words, numbers, and meanings. *International Journal of Personal Construct Psychology, 2*, 65–76.

Young, J.E., Klosko, J.S., & Weishaar, M. (2003). *Schema therapy: A practitioner's guide*. New York: Guilford.

Yowell, C.M. (2002). Dreams of the future: The pursuit of education and career possible selves among ninth grade Latino youth. *Applied Developmental Science, 6*, 62–72.

Zajonc, R.B., & Markus, G. (1975). Birth order and intellectual development. *Psychological Review, 82*, 74–88.

Zeidner, M., & Hammer, A.L. (1992). Coping with missile attack: Resources, strategies, and outcomes. *Journal of Personality, 60*, 709–745.

Zhang, Y., Kohnstamm, G.A., Cheung, P.C., & Lau, S. (2001). A new look at the old "Little Emperor": Developmental changes in the personality of only children in China. *Social Behavior and Personality, 29*, 725–732.

Zheng, W., et al. (2002). The structure of traits delineating personality disorder in a Chinese sample. *Journal of Personality Disorders, 16*, 477–486.

Zuckerman, M. (1969). Theoretical formations. In J.P. Zubek (Ed.), *Sensory deprivation: Fifteen years of research* (pp. 407–432). New York: Appleton-Century-Crofts.

Zuckerman, M. (2005). *Psychobiology of personality, Vol. 2*. New York: Cambridge University Press.

Zuckerman, M., Kieffer, S.C., & Knee, C.R. (1998). Consequences of self-handicapping: Effects on symptom reporting, coping, and academic performance. *Journal of Personality and Social Psychology, 74*, 1619–1628.

Zuckerman, M., Kuhlman, D.M., Joireman, J., Teta, P., & Kraft, M. (1993). A comparison of three structural models for personality: The big three, the big five, and the alternative five. *Journal of Personality and Social Psychology, 65*, 747–768.

Zuckerman, M., & Kuhlman, D.M. (2000). Personality and risk-taking: Common biosocial factors. *Journal of Personality, 68*, 999–1029.

Zuckerman, M., & Tsai, F-F. (2005). Costs of self-handicapping. *Journal of Personality, 73*, 411–442.

Zuroff, D.C., Mongrain, M., & Santor, D.C. (2004).Conceptualizing and measuring

NAME INDEX

SUBJECT INDEX